JESUS REMEMBERED

CHRISTIANITY IN THE MAKING

Volume 1

JESUS REMEMBERED

James D. G. Dunn

WILLIAM B. EERDMANS PUBLISHING COMPANY

GRAND RAPIDS, MICHIGAN / CAMBRIDGE, U.K.

Wm. B. Eerdmans Publishing Co.
255 Jefferson Ave. S.E., Grand Rapids, Michigan 49503 /
P.O. Box 163, Cambridge CB3 9PU U.K.

Printed in the United States of America

08 07 06 05 04 03   7 6 5 4 3 2 1

Library of Congress Cataloging-in-Publication Data

Dunn, James D. G., 1939-
Jesus remembered / James D. G. Dunn.
p.   cm. — (Christianity in the making; v. 1)
Includes bibliographical references and indexes.
ISBN 0-8028-3931-2 (hardcover: alk. paper)
1. Jesus Christ — Person and offices. 2. Jesus Christ —
History of doctrines — Early church, ca. 30-600. I. Title. II Series.
BT203.D86   2003
232 — dc21
2003049024

www.eerdmans.com

For Meta
my love,
my life

Contents

PART TWO: FROM THE GOSPELS TO JESUS

PART THREE: THE MISSION OF JESUS

PART FIVE: THE CLIMAX OF JESUS' MISSION

CONTENTS

Preface

It has long been a hope and intention of mine to provide a comprehensive overview of the beginnings of Christianity. As a student of the New Testament (NT), in both professional and personal capacity, I suppose the ambition has a twofold origin: partly a desire to understand the NT writings in historical context, and not only as theological resource or as literature; and partly an instinctive hermeneutical awareness that the part can be understood only in the light of the whole, just as the whole can be comprehended only through a close understanding of the parts. The desire first took flesh in 1971, when A. R. C. (Bob) Leaney, a wonderfully generous and gentle Head of Department for a recently appointed lecturer, encouraged me to rethink the main NT course in the Theology Department of Nottingham University. With limited teaching resources, and Bob Leaney content to teach what he described as 'a mini-Kümmel' (Introduction to the writings of the NT), the obvious answer seemed to me to be a course entitled 'The Beginnings of Christianity'. The aim was to give students a fairly detailed insight into the life and teaching of Jesus and the initial developments which constituted early Christianity, in both historical and theological perspective.

I already conceived the task in three phases. A whole term (ten teaching weeks) had to be given to Jesus; how could it be otherwise, given the central importance of Jesus for and in Christianity? That left only one other term for the sequel(s). And in practice the discussion of primitive Christianity and of Paul's contribution in particular left very little time for anything beyond the first generation. The lecture course always came to an end when analysis of the second generation of Christianity had barely been entered upon. The situation was unsatisfactory, and only a partial remedy was provided by incorporating much of the missing material into an MA course on 'Unity and Diversity in the New Testament', which was duly written up for publication (1977). Otherwise the regular revisions of the lecture material meant that the third section of 'Beginnings' continued to find itself restricted to two or three brief sketches.

The situation changed significantly with my move to the University of Durham in 1982, where I inherited a core NT course on 'New Testament Theology'. Faced by a similar challenge of too much material to cover in a single course, I had no doubt that the course should focus on the two NT figures of greatest theological significance — Jesus and Paul. It seemed obvious to me then, and still seems obvious to me, that in a Department focusing on the Jewish and Christian traditions of theologizing, detailed historical treatment of the principal focus of all Christian theology (Jesus) was indispensable. Similarly in regard to Paul, arguably the first and most influential of all Christian theologians (by virtue of the canonization of his letters): how could a course in New Testament Theology not give equivalently detailed treatment of Paul's theology? And so my earlier material was reworked to sharpen the theological focus (already a central concern of the earlier course anyway) and to concentrate solely on Jesus and Paul. In a larger Department it was always possible to offer various options which advanced my continuing interest in the second generation of Christianity and the transition to the so-called 'sub-apostolic' age.

This latter interest came to initial fruition in the Durham-Tübingen research seminar on 'The Partings of the Ways, AD 70 to 135', in September 1989, appropriately on the centenary of the death of my great hero, J. B. Lightfoot. The papers were subsequently published (1992) under the title *Jews and Christians,* with the original title of the Symposium as the book's subtitle. There was also the lecture series which I gave in the Gregorian Pontifical University (Rome) in 1990 as Joseph McCarthy Visiting Professor, which was published in fuller version as *The Partings of the Ways between Christianity and Judaism* in 1991. But in the meantime the theology of Paul had become such a major concern that further work towards the fulfilment of my original vision had to be put on hold until I had got Paul out of my system. That time duly arrived, with the publication of my *The Theology of Paul the Apostle* in 1998. At which point, as I delighted to tease my friends, 'I gave up Paul for Jesus'.

Having focused my attention so heavily on Paul for nearly twenty years I had no delusions as to the magnitude of the mountain before me. Even though I had kept fairly well abreast of Jesus and Gospels scholarship during that period I knew well enough that the shift of research interest from Paul to Jesus demanded a massive re-tooling job on my part. Fortunately I was granted by the University in effect two years research leave, first as a Derman Christopherson Fellow (1999-2000), and then as my regular research leave enhanced in recognition of my (second) spell of three years service as Head of the Department. I continued my postgraduate supervisions (almost always a delight and stimulus) but otherwise was freed from academic duties as a member of the Department. I am immensely grateful to the University and to my departmental colleagues for thus encouraging and supporting me and gladly acknowledge that without that leave the challenge of the present volume would have been impossible to take on, let along to meet even to the extent that the following chapters attest.

During the course of the two years, a blessed anticipation *(arrabōn)* of early retirement in due course (take heart, Meta, there is light at the end of the tunnel), I was able to try out several ideas and sections of the book as its structure developed. The attempts to explain and the opportunities to defend its various hypotheses and findings helped (as always) to clarify and sharpen my own think- ing and formulation. I am grateful more than I can say for all the pleasure and stimulus these occasions afforded, for me certainly, and I hope for the others in- volved. For more than two years I have been able to offer a one, two, or three lec- ture series under various titles round the theme 'Looking for Jesus' — in San An- tonio, Texas; as the Hugh Price Hughes Lecture in Hinde Street Methodist Church, London; as the Lund and the Zarley Lectures in North Park, Chicago; in Lincoln Cathedral as part of a series on 'The Uniqueness of Christianity'; in Lynchburg College, Virginia; and in Denver Theological Seminary, Colorado. At the annual symposium on 'The Task of Interpreting Scripture Theologically' at North Park Seminary in October 2000, I was able to develop key themes from chapter 6 under the title *'Ex Akoē Pisteōs'*. The key thesis of the whole volume (chapter 8) was tried out in a wonderful colloquium in Israel, under the inspired leadership of Doris Donnelly, and also in the British New Testament Conference in September 2000 in Bristol, and at the Society of Biblical Literature (SBL) conference in November 2000 at Nashville, under the title 'Jesus in Oral Mem- ory'. Parts of chapter 9 made up a paper for the 'Jesus and Archaeology' confer- ence in Jerusalem, August 2000. Sections of chapter 12 provided a paper for the 'Historical Jesus' seminar at the Society for New Testament Studies annual con- ference in Montreal, August 2001 and for the Festschrift for Peder Borgen. Ma- terial from chapters 9 and 14 contributed to papers on 'Jesus and Holiness' for a Durham interdisciplinary seminar organized by Stephen Barton in November 1999, and to a paper on 'Jesus and Purity' delivered at the SBL conference in Denver, Colorado, in November 2001. Material for chapters 15 to 17 was first worked through thoroughly in contributions to two symposia, one of them the Festschrift for my old friend David Catchpole. And sections from chapter 18 have contributed to yet another Festschrift, this one for my former colleague Sandy Wedderburn.

More interactive and generative of more feedback, the bulk of the first fourteen chapters provided the main feature of the programme of the Durham New Testament Research Seminar for two terms in the first half of 2001. These were particularly stimulating and challenging sessions, and I am grateful to the members of the Seminar for their comments and criticisms, particularly my immediate colleagues, Stephen Barton, Loren Stuckenbruck, Crispin Fletcher Louis, and (as with my *Theology of Paul*) especially Walter Moberly. Charlene Moss saved me from several British English idioms which would have been unfamiliar to speakers of American English. Of my own postgraduates, the overlap of interest, above all with Marta Cserhati, researching 'the third quest of the historical Jesus', and Terence Mournet, researching oral tradition in the Gospels, has been highly instructive and productive. I am grateful not least to Jeffrey Gibson, who persuaded me to post my 'Jesus in Oral Memory' in his XTalk on-line Seminar. The two-week daily dialogue with other members of the Seminar focused not so much on the 'nitty-gritty' issues of the Synoptic data, as I had hoped, but more on the implications of my understanding of the oral traditioning process for subsequent church formation and the emergence of the Gospels. So the benefits of the dialogue will extend into the second volume of the projected three-volume study of Christianity's beginnings. But I found that the experience helped recharge the little grey cells and several of the contributions were very pertinent, especially those of Mark Goodacre, Brian McCarthy, Bob Schacht and Ted Weeden.

I also consulted or sent various parts of the manuscript in first or second draft to friends and colleagues and found their feedback invariably helpful: in Durham itself, Richard Britnell, David Brown, Joe Cassidy, Colin Crowder, Sheridan Gilley, Margaret Harvey and Robert Hayward; elsewhere in the UK, Richard Bauckham, Bob Morgan, Ron Piper, Graham Stanton and Anthony Thiselton; and in North America, Jim Charlesworth, Helmut Koester, John Kloppenborg, and particularly John Meier and Scot McKnight. Many individual points have been nuanced more appropriately as a result, and for that I am very grateful, though at other points, after further consideration, I have restated my earlier view. Needless to say, the remaining misjudgments and infelicities are my own.

Any who have worked in this field will be well aware that each of the following Parts of volume 1 could have been expanded into full-length monographs. It was clear enough to me from the beginning that I could not seriously hope to review all exegetical options or to provide extensive bibliographical documentation of the various opinions even for key texts and motifs. That would have made the volume impossibly long and even more unwieldy than it now is. My primary concern has been rather to draw attention to the principal (mainly textual) data which have to be taken into account when considering whether a tradition can be traced back to Jesus, or as I would prefer to say, to the initial impact made by Jesus' teaching and activity. For both reasons I have made no attempt to consult the immense range of commentaries on the Gospels now available to us, but have concentrated principally on those which go into some detail on the tradition history behind the Gospels and do not hesitate to ask historical questions regarding the origin of these traditions. Questions on how the individual traditions function within each Gospel are for a later volume. It will not surprise those who know the commentary literature, therefore, that I have found the greatest help and most fruitful dialogue with W. D. Davies and Dale Allison on Matthew, Rudolf Pesch on Mark, and Joe Fitzmyer on Luke. Others are certainly drawn in where appropriate, but the frequency of reference to those named indicates the extent of my debt. I have also endeavoured to limit what would otherwise have become an all-inclusive bibliography by focusing entries on the primary subject matter of the volume, but including neither dictionary articles nor most of the once-mentioned articles on individual texts. I hope the footnotes to each chapter are sufficiently detailed to indicate further reading as well as my own engagement with it.

In 1979, when I had nearly completed the manuscript of my inquiry into the origins of the doctrine of the incarnation, I was disappointed to learn that the intended title 'The Beginnings of Christology' had been pre-empted by other authors. In some frustration I turned to John Bowden, Editor of the SCM Press for advice. He responded at once that a better because stronger title would be *Christology in the Making*. I warmed to the title immediately and used it for the 1980 publication. The strength of the phrase still resonates for me, and so, in the (no doubt vain) hope that I will not cause too much confusion on booksellers' shelves, I have christened the three-volume project *Christianity in the Making*. May the reading of volume 1 give as much pleasure and profit as I received in the writing of it.

January 6 (Epiphany), 2002

A major compositional concern in the chapters which follow has been to leave the main text as uncluttered as possible, to facilitate continuity of reading. The footnotes are there to document points made in the text, to justify assertions made too baldly, and to indicate the wider scope of debate and bibliography regarding issues referred to. Those less interested in such finer details should have no qualms in passing over the footnotes with only an occasional glance. They are for those who want to be kept aware of how tentative some of the claims have to be, or to follow up points of detail, or to consult some of the varied (though far from complete) bibliography provided. At least they may give readers less familiar with the myriad debates some assurance that the more controversial opinions voiced in the following pages have not been reached without substantial reflection and consultation. Read well!

CHAPTER 1

Christianity in the Making

Christianity is without doubt the most significant and longest-lasting influence to have shaped the character and culture of Europe (and so also of 'the West') over the last two millennia. To understand Christianity better, its own character and the core elements which made its beliefs and values so influential, remains therefore an important task and a continuing challenge for historical inquiry. Within that larger enterprise, the *beginnings* of Christianity call for special consideration. Partly because the origins of such a major religious and social force are always of interest for the student of history. And partly because Christianity is itself named after the first-century CE figure, Jesus of Nazareth (Jesus Christ), and regards the earliest Christian writings (the New Testament) as definitive ('canonical') for these beliefs and values. To focus thus on Christianity's beginnings is not to claim that only the 'original' is 'authentic', or that 'the apostolic age' was alone 'pure'. It is simply to affirm the continuing relevance of formative factors in the determination of features of Christianity which have been integral to its lasting impact. And for Christianity itself the challenge of setting the texts which attest these beginnings within their historical context and of understanding them better can never be less than a challenge to Christianity's own self-understanding.

The task here envisaged was one more frequently tackled by earlier generations. Subsequent to the influential overviews of F. C. Baur (particularly 1845 and 1854)[1] and the generally disregarded Ernest Renan (1863-81),[2] we could mention, for example, Carl Weizsäcker's *Das apostolische Zeitalter der christlichen Kirche*

---

1. F. C. Baur, *Paul: The Apostle of Jesus Christ* (1845; ET 2 vols. London: Williams and Norgate, 1873, 1875); *The Church History of the First Three Centuries* (1854; ET 2 vols. London: Williams and Norgate, 1878-79).

2. E. Renan, *Histoire des origines du christianisme* in 5 volumes, beginning with his *Vie de Jésus* (1863), ET *The History of the Origins of Christianity* (London: Mathieson, n.d.).

1

(1886),[3] Alfred Loisy, *La Naissance du Christianisme* (1933) and *Les Origines du Nouveau Testament* (1936),[4] and Maurice Goguel's three-volume *Jésus et les Origines du Christianisme* (1932, 1946, 1947).[5] From America came the slighter A. C. McGiffert, *A History of Christianity in the Apostolic Age* (1897).[6] But the most substantive treatments,[7] and nearest models for the current project, are Eduard Meyer's three-volume *Ursprung und Anfänge des Christentums* (1921-23)[8] and particularly Johannes Weiss's *Das Urchristentum* (regrettably incomplete when he died in 1914).[9] These were marked, the last most impressively, by the attempt to draw together the fruits of historical, literary and theological investigations which were so lively at that time. English-speaking scholars have not generally attempted such ambitious overviews or syntheses,[10] and throughout the twentieth century were content to focus on specific issues or to contribute at the level of introductory or semi-popular treatments.[11] The one real exception is the recently undertaken multi-volume treatment by N. T. Wright — *Christian Origins and the Question of God* (so far two volumes, 1992, 1996).[12] Substantial though these volumes are, and much as I agree with major features of the undertaking, however, I have serious reservations about the central hypothesis which so far forms the spine of the work. To have Wright, now bishop of Durham, as a dialogue partner is one of the pleasures of the present project.

The beginning of the third millennium, as (mis)dated from the birth of Je-

3. ET 2 vols. *The Apostolic Age of the Christian Church* (London: Williams and Norgate, 1907, 1912).

4. ET *The Birth of the Christian Religion* and *The Origins of the New Testament* in a single volume (New York: University Books, 1962).

5. *La Vie de Jésus* (Paris: Payot, 1932), ET *The Life of Jesus* (London: George Allen and Unwin, 1933); *La Naissance du Christianisme* (Paris: Payot, 1946), ET *The Birth of Christianity* (London: George Allen and Unwin, 1953); *L'Église primitive* (Paris: Payot, 1947), ET *The Primitive Church* (London: George Allen and Unwin, 1964).

6. Edinburgh: Clark, 1897.

7. Also worthy of mention are the initial volumes of larger-scale projects on church history by H. Lietzmann, *A History of the Church*. Vol. 1: *The Beginnings of the Christian Church* (ET London: Lutterworth, 1937, revised 1949), and J. Lebreton and J. Zeiler, *The History of the Primitive Church* (ET 2 vols; London: Burns, Oates and Washbourne, 1942, 1944).

8. Stuttgart: J. G. Cotta, 1921-23.

9. ET *Earliest Christianity: A History of the Period AD 30-150* (1937; New York: Harper, 1959).

10. McGiffert gave only a brief treatment of Jesus and limited his study to the NT period.

11. The most recent volumes of note are C. Rowland, *Christian Origins: An Account of the Setting and Character of the Most Important Messianic Sect of Judaism* (London: SPCK, 1985), and P. Barnett, *Jesus and the Rise of Early Christianity: A History of New Testament Times* (Downers Grove: InterVarsity, 1999).

12. *The New Testament and the People of God* (London: SPCK, 1992); *Jesus and the Victory of God* (London: SPCK, 1996).

sus, is an appropriate time to gather together the fruits of the last two centuries in a fresh statement and assessment of the *status quaestionis* after two thousand years. More important, however, are the recent developments in the field which call for a more or less complete reevaluation of previous assumptions and approaches. I mention here only the three most significant factors. (a) In terms of methodology, the crisis for the hitherto self-assured historical-critical method of analysing sources and traditions, a crisis occasioned by post-modernism in its various forms, needs to be addressed at some depth. (b) The interaction with social-scientific disciplines, particularly sociology, has shed a good deal of fresh light on the NT texts and Christianity's beginnings, which needs to be incorporated, but critically, into any such overview. (c) The discovery of new texts, particularly the Dead Sea Scrolls and the codices from Nag Hammadi, has undermined the older wisdom which had previously determined scholarly views on the emergence of Christianity in its distinctiveness from its Jewish matrix and within the religious melting pot of the first- and second-century Mediterranean world. Although these texts were discovered more than fifty years ago, their impact continues to ripple through scholarship on earliest Christianity, and the current debates which they occasioned remain confused at many key points. Needless to say, I hope to contribute in some measure to these debates.

There are three great questions for students of Christianity's beginnings: (1) What was it about Jesus which explains both the impact he made on his disciples and why he was crucified? (2) How and why did it come about that the movement which took off from Jesus did not after his death remain within first-century Judaism and became unacceptable to emerging rabbinic Judaism? (3) Was the Christianity which emerged in the second century as a predominantly Gentile religion essentially the same as its first-century version or significantly different in character and kind?

These are not new questions. Already in his *Paul* book, Baur posed the second question in setting out his programme for a history of earliest Christianity, when he claimed that

> the idea (of Christianity) found in the bounds of the national Judaism the chief obstacle to its universal historical realization. How these bounds were broken through, how Christianity, instead of remaining a mere form of Judaism, although a progressive one, asserted itself as a separate, independent principle, broke loose from it, and took its stand as a new enfranchised form of religious thought and life, essentially differing from all the national peculiarities of Judaism is *the ultimate, most important point of the primitive history of Christianity.*[13]

13. Baur, *Paul* 3 (my emphasis).

Baur's formulation of the issue reflects the supreme self-confidence of nineteenth-century German scholarship and the triumphalism of a view of Christianity as the 'absolute' expression of 'the universal, the unconditioned, the essential'[14] which grates intensely for a post-Holocaust sensibility. But, as we shall see further in volume 2, Baur set the agenda for attempts to clarify the history of primitive Christianity for the rest of the nineteenth century. And the issue of Christianity's emergence from within Judaism has reappeared in the second half of the twentieth century, posed all the more sharply by the Holocaust, as one of the absolutely crucial subjects for any analysis of the formative period of both Christianity and Judaism.[15]

The turn of the twentieth century brought the third great issue to the fore, summed up in the phrase, 'the Hellenization of (the earliest form of) Christianity'.[16] This was the principal concern of the history-of-religions school — to locate Christianity as it emerged into the Graeco-Roman world within the context of other religions of the day and to trace the influences from the wider context on that emerging Christianity. The issue is nicely focused on the disparity between the message of Jesus in the Gospels and the gospel of Paul in his letters, where the assumption or conclusion (?) was that several key features of the latter had to be attributed to the influence of mystery cults and early Gnostic ideas.[17] The consequences for our appreciation of Christianity's beginnings are clearly signalled in William Wrede's famous description of Paul as 'the second founder of Christianity', who has 'exercised beyond all doubt the stronger — not the better — influence' than the first founder, Jesus.[18]

Here again are questions best left till volume 2. But one of the key insights of the twentieth century has been the recognition that the historical developments could not be neatly compartmentalized, as though one could simply distinguish Jesus and Jewish Christianity from Paul and Hellenistic/Gentile Christianity, from the Apostolic Fathers and the emerging Great Church, and from Jewish-

---

14. Baur, *History* 4-6, 33, 43, 47.

15. See my *The Partings of the Ways between Christianity and Judaism and Their Significance for the Character of Christianity* (London: SCM, 1991) 1-17. The importance of the plural *(Partings)* has usually been recognized in reactions to this volume; but it is equally important to recognize the importance of the final phrase *(for the Character of Christianity),* intended to draw Christianity's attention to this central feature of its beginnings. The significance for historic (rabbinic) Judaism needs also to be part of the agenda for the ongoing dialogue between Jews and Christians.

16. In his famous lectures, A. Harnack, *What Is Christianity?* (1899-1900; ET Williams and Norgate, [3]1904) defined 'the greatest fact in the history of the Church in the second century' as '*the influx of Hellenism, of the Greek spirit,* and the union of the Gospel with it' (203, his italics).

17. For details see below, vol. 2 (§20).

18. W. Wrede, *Paul* (1904; ET Boston: Beacon, 1908) 180.

Christian and Gnostic heretical forms of Christianity. The breakthrough was made by Walter Bauer's *Rechtgläubigkeit und Ketzerei im ältesten Christentum* (1934, [2]1964),[19] which argued that the earliest forms of Christianity in several major Mediterranean centres may have been what subsequent 'orthodoxy' came to regard as 'heresy'. In other words, the earliest forms of Christianity were much more of a 'mixed bag' than had previously been thought. Was there ever a 'pure' form of Christianity?! Bauer's own thesis is again subject matter for a subsequent volume. But the issues he raised could not be confined to the second century. In one of the most important twentieth-century contributions to the reconstruction of Christianity's beginnings, James M. Robinson and Helmut Koester followed up Bauer's insight in the light of the Nag Hammadi texts and concluded that the same verdict had to be delivered on first-century Christianity as well.[20] Was there ever a single form of Christianity? Is the Christianity of the New Testament simply the deposit of that form of Christianity which endured and/or overcame its (Christian!) rivals?[21]

Both these large-scale issues — the emergence of Christianity from within Judaism, and into the wider Hellenistic world — have inevitably impacted back on the first, on the attempt to understand the mission and message of Jesus himself and its determinative influence. On the one hand, the (re)assertion that Jesus was a Jew has become one of the commonplaces of contemporary NT scholarship. But the more firmly Jesus is located within the Judaism of his day, the more pressing become the questions Why then was he crucified? and How then did the movement which sprang from his mission cease to be part of Judaism (to be Jewish!) so quickly? On the other hand, the likelihood is frequently canvassed today that the pluralism detected by Bauer was a feature of Christianity from the first, that is of the very first hearings of Jesus' own preaching. Or even that the influence of Hellenism which Harnack described as a feature of the second century is already to be traced in Jesus' own message. These last are among the most important issues to be discussed in the following pages (vol. 1). But the point here is that the questions which motivate historical inquiry into Christianity's beginnings can no longer be neatly apportioned to separate volumes. A history of earliest Christianity can no longer treat the mission and message of Jesus simply as prolegomenon, nor confine itself to the period and documents of the NT. Unless

19. ET *Orthodoxy and Heresy in Earliest Christianity* (Philadelphia: Fortress, 1971).

20. J. M. Robinson and H. Koester, *Trajectories through Early Christianity* (Philadelphia: Fortress, 1971).

21. In my *Unity and Diversity in the New Testament: An Inquiry into the Character of Earliest Christianity* (London: SCM, 1977, [2]1990) I followed up Robinson and Koester to the extent of drawing attention to the diversity of earliest Christianity, that is, the diversity *within* the New Testament. But I did not really address the issue of a diversity of which the NT itself was only part.

the major transitions, from Jesus to Paul, from the NT to the early Fathers (and 'heretics'!) are also appreciated, neither the significance of Jesus nor that of Paul, neither the Christianity of the NT writings nor that of the early Fathers can be adequately comprehended or fully grasped.

In other words, what is envisaged in *Christianity in the Making* is the attempt in three volumes to give an integrated description and analysis, both historical and theological, both social and literary, of the first 120 or so years of Christianity (27-150 CE). Volume 1 will, inevitably, focus on Jesus. Part One will examine what has become universally known as 'the Quest of the Historical Jesus', focusing on the crucial insights gleaned in the course of the two-hundred-year-old quest and asking whether or in what degree they are still valid. It will argue that the Gospel traditions provide a clear portrayal of the remembered Jesus since they still display with sufficient clarity for present purposes the impact which Jesus made on his first followers. Part Two will evaluate the sources available to us and describe the historical context of Jesus' mission as concisely as feasible, alert to the current debate regarding these sources and drawing on the most recent archaeological and sociological studies. The most distinctive feature of the present study will be the attempt to freshly assess the importance of the oral tradition of Jesus' mission and the suggestion that the Synoptic Gospels bear testimony to a pattern and technique of oral transmission which has ensured a greater stability and continuity in the Jesus tradition than has thus far been generally appreciated. Parts Three to Five will then attempt to gain an overview of Jesus' mission (as remembered by his first followers), dealing in succession with its main themes, some much controverted, others surprisingly not so; also, inevitably, the questions of what Jesus' hearers thought of him, what he thought of himself, and why he was crucified. The volume will conclude with a discussion of how and why the belief that Jesus had been resurrected arose and what were the claims it embodied.

Volume 2 will begin with a section methodologically equivalent to Parts One and Two of volume 1 — on the quest for the historical 'primitive community' and the value of the sources available, including not just the Acts of the Apostles, but also what can be deduced from the Gospels and the Epistles. In trying to sketch out the earliest history and the emergence of 'the Hellenists' (Acts 6.1), it is important to appreciate the character of the early Nazarene sect within the 'sectarianism' of late Second Temple Judaism. The earliest expansion of the new movement, its causes and course, require careful detective work and sifting of the evidence, not least in regard to the expansion which the Acts does not record. A particular concern at this point will have to be an evaluation of the increasingly vociferous claims that there were diverse and alternative forms of Christianity as early as those attested in the canonical NT.

Given the place of Acts and the Pauline letters within the NT, the dominant

6

figure through the latter half of this period is bound to be Paul. But Paul's life and work need to be built into an integrated picture, and Paul needs to be fitted into the much larger picture of a Nazarene sect 'beginning from Jerusalem'. The emergence of the distinctives which were to mark out Christianity and result in its becoming a separate religion was a much more complex process, involving many others than Paul, but their contributions are much more difficult to bring to light and to tease out. Nevertheless, the (probably) quite close conjunction of Paul's death and the beginning of the first Jewish revolt (66 CE) point to 70 CE, when, properly speaking, Second Temple Judaism came to an end with the destruction of the Temple, as the natural *terminus ad quem* for the second volume.

At the time of writing this Introduction, the form of volume 3 is not yet settled. The intention, however, is to cover what can roughly be classified as the second and third generations of Christianity (70-150). This is the period in which most of the NT texts were written, but the task of correlating them with other data from the same period, particularly Jewish and Graeco-Roman texts and epigraphical data, and of producing a coherent overall picture is extremely daunting. Moreover, 150 takes us into the period when the challenge of Bauer's thesis is at its sharpest and the confrontations between nascent Christianity/ies and its/their chief competitors are already clear. 150 was also Weiss's cut-off date, and though fairly arbitrary it should be sufficient to ensure that the gap between the NT and 'post-apostolic' Christianity has been fully bridged and that the trends and tendencies which formed Christianity's enduring character are sufficiently clear.

And so to Jesus.

PART ONE

FAITH AND THE
HISTORICAL JESUS

CHAPTER 2

Introduction

It began with Jesus — 'it' being Christianity. Whether *he* began it, or *it* looked back to him as its beginning, are matters to be clarified. Either way, and whatever qualifications might prove to be appropriate or necessary in the light of more detailed analysis, the assertion can stand: it began with Jesus. An inquiry into Christianity's beginnings, therefore, must inevitably start with this Jesus, who by common consent flourished in the land of Israel, otherwise known as Palestine, round about the year 30 of the common era (CE).

A historical figure of such immense significance as Jesus has always been and will always be a subject of human curiosity and fascination. In earlier centuries such interest in historical people and events of religious significance was usually expressed primarily in pilgrimage, the ancient equivalent of tourism and sight-seeing. The grand tour of the Holy Land by Queen Helena, mother of Emperor Constantine in the fourth century to identify the sites of Jesus' ministry, thenceforward gave focus to Christian interest in the 'where' of the events of that ministry. The Crusades were motivated by concern to maintain pilgrim access to the places made holy for Christians by what the Christian Gospels recorded as having taken place there. And in an age of widespread illiteracy the details of Jesus' life could be given visual concreteness by artistic reproductions of episodes from the Gospels, as so finely illustrated in the artwork of Chartres Cathedral.

However, the last five hundred years of European history have witnessed a (for the most part) increasing interest in the historical figure of Jesus, as we shall soon see. An important and probably unavoidable consequence has been an increasing tension between such historical interest and the traditional claims of Christian doctrine regarding Jesus, classically expressed in the ecumenical Christian creeds[1] and the artistic representations of Christ the Pantocrator (Al-

1. The Niceno-Constantinopolitan creed, known familiarly as the Nicene creed from its

11

mighty, Ruler of the Universe) so characteristic of Byzantine iconography.[2] This tension continues to the present day, often as a positive tension, but frequently experienced and perceived as a negative or even destructive tension. This too should become clear as we proceed.

The ongoing discussion has had three important dimensions. Since these provide the interweaving warp and woof of the following discussion, it is well to be clear on them, at least in broad terms, before proceeding further. The three can be summed up most simply in the three terms, 'faith, history and hermeneutics'.

(1) By 'faith' I mean that dimension of the discussion formed by Christian belief in Jesus. The traditional terms of that belief have already been indicated in the formal language (and rather daunting conceptuality) of the classic creeds cited in the previous paragraph (n. 1). But the term itself (faith) embraces any conviction that Jesus has provided 'a window into the divine' (almost a definition of an icon),[3] and/or that in some sense his death achieved salvation from sin, and/or that he was raised by God from death to a life beyond death.[4] The point is that such faith inevitably influences and shapes any attempt on the part of one who stands within the Christian tradition (as I do) to make an evaluation of the historical figure. Whether that is a good thing or a bad thing, whether such a faith perspective should or can be bracketed out, or whether such faith can be sufficiently open to critique from without (and from within) are all questions which have bounced back and forth during the last few centuries and will form much of the grist for what follows.

---

use in eucharistic liturgy, affirms: 'We believe . . . in one Lord Jesus Christ, the only-begotten Son of God, begotten from the Father before all ages, light from light, true God from true God, begotten not made, of one substance with the Father, through whom all things came into existence, who because of us men and because of our salvation came down from heaven, and was incarnate from the Holy Spirit and the Virgin Mary and became man . . .'. The same council which endorsed this creed (Chalcedon, 451) also asserted against the teaching of Eutyches that Christ had 'two natures, without confusion, without change, without division, without separation' (*ODCC* 336-37, 1145-46; text of the creed in J. N. D. Kelly, *Early Christian Creeds* [London: Longmans, [2]1960] 297-98).

2. The icon seeks to express the invisible God become visible in Christ, so that what is depicted is 'a humanity suffused with the presence of divinity', 'the "deified" body of Christ', 'the dogma of the two natures of Christ, the divine and the human' (J. Pelikan, *Jesus through the Centuries: His Place in the History of Culture* [New Haven: Yale University, 1985] 92-93).

3. A very early conviction, variously expressed in such passages as Matt. 11.27; John 1.18; and Col. 1.15. The conviction is nicely caught in the teasing title used by J. A. T. Robinson, *The Human Face of God* (London: SCM, 1973).

4. The earliest Christian creeds or confessional formulae (that is, within the first twenty years of Jesus' crucifixion) focus on the significance of Jesus' death and resurrection (data and bibliography in my *Theology of Paul the Apostle* [Grand Rapids: Eerdmans/Edinburgh: Clark, 1998] 174-75).

(2) By 'history' I mean all that is involved in taking seriously the fact that, whatever else he was, Jesus was a figure in history, and, to that extent at least, is amenable to the methods and tools of historical study. What these methods and tools are, what are or should be the working assumptions behind their employment, and whether historical inquiry can or should try to escape completely from the pre-conditioning of some ideology ('faith' or other), these too are questions which form part of the daily diet for protagonists on our theme and must feature prominently in what follows. Here it should simply be noted that the fact of faith, belief regarding Jesus, however expressed, *is itself a historical datum,* one which has itself to be taken into consideration in any historical account of Christianity's beginnings, even when a particular historical method may attempt to bracket out a faith perspective from the assumptions lying behind that method.

(3) By 'hermeneutics' I mean the theory of interpretation, and by extension the science, or perhaps better, *art* of interpreting the data available to us regarding the historical figure of Jesus. The data in question have consisted primarily of the testimony of the NT writings, particularly the Gospels, including, of course, their own faith claims. The wish that there could be other sources has often been expressed, and a significant body of contemporary opinion would claim that that wish has been fulfilled through the discovery of more documents from the earliest centuries CE during the last fifty or so years. This claim too will be a matter for further discussion. But whatever the extent of the data base, the task of interpreting it remains. The hermeneutical task itself has been seen to have many facets in recent years. But the principal concern for the present historical study will be what might be called *the hermeneutical dialogue between faith and history.*[5] Hermeneutics, I suggest, provides a kind of bridge between faith and history. Whether that is in fact the case, whether it can be sustained as such a bridge, and whether, if so, the bridge will be sustainable only in a lopsided way, firmly rooted on one side but with only a shallow hold on the other, are once again questions which lie behind and motivate all that follows.

The task in front of us has usually been described as 'the quest of the historical Jesus', to use the title popularised by the English translation of Albert Schweitzer's magisterial study at the beginning of the twentieth century.[6] This period of Life of Jesus research was described by Schweitzer as 'the greatest

---

5. The faith-history tension is closely related to the tension between the NT as Scripture and as a set of historical documents, but the latter would be more restrictive than the dialogue here envisaged.

6. A. Schweitzer, *Von Reimarus zu Wrede* (1906, but since 1913, *Geschichte der Leben-Jesu-Forschung*); ET *The Quest of the Historical Jesus* (London: Black, 1910). The *Quest* has been republished as the 'first complete edition', with revised translation, Schweitzer's Preface to the sixth German edition (1950), and a Foreword by D. Nineham (London: SCM, 2000). I will distinguish the two English editions as *Quest*[1] and *Quest*[2].

achievement of German theology'.[7] That is an overblown estimate, expressive of the high self-confidence of German biblical scholarship of the time[8] — a self-confidence which, ironically, Schweitzer himself was about to puncture; and its almost exclusive focus on the German 'quest' did too little justice to the interest in such questions in scholarly circles outside Germany. Nevertheless, the estimate did express the sense of intellectual excitement which the quest generated within German scholarship. And the fact remains, for better or worse, that for many decades it was the German questers who drew the scholars of other countries along in their train.

Since Schweitzer's great study, the quest as such has been further analysed and summarised on countless occasions, and there is no need to retrace in detail the paths so familiar to most students of the NT and of previous research into the life of Jesus.[9] However, 'the quest of the historical Jesus' as described by

---

7. Schweitzer, *Quest*[1] 1, *Quest*[2] 3.

8. The opening words (in the preceding paragraph) are: 'When, at some future day, our period of civilisation lies closed and completed before the eyes of later generations, German theology will stand out as a great, a unique phenomenon in the mental and spiritual life of our time' (*Quest*[2] 3).

9. Beyond dictionary articles and popular accounts, however, the roots of the quest and its embeddedness in the broader streams of philosophical thought need to be appreciated — as in C. Brown, *Jesus in European Protestant Thought, 1778-1860* (Durham, NC: Labyrinth, 1985); see also W. Baird, *History of New Testament Research*. Vol. One: *From Deism to Tübingen* (Minneapolis: Fortress, 1992). J. Riches, *A Century of New Testament Study* (Valley Forge: Trinity, 1993) chs. 1, 2, 6, and R. Morgan (with J. Barton), *Biblical Interpretation* (Oxford: Oxford University, 1988) contain many relevant insights. C. Allen, *The Human Christ: The Search for the Historical Jesus* (Oxford: Lion, 1998) provides a well-informed and easy-to-read account. W. Weaver, E. Baasland and J. H. Charlesworth are attempting to 'do a Schweitzer' on the twentieth century, of which only the first volume has been thus far produced: W. Weaver, *The Historical Jesus in the Twentieth Century, 1900-1950* (Harrisburg: Trinity, 1999). For a review of the most recent phase of the quest see especially B. Witherington, *The Jesus Quest: The Third Search for the Jew of Nazareth* (Downers Grove: InterVarsity, 1995); M. A. Powell, *Jesus as a Figure in History: How Modern Historians View the Man from Galilee* (Louisville: Westminster/John Knox, 1998); B. B. Scott, 'New Options in an Old Quest', in B. F. LeBeau, et al., eds., *The Historical Jesus through Catholic and Jewish Eyes* (Harrisburg: Trinity, 2000) 1-49; D. A. Hagner, 'An Analysis of Recent "Historical Jesus" Studies', in D. Cohn-Sherbok and J. M. Court, *Religious Diversity in the Graeco-Roman World: A Survey of Recent Scholarship* (Sheffield: Sheffield Academic, 2001) 81-106; D. S. Du Toit, 'Redefining Jesus: Current Trends in Jesus Research', in M. Labahn and A. Schmidt, eds., *Jesus, Mark and Q: The Teaching of Jesus and Its Earliest Records* (JSNTS 214; Sheffield: Sheffield Academic, 2001) 82-124. The fullest and most recent bibliographical surveys are W. R. Telford, 'Major Trends and Interpretive Issues in the Study of Jesus', in B. Chilton and C. A. Evans, eds., *Studying the Historical Jesus: Evaluations of the State of Current Research* (NTTS 19; Leiden: Brill, 1994) 33-74; C. A. Evans, *Life of Jesus Research: An Annotated Bibliography* (NTTS 24; Leiden: Brill, revised 1996); S. E. Porter, *The Criteria for Authenticity in*

Schweitzer was itself only part of a longer period of historical interest in and inquiry concerning the figure of Jesus, a period which stretches back before Schweitzer and, of course, forward since Schweitzer. That longer period has produced several landmark studies and advances, both classical statements of key issues, historical and methodological, which remain issues to this day, and important findings which still remain valid in large measure and therefore foundational for subsequent studies. These statements and findings need to be brought together, reassessed and restated, not least because the intellectual climate at the end of the twentieth century seems to have been generally hostile towards the idea that such statements and findings should still be able to claim assent today. Such reassessment and restatement will be one of the primary tasks of Part One.

Twenty-five years ago I taught a course on 'Faith and the Historical Jesus'. Over the years and particularly since once again focusing my full attention on the subject, the conviction has been strengthened that the quest is best analysed in terms of the tension and dialogue between faith and history, if we are to appreciate what was seen to be at stake in the various phases of the quest, and still today. In the intervening years I have become more fully aware of the hermeneutical dimension of that tension and dialogue. With that addition or qualification, it still seems to me that the history of the quest can be profitably analysed in terms of, first, 'the flight from dogma' and then 'the flight from history'.

My objectives in Part One are therefore threefold.

1. To recall the roots of the quest: that they reach back well before the Enlightenment. However much, in retrospect, the Enlightenment may have bent the young sapling of renewed historical interest in Jesus and Christianity's beginnings in a particular direction, there is no lack of stimulus and resource for the quest in the developments of pre-Enlightenment scholarship.

2. To note afresh both the genuine advances that have been made in the course of the quest, most of which should not be lightly abandoned, as well as the issues posed (historical, hermeneutical, theological) by the generally acknowledged classical contributions to the quest, most of which remain as issues today. In structuring my review in terms of 'the flight from dogma' and 'the flight from history', I am very conscious of imposing a particular schema on the data. I should emphasise, then, that I regard both 'flights' as uneven trends *(Tendenzen)* rather than consistent programmes or consciously chosen objectives. Also that the allocation of some authors to either 'flight' is more a matter of convenience than of justifiable critique.

Historical-Jesus Research: Previous Discussion and New Proposals (JSNTS 191; Sheffield: Sheffield Academic, 2000) ch. 1 (28-62).

Nevertheless, I hope that the heuristic value of observing the persistence and recurrence of these particular *Tendenzen* will outweigh the defects of the schema.

3. In chapters 3-5 my objective will be primarily descriptive. Only in chapter 6, having recognized the advances made and acknowledged the issues posed by the earlier phases of the quest (and earlier), do I attempt to set out 'my own stall', and to indicate and argue for the historical, hermeneutical, and theological principles which will inform my own attempt to describe the beginnings of Christianity in Jesus of Nazareth.

CHAPTER 3

The (Re-)Awakening of
Historical Awareness

The beginning of the 'quest of the historical Jesus' is usually traced quite properly to the European Enlightenment (c. 1650-1780) and the emergence of 'modernity'. It is important, however, to recognize that interest in historical inquiry
and in the human Jesus began much earlier. The more appropriate place to start is
with the Renaissance (the fourteenth to sixteenth centuries) and the Reformation
(the sixteenth century).

3.1. The Renaissance

The Renaissance is generally regarded as having begun in fourteenth-century Italy with the revival of the study of antiquity called for initially by Petrarch in particular.[1] Of course historical interest and inquiry did not begin with the Renaissance; one should beware both of idealizing the Renaissance and of exaggerating
the transition which it marked. Interest in the past, or perhaps more precisely,
concern to record the present or recent past as a way of informing and legitimating the present, goes back at least to the Greek historians Herodotus and
Thucydides.[2] Historical and biblical scholarship did not begin with the Renaissance.[3] However, it is also true that the Renaissance did bring about a new phase

---

1. D. Weinstein, 'Renaissance', *EncBr* 15.660.
2. E. B. Fryde, 'Historiography and Historical Methodology', *EncBr* 8.947.
3. See, e.g., B. Smalley, 'The Bible in the Medieval Schools', in G. W. H. Lampe, ed.,
The Cambridge History of the Bible. Vol. 2: *The West from the Fathers to the Reformation*
(Cambridge: Cambridge University, 1969) 197-220 (here 216-19).

in historical awareness in western Europe,[4] together with a growing fascination with and admiration for the classical past.[5]

It is at this period that we can see emerging a clear sense of the *pastness* of the past and the *otherness* of the past: the recognition that the past was not only *distant* from the present, but was also *different* from the present.[6] The rediscovery of the Greek classics in their original language (Greek began to be studied again in the West in the late fourteenth century) brought home to Renaissance man that the world unveiled in these texts was very different from that of the late mediaeval period. The manners and customs, the mode of government and law, the way of thinking about the cosmos and society were not as they are now in the present. This awareness naturally included a growing sense that during the intervening decades and centuries *change* had occurred. If these texts and the world of which they spoke were to be properly understood, therefore, such differences and changes had to be recognized and taken into account.

The classical texts had of course been familiar through mediaeval textbooks, digests, and compendia. But the urge to read the classics in their original tongue reinforced the sense of difference and change and gave birth to the new science of *historical philology*. Donald Weinstein describes the situation well.[7]

> It was Petrarch who first understood fully that antiquity was a civilisation apart and, understanding it, outlined a program of classically oriented studies that would lay bare its spirit. The focus of Petrarch's insight was language: if classical antiquity was to be understood in its own terms it would be through the speech with which the ancients had communicated their thoughts. This meant that the languages of antiquity had to be studied as the ancients had used them and not as vehicles for carrying modern thoughts.

What also emerged as essential to the task newly perceived was the further new science of *textual criticism,* the comparison of variant manuscripts, the correction of faulty or dubious passages, and the production of commentaries on the style, meaning and context of an author's thought. This naturally involved not

4. See particularly P. Burke, *The Renaissance Sense of the Past* (London: Edward Arnold, 1969).

5. See further Burke, *Renaissance* ch. 2; C. L. Stinger, *The Renaissance in Rome* (Bloomington: Indiana University, 1985) 59-76.

6. Burke defines the 'sense of history' as including three factors: the sense of anachronism, the awareness of evidence, and the interest in causation. On the first, elaborated as a 'sense of historical perspective, or sense of change, or sense of the past', he comments: 'Medieval men lacked a sense of the past being different in quality from the present'. 'Medieval society, ruled by custom, could not afford the awareness of the difference between past and present and the consequent irrelevance of precedent' (*Renaissance* 1, 19).

7. Weinstein, 'Renaissance' 664.

only mastery of the languages involved and command of a wider swath of classical literature, but also substantial knowledge of the culture which formed the original author's mind and influenced his writing.[8]

These concerns and developments thus gave rise to what can fairly be described as the first principles and methods of modern scholarly research into the history of Christian origins. The first *principle* was that such ancient texts had to be set in their correct historical setting and their language read in accordance with the grammatical and syntactical rules of the time, if they were to be properly understood. This constitutes in effect the first hermeneutical principle which emerged from the Renaissance's 'revival of learning': *historical texts have to be read first and foremost as historical texts.* The first modern scholarly *methods* properly speaking were twofold: (1) *historical philology,* the careful discerning of the meaning of words and sentences in the original language of the text by reference to the way these words and such sentences were used at the time of writing, and (2) *textual criticism,* the skill of reconstructing from the variant manuscripts available, so far as possible, the original texts, by identifying and correcting the corruptions caused by centuries of Christian transmission and editing. It was this principle and these methods which enabled Humanist scholars to expose mediaeval documents masquerading as classical authorities for the forgeries they were. The most famous and frequently cited example is Lorenzo Valla's demonstration on linguistic and historical grounds that the 'Donation of Constantine', which claimed to be a record of the privileges that Emperor Constantine conferred upon Pope Sylvester (313-35), his clergy and his successors, could not be genuine; it is generally reckoned to be an eighth-century fabrication.[9]

We do well to note and acknowledge the deep and continuing indebtedness of all students of ancient texts to the scholarship inaugurated in this period. The enduring fruits of this scholarship are preserved in the dictionaries and lexica and critical editions, constantly being refined in new editions in the light of further manuscript and inscriptional evidence, and forming essential reference works on the shelves of every library and scholar. These contain in compact, easily usable form, the findings of generations of careful and increasingly informed scholarship of the finest quality, magisterial judgments particularly regarding range of word usage and individual idiosyncrasies of style, such as no contemporary computer search could even begin to rival. Twenty-first-century students of these texts need to remember that they are standing on the shoulders of giants. Without

---

8. Ibid.

9. Fryde, 'Historiography' 952, with other examples. Burke cites Valla at length (*Renaissance* 55-58); see further on the development of a critical attitude towards evidence (7-13, 50-69).

having such basic groundwork in place, the rest of us would simply be unable to read and translate these texts in the first place and could have little confidence that the texts themselves available for use are close to what original authors wrote.

Precisely the same concerns motivated the first great advance in scholarship on the writings of the NT. It was the recognition that behind the thousand-year reign of the Latin Vulgate were texts in the original Hebrew and Greek, which led to Erasmus's edition of the Greek New Testament in 1516, from which all modern NT study in the West is derived.[10] Thus began a major enterprise for scholarly inquiry into the past, which is still fundamental to all critical engagement with the NT — the task of recovering the original text as written by the NT writers (so the task was first defined), or (as it is now perceived) the task of achieving as full a consensus as possible in regard to the text of the NT to be used in scholarly circles and as the basis for modern translations.[11] Here too no self-respecting student of the NT will be without a copy of the Bauer lexicon,[12] as an earlier generation had relied oñ Grimm-Thayer.[13] And here too it needs to be recalled that however close to the 'original' the modern *Greek New Testament* is (or is not), the first and unavoidable task of any NT scholar who wishes to speak about or to draw on that text is the task of *translation,* a translation which takes full account of the findings of these earlier generations of historical philology and textual criticism.

3.2. The Reformation

In a broader historical perspective the Reformation forms a seamless extension of the Renaissance. But from a Christian and theological perspective it naturally calls for separate treatment. And indeed we can identify the Reformation as marking a second phase in the developing historical awareness within western

10. E. G. Rupp, 'Desiderius Erasmus', *EncBr* 6.953.

11. See, e.g., W. G. Kümmel, *The New Testament: The History of the Investigation of Its Problems* (1970; Nashville: Abingdon, 1972/London: SCM, 1973) 40-50; and further K. and B. Aland, *The Text of the New Testament* (Grand Rapids: Eerdmans, [2]1989). The product of continuing refinement is K. Aland, et al., eds., *Novum Testamentum Graece* (Stuttgart: Deutsche Bibelstiftung, [26]1979, [27]1993) and/= *The Greek New Testament* (New York: United Bible Societies, [4]1993).

12. W. Bauer, *A Greek-English Lexicon of the New Testament and Other Early Christian Literature,* ET and ed. W. F. Arndt and F. W. Gingrich (Chicago: University of Chicago, 1957), revised and augmented by F. W. Gingrich and F. W. Danker (1979) = BAGD, third edition by F. W. Danker based on Bauer's sixth edition (2000) = BDAG.

13. C. L. W. Grimm and J. H. Thayer, *A Greek-English Lexicon of the New Testament* (Edinburgh: Clark, [4]1901).

Christendom. The Reformers were naturally interested in the *difference* of the past from the present, but not merely for apologetic reasons. They believed that the western church had itself *changed* from the church of Jesus' Apostles and the Fathers — changed not simply as a matter of historical process, but changed too far beyond the legitimation provided by NT, Apostles, and Fathers. For the Reformers, therefore, recognition of that difference was fundamental to their criticism of the changes which they believed had corrupted the church of Rome. In the so-called 'Radical Reformation' this criticism of present beliefs and ecclesiastical structures by reference to the axiomatic purity of the primitive church went much further, as its proponents sought to return to the simplicities of that primitive purity. And the so-called Counter-Reformation in its own way also recognized that historical change carried the unavoidable corollary of *semper reformanda* (always to be reformed). Integral to the internal debate within the western church of the sixteenth century, therefore, was a twofold recognition: first, that the tradition or visible form and practice of the church may at times need correction; and second, that *the past can provide grounds for proper criticism of (the abuses of) the present.*[14]

An integral part of the resulting debate was on the authority of the NT canon, and on how that authority functioned. Or to be more precise, the debate was on how the meaning of the NT writings may be perceived, in order that they may function as authority. Here already in 1496, John Colet, in his lectures on the Pauline letters at the University of Oxford, provided the paradigm for the Reformation, by maintaining that the text should be expounded simply in terms of its *literal sense* (as understood in its historical context) — the *sensus literalis*.[15] Martin Luther likewise insisted on the plain or literal or historical sense and dismissed mediaeval allegorizing as so much rubbish.[16] Most influen-

---

14. For bibliography on the Reformation and Counter-Reformation see *ODCC* 423-24, 1374-75. For the Radical Reformation see G. H. Williams, *The Radical Reformation* (London: Weidenfeld and Nicolson, 1962).

15. This should not be seen as a break with mediaeval interpretation, but as a prioritising of the literal sense, or indeed as a reassertion of the Antiochene Fathers' emphasis on the 'literal' meaning of the text as against the Alexandrines' openness to its polyvalency as expressed through 'allegorical' interpretation. J. H. Bentley, *Humanists and Holy Writ: New Testament Scholarship in the Renaissance* (Princeton: Princeton University, 1983), sums up Colet's significance thus: 'Though routinely hailed as a harbinger of Reformation exegesis, Colet's real achievement was simply to provide a running literal commentary in the patristic fashion, abandoning the late medieval style of exegesis, which often subordinated the scriptures to the needs of scholastic theology' (9-10); I owe the reference to my colleague Arnold Hunt.

16. See, e.g., the extracts in Kümmel, *New Testament*: 'all error arises out of paying no regard to the plain words'; 'This is the method I now employ, the final and best one: I convey the literal sense of Scripture. . . . Other interpretations, however appealing, are the work of fools' (23). See further A. C. Thiselton, *New Horizons in Hermeneutics* (London: Marshall

tial of all was John Calvin's emphasis on the plain meaning of the text, with his sequence of biblical commentaries providing classic examples of philological-historical interpretation.[17]

In what was in effect the first really serious clash between faith (as traditionally conceived) and history (as newly reconceived in Renaissance scholarship) we thus see the first conscious attempt to formulate a hermeneutical principle which reconciles the two. This in effect second principle and model for scholarly interpretation of the NT to emerge in the modern period, therefore, was a refinement of the first — *the primacy of the plain meaning of the text*[18] — always bearing in mind that the 'plain meaning' may include allegory or symbolism when the particular text is 'plainly' allegorical or symbolical.[19] A corollary to this principle was the Reformation conviction regarding the perspicacity of the NT, that is, the sufficiency of the NT to indicate its own interpretation when read in accord with its plain meaning — Scripture as *sui ipsius interpres* (self-

---

Pickering, 1992) 179-84, who also points out that Luther preferred the term 'plain' (or 'natural') meaning, though he did use the term 'literal' (184). In private correspondence (9.10.2000) Thiselton observes: 'Although it is true that he [Luther] dismissed mediaeval allegorising, . . . in his earlier work he was not above such "mediaeval allegorising" himself, and it was part of his developmental process of insight that as his work progressed he came to realise increasingly that such allegorising carried epistemological consequences which were unhelpful for a view of revelation'.

17. 'Calvin is even less tolerant of allegorical interpretation than Luther' (Thiselton, *New Horizons* 185). In the dedication of his commentary on Romans, Calvin explained his understanding of the work of an interpreter. 'Since it is almost his only task to unfold the mind of the writer whom he has undertaken to expound, he misses his mark, or at least strays outside his limits, by the extent to which he leads his readers away from the meaning of his author' (*Epistles of Paul the Apostle to the Romans and to the Thessalonians* [Edinburgh: Oliver and Boyd, 1961] 1). 'Let us know, then, that the true meaning of Scripture is the natural and simple one, and let us embrace and hold it resolutely. Let us not merely neglect as doubtful, but boldly set aside as deadly corruptions, those pretended expositions which lead us away from the literal sense' (*The Epistles of Paul to the Galatians, Ephesians, Philippians and Colossians* [Edinburgh: Oliver and Boyd, 1965] 85). But see also the careful study of K. E. Greene-McCreight, *Ad Litteram: How Augustine, Calvin, and Barth Read the "Plain Sense" of Genesis 1–3* (New York: Lang, 1999) ch. 3.

18. I have been using 'literal' in the still recognisable sense, 'Taking words in their usual or primary sense and employing the ordinary rules of grammar, without mysticism or allegory or metaphor' *(COD)*. But since in today's usage 'literal' often has a slightly pejorative overtone ('merely literal', 'literalist'), it may help avoid some confusion if we stick with the term 'plain' as a synonym.

19. This qualification, if that is what it is, was familiar from the early Patristic debates: 'The "literal" may include the use of metaphor or other figures of speech, if this is the meaning which the purpose of the author and the linguistic context suggest' (Thiselton, *New Horizons* 173, citing John Chrysostom; also 183). With regard to Calvin see further Greene-McCreight, *Ad Litteram* 96 and n. 8 (citing T. H. L. Parker), and the rest of that section (99-106).

interpreting).[20] The corollary, of course, was drawn out in argument with Rome and against Rome's insistence that the authority of the NT was exercised by the magisterium and through the tradition. In direct contrast, the Reformers insisted that the NT exercised its authority by being read in its plain meaning, whether the reading was by pope or priest or layman.

A second corollary of incalculable influence on the cultures of western Europe was the decision that the NT (and the Bible as a whole) should be made widely available (through the recently invented printing press) in the vernacular. We need only recall how influential the Luther Bible has been on modern German and the Tyndale (and later King James) version on modern English for the point to become clear. The first hermeneutical task of translation proved to be a bridge between past and present of importance far beyond the particular concerns of faith.

3.3. Perceptions of Jesus

What effect did all this have on the way Jesus was perceived? Somewhat surprisingly, the answer is Not very much. It might have been expected that the Renaissance would have marked an increased concern to restate the real humanness of Jesus, on the ground that the traditional belief in and emphasis on the deity of Christ had overshadowed his humanity. One need only think again of the portrayal of Christ as the ruler of the world *(Pantocrator)* so characteristic of Byzantine art and piety. In fact, however, in the West there was already a strong strand in late mediaeval spirituality very much concerned with the humanity of Christ and his sufferings. The early mediaeval portrayals of the crucifixion are characteristically formal and somehow unreal, more the expression of Christ's triumph *(Christus triumphans)* than of Christ's sufferings *(Christus patiens)*.[21] So much so that one can hardly avoid asking whether it is a real death which is being portrayed. But in the thirteenth century the growing influence of St. Francis and Franciscan piety saw a corresponding growth of interest in the humanity and passion of Jesus, endowing painting and poetry with 'a new realism'.[22]

The artistic transition is well illustrated in the work of Cimabue (c. 1240-1302), who provided frescoes for the upper church of St Francis at Assisi. In his

20. Kümmel, *New Testament* 22, and further 27-39.

21. G. Aulen maintains that 'Christus Victor' has been the 'classic' theological explanation of how Christ had accomplished human salvation (*Christus Victor: An Historical Study of the Three Main Types of the Idea of Atonement* [London: SPCK, 1931; new edition 1970]).

22. Pelikan, *Jesus* 139-40; D. Adams, 'Crucifix', in J. Turner, ed., *The Dictionary of Art* (London: Macmillan, 1996) 8.211-12; G. Finaldi, *The Image of Christ* (London: National Gallery, 2000) ch. 4.

'Crucifix' (in the 1290s) we begin to see an emotive intensity which causes the viewer to recognize that here was a man who did indeed suffer.[23] But many find the most striking (though by no means the first) example of brutally realistic iconography to be the Isenheim altarpiece of Grünewald, some two hundred years later. Here we are confronted with the historical reality of flagellated flesh and crucifixion in all its horror and grotesqueness. No impassive deity this! It is a historical curiosity, but worth noting nonetheless, that the Isenheim altarpiece of Grünewald was completed and the Greek New Testament of Erasmus produced in the same year, 1516, the year before Luther nailed his famous theses to the church door in Wittenberg (1517) and thus, in the event, launched the Reformation.

Where Renaissance concern to criticize the present in the light of the past made the greatest impact was in raising the question of what Jesus really intended so far as the church was concerned.[24] Here the tension between history (historical scholarship) and (traditional) faith began to become sharper and less comfortable. It was not yet a contrast, not yet a confrontation. The Reformers were reacting against what they perceived as ecclesiastical abuse, not against traditional faith in Christ, or traditional christology. On the contrary, it was important for them to reaffirm the central Christian dogmas regarding Jesus. If anything, they were more vehement against the Socinian denial of the deity of Christ than the Catholics.[25] As the Radical Reformation gave rise to extremes which threatened what the principal Reformers counted important, so any weakening of the christological dogmas would have been perceived not as a reformation of Christianity but as a threat to the very existence of Christianity itself.

The real confrontation between faith and history lay ahead.

23. J. R. Spencer, 'Cimabue', *EncBr* 4.616.

24. Seen particularly in the vigorous attempts by the Reformers to argue that the rock on which Christ promised to build his church (Matt. 16.18) was not Peter himself but Peter's faith in Christ (O. Cullmann, *Peter: Disciple, Apostle, Martyr* [London: SCM, [2]1962] 168).

25. See, e.g., H. L. Short, 'Unitarians and Universalists', *EncBr* 18.859-62 (here 860); Brown, *Jesus* 30-1.

CHAPTER 4

The Flight from Dogma

With the Enlightenment (c. 1650-1780), the tensions between faith and history became more polarised. It is from this period that most would date the beginning of the 'quest of the historical Jesus'. The quest itself has been punctuated by episodes and periods when the tensions between faith and history became unbearable and erupted into open conflict. Our overview will focus first on those phases when scholars of the quest attempted (in one degree or other) to distance themselves from the traditional claims of faith (this chapter), and then on those matching phases when scholars in reaction to the quest attempted to distance themselves from the newer claims of history (chapter 5). Here again I should stress that I am not attempting anything like a complete analysis of the much-analysed quest, but simply highlighting waymarks of particular significance and of continuing relevance for those still interested in pursuing such a quest.

4.1. The Enlightenment and Modernity

a. Scientific Criticism

The Enlightenment is the name usually given to that period in the West when scholars began to 'liberate' themselves from what was perceived as their enslavement and the enslavement of knowledge to established authority and tradition. The case of Galileo came to be archetypal: the fact that, despite his Catholic piety, he had been put on trial for heresy in Rome, found guilty of teaching Copernican 'doctrine' *(sic)* and compelled to recant (1633), epitomised the hegemony which theology was attempting to maintain over the new science and which became something intolerable to the Enlightenment scholar.[1] The philosophical basis was provided by René Descartes (1596-1650), who formulated the model of analytical (scientific, mathematical) reasoning, in which all accepted ideas and opinions are subjected to systematic doubt unless and until one is convinced by self-evident facts.[2] In essence, the Enlightenment signals the emergence of modern science and modern scientific method, where information about the world is to be discovered, not from the Bible or ecclesiastical or classical authority, but from the world itself, by means of careful observation and repeatable experiment.

Biblical scholars and theologians influenced by the Enlightenment followed the same logic. The new science increasingly became the paradigm of knowledge, replacing the old Bible. A concept of 'scientific criticism' began to be propounded whose task was to evaluate the records of the past in the light of modern scientific knowledge, free from what many regarded as the often ignorant and primitive superstitions which had previously clouded the present's perception of the past.[3] A third model for scholarly study of the pastness of Jesus was thus developed, the model of *scientific inquiry*, of investigation of the past following the paradigm provided by the emerging natural sciences.

b. Scientific History

As a concept, 'modernity' overlaps with 'Enlightenment'; it indicates the increasingly scientific perspective and secular frame of reference which has dominated intellectual activity in western Europe since the Enlightenment. But as a phase in Western intellectual history 'modernity' has long outlasted the Enlightenment and indeed stretched well into the 1960s.[4]

For the 'quest of the historical Jesus' the longest lasting effect of 'modernity' has been the application of the scientific paradigm to *history*. History itself came to be redefined as a science, which should proceed scientifically by devel-

1. On Galileo's significance see, e.g., I. G. Barbour, *Issues in Science and Religion* (London: SCM, 1966) 23-34.
2. L. J. Beck, 'Descartes, René', *EncBr* 5.597-602: since the one self-evident fact for he who doubts is that he doubts, and, as doubting, is thinking, the cornerstone of self-evident certainty is given by the famous formula *'Cogito, ergo sum'* ('I think, therefore I am').
3. P. L. Gardiner, 'History, Philosophy of', *EncBr* 8.962.
4. My colleague David Brown points out that both terms are used in narrow and broader senses. Narrowly the Enlightenment denotes only an eighteenth-century movement and modernism a twentieth. 'But both terms are commonly used in a wider sense, and one might as well say in that sense that their influence very much continues into the present, competing with postmodernism' (private communication, dated September 13, 2001).

oping hypotheses and discovering laws which would have explanatory power analogous to that of hypotheses and laws in the physical sciences — hence 'scientific history'.[5] Such 'scientific history' did not really emerge till the nineteenth century. In the earlier phase of modernity, as Ernst Troeltsch puts it, 'Historical facts were only useful "for illustration, not demonstration" and so could be surrendered to scientific criticism'.[6] But in the early nineteenth century historical method emerged as a powerful tool to reconstruct the past. In the 1830s Leopold von Ranke became the model for the master historian, and his famous formula, to describe 'how things really were', became the motto for a scientific and objective history.[7]

Strictly speaking, then, the quest of the 'historical Jesus' as such did not begin till the nineteenth century, when historical method became a tool to penetrate back behind the Christ of the present, the Christ of dogma and elaborated tradition, to the Jesus of the past, the original, the real Jesus. The 'historical Jesus' was, by definition, part of the historical, observable world; so what could be more natural than that the Gospel accounts of him should be analysed as one would analyse any account of the observable world? Thus the third model for scholarly study of the Christian records of Jesus, scientific inquiry, modulated into what became the tool which was to dominate the 'quest of the historical Jesus' for 150 years, *the historical-critical method.*

It is probably as well to take note at once of the hermeneutical assumptions behind the historical-critical method since they proved increasingly to be its Achilles' heel in the second half of the twentieth century.

(1) The first is that there is an objectivity in history (the past) which allows history (the discipline) to be treated on the analogy of the natural sciences; that is, historical facts are objects in history which could be uncovered or recovered by scientific method like so many archaeological artefacts *(Positivism).*

(2) A second assumption has been the correlative one, that the historian could be entirely impartial, strictly objective in his *(sic)* treatment of the historical facts, and could therefore avoid prejudicial value judgments *(Historicism).* Wholly unrecognized (and therefore unquestioned) were the fundamental assumptions that history was the 'grand narrative' of scientific progress, of a unified historical development culminating in the modernization of the Western

---

5. J. Appleby, L. Hunt, and M. Jacob, *Telling the Truth about History* (New York: Norton, 1994) chs. 1-2. See, e.g., E. Troeltsch, 'Historiography', *ERE* 6.716b-23a, particularly 717b-19a.

6. 'The Significance of the Historical Existence of Jesus for Faith', in R. Morgan and M. Pye, eds., *Ernst Troeltsch: Writings on Religion and Theology* (Louisville: Westminster/ John Knox, 1990) 182-207 (here 186).

7. Appleby, Hunt, and Jacob, *Telling the Truth* 67-68, 73-74. Troeltsch could speak of 'purely historical knowledge' ('Historiography' 718b).

world, and that such superimposed hermeneutical frameworks took the prevailing social order for granted and without criticism.[8]

(3) Behind these lay the Enlightenment assumption that human reason is sufficient measure of true and false fact. This was not initially intended as an irreligious or anti-religious sentiment, so long as reason was still understood as God-given. But the increasing secularism of modernity more and more reflected the triumph of autonomous human reason as axiomatic.

(4) Behind this in turn was the assumption, drawn from Isaac Newton's discovery of the universal laws of motion and gravity, that the cosmos is a single harmonious structure of forces and masses (itself an ancient conviction), and that the world is like an intricate machine following immutable laws, a closed system of cause and effect.[9] The inference was that all events are inherently predictable, the effects of causes already observable, and that therefore there is no room for divine intervention. Thus, to postulate divine intervention in any instance would undermine the whole principle of scientific inquiry and of history as a science.

It is easy now to see the weaknesses of these hermeneutical assumptions behind rationalising attempts to build a more effective bridge between the historical figure of Jesus and present faith. But it is important to realise that such assumptions pervaded more or less all scientific scholarship in the nineteenth century and remain influential at a hidden, presuppositional level of much popular scholarship today. At the same time, the need for historical inquiry and the beginnings of the development of historical method should not be linked exclusively to the Enlightenment or modernity. It is also important for the present study to recall again (from chapter 3) that the West's historical awareness and its recognition of the historical distance and difference of the past from the present did not begin with the Enlightenment. On the contrary, they go back at least two or three centuries to the Renaissance and to the West's re-awakening to its classical roots.[10] However much extra 'baggage' may be attached to 'the scientific method' of historical study, its basic rationale holds firm that 'The past is a foreign country: they do things differently there',[11] as does its basic

8. Appleby, Hunt, and Jacob, *Telling the Truth* 232; G. G. Iggers, *Historiography in the Twentieth Century: From Scientific Objectivity to the Postmodern Challenge* (Hanover: Wesleyan University, 1997) 23-30.

9. See again Barbour, *Issues in Science and Religion* 34-37, 56-60. In the early phase of the Enlightenment, a popular image of God was the retired architect, or divine clockmaker, who started the world and thereafter left it to run by the mechanism (natural laws) he had devised (40-43).

10. 'Wherever the culture of the Renaissance took root, there also modern history was evolved' (Troeltsch, 'Historiography' 717b).

11. The much-quoted first line of L. P. Hartley's Prologue to *The Go-Between* (London: Hamish Hamilton, 1953).

conviction of the continuing importance of distinguishing historical from unhistorical.

That said, however, the question remains whether a viable concept and
practice of 'historical method' can also be retrieved from the blinkered historicist
and positivist perspectives of modernity, from the narrowing rationalist and scientific assumptions of the Enlightenment. That is a question to which we shall
have to return (in chapter 6).

4.2. Exit Revelation and Miracle

From the perspective of faith the most dramatic and challenging conclusions to
emerge from the phase of 'scientific criticism' of the Gospel accounts of Jesus related to the fundamental concepts of *revelation* and *miracle*. Whereas reason had
previously been quiescent before the higher claims of revelation and the proofs of
miracle, now the roles were reversed and the claims of revelation and for miracle
were submitted to the judgment of reason. The account of miracle in the biblical
record received its first serious challenge from scientific criticism by Baruch/Ben-
edict Spinoza (1632-77).[12] And the first onslaught on traditional views of Jesus
was made by the English Deists, particularly Thomas Chubb (1679-1747).[13] But
the weight of the challenge to faith[14] can be best illustrated by reference to the two
classic texts which emerged subsequently, from Hermann Reimarus (1694-1768),
whose controversial work was published only posthumously,[15] and David

12. See particularly D. L. Dungan, *A History of the Synoptic Problem* (New York:
Doubleday, 1999) ch. 16 (here 212-13, 229-32).

13. See, e.g., Kümmel, *New Testament* 54-57; Baird, *History* 39-57. Despite his lack of
scholarship, Chubb can be hailed as 'the originator of the quest for the historical Jesus' (Allen,
Human Christ 76). For other points at which the Deists anticipated and influenced Reimarus
see Talbert's Introduction to *Reimarus* (n. 15 below) 14-18, and further Brown, *Jesus* 36-55.

14. David Brown has reminded me that 'faith' was a category which much of the Enlightenment rejected, preferring to speak rather of knowledge or belief; my continued use of the
term indicates my own perspective on this phase of the quest.

15. In seven fragments by G. Lessing (1774-78), of which the last and longest, 'Von dem
Zwecke Jesu und seiner Jünger', is available in ET, 'Concerning the Intention of Jesus and His
Teaching', edited by C. H. Talbert, *Reimarus Fragments* (Philadelphia: Fortress, 1970/London:
SCM, 1971); and G. W. Buchanan, *Hermann Samuel Reimarus: The Goal of Jesus and His Dis-
ciples* (Leiden: Brill, 1970). Typically, Schweitzer regarded Reimarus as the beginning of the
Quest, ignoring the English Deists. Schweitzer's evaluation of the fragment is also overblown:
'This essay is not only one of the greatest events in the history of criticism, it is also a master-
piece of world literature' (*Quest*[2] 15-16). It should be noted, however, that Schweitzer's high estimate of Reimarus followed from his conclusion that Reimarus 'was the first to grasp that the
world of thought in which Jesus moved historically was essentially eschatological' (*Quest*[2] 22).

Friedrich Strauss (1808-74), whose *Life of Jesus*[16] effectively destroyed his academic career.[17]

In both cases the hermeneutical assumptions produced a twofold criterion for analysing the historical value of the Gospels: *contradiction and consistency.*[18] Where texts seemed to contradict other texts[19] or were inconsistent with the universal laws which were now known to govern the course of events, the accounts in these texts should be judged unhistorical on scientific grounds. Here scientific criticism in effect was posed from the outset as a contradiction to the traditional claims of faith, a contradiction still seen as such by most scientifically educated people today.

Reimarus worked with a second criterion, that of *necessity:* an alleged revelation must contain knowledge not attainable by natural reason and be necessary to explain the evidence; that is, the evidence should not be explicable from natural causes.[20] In fact, however, he maintained, cases of alleged revelation were full of contradictions. Thus he was the first systematically to drive a wedge between Jesus and his disciples: in particular, the death of Jesus as a suffering saviour for all mankind contradicts the intention of Jesus and should be regarded as an invention subsequently by his disciples.[21] Jesus' *own* intention had actually been to 'awaken the Jews to the hope of a worldly Messiah' and a speedy deliverance; and his death marked the failure of that hope.[22] Reimarus' analysis of the contradictions in the various NT accounts of Jesus' resurrection has rarely been equalled by later sceptical criticism.[23] As for the alleged miracles on which

16. D. F. Strauss, *The Life of Jesus Critically Examined* (1835-36, [4]1840; ET by George Eliot, 1846, [2]1892; reprinted with Introduction by P. C. Hodgson, Philadelphia: Fortress, 1972/ London: SCM, 1973). Eliot's biographer notes that 'few books of the nineteenth century have had a profounder influence on religious thought in England' (G. Haight, *George Eliot: A Biography* [New York: Oxford University, 1968] 59).

17. Schweitzer, *Quest* ch. 7 ; see also H. Harris, *David Friedrich Strauss and His Theology* (Cambridge: Cambridge University, 1973); J. C. O'Neill, *The Bible's Authority: A Portrait Gallery of Thinkers from Lessing to Bultmann* (Edinburgh: Clark, 1991) 108-16; Baird, *History* 246-58; and the Introductions by Hodgson to Strauss's *Life* and by L. E. Keck to D. F. Strauss, *The Christ of Faith and the Jesus of History* (1865; ET Philadelphia: Fortress, 1977).

18. Talbert, *Reimarus* 13, 25-26; Strauss, *Life* 88-89.

19. Here Reimarus was in effect using the 'plain meaning' of the text as a weapon against Protestant orthodoxy.

20. Talbert, *Reimarus* 13-15. Here anticipated by the Deist John Tolland (Talbert, *Reimarus* 16-17).

21. Talbert, *Reimarus, e.g.,* 129, 134, 151. Here anticipated particularly by Chubb (extract in Kümmel, *New Testament* 55-56).

22. Talbert, *Reimarus* 135-50.

23. Talbert, *Reimarus* 153-200, here anticipated particularly by the Deist Peter Annet (Baird, *History* 49-50).

Christian apologetic had depended for centuries, they actually prove nothing, since the report of a miracle requires as much investigation as that which the miracle is supposed to prove.[24] In contrast, so far as Reimarus was concerned, Christianity's origin and spread could be explained historically on purely natural grounds, as the apostles sought by fraudulent means to revive and maintain their former success prior to Jesus' death.[25]

Here was scientific criticism being used as a scalpel to cut away the accretions of faith, falsifications which went back to Jesus' first disciples. And the challenge was posed systematically for the first, but by no means the last time: what was *Jesus'* aim as distinct from that of subsequent Christian claims regarding Jesus? was Jesus of Nazareth a wholly different figure from the one portrayed in the Gospels? Where claims to revelation could thus be bracketed out, on reasonable grounds, was not a christology 'from below' bound to be very different in character from a christology 'from above'?[26] And not least, what is the present-day reader to make of the contradictions and inconsistencies between the different Gospel accounts of Jesus? After Reimarus any straightforward harmonization of the Gospels was rendered simply incredible.

Between Reimarus and Strauss the miracles of Jesus became the focus of interest, and there were various attempts on rationalist premises to save the historicity of the Gospel accounts. Contradictions could be explained, by postulating, for example, that there were three different healings of blind men at Jericho.[27] The grosser elements of the supernatural could be stripped away, by arguing, for example, that the healing of lepers or blind happened over time rather than instantaneously. Alternatively the entire event could be given a natural explanation: the storm on the sea of Galilee was stilled because the boat rounded a headland;[28] Jesus appeared to be walking on the water but was actually on the shore (the boat was closer to shore than the account records), or was balancing on a raft; the feeding of the 5000 was possible because the young lad of John 6.9 shamed the rest into sharing their picnic boxes (a still popular rationalisation), or (my personal favourite) Jesus stood in front of a cave where other members of the Essene order had previously stored loaves and simply doled them out.[29] Most of these, it

24. Talbert, *Reimarus* 230, here anticipated particularly by the Deist Thomas Woolston (Baird, *History* 45-49).

25. Talbert, *Reimarus* 240-69.

26. By 'christology from below' is usually meant the attempt to assess the significance of Jesus from the data of the Gospels historically evaluated rather than from the creedal assumption that Jesus was God become man.

27. See Strauss's merciless analysis of the solutions then being canvassed (*Life* 441-44).

28. Never mind that the sea of Galilee has no headlands to speak of!

29. The examples are drawn principally from Schweitzer, *Quest*[1] 41, 52 = *Quest*[2] 40, 50-51; see further Brown, *Jesus* 163-72.

should be noted, were not expressions of unfaith: on the contrary, they were attempts to retain faith in a world where science was becoming the established paradigm for all knowledge and therefore provided the governing hermeneutical principle. The fact that rationalisations of the reported miracles of Jesus are still common in the literature and sermons of today reveals both the unease which many Christians continue to feel over at least some of the miracles attributed to Jesus and the continuing influence of the scientific paradigm.

Strauss accepted the same rationalist presupposition that miracles do not happen: to postulate such occasional (arbitrary?) divine intervention would undermine the fundamental principle of scientific inquiry, depending as it does on being able to assume the regularity and consistency of the laws of nature.[30] But he made the acute observation that attempts to retain the miraculous by setting aside details of the account meant abandoning the text without making it any more credible; and attempts to retain the historicity of the account by removing the miracle *in toto* actually *destroyed the whole point and significance of the account.* Where the text clearly intended to relate a miracle, what was gained by denying what the text affirmed? The attempt to save the *history* behind the text was actually destroying the *text* itself. Rather than attempt to explain (away) the history behind the text, the primary endeavour should be to explain how the text came about. Where others began by asking how the *event* related could have taken place, Strauss began by asking whence arose the *narrative* of the miraculous event.[31]

His own solution is summed up in the word *'myth'*, the first time the term enters the quest as a major factor. For Strauss, 'myth' was an expression or embodiment of an idea; in the Gospels, myth is the expression of the first Christians' idea of Christ. It is the idea which gives rise to the account; the narrative is created out of the idea.[32] Such narrative embodiments (myths) of ideas regarding

30. Defence of miracles from the side of faith have typically taken too little account of what divine intervention would involve, given that the interlocking character of natural processes and phenomena may mean that a butterfly's passage in South America can be a contributory factor in a windstorm over Galilee. A subsequent solution has been to abandon the definition of miracle as 'divine intervention', but this still leaves the theological problem of the seeming arbitrariness of God, who can somehow 'manipulate' causes and effects to 'save' some but not others.

31. Strauss states his basic case at once (*Life* 40); good examples on 500-501, 546.

32. Strauss's clearest definition is given in his later *A New Life of Jesus* (1864; ET London: Williams and Norgate, ²1879): 'The Myth, in its original form, is not the conscious and intentional invention of an individual but a production of the common consciousness of a people or a religious circle, which an individual does indeed first enunciate, but which meets with belief for the very reason that such an individual is but the organ of this universal conviction. It is not a covering in which a clever man clothes an idea which arises in him for the use and benefit of the ignorant multitudes, but it is only simultaneously with the narrative, nay, in the very form of the narrative which he tells that he becomes conscious of the idea which he is not yet able to apprehend purely as such' (1.206).

Christ had already been identified in relation to the beginning and end events of Jesus' life; the step Strauss took was to extend this theory of myth to the whole of Jesus' life.[33] Some of the Gospel accounts he designated as historical myths, mythical elements having entwined themselves round a historical event. Jesus' baptism was a good illustration, the historical event of Jesus' baptism having been elaborated by the account of the heavens opening, the heavenly voice and the Spirit descending as a dove. Others he regarded as pure myths, with no correspondence in historical fact. For example, the account of Jesus' transfiguration developed from the idea that Jesus was a new Moses.[34] Behind them all was the idea of Jesus, Jesus perceived by his disciples as Messiah and as therefore fulfilling the expectations for the Messiah then current, albeit modified by the impression left upon the disciples by Jesus' personal character, actions, and fate. In Strauss, however, this idea is transposed into the ideal of God-manhood which transcends the particularity of Christ. It was that ideal which really mattered for Strauss; the historical figure as such was no longer of importance.[35]

The brevity of such an account can never even begin to do justice to the amazingly detailed critique of each of the Gospel narratives which Strauss accomplished. His work needs to be savoured for itself. As Schweitzer observed, those who think that Strauss can be easily dismissed simply demonstrate that they have never read him with care.[36] Because he proved such a controversial figure,[37] his significance is hard to measure adequately. But three points should be noted in particular. (1) Strauss was the first in the hermeneutical debate regarding the Jesus of history to stress *the importance of recognizing the intention of the text* (to narrate a miracle) before any attempt to inquire into the event behind the text — even if he in turn attempted to inquire behind the evident intention to a deeper rationale. It should not escape notice that Strauss's mythical interpretation of the Gospel texts was the Enlightenment equivalent of the patristic and mediaeval resort to other than literal interpretations in order, *inter alia,* to resolve the inconsistencies on the surface level of the text. (2) Strauss's work heightened

33. Strauss, *Life* 65.

34. Strauss, *Life* 86-87, 242-46 (baptism), 540-46 (transfiguration).

35. Strauss, *Life* 780-81. Karl Barth credited Strauss with the distinction of being 'the first to bring to the notice of theology . . . the problem of God's revelation in history' (*From Rousseau to Ritschl* [London: SCM, 1959] 363, also 388).

36. 'If these [rationalist explanations of Jesus' miracles] continue to haunt present-day theology, it is only as ghosts, which can be put to flight by simply pronouncing the name of David Friedrich Strauss, and which would long ago have ceased to walk if the theologians who regard Strauss's book as obsolete would only take the trouble to read it' (Schweitzer, *Quest*[1] 84 = *Quest*[2] 80). Baird classifies Strauss's *Life* as 'the most revolutionary religious document written since Luther's Ninety-Five Theses' (*History* 246).

37. On a plaque in the Tübingen Stift Strauss is commemorated as 'Ärgernis und Anstoss für Theologie und Kirche'.

the embarrassment which typical Enlightenment believers now experienced in regard to the *miracles* of the Gospels. It is little surprise that the reports of Jesus' miracles featured so little in the next hundred years of the critical quest. Strauss had effectively knocked them out of the ring. (3) In their flight from the Christ of dogma, both Reimarus and Strauss had not escaped into anything that might be called objective history, but simply into a different ideology, the ideology of rationalism on the one hand and the ideology of idealism on the other. They therefore stand as cautionary reminders that critical scholarship is never critical enough unless and until it is also *self-critical* and with equal vigour.

It is also important, finally, to recognize that despite their radical criticism, Reimarus and Strauss have remained part of the tradition of scholarly inquiry regarding the Gospels. Such questioning and challenge is inherently healthy and helps keep the scholarly inquiry honest: there are hard questions in all this which cannot and must not be avoided. Reimarus and Strauss should be compulsory texts for any course on Jesus of Nazareth, not simply as part of the story of the quest itself, but because the issues they pose remain issues to this day, and it is good not least for those coming from the faith side of the faith/history dialogue to experience again something of the shock which these texts caused when they were first published. Moreover, dialogue with the heirs of Reimarus and Strauss is one of the activities which helps theology to maintain a place within the public forum of university-level search for knowledge and debate about truth.[38] If theology wants to continue to make any kind of truth claims of relevance beyond the confines of the churches, then it has to make them within that public forum. The alternative is to settle back into an internal ecclesiastical discourse which cannot be understood or effectively communicated outside the *ekklesia*.

4.3. The Liberal Jesus

The heavy emphasis on reason in Enlightenment rationalism was bound to create a reaction. The debate about epistemology (how we know things) had been primarily between the respective roles (and reliability) of reason and sense perception. But there is also the knowing of personal engagement with and relationship with, the knowing of the heart. As Pascal put it early in the Enlightenment's heyday: 'The heart has its reasons which reason knows nothing of'.[39] In church circles, German pietism[40] and the evangelical awakening in England led

38. Cf. Riches, *Century of New Testament Study* 4.

39. Pascal, *Pensées* 4.277.

40. Well illustrated by the pietistic warmth which J. A. Bengel added to the technical skills of textual criticism in the Preface to his *Gnomon Novi Testamenti* (1752).

by John Wesley[41] were already emphasising the importance of religious experience for lively faith. But the wider reaction came to fullest flower in the Romantic revival.

The 'Romantic movement' is the name usually given to a new emphasis placed on the experience of profound inner emotion as the wellspring of inspiration and creativity in artists, on feeling as affording an immediate experience of reality. In the words of the nineteenth-century French poet Charles Baudelaire, 'Romanticism is precisely situated neither in choice of subjects nor in exact truth, but in mode of feeling'.[42] We need think only of the passion in Beeethoven's music, of the emotional intensity of Schubert's Lieder, or of Wordsworth's description of poetry as 'the spontaneous overflow of powerful feelings',[43] to gain a sense of what was felt to be at stake. In literary criticism, including the appropriation of historical writings, the corresponding hermeneutical principle was the objective of entering into the creative experience of inspiration from which the writing was born, calling for a sense of psychological empathy with the author as creator, interpretation as re-creation of the creative act. This at least is the way the matter was formulated by Friedrich Schleiermacher, generally acknowledged to be the founder of modern hermeneutics.[44]

It was principally through Schleiermacher that the influence of Romanticism entered theology; for him it came as a welcome ally to (or replacement for) his youthful pietism. In his apologetic work *On Religion: Speeches to Its Cultured Despisers* (1799) he was able to appeal to the Romantics with the argument that religion is 'the sum of all higher feelings'.[45] And in his major

---

41. Wesley's 'Aldersgate Street experience' in 1738 ('I felt my heart strangely warmed') typified the pietistic/evangelical emphasis on the religion of the heart as against the religion of the head which was more characteristic of the rationalism of a Bishop Butler; for Butler's famous remark to John Wesley, 'Sir, the pretending to extraordinary revelations and gifts of the Holy Spirit is a horrid thing, a very horrid thing', see R. A. Knox, *Enthusiasm* (Oxford: Oxford University, 1950) 450.

42. R. D. Middleton, 'Visual Arts, Western', *EncBr* 19.444.

43. Preface to the second edition (1802) of his *Lyrical Ballads*.

44. F. D. E. Schleiermacher, in his ground-breaking lectures on hermeneutics (1810-34): '. . . understanding a speech always involves two moments: to understand what is said in the context of the language with its possibilities, and to understand it as a fact in the thinking of the speaker'; what he distinguishes later as 'the historical and divinatory, objective and subjective reconstruction of a given statement'; 'By leading the interpreter to transform himself, so to speak, into the author, the divinatory method seeks to gain an immediate comprehension of the author as an individual' (quotations from K. Mueller-Vollmer, *The Hermeneutics Reader* [New York: Continuum, 1994] 74, 83-84, 96; see also Mueller-Vollmer's Introduction 8-12).

45. (ET London: Routledge and Kegan Paul, 1893) 85. 'The sum total of religion is to feel that, in its highest unity, all that moves us in feeling is one; . . . to feel, that is to say, that our being and living is a being and living in and through God' (49-50).

work on *The Christian Faith* (1821-22) he expounded Christianity in terms of the 'feeling of absolute dependence'.[46] Not surprisingly, he proceeds to characterize Jesus as the historical actualization of the ideal, distinguished from the rest of men only by 'the constant potency of his God-consciousness, which was a veritable existence of God in him'.[47] And in the phase of the 'quest of the historical Jesus' which took its lead from Schleiermacher, usually known as Liberal Protestantism in view of its continued reaction against traditional dogma, a major focus was on Jesus' own religious feelings, on Jesus as a 'religious personality'. Back from the religion *about* Jesus to the religion *of* Jesus! This was characteristically expressed in Wilhelm Herrmann's confidence in being able to speak meaningfully about 'the inner life of Jesus' as the basis for the communion of the Christian with God,[48] and in the sustained interest in the 'messianic consciousness' of the 'historical Jesus' as a basis for subsequent christology.[49]

The other major influence on Liberal Protestantism was Immanuel Kant's shift of focus from faith to moral consciousness, man's sense of moral obligation (the categorical imperative).[50] For Kant the proper sphere for religion was not so much metaphysics as morality; it was man's awareness of a moral law that enabled him to postulate a Being who will rectify all in the end.[51] The influence of Kant is evident in the description of the work of the leading Liberal Protestant theologian (Albrecht Ritschl) as 'the theology of moral values'.[52]

This tendency was strengthened in the latter half of the nineteenth century by the influence of Darwin's theory of evolution. Allied to the self-confidence in European civilisation of the period, the general assumption was that evolution is always to 'higher forms' of life, and the corollary was too often uncritically drawn that *moral* evolution is a natural continuation of the biological process. Hence the *laissez-faire* policies of liberal economics, the sense of moral superiority among the European imperialist powers, and the easy assumption of the

46. [2]1830; ET Edinburgh: Clark, 1928, 12-18. Brown prefers to translate *das schlechthinnige Abhängigkeitsgefühl* as 'awareness, sense or consciousness of absolute, utter or ultimate dependence' (*Jesus* 116).

47. *Christian Faith* 377-89. In his lectures on *The Life of Jesus* in 1832 (1864; ET Philadelphia: Fortress, 1975) see 88-104, 263-76.

48. W. Herrmann, *The Communion of the Christian with God* ([2]1892; ET 1906, ed. R. T. Voelkel, Philadelphia: Fortress, 1971/London: SCM, 1972).

49. See particularly W. Baldensperger, *Das Selbstbewusstsein Jesu im Lichte der messianischen Hoffnungen seiner Zeit* (Strassburg: Heitz, 1888).

50. The categorical imperative: 'Act only according to that maxim by which you can at the same time will that it should become a universal law' (documented by Brown, *Jesus* 60).

51. See further Brown, *Jesus* 58-67.

52. The phrase used by H. R. Mackintosh, *Types of Modern Theology: Schleiermacher to Barth* (Edinburgh: Clark, 1937) for his chapter on Ritschl (138-80).

rightness of higher and lower orders in society. The attitude is nicely caught in Coué's famous self-help prescription: 'Every day, in every way, I am getting better and better'.[53]

In terms of 'Life of Jesus' research, the most luscious fruit of the Romantic spirit was Ernest Rénan's *Life* (1863).[54] Not only was it the first of the Liberal lives to be published,[55] but it was the first thorough Catholic treatment,[56] and the first of the histories of Christianity's beginnings to engage fully in the 'quest of the historical Jesus'. The book went through an unprecedented sixty-one editions in France and was quickly translated into all the major European languages.[57] In prose designed to charm and win rather than to argue and persuade, Rénan painted a picture of Jesus in classic Liberal terms. 'The highest consciousness of God which has existed in the bosom of humanity was that of Jesus'. Jesus' 'great act of originality' was that, probably from the first, 'he regarded his relationship with God as that of a son with his father'. 'Boldly raising himself above the prejudices of his nation, he established the universal fatherhood of God'. 'The morality of the Gospels remains . . . the highest creation of human conscience — the most beautiful code of perfect life that any moralist has traced'. 'A pure worship, a religion without priests and external observances, resting entirely on the feelings of the heart, on the imitation of God, on the direct relation of the conscience with the heavenly Father . . .'. 'An absolutely new idea, the idea of worship founded on purity of heart, and on human brotherhood, through him entered the world'.[58]

Towards the end of Liberalism's heyday came the contribution of the doyen of NT Liberal scholars, equally famous but more enduring in influence. These were the lectures on Christianity, delivered by Adolf Harnack without manuscript or notes, to some six hundred students from all the faculties in the University of Berlin at the turn of the century, at the height of his own powers and at the self-

---

53. E. Coué, *De la suggestion et de ses applications* (1915), to be said fifteen to twenty times, morning and evening (p. 17).

54. E. Rénan, *La vie de Jésus* (1863), ET *The Life of Jesus* (London: Trübner, 1864).

55. Schleiermacher's lectures were not published till 1864 (n. 47 above).

56. B. Reardon, *Liberalism and Tradition: Aspects of Catholic Thought in Nineteenth-Century France* (Cambridge: Cambridge University, 1975), described the publication as 'one of the events of the century' (296). The Pope placed it on the Index.

57. In his 1864 *Life* Strauss hailed Rénan as a kindred spirit and 'shook hands with him across the Rhine' (*Quest*[1] 191 = *Quest*[2] 167). Schweitzer described it as 'an event in world literature' (*Quest*[2] 159).

58. Rénan, *Life* 82-83, 87-88, 90. For D. Georgi, Rénan illustrates the tendency of the nineteenth-century quest to portray Jesus as a rural romantic hero 'full of unspoiled naiveté but at the same time full of dignity and wisdom, the ideal image of bourgeois nostalgia' ('The Interest in Life of Jesus Theology as a Paradigm for the Social History of Biblical Criticism', *HTR* 85 [1992] 51-83 [here 78]).

consciously high point of European and German culture.[59] In these lectures Harnack deliberately turned his back on the Christ of dogma. Christianity indeed must be rescued from its dependence on metaphysics and philosophy; the dogma had been too much influenced by Greek philosophy. What was needed now was a rediscovery of the simplicity and freedom of the gospel which Jesus himself had preached. Here for Harnack was 'the essence of Christianity' — the 'historical Jesus' encountered through the Gospels in his own religion and message. And what was that essence? Harnack summed up Jesus' gospel as centring on the fatherhood of God, the infinite value of the human soul, and the importance of love, regularly popularized thereafter as 'the fatherhood of God and the brotherhood of man'.[60] These were Jesus' enduring insights, what was of permanent value when abstracted from the merely transitory. According to Harnack, 'true faith in Jesus is not a matter of credal orthodoxy but of doing as he did'.[61]

What was at stake in all this at the fundamental level of human self-understanding and motivation is profound. Kant, we may say, had made room for morality (and even faith) beyond the limitations of science and knowing.[62] Schleiermacher had added a third category, religion and feeling. How these are to be related and inter-related is the stuff of philosophy, and whether, for example, a reassertion of the importance of the experience of inspiration, of what some now call 'epiphany' (not to mention conscience), can still hold open the door to a realistic concept of revelation, is a question of moment, on which human knowledge and self-understanding, human being and well-being, and not just Christianity itself, are dependent more than is usually appreciated. Since historical knowledge and hermeneutics are also dependent on such questions, questers of the 'historical Jesus' and readers of the Gospels at academic level need to be aware of the deep philosophical assumptions on which particular hypotheses are based and the unresolved epistemological issues and debates continuously rumbling below the surface. In this case, the most important hermeneutical principle at work was in effect the conviction that Jesus, the 'historical Jesus', the Jesus stripped of

59. A. Harnack, *Das Wesen des Christentums* (1900), ET *What Is Christianity?* (London: Williams and Norgate, 1901, [3]1904) compiled from a listener's shorthand record.

60. The 'essence' of Jesus' message variously summarized in *What Is Christianity?* 52-76. Harnack recognised the importance of 'the kingdom of God and its coming' in Jesus' message, but regarded it as 'a spiritual force, a power which sinks into a man within, and can be understood only from within', 'a purely religious blessing, the inner link with the living God', 'the most important experience that a man can have' (63-64). The next few pages show what Harnack thought was the true essence (65-72). Cf. the earlier summaries of Jesus' teaching by Kant and J. G. Herder (Brown, *Jesus* 65, 72; Kümmel, *New Testament* 83).

61. This is W. R. Matthews' summary of *What Is Christianity?* 149-52 in the fifth edition (London: Benn, 1958) x.

62. Kant's *Critique of Pure Reason* opens with the declaration that he wishes to 'abolish knowledge in order to make room for faith' (I owe the reference to my colleague David Brown).

dogmatic accretion, would/must have something to say to modern man, and the consequential desire to provide a mouthpiece for the restatement of that message.[63]

And the result? A Jesus portrayed and understood as a teacher of timeless morality, Jesus as a good example, Jesus as more the first Christian than the Christ — a flight from the Christ of dogma indeed! At the same time, we should not decry the Liberal focus on the moral outcome of religion as the test of its character; such concerns had brought the slave trade to an end and achieved political, social and industrial reforms, although the Liberal tendency to understand morality solely in terms of personal and individual responsibility was the stronger influence, and the *laissez-faire* economics and imperialist hubris of the late nineteenth and early twentieth centuries seem to have been little affected. Moreover, the reassertion of the importance of feeling in religion, of faith as a deeply rooted passion, was surely an important correction to a Protestantism still inclined to be too word-focused and still overly dependent on the Enlightenment paradigm of science and reason. Not least Liberal scholarship deserves credit for its concern to speak meaningfully to its own age. Here too the motivating force in life of Jesus scholarship was not unfaith but desire to speak in the idioms of the time, desire to be heard. The trouble was, we may say, it allowed the spirit of the age to dictate not simply the language but also the agenda.

But the most important achievement of the Liberal quest for Jesus has still to be noted.

4.4. The Sources for Critical Reconstruction of the Life of Jesus

All the thrust of historical scholarship from the Renaissance onwards had been to recover original texts and sources. The Enlightenment had thought to redefine and sharpen the tools of critical scholarship. The Romantic revival had shifted attention to the mysterious character of the fact and moment of inspiration. All this intensified Liberal interest in the Gospels as the only realistic sources for knowledge of the 'historical Jesus'. Jesus himself, after all, had left no writings, no pronouncements or reflections in his own hand or dictated by him, which for Liberal

---

63. 'Liberal scholarship . . . accepted the full burden of historical-critical scholarship without hesitation and without reserve, believing that the historical core of the gospel narratives, when reached, would reveal Jesus as he actually was, and that he would then be revealed as worthy of all honour, respect and imitation, revealed as the founder of a faith which consisted in following him and his teaching closely and purposefully' (N. Perrin, *Rediscovering the Teaching of Jesus* [London: SCM, 1967] 214).

sentiment would have provided the only sure access to his inner life. All that was available was contained in the four Gospels of the NT. But what kind of sources are they? Are they all of the same order and equally reliable? Up until the nineteenth century the four Gospels had been considered equally valid sources for historical information about Jesus. By harmonizing the different accounts and weaving them together a single picture could be formed. But now intensive study led to a revised estimate.

a. John's Gospel

As late as 1832 Schleiermacher was able to use John's Gospel as not only a source but the primary source for his *Life of Jesus*. It was precisely the Fourth Gospel's portrayal of a Jesus deeply conscious of his relation as Son to God as Father which substantiated Schleiermacher's focus on Jesus' 'God-consciousness'.[64] But ironically by the time Schleiermacher's lectures were published (1864) his major prop had been undermined. The differences between John and the other three Gospels, particularly as regards the chronology of the passion, had been a long-standing problem,[65] but considered resolvable even if never fully resolved. But Strauss had posed a serious challenge especially to the authenticity of the Johannine discourses.[66] And in 1847 F. C. Baur produced a powerful case for his conclusion that the Fourth Gospel was never intended to be 'a strictly historical Gospel'.[67]

Given the strength of Baur's critique, the inevitable conclusion could hardly be avoided: John's Gospel is determined much more by John's own theological than by historical concerns. Consequently it cannot be regarded as a good source for the life of Jesus. The conclusion by no means became established straight away.[68] But for those at the forefront of the 'quest of the historical Jesus'

64. 'What John represents as the content of the discourses of Christ must have been what Christ really said, and there is no reason to believe that John introduced any of his own ideas into Christ's discourses' (Schleiermacher, *Life* 262).

65. The differences between John's Gospel and the first three had been emphasized by Griesbach's *Synopsis* in 1776 (see n. 72 below) and by Lessing's reference to John's Gospel as a quite separate category from the other three (1778). 'It belongs to a class all of its own' (H. Chadwick, *Lessing's Theological Writings* [London: Black, 1956] 21 and 79). See also Kümmel, *New Testament* 85-86.

66. Strauss, *Life* 381-86; other extracts in Kümmel, *New Testament* 124-26. See also Strauss's *Christ of Faith* 38-47.

67. F. C. Baur, *Kritische Untersuchungen über die kanonische Evangelien* (Tübingen, 1847); extracts in Kümmel, *New Testament* 137-38.

68. Schweitzer notes several German scholars, including Neander and Ewald, who continued to use the Gospel of John as the authentic framework for the life of Jesus (*Quest*[1] 115-18 = *Quest*[2] 105-107). Typical of the still sustained traditional apologetic in Britain was

the die had been cast.[69] The differences between John and the others, which had previously been glossed over, could no longer be ignored. It was no longer possible to treat all four Gospels on the same level. If the first three Gospels were historical, albeit in qualified measure,[70] then such were these differences that John's Gospel could no longer be regarded as historical. Over the next hundred years the character of John's Gospel as a theological, rather than a historical document, became more and more axiomatic for NT scholarship.[71] Like the miracles of Jesus, though not quite so decisively, the Fourth Gospel had been effectively knocked out of the quest.

b. The Two-Document Hypothesis

The excision of John from the historical source material allowed attention to focus more fully on the other three Gospels. The degree of similarity between these three made their combined contrast with the Fourth Gospel all the more noticeable. It was already appreciated that the considerable overlap of material allowed the three to be set out in parallel and looked at together — hence their common designation as 'Synoptic' (looked at together) Gospels and the title of a book which sets out the three in parallel as a 'Synopsis'.[72] From early centuries it had been assumed that the canonical order of the Gospels was also the historical order, that Matthew was the earliest Gospel, and that Mark had been able to use Matthew, and Luke to use both. But now the urge to find the earliest source or sources for the life of Jesus and the more careful examination of the Synoptic parallels resulted in a crucial conclusion: that in and behind the Synoptic Gospels lay not just one but two primary sources; (1) Mark was the oldest of the three Synoptics and was used by both Matthew and Luke; and (2) Matthew and Luke also used a second source, consisting principally of sayings of Jesus (which came to be designated Q, presumably from the German *Quelle* =

H. P. Liddon, who, in his 1866 Bampton Lectures, *The Divinity of Our Lord and Saviour Jesus Christ* (London: Rivingtons, [2]1868), expounds 'Our Lord's Divinity as witnessed by his consciousness — St John 10.33' (Lecture IV); cf. also B. F. Westcott, *The Gospel According to St. John* (London: Murray, [2]1881). And see Schweitzer, *Quest*[1] 218-19 = *Quest*[2] 185-87.

69. Schweitzer also notes that 'toward the end of the 1870s the rejection of the Fourth Gospel as a historical source was almost universally recognized in the critical camp' (*Quest*[2] 503 n. 21).

70. Baur recognized that each Gospel had its own *Tendenz* (Kümmel, *New Testament* 137-39).

71. Baur's demonstration that the Synoptics are superior as historical sources to John 'belongs to the abiding results of New Testament research' (Kümmel, *New Testament* 139).

72. First used by J. J. Griesbach in 1776 (see Kümmel, *New Testament* 74-75 and n. 88).

'source').[73] The case is generally reckoned to have been firmly established for German scholarship by H. J. Holtzmann in 1863 (when he was just 31),[74] though the case he made for Markan priority was less effective than has usually been appreciated, and the full significance of Q was not grasped initially.[75] In any case, English-speaking readers have generally depended on the much later treatment by B. H. Streeter.[76]

The basic considerations adduced by Holtzmann have remained more or less the same since.[77] For the priority of Mark three features told in particular. (1) The fact that so much of Mark appears also in Matthew and Luke: Holtzmann reckoned that only thirty Markan verses do not appear in the other two Gospels. (2) The order of episodes: when the three Gospels are compared, in each case it appears that the Markan order is primary. (3) The form of the episodes: likewise when the three Gospels are compared, again and again the Markan version seems to be more primitive. For the existence of Q two features proved most significant. (1) The principal fact that some two hundred verses in Matthew and Luke are substantially the same or virtually identical, including some doublets with sayings in Mark.[78] (2) Whereas the Q material has been grouped by Matthew in several composite discourses, it is scattered through Luke.[79] Taken to-

---

73. F. Neirynck attributes the introduction of the term 'Q' into the debate on Synoptic sources (as shorthand for the Logia source) to E. Simon in 1880 ('Note on the Siglum Q', *Evangelica II* [BETL 99; Leuven: Leuven University, 1991] 474); see further D. Lührmann, 'Q: Sayings of Jesus or Logia?', in R. A. Piper, ed., *The Gospel behind the Gospels: Current Studies on Q* (NovTSup 75; Leiden: Brill, 1995) 97-116.

74. H. J. Holtzmann, *Die synoptischen Evangelien: ihr Ursprung und ihr geschichtlicher Charakter* (Leipzig: Englemann, 1863). Holtzmann did not use the symbol 'Q' but referred to the 'Logia' or 'Sayings collection' *(Spruchsammlung)*. For the broader picture, see Dungan, *History* 326-32.

75. J. S. Kloppenborg Verbin, *Excavating Q: The History and Setting of the Sayings Gospel* (Minneapolis: Fortress, 2000) 300-309.

76. B. H. Streeter, *The Four Gospels: A Study of Origins* (London: Macmillan, 1924). Streeter was building on the work of Oxford scholars, particularly J. C. Hawkins, *Horae Synopticae: Contributions to the Study of the Synoptic Problem* (Oxford: Clarendon, 1898, [2]1909), and W. Sanday, ed., *Studies in the Synoptic Problem* (Oxford: Clarendon, 1911), carried on independently of the earlier German work (Holtzmann does not appear in any of their indices, though Sanday was certainly familiar with Holtzmann's work).

77. For convenience I refer to Holtzmann's revised and summary treatment in his *Lehrbuch der historisch-kritischen Einleitung in das Neue Testament* (Freiburg: Mohr-Siebeck, 1886) 367-76.

78. For the documentation of doublets see particularly Hawkins, *Horae Synopticae* 80-107.

79. Holtzmann expressed the point vigorously: 'What is more probable in itself: that Lc deliberately shattered *(muthwillig zerschlagen)* the great structures and scattered the wreckage to the four winds, or that out of his heaps of stones Mt has built those walls' *(Lehrbuch 372)*.

gether, these features are better explained by Matthew's and Luke's dependence on a second source already in Greek[80] (Q), rather than by Luke's dependence on Matthew, Luke having retained the Q material in its Q sequence.[81] In Kümmel's judgment, 'Holtzmann grounded the two source hypothesis so carefully that the study of Jesus henceforth could not again dispense with this firm base'.[82] This is almost wholly true in the case of Markan priority,[83] though the Q hypothesis has never won such wholehearted approval, particularly in English-speaking scholarship. In particular, with an eye to the present-day debate, we might simply note here that Streeter's qualifications regarding Q[84] have been given too little attention.

So far as the 'quest of the historical Jesus' is concerned, the emergence of the two-source or two-document hypothesis should not be regarded as coincidental. The case was already being made by C. H. Weisse in 1838.[85] The timing is significant, since Weisse's contribution followed so closely upon the first edition of Strauss's *Life of Jesus,* and was indeed seen by him as an attempt to meet the challenge posed by Strauss.[86] In other words, the push to find the earliest source(s) for a life of Jesus was in substantial part a response to Strauss, an attempt to circumvent the devastating challenge of Strauss and the road block he had so effectively erected against the use of miracles in the quest.[87] To have identified Mark as the earliest Gospel was in effect to sidestep the old criticisms of contradiction and inconsistency between Gospel accounts; and Q

80. Here the logic is that the level of word-for-word agreement between Matthew and Luke (a survey of the common Synoptic tradition immediately encounters Matt. 3.7-10 and Luke 3.7-9) was unlikely to have been the result of independent translations of an Aramaic original, and much more likely to result from Matthew and Luke drawing on the same text already in Greek. See further below chapter 7, n. 29.

81. The case for Luke having retained the order of Q was made most effectively by Streeter in his contribution to the *Oxford Studies* ('On the Original Order of Q', 141-64); and subsequently by V. Taylor, 'The Order of Q' (1954), and 'The Original Order of Q' (1959), reprinted in his *New Testament Essays* (London: Epworth, 1970) 90-94, 95-118.

82. *New Testament* 151.

83. But see again Kloppenborg Verbin's reservations (n. 75 above).

84. Streeter, *Gospels* 183: (1) 'a substantial portion of the 200 verses in question were probably derived from some other (oral) source than Q'; (2) some passages from Q were probably preserved by Matthew only or Luke only; (3) some of the common material may have been proverbs circulating independently. The author of Q 'wrote to supplement, not to supersede, a living oral tradition' (229).

85. C. H. Weisse, *Die evangelische Geschichte kritisch und philosophisch bearbeitet* (2 vols., Leipzig, 1838).

86. See Kümmel, *New Testament* 149-51.

87. This becomes clear also in Holtzmann's introduction to his 1863 volume, as noted by D. Lührmann, 'The Gospel of Mark and the Sayings Collection', *JBL* 108 (1989) 51-71 (here 51).

appeared to be an early source composed exclusively of *sayings* of Jesus.[88] Here was a sound foundation for the Liberal portrayal of Jesus as a teacher of timeless ethics; the problem of miracle could be ignored. The fact that Q does not appear to have contained an account of Jesus' death also diminished the embarrassment of asking whether Jesus had a theology of his own death as atonement, though it reintroduced with a vengeance the problem posed by Reimarus: whether Christianity's subsequent focus on the cross of Jesus did not transform the simpler ethical message of Jesus into a religion of redemption postulating the necessity of bloody sacrifice.[89] This identification of Q and its character has thus proved to be one of the most important developments in the quest of Jesus, and, as we shall see shortly, its far-reaching ramifications are still being explored.

Initially it was the establishment of Markan priority which had the most far-reaching effects. Linked with the early testimony of Papias, that Mark had written his Gospel as Peter's 'interpreter or translator' *(hermēneutēs)*,[90] and given the high evaluation placed on *original sources,* the inference was easily drawn that not only Mark's priority could be assumed, but also his historicity. The hermeneutical principle at work seems to have been: earliest = historically closest to Jesus = least reworked = most historical.[91] Thus in the latter part of the nineteenth century Mark came to be regarded as offering a reliable chronological outline of Jesus' ministry and became in effect the basic source book for lives of Jesus.[92] The Markan outline of a 'Galilean springtime' cut short by the gathering autumnal shadows of the cross thus became the normative pattern of the Liberal

88. Early reconstructions of Q did not include the miracle of Matt. 8.5-13/Luke 7.1-10, it being attributed by Weisse and Holtzmann to Ur-Markus (Kloppenborg Verbin, *Excavating Q* 329).

89. Harnack's own conclusions regarding Q are revealing: '. . . this compilation of sayings which alone affords us a really exact and profound conception of the teaching of Jesus, and is free from bias, apologetic or otherwise. . . . This source is the authority for that which formed the central theme of the message of our Lord — that is, the revelation of the knowledge of God, and the moral call to repent and believe, to renounce the world and to gain heaven — this and nothing else' (*The Sayings of Jesus* [London: Williams and Norgate, 1908] 250-51).

90. According to Papias, 'The Elder used to say this: "Mark became Peter's interpreter/translator *(hermēneutēs)* and wrote down accurately all that he remembered, not, however, in order *(hosa emnēmoneusen, akribōs egrapsen, ou mentoi taxei),* of the things said or done by the Lord"' (Eusebius, *HE* 3.39.15).

91. B. F. Meyer, *The Aims of Jesus* (London: SCM, 1979) observes: 'It was the simplistic equation of "early sources" with guileless history that led to the exaggeration of the importance of the synoptic problem' (38).

92. A good example is F. C. Burkitt, *The Gospel History and Its Transmission* (Edinburgh: Clark, 1906) ch. 3; also *The Earliest Sources for the Life of Jesus* (London: Constable, ²1922) ch. 3.

lives of Jesus.[93] Such use of Markan priority soon came under question, but the basic finding, Markan priority itself, the conclusion that Mark is the earliest of all the Gospels and source of the other two Synoptics, has remained a very solid accomplishment of Gospel scholarship, which has rightly retained its value and importance for 'life of Jesus' research.

4.5. The Collapse of the Liberal Quest

The assumption that historical and source criticism were uncovering the 'historical Jesus', a Jesus attractive to the Liberal sentiments of the late nineteenth century, was rudely shattered in the decades spanning the turn of the century. Two principal causes have been identified as undermining the quest.

a. Enter Eschatology

One was the reintroduction of eschatology into the picture.[94] The point of entry was Jesus' teaching on the kingdom of God. In late-nineteenth-century Liberal Protestantism the kingdom had been understood in purely ethical terms. Ritschl defined it thus:[95]

> The kingdom of God consists of those who believe in Christ, inasmuch as they treat one another with love without regard to differences of sex, rank or race, thereby bringing about a fellowship of moral attitude and moral proprieties extending through the whole range of human life in every possible variation.

In other words, for Ritschl the kingdom of which Jesus spoke was 'the highest good' of humankind in this world, was ethical in character (the product of action

---

93. See Schweitzer, *Quest* ch. 14, particularly *Quest*[1] 203-204 = *Quest*[2] 176-77 (on the influence of the brief outline of the life of Jesus with which Holtzmann ended his 1863 study of the Synoptics), and *Quest*[1] 210-11 = *Quest*[2] 181-82. J. S. Kloppenborg, 'The Sayings Gospel Q and the Quest of the Historical Jesus', *HTR* 89 (1996) 307-44, points out how surprising it was that so little attention was paid at this stage to 'the second main source', Q (311-12).

94. It was the principal concern of Schweitzer's *Quest* to demonstrate that eschatology was the key to understanding Jesus' mission, a key which Reimarus and Strauss had recognized, but which generally had been neglected or rejected.

95. A. Ritschl, *Die christliche Lehre von der Rechtfertigung und Versöhnung* vol. 3 (Bonn, [3]1888) 271, ET *The Christian Doctrine of Justification and Reconciliation* (Edinburgh: Clark, 1902) 285. See also Ritschl's *Instruction in the Christian Religion* (1875) §§5-9, conveniently available in G. W. Dawes, ed., *The Historical Jesus Quest: Landmarks in the Search for the Jesus of History* (Leiderdorp: Deo, 1999) 154-71 (here 154-58).

motivated by love), and was already present in the community of disciples. So far as Ritschl was concerned, the historical mission of Jesus was to 'bring in' or establish the kingdom of God on earth, the task of his disciples to extend it.[96]

This optimistic complacency was shattered by Johannes Weiss, ironically Ritschl's own son-in-law.[97] Weiss insisted that Jesus' talk of the kingdom had to be understood against the background of the intertestamental Jewish apocalypses, a primary feature of which is the sharp *dis*continuity perceived between the present age and the age to come. In particular, this signified to Weiss that the kingdom was *other*-worldly; not something brought about by human means, but wholly dependent on an act of divine intervention. It was *eschatological* — not a developing ethically pure society but that which brings the present order to an end. And it was *future* — not yet, and not yet in the society of the disciples.[98] In short, Jesus proclaimed the kingdom of God as an *event,* which *God* would bring about in the near *future.*[99]

Schweitzer himself pushed the eschatological emphasis further. For him eschatology was the key to the whole public ministry of Jesus, not just his teaching.[100] According to Schweitzer, Jesus was a man obsessed with eschatology, fanatically convinced that the end was at hand, the kingdom of God at the threshold. As his ministry progressed, Jesus came to believe that he himself was the agent of the end, whose death would trigger the final intervention of God. The superb quality of Schweitzer's writing (though here he was carried away by his rhetoric), but also the shock which his thesis brought to the quest,

96. This essentially Liberal concept of the kingdom lingered long into the twentieth century — e.g., in T. W. Manson, *The Teaching of Jesus* (Cambridge: Cambridge University, 1931) 130-36 ('The Kingdom of God in its essence is . . . a personal relation between God and the individual' — 135) — and still in the dedications of church collections which pray that the offerings may be used 'for the extension (or establishment) of thy kingdom'.

97. J. Weiss, *Die Predigt Jesu vom Reiche Gottes* (Göttingen, 1892); ET ed. R. H. Hiers and D. L. Holland, *Jesus' Proclamation of the Kingdom of God* (Philadelphia: Fortress/London: SCM, not till 1971). The second edition of 1900 was much fuller, but the impact of the first edition was all the greater by its brevity (see Hiers and Holland's 'Introduction' 49-53; Kümmel, *New Testament* 439 n. 295).

98. 'As Jesus conceived it, the Kingdom of God is a radically superworldly entity which stands in diametric opposition to this world. . . . there can be no talk of an innerworldly development of the Kingdom of God in the mind of Jesus!' (Weiss, *Jesus' Proclamation* 114; see also, e.g., 73-75, 78, 82, 91, 102-103, and his summary on 129-30).

99. Harnack defended his essentially Ritschlian view of the kingdom in Jesus' preaching by dismissing the Jewish apocalyptic expectancy to which Weiss drew attention as 'a religion of miserabilism', 'a miserabilism which clings to the expectation of a miraculous interference on God's part, and in the meantime, as it were, wallows in wretchedness' (*What Is Christianity?* 16-17, 45). This was typical of Liberal disparagement of the idea that Jesus could have expected imminent divine intervention.

100. Schweitzer, *Quest*[1] 348-49; as a new chapter *Quest*[2] 315.

is memorably summed up in a much quoted summary paragraph from the first edition:[101]

> There is silence all around. The Baptist appears, and cries: 'Repent, for the Kingdom of Heaven is at hand'. Soon after that comes Jesus, and in the knowledge that He is the coming Son of Man lays hold of the wheel of the world to set it moving on that last revolution which is to bring all ordinary history to a close. It refuses to turn, and He throws Himself upon it. Then it does turn; and crushes Him. Instead of bringing in the eschatological conditions He has destroyed them. The wheel rolls onward, and the mangled body of the one immeasurably great Man, who was strong enough to think of Himself as the spiritual ruler of mankind and to bend history to His purpose, is hanging upon it still. That is His victory and His reign.

Whether the (re)discovery of the eschatological Jesus should be regarded as quite such a stunning blow to the Liberal quest is very much open to question. Schweitzer's own reconstruction was very much in the Liberal mode, at least so far as his critical use of the Gospel sources and his willingness to speak of Jesus' messianic self-consciousness were concerned. But the findings of Weiss and Schweitzer certainly posed a huge problem for the quest. How could such a Jesus be expected to appeal to nineteenth-century sensibilities? The Liberal Jesus had almost been designed to effect such an appeal. But who would wish to follow or take as an example a failed eschatological prophet or apocalyptic fanatic? Weiss and Schweitzer themselves offered no answer to the problem they thus posed. On the contrary, the concluding section of Weiss's book rather disappointingly retreats into Liberal pieties.[102] Schweitzer, not dissimilarly, in his closing paragraph, resorts to a kind of mysticism,[103] and he evidently found the inspiration

---

101. Schweitzer, *Quest*[1] 368-69. In his subsequent editions Schweitzer omitted (*Quest*[2] 333) a lengthy section including this famous passage (*Quest*[1] 364-69). It is regrettable that English readers of the 1910 translation remained unaware of Schweitzer's second thoughts regarding the passage (1913). I include the passage here partly because of its influence on English-speaking scholarship and partly to draw attention to the fact that it did not reflect Schweitzer's maturer thought.

102. 'That which is universally valid in Jesus' preaching, which should form the kernel of our systematic theology, is not his idea of the Kingdom of God, but that of the religious and ethical fellowship of the children of God' (*Jesus' Proclamation* 135). See also the Introduction to Weiss's *Jesus' Proclamation* by Hiers and Holland (16-24).

103. 'He comes to us as one unknown, without a name, as of old, by the lakeside, he came to those men who did not know who he was. He says the same words, "Follow me!" and sets us to those tasks which he must fulfil in our time. He commands. And to those who hearken to him, whether wise or unwise, he will reveal himself in the peace, the labours, the conflicts and the sufferings that they may experience in his fellowship, and as an ineffable mystery they

for his later philanthropy in his philosophy of 'reverence for life'.[104] And others found that the old Liberal individualism still provided a satisfactory exegesis of Jesus' kingdom preaching.[105]

More to the point is the observation made by Schweitzer a few pages earlier that 'the historical Jesus will be to our time a stranger and an enigma'.[106] It is this which best sums up the impact of Weiss's and Schweitzer's eschatological or apocalyptic Jesus. In their desire to find a Jesus who spoke to nineteenth-century man, the nineteenth-century questers had largely succumbed to the temptation to find a nineteenth-century Jesus, a Jesus who represented their own views and expressed their own priorities.[107] They had made the 'historical Jesus' in their own image.[108] They had modernized Jesus.[109] In this one observation, then, Schweitzer provided an acid test of historical responsibility. As had been recognized half a millennium earlier, history is bound to be distant and different from the present. Confrontation with a figure across the historical gulf of culture and

---

will learn who he is. . . .' (*Quest*[2] 487; *Quest*[1] 401). Similarly two pages earlier in the first edition: 'It is not Jesus as historically known, but Jesus as spiritually arisen within men, who is significant for our time and can help it. Not the historical Jesus, but the spirit which goes forth from Him and in the spirits of men strives for new influence and rule, is that which overcomes the world' (*Quest*[1] 399). The passage was also omitted in later revisions; but in the Preface to the 1950 edition Schweitzer writes: 'It was Jesus who began to spiritualize the ideas of the kingdom of God and the Messiah. He introduced into the late-Jewish *(sic)* conception of the kingdom his strong ethical emphasis on love. . . . As the spiritual ruler of the spiritual kingdom of God on earth he is the Lord who wills to rule in our hearts' (*Quest*[2] xliv). Schweitzer's resort to a form of mysticism to bridge the gulf he had opened up is also evident in his study of Paul, *The Mysticism of Paul the Apostle* (London: Black, 1931).

104. See, e.g., 'Schweitzer, Albert', *ODCC* 1470.

105. See n. 96 above.

106. Schweitzer, *Quest*[1] 397 = *Quest*[2] 478.

107. J. Jeremias, *Das Problem des historischen Jesus* (Stuttgart: Calwer, 1960), ET *The Problem of the Historical Jesus* (Philadelphia: Fortress, 1964), summed it up rather cavalierly: 'The rationalists pictured Jesus as a preacher of morality, the idealists as the Ideal Man; the aesthetes extolled him as the master of words and the socialists as the friend of the poor and as the social reformer, while the innumerable pseudo-scholars made of him a fictional character. Jesus was modernized. These lives of Jesus are mere products of wishful thinking. The final outcome was that every epoch and every theology found in the personality of Jesus the reflection of its own ideals, and every author the reflection of his own views' (5-6).

108. Much quoted is the comment of George Tyrrell, *Christianity at the Crossroads* (London: Longmans Green, 1909): 'The Christ that Harnack sees, looking back through nineteen centuries of Catholic darkness, is only the reflection of a liberal Protestant face, seen at the bottom of a deep well' (49).

109. As Schweitzer himself observed; see *Quest*[1] 4, 308-11 = *Quest*[2] 6, 275-78: 'He is himself only a phantom created by the Germanic mind in pursuit of a religious will-o'the wisp' (*Quest*[1] 309 = *Quest*[2] 276). See also H. J. Cadbury, *The Peril of Modernizing Jesus* (London: Macmillan, 1937; SPCK, 1962).

society, of assumptions and aspirations, should always cause us something of a shock. Indeed, the *absence* of some element of strangeness probably indicates that the depth of historical distance and the degree of historical difference have been underestimated. Weiss and Schweitzer brought home the fact that Jesus had been domesticated, and in consequence could be presented somewhat as a superior kind of nineteenth-century Sunday school teacher. In short, the Liberal attempt to get behind the Christ of dogma to the Jesus of history had simply produced bad history — nowhere more clearly pointed up than in the aside of William Temple: 'Why anyone should have troubled to crucify the Christ of Liberal Protestantism has always been a mystery'.[110]

b. Re-Enter Faith!

The more effective block on the Liberal quest was the surprising re-emergence of faith as a factor which could not be ignored, the sobering realization that a historical inquiry into the life of Jesus had after all to take account of faith. After giving way to the claims of history for so long, faith at last bit back!

The case was put no more boldly than by Martin Kähler in his *Der sogennante historische Jesus und der geschichtliche biblische Christus* (1892).[111] The title makes Kähler's point for him. It distinguishes the two German words *Historie* and *Geschichte,* both meaning 'history'. *Historie* he understands as the bare data, independent of any significance which might be placed on them. *Geschichte,* on the other hand, denotes history in its significance, historical events and persons which attract attention by reason of the influence they have exercised. The English translator's distinction between 'historical', with the suggested overtone of *merely* historical, and 'historic', denoting lasting fame, catches something of the same distinction. Kähler's central claim, then, is that the Christ of the Bible is *Jesus seen in his significance.*[112] For Kähler there is no such thing in the Bible as 'the historical Jesus', a figure devoid of significance (hence 'So-called Historical Jesus'). The Liberal lives of Jesus had attempted to get back to a Jesus behind the Gospel texts, by stripping away the interpretative

110. W. Temple, *Readings in St. John's Gospel* (London: Macmillan, 1945) xxiv. See also M. D. Chapman, *The Coming Christ: The Impact of Eschatology on Theology in Edwardian England* (JSNTS 208; Sheffield: Sheffield Academic, 2001).

111. ET *The So-Called Historical Jesus and the Historic Biblical Christ,* ed. C. E. Braaten (Philadelphia: Fortress, 1964).

112. 'From a purely historical point of view the truly historic element in any great figure is the discernible personal influence which he exercises upon later generations'; 'The real Christ, that is, the Christ who has exercised an influence in history . . .' (Kähler, *So-Called Historical Jesus* 63, 66).

layers and (presumed) distortions. Kähler responded by arguing that this could not be done: the Gospels' picture of Jesus is impregnated with interpretation throughout.[113] It simply is not possible to get back from the Gospels to a Jesus who may or may not have been significant. In trying to do so the questers were in effect drawing on a further source to fill in the gaps, a fifth Gospel, as it were — that is, themselves, their own minds and imaginations.[114] On this perspective, the whole quest was nothing more than 'a blind alley', wherein the so-called 'historical Jesus' was not to be found.[115] This forthright challenge by Kähler did not make much of an immediate impact, but it was a fundamental theological consideration in Bultmann's abandonment of the quest and remained influential through the middle decades of the twentieth century.

Wrede made a correlated but much more immediately crippling observation: that the Gospels so much relied on as sources for objective history were in fact also, indeed primarily *documents of faith*. They were not portrayals of Jesus as he was, but of Jesus as his disciples subsequently saw him. This larger claim was the result of Wrede's more narrowly focused study of 'the messianic secret' in the Synoptic Gospels, and of his conclusion that the secrecy motif in Mark in particular was a theological motif inserted by the Evangelist to explain why Jesus' messiahship had not been recognized by his own people.[116] The unavoidable corollary was that Mark had *not* intended to write a historical account of Jesus' ministry and teaching; the shape and content of Mark, and by extension of the other Synoptics also, had been determined by theological considerations. In which case, the sharp distinction between historical Synoptics and a theological John had to be abandoned; the Synoptics were also theological, and in their own manner and degree just as theological as John. In which case also, the possibility of using Mark as a straightforward source for the history of Jesus' ministry was gone. This finding by Wrede, of the Synoptics as theological tracts, became almost axiomatic for twentieth-century scholarship and an effective block on any renewal of the 'quest of the historical Jesus' on Liberal assumptions for most of the twentieth century.

In the same connection we should note also a point made by Schweitzer in his own response to Wrede. He climaxes his account of the quest with the contri-

---

113. 'Every detail of the apostolic recollection of Jesus can be shown to have been preserved for the sake of its religious significance' (Kähler, *So-Called Historical Jesus* 93).

114. Kähler, *So-Called Historical Jesus* 55 (Braaten's 'Introduction' 20). Hence also the criticisms in nn. 107-109 above.

115. Kähler, *So-Called Historical Jesus* 46.

116. W. Wrede, *Das Messiasgeheimnis in den Evangelien: Zugleich ein Beitrag zum Verstandnis des Markusevangeliums* (Göttingen, 1901); ET *The Messianic Secret* (Cambridge: Clarke, not till 1971). See C. Tuckett, ed., *The Messianic Secret* (London: SPCK, 1983), and further below §15.2c.

butions by Wrede and himself, as a choice between 'thoroughgoing scepticism' (Wrede) and 'thoroughgoing eschatology' (Schweitzer).[117] And of the points he makes against Wrede, one of the sharpest is that indications of dogmatic influence in the Synoptics' account of Jesus' preaching are not necessarily to be taken as a sign of subsequent Christian theologising, but may be indicative of Jesus' *own* mode of thinking. Eschatology itself was nothing other than 'dogmatic history', expectation of the future course of events as determined by an eschatological perspective.[118] The 'messianic secret' may well have been Jesus' own device, on the same assumption; 'for Jesus the overall necessity of his death is grounded in dogma, not in external historical facts'.[119] Where Wrede said, 'Dogmatic, and therefore unhistorical', the thoroughgoing eschatological school replied, 'Dogmatic, and therefore historical'.[120]

Whatever we make of Schweitzer's particular claim, and we will return to it later,[121] the fundamental observation remains: that the presence of dogmatic influence in the Synoptic tradition should not be regarded in and of itself as proof of later Christian reflection; the dogma may have been one that Jesus himself cherished. The observation surprisingly complements that of Kähler (to whom Schweitzer makes no reference): any assumption that the presence of faith or theology or dogma constitutes a sure sign of a later perspective is simply fallacious; *the faith, theology or dogma may have been that of Jesus himself,* and any assumption that the 'historical Jesus' must have been innocent of all such should have been self-evidently incredible. It is a pity that the antithetical polarisation of the Jesus of history and the Christ of faith prevented this observation of Schweitzer's from having the influence it deserved.

c. The *Coup de Grâce*

It is no doubt true that the most devastating blow of all to Liberalism, and thus also to the Liberal quest, came from the First World War. The fact that the high cultures of Europe could descend so far into the bloody horror of the Somme and the muddy hell of Passchendaele swept the carpet from under Liberalism's agenda for the emerging generation. The evidence of human bestiality and bru-

117. Schweitzer, *Quest* ch. 19; he was referring to his own *Das Messianitäts- und Leidensgeheimnis: Eine Skizze des Lebens Jesu* (1901); ET *The Mystery of the Kingdom of God: The Secret of Jesus' Messiahship and Passion* (New York: Macmillan, 1914).
118. Schweitzer, *Quest*: 'Eschatology is simply "dogmatic history", which breaks in upon the natural course of history and abrogates it' (*Quest*[1] 349; *Quest*[2] 315)
119. Schweitzer, *Quest*[1] 390 = *Quest*[2] 350; see also *Quest*[2] 327, 330, 334, 337-38, 342.
120. Schweitzer, *Quest*[1] 385 = *Quest*[2] 346.
121. See below particularly §§12.3b, 12.6c-d, 17.3, 5.

tality had a shattering effect on the confident Liberal optimism in humankind's moral evolution. Not surprisingly the post-war theological response came in quite different terms, the proclamatory word of Barth's neo-orthodoxy and the stoical 'decisionism' of Bultmann's existentialism, neither of which was very much interested in the 'historical Jesus' or in further questing for him.[122]

4.6. Jesus in Sociological Perspective

The forty years from the outbreak of the First World War mark something of a hiatus or diversion in 'life of Jesus' research, dominated as the period was by the reassertion of a dogmatic christological perspective (Barth) and an (in effect) equally dogmatic kerygmatic perspective (Bultmann). Consequently, it will make better sense to delay till the next section (see §§5.3 and 4 below) consideration of both the contribution of Bultmann and the wrestlings of the immediate post-Bultmannian generation with Bultmann's heritage in terms of the tension between history and faith. That the Bultmann epoch does indeed constitute something of an interruption both in the flight from dogma and in the quest itself, however, is also confirmed by the fact that from the mid-1970s onwards the concerns which had dominated the old Liberal quest reasserted themselves — in two forms.

For all its defects and failures, the Liberal quest had attempted to see Jesus within his historical context, and it was motivated by a genuine ethical concern. The former objective found a close ally in the emergence of the history-of-religions school at the beginning of the twentieth century. This latter was an extension of the Liberal reaction against dogma in that it turned away from the traditional preoccupation of Christianity as primarily a doctrinal system and sought to understand the emergence of Christianity as one among the many religious movements of the first-century Greco-Roman world.[123] In the event, inquiry focused mostly on the 'Hellenization' of Christianity (to use Harnack's term),

122. Perrin points out, however, that we can only really speak of the collapse of the Liberal quest in reference to Germany; the Liberal position on the question of our knowledge of the historical Jesus and on the relationship of that knowledge to Christian faith was maintained in Britain and America for another fifty years (*Rediscovering* 214-15). See further Weaver, *Historical Jesus* xi-xii and chs. 4-6 *passim*.

123. W. Wrede's programmatic essay caught the mood — 'The Task and Method of "New Testament Theology"' (1897), ET in R. Morgan, *The Nature of New Testament Theology* (London: SCM, 1973) 68-116. It should be noted that the motivation in the emerging sociological perspective was not so much hostility to dogma as concern that the older dogmatic perspective was too narrow and for that reason distorted twentieth-century perception of the historical reality. This section fits least comfortably within the overarching theme of the present chapter.

building on the old Liberal assertion of a major transition (mutation?) from Jesus the teacher of timeless moral ideals to Paul the proponent of a religion patterned on the mystery cults of the time.[124] Schweitzer could be said to have shared the same history-of-religions motivation, in that he set Jesus within the context of Jewish apocalypticism. But in so doing, as we noted above, he left questers with a conundrum (how could a failed apocalyptic prophet provide a credible religious model for the twentieth century?), to which Bultmann's existentialism provided only temporary solution.

At the same time Liberalism's ethical concern was strengthened by the first attempts to draw on the emerging social sciences, particularly sociology.[125] The infant enterprise survived the war, but its new step-father (kerygmatic theology) was hardly well disposed towards it, and its early flourishing in Marxist contributions[126] no doubt increased Western scholarly suspicion towards it. It is true that the early form critics recognized a social dimension to the forms *(Sitz im Leben),* but only in a limited way — the life of the forms within the congregations, not the life of the churches within a wider social context.[127] And although the older Liberal agenda lived on in the Chicago School into the 1920s and 30s,[128] it did not make any real impact beyond America.

It was only in the mid-1970s that the infant attained full adulthood. This coming of age was partly the result of the social sciences having become fully established within expanding university systems in the West,[129] and partly the result of increasing European disengagement with its colonial past and the con-

124. See chapter 1 above at nn. 16 and 18.

125. Also characteristic of the history-of-religions method was Troeltsch's observation that 'the Christian idea will never become a powerful reality without community and cult' ('The Significance of the Historical Existence of Jesus' 196). See further Troeltsch's *The Social Teaching of the Christian Churches* (1912; ET London: George Allen and Unwin, 1931). G. Theissen, 'Social Research into the New Testament', *Social Reality and the Early Christians* (Minneapolis: Augsburg Fortress, 1992/Edinburgh: Clark, 1993) 1-29, notes that Troeltsch 'wished to supplement the "ideological" view of Christianity carried through in the history of dogma by a "sociological" way of looking at things. But he restricted himself to the social doctrines of the churches and sects' (8, n. 8). Theissen also points out that Troeltsch lived in the same house in Heidelberg as Max Weber and that they influenced each other mutually (7).

126. Particularly K. Kautsky, *Foundations of Christianity* (1908, [11]1921; ET London: George Allen and Unwin, 1925).

127. Theissen, 'Social Research' 8-13. See further below §8.6a and vol. 2.

128. Most notably S. J. Case, *Jesus: A New Biography* (Chicago: University of Chicago, 1927), and S. Matthews, *Jesus on Social Institutions* (New York: Macmillan, 1928); see further Weaver, *Historical Jesus* 127-36.

129. The expansion of the British university system in the 1960s was marked by the transition from 'Theology' or 'Divinity' as the appropriate title for departments or faculties to 'Religious Studies'.

comitant emergence of liberation theology.[130] The revival and mature flourishing of the sociological quest is evident in two contributions in particular.

a. Gerd Theissen

To Gerd Theissen must go the credit for making the first effective attempt to study NT texts from a sociological perspective.[131] With regard to Jesus, he argued that 'The sayings tradition is characterized by an ethical radicalism that is shown most noticeably in the renunciation of a home, family, and possessions'.[132] In a larger sequel he broadened his perspective from a sociology of literature to a study of the sociology of the Jesus movement, whose objective he defined as 'to describe typical social attitudes and behaviour within the Jesus movement and to analyse its interaction with Jewish society in Palestine generally'.[133] The resultant picture is broader too, with a chapter on 'the wandering charismatics', but one also on their 'sympathizers in the local communities', thus providing a more balanced portrayal than in the earlier lecture. Nonetheless, the focus is still on the former, the tone set by the opening claim of the chapter on the wandering charismatics: 'Jesus did not primarily found local communities, but called into being a movement of wandering charismatics'. The local communities in turn 'are to be understood exclusively in terms of their complementary relationship to the wandering charismatics'.[134] The primary importance of these radical itinerants is further emphasized in that it was they who shaped and handed down the earliest Jesus tradition.[135] The nearest parallels to this 'movement of outsiders' were the numerous wandering Cynic philosophers and preachers.[136]

As is the case with many ground-breaking contributions, Theissen's socio-

---

130. See particularly J. Sobrino, *Jesus the Liberator: A Historical-Theological Reading of Jesus of Nazareth* (ET Maryknoll: Orbis, 1993).

131. 'The sociology of literature investigates the relations between written texts and human behaviour' — the opening words of 'Wanderradikalismus: Literatursoziologische Aspekte der Überlieferung von Worten Jesu im Urchristentum', *ZTK* 70 (1973) 245-71; ET 'The Wandering Radicals: Light Shed by the Sociology of Literature on the Early Transmission of Jesus Sayings', *Social Reality* 33-59 (here 33). There followed a sequence of studies on Paul (1 Corinthians) which had a similar impact on Pauline studies; see further vol. 2.

132. 'Wandering Radicals' 37-40.

133. *Soziologie der Jesusbewegung: Ein Beitrag zur Entstehungsgeschichte des Urchristentums* (Munich: Kaiser, 1977), ET *The First Followers of Jesus: A Sociological Analysis of the Earliest Christianity* (London: SCM, 1978) = *Sociology of Early Palestinian Christianity* (Philadelphia: Fortress, 1978) 1.

134. *First Followers* 8, 22.

135. *First Followers* 8, 10.

136. *First Followers* 14-15; also 'Wandering Radicals' 43-44.

logically determined reconstruction of Christianity's beginnings is vulnerable to heavy criticism.[137] In particular, he has given the tradition of Jesus commissioning his disciples in mission (Mark 6.6-13 pars.) a definitive role for the Jesus movement as a whole.[138] He fails to ask about the rhetoric of various passages on the cost of discipleship (e.g., Luke 14.26) and interprets them too literally.[139] His interpretation is at times rather tendentious; for example Matt. 19.28 indicates that the task of the twelve 'lay among the twelve (scattered) tribes of Israel'; and Acts 13.1 shows Antioch to be 'the "home" of a group of wandering charismatics'.[140] And his understanding of tradition as kept alive by wandering charismatics rather than in and by settled communities seems to owe more (unrecognized) to a romantic conception of wandering bards than to a sociology of community tradition (see chapter 8 below). In short, it is only by setting various sayings of Jesus into the context which Theissen proposes that he is able to interpret them as he does. Whereas, as we shall see, such sayings do not diminish in radical force when understood as a call to reshape the social conventions of Jesus' day. Nevertheless, Theissen's reconstruction of an earliest stage of the Jesus tradition kept alive by homeless itinerants, with clear parallels in world-renouncing itinerant Cynic philosophers, has had far-reaching influence, particularly on the neo-Liberal Jesus to be described below in §4.7.[141]

Shortly following Theissen, John Gager's *Kingdom and Community* made a substantial stir, but its treatment of Jesus was too much dependent on an analytic model drawn on the template of later millenarian movements (particularly Melanesian cargo cults) to be of lasting significance.[142] Other works have been

137. For a critique from a sociological perspective see particularly J. H. Elliott, 'Social-Scientific Criticism of the New Testament and Its Social World', *Semeia* 35 (1986) 1-33; R. A. Horsley, *Sociology and the Jesus Movement* (New York: Continuum, 1989, ²1994) 30-42. Horsley characterizes Theissen's presentation of the Jesus movement as 'a modern domestication of the Gospel materials' (39).

138. Theissen is also overly dependent on *Didache* 11, repeating the mistakes made in the debate about Charisma and Office *(Charisma* and *Amt)* occasioned by the publication of the *Didache* at the end of the nineteenth century (see my *Theology of Paul* 566-67); Crossan, *The Birth of Christianity* (HarperSanFrancisco, 1998) Part VIII, pushes still further down the same line (see below, chapter 14 n. 72). Similarly, his concept of 'charisma' owes more to Weber than to Paul, for whom charisma was an essentially community function (Rom. 12.4-6; 1 Cor. 12.4-27).

139. See further Horsley, *Sociology* 43-50; 'this uncritical use of individual texts in support of contentions that most in fact do not attest' (45).

140. *First Followers* 9.

141. See below, chapter 7, n. 96. Theissen was to some extent anticipated by P. Hoffmann, *Studien zur Theologie der Logienquelle* (Münster: Aschendorff, 1972, ²1975) 332-34.

142. J. G. Gager, *Kingdom and Community: The Social World of Early Christianity*

as significant for their influence on contemporary use of the Gospel portrayal of Jesus, particularly in terms of liberation theology, as they have been for their contributions to the 'quest of the historical Jesus' as such — if not more.[143]

b. Richard Horsley

The other most important voice in calling for a realistic historical sociology of the Jesus movement has been Richard Horsley. Reviving an emphasis which has surfaced periodically in 'Life of Jesus' research,[144] Horsley protests vigorously against the depoliticisation of Jesus and his mission and questions the theological presuppositions which have dominated most previous discussion.[145] In particular, traditional interpretations of Jesus individualized his teaching and assumed that 'religion' and 'politics' are two quite separate categories; whereas the tradition for Jesus was that of the political prophets, Elijah and Elisha, and he was executed as a political agitator or criminal, charges of which he was hardly entirely innocent.[146] In Jesus' teaching, the kingdom of God should not be understood in terms of the older apocalyptic eschatology as the end of the world ('cosmic catastrophe'), but as 'a political metaphor and symbol' of the restoration of society and the renewal of social life; Jesus' concern was for nothing less than 'the renewal of Israel' conceived in 'some fairly definite and distinctive patterns of social relationship'.[147] What was in view, then, was not particular groups or wandering charismatics, but local communities, conceived in familial but non-patriarchal terms (Mark 3.35), communities without hierarchy (Matt. 23.8-9) whose members took economic responsibility for one another ('forgive us our

---

(Englewood Cliffs: Prentice-Hall, 1975) 20-37. It also worked with a conception of Jesus as a millenarian prophet (28-32) which was just about to go out of fashion among those from whom Gager might have expected support (see further below, §4.7).

143. Notably L. Boff, *Jesus Christ Liberator: A Critical Christology for Our Time* (Maryknoll: Orbis, 1978); J. L. Segundo, *The Historical Jesus of the Synoptics* (1982; ET Maryknoll: Orbis, 1985); E. Schüssler Fiorenza, *In Memory of Her: A Feminist Theological Reconstruction of Christian Origins* (New York: Crossroad, 1983) 105-59; see also her 'Jesus and the Politics of Interpretation', *HTR* 90 (1997) 343-58. They regard traditional dogmatic concerns as a cloak for colonial and patriarchal oppression.

144. From Reimarus (§4.2) to S. G. F. Brandon, *Jesus and the Zealots: A Study of the Political Factor in Primitive Christianity* (Manchester: Manchester University, 1967).

145. R. A. Horsley, *Jesus and the Spiral of Violence: Popular Jewish Resistance in Roman Palestine* (San Francisco: Harper and Row, 1987).

146. Horsley, *Jesus* 151-53, 156-57, 160-64; also ch. 10.

147. Horsley, *Jesus* 168-72, 192-208. Horsley has deeply influenced R. D. Kaylor, *Jesus the Prophet: His Vision of the Kingdom on Earth* (Louisville: Westminster/John Knox, 1994) particularly ch. 3.

debts') and willingly helped one another, even the local adversary ('love your enemies'), communities which worked out conflicts without resort to the courts (Matt. 18.15-22) and regarded themselves as independent from the Temple and the attendant political-economic-religious establishment (Matt. 17.24-27) and without obligation to pay Roman tribute (Mark 12.17).[148] 'The kingdom of God apparently had no need of either a mediating hierocracy or a temple system'.[149]

Horsley has restated and buttressed his arguments in a sequence of further studies,[150] but the main thesis and its principal components were already clear in the initial statement. Its egalitarian utopianism is certainly attractive for anyone dismayed by the longevity and persistence of traditionally oppressive hierarchies, and the thesis is more soundly based than Theissen's portrayal of Jesus' first followers as itinerant charismatics. But its very attractiveness inevitably raises the question whether Horsley has been able to avoid the mistake of those old Liberals who projected on Jesus their own priorities in portraying him as a social reformer.[151] Some of the same problems arise. Like the Liberals he remains ambivalent about the references in the Jesus tradition to a future coming of God/the Son of man in judgment and full realization of the kingdom.[152] And as with the Liberals, the transition to the expanding mission of Paul remains problematic to envisage, since the Jesus tradition takes us only to continuing Galilean village communities.[153] Moreover, it is difficult to avoid the impression of special pleading at some key points: particularly in the suggestion that Jesus' exorcisms implied that 'the days of Roman domination were numbered', and in the surprising *tour de force* against the consensus view that Jesus associated or ate with tax-collectors and sinners.[154] Nevertheless, Horsley's warning not to abstract Jesus' teaching from the religious-social-political context of his time must be heeded, and Horsley will inevitably be an important dialogue partner in the following pages.[155]

---

148. Horsley, *Jesus* chs. 8-10.

149. Horsley, *Jesus* 325.

150. Particularly *Sociology;* also *Archaeology, History and Society in Galilee: The Social Context of Jesus and the Rabbis* (Valley Forge: Trinity, 1996); R. A. Horsley and J. A. Draper, *Whoever Hears You Hears Me: Prophets, Performance, and Tradition in Q* (Harrisburg: Trinity, 1999).

151. See above, n. 107.

152. Horsley. *Jesus* 175-77, 320.

153. The problem becomes clearer in the two later volumes (n. 150 above).

154. Horsley, *Jesus* 181-90 (here 190), 212-23. See also below §13.5 and n. 216, chapter 15, n. 279.

155. Pertinent, however, is the observation of L. E. Keck, *Who Is Jesus? History in Perfect Tense* (Columbia: University of South Carolina, 2000), that 'today's sense of the task is no longer that of locating second-temple-era materials that illumine aspects of Jesus but rather that of first reconstructing as fully as possible the Galilee that he knew and then detecting where Jesus should be placed *in* it so that he becomes an integral part *of* it' (36).

4.7. Re-Enter the Neo-Liberal Jesus

One of the most surprising facts of recent 'life of Jesus' research is that after about seventy years of silence, the old Liberal Jesus has revived (or should we say, returned from exile?). Despite having had the last rites pronounced over him at the beginning of the twentieth century, the Liberal Jesus has risen again, apparently hale and hearty. That this should have happened in North America makes it more understandable, since the church-state division there has encouraged a self-conscious and self-perpetuating liberal individualism in higher education which tends to regard freedom from and reaction against church and theology as one of its defining characteristics. This resurrected Jesus is not quite in the same form, of course, but the distinctive features of the old Liberal quest are all clearly discernible: the flight from dogma, the claim to new sources which make possible a reconstruction of the 'historical Jesus', the focus on Jesus' teaching, and the stripping away once again of the embarrassing apocalyptic features which Weiss and Schweitzer had moved to centre stage.[156] In the closing decades of the twentieth century each emphasis had its particular spokesman. But the overall outcome is a rather familiar figure — the neo-Liberal Jesus, the challenge of whose teaching can be summed up not so much (as before) in fundamental moral principles as in the challenge of subversive wisdom.[157]

The most outspoken in his flight from dogma and traditional authority is Robert Funk. He has made no secret of his intention to mount 'a frontal assault on a pervasive religious illiteracy that blinds and intimidates even those, or perhaps especially those, in positions of authority in the church and in our society'.[158] Entirely in the spirit of the original quest, he takes the distinction between the historical Jesus and the Christ of faith as axiomatic and sees it as the goal of his endeavours, and those of the Jesus Seminar, which he established, to liberate the real Jesus not only from the Christ of the creeds but also from the Je-

---

156. The parallel stretches further when we take into consideration the Kähler-like response of L. T. Johnson, *The Real Jesus* (HarperSanFrancisco, 1996), and the Schweitzer-like ripostes of D. C. Allison, *Jesus of Nazareth: Millenarian Prophet* (Minneapolis: Fortress, 1998), and, at a more popular level, B. D. Ehrman, *Jesus: Apocalyptic Prophet of the New Millennium* (Oxford: Oxford University, 1999); see now also M. Reiser, 'Eschatology in the Proclamation of Jesus', in Labahn and Schmidt, eds., *Jesus, Mark and Q* 216-38.

157. 'Neo-Liberal' is my own designation. Similar evaluations are made by H. Koester, 'Jesus the Victim', *JBL* 111 (1992) 3-15 (here 5); L. E. Keck, 'The Second Coming of the Liberal Jesus?', *Christian Century* (August 24-31, 1994) 784-87. Despite his own closeness to Liberal precedents (Jesus as social reformer), Horsley mounts a similar critique, particularly in 'The Teachings of Jesus and Liberal Individualism', in Horsley and Draper, *Whoever* 4-5, 15-28. On the relation of the 'neo-Liberal' quest to the 'third quest' see below, chapter 5, n. 100. I put no great weight on the 'labels' I use.

158. R. W. Funk, *Honest to Jesus* (San Francisco: HarperSanFrancisco, 1996) 6-7.

sus of the Gospels.[159] Similarly Paul Hollenbach seeks the Jesus of history 'in order to overthrow, not simply correct the "mistake called Christianity"'.[160] The nearest equivalent in Germany is Gerd Lüdemann, who has been a devoted practitioner of the historical method, but who now regards 'as illegitimate any return to the preaching of Jesus as a foundation for Christian faith'.[161]

The search for new sources has found a doughty champion in Dominic Crossan,[162] who has broken right through the constraints imposed by the four canonical Gospels, hitherto regarded as the only substantive sources, and has produced an amazing cornucopia of sources for traditions about Jesus — no less than fifty-two![163] Of course, most of them provide testimony to only a few sayings of Jesus or episodes from Jesus' life. But the heart of Crossan's claim is that there are three major sources which can be dated confidently to the period 30-60 CE.[164] The first of these is the *Gospel of Thomas,* the most important document among the cache discovered at Nag Hammadi in Egypt in 1945. A Coptic translation of an earlier Greek document, it has usually been regarded as a Gnostic reworking of earlier sayings material, many of which are found also in Q. But

159. Funk, *Honest* 10-11, 19-21; 'The first test concerns whether or not the quest gives credence to the distinction between the historical Jesus and the Jesus of the gospels' (64). Similarly R. W. Funk, et al., *The Five Gospels: The Search for the Authentic Words of Jesus* (New York: Macmillan, 1993) 3-4. In the poster for his lecture tour in the UK, 'Jesus Seminar on the Road — UK 2000', Funk is cited thus: 'The purpose of the quest of the historical Jesus is to set Jesus free from the scriptural and experiential prisons in which we have incarcerated him. . . . the pale, anaemic, iconic Jesus suffers by comparison with the stark reality of the genuine article' — more or less a quotation from *Honest* 300.

160. P. Hollenbach, 'The Historical Jesus Question in North America Today', *BTB* 19 (1989) 11-22 (here 20).

161. G. Lüdemann, *The Great Deception and What Jesus Really Said and Did* (London: SCM, 1998) x; the book was a 'taster' for his *Jesus after Two Thousand Years: What He Really Said and Did* (Lüneburg: Klampen, 2000; ET London: SCM, 2000), where he acknowledges the stimulus which his own project received from the Jesus Seminar and its publications (vii). The value of Lüdemann's succinct summary of the reasoning of a fairly sceptical wing of German scholarship on individual Gospel traditions should not be underestimated. Similarly the views of the Jesus Seminar, as summarized in Funk's *Five Gospels* and *The Acts of Jesus* (San Francisco: HarperSanFrancisco, 1998), whatever may be said of the methods used, bear testimony to an important segment of scholarly opinion. In my own analysis of the Jesus tradition I will make constant reference to them.

162. J. D. Crossan, *The Historical Jesus: The Life of a Mediterranean Jewish Peasant* (San Francisco: Harper, 1991).

163. Crossan, *Historical Jesus* 427-50. See also R. J. Miller, ed., *The Complete Gospels* (San Francisco: HarperSanFrancisco, 1994), which provides the annotated texts of twenty-one Gospels.

164. Crossan, *Historical Jesus* 427-29; cf. Funk, *Honest* 124-25, who, like Harnack (n. 89 above), has found in Q the means to get behind the Pauline gospel (which already influenced Mark) to the gospel of Jesus himself (41-42).

Crossan follows those who see in Thomas primitive features, independent of Q, and argues that the earlier of its two layers can be dated to about 50.[165] The second source is Q itself, dated to the 50s, but now stratified into three layers of development: 1Q, a sapiental layer; 2Q, an apocalyptic layer; and 3Q, an introductory layer.[166] The third new major source for the earliest layer of Jesus tradition is the *Cross Gospel,* a linked narrative of Jesus' crucifixion and resurrection, which Crossan himself has constructed out of the *Gospel of Peter,* itself to be dated to the mid second century CE, and postulated by Crossan as the source for the canonical passion narratives.[167] Other sources Crossan locates within a second stratum (60-80 CE). Of these the most important are the Secret Gospel of Mark (the first version of Mark 10.32-46a), and what he calls the 'Dialogue Collection', a collection of sayings independent of the Synoptic tradition, on which the Nag Hammadi *Dialogue of the Saviour* was able to draw.[168]

A more reliable foundation in new sources is offered by Helmut Koester, who has dissociated himself from the work of the Jesus Seminar and who sums up many years of work in this area with his magisterial treatment of *Ancient Christian Gospels.*[169] He comes to similar conclusions regarding the *Gospel of Thomas* (first century), Q (earliest stage 40-50),[170] Secret Mark ('not too far removed from the date of . . . Mark'), and the 'dialogue gospel' (during the last decades of the first century CE),[171] though he 'differs fundamentally' from Crossan's hypothesis of a 'Cross Gospel'.[172]

---

165. He dates a second layer possibly as early as the 60s or 70s. Other members of the Jesus Seminar are content to settle for a date for *Thomas* of 70-100 (Miller, ed., *Complete Gospels* 303). P. Jenkins, *Hidden Gospels: How the Search for Jesus Lost Its Way* (New York: Oxford University, 2001) cites L. M. White's observation that the early dating of *Thomas* is 'actually the lynchpin for most of the arguments of the Jesus Seminar' (62); he also mounts a scathing critique on uncritical media interest in eccentric Jesus scholarship (ch. 8).

166. Following J. S. Kloppenborg, *The Formation of Q* (Philadelphia: Fortress, 1987), who detects three compositional strata in extant Q — a primary sapiential layer, composed of six 'wisdom speeches' (Q^1); a second apocalyptic layer, made up of five judgment speeches (Q^2); and a final but not very substantial revision (Q^3) (see, e.g., 317, 243, 170). The argument is refined in his *Excavating Q,* chs. 2-3.

167. J. D. Crossan, *The Cross That Spoke: The Origins of the Passion Narrative* (San Francisco: Harper and Row, 1988).

168. Cf. Funk, *Honest to Jesus* 99, 117-18, 124-25.

169. H. Koester, *Ancient Christian Gospels: Their History and Development* (London: SCM/Philadelphia: Trinity, 1990); see also his *Introduction to the New Testament* vol. 2 (Philadelphia: Fortress, 1982) 147-55. Cf. Funk, *Honest* 70-74.

170. Likewise following Kloppenborg, *Formation* (*Ancient Christian Gospels* 87, 134-35).

171. Koester, *Ancient Christian Gospels* 75-128 *(Thomas),* 128-71 (Q), 293-303 (Secret Mark), 'dialogue gospel' (173-87).

172. Koester, *Ancient Christian Gospels* 218-20, 220 n. 2, and 231 n. 3.

The most consistent advocate of a non-eschatological Jesus has been Marcus Borg. In his revised doctoral thesis (completed in 1972 under G. B. Caird) he examined the Synoptic 'threat' tradition and argued that, despite the dominant tradition of scholarship since Schweitzer, the only imminent catastrophe in view was the destruction of Israel. So too, the coming Son of Man sayings are evidence of the developing images and beliefs of the early Christians rather than of any sense on the part of Jesus of an imminent end to history.[173] Since then the renunciation of Schweitzer has become a mark of the neo-Liberal quest. Funk can indeed claim that 'the liberation of the non-eschatological Jesus of the aphorisms and parables from Schweitzer's eschatological Jesus is the fifth pillar of contemporary scholarship'.[174] And of course, the argument that the apocalyptic elements in Q are revisions of an original wisdom Q[175] has greatly reinforced the trend. The extent of the flight from Schweitzer is indicated by the fact that Tom Wright, no friend of the Jesus Seminar,[176] but also owning his debt to Caird, has become quite as strong a critic of Schweitzer as anyone. He has particularly pressed the point that apocalyptic language has to be understood metaphorically in reference to historical and political events rather than literally in reference to 'the end of the world'. Neither Jesus nor his Jewish contemporaries were expecting the end of the space-time universe. Schweitzer's was 'a bizarre literalistic reading of what the first century knew to be thoroughly metaphorical'.[177]

The pictures which emerge are riveting: a Jesus who was 'a Galilean devi-

173. M. J. Borg, *Conflict, Holiness and Politics in the Teachings of Jesus* (New York: Mellen, 1984) 201-27. See also his 'An Orthodoxy Reconsidered: The "End-of-the-World Jesus"', in L. D. Hurst and N. T. Wright, eds., *The Glory of Christ in the New Testament,* G. B. Caird FS (Oxford: Clarendon, 1987) 207-17; also *Jesus in Contemporary Scholarship* (Valley Forge: Trinity, 1994) 7-9, 30-31, chs. 3 and 4; e.g., 'without the coming Son of man sayings, there is no reason to think of the kingdom of God as the imminent end of the world' (*Jesus in Contemporary Scholarship* 54).

174. Funk, ed., *Five Gospels* 4. B. B. Scott, who describes himself as 'a charter member' of the Jesus Seminar, observes that the presumption against the authenticity of apocalyptic material in the Jesus tradition was strengthened by the fact that 'many of those who supported the apocalyptic position gradually quit attending the Seminar sessions' ('New Options in an Old Quest' 34-37). It should be noted that Koester distances himself from the Jesus Seminar's neo-Liberalism at this point: he questions whether the early stage of Q can really be defined as noneschatological, and notes that *Thomas* presupposes a tradition of eschatological sayings of Jesus ('Jesus the Victim' 7; see also above, n. 157).

175. Above, n. 166.

176. Wright, *Jesus* 29-35; also 'Five Gospels but No Gospel: Jesus and the Seminar', in B. Chilton and C. A. Evans, eds., *Authenticating the Activities of Jesus* (NTTS 28.2; Leiden: Brill, 1999) 83-120; for critique of the Jesus Seminar see also Witherington, *Jesus Quest* ch. 2.

177. Wright, *Jesus* 81, 95-97, 202-11. Also Horsley, *Jesus* 157-60, 168-72, though not so trenchantly. Cf. Morgan, *Biblical Interpretation:* 'Religious symbols . . . are not to be analysed as information about the end of the world' (245).

ant', 'a free spirit', 'the proverbial party animal', 'a vagabond sage', 'a simple sage', 'a subversive sage', 'the subverter of the everyday world around him' (Funk);[178] Jesus as a liberation theologian;[179] a Jesus almost completely shorn of kingdom of God language and Jewish concerns, emerging instead as a teacher of aphoristic wisdom heavily influenced by the Cynic philosophy of Hellenized Galilee;[180] 'a social gadfly, an irritant on the skin of conventional mores and values', a Cynic Jesus.[181] Much more carefully delineating on his broad canvas and giving welcome renewed attention to the stories of Jesus' healings, Crossan nevertheless ends up with Jesus as 'a peasant Jewish Cynic' calling for a radical egalitarianism and proclaiming 'the brokerless kingdom of God'.[182] Borg has developed a more richly rounded picture of Jesus,[183] but stands within the Jesus Seminar in characterising Jesus as 'a teacher of a culturally subversive wisdom . . . who taught a subversive and alternative wisdom'.[184] This is not the nineteenth-century Liberal redivivus. But it is a Jesus stripped of the elements of (later) faith which modernity has found so problematic. Nor is it the kindly nineteenth-century Sunday School teacher who has thus been recovered. But it is a Jesus who could well be imagined in many a twentieth-century faculty staff room or as an independent 'loose cannon' academic, with his unsettling anecdotes, disturbing aphorisms, and provocative rhetoric.[185] Consequently, the same question arises once again which

178. Quotations from Funk, *Honest* 204, 208, 212, 252-53, 302.

179. J. M. Robinson, 'The Jesus of Q as Liberation Theologian', a paper delivered to the Jesus Seminar in 1991, published in Piper, ed., *The Gospel behind the Gospels* 259-74.

180. B. L. Mack, *A Myth of Innocence: Mark and Christian Origins* (Philadelphia: Fortress, 1988) ch. 2; e.g., 'Jesus' wisdom incorporated the pungent invitation to insight and the daring to be different that characterized the Cynic approach to life' (69); similarly 'Q and a Cynic-Like Jesus', in W. E. Arnal and M. Desjardins, eds., *Whose Historical Jesus?* (SCJ 7; Waterloo: Wilfrid Laurier University, 1997) 25-36.

181. L. E. Vaage, *Galilean Upstarts: Jesus' First Followers According to Q* (Valley Forge: Trinity, 1994) 102.

182. Crossan, *Historical Jesus* 421-22. As Witherington notes, Crossan's more popular version, *Jesus: A Revolutionary Biography* (San Francisco: HarperSanFrancisco, 1994) 121-22 seems to modify the earlier 'Jewish Cynic peasant model' (*Jesus Quest* 89). The qualifications increase in Crossan, *Birth* 280-81, 333-35, 412-13. Fuller critique in Witherington, *Jesus Quest* 64-92; Wright, *Jesus* 44-65.

183. In *Jesus: A New Vision* (San Francisco: Harper and Row, 1987) Borg developed his earlier portrayal by adding characterisation of Jesus as a holy person conscious of Spirit empowering and Jesus as a sage or teacher of wisdom (see Borg's own account in *Jesus in Contemporary Scholarship* 26-28). Like Horsley (see §4.6 above), he also emphasizes Jesus' social world. He summarizes his portrayal of Jesus in M. Borg, ed., *Jesus at 2000* (Boulder: Westview, 1997) 11: Jesus was (1) a Spirit person, (2) a healer, (3) a wisdom teacher, (4) a social prophet, (5) a movement initiator.

184. Borg, *Jesus: A New Vision* 115-16; *Jesus in Contemporary Scholarship* 9-10.

185. Funk himself notes that 'the use of "itinerant" or "transient" [in relation to Jesus]

proved so fatal to the nineteenth-century Liberal Jesus: whether this neo-Liberal Jesus is any less a construct and retrojection of late-twentieth-century ideals and aspirations than was the Liberal Jesus of late-nineteenth-century ideals and aspirations.[186] And Temple's jibe still has resonance: is it any less of a mystery why anyone should have troubled to crucify the Christ of neo-Liberalism?[187] These issues will also remain with us as we proceed.

More questionable is Crossan's confidence in his new sources, in his ability to set them all into sequential strata, and even more in his ability to attribute particular traditions to these different strata.[188] But Crossan is only a somewhat extreme exponent of a more widely supported trend in favour of recognizing that later documents have preserved earlier traditions. And the importance of the discovery of the *Gospel of Thomas* in particular should not be understated.[189] For in it, for the first time, we have a complete, unified, and coherent sayings Gospel. At a stroke, then, *Thomas* has given a degree of credibility to the hypothesis of a sayings source (Q) for Matthew and Luke which the hypothesis never previously enjoyed.[190] Moreover, the degree of overlap between Q material and *Thomas,* and the fact that we have evidence of an earlier Greek version of *Thomas,*[191] point to some kind of 'trajectory' from or through Q to *Thomas* which is different from the incorporation of Q by Matthew and Luke into their Gospels.[192] It also

---

may merely echo academic empathy for our own rootless age' (*Honest* 87). Mack speaks of 'the telltale remnants of a rather playful mode of response', and notes as characteristic of this manner of conversation 'wit, skillful manipulation of the limits of conventional logic, and delight in repartee . . .' (*Myth* 62).

186. Crossan is fully aware of the danger: 'It is impossible to avoid the suspicion that historical Jesus research is a very safe place to do theology and call it history, to do autobiography and call it biography' (*Historical Jesus* xxviii).

187. See above, n. 110.

188. Note the sharp critique by C. M. Tuckett, 'The Historical Jesus, Crossan and Methodology', in S. Maser and E. Schlarb, eds., *Text und Geschichte,* D. Lührmann FS (Marburg: Elwert, 1999) 257-79; criticisms include Crossan's privileging of *Thomas* and Q and his arbitrariness in failing to acknowledge that there may be 'sources' other than Mark and Q behind Matthew and Luke and a 'miracles collection' behind Mark (262-65, 273).

189. Many versions are available; see chapter 7, n. 104 below.

190. The parallels between *Thomas* and the four canonical Gospels are conveniently listed by J. K. Elliott, *The Apocryphal New Testament* (Oxford: Clarendon, 1993) 133-35. The sayings material has been set out in parallel by W. D. Stroker, *Extracanonical Sayings of Jesus* (Atlanta: Scholars, 1989), and J. D. Crossan, *Sayings Parallels: A Workbook for the Jesus Tradition* (Philadelphia: Fortress, 1986).

191. The Oxyrhynchus papyri were recovered between 1897 and 1904. Following the discovery of the *Gospel of Thomas* it was realised that Pap. Oxy. 1 contains *Thomas* 26-33 and 77, Pap. Oxy. 654 contains *Thomas* 1-7, and Pap. Oxy. 655 contains *Thomas* 36-39.

192. Noted originally by J. M. Robinson, 'LOGOI SOPHON: On the Gattung of Q' (1964), ET in Robinson and Koester, *Trajectories* 71-113.

follows that the call, originally made by Wrede,[193] for inquiry into Christian origins to ignore the boundaries formed by the canon, hitherto of little real effect, has now to be given serious attention as never before.[194] These two facts revolutionise the issue of sources for knowledge of Jesus' own preaching and teaching, and the use to be made of Q and *Thomas* in particular will require fuller consideration later (chapter 7).

The reappearance of a deapocalypticised Jesus constitutes a protest against the influence of Weiss and Schweitzer, who had previously been credited with putting in place one of the most important parameters for twentieth-century 'historical Jesus' research. The importance of the protest lies in the fact that non-apocalypticism has become one of the hallmarks of the neo-Liberal Jesus: it is the absence of apocalyptic sayings in the *Gospel of Thomas* which allows it to be dated early; and the possibility of separating out a non-apocalyptic layer in Q results similarly in a non- or pre-apocalyptic $1Q/Q^1$.[195] In each case the finding is taken to confirm that Jesus' own preaching was non-apocalyptic, though it is hard to see how the argument escapes the criticism of *petitio principii* (begging the question). The loss of Schweitzer's 'stranger and enigma' yardstick for responsible critical reconstruction of the 'historical Jesus' is probably even more serious. The attractiveness of the neo-Liberal Jesus to an unrepresentative strand in NT scholarship, a counter-culture Jesus who serves as an iconic precedent for all anti-establishment restiveness, or a Jesus who was more sophisticatedly subversive than an apocalyptic prophet,[196] should have provided warning enough. The historical distance and difference has once again been elided. Jesus has once again been modernized; or should we rather say, post-modernized!

It is somewhat unnerving thus to find the quest beginning in effect to repeat itself and the governing idea reappearing so strongly, that lurking somewhere behind the Synoptic tradition there is a 'historical Jesus', untrammelled by what late-twentieth-century sensibilities regard as unacceptable dogmas, just waiting to be found and to function as a corrective to later distortions. Quite apart from the issues which it has posed afresh, then, the neo-Liberal quest provides a strong

193. Wrede, 'The Task and Methods of "New Testament Theology"' 68-116.

194. So particularly H. Koester, 'GNOMAI DIAPHOROI: The Origin and Nature of Diversification in the History of Early Christianity', *HTR* 58 (1965) 279-318, reprinted in Robinson and Koester, *Trajectories* 114-57 (here 115, 119); also his discussion of the genre 'gospel' in *Ancient Christian Gospels* 43-48.

195. Particularly Koester, e.g., 'One Jesus and Four Primitive Gospels', *HTR* 61 (1968) 203-47, reprinted in Robinson and Koester, *Trajectories* 158-204 (here 171); also *Ancient Christian Gospels* 87.

196. Borg evidently wishes to distance Jesus from the sort of Christian groups today which 'most of us know' and 'for whom the imminent expectation of the second coming and the final judgment is central' (*Jesus in Contemporary Scholarship* 78, 82-83).

reminder that the tension, or perhaps better, confrontation between faith and history is still strong and that the flight from dogma continues to be a motivating force in attempts to reconstruct the historical Jesus.

4.8. Conclusion

To sum up, the flight from dogma has left us a number of markers for future consideration: the importance of the gap between Jesus and his followers, Paul in particular (Reimarus, Harnack); the problem of miracle and the importance of taking the intention of the miracle narratives seriously (Strauss); the necessity to check tradition against its original sources and therefore to recover these sources (Liberals and neo-Liberals); the importance of some experiential rapport between the interpreter and the text (Schleiermacher) and of taking seriously the ethical outcome of beliefs (Liberals); the danger of modernizing Jesus and of failing to recognize his otherness, with particular reference to his eschatological preaching (Schweitzer); the importance of recognizing that faith played an important part in shaping the tradition from its earliest stages (Kähler); the need to take account of the social context of Jesus and of the movement he initiated (Theissen, Horsley); the necessity to extend our search for sources of Jesus' teaching beyond the boundaries of the canon (Koester, Crossan). Other items could be added, but these certainly provide a substantial agenda to be going on with.

And all this is still only one side of the story.

CHAPTER 5

The Flight from History

The quest for the historical figure known as Jesus of Nazareth has been marked throughout by tension between faith and history. Initially the faith in question was conceived as dogma, the developed and formalized faith of the Christian churches, perceived as forming a kind of suffocating layer which separated present from past, or even a kind of prison from which the historical Jesus needed to be liberated. At first history was seen as the great liberator. Careful historical research, it was assumed, would enable the present to reconstruct the past clearly enough to expose to modern gaze the real (historical) Jesus. And even when faith returned to a more experiential and less cerebral form, it was still assumed that historical inquiry would enable a fresh encounter between the faith of the 'historical Jesus' and the faith of the present-day believer. The surprising confidence of the neo-Liberal quest bespeaks the same liberal optimism, that the tools of historical inquiry are wholly adequate for the job of finding a wise teacher behind the theologized Gospel portrayal, behind the dogmatic Christ of classic Christian faith. It is matched only by the same confidence in their ability to decompose documents, not least later Gnostic Gospels, into definite compositional layers and more 'original' tradition.

But there is the other side of the tension still to be considered, a second plot line running through the story of the quest. History has by no means always been seen as a positive force. And what it is that history, that is, historical inquiry, can actually do, what historical research can actually be expected to produce, are questions too little asked by too many of those involved in the quest. It is this second feature of the quest, including the hermeneutical questions it has posed, to which we now turn.

5.1. The Historical-Critical Method

Two people are usually given credit for stating and defining most clearly the principles on which critical historical study is postulated and the sobering consequences which follow.[1]

The first is Gotthold Lessing (1729-81).[2] As the publisher of Reimarus's *Fragments,* Lessing was vulnerable to criticism,[3] and though he was no less a rationalist himself, he attempted to meet the challenge posed by Reimarus at a more profound level. He did so in one of his most famous pamphlets, *On the Proof of the Spirit and of Power* (1777),[4] by distinguishing between the reports of miraculous events and the events themselves, and thus in effect drove a wedge between faith and history. In brief, Lessing offers his own version of what was then a widely perceived distinction between two kinds of truth:[5] *religious* truths which no rational man would dispute, including the existence of God and the immortality of the soul (this was the rationalist creed), and *historical* truths, subject to historical inquiry, and capable of providing no basis for religious faith. The former are innate, self-evident, necessary; the latter are contingent, accidental, always uncertain, since the historian can deal only in the probabilities of reconstruction out of human testimonies. Hence Lessing's much-quoted dictum: 'accidental truths of history can never become the proof of necessary truths of reason'. And consequently there comes into focus what Lessing calls 'the ugly, broad ditch', between historical (un)certainty and the certainty of the necessary truths of reason, 'which I cannot get across, however often and however earnestly I have tried to make the leap'.[6] In other words, to

---

1. A fuller treatment would have to take account of the pioneer work of Richard Simon (1638-1712), often regarded as the founder of modern biblical criticism (Kümmel, *New Testament* 41-47; Baird, *History* 17-25), and particularly of Spinoza (surprisingly ignored by Kümmel and mentioned only briefly by Baird; but see Dungan, *History* ch. 16, particularly 212-16, 227-42 — Dungan's own estimate of Spinoza's importance [6-7]; the key chapter from Spinoza's *Tractatus Theologico-Politicus* [1670], on the interpretation of Scripture, is reproduced by Dawes, *Historical Jesus Quest* 5-26).

2. For analysis and evaluation of Lessing see Chadwick, *Lessing's Theological Writings* 30-49; Brown, *Jesus* 16-29; Baird, *History* 165-69; O'Neill, *Authority* 13-27.

3. Schweitzer, e.g., cites Semler's attempt to ridicule Reimarus's editor (*Quest*[1] 15-16; *Quest*[2] 16).

4. ET in Chadwick, *Lessing's Theological Writings* 51-56. The pamphlet was thus published between Lessing's publication of Reimarus's Fragment 'On the Resurrection Narrative' (1777) and that of the Fragment 'On the Intentions of Jesus and His Disciples' (1778). See also Talbert's Introduction to *Reimarus* 29-34.

5. Chadwick notes Lessing's debt to Leibniz and the English Deists (*Lessing's Theological Writings* 30-36).

6. Chadwick, *Lessing's Theological Writings* 53, 55. See further Barth, *Rousseau to*

transpose Lessing's language to the terms of the present study, it is impossible to 'prove' faith from history.

However, it was Ernst Troeltsch who at the end of the nineteenth century posed the dilemma of the historical-critical method most sharply.[7] Troeltsch identified three principal characteristics of 'the historical method': *probability, analogy* and *correlation.*[8] By 'probability' he had in view Lessing's chief characterisation of historical truth (at best probable, never certain), 'the final result being never more than probably correct'. By 'analogy' he meant the necessary assumption that the past was analogous to the present, that the laws of nature operated then as now, that human beings were constituted and interacted in ways that we today can understand from our own experience; otherwise how could we even begin to make sense of accounts of events and human actions which have come down to us?[9] And by 'correlation' he had in mind the interrelatedness of all events and processes ('No man is an island'), which means that no single event could be extracted from that correlation and explained apart from it — Troeltsch's version of the Enlightenment's vision of the cosmos as an interlocking machine and closed system, what he subsequently called 'the web of causality'.[10]

The problem is, as Troeltsch well recognized, that since everything in history is, properly speaking, historical, it becomes impossible to escape the consequent ravages of the historical method as defined by Troeltsch. 'Once it is applied to biblical scholarship and church history, (the historical method) is a leaven which transforms everything and which finally causes the form of all pre-

---

Ritschl 133-38. O'Neill describes this as 'a move that marks a turning point in the history of European thought' (*Authority* 19).

7. E. Troeltsch, 'Über historische und dogmatische Methode in der Theologie', *Gesammelte Schriften* 2 (Tübingen: Mohr, 1913) 729-53, ET 'Historical and Dogmatic Method in Theology', *Religion in History: Ernst Troeltsch* (Edinburgh: Clark, 1991), reprinted in Dawes, ed., *Historical Jesus Quest* 29-53. For the influence of Troeltsch, see, e.g., D. E. Nineham (discussed by A. C. Thiselton, *The Two Horizons* [Exeter: Paternoster, 1980] 53-60); also Nineham's Foreword to Schweitzer's *Quest*[2] xiv, xxiii, xxix; V. A. Harvey, *The Historian and the Believer* (London: SCM, 1966), who takes Troeltsch as his starting point; and J. Bowden, *Jesus: The Unanswered Questions* (London: SCM, 1988) 148-60.

8. I cheat a little: Troeltsch defines his first 'essential aspect' as 'the habituation on principle to historical criticism', but he immediately makes it clear what that means — that 'in the realm of history there are only judgments of probability' ('Historical and Dogmatic Method' 32).

9. 'Agreement with normal, customary, or at least frequently attested happenings and conditions as we have experienced them is the criterion of probability for all events that historical criticism can recognize as having actually or possibly happened. The observation of analogies between similar events in the past provides the possibility of imputing probability to them and of interpreting what is unknown about the one by reference to what is known about the other' (Troeltsch, 'Historical and Dogmatic Method' 32-33).

10. Troeltsch, 'Historiography' 717.

vious theological methods to disintegrate'; 'it relativizes everything'.[11] In other words, anything and everything in history cannot avoid being subjected to the scrutiny of the historical-critical method, and therefore falls prey to the loss of that certainty which faith so much prizes. To change the metaphor, the acids which the historical method uses to clean away the surface varnish and later reworkings of the original painting eat not only into such later accretions but into the original painting and the very canvas itself.

Of course, in one sense, Troeltsch was simply restating the problem of all historical inquiry and underscoring the humility and tentativeness which all attempts at historical reconstruction should exercise. Here undoubtedly the observations and arguments of Lessing and Troeltsch need to be taken seriously if historical statements regarding Jesus are to carry any weight. So too with Troeltsch's second characteristic, the principle of analogy. In fact it was a standard principle in nineteenth-century Romantic historiography: the conviction that understanding is only possible because of the homogeneity of human nature, that throughout history 'all men think, feel, will as we ourselves would in a like situation'.[12] In the words of the great nineteenth-century historian J. G. Droysen, 'With respect to men, human utterances, and forms, we are, and feel ourselves to be, essentially similar and in a condition of mutuality'.[13] The third principle found its fullest exposition in the history-of-religions method, which set the investigation and evaluation of Christianity within the framework of the history of religion and culture and sought to understand its emergence, including Jesus, as part of a general historical process.[14] Yet one cannot help wondering whether the last two principles (analogy and correlation) are not inevitably too restrictive. In particular, can they recognize the *novum,* the genuinely new?[15] And anyway, are they not too much bound up with a nineteenth-century Newtonian view of the world and of causation which the twentieth century was soon to leave behind? To such questions we will have to return.

11. 'Historical and Dogmatic Method' 31, 37 (the first following the translation of Bowden, *Jesus* 153).

12. The quotation is from H. N. Tuttle's analysis of Dilthey, quoted by Thiselton, *Two Horizons* 69.

13. Cited by H.-G. Gadamer, *Truth and Method* (New York: Crossroad, [2]1989) 217.

14. Riches cites Otto Pfleiderer in particular (*Century of New Testament Study* 7-8, 11).

15. 'At every point there do indeed emerge unique and autonomous historical forces that, by virtue of our capacity for empathy, we perceive to be related to our common humanity. At the same time, however, these unique forces also stand in a current and context comprehending the totality of events, where we see everything conditioned by everything else so that there is no point within history which is beyond this correlative involvement and mutual influence' (Troeltsch, 'Historical and Dogmatic Method' 33); see also 'Historiography' 719b-720a.

5.2. The Search for an Invulnerable Area for Faith

However we may now evaluate the fundamental statements about historical method by Lessing and Troeltsch, the fact is that the strict application of historical method became a major problem for those who wished to maintain some sort of faith standpoint. The response was a flight from history, less trumpeted than the Enlightenment's flight from dogma, but just as critical for the understanding and expression of faith.

Lessing's (or the Enlightenment) solution, as we have seen, was to postulate an area for faith ('necessary truths of reason')[16] incapable of historical investigation, to maintain that religious truth is of a different order from historical truth, and that the former in no way needs or depends on the latter. But the theory of innate ideas ('necessary truths of reason') could not last;[17] the truths self-evident to all 'men of reason' soon proved to be neither self-evident nor necessary. Nor have either Reimarus's rationalist Jesus or Strauss's idea of God-manhood commanded lasting assent. Historical method had proved merely reductive of faith; even the much diminished faith that remained had not escaped its withering power after all.

As the epistemological debate moved on, the nineteenth-century Protestant Liberals attempted to locate the safe area for faith in Schleiermacher's religious consciousness, which is not in the end amenable to historical analysis, or in Kant's sense of moral obligation, from which a religious ethic could be derived independently of the NT. The climactic result was in effect the stripping away of all historical accidentals from the eternal verities taught (as it happened!) by Jesus. The urge to find an area for faith invulnerable to historical questioning (in Kähler's phrase, a *sturmfreies Gebiet,* a 'storm-free area') was a major motivating factor particularly for one of Bultmann's teachers in the late nineteenth century, Wilhelm Herrmann, and for Kähler himself.

In his influential study, Herrmann claimed to recognize the force of Lessing's caveats on the weight attachable to historical judgment,[18] but argued that a secure base can nonetheless be found in religious experience, the experience of faith: the power of Jesus' inner life reaches across the centuries; 'Jesus Himself and His power over the heart is actually the vital principal [*sic*] of our religion'.[19] This emphasis on the reality and power of religious experience, over

---

16. I note again that 'faith' is my term.

17. It had already been heavily criticized by Locke in his *Essay Concerning Human Understanding* (1690) and was about to be subjected to Kant's *Critique of Pure Reason* (1781).

18. Herrmann, *Communion* 72.

19. Herrmann, *Communion* 109; '. . . whenever we come to see the Person of Jesus, then, under the impress of that inner life that breaks through all the veils of the story, we ask no more questions as to the trustworthiness of the Evangelists' (75); 'When we speak of the historical

against an understanding of faith primarily in terms of uniform dogma, is to be welcomed; Herrmann's focus on the experience of faith was influential on both Barth and Bultmann, and his emphasis on the faith of Jesus anticipated the later interest in the subject in the second half of the twentieth century. But the will-o'-the-wisp of Jesus' 'inner life' was hardly a secure area of retreat from the threats of historical method.[20]

More effective and of more lasting influence was the contribution of Kähler. He took the challenge of historical criticism more seriously, and instead of ducking the challenge he accepted it in full. 'We do not possess any sources for a "Life of Jesus" which a historian can accept as reliable and adequate'. Historical scholarship leaves us with 'mere probabilities'. The sources contain nothing capable of sustaining a biography of Jesus.[21] Despite Lessing, the effective assumption in life of Jesus research had been that faith must rest on the historical Jesus, that is, on Jesus insofar as he could be uncovered and reconstructed by historical-critical research. But the multiplicity of different reconstructions only made faith harder and not easier.[22] More to the point, only a few scholars have the specialist training to carry through such reconstruction. Is faith, then, to depend on the findings of a few scholars? Are critical historians to become the new priests and pope of Christian faith? No! To tie faith to the historical accuracy of this or that detail would wholly undermine faith. Faith looks only to the historic Christ, the biblical Christ, 'the Christ who is preached'.[23] 'The biblical Christ is the "invulnerable area" from which faith can gain its certainty without relying on the heteronomous guarantees of external authorities'.[24]

This move to link faith with the preached Christ anticipated Bultmann, and the shift from a reconstructed Jesus *behind* the Gospels to the Christ *of* the Gospels anticipated the more recent focus on the Gospels themselves rather than on

---

Christ we mean that personal life of Jesus which speaks to us from the New Testament' (77); 'Doubt as to its actual historicity can really be overcome only by looking to the contents of what we learn to know as the inner life of Jesus' (113); 'The traditional record may appear doubtful; but the essential content of that record, namely, the inner life of Jesus, has the power to manifest itself to the conscience as an undeniable fact. That means everything' (235-36). A second 'objective fact' for Herrmann 'is that we hear within ourselves the demand of the moral law' (103).

20. Troeltsch was dismissive: 'The whole position is untenable in the face of historical criticism' ('The Significance of the Historical Existence of Jesus' 192; see also 198).

21. Kähler, *So-Called Historical Jesus* 48, 50-52. 'The inner development of a sinless person is as inconceivable to us as life on the Sandwich Islands is to a Laplander' (53).

22. 'Historical facts which first have to be established by science cannot *as such* become experiences of faith. Therefore, Christian faith and a history of Jesus repel each other like oil and water . . .' (Kähler, *So-Called Historical Jesus* 74).

23. Kähler, *So-Called Historical Jesus* 66, 72-73, 109-10 (Braaten's 'Introduction' 26-27).

24. Braaten's 'Introduction' 29.

the history behind the Gospels. But if the hope was to present a single Christ over against the multiply diverse reconstructions of the historical Jesus, it ignores the interpretative problems and hermeneutical reality which confront readers of the NT and hearers of its message(s). For even in the NT there are several 'Christs of faith',[25] and if we are talking of the experience of faith in encounter with the preached Christ, then the diversity of experiences may be as problematical as the diversity of historical Jesuses. Is the biblical Christ, then, quite such an invulnerable area for faith? And is history so dispensable as Kähler implies? Kähler's 'Yes' to these questions began to be seriously questioned only in the second half of the twentieth century. In the meantime the flight from history continued.

5.3. Rudolf Bultmann (1884-1976)

By common consent, Karl Barth (1886-1968) rang the death knell on Liberal Protestantism. It gave no message for a war-torn Europe; the message of optimistic moralism was no gospel. In contrast, Paul's letter to the Romans spoke a gospel of divine sovereignty and transcendence, of human finitude and sinfulness, and of God's initiative in revelation and grace. The good news is conveyed through the kerygma about Christ, the proclamation that God has drawn near in Jesus, not in a Jesus discovered by historical analysis. In his epoch-making *Epistle to the Romans* Barth strongly reaffirmed Kähler's position: 'In history as such there is nothing so far as the eye can see which can provide a basis for faith'.[26]

In a famous correspondence between Harnack and Barth (1923),[27] Harnack accused Barth of abandoning scientific theology, and of surrendering the gains of the previous decades. Barth replied that historical criticism has its rightful place, but that it also has its limitations: it can deal only with the words of Paul; it cannot get to the word of God within Paul's words. Harnack claimed that theology can be defined historically, the simple gospel of Jesus historically rediscovered as over against the intellectualisation imposed on it through the in-

---

25. See my *Unity and Diversity* 216-26.

26. Cited by H. Zahrnt, *The Historical Jesus* (London: Collins, 1963) 68. Influential also was the comment of the Danish philosopher Søren Kierkegaard (1813-1855): 'If the contemporary generation [of Jesus] had left nothing behind them but these words: "We have believed that in such and such a year the God appeared among us in the humble form of a servant, that he lived and taught in our community, and finally died", it would have done all that was necessary' (*Philosophical Fragments* [Princeton: Princeton University, [2]1962] 130). See also L. E. Keck, *A Future for the Historical Jesus* (Nashville: Abingdon, 1971) 49-50, 84-85.

27. For details see J. M. Robinson, *A New Quest of the Historical Jesus* (London: SCM, 1959) 45. See further H. M. Rumscheidt, *Revelation and Theology: An Analysis of the Barth-Harnack Correspondence of 1923* (Cambridge: Cambridge University, 1972).

fluences of Greek philosophy. Barth replied that Harnack was reducing Christianity to the human level; theology was concerned rather with the transcendent God and his approach in Christ, not with the religious life as exemplified in Jesus. Taking up 2 Cor. 5.16, Barth affirmed that we know Christ no longer according to the flesh: this is the Jesus with whom critical scholarship is concerned, and over whom it disagrees; rather it is the Christ of faith with whom we have to do, who confronts us now in the Word of God. This debate had a decisive influence on Bultmann, who abandoned the Liberalism in which he had been trained and embraced Barth's kerygmatic theology.[28]

Bultmann's principal contribution to our story lies in his development of what quickly became known in the English-speaking world as 'form criticism'.[29] In this he was building on the work of two immediate predecessors. Julius Wellhausen had demonstrated that in each of the Synoptic Gospels one can distinguish between old tradition and the editorial contribution of the Evangelists. It is the editorial work and concerns of the Evangelist which have given each Gospel its present form, whereas the earlier tradition consists chiefly of single brief units.[30] K. L. Schmidt had gone on to examine the connecting links which join together the separate episodes in Mark's Gospel. He concluded that almost all the references to time and place are to be found in the verses which connect the single narratives into the larger whole; that is, they are part of the editorial work of the Evangelist. It also follows that the original tradition was made up almost entirely of brief, single units which lack note of time or indication of place; that is, which lack historical reference. The impression that Mark gives of being a continuous historical narrative is given entirely by the editorial links.[31] These conclusions became foundational for Bultmann: (i) the distinction between earlier tradition and editorial work, (ii) the nature of the earlier tradition — single units, and (iii) the lack of historical interest within the earlier tradition.[32]

28. Robinson, *New Quest* 46.

29. The English term is not a translation, but is modeled on the parallel of 'text criticism' and 'source criticism'. The German term *Formgeschichte* was coined by M. Dibelius, *Die Formgeschichte des Evangeliums* (1919), ET *From Tradition to Gospel* (London: Nicholson and Watson, 1934) and denotes the 'history of the form', thus focusing much more on the process than on the forms themselves. The difference in emphasis had unfortunate consequences.

30. Summed up in his *Einleitung in die drei ersten Evangelien* (Berlin: Reimer, 1905): 'The ultimate source of the Gospels is oral tradition, but this contains only scattered material. The units, more or less extensive, circulate in it separately. Their combination into a whole is always the work of an author and as a rule the work of a literary artist *(Schriftsteller)*' (43).

31. K. L. Schmidt, *Der Rahmen der Geschichte Jesus: Literarkritische Untersuchungen zur ältesten Jesusüberlieferung* (Berlin: Trowitzsch, 1919).

32. Bultmann acknowledges his debt to Wellhausen and Schmidt in his 'The New Approach to the Synoptic Problem' (1926), *Existence and Faith* (London: Collins, Fontana, 1964) 39-62 (here 42-44).

These conclusions allowed the earliest form critics to take a decisive step forward. The Liberal quest of the historical Jesus had been content with having uncovered the two earliest sources of Jesus tradition (Mark and Q). But Wrede's insistence on the theological character of Mark (see above, §4.5b) had undermined the previous confidence in Mark as a source for historical information. Now Dibelius and Bultmann offered the prospect of getting behind the earliest sources. Dibelius defined the twofold objective of *Formgeschichte* thus: 'it seeks to explain the origin of the tradition about Jesus, and thus to penetrate into a period previous to that in which our Gospels and their written sources were recorded . . . (and) to make clear the intention and real interest of the earliest tradition'.[33] Bultmann similarly defines the aim of form criticism: 'to rediscover the origin and the history of the particular units and thereby to throw some light on the history of the tradition before it took literary form'.[34] At first this might seem to give renewed hope to questers: to get back to the earliest stages of the traditions regarding Jesus must surely bring one closer to the historical figure of Jesus. But had such a hope been entertained, Bultmann would soon have dashed it.

The way had already been closed off by the observation that the earlier forms display no historical interest in locating particular episodes or sayings at specific points within Jesus' ministry. Which is also to say that there was no interest in these earlier stages of the Jesus tradition in tracing out any development in Jesus or in his self-consciousness.[35] But that also means that there is no biographical interest in or intent behind the tradition in its earlier forms. This is the basis for Bultmann's much-quoted dictum:[36]

> I do indeed think that we can know almost nothing concerning the life and personality of Jesus, since the early Christian sources show no interest in either, are moreover fragmentary and often legendary; and other sources about Jesus do not exist. . . . [W]hat has been written in the last hundred and fifty years on the life of Jesus, his personality and the development of his inner life, is fantastic and romantic.

33. Dibelius, *Tradition* v.

34. R. Bultmann, *The History of the Synoptic Tradition* (1921, [2]1931; ET Oxford: Blackwell, 1963) 4.

35. A classic example is the Synoptic accounts of Jesus' baptism. They recount an event which happened to Jesus, not an experience of Jesus. Dibelius expressed the point sharply: 'It is not credible that the origin of the whole narrative goes back to what Jesus himself told of his inner experience at the baptism, otherwise the section would have been preserved as a word of Jesus' (*Tradition* 274). Despite this, most lives of Jesus have felt free to speculate about the sense of vocation which Jesus received on that occasion; see further below §11.5b.

36. R. Bultmann, *Jesus and the Word* (1926; ET New York: Scribners, 1935) 8.

It is important to recognize here, however, that what Bultmann was decrying was the pointless inquiry after Jesus' *personality* and *inner life*. He was much more confident about reaching back to the message of Jesus. Four pages later he also says: 'Little as we know of his life and personality, we know enough of his *message* to make for ourselves a consistent picture'.[37] Yet what did this mean? Bultmann envisages the Jesus tradition as 'a series of layers', Hellenistic and Greek, Palestinian and Aramaic, within which again 'different layers can be distinguished'. By means of critical analysis 'an oldest layer' can be determined, 'though it can be marked off with only relative exactness'. Even then 'we have no absolute assurance that the exact words of this oldest layer were really spoken by Jesus', since there is the possibility of still earlier development in the tradition 'which we can no longer trace'.[38] In other words, the earliest layer, to which Bultmann in fact traces about twenty-five sayings of Jesus (some forty-one verses), gives us a sufficient impression of the teaching of the man who stands behind the oldest Palestinian community which preserved that first layer.[39] And on that understanding, Bultmann proceeded to give an impressive sketch of the teaching of Jesus, or, as he notes some might prefer, of 'Jesus'. Of Jesus' teaching only, it should also be noted; almost a century later, the impact of Strauss was still being felt.

The other roadblock for any would-be questers which Bultmann's exposition of form criticism erected was his observation that 'what the sources offer us is first of all the message of the early Christian community'.[40] In this, of course, he follows Wrede and Wellhausen.[41] But for Bultmann the observation applies equally to the earlier layers of tradition. This is where the key phrase *Sitz-im-Leben* ('life-setting') became crucially significant: the tradition as we have it bears witness first and foremost to the 'life-setting' which gave the tradition its present form. It was the usefulness of the tradition to the life of the earliest churches which gave the tradition its shape, and from that shape we can deduce the concerns of the earliest churches more directly than any deduction we may draw regarding Jesus' own message. What this meant in practice for Bultmann was, first of all, the recognition that many of the sayings would have been modified in the course of transmission. The point is that the traditions of Jesus' teaching were preserved not for any archival value, but because of their continuing value to the early community. And since the needs and circumstances of the earliest churches would differ from those of Jesus, the tradition would inevitably

37. Bultmann, *Jesus* 12.
38. Bultmann, *Jesus* 13.
39. 'The Study of the Synoptic Gospels', *Form Criticism* (with K. Kundsin, 1934; New York: Harper, 1962) 11-76 (here 60-63).
40. Bultmann, *Jesus* 12.
41. Bultmann, 'New Approach' 41-43; note Robinson's gloss in *New Quest* 35.

have been adapted and shaped. It also meant, secondly, that 'many sayings [within the Jesus tradition] originated in the church itself'. Here Bultmann envisages material being drawn in from Judaism and wider religious traditions, or early Christian prophets speaking a word of (the risen) Jesus, in each case, presumably, words which spoke to the community's needs and which were considered by the community as worthy of inclusion in the Jesus tradition.[42] This working hypothesis provided Bultmann with one of his key critical tools: 'whatever betrays the specific interests of the church or reveals characteristics of later development must be rejected as secondary'.[43]

More to the immediate point, none of these negative conclusions (negative for questers) really mattered. For form criticism gave Bultmann the confirmation (provided, ironically, by his historical method) that his theological shift, in following Barth, was correct. The early church was also not interested in the historical figure of Jesus, that is, in the life and personality of the Jesus who walked and taught in Galilee. Kähler was right: the only Jesus who meets us through the pages of the Gospels, even when we have completed our form-critical analysis, is the Christ of faith. Barth's claim that all hangs on the word of God in preaching depends not only on Paul, but is confirmed also by the Gospels. This Christ of faith can be encountered in the here and now and is not at all dependent on a reconstructed historical Jesus, were that even possible. The conclusion that it is not possible carries critical historical weight, but no significance for faith. Faith does not depend, and should not be made to depend, on history. In an outcome that reflects the influence of Herrmann as well as Kähler, Bultmann was in effect able to find a secure refuge for faith in the moment of existential encounter with the word of proclamation, an area for faith invulnerable indeed to the challenge and acids of historical criticism.

In all this Bultmann was able to bridge, or rather disregard, the gulf between his negative historical-critical findings and his very positive faith in the kerygmatic Christ by means of an existentialist hermeneutic. He makes this clear in a revealing passage in *Jesus and the Word*.[44]

> When I speak of the teaching or thought of Jesus, I base the discussion on no underlying conception of a universally valid system of thought [like his ra-

42. See further below §8.2.

43. Bultmann, *Jesus* 13.

44. Bultmann, *Jesus* 11. He was more explicit in his famous 1941 address on 'Neues Testament und Mythologie: Das Problem der Entmythologisierung der neutestamentlichen Verkündigung', in which he directly addressed the problem of interpreting the thought-world of the NT writers and unfolded his programme of demythologizing: 'Our task is to produce an existentialist interpretation of the dualistic mythology of the New Testament . . .' (ET 'New Testament and Mythology', in H. W. Bartsch, ed., *Kerygma and Myth* [London: SPCK, 1957] 1-44 [here 16]).

tionalist and Liberal predecessors]. . . . Rather the ideas are understood in the light of the concrete situation of a man living in time; as his interpretation of his own existence in the midst of change, uncertainty, decision; as the expression of a possibility of comprehending this life; as the effort to gain clear insight into the contingencies and necessities of his own existence. When we encounter the words of Jesus in history, *we* do not judge *them* by a philosophical system with reference to their rational validity; *they* meet *us* with the question of how we are to interpret our own existence. That we be ourselves deeply disturbed by the problem of our own life is therefore the indispensable condition of our inquiry.

Here, as with Herrmann and Kähler, one cannot but be impressed by the degree of personal involvement with the subject matter so evident in all Bultmann's theology; that is what makes it such good theologising. But even so, we can hardly avoid asking whether Bultmann's existentialist hermeneutic is any more valid than Reimarus's rationalist hermeneutic or Harnack's Liberal hermeneutic. Once again the flight from history caused no problem for what was essentially a fideistic position (standpoint of faith), because faith had been rearticulated, or better redefined, in terms of a contemporary philosophy[45] whose appeal was hardly more enduring than the problematic historical-critical method itself. 'He who marries the spirit of the age will soon find himself a widower'.

5.4. The Second Quest

Despite the huge influence of Bultmann, it was his pupils who most effectively raised again the question whether some sort of quest of the historical Jesus ought to be resumed. The old quest had been effectively declared both impossible and illegitimate.[46] It was *impossible* because 'the Gospels are primary sources for the history of the early Church, and only secondarily sources for the history of Jesus'; 'the twentieth century presupposes the kerygmatic nature of the Gospels, and feels really confident in asserting the historicity of its details only where their origin cannot be explained in terms of the life of the Church'. It was *illegitimate* because such historical inquiry runs counter to faith: 'whereas the kerygma calls for existential commitment to the meaning of Jesus, the original quest was an attempt to avoid the risk of faith by supplying objectively verified proof for its "faith"'.[47] To the two questions *Can* we know anything about the life of the his-

45. See, e.g., Bultmann's interpretation of the cross and resurrection of Jesus ('New Testament and Mythology' 35-43).
46. Robinson, *New Quest* ch. 2.
47. Robinson, *New Quest* 35, 37-38, 44.

torical Jesus? and *Need* we know anything about the life of Jesus? Bultmann had delivered a resounding No![48] But that No! soon came into question itself.

It was the issue of theological legitimacy which sparked off the reaction. In a famous lecture in 1953, Ernst Käsemann made two important observations. First, there is a danger in posing a too sharp discontinuity between the historical Jesus and the Christ of faith; for the earliest Christians the identity of the exalted Lord and the earthly Jesus was of first importance. Failure to appreciate the historical particularity of the man from Nazareth, to whom the eschatological event was bound, ran the danger of dissolving the event itself into a myth, the danger of docetism.[49] 'To cleave firmly to history is one way of giving expression to the *extra nos* of salvation'. Moreover, second, the Synoptics themselves allowed considerable intrinsic importance to the past; their very format indicated that they saw the life-history of Jesus as constitutive for faith.[50] Or as the point was later developed, the Gospels are also kerygma, documents of the church's faith, but they did not simply repeat the message *that* Jesus had lived and died; rather, they were considerably concerned with the *what* of the pre-Easter history of Jesus — a history, of course, seen from the standpoint of faith, but the history of Jesus nonetheless.[51] Consequently, if what we know of the historical figure of Jesus proved to be inconsistent with the kerygma proclaimed by the Gospels, that would be serious.[52] Here history reappears as a potential threat to faith: it may not be able to prove faith, but it may once again cause embarrassment to the (would-be) believer who takes its findings seriously.

Bultmann had also distanced Jesus from the faith/theology of the church. In the opening sentence of his *Theology of the New Testament,* Bultmann asserts that 'The message of Jesus belongs to the presuppositions of the theology of the New Testament and is not part of that theology itself'.[53] The kerygma began at Easter. So, when he wrote his *Primitive Christianity in Its Contemporary Setting,* he included the proclamation of Jesus under the heading of 'Judaism'.[54] A sen-

---

48. In an influential conclusion to his *Einleitung,* Wellhausen had already made the point: 'We cannot get back to him, even if we wanted to' (115).

49. 'Docetism' (from *dokeō,* 'seem') describes the belief evident towards the end of the first century (cf. 1 John 4.1-3; 2 John 7) and strongly held in Gnostic circles that Jesus' humanity and sufferings were apparent ('seeming') rather than real.

50. E. Käsemann, 'The Problem of the Historical Jesus' (1954), *Essays on New Testament Themes* (London: SCM, 1964) 15-47 (here 25, 31-34, 46; quotation from 33).

51. G. Bornkamm, *Jesus of Nazareth* (1956; ET London: Hodder and Stoughton, 1960) 22-26; Robinson, *New Quest* ch. 4 (particularly 85-92). 'Kerygma without narrative is sheer church assertion; narrative without witness is ambiguity and offense' (Keck, *Future* 134).

52. Perrin, *Rediscovering* 231, 244.

53. R. Bultmann, *Theology of the New Testament* vol. 1 (1948; ET London: SCM/New York: Scribner, 1952) 3.

54. (ET London: Thames and Hudson, 1956) 71-79.

tence attributed to Wellhausen expresses the point in a neat epigram: 'Jesus was the last of the Jews and Paul the first Christian'.[55] But in response to the criticism of the new questers, Bultmann conceded that Jesus' proclamation is also kerygma, is already kerygma; the kerygma of the post-Easter community is already implicit in the pre-Easter ministry of Jesus; Jesus' message is 'after all a hidden or secret Christian preaching'.[56] This concession was of major importance. Central to the distinction between the proclamation of Jesus and the kerygma of the church had been the assertion that Jesus proclaimed the kingdom, whereas the church proclaimed Jesus; in Bultmann's formulation, 'the proclaimer became the proclaimed'. So a key issue for the new quest was whether in some sense Jesus proclaimed *himself;* to what extent was a christology implicit in Jesus' own message? In this case, ironically, the potential is reversed; now the historical Jesus might provide grounds for faith in Christ. Despite Barth, the possibility of a christology 'from below' reappears, including the possibility of a 'high' christology.[57]

Through such discussion the *theological legitimacy* of the quest was reasserted.[58] But what about the other stumbling block posed by Kähler and Bultmann — the conclusion that the quest was *impossible* to fulfil? Here the initial response was surprisingly positive. Form-critical analysis need not be so negative in its findings after all! Thus Käsemann was able to identify 'the distinctive element in the mission of Jesus' as the amazing authority Jesus claimed for himself over against Moses and the Torah.[59] Bornkamm adds to that the note of eschatological fulfilment in Jesus' proclamation. In a further rebuttal of Bultmann, he insists in effect that in an eschatological schema of old age and new age, Jesus cannot be put on the former side of the division. It is the Baptist who is forerunner; whereas 'Jesus calls: The shift in the aeons is here, the kingdom of God is already dawning'.[60] In turn, Ernst Fuchs, another Bultmann pupil, focused attention on Jesus' *conduct* as 'the real context of his preaching', thus reversing a

55. I have not been able to trace the quotation (it is referred to by O. Betz, *What Do We Know about Jesus?* [ET London: SCM, 1968] 17), but the concluding remarks of Wellhausen's *Einleitung* express the same opinion (113-15).

56. Cited by Robinson, *New Quest* 21.

57. Cf. particularly W. Pannenberg, *Jesus — God and Man* (London: SCM, 1968) 21-30: 'faith primarily has to do with what Jesus *was*. Only from that can we know what he is for us today and how proclamation about him is possible today. Christology is concerned, therefore, not only with *unfolding* the Christian community's confession of Christ, but above all with *grounding* it in the activity and fate of Jesus in the past' (28). See also J. Roloff, *Das Kerygma und der irdische Jesus* (Göttingen: Vandenhoeck und Ruprecht, 1970) 25-40, indeed the whole thesis (conclusion 270-73).

58. See also Keck, *Future* 50-58.

59. Käsemann, 'Problem' 37-45.

60. Bornkamm, *Jesus* 67; followed by Robinson, *New Quest* 118-19.

tendency to concentrate exclusively on Jesus' teaching which had prevailed since Strauss, and bringing to attention the importance of Jesus' table-fellowship with tax-collectors and sinners (Matt. 11.19 par.).[61] The most striking product of the new phase, however, was Joachim Jeremias's full exposition of *The Proclamation of Jesus*.[62] Although not a member of the Bultmann school, with which the new quest in Germany was principally associated, Jeremias's work on the parables of Jesus stands as the best example of form-critical method,[63] and his demonstration that Jesus prayed to God as 'Abba', despite his own overstatement, has remained, somewhat surprisingly, one of the securest findings of the new quest.[64] But in his *Proclamation of Jesus* Jeremias provided about as sound a reconstruction of that proclamation as one could hope for, particularly because he took seriously the need to demonstrate the Aramaic basis for the sayings of Jesus.[65]

What looked like a sufficiently adequate rejoinder to Bultmann's conclusion that the original quest was also impossible seemed to be emerging. But the bright dawn of a new day was soon clouded over by fresh controversy and uncertainty. A methodological problem of uncharted dimensions quickly began to emerge. Since so much of the new quest was dependent on the recognition of a number of key sayings in the Jesus tradition as authentic words of Jesus, the question inevitably came to the fore: How do we identify such sayings? What criteria are there for tracing tradition all the way back (through Bultmann's layers) to Jesus himself?

The criterion which gained greatest prominence had been used by both Bultmann[66] and Käsemann,[67] but it was Norman Perrin who formulated it most explicitly as the 'criterion of dissimilarity': 'the earliest form of a saying we can reach may be regarded as authentic if it can be shown to be dissimilar to charac-

---

61. Robinson, *New Quest* 14-15. E. Fuchs, 'The Quest of the Historical Jesus', *Studies of the Historical Jesus* (London: SCM, 1964) 11-31 (here 21, but Robinson's rendering of the German is better). Fuchs is also significant as the one who reintroduced into the discussion the importance of Jesus' own faith ('Jesus and Faith', *Studies* 48-64).

62. J. Jeremias, *New Testament Theology*. Vol. One, *The Proclamation of Jesus* (1971; ET London: SCM, 1971). The projected further volumes of the *Theology* never materialised. In the same year Jeremias's earlier dialogue-partner, C. H. Dodd, also brought his work on Jesus to a climax, but in a more popular format, with his *The Founder of Christianity* (London: Collins, 1971).

63. J. Jeremias, *The Parables of Jesus* (1947, [6]1962; ET London: SCM, [2]1963).

64. J. Jeremias, *The Prayers of Jesus* (1966; ET London: SCM, 1967) ch. 1.

65. As his *Parables* book had acknowledged his debt to C. H. Dodd (see below §12.4g and at n. 453), so Jeremias's *Proclamation* gave credit to another important British scholar, Manson's *Teaching of Jesus*, whose contribution otherwise was largely lost to sight in the wake of Bultmann's influence.

66. Most succinctly in his 'New Approach' 43; see also above at n. 43.

67. Käsemann, 'Problem' 37.

teristic emphases both of ancient Judaism and of the early Church'.[68] The point was not that only sayings which satisfied this criterion should be recognized as authentic, but rather that such sayings will be the only ones we can *know* to be genuine.[69] Perrin backed up this first criterion with a second, 'the criterion of coherence',[70] and with some hesitation a third, 'the criterion of multiple attestation'.[71] As the discussion of criteria broadened out beyond the confines of the new quest properly so called, others have been offered, not necessarily as alternatives, but in addition. For example, Jeremias in effect offered the criterion of characteristic style traceable back to Aramaic forms;[72] J. P. Meier has given some prominence to 'the criterion of embarrassment';[73] Theissen (with Dagmar Winter) presses the criterion of historical plausibility;[74] Georg Strecker argues for the 'criterion of development';[75] Stephen Patterson suggests the criterion of memorability;[76] and Stanley Porter has put forward the triple criteria of Greek language and context, Greek textual variance, and discourse features.[77]

Few, however, are wholly satisfied with these criteria. If the criterion of dissimilarity is applied consistently, and only that material is added which coheres with the limited findings of the first trawl through the Jesus tradition, then the historical Jesus who emerges is bound to be a strange creature, with anything which links him to the religion of his people or to the teaching of his followers automatically ruled out of court, 'a unique Jesus in a vacuum'.[78] Besides, as

68. Perrin, *Rediscovering* 39.

69. R. S. Barbour, *Traditio-Historical Criticism of the Gospels* (London: SPCK, 1972).

70. 'Material from the earliest strata of the tradition may be accepted as authentic if it can be shown to cohere with material established as authentic by means of the criterion of dissimilarity' (*Rediscovering* 43).

71. '. . . authentic material which is attested in all, or most, of the sources which can be discerned behind the synoptic gospels' (*Rediscovering* 45); see further Porter, *Criteria* 82-89.

72. Jeremias, *Proclamation* Part One. See also M. Casey, *Aramaic Sources of Mark's Gospel* (SNTSMS 102; Cambridge: Cambridge University, 1998); also 'An Aramaic Approach to the Synoptic Gospels', *ExpT* 110 (1999) 275-78.

73. J. P. Meier, *The Marginal Jew: Rethinking the Historical Jesus* Vol. One (New York: Doubleday, 1991) 168-71.

74. G. Theissen and D. Winter, *Die Kriterienfrage in der Jesusforschung: Vom Differenzkriterium zum Plausibilitätskriterium* (Freiburg: Universitätsverlag, 1997) 175-217; also G. Theissen, 'Historical Scepticism and the Criteria of Jesus Research', *SJT* 49 (1996) 147-76. Cf. A. E. Harvey, *Jesus and the Constraints of History* (London: Duckworth, 1982).

75. G. Strecker, *Theology of the New Testament* (1996; ET Berlin: De Gruyter, 2000) 251.

76. S. J. Patterson, *The God of Jesus: The Historical Jesus and the Search for Meaning* (Harrisburg: Trinity, 1998) 265-72 (here 269).

77. Porter, *Criteria* Part II.

78. E. Schillebeeckx, *Jesus: An Experiment in Christology* (1974; ET London: Collins, 1979) 94.

Morna Hooker pertinently asked, do we know enough about either the Judaism of Jesus' time or earliest Christianity for the criterion to be applied with any confidence?[79] Or as Lee Keck wisely observes: 'Instead of the *distinctive* Jesus we ought rather to seek the *characteristic* Jesus'.[80] The criterion of coherence may simply reinforce an imbalanced core and bracket out incoherencies typical of real life.[81] Multiple attestation may be of little more help, since, conceivably, the variations between, say Mark and Q, go back to a common post-Easter source.[82] Alternatively, the identification of several other sources may seem at first to boost the importance of this criterion (Crossan),[83] but the tendentiousness of the claims involved simply produces a fresh spatter of question marks against the results obtained.[84] The criterion of Aramaisms is similarly problematic, in that the criterion of itself cannot distinguish between an Aramaic-speaking Jesus and an Aramaic-speaking church.[85] The criterion of embarrassment runs the same gauntlet as the criterion of dissimilarity: should the relatively few embarrassing sayings be regarded as any more characteristic of Jesus or as any more capable of catching the essence of Jesus' proclamation than dissimilar sayings?[86] Theissen's criterion of historical plausibility is more a restatement of historical method than a criterion. And Porter's criteria depend on the highly disputed argument that Jesus used Greek (he finds seven instances) and on being able clearly to determine that a discourse was given *in toto* by Jesus rather than composed out of earlier Jesus tradition.

Whither then this new phase of the quest? It would be untrue to say that 'the second quest' has ended,[87] whether 'with a bang' or 'with a whimper'. That there has been a 'bang', equivalent to the bangs which caused the first quest to implode, we shall see shortly (see §5.6 below). But there are still those who pursue the quest largely in the old terms, with confidence in the historical method unshaken. Joachim Gnilka and Jürgen Becker see no need to provide more than a

79. M. D. Hooker, 'Christology and Methodology', *NTS* 17 (1970-71) 480-87; also 'On Using the Wrong Tool', *Theology* 75 (1972) 570-81. See further Porter, *Criteria* 73-76.

80. Keck, *Future* 33 (my emphasis).

81. J. T. Sanders, 'The Criterion of Coherence and the Randomness of Charisma: Poring through Some Aporias in the Jesus Tradition', *NTS* 44 (1998) 1-25.

82. The problem is nicely posed by Allison, *Jesus of Nazareth* 2-10.

83. See above §4.7 and further below §§7.6 and 7.8.

84. See again Allison, *Jesus of Nazareth* 10-33.

85. See further Porter, *Criteria* 92-99.

86. See also Crossan, *Birth of Christianity* 144-45; Porter, *Criteria* 106-10. Meier is fully aware of the weakness of the criterion (*Marginal Jew* 1.171, 184; also 'The Present State of the "Third Quest" for the Historical Jesus: Loss and Gain', *Biblica* 80 [1999] 459-87 [here 475-76]).

87. E.g., Funk thinks 'the brief life of the new quest came to a close around 1975' (*Honest to Jesus* 63); and Patterson thinks it lasted only about ten years (*The God of Jesus* 41-42).

few introductory pages on methodology.[88] Both share the original assumptions of form-critical method, particularly as to the earliest form of the tradition (individual units), with the most cursory of references to the phase of oral transmission.[89] Both continue to give pride of place to the criterion of dissimilarity in evaluating individual sayings.[90] And the issues raised by the North American neo-Liberals, particularly as regards the *Gospel of Thomas,* are at best only hinted at.[91] At this point the gulf between European and North American, or, better, between English-language and German-language scholarship becomes as wide as ever it has been before.[92]

At the same time, both sides of the Atlantic have produced important works which draw on the best of the earlier methods and which serve as a bridge to the latest phase of the quest. I have in mind John Meier's massive (now three-volume) study of *A Marginal Jew*[93] and Gerd Theissen and Annette Merz's *The Historical Jesus.*[94] Unlike Gnilka and Becker, they both devote considerable attention to the question of sources,[95] and, like Gnilka, they attend to questions of social context.[96] Meier's emphasis on criteria to determine the historicity of particular words and deeds of Jesus,[97] and his otherwise brief methodological observations,[98] reflect more the techniques of the new quest. But his third volume in particular, which is totally dedicated to detailing the various relationships and interactions between the Jew named Jesus and his Jewish followers and competi-

88. J. Gnilka, *Jesus von Nazaret: Botschaft und Geschichte* (Freiburg: Herder, 1993), ET *Jesus of Nazareth: Message and History* (Peabody: Hendrickson, 1997) 12-25; J. Becker, *Jesus of Nazareth* (Berlin: de Gruyter, 1998) 1-17. But special mention should be made of Schillebeeckx's *Jesus,* the most ambitious and successful attempt by a historical and systematic theologian to master and integrate specialist NT scholarship into a larger perspective on the early developments in dogmatic christology.

89. Gnilka, *Jesus* 13, 15; Becker, *Jesus* 7.

90. Gnilka, *Jesus* 20; Becker, *Jesus* 13-14.

91. Gnilka, *Jesus* 15; Becker, *Jesus* 9, 16 n. 15.

92. Similarly Strecker's *Theology* does not look beyond the immediate post-Bultmannian phase of the Quest (241-43, 249-53)

93. Vol. 1 — *The Roots of the Problem and the Person* (above n. 73); vol. 2 — *Mentor, Message, and Miracles* (New York: Doubleday, 1994); vol. 3 — *Companions and Competitors* (New York: Doubleday, 2001). Meier provided a brief summary of his conclusions to date in 'Reflections of Jesus-of-History Research Today', in J. H. Charlesworth, ed., *Jesus' Jewishness: Exploring the Place of Jesus in Early Judaism* (New York: Crossroad, 1991) 84-107.

94. G. Theissen and A. Merz, *The Historical Jesus* (London: SCM, 1998).

95. Meier, *Marginal Jew* 1 chs. 2-5; Theissen and Merz, *Historical Jesus* chs. 2-3.

96. Meier, *Marginal Jew* 1 chs. 9-10; Theissen and Merz, *Historical Jesus* chs. 5-7.

97. Meier, *Marginal Jew* 1 ch. 6.

98. Meier, *Marginal Jew* 1.4-6, 9-12, though with an interesting discussion of basic concepts ('The real Jesus and the historical Jesus'), including Kähler's distinction between 'historical' and 'historic' (22-40).

tors, puts him firmly in the 'third quest' (see §5.5 below). Theissen and Merz's discussion of 'Historical Scepticism and the Study of Jesus' is more far-reaching, though summary in form,[99] but the Jewishness of Jesus as such is not a particular focus of the volume. Even so, if I have to recommend a single volume on 'the historical Jesus' for student use, this is it.

The trouble in all this is that, with the exception of Theissen, issues of fundamental perspective and method, some posed by the sociological approach and the neo-Liberal quest (see above, §§4.6-7), others left over from the reconceptualisation of the task by the early form critics (§3 above), have been too much neglected. What should be the starting point for an approach to the Jesus tradition for those in 'quest of the historical Jesus'? Have the implications of Jesus' particular social setting in Galilee been adequately taken into account? What should count as sources for the earliest phases of the Jesus tradition? And with what conception of the traditioning process should we operate? Or in a word, can the roadblock of 'impossibility' be so easily dismantled as the second questers seem to assume?

5.5. A Third Quest?

In the closing decades of the twentieth century the most hopeful advance in life of Jesus research was the recognition that the quest must primarily have in view *Jesus the Jew* and a clearer and firmer grasp of the consequences. What distinguishes this 'third quest of the historical Jesus'[100] is the conviction that any attempt to build up

99. Theissen and Merz, *Historical Jesus* ch. 4.

100. The title was introduced by N. T. Wright in his updating of Stephen Neill's *The Interpretation of the New Testament, 1861-1986* (Oxford: Oxford University, 1964, ²1988) 379. On the continuities and discontinuities between the 'second' and 'third' quests see Du Toit, 'Redefining Jesus' 98-110. The description ('third quest') is sometimes used to cover also what I have called the neo-Liberal quest (as by Witherington, *Jesus Quest;* Scott, 'New Options' 7 ['third stage']); and in his emphasis that Jesus looked for 'the renewal of Israel' Borg certainly overlaps with characteristic 'third quest' concerns (§4.7 above, as also Horsley, §4.6). Meier's emphasis on the Jewishness of Jesus (albeit 'a marginal Jew') also qualifies him as third-quester; in *Marginal Jew* 3.8 he points out that he uses the term ('marginal Jew') to *avoid* a set definition of Jesus and in imitation of Jesus' own 'riddle-speech'. Funk notes the key question to be 'what role to assign Jesus the Jew in the Jewish sect known as Christianity' (*Honest to Jesus* 32, 58-59), but subsequently distances himself from 'the third quest' (65), though his dismissal of 'third questers' ('faith seems to make them immune to the facts') seems to ignore the fact that none of his 'facts' is undisputed.

However, I invest no significance or importance in such numbering of the quests. C. Marsh, 'Quests of the Historical Jesus in New Historicist Perspective', *Biblical Interpretation* 5 (1997) 403-37, distinguishes nine quests in all: (1) The Positivist Quest (eschatological

a historical picture of Jesus of Nazareth should and must begin from the fact that he was a first-century Jew operating in a first-century milieu. After all, when so much is historically uncertain, we can surely assume with confidence that Jesus was brought up as a religious Jew. There is no dispute that his mission was carried out within the land of Israel. And his execution on the charge of being a messianic pretender ('king of the Jews') is generally reckoned to be part of the bedrock data in the Gospel tradition.[101] What more natural, one might think, what more inevitable than to pursue a quest of the historical Jesus the Jew?[102]

Such an objective seems very obvious, but it is one which generations of scholarship seem to have resisted. Indeed, one of the most astonishing features of two hundred years of earlier quests is the way in which they have consistently attempted to distance Jesus as quickly and as far as possible from his Jewish milieu. Although Reimarus set Jesus within Judaism (Christianity was founded by the apostles), his importance, according to Kümmel, is that he raised the question, 'what role in the emancipation of Christianity from Judaism is to be attributed to Jesus'.[103] Susannah Heschel observes that liberal theologians painted 'as negative a picture as possible of first-century Judaism' in order 'to elevate Jesus as a unique religious figure who stood in sharp opposition to his Jewish surroundings'.[104] A unique religious consciousness, unaffected by historical circumstances, in effect cut Jesus off from Judaism. Renan, for example, could write: 'Fundamentally there was nothing Jewish about Jesus'; after visiting Jerusalem, Jesus 'appears no more as a Jewish reformer, but as a destroyer of Judaism . . . Jesus was no longer a Jew'.[105] And for Ritschl, Jesus' 'renunciation of Judaism and its law . . . became a sharp dividing line between his teachings and

---

Jesus); (2) The Positivist Quest (non-eschatological Jesus); (3) The Romantic Quest; (4) The Form-critical Quest; (5) The Quest of the non-Jewish Jesus; (6) The Traditio-historical Quest; (7) The Existentialist Quest; (8) The Jewish-Christian Quest; (9) The Postmodern Quest (410-15). See also J. Carleton Paget, 'Quests for the Historical Jesus', in M. Bockmuehl, ed., *The Cambridge Companion to Jesus* (Cambridge: Cambridge University, 2001) 138-55 (147-52). For a German perspective on the 'third quest' see Theissen and Winter, *Kriterienfrage* 145-71.

101. See below §§15.3a and 17.2.

102. The case is well made by Wright, *Jesus* ch. 3.

103. Kümmel, *New Testament* 90; Brown points out that 'Reimarus's interest in the Jewish background (of Jesus) extended no further than his interest in reducing Jesus' mission to a messianic political coup' (*Jesus* 53).

104. S. Heschel, *Abraham Geiger and the Jewish Jesus* (Chicago: University of Chicago, 1998) 9, 21. On the anti-Jewishness of nineteenth-century NT scholarship see particularly 66-75, 106-107, 117-18, 123, 153-57, 190-93, 212-13, 227. See also H. Moxnes, 'Jesus the Jew: Dilemmas of Interpretation', in I. Dunderberg, et al., eds., *Fair Play: Diversity and Conflicts in Early Christianity,* H. Räisänen FS (Leiden: Brill, 2002) 83-103 (here 83-89, 93-94).

105. Heschel, *Abraham Geiger* 156-57.

those of the Jews'.[106] Schweitzer's own account of the quest simply failed to take account of the substantial debate between Jewish and Christian scholarship on the theme of Jesus the Jew.[107] The irony of Liberalism at this point is that it not only sought to 'liberate' Jesus from the distorting layers of subsequent dogma, but it also sought to present Jesus as the one who 'liberated' the quintessential spirit of religion from the 'outmoded garb' of Jewish cult and myth.[108]

In the twentieth century, in a not wholly dissimilar way, Bultmann's existential Christ of faith could make the quantum leap into the present moment of encounter without any dependence on his historical (Jewish) background.[109] It remained fairly commonplace in German theology even after the Second World War to describe Second Temple Judaism as *Spätjudentum* (late Judaism)[110] — that is, Judaism ceased to have significance thereafter — and to describe Jesus as doing away with Judaism or bringing Judaism to an end.[111] In the second quest the principal criterion, the criterion of dissimilarity, tried to make a virtue out of what second questers perceived as a necessity by reconstructing their picture of Jesus out of what *distinguished* Jesus *from* his historical context and set him over against his Jewish milieu.[112] And the neo-Liberal quest differs from the old Lib-

---

106. Heschel, *Abraham Geiger* 123. Note also the response to Weiss by W. Bousset, *Jesus im Gegensatz zum Judentum: ein religionsgeschichtlicher Vergleich* (Göttingen: Vandenhoeck und Ruprecht, 1892): 'In late Judaism there is no really living power, no creative spirit. . . . Jesus' message above all and first of all must be understood in light of its contrast to Judaism . . .' (6-7), cited by Kümmel, *New Testament* 230-31.

107. Heschel, *Abraham Geiger* 3, 127.

108. In effect working out the programmatic understanding of Christianity and its beginnings as indicated by Baur already in his *Paul* 3 (cited above in chapter 1 at n. 13). On Hegel's anti-Judaism see Brown, *Jesus* 88-90. Dungan also points out that the triumph of Markan priority in effect dethroned the Jewish Matthew from its former pre-eminence (*History* 339).

109. Despite his recognition that the proclamation of Jesus belonged under the heading of 'Judaism' (see above at n. 54).

110. See C. Klein, *Anti-Judaism in Christian Theology* (1975; ET London: SPCK/Philadelphia: Fortress, 1978) here ch. 2; still in F. Hahn, *Christologische Hoheitstitel* (Göttingen: Vandenhoeck, [5]1995) 133, 351; Becker, *Jesus,* e.g., 88, 224 n. 146.

111. See, e.g., Pannenberg, *Jesus* 255; L. Goppelt, *Theology of the New Testament.* Vol. 1: *The Ministry of Jesus in Its Theological Significance* (1975; ET Grand Rapids: Eerdmans, 1981) 97 ('Jesus actually superseded Judaism at its very roots through a new dimension'). See further J. T. Pawlikowski, *Christ in the Light of the Christian-Jewish Dialogue* (New York: Paulist, 1982) 37-47. Heschel gives a very unsympathetic reading of a 1992 contribution by Käsemann to a debate on Christian identity in Christian-Jewish dialogue: 'Käsemann writes that calling Jesus' teaching Jewish is insulting and renders Christianity meaningless' (*Abraham Geiger* 232, referring to E. Käsemann, 'Protest!', *EvT* 52 [1992] 177-78, but this is not an actual quotation from Käsemann). The debate was initiated by J. Seim, 'Zur christlichen Identität im christlich-jüdisch Gespräch', *EvT* 51 (1991) 458-67; Seim responds in *EvT* 52 (1992) 185-87.

112. See further above §5.4. H. Merklein, *Jesu Botschaft von der Gottesherrschaft* (SBS

eral quest at this point only by its argument that the influence of Hellenization, which in Harnack's view marked out the difference of the early church from Jesus, is already to be found in Jesus' own teaching; despite the acknowledgment of Jesus' Jewishness, the Tendenz is to play up the similarities between Jesus' teaching and Hellenistic culture and the differences from his native Jewish culture.[113] In the history of Jesus research nothing has evidenced the flight from history more devastatingly than the persistent refusal to give any significance to the Jewishness of Jesus.

Of course a Jewish perspective on Jesus was by no means unknown before the 1980s,[114] though these earlier studies proved curiously ineffective in regard to the mainstreams of Jesus research. And the contribution of Geza Vermes in particular has had a subtle and significant influence;[115] he has been in effect the John the Baptist of the third quest. But what has proved decisive in the new shift of perspective has been the growing groundswell of reaction, in NT scholarship as in Christian scholarship generally, against the denigration of Judaism which has been such a deeply rooted and longstanding feature of Christian theology. The repentance and penitence required by the Shoah/Holocaust, though in some circumstances in danger of being overplayed, have still to be fully worked through at this point. The mindset which figures Judaism as the religion of law to be set over against Christianity as the gospel, with the chief task being to show how Jesus belongs with the latter rather than the former, still seems to operate at a deep subconscious level. The portrayal of the Pharisees as archetypal legalists

---

111; Stuttgart: KBW, 1983) argues that for the Baptist and Jesus Israel had lost its prerogative of being the chosen people of God and had become 'a community deprived of salvation (Unheilskollektiv)', but he removes the talk of 'Unheilskollektiv' in the later edition (³1989).

113. So, particularly, Mack: 'One seeks in vain [in original Jesus' teaching] a direct engagement of specifically Jewish concerns' (*Myth* 73); the Jewish apocalyptic prophet is replaced by the Hellenized Cynic teacher. See also the critique of Horsley and Draper, *Whoever Hears* 4-5, 9; Meier, *Marginal Jew* 3.3-4.

114. For the nineteenth century note particularly Abraham Geiger and further Heschel, *Abraham Geiger* 130-37, 148-50, 235-38. For the twentieth century note particularly J. Klausner, *Jesus of Nazareth: His Life, Times and Teaching* (London: George Allen and Unwin, 1925); R. Meyer, *Der Prophet aus Galiläa. Studie zum Jesusbild der drei ersten Evangelien* (1940; reissued Darmstadt: Wissenschaftliche Buchgesellschaft, 1970); S. Ben-Chorin, *Brüder Jesus: Der Nazarener in jüdischer Sicht* (Munich, 1967); D. Flusser, *Jesus* (1969; revised Jerusalem: Magnes, 1998). D. A. Hagner, *The Jewish Reclamation of Jesus: An Analysis and Critique of the Modern Jewish Study of Jesus* (Grand Rapids: Zondervan, 1984) describes the various attempts to evaluate Jesus from a Jewish perspective (ch. 1), claiming that 'the Jewish reclamation of Jesus has been possible only by being unfair to the Gospels' (14); 'it is always Jesus the Jew they are interested in and not the Jesus of Christianity' (38). See also Moxnes, 'Jesus the Jew' 89-96, 98-101.

115. G. Vermes, *Jesus the Jew* (London: Collins, 1973).

and bigots retains a disquietingly stubborn popularity.[116] And, as just noted, the assumption that Judaism's only function was to prepare for Christianity (thus 'late Judaism') still persists. Oddly enough, however, despite other potent earlier contributions on Jesus the Jew[117] and the recognition that some fresh methodological reflection was necessary to break the impasse of the second quest,[118] it was E. P. Sanders' work on *Paul* which caused the penny finally to drop in New Testament scholarship.[119] If traditional New Testament scholarship had misrepresented the Judaism with which *Paul* had to do, how much more was it necessary for *Jesus'* relationship to his ancestral Judaism to be reassessed. In that sense, Sanders' *Jesus and Judaism* (1985)[120] has to be reckoned as the real beginning of the third quest.[121]

The prospects for such a (third) quest have also been considerably improved by the fresh insights into the character of Second Temple Judaism which have been granted to scholarship during the last fifty years. Here the discovery of the Dead Sea Scrolls has pride of place. More than anything else they have broken open the idea of a monolithic, monochrome Judaism, particularly as set over against the distinctiveness of newly emerging Christianity. It has now become possible to envisage Jesus, as also 'the sect of the Nazarenes' (Acts 24.5, 14; 28.22), within the diversity of late Second Temple Judaism in a way which was hardly thinkable before. This breakthrough has been accompanied and reinforced by other important developments — particularly the breakdown of the previously quite sharp distinction between Judaism and Helle-

116. See below, §9.3a.

117. See n. 114 above.

118. We should recall Jeremias' *Proclamation,* notable for its appreciation of Jesus as an Aramaic speaker. Meyer's *Aims of Jesus* was an important precursor of Sanders (n. 120 below), but his work was equally if not more significant in highlighting the importance of a better hermeneutic for would-be questers (see further below, chapter 6). J. Riches, *Jesus and the Transformation of Judaism* (London: Darton, Longman and Todd, 1980) anticipates some of Borg's emphases, though his central motif ('the transformation of Judaism') is problematic (a reworking of Judaism's fundamental beliefs). The attempt of Harvey, *Jesus and the Constraints of History,* to give a new turn to the discussion by the notion of 'historical constraints' works well initially (political constraints, the crucifixion) but progressively less so as he proceeds. And B. Chilton, *A Galilean Rabbi and His Bible: Jesus' Own Interpretation of Isaiah* (London: SPCK, 1984), proposes a quite narrowly focused thesis, as indicated by his subtitle.

119. E. P. Sanders, *Paul and Palestinian Judaism* (London: SCM, 1977).

120. London: SCM; see his critique of previous studies (23-51), starting with a scathing denunciation of W. Bousset's *Jesus* (London: Williams and Norgate, 1906) (*Jesus and Judaism* 24-26).

121. So also Scott, 'New Options' 11, and Meier, 'Present State of the "Third Quest"' 462; it was Sanders' work which brought the third quest to German attention (Theissen and Winter, *Kriterienfrage* 152).

nism,[122] the recognition that the portrayals of rabbinic Judaism in Mishnah and Talmud may not simply be projected backwards into the first century,[123] the renewed interest in the rich range of apocryphal and pseudepigraphical Jewish literature as further testimony to the diversity of Second Temple Judaism,[124] and the increasing sophistication in evaluating the steadily mounting archaeological data from the Israel (particularly Galilee) of Jesus' time.[125] In short, it is no exaggeration to say that scholarship is in a stronger position than ever before to sketch a clearer and sharper picture of Judaism in the land of Israel at the time of Jesus and as the context of Jesus' ministry. As Nils Dahl observes: 'Everything that enlarges our knowledge of this environment of Jesus (Palestinian Judaism) indirectly extends our knowledge of the historical Jesus himself'.[126]

Not least of importance is the fact that the New Testament documents themselves can and should be counted as part of the evidence for the character and diversity of first-century Jewish literature. Paul is the only Pharisee from whom we have first-hand documentation from before 70 CE. And if the letters of Paul have to be counted as Jewish literature in an important sense,[127] then how much more the Gospels. Even if one or more of the Gospels has to be attributed to a Gentile author, the traditions which they contain (we need only reckon with the Synoptic Gospels at this point) can hardly fail to be classified as 'Jewish'.[128]

The most significant attempts to portray Jesus within late Second Temple Judaism in this renewed (third) quest thus far have been those of Sanders and

122. M. Hengel, *Judentum und Hellenismus* (WUNT 10; Tübingen: Mohr Siebeck, ³1988); ET *Judaism and Hellenism* (London: SCM, 2 vols., 1974).

123. The many works of J. Neusner have been important here; see particularly *The Rabbinic Traditions about the Pharisees before AD 70* (Leiden: Brill, 1971); also *From Politics to Piety: The Emergence of Rabbinic Judaism* (Englewood Cliffs: Prentice Hall, 1973); also *Judaism: The Evidence of the Mishnah* (Chicago: University of Chicago, 1981); see also on the one hand P. S. Alexander, 'Rabbinic Judaism and the New Testament', *ZNW* 74 (1983) 237-46, and on the other C. A. Evans, 'Early Rabbinic Sources and Jesus Research' in B. Chilton and C. A. Evans, *Jesus in Context: Temple, Purity and Restoration* (Leiden: Brill, 1997) 27-57.

124. See below, chapter 9, n. 11.

125. See particularly J. H. Charlesworth, *Jesus within Judaism: New Light from Exciting Archaeological Discoveries* (New York: Doubleday, 1988); also *Jesus and Archaeology* (Grand Rapids: Eerdmans, forthcoming); J. L. Reed, *Archaeology and the Galilean Jesus* (Harrisburg: Trinity, 2000); see further below, §§9.6-7.

126. N. A. Dahl, 'The Problem of the Historical Jesus' (1962), *Jesus the Christ: The Historical Origins of Christological Doctrine* (Minneapolis: Fortress, 1991) 81-111 (here 96).

127. So, e.g., A. F. Segal, *Paul the Convert: The Apostolate and Apostasy of Saul the Pharisee* (New Haven: Yale University, 1990): 'Paul should be treated as a major source in the study of first-century Judaism' (xi).

128. Cf., e.g., the remarks of C. G. Montefiore, *The Synoptic Gospels* (London: Macmillan, 1909, ²1927) cxxxiv-cxlv.

Wright.[129] Sanders gives only cursory attention to questions of method, so that the main thrust of his work has been twofold. First, he sees the key to understanding Jesus' intentions in Israel's own 'restoration eschatology'; Jesus himself looked for the restoration of Israel.[130] Second, Jesus did not pit himself against Judaism, against the law or the Pharisees; set within the matrix of Second Temple Judaism, Jesus remains there throughout.[131] Wright likewise makes a double thrust.[132] He takes off from Sanders' insight regarding 'restoration eschatology' and develops it in more specific terms as Israel's hope for return from exile, a theme which has become for him something of an *idée fixe*.[133] Moreover, as already noted, he shares with Borg the conviction that Schweitzer got it wrong: Jesus did not expect the end of the world; apocalyptic language is metaphorical;[134]

129. See also Charlesworth, *Jesus within Judaism;* Charlesworth, ed., *Jesus' Jewishness;* B. H. Young, *Jesus the Jewish Theologian* (Peabody: Hendrickson, 1995); Allison, *Jesus of Nazareth;* Ehrman, *Jesus;* P. Fredriksen, *From Jesus to Christ* (New Haven: Yale University, 1988) ch. 6; also *Jesus of Nazareth, King of the Jews: A Jewish Life and the Emergence of Christianity* (New York: Knopf, 1999); S. McKnight, *A New Vision for Israel: The Teachings of Jesus in National Context* (Grand Rapids: Eerdmans, 1999); J. Schlosser, *Jésus de Nazareth* (Paris: Noesis, 1999); B. Chilton, *Rabbi Jesus: An Intimate Biography* (New York: Doubleday, 2000). Fredriksen is heavily influenced (in both volumes) by Sanders, and McKnight by Wright. Chilton's *Rabbi Jesus,* appealing in the raw Jewishness of its portrayal (Jesus as an illiterate but dynamic peasant mystic afire with a passion for Israel's purity), is constructed too fancifully from a few hints in biblical and non-biblical sources of at best doubtful relevance — 'more boldly original than historically persuasive' is the judgment of Keck, *Who Is Jesus?* 43. Keck's review of 'The Jesus Quest and the Jewish Jesus' (23-47) is full of sharply insightful comment.

130. Sanders, *Jesus,* Part One, 'The Restoration of Israel' (61-119); Sanders' treatment was more focused and proved more effective (in impact) than Meyer's (*Aims* 133-37, 153-54, 161, 223-41). In McKnight's view, 'The most important development in recent studies of the historical Jesus has been the recognition that Jesus had a mission to the nation of Israel' (opening sentence of his *New Vision* viii).

131. Sanders, *Jesus,* particularly chs. 6, 9, and 10 (174-211, 245-93).

132. Characteristic of the third quest is Wright's insistence that the much-discussed 'criterion of double dissimilarity' must be complemented by a 'criterion of double similarity: when something can be seen to be credible . . . within first-century Judaism, and credible as the implied starting point . . . of something in later Christianity, there is a strong possibility of our being in touch with the genuine history of Jesus' (*Jesus* 132).

133. Wright, *The New Testament and the People of God* 268-72, 299-301; *Jesus* 126-31, 227, 230-34 (even the parable of the sower 'tells the story of Israel, particularly the return from exile'), 255-56, 268-69 ('forgiveness of sins is another way of saying "return from exile"'), 340 and 364 (the expected destruction of Jerusalem indicates that 'the exile was coming to an end at last'), 557 (the Last Supper 'pointed to the return from exile'). For critique see below, §12.6c(2).

134. Wright, *New Testament* 298-99, 306-307, 332-33; *Jesus* 56-57 (against Crossan), 75 (Borg), 81 (cited above, chapter 4 at n. 177), 95-97, 114, 513 ('"Apocalyptic" . . . uses "cosmic" or "other-worldly" language to describe [what we think of as] "this-worldly" realities, and

the climax for which Jesus looked was YHWH's return to Zion (enacted in his own return to Jerusalem and in the expected destruction of Jerusalem).[135] The issues thus raised by Sanders and Wright are fundamental for any quest for Jesus the Jew. They will be important dialogue partners in subsequent chapters.

Yet even as another group of historical critics set out on another quest of the historical Jesus, the fundamental question is being posed more sharply than ever: Is the historical method after all capable of penetrating back to a 'historical Jesus'? Almost without many second and third questers noticing, the spring tide of postmodernism has built up against the dykes of the historical method, threatening to obliterate most of the familiar landmarks on which historical critics have depended for finding their way. Following the interlude of the new quest, the flight from history has resumed with a vengeance. And though the third questers have set out to remedy what has been the most blatant disregard of history in the quest (the Jewishness of Jesus), they too are in danger of being overtaken by the postmodern wave of a-historicism.

5.6. Postmodernism

'Postmodernism' is the term coined to indicate a paradigm shift in Western thinking, like the paradigm shifts of the Renaissance and the Enlightenment, a transformation in intellectual conceptualisation and ways of thinking which, again like the Renaissance and the Enlightenment, is amorphous and diffuse in character but all too real in its influence. In a major epistemological revolution earlier in the twentieth century the older subject-object antithesis and discontinuity had already come under radical question. The Cartesian philosophical assumption, that 'I' as a self-conscious subject can describe and define what I observe with complete objectivity, had underpinned the nineteenth-century scientific method. The existentialism of the inter-war period had also reflected a significant shift in emphasis in observation of reality from the externality of the observed to the involvement of the observer in the act of observing.[136] But as the Newtonian

---

to invest them with [what we think of as] their "theological" or "spiritual" significance'. 'No Jews whose opinions are known to us thought that their god was about to bring the space-time world, including land and Temple, to a sudden end'. 'Their expectations remained national, territorial and Temple-centred').

135. Wright, *Jesus,* ch. 13 ('The Return of the King', 612-53), although he also argues that 'Israel's god was already becoming king, in the events of Jesus' ministry' (454).

136. My colleague David Brown notes that the philosophical climates were different in England and in mainland Europe. 'Existentialism never really took off in England, and belief in the objectivity of knowledge even today remains much stronger among English philosophers than it would be on the continent'.

worldview more and more gave way to the world of Einsteinian relativity and the essential uncertainties of quantum physics, so the possibility of the older scientific objectivity came to be seen as less and less realistic — still more or less effective for most of the time but wholly inadequate, even misconceived, at both the macrocosmic and microcosmic level. Biologists who retain the old nineteenth-century optimism that they are able to discover everything there is to know about life may still believe that they represent a scientific method of universal validity for all 'scientific' research, but 'science' no longer speaks with a united voice on the subject. The reverberations of this shift in the self-understanding of scientific method are still rippling through those other disciplines which have been accustomed to acknowledge that the sciences provide a methodological paradigm for academic research.

Postmodernism is the outworking in the humanities and particularly in literary criticism (from the 1970s) of this new appreciation of the *relativity* of all things and processes. In the discipline of history it has resulted in the abandonment not only of the idea of strictly objective knowledge, of 'facts' independent of interpretation, but also of the concept of linear time and so also of a single unified historical development or, in a word, of a 'grand narrative'.[137] In the 'linguistic turn' of postmodernism, history has been reclaimed from the patronage of the sciences and restored to its ancient place as literature, but with the old distinctions between fact and fiction, history and poetry now again blurred, and the assumption that historical texts refer to a reality outside of themselves called into question.[138] The main impact of postmodernism, however, has been to call into question the traditional hegemony of the author, to liberate the meaning of texts from their originating context, and to bring the reader to centre-stage in the hermeneutical process. Already in the so-called 'New Criticism' of the mid-twentieth century, the classical idea that the author's intention is the criterion of meaning had been called in question. Rather, it was asserted, the text should be regarded as 'autonomous', self-contained, to be appreciated in its own terms. This emphasis was reinforced by the exposure of 'the intentional fallacy': the intention of the author was a private state of mind, which lay behind the text; the text should be allowed to speak for itself.[139] It is just this autonomy of the text from its author which makes it possible for 'the "matter" of the text [to] escape from the finite intentional horizon of its author' to impact within the reader's world of meaning, a 'decon-

137. Iggers, *Historiography* 56-57; K. Jenkins, 'Introduction' to *The Postmodern History Reader* (London: Routledge, 1997) 5-9, 17-18.

138. Iggers, *Historiography* 100; see also Appleby, Hunt, and Jacob, *Telling the Truth* ch. 6.

139. Thiselton, *New Horizons* 58-59, citing R. Wellek and A. Warren, *Theory of Literature* (1949), and W. K. Wimsatt and M. Beardsley, 'The Intentional Fallacy' (1954).

textualizing' of the text which allows it to be 'recontextualized' in the act of reading.[140]

In study of the Gospels the equivalent response to the traditional historical-critical focus on the world behind the text came to expression in another new 'criticism' (in sequence after source criticism, form criticism, and redaction criticism), namely 'narrative criticism', which emerged in the 1980s.[141] In twentieth-century development of Gospel studies it was more a second phase of the reaction against form criticism's fragmentation of the stuff of the Gospels, and a deliberate attempt to go beyond the first phase of reaction, that is, redaction criticism, which focused too narrowly on the points where the Evangelist had redacted his sources. Like the New Criticism, narrative criticism emphasized the wholeness and unity of the text/Gospel as such, with a similar emphasis on the autonomy of the text. Thus, in what has been regarded as the first expression of 'narrative criticism', David Rhoads speaks of the 'autonomous integrity' of Mark's story world. 'Narrative criticism brackets . . . historical questions and looks at the closed universe of the story-world'.[142] Significantly, in focusing thus on the text as such, narrative critics have found it necessary to reintroduce the concept of 'author', but not the author behind the text (the 'real author'), rather the 'implied author', that is, the author inferred from the narrative itself, drawing on the concepts of 'implied author' and 'implied reader' introduced to the discussion by Wolfgang Iser.[143]

More characteristic of postmodernism's impact on Gospel studies has been

140. P. Ricoeur, 'The Hermeneutical Function of Distanciation', *From Text to Action: Essays in Hermeneutics II* (Evanston: Northwestern University, 1991) 75-88 (here 83-84).

141. See particularly S. D. Moore, *Literary Criticism and the Gospels* (New Haven: Yale University, 1989) Part I; M. A. Powell, *What Is Narrative Criticism?* (Minneapolis: Fortress, 1990); D. Rhoads and K. Syreeni, eds., *Characterization in the Gospels: Reconceiving Narrative Criticism* (JSNTS 184; Sheffield: Sheffield Academic, 1999), including Rhoads's concluding chapter, 'Narrative Criticism: Practices and Prospects' 264-85.

142. D. Rhoads, 'Narrative Criticism and the Gospel of Mark', *JAAR* 50 (1982) 411-34 (here 413), cited by Moore, *Literary Criticism* 8-9; though note Rhoads's later observation that 'there is no storyworld apart from social context, and there is no storyworld apart from the reading experience' ('Narrative Criticism' 269). Particularly influential has been H. W. Frei, *The Eclipse of Biblical Narrative: A Study in Eighteenth and Nineteenth Century Hermeneutics* (New Haven: Yale University, 1974).

143. Thiselton, *New Horizons* 516-22, referring to W. Iser, *The Implied Reader: Patterns of Communication in Prose Fiction from Bunyan to Beckett* (Baltimore: Johns Hopkins University, 1974); also *The Act of Reading: A Theory of Aesthetic Response* (Baltimore: Johns Hopkins University, 1978). The most influential narrative-critical exposition of a Gospel has been R. A. Culpepper's *Anatomy of the Fourth Gospel: A Study in Literary Design* (Philadelphia: Fortress, 1983; see, e.g., Morgan, *Biblical Interpretation* 230-34). Moore dialogues particularly with R. C. Tannehill, *The Narrative Unity of Luke-Acts: A Literary Interpretation.* Vol. 1: *The Gospel According to Luke* (Philadelphia: Fortress, 1986) (*Literary Criticism,* index 'Tannehill').

the shift from author to reader, from reading behind the text to reading in front of the text, from text as window to text as mirror. This hermeneutical shift is epitomised in reader-response theory, which no longer sees meaning simply 'in' the text, let alone in reference 'behind' the text, but meaning as created by the reader in the act of reading. Texts do not make meaning; readers make meaning. Texts do not dictate to readers; readers dictate to texts. In Stephen Moore's words, 'Prior to the interpretive act, there is nothing definitive in the text to be discovered'.[144]

> Meaning is not in the past (when the text was produced) or in the text as an object, but meaning is produced in the reader's present when the text is read (Murfin, 142). For reader-response critics meaning is not a content in the text which the historian simply discovers; meaning is an experience which occurs in the reading process.[145]

There is an obvious threat in all this to any ideas of canons for agreed meanings. If all meaning is contingent to each individual act of reading, then it would appear that every man, every woman makes his or her own meaning, and there are no generally acceptable criteria to enable us to judge whether one reading is good or bad, wise or foolish, or better than another. In postmodernism pluralism is all. However, in the debate over reader-response theory two constraints have been put forward. One is the perception of reader-response as more of a dialogue between text and reader, where the text has to be 'heard' and listened to, lest reader-response deteriorate into the straightforward manipulation of the text to speak to the reader's agenda. In his debate with Stanley Fish, Iser in particular wishes to maintain an objective status for the text, that there is a 'given' to be 'mediated': 'the "something" which is to be mediated exists prior to interpretation, acts as a constraint on interpretation'.[146]

The other is Fish's own recognition that reading is not a wholly isolated, individual experience. In his most influential work, he has emphasized that any reading is conditioned to at least some extent by the reading or interpretive community to which the individual reader belongs.[147] This emphasis is fairly easily integrateable with Hans-Georg Gadamer's emphasis that the interpreter and the act of interpretation are themselves caught up in the flow of history, that historical text and inter-

---

144. Moore, *Literary Criticism* 121. See further 71-107.

145. G. Aichele, et al., *The Postmodern Bible* (New Haven: Yale University, 1995) 42, citing R. C. Murfin, 'What Is Reader-Response Criticism?', in *Heart of Darkness,* ed. R. C. Murfin (New York: St. Martin's, 1989) 139-47. See further Aichele 24-38.

146. Aichele, *Postmodern Bible* 41, citing W. Iser, 'Talk Like Whales: A Reply to Stanley Fish', *Diacritics* 11 (1981) 82-87 (here 84).

147. S. Fish, *Is There a Text in This Class? The Authority of Interpretive Communities* (Cambridge: Harvard University, 1980).

preter are both part of a historical continuum (*Wirkungsgeschichte,* 'history of effect'). Consequently, the interpreter cannot stand above the tradition which links him or her to the past under study, but can only begin to understand adequately as being part of and through that tradition.[148] This solution, applied to the Gospels, does not, of course, restore the old objectivity of the Gospels' meaning. But it does indicate a stronger possibility of recognizing a firmness to their perceived significance; it does prevent a falling apart into complete subjectivity and relativity; and from a Christian perspective in particular, it does attune with the more traditional thought of a trust-sustaining consensus *(sensus communis = sensus fidelium)* within which matters of faith and conduct can be discussed and determined.

Such attempts to maintain some degree of stability in the meaning heard from texts is regarded by the more radical postmodernists as a failure of nerve.[149] For them the challenge of postmodernism strikes more deeply. Postmodernism questions not only the objectivity of a text's meaning but the objectivity of meaning itself.

> By sweeping away secure notions of meaning, by radically calling into question the apparently stable foundations of meaning on which traditional interpretation is situated, by raising doubts about the capacity to achieve ultimate clarity about the meaning of a text, postmodern readings lay bare the contingent and constructed character of meaning itself.[150]

For deconstructionist critics there is no text, only interpretations, indeed, a 'succession of infinitely different interpretations'. Every text falls into 'the epistemological abyss'.[151] Moore sums up his review at this point by a fitting citation of Troeltsch's famous remark (above at n. 11),[152] with the clear implication that hermeneutical method is now caught in precisely the same bind as historical method, so that the NT scholar who depends on either should abandon all hope of producing any solid theological conclusions from either. This destabilizing of the very concept of meaning has, it is freely acknowledged, a political agenda: to liberate the meaning of the text from the dominant meanings (interpretations) of the past, perceived by many (feminist and liberation readings in particular) as oppressive and coercive.[153] Whether this line of argument leads un-

---

148. Gadamer, *Truth* 300-307; see further below §6.4e.
149. Aichele, *Postmodern Bible* 38-67.
150. Aichele, *Postmodern Bible* 2-3.
151. Moore, *Literary Criticism* 119-31.
152. Moore, *Literary Criticism* 129.
153. Aichele, *Postmodern Bible* 3-5 and *passim.* The parallel (alliance?) here with the neo-Liberal attempt to save Jesus from institutional Christianity (§4.7 above) should not escape notice.

avoidably to the breakdown of even the possibility of any real communication of intention, to an anarchy of subjectivism or simply to an unavoidable pluralism of equally legitimate readings, are questions still under dispute. At any rate, the idea of the stability of a text's meaning has been put in question, and for radical postmodernists any suggestion of a normative meaning of any text has been effectively pushed from the field of play.

The loss of confidence in historical method in postmodern circles is thus complete. And so far as the quest of the historical Jesus is concerned, its results, particularly when the various Jesuses of the neo-Liberal quest are included, simply confirm the failure of traditional historical methodology. The simple and rather devastating fact has been that Gospels researchers and questers of the historical Jesus have failed to produce agreed results. Scholars do not seem to be able to agree on much beyond a few basic facts and generalisations; on specific texts and issues there has been no consensus. The lengthy debate from the 1960s onwards about appropriate criteria for recognition of the actual words of Jesus has not been able to produce much agreement about the criteria, let alone their application. All this is seen as simply demonstrating the inadequacies of the historical method as traditionally conceived and reconfirms the 'impossibility' verdict passed on the old quest.

No wonder, then, that the flight from history has been so complete, from historical context to the world of the text, from historical author to contemporary reader, from intended meaning to the experience of reading, from stable meaning to the endless interplay of interpretation. In such circumstances, can the 'quest of the historical Jesus' ever hope to succeed?

CHAPTER 6

History, Hermeneutics and Faith

6.1. An Ongoing Dialogue

As thus far described, the situation at the beginning of the twenty-first century is one of even greater confusion than when Schweitzer surveyed the equivalent scene at the beginning of the twentieth century. On the one hand, the rampant neo-Liberal quest seems to have superseded and called in question some of the key results of nineteenth- and twentieth-century Gospels and life of Jesus research. And on the other, postmodernism seems to have pulled the rug completely from under the feet of even the possibility of historical research producing results which could command wide assent. The possibility of a 'third quest' is one I shall pursue further in what follows. But before we do so it is advisable to take stock of the gains and losses and outstanding challenges from the more than five hundred years of tension between faith and history in regard to Jesus of Nazareth so far reviewed. The questions posed by Reimarus and Strauss, by Lessing and Troeltsch, by Kähler and Wrede, by Bultmann and Robinson, by Funk and Crossan, by Iser and Fish are still there, and unless they can be answered satisfactorily at this point any progress is likely soon to encounter new variations of the same old roadblocks as before.

If our analysis has confirmed that history (the discipline) and faith have made uncomfortable bedfellows, each usually trying to push the other out of the bed, it has also demonstrated that history and hermeneutics are close companions, Siamese twins perhaps. That will no doubt be part of the reason for the failure of history and faith to bed well together: hermeneutics is the too little acknowledged third partner — a somewhat uncomfortable *ménage à trois*. But unless the interdependence of history and hermeneutics is acknowledged, there can be no progress; as Gadamer puts it, 'the foundation for the study of history is hermeneutics'.[1]

---

1. Gadamer, *Truth* 198-9.

Any attempt to reassert the importance of history for faith and to restate sound principles of historical method will therefore have to engage with the hermeneutical problems thrown up not least by postmodernism. Fortunately it neither should be necessary nor is it desirable to enter into the complexities and subtleties of the classic discussions, on the distinctions between 'meaning' and 'significance', between 'understanding' and 'explanation' and between 'sign' and 'significance', or on the meaning of 'meaning'. But a number of key principles do seem to have emerged in the period reviewed and these are worth restating, however tentatively (since I have little expertise in the philosophical technicalities involved), before we proceed further.

It should be noted at the outset, however, that all these principles are interlocking, and while they have to be stated separately, their interrelatedness means that each qualifies the other in some measure. An effective historical method and use of historical texts cannot be reduced to a single principle. We are faced with the unavoidable task of balancing and integrating different and at times competing emphases. But that is what we call 'life'; why should the interplay of history, hermeneutics, and faith be any different?

6.2. The Necessity of Historical Inquiry

We start at the same point with which we began. The historical figure of Jesus will always stimulate curiosity on the part of those who are interested in the great men and women of history. Those who want to understand better the historical, social, and ideological forces which have shaped their culture will always want to inquire more closely about the man whose title (Christ) is borne by the most important and long-lasting influence (Christianity) on the European intellectual and artistic as well as religious and ethical traditions. And since individuals are shaped by their culture, the insatiable human curiosity to 'know thyself' means that interest in Jesus is even part of the quest for self-understanding and self-identity, for the individual's own deep roots. Already late mediaeval Western piety wanted to know again the reality of Christ's sufferings, and the Renaissance and Reformation brought a new concern to get the history of Jesus right. So still today: 'What was he like? What was he really like?' are questions which rise unbidden where such historical interest is engaged. Such questions are unlikely to be silenced by the claims that previous answers have been highly tendentious, or that the evidence is fragmentary and tainted. Nor will they likely be satisfied by being referred to a story world detached from the real world. Did Jesus really do that? Did Jesus really say that? are not simply childish questions, but express the human curiosity which is at the root of all human inquiry and accumulation of knowledge.

For those within the Christian tradition of faith, the issue is even more important. Christian belief in the incarnation, in the events of long ago in Palestine of the late 20s and early 30s AD as the decisive fulcrum point in human history, leaves them no choice but to be interested in the events and words of those days. For the incarnation, by definition, means the commitment of God to self-manifestation in Jesus at a particular time and place within human history, and thus places a tremendous weight of significance on certain events in Palestine in the years 28-30 (or thereabouts) of the common era. Christians cannot but want to know what Jesus was like, since he shows them what God is like. The fact that our knowledge of these events and words is fragmentary and uncertain makes no difference. As Kähler and Bultmann insisted, faith need not, indeed should not, be dependent on the scholarly arguments about this verse or that passage. But the new questers of the third quarter of the twentieth century showed that faith could and does have a theologically legitimate interest in the history of Jesus. Honest historical inquiry may be granted insights regarding Jesus which are crucially (in)formative of honest (self-critical) faith. Scholarship in its search for truth, however flawed its perception of that truth, can stimulate and feed, discipline, and even correct faith (when faith makes statements of fact beyond its competence). A faith which regards all critical scrutiny of its historical roots as inimical to faith can never hold up its head or lift up its voice in any public forum.[2]

6.3. What Can History Deliver?

The task of the historian is to explain not only what happened, but why it happened and why it happened in the way it did. But the attempt to treat history as a 'science' has suffered from too uncritical assumptions and over-optimistic expectations. So, it is fair to ask whether it can deliver at all and if so what. The above overview has highlighted several important pointers.

a. Historical Distance and Difference

As became evident already in the Renaissance and Reformation, the test of a historical scrutiny of the past is the realisation it brings of the *otherness* of the past.

2. 'The fact that Jesus can be made an object of historical-critical research is given with the incarnation and cannot be denied by faith, if the latter is to remain true to itself' (Dahl, 'Problem' 101). Koester notes pointedly: 'Be it simple curiosity, be it in the service of a serious religious search, or be it in the interest of a vital ideological commitment, to have Jesus on one's side is evidently important even in the postmodern late twentieth century' ('Jesus the Victim' 8). See further R. Morgan, 'The Historical Jesus and the Theology of the New Testament', in Hurst and Wright, eds., *Glory of Christ* 187-206.

It is this historical distance and difference which prevents the present from domesticating the NT and either muffling or dictating its message. As Schweitzer observed a century ago, if Jesus does not come to us, in some degree at least, as a stranger and an enigma, then we can be sure that we have modernized Jesus, and to that extent at least have failed to grasp what Jesus of Nazareth was about. As the Reformation, by setting the apostolic age in its historical context, provided a corrective to the abuses of mediaeval Catholicism, so Schweitzer, by setting Jesus more realistically in his historical context, provided a corrective to a portrayal of Jesus too much shaped in accordance with nineteenth-century western European sensibilities. The point is that the otherness of Jesus is, in part at least, a historical otherness, the otherness in particular of Jesus the Jew — again something we 'moderns' have forgotten to our cost. Without that sense of Jesus 'born under the law' (Gal. 4.4), of Christ 'become servant of the circumcision' (Rom. 15.8), with historical awareness of what that meant in terms of the particularities of history, then the humanity of Christ is likely to be lost again to view within Christianity and swallowed up in an essentially docetic affirmation of his deity. Although the failures of earlier lives of Jesus at this point (see particularly §5.5 above) are now widely acknowledged, the instinctive compulsion to extricate Jesus from his historical context and to assume his timeless relevance still has to be resolutely resisted.

b. Probability Not Certainty

The fundamental methodological observations made by Lessing and Troeltsch must also be given full weight. The key and most enduring point can be restated simply in terms of the distinction, familiar to historians, between event, data, and fact.[3] The historical 'event' belongs to the irretrievable past. All the historian has available are the 'data' which have come down through history — personal diaries, reminiscences of eyewitnesses, reports constructed from people who were present, perhaps some archaeological artefacts, as well as circumstantial data about climate, commercial practice, and laws of the time, and so forth.[4] From these the historian attempts to reconstruct the 'facts'. The facts are not to be identified as data; they are always an *interpretation* of the data.[5] Nor should the fact

3. As I learned it from R. G. Collingwood, *The Idea of History* (Oxford: Oxford University, 1946; Oxford Paperback 1961), e.g., 133, 176-77, 251-52.

4. Droysen's observation is pertinent here: 'The data for historical investigation are not past things, for these have disappeared, but things which are still present here and now, whether recollections of what was done, or remnants of things that have existed and of events that have occurred' (extract from his *Historik* [1857] in Mueller-Vollmer, *Hermeneutics Reader* 120).

5. Contrast Fredriksen, who exemplifies a common popular perception regarding 'facts'

be identified with the event itself, though it will always be in some degree of approximation to the event.[6] Where the data are abundant and consistent, the responsible historian may be confident of achieving a reasonably close approximation. Where they are much more fragmentary and often inconsistent, confidence of achieving a close approximation is bound to be much less. It is for this reason that the critical scholar learns to make carefully graded judgments which reflect the quality of the data — almost certain (never simply 'certain'), very probable, probable, likely, possible, and so on.[7] In historical scholarship the judgment 'probable' is a very positive verdict.[8] And given that more data may always emerge — in ancient history, a new inscription or, prize of prizes, a new cache of scrolls or documents — any judgment will have to be provisional, always subject to the revision necessitated by new evidence or by new ways of evaluating the old evidence.[9] This insight was already the basis of the Deists' and Reimarus' rejection of proof from miracle: could there be sufficient data to put the claim to miracle beyond dispute? As David Hume had earlier pointed out, it is more prob-

---

and who defines 'facts' as I define 'data': 'We have facts. . . . Facts are always subject to interpretation . . . but they also exist as fixed points in our investigation' (*Jesus* 7). The same distinction between 'data' and 'facts' applies also to scientific method generally: 'the data of science are never "bare facts"'; 'there are no uninterpreted facts' (Barbour, *Issues in Science and Religion* 139).

6. Such a distinction can hope to work, of course, only with 'simple' events (Did x shoot y?); but then we should probably not speak of complex events such as a career, a battle, or the destruction of Jerusalem as though it was a single 'event'.

7. Cf. P. A. Boeckh's distinction between the 'plausible', the 'presumable', and the 'credible' (in Mueller-Vollmer, *Hermeneutics Reader* 145-46).

8. In a famous libel trial in UK during the early months of 2000 the historical facticity of the Holocaust was at issue: whether there was a systematic plan to destroy European Jews, whether there were gas chambers at Auschwitz, and whether Hitler was directly responsible. Most would regard the probability of these facts as overwhelming; but without certainty the room for doubt can be exploited by Holocaust deniers. As Martin Gilbert (biographer of Winston Churchill) observed, in the libel action brought by David Irving, history itself was on trial (*The Guardian*, Saturday, February 5, 2000, p. 3). There was an interesting sequel some months later when Jörg Haider of the Austrian Freedom Party lost a libel case over his reference to Nazi concentration camps as 'punishment centres'. His claim that the reference was 'correct and respectable' and that the expression was commonly used was rejected by the judge with the comment: 'The term punishment centre comes from a single document from the Third Reich in 1941 in which it referred to mass extermination camps as punishment centres. That is the only place the term has come from. The term is historically incorrect. A leading politician in 1995 . . . should have had a better grasp of historical reality' (*Daily Telegraph*, September 27, 2000).

9. Since the task of a criminal law court is often likened to that of the critical historian, we may appropriately compare the sequence of successful appeals against several notorious sentences in British courts over the past fifteen years on the basis of revised scientific evaluation of the evidence on which guilt had been determined.

able that the account of a miracle is an untrue account than that the miracle re-counted actually took place.[10] That was precisely why the claim to miracle be-came more problem than proof. The older defence that the biblical miracles belonged to a unique period was no longer sufficient to protect them from critical questioning.

All this created a crisis for faith. But why? Because it challenged the cer-tainty of faith. The safe alternative for Lessing was the certainty provided by the 'necessary truths of reason'. The Liberal flight from history was also a search for an 'invulnerable area' for faith. Bultmann similarly posed the certainty of faith in antithesis to the uncertainty of historical knowledge.[11] But a crucial question was too little asked: whether we should expect *certainty* in matters of *faith,* whether an invulnerable 'certainty' is the appropriate language for faith, whether faith is an 'absolute'. It was the Enlightenment assumption that necessary truths of rea-son are like mathematical axioms, and that what is in view is the certain QED of mathematical proof, which has skewed the whole discussion. But faith moves in a totally different realm from mathematics. The language of faith uses words like 'confidence' and 'assurance' rather than 'certainty'.[12] Faith deals in trust,[13] not in mathematical calculations, nor in a 'science' which methodically doubts every-thing which can be doubted.[14] Nor is it to be defined simply as 'assent to propo-sitions as true' (Newman). Walking 'by faith' is different from walking 'by sight' (2 Cor. 5.7).[15] Faith is commitment, not just conviction.

10. See, e.g., E. and M. Keller, *Miracles in Dispute: A Continuing Debate* (London: SCM, 1969) ch. 5 ('David Hume and Sound Judgment: A Wise Man Proportions His Belief to the Evidence'), discussing Hume's *Inquiry Concerning Human Understanding* Section X. One need only consider the typical reaction by most today, including most Christians, to claims of miraculous healings by 'televangelists' or miraculous phenomena linked to statues of the Virgin Mary or of Hindu gods, to see the force of Hume's argument.

11. Keck, *Future* 55-56, 57-58.

12. Theissen begins his 'attempt to leap across Lessing's yawning gulf' by asserting: 'Faith is absolute certainty' ('Historical Scepticism' 147). It is interesting to note that the word 'certainty' is used only once in NRSV NT (Acts 2.36) where it translates the Greek adverb *asphalōs*. The term itself has the basic connotation of 'security' (*asphaleia,* Acts 5.23; 1 Thess. 5.3; *asphalōs,* Mark 14.44; Acts 16.23), 'reliable' (*asphalēs,* Luke 1.4; Acts 21.34; 22.30; 25.26; Phil. 3.1; Heb. 6.19).

13. This is the term ('trust') which Keck prefers in his reworking of the issues (*Future* 68-83), though his further outworking of the theme in terms of 'trusting Jesus' as a figure in the past (177-83) is more problematic as either implying an exemplarist christology ('the trusted person a model for his own life') or as presupposing the resurrection (184-89).

14. Echoing Gadamer, *Truth* 238-39. Cf. the profound illustration of faith which Paul finds in Abraham (Rom. 4.16-21).

15. Unfortunately the 'definition of faith' in Heb. 11.1 is much disputed as to its meaning and does not bring added clarity to the issue; see, e.g., the recent discussions in H. W. Attridge, *Hebrews* (Hermeneia; Philadelphia: Fortress, 1989) 307-10; W. L. Lane, *Hebrews* (WBC 47;

Faith as trust is never invulnerable to questions.[16] Rather, faith lives in dialogue with questions. Faith-without-doubt is a rare commodity, which few (if any) have experienced for any length of time.[17] On the contrary, doubt is the inoculation which keeps faith strong in face of unbelief. Whereas it is the 'lust for certainty' which leads to fundamentalism's absolutising of its own faith claims and dismissal of all others. In fact, of course, little or nothing in real life is a matter of certainty, including the risks of eating beef, or of crossing a road, or of committing oneself to another in marriage. In each case, particularly in the case of personal relationships, the language of trust, confidence, and assurance is much the more appropriate.[18] In which case faith can live a good deal more comfortably with the uncertainties of human testimony than Lessing or Troeltsch thought.[19] In a day when all evaluation of social relationships is dependent to a considerable extent on statistical survey and analysis, the fact that we live by probabilities rather than by certainties is less of a problem than it has ever been.[20]

c. Analogy

Troeltsch's second characteristic of the historical-critical method is the necessary complement to the recognition of historical otherness (§6.3a above). The recognition of a natural homogeneity and similarity between the historian and the historian's subject matter is what prevents history from lapsing into a bare catalogue of sequences of events. This insight was fundamental to Wilhelm Dilthey's attempt to distinguish the methodology of the human sciences from that of the natural sciences. 'Lived experiences' of the past can be 're-lived'; even 'what is alien and past' (§6.3a above) can be relived by historical under-

---

Dallas: Word, 1991) 325-26; P. Ellingworth, *Hebrews* (NIGTC; Grand Rapids: Eerdmans, 1993) 564-66.

16. 'Trust is not the inevitable last step in a series of historical inferences' (Keck, *Future* 126).

17. Even in the case of the final resurrection appearance of Jesus recorded in Matthew's Gospel, Matthew records that 'some doubted' (Matt. 28.17); see further below, §18.4b.

18. For Newman 'certainty', or subsequently 'certitude', was essential in religion; see his *An Essay in Aid of a Grammar of Assent,* ed. I. T. Ker (Oxford: Clarendon, 1985) index 'Certitude'. But my colleague Sheridan Gilley points out that for Newman 'certitude' is 'ultimately personal, the sort of certitude that we have in our personal relations, in which we trust, love and have faith in God and one another' (personal communication dated March 14, 2001).

19. Thiselton cites A. D. Galloway, 'Merely probable knowledge is psychologically compatible with the trustful certainty of faith. . . . There is nothing illogical or unreasonable in the combination of such trust with merely probable knowledge' (*Two Horizons* 83).

20. Even more than when Bishop Butler first made the point, 'probability is the very guide of life' (Introduction to his *The Analogy of Religion* [1736]).

standing.[21] It is important to realise that this sense of the historian's ability to empathise with the past was central in what was perceived as the emergence of 'historical consciousness' in Romanticism.[22] Historical consciousness could rise above its own relativity. To 'know' the historical past is not simply to know it as a historical phenomenon to be understood only in its own terms, but to know it as belonging to what is in the end of the day the same world,[23] as one who enters a foreign country and after moving beyond the initial strangeness begins to appreciate the shared patterns of humanness, of culture and community. It is equally important to note that we are not talking here of faith as such. It is possible for the historian to enter empathetically into the faith experience of the first followers of Jesus even when the historian does not share that particular faith. That is why the quest of the historical Jesus is not simply a matter of faith looking for its mirror-image or confirmation in the past. Precisely because all three factors so far outlined are involved, a faith perspective can be and has to be self-critical. At the same time, historical method which lacks empathy with the subject matter is unlikely to enter far into the lived experience of the historical characters being studied.[24]

On the other hand, it is important to note the limiting feature of the principle of analogy. Gadamer cites Friedrich Schlegel:[25]

> The two basic principles of so-called historical criticism are the postulate of the commonplace and the axiom of familiarity. The postulate of the commonplace is that everything that is really great, good, and beautiful is improbable, for it is extraordinary or at least suspicious. The axiom of familiarity is that things must always have been just as they are for us, for things are naturally like this.

This passage clearly signals the danger that these postulates, spelling out the principle of analogy, may reduce all that is recognizable in human experience to the lowest common denominator. Can it, we may ask, for example, give suffi-

---

21. See the extracts from volume 7 of Dilthey's *Gesammelte Schriften* (Göttingen: Vandenhoeck, 1926), in Mueller-Vollmer, *Hermeneutics Reader* 149-64, particularly 159-61; Dilthey recognized that 'all understanding contains something irrational because life is irrational; it cannot be represented by a logical formula' (162).

22. Hence my use of the different phrase, 'historical awareness', to characterize the developments of the Renaissance (chapter 3 above).

23. Gadamer, *Truth* 290. See further Gadamer's treatment of Dilthey (218-64); also P. Ricoeur, 'The Task of Hermeneutics', *From Text to Action: Essays in Hermeneutics II* (Evanston: Northwestern University, 1991) 58-63.

24. Gadamer cites Dilthey as declaring 'that only sympathy makes true understanding possible' (*Truth* 232).

25. Gadamer, *Truth* 361.

cient recognition to rarely paralleled genius? What about the *novum,* the genuinely 'new' within the historical process?[26] The old proof from miracle argument
for Christianity may have become problematic, but even so we still have to ask,
can the principle of analogy allow for the wholly unusual?[27] Is the range of human experience, regularly taken to indicate the scope of analogy (Western self-
consciousness), broad enough?[28] It will hardly need saying that such issues cannot be ignored when the subject matter is one (Jesus) for whom claims to uniqueness have been fundamental in assessing the significance of the historical person.

d. The Illusion of Objectivity

As already indicated, a further weakness of Troeltsch's analysis of historical
method is that Troeltsch was still a child of the nineteenth-century scientific paradigm, which continued to perceive reality in terms of a closed system in which
all laws would eventually be discovered and all causes and effects could be measured. So long as the scientific method as understood in the nineteenth century
provided the model for the historical method, the idea of historical facts as objective artefacts, and the goal of historical objectivity could be held up as a viable
aim.[29] But the twentieth century's recognition of indeterminacy in explanation
and of complementary and conflicting explanations possible at both microcosmic and macrocosmic level has confirmed that Troeltsch's perception of reality was too restricted. Consequently the definition of historical method expressed
in terms of such a restricted world view is itself too restricted; or rather, the

---

26. Thiselton appositely cites A. B. Gibson's striking comment that 'on the basis of a
Humean epistemology or a thoroughly empiricist world-view "anything that happens for the
first time is to be discredited"' (*Two Horizons* 79). See further Thiselton's critique of Troeltsch
(69-84). Troeltsch's attempt to deal with the problem he had posed, in *The Absoluteness of
Christianity and the History of Religions* (1901; ET Louisville: John Knox, 1971), is characteristic of European Liberalism in its personalistic individualism, evolutionary optimism, and religious imperialism.

27. 'For a critical history of Jesus, the principle of analogy is invoked on the basis that
Jesus was a man; it has nothing to say about his being "a mere man"' (Meyer, *Aims* 17-18).

28. To return to the inverse parallel of Hitler, Ron Rosenbaum takes Schweitzer's *Quest*
as the model for his review of the many attempts to explain Hitler, noting the unwillingness of
many to accept that Hitler's evil may *not* be understandable, that it may at the end of the day
simply not be capable of rational explanation (*Explaining Hitler: The Search for the Origins of
His Evil* [London: Macmillan, 1999] xxiv, xxviii-xxix, xli).

29. '. . . purely objective causal explanation . . . constitutes the distinctive character of
history as a pure theoretical science' (Troeltsch, 'Historiography' 720a). As already noted,
Troeltsch's conception of the 'unique' is held within his conception of scientific causality, albeit as 'the product of individual causes in their infinite complexity' (720a).

claims made for the historical-critical method in such circumstances are un-avoidably excessive, as pretending to pronounce on what, as has since become clearer, it is not capable of comprehending. The idea of what a hermeneutic of scientific inquiry might mean has had to change, though the corollary is still too little acknowledged.

Bultmann fell into the same trap. Even though the scientific paradigm shift occasioned by Einstein's theory of relativity was well under way,[30] he still continued to assert (1957) that 'the historical method includes the presupposition that history is a unity in the sense of a closed continuum of effects in which individual events are connected by the succession of cause and effect'.[31] It was the *objectivity* which the scientific method assumed as possible of achievement against which he so fiercely reacted in his demythologizing programme.[32] But as Paul Ricoeur points out in his 'Preface to Bultmann', Bultmann was thereby in effect ignoring the objectifying character of *all* language, the language of faith as well as the language of myth.[33] Ironically, Bultmann's existentialism was a way of *avoiding* the problem of objectifying language rather than a way of dealing with it. Here again Gadamer appositely cites Edmund Husserl:

> The naïvete of talk of 'objectivity' which completely ignores experiencing, knowing subjectivity, subjectivity which performs real, concrete achievements, the naïvete of the scientist concerned with nature, with the world in general, who is blind to the fact that all the truths that he acquires as objective, and the objective world itself that is the substratum in his formulas is his own *life construct* that has grown within him, is, of course, no longer possible, when *life* comes on the scene.[34]

None of this is to deny the importance of the otherness of the past (§6.3a above), or that historical data have a recognizable objectivity. It is, however, to recognize that the movement from data to fact (§6.3b above) is a good deal more

---

30. I refer particularly to Heisenberg's 'uncertainty principle' and Niels Bohr on the indeterminacy of quantum physics.

31. R. Bultmann, 'Is Exegesis without Presuppositions Possible?', *Existence and Faith* (ET 1961; London: Collins, 1964) 342-51 (here 345).

32. See, e.g., Keck, *Future* 50-52; J. D. G. Dunn, 'Demythologizing — The Problem of Myth in the New Testament', in I. H. Marshall, ed., *New Testament Interpretation: Essays on Principles and Methods* (Exeter: Paternoster, 1977) 285-307.

33. P. Ricoeur, 'Preface to Bultmann' (i.e., to the French edition of *Jesus and the Word* and *Jesus Christ and Mythology,* 1968), *Essays on Biblical Interpretation* (Philadelphia: Fortress, 1980) 49-72: 'Bultmann seems to believe that a language which is no longer "objectifying" is innocent. But in what sense is it still a language? And what does it signify?' (65-67).

34. Gadamer, *Truth* 249 (Husserl was writing with regard to Hume); see also 261.

complex than is usually appreciated. Where it involves language (description of an artefact, a written document) we need to be aware that language has differing degrees of referentiality.[35] More to the present point, it involves interpretation, involves the interpreter, so that even if the observation of data can be likened in some measure to the old ideal of scientific research, the act and process of interpretation cannot.[36] Alternatively expressed, historicism (historical positivism) could think in terms of 'brute facts' in abstraction from interpretation. But the facts[37] that matter in history, the facts that carry history forward, are never 'bare facts', empty of significance. Facts, other than the merely ephemeral, are always experienced as significant, facts-in-their-significance,[38] a 'fact' ignored by questers who, desirous of academic respectability for their work, continue to appeal to the Enlightenment paradigm of scientific objectivity.[39] The same point is inescapable when we recognize the role of analogy in historical method (§6.3c above). Here too, to acknowledge that historical method depends on analogy is not at all to deny the objectivity of that which is known but simply to underline the inevitable subjectivity in the knowing of that which is known, whether past or present.

35. G. B. Caird, *The Language and Imagery of the Bible* (London: Duckworth, 1980) ch. 12 ('Language and History').

36. Curiously, in one of the most illuminating treatments of 'the challenge of poetics to (normal) historical practice', R. Berkhofer (in Jenkins, ed., *Postmodern History* 139-55) regards the movement from 'evidence' to 'facts' to 'synthesis' as firm lines (empirically based) still linking the frames of representation and referentiality (148). G. Himmelfarb, 'Telling It as You Like It: Postmodernist History and the Flight from Fact' (Jenkins, ed., *Postmodern History* 158-74) protests with some justification that modernist history is not so uncritically positivist as postmodernists often imply: 'the frailty, fallibility and relativity of the historical enterprise . . . are not the great discoveries of postmodernism' (159, see also 160, 165-66).

37. 'Fact' is here being used in its popular sense. My own preferred formulation would speak in terms of events and data (§6.3b above); 'facts' as I use the term are interpreted data.

38. Cf. Collingwood, *Idea of History* 131-33; Thiselton, *Two Horizons* 80-81, referring to Pannenberg.

39. Crossan, despite the otherwise revolutionary character of his approach, bases his analysis of the Jesus tradition on a surprisingly 'objective' stratification of that tradition; H. Childs, *The Myth of the Historical Jesus and the Evolution of Consciousness* (SBLDS; Atlanta: SBL, 2000) criticises Crossan for 'a subtle and unwitting positivism' (ch. 2, here 55). And Wright's concern to avoid 'having loose ends . . . flapping around all over the place' (*Jesus* 367) is surprisingly modernist in character. Even Meier, who recognizes that 'the quest for objectivity' is unrealistic (*Marginal Jew* 1.4-6), retains the ideal of an exegete using 'purely historical-critical methods' (1.197; also 'Present State of the "Third Quest"' 463-64). See further the shrewd critique of A. G. Padgett, 'Advice for Religious Historians: On the Myth of a Purely Historical Jesus', in S. T. Davis, et al., eds., *The Resurrection: An Interdisciplinary Symposium on the Resurrection of Jesus* (Oxford: Oxford University, 1997) 287-307.

e. 'Critical Realism'

'Critical Realism' is a term brought to NT study by Ben Meyer[40] from his long engagement with the works of Bernard Lonergan. It sums up Lonergan's theory of knowledge: 'knowing' is not just seeing; rather, it is a conjunction of experience, understanding, and judging.[41] 'Critical realism' expresses the synthesis that he wants to maintain over against the antitheses of naïve realism on the one hand and idealism on the other, against the former's overemphasis on the objectivity of that which is known and the latter's overemphasis on the subjectivity of the knowing.[42] In applying this epistemology to history, Lonergan shows just how complex is the process between data and fact.[43] 'Critical realism' is formulated particularly against the 'naïve realism' of the old historical positivism, against what Lonergan calls 'the principle of the empty head',[44] that is, the idea 'that objectivity is arrived at through the subtraction of subjectivity', 'objectivity in the world of immediacy simple-mindedly applied to the world mediated by meaning'.[45] Meyer formulates Lonergan's argument thus: 'The hallmark of critical realism is its insistence on the empirical (data), the intelligent (questioning and answering), the rational (the grasp of evidence as sufficient or insufficient, the personal act of commitment) as — all of them together — entering into true judgment'.[46] Wright has taken up Meyer's concerns in turn and proposes his own form of 'critical realism':

> This is a way of describing the process of 'knowing' that acknowledges the *reality of the thing known, as something other than the knower* (hence 'real-

---

40. B. F. Meyer, *Critical Realism and the New Testament* (Princeton Theological Monographs 17; Allison Park: Pickwick, 1989); also *Reality and Illusion in New Testament Scholarship: A Primer in Critical Realist Hermeneutics* (Collegeville: Liturgical Press, 1994). Meyer's debt to Lonergan was already evident in his *Aims* 16-18.

41. Most compactly expressed in B. Lonergan, 'Cognitional Structure', *Collection: Papers by Bernard Lonergan* (Toronto: University of Toronto, [2]1988) 205-21. 'The criteria of objectivity are not just the criteria of ocular vision; they are the compounded criteria of experiencing, of understanding, of judging, and of believing. The reality known is not just looked at; it is given in experience, organized and extrapolated by understanding, posited by judgment and belief' (*Method in Theology* [London: Darton, Longman and Todd, 1972] 238).

42. For the wider use of the term in philosophy see C. F. Delaney, 'Critical Realism', in R. Audi, ed., *The Cambridge Dictionary of Philosophy* (Cambridge: Cambridge University 1995) 169-70; A. Collier, 'Critical Realism', *Routledge Encyclopedia of Philosophy* (1998) 2.720-22 ('Critical realism holds there is more to "what is" than "what is known" . . .').

43. *Method* chs. 8-9.

44. As in *Method* 157, 204, 233.

45. Meyer, *Reality and Illusion* 109, 135.

46. Meyer, *Reality and Illusion* 142, and see earlier 68-70.

ism'), while also fully acknowledging that the only access we have to this reality lies along the spiralling path of *appropriate dialogue or conversation between the knower and the thing known* (hence 'critical').[47]

The historians Appleby, Hunt, and Jacob argue in similar terms for 'practical realism' as 'an interactive relationship between an inquiring subject and an external object',[48] a 'qualified objectivity . . . disentangled from the scientific model of objectivity'. They concede the impossibility of neutral research but maintain 'the viability of stable bodies of knowledge that can be communicated, built upon, and subjected to testing'.[49]

I align myself with the basic thrust of Lonergan's epistemology and its application to history. Even the data themselves are never 'raw': they have already been 'selected' by the historical process; they are 'selected' again by the way they have been discovered and brought to present notice; they come with a context, or various contexts already predisposing interpretation; the interpreter's framework of understanding or particular thesis causes certain data to appear more significant than others; and so on. But all that being said, there is an otherness, an 'over-against-us' character to the data, and also to the events to which they bear witness. And the task of seeking to describe and evaluate the data and to reach some sort of judgment regarding the facts, which is not merely subjective but may command proper critical respect, is not only viable, but in the case of the great event(s) of Jesus necessary. In particular, the model of historical study as a *dialogue* between present and past, between historian and history, is one which has always appealed to me, not least because it recognizes that the historian not only asks the questions, but, in genuine engagement with the subject matter, often finds him/herself put in question. In what follows, therefore, I will attempt to practise the historian's art somewhat on the model of 'critical realism'.

All this becomes still more relevant when the subject matter is mediated to us primarily through historical *texts*.

6.4. Hermeneutical Principles

The 'linguistic turn' of postmodernism has refocused the historian's task on 'text' rather than 'event'. Besides which, any attempt to recover the historical figure of Jesus is more or less exclusively a matter of dealing with ancient texts. So questions about history elide almost imperceptibly into questions about interpre-

---

47. Wright, *The New Testament and the People of God* 31-46 (here 35 — Wright's emphasis).

48. *Telling the Truth* 251, 254, 259, 285.

49. *Telling the Truth* 254-61 (here 254).

tation. Here too the above survey has produced some enduring insights on which it is still important to build.

a. Historical Text as Historical Text

If the Renaissance and Reformation recognition of the distance and difference of the past continues to provide a fundamental perspective for historical inquiry, so too their reappropriation of the fact that the original texts of the NT were not first composed in the *lingua franca* of western Europe (Latin) likewise continues to provide a fundamental hermeneutical principle. In other words, the necessity and character of *translation* become a basic factor in any contemporary use of these texts to speak about Jesus. Modern readings of the NT in North America in particular sometimes seem to forget that the NT texts were not first written in English. In reality, to anyone who lacks knowledge of Greek, the texts are little more than indecipherable squiggles on the page. In order that they may be read in the first place, these squiggles must be identified as Greek, and as ancient Greek. And in order that they may be conveyors of any meaning these ancient Greek words need to be read within the context of the language usage of the time.[50] Historical philology is still essential and unavoidable.[51] It inevitably follows that the Greek text (even in its modern, eclectic form) is normative in regard to any and every translation; unless the Greek text is recognized as determining and limiting the range and diversity of translation, then the translation loses its claim to legitimacy as a translation.

Transpose this into the language of the current hermeneutical debate and the consequences begin to become clearer. The point can be put simply: there are such things as bad, or even (dare one say it?) *wrong* translations.[52] Presumably

50. Here again I acknowledge my debt to Collingwood, *Idea of History* 244.

51. Schleiermacher summed up the gains of previous discussion by defining the two canons for 'grammatical interpretation': 'First canon. A more precise determination of any point in a given text must be decided on the basis of the use of language common to the author and his original public'; 'Second canon. The meaning of each word of a passage must be determined by the context in which it serves' (*Hermeneutics: The Handwritten Manuscripts by F. D. E. Schleiermacher,* ed. H. Kimmerle [ET Missoula: Scholars, 1977]) excerpted by Mueller-Vollmer, *Hermeneutics Reader* 86, 90. Similarly Bultmann: 'every text speaks in the language of its time and of its historical setting. This the exegete must know; therefore, he must know the historical conditions of the language of the period out of which the text he is to interpret has arisen' ('Exegesis without Presuppositions' 344).

52. An interesting feature of the libel action brought by David Irving (n. 8 above) was the number of points at which the case hung on allegations of Irving's mistranslation of German documents. In his Judgment, Mr Justice Gray found the allegations to be well founded (most explicitly §13.31).

postmodern teachers of ancient languages and texts do not dissent from this, and postmodern examiners of such translations mark them down like any other teacher. In the case of readings of the NT, the normativity of the Greek text implies that there can be bad readings, 'bad' because they are based on poor translations. Put another way, it is simply important to recognize *the character of historical texts as historical texts.* For the Greek text read as a historical text (interpretations as well as translations taking account of accidence, syntax, and idiom of the day) inevitably functions as a norm for legitimacy of modern readings too.[53] Without that basic recognition, the particular text becomes no more than a lump of potter's clay, vulnerable to being shaped entirely by the whim of the interpreter (potter). In other words, the very identity of the text is at stake, and historical study and scholarly method are unavoidable if the NT and the Gospels are to be read at all.

To avoid unnecessary confusion, it should be stated explicitly that, of course, there is no such thing as a single correct translation of a foreign-language text, far less a perfect translation. Anyone who has had to engage in translation knows that there is no translation without interpretation, that interpretation is an inescapable part of translation.[54] Individual words in both languages have ranges of meaning (polysemic, multivalent), and there is no word in one language whose range and cultural overtones exactly match those of a word in the other language. In translation, choices have to be made between words and idioms which are equally as close and equally as distant from the words and idioms of the original-language text. The abundant diversity of modern translations of the Bible is all the illustration needed.[55] None of this, however, alters the point that the original-language text is what is to be translated/interpreted, and that each translation has to justify itself as a translation of that text. The historical text cannot determine the exact translation, but unless the text functions as some kind of norm for the translation, unless it is seen to provide a limiting factor on the diversity of acceptable translations, then translation itself becomes irresponsible.

---

53. Worth noting is the comment of Gabrielle Spiegel: 'texts represent situated uses of language. Such sites of linguistic usage, as lived events, are essentially local in origin and therefore possess a determinate social logic of much greater density and particularity than can be extracted from totalizing constructs like "language" and "society"' (in Jenkins, ed., *Postmodern History* 198).

54. The word 'hermeneutics' comes from the Greek *hermēneia,* which can mean both 'translation' and 'interpretation'.

55. Consider, e.g., the range of translations offered for *hypostasis* in Heb. 11.1 — including 'assurance', 'conviction', 'substance', 'guarantee', 'objective reality', 'foundation', and 'realization' (reviewed by Ellingworth, *Hebrews* 564-65; and further n. 15 above).

b. What Rights Does the Text Have?

In the middle decades of the twentieth century, as noted already, the so-called 'New Criticism' introduced the idea of the 'autonomy' of a text.[56] The intention was to free the text from the assumption that its meaning must be defined as the meaning intended by the author.[57] We have still to address the question of meaning, but even at this point it is probably worth registering a word of caution against a too casual talk of a text's autonomy. For the imagery evoked is unfortunate. As though the interpreter somehow 'liberated' a text from its historical context; whereas to set it in that context was somehow to violate its autonomy. But the 'autonomy' of a text is another illusion. For a text will always be read in context, whether the historical context of the text, or of its later editions, or the contemporary context of the reader. The text is not like a free-floating balloon to be pulled to earth every so often, its message read, and then released back again into the atmosphere, as though that was its natural setting. As text it was always earth-bound from the first. The reality is that the less attention given to the text's own context, the more likely the text is to be abused by the hermeneutical process.

To change the imagery to that of rights. At one point Robert Morgan, who favours the concept of textual determinacy but is ever conscious that all such affirmations need to be carefully nuanced, asserts that 'Texts, like dead men and women, have no rights . . .'.[58] But is that a nuance too far? After all, the rights of dead men and women are protected by inheritance law. Their reputations (the right to how they are remembered, their significance) will be defended by those who cherish their memory. Perhaps the rights of a text are better compared to those of a child. As the rights of a child include the right to know its parentage and place of origin, so the rights of a text include the right to its own identity as determined by its composer or by the process which resulted in its enduring text form. Here again there are obvious qualifications to be registered. Some texts, particularly proverbs and aphorisms, were never limited to a particular context and their enduring value is independent of a specific context of usage. But others, like the letters of Paul, were clearly written in particular historical contexts and with particular historical circumstances in view. Any reading which disregards or discounts what evidence we have of these contexts and these circumstances is more than likely to misread the text.

56. Thiselton, *New Horizons* 58-60.

57. So again Ricoeur: 'The autonomy of the text already contains the possibility that what Gadamer calls the "matter" of the text may escape from the intentional horizon of its author' ('The Hermeneutical Function of Distanciation' 83).

58. Morgan, *Biblical Interpretation* 7.

Each of the Synoptic Gospels comes somewhere in between the direct contextual communication of the Pauline letters and the indirect non-contextual communication of proverbs. But from the first the Gospels have been recognized as intentional in form and content — as 'gospels'! And certainly since Wrede the fact that each Evangelist has structured the earlier tradition to convey his own rendering of the Jesus tradition has been taken as axiomatic. To what extent similar theological intention can be discerned in the earlier forms of the tradition is a good deal less clear. But the principle of respecting the text and allowing the text so far as possible, using all the tools of historical criticism, to speak in its own terms is still valid. Any less a goal for exegesis would be self-condemned.[59] How far that takes us back to Jesus, of course, is a question still to be addressed.

c. The Priority of Plain Meaning

If we take seriously the fact that the NT texts are historical texts, it follows that the old case for historical philology and the hermeneutical principle of plain meaning can still demand respect. To be sure, plain meaning as appealed to by such as Calvin was not always the literal or verbal sense *tout simple,* but a meaning determined in part by Calvin's faith, by the rule of faith — 'plain' to those who shared Calvin's faith. 'Plain meaning' as it has operated in practice is already in some measure a product of the reader's perspective, a negotiated outcome.[60] We will explore the point further below. Here my concern is to emphasize that the precedence accorded to the text has to include the primary task of *listening* to the text, the goal of letting it speak so far as possible in its own terms. *Some* concept of 'plain meaning' has to be granted if the text is to be properly respected and if there is to be a genuine hermeneutical dialogue between text and reader. I want to keep room for the experienced reality of a text being heard in its plain meaning as breaking through previous understandings and calling for their revision — for the great conversions of a St Anthony hearing Jesus' words to the rich young ruler for the first time in their plain sense, as well as for the myriad minor conversions which constitute typical growth in knowledge and wisdom.

It is true that postmodernism has put a question mark against the meaning of

59. It 'has always been a principle of all textual interpretation: namely that a text must be understood in its own terms' (Gadamer, *Truth* 291).

60. Greene-McCreight concludes that a plain sense reading 'involves negotiating between the constraints of verbal sense and Ruled reading . . . respecting the verbal and textual data of the text as well as privileging the claims about God and Jesus Christ which cohere with the Rule of faith'. 'The "plain sense" reading will result from a conjunction of verbal sense and prior understanding of the subject matter of the text provided by the conception of the Christian faith supplied by the apostolic tradition' (*Ad Litteram* ix, 244).

'meaning' itself, or, to be more precise, against the idea of stability of meaning or of specific meaning being effectively communicated from (or through) text to reader. But the very concept of effective communication, on the basis of which the overwhelming majority of lectures and speeches are delivered, books and letters written, depends on the assumption that words and sentences constructed with a view to communicate an intention can usually hope for a large measure of success in so communicating. Despite theorists denying the referentiality of texts outside of themselves, nowhere have practising historians given up the belief that language refers to reality; texts are still viewed as vehicles for communication of consciously held ideas.[61] The general principle is not affected by the fact that some communicators are bad at communicating, or by the recognition of a communicator's ambiguity or (deliberate) deceptiveness, rhetoric or individual style, humour or irony. The principle of 'plain meaning' can embrace such features, since it seeks to take as full account of historical context, genre, and particular circumstances as necessary. Nor is the principle undermined by recognition that on innumerable finer points or nuances there will be considerable scope for disagreement among auditors and readers. Without the conviction that at least the main point and thrust of what we wish to communicate is in fact communicated, no communication could hope to rise above the first stumbling phrases of someone trying to speak in a new foreign language. The irony (or should we say self-condemnation) of arguments intended to 'prove' the incapacity of texts to communicate intended meaning seems somehow to escape some practitioners.[62] On this logic we should abandon all laws of copyright and 'intellectual property' and strike the term (and the academic 'sin' of) 'plagiarism' from our vocabulary and university rule books.

If, then, it is possible to construe meaning from a verbal communication today, and to gain a broad consensus assent as to what the main thrust of that meaning is, then it is in principle possible to construe the equivalent meaning in an ancient communication and to gain some breadth of consensus regarding that meaning as the communication was first spoken and heard or first written and read. Such consensus will not extend to every detail by any means, just as it will not depend on a translation as 'fixed' as the original text; nor could it foreclose

61. Iggers, *Historiography* 118-33, 139-40, 144-45. Iggers can even conclude with the outspoken assertion: 'The alternative to an albeit chastened Enlightenment is barbarism' (147).

62. Meyer appeals effectively to the phenomenon of 'self-reversal' (Lonergan), referring *inter alia* to 'Richard Rorty's four-hundred-page philosophic argument purporting to show the non-cognitive character of philosophy and hence the futility of philosophic argument' (*Reality and Allusion* 40-47 [here 43], 131-36); cf. Moore, *Literary Criticism* 145-48. R. Ingarden warns of the failure to recognize the social nature of language. 'It is simply not true that each of us forms the meanings of words for himself alone, in complete isolation, "privately"' (from *The Cognition of the Literary Work of Art* [1973], abstracted in Mueller-Vollmer, *Hermeneutics Reader* 198-200).

on or close off other meanings heard or read from the communication in its continuing existence as text; but the hermeneutical principle of plain meaning in historical context as the primary reading or first goal in interpretation still stands.[63]

Of course, the ancient communicator, unlike the present-day communicator, cannot be engaged in dialogue regarding the meaning of his words, so that the hermeneutical equivalent of the Lessing (or uncertainty) principle will reduce the consensus. But here, in hermeneutics as with historical method, we are not dealing with meaning as an objective artefact, and our 'reconstruction' of historical meaning in historical context will be an exercise in probabilities and approximations, whose success will depend on how much data (historical philology) are available to us. In fact, most passages in the NT have a fair degree of stability of meaning in terms of the words and idioms and syntax of their time of composition. And the interpreter who is able to draw on the fruits of classical philology and to recognize the text's genre is more likely to gain access to that stable meaning as intended by its author than are other interpreters. Again, this is not to deny that other readings in other, subsequent contexts of the text, including the text in translation, are possible and valid. It is simply to assert again that the normativity of the historical text in historical context should be acknowledged. Alternatively expressed, historical criticism does not dictate the meaning of a historical text, but exegesis should be accorded some right to indicate the limits beyond which readings of the text become implausible and illegitimate.

To restate the point (§6.4b above) in terms of meaning and with still different imagery, if we liken a historical text to a plant, then it is vital that we take account of the fact that it is embedded in a certain soil, with roots and tendrils reaching often deep into that soil. To uproot the plant and attempt to transpose it into a different bed without regard to its rootedness is likely to kill it. A historical text is like such a plant. The plain 'meaning' cannot be fully read off the text without regard to its rootedness in its originating context. The reference is not only to the situation/social context of writer and first readers/auditors, but also to the overtones that the words and phrases and idioms would have carried in these contexts (the root tendrils) and to the allusions and echoes, intended but also unintended, which the language of the text would have conveyed when it enacted the purpose for which it was written. That already makes for a tremendous 'richness' in the text, which means that 'plain meaning' is never a matter of understanding a text in terms merely of its grammatical and syntactical structure. But it also serves as a

63. Cf. Morgan, *Biblical Interpretation* 181-82, 198, 156-57. For a recent vigorous defence of 'literal sense', 'authorial intention', and even 'objective interpretation' see F. Watson, *Text and Truth: Redefining Biblical Theology* (Edinburgh: Clark, 1997) 95-126. Anthony Thiselton refers me particularly to R. Searle, 'Literal Meaning', *Expression of Meaning* (Cambridge: Cambridge University, 1979) 117-36, and N. Wolterstorff, *Divine Discourse* (Cambridge: Cambridge University, 1995) 183-201.

caution against a too hasty uprooting of the text from its historical context and assumption that such a text transplanted in a different context (as, for example, in
service of a later dogmatic pronouncement) will still be the same text.

It should be noted that I am not talking here in terms of 'intended meaning'
as that has mostly been understood. Criticism of the 'intentional fallacy' was a
reaction against Romanticism's hope to enter into the creative experience of
authorial composition, the intention seen as behind the text, bringing the text into
being.[64] The goal of 'plain meaning', however, focuses on the text itself. To reassert the importance of the 'plain meaning', therefore, is not to deny the importance of authorial intention. Rather it is to focus on authorial intention *as
entextualised*.[65] It is the text as embodying that intention, as a communicative act
between author and intended readers/auditors, to which attention is given. In discussion of biblical texts too much importance has traditionally been placed on
the 'moment' of inspiration, and not enough on the 'moment' of reception. The
text was (and is) precisely what mediates between the two. The writer did not
write into a vacuum, but with a view to how his text was heard.[66] Reader-
response did not begin in the twentieth century! It was already one half of the
communicative act which was the text. It should not surprise us, then, that a need
has been felt within contemporary hermeneutical theory to reintroduce the author
in terms of 'the implied author'.[67] This is simply to acknowledge that in most
cases the text itself bears testimony to its own integral intentionality. Since we
may assume, on most occasions, that the implied intention is the intention which
the real author wished to imply, the outcome may be little different.

d. The Hermeneutical Circle

Hermeneutics has long been fascinated by the fact and problem of the
hermeneutical circle. In its initial form it was the circularity of part and whole,
already noted by Schleiermacher: the parts can only be understood in terms of
the whole; but understanding of the whole is built up from the parts. As

64. See above, chapter 4, n. 44.

65. Meyer, *Reality and Illusion* 94-98. Authorial intention 'is to be understood not as
some subjective occurrence lying behind the text but as the principle of the text's intelligibil-
ity', 'as primarily embodied in the words the author wrote' (Watson, *Text and Truth* 112, 118).

66. It should be added, of course, that Paul's letters (the most obvious examples in the
NT of intentional texts) were not always effective communication, in that the response they
elicited was not as he would have wished. But the fact that so many of them (some were lost)
were respected, retained, no doubt read and reread, pondered, circulated, collected, and finally
gathered to become part of the NT canon attests their overall effectiveness.

67. Above chapter 5, n. 143.

Schleiermacher was well aware, the 'whole' was not simply the whole particular writing, but the whole language and historical reality to which the particular text belonged.[68] It is called a circle, because the hermeneutical process is unavoidably a movement back and forth round the circle, where understanding is ever provisional and subject to clarification and correction as the whole is illuminated by the parts and the part by the whole. As Schleiermacher's pupil, P. A. Boeckh, went on to point out, this hermeneutical circle 'cannot be resolved in all cases, and can never be resolved completely'. Boeckh continues:

> every single utterance is conditioned by an infinite number of circumstances, and it is therefore impossible to bring to clear communication. . . . Thus the task of interpretation is to reach as close an approximation as possible by gradual, step-by-step approximation; it cannot hope to reach the limit.[69]

The similarity to the procedures of historical study indicated above (§6.3) should be obvious.

By way of immediate corollary, it is worth observing that narrative criticism has attempted in effect to narrow the hermeneutical circle of whole and parts, by limiting the whole to the text itself.[70] In narrative criticism, in order to make sense of a part, verse, or passage of a Gospel, the hermeneutical circle need only take in the whole of the Gospel itself. But all that has already been said should be enough to show the weakness of this model of the hermeneutical circle. The reality is that the historical text draws on (and its communicative potential depends on) wider linguistic usage of the time; it makes references and allusions to characters and customs which are not explained within 'the closed universe'[71] of the text; it cannot be adequately understood without some awareness of the society of the time.[72] For example, without knowledge of the extra-textual social tensions between Jews and Samaritans, a central thrust of the parable of the Good Samaritan (Luke 10) will be lost.[73] Without a knowledge of who

68. In Mueller-Vollmer, *Hermeneutics Reader* 84-85. Gadamer notes that 'this circular relationship between the whole and the parts . . . was already known to classical rhetoric, which compares perfect speech with the organic body, with the relationship between head and limbs' (*Truth* 175).

69. In Mueller-Vollmer, *Hermeneutics Reader* 138.

70. See above, §5.6.

71. See chapter 5, n. 142 above.

72. B. J. Malina, *The Social Gospel of Jesus* (Minneapolis: Fortress, 2001) 1-13 speaks for the recent sociological perspective on the Jesus tradition when he suggests that 'The Bible is necessarily misunderstood if one's reading of it is not grounded in an appreciation of the social systems from which its documents arose' (5).

73. See further K. E. Bailey, *Poet and Peasant: A Literary-Cultural Approach to the Parables in Luke* (Grand Rapids: Eerdmans, 1976) ch. 2.

Moses and Elijah are, information not provided by the text, the reader will miss a fundamental dimension of the significance of the account of Jesus' transfiguration (Mark 9.2-8 pars.). The surprising evocation of the Newtonian world view ('closed universe') in a hermeneutic trying to distance itself from the historical-critical method prompts a wry smile.

A second form of the hermeneutical circle sends the interpreter back and forth between the matter of the text and the speech used to convey it, between Word and words, *Sache und Sprache,*[74] between *langue* and *parole,* signified and signifier.[75] This form of the hermeneutical procedure has been played out throughout the period reviewed in the preceding chapters, particularly in the way in which again and again a definitive subject matter perceived through the text has been used to critique the wording of the text itself. One thinks, for example, of the gospel *(was treibet Christus)* serving as the critical scalpel for Luther,[76] or the universal ideals of Jesus indicating an 'essence' from which the merely particular could be stripped,[77] or Bultmann's 'kerygma' providing the key for his demythologizing programme,[78] or 'justification by faith' acting as the 'canon within the canon' for Käsemann.[79] Or in recent Jesus research an instructive example is Wright's repeated appeal to a metanarrative of Israel in exile and hoped-for return from exile as providing a hermeneutical echo chamber in which the various sayings of Jesus and stories about Jesus resonate with a meaning hardly evident on the face of the text.[80]

The third form of the hermeneutical circle is that between reader and text. The interaction between reader and text was already implicit in the recognition of a 'psychological' dimension to hermeneutics,[81] and in the historical principle of 'analogy' (above §6.3c). Bultmann elaborated the point in his insistence

---

74. Meyer, *Aims* 96. *Sachkritik* (the English 'content criticism' is not really adequate) builds on the older theological distinction between the Word of God and the words of Scripture through which it is heard (but is not to be simply identified with them) by distinguishing between the real intention *(die Sache,* the matter or subject) of a text and the language in which it is expressed *(die Sprache). Sachkritik* is linked particularly with the name of Bultmann (see, e.g., Thiselton, *Two Horizons* 274).

75. Referring to Ferdinand de Saussure's influential distinction between the language system *(langue)* and concrete acts of speech *(parole)* and his idea of the text as an encoded sign-system — hence 'semiotics', the theory of signs (see Thiselton, *New Horizons* 80-86).

76. Luther's famous criticism of the epistle of James: 'What does not teach Christ is not apostolic, even though St. Peter or Paul taught it' (Kümmel, *New Testament* 25).

77. See above, §4.3.

78. See above, §5.3.

79. E.g., E. Käsemann, ed., *Das Neue Testament als Kanon* (Göttingen: Vandenhoeck, 1970) 405.

80. Wright, *Jesus passim.*

81. Schleiermacher and Droysen, in Mueller-Vollmer, *Hermeneutics Reader* 8-11, 128.

(which students of the NT still needed to hear) that 'there cannot be any such thing as presuppositionless exegesis'. 'A specific understanding of the subject matter of the text, on the basis of a "life-relation" to it, is always presupposed by exegesis', hence the term, 'pre-understanding'.[82] The point is sometimes missed when more conservative biblical scholars deem it sufficient to declare their presuppositions before embarking on what most of their fellow scholars would regard as uncritical exegesis, as though the declaration of presuppositions somehow vindicated the exegesis itself (since 'Everyone has presuppositions'). But the point is not simply that any reading of a text is shaped by the pre-understanding brought to it. The point is rather that as the exegete moves round the hermeneutical circle between pre-understanding and text, the text reacts back upon the pre-understanding, both sharpening it and requiring of it revision at one or another point, and thus enabling a fresh scrutiny of the text, necessitating in turn a further revision of pre-understanding, and so on and on.

The most vicious form of the hermeneutical circle, however, has proved to be that between reader and text as it has been developed within postmodern literary criticism. Indeed, deconstructionist hermeneutics attempt in effect to undermine the whole procedure envisaged in the hermeneutical circle by suggesting that the reality is an infinite series of interlocking circles, where the search for meaning is never ending and the play between signifier and signified goes on *ad infinitum*. The image conjured up is of a computer game without an end, or of an internet search into the infinity of cyberspace as web pages direct to other web pages in an endless sequence, or indeed of a computer hacker who has succeeded in so overloading a system that it crashes, or perhaps again of an academic colleague who always insists on the impossibility of any effective discussion of an academic subject or political policy without first resolving the problem of what human consciousness is. Intellectually challenging as such exercises are, they do not much assist in the living of life, the advance of knowledge, or the building of community. To conceive the hermeneutical process as an infinitely regressive intertextuality is a counsel of despair which quickly reduces all meaningful communication to impossibility and all communication to a game of 'trivial pursuit'.

Perhaps it has been the image of a 'circle' which has misled us, since it invites the picture of an endless 'going round in circles'. In fact, however, from its earliest use, the hermeneutical circles were always perceived as a progressive exercise, in which the circles, as it were, became smaller. Alternatively expressed, the circle was seen more as a spiral, the circle in effect as a three-dimensional cone, so that successive circlings resulted in a spiralling towards a common centre. Wilhelm von Humboldt expressed the point well (though with nineteenth-

---

82. Bultmann, 'Exegesis without Presuppositions' 343-44, 347. See also Gadamer's striking 'defence' of prejudice (*Truth* 270-71, 276-68).

century overconfidence) when he talked of history as 'a critical practice through which [the historian] attempts to correct his preliminary impressions of the object until, through repeated reciprocal action, clarity as well as certainty emerge'.[83] Once again, the likeness of the hermeneutical method to the historical method described above (§6.3) is to be noted. As a reader of historical texts (the Gospels and Epistles of the NT), therefore, I (and most others engaged in the same exercise) do not despair over the hermeneutical circle but find that the reality of a self-critical critical scrutiny of these texts can and does provide a growing appreciation and understanding of why they were written and what they must have conveyed to their first auditors and readers. The meaning intended by means of and through the text is still a legitimate and viable goal for the NT exegete and interpreter.

e. 'Historically Effected Consciousness'

Worth particular mention, because of its influence within contemporary hermeneutics as they have impacted on biblical criticism,[84] is Gadamer's concept of *Wirkungsgeschichte,* the 'history of effect' of a text. Here the hermeneutical circle is correlated with the older hermeneutical recognition of hermeneutics as the interplay between the polarities of familiarity and strangeness. The point is that the gap between text and reader is not empty; it is filled by the effect which the text has exercised in the in-between time between 'an historically intended, distanced object and belonging to a tradition'. Consequently Gadamer questions 'the naïve assumption of historicism' that the temporal distance is something which must be overcome. Rather it should be seen 'as a positive and productive condition enabling understanding'. The intervening tradition is part of us.[85] Gadamer's point is not to be reduced simply to the recognition that the interpreter stands within a history influenced by the text. The key term is actually the more elaborate phrase, *wirkungsgeschichtliches Bewusstsein,* 'historically effected consciousness'. Here it is important to recognize the distinction between the English verbs 'affect' and 'effect': to 'affect' someone is to move or touch or influence that person; to 'effect' is to bring about or bring into being a certain result or outcome.[86] Gadamer's point, then, is that the interpreter's consciousness, or pre-understanding we might say, is not simply influenced by the text; rather, it has in some measure been brought into being by the text; it is itself in some de-

---

83. From Mueller-Vollmer, *Hermeneutics Reader* 112-13.
84. See, e.g., Watson, *Text and Truth* particularly 45-54.
85. Gadamer, *Truth* 295, 297, 282.
86. As Gadamer's translators note (*Truth* xv).

gree a product of the text; it is a consciousness of the text to be interpreted. It is because the interpreter's consciousness has been thus 'effected' that it can be 'effectual in finding the right questions to ask'.[87]

Still more influential[88] has been Gadamer's conception of the two 'horizons' involved in hermeneutics, 'the horizon in which the person seeking to understand lives and the historical horizon within which he places himself'. But it is not enough to think of the hermeneutical process as a transposition from the familiar contemporary horizon to the alien horizon of the text. For the horizons, particularly that of the interpreter, are neither static nor closed; they shift, they are revisable. 'The horizon of the present is continually in the process of being formed . . . (and) cannot be formed without the past'. Hence, 'understanding is always the fusion of these horizons supposedly existing by themselves'.[89]

The value of this way of re-envisaging the hermeneutical circle is two-fold.[90] First, it recognizes and affirms the fact of distance and difference between the interpreter and the text. Even in the 'fusion of horizons' *(Horizont-verschmelzung)* the distinctiveness and difference of the other horizon are not to be lost to sight. Second, the hermeneutical process is seen to be more than simply Romanticism's empathetic feeling with the author; it is rather a movement of growing recognition both of the text's otherness and yet also of its effect (great or small, for good or ill) on the interpreter's own self-identity. The fusion of horizons is another way of saying that the reciprocally revisionary character of the hermeneutical circle is a spiral not only into an enlarging/deepening understanding of the text; it is also a spiral into an enlarging/deepening understanding of oneself.

No wonder, then, that Gadamer has proved to be such an ally to those who want to maintain that faith is not in principle at odds with the hermeneutical process in its application to study of the NT, conceived as it has been in terms of Enlightenment historicism or through analogy as determined by 'modern' consciousness. Gadamer has made us aware of dimensions of self-consciousness without which a critical hermeneutic cannot be sufficiently self-critical.[91]

---

87. Gadamer, *Truth* 340-41, 301.

88. Illustrated particularly by Thiselton's two major studies, *Two Horizons* and *New Horizons*.

89. Gadamer, *Truth* 302-307.

90. Cf. Ricoeur's reflections arising from Gadamer's work, in the closing section of 'The Task of Hermeneutics' and in 'The Hermeneutical Function of Distanciation', which followed (*Text to Action* 73-88).

91. Not surprisingly, Ben Meyer was the first to recognize the significance of Gadamer for historical study of Jesus (*Aims* 59).

f. Reading as Encounter

If I prefer the image of hermeneutics as a 'dialogue' it is not to deny or ignore the important points which emerge from considering the hermeneutical circle. I simply find the image of dialogue as personal encounter more appealing, partly because it gives weight to the idea of hermeneutics as in some sense a process of personal formation, and partly because it recognizes the text as communicative act. Hermeneutics is best conceived as a dialogue where both partners must be allowed to speak in their own terms, rather than as an interrogation of the text where the text is only allowed to answer the questions asked. To put the same point another way, for a dialogue to be fruitful there must also be genuine engagement of the interpreter with the text. Here again we have consciously to move on from the old scientific paradigm of dispassionate, clinical research, as though the text was a corpse in the pathology lab waiting to be dissected by the scalpels of the historical method. The point was already recognized emotionally in Pietism and the Romantic revival, theologically in Barth's theology of encounter with the kerygmatic word and Bultmann's existentialism and hermeneutically in the more conservative forms of reader-response criticism, in Ricoeur's conception of a second naivete,[92] and in George Steiner's exposition of 'real presence'.[93] Even deconstruction can be seen as an attempt to ensure that the hegemony wrested from the author is not simply assumed by the reader; *the text itself* deconstructs all interpretations! The point is that without the interpreter's openness to being addressed by the text, the interpreter can scarcely hope to avoid abusing the text. Unless the text is, at least in some sense, allowed to set its own agenda, it is questionable whether it is being heard at all.

In short, if we sum up the hermeneutical issues by responding to the postmodern question 'Is there meaning in the text?', the answer has to be either a qualified Yes or a qualified No. It is not that the encounter is a 'picnic' to which the text brings the words and the reader the meaning, to pick up Northrop Frye's engaging metaphor. The truth has to be somewhere in between, indeed precisely in the integration of these two too simplistically separated terms, in the 'fusion' of these two polarities. The text in its language and syntactical relationships already has a potentiality for meaning, a potentiality which becomes active and effective in the encounter of reading, whether the first reading or the thousandth reading. As with the critically realist approach to the history of Christianity's be-

---

92. P. Ricoeur, *The Symbolism of Evil* (Boston: Beacon, 1969) 351. See further Ricoeur, *Essays* 6, 23; also 'Preface to Bultmann' 67-69; also 'Hermeneutical Function of Distanciation' 84-88; Thiselton, *New Horizons* 359-60.

93. G. Steiner, *Real Presences: Is There Anything in What We Say?* (London: Faber and Faber, 1989).

ginnings, so with the hermeneutics of reading the NT, there is neither an absolutely objective meaning 'in' the text, nor an absolutely subjective meaning imported to the text by the reader. The text must be listened to as well as read. 'The
voice that speaks from the past . . . itself poses a question and places our meaning
in openness'.[94]

6.5. When Did a Faith Perspective
First Influence the Jesus Tradition?

I have argued that the key issue in any attempt to talk historically about Jesus of
Nazareth has been and continues to be the tension between faith and history, or
more accurately now, the hermeneutical tension between faith and history. Most
of what has so far been discussed in this chapter bears on that issue, and the
above overview leaves us with a number of important insights, which we need
now to harvest.

a. What Is the Historical Jesus?

The Enlightenment ideal of historical objectivity also projected a false goal onto
the quest of the historical Jesus. For from its inception, questers have made the
assumption that behind the text of the Gospels, behind the traditions which they
incorporate, there is a 'historical Jesus', an objective historical datum who will
be different from the dogmatic Christ or from the Jesus of the Gospels and who
will enable us to criticize the dogmatic Christ and the Jesus of the Gospels.[95]

　　An important factor in all this has been the confusion injected into the
quest by the key phrase itself — 'historical Jesus'. It is true that whenever a definition is offered for the phrase, the person offering the definition is clear that the
'historical Jesus' is *the Jesus constructed by historical research.*[96] Despite that,

---

　　94. Gadamer, *Truth* 374.

　　95. The archaeological imagery used by Funk is revealing when he describes the first of
'two pillars of modern biblical criticism' as 'the distinction between the historical Jesus, to be
uncovered by historical excavation, and the Christ of faith encapsulated in the first creeds' (*Five
Gospels* 3). Similarly Mack's description of his own and earlier 'archaeological efforts' (*Myth*
xi-xiii, 5). The image is given paradigmatic status in Kloppenborg Verbin's most recent title
(*Excavating Q*) and in the finely executed partnership of J. D. Crossan and J. L. Reed, *Excavating Jesus: Beneath the Stones, behind the Texts* (SanFrancisco: HarperSanFrancisco, 2001)
particularly xvii-xviii, 8, 12-14. See also below chapter 8, n. 302.

　　96. E.g., Robinson, *New Quest* 26; Keck, *Future* 20, 35 ('the historical Jesus is the historian's Jesus, not a Kantian *Ding an sich*'); Meier, *Marginal Jew* 1.21-26.

however, the phrase is used again and again in a casual way to refer to the Jesus of Nazareth who walked the hills of Galilee, and it is that sense which predominates overall. Or to be more precise, the phrase 'the historical Jesus' as typically used is something of an amalgam of the two senses. The quest has generally assumed its capacity to construct (from the available data) a Jesus who will be the real Jesus: the historical Jesus (reconstructed) will be the historical Jesus (actual); again and again the one sense elides indistinguishably into the other.[97] It is this confusion which largely lies behind the surprising confidence of the nineteenth- and late-twentieth-century questers that a Jesus reconstructed from the sources available would be a sound base (the actual Jesus) for a critique of the Jesus of these sources.[98] It needs to be said once again, then, that the 'historical Jesus' is properly speaking a nineteenth- and twentieth-century construction using the data provided by the Synoptic tradition, *not* Jesus back then and *not* a figure in history whom we can realistically use to critique the portrayal of Jesus in the Synoptic tradition.

b. Kähler's Point

It is here that Kähler's key observation needs to be reasserted.[99] The idea that a Jesus *reconstructed from the Gospel traditions* (the so-called 'historical Jesus'), *yet significantly different from the Jesus of the Gospels,* is the Jesus who taught in Galilee (the historical Jesus!) is an illusion. The idea that we can see through the faith perspective of the NT writings to a Jesus who did *not* inspire faith or who inspired faith in a *different* way is an illusion. There is no such Jesus. That there *was* a Jesus who *did* inspire the faith which in due course found expression in the Gospels is not in question. But that we can somehow hope to strip out the theological impact which he actually made on his disciples, to uncover a different Jesus (the real Jesus!), is at best fanciful. It is not simply that 'we reach Jesus only

97. This reflects, of course, the wider confusion between 'history' = the past and 'history' = the historian's attempt to reconstruct the past. A similar confusion between real reader, ideal reader, and implied reader often vitiates much reader-response criticism (above §6.4), as also confusion with regard to what 'Q' refers to in criticism of the Synoptic Gospels (see below, §7.4).

98. This is why the move of the neo-Liberals to provide new sources and to point to major differences between sources is so important: the more differentiated the data, the greater the possibility of reconstructing a historical Jesus different from all the later representations. Which is also why the question of sources must be the next item on our agenda (chapter 7 below).

99. Perhaps I should stress that I am taking up only this key point from Kähler, not his larger agenda as a late-nineteenth-century systematic theologian.

through the picture his disciples made of him',[100] it is also that the only Jesus we reach through that picture is the Jesus who inspired that picture.

Of course we do have some echoes of an outsider's perspective in Roman and rabbinic sources.[101] But we simply do not have portrayals of Jesus as seen through the eyes of the high priests or the Roman authorities or the people of the land. We do not have a 'neutral' (!) portrayal of Jesus.[102] All we have in the NT Gospels is Jesus seen with the eye of faith. We do not have a 'historical Jesus', only the 'historic Christ'. As Kähler noted, the proof of the pudding is in the diverse Jesuses constructed by questers generally, not least the Liberal and now neo-Liberal Jesuses. In each case, the distinctiveness of the 'objective Jesus' is largely the creation of the historical critic. The irony indeed is that the typical 'historical Jesus' is as much a theological Jesus as is any Gospel portrayal, since the constructed Jesus has been almost always an amalgam of the historian's own ideals (the fifth Gospel according to Kähler) and the critically (selectively) worked data.[103] Whether the new sources trumpeted by the neo-Liberal questers make a significant difference to Kähler's point is again an issue to which we will have to return.

c. Form Criticism's Missed Opportunity

Form criticism opened up a new possibility of penetrating behind the earliest written sources. It also recognized that faith had shaped these earlier forms. But its practitioners were distracted from the implications of this recognition for 'Life of Jesus' research by focusing on the way faith had shaped the forms toward their final form in the Gospels. They neglected to inquire very far about the faith stimulus which *started* the traditioning process. Or else they took Easter faith as the starting point for the tradition, assuming that the portrayal of Jesus is entirely post-Easter in creation and the product of developed faith. In a sense we

100. H.-I. Marrou, *De la connaissance historique* (Paris: Editions du Seuill, 1954) 108, cited by Reiser, 'Eschatology' 221.

101. See below, §7.1.

102. Beyond, arguably, Josephus' brief references to Jesus (see again §7.1 below).

103. To clarify the point: I do not mean that the tendencies of individual Evangelists cannot be identified and allowed for. My point is rather that the basic tendency of faith saturates the tradition and that any steps to isolate an unsaturated residuum are inevitably 'contaminated' by the procedures used and 'distorted' by the spectacles through which the Gospel tradition is read. Nor do I abandon the practice of 'critical realism' (§6.3e). My point is rather that the only Jesus we can realistically expect to emerge from the critical dialogue with our sources is the Jesus who made the impact on the disciples which we encapsulate in the word 'faith'. The point is developed in the following pages.

have suffered from the false idea that 'form criticism' is the translation of *Form-geschichte,* in that study of the history of transmission of the tradition (from the first) has been too often subverted into a study of the forms themselves. So too the recognition that forms have a *Sitz-im-Leben* (life-setting) diverted attention too much from the process of transmission to the communities which gave the forms their shape. To these matters we will have to return in §§8.3-6.

The weakness of form criticism as a tool in the quest is illustrated by the ease with which it succumbed to the same illusion that Kähler identified: the assumption that there is a recoverable reality (an 'original' form) behind the text untouched by faith. So it could include the working assumption that many of the individual forms in effect were given their initial shape and had a vital life outside the communities of faith, as though the forms were to be found in story-telling round the campfires of travellers or in the casual conversations of the marketplace,[104] as though the Evangelists hunted out tales about Jesus in the way that European composers in the first half of the twentieth century hunted out the folksongs and folk tunes of their people for their own compositions. But again we have to ask whether we have in the Synoptic tradition *any* data which are untouched by faith from the outset.

d. Disciple-Response

It is at this point that we can draw further upon the insights of postmodern literary criticism — that the meaning of a text is in some sense the product of a creative encounter between text and reader. For though the point being made is usually with regard to the present-day reader's reception of literary texts, it actually applies also to the tradition process itself which lies behind the Synoptic Gospels. Here Gadamer's concept of the *Wirkungsgeschichte* of a text or tradition is also to the point, since it applies also to the moment in which the tradition was itself created. There is in fact *no* gap to be bridged between a Jesus historically conceived and the subsequent tradition which has effected consciousness; all we

104. Cf. particularly E. Trocmé, *Jesus and His Contemporaries* (London: SCM, 1973): 'the setting in which the miracle stories originated and were handed down for a time is not a Christian one, but must be sought in . . . the village society of north-eastern Galilee or the area immediately surrounding Lake Tiberias. Story-tellers at markets and during winter evenings found a ready audience for narratives with no literary pretensions, but too sensational to leave a popular audience unmoved. . . . We owe to him [Mark] the introduction of these narratives into a Christian setting' (104). The point is elaborated by G. Theissen, *The Gospels in Context: Social and Political History in the Synoptic Tradition* (Minneapolis: Fortress, 1991) 97-112; see also his stimulating novellistic treatment, *The Shadow of the Galilean: The Quest of the Historical Jesus in Narrative Form* (London: SCM, 1987).

have is disciples effected by Jesus and the disciples thus 'effected' expressing their 'effection' by formulating the tradition which effects.[105] The traditions which lie behind the Gospels (for the moment we will leave aside the question of what proportion of these traditions) began from the various encounters between Jesus and those who by virtue of these encounters became disciples. The earliest traditions are the product of disciple-response. There is not an objectified meaning to be uncovered by stripping away the accretions of disciple faith. The tradition itself in its earliest form is in a crucially important sense the creation of faith; or to be more precise, it is the product of the encounters between Jesus and the ones who became his disciples. The hearing and witnessing of the first disciples was already a hermeneutical act, already caught in the hermeneutical circle. The twenty-first-century exegetes and interpreters do not begin the hermeneutical dialogue; they continue a dialogue which began in the initial formation of the tradition.[106]

The point for us now, therefore, is that the saying or account attests the *impact* made by Jesus.[107] But that does not enable us to get behind that impact to a Jesus who might have been heard otherwise. For the original impulse behind these records was, to put the point more accurately, *sayings of Jesus as heard and received,* and *actions of Jesus as witnessed and retained in the memory* (both parts of each phrase being important). We have to add in both cases, *and as reflected on thereafter,* of course. However, what we have in these traditions is not just the end-product of that reflection. It is rather the faith-creating word/event,

---

105. Cf. Ricoeur's observation that the phenomenon of distance and difference refers not simply to the modern reading of an ancient text: 'The distance is given at the beginning. It is the very first distance between the hearer and the witness of the event' ('Preface to Bultmann' 56).

106. Watson seems to think only in terms of a significance seen retrospectively (*Text and Truth* 52-53).

107. For want of a better way of describing it, in what follows I speak of the 'impact' of Jesus. Similarly P. Barnett, *Jesus and the Logic of History* (Grand Rapids: Eerdmans, 1997) speaks of 'the percussive impact of Jesus the Teacher' (56, 102, 127); cf. his *Jesus and the Rise of Early Christianity* ch. 2. Patterson emphasises '(the original) impression' made by Jesus, the 'experience' 'created' by Jesus in his disciples (*The God of Jesus* 10, 46-50, 53-54, 56-58, 87, 90, 113, 118, 130-31); he cites Willi Marxsen, 'Christian faith began with the event of being moved by Jesus' (56, n. 1). We should also recall that form-critical analysis of the Jesus tradition was predicated on the assumption that the tradition was retained as live tradition, precisely in that the tradition continued to influence and shape the lives of the earliest disciples and communities. It is more or less self-evident that teaching like Matt. 7.24-27/Luke 6.47-49 and Mark 8.34-38 pars. must have made a faith-creating impact on those who passed on the teaching. There are obvious links in all this to the hermeneutical conception of language as event ('language-event'); for discussion see Thiselton, *Two Horizons* 335-56; and on 'speech-act' theory, *New Horizons* 283-312, 361-68.

as itself a force shaping faith and as retained and rehearsed by the faith thus created and being created. In other words, the Jesus tradition gives immediate access not to a dispassionately recorded word or deed, nor only to the end product (the faith of the 50s, 60s, 70s, or 80s), but also to the process between the two, to the tradition which began with the initial impact of Jesus' word or deed and which continued to influence intermediate retellers of the tradition until crystallized in Mark's or Matthew's or Luke's account.[108] In short, we must take seriously the character of the tradition as disciple-response, and the depth of the tradition as well as its final form.[109]

e. The Remembered Jesus

We can therefore press Kähler's point still further to one of fundamental principle. The Synoptic tradition provides evidence not so much for what Jesus did or said in itself, but for what Jesus was *remembered* as doing or saying by his first disciples, or as we might say, for the *impact* of what he did and said on his first disciples. Bearing in mind the point just made, we may say that it is precisely the process of 'remembering' which fuses the horizons of past and present, by making the past present again *(Vergegenwärtigung).*[110] What we actually have in the earliest retellings of what is now the Synoptic tradition, then, are the memories

108. Cf. particularly the repeated emphasis of H. Schürmann on the pre-Easter beginnings of the Synoptic tradition — 'Die vorösterlichen Anfänge der Logientradition: Versuch eines formgeschichtlichen Zugangs zum Leben Jesu', in H. Ristow and K. Matthiae, eds., *Der historische Jesus und der kerygmatische Christus* [Berlin: Evangelische, 1961] 342-70); also *Jesus: Gestalt und Geheimnis* (Paderborn: Bonifatius, 1994) 85-104, 380-97: 'With the help of form-critical principles it can be shown . . . that the beginnings of the logia tradition must lie in the pre-Easter circle of disciples, and therewith in Jesus himself. Therewith would a form-critical access be opened to the "historical Jesus", for the "historical Jesus" is now himself a factor in the history of the tradition (as its initiator)' (103).

109. The argument here is similar to that between J. A. Sanders and B. S. Childs on 'canonical criticism', in which I side with Sanders; see my 'Levels of Canonical Authority', *HBT* 4 (1982) 13-60 (particularly 15 and n. 14), reprinted in *The Living Word* (London: SCM, 1987) 141-74, 186-92 (particularly 142-43 and n. 14).

110. Cf. particularly J. Schröter, *Erinnerung an Jesu Worte: Studien zur Rezeption der Logienüberlieferung in Markus, Q und Thomas* (WMANT 76; Neukirchen-Vluyn: Neukirchener, 1997) 3-4; 'Recall of the Jesus tradition can be understood accordingly as a selective process by which the actual present becomes meaningful by reference to the person of Jesus' (463-64). See further Schröter's 'Markus, Q und der historische Jesus', *ZNW* 89 (1998) 173-200; also 'Die Frage nach dem historischen Jesus und der Charakter historischer Erkenntnis', in A. Lindemann, ed., *The Sayings Source Q and the Historical Jesus* (Leuven: Leuven University, 2001) 207-54, where the overlap of our programmatic concerns is clear (especially 213-34, 252-53).

of the first disciples — not Jesus himself, but the remembered Jesus.[111] The idea
that we can get back to an objective historical reality, which we can wholly separate and disentangle from the disciples' memories and then use as a check and
control over the way the tradition was developed during the oral and earliest written transmission, is simply unrealistic.[112] This observation would have been
more obvious had more attention been given to the narrative tradition, as distinct
from the sayings tradition, over the past 150 years. For narratives about Jesus
never began with Jesus; at best they began with eyewitnesses. From the first we
are confronted not so much with Jesus but with how he was perceived. And the
same is actually true of the sayings tradition: at best what we have are the teachings of Jesus as they impacted on the individuals who stored them in their memories and began the process of oral transmission.

In one sense, of course, we are simply recognizing the nature of the evidence which any biographer has to weigh who has no access to any writings of
the biography's subject. That is to say, a portrayal of Jesus as seen through the
eyes and heard through the ears of his first disciples is neither an illegitimate nor
an impossible task, and such a portrayal, carefully drawn in terms of the evidence
available, should not be dismissed or disparaged as inadmissible. As Lee Keck
observes: 'the perception of Jesus that he catalyzed is part of who Jesus was'.[113]
After all, it is precisely the impact which Jesus made and which resulted in the
emergence of Christianity which we (not just Christians) want to recover. Of
course it would be wonderful and intriguing if we could portray Jesus as seen by
Pilate or Herod, by Caiaphas or the house of Shammai. But we simply do not
have sufficient evidence for that, and even if we had, what would it tell us about

111. 'We do not escape the fact that we know Jesus only as the disciples remembered
him' (Dahl, 'Problem' 94). 'An act of remembrance — the remembrance of a real and well-
known person — is a built-in feature of the faith that inspired the writing of the gospels' (Dodd,
Founder 28-29). Meyer also emphasises 'the overarching fact . . . that Palestinian Christianity
was nourished on the memory of Jesus' (*Aims* 69, 72-73). Others who recognize the importance
of disciples' recollection in the traditioning process include, e.g., Schillebeeckx, *Jesus* 45-47,
72, 226-29; Goppelt (*Theology* 1.6); and Charlesworth (*Jesus* 24). John Knox frequently referred to the Church's memory of Jesus, but in too broad and ill-defined a manner to be helpful
here; see the critique of P. Carnley, *The Structure of Resurrection Belief* (Oxford: Clarendon,
1987) 268-75, 280-94. As the title of the present volume indicates, the *remembered* Jesus will
be a leitmotif of the present study.

112. Dahl continues (in the passage quoted in n. 111): 'Whoever thinks that the disciples
completely misunderstood their Master or even consciously falsified his picture may give fan-
tasy free reign *(sic)*' ('Problem' 94).

113. Keck, *Who Is Jesus?* 20. Worth pondering also is his further comment: 'All too often historians of early Christianity use Jesus' words about what is to be done as evidence of
what early Christians did, instead of using it as evidence for the norm from which they were de-
viating but needed to be brought back into alignment' (165).

the beginnings of Christianity, about the character and impact of a mission which transformed fishermen and toll-collectors into disciples and apostles? In terms of pivotal individuals on whom the history of the world has turned, it is the latter in whom we are most interested. And the Synoptic tradition is precisely what we need for the task.

f. When Did Faith Begin?

The significance of the step being advocated here, therefore, should not be missed. For it is tantamount to asserting that faith goes back to the very *origins* of the Jesus tradition, that the Jesus tradition emerged *from the very first* as the expression of faith. In so saying I do not mean that the tradition was formulated only in the light of Easter faith, as Wrede and the kerygmatic theologians have assumed. I am referring to the first stirrings of faith which constituted the initial, pre-Easter disciple-response. I am asserting that the teaching and events of Jesus' ministry did not suddenly become significant in the light of Easter — much more significant, no doubt, as various markers in the Gospels indicate,[114] but not significant for the first time.[115] The suggestion that the remembered Jesus was wholly insignificant, unfascinating and unintriguing, having no real impact prior to his death and resurrection, is simply incredible. Peter and the others did not first become disciples on Easter day. There was already a response of faith, already a bond of trust, inspired by what they first and subsequently heard and saw Jesus say and do. Not yet explicitly faith in Jesus, but the Evangelists do not hesitate to describe the disciples' pre-Easter response to Jesus in terms of *faith*.[116] Only so can we explain how the Jesus tradition is so rich and full as it is — hardly the deposit of casual and vague memories first jerked into faith by Easter. In short, the tension between faith and history has too often been seen as destructive of good history. On the contrary, however, it is the recognition that Jesus can be perceived *only* through the impact he made on his first disciples (that is, their faith) which is the key to a historical recognition (and assessment) of that impact. Whether that key works and how well it works are matters for further exploration in chapter 8.

114. E.g., Mark 9.9; John 2.22.

115. As E. Lohse, 'Die Frage nach dem historischen Jesus in der gegenwärtigen neutestamentlichen Forschung', *Die Einheit des Neuen Testaments* (Göttingen: Vandenhoeck und Ruprecht, 1973) 29-48, points out, it is the Evangelists themselves who insist that 'the "beginning" of the gospel lies not first in the confession and preaching of the post-Easter community, but in the historical Jesus' (35-36), referring to Mark 1.1 and Acts 10.37ff. (see also below, §11.2c).

116. See further below, §13.2b.

It should not go unobserved that if this insight is justified it provides some sort of solution to the long-perceived gulf between history and faith. For in the historical moment(s) of creation of the Jesus tradition we have *historical faith*. The problem of history and faith, we might say, has been occasioned by the fact that further down the stream of faith and history the two have seemed so difficult to reconcile. But if it is in fact possible to trace the two streams, history and faith, back to the origins of the Jesus tradition, we find that we can step back and forth across the rivulets (pressing the analogy of a river's sources) with much less difficulty. Of course we are only at the *beginning* of faith at this point; but it is the beginning of *faith*. And nothing that has been so far said is intended to deny or discount the fact that the tradition developed, that there were accretions of faith, that post-Easter retellings conveyed post-Easter faith, that the tradition was elaborated in the passing on. All I am saying at this point is that the actual Synoptic tradition, with its record of things Jesus did and said, bears witness to a continuity between pre-Easter memory and post-Easter proclamation, a continuity of faith. However great the shock of Good Friday and Easter for the first disciples, it would be unjustified to assume that these events marked a discontinuity with their initial disciple-response, that they brought about complete disruption of their earlier disciple faith and that the traditioning process began only from that point on.[117] The mechanics of this process will occupy us later (§8.3-6).

g. The Diversity of Faith

Another aspect of postmodern criticism should not be ignored, namely the pluralism endemic to the recognition that readers respond differently to texts and so produce multiple meanings. Applied to the beginnings of the Jesus tradition, that insight reminds us that Jesus would have impacted variously on different individuals.[118] Or in terms of the present discussion, there would have been diversity of faith from the very first.[119] That is not, or should not be, a problem. For the evidence of the Synoptic tradition is of a homogeneity of impression made by Jesus on those who first created and then transmitted that tradition. As with the claim

117. Wellhausen already expressed the presupposition which became characteristic of the form-critical approach to the gospel tradition: 'Without this *later influence* (Nachwirkung) in the community we can visualize nothing of the religious personality of Jesus. It always appears only in a *reflection* (Reflex), *broken* (gebrochen) by the medium of the Christian faith' (*Einleitung* 114, my emphasis).

118. On the diversity of discipleship/disciple response to Jesus see further below, chapter 13.

119. 'Theological diversity in primitive Christianity is not a secondary phenomenon but a primary one' (Kloppenborg, 'Sayings Gospel Q' 320).

that the historical text as historical text provides parameters for the meanings to be read out from it (§6.4a), so the overall homogeneity of the Synoptic tradition points to the consistency of the impact made by Jesus as attested by that tradition. To put it another way, it is the consistency of disciple-response which gives the tradition its consistency.[120] At the same time it is important to remember, given the diversity (and fissiparity) of subsequent Christianity, that the circle of discipleship was not uniform from the beginning and that a diversity of responses could be and was contained within the homogeneity of the overall response, within the discipleship which gave rise in due course to the earliest churches. If Jesus was always the unifying factor, and disciple-faith in him, it was a unity embracing and holding together a diversity of faith responses from the first.

But were there not other responses which fell short of discipleship, or which understood discipleship differently, or which stopped short of Good Friday and Easter? There are certainly hints of such in our traditions,[121] and neo-Liberalism wants to find evidence of such in the Gospel of Thomas and other documents. Whether such claims can be sustained by the evidence of these sources is an issue which we have still to discuss.[122] But it is already clear that the disciple-response which created the Synoptic tradition and from which mainstream Christianity emerged is that with which we primarily have to do.[123] Whatever we may think regarding Gnostic Christianity as a legitimate (or otherwise) response to Jesus, the fact is that Q was not retained within mainstream Christianity except as integrated with the Gospel format initiated by Mark, and *Thomas* was rejected by the emerging great Church. The very concern of some scholars to justify use of the *Gospel of Thomas* by seeking to demonstrate its consistency with a stripped-down Synoptic tradition is actually a backhanded recognition of the normativeness of the Synoptic tradition. So while we will want to be alert to the likely (and possibly uncomfortable) breadth of the diversity of the earliest faith-response to Jesus, it will inevitably be the Synoptic tradition which commands our primary attention. And our first concern will be to trace the early outlines of the principal thoroughfare which led through Good Friday and Easter, the first stirrings of Christianity in the making.

120. Cf. Dodd: 'The first three gospels offer a body of sayings on the whole so consistent, so coherent, and withal so distinctive in manner, style and content, that no reasonable critic should doubt, whatever reservations he may have about individual sayings, that we find here reflected the thought of a single, unique teacher' (*Founder* 21-22); Schillebeeckx: 'this pluralism which at rock bottom is "held together" by Jesus as he lived on earth and was apprehended by other people' (*Jesus* 51).

121. E.g. Mark 9.38-41; Acts 19.1-7.

122. See below, particularly §§7.4, 6.

123. The relevance and importance of John's Gospel for our task is more disputed; see further below, §7.7.

6.6. Two Corollaries

Finally, two corollaries which emerge from the preceding discussions are of interest at least to Christian scholarship.

a. One is the issue of norms. At various points I have indicated that the interpreter of the Jesus tradition has to acknowledge a degree of normativity to particular forms of that tradition: the Greek text is normative for translations and thus also interpretations of that text; the 'plain meaning' of the text (as defined earlier) has primary claim to be the voice of the text in the dialogue of meaning; the Synoptic form of the Jesus tradition is normative for any attempt to illuminate the very first stirrings of Christianity in the making. I use the terms 'norm' and 'normative' here in the sense of 'definitive', 'determinative', setting the boundaries for acceptable re-expressions. This is not an attempt to insist on a univocalicity of interpretation (as though there could be only one correct hearing of a text). Nor is it an attempt to privilege origins illegitimately. It is simply a reminder that, for better or worse, these are the definitive and determinative texts for any talk of Jesus which aspires to historical integrity.

The point first arose, and in an archetypical way, with the Reformation's criticism of the abuses of mediaeval Catholicism on the basis of Scripture. The principle thus emerged that only by recognizing the historical otherness of the NT witness to Jesus can we free ourselves to hear the NT speaking within the tradition and when necessary over against the tradition. It was precisely this recognition which resulted in the attempt to formulate methods of inquiry back into the earliest forms of the tradition. In that inquiry it became necessary to acknowledge that within the flow of tradition, of which Scripture is itself a part, the NT must be accorded some sort of critical role. Precisely by virtue of the NT's pivotal testimony to the incarnation, the NT was bound to function as the *norma normans,* the canon within the canon of Scripture and tradition; otherwise that pivotal testimony would be devalued and its canonical status be effectively lost.[124] Of course, it certainly does *not* follow that determining or exercising the critical role of the NT should therefore lie in the hands of biblical scholars, though, given not least what has been said just above, it would be surprising if they did not have some part to play in the process — both as scholars and as Christians. It is this readiness for self-criticism in the light of tradition, and not simply on the part of scholars, which marks out the western church — its willingness to recognize and acknowledge when it has departed from its norm, whether in the condemnation of a Galileo or in its centuries-long tradition of

124. Cf. the criticism of Vatican II's 'Dogmatic Constitution on Divine Revelation' acknowledged by J. Ratzinger in H. Vorgrimler, ed., *Commentary on the Documents of Vatican II,* Vol. 3 (London: Burns and Oates/New York: Herder and Herder, 1968) 192-93.

anti-Semitism[125] — a dialogue of criticism which remains something of a barrier and bewilderment for the Christianity of East and South.

b. The other is what we might call the challenge of faith and to faith to continue to speak in a forum wider than that of church, or indeed of lecture room. Whatever may be said now of the Renaissance Christian and the Enlightenment scholarship of Strauss and Lessing, whatever we may think of the Liberal and neo-Liberal quest or Bultmann's demythologizing programme, they were all united by a common concern: that the foundational documents of the Christian tradition should still be heard to speak meaningfully to the present day, that Christian education should not be some hole-in-the-corner enterprise hidden away from the rest of the educational process, that theology should be seen to have a legitimate position in the academic concourse and still important contributions to make to human knowledge and well-being.[126]

I mention this here because there is a certain danger in the emphases of such as Fish and Gadamer that the meaningfulness of the Jesus tradition will be and can be appreciated only within the interpretive community (that is, the church), within the living tradition (that is, the Christian tradition). The risk is of locking up the Gospels once again within the churches, with a meaning heard clearly enough within the worshipping community but unable to speak to the world outside, unable to dialogue effectively with other forms of knowledge given to us, and unable to be heard or understood because meaning is thought to reside (only?) in a reading within the continuum and community of meaning. To seek thus to escape postmodernism's pluralism and relativity would significantly diminish the possibility of effective Christian apologetics and evangelism. At the same time, as we have seen, any attempt to present a Jesus stripped of the garments of faith is doomed to failure, given the character of the Jesus tradition from the first. The challenge, then, is whether a Jesus presented by faith and through faith can still be heard outside the churches, in the forums of the world's discourses.

---

125. It should, however, be confessed that the historical method as applied in the nineteenth century did *not* prevent anti-Judaism in Christian presentation of Jesus; the recognition of subjectivity in interpretation did not extend sufficiently to take account of anti-Jewish bias (Heschel, *Abraham Geiger* 73, 122).

126. 'The historical Jesus helps to keep the church honest through the constant pressure of having to do with a real human, historic figure' (Keck, *Future* 127).

PART TWO

FROM THE GOSPELS TO JESUS

CHAPTER 7

The Sources

In Part One I have attempted to highlight the chief moments in the quest for Jesus, particularly over the last two hundred years, but earlier also, and particularly in terms of the tensions between history and faith which have left such lasting marks (or scars!) on biblical scholarship. I have drawn attention to the classic or definitive treatments which incisively posed issues that still remain with us or which first formulated breakthroughs whose significance still endures. And in chapter 6 I have offered my own summing up of the lessons to be learned from the interplay of history, hermeneutics, and faith, both in response to the challenges old and new of the last fifty years and as indicating the perspective from which I seek to pursue the historical and hermeneutical tasks of this volume.

The survey also posed other fundamental issues of method which are often neglected by those still pursuing the quest in the terms laid down by the post-Bultmannian generation.[1] What should be the starting point for an approach to the Jesus tradition for those in 'quest of the historical Jesus'? In particular, what should count as sources for the earliest phases of the Jesus tradition? With what conception of the traditioning process should we operate? And have the implications of Jesus' 'Jewishness' and of his particular historical setting in Galilee been adequately taken into account? These questions had to be 'put on hold' till the challenge of postmodernism had been posed and the basic principles which determine the very conception of our task had been examined. But now these ques-

---

1. The only ones who on the way to writing a Jesus book have made a serious attempt to address fundamental issues of method in recent years are Meyer, *Aims* 76-110, Wright, *New Testament* 31-144, and Theissen and Winter, *Kriterienfrage*. Sanders' attempt to shift the focus of the quest from the sayings of Jesus to the 'facts about Jesus' (*Jesus* 3-22 [here 5]) has been influential. Crossan's practice assumes more than it explains (but see his *Birth* 137-73); his hope had been to inaugurate a full-blown debate on methodology (139).

tions can be pursued and will form the agenda for Part Two — sources (chapter 7), tradition (chapter 8), and historical context (chapter 9) — as we re-envisage the historical realities behind the Gospels and attempt to get back in some sense from the Gospels to Jesus.

The first task in any historical investigation is to ascertain what the *sources* are on which the historian can draw, and to ask how reliable these sources are. In this case our sources are almost entirely limited to those which evidence direct influence from Jesus at one remove or another. The few external sources can be reviewed quite briefly. As to the Christian (and near Christian) sources themselves, the above survey indicated two periods of intensive debate on the source question: the Liberal phase focused attention particularly on 'the Synoptic problem'; and the most recent, still continuing neo-Liberal phase has raised the status of non-canonical sources. We will not forget the intermediate phase (roughly 1920 to 1980) when form criticism supplanted source criticism as the principal engine of Gospels research. But that is an important part of the subject matter of chapter 8.

The issues are clear. I have already concluded (chapter 6) that the pre- and post-Enlightenment advances in historical and hermeneutical awareness still provide some sound principles for any quest of the historical figure of Jesus. Can we also say that the advances in source criticism during the heyday of Liberalism (the two source/document hypothesis for the Synoptics, and the much lower value accorded to John's Gospel as a source for information on Jesus' ministry) still provide sound working hypotheses for any attempt to assess the historical value of the traditions regarding Jesus? The arguments of Kloppenborg in particular, followed by the neo-Liberal questers, that the Q source can be readily stratified, and those of Koester in particular, that there are other Gospel sources on which to draw, have not commanded anything like the same consent as the older source hypotheses and certainly require further scrutiny. Nevertheless, the increasing recognition of Q as a coherent document with a distinctive theological profile, and the possibility of tracing different trajectories through earliest Christianity, pose challenging questions to traditional claims of coherence and continuity between Jesus and what came after. The ramifications of these hypotheses for any continuing 'quest of the historical Jesus' are so important that it will be necessary to give them careful attention.

But first, it is important to remind ourselves of the testimony regarding Jesus outside specifically Christian sources and the earliest evidence for Jesus as a historical person.

The Sources

7.1. External Sources

It has always been recognized that there are references to Jesus outside the more immediate Christianly influenced traditions. They are periodically reviewed, usually with the same results.[2]

Josephus the Jewish historian in his *Jewish Antiquities* (written in the 90s) refers to Jesus twice. The first passage has clearly been subject to Christian redaction, but there is a broad consensus[3] that Josephus wrote something like the following:

> At this time there appeared Jesus, a wise man. For he was a doer of startling deeds, a teacher of people who received the truth with pleasure. And he gained a following both among many Jews and among many of Greek origin. And when Pilate, because of an accusation made by the leading men among us, condemned him to the cross, those who had loved him previously did not cease to do so. And up until this very day the tribe of Christians (named after him) has not died out (*Ant.* 18.63-64).

The second passage is briefer and presumably alludes back to the earlier passage. It is an account of the summary execution of James (in 62 CE), who is described as 'the brother of Jesus who is called Messiah' (*Ant.* 20.200). Few have doubted that it came from Josephus' pen.

In the course of his treatment of the great fire of Rome during Nero's reign (64 CE), *Tacitus* the Roman historian (writing early in the second century) refers to the scapegoats on whom blame was put, known by the common people as 'Christians'. He explains: 'Their name comes from Christ, who, during the reign of Tiberius, had been executed by the procurator Pontius Pilate' (*Annals* 15.44). To be noted is the fact that the formulation has no distinctive Christian features. And had the information come to Tacitus from Christian sources we would have expected some disclaimer ('whom they called Christ') and reference to crucifix-

---

2. Meier, *Marginal Jew* 1.56-111, has provided a full and discriminating discussion of these passages, and nothing more need be added at this point. I follow his translations, which are superior to those of the Loeb editions. See also, e.g., C. A. Evans, 'Jesus in Non-Christian Sources', in B. Chilton and C. A. Evans, eds., *Studying the Historical Jesus* (Leiden: Brill, 1994) 443-78; Theissen and Merz, *Historical Jesus* 63-89; R. E. Van Voorst, *Jesus outside the New Testament* (Grand Rapids: Eerdmans, 2001), with extensive bibliography (219-34).

3. See particularly G. Vermes, 'The Jesus Notice of Josephus Re-Examined', *JJS* 38 (1987) 1-10, who points out that the two key phrases ('a wise man', 'a doer of startling deeds') are characteristic of Josephus and (so far as the possibility of an interpolation is concerned) improbably Christian. See further Charlesworth, *Jesus* 91-98, and Van Voorst, *Jesus* 89-99.

ion rather than simply execution. As it is, Tacitus clearly regarded 'Christ' as a proper name, whose followers were known as *Christiani.*[4]

Suetonius, also writing early in the second century, makes a similar but confused reference to an episode in 49 CE. 'Since the Jews were constantly causing disturbances at the instigation of Chrestus, he [Claudius] expelled them from Rome' (*Claudius* 25.4). Most infer that Suetonius misheard the name (the pronunciation of *Christus* and *Chrestus* would have been very similar) and misunderstood the report as a reference to someone (Chrestus) active in the Jewish community at the time. The broad consensus is that the disturbances referred to had been occasioned by some strong reactions within certain synagogues to Jewish merchants and visitors preaching about Jesus as the Christ. The confusion involved is hardly the work of artifice or contrivance, but certainly weakens the historical value of the text.

Of the possible references to Jesus in *Jewish* rabbinic sources, the most plausible echo of early pre-rabbinic (Pharisaic) reaction to Jesus is *b. Sanhedrin* 43a, referring to Yeshu (Jesus) who was hanged on the eve of Passover and describing him as a magician who beguiled Israel and led it astray. But the whole enterprise of reading first-century details from often much later rabbinic traditions is too fraught with difficulty for us to put too much weight on them.[5]

Such references are important if only because about once every generation someone reruns the thesis that Jesus never existed and that the Jesus tradition is a wholesale invention.[6] But they provide very little hard information and it will suffice to refer to them at the two or three relevant points in what follows.

7.2. The Earliest References to Jesus

In view of some continuing uncertainty as to the sources used by Josephus and Tacitus it is probably worth simply recording the earliest references to Jesus as a historical personage. They come from Paul's letters, the earliest Christian documentation which has come down to us.

The first is 1 Cor. 15.3 where Paul recites the foundational belief which he himself had received and which was evidently taught to converts as the earliest Christian catechetical instruction: 'that Christ died . . .'. The point is that Paul

4. On the other hand, we can hardly be entirely confident that Tacitus had access to official records (Van Voorst, *Jesus* 49-52).

5. See further J. Maier, *Jesus von Nazareth in der talmudischen Überlieferung* (Darmstadt: Wissenschaftliche Buchgesellschaft, 1978); Van Voorst, *Jesus* 104-29.

6. Most recently G. A. Wells has continued a long-running but lone campaign in *The Jesus Myth* (Chicago: Open Court, 1999). For earlier treatments in the same vein see Weaver, *Historical Jesus* ch. 2.

was probably converted about two years following the event confessed[7] and probably received this foundational instruction at that time. In other words, in the early 30s Paul was being told about a Jesus who had died two or so years earlier.

The second comes from Gal. 1.18-20, where Paul records his first visit to Jerusalem after his conversion. If his conversion is to be reckoned about two years after Jesus' crucifixion, then his visit to Jerusalem will have to be dated no more than about five years after the crucifixion (mid-30s). On that visit he recalls that he met with 'James, the Lord's brother'. Later on he refers to 'the brothers of the Lord' (1 Cor. 9.5). This accords, it should be noted, with the second Josephus reference cited above (*Ant.* 20.200). It is a work of some desperation which denies the obvious deduction from these references, that there was a man called Jesus whose brothers were well known in the 30s to 60s.[8]

In assessing the impact of Jesus the teacher on early Christianity, before as well as after Easter, Paul Barnett stresses the value of the NT letters, particularly those of Paul.[9] This is a salutary reminder that we should neither ignore these earliest of NT writings, nor start from the assumption that a great gulf is fixed between the Jesus tradition and Paul. It is true, of course, that if we had nothing but Paul's letters to depend on for our knowledge of Jesus' Galilean and Judean mission we would know very little about him.[10] Nevertheless, in letters not intended to provide biographical details, the number of allusions is probably enough to confirm both Paul's knowledge of and interest in Jesus prior to his death and resurrection.[11]

7.3. Mark

Despite various attempts to overturn the Holtzmann hypothesis, the Markan hypothesis still stands secure.[12] For the great majority of specialists in critical study

---

7. See below, vol. 2.

8. On this point particularly Wells displays an unyielding determination to interpret all data in favour of his thesis, whatever the probabilities (*Jesus Myth* 52-53); such a tendentious treatment is less deserving of the description 'historical' than Jesus.

9. Barnett, *Jesus and the Logic of History* ch. 3.

10. Barnett lists fifteen details gleaned from Paul (*Jesus and the Logic of History* 57-58): (1) descent from Abraham, (2) direct descent from David, (3) 'born of a woman', (4) lived in poverty, (5) born and lived under the law, (6) a brother called James, (7) a humble life style, (8) ministered primarily to Jews, (9) instituted a memorial meal before his betrayal, and (10) cruelly treated at that time; the other five cover Jesus' death, burial, and resurrection, with two other items gleaned from the Pastorals.

11. See my *Theology of Paul* 182-99 and further below, §§7.9; 8.1e.

12. J. A. Fitzmyer, 'The Priority of Mark and the "Q" Source in Luke', in D. G. Miller, ed., *Jesus and Man's Hope* (Pittsburgh: Pittsburgh Theological Seminary, 1970) 131-70, and

of the Gospels, by far the most obvious explanation of the data is that Mark was a primary source used by both Matthew and Luke.[13] Of the traditional three considerations marshalled (§4.4b), the argument from order has proved least satisfactory.[14] But the stunning fact continues to be the extent of the overlap of material particularly between Mark and Matthew.[15] So much so that there is hardly anything distinctive in Mark which is not also in Matthew.[16] By itself this clearly indicates literary interdependence, without revealing which way the line of dependence ran. In the older views it had been assumed that Mark was some kind

G. M. Styler, 'The Priority of Mark', in C. F. D. Moule, *The Birth of the New Testament* (London: Black, 1962, [3]1981) 285-316, have become classic restatements. The most resolute critic of the two-source hypothesis has been W. R. Farmer, particularly in his *The Synoptic Problem* (New York: Macmillan, 1964, [2]1976), who was able to demonstrate the question-begging form of many of the by then traditional arguments (as formulated particularly by Streeter); see Dungan's fuller account (*History* 371-90). Farmer's attack on the substance of the arguments has been much less effective; see especially C. M. Tuckett, *The Revival of the Griesbach Hypothesis: An Analysis and Appraisal* (SNTSMS 44; Cambridge: Cambridge University, 1983). For a careful restatement of the case, which takes into account Farmer's criticisms, see Kloppenborg Verbin, *Excavating Q* ch. 1 (including a salutary reminder on the necessity of hypotheses and on what constitutes a 'good hypothesis' — 50-54). See also R. H. Stein, *The Synoptic Problem: An Introduction* (Grand Rapids: Baker, 1987) Part I.

13. See, e.g., the recent introductions by U. Schnelle, *The History and Theology of the New Testament Writings* (1994; ET London: SCM, 1998) 166-72; Theissen and Merz, *Historical Jesus* 25-27; R. E. Brown, *An Introduction to the New Testament* (New York: Doubleday, 1997) 114-15. Farmer has won some support in North America for the 'Two-Gospel (= Griesbach) hypothesis', as distinct from the 'Two-Source hypothesis', but hardly any elsewhere.

14. D. J. Neville, *Arguments from Order in Synoptic Source Criticism: A History and Critique* (Macon: Mercer University, 1994); see also particularly C. M. Tuckett, 'Arguments from Order: Definition and Evaluation', in C. M. Tuckett, ed., *Synoptic Studies: The Ampleforth Conferences of 1982 and 1983* (JSNTS 7; Sheffield: JSOT, 1984) 197-219.

15. On Holtzmann's reckoning, more than 95% of Mark appears also in either Matthew or Luke (see above, §4.4b). Streeter made much of the fact that 90% of Mark's subject matter reappears in Matthew 'in language very largely identical with that of Mark' (*Four Gospels* 151, 159). For examples of the closeness between the texts of Mark and Matthew in particular, which can hardly be explained by other than literary dependence, see Mark 1.16-20/Matt. 4.18-22; Mark 2.18-22/Matt. 9.14-17/Luke 5.33-39; Mark 8.1-10/Matt. 15.32-39; Mark 8.31–9.1/ Matt. 16.21-28/Luke 9.22-27; Mark 10.13-16/Matt. 19.13-15/Luke 18.15-17; Mark 10.32-34/ Matt. 20.17-19/Luke 18.31-34; Mark 11.27-33/Matt. 21.23-27/Luke 20.1-8; Mark 13.3-32/ Matt. 24.3-36/Luke 21.7-33. A similar degree of literary interdependence, but with significant Matthean editing, is evident in Mark 2.23–3.6/Matt. 12.1-14; Mark 6.45-52/Matt. 14.22-33; and Mark 8.27-30/Matt. 16.13-20.

16. The Markan material not in either Matthew or Luke consists of three short episodes (4.26-29; 7.31-37; 8.22-26) and three quite short texts (3.20; 9.49; 14.51) (W. G. Kümmel, *Introduction to the New Testament* [1973; ET Nashville: Abingdon/London: SCM, 1975] 56; greater detail in Streeter, *Four Gospels* 195-96).

of abbreviation of Matthew. But Synoptic analysis indicates that in much of the common material Mark's episodes are actually longer than Matthew's.[17] Such a finding is more obviously to be explained by Matthew abbreviating Mark's prolixity in order to make room for all the other sayings material which he had to hand, rather than by Mark expanding individual episodes while omitting all the extra teaching provided by Matthew, including, for instance, the Sermon on the Mount (Matthew 5–7) and the kingdom parables of Matthew 13. Why would an Evangelist who stresses the role of Jesus as Teacher[18] omit so much of the teaching set out in Matthew's Gospel?[19] In addition, the more detailed differences between Matthew and Mark, in the great majority of cases, are best explained as Matthew's improvement on Mark's style or Matthew's avoidance of dubious implications which could be drawn from Mark's language.[20] Here no more than in historical study do we deal in certainties; but much the most probable explanation of the available evidence continues to postulate Markan priority.

Doubts persist as to whether the NT Mark as such was the source used by the other two Synoptic Evangelists. Should we speak rather of an earlier Mark (Ur-Markus), or of different editions of Mark?[21] Most have been content to affirm that the Matthean and Lukan source was as near to the canonical Mark as

17. The linked stories of the Gerasene demoniac (Mark 5.1-20/Matt. 8.28-34/Luke 8.26-39) and Jairus' daughter and the woman with the haemorrhage (Mark 5.21-43/Matt. 9.18-26/Luke 8.40-56) look like examples of heavy abbreviation of Markan redundancy, especially by Matthew. Similarly with Matthew's treatment of the death of John the Baptist (Mark 6.17-29/Matt. 14.3-12) and possibly with Matthew's and Luke's treatment of the healing of the epileptic boy (Mark 9.14-29/Matt. 17.14-21/Luke 9.37-43; see below, §8.4c[iii]).

18. See below, §8.1b.

19. See further Stein, *Synoptic Problem* 49-51.

20. E.g., most would consider it more likely that Matthew has modified Mark in each of the two following cases, rather than vice-versa.

Matt. 13.58	Mark 6.5
And he *did not do many* deeds of power there, because of their unbelief.	And he *could do no* deed of power there, except that he laid his hands on a few sick people and cured them. And he was amazed at their unbelief.

Matt. 19.16-17	Mark 10.17-18
Then someone came to him and said, 'Teacher, what *good deed* must I do to have eternal life?' And he said to him, '*Why do you ask me about what is good?* There is only one who is good.'	A man ran up and knelt before him, and asked him, '*Good* Teacher, what must I do to inherit eternal life?' Jesus said to him, '*Why do you call me good?* No one is good but God alone.'

See the full data collected by Hawkins, *Horae Synopticae* 117-25; also Stein, *Synoptic Problem* 52-67; and below, chapter 8 n. 214.

21. So, e.g., Koester, *Ancient Christian Gospels* 284-86; Theissen and Metz, *Historical Jesus* 26. Earlier discussion is reviewed in Kümmel, *Introduction* 61-63.

makes no difference. But the suggestion of different 'editions' invites a word of caution. Certainly, as textual criticism has made us all too aware, any act of copying will have introduced variants, both deliberate and unintended. No one doubts that documents were absorbed and redacted by others, or, for example, that the ending of Mark (16.9-20) was later added by scribes. But what seems to be in view, on Koester's reconstruction at any rate, includes more extensive recensions of the same work. This raises the question whether the processes at this point are being conceived too much in terms of the modern literary pattern of several editions of a book. Should we not rather be attempting to adjust our thinking away from the literary mindset of the modern world and to re-envisage the situation in terms of oral tradition? The point then being that much of the traditioning process would include oral variations of the traditions used by Mark, as also oral memories of those who heard readings from Mark's version of the Jesus tradition. More attention needs to be given to the possibility that Evangelists were able to select the version of tradition they used from more than one version, written or oral. We will return to this question later (§§8.3-6).

A very large consensus of contemporary scholarship dates Mark somewhere in the period 65-75 CE.[22] The ancient tradition (from Papias) that the Gospel was composed by Mark, from his recollections of Peter's preaching,[23] fits to some extent with other references[24] and makes better sense in the context of oral transmission than most seem to appreciate,[25] but the evidence is too sparse for sound hypothesis building. And the issue of where Mark was written and for whom it was written remains unresolved,[26] being also caught up in the question of whether we can (or should) identify a particular community/church with the Gospel — another question to which we shall have to return.[27] So far as the value of Mark as a source is concerned, we shall have to be content with the firm consensus that Mark is the earliest written Gospel to have survived intact, that it appeared about forty years after Jesus' death, and that it contains traditions about Jesus which must have circulated in the generation prior to that date.

22. See, e.g., M. Hengel, *Studies in the Gospel of Mark* (London: SCM, 1985) ch. 1; M. D. Hooker, *Mark* (BNTC; London: Black, 1991) 5-8; Schnelle, *History* 200-202; Brown, *Introduction* 161-64.

23. See above, chapter 4 n. 90.

24. 1 Pet. 5.13 (Mark as Peter's 'son'); Justin refers to 'Peter's memoirs' as containing a passage which is found only in Mark 3.16-17 (*Dialogue* 106.3); cf. also Phlm. 24; Col. 4.10.

25. See below, chapter 8 n. 216.

26. See, e.g., the review in W. R. Telford, *Mark* (NTG; Sheffield: Sheffield Academic, 1995) 23-26, 150-51. We will have to return to the subject in vol. 3.

27. See further below, §§7.4b and 8.6d.

7.4. Q

The attention given to Mark at the end of the nineteenth century is paralleled by the amount of attention lavished on Q in the closing decades of the twentieth century. Consequently we must pay particular attention to Q and to the issues raised in recent discussions, not least because of Q's potential significance for any inquiry into the mission and message of Jesus.

a. A Q Document?

The second conclusion of the two-document hypothesis has not achieved such an overwhelming consensus among NT scholars, but still remains a persuasive working hypothesis for the substantial majority.[28] The close verbal similarities between many Matthean and Lukan, non-Markan, passages are difficult to explain otherwise than on the hypothesis of literary dependence when the tradition had already been put into Greek.[29] That Matthew and Luke drew at least these passages independently from a Greek source Q continues to provide the best working hypothesis; though it is also worthy of note that for some reason, the only alternative offered has been that Luke drew his 'Q' material from Matthew, with the possibility hardly considered that Luke was written prior to Matthew and provided the source for Matthew's 'Q' material.[30]

28. See particularly the arguments of Kloppenborg, *Formation* ch. 2; also *Excavating Q* 87-111; C. M. Tuckett, *Q and the History of Early Christianity* (Edinburgh: Clark, 1996) ch. 1; these include the unavoidable conclusion that Q was written in Greek (*Formation* 51-64; *Excavating Q* 72-80; *Q* 83-92) and Kloppenborg's important restatement of the argument concerning the order of Q (*Formation* 64-80). D. Catchpole, *The Quest for Q* (Edinburgh: Clark, 1993) argues overall persuasively that in sixteen shared pericopes Luke has preserved the original form (1-59). The International Q Project has now produced J. M. Robinson, P. Hoffmann, and J. S. Kloppenborg, eds., *The Critical Edition of Q: Synopsis* (Leuven: Peeters, 2000). For earlier presentations see A. Polag, *Fragmenta Q: Textheft zur Logienquelle* (Neukirchen-Vluyn: Neukirchener, 1979), followed by I. Havener, *Q: The Sayings of Jesus* (Collegeville: Liturgical, 1987); J. S. Kloppenborg, *Q Parallels: Synopsis, Critical Notes and Concordance* (Sonoma: Polebridge, 1988); Miller, ed., *Complete Gospels* 253-300.

29. The best examples are: Matt. 3.7-10, 12/Luke 3.7-9, 17; Matt. 6.24/Luke 16.13; Matt. 6.25-33/Luke 12.22-31; Matt. 7.1-5/Luke 6.37-42; Matt. 7.7-11/Luke 11.9-13; Matt. 8.19-22/Luke 9.57b-60a; Matt. 11.2-11, 16-19/Luke 7.18-19, 22-28, 31-35; Matt. 11.21-27/ Luke 10.12-15, 21-22; Matt. 12.39-45/Luke 11.29-32, 24-26; Matt. 13.33/Luke 13.20-21; Matt. 24.45-51/Luke 12.42-46.

30. Possibly a carry-over from the old assumption that the first Gospel was written by one of Jesus' twelve disciples and that Luke, the author of the third Gospel, must have been more remote from what he recorded. Or, more likely, the influence of Luke 1.1, indicating that Luke was aware of 'many' predecessors. But Flusser is convinced that Luke is the oldest Gos-

More serious has been the failure to reckon fully with the complications involved in the 'Q' hypothesis which continue to bedevil its developed use. One is the fact that the letter 'Q', strictly speaking, can be used both for the material which is actually common to Matthew and Luke and for the document from which that material *ex hypothesi* has been drawn.[31] The other is that, as Streeter and most commentators have noted, we can hardly exclude the likelihood that Matthew drew on some material from this document which Luke ignored and vice-versa.[32] In other words, the very definition of 'Q' (material common to Matthew and Luke) prevents us from seeing the true extent of the hypothesized source.[33] These concerns are met to a fair extent by arguing,[34] first, that the 'Q'/'q' material has a coherence and unity which implies a coherent compositional strategy;[35] and second, that, on the parallel of Matthew's and Luke's use of Mark, it can be judged likely that Matthew and Luke made use of the bulk of 'Q' (that 'q' is most of 'Q').[36] However, the fact remains that 'q' material varies in agreement of wording very substantially, from nearly 100%

---

pel (*Jesus* 21-22, 221-50). And see now M. Hengel, *The Four Gospels and the One Gospel of Jesus Christ* (London: SCM, 2000) ch. 7, particularly 169-86, 205-207, who argues precisely for Matthew's dependence on Luke (as well as on Mark), and who concludes that it is simply impossible to reconstruct a sayings source (Q) (178, 206).

31. It might have been wiser to denote the actual common material as 'q', reserving 'Q' for the hypothesized written source, but it is too late to introduce such a refinement.

32. Examples suggested include Matt. 10.5b (Catchpole, *Quest* 165-71); 10.23 (H. Schürmann, 'Zur Traditions- und Redaktionsgeschichte von Mt 10,23', *BZ* 3 [1959] 82-88); 11.28-30 (J. D. Crossan, *Fragments: The Aphorisms of Jesus* [San Francisco: Harper and Row, 1983] 191-93); Luke 4.16-30 (H. Schürmann, *Lukasevangelium* [HTKNT 2 vols.; Freiburg: Herder, 1969, 1994] 1.242; Tuckett, *Q* 227-28); 15.8-10 (Kloppenborg, *Excavating Q* 96-98); and 17.20-37 (R. Schnackenburg, 'Der eschatologische Abschnitt, Luke 17.20-37', in A. Descamps and R. P. A. de Halleux, eds., *Mélanges bibliques,* B. Rigaux FS [Gembloux: Duculot, 1970] 213-34).

33. Note, e.g., the questions raised by A. Lindemann, 'Die Logienquelle Q: Fragen an eine gut begründete Hypothese', in Lindemann, ed., *Sayings Source Q* 3-26 (here 4-13, 26).

34. Kloppenborg, *Formation* 80-95; Tuckett, *Q* 92-96.

35. See particularly A. D. Jacobson, 'The Literary Unity of Q', *JBL* 101 (1982) 365-89, reprinted in J. S. Kloppenborg, ed., *The Shape of Q* (Minneapolis: Fortress, 1994) 98-115; also Jacobson, *The First Gospel: An Introduction to Q* (Sonoma: Polebridge, 1992) ch. 4. The argument was already made by T. W. Manson, *The Sayings of Jesus* (London: SCM, 1949) 15-16; cf. Streeter, *Four Gospels* 289-91.

36. But if Luke contains only about 60% of Mark, the argument becomes a little thin, despite Kloppenborg's suggestion that Luke valued Q more highly than Mark, from which he deduces that Luke would have preserved more of Q than he did of Mark (*Formation* 82). C. A. Evans shows how diminished would be our appreciation of Mark if we had to depend only on what was common to both Matthew and Luke ('Authenticating the Words of Jesus', in B. Chilton and C. A. Evans, eds., *Authenticating the Words of Jesus* [Leiden: Brill, 1999] 3-14 [here 6-10]).

to around 8%,[37] so that the confidence in the existence of 'Q', based as heavily as the hypothesis is on the passages towards the 100% end of the scale, must inevitably be weaker in regard to passages towards the 8% end of the scale.[38] Alternatively expressed, given the amount of editorial modification which Matthew and Luke must be assumed to have made (again on the parallel of their use of Mark), it becomes exceedingly difficult to move from 'q' to 'Q' with much confidence on many textual details.[39] Streeter's further suggestion,[40] that a substantial portion of the common ('q') material was actually derived from oral tradition (not 'Q'), has fared little better, but deserves more attention, since it allows the possibility that Matthew or Luke knew variant oral forms of some 'Q' traditions and on several occasions at least preferred the oral version. We shall have to return to the issue raised here later.[41]

b. A Q Community?

None of this need be too serious, were it not that there are those who wish to press for more far-reaching conclusions with regard to Q.[42] I have in mind particularly the influential thesis of John Kloppenborg and those who follow it. For one thing, Kloppenborg shares the widespread conviction that behind Q stands a Q community.[43] That in itself is hardly objectionable: a sociological perspective

37. Statistics in R. Morgenthaler, *Statistische Synopse* (Zürich: Gotthelf, 1971) 258-61; examples and table in Kloppenborg Verbin, *Excavating Q* 56-64. The point is given particular emphasis by T. Bergemann, *Q auf dem Prüfstand: Die Zuordnung des Mat/Lk-Stoffes zu Q am Beispiel der Bergpredigt* (FRLANT 158; Göttingen: Vandenhoeck und Ruprecht, 1993).

38. The extensive use of double square brackets (denoting uncertainty as to the Q reading) in passages outside those listed above (n. 29) by Robinson/Hoffmann/Kloppenborg, *Critical Edition,* underlines the point.

39. E.g., which 'q' version of Matt. 12.28/Luke 11.20 came from 'Q'? Plausibility judgments have to be made concerning both Matthew's and Luke's theologies, as well as Q's, before a decision can be reached, and the case can be argued either way with more or less equal facility (see below, chapter 12 n. 365).

40. See above, chapter 4 n. 84.

41. See below, §8.5.

42. Having made my point, I will revert to the simple nomenclature Q rather than persist with 'Q'. I will follow the convention of citing Q passages according to Luke; e.g., Q 3:7-10 = Luke 3:7-10/Matt. 3:7-9.

43. H. E. Tödt, *The Son of Man in the Synoptic Tradition* ([2]1963; ET London: SCM, 1965) 246-69 is usually credited with starting this trend. For example, Kloppenborg cites S. Schulz, 'Die Gottesherrschaft ist nahe herbeigekommen (Mt 10,7/Lk 10,9). Der kerygmatische Entwurf der Q-Gemeinde Syrien', in *Das Wort und die Wörter,* G. Friedrich FS (Stuttgart: Kohlhammer, 1973) 57-67: 'Behind Q there is a special sphere of tradition with an independent kerygmatic tradition, i.e., a distinct community which preserved and continued to proclaim Jesus' message in the post-

has quite properly reinforced the earlier insight of form criticism that tradition can hardly be thought of as other than community tradition.[44] Though the question should not be ignored, whether such a document was simply a deposit of a community's tradition or may have been addressed *to* a community (in exhortation or rebuke) by a particular author.[45] There is some tension here, not always perceived or clarified, between Q as simply a collection of community tradition and Q as a carefully constructed composition.

More serious, however, is the assumption that Q somehow *defines* its community: it is a 'Q community' or 'Q-group' in the sense that the Q material is its *only* Jesus tradition; it holds to this material in distinction from (defiance of?) other communities who presumably are similarly defined by their document.[46] There are several flaws in the logic here.

First is what we might call *the 'one document per community' fallacy.* It simply will not do to identify the character of a community with the character of a document associated with it.[47] Such a document will no doubt indicate concerns and emphases in the community's teaching. But only if we can be confident that the single document was the community's sole document (or traditional material) could we legitimately infer that the concerns and beliefs of the community did not extend beyond those of the document. And we cannot have such confidence. On the same logic we could speak of 'wisdom villages' in the land of Israel which knew no prophetic books, or prophetic communities at odds with Torah communities. The Dead Sea Scrolls should surely have banished forever the idea that communities possessed and treasured only one document or only one genre of tradition. Where documents have different purposes, the lack of cross-reference between them tells us nothing as to whether both docu-

---

Easter situation' (58; *Formation* 26). See also Kloppenborg, 'Literary Convention, Self-Evidence and the Social History of the Q People', *Semeia* 55 (1992) 77-102; Vaage, *Galilean Upstarts.* Hoffmann prefers to speak of a 'Q-group' rather than a 'Q community' (*Studien* 10), but so long as the developed ecclesiastical overtones of 'church' are kept under control, the issues are not significantly different (cf. Kloppenborg Verbin, *Excavating Q* 170-71).

44. See below, §8.1a and further §8.6a, d.

45. Tuckett, *Q* 82.

46. In *Excavating Q,* Kloppenborg Verbin makes the point more subtly by pressing the distinction between 'diversity' and 'difference' (354-63): 'Q's "differentness" is substantial and that difference has the potential of undermining some of the tidy models for imagining theological continuity' (363).

47. Kloppenborg, *Formation* 25; 'Q represents a theologically autonomous sphere of Christian theology' (27), 'a discrete group in which Q functioned as the central theological expression' (39). Koester, *Ancient Christian Gospels:* 'Both documents [the *Gospel of Thomas* and Q] presuppose that Jesus' significance lay in his words, *and in his words alone*' (86, my emphasis). See also B. Mack, *The Lost Gospel: The Book of Q and Christian Origins* (San Francisco: HarperCollins, 1993) 213-14, 245-47.

ments were known or unknown to the writers or recipients of each.[48] The life and identity of any community of Jesus' earliest followers was unlikely to be dependent solely on the written traditions it possessed, let alone a single document.[49] Thus, the absence of various themes from Q (e.g., purity issues, Torah)[50] should not be taken necessarily as evidence of the Q community's limited concerns, but may rather indicate that Q does not represent the whole concerns of the Q people.

Second, allied to the one document per community fallacy is a particularly important argument from silence. The absence of indications that Q was influenced by the Passion kerygma or narratives is taken by some to imply that the Q community did not know either Passion kerygma or Passion stories and maintained a christology at odds with the christology of the canonical Gospels.[51] Of course it is incredible that there were groups in Galilee who cherished the memory of Jesus' teaching but who either did not know or were unconcerned that Jesus had been executed. In fact, Q does show awareness of Jesus' death.[52] So the argument reduces to points in Q's collection where Q *might* have borrowed some element from the Passion kerygma but consistently failed to do so[53] — an *argumentum ex silentio* indeed. But there are different ways of presenting and understanding Jesus' death in the NT writings; they are not mutually exclusive, nor do they testify to ignorance of others.[54] It is well known, for example, that the evangelistic sermons in Acts do not attribute a soteriological function to Jesus' death;[55] their pat-

48. Lindemann observes that Q belongs to a different *Gattung* from Mark, that is a *Gattung* other than 'Gospel' ('Logienquelle Q' 13-17).

49. See further H. W. Attridge, 'Reflections on Research into Q', *Semeia* 55 (1992) 223-34 (here 228-29); D. C. Allison, *The Jesus Tradition in Q* (Harrisburg: Trinity, 1997) 43-46: 'The truth is that while Q may omit some things, it does not include anything really at odds with what Matthew or Luke held dear' (45); 'We know for a fact that Q's authors believed in much that Q does not tell us about' (46).

50. Kloppenborg Verbin, *Excavating Q* 199.

51. Particularly Mack, *Lost Gospel* 4.

52. Kloppenborg Verbin cites Q 6.22-23; 13.34-35; 11.49-51; and 14.27 (*Excavating Q* 369-71). Cf. the fact that Q alludes to many more miracles (Q 7.22; 10.13; 11.20) than it actually records (did Matt. 8.13/Luke 7.10 and Matt. 9.33/Luke 11.14 appear in Q?). Kloppenborg suggests 'that the appeal to wonder-working would be largely irrelevant to the formative stratum [of Q], since it is not concerned to defend a particular portrait of Jesus, but to promote an ethic based on the providential care and loving surveillance of God' ('Sayings Gospel Q' 330). One might simply observe that the limited purpose of a particular collection of Jesus' sayings should not be taken as indication that this purpose encompassed the full extent of the concerns and knowledge of Jesus tradition on the part of those who compiled or used the collection.

53. Kloppenborg Verbin, *Excavating Q* 374.

54. Paul uses several metaphors, by no means all entirely consistent with each other (see my *Theology of Paul*, chapter 9).

55. See, e.g., my *Unity and Diversity* 17-18.

tern of suffering-vindication, in fact, is rather close to what is implied in the Q allusions to Jesus' death.

Third, a further fallacy is the assumption that communities of disciples were isolated from one another and that documents were written only for the use of the scribe's own community — as though teachers who had been teaching the same range of tradition for many years suddenly found it necessary to commit it to writing for the community already long familiar with that tradition through their teaching. But the evidence of our earliest sources is that communities maintained communication with one another; and it is more probable that tradition was written down in order to facilitate communication at a distance.[56] It is hardly likely that Luke was the only one who knew that 'many (had) taken in hand to compile an account of the things that had been accomplished among *us*' (Luke 1.1). And we simply do not know how widely Q was circulated. The fact that both Matthew and Luke had access to copies points in a different direction.

In short, while the hypothesis that Q represents teaching material of/for one or several communities is entirely plausible, the further hypotheses that there were distinctively 'Q communities', in effect isolated from other early Christian communities, depends on deductions which go well beyond what the data of Q itself indicate.[57]

c. A Redactional Q?

The other matter on which it is necessary to take issue with Kloppenborg is his argument that Q can be stratified into an earliest sapiential layer (Q^1),[58] and a secondary prophetic redactional layer (Q^2),[59] more or less equivalent to Koester's apocalyptic redactional layer.[60] Certainly the case for seeing Q as structured

56. See again below, §8.6d.

57. Cf. Lindemann, 'Logienquelle Q' 17-18. E. P. Meadors, *Jesus the Messianic Herald of Salvation* (Tübingen: Mohr Siebeck, 1995) notes the improbability of both Matthew and Luke combining sources which were christologically incompatible (15); his central thesis is that the two sources, Mark and Q, are 'utterly compatible with one another' (particularly ch. 9, and conclusion 316).

58. Kloppenborg sees Q^1 as made up of six clusters of sayings: (1) 6.20b-23b, 27-35, 36-45, 46-49; (2) 9.57-60 (61-62); 10.2-11, 16 (23-24?); (3) 11.2-4, 9-13; (4) 12.2-7, 11-12; (5) 12.22b-31, 33-34 (13.18-19, 20-21?); (6) 13.24; 14.26-27; 17.33; 14.34-35 (*Excavating Q* 146).

59. Q 4.1-13; 11.42c; 16.17 are attributed to the final redaction (Q^3) (*Excavating Q* 152-53).

60. Koester notes that Kloppenborg assigns to the secondary stage not only sayings about the judgment of this generation and about the coming of the Son of Man but also the entire sections in which these sayings are embedded (Q 3.7-9, 16-17; 4.1-13; 12.39-59; 17.23-37; and the Q materials in Luke 7.1-35 and 11.14-52). Koester argues for 'a more explicit eschato-

round the motif of coming judgment and on the lines of Deuteronomistic theology is impressive.[61] As is also the evidence marshalled of interpolations into earlier material.[62] I do not particularly wish to dissent from the working hypothesis that Q was a carefully structured document. What remains unclear to me, however, is what we might call the status of the Q^1 material.

One principal focus of discussion thus far has been the question of *genre*. Kloppenborg initially left himself somewhat vulnerable on this front in talking of sayings appropriate to different genres, and seeming to assume, for example, that a wisdom genre may not 'permit' apocalyptic forms.[63] Such an argument would fall into the same trap as that of the early form critics who postulated the concept of 'pure' forms, and consequently found it necessary to classify various of the actual Synoptic pericopes as 'mixed' forms.[64] But Kloppenborg is well aware of examples of 'mixed genres' in the literature of the period,[65] and that the second stage compiler, on his own hypothesis, evidently had no qualms in combining the

---

logical orientation of the earliest composition of Q' ('The Sayings of Q and Their Image of Jesus', in W. L. Petersen, et al., eds., *Sayings of Jesus: Canonical and Non-canonical,* T. Baarda FS [NovTSup 89; Leiden: Brill, 1997] 137-54 [here 145]); 'the image of Jesus that is accessible through the most original version of Q is that of an eschatological prophet' (153).

61. See Kloppenborg Verbin, *Excavating Q* 118-24; he now sees the story of Lot as a further structural element (118-21).

62. Q 6.23c; 10.12, 13-15; 12.8-10 (*Excavating Q* 147-50).

63. I echo Kloppenborg's language (*Formation* 31).

64. See particularly Allison, *Jesus Tradition* 4-7, 41-42; A. Kirk, *The Composition of the Sayings Source: Genre, Synchrony and Wisdom Redaction in Q* (NovTSup 91; Leiden: Brill, 1998) 64-86: 'the question of the degree of coherence and cohesion actually present in a given text must not be begged' (67); 'mixing genres in literature often seems the rule rather than the exception' (270); 'mixing of genres does not necessitate a redaction-*history* judgment if the genres in question are integrated with respect to each other and to the total textual *Gestalt*' (400). It is somewhat surprising that Kloppenborg has not interacted more fully with Kirk (his pupil) in his *Excavating Q*. Cf. also Horsley in Horsley and Draper, *Whoever* 69-75: 'if even "those sections of Q that supposedly do reflect apocalyptic idiom" are restrained and selective and the nonapocalyptic "sapiential" sections of Q are also pervaded by an "eschatological tenor", it would seem that precious few apocalyptic forms and motifs remain as the differentiating features' (72, citing Kloppenborg); 'If Wisdom appears in "apocalyptic" or prophetic sayings and "sapiential" sayings use apocalyptic language against the sages, then the criteria of categorization require critical attention' (74).

64. Kloppenborg, *Formation* 96-101.

65. E.g., CD and 1QS from the DSS, or *T. 12 Patr.* from Jewish pseudepigrapha and Revelation from the NT; see further D. J. Harrington, *Wisdom Texts from Qumran* (London: Routledge, 1996). Kloppenborg, noting that Proverbs contains some prophetic motifs and that Isaiah has absorbed sapiential elements, is initially critical of Koester for assuming that apocalyptic Son of Man and future-oriented eschatology sayings run counter to the tendencies of the 'wisdom gospel' genre and 'for that reason are judged to be secondary' (*Formation* 37-39; referring to Koester, 'GNOMAI DIAPHOROI').

different material (genres) of Q^1 and Q^2.[66] So critics at this point should not themselves make the mistake of which they accuse Kloppenborg, that is, of assuming that the designation of a 'sayings' genre as a *'sapiential'* sayings genre would necessarily be restricted to exclusively 'wisdom' sayings.[67] The deficiency of such categorisation is rather, as Christopher Tuckett has repeatedly observed, that the range of material included by Kloppenborg in this genre gives such a breadth of definition to 'wisdom' as to diminish its usefulness as a distinguishing category.[68] The likening of Q to a collection of Cynic chreiae,[69] a suggestion taken up and pushed further by others,[70] has confused the issue still further.[71] And to speak of a gnosticizing tendency in the sapiential genre[72] is to confuse later development with original motivation,[73] and to propagate a concept

66. Cf. C. M. Tuckett, 'On the Stratification of Q: A Response', *Semeia* 55 (1992) 213-22 (here 215-16). See Kloppenborg's further clarification in *Excavating Q* 380-82, 385-88, 394 n. 60.

67. For Kloppenborg's robust response to Horsley in particular, see *Excavating Q* 150-51 n. 71.

68. Tuckett, *Q* particularly 345-48, 353-54; similarly Horsley in Horsley and Draper, *Whoever* 77-78 and further 75-82. Schröter also points out that the vagueness of 'Logoi/Sayings' hardly makes it a suitable criterion to distinguish a specific genre (*Erinnerung* 95-96).

69. Kloppenborg, *Formation* 306-16, 322-25; but he has repeatedly pointed out that he is thinking in terms of form not of content.

70. Especially F. G. Downing, *Cynics and Christian Origins* (Edinburgh: Clark, 1992) ch. 5; also 'The Jewish Cynic Jesus' in Labahn and Schmidt, eds., *Jesus, Mark and Q* 184-214; Mack, *Lost Gospel* 45-46, 114-23; also *The Christian Myth: Origins, Logic and Legacy* (New York: Continuum, 2001) ch. 2; Vaage, *Galilean Upstarts;* also 'Q and Cynicism: On Comparison and Social Identity', in Piper, ed., *The Gospel behind the Gospels* 199-229; also 'Jewish Scripture, Q and the Historical Jesus: A Cynic Way with the Word', in Lindemann, ed., *Sayings Source Q* 479-95. See also Theissen, *First Followers* 14-15; Crossan, *Historical Jesus,* e.g., 338.

71. For Tuckett's critique see 'A Cynic Q?', *Biblica* 70 (1989) 349-76; also *Q* 368-91. See also the critiques of H. D. Betz, 'Jesus and the Cynics: Survey and Analysis of a Hypothesis', *JR* 74 (1994) 453-75; J. M. Robinson, 'The History-of-Religions Taxonomy of Q: The Cynic Hypothesis', in H. Preissler and H. Seiwert, eds., *Gnosisforschung und Religionsgeschichte,* K. Rudolph FS (Marburg: Elwert, 1994) 247-65; P. R. Eddy, 'Jesus as Diogenes? Reflections on the Cynic Jesus Thesis', *JBL* 115 (1996) 449-69. Robinson criticizes Vaage not so much for finding Cynic parallels to selected texts in the formative stratum of Q as for the texts' 'cynical interpretation that forms a Procrustean bed into which the Q movement is forced' (*'Galilean Upstarts:* A Sot's Cynical Disciples?', in Petersen, et al., eds., *Sayings of Jesus* 223-49 [here 249]). In his most recent contribution, Kloppenborg Verbin criticizes the critics of the Cynic Q for their theological subtexts, and prefers to speak of 'a cynic-like Q' (*Excavating Q* 420-42). See also chapter 9 nn. 203-204 below.

72. As does Robinson, 'LOGOI SOPHON'; Tuckett's critique in n. 71 above includes Robinson (*Q* 337-43).

73. Cf. D. Lührmann's critique of Robinson on this point (*Die Redaktion der Logienquelle* [WMANT 33; Neukirchen-Vluyn: Neukirchener, 1969] 91).

of genre as having an inherent character analogous to the genetic determinism advocated by some contemporary biologists. All in all, the attempt to classify and demarcate genre types has not proved very helpful in the discussion of Q.

More to the point is the question of *redaction* itself. Here we need to remind ourselves of the methodological problems in such an analysis.[74] If we take the parallel of Mark, it has proved difficult enough to determine redaction in Mark's case. There are, after all, no firm rules which enable modern commentators to distinguish clearly (outside the more obviously editorial linking passages) what Mark has retained or added: for example, regularity of word and motif in Mark tells us nothing as to whether the word or motif occurred regularly, occasionally or not at all in Mark's sources.[75] And if identification of redaction is difficult in a case where the text of the document (Mark) is firm, how much more difficult in the case of Q whose text is always a matter of argument and hypothesis.[76] How in particular is one to distinguish redaction from (initial) composition?[77] If a redactor was not troubled by the presence of aporiae and tensions in

74. Kloppenborg offers his 'methodological considerations' in *Formation* 96-101; also *Excavating Q* 114-18.

75. Cf. particularly P. Dschulnigg, *Sprache, Redaktion und Intention des Markus-Evangeliums* (SBB 11; Stuttgart: Katholisches Bibelwerk, 1986). Despite, e.g., R. H. Stein, 'The Proper Methodology for Ascertaining a Markan Redaction History', *NovT* 13 (1971) 181-98; E. J. Pryke, *Redactional Style in the Marcan Gospel* (SNTSMS 33; Cambridge: Cambridge University, 1978). A good example is the issue of a pre-Markan Passion narrative (see below, §17.1).

76. The result has been, apart from those following Kloppenborg, that more or less every redactional study of Q comes up with its own compositional history; cf., e.g., S. Schulz, *Q: Spruchquelle der Evangelisten* (Zürich: Theologischer, 1972); M. Sato, *Q und Prophetie: Studien zur Gattungs- und Traditionsgeschichte der Quelle Q* (WUNT 2.29; Tübingen: Mohr Siebeck, 1988); Allison, *Jesus Tradition* 8-37. It is true, however, that there is a substantial Kloppenborg consensus regarding the redactional character of the theme of judgment against 'this generation'. But see below, chapter 12. n. 397.

77. Note particularly Tuckett's criticisms at this point (*Q* 52-82): e.g., 'Lührmann's *"Redaktion"* is not so very different from the *"Sammlung"* from which he would distinguish it' (56); 'Jacobson's "compositional" stage is very similar to Lührmann's final redactional stage' (63). Contrast also, Jacobson's conclusion that 'an older Son of Man layer', a 'block of apocalyptic paraenesis, buttressed . . . by the imminent expectation of the Son of Man' underlies the 'later layer of Deuteronomistic-Wisdom material' ('Unity' 114-15; similarly Lührmann, *Redaktion* 93-100), with Koester's argument that an earlier wisdom/prophetic layer has been modified by the inclusion of Son of Man sayings ('GNOMAI DIAPHOROI' 138; also *Ancient Christian Gospels* 133-62). Bultmann, it should be recalled, concluded that announcements regarding the coming Kingdom of God went back to Jesus, whereas many of the wisdom sayings were plundered from Jewish wisdom ('New Approach' 57-58; 'Study' 55-57). Kloppenborg's earlier article, 'Tradition and Redaction in the Synoptic Sayings Source', *CBQ* 46 (1984) 34-62, provides several reminders of the breadth of disagreement and of the many imponderables in the quest for Q redaction. J. M. Robinson, 'The Q Trajectory: Between John and Matthew

his final text, would an initial compositor of Q have felt any different?[78] How can one both argue for the coherence and unity of Q (as proof of its existence), and at the same time argue that internal tensions indicate disunity, without the one argument throwing the other into question?[79] Textual tensions are no clear proof of redactional layers (what author ever succeeded in removing all tensions from his/ her final product, or attempted to do so?).[80] Clinical technique here is in danger of running ahead of common sense. That said, I do not deny the plausibility of detecting at least some redaction in the composition of Q (above n. 62).

My questions begin to multiply however when we turn our focus on to Q^1. Kloppenborg does not explicitly address the issue of whether Q^1 was also a document, certainly not in the way he addresses the issue of whether Q itself was a document.[81] All he actually demonstrates is the plausibility of detecting clusters of sayings which have been taken over (and redacted) at the stage of composing Q (or Q^2). He does not actually demonstrate that Q^1 ever functioned as a single document or stratum in his excavations into Q. And on closer examination it is hard to detect a unifying theme or redactional motif which links them together (as, arguably, is the case with the motif of coming judgment in Q itself). What we seem to have, rather, is six(?) clusters of Jesus' teaching: (1) the somewhat disparate material gathered into 'the Sermon on the Plain' (Q 6.20-23, 27-49); (2) teaching on discipleship and mission (9.57-62; 10.2-11, 16); (3) teaching on prayer (11.2-4, 9-13); (4) encouragement to fearless confession (12.2-7, 11-12);

via Jesus', in B. A. Pearson, ed., *The Future of Early Christianity,* H. Koester FS (Minneapolis: Fortress, 1991) 173-94 provides a lucid account of the two main competing perspectives in attempts to reconstruct Q's history ('trajectory').

78. In Koester's view the apocalyptic material 'conflicts' with the emphasis of the wisdom and prophetic material (*Ancient Christian Gospels* 135). Kloppenborg speaks of 'aporiae created by redactional activity' or of a group of sayings 'modified by the insertion of a secondary expansion or commentary . . .' (*Formation* 97, 99); but that simply begs the question, as Kloppenborg seems to realise (*Formation* 99).

79. Jacobson, 'Unity', is particularly vulnerable at this point (cf. Tuckett, *Q* 63-64). Here again Streeter's words of caution have been too much ignored (*Four Gospels* 235-38).

80. The pendulum may have begun to swing against Kloppenborg in recent treatments of Q which argue for a single compositional stage: Schröter, *Erinnerung* particularly 216-17, 292-93, 368-69, 449-50, 468-72; Kirk, *Composition of the Sayings Source:* 'No warrants exist for supposing that a single one [of Q's twelve speeches] formed gradually or incrementally or is a sedimentized witness to some multi-layered archaeology of early Christianity' (269); Horsley in Horsley and Draper, *Whoever* 23-24, 61-62, 83-93, 148; P. Hoffmann, 'Mutmassungen über Q: zum Problem der literarischen Genese von Q', in Lindemann, ed., *Sayings Source* Q 255-88 (conclusion 286); D. Lührmann is also dubious about Kloppenborg's suggested composition history of Q ('Die Logienquelle und die Leben-Jesu-Forschung', in Lindemann, ed., *Sayings Source Q* 191-206 [here 204]).

81. He does, however, assume it (*Excavating Q* 159, 197, 200, 208-209); see also 154-59 on the genre of Q^1.

(5) the right priorities (12.22-31, 33-34); (6) more teaching on discipleship (13.24; 14.26-27; 17.33; 14.34-35). There is no reason, however, why this material should be taken as a single document.[82] It looks in fact more like the sort of teaching material which was no doubt rehearsed in the Q communities in their regular gatherings, some individual items already grouped (different clusters) for convenience and as good pedagogical practice.[83] If we follow this line of reasoning, then the rationale for two distinct compositional layers is undermined, and the related hypothesis that a single document (Q[1]) represented the sole concerns and interests of the Q people (cf. §7.4b) makes even less sense.[84] The evidence is fully satisfied by the alternative hypothesis of a single compositional act, when the Q author/editor pulled together these different clusters, adapted them (the redactional interpolations), and knitted them into the larger single collection Q (or Q[2]).[85]

82. Similarly Hoffmann's conclusion ('Mutmassungen über Q' 266). The considerations adduced by Kloppenborg (*Excavating Q* 144-46, referring back to *Formation* ch. 5) hardly demonstrate 'in all likelihood . . . a discrete redactional stratum': (1) A common structure: but to describe the first item in each cluster as a 'programmatic saying' overstates the case; since it is all teaching material with the character of personal address ('you'), it naturally evinces a 'rhetoric of persuasion', but that hardly marks it out as distinctive; and the designation of the last item in each cluster as one which 'underscores the importance of the instructions' applies even on Kloppenborg's reckoning to only four of the six clusters. (2) To describe the content as 'an interlocking set of concerns which have to do with the legitimation of a somewhat adventuresome social practice' implies a higher degree of intention and coherence bonding the clusters than is actually evident.

83. This hypothesis makes as good if not better sense of the case for 'complexes of logia' or 'collections of aphoristic sayings' behind Q, as suggested by D. Zeller, *Die weisheitlichen Mahnsprüche bei den Synoptikern* (Forschung zur Bibel 17; Würzburg: Echter, 1977) 191-92, and argued particularly by R. A. Piper, *Wisdom in the Q-tradition: The Aphoristic Teaching of Jesus* (SNTSMS 61; Cambridge: Cambridge University, 1989); but Zeller gives a negative answer to the question 'Eine weisheitliche Grundschrift in der Logienquelle?', in F. Van Segbroeck et al., eds., *The Four Gospels 1992: Festschrift Frans Neirynck* (Leuven: Leuven University, 1992) 389-401. The recognition of a tendency to cluster sayings of Jesus has been a feature of Q research — J. M. Robinson, 'Early Collections of Jesus' Sayings', in J. Delobel, ed., *Logia: Les Paroles de Jésus — The Sayings of Jesus* (BETL 59; Leuven: Peeters, 1982) 389-94; Crossan, *Fragments;* P. H. Sellew, *Dominical Discourses: Oral Clusters in the Jesus Sayings Tradition* (Philadelphia: Fortress, 1989); R. A. Horsley, 'Q and Jesus: Assumptions, Approaches and Analyses', in J. S. Kloppenborg and L. E. Vaage, eds., *Early Christianity, Q and Jesus, Semeia* 55 (1992) 175-209.

84. The argument, e.g., that the absence of such concerns as purity distinctions and Torah indicates the limitation of the Q people's range of interest, or that they saw Jesus more as a sage than a prophet (*Excavating Q* 199, 397-98), begins to make sense only if Q[1] represented the complete range of concerns of the Q people.

85. See further Tuckett, *Q* 71-74; F. G. Downing, 'Word-processing in the Ancient World: The Social Production and Performance of Q', *JSNT* 64 (1996) 29-48, reprinted in

Again these matters would not be too serious except that such analysis presupposes, once again, that the different layers represent different understandings of Jesus, 'asymmetrical kerygmas',[86] different circles of discipleship.[87] Tensions within Q become tensions between redactional levels, between different *Sitze-im-Leben,* added to the tensions between Q and the circles which focused on the cross and resurrection.[88] All this is then taken as providing proof that the earliest responses to Jesus were far more diverse than had previously been recognized, and that the historical Jesus was first remembered as a teacher of wisdom. But, as Kloppenborg himself has pointed out, 'tradition-history is not convertible with *literary* history': tradition brought in at a redactional stage might be as old as or older than the tradition redacted.[89]

Overall, it is difficult to avoid the conclusion that the leap from Matthew's and Luke's common material ('q') to 'Q', to a 'Q community' with markedly different stages in its development, and thence to a wisdom-teaching/non-apocalyptic Jesus is too much lacking in visible means of support. The various attempts to build hypothesis upon presupposition upon hypothesis can scarcely inspire confidence in the outcome. In what follows, therefore, I will use the Q hypothesis as a working hypothesis, but not assume a stratified Q (Q^1, Q^2, Q^3). It will also be important to recall Streeter's qualification that 'a substantial portion of the 200 verses in question were probably derived from some other (oral) source than Q'.[90] The issue will be investigated further below (§8.5).

Doing Things with Words in the First Christian Century (JSNTS 200; Sheffield: Sheffield Academic, 2000) 75-94 (here 85-94). Horsley in Horsley and Draper, *Whoever* 62-67, sums up his genre critique: 'The common features that supposedly characterize the sayings clusters assigned to the different strata either fail to appear in the clusters or do not appear consistently across the various clusters. The hypothesized layers cannot in fact be differentiated according to the stated criteria of these features' (67).

86. Kloppenborg, *Formation* 21-22; Koester, *Ancient Christian Gospels* 160: 'Q's theology and soteriology are fundamentally different' from the theology represented by the Pauline kerygma.

87. So particularly Schulz, who thinks it possible to distinguish a Palestinian Jewish Christian group on the Syrian border from a later Hellenistic Jewish Christian group in Syria itself (*Q* 47, 57, 177, etc.).

88. Contrast Schröter, though his critique is still too dependent on the genre argument (*Erinnerung* 35); 'Since a genre can be connected with reality in multiple ways, it follows conversely that the union of more genres in one text in no way compels the conclusion that these stemmed originally out of disparate situations' (59, similarly 142).

89. Kloppenborg, *Formation* 244-45; also *Excavating Q* 151; similarly Attridge, 'Reflections' 228.

90. See above, chapter 4 n. 84.

d. Date and Place

Given the imponderable uncertainties about Q itself, the questions of the date, place, and reasons for its composition may be too much a matter of *obscurum per obscurius.* The only real clarity is that Matthew and Luke used the document Q; so any date prior to their composition (80-95) is technically possible. Hoffmann and Kloppenborg date the final redaction of Q to about the final stages of the first Jewish revolt or just after.[91] Allison notes that allusions have been detected to certain Jewish 'sign prophets' known from Josephus (Catchpole, referring particularly to Q 17.23-24),[92] suggesting a date sometime after 45; or to Caligula's attempt to have a statue or bust of himself erected in the Jerusalem Temple (Theissen, referring to Q 4.5-7),[93] suggesting a date subsequent to 39/40. And Allison himself thinks his Q[1] probably appeared in the 30s, with final Q in the 40s or 50s.[94]

As to Q's *Sitz im Leben,* the strongest case has undoubtedly been made for Galilee.[95] The influence of Theissen (§4.6) is evident on those who see an early collection of Q material (Q[1]?) as providing guidance for itinerant missionaries.[96]

91. P. Hoffmann, 'The Redaction of Q and the Son of Man', in Piper, ed., *The Gospel behind the Gospels* 159-98; Kloppenborg, *Excavating Q* 80-87.

92. D. R. Catchpole, 'The Question of Q', *Sewanee Theological Review* 36 (1992) 3-44.

93. Theissen, *The Gospels in Context* 206-21.

94. Allison, *Jesus Tradition* 49-54; possibly in Aramaic (47-49, 62-66).

95. See particularly Kloppenborg Verbin, *Excavating Q* chs. 4-5, and the impressive argument of J. L. Reed, 'The Sayings Source Q in Galilee', *Archaeology and the Galilean Jesus* 170-96. But challenged now by M. Frenschkowski, 'Galiläa oder Jerusalem? Die topographischen und politischen Hintergründe der Logienquelle', in Lindemann, ed., *Sayings Source Q* 535-59. We will have to return to the question in vol. 2; for the present volume see further below, §9.6b. It is curious that the indications of Q material's Galilean context should be counted as good evidence for Q communities in Galilee, of which we know next to nothing, but not as good evidence for Jesus' mission, whose Galilean context is undisputed.

96. Zeller, *Mahnsprüche* 192, 196-97; U. Luz, *Matthäus* (EKK 3 vols. so far; Zürich: Benziger/Neukirchen: Neukirchener, 1985, 1990, 1997) 1.371; L. Schottroff and W. Stegemann, *Jesus and the Hope of the Poor* (Maryknoll: Orbis, 1986) 38, 47-49; R. Uro, *Sheep among the Wolves* (Helsinki: Suomalainen Tiedeakatemia, 1987) 241; Vaage, *Galilean Upstarts* 38-39; Allison, *Jesus Tradition* 30-32; J. D. Crossan, 'Itinerants and Householders in the Earliest Jesus Movement', in W. E. Arnal and M. Desjardins, eds., *Whose Historical Jesus?* (SCJ 7; Waterloo: Wilfrid Laurier University, 1997) 7-24. S. J. Patterson, *The Gospel of Thomas and Jesus* (Sonoma: Polebridge, 1993) chs. 5-6 argues that the 'wandering radicalism' (Theissen) was preserved in the *Gospel of Thomas* by 'a group of Thomas itinerants' who 'wandered' into Syria from Palestine (156-57); 'if in synoptic texts one must read the tradition largely through the lens of "local sympathizers", in the Gospel of Thomas one reads it through the lens of the "wandering charismatics"' (170). See the review of the discussion by W. E. Arnal, *Jesus and the Village Scribes* (Minneapolis: Fortress, 2001) ch. 2, who subjects the hy-

But disagreement about Q's compositional/redactional history makes further clarification of Q's *Sitz im Leben* more difficult. What does emerge, however, is some sense of tradition history, of the process by which these traditions were transmitted. This is a process which Catchpole and Allison, for example, would suggest began with Jesus himself,[97] which indeed is probably the case, though the fact that they think of that process in terms of literary editing (rather than of oral transmission) is a further example of a blind spot which still needlessly restricts contemporary perspective on the earliest stages of the history of the Jesus tradition.

7.5. Matthew and Luke

For the sake of completeness we should remember that not only Mark and Q are sources for the Jesus tradition, but also Matthew and Luke.[98] And not just for the fact that they provide proof of the two-source hypothesis and for the way they used Mark and Q,[99] but also for the traditions which are peculiar to Matthew and Luke (usually designated 'M' and 'L').[100] Since these latter attest tradition quite as substantial in quantity as Mark or Q themselves, the status of that material can hardly be ignored. We need only think of the Matthean and Lukan birth narratives (Matthew 1–2; Luke 1–2), of Matt. 10.5 and 23, or of the familiar Lukan parables of the Good Samaritan and the Prodigal Son (Luke 10.30-37; 15.11-32) to realise how much is at stake here. The status of such singly attested traditions is a question we will have to take up at various points in what follows.[101] For the present two points are worth making.

---

pothesis to a withering critique: 'sociologically, the hypothesis is theoretically vacuous' (9); 'it is not normally grounded in a careful investigation of the social realia of the period' (72); 'the texts . . . do not evince itinerary until one has assumed itinerary' (69, 91-95); the Q people were probably 'village scribes involved in the administration of formerly autonomous village life', who alone would have the ability to write such a document (170-72); the metaphor and rhetoric of uprootedness has been mistaken (183-93).

97. Catchpole, *Quest* 188; Allison, *Jesus Tradition* 60-62.

98. As already noted, both Gospels are usually dated in the period 80-95; see, e.g., Schnelle, *History* 222, 243; Brown, *Introduction* 216-17, 273-74; W. D. Davies and D. C. Allison, *Matthew* (ICC, 3 vols.; Edinburgh: Clark, 1988, 1991, 1997) 1.127-38; J. A. Fitzmyer, *Luke* (AB 28A, two vols.; New York: Doubleday, 1981, 1985) 53-57. I shall, of course, look more closely later on at both the processes of tradition accumulation, organisation, and editing which lie behind these Gospels (vol. 2) and the Gospels in their own right (vol. 3).

99. See, e.g., G. N. Stanton, 'Matthew as a Creative Interpreter of the Sayings of Jesus' (1982), in P. Stuhlmacher, ed., *The Gospel and the Gospels* (Grand Rapids: Eerdmans, 1991) 257-72.

100. These are listed by Streeter, *Four Gospels* 198.

101. See further below, particularly §§11.1 and 13.7.

One is that the Matthean and Lukan *Sondergut* (distinctive material) attests a much richer body of Jesus tradition than any single Synoptic Evangelist used or was able to use. That itself tells us something about the traditioning process: that not every church knew or thought it necessary to know all there was to know about Jesus; and that the Evangelists were probably at least in some measure selective in their use of Jesus tradition. Would that we knew how wide was the 'pool' of Jesus tradition and how widely known. But we don't. At least, however, we need to be conscious of the likely breadth and dispersal of the Jesus tradition and suspicious of the too simplistic rule of thumb that tradition only once attested is therefore necessarily of less value as a remembrance of Jesus.[102]

The other point is once again a plea to avoid thinking of the Matthean and Lukan *Sondergut* solely in literary terms, as though Matthew and Luke depended for their knowledge of Jesus tradition exclusively on written sources.[103] Such a way of envisioning the traditioning process simply attests the failure of historical imagination to accept instruction from history. Scholars of the twenty-first century must take more seriously than their twentieth-century predecessors the fact that first-century Israel was an oral culture and the probability that the Jesus tradition was processed in oral form through the first two generations of Christians (and beyond), prior to, including Q, and alongside the written Gospels. The importance of this observation will become clearer in chapter 8.

7.6. The *Gospel of Thomas*

The amount of credibility invested in the *Gospel of Thomas* by Koester and the neo-Liberal questers makes the issue of *Thomas*'s value as a source for the teaching of Jesus particularly sensitive.[104] From early days following its initial publi-

---

102. With reference particularly to Crossan, *Historical Jesus;* and though he does not need to be reminded of the point (xxxi-xxxiii), nevertheless his working criterion (use only if attested more than once) is bound to skew the portrayal of Jesus in at least some degree.

103. Despite his frequent warnings not to regard Q material solely as written tradition, Streeter seems to fall into the trap he warns against elsewhere of regarding the material unique to Matthew (M) and Luke (L) as separate documents; hence his 'Four Document Hypothesis' (*Four Gospels* ch. 9). See further below, chapter 10, n. 24.

104. Translation from the Coptic by H. Koester and T. O. Lambdin in J. M. Robinson, ed., *The Nag Hammadi Library in English* (Leiden: Brill, ³1988) 124-38; by B. Blatz in W. Schneemelcher and R. McL. Wilson, *New Testament Apocrypha* (Cambridge: James Clarke, revised edition 1991) 110-33; and by J. K. Elliott, *Apocryphal New Testament* 123-47 (with extensive bibliography). Also R. Cameron, *The Other Gospels: Non-Canonical Gospel Texts* (Guildford: Lutterworth, 1983) 23-37; Miller, ed., *Complete Gospels* 301-22; Funk, ed., *Five Gospels* 471-532.

cation (1959), opinion has been almost equally divided as to whether the *Gospel of Thomas* knew and drew from the Synoptics (and John) or is a witness to an early form of the Jesus tradition prior to the Synoptics and independent of the Synoptics as such.[105] The evidence is not decisive either way. The problem is the complexity of the traditioning process which such comparisons open up. In each case we have to consider the possibility of interaction between *Thomas* in its Greek form (attested by the Oxyrhynchus papyri)[106] or its subsequent Coptic form and any of three or four levels — the traditions (oral or written) on which each document drew, the documents themselves (Mark, Q, Matthew, Luke, John), second-hand oral knowledge of individual traditions as they appear in each document but as a result of one or more hearings of the document being read (second orality),[107] or even subsequent assimilation by scribes of one text form to another.[108] It is awareness of such complexity which causes Tuckett to suggest, at the end of a paper in which he argues that five *Thomas* logia show knowledge of Lukan redaction (*GTh* 5, 16, 55) and Markan redaction (*GTh* 9, 20), that 'the problem of the relationship between Th[omas] and the synoptics is probably ultimately insoluble'.[109] At the very least, then, *Thomas* provides evidence of the different forms or versions which particular sayings could and did take, and possibly from an early stage of the traditioning process.

That said, however, certain caveats have to be lodged. First, the question of the value of *Thomas* as a source for our knowledge of Jesus' teaching has been caught up in the continuing search for evidence of pre-Christian Gnosticism. The point is that the *Gospel of Thomas* is best categorized as a 'Gnostic' (or gnostic)

---

105. Bibliography in Koester, *Ancient Christian Gospels* 84-85; Meier, *Marginal Jew* 1.128-30. That *Thomas* is the product of a tradition history 'basically independent of the synoptic tradition' is the central thesis of Patterson, *Thomas and Jesus* chs. 2-3, who concludes that 'Thomas is the offspring of an autonomous stream of early Christian tradition' (110); though given the substantial overlap between *Thomas* and the Synoptic tradition 'autonomous' is a questionable judgment (see also below, §8.6d).

106. See above, chapter 4 n. 191. See further Schneemelcher and Wilson, *New Testament Apocrypha* 117-18, 121-23; Elliott, *Apocryphal New Testament* 128-33 (with bibliography), 135-36, 139-41.

107. See particularly R. Uro, 'Thomas and Oral Gospel Tradition', in R. Uro, ed., Thomas *at the Crossroads: Essays on the* Gospel of Thomas (Edinburgh: Clark, 1998) 8-32.

108. Cf. Patterson, *Thomas and Jesus* 92-93.

109. C. Tuckett, 'Thomas and the Synoptics', *NovT* 30 (1988) 132-57. Meier is overconfident in his conclusion that the *Gospel of Thomas* 'knew and used at least some of the canonical Gospels, notably Matthew and Luke' (*Marginal Jew* 1.139, referring to his earlier discussion, 134-37); he is supported in this by M. Fieger, *Das Thomasevangelium* (NTAbh 22; Münster, 1991; Meier, 'Present State of the "Third Quest"' 464); similarly J. H. Charlesworth and C. A. Evans, 'Jesus in the Agrapha and Apocryphal Gospels', in Chilton and Evans, eds., *Studying the Historical Jesus* 479-533 (here 496-503).

document.[110] If then the distinctive *Thomas* tradition is early, it could provide a strong basis for the argument that a Gnostic response to and use of Jesus' teaching was among the earliest responses to Jesus; in a word, Gnostic Christianity would be as old (and thus as 'respectable'), or at least as deeply rooted in the Jesus tradition, as the Christianity of the canonical Gospels. However, the earlier stage of the search, the search for a pre-Christian Gnostic redeemer myth,[111] proved unsuccessful and ran out of steam in the 1960s. And the older view, that Gnosticism is more accurately defined as a second-century Christian heresy,[112] or at least that the Gnostic redeemer myth was itself parasitic upon early Christianity's own christology,[113] should be accorded fresh recognition. The problem with using the term 'gnostic' for the various soteriologies of the first century (or earlier) is the same as with the use of 'wisdom' for a variety of sayings collections.[114] Is the term appropriate even when the features described as Gnostic/gnostic are so heavily diluted as to cease to be distinctive of Gnosticism?[115] And the alternative of 'pre-Gnostic' or 'proto-Gnostic' is little better as a description of mid-first-century Christianity.[116] The point is that the *Gospel of Thomas*

110. E.g., Koester, *Ancient Christian Gospels* 83, 124-28, referring particularly to *GTh* 3, 29, 50, 56, 83, 84; Patterson, *Thomas and Jesus* 226-28; Lüdemann has no doubt that the message of *Thomas* 'corresponds with that of the early Christian Gnostics' (*Jesus* 589). *Pace* J. D. Crossan, *Four Other Gospels* (Minneapolis: Winston, 1985), who argues that *Thomas* 'is primarily concerned with asceticism rather than gnosticism' (28-35): the alternatives are not mutually exclusive. On the problems of defining *Thomas* more precisely as 'Gnostic' see A. Marjanen, 'Is *Thomas* a Gnostic Gospel?', and R. Uro, 'Is *Thomas* an Encratite Gospel?, in R. Uro, ed., Thomas *at the Crossroads* 107-39 and 140-62, with further bibliography 108-109 nn. 5-11.

111. The pre-Christian Gnostic redeemer myth was hypothesized by Bultmann in particular as a source for Paul's christology (*Theology* 1.164-68), a thesis which was hugely influential through the middle of the twentieth century but is now widely regarded as *passé* (see, e.g., those cited in my *Theology of Paul* 282 n. 68 and 550 n. 97). See below, vol. 2.

112. S. Petrement, *A Separate God: The Christian Origins of Gnosticism* (San Francisco: HarperCollins, 1994).

113. So already R. M. Grant, *Gnosticism: An Anthology* (London: Collins, 1961): 'The most obvious explanation of the origin of the Gnostic redeemer is that he was modelled after the Christian conception of Jesus. It seems significant that we know no redeemer before Jesus, while we encounter other redeemers (Simon Magus, Menander) immediately after his time' (18). See further those cited in my *Christology in the Making* (London: SCM, [2]1989) 305 n. 3.

114. See above, n. 68.

115. K. Rudolph defines Gnosis/Gnosticism about as broadly as is possible: 'a dualistic religion . . . which took up a definitely negative attitude towards the world and the society of the time, and proclaimed a deliverance ("redemption") of man precisely from the constraints of earthly existence through "insight" into his essential relationship . . . with a supramundane realm of freedom and rest' (*Gnosis: The Nature and History of an Ancient Religion* [1977; ET Edinburgh: Clark, 1983] 2).

116. We might as well describe Second Temple Judaism as pre- or proto-Christian, or

seems to attest the developed form of the Gnostic redeemer myth (*GTh* 28).[117] And the overall perspective of the document can be fairly described as that of second-century Gnosis.[118] In consequence, therefore, we should not be surprised if we find that any earlier traditions have been redacted in a Gnostic direction.

Second, there is another persistent fallacy operative in this area, that *'independent'* means *'more original'*. Where elements in the Nag Hammadi documents cannot be derived from Christian tradition, the corollary is regularly drawn that these elements pre-date Christianity (proof that Gnosticism is as old as Christianity). But the ancient Mediterranean world was a melting pot for many religious traditions and philosophies. So, 'independent' may simply mean 'independent of Christianity' rather than 'earlier than Christianity'. In our present case, the different version of the Jesus tradition attested by the *Gospel of Thomas* is often assumed to be the more original.[119] But all that analysis demonstrates is that the versions are different.[120] The possibility remains open that that is all there is to it (attesting the diversity of ways in which the tradition was told and retold in Christian congregations), as well as the possibility of redaction either or both ways. This again is a subject to which we will have to return (chapter 8).

In particular, Koester's treatment of the *Gospel of Thomas* leaves him vulnerable to the charge of *petitio principii*. For again and again he assumes rather than demonstrates that the *Gospel of Thomas* bears witness to an early, non-apocalyptic layer of Jesus tradition.[121] But it is perfectly comprehensible that a Gnostic redaction, for which a 'realized eschatology' was central, should have omitted and 'corrected' all tradition which attested a future eschatology and hope of a coming Son of Man.[122] And if, on other grounds, a future eschatology seems to belong to the bedrock of the Synoptic tradition,[123] then the more probable conclusion will have to be that the *Gospel of Thomas* does indeed attest to a

---

mediaeval Christianity as pre- or proto-Protestant, for all the value these designations would contain as descriptions of Second Temple Judaism and mediaeval Christianity.

117. Cf. the 'Hymn of the Pearl' in *Acts of Thomas* 108-13.

118. Note, e.g., *GTh* 3.4-5; 37.2-3; 50; 77; 84; 87.

119. Crossan gives the same warning: 'independent does not necessarily mean earlier' (*Four Other Gospels* 35).

120. Of the cases cited by Koester, *Ancient Christian Gospels* 89-124, note, for example, *GTh* 9, 20, 21b, 39, 63, 64, 76, 99, 100, 109 (Koester 92, 97-99, 103-104, 108-10, 112).

121. Koester, 'GNOMAI DIAPHOROI' 137-39; also 'One Jesus' 171, 186-87; also *Ancient Christian Gospels* 92-99. In the last case, the comparison with John is similarly tendentious in claiming that John avoided the Gnostic implications (as indicated by *Thomas*) of the tradition he was using (115-23).

122. As Koester acknowledges (*Ancient Christian Gospels* 97). But we should again note that Koester also agrees that 'the Gospel of Thomas presupposes, and criticizes, a tradition of the eschatological sayings of Jesus' ('Jesus the Victim' 7 n. 17).

123. See below, §12.4.

gnostically motivated *excision* of that motif from the earlier tradition. In fact, it is only a tendentious analysis of both Q and *Thomas* which has been able to make a case for a non-apocalyptic earliest stratum of Jesus tradition.[124] The tradition history of the son of man/Son of Man sayings in particular invites, rather, a more sophisticated analysis which tells much more in favour of their presence in the earliest stages of the tradition.[125]

In what follows, then, we shall expect to find that the *Gospel of Thomas* attests different forms which the Jesus tradition took. But where *Thomas* differs markedly from the consensus of the Synoptic tradition in terms of particular motifs, the likelihood will usually be that the Synoptic tradition is closer to the earliest remembered sayings of Jesus than is the *Gospel of Thomas*. Which also means that issues of date may be largely irrelevant to our concerns. For while the question must always remain open that a particular *Thomas* saying has preserved an early/earlier version of the saying than the Synoptic tradition or that an unparalleled *Thomas* saying is as early as the earliest Synoptic tradition, it will always be the undoubtedly early Synoptic tradition which provides the measure by which judgment is made on the point.[126] The insistence on the need to date the *Gospel of Thomas* itself early (as by Crossan and Koester)[127] once again implies a theory of tradition history too much in terms of literary strata/editions rather than of oral retellings/performances.

7.7. The Gospel of John

Baur's dismissal of John's Gospel as a historical source held increasingly undisputed sway in scholarly circles for about a hundred years. And though the sharp distinction between John and the Synoptics as between theology and history was undermined by Wrede,[128] few scholars would regard John as a source for information regarding Jesus' life and ministry in any degree comparable to the Synop-

---

124. See further Horsley in Horsley and Draper, *Whoever* 76 n. 62, 78-81.

125. See below, §§16.4-5. However Koester does recognize the influence which the oral tradition may have continued to exert (*Ancient Christian Gospels* 99, 109); see also below, §8.3d.

126. This remains true even when we take seriously C. W. Hedrick's warning against 'The Tyranny of the Synoptic Jesus', in C. W. Hedrick, ed., *The Historical Jesus and the Rejected Gospels, Semeia* 44 (1988) 1-8, since any portrayal of Jesus is better based on clusters and themes in the Jesus tradition rather than on individual sayings (see further below, §10.2).

127. See above, §4.7; Patterson suggests a date for *Thomas* in the vicinity of 70-80 CE (*Thomas and Jesus* 120).

128. But Baur already argued that each of the Gospels is systematically tendentious in character (see chapter 4 n. 70).

tics.[129] It is worth noting briefly the factors which have been considered of enduring significance on this point. One is the very different picture of Jesus' ministry, both in the order and significance of events (particularly the cleansing of the Temple and the raising of Lazarus) and the location of Jesus' ministry (predominantly Jerusalem rather than Galilee). Another is the striking difference in Jesus' style of speaking (much more discursive and theological, in contrast to the aphoristic and parabolic style of the Synoptics). As Strauss had already pointed out, this style is consistent, whether Jesus speaks to Nicodemus, or to the woman at the well, or to his disciples, and very similar to the style of the Baptist, as indeed of 1 John. The inference is inescapable that the style is that of the *Evangelist* rather than that of *Jesus*.[130] Probably most important of all, in the Synoptics Jesus' principal theme is the kingdom of God and he rarely speaks of himself, whereas in John the kingdom hardly features and the discourses are largely vehicles for expressing Jesus' self-consciousness and self-proclamation. Had the striking 'I am' self-assertions of John been remembered as spoken by Jesus, how could any Evangelist have ignored them so completely as the Synoptics do?[131] On the whole, then, the position is unchanged: John's Gospel cannot be regarded as a source for the life and teaching of Jesus of the same order as the Synoptics.

The one major revision required to what we might call the Baur consensus on the historical value of John's Gospel has been the masterly study by C. H. Dodd on the subject.[132] Dodd made a strong case for recognizing that both narrative and discourse material contain good, early tradition.[133] In particular, John's account of the beginnings of Jesus' ministry probably contains information which the Synoptics passed over; geographical details provided by John are best explained as remembered details; and many are persuaded by John's assessment of the length of Jesus' ministry (three Passovers), the indication of more frequent visits by Jesus to Jerusalem, and the chronology of the last week of Jesus' life.[134] As for the discourse material, the number of sayings embedded within the discourses, which have parallels in the Synoptics, is best explained by the fact that

129. Though few are as dismissive as M. Casey, *Is John's Gospel True?* (London: Routledge, 1996).

130. Strauss, *Life* 384-86.

131. For further illustration see my *The Evidence for Jesus* (London: SCM, 1985) ch. 2.

132. C. H. Dodd, *Historical Tradition in the Fourth Gospel* (Cambridge: Cambridge University, 1963).

133. I summarize the evidence, with some elaboration, in my 'John and the Oral Gospel Tradition', in H. Wansbrough, ed., *Jesus and the Oral Gospel Tradition* (JSNTS 64; Sheffield: JSOT, 1991) 351-79 (here 355-58).

134. See also F. J. Moloney, 'The Fourth Gospel and the Jesus of History', *NTS* 46 (2000) 42-58. The references to Passover are John 2.13, 23; 6.4; 11.55; 12.1; 13.1; 18.28, 39; 19.14.

the Fourth Evangelist knew and used a Synoptic-like tradition.[135] Indeed, again and again it looks as though the Johannine discourses are based on particular sayings of Jesus, similar to the Synoptic sayings in character.[136] Moreover, the regular Johannine pattern of miracle ('sign') followed by discourse, and the 'farewell discourses' of John 14–17 strongly suggest that what we have in the Fourth Gospel is the Evangelist's meditations on significant words and deeds of Jesus.

In short, John provides another window on how the Jesus tradition was used already within the first century, and indeed, within the first two generations of Christianity.[137] But one can recognize *both* that the tradition has been heavily worked upon *and* that it is well rooted within earlier Jesus tradition.[138] The point so far as the teaching material is concerned is, once again, that the recognition of both features is determined by comparison with the Synoptic tradition. That is to say, the Synoptic tradition provides something of a norm for the recognition of the oldest traditions. In what follows, therefore, we shall certainly want to call upon John's Gospel as a source, but mostly as a secondary source to supplement or corroborate the testimony of the Synoptic tradition.

7.8. Other Gospels

So far as testimony to earliest memories of Jesus' teaching and life is concerned, the value of the other Gospels cited by Crossan and Koester becomes progressively slighter.

a. The appropriately named *'Dialogue Gospel'* is plausibly deduced to be a source for the Nag Hammadi document known as the *Dialogue of the Saviour.*[139]

---

135. The debate continues as to whether John knew and used any of the Synoptics; see the review of the debate by D. M. Smith, *John among the Gospels: The Relationship in Twentieth-Century Research* (Minneapolis: Fortress, 1992). In my own view, Dodd was right: the indications of John's knowledge of earlier Gospels are as readily or better explained by John's knowledge of an oral tradition which shared those features.

136. Koester, *Ancient Christian Gospels* 256-67, argues that John knows and refutes the pre-Johannine Gnostic understanding of these sayings (263-67), but all that the evidence indicates is a different interpretation of similar material; and, once again, 'different' does not mean 'earlier'.

137. The Gospel of John itself is usually dated to about 100 CE; see, e.g., Koester, *Ancient Christian Gospels* 267; Schnelle, *History* 476-77; Brown, *Introduction* 374-76. Few have been persuaded by the attempt of J. A. T. Robinson, *Redating the New Testament* (London: SCM, 1976) to date John's Gospel prior to 70 CE.

138. See further my 'Let John Be John: A Gospel for Its Time', in P. Stuhlmacher, ed., *Das Evangelium und die Evangelien* (Tübingen: Mohr Siebeck, 1983) ET *The Gospel and the Gospels* (Grand Rapids: Eerdmans, 1991) 293-322.

139. Translation of the Coptic by H. Koester and E. H. Pagels, in Robinson, ed., *Nag*

The *Dialogue Gospel* is itself clearly Gnostic (particularly §§26, 28, 55, 84) and draws on material known to us only through the *Gospel of Thomas*.[140] Tuckett finds clear evidence that the *Dialogue Gospel* shows awareness of Matthew's and probably also Luke's finished Gospels.[141] More interesting are the parallels with John's Gospel, not only in content but also in the implication that the *Dialogue Gospel* also constituted developing reflection on earlier tradition of Jesus' sayings (most clearly evident in §§8, 9, 53). But Koester once again betrays his *Tendenz* when he argues that John knew 'the more traditional Gnostic dialogue, which the *Dialogue of the Savior* has preserved in its more original form'.[142] For the evidence suggests rather that the *Dialogue Gospel* (source of the Nag Hammadi *Dialogue of the Saviour*) is already a well-developed reflection on earlier tradition, whose earlier form is only occasionally visible. Rather like the *Gospel of Thomas* and the Gospel of John, therefore, the *Dialogue Gospel* provides evidence of the different ways the sayings tradition was developed. But even more than in the case of *Thomas* it is doubtful whether the distinctive features of the *Dialogue Gospel* provide earlier or more original versions of Synoptic traditions. And much less than in the case of the Gospel of John does it provide evidence of rootedness in the earliest forms of the Jesus tradition.

b. The case regarding the *Apocryphon* (or *Letter*) *of James*[143] is similar but even less strong. Koester again pushes the evidence too hard when he argues that *Apoc. Jas.* represents an earlier stage in the sayings tradition presupposed in the discourses of John's Gospel.[144] The document is clearly Gnostic in character

---

Hammadi Library 244-59, and by B. Blatz in Schneemelcher and Wilson, eds., *New Testament Apocrypha* 1.300-11; also Cameron, *Other Gospels* 38-48; Miller, ed., *Complete Gospels* 343-56. The codex is badly damaged and the text often fragmentary, but the dialogue between the Lord, Judas, Matthew, and Mary suggested by Koester makes a coherent whole and accounts for about two-thirds of the Nag Hammadi document (§§4-14, 19-20, 25-34, 41-104; *Dial. Sav.* 124.23–127.19; 128.23–129.16; 131.19–133.21[?]; 137.3–146.20).

140. Catalogued in Koester, *Ancient Christian Gospels* 176-85, and see his conclusion (186-87).

141. C. M. Tuckett, *Nag Hammadi and the Gospel Tradition* (Edinburgh: Clark, 1986) 128-35, referring particularly to §53 (Matt. 6.34; 10.10, 24) and §§3, 16, and 90 (Luke 21.8; 17.20-21; 11.1).

142. *Ancient Christian Gospels* 180.

143. Translation by F. E. Williams in Robinson, ed., *Nag Hammadi Library* 29-37, and D. Kirchner in Schneemelcher and Wilson, *New Testament Apocrypha* 1.285-99; Elliott, *Apocryphal New Testament* 673-81 (with bibliography); analysis in R. Cameron, *Sayings Traditions in the Apocryphon of James* (Philadelphia: Fortress, 1984), and Koester, *Ancient Christian Gospels* 187-200.

144. *Ancient Christian Gospels* 191-96, 200, largely following Cameron, *Sayings Traditions*. Since the earlier tradition cannot be separated out as a unified first-century source, Crossan includes *Apoc. Jas.* only in his fourth stratum (120-150 CE) (*Historical Jesus* 432).

(e.g. 10.1-6; 12.4-9) and the parallels could very well be explained as echoes of tradition known from the canonical Gospels.[145]

c. *'The Secret Gospel of Mark'*[146] refers to a version of Mark's Gospel which Clement of Alexandria regarded as a 'more spiritual' elaboration of canonical Mark, and which the Carpocratians (a second-century Gnostic sect) further amplified.[147] The two extracts follow Mark 10.34 and 10.46a respectively: the former and longer recounts the raising of a young man and appears to be a variation of the raising of Lazarus in John 11; the latter recounts briefly Jesus' encounter with the young man's sister and mother and Salome. Crossan and Koester, however, both argue that canonical Mark is derived from *Secret Mark*, the two extracts adding to the store of pre-canonical Gospel tradition and confirming the diversity of that earlier tradition.[148] On the parallels between the Secret Gospel and John 11, Koester thinks it 'impossible that *Secret Mark* is dependent upon John 11';[149] but he does not even consider the possibility that the *Secret Mark* version is an allusive echo of John's account. With such logic, the recognition of any allusion to earlier documents would be equally 'impossible'. On the several parallels between *Secret Mark* and phrases from different parts of Mark, Crossan thinks it probable that 'canonical Mark scattered the dismembered elements of those units throughout his gospel'.[150] But that is a highly implausible scenario; it is much more likely that *Secret Mark* is a composition drawing on remembered phrases from other stories in canonical Mark.[151] The

145. Tuckett, *Nag Hammadi* 88-97. Cf. particularly 4.23-30 with Mark 10.28-30 and Matt. 6.13. The echoes of John's Gospel are strong: the ascending-descending motif in 14.19–15.35; and cf. *Apoc. Jas.* 7.1-6 with John 16.29 and *Apoc. Jas.* 12.41–13.1 with John 20.29. Is there an echo of Gal. 3.13 in *Apoc. Jas.* 13.23-25?

146. H. Merkel, in Schneemelcher and Wilson, *New Testament Apocrypha* 1.106-9; Elliott, *Apocryphal New Testament* 148-49 (with bibliography); also Cameron, *Other Gospels* 67-71; Miller, ed., *Complete Gospels* 408-11; analysis in Koester, *Ancient Christian Gospels* 293-303.

147. See Crossan's helpful account in *Four Other Gospels* 98-100.

148. Crossan, *Historical Jesus* 328-32, 411-16.

149. *Ancient Christian Gospels* 296, despite Crossan's recognition of the unwisdom of such an emphatic and unyielding term ('impossible'), citing R. E. Brown, 'The Relation of "The Secret Gospel of Mark" to the Fourth Gospel', *CBQ* 36 (1974) 466-85 (here 470, 474) (*Four Other Gospels* 104-105).

150. Crossan, *Four Other Gospels* 108; further *Historical Jesus* 415-16; there are parallel phrases in Mark 10.47; 10.13-14; 14.51; 1.41; 5.41; 9.27; 10.21, 22; 9.2; 14.51-52; 4.11; 3.33-34.

151. Similarly F. F. Bruce, *The 'Secret' Gospel of Mark* (London: Athlone, 1974): 'an obvious pastiche . . . a thoroughly artificial composition, quite out of keeping with Mark's quality as a story-teller' (12); Merkel, *New Testament Apocrypha* 1.107; Charlesworth and Evans, 'Jesus in the Agrapha' 526-32. Nor is it self-evident that the absence of some of these phrases from Matthew and Luke indicates that they appear in Mark as 'secondary redaction' (Koester, *Ancient Christian Gospels* 298); Matthew and Luke regularly omit or qualify phrases and motifs in their use of Mark.

fallacy here, as elsewhere, is to assume that what is in view must be some kind of literary editing process, whereas many traditions even when already written down would still have been remembered orally.

d. As for the so-called *'Cross Gospel'* disinterred from the *Gospel of Peter* by Crossan and regarded by him as a source for all four canonical Gospels and combined with an 'intercanonical stratum' to make up the *Gospel of Peter* it-self,[152] very little need be said. Crossan's failure to persuade Koester has already been noted,[153] and his response to Raymond Brown's critique of his own earlier treatment[154] does not change the position much at all.[155] It is certainly true that the *Gospel of Peter* itself[156] may bear witness to accounts of Jesus' Passion which circulated orally apart from the canonical Gospels and on which both the canonical Gospels and Peter were able to draw, each to retell in his own way and with his own variation and elaboration.[157] On the other hand, Ron Cameron's suggestion that 'the document as we have it antedates the four gospels of the New Testament and may have served as a source for their respective authors'[158] pushes the 'independent therefore earlier' fallacy to an extreme.[159]

152. *The Cross That Spoke* 17, 20.

153. Above, chapter 4 n. 172.

154. R. E. Brown, 'The Gospel of Peter and Canonical Gospel Priority', *NTS* 33 (1987) 321-43, in response to Crossan, *Four Other Gospels* 123-81; also Brown, *The Death of the Messiah* (New York: Doubleday, 1994) 1317-49. See also J. B. Green, 'The Gospel of Peter: Source for a Pre-Canonical Passion Narrative?', *ZNW* 78 (1987) 293-301; F. Neirynck, 'The Apocryphal Gospels and the Gospel of Mark', *BETL* 86 (1989) 123-75, reprinted in *Evangelica II* (Leuven: Leuven University, 1991) 715-62 (here 744-49); A. Kirk, 'Examining Priorities: Another Look at the *Gospel of Peter*'s Relationship to the New Testament Gospels', *NTS* 40 (1994) 572-95; Charlesworth and Evans, 'Jesus in the Agrapha' 503-14.

155. Crossan, *Birth* 55-58, 481-525.

156. Translations by C. Maurer in Schneemelcher and Wilson, *New Testament Apocrypha* 1.223-7, and Cameron, *Other Gospels* 78-82; and by Elliott, *Apocryphal New Testament* 154-58 (with bibliography 151-54); Miller, ed., *Complete Gospels* 399-407; analysis in Koester, *Ancient Christian Gospels* 216-40; the Greek text is appended in Neirynck, *Evangelica II* 763-67.

157. Cf. Koester, *Ancient Christian Gospels* 220-30, 240, with reference to the Passion narrative; Brown, 'Gospel of Peter' 333-38, whose reminder of 'a second orality', when knowledge of already written Gospels would still depend on hearing and oral communication (335), is apposite. On the suggestion of a common old tradition, note the hesitations of Schneemelcher, *New Testament Apocrypha* 1.219. Neirynck, *Evangelica II* 735-40, is confident that dependence on Mark can be demonstrated for the resurrection narrative (*Gospel of Peter* 50-57), a conclusion from which Koester does not demur (239).

158. Cameron, *Other Gospels* 78. Crossan's earlier suggestion that literate Galilean Christians might have assumed that Herod Antipas could be responsible for ordering a crucifixion in Jerusalem and the people (not soldiers) be responsible for carrying it out (as the *Gospel of Peter* narrates) is hardly credible (*Historical Jesus* 287).

159. Two phrases have usually been regarded as docetic (10 — at his crucifixion Jesus

e. Other sources dealt with by Crossan and Koester can be mentioned briefly. It is difficult to assess the significance of Papyrus Egerton 2 with its striking parallels to John 5.39-46; 9.29; and 10.31, 39 and Mark 1.40-44; 12.13-15; and 7.6-7.[160] The parallels to Mark and John may be explained in several ways, of which use of traditions earlier than and independent of Mark and John is only one.[161] Certainly Pap. Eg. 2 may provide further witness to the different versions in which stories about Jesus were circulated; but it is equally possible that the parallels are the result of hearing these Gospels read or of oral circulation of what these Gospels narrated.[162] Once again, we must take care lest we unconsciously assume a literary interdependency or a deliberate scissors and paste redaction.

f. For completeness we should also mention the often canvassed possibility that collections of miracle stories lie behind Mark[163] and John.[164] Other questions, as to whether Mark was able to draw on further pre-formed tradition, for example, groupings of parables (Mark 4) and apocalyptic material (Mark 13), as also the question of an already extensive Passion narrative prior to Mark, are

---

'was silent, as if he felt no pain'; 19 — Jesus' final cry on the cross, 'My power, O power, thou hast forsaken me!'); but here too note the hesitations of Schneemelcher, *New Testament Apocrypha* 1.220-21.

160. J. Jeremias and W. Schneemelcher in Schneemelcher and Wilson, *New Testament Apocrypha* 1.96-99; Elliott, *Apocryphal New Testament* 37-40 (with bibliography); analysis in Koester, *Ancient Christian Gospels* 205-16.

161. Koester, *Ancient Christian Gospels* is too confident that the direction of influence is more likely to have been from Pap. Eg. 2 to John than vice-versa (208-11); e.g., talk of Jesus' 'hour . . . not yet come' is distinctively Johannine (John 7.30), and reference to the 'hour' in Mark 14.35 is much more remote (211). Similarly overconfident is Cameron, *Other Gospels* 71-73.

162. Schneemelcher, *New Testament Apocrypha* 97; Elliott, *Apocryphal New Testament* 38; Charlesworth and Evans, 'Jesus in the Agrapha' 514-25 (here 521-22); Miller, ed., *Complete Gospels* 412; and particularly F. Neirynck, 'Apocryphal Gospels and Mark' 753-59 (with additional notes (771-72); also 'Papyrus Egerton 2 and the Healing of the Leper', *ETL* 61 (1985) 153-60, reprinted in *Evangelica II* 773-79 with additional notes (1985 and 1991) added (780-83). The suggestion that Pap. Eg. 2 indicates a pre-canonical combination of Johannine and Synoptic materials (Crossan, *Four Other Gospels* 75) is much less likely.

163. See particularly P. A. Achtemeier, 'Towards the Isolation of Pre-Markan Catenae', *JBL* 89 (1970) 265-91; also 'The Origin and Function of the Pre-Markan Miracle Catenae', *JBL* 91 (1972) 198-221; Koester, *Ancient Christian Gospels* 201-203, 286-87.

164. Crossan, *Historical Jesus* 429-30; Koester, *Ancient Christian Gospels* 203-205, 251-53, 286-87. Miller, ed., *Complete Gospels* 175-93, attempts a reconstruction of the Signs Gospel hypothesized to lie behind John, based on the work of R. T. Fortna, *The Fourth Gospel and Its Predecessor* (Philadelphia: Fortress, 1988). The significance of such collections (aretalogies) as early ways of presenting Jesus ('Jesus as the Divine Man') was already signalled by Koester in his 'One Jesus and Four Primitive Gospels' 187-93.

matters which may be noted here but are best held for consideration until we look more closely at the traditioning process (§8.6).

7.9. Knowledge of Jesus' Teaching and Agrapha

To complete the review of sources for the teaching of Jesus we should also refer to specific references to such teaching in Paul (1 Cor. 7.10-11; 9.14; 11.23-25) and to the likelihood that Paul and other early letter writers alluded to the traditions of Jesus' teaching on several occasions. The question however is somewhat complex and is best left till later (§8.1e).

Also to be mentioned are the agrapha (unknown sayings) of Jesus attributed to him in the rest of the New Testament (particularly Acts 20.35), in variant readings in the Gospels (particularly Luke 6.4 D), and in Patristic sources (notably *GTh* 82, cited by Origen, *on Jer. Hom.* 3.3).[165] They do not add much to the overall picture, their credibility as sayings of Jesus largely depending on their compatibility with the more familiar Synoptic traditions. But they do constitute a further reminder that there must have been a fairly lively oral tradition of Jesus' sayings which continued to be circulated apart from the canonical Gospels. It is a fuller consideration of that tradition to which we must now turn.

---

165. Overlapping collections by O. Hofius in Schneemelcher and Wilson, *New Testament Apocrypha* 1.88-91, and Elliott, *Apocryphal New Testament* 26-30 (with bibliography); see also Charlesworth and Evans, 'Jesus in the Agrapha' 479-95; W. G. Morrice, *Hidden Sayings of Jesus: Words Attributed to Jesus outside the Four Gospels* (London: SPCK, 1997).

CHAPTER 8

The Tradition

Few if any today assume that the written sources take the reader back directly to the Jesus who worked and taught in Galilee three or more decades earlier. But equally, few if any doubt that behind the written sources there was earlier tradition.[1] The question is whether this earlier tradition fully or only partially bridges the period between Jesus and our present sources. Form criticism provided a partial answer, but, as we saw, its early thrust seems to have been redirected into an unending debate about criteria. And the neo-Liberal quest for new sources seems to be falling into the old trap of thinking in terms only of written sources. But what of the earlier tradition? As David Du Toit observes, there are both 'a complete lack of consensus on one of the most fundamental questions of the whole enterprise, namely on the question of the process of transmission of the Jesus traditions', and an 'urgent need to develop a comprehensive theory of the process of transmission of tradition in early Christianity'.[2] In fact, however, there are a perspective on the Jesus tradition which has only recently been properly recognized, and a rich potential in a fresh understanding of the Jesus tradition as *orally* transmitted which has hardly begun to be fully tapped. In this chapter I want to take the first steps towards developing a theory of transmission which would meet the need indicated by Du Toit.

---

1. Since I make considerable use of this term ('tradition'), I should define how I am using it. Expressed in very general terms, 'tradition' denotes both content and mode of transmission: the content is typically beliefs and customs which are regarded as stemming from the past and which have become authoritative; the mode is informal, typically word of mouth. At one end of its spectrum of usage 'tradition' has to be distinguished from individual memory, though it could be described as corporate memory giving identity to the group which thus remembers. At the other end it has to be distinguished from formal rules and written law, though its being written down need not change its character, initially at any rate.

2. Du Toit, 'Redefining Jesus' 123-24.

8.1. Jesus the Founder of Christianity[3]

We have already noted the irony that for most of its existence, the 'quest of the historical Jesus' was not historical enough in that it attempted to distance Jesus, by one means or another, from his historical context as a Jew. As many of the rationalists, savaged by Strauss, had attempted to 'save' the miracle-working Jesus by allowing a little bit of miracle, so most of the Liberals had attempted to 'save' the real Jesus by 'inoculating' the quest with a little bit of history. At the same time, the other strand in 'life of Jesus' research, from Reimarus to the neo-Liberals, has attempted to 'save' Jesus from Christian dogma by distancing him from the movement which followed his death and which became Christianity. In the most common scenario, it was Paul who counts (or is to be blamed!) as the real founder of Christianity.[4] This has been one of the real peculiarities of the quest, that it has attempted to find a Jesus who was neither a Jew nor founder of Christianity, or who was contingently one but not the other.[5] But in seeking to avoid the Christianized Jesus as well as the Jewish Jesus, all that remained, all that could remain, was the idiosyncratic Jesus, who could hardly be other than an enigma to Jew and Christian alike, and who reflected little more than the quester's own idiosyncracies.

In fact, the obvious way forward is simply to reverse the logic. If the starting assumption of a fair degree of continuity between Jesus and his native religion has *a priori* persuasiveness, then it can hardly make less sense to assume a fair degree of continuity between Jesus and what followed.[6] The initial considerations here are straightforward.

a. The Sociological Logic

Several indicators have long been familiar. For one thing, it has long been recognized that the historian needs to envisage a Jesus who is 'big' enough to explain the beginnings of Christianity.[7] For another, the first followers of Jesus were

---

3. For convenience I use the title of Dodd, *Founder,* similarly B. F. Meyer, 'Jesus Christ', *ABD* 3.795, though of course, the use of 'Christianity' as a term for what Jesus 'founded' is anachronistic.

4. See again Wrede cited above chapter 1 at n. 18.

5. The attitude was typified by the second quest's criteria of double dissimilarity which set the distinctiveness of Jesus over against both Judaism and church (see above §5.4 at n. 68). T. Holmén, 'Doubts about Double Dissimilarity: Restructuring the Main Criterion of Jesus-of-History Research', in Chilton and Evans, eds., *Authenticating the Words of Jesus* 47-80, argues that 'dissimilarity to Christianity alone suffices as an argument for authenticity' (74-75).

6. Cf. Wright's argument for a criterion of double similarity (above chapter 5 n. 132).

7. Sanders put the point well by referring to the second half of 'Klausner's test': a good hypothesis regarding Jesus will explain why the movement initiated by him eventually broke

known as 'Nazarenes' (Acts 24.5), which can be explained only by the fact that they saw themselves and were seen as followers of 'Jesus the Nazarene';[8] and then as 'Christians' (Acts 11.26),[9] which again must be because they were known to be followers of the one they called the 'Christ'. Moreover, Jesus is explicitly referred to once or twice in the early tradition as the 'foundation' *(themelion),* which Paul laid (including Jesus tradition?),[10] and on which the Corinthians were to build their discipleship (1 Cor. 3.10-14); or as the 'corner stone' *(akrogōniaios)* which began the building and established its orientation (Eph. 2.20; 1 Pet. 2.6).[11]

Sociological reflection on what this self-identification on the part of the Christians would have involved yields further fruit. Here, after all, were small house groups who designated themselves by reference to Jesus the Christ, or Christ Jesus. Sociology and social anthropology teach us that such groups would almost certainly have required a foundation story (or stories) to explain, to themselves as well as to others, why they had formed distinct social groupings, why they were designated as 'Nazarenes' and 'Christians'. It is hardly likely that a bare kerygmatic formula like 1 Cor. 15.3-8 would have provided sufficient material for self-identification.[12] Even the initiatory myths of the mystery cults told more elaborate stories.[13] Stories of such diverse figures as Jeremiah and Diogenes were preserved by their disciples as part of the legitimation for their own commitment.[14] And if Moses is to be regarded as the nearest equivalent (as founder of the religion of Israel), then we need simply recall that Exodus to Deuteronomy are framed and interspersed by the story of Moses' life. Of course, counter-examples can be named: we know very little of Qumran's Teacher of Righteousness.[15] On the other hand, the Teacher of Righteousness never gave his

---

with Judaism *(Jesus* 18). Wright reiterates the point in his own terms: e.g., 'Jesus must be understood as a comprehensible and yet, so to speak, crucifiable first-century Jew, whatever the theological or hermeneutical consequences' *(Jesus* 86).

8. See below chapter 9 n. 272.

9. See further below, vol. 2.

10. See below §8.1b-e.

11. The term *akrogōniaios* designates 'the foundation stone at its farthest corner, with which a building is begun — it firmly fixes its site and determines its direction' (H. Krämer, *EDNT* 1.268).

12. Against those who assume that the kerygma of cross and resurrection not only overshadowed the traditions of Jesus' pre-Good Friday ministry but also in effect expunged them from the corporate memory.

13. See, e.g., Plutarch's treatment of the myth of Isis and Osiris, J. G. Griffiths, *Plutarch's de Iside et Osiride* (Cardiff: University of Wales, 1970).

14. Jeremiah, e.g., 1.1-10 (dates and call); 19.14–20.6; 28; 32; 36–42. Dio Chrysostom, *Sixth Discourse: Diogenes, or on Tyranny* (Loeb 1.250-83); Diogenes Laertius, *Lives* 6.20-81.

15. The basic treatment is still G. Jeremias, *Der Lehrer der Gerechtigkeit* (SUNT 2; Göttingen: Vandenhoeck und Ruprecht, 1963).

name to the movement he initiated, whereas the first Christians could explain themselves only by reference to him whom they called '(the) Christ'. But if the Gospels tell us anything they surely tell us that the first Christians felt the need to explain themselves by telling stories about Jesus, what he said and what he did.[16]

b. Teachers and Tradition

This *a priori* logic is supported by the evidence that the passing on of *tradition* was part of church founding from the first. Paul was careful to refer his churches back to such foundation traditions on several occasions;[17] the evidence is hardly to be explained as references solely to kerygmatic or confessional formulae. Rather, we find that it includes community tradition (1 Cor. 11.2, 23), teaching on how the new converts should live (e.g., Phil. 4.9; 1 Thess. 4.1; 2 Thess. 3.6), and traditions of Jesus in accordance with which they should conduct their lives (Col. 2.6-7; *kata Christon* in 2.8).[18]

If further confirmation is needed, it is provided by the prominence of *teachers* within the earliest Christian churches.[19] Teachers, indeed, seem to have been the first regularly paid ministry within the earliest Christian movement (Gal. 6.6; *Did.* 13.2). Why teachers? Why else than to serve as the congregation's repository of oral tradition? What else would Christian teachers teach? A Christian interpretation of the Scriptures, no doubt. But also, we can surely safely assume, the traditions which distinguished house churches from local house synagogues or other religious, trade, or burial societies.[20]

We should pause at this point to recall just how crucial teachers were to ancient communities. All who read these pages will have been bred to a society

16. Moule is one of remarkably few who recognized this fundamental (human) need in his *Birth of the New Testament;* chs. 3-6, each entitled 'The Church Explains Itself' in different ways.

17. 1 Cor. 11.2, 23; 15.1-3; Phil. 4.9; Col. 2.6-7; 1 Thess. 4.1; 2 Thess. 2.15; 3.6.

18. See my *Colossians and Philemon* (NIGTC; Grand Rapids: Eerdmans, 1996) 138-41, 151; and further my *Theology of Paul* 194-95.

19. Acts 13.1; Rom. 12.7; 1 Cor. 12.28-29; Eph. 4.11; Heb. 5.12; Jas 3.1; *Did.* 15.1-2.

20. See also A. F. Zimmermann, *Die urchristlichen Lehrer* (WUNT 2.12; Tübingen: Mohr Siebeck, 1984), though he pushes too hard his thesis that in the early community *(Urgemeinde)* the teachers formed a Jewish-Christian-Pharisaic circle. From what we know of more formal teaching in the schools, we can be sure that oral instruction was the predominant means: 'it is the "living voice" of the teacher that has priority' (L. C. A. Alexander, 'The Living Voice: Scepticism Towards the Written Word in Early Christianity and in Graeco-Roman Texts', in D. J. A. Clines, et al., eds., *The Bible in Three Dimensions: Essays in Celebration of Forty Years of Biblical Studies in the University of Sheffield* [Sheffield: Sheffield Academic, 1990] 221-47 [here 244]).

long accustomed to being able to rely on textbooks, encyclopaedias, and other reference works. But an ancient oral society had few if any such resources and had to rely instead on individuals whose role in their community was to function as what Jan Vansina describes as 'a walking reference library'.[21]

Nor should it be forgotten that, at least according to the tradition, Jesus himself was regarded as a 'teacher' *(didaskalos),*[22] and was so regarded by his disciples.[23] Jesus may even have regarded himself as such (Matt. 10.24-25/Luke 6.40). That the disciples of Jesus are consistently called 'disciples', that is 'those taught, learners' (Hebrew *talmidim;* Greek *mathētai*) — should also be included.[24] The relation between Jesus and his disciples was remembered as one between teacher and taught, with the implication that, as such, the disciples understood themselves to be committed to remember their teacher's teaching.[25]

c. Witnessing and Remembering

Two important motifs in the NT also confirm the importance for the first Christians of retelling the story of Jesus and of taking steps actively to recall what Jesus said and did.

One is the motif of *'bearing witness'.* The motif is particularly prominent in Acts and John. In Acts it is stressed that the role of the first disciples (or apostles in particular) was to be 'witnesses' *(martyres)* of Jesus (1.8). Particularly in mind were the events of Jesus' crucifixion and resurrection (2.32; 3.15; 5.32; 10.41; 13.31).[26] But it is clear from 1.22 and 10.37-39 that Luke understood the witnessing to include Jesus' ministry 'beginning from the baptism of John'. Paul preeminently is presented as a 'witness' of Jesus (22.15, 18; 23.11; 26.16). In John's Gospel the importance of witness-bearing to Jesus is equally stressed.

21. J. Vansina, *Oral Tradition as History* (Madison: University of Wisconsin, 1985) 37.

22. Mark 5.35/Luke 8.49; Mark 9.17/Luke 9.38; Mark 10.17/Matt. 19.16/Luke 18.18; Mark 10.20; Mark 12.14, 19, 32/Matt. 22.16, 24, 36/Luke 20.21, 28, 39; Matt. 8.19; 9.11; 12.38; 17.24; Luke 7.40; 10.25; 11.45; 12.13; 19.39.

23. Mark 4.38; 9.38; 10.35; 13.1/Luke 21.7; Mark 14.14/Matt. 26.18/Luke 22.11; though it is noticeable that Matthew and Luke seem to have avoided the term (for the most part) on the lips of the disciples, presumably as not being sufficiently exalted.

24. *Mathētēs* ('disciple') is used frequently in the Gospels — Matthew 73, Mark 46, Luke 37, John 78.

25. R. Riesner, *Jesus als Lehrer* (WUNT 2.7; Tübingen: Mohr Siebeck, 1981) has particularly emphasized this feature of the tradition (particularly 246-66, 357-79, 408-53); also 'Jesus as Preacher and Teacher', in Wansbrough, ed., *Jesus and the Oral Gospel Tradition* 185-210. See further below §15.8.

26. The implication of 1 Cor. 15.6 is that most of the 'more than five hundred' to whom Jesus had appeared were still alive, and thus able to confirm the witness of the kerygma.

John the Baptist is the model witness (1.7-8, 15, 19, 32, 34; 3.26, 28; 5.32), but also the woman at the well (4.39) and the crowd (12.17). The immediate disciples have a special responsibility to bear witness *(martyreō)* to Jesus, assisted by the Spirit (15.26-27), a responsibility which the Evangelist was deemed to be carrying out by means of his Gospel (19.35; 21.24).[27]

The motif runs over into the Johannine epistles (1 John 1.2; 4.14), where it is strengthened by two complementary motifs. One is the 'from the beginning' *(ap' archēs)* theme: what is borne witness to is 'that which was from the beginning' (1.1), what the witnesses heard 'from the beginning' (2.24), particularly the command to love one another (2.7; 3.11; 2 John 5-6); in John 15.26-27 it is made clear that 'from the beginning' embraces the whole of the original disciples' time with Jesus (as with Acts 1.22). Luke had the same concern when he promised to narrate what had been 'delivered to us by those who from the beginning were eyewitnesses[28] and ministers of the word' (Luke 1.1-2; cf. Mark 1.1).[29]

The other complementary theme emphasizes the importance of a continuity of 'hearing' from first disciples to converts, and of the converts both retaining what they had 'heard' and living in accord with it — again not only in the Johannine epistles,[30] but also in Heb. 2.1, 3 and in the later Paulines.[31] All this indicates a strong sense within first-century Christianity of the need to ensure a continuity of tradition from first witnesses to subsequent disciples and of a life lived in consistency with that tradition.

More striking still is the motif of *'remembering'*, also important for identity formation.[32] Already Paul stresses the importance of his converts remembering him and the 'traditions' which he taught them (1 Cor. 11.2; 2 Thess. 2.5). And close to the heart of the Lord's Supper tradition which Paul passed on was the exhortation to remember Christ — 'Do this in remembrance of me' *(eis tēn emēn anamnēsin)* (1 Cor. 11.24-25; Luke 22.19) — by no means a merely cognitive act of recollection.[33] 2 Timothy retains the motif with reference to well-established

27. Note also 1 Pet. 5.1; Rev. 1.2, 9; 6.9; 12.11, 17; 19.10; 20.4.

28. S. Byrskog, *Story as History — History as Story: The Gospel Tradition in the Context of Ancient Oral History* (WUNT 123; Tübingen: Mohr Siebeck, 2000) has given particular emphasis to the importance of eyewitness testimony ('autopsy') as source for the Gospel traditions (see, e.g., 69-70, 103-104, 106-107, 162, 247, 292).

29. It is often noted that use of 'the word' *(logos)* in Luke 1.2 approaches the Johannine concept of Jesus as 'the word' (John 1.14; 1 John 1.1).

30. 1 John 1.1, 3, 5; 2.24; 3.11; 2 John 6.

31. Particularly Eph. 4.21; 2 Tim. 1.13; 2.2. See also §13.1 below.

32. Schröter draws on A. Assmann, *Das kulturelle Gedächtnis: Schrift, Erinnerung und politische Identität in frühen Hochkulturen* (München, 1992) in stressing 'the concept of *remembering* as an identity-establishing and thus also cultural phenomenon' (*Erinnerung* 462-63).

33. See particularly O. Hofius, 'The Lord's Supper and the Lord's Supper Tradition: Re-

traditions (2.8, 14), the first (2.8) echoing the (presumably well-known) formula with which Paul reassured the Roman believers regarding his own gospel (Rom. 1.3-4).[34] The importance of post-Easter believers remembering Jesus' words is a repeated theme in Luke-Acts and John;[35] the equivalence of John 14.26 and 15.27 indicates that 'remembering all I have said to you', and 'witnesses with me from the beginning', are two sides of the same coin. 2 Peter confirms that remembering the teaching first given was a central concern in early Christianity (1.15; 3.2); similarly Rev. 3.3. *1 Clement* uses the phrase 'remember(ing) the words of the Lord Jesus' to introduce a brief catena of Jesus' sayings on two occasions (13.1-2; 46.7-8), as does Polycarp with a similar introductory formula, 'remembering what the Lord taught when he said' (*Phil.* 2.3). Here we should also simply note the famous Papias tradition, which repeatedly emphasises the importance of 'remembering' in the transmission of the earliest traditions stemming from the first disciples (Eusebius, *HE* 3.39.3-4, 15; 6.14.6), and Justin's concern to 'bring to remembrance' teachings of Jesus (*Dial.* 18.1; *1 Apol.* 14.4).[36]

Cameron argues that 'the formulaic employment of this term ("remembering") to introduce collections of sayings of Jesus is a practice which began with the relatively free production of sayings traditions . . .'.[37] And it is certainly true that the motif includes some freedom in the transmission of the sayings in view.[38] But the idea of remembering Jesus tradition is as early as our earliest references to such tradition (Paul). And it is notable that John, despite his freedom in producing dialogues of Jesus, seems for the most part to have restricted the remembering motif to sayings which have clear Synoptic parallels, that is, which were well rooted in Jesus tradition.[39] It is more likely, then, that the use of the motif in the

---

flections on 1 Corinthians 11.23b-25', in B. F. Meyer, ed., *One Loaf, One Cup: Ecumenical Studies of 1 Cor. 11 and Other Eucharistic Texts* (Macon, Ga.: Mercer University, 1993) 75-115 (here 103-11); W. Schrage, *Der erste Brief an die Korinther* (EKK VII, 4 vols.; Zürich: Benziger, 1991, 1995, 1999, 2001) 3.41-42.

34. For more detail see my *Romans* (WBC 38; Dallas: Word, 1988) 5-6.

35. Luke 24.6, 8; Acts 11.16; 20.35; John 2.22; 12.16; 14.26; 15.20; 16.4.

36. As is well known, Justin called the Gospels 'memoirs, recollections *(apomnēmoneumata)*' of the apostles (*1 Apol.* 66.3; *Dial.* 100.4). The point was properly emphasized in a neglected essay by N. A. Dahl, 'Anamnesis: Memory and Commemoration in Early Christianity' (1946), *Jesus in the Memory of the Early Church* (Minneapolis: Augsburg, 1976) 11-29.

37. *Sayings Traditions* ch. 3 (here 112).

38. Cf. Koester, *Ancient Christian Gospels* 70. But Cameron also notes Polycarp's 'tendency to bring such collections into conformity with the written gospels of his church' (*Sayings Traditions* 113); or, once again, is it rather the case that the tradition was known in variant forms?

39. John 2.19-22 (Mark 14.58 par.); John 12.14-16 (Mark 11.1-10 pars.); John 15.20 (Matt. 10.24-25); the only exception is John 16.4.

Apocryphon of James (Cameron's main focus) was an attempt to manipulate a well-established and deeply rooted concern (to remember Jesus' teaching) by using it to commend a sayings tradition laced with 'secret' (Gnostic) elements.[40]

In short, the witnessing and remembering motifs strengthen the impression that more or less from the first those who established new churches would have taken care to provide and build a foundation of Jesus tradition. Particularly important for Gentiles taking on a wholly new life-style and social identity would be guidelines and models for the different character of conduct now expected from them. Such guidelines and models were evidently provided by a solid basis of Jesus tradition which they were expected to remember, to take in and live out.

d. Apostolic Custodians

The idea of the 'apostles' as themselves the foundation of the church, or of the new Jerusalem, appears already in Eph. 2.20 and Rev. 21.14. More striking is the fact that a clear emphasis of the early chapters of Acts is the role of the apostles as ensuring continuity between what Jesus had taught and the expanding mission of the movement reinvigorated afresh at Pentecost. The implication of the opening words is that Acts is a continuation of 'all that Jesus began to do and teach' as recorded in 'the first part of his work', the Gospel of Luke (Acts 1.1). The instruction given to the apostles (1.2), the implication continues, had just the same continuity in view.[41] Hence, when the traitor Judas is replaced by a new twelfth apostle, the criterion for his election is that he should have been one of their number throughout the ministry of Jesus, 'beginning from the baptism of John' (1.21-22). Hence also the emphasis in 2.42, where the first mark of the new post-Pentecost community is its continuation in and firm attachment to *(proskartereō)* 'the teaching of the apostles'.

Such an emphasis might be regarded as a late perspective, when, arguably, continuity questions would have become (more) important. But there are indications that such continuity was seen as important from the first. These indications focus on the importance of Peter, James, and John to which our texts testify. They were evidently reckoned as the first men among the leaders of the initial Jerusalem community (Acts 1.13) — Peter certainly (1.15; 2.14; 5.1-10, 15, 29),

---

40. 'Now the twelve disciples [were] sitting all together at [the same time], and remembering what the Savior had said to each one of them, whether secretly or openly, they were setting it down in books' (*Apoc. Jas.* 2.1 Cameron).

41. More than any other Evangelist, Luke emphasizes the role of the disciples as 'apostles' (Luke 6.13; 9.10; 17.5; 22.14; 24.10).

with John as his faithful shadow (3.1-11; 4.13, 19; 8.14), and James by implication (12.2). Fortunately for any concerned at such over-dependence on Acts, Paul's testimony confirms that a Jerusalem triumvirate (with James the brother of Jesus replacing James the executed brother of John) were generally accounted 'pillars' (Gal. 2.9). The imagery clearly implies that already, within twenty years of the beginnings of the new movement, these three were seen as strong supports on which the new community (temple?) was being built.[42] This correlates well with the remembrance of the Jesus tradition that Peter and the brothers Zebedee had been closest to Jesus[43] and thus were accounted principal witnesses to and custodians of Jesus' heritage.

Paul's concept of apostleship is somewhat different from Luke's. But it coheres to the extent that Paul regarded his apostolic role to consist particularly in founding churches (Rom. 15.20; 1 Cor. 3.10; 9.1-2). And, as we have seen, a fundamental part of that role was to pass on foundation tradition (above §8.1b).

e. How the Jesus Tradition Was Used

The circumstantial and cumulative evidence cited above is not usually given the weight I am placing upon it, because Paul in particular seems to show so little interest in the ministry of Jesus and so little knowledge of Jesus tradition.[44] We cannot assume that he ever encountered Jesus personally or had been in Jerusalem during the time of Jesus' mission.[45] On the other hand, Paul would surely have used the two weeks spent in Peter's company (three years after his conversion) to fill out his knowledge of Jesus and of the traditions of Jesus' mission and teaching from Jesus' leading disciple (Gal. 1.18).[46] Nevertheless, the fact remains that Paul cites Jesus explicitly on only three occasions, all curiously in 1 Corinthians (7.10-11; 9.14; 11.23-25), though he also implies that had he known Jesus tradition relevant to other issues of community discipline he would

42. See my *The Partings of the Ways between Christianity and Judaism* (London: SCM, 1991) 60; and further below §13.3.

43. Mark 5.37/Luke 8.51; Mark 9.2 pars.; 13.3; 14.33/Matt. 26.37.

44. Funk, e.g., stands in a line of argument stretching from Reimarus and through Baur in claiming that Paul was 'alienated from the original disciples and, as a consequence, from the written gospel tradition' (*Honest* 36).

45. At the same time, it can scarcely be credited that Paul received his training as a Pharisee away from Jerusalem (see below, vol. 2); if so, given the timescale between Jesus' death and Paul's conversion (perhaps only two years), the probability that he was indeed present in Jerusalem during the climax of Jesus' mission becomes quite strong. The evaluation of this possibility still suffers from the influence of the reading of 2 Cor. 5.16 common in the early decades of the twentieth century (see above §5.3; and further Dunn, *Theology of Paul* 184-85).

46. See again my *Theology of Paul* 188; and above §7.2.

have cited it (1 Cor. 7.25; 14.37).[47] At the same time, there are various echoes of Synoptic tradition in Paul's letters,[48] but none which he refers explicitly to Jesus; nor does he cite Jesus' authority to give the teaching more weight.

Does this evidence suggest Paul's own lack of interest in 'remembering' what Jesus said and that it was Jesus who said it? Those who argue for an affirmative answer seem to forget that the pattern we find in Paul's letters is repeated elsewhere within earliest Christianity, particularly in the letters of James and 1 Peter.[49]

47. 1 Thess. 4.15-17 is also frequently taken as a deliberate citation of a Jesus saying, though I doubt it (see my *Theology of Paul* 303-304).

48. Arguably among the most striking are:

Rom. 1.16	Mark 8.38/Luke 9.26
Rom. 2.1/14.10	Luke 6.37/Matt. 7.1-2
Rom. 8.15-17/Gal. 4.4-6	Abba
Rom. 12.14	Luke 6.27-28/Matt. 5.44
Rom. 12.17/1 Thess. 5.15	Matt. 5.39/Luke 6.29
Rom. 12.18	Mark 9.50
Rom. 13.7	Mark 12.17 pars.
Rom. 13.9	Mark 12.31 pars.
Rom. 14.13	Mark 9.42 pars.
Rom. 14.14	Mark 7.15
Rom. 14.17	kingdom of God
1 Cor. 2.7	Matt. 13.35
1 Cor. 13.2	Matt. 17.20
1 Thess. 5.2, 4	Matt. 24.43/Luke 12.39
1 Thess. 5.13	Mark 9.50

On the Romans passages see my *Romans* (WBC 38; Dallas: Word, 1988) *ad loc.;* see also Koester, *Ancient Christian Gospels* 52-57; other bibliography in my *Theology of Paul* 182. On the possibility that Paul knew Q (material) see Allison, *Jesus Tradition* 54-60 (with further bibliography). For Colossians see Col. 2.22 (Mark 7.7/Matt. 15.9); 3.13 (Matt. 6.12, 14-15; 18.23-35); 4.2 (Mark 13.35, 37; Matt. 24.42; 25.13).

49. James	1.5	Luke 11.9/Matt. 7.7
	2.5	Luke 6.20b/Matt. 5.3
	4.9	Luke 6.21b/Matt. 5.4
	4.10	Luke 14.11/Matt. 23.12
	5.1	Luke 6.24-25
	5.2-3a	Matt. 6.20/Luke 12.33b
	5.12	Matt. 5.34-37
1 Peter	2.12b	Matt. 5.16b
	2.19-20	Luke 6.32-33/Matt. 5.46-47
	3.9, 16	Luke 6.28/Matt. 5.44
	3.14	Matt. 5.10
	4.14	Luke 6.22/Matt. 5.11

For convenience I follow Koester's analysis (*Ancient Christian Gospels* 63-75). We should also note that 1 John must have known and valued the Johannine Jesus tradition; but we would hardly

Only occasionally is Jesus cited as the authority for the sayings quoted.[50] Usually the teaching which echoes the Jesus tradition is simply part of more extensive paraenesis, without explicit attribution to Jesus.

What are we to make of this? Given that James and 1 Peter probably take us into the second generation of Christianity, when the Synoptic tradition and the Synoptic Gospels themselves would be becoming known, it is very unlikely that in every case the authors were unaware that the teaching originated with Jesus. More plausible is the suggestion I have made elsewhere,[51] that we see in these data one of the ways the Jesus tradition was remembered and used. It is generally recognized that when groups become established over a lengthy period they develop in effect their own identity- and boundary-forming language, that is, at the very least, the use of abbreviations, a kind of shorthand and code words which help bond them as a group and distinguish insiders from outsiders (who do not know the language).[52] The whole point is that in in-group dialogue such in-references are *not* explained; on the contrary, it is the recognition of the code word or allusion which gives the insider-language its bonding effect; to unpack the reference or allusion (for a stranger) in effect breaks the bond and lets the outsider into the group's inner world.[53] My suggestion, then, is that the Jesus tradition formed such an insider's language among the earliest Christian communities; Paul's use of it in Romans (to a church he had never visited) implies his confidence that this language was a language common to all Christian churches, given by the founding apostle when he/she passed on the Jesus tradition to the new foundation (§§8.1a and b above).[54] In terms of the argument to be developed

---

know it from 1 John itself! On 'The Sayings of Jesus in the Letter of James' see W. H. Wachob and L. T. Johnson in Chilton and Evans, eds., *Authenticating the Words of Jesus* 431-50.

50. Acts 20.35; 1 Clem. 13.1-2; 46.7-8.

51. See my 'Jesus Tradition in Paul', in Chilton and Evans, *Studying the Historical Jesus* 155-78 (particularly 176-78); also *Theology of Paul* 651-53.

52. This would fit with the suggestions that the writers were able to draw on collections of sayings like those in the Lukan 'Sermon on the Plain' used for catechetical purposes (cf. D. C. Allison, 'The Pauline Epistles and the Synoptic Gospels: The Pattern of the Parallels', *NTS* 28 [1982] 1-32; Koester, *Ancient Christian Gospels* 54, 65-68). *Didache* perhaps indicates a pattern more widely followed: under the heading of 'the Lord's teaching' (1.1) extensive teaching is then given with only occasional reference to Jesus as its source; see also W. Rordorf, 'Does the *Didache* Contain Jesus Tradition Independently of the Synoptic Gospels?', in Wansbrough, ed., *Jesus* 394-423; I. Henderson, '*Didache* and Orality in Synoptic Comparison', *JBL* 111 (1992) 283-306; J. A. Draper, 'The Jesus Tradition in the *Didache*', in J. A. Draper, ed., *The Didache in Modern Research* (Leiden: Brill, 1996) 72-91; also Crossan's analysis in *Birth* 387-95.

53. See also Allison, *Jesus Tradition in Q* 111-19.

54. In the treatments cited above (n. 51) I also observe that in the only two passages where Paul cites the authority of Jesus in paraenesis (1 Cor. 7.10-11; 9.14) he goes on to qualify

below, we have to assume a wider knowledge of the Jesus story among the recipients of Paul's letters, which his auditors would be able to draw upon to bridge the 'gaps of indeterminacy' in his letters.[55]

In short, the fact that almost all the references to Jesus tradition in the writings of earliest Christianity are in the form of allusion and echo should be taken to confirm (1) that such letters were not regarded as the medium of initial instruction on Jesus tradition to new churches, and (2) that churches could be assumed to have a relatively extensive knowledge of Jesus tradition, presumably passed on to them when they were first established.[56]

f. The Gospels as Biographies

Bultmann led questers up another false trail by his strong assertion that 'There is no historical-biographical interest in the Gospels'.[57] The influence of this view, that the Gospels are not biographies of Jesus, persists to the present day.[58] However, it is too little recalled that on this point Bultmann was reacting against the Liberal questers' confidence that they could penetrate back into Jesus' self-consciousness and could trace the development of his self-understanding as Messiah (messianic self-consciousness).[59] Kähler had already responded to the Liberal questers by observing that the real sources for such attempts were the questers' own imaginations, an unfortunate extension of the historical principle

---

that teaching in some way; ironically he has to cite Jesus explicitly precisely *because* he is qualifying what Jesus was known to have said. In contrast, the allusive reminder of Jesus' teaching elsewhere effectively indicates that the authority of that teaching required neither justification nor qualification.

55. See below, §8.3g. The growing recognition that Paul's letters depend in at least some measure for their coherence on underlying 'stories' which he assumed is indicated by B. W. Longenecker, ed., *Narrative Dynamics in Paul: A Critical Assessment* (Louisville: Westminster John Knox, 2002).

56. See further C. F. D. Moule, 'Jesus in New Testament Kerygma' (1970), *Essays in New Testament Interpretation* (Cambridge: Cambridge University, 1982) 37-49, who quotes J. Munck with effect: 'It is important at the outset to realize that though we have none of Paul's sermons, they must have differed in form at least from his letters' (41 n. 12).

57. Bultmann, *History* 372.

58. Albrecht Dihle begins his article on 'The Gospels and Greek Biography' in Stuhlmacher, ed., *The Gospel and the Gospels* 361-86, by recalling that 'every theological student is warned in his first semester against reading the four canonical Gospels as biographies of Jesus' (361).

59. Hence Bultmann's much quoted view 'that we can know almost nothing concerning the life and personality of Jesus, since the early Christian sources show no interest in either' (cited above §5.3 at n. 36; see also chapter 4 n. 49).

of analogy (§6.3c). The point was, as Kähler makes clear, that the original questers were attempting to write biographies on the model of the nineteenth-century biography, with its interest in the personal life and development of the biographical subject.[60] So what Bultmann was actually decrying was the attempt to write a *modern* biography of Jesus.

Since the 1970s, however, the question of the Gospels' genre has come under increasingly close scrutiny, and it has become much clearer that the Gospels are in fact very similar in type to *ancient* biographies (Greek *bioi;* Latin *vitae*).[61] That is, their interest was not the modern one of analysing the subject's inner life and tracing how an individual's character developed over time. Rather, the ancient view was that character was fixed and unchanging;[62] and the biographer's concern was to portray the chosen subject's character by narrating his words and deeds.[63] Which is just what we find in the Synoptic (indeed all the canonical) Gospels,[64] though not, it should be noted, in the other Gospels now frequently drawn into the neo-Liberal quest.[65] Moreover, it is clear that common purposes of ancient *bioi* were to provide examples for their readers to emulate, to give information about their subject, to preserve his memory, and to defend and promote his reputation.[66] Here again the Gospels fit the broad genre remarkably well.[67] Of course, it remains true that the Gospels were never simply biographical; they were propaganda; they were kerygma. But then neither were ancient biographies wholly dispassionate and objective (any more than modern biographies).[68] In other words, the overlap between Gospel and ancient biography remains substantial and significant.

In short, the genre itself tells us at once that there was a considerable historical interest in the formulating, retelling, and collecting into Gospel format of the material which now comprises the Synoptic Gospels.[69] This should hardly

60. Kähler, *Historical Jesus* 55, 63.

61. See particularly D. Aune, *The New Testament in Its Literary Environment* (Philadelphia: Westminster, 1987) chs. 1 and 2; R. A. Burridge, *What Are the Gospels? A Comparison with Graeco-Roman Biography* (SNTSMS 70; Cambridge: Cambridge University, 1992), both with further bibliography; Burridge reviews the earlier protests against the critical dogma (the Gospels not biographies) in ch. 4; D. Frickenschmidt, *Evangelium als Biographie. Die vier Evangelien im Rahmen antiker Erzählkunst* (Tübingen: Francke, 1997).

62. Aune, *Literary* 28, 63; though note also Burridge, *Gospels* 183-84.

63. Aune, *Literary* 30; Burridge, *Gospels* 144, 150-52, 176-77, 186-88.

64. Aune, *Literary* 57; Burridge, *Gospels* particularly 205-206, 211-12.

65. See above, §§4.7 and 7.8.

66. Aune, *Literary* 36, 62; Burridge, *Gospels* 150-52, 186-88.

67. Aune, *Literary* 57-58; Burridge, *Gospels* 214-17.

68. Recall again the attempts to 'explain' Hitler (above, chapter 6 n. 28).

69. F. G. Downing has argued that in terms of the features of the ancient *bios* (biography) adduced by Burridge, Q itself can be designated a *bios* ('Genre for Q and a Socio-Cultural

surprise us. As Richard Burridge points out: 'biography is a type of writing which occurs naturally among groups of people who have formed around a certain charismatic teacher or leader, seeking to follow after him'. And later on he quotes Momigliano's comment that 'The educated man of the Hellenistic world was curious about the lives of famous people'.[70] Which brings us back more or less to where we started (chapter 2, §6.2).

To sum up, there is substantial circumstantial evidence on two points. First, that the earliest churches would have wanted to remember and actually did remember and refer to Jesus tradition, provided for them as foundational tradition by their founding apostle(s). And second, that the Gospels attest to a lively interest among the first Christians in knowing about Jesus, in preserving, promoting, and defending the memory of his mission and in learning from his example.

8.2. The Influence of Prophecy

The picture which is emerging from the above survey is of church-founding apostles passing on Jesus tradition, of teachers reinforcing their church's corporate memory of Jesus tradition, and of early letter writers alluding to and evoking that Jesus tradition in their paraenesis. This picture is most seriously challenged by the common assumption that prophetic utterances in the early churches were often added to the Jesus tradition. The claim is not simply that earlier tradition was modified, radically or otherwise, by church teaching. It is also that prophetic utterances were heard as words of Jesus, accepted as such and included in the church's store of Jesus tradition, to be spread about more widely in due course, no one thinking it necessary to continue to identify them as prophecies (words of the exalted Jesus). Thus Bultmann:

> The Church drew no distinction between such utterances by Christian prophets and the sayings of Jesus in the tradition, for the reason that even dominical sayings in the tradition were not the pronouncements of a past authority, but sayings of the risen Lord, who is always a contemporary for the Church.[71]

Context for Q: Comparing Sorts of Similarities with Sets of Differences', *JSNT* 55 [1994] 3-26, reprinted in Downing, *Doing Things with Words* 95-117). Kloppenborg Verbin is sympathetic (*Excavating Q* 161-62, 380); in Aune's terms, 'Q would have strong biographical tendencies' (406 n. 74).

70. Burridge, *Gospels* 80-81, 150-51.

71. Bultmann, *History* 127-28. 'In the primitive community at Jerusalem the spirit of Jesus continued to be active, and his ethical teaching was progressively elaborated and expressed in utterances which were then transmitted as the sayings of Jesus himself' ('New Approach' 42).

And Käsemann did not hesitate to speculate that 'countless "I" sayings of the Christ who revealed himself through the mouth of prophets gained entry into the Synoptic tradition as sayings of Jesus'.[72] The most thorough study of the topic, by Eugene Boring,[73] concludes that a substantial amount of the Jesus tradition has been influenced by prophetic usage or stems directly from prophetic utterances. For example, according to Boring, fifteen Q sayings probably originated as prophetic utterances; though in Mark at most eleven 'sayings-units' (excluding 13.5b-31, only five sayings units) are probably from Christian prophets.[74]

How well is this hypothesis founded? On the one hand, it should certainly be accepted that there was a considerable prophetic vitality in the early churches, much cherished by Paul in particular.[75] Specific prophetic utterances are attributed to the inspiring Spirit (Acts 13.2; 20.23; 21.4, 11) and at least in some cases are attributed to the risen Lord (1 Thess. 4.15[?];[76] Revelation 2–3). This would fit well with what we read in the *Odes of Solomon*[77] — presumably the risen Christ being thought to speak through the Odist: 'And I have arisen and am among them, And I speak through their mouth' (42.6).[78] We also know from Celsus that prophets were accustomed to speak their prophecies in 'I' terms (Origen, *contra Celsum* 7.9).[79] Given this background, one might well acknowledge the likelihood of prophetic utterances having been included within the Jesus tradition. The most obvious example would probably be Matt. 18.20; but other plausible examples could include Matt. 11.28-30 and Luke 11.49-51; 22.19b.[80]

---

72. E. Käsemann, 'Is the Gospel Objective?', *Essays on New Testament Themes* (London: SCM, 1964) 48-62 (here 60). The only formal category identified by Käsemann was 'sentences of holy law' in his influential essay, 'Sentences of Holy Law in the New Testament' (1954), *New Testament Questions of Today* (ET London: SCM, 1969) 66-81. But note the penetrating criticism of D. E. Aune, *Prophecy in Early Christianity and the Mediterranean World* (Grand Rapids: Eerdmans, 1983) 166-68, 237-40.

73. M. E. Boring, *Sayings of the Risen Jesus: Christian Prophecy in the Synoptic Tradition* (SNTSMS 46; Cambridge: Cambridge University, 1982).

74. Boring, *Sayings* 179-80, 196. He lists Q/Luke 6.22-23; 10.3-16, 21-22; 11.29b-30, 39-52; 12.8-12; 13.34-35; 16.17; 22.28-30; Mark 3.28-29; 6.8-11; 8.38; 9.1; 13.26.

75. Rom. 12.6; 1 Cor. 12.10, 28-29; 14.1, 3-6, 22, 24-25, 29-32, 39; 1 Thess. 5.20; see further J. D. G. Dunn, *Jesus and the Spirit: A Study of the Religious and Charismatic Experience of Jesus and the First Christians as Reflected in the New Testament* (London: SCM, 1975) 225-33; Boring, *Sayings* 26-52; Aune, *Prophecy* 190-217.

76. But see n. 47 above.

77. Charlesworth dates the *Odes* to about 100 CE (*Old Testament Pseudepigrapha* 2.726-27).

78. Bultmann puts much weight on *Od. Sol.* 42.6 (*History* 127-28 n.).

79. See further Boring, *Sayings* 128-30.

80. J. D. G. Dunn, 'Prophetic "I"-Sayings and the Jesus Tradition: The Importance of Testing Prophetic Utterances within Early Christianity', *NTS* 24 (1977-78) 175-98, reprinted in

On the other hand, despite the quite frequent references to prophets in the early Christian tradition, there is no clear indication at any point that they spoke or were expected to speak in the voice of Jesus within the gathered Christian assembly. Revelation 2–3 is hardly a model for what is envisaged. It would be surprising, for example, if no prophet in a Pauline church ever uttered a prophecy regarding circumcision; yet such an utterance is completely lacking in the Jesus tradition.[81] The role of prophets, vital as it was in Paul's eyes, was much more circumscribed or modest (1 Cor. 14.3) than the above hypothesis envisages.[82] Moreover, in the Jewish and Christian tradition prophecies are normally given in the name of the prophet, even when the prophet is confident that he speaks for God. Thus, no OT prophetic book names Yahweh as its author;[83] Luke always names the prophet concerned (Acts 11.27-28; 13.1; 21.9-14) and distinguishes Spirit speech (Acts 13.2; 21.11) from utterances of the exalted Christ (Acts 18.9-10; 23.11);[84] and Paul makes a point of distinguishing his own inspired opinion from the Jesus tradition (1 Cor. 7.10, 25, 40).[85] All this suggests that Bultmann and Boring are overeager to find evidence of prophetic activity in the Synoptic tradition.[86] The broader evidence suggests rather that such utterances were the exception rather than the rule.

When Boring's examples of prophetic utterance are analysed it becomes clear that the criteria used are hardly adequate to distinguish an (occasional?) prophetic utterance of Jesus from an early Christian prophecy (e.g. Luke 11.39-52).[87] Boring's logic works only if Jesus did not send out his disciples on mission, did not expect persecution for his disciples (even with the precedent of John the Baptist looming large), and did not regard his own message as having final eschatological

---

The Christ and the Spirit. Vol. 2: Pneumatology (Grand Rapids: Eerdmans, 1998) 142-69 (here 146). Aune disputes the case for Luke 11.49 (Prophecy 236-37).

81. It is probably significant for our assessment of the Gospel of Thomas that teaching on circumcision is, however, attributed to Jesus in GTh 53.

82. Note the tendentiousness of Boring's definition of the early Christian prophet as 'an immediately-inspired spokesman for the risen Jesus' which, despite his awareness of the danger, elides into the 'distinctive' Christian idea of the prophet speaking words of the exalted Jesus; 'the risen Jesus plays the role of Yahweh in the prophetic configuration' (Sayings 16-22).

83. F. Neugebauer, 'Geistssprüche und Jesuslogien', ZNW 53 (1962) 218-28 (here 222).

84. D. Hill, 'On the Evidence for the Creative Role of Christian Prophets', NTS 20 (1973-74) 262-74 (here 268-70); see further Hill's New Testament Prophecy (London: Marshall, Morgan and Scott, 1979) 160-85. See also Boring, Sayings 229.

85. See further my 'Prophetic "I"-Sayings' 147-50.

86. P. Stuhlmacher, Biblische Theologie des Neuen Testaments. Band 1: Grundlegung von Jesus zu Paulus (Göttingen: Vandenhoeck und Ruprecht, 1992) 45-46 cites Aune's pertinent conclusion: 'the historical evidence in support of the theory lies largely in the creative imagination of scholars' (Prophecy 245).

87. Boring, Sayings 153-58.

significance.[88] Here again too little recognition is being given to the originally oral character of the Jesus tradition, with the scope for reworking and elaboration of the tradition which that entailed. And though Boring fully recognizes that the prophet may well have interpreted earlier sayings of Jesus,[89] he is too quick to characterize such retelling of the tradition as distinctively prophetic.[90]

But were there major intrusions/additions of completely new motifs and emphases? Were there insertions which subverted the thrust of the original material/earlier tradition? Did the traditioning process 'change the direction' of the earlier material? Here the evocation of a vigorous prophetic practice in the earliest churches may well count against rather than for Bultmann's original hypothesis. For a uniform feature both in older Jewish and in early Christian prophecy is the recognition that inspiration could give rise to *false* prophecy. A prophetic utterance was *not* simply accepted at face value as a word from God. The need to *test* prophecy and to have tests for prophecy was recognized more or less from the beginning of Israel's reliance on prophecy.[91] Among Jesus' contemporaries, both Qumran and Philo were well aware of the problem.[92] So too Josephus does not hesitate to designate certain as 'false prophets' *(pseudoprophētēs)* in his *Antiquities*,[93] and the 'sign prophets' he describes during the first century CE he also describes as 'impostors' and 'deceivers'.[94] And as soon as we begin to read of prophets operating in the earliest churches we find the same concern reflected. Already in what may be the earliest writing in the NT Paul counsels: 'Do not despise prophecy, but test everything, hold to the good and avoid every form of evil' (1 Thess. 5.20-22). 'Evaluation' of prophetic utterance is a standard part of a church's monitoring of prophecy (1 Cor. 12.10; 14.29).[95] And the concern runs through the NT into the second-century churches.[96] The instruction of 1 John

88. With reference to Boring's treatment of Luke 6.22-23 and 10.3-16 (*Sayings* 138-41, 143-48), 12.11-12 (164-65) and 12.8-9 and 22.28-30 (165-67, 176-79) respectively.

89. Boring, *Sayings* ch. 7.

90. Aune, *Prophecy* 242-44. See further below §8.6.

91. E.g., Deut 13.1-5; 1 Kings 22.1-38; Isa. 28.7; Jer. 28.9. The ancient proverb, 'Is Saul also among the prophets?' (1 Sam. 10.12; 19.24) reflects an early recognition of the ambiguity of the prophetic experience.

92. E.g., CD 12.2-3; 1QH 12[4].15-20; *Spec. Leg.* 1.315; 4.48-52.

93. *Ant.* 8.236, 241-42, 318, 402, 406, 409; 9.133-34, 137; 10.66, 104, 111.

94. 'Impostor *(goēs)*' — *War* 2.261, 264; *Ant.* 20.97, 160, 167, 188. 'Deceiver *(apataō, apateōn)*' — *War* 2.259; 6.287; *Ant.* 20.98, 167, 188. See further R. Gray, *Prophetic Figures in Late Second Temple Jewish Palestine: The Evidence from Josephus* (Oxford: Oxford University, 1993) 143-44.

95. Aune recognizes the importance of such testing/evaluation (*Prophecy* 217-29), but concludes that it was not 'normal procedure' (220, 222), despite 1 Thess. 5.21-22 and 1 Cor. 14.29.

96. *Did.* 11.7-8; 12.1; Hermas, *Mand.* 11.7, 11, 16.

was evidently standard 'good practice' in the earliest churches: 'Believe not every spirit, but test the spirits . . .' (1 John 4.1).[97]

Once this point has been grasped, it gives rise to an important corollary of relevance for the present discussion.[98] The corollary is that wherever prophecy was active in the earliest churches it is likely to have been accompanied by what we might call a hermeneutic of suspicion. The prophetic utterance would *not* automatically have been assumed to be inspired by the Spirit of Jesus, or the words to be words of (the exalted) Christ. The awareness that such utterances must be tested seems to have been continuous through Israel's prophetic experience and into Christianity's prophetic experience.[99]

The next step in the logic is the decisive one. What test would be applied to such utterances? One of the consistent answers is in effect the test of already recognized and established tradition. It was denial of or departure from foundational tradition which most clearly attested a *false* prophecy, which should therefore *not* be given any credence. The test is already articulated within the Torah: the prophet who called Israel to go after other gods should not be listened to (Deut. 13.1-3). And the prophets prophesied essentially in support of that formative tradition.[100] In the NT the test of authoritative tradition is articulated most clearly by Paul in 1 Cor. 12.3 (the test of the key kerygmatic confession, 'Jesus is Lord'),[101] and by 1 John 4.2-3 (the test of the developed confession).

It could indeed be said that Paul's own claims to be an apostle, with a distinctive new or different emphasis in his gospel, had to be put to the same test and had to pass it if his apostleship and missionary work were not to be judged unacceptable variations of the gospel of Jesus Christ. This is the clear implication of Galatians 1–2, where Paul, having insisted on the independence of his apostolic authority from the Jerusalem apostles, nevertheless found it necessary to go

97. Note how the need for and fact of testing prophecies are in effect assumed in a range of NT passages (Matt. 7.15-23; 1 Cor. 2.12-14; 14.37-38; 2 Thess. 2.2-3; Heb. 13.7-9; Rev. 2.20).

98. This is the main point of my 'Prophetic "I"-Sayings'.

99. Boring recognizes the importance of the subject (*Sayings* 64-69) but does not pursue the issue of criteria (119-20).

100. 'In the Judaism from which early Christianity was born, the prophets were not thought of as inspired innovators, who brought radically new revelation, but as strong links in the chain of tradition, who only presented afresh what was already Israel's traditional lore' (Boring, *Sayings* 71).

101. That 'Jesus is Lord' was one of the earliest Christian (baptismal) confessions is attested in Rom. 10.9. Most would regard Rom. 12.6 as making the same point: prophecy had to be 'in accordance with the analogy *(analogia)* of faith', 'in agreement with (or proportion to) the faith' (BAGD, *analogia*); cf. 6.17 ('the pattern [*typos*] of teaching'); 12.3 ('the measure [*metron*] of faith'). Aune points out that 'the test of congruence with kerygmatic tradition' was applied also in Gal. 1.6-9 and 2 Thess. 2.2 (*Prophecy* 235).

up to Jerusalem to lay his gospel before the leading apostles, 'lest somehow I was running or had run in vain' (2.2).[102] Despite his confidence that he was called by Christ, Paul recognized the necessity that his claim to exceptional revelation (1.12) had to be tested and accepted by those who represented the temporal continuity with Jesus. Which also implies that Paul's repeated insistence that he was indeed an apostle was in effect a claim to belong to that body which had responsibility to authenticate as well as to preach the gospel (1 Cor. 15.8-11). In the light of all this, it must be judged unlikely that Paul for one would have accepted any prophetic utterance as a word of Jesus simply because it was an inspired (prophetic) utterance.

When this insight (the importance of testing prophecies by reference to the already established tradition) is brought to the issue of prophetic utterances becoming incorporated into the Jesus tradition, the results are quite far-reaching. For it means, first, that *any prophecy claiming to be from the exalted Christ would have been tested by what was already known to be the sort of thing Jesus had said.* This again implies the existence in most churches of such a canon (the word is not inappropriate) of foundational Jesus tradition.[103] But it also implies, second, that only prophetic utterances which *cohered* with that assured foundational material were likely to have been accepted as sayings of Jesus. Which means, thirdly, that — and the logic here needs to be thought through carefully — any *distinctive* saying or motif within the Jesus tradition as we now have it is likely to have come from the original teaching of Jesus, since otherwise, if it originated as a prophetic utterance, it is unlikely to have been accepted as a saying of Jesus by the church in which it was first uttered.[104] In other words, we have here emerging an interesting and potentially important fresh criterion for recognizing original Jesus tradition

102. For fuller exposition of the delicate balance between his own sense of apostolic authority and the authority of the Jerusalem leadership, see my 'The Relationship between Paul and Jerusalem according to Galatians 1 and 2', *NTS* 28 (1982) 461-78, reprinted in *Jesus, Paul and the Law: Studies in Mark and Galatians* (London: SPCK, 1990) 108-28; also *The Epistle to the Galatians* (BNTC; London: Black, 1993) here 93-94.

103. Dibelius also envisaged collections of Jesus' sayings which acted as a 'regulatory' control and prevented more than a few inspired words entering the Jesus tradition (*Tradition* 240-43) but never explained the rationale of what he had in view. Note also Boring's insistence that tradition and Spirit went together in early Christianity, and his conclusion that Mark was 'suspicious of Christian prophecy' (*Sayings* 72, 79, 198).

104. As illustrations we may cite two of Boring's examples (*Sayings* 159-64, 173-74). With reference to Luke 12.10, is it likely that the community would have accepted a prophetic utterance which gave the prophet's or the community's own inspiration higher priority than the exalted Jesus? (see also below §15.7h; cf. Aune's critique of Boring's key example of Mark 3.28-29 in *Prophecy* 240-42). With reference to Luke 16.17, if it is the case that Jesus was remembered as relaxing the law, would a prophetic saying have been accepted which insisted on the eternal validity of the letter of the law (see further below §14.4)?

— a reverse criterion of coherence: the *less* closely a saying or motif within the Jesus tradition coheres with the rest of the Jesus tradition, the *more* likely is it that the saying or motif goes back to Jesus himself!

In short, Bultmann's assumption of a vigorous prophetic activity in the earliest churches adding substantially to the Jesus tradition is hardly borne out by what we know about such prophetic activity. And our knowledge of how prophecies were received in the earliest churches raises a substantial question mark against any claim that distinctive or characteristic features of the Jesus tradition originated in prophetic activity. On the contrary, the likelihood is that the first Christian churches would have been alert to the danger of diluting or contaminating their vital foundational tradition by incorporating into it any material incoherent with its principal emphases.

8.3. Oral Tradition

Does what we know about the traditioning processes within earliest Christianity bear the weight of inferences being drawn from the above considerations? On this point all participants in the discussion are agreed that the acid test has to be the evidence of the Jesus tradition itself. That said, however, there has been a huge and persisting gap in the analysis of that evidence. I refer to the repeated failure to take seriously the fact that in the initial stages of the traditioning process the tradition must have been *oral* tradition;[105] and thus also the failure to investigate the character of the tradition in its oral phase, and to ask what its orality must have meant for the transmission of that material. I do not deny that the subject has been raised during the period covered by the various quests of the 'historical Jesus'. Unfortunately, however, when it has been raised, the issue has usually been sidetracked into other questions and its significance for our understanding of the tradition history of the Jesus tradition lost to sight.

a. J. G. Herder

Within the history reviewed above, J. G. Herder (1744-1803) is usually given the credit for first raising the issue. Herder was unhappy with Lessing's idea that behind the Synoptic Gospels lay an original Aramaic gospel of the Nazarenes: 'Neither apostolic nor church history knows of any such Primal Gospel'. What

---

105. W. Schmithals is a lone voice in his highly implausible view, recently repeated, that the Synoptic tradition was literary from the first ('Vom Ursprung der synoptischen Tradition', *ZTK* 94 [1997] 288-316).

did lie behind them was indeed a 'common Gospel', but it was an *oral* gospel.[106] Herder's description of this material foreshadows later treatments, not least his description of the orally transmitted material as 'an oral saga'.[107]

> In the case of a free, oral narrative, not everything is equally untrammeled. Sentences, long sayings, parables are more likely to retain the same form of expression than minor details of the narrative; transitional material and connecting formulae the narrator himself supplies. . . . The common Gospel consisted of individual units, narratives, parables, sayings, pericopes. This is evident from the very appearance of the Gospels and from the different order of this or that parable or saga. . . . The fact that it consists of such parts vouches for the truth of the Gospel, for people such as most of the apostles were, more easily recall a saying, a parable, an apothegm that they had found striking than connected discourses.

Unfortunately these potentially fruitful insights were absorbed into and lost to sight in the quest for sources of the Synoptic Gospels which became the dominant concern of nineteenth-century Gospels research.[108]

b. Rudolf Bultmann

It was not until the rise of form criticism early in the twentieth century that the question of the earliest Jesus tradition's oral character reemerged.[109] In his Preface to the 1962 publication of one of his essays on form criticism, Bultmann began with a summary definition: 'The purpose of Form Criticism is to study the history of the oral tradition behind the gospels'.[110] And in his summary description of how oral tradition was transmitted he made an observation similar to that of Herder: 'Whenever narratives pass from mouth to mouth the central point of the narrative and general structure are well preserved; but in the incidental details change takes place . . .'.[111] Unfortunately, once again, the possibilities of work-

106. I draw on Kümmel's abstract, despite his somewhat misleading description (*New Testament* 79-82).

107. Extracts from J. G. Herder, *Collected Works* (ed. B. Suphan) Vol. XIX, in Kümmel, *New Testament* 81-82. B. Reicke, *The Roots of the Synoptic Gospels* (Philadelphia: Fortress, 1986) 11-12, makes special mention of J. C. L. Gieseler, *Historisch-kritischer Versuch über die Entstehung und die frühesten Schicksale der schriftlichen Evangelien* (Leipzig: Englemann, 1818).

108. Kümmel's own treatment represents the same priorities. See further below, chapter 10 n. 24.

109. Already signalled by Wellhausen (cited above, chapter 5 n. 30).

110. *Form Criticism* (with K. Kundsin) 1.

111. 'New Approach' 47.

ing fruitfully with a realistic conceptualisation of oral tradition and how it functioned were more or less strangled at birth by several assumptions which distorted Bultmann's reconstruction of the oral traditioning processes.

Two in particular are worth noting. (1) Bultmann focused on the forms and assumed that certain 'laws of style' determined the transmission of the forms. These laws, apparently drawn from some acquaintance with studies in folklore elsewhere,[112] included the further assumptions of a 'pure' form,[113] of a natural progression in the course of transmission from purity and simplicity towards greater complexity,[114] and of a development in the tradition determined by form rather than content.[115] (2) More significant was Bultmann's assumption of a *literary* model to explain the process of transmission. This becomes most evident in his conceptualisation of the whole tradition about Jesus as 'composed of a series of layers'.[116] The imagined process is one where each layer is laid or builds upon another. Bultmann made such play with it because, apart from anything else, he was confident that he could strip off later (Hellenistic) layers to expose the earlier (Palestinian) layers.[117] The image itself, however, is drawn from the

---

112. *History* 6-7; though note the criticism of E. P. Sanders, *The Tendencies of the Synoptic Tradition* (SNTSMS 9; Cambridge: Cambridge University, 1969) 18 n. 4.

113. 'The "pure form" *(reine Gattung)* represents a mixture of linguistic and history-of-language categories, which is to be assigned to an out-of-date conception of language development' *(eine Vermischung linguistischer und sprachhistorischer Kategorien . . . die einer heute überholten Auffassung der Sprachentwicklung zuzuweisen ist)* (Schröter, *Erinnerung* 59; also 141-42). See also G. Strecker, 'Schriftlichkeit oder Mündlichkeit der synoptischen Tradition?', in F. van Segbroeck, et al., eds., *The Four Gospels 1992, Festschrift Frans Neirynck* (Leuven: Leuven University, 1992) 159-72 (here 161-62, with other bibliography in n. 6).

114. But see Sanders' critique in *Tendencies,* in summary: 'There are no hard and fast laws of the development of the Synoptic tradition. On all counts the tradition developed in opposite directions. It became both longer and shorter, both more and less detailed, and both more and less Semitic . . .' (272).

115. See, e.g., his assertions in 'New Approach' 45-47 and 'Study' 29, and the fuller analysis of *History;* and critique of the assumption by W. H. Kelber, *The Oral and the Written Gospel* (Philadelphia: Fortress, 1983) 2-8. G. Theissen, *Miracle Stories of the Early Christian Tradition* (1974; ET Edinburgh: Clark, 1983) 1-24, illustrates well how classical form criticism merges into literary criticism (genre, structural, and narrative criticism), but his own awareness of the dynamic of the traditioning process (also in reaction to the model of archaeological strata in a text) depends too much on an ideal(isation) of 'genre' ('actualisations of structurally predetermined possibilities'), not dissimilar to the early form critics' ideal(isation) of 'form' (17-22, 172).

116. Bultmann, *Jesus* 12-13 (see above §5.3 at n. 38). The persistence of the imagery is indicated in Funk: 'the narrative gospels are made up of layered traditions, some oral, some written, piled on top of each other. At the bottom — in the earliest stratum . . .' (*Acts of Jesus* 24).

117. Ibid.

literary process of editing, where each successive edition (layer) is an edited version (for Bultmann, an elaborated and expanded version) of the previous edition (layer). But is such a conceptualisation really appropriate to a process of oral retellings of traditional material? Bultmann never really addressed the question, despite its obvious relevance.[118]

Here again, then, we have to speak of form criticism's missed opportunity (as in §6.5c). The main body of discussion following Bultmann stayed with the literary model, and the focus shifted more to the communities which shaped the tradition or to the easier question of its later shaping in redaction criticism.[119] There were three main exceptions.

c. C. F. D. Moule

Moule did not focus his attention on the character or processes of oral tradition, so his contribution is somewhat tangential to the present concerns. Nevertheless, his insights into the formation of the Gospels are of considerable relevance — two in particular.

First, he observed that the Gospels retain a clear distinction between pre-Easter and post-Easter perceptions of Jesus.[120] His pupil, Eugene Lemcio, has elaborated the point. The Synoptic Gospels particularly retain a clear sense of before and after Easter in the *content* of the Jesus tradition which they retell. The *context* of the retelling everywhere implies a post-Easter perspective. But only occasionally is this perspective evident in the content of the tradition as such. So, for example, the call for faith in or assumption of the story-teller's faith in Jesus is implicit in the context of the retelling, but is not interjected into the Jesus tradition itself.[121] If this is indeed the case for the much retold and developed retelling

118. In his current research at Durham University on oral tradition and the Gospels, Terence Mournet notes that the same assumption of exclusively literary dependence between the different strands of the Synoptic tradition vitiates Farmer's *Synoptic Problem* attempt to overthrow the two-document hypothesis and Sanders' *Tendencies* critique of Bultmann and Dibelius. The same criticism could be levelled at the attempt by M. Goulder, *Luke: A New Paradigm* (2 vols; JSNTS 20; Sheffield: Sheffield Academic, 1989) to dispense with Q (particularly ch. 2).

119. The most successful and influential was H. Conzelmann, *Die Mitte der Zeit* (Tübingen: Mohr-Siebeck, 1953, [2]1957, [5]1964; ET *The Theology of St. Luke* (London: Faber and Faber, 1961).

120. C. F. D. Moule, 'The Intention of the Evangelists' (1959), *The Phenomenon of the New Testament* (London: SCM, 1967) 100-114.

121. E. E. Lemcio, *The Past of Jesus in the Gospels* (SNTSMS 68; Cambridge: Cambridge University, 1991); see particularly 8-18, 109-14. I restate Lemcio's argument in my own terms. Cf. Schürmann cited above chapter 6 n. 108.

of the tradition (by the Synoptic authors), how much more can we infer it to have been true of the earlier retelling of the tradition on which Mark, Matthew and Luke were dependent.

Second, in his too little regarded *Birth of the New Testament,* Moule attempted to highlight the vitality of the form-history process in the life of the churches, and 'to place in their setting in life and thought the processes which led up to the writing of early Christian books'.[122] Here again, however, his concern was primarily to explain the genesis of Christian literature, not the character and processes of oral tradition, though some of his observations are entirely relevant to our inquiry.[123]

d. Helmut Koester

The second significant development beyond Bultmann was that of Bultmann's last doctoral pupil. From the outset of his academic career Koester has emphasized the fact that the Jesus tradition existed in oral streams ('free tradition') well into the second century.[124] And the insight has been maintained consistently in his subsequent work until the present,[125] repeatedly cautioning against the assumption of a purely literary and linear development of the tradition. All this time, however, his voice, like Moule's, has been too little heeded on this point, to the discipline's loss, partly, no doubt, because he himself has never given it the prominence which the insight deserved.[126] More to the point, he has not developed a model of oral transmission, and has paid too little attention to the dynamic of the oral traditioning process beyond the support it gives to his thesis that other (later) Gospels contain early forms of the tradition.[127]

122. Moule, *Birth* 3.

123. See particularly his recognition that Papias (Eusebius, *HE* 3.39.15) conceived of Peter retelling the teaching of Jesus '"*pros tas chreias,* with reference to the needs" (i.e. as occasion demanded, as need arose)' (*Birth* 108, 120-21); his observation on 'the more fluid interchange of forms (in worship), such that snatches of prayer and hymnody flow in and out of the texture of pastoral exhortation' (270), also parallels the recognition among folklorists of the fluidity of oral performances (below §8.3f).

124. H. Koester, *Synoptische Überlieferung bei den apostolischen Vätern* (Berlin: Akademie-Verlag, 1957).

125. See, e.g., H. Koester, 'Written Gospels or Oral Traditions?', *JBL* 113 (1994) 293-97.

126. One indication is the fact that none of the contributors to his Festschrift (Pearson, ed., *Future of Early Christianity*) pays much attention to this important aspect of his scholarly work.

127. See above §§7.6, 8. The same criticism can be pressed more strongly against Funk's *Five Gospels* in that the volume has focused too much on the end product of the as-

e. Birger Gerhardsson

The third response to Bultmann deserving of special note has attracted much more attention. It is the protest by Harald Riesenfeld and his pupil Birger Gerhardsson that Bultmann had indeed ignored the most obvious precedents for the transmission of tradition in Palestine.

Riesenfeld noted that the technical terms used for transmission of rabbinic tradition underlie the Greek terms used in the NT for the same process *(paralambanein* and *paradidonai)* and deduced that the early Christian traditioning process, like the rabbinic, was a 'rigidly controlled transmission' of words and deeds of Jesus, 'memorized and recited as holy word'. The idea of a community-shaped tradition was too inaccurate. Rather we must think of tradition derived directly from Jesus and transmitted by authorised teachers 'in a far more rigid and fixed form'.[128]

Gerhardsson developed Riesenfeld's central claim by a careful study of rabbinic tradition transmission, as the nearest parallel for the Palestinian Jesus tradition, and reinforced his teacher's main claim.[129] Unlike the form critics, Gerhardsson recognized the need to investigate the actual techniques of oral transmission. The key word, he confirmed, is 'memorization',[130] memorization by means of constant repetition, the basic technique of all education then and since (in fact, until relatively recently in the West).[131] In Rabbinic Judaism the pupil had the duty 'to maintain his teacher's exact words', as the basis for any subsequent comment(ary) of his own.[132] Principally on the basis of the importance of 'the word of the Lord' in earliest Christianity, as attested by Luke and

---

sumed process; in its red, pink, grey, and black designations of particular sayings the Jesus Seminar also has shown too little interest in and empathy with the dynamic of the process.

128. H. Riesenfeld, 'The Gospel Tradition and Its Beginning' (1957), *The Gospel Tradition* (Philadelphia: Fortress, 1970) 1-29 (here 16, 26, 24).

129. B. Gerhardsson, *Memory and Manuscript: Oral Tradition and Written Transmission in Rabbinic Judaism and Early Christianity* (Lund: Gleerup, 1961), refined in a succession of further publications: *Tradition and Transmission in Early Christianity* (Lund: Gleerup, 1964); *The Origins of the Gospel Traditions* (Philadelphia: Fortress, 1979); *The Gospel Tradition* (Lund: Gleerup, 1986); the last two are reprinted in *The Reliability of the Gospel Tradition* (Peabody: Hendrickson, 2001); also 'Illuminating the Kingdom: Narrative Meshalim in the Synoptic Gospels', in Wansbrough, ed., *Jesus* 266-309.

130. E.g., 'The general attitude was that words and items of knowledge must be memorized: *tantum scimus, quantum memoria tenemus* [we know only as much as we retain in our memory]' (*Memory* 124).

131. 'Cicero's saying was applied to its fullest extent in Rabbinic Judaism: *repetitio est mater studiorum*. Knowledge is gained by repetition, passed on by repetition, kept alive by repetition. A Rabbi's life is one continual repetition' (*Memory* 168).

132. Gerhardsson, *Memory* 130-36 (here 133); also chs. 9-10.

Paul, Gerhardsson went on to deduce that Jesus 'must have made his disciples learn certain sayings off by heart; if he taught, he must have required his disciples to memorize'; 'his sayings must have been accorded even greater authority and sanctity than that accorded by the Rabbis' disciples to the words of their teachers'. Consequently, when the Evangelists edited their Gospels they were able to work 'on a basis of a fixed, distinct tradition from, and about, Jesus'.[133]

Unfortunately these contributions were widely dismissed, in large part because the appeal to rabbinic precedent was deemed (unfairly) to be anachronistic.[134] More to the point, unlike the rabbinic tradition, the Gospel tradition does not depict Jesus teaching by repetition.[135] And more important for present purposes, the claims of both Riesenfeld and Gerhardsson seem to envisage a far more rigid and fixed tradition than could readily explain the obvious disparities between the same tradition as used by the Evangelists.[136] Of course, there was bound to be at least an element of memorization in Jesus' teaching technique and in the disciples' remembering; the aphorisms characteristic of Jesus' teaching lent themselves to such memorization. Still, the question remains whether Jesus intended to initiate a chain of teaching maintained by the process of memorization. And even when we allow for the evidence marshalled above (particularly §8.1b and d), the process envisaged for the transmission of the Jesus tradition seems to be too controlled and formal to explain the *divergencies* in the tradition as it has come down to us.[137] The possibility of finding the key to the tradition history from Jesus to the Synoptics in the processes of oral transmission had once again eluded scholarly grasp.[138]

133. Gerhardsson, *Memory* 328, 332, 335; similarly *Origins* 19-20, 72-73; *Gospel* 39-42. Riesner also emphasizes the role of learning by heart *(Auswendiglernen)* in Jesus' teaching *(Jesus* 365-67, 440-53; also 'Jesus' in Wansbrough, ed., *Jesus* 203-204). D. L. Balch, 'The Canon: Adaptable and Stable, Oral and Written. Critical Questions for Kelber and Riesner', *Forum* 7.3/4 (1991) 183-205, criticizes Riesner for assuming 'a print mentality' which was not true of 'passing on tradition of great philosophers' teachings' (196-99).

134. Cf. J. Neusner's apology for his earlier review in his Foreword to the recent reprint of *Memory* and *Tradition (Reliability of the Gospel Tradition).*

135. Kelber, *Oral* 14. Note also Hengel's criticism referred to below (chapter 14 n. 64).

136. Schröter, *Erinnerung* 29-30. Gerhardsson did not examine the Synoptic tradition itself in *Memory,* though he went a considerable way towards filling the gap twenty-five years later in his *Gospel.*

137. Gerhardsson could speak of 'a logos fixed by the college of Apostles', with reference to the tradition of 1 Cor. 15.3ff. *(Memory* 297). As his later work shows, Gerhardsson hardly needed to be reminded of the differences between accounts of the same material in the Synoptics. But the key point remains that the model of 'memorization' is not well fitted to account for such differences.

138. Byrskog, a pupil of Gerhardsson, has developed a different model to bridge the gap between original events and Gospel accounts — the model of oral history *(Story as History,*

f. Werner Kelber

To Werner Kelber is due the credit for being the first NT scholar to take seriously the distinctive character of oral tradition as illuminated by a sequence of studies from classicists, folklorists, and social anthropologists.[139] Characteristics include 'mnemonic patterns, shaped for ready oral recurrence', 'heavily rhythmic, balanced patterns, in repetitions or antitheses, in alliterations and assonances, in epithetic and other formulary expressions, in thematic settings, . . . in proverbs'. Typical of oral performances were variations on what nevertheless were recognizable versions of the same story, with some more or less word-for-word repetition in places, both fixed and flexible formulaic elements, and so on.[140] Kelber drew attention to similar features which had already been observed in the Jesus tradition: 'the extraordinary degree to which sayings of Jesus have kept faith with heavily patterned speech forms, abounding in alliteration, paronomasia, appositional equivalence, proverbial and aphoristic diction, contrasts and antitheses, synonymous, antithetical, synthetic, and tautologic parallelism and the like', miracle stories 'typecast in a fashion that lends itself to habitual, not verbatim, memorization'.[141] And in his description of oral transmission he fully acknowledges his indebtedness to earlier studies. 'Oral thinking consists in formal patterns from the start'; 'formulaic stability'

---

particularly 46). But the model assumes later historians (like Luke) seeking out and inquiring of those, like Peter, the women at the cross and tomb, and the family of Jesus (65-91), who could remember the original events and exchanges (cf. Luke 1.1-4). Byrskog, in fact, has no real conception of or indeed role for oral transmission as itself the bridging process.

139. The earlier contribution by the Seminar on 'Oral Traditional Literature and the Gospels' passed largely unnoticed, mainly, I suppose, because it functioned in service of the theme for the overall Colloquy on *The Relationships among the Gospels* (ed. W. O. Walker; San Antonio: Trinity University, 1978) 31-122. L. E. Keck reviews earlier work and summarizes the Seminar's discussion ('Oral Traditional Literature and the Gospels: The Seminar', *Relationships* 103-22). In contrast, Kelber's book provoked a lively discussion in L. H. Silberman, ed., *Orality, Aurality and Biblical Narrative*, Semeia 39 (Atlanta: Scholars, 1987), and J. Dewey, ed., *Orality and Textuality in Early Christian Literature*, Semeia 65 (Atlanta: Scholars, 1995).

140. W. J. Ong, *Orality and Literacy: The Technologizing of the Word* (1982; London: Routledge, 1988) 33-36, 57-68. The work of A. B. Lord, *The Singer of Tales* (Cambridge: Harvard University, 1978) has been seminal (here especially ch. 5). Note also R. Finnegan, *Oral Poetry: Its Nature, Significance and Social Context* (Cambridge: Cambridge University, 1977) ch. 3, especially 73-87; also 90-109. See also A. B. Lord, 'The Gospels as Oral Traditional Literature', in Walker, *Relationships* 33-91 (here 37-38, 63-64, 87-89); and the overview by D. E. Aune, 'Prolegomena to the Study of Oral Tradition in the Hellenistic World', in Wansbrough, ed., *Jesus* 59-106 (with bibliography).

141. Kelber, *Oral* 27; see also 50-51. Of course, Gerhardsson notes similar characteristics in rabbinic oral transmission (*Memory* 148-56, 163-68).

and 'compositional variability' go hand in hand — 'this mid-state between fixed and free'.[142] Oral transmission 'exhibits "an insistent, conservative urge for preservation" of essential information, while it borders on carelessness in its predisposition to abandon features that are not met with social approval'.[143] 'Variability and stability, conservatism and creativity, evanescence and unpredictability all mark the pattern of oral transmission' — the 'oral principle of "variation within the same"'.[144]

The chief thrust of Kelber's book, however, is to build on the distinction between oral and written, between oral performance and literary transmission, which he draws from Walter Ong in particular.[145] The distinction is important, not least since it requires modern literary scholars to make a conscious effort to extricate their historical envisaging of the oral transmission of tradition from the mind-set and assumptions of long-term literacy.[146] Equally important is the immediacy of an oral communication in contrast to written, the direct and personal engagement of speaker and auditor not possible in writing, what Kelber calls the 'oral synthesis'.[147] This is partly what I have in mind when I talk of the 'impact' made by Jesus on his disciples (§§6.5d-f). The contrast can be overplayed: for example, the recognition that in the ancient world documents were written to be *heard,* that is, read out and listened to rather than read, is commonplace in all these disciplines;[148] the fact

142. Kelber, *Oral* 27-28, the last phrase quoted from B. Peabody, *The Winged Word: A Study in the Technique of Ancient Greek Oral Composition as Seen Principally through Hesiod's* Works and Days (Albany: State University of New York, 1975) 96.

143. Kelber, *Oral* 29-30, quoting Lord, *Singer of Tales* 120. Lord also characterises the change from oral to literary composition as 'the change . . . from stability of essential story, which is the goal of oral tradition, to stability of text, of the exact words of the story' (*Singer* 138).

144. Kelber, *Oral* 33, 54; quoting E. A. Havelock, *Preface to Plato* (Cambridge: Harvard University, 1963) 92, 147, 184, *passim.*

145. See also W. H. Kelber, 'Jesus and Tradition: Words in Time, Words in Space', in Dewey, ed., *Orality and Textuality* 139-67. T. M. Derico, *Orality and the Synoptic Gospels: An Evaluation of the Oral-Formulaic Theory as Method for Synoptic Tradition Criticism* (Cincinnati Bible Seminary MA, 2000) offers an extensive critique of Kelber (ch. 4).

146. Ong begins by noting: 'We — readers of books such as this — are so literate that it is very difficult for us to conceive of an oral universe of communication or thought *except as a variation of a literate universe*' (*Orality* 2, my emphasis). As noted above, the mistake has been common in source and form criticism of the Gospels.

147. Kelber, *Oral* 19, referring to W. J. Ong, *The Presence of the Word: Some Prolegomena for Cultural and Religious History* (New Haven: Yale University, 1967; paperback Minneapolis: University of Minnesota, 1981) 111-38.

148. See further P. J. Achtemeier, *'Omne verbum sonat:* The New Testament and the Oral Environment of Late Western Antiquity', *JBL* 109 (1990) 3-27; Downing, 'Word-processing in the Ancient World' 75-89 (with more bibliography); Horsley and Draper, *Whoever* 132-34, 144-45, in dependence on R. Thomas, *Literacy and Orality in Ancient Greece* (Cambridge: Cambridge University, 1992); Byrskog, *Story as History* 139-44.

that letters can be a fairly effective substitute for personal absence has become important in recent study of Paul's letters;[149] and the encounter with its written version can be as creative as a hearing of the original speech — indeed, in reader-response criticism each reading of a text is like a fresh performance of it.[150] Even so, for anyone who has experienced a (for them) first performance of a great musical work, like Beethoven's Ninth or Verdi's Requiem, the difference between hearing in the electric atmosphere of the live performance and hearing the recorded version played later at home (let alone simply reading the score) is unmistakable.[151]

There are other important observations made by Kelber. He takes up the key observation of Albert Lord[152] in warning against the ideal of 'original form'; 'each oral performance is an irreducibly unique creation'; if Jesus said something more than once there is no 'original'.[153] This is true, although the impact made by each retelling by Jesus on those who heard and retained the teaching should be distinguished from the effect of their own reteaching on others. Kelber also rightly notes that oral retelling of Jesus' words will already have begun during Jesus' lifetime; the Bultmannian thesis of a tradition which began to be transmitted only after Easter is highly questionable.[154] Moreover, in Kelber's work, very noticeably, *narratives,* the retold stories about Jesus, reemerge into promi-

---

149. Influential here has been R. W. Funk, 'The Apostolic Parousia: Form and Significance', in W. R. Farmer, et al., eds., *Christian History and Interpretation,* J. Knox FS (Cambridge: Cambridge University, 1967) 249-68.

150. The idea has been much taken up, e.g., by N. Lash, 'Performing the Scriptures' in his *Theology on the Way to Emmaus* (London: SCM, 1986), 37-46, and Frances Young, *The Art of Performance: Towards a Theology of Holy Scripture* (London: Darton, Longman and Todd, 1990).

151. 'The reader is absent from the writing of the book, the writer is absent from its reading' (Kelber, *Oral* 92, quoting P. Ricoeur, *Interpretation Theory: Discourse and the Surplus of Meaning* [Fort Worth: Texas Christian University, 1976] 35).

152. Lord, *Singer:* 'In a sense each performance is "an" original, if not "the" original. The truth of the matter is that our concept of "the original", of "the song", simply makes no sense in oral tradition' (100-101).

153. Kelber, *Oral* 29; also 59, 62; also 'Jesus and Tradition' 148-51, though his argument is too dependent on generalisations from 'oral aesthetics', not closely enough related to the particularities of first-century Palestine (cf. J. M. Foley, 'Words in Tradition, Words in Text: A Response', in Dewey ed., *Orality and Textuality* 169-80 [here 170-72]). Finnegan also glosses Lord: 'There is no correct text, no idea that one version is more "authentic" than another: each performance is a unique and original creation with its own validity' (*Oral Poetry* 65). She credits Lord with bringing this point home most convincingly (79), though by way of critique she points out that memorization also plays a part (79, 86).

154. Kelber, *Oral* 20-21, citing appositely the demonstration by Schürmann of sayings on kingdom, repentance, judgment, love of enemy, eschatological preparedness, etc., which show no trace of post-Easter influence ('Die vorösterlichen Anfänge der Logientradition'); see again above chapter 6 n. 108.

nence from the marginalisation imposed upon them by the almost exclusive focus of scholarly interest on the sayings of Jesus.[155] Not least of importance, given Kelber's developed thesis, is his recognition that Mark (his main focus in the Gospels) retains many of the indices of orality — for example, its 'activist syntax' and colloquial Greek, its use of the storyteller's 'three', and its many redundancies and repetitions; 'Mark may be treating an oral story in order for it to remain functional for the ear more than for the eye'.[156] Mark's Gospel may be *frozen* orality,[157] but it is frozen *orality*.[158]

Unfortunately, Kelber pushes his thesis about Mark marking a major transition from oral to written far too hard and seriously diminishes its overall value. The first step in his thesis development is that the written Gospel disrupts the 'oral synthesis'; it 'arises not from orality *per se,* but out of the debris of deconstructed orality'; it indicates 'alienation from the oral apparatus'; it 'accomplishes the death of living words for the purpose of inaugurating the life of textuality'.[159] The transition is overdramatized: it is widely recognized that in a predominantly oral culture, oral versions of a tradition would continue after it had been transcribed and that knowledge of the written version would usually be in an oral medium.[160]

155. Kelber, *Oral* ch. 2.

156. Kelber, *Oral* 65-68. See also Theissen, *Miracle Stories* 189-95.

157. Kelber, *Oral* 91, 94.

158. The oral character of Mark's narrative has since been strongly emphasized by T. P. Haverly, *Oral Traditional Literature and the Composition of Mark's Gospel* (Edinburgh PhD, 1983); and especially by J. Dewey, 'Oral Methods of Structuring Narrative in Mark', *Interpretation* 43 (1989) 32-44; also 'The Gospel of Mark as an Oral-Aural Event: Implications for Interpretation', in E. S. Malbon and E. V. McKnight, eds., *The New Literary Criticism and the New Testament* (JNSTS 109; Sheffield: Sheffield Academic, 1994) 145-63. Note also Lord's earlier evaluation of 'The Gospels as Oral Traditional Literature' (Walker, *Relationships* 58-84 [particularly 79-80, 82], 90-91). The conclusion of the Symposium on *Jesus and the Oral Gospel Tradition* (ed. H. Wansbrough) can cut both ways: 'We have been unable to deduce or derive any marks which distinguish clearly between an oral and a written transmission process. Each can show a similar degree of fixity and variability' (12). Strecker rightly emphasises the continuity in transmission of the tradition from oral to written ('Schriftlichkeit' 164-65). Cf. Schröter, *Erinnerung* 55, 60.

159. Kelber, *Oral* 91-96, 130-31, 184-85 (quotations from 95, 98, 131). Compare and contrast the more balanced judgment of G. N. Stanton, 'Form Criticism Revisited', in M. Hooker and C. Hickling, eds., *What about the New Testament?,* C. Evans FS (London: SCM, 1975) 13-27: 'There is no reason to doubt that it was not the writing of Mark's gospel, but the later slow acceptance of Mark as a fixed and authoritative text which led to the death of oral traditions about Jesus' (20). Kelber subsequently shows himself more dubious regarding what he calls 'the great divide thesis, which pits oral tradition vis-à-vis gospel text' ('Modalities of Communication, Cognition and Physiology of Perception: Orality, Rhetoric, Scribality', *Semeia* 65 [1995] 194-215 [here 195]).

160. See, e.g., Ø. Andersen, 'Oral Tradition', in Wansbrough, ed., *Jesus* 17-58 (here 43-53).

At the same time, it is true that only with a written text can we begin to speak of an editing process, such as Bultmann envisaged; prior to that, in repeated oral performances the dynamics are different, more of the order of 'theme and variations' than of Gerhardsson's 'memorization'.[161] This is why talk of 'sources', appropriate in considering the origin of a written text, can be inappropriate with oral tradition. It is also why, I may add, even talk of 'oral transmission' can mislead such discussions, since it envisages oral performance as intended primarily to transmit (transfer) rather than, say, to celebrate tradition.[162]

However, Kelber pushes on to argue that Mark's textualizing of the tradition amounts to an 'indictment of oral process and authorities', an 'emancipation from oral norms', an objection to 'the oral metaphysics of presence'. Thus Mark repudiates the first disciples, Jesus' family, and ongoing prophetic activity as oral authorities to be discredited; the first disciples are 'effectively eliminated as apostolic representatives of the risen Lord'.[163] Kelber calls in Paul as apostle of orality and sets him over against Mark's Gospel as written text, with the classic gospel/law antithesis reworked as an antithesis between oral gospel and written law, spirit and (written) letter, 'under the law' as under textuality.[164] In all this a different christology is at stake: the Passion narrative as a literary phenomenon implies a distanciation from an oral christology; Q, with its 'fundamentally oral disposition' and inclusion of prophetic utterances, maintains the living voice of Jesus, whereas Mark elevates 'the earthly Jesus at the price of silencing the living Lord' by 'relegating all sayings to the former while silencing the voice of the latter'.[165]

Here is a thesis too quickly gone to seed. To find Paul as apostle of orality lumped with Q is a refreshing change. But Paul himself would almost certainly have been baffled by the thrust of such an argument. As one who vividly recalls his preaching in his letters (e.g. Gal. 3.1) and who both preached the kerygma of the first witnesses (1 Cor. 15.1-11) and depended on the Spirit's inspiration for the effect of his preaching of the crucified Christ (1 Cor.

---

161. The more serious danger in writing down a tradition, as Lord observed, is 'when the singer believes that they [the written versions] are *the* way in which the song *should* be presented' (*Singer* 79).

162. For this reason I often use the inelegant verbal noun formation 'traditioning' to indicate a process of which 'transmission' *per se* may be only a part.

163. Kelber, *Oral* 96-105, 129 (quotations from 98, 99-100, 129).

164. Kelber, *Oral* 141-51, 151-68.

165. Kelber, *Oral* 185-99, 199-207 (quotations from 201, 207). In the 'Introduction' to the republication of his *Oral* (Indiana University, 1996), Kelber concedes some ground to his critics: he forced 'the polarity of orality versus textuality' (xxi); he has become more aware of 'composition in dictation' and 'cultural memory', essentially oral processes (xxii-xxiii). But he still maintains 'Mark's polemic against the disciples . . . as an estrangement from the standard-bearers of oral tradition' (xxv).

2.4-5), Paul would certainly not have recognized such distinctions.[166] Kelber forgets not only the continuity between oral and first writing (as initially written orality), which he had earlier acknowledged, but he ignores the points made above, that in an age of high illiteracy documents were written to be *heard* and that a reading can also be likened to a performance. In claiming that, in contrast to Mark's Gospel, 'Q effects a direct address to present hearers',[167] he ignores the fact that Q is generally regarded as a *written* source (above §7.4). He also forgets the living character of tradition, that written as well as oral tradition can effect a re-presentation (making present again) of ancient teaching and events,[168] particularly in liturgy, as in Paul's recollection of Jesus' words in regard to the Lord's Supper (1 Cor. 11.23-26). Regrettably then, once again, the potential significance of recognizing the distinct character of the oral traditioning process in the case of the Jesus tradition has been subverted by another agenda and lost to sight.

g. R. A. Horsley and J. Draper

As Kelber made fruitful use of earlier work on the oral epic, so Horsley and Draper have benefited from the subsequent work of J. M. Foley in the same area.[169] Foley has advanced the debate on how oral performance functions (and functioned) by drawing upon the 'receptionalist' theories of contemporary literary criticism, particularly those of Iser and H. R. Jauss, to fill out what Foley calls 'traditional referentiality'. The key point is that a text has to be heard within the appropriate 'horizons of expectation' (Jauss); any text has 'gaps of indeterminacy' (Iser) which can be bridged only from the hearer's prior understanding of the text, author, and tradition. In other words, 'traditional referentiality' invokes 'a context that is enormously larger and more echoic than the text or work itself'; 'the traditional phraseology and narrative patterns continue to provide ways for the poet to convey meaning, to tap the traditional reservoir'. To elaborate the point Foley uses the term 'metonymy' and the concept of 'metonymic reference'

---

166. Cf. F. Vouga, 'Mündliche Tradition, soziale Kontrolle und Literatur als theologischer Protest', in G. Sellin and F. Vouga, eds., *Logos und Buchstabe: Mündlichkeit und Schriftlichkeit im Judentum und Christentum der Antike* (Tübingen: Francke, 1997) 195-209 (here 205-206, and further 205-208).

167. Kelber, *Oral* 201.

168. Deut. 6.20-25: '*we* were Pharaoh's slaves . . . and the Lord brought *us* out of Egypt . . .'.

169. J. M. Foley, *Immanent Art: From Structure to Meaning in Traditional Oral Epic* (Bloomington: Indiana University, 1991); also *The Singer of Tales in Performance* (Bloomington: Indiana University, 1995).

to designate 'a mode of signification wherein the part stands for the whole', in which a text 'is enriched by an unspoken context that dwarfs the textual artifact'.[170] He can thus speak of 'the unifying role of tradition', able to give consistency within the diversity of performance because of the traditional referentiality of the text. Oral traditional texts imply an audience with the background to respond faithfully to the signals encoded in the text, to bridge the gaps of indeterminacy and thus to 'build' the implied consistency.[171] In short, performance is the enabling event, tradition the enabling referent.[172]

Horsley applies Foley's thesis to Q: Q should be seen as the transcript of one performance among many of an oral text, 'a libretto that was regularly performed in an early Jesus movement'; its metonymic context of reception would be Israelite (as distinct from Judean) cultural traditions.[173] Draper likewise takes up the idea of metonymic referencing, noting that it will be culturally determined and that a single word or phrase will often summarize in telescoped form a whole aspect of the culture and tradition of the people; he goes on to read Q 12.49-59 as an example, concluding that its metonymic reference is not apocalyptic but prophetic-covenantal.[174]

Horsley and Draper have their own particular axes to grind (haven't we all?). But the blend of insights from earlier oral tradition theory with contemporary literary theory provided by Foley is of wider significance and its potential has still to be fully explored in regard to the Jesus tradition. I hope the present work will constitute a step in that direction.

h. Kenneth Bailey

What has been missing in all this has been a sufficiently close parallel to the oral traditioning which presumably was the initial mode of and vehicle for the Jesus

---

170. Foley, *Immanent Art* chs. 1 and 2 (particularly 6-13 and 42-45; quotations from 7 and 40-41). The argument is developed in *Singer of Tales in Performance* chs. 1-3.

171. Foley, *Immanent Art* 44, 47-48. He can even argue that the responsibility of the 'reader' of an oral traditional text is 'to attempt to become as far as possible the audience implied by that text . . .' (54-55).

172. A central thesis of *Singer of Tales in Performance* 28. See also Vansina, *Oral Tradition as History,* on 'Performance': 'The tale must be well known to the public if the performance is to be a success for the audience must not be overly preoccupied with the task of trying to follow painstakingly what is being told in order to enjoy the tale. They must already know the tale so that they can enjoy the rendering of its various episodes, appreciate the innovations, and anticipate the thrills still to come. So every performance is new, but every performance presupposes something old: the tale itself' (35).

173. Horsley and Draper, *Whoever* 160-74.

174. Horsley and Draper, *Whoever* 181-94.

tradition. As Kelber himself noted,[175] however helpful the lessons learned from the study of Homeric epics and Yugoslavian sagas, we cannot simply assume that they provide the pattern for oral transmission of Jesus tradition within the thirty or so years between Jesus and the first written Gospel. The nearest we have to fill the gap are the anecdotal essays by Kenneth Bailey in which he has reflected on more than thirty years experience of Middle East village life.[176] These villages have retained their identity over many generations, so that, arguably, their oral culture is as close as we will ever be able to find to the village culture of first-century Galilee. Bailey puts forward the idea of *'informal controlled tradition'*, to distinguish it from the models used by both Bultmann ('informal, uncontrolled tradition') and Gerhardsson ('formal controlled tradition'). In informal controlled tradition the story can be retold in the setting of a gathering of the village by any member of the village present, but usually the elders, and the community itself exercises the 'control'.[177]

Bailey characterizes the types of material thus preserved under various headings. (1) Pithy proverbs; he describes 'a community that can create (over the centuries) and sustain in current usage up to 6,000 wisdom sayings'. (2) Story riddles; 'in that story the hero is presented with an unsolvable problem and comes up with a wise answer'. (3) Poetry, both classical and popular. (4) Parable or story; 'Once there was a rich man who . . .', or 'a priest who . . .', and so on. (5) Well-told accounts of the important figures in the history of the village or community; 'if there is a central figure critical to the history of the village, stories of this central figure will abound'.[178]

Particularly valuable are Bailey's notes on how the community controlled its tradition. He distinguishes different levels of control. (i) No flexibility — po-

---

175. Kelber, *Oral* 78-79.

176. K. E. Bailey, 'Informal Controlled Oral Tradition and the Synoptic Gospels', *Asia Journal of Theology* 5 (1991) 34-54; also 'Middle Eastern Oral Tradition and the Synoptic Gospels', *ExpT* 106 (1995) 363-67. I describe these as anecdotal, but will note several points at which Vansina's ethno-historical researches in Africa (*Oral Tradition as History* and his earlier *Oral Tradition: A Study in Historical Methodology* [London: Routledge and Kegan Paul, 1965]) bear out Bailey's findings. Terence Mournet refers me also to I. Okpewho, *African Oral Literature: Backgrounds, Character and Continuity* (Bloomington: Indiana University, 1992). Wright is one of very few scholars to have taken note of Bailey's work (*Jesus* 133-37).

177. Bailey, 'Informal' 35-40; 'Oral Tradition' 364. Bailey had already made the point in his *Poet and Peasant:* 'Not only is the life of such [Middle Eastern] peasants remarkably archaic but their intellectual life is in the form of poems and stories preserved from the past. Men gather nightly in the village for what is called "haflat *samar*" (social gathering for *samar*), which is cognate with the Hebrew *shamar,* "to preserve". They are gathering to preserve the intellectual life of their community by the recitation of poems and the retelling of stories . . .' (31-32).

178. Bailey, 'Informal' 41-42; 'Oral Tradition' 365.

ems and proverbs.[179] (ii) Some flexibility — parables and recollections of people and events important to the identity of the community. 'Here there is flexibility and control. The central threads of the story cannot be changed, but flexibility in detail is allowed'. (iii) Total flexibility — jokes and casual news. *'The material is irrelevant to the identity of the community* and is not judged *wise* or *valuable'*.[180]

> In the *haflat samar* the *community* exercises control over the recitation. These poems, proverbs and stories form their identity. The right telling of these stories is critical for that identity. If someone tells the story "wrong", the reciter is corrected by a chorus of voices. Some stories may be new. But the stories that matter are the accounts known by all. The occasion is informal but the recitation is *controlled*.[181]

He illustrates more recent tradition by retelling stories about John Hogg, the primary founder of the new Egyptian evangelical community in the nineteenth century. These were orally transmitted and sustained stories which had been drawn on for Dr Hogg's biography (published in 1914) and which were still being retold in almost same way when Bailey dipped into the tradition in 1955-65.[182]

He also tells two stories from his own experience.[183] One concerns a fatal accident that took place at a village wedding, where it was customary to fire hundreds of rifle rounds into the air in celebration. On his way (back) to the village Bailey heard the story from several people, including the boatman taking him

---

179. The same observation is made by Vansina, *Oral Tradition as History* 48-49.

180. Bailey, 'Informal' 42-45 (his emphasis).

181. Bailey, 'Oral Tradition' 365; 'Stories critical for the community's identity can be repeated in public only by those deemed worthy to repeat them' (364). Vansina also notes that the more important a tradition to a community's identity, the greater the control likely to be exercised over its recitation and transmission (*Oral Tradition* 31-39) and concludes, 'Various methods of transmission may be used, some of which are capable of ensuring that the proto-testimony does not alter much in the course of transmission' (46; see also 78, 199). 'Communication of oral tradition is part of the process of establishing collective representations' (*Oral Tradition as History* 124; see also 41-42, 96-100).

182. Bailey, 'Informal' 45-47; 'Oral Tradition' 366. To be noted is the fact that 'community' here does not equate to 'individual village', since the evangelical community would be scattered over many villages. Bailey's claims regarding the stability of the stories told about Hogg have been seriously challenged, particularly by T. Weeden in http://groups.yahoo.com/group/crosstalk2/message/8301 and /8730. In personal correspondence Bailey has expressed his regret at some overstatement in regard to the Hogg traditions, but insists that his hypothesis is based primarily on his own experience of the *haflat samar.* Weeden's further critique of Bailey's anecdotes and their significance misses much of Bailey's point, is unduly censorious, and weakens Bailey's case hardly at all.

183. Bailey, 'Informal' 48-50.

across the Nile, a boy on the far bank, and other villagers including the village mayor. Each retelling included different details, but the climax of the story was almost word for word:

> Hanna [the bridegroom's friend] fired the gun. The gun did not go off. He lowered the gun. The gun fired [passive form]. The bullet passed through the stomach of Butrus [the bridegroom]. He died. He did not cry out, 'O my father', nor 'O my mother' (meaning he died instantly without crying out). When the police came we told them, 'A camel stepped on him'.

The point was that the community had quickly determined that the death was an accident and the story had been crystallized to make this clear ('The gun fired', not 'He fired the gun').[184] By the time Bailey heard it (a week after the event) the story had been given its definitive shape.[185]

His other story is of his own experience of preaching. Often he would tell a story new to the community. As soon as the story was finished the congregation would enact 'a form of oral shorthand'.

> The elder on the front row would shout across the church to a friend in a loud voice, 'Did you hear what the preacher said? He said . . .' and then would come a line or two of the story including the punch line. People all across the church instinctively turned to their neighbours and repeated the central thrust of the story twice and thrice to each other. They wanted to retell the story that week across the village and they had to learn it on the spot.

184. The police accepted the community's version ('A camel stepped on him'), not because they did not know what had happened but because they accepted the community's judgment that the shooting was an accident. Vansina cites a case from his field research in the Congo where a group testimony was rehearsed beforehand so that there would be no disagreement when the testimony was given in public (*Oral Tradition* 28) — that is, a tradition preserved by a group and under corporate control. The point is taken up by E. L. Abel, 'The Psychology of Memory and Rumor Transmission and Their Bearing on Theories of Oral Transmission in Early Christianity', *JR* 51 (1971) 270-81 (here 276).

185. Bailey notes that he had first heard the story some thirty years earlier, but the central core was 'still indelibly fixed' in his mind because it was so firmly implanted in his memory that first week ('Informal' 49). If I may add my own pennyworth, I met Kenneth Bailey in 1976, when he told me the same two stories. They made such an impression on me that I have retold them several times during the intervening years. When I eventually came across the article cited (in 1998) I was fascinated to note that my own retelling had maintained the outline and the key features of the core elements, although in my retelling the supporting details had been reshaped. This oral transmission covered more than twenty years, after a single hearing of the stories, by one who normally forgets a good joke almost as soon as he has heard it! Martin Hengel gives two personal reminiscences where the 'oral tradition' stretches back over 55 and more than 150 years (*Studies in the Gospel of Mark* 109-10).

The hypothesis which Bailey offers on the basis of his reflections on these experiences is that informal, controlled oral tradition is the best explanation for the oral transmission of the Jesus tradition. Up until the upheaval of the first Jewish revolt (66-73) informal controlled oral tradition would have been able to function in the villages of Palestine. But even then, anyone twenty years and older in the 60s could have been 'an authentic reciter of that tradition'.[186]

To say it again, Bailey's essay is anecdotal and not the result of scientific research.[187] Even so, the character of oral tradition which it illustrates accords well with the findings of other investigations of oral tradition and is self-evidently far closer to the sort of oral traditioning which must be posited for the Jesus tradition than the studies on which Kelber has been able to draw. Bailey's experience also confirms that the previous paradigms offered by Bultmann and Gerhardsson are inadequate for our own understanding of the oral transmission of the Jesus tradition. In particular, the paradigm of literary editing is confirmed as wholly inappropriate: in oral tradition one telling of a story is in no sense an editing of a previous telling; rather, each telling starts with the same subject and theme, but the retellings are different; each telling is a performance of the tradition itself, not of the first, or third, or twenty-third 'edition' of the tradition. Our expectation, accordingly, should be of the oral transmission of Jesus tradition as a sequence of retellings, each starting from the same storehouse of communally remembered events and teaching, and each weaving the common stock together in different patterns for different contexts.

Of special interest is the degree to which Bailey's thesis both informs and refines the general recognition among students of the subject that oral tradition is typically flexible, with constant themes, recognizable versions of the same story, some word-for-word repetition, and both fixed and variable formulaic elements depending on the context of the performance. What he adds is significant; in particular the recognition of the likelihood that (1) a community would be concerned enough to exercise some control over its traditions; (2) the degree of control exercised would vary both in regard to form and in regard to the relative importance of the tradition for its own identity; and (3) the element in the story regarded as its core or key to its meaning would be its most firmly fixed element.[188]

---

186. Bailey, 'Informal' 50; similarly 'Oral Tradition' 367.

187. T. M. Derico hopes to carry out more scientifically controlled fieldwork (*On the Selection of Oral-Traditional Data: Methodological Prolegomena for the Construction of a New Model of Early Christian Oral Tradition* [St. Andrews MPhil, 2001], though the advent of television into the village communities of the Middle East may mean that the generations-old pattern of oral tradition is already being lost beyond recall.

188. Cf. Lord's examples of songs with a 'more or less stable core' (*The Singer Resumes the Tale* [Ithaca: Cornell University, 1995] 44, 47, 61-62).

The crucial question, of course, is whether such an understanding of oral tradition provides an explanatory model for the Jesus tradition, and in particular, whether we can find the marks of such 'informal, controlled oral tradition' in the Synoptic tradition itself. I believe it does and think we can.

8.4. The Synoptic Tradition as Oral Tradition: Narratives

We certainly do not know enough about oral traditioning in the ancient world to draw from that knowledge clear guidelines for our understanding of how the Jesus tradition was passed down in its oral stage. Any inquiry on this subject is bound to turn to the Jesus tradition itself to ask whether there is sufficient evidence of oral transmission and what the tradition itself tells us about the traditioning process. We need to bear in mind, of course, that the only evidence we have is already literary (the Synoptic Gospels) and therefore also the possibility that the mode of transmission has been altered. On the other hand, Kelber readily acknowledges the oral character of much of Mark's material, and the boundaries between oral Q and written Q seem to be rather fluid, as we shall see. We shall therefore focus on Mark and Q material in the next two sections (§§8.4-5).

For convenience we will look first at the *narrative traditions*. Here at least we do not have the problem of deciding whether such traditions came from Jesus (as we inevitably ask in respect of sayings attributed to Jesus). At best such traditions derive from those who were with Jesus and who witnessed things he did and said.

a. The Conversion of Saul

The first example comes not from the Synoptics themselves, but from Luke's second volume, Acts. All that is necessary for the example to be relevant for an inquiry into Jesus tradition is the assumption that Luke handled such a tradition in Acts in the same way that he handled traditions in his Gospel.[189] The value of the example is threefold. (i) The three accounts (Acts 9.1-22; 22.1-21; 26.9-23) all come from a single author (Luke), so we avoid some of the unknowns opera-

---

189. The three accounts of Paul's conversion in Acts are occasionally treated synoptically (e.g., C. W. Hedrick, 'Paul's Conversion/Call: A Comparative Analysis of the Three Reports in Acts', *JBL* 100 [1981] 415-32; C. K. Barrett, *Acts 1–14* [ICC; Edinburgh: Clark, 1994] 439-45), but their value as examples of the way oral tradition functioned has thus far not really been appreciated.

tive when two or three different authors deal with the same episode; there is no need to hypothesize different sources. (ii) They are manifestly all accounts of the same event (Saul's conversion), so the harmoniser's hypothesis of different episodes to explain differences between parallel accounts is not open to us. (iii) And yet they are strikingly different in their detail; so if the *same* author can tell the *same* story in such *different* ways, it must tell us much about his own attitude to re-telling traditional material, and possibly about the early Christian traditioning process more generally.[190]

When we examine the three accounts more closely there quickly becomes evident a striking parallel to the patterns of oral tradition observed above (§§8.3f-h). There are several constants: the chief character — Saul; the setting — a journey to Damascus to persecute followers of Jesus; the circumstances — a (bright) light from heaven, Saul fallen to the ground, Saul's companions; the heavenly voice. But beyond that the details vary considerably. Did Saul's companions all fall to the ground (26.14), or only Saul himself (9.4, 7)? Did they hear the voice of Jesus (9.7), or not (22.9)? Saul's blindness, so prominent in chs. 9 and 22, is not mentioned in ch. 26. Likewise, Ananias has considerable prominence in chs. 9 and 22, but is nowhere mentioned in ch. 26. The other constant, the commission to go to the Gentiles, comes once to Saul directly on the road (26.16-18), once through Ananias (9.15-17), and once later in Jerusalem (22.16-18). Most striking of all is the fact that what was evidently accounted the core of the story, the exchange between Saul and the exalted Jesus, is *word for word the same in each account,* after which each telling of the story goes its own distinctive way:[191]

190. The passages are thus a good example of Lord's observation that even from the same singer, stability from one performance to another is likely to lie not at the word for word level of the text, but at the levels of theme and story pattern (*Singer* ch. 5). Similarly Finnegan: 'that variability is not just a feature of lengthy oral transmission through time and space but is inherent both in different renderings of one literary piece within the same group and period and even in texts by the same person delivered at no great interval in time. In such cases, memorisation of basic themes or plots is involved, but a generalised explanation of the oral poetry in terms of particular texts exactly memorised does not easily fit the abundant variability demonstrated in tape-recorded (as well as dictated) texts' (*Oral Poetry* 57).

191. In the following extracts I will underline the verbal agreements between the different versions. The degree of agreement would be clearer if I used Greek, but that would reduce the wider usefulness of the documentation. To bring out the closeness of the Greek I have used my own translations.

9.3 As he was <u>travelling</u> and approaching <u>Damascus</u>,	22.6 'While I was <u>travelling</u> and approaching <u>Damascus</u>,	26.12 'I was <u>travelling</u> to <u>Damascus</u> with the authority and commission of the chief priests, 13 when at midday along the road, your Excellency, I saw <u>a light from heaven</u>, brighter than the sun, shining around me and my companions. 14 When we had all fallen <u>to the earth</u>, I <u>heard a voice saying</u> to me in the Hebrew language, "<u>Saul</u>, <u>Saul, why are you persecuting me</u>? It hurts you to kick against the goads". 15 I asked, "<u>Who are you, Lord?</u>" The Lord said, "<u>I am Jesus</u> <u>whom you are persecuting</u>.
	about noon	
suddenly <u>a light from heaven</u>	<u>a great light from heaven</u> suddenly	
flashed around him.	shone about me.	
4 He <u>fell</u> <u>to the earth</u> and <u>heard a voice saying</u> to him, "<u>Saul</u>, <u>Saul, why are you persecuting me?</u>	7 I <u>fell</u> to the ground and <u>heard a voice saying</u> to me, "<u>Saul</u>, <u>Saul, why are you persecuting me?</u>	
5 He asked, "<u>Who are you, Lord?</u>" The reply came, "<u>I am Jesus</u>, <u>whom you are persecuting</u>.	8 I answered, "<u>Who are you, Lord?</u>" Then he said to me, "<u>I am Jesus</u> of Nazareth <u>whom you are persecuting</u>". 9 Now those who were with me saw the light but did not hear the voice of the one who was speaking to me. 10 I asked, "What am I to do, Lord?" The	
6 But <u>get up and</u> enter the city, and you will be told what you are to do".	Lord said to me, "<u>Get up and</u> go to Damascus; there you will be told everything that has been assigned to you to do"'.	16 But <u>get up and</u> stand on your feet; . . ."'.

Here, then, we have an excellent example of the oral principle of 'variation within the same', and specifically of Bailey's finding that the key point in the story will be held constant, while the supporting details can vary according to the circumstances. In this case in particular, the second account is clearly angled to bring out Saul's Jewish identity (22.3, 17; also Ananias — 22.12) and the account of the heavenly commission delayed for dramatic effect (22.17-21), whereas the third account functions as part of Paul's defence by implying that Paul's commission was part of Israel's commission (26.18, 23).[192] In short, what becomes evident here is the fact that Luke was himself a good story-teller and that his retelling the story of Paul's conversion is a good example not simply of the use of oral tradition in a written work, but of the oral traditioning process itself.

b. The Centurion's Servant

Within the Gospel tradition itself, one of the most intriguing episodes is the one recorded in Matt. 8.5-13 and Luke 7.1-10 (with a likely parallel in John 4.46b-54). The first point of interest is that the pericope is usually credited to Q, despite it being a narrative and despite there being no parallel to such an episode being

192. Note the echoes of Isa. 42.6, 16 and 49.6.

included within other sayings Gospels.[193] But why should a pericope be attributed to the document Q simply because it belongs to the non-Markan material common to Matthew and Luke ('q')?[194] Did Matthew and Luke have no common (oral) tradition other than Q? That hardly seems likely as an *a priori*. In fact, the logic behind the Q hypothesis is that the degree of *closeness* between Matthew and Luke ('q') can be explained only by postulating a common written source ('Q'). Whereas the divergence between Matthew and Luke in the first half of the story is substantial, to put it no more strongly. Of course, it is possible to argue, as most do, that Matthew or Luke, or both, have heavily edited the Q version; but when 'q' properly speaking covers only part of the pericope, the argument for the existence of 'Q' at this point becomes very slippery.

Is common oral tradition a more plausible hypothesis? Let us not assume that Matthew's and Luke's only source for such non-Markan Jesus tradition was a written document (Q). When we then examine the matter more closely the oral tradition hypothesis does indeed seem to make as good if not better sense.

Matt. 8.5-13	Luke 7.1-10
7.28 Now when Jesus had ended all these words . . . . 5 When <u>he entered Capernaum,</u> <u>a centurion</u> came to him, appealing to him 6 and saying, "Lord, my servant is lying at home paralyzed, in terrible distress". 7 And he said to him, "I will come and cure him".	1 After Jesus had completed all his sayings in the hearing of the people, <u>he entered Capernaum.</u> 2 <u>A centurion</u> there had a slave whom he valued highly, and who was ill and close to death. 3 When he heard about Jesus, he sent some Jewish elders to him, asking him to come and heal his slave. 4 When they came to Jesus, they appealed to him earnestly, saying, "He is worthy of having you do this for him, 5 for he loves our people, and it is he who built our synagogue for us". 6 And Jesus went with them, but when he was not far from the house, the centurion sent friends to
8 The centurion answered, "<u>Lord,</u> <u>I</u> <u>am not fit to have you come under my roof;</u> <u>but</u> only <u>speak the word, and</u> <u>my servant</u> will <u>be healed. 9 For I also am a man</u> <u>under authority, with soldiers under me; and I say</u> <u>to one, 'Go', and he goes, and to another, 'Come',</u> <u>and he comes, and to my slave, 'Do this', and the</u> <u>slave does it". 10 When Jesus heard</u> him, <u>he was</u> <u>amazed and</u> <u>said</u> to those who <u>followed him,</u> "Truly <u>I tell you,</u> in <u>no</u> one <u>in</u> <u>Israel have I found such faith.</u> 11 I tell you,	say to him, "<u>Lord,</u> do not trouble yourself, for <u>I</u> <u>am not fit to have you come under my roof;</u> 7 therefore I did not consider myself worthy to come to you. <u>But</u> <u>speak the word, and</u> let <u>my servant</u> <u>be healed. 8 For I also am a man</u> <u>under authority, with soldiers under me; and I say</u> <u>to one, 'Go', and he goes, and to another, 'Come',</u> <u>and he comes, and to my slave, 'Do this', and the</u> <u>slave does it". 9 When Jesus heard</u> this <u>he was</u> <u>amazed</u> at him, <u>and</u> turning to the crowd that <u>followed him,</u> he <u>said,</u> "<u>I tell you,</u> <u>not</u> even <u>in</u> <u>Israel have I found such faith".</u>

193. The point is simply assumed, e.g., by Bultmann, *History* 39; Miller, *Complete Gospels* 262-63 (others in Kloppenborg, *Q Parallels* 50). Early reconstructions of Q did not include Matt. 8.5-13/Luke 7.1-10 (chapter 4 n. 88).

194. The most weighty consideration is that Matthew and Luke both agree in positioning the episode after the Sermon on the Mount/Plain — Matt. 7.28/Luke 7.1 (Harnack, *Sayings of Jesus* 74; Lührmann, *Redaktion* 57). But is that sufficient?

| many will come from east and west and will eat with Abraham and Isaac and Jacob in the kingdom of heaven, 12 while the heirs of the kingdom will be thrown into the outer darkness, where there will be weeping and gnashing of teeth". 13 And to the centurion Jesus said, "Go; let it be done for you according to your faith". And the servant was healed in that hour. | Luke 13.28-29 |
| | 10 When those who had been sent returned to the house, they found the slave in good health. |

The episode is clearly the same: it is the story of the healing at a distance of the seriously ill servant of a centurion who lived in Capernaum. Within that framework we find the same striking features: (i) a core of the story where the agreement is almost word for word (Matt. 8.8-10/Luke 7.6b-9); (ii) details which vary on either side of the core to such an extent that the two versions seem to contradict each other (in Matthew the centurion comes to plead with Jesus personally; in Luke he makes a point of not coming).

Evidently the exchange between Jesus and the centurion made a considerable impression on the disciples of Jesus: the combination of humility and confidence in Jesus on the part of such a figure, and Jesus' surprise at its strength would have been striking enough.[195] Equally noticeable is the way in which Matthew and Luke have each taken the story in his own way. Matthew emphasizes the theme of the centurion's *faith,* by inserting the saying (Matt. 8.11-12) which Luke records in Luke 13.28-29 (the centurion as precedent for Gentile faith),[196] and by rounding off his telling with a further commendation by Jesus of the centurion's faith (Matt. 8.13). Luke emphasizes the theme of the centurion's *worthiness* by having the elders testify of his worthiness *(axios)* (7.4-5) in counterpoise to the centurion's expression of unworthiness *(oude exiosa)* (7.7a). Nor should we ignore the fact that both Matthew and Luke draw their different emphases from the same core — faith (Matt. 8.10), worthiness/fitness (*hikanos,* Luke 7.6).

Here I would suggest is a fine example of oral traditioning, or if it is preferred, of Evangelists writing the story in oral mode.[197] The story was no doubt

195. Contrast the Jesus Seminar: 'Since the words ascribed to Jesus vary, and since there is nothing distinctive about them, we must assume they were created by story-tellers' (Funk, *Five Gospels* 300). But the argument is self-defeating: would story-tellers create such unmemorable words, and why then would they be held constant in other re-tellings?

196. Funk's discussion is quite confused as to whether Matt. 8.11-12 could have existed separately from Matthew's narrative context (*Five Gospels* 160), despite the recognition that its 'Q' parallel (Luke 13.28-29) need not presuppose a Gentile mission (348), whereas Kloppenborg argues that the 'tendentious development of the healing story into an apology for Gentile inclusion occurred already in the oral stage' prior to Q (*Formation* 120).

197. Contrast the redactional approach, as exemplified by U. Wegner, *Der Hauptmann von Kafarnaum* (WUNT 2.14; Tübingen: Mohr Siebeck, 1985), and Catchpole, *Quest* ch. 10, which characteristically assumes the literary paradigm throughout and evokes the picture of Matthew and Luke carefully editing an original Q more or less word by word.

one which belonged to several communities' store of Jesus tradition. The story's point hangs entirely on the central exchange between Jesus and the centurion; that is maintained with care and accuracy. We may deduce that the story was important for these communities' identity, not least for their own sense of respect for and openness to Gentiles.

What, however, about John 4.46-54?

> 46Then he came again to Cana in Galilee where he had changed the water into wine. Now there was a royal official *(basilikos)* whose son lay ill in Capernaum. 47When he heard that Jesus had come from Judea to Galilee, he went and begged him to come down and heal his son, for he was at the point of death. 48Then Jesus said to him, 'Unless you see signs and wonders you will not believe'. 49The official said to him, 'Sir, come down before my little boy dies'. 50Jesus said to him, 'Go; your son will live'. The man believed the word that Jesus spoke to him and started on his way. 51As he was going down, his slaves met him and told him that his child was alive. 52So he asked them the hour when he began to recover, and they said to him, 'Yesterday at one in the afternoon the fever left him'. 53The father realized that this was the hour when Jesus had said to him, 'Your son will live'. So he himself believed, along with his whole household.

Agreement in no less than eleven points of detail is probably enough to substantiate the conclusion that this story of the healing at a distance of the seriously ill servant of a person of rank in Capernaum is another version (more distant echo?) of the same episode that we find in Matthew 8 and Luke 7.[198] Particularly noticeable, however, are the facts that the official is not (no longer) identified as a Gentile and that the Matthean/Lukan core is not (no longer) there. On the other hand, the key emphasis on the person's faith is present, and Jesus' response to that faith (despite some initial hesitation); John strengthens the theme and uses it to develop his own warning against a faith based merely on miracle (John 4.48).[199]

What to make of this in terms of early Christian oral transmission? The simplest answer is that two versions of the same episode diverged in the course of various retellings. It could be that the idea of the official as a *Gentile* centurion

---

198. See further Dodd, *Historical Tradition* 188-95; Wegner, *Hauptmann* 37-57, 73-74; Dunn, 'John and the Oral Gospel Tradition', in Wansbrough, ed., *Jesus* 359-63. The Jesus Seminar thought the Johannine version was closer to the 'original form' (Funk, *Acts of Jesus* 46).

199. For John's theology of different levels of faith, see, e.g., R. E. Brown, *John* (AB 29, 2 vols.; New York: Doubleday, 1966) 530-31. Dodd saw the contrast as between the Synoptics' interest in the remarkable faith of a Gentile, whereas 'in John the central interest lies in the life-giving power of the word of Christ' (*Historical Tradition* 194). Crossan, however, overstates the contrast between the two versions (Matthew/Luke and John) when he talks of the story being pulled in 'two contradictory directions' (*Historical Jesus* 327).

was introduced in the course of the retelling.[200] Alternatively, and if anything more probable, it could be that in the second (Johannine) stream of tradition the identity of the official as a Gentile was seen as a subsidiary detail to the main emphasis on his faith, and so was neglected in the retellings.[201] Either way, the differences are so great that the hypothesis of literary dependence becomes highly improbable;[202] on the contrary, the two versions (Matthew/Luke and John) provide good evidence of stories of Jesus being kept alive in oral tradition.[203] And either way we can see something of both the retentiveness of the oral traditioning process and its flexibility in allowing traditions to be adapted to bring out differing emphases.

c. Markan Narratives

I have already given examples of where Synoptic analysis points to the firm conclusion of Matthean and Lukan dependency on Mark (§7.3). But in other cases the variation in detail is such that the straightforward hypothesis of literary dependence on Mark becomes very strained. Consider the following narratives: the stilling of the storm (Mark 4.35-41/Matt. 8.23-27/Luke 8.22-25); the Syrophoenician woman (Mark 7.24-30/Matt. 15.21-28); the healing of the possessed boy (Mark 9.14-27/Matt. 17.14-18/Luke 9.37-43); the dispute about greatness (Mark 9.33-37/Matt. 18.1-5/Luke 9.46-48); and the widow's mite (Mark 12.41-44/Luke 21.1-4).

200. Since Herod's army was modelled on the Roman pattern, the 'centurion' of the Synoptic account could conceivably have been a Jew.

201. *Basilikos* (John 4.46) denotes a royal official, not necessarily a Jew; Herod Antipas could have appointed some experienced foreigners (like a centurion) to his military staff.

202. *Pace* F. Neirynck, 'John 4.46-54: Signs Source and/or Synoptic Gospels', *Evangelica II* (Leuven: Leuven University, 1991) 679-88, who assumes that only redaction of literary sources can be invoked to explain the differences.

203. Cf. E. Haenchen, *Johannesevangelium* (Tübingen: Mohr-Siebeck, 1980) 260-61, summarizing his treatment in 'Johanneische Probleme', *Gott und Mensch* (Tübingen: Mohr-Siebeck, 1965) 82-90.

i. The Stilling of the Storm

Matt. 8.23-27	Mark 4.35-41	Luke 8.22-25
23 And when he got into the boat, his disciples followed him. 24 A great storm arose on the sea, so great that the boat was being swamped by the waves; but he was asleep. 25 And they went and <u>woke him up</u>, saying, "Lord, save us! <u>We are perishing!</u>" 26 And he said to them, "Why are you afraid, you of little <u>faith</u>?" Then <u>he got up and rebuked the winds and the sea;</u> <u>and there was a</u> dead <u>calm.</u> 27 The men were amazed, saying, "What sort of man <u>is this, that even the winds and the sea obey him?</u>"	35 On that day, when evening had come, he said to them, "Let us go across to the other side". 36 And leaving the crowd behind, they took him with them in the boat, just as he was. Other boats were with him. 37 A great <u>stormwind</u> arose, and the waves beat into the boat, so that the boat was already being filled. 38 But he was in the stern, sleeping on the cushion; and they <u>woke him up</u> and said to him, "Teacher, do you not care that <u>we are perishing?</u>" 39 <u>He got up and rebuked the wind,</u> and said to the sea, "Be quiet! Silence!" Then the wind ceased, <u>and there was a</u> dead <u>calm.</u> 40 He said to them, "Why are you <u>afraid</u>? Have you still no <u>faith</u>?" 41 And they were filled with great awe and said to one another, "Who then <u>is this, that even the wind and the sea obey him?</u>"	22 One day he got into a boat with his disciples, and he said to them, "Let us go across to the other side of the lake". So they put out, 23 and while they were sailing he fell asleep. A <u>stormwind</u> swept down on the lake, and the boat was filling up, and they were in danger. 24 They went to him and <u>woke him up</u>, saying, "Master, Master, <u>we are perishing!</u>" And <u>he got up and rebuked the wind</u> and the raging waves; they ceased, <u>and there was a</u> <u>calm.</u> 25 He said to them, "Where is your <u>faith</u>?" They were <u>afraid</u> and amazed, and said to one another, "Who then <u>is this, that</u> he commands <u>even the winds and</u> the water, and they <u>obey him?</u>"

Here again we have the characteristic features of different retellings of a single story about Jesus. The key points remain constant: Jesus with his disciples in a boat (on the lake); a great storm and Jesus asleep (differently described); the disciples rouse Jesus, he rebukes the wind and sea and a calm results; Jesus questions the disciples' lack of faith and they express wonder. The key lines are clearly: 'he got up and rebuked the wind(s), and there was a calm'; 'who is this that even the wind(s) obey him?'[204] Round this core the story could be told and retold, the details varied in accordance with the context of retelling and with any particular angle the storyteller wished to bring out.[205]

Once again it is quite possible to argue for a purely literary connection —

204. It is widely recognized that the story is structured on the pattern of the story of Jonah, with the key lines distinctive to bring out the point, How much greater than Jonah is here; see, e.g., Davies and Allison, *Matthew* 2.70.

205. In particular Matthew's retelling emphasizes the themes of discipleship/following (*akolouthein* — 8.19, 22, 23) and of 'little faith' (*oligopistos/ia*), distinctive to Matthew (8.26; cf. 6.30; 14.31; 16.8; 17.20). See also below §13.2b.

Matthew and Luke drawing upon and editing Mark's (for them) original. The problem with the purely literary hypothesis is that most of the differences are so inconsequential. Why, for example, as literary editors would it be necessary for them to vary the description of the danger of the boat being swamped (each uses different verbs) and to vary the account of Jesus sleeping and the references to the disciples' fear and lack of faith? Is it not more plausible to deduce that Matthew and Luke knew their own (oral) versions of the story and drew on them primarily or as well? Alternatively, it could be that they followed Mark in oral mode, as we might say; that is, they did not slavishly copy Mark (as they did elsewhere), but having taken the point of Mark's story they retold it as a storyteller would, retaining the constant points which gave the story its identity, and building round the core to bring out their own distinctive emphases.

ii. The Syrophoenician Woman

Matt. 15.21-28	Mark 7.24-30
21 Jesus left that place and went off to the district of <u>Tyre</u> and Sidon. 22 Just then a Canaanite <u>woman</u> from that region came out and started shouting, "Have mercy on me, lord, son of David; my daughter is tormented by a demon". 23 But he did not answer her at all. And his disciples came and urged him, saying, "Send her away, for she keeps shouting after us". 24 He answered, "I was sent only to the lost sheep of the house of Israel". 25 But she came and knelt before him, saying, "Lord, help me". 26 He answered, "It is not fair to take the children's food and throw it to the dogs". 27 She said, "Certainly, lord, for also the dogs eat from the crumbs that fall from their masters' table". 28 Then Jesus answered her, "Woman, great is your faith! Let it be done for you as you wish". And her <u>daughter</u> was healed from that hour.	24 From there he set out and went away to the region of <u>Tyre</u>. He entered a house and did not want anyone to know he was there. Yet he could not escape notice, 25 but a <u>woman</u> whose little daughter had an unclean spirit immediately heard about him, and she came and bowed down at his feet. 26 Now the woman was a Gentile, of Syrophoenician origin. She begged him to cast the demon out of her daughter. 27 He said to her, "Let the children be fed first, for <u>it is not fair to take the children's food and throw it to the dogs</u>". 28 But she answered him, "<u>Certainly, lord, and the dogs under the table eat from the crumbs</u> of the children". 29 So he said to her, "For saying that, you may go, the demon has left your <u>daughter</u>". 30 So she went to her home, and found the child lying on the bed, and the demon gone.

The picture here is very similar. The story is again clearly the same: an event which took place in the district of Tyre; a non-Israelite woman with a demon-possessed daughter; healing at a distance. Most striking is the fact that the two versions share very few words in common apart from the core section (underlined). The core of the story is manifestly the exchange between Jesus and the woman, held constant, more or less verbatim (Mark 7.27-28/Matt. 15.26-27). Apart from that the retelling is completely variable: in particular, Mark emphasizes the woman's Gentile identity, while Matthew both plays up the resulting tension and the woman's faith. As with the story of the centurion's servant above, the fact that the healing was successful is almost an afterthought in each telling.

Here too the same feature is evident as in the stilling of the storm: the variation between the two versions is such that the hypothesis of literary dependence becomes very implausible. A connection at the level of oral retelling is much the more probable. Either Matthew knew the story through the tradition of oral performance and drew directly from that tradition, or he himself retold Mark's story as a storyteller would. We should note that it would be misleading to say that Matthew knew a different *version* of the story.[206] For that would be to slip back into the idiom of literary editions, as though each retelling of the story was a fresh 'edition' of the story; whereas the reality with which we are confronted is more like spontaneously different variations (retellings) on a theme (the identifiable subject matter and core).

iii. The Healing of the Possessed Boy

Matt. 17.14-18	Mark 9.14-27	Luke 9.37-43
14 And when they <u>came</u> to the <u>crowd,</u>	14 And when they <u>came</u> to the disciples, they saw a great <u>crowd</u> about them, and scribes arguing with them. 15 And immediately all the crowd, when they saw him, were greatly amazed, and ran up to him and greeted him. 16 And he asked them, 'What are you discussing with them?' 17 And one of the crowd answered him,	37 On the next day, when they had <u>come</u> down from the mountain, a great <u>crowd</u> met him.
a man came up to him and kneeling before him said, 15 'Lord, have mercy on <u>my son,</u>	'Teacher, I brought <u>my son</u>	38 And behold, a man from the crowd cried, 'Teacher, I beg you to look upon <u>my son,</u> for he is my only child; 39 and behold, a spirit
for he is an epileptic and he suffers terribly; for often he falls into the fire, and often into the water. 16 And I brought him to <u>your disciples,</u> <u>and</u> they could <u>not</u> heal him'. 17 And Jesus <u>answered,</u> '<u>O faithless</u> and perverse <u>generation, how long am I to be</u> with <u>you?</u> How long am I <u>to put up with you?</u> Bring him here to me'.	to you, for he has a dumb spirit; 18 and wherever it seizes him, it dashes him down; and he foams and grinds his teeth and becomes rigid; and I asked <u>your disciples</u> to cast it out, <u>and</u> they were <u>not</u> able'. 19 And he <u>answered</u> them, '<u>O faithless</u> <u>generation, how long am I to be</u> with <u>you?</u> How long am I <u>to put up with you?</u> Bring him to me'. 20 And they brought the boy to him; and when the spirit saw him, immediately it <u>convulsed</u> the boy, and he fell on the ground and rolled about, foaming at the mouth.	seizes him, and he suddenly cries out; it convulses him till he foams, and shatters him, and will hardly leave him. 40 And I begged <u>your disciples</u> to cast it out, <u>and</u> they could <u>not</u>'. 41 Jesus <u>answered,</u> '<u>O faithless</u> and perverse <u>generation, how long am I to be</u> with <u>you</u> and <u>to put up with you?</u> Lead your son here'. 42 While he was coming, the demon tore him and <u>convulsed</u> him.

206. Characteristic of discussion dominated by the literary paradigm is the assumption that variations between the two versions can be explained only in terms of conflation of sources; see, e.g., V. Taylor, *Mark* (London: Macmillan, 1952) 347.

	25 And when Jesus saw that a crowd came running together,	
18 And Jesus <u>rebuked</u> him,	he <u>rebuked</u> the unclean spirit, saying to it, 'You dumb and deaf spirit, I command you, come out of him, and never enter him again'. 26 And after crying out and convulsing him	But Jesus <u>rebuked</u> the unclean spirit,
and the demon <u>came out</u> of him,	terribly, it <u>came out</u>, and the boy was like a corpse; so that most of them said, 'He is dead'. 27	and healed the boy, and gave him back to his father. 43 And
and the boy was cured from that hour.	But Jesus took him by the hand and lifted him up, and he arose.	all were astonished at the majesty of God.

Here again we find what is clearly the same story — the healing, as is generally recognized from the description, of an epileptic boy.[207] And here again the verbal agreement across the three accounts is very modest, hardly inviting the explanation that Matthew and Luke derived their versions solely as an exercise in literary editing of Mark's account. If indeed Mark's long version was the only version they knew, then they have severely abbreviated it by retelling it in oral mode, feeling free to vary introduction, description of the boy's condition and cure, and conclusion, and holding constant only the core of Jesus' verbal rebuke. Alternatively, the degree of verbal agreement between Matt. 17.16b-17/Luke 9.40b-41[208] could indicate that Matthew and Luke happened to know another (oral) version which they echoed at that point.

iv. The Dispute about Greatness

Matt. 18.1-5	Mark 9.33-37	Luke 9.46-48
	33 Then they came to Capernaum; and when he was in the house he asked them, "What were you arguing about on the way?" 34 But they were silent,	
1 At that time the disciples came to Jesus and asked, "<u>Who</u> is <u>greater</u> in the kingdom of heaven?"	for on the way they had argued with one another about <u>who</u> was <u>greater</u>. 35 He sat down, called the twelve, and said to them, "Whoever wants to be first must be last of all and servant of all".	46 An argument arose among them as to <u>who</u> of them was <u>greater</u>.
2 He called <u>a little child, and put it</u> among them, 3 and said, "Truly I tell you, unless you turn and become like little children, you will never enter the kingdom of heaven. 4 Whoever humbles himself like	36 Then he took <u>a little child and put it</u> among them; and taking it in his arms, he said to them,	47 But Jesus, aware of their inner thoughts, took <u>a little child and put it</u> by his side, 48 and said to them,

207. See below chapter 15 n. 278.

208. One of the famous 'minor agreements' between Matthew and Luke over against Mark.

this little child is greater in the kingdom of heaven. 5 And whoever welcomes one such little child in my name welcomes me".	37 "Whoever welcomes one of such little children in my name welcomes me, and whoever welcomes me welcomes not me but the one who sent me".	"Whoever welcomes this little child in my name welcomes me, and whoever welcomes me welcomes the one who sent me; for he who is lesser among all of you, that one is great".

The basic picture is the same as before. The constants are clear: the disciples' dispute about who was greater; Jesus' rebuke by drawing a little child into the company; and the core saying which climaxes the story. Each retelling elaborates the basic outline in the Evangelist's own way (Mark 9.35; Matt. 18.3-4; Luke 9.48c). Mark and Luke were able also to use the fuller tradition of Jesus' speaking about 'the one who sent me' (Mark 9.37b/Luke 9.48b). And here again the low degree of verbal interdependence tells against literary interdependence, whereas the mix of constancy and flexibility is more suggestive of an oral mode of performance.[209]

v. The Widow's Pence

Mark 12.41-44	Luke 21.1-4
41 He sat down opposite the treasury, and watched how the crowd put money into the treasury. Many rich people put in large sums. 42 A poor widow came and put in two small copper coins, which are worth a penny. 43 Then he called his disciples and said to them, "Truly I tell you, this poor widow has put in more than all those who are contributing to the treasury. 44 For all have contributed out of their abundance; but she out of her poverty has put in all she had, her entire life".	1 He looked up and saw rich people putting into the treasury their gifts; 2 he also saw a needy widow putting in two small copper coins. 3 He said, "Of a truth I tell you, this poor widow has put in more than all of them; 4 for all those have contributed out of their abundance for the gifts, but she out of her poverty has put in all the life she had".

The episode is brief, being almost entirely taken up with the identifying details (the contrast between the rich people's giving and the two small copper coins of the poor widow), and with Jesus' observation which evidently made the episode so memorable (and which was consequently retained close to word for word). With such a brief pericope the scope for explanation in terms of Luke's editing of Mark is stronger. But even so, the flexibility of detail in the build-up to the climactic saying bespeaks more of oral than of literary tradition.

209. Here again Taylor's discussion in terms of 'fragments loosely connected at 35 and 36' and 'fragmentary stories' (*Mark* 403-404) betrays the assumption that there must have been an original story or original stories of which only fragments remain, and thus also his failure to appreciate the character of oral tradition.

Other examples could be offered.[210] None of this is intended to deny that Matthew and Luke knew Mark as such and were able to draw on his version of the tradition at a literary level and often did so; in terms of written sources, the case for Markan priority remains overwhelmingly the most probable (§7.3). Nor have I any wish to deny that Matthew and Luke regularly edited their Markan *Vorlage*. Sometimes by substantial abbreviation.[211] Sometimes by adding material to make a better[212] or a further point.[213] Sometimes to clarify or avoid misunderstandings.[214] At the same time, however, it would be improper to ignore the fact that in a good number of cases, illustrated above, the more natural explanation for the evidence is *not* Matthew's or Luke's literary dependence on Mark, but rather their own knowledge of oral retellings of the same stories (or, alternatively, their own oral retelling of the Markan stories).

Students of the Synoptic tradition really must free themselves from the as-

210. The healing of Peter's mother-in-law (Mark 1.29-31/Matt. 8.14-15/Luke 4.38-39); the cleansing of the leper (Mark 1.40-45/Matt. 8.1-4/Luke 5.12-16); Jesus' true family (Mark 3.31-35/Matt. 12.46-50/Luke 8.19-21); precedence among the disciples (Mark 10.35-45 = Matt. 20.20-28; but Luke 22.24-27); the healing of the blind man/men (Mark 10.46-52/Matt. 20.29-34/Luke 18.35-43). Why do the lists of the twelve close disciples of Jesus vary as they do (Mark 3.16-19/Matt. 10.2-4/Luke 6.13-16)? Presumably because in the process of oral transmission, confusion had arisen over the names of one or two of the least significant members of the group (see below §13.3b). The sequence of Mark 12.1-37/Matt. 21.33-46, 22.15-46/Luke 20.9-44 could be orally related, but the extent and consistency of verbal link suggest a primarily literary dependence of Matthew and Luke on Mark. The constancy of verbal link among the three accounts of the feeding of the five thousand likewise probably indicates an editing rather than a retelling process (Mark 6.32-44/Matt. 14.13-21/Luke 9.10-17); but John's version (John 6.1-15), where almost the sole verbal links are the numbers (cost, loaves and fishes, participants, baskets of fragments), surely indicates oral retelling. The character of the sequel (Mark 6.45-52/Matt. 14.22-33/John 6.16-21) points clearly in the same direction. And though Matthew's dependence on Mark for the passion narrative is clear, the alternative version used by Luke may well indicate a tradition passed down orally independent of the Mark/Matthean (literary) version (see further below §17.1).

211. See above chapter 7 n. 17. Lord notes that performances of often very different lengths are a mark of oral tradition (*Singer of Tales* 109-17).

212. E.g., Matt. 12.5-7, 11-12a adds precedents more apposite to the two cases of Sabbath controversy than were provided in Mark 2.23-28 and 3.1-5 (Matt. 12.1-8 and 9-14); cf. Luke 13.10-17; see below §14.4a.

213. E.g., the Matthean additions to explain why Jesus accepted baptism from the Baptist (Matt. 3.14-15) and in his presentation of Peter as the representative disciple (Matt. 14.28-31; 16.17-19), and the Lukan addition of a second mission (of the seventy[-two]) in Luke 10.1-12, presumably to foreshadow the Gentile mission (cf. 14.23 in §8.5e below).

214. Cf., e.g., Mark 6.3a, 5a with Matt. 13.55a, 58; Mark 10.17-18 with Matt. 19.16-17 (cited above chapter 7 n. 20, with further bibliography). In both cases Matthew's respect for the Markan wording is clear, even when he changed it, presumably to prevent any unwelcome implication (see my *Evidence for Jesus* 18-22).

sumption that variations between parallel accounts can or need be explained *only* in terms of literary redaction. After all, it can hardly be assumed that the first time Matthew and Luke heard many of these stories was when they first came across Mark's Gospel. The claim that there were churches in the mainstream(s) represented by Matthew and Luke who did not know any Jesus tradition until they received Mark (or Q) as documents simply beggars belief and merely exemplifies the blinkered perspective imposed by the literary paradigm. To repeat: the assumption, almost innate to those trained within western (that is, literary) culture, that the Synoptic traditions have to be analysed in terms of a linear sequence of written editions, where each successive version can be conceived only as an editing of its predecessor, simply distorts critical perception and skews the resultant analysis. The transmission of the narrative tradition has too many oral features to be ignored.[215]

The more appropriate conclusions are twofold. (1) The variations between the different versions of the same story in the tradition do not indicate a cavalier attitude to or lack of historical interest in the events narrated. In almost every case examined or cited above it is clearly *the same story* which is being retold. Rather, the variations exemplify the character of oral retelling.[216] In such oral transmission the concern to remember Jesus is clear from the key elements which give the tradition its stable identity,[217] just as the vitality of the tradition is indicated by the performance variants. These were not traditions carried around in a casket like some sacred relic of the increasingly distant past, their elements long rigid by textual rigor mortis. But neither were they the free creation of teachers or prophets with some theological axe to grind. Rather they were the lifeblood of

215. To evoke Occam's razor here, on the ground that direct literary interdependence of a limited number of written documents is the simplest solution, is to forget the complex hypotheses which have to be evoked to explain why the later author should depart so freely from the detail of a tradition already fixed in writing. The hypothesis of performance of tradition in oral mode, rather than transmission of tradition in literary mode, is actually the simpler explanation of the Synoptic data, even though it is much more difficult (impossible) to trace any sequence of performances apart from those attested by the Gospel tradition itself (which is presumably why the hypothesis has never been given much consideration). See also §10.3 below.

216. It should be noted that this deduction from the tradition itself coheres with Papias's account both of Peter's preaching and of Mark's composition: that Peter 'gave/adapted (*epoieito* — could we say 'performed') his teaching with a view to the needs (*pros tas chreias* — that is, presumably, of the audiences), but not as making an orderly account (*suntaxin*) of the Lord's sayings, so that Mark did no wrong in thus writing down some things (*enia*) as he recalled them' (Eusebius, *HE* 3.39.15).

217. 'The different versions [of a scene] generally agree rather closely in the report of what Jesus said, but use more freedom in telling the story which provides the occasion for it' (Dodd, *Founder* 35-36); cf. Vansina, who notes that 'the stability of the message' is likely to be as great or greater in the case of narratives than in the case of epics (*Oral Tradition as History* 53-54).

the communities in which they were told and retold. What Jesus did was important to these communities for their own continuing identity.[218]

(2) In the material documented above, the differences introduced by the Evangelists, whether as oral diversity or as literary editing, are consistently in the character of abbreviation and omission, clarification and explanation, elaboration and extension of motif. The developments often reflect the deeper faith and insight of Easter; that is true. But they do not appear to constitute any radical change in the substance or character or thrust of the story told.[219] Of course, we have only sampled the Jesus tradition to a limited extent, and we will have to check these first findings as we proceed. But at least we can say that thus far the hypothesis offered in §6.5e and developed in §§8.1-2 is being substantiated by the evidence; on the whole, *developments in the Jesus tradition were consistent with the earliest traditions of the remembered Jesus.*

8.5. The Synoptic Tradition as Oral Tradition: Teachings

I choose the term 'teachings' rather than 'sayings', since the latter is too casual. It allows, possibly even fosters the impression of serendipity — sayings of Jesus casually overheard and casually recalled, as one today might recall impressions of one's school or college days in a class reunion thirty years later. But as we have already noted (§8.1b), Jesus was known as a teacher, and the disciples understood themselves as just that, 'disciples' = 'learners' *(mathētai).* The recollection of Jesus' teaching was altogether a more serious enterprise from the start. Moreover, if I am right, the earliest communities of Jesus' disciples would have wanted to retain such teaching, as part of their own foundation tradition and self-identification, a fact which Paul and other early Christian letter writers were able to exploit when they incorporated allusions to Jesus' teaching in their own paraenesis (§8.1e). We need not assume a formal process of memorization, such as Gerhardsson envisaged. But a concern to learn what the master had taught, and to exercise some control over the degree of variations acceptable in the passing on of that teaching, can both be assumed on a priori grounds (§8.2) and find at least some confirmation in the oral traditioning processes envisaged by Bailey.

---

218. It is probably significant that the two traditions of the same event which diverge most markedly are those relating to the death of Judas (Matt. 27.3-10; Acts 1.15-20); in comparison with the death of Jesus, the fate of Judas was of little historical concern.

219. It is more likely that Matt. 10.5 (restriction of the disciples' mission to Israel) recalls Jesus' own instruction than that Jesus was known to commend a Gentile mission and Matt. 10.5 emerged as a prophetic protest within the Judean churches; in fact, Jesus' commendation of Gentile mission is at best an inference to be drawn from certain episodes in the tradition. See further below §13.7.

a. Aramaic Tradition

We may start by recalling that the tradition as it has come down to us has already been translated once, from Aramaic to Greek. Here is another curious blind spot in most work on Jesus' teaching, in all phases of the 'quest for the historical Jesus'. I refer to the repeated failure to ask about the Aramaic form which Jesus' teaching presumably took.[220] Without such inquiry any assertions about earliest forms of the teaching tradition are bound to be suspect in some measure. Not that such a criterion (Can this saying be retrojected back into Aramaic?) should be applied woodenly; translation aimed to achieve dynamic equivalence could easily produce a Greek idiom quite different from the nearest Aramaic equivalent.[221] What is of more immediate importance for us here are the important observations by Aramaic experts with regard to the character of the teaching tradition. All have noted that the tradition, even in its Greek state, bears several marks of oral transmission in Aramaic. Already in 1925 C. F. Burney had drawn attention to the various kinds of parallelism (synonymous, antithetic, synthetic)[222] and rhythm (four-beat, three-beat, *kina* metre) characteristic of Hebrew poetry.[223] And Matthew Black noted many examples of alliteration, assonance, and paronomasia.[224] This is all the stuff of oral tradition, as we noted above (§8.3f). Joachim Jeremias climaxed a lifetime's scholarship by summarising the indications that many of the words appearing in Jesus' teaching had an Aramaic origin, and that the speech involved had many characteristic features, including 'divine passive', as well as the features already noted by Burney and Black.[225]

220. See below §9.9b and n. 287.

221. Note the warning of M. Casey, 'The Original Aramaic Form of Jesus' Interpretation of the Cup', *JTS* 41 (1990) 1-12, particularly 11-12; repeated in *Aramaic Sources of Mark's Gospel* (SNTSMS 102; Cambridge: Cambridge University, 1998) 241. G. Schwarz, *'Und Jesus sprach': Untersuchungen zur aramäischen Urgestalt der Worte Jesu* (BWANT 118; Stuttgart: Kohlhammer, [2]1987) is vulnerable to criticism at this point.

222. Riesner estimates 'about 80 per cent of the separate saying units are formulated in some kind of *parallelismus membrorum*' ('Jesus as Preacher and Teacher' 202).

223. C. F. Burney, *The Poetry of Our Lord* (Oxford: Clarendon, 1925); see also Manson, *Teaching* 50-56.

224. M. Black, *An Aramaic Approach to the Gospels and Acts* (Oxford: Clarendon, [3]1967) 160-85; though note J. A. Fitzmyer's strictures ('The Study of the Aramaic Background of the New Testament', *A Wandering Aramean: Collected Aramaic Essays* [Missoula: Scholars, 1979] 1-27 [here 16-17]). See also Riesner, *Jesus als Lehrer* 392-404.

225. Jeremias, *Proclamation* 3-29. Still valuable is the classic study by G. Dalman, *Die Worte Jesu mit Berücksichtigung des nachkanonischen jüdischen Schriftums und der aramäischen Sprache* (Leipzig: Hinrichs, 1898); ET *The Words of Jesus Considered in the Light of Post-Biblical Jewish Writings and the Aramaic Language* (Edinburgh: Clark, 1902).

This evidence should be given more weight than has usually been the case. Of course, such features are common to written as well as oral tradition. And an Aramaic phase may only be evidence of an early (post-Easter) stage of transmission when the tradition was still circulating in Aramaic. But if the tradition is *consistently* marked by *particular* stylistic features, as the Aramaic specialists conclude, then it has to be judged more likely that these are *the characteristics of one person,* rather than that the multitude of Aramaic oral tradents had the same characteristics. The possibility that we can still hear what Jeremias called 'the *ipsissima vox'* (as distinct from the *ipsissima verba*) of Jesus coming through the tradition should be brought back into play more seriously than it has in the thirty years since Jeremias last wrote on the subject.[226]

As with the narrative tradition, so with the teaching tradition, various examples are readily forthcoming. We begin with two examples from within earliest Christianity's liturgical tradition. In this case the studies in orality have confirmed what might anyway have been guessed: that tradition functioning as 'sacred words' within a cult or liturgy is generally more conservative in character; the transmission (if that is the best term) is in the nature of sacred repetition in celebration and affirmation of a community's identity-forming tradition.

b. The Lord's Prayer (Matt. 6.7-15/Luke 11.1-4)

Matt. 6.7-15	Luke 11.1-4
7 "When you are praying, do not heap up empty phrases as the Gentiles do; for they think that they will be heard because of their many words. 8 Do not be like them, for your Father knows what you need before you ask him.	
	1 He was praying in a certain place, and after he had finished, one of his disciples said to him, "Lord, teach us to pray, as John taught his disciples". 2 He said to them, "When you pray, say: Father, hallowed be your name. Your kingdom come.
9 Pray then in this way: Our <u>Father</u> who are in heaven, <u>hallowed be your name. 10 Your kingdom come.</u> Your will be done, on earth as it is in heaven. 11 <u>Give us today our daily bread. 12 And forgive us our</u> debts, as <u>we</u> also have <u>forgiven</u> our debtors. <u>13 And do not bring us to the time of trial,</u> but rescue us from the evil one. 14 For if you forgive others their trespasses, your heavenly Father will also forgive you; 15 but if you do not forgive others, neither will your Father forgive your trespasses".	3 <u>Give us</u> each <u>day our daily bread. 4 And forgive us our</u> sins, for <u>we</u> ourselves also <u>forgive</u> everyone indebted to us. <u>And do not bring us to the time of trial"</u>.

226. Funk talks of Jesus' 'voice print', including antithesis, synonymous parallelism, reversal, paradox, and others more distinctive to Funk's own standpoint (*Honest* 144-45, 149-58).

What is the explanation for such variation? It would be odd indeed if Matthew and Luke derived this tradition from a common written source (Q).[227] Why then the variation, particularly within the prayer itself? Here again the curse of the literary paradigm lies heavy on discussion at this point: the assumption that this tradition was known only because it appeared in writing in a Q document![228] The much more obvious explanation is that this was a tradition maintained in the living liturgy of community worship (as the first person plural strongly suggests). Almost certainly, the early Christian disciples did not know this tradition only because they had heard it in some reading from a written document. *They knew it because they prayed it,* possibly on a daily basis.[229] In this case, in addition to the curse of the literary paradigm, the fact that so many academic discussions on material like this take place in isolation from a living tradition of regular worship, probably highlights another blind spot for many questers.

The point is that liturgical usage both conserves and adapts (slowly).[230] As Jeremias argued, the most likely explanation for the two versions of the Lord's Prayer is two slightly diverging patterns of liturgical prayer, both versions showing signs of liturgical adaptation: in Matthew the more reverential address and an opening phrase more readily said in congregational unison, and the additions at the end of each half of the prayer to elaborate the brevity and possibly clarify the petition to which the addition has been made; in Luke particularly the modification for daily

227. As Streeter observed (*Four Gospels* 277-78).

228. Typical is the opinion of D. E. Oakman, 'The Lord's Prayer in Social Perspective', in Chilton and Evans, eds., *Authenticating the Words of Jesus* 137-86, that 'the differences in form are best acounted for by differing scribal traditions and interests' (151-52). For a full documentation of the difference of opinions on whether the Prayer was in Q see S. Carruth and A. Garsky, *Documenta Q: Q 11:2b-4* (Leuven: Peeters, 1996) 19-33.

229. The likelihood of a primarily oral rather than literary transmission is however quite widely recognized, particularly when *Did.* 8.2 is included in the discussion; it is 'most unlikely that a Christian writer would have to copy from any written source in order to quote the Lord's Prayer' (Koester, *Ancient Christian Gospels* 16); cf. also Luz, *Matthäus* 1.334; Crossan, *Historical Jesus* 293; J. P. Meier, *A Marginal Jew* vol. 2 (New York: Doubleday, 1994) 357-58. H. D. Betz, *The Sermon on the Mount* (Hermeneia: Minneapolis: Fortress, 1995) 370-71: 'It is characteristic of liturgical material in general that textual fixation occurs at a later stage in the transmission of these texts, while in the oral stage variability within limits is the rule. These characteristics also apply to the Lord's Prayer. The three recensions, therefore, represent variations of the prayer in the oral tradition. . . . (T)here was never only *one original written* Lord's Prayer. . . . (T)he oral tradition continued to exert an influence on the written text of the New Testament well into later times' (370). In *Didache* 8.3 it is commended that the prayer be said three times a day (a good Jewish practice). For the relevance of Rom. 8.15 and Gal. 4.6 see below chapter 14 n. 36 and §16.2b.

230. Ritual formulae tend to be more fixed (Vansina, *Oral Tradition* 146-47). Orthodoxy still celebrates the liturgies of St John Chrysostom and St Basil of Caesarea.

prayer ('each day').[231] That the process of liturgical development/modification continued is indicated by the later addition of the final doxology ('for yours is the kingdom and the power and the glory for ever, amen') to Matthew's version.[232] It is not without relevance to note that such liturgical variation within what is manifestly the same prayer continues to this day. For example, in Scotland pray-ers tend to say 'debts', in England 'trespasses'. And contemporary versions jostle with traditional versions in most modern service books. Since liturgy is in effect the most like to oral tradition in modern western communities (regular worshippers rarely need to 'follow the order' in the book) the parallel has some force.

One other point worth noting is that both introductions (Matt. 6.9a; Luke 11.1-2a) confirm what was again likely anyway: that this prayer functioned as an identity marker for the first disciples.[233] Christians were recognizable among themselves, as well as to others, as those who said 'Father' or 'Our Father' to God, whereas the typical prayer of Jewish worship had more liturgical gravitas.[234] Moreover, both versions of the tradition attribute the prayer explicitly to Jesus and report the prayer as explicitly given to his disciples by Jesus.[235] That no doubt was why the prayer was so cherished and repeated. It would be unjustifiably sceptical to conclude despite all this that the prayer was compiled from individual petitions used by Jesus[236] and/or emerged only later from some unknown disciple.[237] Its place in the early tradition indicates rather the influence of some widely and highly regarded person; among whom Jesus himself is the most obvious candidate for the speculator.[238]

231. See further Jeremias, *Prayers of Jesus* 89-94; also *Proclamation* 195-96. Fitzmyer, though agreeing with much of Jeremias' case, thinks the Matthean variations are Matthean redaction (*Luke* 897); but the hypothesis of liturgical development rather than of unilateral literary redaction makes better sense.

232. Text-critical data in B. M. Metzger, *A Textual Commentary on the Greek New Testament* (London: United Bible Societies, 1971, corrected 1975) 16-17. *Did.* 8.2-3 indicates an intermediate phase when the doxology was only 'Yours is the power and the glory for ever'.

233. Jeremias, *Proclamation* 196-97.

234. For example, the benediction before the meal begins, 'Blessed art thou, Lord our God, king of the universe'. G. Vermes, *The Religion of Jesus the Jew* (London: SCM, 1993), observes that 'the customary Jewish prayer terminology, "Lord, King of the universe", is nowhere associated with Jesus' (136). See further §14.2b and §14.3d.

235. It goes back into good Aramaic; see Jeremias, *Proclamation* 196; Fitzmyer, *Luke* 901; Davies and Allison, *Matthew* 1.593.

236. Funk, *Five Gospels* 148-50; the discussion is vitiated by the assumption of literary dependence.

237. Crossan, *Historical Jesus* 294.

238. 'Had it been usual to put prayers in the mouth of Jesus, we would have had more Jesus prayers than just this one, which indeed is not specifically a Christian prayer' (Lüdemann, *Jesus* 147); similarly Meier, *Marginal Jew* 2.294; Becker, *Jesus* 265-67.

c. The Last Supper

The obvious second example is the record of Jesus' last supper with his disciples, which evidently became a matter of regular liturgical celebration (1 Cor. 11.23-26). The tradition here is fourfold.

A Matt. 26.26-29	Mark 14.22-25
26 While they were eating, Jesus took a loaf of bread, and after blessing it he broke it, giving it to the disciples, and said, "Take, eat; this is my body". 27 Then he took a cup, and after giving thanks he gave it to them, saying, "Drink from it, all of you; 28 for this is my blood of the covenant, which is poured out for many for the forgiveness of sins. 29 I tell you, from now on I will not drink of this fruit of the vine until that day when I drink it new with you in the kingdom of my Father".	22 While they were eating, he took a loaf of bread, and after blessing it he broke it, gave it to them, and said, "Take; this is my body". 23 Then he took a cup, and after giving thanks he gave it to them, and all of them drank from it. 24 He said to them, "This is my blood of the covenant, which is poured out on behalf of many. 25 Truly I tell you, no more will I drink of the fruit of the vine until that day when I drink it new in the kingdom of God".

B Luke 22.17-20	1 Cor. 11.23-26
17 Then he took a cup, and after giving thanks he said, "Take this and divide it among yourselves; 18 for I tell you that from now on I will not drink of the fruit of the vine until the kingdom of God comes". 19 Then he took a loaf of bread, and when he had given thanks, he broke it and gave it to them, saying, "This is my body, which is given for you. Do this in remembrance of me". 20 Also the cup likewise after supper, saying, "This cup is the new covenant in my blood which is poured out for you".	23 For I received from the Lord what I also handed on to you, that the Lord Jesus on the night when he was betrayed took a loaf of bread, 24 and when he had given thanks, he broke it and said, "This is my body which is for you. Do this in remembrance of me". 25 Likewise also the cup after supper, saying, "This cup is the new covenant in my blood. Do this, as often as you drink it, in remembrance of me". 26 For as often as you eat this bread and drink the cup, you proclaim the Lord's death until he comes.

The tradition has been preserved in two clearly distinct forms, one in Mark and Matthew (A), the other in Luke and Paul (B). In A Jesus 'blesses' the bread; in B he 'gives thanks'. B adds to the word over the bread, 'which is (given) for you. Do this in remembrance of me'. Over the cup A has 'This is my blood of the covenant which is poured out (for) many', whereas B has 'This cup is the new covenant in my blood'. This variation is most obviously to be explained in terms neither of literary dependence, nor of one or the other form being more easily retrojected into Aramaic,[239] but in terms of two slightly variant liturgical practices. For example, the fact that in the A version the words over the bread and the

---

239. Fitzmyer notes that both forms can be retrojected into contemporary Aramaic 'with almost equal ease and problems' (*Luke* 1394-95); see again Casey, 'Original Aramaic Form'; also *Aramaic Sources* 241.

wine are set in parallel ('This is my body; this is my blood') probably indicates a liturgical shaping to bring out the parallelism. Whereas the B version maintains the framework of a meal, with the bread word presumably said at the beginning (in accordance with the normal pattern of the Jewish meal) and the cup bringing the meal to a close ('after supper'). In A the modification puts the focus more directly on the wine/blood, whereas in B the focus is more on the cup.[240]

Here again it would be somewhat farcical to assume that this tradition was known to the various writers only as written tradition and only by hearing it read occasionally from some written source. The more obvious explanation, once again, is that these words were familiar within many/most early Christian communities because they used them in their regular celebrations of the Lord's Supper: *this was living oral tradition* before and after it was ever written down in semi-formal or formal documentation. Here too it was a matter of fundamental tradition, the sort of tradition which Paul took care to pass on to his newly formed churches (1 Cor. 11.23),[241] the sort of tradition which gave these churches their identity and by the performance of which they affirmed their identity (cf. again 1 Cor. 10.21). It was tradition remembered as begun by Jesus himself, and remembered thus from as early as we can tell.[242]

---

240. See further my *Unity and Diversity* 165-67, and those cited there in n. 23; R. F. O'Toole, 'Last Supper', *ABD* 4.234-41 (here 237-39); Theissen and Merz, *Historical Jesus* 420-23.

241. The fact that Paul ascribes the tradition to 'the Lord' (1 Cor. 11.23) should not be taken to indicate a revelation given to Paul after his conversion (as particularly most recently H. Maccoby, 'Paul and the Eucharist', *NTS* 37 [1991] 247-67). The language is the language of tradition ('I received' — *parelabon;* 'I handed on to you' — *paredōka*), and 'the Lord' from whom Paul received it is 'the Lord Jesus [who] on the night in which he was betrayed took bread . . .' (11.23). See further the still valuable discussion of O. Cullmann, 'The Tradition', *The Early Church: Historical and Theological Studies* (London: SCM, 1956) 59-75, who notes *inter alia* that 1 Cor. 7.10 also refers the tradition of Jesus' teaching on divorce to 'the Lord' ('To the married I give charge, not I but the Lord . . .') (68). In an XTalk on-line Seminar exchange Maccoby repeated his claim that 'the Eucharistic elements betray their lack of orality not only by their lack of semitisms' (ignoring Fitzmyer's observation above — n. 239) and referred to the 'glaring contradictions between the various Gospels'. What Maccoby calls 'glaring contradictions' I see only as performance variation — well within the range of performance variation in the Jesus tradition elsewhere.

242. The silence of *Didache* 9 ('concerning the Eucharist') as to any 'words of institution' need not imply that *Didache* reflects an earlier stage (than Mark or 1 Cor. 11) in the liturgical development (as Crossan, *Historical Jesus* 360-67 argues). It could well be that *Didache* assumes the traditional core and attests simply the addition of thanksgiving *(eucharistein)* prayers deemed appropriate in a more liturgically solemnized act (as also *Didache* 10). John's Gospel says nothing of a last supper, but reflects knowledge of bread and wine words in John 6.52-58. See the brief discussion and review (with bibliography) in Davies and Allison, *Matthew* 3.465-69. On the *Didache* and the eucharist see the essays by J. A. Draper, J. Betz, and E. Mazza, in Draper, ed., *Didache* 1-42 (26-31), 244-75, 276-99.

It is, of course, a fair question as to whether in the earliest form Jesus was remembered as celebrating a Passover meal[243] or instituting a ritual to be repeated. On the latter issue, the A version does not in fact say so; and the call for or assumption of repetition is a distinctive feature both of B and of the elaboration in 1 Cor. 11.25b-26.[244] Moreover the evidence of redaction is apparent elsewhere.[245] Nevertheless the characteristics of oral tradition remain clear: a concern to maintain the key elements of the words used by Jesus as carefully as necessary, with a flexibility (including elaboration) which in this case no doubt reflects the developing liturgical practices of different churches.

d. Sermon on the Mount/Plain

A curious feature of the Sermon on the Mount tradition is the variableness in the closeness between the Matthean and Lukan versions. In what we might call (for the sake of convenience) the third quarter of Matthew's Sermon, the degree of closeness is such that the passages qualify as good evidence for the existence of a Q document.[246] But in the other three-quarters the verbal parallel is much less close, so much so as to leave a considerable question as to whether there is evidence of any literary dependence.[247] If, alternatively, we look at the Sermon on the Plain (Q/Luke 6.20b-23, 27-49) and other Q parallels, the equally striking fact emerges that the closeness of the parallels with Matthew is quite modest, again leaving open the question of literary dependence.[248] In most cases much

243. See below §17.1c.

244. These considerations (including the focus more on the cup than on the wine) ease the problem of conceiving how a Jew could require his disciples to drink blood (e.g., Theissen and Merz, *Historical Jesus* 421-23; Funk, *Acts of Jesus* 139). In any case, it needs to be remembered that an act of prophetic symbolism (see below §15.6c at n. 231) was in view from the first: they ate bread (not flesh); they drank wine (not blood); see now J. Klawans, 'Interpreting the Last Supper: Sacrifice, Spiritualization, and Anti-Sacrifice', *NTS* 48 (2002) 1-17.

245. Particularly Matthew's addition of the phrase 'for the forgiveness of sins' (Matt. 26.28), the very phrase he seems deliberately to have omitted in 3.2 (cf. Mark 1.4/Luke 3.3). See further below §11.3b.

246. Matt. 6.22-23/Luke 11.34-36; Matt. 6.24/Luke 16.13; Matt. 6.25-34/Luke 12.22-32; Matt. 7.1-2/Luke 6.37a, 38b; Matt. 7.3-5/Luke 6.41-42; Matt. 7.7-11/Luke 11.9-13; Matt. 7.12/Luke 6.31.

247. Despite which, most discussions simply assume redactional use of Q; see, e.g., Fitzmyer, *Luke,* Davies and Allison, *Matthew,* and Kloppenborg, *Q Parallels, ad loc.* Streeter recognized the likelihood of 'oral tradition in more than one form', but argues that differences have to be explained by Matthew's 'conflation' of Q and M — that is, by literary editing (*Four Gospels* 251-53).

248. Bergemann, *Q auf dem Prüfstand,* concludes that Luke 6.20b-49 was not part of

the more plausible explanation is of two orally varied versions of the same tradition. As before, the evidence does not determine whether one or the other (or both) has simply drawn directly from the living oral tradition known to them, or whether one or the other has borrowed in oral mode from the Q document. Either way the evidence is more of oral dependence than of literary dependence. Consider the following examples.

Matt. 5.13	Luke 14.34-35
13 You are the salt of the earth; but if salt has lost its taste, how can it be restored? It is no longer good for anything, but is thrown out to be trampled under foot.	34 Salt is good; but if even salt has lost its taste, how can it be seasoned? 35 It is fit neither for the earth nor for the manure heap; they throw it out.

Matt. 5.25-26	Luke 12.57-59
25 Come to terms quickly with your accuser while you are on the way (to court) with him, lest your accuser hand you over to the judge, and the judge to the guard, and you will be thrown in prison. 26 Truly I tell you, you will never get out from there until you have paid back the last penny.	57 And why do you not judge for yourselves what is right? 58 Thus, when you go with your accuser before a magistrate, on the way (to court) make an effort to settle with him, lest you be dragged before the judge, and the judge hand you over to the officer, and the officer throw you in prison. 59 I tell you, you will never get out from there until you have paid back the very last halfpenny.

Matt. 5.39b-42	Luke 6.29-30
But whoever hits you on your right cheek, turn to him the other also; 40 and to the one who wants to sue you and take your tunic, let him have your cloak also; 41 and whoever forces you to go one mile, go with him a second. 42 Give to the one who asks you, and do not turn away the one who wants to borrow from you.	29 To the one who strikes you on the cheek, offer the other also; and from the one who takes away your cloak do not withhold your tunic also. 30 Give to everyone who asks you; and from the one who takes what is yours, do not ask for them back.

Matt. 6.19-21	Luke 12.33-34
19 Do not store up for yourselves treasures on earth, where moth and rust consume and where thieves break in and steal; 20 but store up for yourselves treasures in heaven, where neither moth nor rust consumes and where thieves do not break in and steal. 21 For where your treasure is, there will be also your heart.	33 Sell your possessions, and give alms. Make purses for yourselves that do not wear out, an unfailing treasure in the heavens, where no thief comes near and no moth destroys. 34 For where your treasure is, there also your heart will be.

Q. Kloppenborg Verbin's response (*Excavating Q* 62-65) fails to reckon with the variability in agreement *within* individual pericopes and the phenomenon of stable core elements, to which I am here drawing attention.

Matt. 7.13-14	Luke 13.24
13 <u>Enter through the narrow</u> gate; for the gate is wide and the road is easy that leads to destruction, and there are <u>many</u> who <u>enter</u> through it. 14 For the gate is narrow and the road is hard that leads to life, and there are few who find it.	24 Strive to <u>enter through the narrow</u> door; for <u>many</u>, I tell you, will try to <u>enter</u> and will not be able.

Matt. 7.24-27	Luke 6.47-49
24 <u>Everyone</u> then who <u>hears</u> these <u>my</u> <u>words</u> <u>and acts on them</u> will be <u>like</u> a wise man who <u>built</u> his <u>house</u> on rock. 25 Torrential rain fell, the <u>floods</u> came, and the winds blew and beat on <u>that house</u>, but it did not fall, because it had been founded on rock. 26 And everyone <u>who hears</u> these words of mine <u>and does not act</u> on them will be <u>like</u> a foolish man who <u>built</u> his <u>house on</u> sand. 27 Torrential rain fell, and the <u>floods</u> came, and the winds blew and beat against that house, and it <u>fell</u> — and <u>great</u> was its fall!	47 <u>Everyone</u> who comes to me and <u>hears</u> <u>my</u> <u>words</u> <u>and acts on them,</u> I will show you what he is <u>like.</u> 48 He is like a man <u>building</u> a <u>house,</u> who dug deeply and laid the foundation <u>on rock;</u> when a <u>flood</u> arose, the river burst against <u>that house</u> but could not shake it, because it had been well built. 49 But he <u>who hears</u> <u>and does not act</u> is <u>like</u> a man <u>building</u> a <u>house on</u> the ground without a foundation. When the <u>flood</u> burst against it, immediately it <u>fell,</u> and <u>great</u> was the ruin of that house.

In each case two features are evident: the teaching is the same in substance; the main emphases are carried by key words or phrases (salt, lost its taste, thrown out; accuser, [danger of being] thrown in prison, 'I tell you, you will never get out until you have paid back the last [half]penny';[249] cheek, other, cloak/tunic also, 'Give to him who asks you';[250] treasure in heaven [invulnerable to] moth or thief, 'where your treasure is there also will your heart be';[251] 'Enter through the narrow [gate]'; hearing and acting, house built on rock, flood, house built on poor foundation, fall); otherwise the detail is quite diverse.[252] It is hard to imagine such sayings being simply copied from the same document.[253] The alternative suggestion that there were several editions of Q (Matthew copying from one,

249. *Did.* 1.5 makes use of this last saying: 'he will not get out from there, until he has paid back the last penny'.

250. *Did.* 1.4-5 may well reflect knowledge of Matthew's version. In the *Gospel of Thomas* the saying has been formulated with a slightly different thrust: 'If you have money, do not lend it at interest, but give it to someone from whom you will not get it back' (*GTh* 95).

251. See further below chapter 13 n. 158.

252. I have left Matt. 5.43-48/Luke 6.27-28, 32-36 till §14.5 below.

253. The difficulty of reconstructing Q in these cases is evident in Robinson/Hoffmann/ Kloppenborg's *Critical Edition*. E.g., in what Kloppenborg regards as the first cluster in his Q[1] (Q 6.20-23b, 27-49), 6.27-35 is all like 6.29-30, illustrated above. However, it is less likely that the considerable variations are the result of editing a document (Q). The more obvious explanation is that Matthew knew different versions and that he was free to present the overlap material (q) in the spirit of the free-er oral retelling. Similarly with Q 6.36, 43-44, 46. On the Q hypothesis, it is Matthew who has broken up and scattered Q 6.37-40 (Matt. 7.1-2; 15.14; 10.24-25).

Luke from another) smacks of desperation, since the suggestion undermines the arguments for the existence of a Q document in the first place. Similarly with the suggestion that Matthew was free in his editing of Q (= Luke) or vice-versa.[254] Here once again the literary paradigm will simply not serve. These are all teachings remembered as teachings of Jesus in the way that oral tradition preserves such teaching: the character and emphasis of the saying is retained through stable words and phrases, while the point is elaborated in ways the reteller judged appropriate to the occasion.

e. Other Q/q Tradition

The picture is little different for traditions shared by Matthew and Luke elsewhere in the record of Jesus' teaching. Once again there are passages where the wording is so close that a literary dependence is the most obvious explanation.[255] But once again, too, there are parallel passages which simply cry out to be explained in terms of the flexibility of oral tradition.

Matt. 10.34-38	Luke 12.51-53; 14.26-27

34 Do not think that I came to bring peace to the earth; I came not to bring peace, but a sword.
 	
                              35 For I came to set a man against his father,
and a daughter against her mother,
                              and a daughter-in-law against her mother-in-law;   36 and a man's foes will be members of his own household.
37 Whoever loves father or mother more than me is not worthy of me; and whoever loves son or daughter more than me is not worthy of me;
                              38 and he who does not take up his cross and follow after me is not worthy of me.
	12.51 Do you consider that I am here to give peace on the earth? No, I tell you, but rather division! 52 From now on five in one household will be divided; three against two and two against three 53 they will be divided, father against son and son against father, mother against daughter and daughter against mother, mother-in-law against her daughter-in-law and daughter-in-law against mother-in-law.
	
	14.26 Whoever comes to me and does not hate his father and mother, and wife and children, and brothers and sisters, yes, and even his own life, cannot be my disciple. 27 Whoever does not carry his own cross and come after me cannot be my disciple.

254. E.g., the reconstructions of Q by Polag, *Fragmenta Q,* seem to assume that sometimes Luke, sometimes Matthew, has preserved Q; as a result he both masks the disparity between the two versions and still leaves it a puzzle why either or both diverged from the written text of Q. E.g., in the first case, on the usual literary redactional principles, it is more likely that Luke 14.34a echoes Mark 9.50a than that Luke = Q.

255. Matt. 8.19b-22/Luke 9.57b-60a; Matt. 11.7-11, 16-19/Luke 7.24-28, 31-35; Matt. 11.25-27/Luke 10.21-22; Matt. 12.43-45/Luke 11.24-26; Matt. 23.37-39/Luke 13.34-35; Matt. 24.45-51/Luke 12.42-46.

Matt. 18.15, 21-22	Luke 17.3-4
15 "If your brother sins against you, go and point out the fault when you and he are alone. If he listens to you, you have regained your brother". 21 Then Peter came and said to him, "Lord, if my brother sins against me, how often should I forgive him? As many as seven times?" 22 Jesus said to him, "I tell you, not seven times, but seventy-seven times".	3 Be on your guard! If your brother sins, rebuke him, and if he repents, forgive him. 4 And if someone sins against you seven times a day, and turns back to you seven times and says, "I repent", you must forgive him.

Matt. 22.1-14	Luke 14.15-24
1 Once more Jesus spoke to them in parables, saying: 2 "The kingdom of heaven may be compared to a king who gave a wedding banquet for his son. 3 He sent his slaves to call those who had been invited to the wedding banquet, but they would not come. 4 Again he sent other slaves, saying, 'Tell those who have been invited: Look, I have prepared my dinner, my oxen and my fat calves have been slaughtered, and everything is ready; come to the wedding banquet'. 5 But they made light of it and went away, one to his farm, another to his business, 6 while the rest seized his slaves, mistreated them, and killed them. 7 The king was angered. He sent his troops, destroyed those murderers, and burned their city. 8 Then he said to his slaves, 'The wedding is ready, but those invited were not worthy. 9 Go therefore into the streets, and invite everyone you find to the wedding banquet'. 10 Those slaves went out into the streets and gathered all whom they found, both good and bad; so the wedding hall was filled with guests. 11 But when the king came in to see the guests, he noticed a man there who was not wearing a wedding robe, 12 and he said to him, 'Friend, how did you get in here without a wedding robe?' And he was speechless. 13 Then the king said to the attendants, 'Bind him hand and foot, and throw him into the outer darkness, where there will be weeping and gnashing of teeth'. 14 For many are called, but few are chosen".	15 One of the dinner guests, on hearing this, said to him, "Blessed is anyone who will eat bread in the kingdom of God!" 16 Then Jesus said to him, "A certain person gave a great dinner and invited many. 17 At the time for the dinner he sent his slave to say to those who had been invited, 'Come; for it is now ready'. 18 But they all alike began to make excuses. The first said to him, 'I have bought a farm, and I must go out and see it; please accept my regrets'. 19 Another said, 'I have bought five yoke of oxen, and I am going to try them out; please accept my regrets'. 20 Another said, 'I have married a wife, and therefore I cannot come'. 21 So the slave returned and reported this to his master. Then the owner of the house became angry and said to his slave, 'Go out at once into the roads and lanes of the town and bring in the poor, the crippled, the blind, and the lame'. 22 And the slave said, 'Sir, what you ordered has been done, and there is still room'. 23 Then the master said to the slave, 'Go out into the roads and lanes, and compel them to come in, so that my house may be full. 24 For I tell you, none of those who were invited will taste my dinner'".

In each of the above cases we clearly have the same theme. But the agreement and overlap in wording between the Matthean/Lukan parallels is so modest, even minimal, that it becomes implausible to argue that the one was derived from the other or from a single common source at the literary level. The hypothesis that Matthew and Luke drew directly from Q (= Luke?)[256] simply does not make enough sense of the data, whereas the similarity of theme and point being made fits well with the flexibility and adaptability of oral retelling.[257] In each case the Evangelist seems to have expressed and/or elaborated the common theme in his own way: Matt. 10.37-38 (worthiness); Luke 14.26-27 (discipleship); Matt. 18.15, 21-22 (church discipline); Matt. 22.7, 11-14 (destruction of Jerusalem, lack of wedding robe), Luke 14.21-22, 23 (the church's twofold mission). But such retellings are well within the parameters of orally passed on teaching.[258] We can conclude without strain that Jesus was remembered as warning about the challenge of discipleship and the family divisions which would likely ensue, as encouraging generous and uncalculating forgiveness, and as telling a story (or several stories) about a feast whose guests refused to come (the variation in reasons given is typical of story-telling) and who were replaced by people from the streets.[259]

256. See again, e.g., Fitzmyer, *Luke,* and Kloppenborg, *Q Parallels, ad loc.;* Catchpole, *Quest* 323-24. The parable of the talents/pounds (Matt. 25.14-29/Luke 19.11-27) could also have been cited, where the difficulty in reconstructing Q is again clear (Robinson/Hoffmann/ Kloppenborg, *Critical Edition* 524-57; A. Denaux, 'The Parable of the Talents/Pounds [Q 19,12-27]: A Reconstruction of the Q Text', in Lindemann, ed., *Sayings Source Q* 429-60).

257. The *Gospel of Thomas* has variant traditions of the first and last of the three examples above (Matt. 10.34-36/Luke 12.51-53/*GTh* 16; Matt. 10.37-38/Luke 14.26-27/*GTh* 55, 101 [but with typical *Thomas* embellishment]; Matt. 22.1-14/Luke 14.15-24/*GTh* 64 [but the thrust slightly redirected — see below §12.4 n. 203); Mark 8.34 also knows a variant version of Matt. 10.38/Luke 14.27/*GTh* 55.2b, which Matt. 16.24 and Luke 9.23 follow. Whereas in the second example *Didache* again seems to know Matthew (*Did.* 15.3; Matt. 18.15-35), as probably does *Gos. Naz.* 15 (Matt. 18.21-22).

258. Cf. Gerhardsson, 'Illuminating the Kingdom', who concludes that the differences between the parables (narrative *meshalim*) demonstrate 'deliberate alterations of rather firm texts' (291-98), though the assumption of the literary paradigm should also be noted.

259. The judgments rendered by the Jesus Seminar on these passages well illustrate the highly dubious criteria and tendentious reasoning by which they reached their conclusions, including: a rather naive idea of consistency (Matt. 10.34-36 seems to 'contradict' Jesus' teaching on unqualified love; see further chapter 14 n. 242 below); Jesus was less likely to echo Scripture than the Christian community (reason unexplained); use made of material indicates its originating purpose (Luke 17.3-4 as the reflection of 'a more mature community than is likely to have been the case with Jesus' followers during his lifetime'); the fallacy of 'the original form' (the rationale of the procrustean bed of the literary paradigm) (Funk, *Five Gospels* 174, 216-17, 362, 234-35). But to discuss 'authenticity' by reference simply to such considerations as precise wording, tensions with other sayings and appropriateness to later contexts, totally

To sum up, our findings in regard to the traditions of Jesus' teaching accord well with those regarding the narrative traditions. I have no wish to deny the existence of a Q document, any more than to deny the priority of Mark.[260] But again and again in the case of 'q'/'Q' material we are confronted with traditions within different Synoptics which are clearly related (the same basic teaching), and which were evidently remembered and valued as teaching of Jesus. At the same time, in the cases examined above the relation is not obviously literary, each version derived by editing some written predecessor. The relation is more obviously to be conceived as happening at the oral level. That could mean that these traditions were known to the Evangelists not (or not only) in a written form, but in the living tradition of liturgy or communal celebration of the remembered Jesus. Or it could mean that they knew the tradition from Q, but regarded Q as a form of oral retelling (that is, they had heard Q material being read/performed), so that their own retelling retained the oral characteristics of the traditioning process. The two alternatives are not mutually exclusive, of course, but it can hardly be denied that the consequences for the definition of the scope and content of the Q document are considerable. It is important that future Q research should take such considerations on board.[261]

As with the narrative tradition, the sample of teaching tradition examined above seems to confirm the implications drawn from the oral character of its formulation. (1) There was teaching of Jesus which had made such an impact on his first hearers that it was recalled, its key emphases crystallized in the overall theme and/or in particular words and phrases, which remained constant in the process of rehearsing and passing on that teaching in disciple gatherings and churches.[262] All of the teaching reviewed would have been important to their

---

fails to consider the implications of oral transmission: a saying, like a story, could retain its identity by constancy of theme and particular words or phrases, while at the same time being adapted and reapplied to developing situations in the ongoing life of the earliest churches.

260. See above §8.4 conclusion.

261. It should not be assumed that the publication of *The Critical Edition of Q* (Robinson/Hoffmann/ Kloppenborg) has settled the content or scope of the Q document. And it should certainly not be concluded that Q material existed solely in written or documentary form.

262. Cf. Crossan: 'the basic unit of transmission is never the ipsissima verba of an aphoristic saying but, at best and at most, the *ipsissima structura* of an aphoristic core'; 'In oral sensibility one speaks or writes an aphoristic saying, but one remembers and recalls an aphoristic core' (*Fragments* 40, 67). Cf. also the concept of an 'originating structure' of a parable in B. B. Scott, *Hear Then the Parable: A Commentary on the Parables of Jesus* (Minneapolis: Fortress, 1989): 'It is futile to seek the original words of a parable. The efforts of those who preserved the parables should not be viewed as the efforts of librarians, archivists, or scribes preserving the past, but of storytellers performing a parable's structure. We must distinguish between performance, which exists at the level of *parole,* actual spoken or written language, and structure, which exists at the level of *langue,* an abstract theoretical construction' (18-19).

identity as disciples and communities of disciples and for the character of their shared life. Such teaching would no doubt have been treasured and meditated upon in the communal gatherings, much as Bailey has suggested.

(2) The variations in the reteaching indicate a readiness to group material differently, to adapt or develop it, and to draw further lessons from it, consistent with the tradition of initial impact made by Jesus himself and in the light of the developing circumstances of the churches which treasured the teaching. Once again the point is that the tradition was *living tradition,* celebrated in the communal gatherings of the earliest churches. There was no concern to recall all the exact words of Jesus; in many cases the precise circumstances in which the teaching was given were irrelevant to its continuing value. But neither is there any indication in the material reviewed that these were sayings interjected into the tradition by prophets or free (literary) creation, or that the development of particular teachings subverted their original impact.[263] These were remembered as teaching given by Jesus while he was still with his disciples, and treasured both as such and because of its continuing importance for their own community life and witness.

8.6. Oral Transmission

In the light of the above we can begin to sketch in the likely process of traditioning in the case of the Jesus tradition.[264] The fact that it coheres so well with the 'in principle' sketch of §6.5 and the a priori considerations of §§8.1-2 is significant.

---

263. Draper also argues that the thesis of some of Jesus' sayings 'created entirely de novo . . . conflicts with the processes of oral transmission. Such entirely innovative "words of the Risen Jesus" are inherently unlikely' (Horsley and Draper, *Whoever* 183). Horsley however assumes that prophets would have been responsible for the celebration of the tradition (*Whoever* 300-310) without enquiring what the role of teachers might have been.

264. B. W. Henaut, *Oral Tradition and the Gospels: The Problem of Mark 4* (JSNTS 82; Sheffield: JSOT, 1993) is tendentiously concerned to argue the virtual impossibility of recovering any oral tradition behind the Gospels: all differences, no matter how great, can be explained in terms of literary redaction, and oral tradition was wholly fluid and contingent on the particularities of each performance. But his conception of the oral tradition process is questionable — as though it were a matter of recovering a history of tradition through a set of sequential performances (e.g., 118; here we see the problem in talking of 'oral transmission' — above §8.3f at n. 162). And he gives too little thought to what the stabilities of oral remembrances of Jesus might be as distinct from those in the epics and sagas studied by Parry and Lord. H. W. Hollander, 'The Words of Jesus: From Oral Tradition to Written Record in Paul and Q', *NovT* 42 (2000) 340-57, follows Henaut uncritically (351-55): he has no conception of tradition as reflecting/embodying the impact of anything Jesus said or did; and he thinks of oral tradition as essentially casual, without any conception that tradition could have a role in forming community identity and thus be important to such communities.

a. In the Beginning

In the beginning, already during Jesus' own ministry, as soon as disciples began to gather round him, we can envisage initial impressions and memories being shared among the group. 'Do you remember what he did/said when he . . . ?' must have been a question often asked as the embryonic community began to feel and express its distinctiveness.[265] No doubt in similar ways their village communities had celebrated their identity and history in regular, even nightly gatherings. And as soon as the disciples of Jesus began to perceive themselves as (a) distinctive group(s) we may assume that the same impulse characteristic of oral and village culture would have asserted itself. As Jesus' immediate group moved around Galilee, encountering potential and then resident groups of disciples or sympathisers in various villages, the natural impulse would be the same. We can assume, of course, that Jesus was giving fresh teaching (as well as repeat teaching) all the while. But in more reflective gatherings, or when Jesus was absent, the impulse to tell again what had made the greatest impact on them would presumably reassert itself.[266]

Three features of this initial stage of the process are worth noting. First, if Bailey's anecdotal accounts bring us closer than any other to the oral culture of Galilee in the second quarter of the first century CE, then we may assume that the traditioning process *began* with the initiating word and/or act of Jesus. That is to say, the impact made by Jesus would not be something which was only put into traditional form (days, months, or years) later. The impact would *include* the formation of the tradition to recall what had made that impact. In making its impact the impacting word or event *became* the tradition of that word or event.[267] The stimulus of some word/story, the excitement (wonder, surprise) of some event would be expressed in the initial shared reaction;[268] the structure, the identifying elements and the key words (core or climax) would be articulated in oral form in

265. Cf. Funk, *Acts of Jesus:* 'The followers of Jesus no doubt began to repeat his witticisms and parables during his lifetime. They soon began to recount stories about him . . .' (2).

266. Keck objects to speaking of Jesus as starting a 'movement' — 'an anachronistic modern invention, the "secular" alternative to the idea that Jesus founded the church' (*Who Is Jesus?* 48-50). But he is over-reacting to claims that Jesus sought to reform society and hardly does justice to the group dynamics set in motion by a mission such as Luke reports (Luke 8.1-3). Was the impact made by Jesus always individual and never involved groups other than the core disciples? Keck evidently envisages only a latent impact triggered into effect by subsequent post-Easter evangelism.

267. Cf. C. K. Barrett, *Jesus and the Gospel Tradition* (London: SPCK, 1967): '. . . the tradition originated rather in the impression made by a charismatic person than in sayings learnt by rote'; 'it was preserved because it could not be forgotten' (10, 16).

268. Or should we be determined, come what may, to find a Jesus (reconstruct a 'historical Jesus') who neither stimulated nor excited?

the immediate recognition of the significance of what had been said or happened. Thus established more or less immediately, these features would then be the constants, the stable themes which successive retellings could elaborate and round which different performances could build their variations, as judged appropriate in the different circumstances.[269] Subsequently we may imagine a group of disciples meeting and requesting, for example, to hear again about the centurion of Capernaum, or about the widow and the treasury, or what it was that Jesus said about the tunic and the cloak, or about who is greater, or about the brother who sins.[270] In response to which a senior disciple would tell again the appropriate story or teaching in whatever variant words and detail he or she judged appropriate for the occasion, with sufficient corporate memory ready to protest if one of the key elements was missed out or varied too much. All this is wholly consistent with the character of the data reviewed above.[271]

It also follows, second, that those accustomed to the prevalent individualism of contemporary culture (and faith) need to make a conscious effort to appreciate that the impact made by Jesus in the beginning was not a series of disparate reactions of independent individuals.[272] Were that so we might well wonder how any commonality of tradition could emerge as individuals began to share their memories, perhaps only after a lengthy period. Postmodern pluralism would have been rampant from the first! But tradition-forming is a *communal* process,

269. Funk agrees: under the heading 'Performance as gist; nucleus as core', he observes the 'general rule in the study of folklore that oral storytellers reproduce the gist of stories in their oral performances . . . [the Synoptic Evangelists] tend to reproduce the nucleus of a story — the core event — with greater fidelity than the introduction or conclusion. . . . As a consequence, historical reminiscence is likely to be found in the nucleus of stories, if anywhere . . .' (*Acts of Jesus* 26). See also above, n. 262, and cf. B. Witherington, *The Christology of Jesus* (Minneapolis: Fortress, 1990) 7-22.

270. It is hardly realistic to assume that the only initial memories were of Jesus' teaching, and thus to deduce that stories about events during Jesus' ministry were not part of the Jesus tradition from the first and only emerged as a subsequent 'narrativization' of themes from the sayings tradition; *pace* W. Arnal, 'Major Episodes in the Biography of Jesus: An Assessment of the Historicity of the Narrative Tradition', *TJT* 13 (1997) 201-26.

271. Crossan argues that the continuity between Jesus and his subsequent followers was 'not in mnemonics but in mimetics, not in remembrance but in imitation' ('Itinerants and Householders' 16), as though the two formed an antithetical either-or, and as though the mimesis recalled a lifestyle somehow independent of the teaching which had provided the theological rationale for that lifestyle. There is more substance, however, in his subsequent observation that 'it is the continuity of life-style between Jesus and itinerants that gives the oral tradition its validity' (16).

272. Cf. Horsley's scathing critique of Liberalism's focus on the individual and of Mack's *Lost Gospel* (Horsley and Draper, *Whoever* 15-22). Elsewhere Crossan (*Birth of Christianity* 49-93) and Funk (*Honest* 244) also seem to think of oral tradition solely in terms of individuals' casual recollection.

not least because such tradition is often constitutive of the community as community.[273] As it was a shared experience of the impact made by Jesus which first drew individuals into discipleship, so it was the formulation of these impacts in shared words which no doubt helped bond them together as a community of disciples.[274] 'Already the pre-Easter circle of disciples was a "confessing community" *(Bekenntnisgemeinschaft)* of committed disciples *(nachfolgenden Jüngern)*, who confessed Jesus as the final revealer and interpreter of the word of God'.[275]

At the same time, the points made in §6.5 should not be forgotten. The character of the tradition as shared memory means that in many instances we do not know precisely what it was that Jesus did or said. What we have in the Jesus tradition is the consistent and coherent features of the shared impact made by his deeds and words, not the objective deeds and words of Jesus as such. What we have are examples of oral retelling of that shared tradition, retellings which evince the flexibility and elaboration of oral performances. There is surely a Jesus who made such impact, the remembered Jesus, but not an original pure form,[276] not a single original impact to which the historian has to try to reach

---

273. Strecker reminds us that the concept 'Sitz im Leben' ('setting in life') is primarily a sociological category: 'The "Sitz im Leben" of a text is generally to be sought in the life of the community, especially in the worship and in the catechetical instruction. In distinction to the literary tradition *(Tradition)*, the oral tradition *(Überlieferung)* is primarily prescribed for performance in the Christian community and structured accordingly' ('Schriftlichkeit' 163; also 169); cf. Kloppenborg's recognition that the concerns of Q were community-oriented ('Literary Convention' 86-91).

274. This is not to deny that stories about Jesus would have circulated outside the early Christian communities. But I reject the implication of Trocmé and Theissen (chapter 6 n. 104) that Mark or others had to go outside the Christian storytelling and traditioning processes in order to find miracle stories about Jesus; so explicitly Theissen — 'Their "tellers" are not a special group within the Christian community, but people in the community at large . . .' *(Gospels in Context* 103). But absence of 'specifically Christian motifs' need indicate only that the tradition was maintained without 'specifically Christian' elaboration through the time that it was written down.

275. Schürmann, *Jesus* 429; followed by Stuhlmacher, *Biblische Theologie* 44-45. In his most recent contribution on Q, Kloppenborg Verbin explicitly accepts 'the fundamental conservatism of the compositional process' (in debate with Kelber and Schröter), agrees that ancient composition was 'consistently oral and collaborative' (citing Downing), and speaks of 'the "canon" of what was sayable of Jesus' ('Discursive Practices in the Sayings Gospel Q and the Quest of the Historical Jesus', in Lindemann, ed., *Sayings Source Q* 149-90 [here 169-74]).

276. If Jesus told at least some of his parables and delivered some of his teaching on more than one occasion, then neither was there a single original context for such teaching. J. Liebenberg, *The Language of the Kingdom and Jesus* (BZNW 102; Berlin: de Gruyter, 2001) points out that the polyvalency of the parables subverts all attempts to identify an original meaning or context (508-13); see also his earlier crtitique of Bultmann's concept of an original

back to in each case.[277] The remembered Jesus may be a synthesis of the several impacts made on and disciple responses made by Jesus' earliest witnesses, but the synthesis was already firm in the first flowering of the tradition.[278]

Third, it follows also and is perhaps worth repeating that the traditioning process should not be conceived of as initially casual and only taken seriously by the first disciples in the post-Easter situation. As just implied, community formation was already at an embryonic stage from the first call of Jesus' immediate circle of disciples; 'formative tradition' would have had an indispensable part in that process.[279] To the extent that the shared impact of Jesus, the shared disciple-response, bonded into groups of disciples or adherents those thus responsive to Jesus' mission, to that extent the dynamics of group formation would be operative. In that process it is scarcely conceivable that the shared memories of what Jesus had said and done (already 'Jesus tradition'!) did not play an important part, both in constituting the groups' identity (what other distinguishing features had they?), and in outlining the boundaries which marked them off as groups (however informal) from their fellow Jews (here, no doubt, the pronouncement and controversy stories had an early, even pre-Easter role; why not?).

Nor should we forget the continuing role of eyewitness tradents, of those rec-

---

form or *selbständige Traditionsstücke* 'as if one could pinpoint elements in the synoptic tradition which were originally created to exist in and for themselves' (432-48). He also challenges the 'dictum in New Testament scholarship that the first transmitters of these stories [parables] were unable to understand them and therefore almost by necessity had to change them in order to make them intelligible for themselves and/or their readers/listeners' (82). But he does not give enough weight to the degree to which parables' narrative structure and context of use (as well as what he calls their 'generic-level structures') evidently functioned to limit their polyvalency and to provide the communities with guidelines on how the parable should be heard (cf. particularly 445-46, 499-503).

277. Kloppenborg speaks appropriately of the 'performative diversity at the earliest stages of the Jesus tradition' ('Sayings Gospel Q' 334).

278. A. Goshen-Gottstein, 'Hillel and Jesus: Are Comparisons Possible?', in J. H. Charlesworth and L. L. Johns, eds., *Hillel and Jesus* (Minneapolis: Fortress, 1997) 31-55, notes the lack of biographical interest in rabbinic tradition in regard to the rabbis (cf. the Teacher of Righteousness at n. 15 above), who were not remembered for their lives or example, and whose teaching was remembered only as part of a much larger, collective enterprise. In contrast, it is evident that Jesus was remembered as the beginning of a new line of tradition (not just as one sage among others), and the impact of his life as well as his teaching resulted in his actions as well as his words being remembered and gave the Jesus tradition a biographical dimension from the start (see also §8.1f above).

279. Cf. the picture which P. S. Alexander, 'Orality in Pharisaic-Rabbinic Judaism at the Turn of the Eras', in Wansbrough, ed., *Jesus* 159-84, adduces for the disciple-circle round a rabbi in the early tannaitic period forming a small, quasi-religious community, eating communally, sharing a common purse, and being taught by the rabbi (166-67), a picture which may not be as anachronistic as might at first appear (182-84).

ognized from the first as apostles or otherwise authoritative bearers of the Jesus tradition (§8.1d). Such indications as there are from the pre-Pauline and early Pauline period suggest already fairly extensive outreach by such figures, both establishing and linking new churches, and a general concern to ensure that a foundation of authoritative tradition was well laid in each case.[280] In focusing particular attention on the communal character of the early traditioning process we should not discount the more traditional emphasis on the individual figure of authority respected for his or her own association with Jesus during the days of his mission.[281]

Within the Jesus tradition itself we should recall the clear memory that Jesus sent out his disciples as an extension of his own mission (Mark 6.7-13 pars.).[282] Mark tells us that the twelve were chosen 'to be with him and that he might send them out to preach . . .' (Mark 3.14). What would they have said when they preached? The implication of the text is clear, and the inference from the fact of a shared mission hard to avoid, that their preaching would have at least included teaching which Jesus had given them.[283] Also that Jesus would have taught them what to say — not in a verbatim mode, but in a mode which would convey the disciple-effecting impact which they themselves had experienced. We may be confident that a good deal at least of the retellings of Jesus tradition now in the Synoptic Gospels were already beginning to take shape in that early pre-Easter preaching of the first disciples.[284]

---

280. Paul himself provides the best evidence in each case: he is able to take it for granted, as widely accepted, that an 'apostle' is a church-founder (particularly 1 Cor. 9.1-2); the implication of such passages as Acts 9.32-43; 15.3 and Gal. 1.22 is that the earliest churches already formed a network; and the indications of such passages as 1 Cor. 11.2; 15.1-3 and Gal. 1.18 confirm the importance of basic instruction in what was already designated tradition.

281. In personal correspondence Richard Bauckham emphasizes the significance of Byrskog's work at this point.

282. On historicity, see particularly Meier, *Marginal Jew* 3.154-63. We noted earlier that a strong body of opinion regarding Q sees the earliest stage of its collection/composition (Q¹?) as intended to provide guidance for itinerant missionaries on the pattern of Jesus' own mission (chapter 7 nn. 96-97); similarly Schürmann, 'vorösterlichen Anfänge'; and see later (§14.3b).

283. Theissen envisages the disciple missionaries as messengers of Jesus because they passed on Jesus' words ('Wandering Radicals' 42-43).

284. The point has been argued by E. E. Ellis on several occasions, most recently in 'The Historical Jesus and the Gospels', in J. Ådna, et al., eds., *Evangelium — Schriftauslegung — Kirche*, P. Stuhlmacher FS (Tübingen: Mohr Siebeck, 1997) 94-106, reprinted in his *Christ and the Future in New Testament History* (NovTSup 97; Leiden: Brill, 2000) 3-19; also *The Making of the New Testament Documents* (Leiden: Brill, 1999) 20-27; but he weakens his case by unnecessarily questioning whether there was an initial oral stage of transmission (*Christ* 13-14) and arguing for 'at least some written transmission from the beginning' (*Making* 24), that is, already during Jesus' ministry (*Christ* 15-16; *Making* 32, 352). Similarly A. Millard, *Reading and Writing in the Time of Jesus* (BS 69; Sheffield: Sheffield Academic, 2000) argues that notes may well have been made by one or more of the literate among Jesus' hearers which could have

This is *not* to accept Theissen's thesis that the Jesus tradition was the preserve of wandering charismatics, and that they were primarily responsible for maintaining and circulating it. As already observed, community formation and tradition formation go hand in hand. And the Q material, on which the thesis is principally based, itself betrays settings for the tradition in towns and villages.[285] In this particular phase of discussion, there is a danger of thinking of the tradition in effect simply as 'gospel' and of its transmission simply in terms of evangelistic preaching.[286] But as early form critics recognized, the Jesus traditions are traditions which have come down to us because they were in regular and repeated use. That is, the principal conduit for their transmission was not a single, once-only proclamation by evangelists in missionary situations, but the communities which had been called into existence by such preaching, which identified themselves by reference to such tradition, and which referred to the tradition in their regular gatherings to inform and guide their common life and in relation to their neighbours. It was this breadth of tradition which provided the context of reception for individual performances of items of the tradition, shaping the congregation's 'horizon of expectation' and enabling them to fill in the 'gaps of indeterminacy'.[287] This I believe is a fair statement of what must have been the case, which remains persuasive even if we do not know how extensive was the body of Jesus tradition held by individual communities; the influx of new converts, the reception of further tradition and the creative reworking of the tradition already received need not modify the basic picture to any significant extent.

Did Easter and the transition from Galilean village to Hellenistic city, from

---

served as sources for Mark (223-29); though he also observes that Paul shows no awareness of any written records of Jesus' mission (211). Ellis's conception of oral transmission is very restricted to a choice between 'folkloric origin' and the 'controlled and cultivated process' of the rabbinic schools (*Christ* 14-15; cf. Millard, *Reading and Writing* 185-92); and neither seems to be aware of Bailey's contribution. See also n. 264 above. I have already pointed out (n. 138 above) that Byrskog's use of 'oral history' as an analogy to the process resulting in the Gospels seems effectively to ignore the likelihood or character of an oral stage such as is envisaged here.

285. Peter Richardson concludes his study of 'First-Century Houses and Q's Setting', in D. G. Horrell and C. M. Tuckett, eds., *Christology, Controversy and Community*, D. R. Catchpole FS (NovTSup 99; Brill: Leiden, 2000) 63-83: 'Q was set naturally in towns [and cities?], not within the activities of wandering charismatics' (83).

286. To be fair, Crossan in particular sees 'the primary crucible for the tradition of Jesus sayings' in 'the delicate interaction between itinerant and householder' ('Itinerants and Householders' 24); but insofar as the thesis applies to Q, the hypothesized tension between itinerants and householders is provided more by the hypothesis than by the text.

287. See also Vouga, 'Mündliche Tradition' 198-202, who draws particularly on Vansina's *Oral Tradition as History*. Liebenberg consistently speaks of different 'performances' of the parables — e.g., of the sower (*Language* 350-414).

Aramaic to Greek not make any difference, then? Yes, of course it did. Easter shaped the perspective within which this first tradition was remembered. The transition from village to city shaped the tradition for changing circumstances. The transition from Aramaic to Greek (already implied by the description of 'Hellenists' = Greek-speakers in Acts 6.1) would introduce the shifts in nuance which any translation involves.[288] But the oral Jesus tradition itself provided the continuity, the living link back to the ministry of Jesus, and it was no doubt treasured for that very reason; the very character of the tradition, retaining as it does so many of its Galilean village[289] and pre-Easter themes,[290] not to mention its Aramaic resonances (§8.5a), makes that point clear enough. Here again we may learn from postmodernism's emphasis on the reception rather than the composition of text. If it is indeed the case that the hearer fills in the 'gaps in signification' from the tradition (Iser), that an audience interprets a particular performance from their shared knowledge (Foley), then we can be fairly confident that the Jesus tradition was an essential part of that shared knowledge, enabling the hearers in church gatherings to 'plug in' to particular performances of the oral tradition and to exercise some control over its development. We see this happening, I have already suggested, in the variations Paul plays upon several elements in the Jesus tradition which he echoes in his letters (§8.1e above).

b. Tradition Sequences

Another questionable assumption which has dominated the discussion since the early form critics is that in the initial stage of the traditioning process the tradition consisted of individual units.[291] That may indeed have been the case for the

---

288. It is not necessary to assume that the 'Hellenists' emerged only after Easter; there may have been Greek-speaking disciples during Jesus' Galilean and Jerusalem missions (cf. Mark 7.26; John 12.20-22) and traditions already being transposed into Greek. The only formal difference in the traditioning process itself seems to have been the emergence of the recognized role of *teacher* (§8.1b), with the implication of a more structured ordering of the tradition as indicated in §8.6b below.

289. A repeated emphasis of Horsley and Draper, *Whoever;* see also G. Theissen, *Lokalkolorit und Zeitgeschichte in den Evangelien: Ein Beitrag zur Geschichte der synoptischen Tradition* (NTOA 8; Freiburg, Schweiz: Universitätsverlag, 1989), who, as the subtitle implies, explores the issue as a way of illuminating the period of oral tradition (1-16, and ch. 1); see also below §9.7.

290. See again Schürmann, 'vorösterlichen Anfänge'.

291. Kloppenborg, following in the train of successive form-critical analyses, perceives the composition process as 'the juxtaposition of originally independent units' (*Formation* 98). Similarly E. P. Sanders takes it for granted that in the beginning 'preachers and teachers used a small unit of material' (*The Historical Figure of Jesus* [London: Penguin, 1993] 59). Funk as-

very beginning of the process, and the *Gospel of Thomas* gives it some credibility for the continuing tradition. But editorial fingerprints on collections of Jesus tradition in the present Synoptics do not constitute sufficient evidence that each of the collections was first composed by those who thus handled them. There is also good evidence of sayings being grouped and stories linked from what may have been a very early stage of the transmission process — even, in some cases, that Jesus may have taught in connected sequences which have been preserved. To group similar teachings and episodes would be an obvious mnemonic and didactic device for both teachers and taught, storytellers and regular hearers, more or less from the beginning.[292]

We may think, for example, of the sequence of beatitudes brought together in oral tradition or Q (Matt. 5.3, 4, 6, 11, 12/Luke 6.20b, 21b, 21a, 22, 23), and elaborated differently by Matthew and Luke (Matt. 5.3-12, Luke 6.20b-26). Or Jesus' responses to would-be disciples (Matt. 8.19-22/Luke 9.57-62).[293] Or the sequence of mini-parables (the wedding guests, new and old cloth, new and old wineskins) in Mark 2.18-22 (followed by Matt. 9.14-17 and Luke 5.33-39). Or the sequence of teaching on the cost of discipleship and danger of loss (Mark 8.34-38; again followed by Matt. 16.24-27 and Luke 9.23-26), where Q/oral tradition has also preserved the sayings separately.[294] Similarly with the sequence of sayings about light and judgment in Mark 4.21-25 (followed by Luke 8.16-18), with equivalents scattered in Q and the *Gospel of Thomas*.[295]

We will have occasion to analyse some of the most fascinating of the sequences later on: the 'parables of crisis' in Matt. 24.42-25.13 pars. (§12.4g), Jesus and the Baptist in Matt. 11.2-19 par. (§12.5c), and Jesus' teaching on his ex-

---

sumes that 'the imprint of orality' is evident only in 'short, provocative, memorable, oft-repeated phrases, sentences, and stories' — 'a sixth pillar of modern gospel scholarship' (*Five Gospels* 4); 'only sayings that were short, pithy, and memorable were likely to survive' (*Honest* 40, 127-29; similarly *Acts of Jesus* 26). This assumption predetermines that 'the Jesus whom historians seek' will be found only in such brief sayings and stories. He lists 101 words (and deeds) judged to be 'authentic' in his *Honest* 326-35.

292. Here again I should perhaps stress that I am thinking not just of the more formal occasions of retelling and reteaching in 'cult narrative' and catechism, well indicated by Moule, *Birth*, and H. Koester, 'Written Gospels or Oral Tradition?', *JBL* 113 (1994) 293-97 (here 293-94).

293. Or indeed any of the six clusters identified by Kloppenborg as belonging to Q[1], which I have already suggested are better understood as different traditional materials grouped by teachers for purposes of more effective and coherent teaching than as a single 'stratum' (above §7.4c and n. 83).

294. Matt. 10.38/Luke 14.27; Matt. 10.39/Luke 17.33; Matt. 10.33/Luke 12.9.

295. Matt. 5.15/Luke 11.33/*GTh* 33.2; Matt. 10.26/Luke 12.2/*GTh* 5.2, 6.4; Matt. 7.2/Luke 6.38b; Matt. 25.29/Luke 19.26/*GTh* 41. See further below chapter 13; also Crossan, *Fragments* ch. 5; M. Ebner, *Jesus — ein Weisheitslehrer? Synoptische Weisheitslogien im Traditionsprozess* (Freiburg: Herder, 1998) ch. 1.

orcisms in Matt. 12.24-45 pars. (§12.5d). Even more fascinating, but almost impossible to set out in tabular form, is the tradition of the sending out of the disciples on mission, where it is evident from Mark 6.7-13 and the parallels in Matt. 9.37–10.1, 7-16 and Luke 9.1-6; 10.1-12 that there were at least two variations, one used by Mark and another oral (Q?) version.[296] The variations make it probable that the material was used and re-used, probably beginning with Jesus' own instructions for mission, but developed and elaborated in terms of subsequent experience of early Christian mission.[297]

As for Q itself, we may recall the earlier observation that it is almost impossible to devise a secure method for distinguishing redaction from (initial) composition in a hypothetically reconstructed document (above §7.4c). The point can be pushed further by arguing that Q was itself composed as a sequence of discourses.[298] But Kloppenborg's finding that Q's sayings have been gathered into 'coherent or topical groupings' is also to the point.[299] And the composition of Mark itself can be understood as setting in appropriate sequence a number of groupings already familiar in the oral traditioning process:[300]

24 hours in the ministry of Jesus	Mark 1.21-38
Jesus in controversy (in Galilee)	Mark 2.1-3.6
Parables of Jesus	Mark 4.2-33
Miracles of Jesus round the lake	Mark 4.35-5.43; 6.32-52
Marriage, children, and discipleship	Mark 10.2-31
Jesus in controversy (in Jerusalem)	Mark 12.13-37
The little apocalypse	Mark 13.1-32
The passion narrative	Mark 14.1-15.47

Of course most of this is unavoidably speculative, even more so if we were to guess at whether and how passages like Mark 4.2-33 (parables of Jesus) and Mark 13.1-32 (the little apocalypse) grew by a process of aggregation from ear-

296. See particularly Schröter, *Erinnerung* 211, 236-37. On the possibility that Paul knew a form of the missionary discourse related to Q 10.2-16 see especially Allison, *Jesus Tradition in Q* 105-11.

297. See above §7.4d at nn. 96-97, but also the qualification in Kloppenborg Verbin, *Excavating Q* 183; also M. Hengel, *The Charismatic Leader and His Followers* (Edinburgh: Clark, 1981) 74-76. Does the fact that *Thomas* has only two disjoint parallels (*GTh* 14.2/Luke 10.8-9; *GTh* 73/Matt.9.37-38/Luke 10.2) imply a fading of a compulsion to mission?

298. See above chapter 7 n. 80.

299. *Formation* 90-92; *Excavating Q* 168-69, 206-209.

300. Cf. particularly, H. W. Kuhn, *Ältere Sammlungen im Markusevangelium* (Göttingen: Vandenhoeck, 1971). Worthy of note is Lord's observation that 'Oral traditional composers think in terms of blocks and series of blocks of tradition' ('Gospels' in Walker, ed., *Relationship* 59).

lier, smaller groupings. The point is that we should not assume that such compositional procedures came into the process only at a later stage of the process or only when the tradition was written down.

c. Not Layers but Performances

One of the most important conclusions to emerge from this review of the oral character of so much of the Jesus tradition, and of the likely processes of oral transmission, is that the perspective which has dominated the study of the history of Synoptic tradition is simply wrong-headed. Bultmann laid out the playing field by conceiving of the Jesus tradition as 'composed of a series of layers'.[301] The consequence of this literary paradigm was that each retelling of episodes or parts of the Jesus tradition was bound to be conceived on the analogy of an editor editing a literary text. Each retelling was like a new (edited) edition. And so the impression of each retelling as another layer superimposed upon earlier layers became almost inescapable, especially when the literary imagery was integrated with the archaeological image of the ancient tell, where research proceeds by digging down through the historical layers.[302] The consequence has been widespread disillusion at the prospect of ever being able successfully to strip off the successive layers of editing to leave some primary layer exposed clearly to view. Equally inevitable from such a perspective were the suspicion and scepticism met by any bold enough to claim that they had been successful in their literary archaeology and had actually uncovered a large area of Jesus' bedrock teaching.

But the imagery is simply inappropriate.[303] An oral retelling of a tradition is not at all like a new literary edition. It has not worked on or from a previous retelling. How could it? The previous retelling was not 'there' as a text to be consulted. And in the retelling the retold tradition did not come into existence as a kind of artefact, to be examined as by an editor and re-edited for the next retell-

301. Bultmann, *Jesus* 12-13.

302. As again by Crossan in his talk of 'scientific stratigraphy' (*Historical Jesus* xxviii, xxxi-xxxii). See also above chapter 6 n. 95. Bruce Chilton made an earlier protest against this 'literary fallacy' — *The Temple of Jesus: His Sacrificial Program within a Cultural History of Sacrifice* (University Park: Pennsylvania State University, 1992) 114-15, 120, referring to his *Profiles of a Rabbi: Synoptic Opportunities in Reading about Jesus* (BJS 177; Atlanta: Scholars, 1989).

303. Cf. Liebenberg: 'Although it is true that all one has to work with are the canonical and non-canonical gospel texts, it remains methodologically unsound to work with a theory of the gospel tradition which gives pride of place to these texts, when it is known that they came into being in a predominantly oral milieu, and more significantly, that the first twenty to thirty years after the life of Jesus the stories and aphorisms attributed to him were transmitted and performed orally' (*Language* 518).

ing. In oral transmission a tradition is performed, not edited. And as we have seen, performance includes both elements of stability and elements of variability — stability of subject and theme, of key details or core exchanges, variability in the supporting details and the particular emphases to be drawn out. That is a very different perspective. And it allows, indeed requires, rather different conclusions. These include the likelihood that the stabilities of the tradition were sufficiently maintained and the variabilities of the retellings subject to sufficient control for the substance of the tradition, and often actual words of Jesus which made the first tradition-forming impact, to continue as integral parts of the living tradition, for at least as long as it took for the Synoptic tradition to be written down. In other words, whereas the concept of literary *layers* implies increasing remoteness from an 'original', 'pure', or 'authentic' layer, the concept of *performance* allows a directness, even an immediacy of interaction, with a living theme and core even when variously embroidered in various retellings.[304]

The concept of oral transmission, as illustrated from the Synoptic tradition itself, therefore, does not encourage either the scepticism which has come to afflict the 'quest of the historical Jesus' or the lopsided findings of the neo-Liberal questers. Rather it points a clear middle way between a model of memorization by rote on the one hand and any impression of oral transmission as a series of evanescent reminiscences of some or several retellings on the other. It encourages neither those who are content with nothing short of the historicity of every detail and word of the text nor those who can see and hear nothing other than the faith of the early churches. It encourages us rather to see and hear the Synoptic tradition as the repertoire of the early churches when they recalled the Jesus who had called their first leaders and predecessors to discipleship and celebrated again the powerful impact of his life and teaching.

d. Oral Tradition to Written Gospel

We need not follow the course of oral transmission beyond the transition from oral tradition to written Gospel. The significance of that transition can be exaggerated, as we noted above in reviewing the work of Kelber (§8.3f): Jesus tradi-

---

304. I have struggled to find a suitable image to replace that of 'layers' (edited editions), and played with the model of forms somewhat like space satellites circling round the remembered Jesus, with the forms of the 60s and 70s not necessarily further from Jesus than those of the 40s and 50s. The image is not very good, but it can be elaborated to depict John's Gospel as on a higher orbit, or to include the possibility of forms drifting out of the gravity of the remembered Jesus or being caught by a countervailing gravity. The earlier image of a trajectory could be fitted to this also — e.g., Q material on a trajectory leading to a *Gospel of Thomas* no longer held within the original gravity field.

tion did not cease to circulate in oral form simply because it had been written down; hearings of a Gospel being read would be part of the oral/aural transmission, to be retold in further circles of orality;[305] the written text was still fluid, still living tradition.[306] But there are two other aspects, misleading impressions or unexamined assumptions, which have encouraged false perspectives on the subject and which should be highlighted here.

One is the impression that the oral Jesus tradition was like two (or several) narrow streams which were wholly absorbed into the written Gospels through their sources. So much of the focus in Gospel research has been on the question of sources for the Gospels that it has been natural, I suppose, for oral tradition to be conceived simply as source material for the Gospels, without any real attempt being made to conceptualize what oral communities were like and how the oral tradition functioned prior to and independently of written collections and Gospels. As already noted, some narrative criticism and some discussions of Synoptic pericopes at times almost seem to assume that when a copy of Mark or Matthew or Luke was initially received by any church, that was the first time the church had heard the Jesus tradition contained therein. But this is to ignore or forget one of the key insights of form criticism in the beginning, namely the recognition that the tradition took various forms because the forms reflected the way the tradition was being used in the first churches. In fact, it is almost self-evident that the Synoptists proceeded by gathering and ordering Jesus tradition which had already been in circulation, that is, had already been well enough known to various churches, for at least some years if not decades. Where else did the Evangelists find the tradition? Stored up, unused, in an old box at the back of some teacher's house? Stored up, unrehearsed, in the failing memory of an old apostle? Hardly! On the contrary, it is much more likely that when the Synoptic Gospels were first received by various churches, these churches *already* possessed (in communal oral memory or in written form) their own versions of much of the material. They would be able to compare the Evangelist's version of much of the tradition with their own versions. This conclusion ties in well with the considerations adduced above (§8.1). And as we have seen above, the divergences between different versions of the Synoptic tradition imply a lively and flexible oral tradition known to the Evangelists and presumably also to the churches with which they were associated.

This line of thought links in with the other assumption which has become debilitatingly pervasive: that each document belongs to and represents the views

---

305. As Koester was already pointing out in his first monograph *(Synoptische Überlieferung)*.

306. See particularly D. C. Parker, *The Living Text of the Gospels* (Cambridge: Cambridge University, 1997), whose warning against searching for an original text mirrors the warning of specialists in oral tradition against searching for an original form.

of only one community, and that the tensions within and among documents indicate rival camps and already different Christianities. The assumption derives again from the first insights of form criticism: that the forms of the tradition reflect the interests of the churches which used them. This was reinforced by the sociological perspective of the final quarter of the twentieth century: literature as the expression not so much of a single mind as of a social context. But these insights have been narrowed (and distorted) in a quite extraordinary way, to claim in effect that each text was written by and for a particular community — a Q community, a Mark community, a Matthean community, and so on.[307] I have already challenged this assumption with regard to Q (§7.4b), and by implication for the Gospels generally. But the assumption covers also the streams of tradition which entered into the Gospels. The assumption, in other words, is of differing and conflicting streams of tradition more or less from the first, celebrating in effect different Jesuses — a prophetic and/or apocalyptic Jesus, Jesus the wisdom teacher, the Jesus of aretalogies (divine man), and so on.[308]

307. R. Bauckham, 'For Whom Were the Gospels Written?', in R. Bauckham, ed., *The Gospels for All Christians: Rethinking the Gospel Audiences* (Grand Rapids: Eerdmans, 1998), provides a number of examples (13-22). He suspects that 'those who no longer think it possible to use the Gospels to reconstruct the historical Jesus compensate for this loss by using them to reconstruct the communities that produced the Gospels' (20). See also S. C. Barton's strictures in the same volume ('Can We Identify the Gospel Audiences?', *Gospels for All* 173-94) on the use of 'community' and on our ability to identify beyond generalizations the social context in which the Gospels were written.

308. Cf. particularly Koester, 'One Jesus and Four Primitive Gospels'; also 'The Structure and Criteria of Early Christian Beliefs', in Robinson and Koester, *Trajectories* 205-31; Lührmann, *Redaktion* 95-96; Mack, *Myth* 83-97. Koester's reflections on 'The Historical Jesus and the Historical Situation of the Quest: An Epilogue', in Chilton and Evans, eds., *Studying the Historical Jesus* 535-45, exemplifies how dubious the reasoning has become: (1) 'The history of Christian beginnings *demonstrates* that it was most effective to establish and to nurture the community of the new age without any recourse to the life and work of Jesus of Nazareth' ('Historical Jesus' 535, my emphasis). *Assumption:* 'the community of the new age' did not know or value any Jesus tradition. (2) 'There were followers of Jesus, who were not included in the circle of those churches for which the central ritual and the story of Jesus' suffering and death was the unifying principle. Instead, they believed that their salvation was mediated through the words of wisdom that Jesus had spoken. In the Synoptic Sayings Source a community appears that had combined this belief in Jesus with the expectation of his return as the Son of Man' ('Historical Jesus' 537). *Assumptions:* one document per church; silence regarding means ignorance of or opposition to; differing emphases are irreconcilable in a single document. (3) Some of those addressed in 1 Corinthians seem to have understood Jesus' sayings 'as the saving message of a great wisdom teacher'; the earliest compositional strata of Q seem to have understood 'Jesus' words of wisdom as a revelation providing life and freedom' ('Historical Jesus' 540). *Assumptions:* Corinthian 'wisdom' was based on Jesus' teaching, and implies a christology; 1 Corinthians 1-4 requires more than a rhetorical and socio-political understanding of that wisdom; Q wisdom was soteriological rather than paraenetic.

Richard Bauckham has recently challenged this assumption with regard to the written Gospels. His counter-thesis is that 'the Gospels were written for general circulation around the churches and so envisaged a very general Christian audience. Their implied readership is not specific but indefinite: any and every Christian community in the late first-century Roman Empire'.[309] The claim may be stated in an exaggerated form (for *all* Christians?), but we should not discount the likelihood that Evangelists wrote out of their more local experience primarily with a view to a much larger circle of churches, in Syria-Cilicia, for example. And Bauckham needs to give more weight to the likelihood that particular communities were the Evangelist's *source* for Jesus tradition, as distinct from communities as the Evangelist's *target* in writing his Gospel. But he is justified in dismissing the idea that the Evangelist would have written his Gospel for the community in which he lived.[310] And he rightly challenges any suggestion that the tradition-stock available to any one Evangelist was limited to his own community or circle of churches.[311]

The point here is that Bauckham is certainly correct to highlight the evidence that the first churches were by no means as isolated from one another and at odds with one another as has been so often assumed. If Paul's letters (and Acts) are any guide, the first churches consisted rather of 'a network of communities in constant communication', linked by messengers, letters, and visits by leading figures in the new movement.[312] This ties in with what was noted above: that church founding included the initial communication of foundation tradition and that Paul could assume common tradition, including knowledge of Jesus tradition, even in a church which he had never previously visited (Rome). And though there were indeed severe tensions between Paul and the Jerusalem leadership, Paul still regarded the lines of continuity between the churches in Judea and those of the Gentile mission as a matter of first importance.[313] In short, the suggestion that there were churches who knew only one stream of tradition — Jesus only as a miracle worker, or only as a wisdom teacher, etc. — has been given far

309. Bauckham, 'For Whom?' 1.

310. Bauckham, 'For Whom?' 28-30; 'Why should he go to the considerable trouble of writing a Gospel for a community to which he was regularly preaching?' (29).

311. In private correspondence.

312. Bauckham, 'For Whom?' 30-44; also M. B. Thompson, 'The Holy Internet: Communication between Churches in the First Christian Generation', in Bauckham, ed., *Gospels* 49-70. Bauckham justifiably asks, 'Why do scholars so readily assume that the author of a Gospel would be someone who had spent all his Christian life attached to the same Christian community?' (36). Bauckham's thesis has now been criticized by D. C. Sim, "The Gospels for All Christians? A Response to Richard Bauckham', *JSNT* 84 (2001) 3-27. I will address this debate in volume 2.

313. Gal. 1.22; 1 Thess. 2.14; 2 Cor. 1.16.

too much uncritical credence in scholarly discussions on the Gospels and ought
to have been dismissed a lot sooner.

8.7. In Summary

This has been a lengthy chapter, so let me sum up what has emerged about the Jesus tradition prior to its being written down.

First (§8.1), I noted the strong circumstantial case for the view that, from the
beginning, new converts would have wanted to know about Jesus, that no church
would have been established without its store of foundation (including Jesus) tradition, and that the churches were organised to maintain and to pass on that tradition. The importance of remembering Jesus and learning about him and of responsible teachers is attested as early as we can reach back into earliest Christianity, in
Jewish as well as Gentile churches. The apparent silence of Paul and the character
of the Gospels themselves provide no substantive counter-argument.

Second (§8.2), the assumption that prophecy within the earliest churches
would have added substantial material to the Jesus tradition has been misleading.
It is not borne out to any great extent by what we know of early church prophetic
activity. On the contrary, recognition of the danger of *false* prophecy would almost certainly have been as widespread as prophecy itself, and the first churches
would probably have been alert to the danger of accepting any prophetic utterance which was out of harmony with the Jesus tradition already received.

When we turned, third (§8.3), to examine the relevance of oral tradition to
our quest, we noted the widespread recognition among specialists in orality of
the character of oral transmission as a mix of stable themes and flexibility, of
fixed and variable elements in oral retelling. But we also noted that such insights
have hardly begun to be exploited adequately in the treatment of Jesus tradition
as oral tradition. However, Bailey's observations, drawn from his experience of
oral traditioning processes in Middle Eastern village life, have highlighted points
of potential importance, particularly the rationale which, in the cases in point,
determined the distinction between the more fixed elements and constant themes
on the one hand, and the flexible and variable elements on the other. Where stories or teaching was important for the community's identity and life there would
be a concern to maintain the core or key features, however varied other details
(less important to the story's or teaching's point) in successive retellings.

Our own examination, fourth (§§8.4, 5), of the Jesus tradition itself confirmed the relevance of the oral paradigm and the danger of assuming (consciously or otherwise) the literary paradigm. The findings did not call into serious question the priority of Mark or the existence of a document Q. But, in each
of the examples marshalled, the degree of variation between clearly parallel tra-

ditions and the inconsequential character of so much of the variations have hardly encouraged an explanation in terms of literary dependence (on Mark or Q) or of literary editing. Rather, the combination of stability and flexibility positively cried out to be recognized as typically oral in character. That probably implies in at least some cases that the variation was due to knowledge and use of the same tradition in oral mode, as part of the community tradition familiar to Matthew and Luke. And even if a pericope was derived from Mark or Q, the retelling by Matthew or Luke is itself better described as in oral mode, maintaining the character of an oral retelling more than of a literary editing.[314]

In both cases (narratives and teachings) we also noted (1) a concern to remember the things Jesus had done and said. The discipleship and embryonic communities which had been formed and shaped by the impact of Jesus' life and message would naturally have celebrated that tradition as central to their own identity as disciples and churches. We noted also (2) that the memories consisted in stories and teachings whose own identity was focused in particular themes and/or particular words and phrases — usually those said by Jesus himself. And (3) that the variations and developments were not linear or cumulative in character, but the variations of oral performance. The material examined indicated neither concern to preserve some kind of literalistic historicity of detail, nor any readiness to flood the tradition with Jewish wisdom or prophetic utterance.

Finally (§8.6), we have observed that the pattern of the oral traditioning process was probably established more or less from the beginning (before the first Easter) and was probably maintained in character through to (and beyond) the writing down of the tradition. The first impact (sequence of impacts) made by Jesus resulted in the formation of tradition, which was itself formative and constitutive of community/church through Easter, beyond Galilee and into Greek, and was preserved and celebrated through regular performance (whether in communal or specifically liturgical gatherings) or reviewed for apologetic or catechetical purposes. In other words, what we today are confronted with in the Gospels is not the top layer (last edition) of a series of increasingly impenetrable layers, but the living tradition of Christian celebration which takes us with surprising immediacy to the heart of the first memories of Jesus.

On the basis of all this we can begin to build a portrayal of the remembered Jesus, of the impact made by his words and deeds on the first disciples as that impact was 'translated' into oral tradition and as it was passed down in oral performance within the earliest circles of disciples and the churches, to be enshrined in due course in the written Synoptic tradition.

314. R. F. Person, 'The Ancient Israelite Scribe as Performer', *JBL* 117 (1998) 601-609, argues that the scribes understood their task as re-presenting the dynamic tradition of their communities, as illustrated from some of the scribal interventions in 1QIsa[a].

CHAPTER 9

The Historical Context

As access to (written) sources and ability to evaluate (oral) tradition are fundamental for a historical investigation, so also is an appreciation of the context of
the historical figure on whom the investigation seeks to focus. In this case the
historical context is, in the first place, the geographical context of Galilee and
Judea in the early decades of the first century of the common era.[1] The historical context also includes, of course, the social and political context: Jesus was
an artisan from a Galilean village, and the land had been conquered by the
Romans. But the principal context which needs to be illuminated is the national
and religious context. Central to this investigation, we have already stressed
(§5.5), is the recognition that Jesus was a Jew. Our first task must therefore be to
sketch in what that would have meant. The primary context for Jesus the Jew
was Judaism.[2]

9.1. Misleading Presuppositions about 'Judaism'

The description of Judaism at the time of Jesus is beset with problems of definition, not least those of anachronistic definition. If we are to gain a clear perspective on the Judaism (of the time) of Jesus, these problems need to be faced
squarely, since otherwise the historical context within which we locate Jesus may
be seriously distorted, and we may be led up a number of false trails.

An older generation of scholarship, both Jewish and Christian, thought in

---

1. What Renan famously called 'a fifth Gospel' (*Life* 31).
2. What follows (§§9.1-5) is a revised version of my earlier 'Judaism in the Land of Israel in the First Century', in J. Neusner, ed., *Judaism in Late Antiquity,* Part 2: *Historical Syntheses* (Leiden: Brill, 1995) 229-61.

terms of 'normative Judaism',[3] the assumption being that the Judaism represented in rabbinic tradition (Mishnah, Talmuds, etc.) already served as the norm determinative for Judaism in the first century.[4] Scholars were, of course, aware of Jewish pseudepigrapha, several of which date from the second century BCE or earlier,[5] and of Philo, the Alexandrian Jewish philosopher who died about 50 CE.[6] But these writings were preserved for posterity by Christians and not by the rabbis and so could the more easily be regarded as variations on or deviations from a Pharisaic/rabbinic norm.[7] There was also some reflection on the possibility that diaspora Judaism was a different branch of the species from Palestinian Judaism, perhaps thus providing a solution to the conundrum of what Judaism it was that the Christian Paul set his face so firmly against.[8] But the thesis simply reinforced the sense that diaspora Judaism was a divergent (and inferior) form of Judaism, whose degree of divergence itself provided a large part of the explanation of why Pauline Christianity and normative/Palestinian Judaism went their separate ways.

In the mid-twentieth century, however, the assumption of a Pharisaic/rabbinic normative Judaism recognized as such in first-century Israel was shattered by the discovery of the Dead Sea Scrolls. Although the delay in publishing many of the more obviously sectarian scrolls diminished their initial impact, they clearly include Jewish documents which predate Christianity and could never have been affected by Christianity.[9] More to the point, their self-asserted sectarian character is evident,[10] and can hardly fail to be attributed to a kind of Judaism

---

3. The term is particularly linked to G. F. Moore, *Judaism in the First Three Centuries of the Christian Era* (3 vols.; Cambridge: Harvard University, 1927-30); see, e.g., Sanders, *Paul and Palestinian Judaism* 34 and n. 11.

4. The assumption prevails, e.g., in J. Jeremias, *Jerusalem in the Time of Jesus* (London: SCM, 1969), and in S. Safrai and M. Stern, eds., *The Jewish People in the First Century* (CRINT I; Assen: van Gorcum, 2 vols. 1974, 1976). The scholarship of the period is typified by reliance on the great collection of rabbinic material by H. Strack and P. Billerbeck, *Kommentar zum Neuen Testament* (Munich: Beck, 4 vols., 1926-28).

5. Particularly R. H. Charles, ed., *The Apocrypha and Pseudepigrapha of the Old Testament* (Oxford: Clarendon, 2 vols. 1913); W. Bousset and H. Gressmann, *Die Religion des Judentums im späthellenistischen Zeitalter* (HNT 21; Tübingen: Mohr Siebeck, 1925, [4]1966).

6. See P. Borgen, 'Philo of Alexandria' in M. E. Stone, ed., *Jewish Writings of the Second Temple Period* (CRINT II.2; Assen: Van Gorcum, 1984) 233-82; also 'Philo of Alexandria', *ABD* 5.333-42; J. Morris, in Schürer, *History* III.2, 809-89.

7. See, e.g., the disagreement among Bousset, Gressmann, and Moore on this question (discussed by Sanders, *Paul and Palestinian Judaism* 34 and 55-56).

8. Particularly C. G. Montefiore, *Judaism and St. Paul* (London: Goschen, 1914), and H. J. Schoeps, *Paul: The Theology of the Apostle in the Light of Jewish Religious History* (London: Lutterworth, 1961).

9. See below n. 78.

10. See particularly H. Stegemann, *The Library of Qumran* (1993; ET Grand Rapids: Eerdmans, 1998) 104-18.

which flourished in the heart of the land of Israel up to the 60s of the first century
CE. This in turn has resulted in a renewed interest in the pseudepigrapha[11] and an
increasing recognition that they too have to be described as representing different
forms of Judaism. At the same time the extent of Pharisaic influence in first-
century Israel has been radically questioned,[12] and the sharpness of any distinction between 'Judaism' and 'Hellenism' which had allowed a clear demarcation
between 'Palestinian Judaism' and 'Hellenistic Judaism' has been considerably
blurred.[13] Within a broader framework we could perhaps also note that the liberal
thrust of so much western scholarship, reinforced more recently by postmodern
suspicion, has progressively undermined the very idea of a 'norm'.

In consequence the last two decades of the twentieth century witnessed an
increasing tendency to emphasize the diverse character of first-century Judaism
and to speak of several 'Judaisms' (plural), leaving the question of their legitimacy as forms of 'Judaism' unasked as being either misleading or improper.[14]
Still too little explored, however, is the further or alternative question how this
quite proper modern, phenomenological description of different Judaisms relates
to the *self-perception* of each of these several Judaisms in their own day, not to
mention their own evaluation of the other Judaisms.

The main alternative option at this point for a historian of the period is to
speak of 'Palestinian Judaism'. It is true that the name 'Palestine' came into formal use for the territory only in the second century CE, when, following the failure of the second Jewish Revolt (132-135), the Roman colony of Aelia
Capitolina was reestablished, and Judea was renamed Syria Palaestina. But the
usage itself is very old and common among Greco-Roman writers. Herodotus in
the fifth century BCE already speaks of 'the Syrians of Palestine' (*Hist.* II.10.3),

---

11. See particularly J. H. Charlesworth, ed., *The Old Testament Pseudepigrapha* (2
vols.; London: Darton, Longman and Todd, 1983, 1985) = OTP; also Charlesworth, *Jesus* ch. 2;
H. F. D. Sparks, ed. *The Apocryphal Old Testament* (Oxford: Clarendon, 1984).

12. Differently by Neusner, *Rabbinic Traditions;* also *From Politics to Piety;* and by
Sanders, particularly *Judaism: Practice and Belief, 63 BCE–66 CE* (London: SCM, 1992) ch. 18.

13. See chapter 5 n. 122; see also below n. 288.

14. E.g., S. Sandmel, *The First Christian Century in Judaism and Christianity* (New
York: Oxford University, 1969) ch. 2 'Palestinian Judaisms'; J. Neusner et al., eds., *Judaisms
and Their Messiahs at the Turn of the Christian Era* (Cambridge: Cambridge University, 1987);
J. Neusner, *Studying Classical Judaism: A Primer* (Louisville: Westminster, 1991) 27-36; A. F.
Segal, *The Other Judaisms of Late Antiquity* (Atlanta: Scholars, 1987); J. Murphy, *The Reli-
gious World of Jesus: An Introduction to Second Temple Palestinian Judaism* (Hoboken, NJ:
Ktav, 1991) 39. 'Whereas rabbinic Judaism is dominated by an identifiable perspective that
holds together many otherwise diverse elements, early Judaism appears to encompass almost
unlimited diversity and variety — indeed, it might be more appropriate to speak of early
Judaisms' (R. A. Kraft and G. W. E. Nickelsburg, *Early Judaism and Its Modern Interpreters*
[Atlanta: Scholars, 1986] 2).

and though there is a question as to whether he was referring only to the coastal strip south of Phoenicia (the territory of the Philistines), Josephus had no doubt that Herodotus meant the Jews/Judeans (*Ap.* 1.168-71). And Aristotle in the fourth century BCE refers to the Dead Sea as 'the lake in Palestine' (*Meteorologica* II, p. 359a).[15] So 'Palestinian Judaism' is an accurate enough historical description for the Judaism of the first century CE, whatever the sensitivities occasioned for modern scholarship by the political realities of present-day Israel and Palestine. 'Judaism in the land of Israel' would be equally acceptable and give more weight to Israel's covenant perspective.

Equally problematic has been the temporal connotations attached to 'Judaism'. As already noted (§5.5), an older scholarship spoke of first-century Judaism as *Spätjudentum* (*late* Judaism), a usage which persisted into the late 1960s. This was an astonishing designation since it reduced Judaism to the role of serving solely as forerunner to Christianity and left a question mark over how one should describe the next nineteen centuries of Judaism! The still more common 'intertestamental Judaism' reduced the significance of this 'Judaism' to bridging the gap between the (Christian) Testaments and implied a coherence ('Judaism') for the documents chiefly referred to, which is by no means clear. The natural reaction has been to choose the opposite adjective and to speak of 'early Judaism', or 'formative Judaism'.[16] The actual period covered is of uncertain length, particularly its starting point — whether from Ezra, or from the Greek period (300 BCE), the most favoured option, or from the close of the Jewish canon (from Bible to Mishnah), or from the Maccabees, or from the emergence of the Pharisees as a religious force, or indeed from the beginnings of the reformulation of Judaism after 70 CE. The end point is more obviously 200 CE, on the grounds that the codification of the Mishnah (about 200) marks the beginning of rabbinic Judaism proper.[17] The designation 'early Judaism', however, runs a risk similar to that of the objectionable *Spätjudentum,* since it can be taken to imply that the only significance of first-century Judaism was as a precursor to rabbinic Judaism.

The further alternative of designating the period 300 BCE to 200 CE as

---

15. See *GLAJJ* 1.2-3, 7, 349 (§§1, 3,142) with commentary.

16. So, e.g., the title of the volume edited by Kraft and Nickelsburg, *Early Judaism;* Neusner has also promoted the term 'Formative Judaism' in the series produced by him under that title. In contrast, the series of volumes edited by W. S. Green *(Approaches to Ancient Judaism)* use 'Ancient Judaism' to cover everything from the post-exilic period to the early rabbis. M. Z. Brettler, 'Judaism in the Hebrew Bible? The Transition from Ancient Israelite Religion to Judaism', *CBQ* 61 (1999) 429-47, suggests speaking of the biblical period as 'emergent' or 'earliest' Judaism.

17. For the equivalent questions regarding the beginning of 'the rabbinic period', see I. M. Gafni, 'The Historical Background', in S. Safrai, ed., *The Literature of the Sages* (CRINT II.3.1; Assen: Van Gorcum, 1987) 1-34.

'Middle Judaism'[18] has the advantage of distinguishing the Greco-Roman period from what went before (the 'ancient Judaism' of the sixth to fourth centuries BCE). But it raises in turn the issues of when we should start speaking of 'Judaism' proper, whether 'Judaism' is a concept or simply a label, and the justification for and significance of marking off the pre-exilic period ('the religion of Israel') so sharply from the still biblical 'Judaism' of the return from exile.[19] Probably the least objectionable and problematic term to use is 'Second Temple Judaism': it does not purport to denote 'Judaism' as such but the 'Judaism' which spanned the 600 or so years from the rebuilding of the Temple in the late sixth century BCE to its destruction in 70 CE, a Judaism focused round the Jerusalem Temple.

All this potential perplexity points up the need to proceed cautiously if we are to avoid the danger of imposing categories and grids which might distort the evidence more than display it. In view of the confusion of definitions which has weakened earlier debate we should obviously begin with some clarification of the term 'Judaism' itself (§9.2). We can then indicate something of the range of beliefs and practices which that term, or more precisely, Palestinian Judaism or Second Temple Judaism, may properly be used to categorise (§9.3). It will also be necessary to highlight the factionalism which was such a mark of the Judaism of the second half of the Second Temple period (§9.4), in the light of which it will be still more pressing to clarify what it was that makes it possible to use the same category, 'Judaism', for all the 'Judaisms'. What was the common ground which they shared (§9.5)? Finally we need to ask what difference it might have made that Jesus was brought up in Galilee (§§9.6-7) and remind ourselves of the politics of the period and how they would have influenced conditions in the time of Jesus (§9.8). All this should give us a clearer idea of what the description of someone as a 'Jew', whether Jesus or any other Jew, would have signified in the first century CE.[20] The immediate results are summed up in a brief outline of Jesus' life and mission (§9.9).

18. G. Boccaccini, *Middle Judaism: Jewish Thought, 300 BCE to 200 CE* (Minneapolis: Fortress, 1991).

19. *The Anchor Bible Dictionary* completes its articles on the 'History of Israel' with the Persian period and begins its treatment of 'Judaism' with the Greco-Roman period (*ABD* 3.526-76, 3.1037-89).

20. Cf. D. J. Harrington, 'The Jewishness of Jesus: Facing Some Problems' (1987), in Charlesworth, ed., *Jesus' Jewishness* 123-36: 'Our increased understanding of the diversity within Palestinian Judaism in Jesus' time makes it difficult to know precisely what kind of Jew Jesus was and against which background we should try to interpret him'; 'the more we know, the less we know' (136, 128). Similarly T. Holmén, 'The Jewishness of Jesus in the "Third Quest"', in Labahn and Schmidt, eds., *Jesus, Mark and Q* 143-62. Meier: 'the phrase Jesus the Jew has become an academic cliché. The real challenge is to unpack that phrase and specify what sort of first-century Jew Jesus was' ('Present State of the "Third Quest"' 467). Meier pre-

I should probably stress right away that the sketch which follows makes no pretensions to provide a complete overview of Second Temple Judaism; that would distract too much from the primary task, even if space permitted. My concern is rather threefold. First, to indicate something of the *comprehensiveness* of Judaism, not simply as a religion but also as what might be called a national ideology, or better, as a religion which encompassed the whole of life, education and family life, the law of the land and social relationships, not to mention economics and politics. Second, to give an impression both of the *diversity* of Second Temple Judaism and of what held it together as 'Judaism'. The hope, obviously, is, thirdly, that thereby readers may be the better able to situate Jesus within Second Temple Judaism, within its comprehensiveness and its diversity, and to identify more readily the points of distinctiveness and tension within his mission.

9.2. Defining 'Judaism'

a. 'Judaism'

What then is 'Judaism'? When did 'Judaism' begin? If the answers were to depend solely on word occurrence in our literary sources, the answers would be clear. For the Greek term *Ioudaismos* first appears in literature in 2 Maccabees, in three passages — 2.21; 8.1; and 14.38. 2.21 describes the Maccabean rebels as 'those who fought bravely for Judaism' *(hyper tou Ioudaismou);* 8.1 their supporters as 'those who had continued in Judaism' *(tous memenēkotas en tō Ioudaismō);* and 14.38 the martyr Razis as one who had formerly been accused of Judaism and who had eagerly risked body and life *hyper tou Ioudaismou.* Reflecting the same traditions, 4 Macc. 4.26 describes the attempt of the Syrian overlord Antiochus Epiphanes 'to compel each member of the nation to eat defiling foods and to renounce Judaism'.

The only other literary evidence from our period (before the end of the first century CE) is Gal. 1.13-14, where Paul speaks of his former conduct 'in Judaism' *(en tō Ioudaismō),* and recalls how he had at that time persecuted 'the church of God' and had progressed *en tō Ioudaismō* beyond many of his contemporaries among his people *(en tō genei mou).* In addition however we should note

---

fers to speak of Jesus as a 'marginal Jew' rather than of 'Judaisms' (468). One might ask whether the description 'marginal Jew' situates Jesus the Jew firmly enough within Second Temple Judaism; but Meier does take the Jewishness of Jesus seriously (466-69, 483-86). From his socioeconomic perspective Crossan defends Meier's usage, though he prefers to speak of Jesus as 'a marginalized peasant' *(Birth* 350-52). But see also G. Theissen, 'Jesus im Judentum. Drei Versuche einer Ortsbestimmung', *Kirche und Israel* 14 (1999) 93-109. And note Moxnes's closing observations ('Jesus the Jew' 101-103).

a funerary inscription from our period in Italy, which praises a woman 'who lived a gracious life within Judaism' (*en tō Ioudaismō, CIJ* 537).[21]

Two points call at once for comment. First, in the earliest phase of its usage there are no examples of the term being used by non-Jews. 'Judaism' begins as a *Jewish term of self-reference*. But equally noticeable is the fact that all four sources just cited reflect the perspective of *Hellenistic* (or diaspora or Greek-speaking) Judaism. Thus, it is significant that the term occurs in 2 Maccabees, composed in Greek and a self-confessed 'epitome' of the five-volume work of Jason of Cyrene (2.26, 28), and not as a translation of some Hebrew term in 1 Maccabees. Indeed, K. G. Kuhn can find only one passage in rabbinic literature and perhaps Palestinian usage where *yhwdoth* = *Ioudaismos* occurs, but, interestingly, in a description of the Jews in Babylon who did not change their God or their religious laws but held fast *byhwdoth* ('in their Judaism') (*Esther Rab.* 7.11).[22] Here we should simply note the further element of anomaly in our definitions in that we are using a term ('Judaism') to describe the religion of Jews in the land of Israel in the first century which *those native to the land evidently did not use for themselves*.

Second, in all cases the term 'Judaism' was being used in self-definition to mark out the character of belief and practice which *distinguished* the referent from the surrounding culture and ethos. Such diaspora Jews lived 'within Judaism' as 'a sort of fenced off area in which Jewish lives are led'.[23] Indeed, in 2 Maccabees the term is obviously coined as a counter to *hellēnismos*, 'Hellenism' (2 Macc. 4.13) and *allophylismos*, 'foreignness' (2 Macc. 4.13; 6.24). That is to say, for the author of 2 Maccabees, 'Judaism' is the summary term for that system embodying national and religious identity which was the rallying point for the violent rejection by the Maccabees of the Syrian attempt to assimilate them by the abolition of their distinctive practices (particularly circumcision and food laws — 1 Macc. 1.60-63; so also 4 Macc. 4.26). From the beginning, therefore 'Judaism' has a *strongly nationalistic overtone* and denotes a powerful integration of religious and national identity which marked Judaism out in its *distinctiveness* from other nations and religions.[24]

This is confirmed by the other literary usage cited above — Gal. 1.13-14. For

---

21. Y. Amir, 'The Term *Ioudaismos:* A Study in Jewish-Hellenistic Self-Identification', *Immanuel* 14 (1982) 34-41.

22. K. G. Kuhn, 'Israel', *TDNT* 3.363 and 364 n. 49.

23. Amir, *Ioudaismos* 39-40.

24. D. R. Schwartz, 'On the Jewish Background of Christianity', *Studies on the Jewish Background of Christianity* (WUNT 60; Tübingen: Mohr Siebeck, 1992) 11, plays down the nationalist dimension of 'Judaism' in its reaction to 'Hellenism'; 'Hellenism' may indeed have defined itself by its culture more than by descent or place of origin, but the reaction is hardly to be described as simply 'in kind'.

the life described there as 'in/within Judaism' is marked by the same total commitment to traditional religious practices and by the same hostility to anything which would dilute or defile Israel's distinctiveness. The fierceness of this reaction is indicated particularly by the terms 'zeal' (Phil. 3.6) and 'zealot' (Gal. 1.14). These terms are prominent in describing Maccabean motivation,[25] where Phinehas is presented as the great role model (1 Macc. 2.26, 54; 4 Macc. 18.12) and the war-cry is 'zeal for the law' (1 Macc. 2.26, 27, 50, 58; 2 Macc. 4.2). And Paul implicitly aligns himself with such fiercely nationalistic response by attributing his motivation as a persecutor of the church to the same 'zeal' (Phil. 3.6). It is equally significant that he sets his life 'in/within Judaism' in sharp contrast to his commission as apostle to the Gentiles (Gal. 1.13-16), implying clearly that it was the hostility to things 'Gentile' in his 'Judaism' on which he had now turned his back.[26]

In short, so far as its earliest usage is concerned, the term 'Judaism' describes the system of religion and way of life within which diaspora Jews lived so as to maintain their distinctive identity, and also the national and religious identity which was given its more definitive character by vigorous resistance to the assimilating and syncretistic influences of wider Hellenism.

b. 'Jew', 'Israel'

This finding seems to be strengthened by comparison with the much more widespread use of the terms 'Jew' and 'Israel'. The term 'Jew' *(Ioudaios)* begins of course as a way of identifying someone from Judea *(Ioudaia)*.[27] Indeed, for its early usage *Ioudaios* should be translated 'Judean', rather than 'Jew'.[28] And even

---

25. *Zēlos* in 1 Macc. 2.54, 58; *zēloun* in 1 Macc. 2.24, 26, 27, 50, 54, 58; *zēlōtēs* in 2 Macc. 4.2; 4 Macc. 18.12.

26. See further my *Galatians* (BNTC; London: Black, 1993) *ad loc.;* also *Theology of Paul* 346-54; see further below, vol. 2.

27. 'This name *(Ioudaioi),* by which they have been called from the time when they went up from Babylon, is derived from the tribe of Judah; as this tribe was the first to come to those parts, both the people themselves and the country have taken their name from it' (Josephus, *Ant.* 11.173).

28. When 'Judean' transposed into the less territorially specific 'Jew' is an important question, still highly relevant, for example, in discussion of the reference of *hoi Ioudaioi* in the Gospel of John. S. J. D. Cohen, *The Beginnings of Jewishness: Boundaries, Varieties, Uncertainties* (Berkeley: University of California, 1999) concludes that prior to the Hasmonean period *Ioudaios* should always be translated 'Judean', and never as 'Jew' (70-71, 82-106); the shift from a purely ethno-geographical term to one of religious significance is first evident in 2 Macc. 6.6 and 9.17, where for the first time *Ioudaios* can properly be translated 'Jew'; and in Greco-Roman writers the first use of *Ioudaios* as a religious term appears at the end of the first century CE (90-96, 127, 133-36). Given the crucial transformative effect of the Maccabean re-

in later usage, referring, for example, to Jews long settled in the diaspora, the basic sense of 'the Jews' as the nation or people identified with the territory of Judea is still present.[29] But since Judea was a temple state, religious identity was inextricably bound up with ethnic identity — 'the Jews' as worshippers of the God whose temple was in Jerusalem.[30] It was precisely this initial ambivalence and subsequent shift to a more religious significance which made it possible for the idea of non-Judeans becoming Jews, as in the famous case of Izates, king of Adiabene in the mid-first century CE (Josephus, *Ant.* 20.38-46).[31]

The point for us, however, is the one again made so effectively by Kuhn: that is, that '"Israel" is the name which the people uses for itself, whereas "Jews" is the non-Jewish name for it'.[32] In other words, 'Jew' is more the term used, by (Hellenistic) Jews (Philo, Josephus, Aristeas, Eupolemus, Artapanus, Hecataeus) as well as others, to distinguish the people so designated from other peoples, whereas 'Israel' is a self-affirmation by reference to its own distinctively apprehended heritage. Thus we find, for example, the use of 'Jews' in 1 Maccabees where the context is official and the tone diplomatic, but 'Israel' when it is a matter of self-designation;[33] in the Gospels 'king of the Jews' is Pilate's terminology, but 'king of Israel' that of the high priests;[34] Paul speaks regularly of 'Jew(s) and Greek(s)' as a way of categorising the whole of humanity,[35] while preferring to

---

bellion, however, it is questionable whether Cohen should push his thesis to include the claim that '*Ioudaismos* should be translated not as "Judaism" but as Judeanness' (106). BDAG has controversially elected to argue consistently for 'Judean' as the best translation (and even 'Judeanism'), but fails to take into account the shift in reference just outlined. For the question's more immediate relevance to our present concerns see below §9.6.

29. See BAGD/BDAG, *Ioudaia;* G. Harvey, *The True Israel: Uses of the Names Jew, Hebrew and Israel in Ancient Jewish and Early Christian Literature* (Leiden: Brill, 1996) ch. 2.

30. Hence the well-known but still surprising willingness of the Roman authorities to permit diaspora Jews to send their temple dues to Jerusalem.

31. Izates realized that 'he would not be genuinely a Jew *(einai bebaiōs Ioudaios)* unless he was circumcised', but was initially dissuaded from circumcision itself on the advice of his mother that his people 'would not tolerate the rule of a Jew over them' (*Ant.* 20.38-39). See further Cohen, *Beginnings of Jewishness* 78-81 and ch. 5 ('Crossing the Boundary and Becoming a Jew'). R. S. Kraemer, 'On the Meaning of the Term "Jew" in Greco-Roman Inscriptions', *HTR* 82 (1989) 35-53, finds evidence of non-Jews who affiliated with Judaism taking on the term 'Jew' either for themselves or for their children.

32. Kuhn, 'Israel' 360; see analysis and discussion on 359-65; see further *EncJud* 10.22. Kuhn's conclusions have been confirmed by P. Tomson, 'The Names Israel and Jew in Ancient Judaism and in the New Testament', *Bijdragen* 47 (1986) 120-40, 266-89, and have not been disturbed by Harvey, *True Israel,* whose focus is different (he objects to the idea that 'Israel' was limited as a title to a perceived 'pure or true Israel').

33. Kuhn, 'Israel' 360-61.

34. Mark 15.2, 9, 12, 26; 15.32 pars.

35. E.g., Rom. 2.9-10; 3.9; 10.12; 1 Cor. 12.13; Gal. 3.28.

say of himself 'I am an Israelite';[36] and in the rabbinic writings 'Israel' and not 'Jews' is the almost universal self-designation.[37] 'Jews', in other words, naturally evokes the counterpart, 'Gentiles', each defining itself by its exclusion of the other — 'Jews' = non-Gentiles, 'Gentiles' = non-Jews.[38] In contrast, 'Israel' is defined by the insider, not the outsider, and more by reference to its internal history (as heirs of the promises made to the patriarchs), than by reference to the history of nations and peoples. In short, *'Jew' betokens the perspective of the spectator* (Jewish included), *'Israel' that of the participant.*[39]

We might simply add that the picture is confirmed by the use of the verbal equivalent to 'Judaism' and 'Jew', equally infrequent in our sources as the former — *ioudaizein,* 'to live like a Jew'.[40] In each case it probably describes the action of a non-Jew in adopting what were regarded as distinctive Jewish customs (sabbath, food-laws, etc.) though not to the extent of being circumcised (becoming a proselyte).[41] In contrast, there is no verbal form of 'Israel/Israelite'. The 'judaizer' starts from outside, his very action presupposes the distinction between Jew and Gentile, he begins to cross a boundary, whereas the 'Israelite' starts from inside and so has no need to take an action equivalent to *ioudaizein.*[42]

The upshot of all this is that great care must be taken in using the term 'Judaism' to categorize the religious identity of the principal inhabitants of the land of Israel in the first century. Of course our modern use need not be determined or restricted by ancient usage. But we do need to be more alert than usual as historians to the fact that any modern attempt to describe first-century Judaism will inevitably reinforce something of the spectator perspective and concern for differentiation from others implicit in the ancient usage. *The very term itself makes it difficult for us to gain an insider's view of Judaism at the time of Jesus.* And if we want to see Jesus and earliest Christianity in context, that is, in some sense

36. Rom. 11.1; 2 Cor. 11.22. In contrast, it is the Gentile Luke who has Paul say of himself 'I am a Jew' not only to the Roman tribune but also to the Jerusalem crowd, speaking in Aramaic (Acts 21.39; 22.3). See further my 'Who Did Paul Think He Was? A Study of Jewish-Christian Identity', *NTS* 45 (1999) 174-93.

37. S. Zeitlin, *The Jews: Race, Nation, or Religion?* (Philadelphia: Dropsie, 1936) 31-32, recalling that after the failure of the bar Kokhba revolt the Jews ceased to exist as a nation.

38. Since '(the) Gentiles' is a way of translating *(ha)goyim = (ta) ethnē* = '(the) nations', the contrast really says 'Jews and all other nations', Jews in distinction from all the rest.

39. Similarly Kuhn and Tomson (above n. 32).

40. Only five known occurrences prior to the second century CE — Esther 8.17 LXX; Theodotus in Eusebius, *Praep. Evang.* 9.22.5; Gal. 2.14; Josephus, *War* 2.454, 463; Plutarch, *Life of Cicero* 7.6.

41. See further Cohen, *'Ioudaizein,* "to Judaize"', *Beginnings of Jewishness* ch. 6.

42. This more historically accurate use of the term 'judaizer' should therefore be distanced from the historically inaccurate use of the term (since Baur) to denote conservative Jewish Christians in their opposition to Paul's circumcision-free Gentile mission; see below, vol. 2.

'within Judaism' or emerging from 'within Judaism', we will have to be conscious of the strong nationalist overtones in the term's early use, and of the degree to which national and religious identity were fused in the one word — including not only differentiation from but also a certain hostility to the other nations and their religious practices.

9.3. The Diversity of Judaism — Judaism from Without

What counts as Judaism in Palestine in the first century? What falls within the scope of 'Judaism' in the late Second Temple period? How broad and encompassing was or can 'Judaism' be (from our perspective) as a historical description? A natural and popular response has been to look at the different groups and writings of the period. And though this approach is open to objection, as we shall see, a description of these groups and writings does form an important part of our understanding of first-century Judaism, particularly of its diversity. In this section, then, our first objective is, briefly, to give some indication of the range of practice and belief covered by (Palestinian/late Second Temple) 'Judaism' as a phenomenological description.[43] In each case the key question is: If this too is 'Judaism', what does that tell us about 'Judaism'? Although much of the evidence available is fragmentary, often hostile and sometimes minimal, in most cases we have enough information to work with, and modern treatments have improved markedly in quality and reliability over the last two decades.

a. The Four 'Sects'

The usual starting point has been Josephus' 'four philosophies' or 'sects' *(haireseis)*[44] — not unnaturally since Josephus' way of introducing them seems to imply that these were the only groupings among the Jews worthy of attention on the part of his readers (*War* 2.119-166; *Ant.* 18.11-25).[45] To begin with

---

43. The objective is limited: I have no intention of attempting a full description of the groups and elements which made up Second Temple Judaism.

44. Note the various discussions on the use of terms like 'sect' in S. J. D. Cohen, *From the Maccabees to the Mishnah* (Philadelphia: Westminster, 1987) ch. 5; A. J. Saldarini, *Pharisees, Scribes and Sadducees in Palestinian Society* (Edinburgh: Clark, 1988) particularly 70-73, 123-27 (Saldarini prefers the translation 'schools of thought'); M. Hengel and R. Deines, 'E. P. Sanders' "Common Judaism", Jesus, and the Pharisees', *JTS* 46 (1995) 1-70 (here 43-45); a fuller version in Hengel, *Judaica et Hellenistica: Kleine Schriften I* (WUNT 90; Tübingen: Mohr Siebeck, 1996) 392-479.

45. In reference to the debate as to whether Josephus really thought of four rather than

Josephus also makes good sense since Josephus is as close to the events as we could hope for (he wrote between the early 70s and the early 100s);[46] and he is more informative than we might have expected (he was attempting to describe and defend his native religion to his influential Roman patrons). That such an apologetic treatment will be biased and selective need hardly be said. But the fact remains that the spectator perspective of Josephus is likely to give a fuller and sounder basis for a description of first-century Judaism than any other, and there are sufficient other sources for us to be able to recognize much if not most of Josephus' bias.[47] In each case, however, there are major questions unresolved and continuing debate of great vigour.

(1) *Pharisees* naturally come first: Josephus always gives them first place in his lists, and they were almost certainly the principal forerunners of subsequently prevailing rabbinic Judaism.[48] Older treatments of them are generally unreliable, partly because of a Christian bias which saw them as chief representatives of a legalism which served, by way of contrast, to highlight the gracious character of the Christian message,[49] and partly because of uncritical use (by both Jewish and Christian scholars) of the later rabbinic traditions as evidence of what the first-century Pharisees already believed and practised.[50] The first of

---

three philosophies or sects we might simply note that he describes the movement which he claims began with Judas of Galilee both as a 'sect' (*War* 2.118) and as a 'philosophy' (*Ant.* 18.9, 23).

46. On Josephus see Schürer, *History* 1.43-63; H. W. Attridge, 'Josephus and His Works', in Stone, *Jewish Writings* 185-232; L. H. Feldman, 'Josephus', *ABD* 3.981-98.

47. Cf. particularly E. P. Sanders, *Judaism* 5-7; on using Josephus as a historical source see also S. Mason, 'Revisiting Josephus's Pharisees', in J. Neusner and A. J. Avery-Peck, eds., *Judaism in Late Antiquity*. 3.2: *Where We Stand: Issues and Debates in Ancient Judaism* (Leiden: Brill, 1999) 23-56.

48. As most deduce (or assume) (e.g., Gafni, 'Historical Background' 7-8), despite the problems and misgivings articulated, e.g., by Saldarini, *Pharisees* 7-9 and ch. 10; G. Stemberger, *Jewish Contemporaries of Jesus: Pharisees, Sadducees, Essenes* (1991; ET Minneapolis: Fortress, 1995) particularly 140-47; further bibliography in Meier, *Marginal Jew* 3.357-58.

49. See Heschel's string of examples (*Abraham Geiger* 75-76, 79, 86, 127, 192, 199, 210-11, 215, 222, 232); H.-G. Waubke, *Die Pharisäer in der protestantischen Bibelwissenschaft des 19. Jahrhunderts* (Tübingen: Mohr Siebeck, 1998); also Klein's review in *Anti-Judaism* ch. 4; Sandmel's critique of M. Black, 'Pharisees', *IDB* 3.774-81 (*First Christian Century* 101-102); and M. Weinfeld's critique particularly of Wellhausen ('Hillel and the Misunderstanding of Judaism in Modern Scholarship', in Charlesworth and Johns, eds., *Hillel and Jesus* 56-70).

50. See above n. 4. For a review of scholarly literature on the Pharisees since 1874 see R. Deines, *Die Pharisäer: Ihr Verständnis im Spiegel der christlichen und jüdischen Forschung seit Wellhausen und Graetz* (WUNT 101; Tübingen: Mohr Siebeck, 1997). For recent bibliography see Meier, *Marginal Jew* 3.342-45.

these misperceptions has been shattered in English-speaking scholarship particularly by Sanders,[51] the second by Neusner in his careful layering of the traditions to expose those which can be traced back to the first century with the greatest confidence.[52] The further questions prompted by Sanders and Neusner have provided much of the agenda for subsequent debate.

Of ongoing issues, the most fundamental is whether we know enough about the Pharisees to draw a rounded picture of them. As we have learned more about Second Temple Judaism, the more it has become apparent that we know *less* about the Pharisees than we previously took for granted;[53] though to know that we know less is still to know more! In similar vein, Sanders may be justified in objecting to Neusner's use only of attributed rabbinic traditions to inform his picture of Pharisaic debates. But Sanders is himself open to criticism for bracketing out the evidence of the Gospels. And more should certainly be made of Paul, the only self-attested Pharisee writing in the pre-70 period.[54] Even though the testimony of the rabbinic traditions is at best confusing, we can still sketch in several distinctive and characteristic features.

A second main bone of contention is the importance of purity for the Pharisees, and whether they were primarily a purity sect. Sanders objects to Neusner's strong emphasis on this feature, though he concedes a good deal of key ground while disputing its significance.[55] But he forgets that where particular religious practices are integral to a group's identity, even 'minor gestures' can become make or break points of division.[56] And more weight should surely be given to

51. Sanders, *Paul and Palestinian Judaism;* also *Jesus and Judaism,* index 'Pharisees'; also *Judaism.*

52. Neusner, *Rabbinic Traditions;* also *Politics to Piety;* also *Judaism.*

53. See particularly J. Sievers, 'Who Were the Pharisees?', in Charlesworth and Johns, eds., *Hillel and Jesus* 137-55; he points out, e.g., that 'rabbinic literature never identifies any named individual as a Pharisee' (139). Given the complexities of the Quest reviewed above (Part One), Keck's cautionary reminder should be pondered: 'the quest of the historical Pharisee is even more complex and controversial than the quest of the historical Jesus' (*Who Is Jesus?* 34).

54. See J. D. G. Dunn, 'Pharisees, Sinners and Jesus', in J. Neusner, et al., eds., *The Social World of Formative Christianity and Judaism,* H. C. Kee FS (Philadelphia: Fortress, 1988) 264-89, reprinted in my *Jesus, Paul and the Law: Studies in Mark and Galatians* (London: SPCK, 1990) 61-86 (here 67-69); Saldarini, *Pharisees* ch.7, though any deduction from Paul's life to the effect of Pharisaic influence in Syria and Cilicia (137) is very dubious (see further below Vol. 2).

55. E. P. Sanders, *Jewish Law from Jesus to the Mishnah: Five Studies* (London: SCM, 1990) ch. 3; also *Judaism,* particularly 431-40 ('minor gestures' — *Jewish Law* 232, 235; *Judaism* 440). For Neusner's own reply see his 'Mr Maccoby's Red Cow, Mr Sanders's Pharisees — and Mine', *JSS* 23 (1991) 81-98; also 'Mr. Sanders's Pharisees and Mine', *BBR* 2 (1992) 143-69.

56. As Kraft and Nickelsburg note: 'In such instances, differences in interpretation and disputes about law are raised to the level of absolute truth and falsehood and have as their con-

the Pharisees' very name, generally agreed to signify 'separated ones',[57] and thus indicating a wider perception of the Pharisees as a group who defined themselves by their concern to keep themselves apart — a primarily purity concern.[58]

A third, closely related issue concerns the political and social influence of the Pharisees. Sanders focuses his polemic against the idea that the Pharisees 'ran Judaism',[59] but otherwise recognizes that they did exercise at least some political influence at the time of Jesus.[60] More weight, however, needs to be given

---

sequences salvation and damnation' (*Early Judaism* 18). Similarly Hengel and Deines: 'On the inside . . . there were sometimes bitter fights, precisely over the concrete halakhah' ('Sanders' Judaism' 8; also 45-47). See also below n. 138. T. Holmén, *Jesus and Jewish Covenant Thinking* (Leiden: Brill, 2001) likewise notes that a shared concern (among different groups) to keep the covenant resulted in particular issues and topics becoming definitive of covenant keeping and indicative of covenant loyalty (48-49), not least circumcision and Sabbath (70-79).

57. P*e*rushim, from *parash*, 'to separate'; see Schürer, *History* 2.396-97; Cohen, *Maccabees* 162; Saldarini, *Pharisees* 220-25. Meier, *Marginal Jew* 3.366-67 doubts whether such firm inferences can be drawn.

58. See further Saldarini, *Pharisees* 212-16, 233-34, 285-87, 290-91; Stemberger, *Jewish Contemporaries* 75-82; Hengel and Deines, 'Sanders' Judaism' 41-51; H. K. Harrington, 'Did the Pharisees Eat Ordinary Food in a State of Ritual Purity?', *JSJ* 26 (1995) 42-54; J. Schaper, 'Pharisees', in W. Horbury, et al., eds., *Judaism*. Vol. 3: *The Early Roman Period* (Cambridge: Cambridge University, 1999) 402-27 (here 420-21). The old view that the Pharisees sought to extend the holiness of the Temple throughout the land of Israel on the basis of Exod. 19.5-6 is probably still warranted (Schürer, *History* 2.396-400; A. F. Segal, *Rebecca's Children: Judaism and Christianity in the Roman World* [Cambridge: Harvard University, 1986] 124-28; others in Sanders, *Jewish Law* 152). J. Milgrom, *Leviticus* (AB 3, 2 vols.; New York: Doubleday, 1991) makes an important contribution to the debate between Neusner and Sanders when he observes that 'the priestly laws of impurity (Leviticus 11–15) rest on the postulate that impurity incurred anywhere is potentially dangerous to the sanctuary', and that 'the priestly legislators are very much concerned with the need to eliminate, or, at least, control the occurrence of impurity *anywhere in the land* — whether in the home, on the table, or in the bed' (1.1007). T. Kazen, *Jesus and Purity Halakhah: Was Jesus Indifferent to Impurity?* (ConBNT 38; Stockholm: Almqvist and Wiksell, 2002) argues that Pharisees represented an 'expansionist purity practice in Second Temple Judaism' (72-87, and index 'expansionism'). See also below §14.4c-d.

59. *Judaism* 395-412; see further below §9.7b.

60. Sanders's review of the evidence concludes that following their loss of the political power which they enjoyed during the reign of Salome Alexandra (76-67 BCE), the Pharisees did not entirely withdraw from the political arena but were active as far as they could be, a 'moderate but usually ineffective opposition', and some of them were certainly involved in the disturbances prior to the death of Herod the Great, in the uprising of Judas the Galilean in 6 BCE, and in the outbreak of revolt of 66 CE (*Judaism* 380-95; similarly Saldarini, *Pharisees* 98-106, 132-33; Stemberger, *Jewish Contemporaries* 117-22; more combatively Hengel and Deines, 'Sanders' Judaism' 55-67; Schaper, 'Pharisees' 419 [note also 412]). Mason justifiably warns against inferring too much from Josephus's silence regarding the Pharisees in the very thin coverage Josephus provides for the period 6-66 CE ('Revisiting' 47-48).

to the probability that the Pharisees exercised substantial influence on the people.[61] Josephus reports that they handed down various traditions 'to the people' (*Ant.* 13.297), which suggests that their degree of exclusivism was motivated by a concern for the holiness (purity) of the whole people.[62] Their influence is borne out by the widespread concern for purity, reflecting characteristic Pharisaic concerns, attested by archaeological discoveries of *miqwaoth* and stone vessels widespread throughout the land.[63] As also by the popularity of the heroic story of Judith, which in its concern for purity could be described as 'early or proto-Pharisaic'.[64]

A quite different and influential line has been argued by Anthony Saldarini: that Pharisees belonged to the 'retainer' class in Jewish society, who served the needs of the ruler and governing class, and were therefore in some degree dependent on the rich and powerful.[65] The thesis is based on Gerhard Lenski's analysis of agrarian empires in terms of class structure and, as with Crossan's similar use of Lenski,[66] runs the risk of imposing another 'grand narrative' on the particularities and peculiarities of Second Temple Judaism. In particular, the portrayal of Pharisees as a class working for the wealthy aristocracy and representing the interests of the Temple authorities does not fit well with Josephus' portrayal of the esteem in which they were held by the people, and with their own attested concerns. At the same time we should certainly not fall into the trap of thinking of quite distinct groups (sects, classes), or of groups always acting either in isolation or in unison, and many Pharisees no doubt did serve as a scribal bureaucracy.

Where the Pharisees stood out most clearly among their contemporaries, however, was in their concern to keep the law with scrupulous accuracy and exactness *(akribeia)*,[67] and in their development of a distinctive halakhic interpre-

---

61. This is the main burden of Hengel's and Deines' critique of Sanders.

62. Hengel and Deines, 'Sanders' Judaism' 30-31, 46-47, in contrast to the high degree of exclusivism shown by the Qumran people. See also Meier, *Marginal Jew* 3.405-406.

63. Hengel and Deines, 'Sanders' Judaism' 34-35. See further below §9.6a, particularly at n. 176.

64. Hengel and Deines, 'Sanders' Judaism' 48-49.

65. Saldarini, *Pharisees* particularly 39-48, 295-97; the thesis has proved attractive particularly to Horsley, *Jesus* 17, 63 ('among the "retainers" through whom society was governed'), 70 ('representatives of the Temple-government in dealing with local affairs'); also *Galilee: History, Politics, People* (Valley Forge: Trinity, 1995) 150 and n. 37; also *Archaeology* 152 and n. 59; similarly with Borg, *Jesus in Contemporary Scholarship* 101-103.

66. Crossan, *Birth* ch. 11. See below chapter 12 nn. 405 and 411.

67. Josephus, *War* 1.110; 2.162; *Ant.* 17.41; *Life* 191; Acts 22.3; 26.5; see particularly A. I. Baumgarten, 'The Name of the Pharisee', *JBL* 102 (1983) 411-28 (here 413-17). Sanders does not dispute this point (*Jesus and Judaism* 275).

tation of Torah,[68] 'the traditions of their fathers',[69] the so-called 'oral law'.[70] Here it is important to recall that the Pharisees were not a uniform, far less monolithic, party. Most famous at the time of Jesus were the many disputes on points of halakhic detail between the 'schools' of Hillel and Shammai, remembered respectively for the mildness and the severity of their rulings.[71] To acknowledge this is to make no concession to the old accusation of Pharisaic 'legalism', since Pharisees were characteristically more flexible in their rulings than Qumran, and the Hillelites more lenient in their rulings on divorce than Jesus (§14.4e). At the same time, their devotion to Torah is not open to question. Consequently, it is no great surprise that the Judaism which survived the disaster of 70 CE, the Judaism most closely related to the Pharisees, was a Judaism of rabbi, Torah, and Halakhah.

(2) Little can be said of the *Sadducees* because of the paucity of evidence.[72] They are usually thought to have differed from the Pharisees by rejecting the 'oral law' (on the basis of *Ant.* 13.297 and 18.17), though a minority of commentators see the basic issue separating Sadducee from Pharisee as that, once again, of purity.[73] A considerable overlap is also generally assumed between the Sadducees and the aristocratic families from whom the high priests

68. 'Halakhah', from the Hebrew root *hlk*, 'to walk', refers individually and collectively to the rules/rulings (derived from the written Torah) which determine how individuals should act ('walk') in particular situations — in effect, case law. See further G. G. Porton, 'Halakah', *ABD* 3.26-27; S. Safrai, 'Halakha', in Safrai, ed., *Literature of the Sages* 121-209.

69. E.g., *Ant.* 13.297, 408; 17.41; *Life* 198; Mark 7.3, 5; Gal. 1.14.

70. On the oral law see again Hengel and Deines, 'Sanders' Judaism' 17-39; also S. Safrai, 'Oral Tora', in Safrai, ed., *Literature of the Sages* 35-119; discussion also in H. L. Strack and G. Stemberger, *Introduction to the Talmud and Midrash* (ET San Francisco: HarperCollins, 1991) 35-49 (with bibliography). On the Pharisaic distinctives see further Meier, *Marginal Jew* 3.313-30.

71. See, e.g., Schürer, *History* 2.363-66, with bibliography (n. 29) and reference to the Mishnaic passages which mention differences between the two schools (n. 39); Hengel and Deines, 'Sanders' Judaism' 39-41. There was also probably disagreement on the level of political involvement thought to be appropriate, whether to cooperate with the Roman authorities or to oppose them (M. Hengel, *The Pre-Christian Paul* [London: SCM, 1991] 44-45). Crossan and Reed think 'it was probably the Hillelite Pharisees who instigated theoretically and organised practically' the nonviolent but martyrdom-ready resistance described by Josephus in *War* 2.169-74, 185-203 and *Ant.* 18.55-59, 261-309 (*Excavating Jesus* 143-45).

72. Bibliography in Meier, *Marginal Jew* 3.444.

73. G. G. Porton, *ABD* 5.892-93. 'In the Mishnah and Tosefta most of the disputes between the Sadducees and Pharisees (and others) concern interpretations of the laws of ritual purity' (Saldarini, *Pharisees* 233). See also Meier, *Marginal Jew* 3.399-406, who points out that the Sadducees must have had their own halakhah and suggests that, in contrast to the Pharisees, the Sadducees were content to defend and observe their special traditions 'without claiming that their special traditions were obligatory for all Jews'.

were drawn and who controlled the Temple.[74] Since Judea was a temple state, that placed the levers of political, religious, economic, and social power firmly in their hands, to the extent permitted by Rome and the Herods.[75] This is a fact of considerable importance for any study of Jesus in his historical setting: it not only reminds us that the Judaism of Jesus' time was a socio-political-religious complex; but it also means that so far as Jewish involvement in the death of Jesus is concerned we can speak realistically only of the high priestly faction.[76] At the same time, despite their wealth and degree of Hellenisation, their very name suggests,[77] somewhat surprisingly, an origin similar to that of the Essenes, that is, in partisan protest on behalf of the legitimate (Zadokite) priesthood, whose prerogative had been usurped by the Hasmoneans. At all events their prominence and power prior to 70 CE are clear testimony to the importance of the Temple in first-century Judaism.

(3) As for the *Essenes,* there is a substantial consensus that Qumran was an Essene community and that the great bulk of the Dead Sea Scrolls came from their library.[78] But the evidence of Josephus (*War* 2.124) and Philo (*Prob.* 76) is probably sufficient to demonstrate that Qumran was only one branch of the Essenes and that other Essene groups lived in various towns, including possibly Jerusalem itself.[79] And the disparity of the material in the scrolls is becoming steadily clearer, with only some representative of the Qumran community's own

74. See Sanders, *Judaism* ch. 15. 'Priests themselves were a clan rather than a sect or party' (Fredriksen, *Jesus* 63).

75. See further K. C. Hanson and D. E. Oakman, *Palestine in the Time of Jesus* (Minneapolis: Fortress, 1998) 139-54; Meier, *Marginal Jew* 3.394-99. On the character, status, and powers of 'the Sanhedrin' see particularly Sanders, *Judaism* 472-88; even if Sanders is again in danger of overstating his case (Hengel and Deines, 'Sanders' Judaism' 58), it remains unclear whether *sunedrion* in a passage like *Ant.* 14.171-76 should be translated as 'the Sanhedrin' rather than as 'the Council'.

76. See, e.g., Dunn, *Partings* 51-53 and those cited there. See further below §17.2.

77. If indeed the 'Sadducees' took their name from Zadok the priest (Schürer, *History* 2.405-407; Porton, *ABD* 5.892; G. Stemberger, 'The Sadducees', in Horbury, et al., eds., *Judaism* 3.428-43 [here 430-34]; Meier, *Marginal Jew* 3.450-53).

78. Several editions of the complete scrolls have been recently published. I have used mainly F. García Martínez and E. J. C. Tigchelaar, *The Dead Sea Scrolls Study Edition* (Leiden: Brill/Grand Rapids: Eerdmans, 1997), and G. Vermes, *The Complete Dead Sea Scrolls in English* (London: Penguin, 1997). The most useful introductions are currently F. M. Cross, *The Ancient Library of Qumran* (Sheffield: Sheffield Academic, [3]1995), and J. C. Vanderkam, *The Dead Sea Scrolls Today* (Grand Rapids: Eerdmans, 1994). For a description of the archaeology of Qumran see R. Donceel, 'Qumran', *OEANE* 4.393-96.

79. B. Pixner makes the case for the existence of an 'Essene quarter' within the 'gate of the Essenes' on Mount Zion; see, e.g., his 'Jesus and His Community: Between Essenes and Pharisees', in Charlesworth and Johns, eds., *Hillel and Jesus* 193-224 (here 196-200).

beliefs, and probably the *Covenant of Damascus* (CD) representative of the more widely dispersed Essenes.[80]

The Qumran community is the clearest example of a 'sect' (in the modern sense of the word) within first-century Judaism[81] — its distinctiveness as such becoming more apparent as the more sectarian of the Dead Sea Scrolls (from Cave 4) have been published, including strong predestinarian, dualistic and mystical features.[82] The community evidently regarded itself as an alternative to the Jerusalem Temple (hence its withdrawal to the wilderness),[83] determined membership by reference to its own understanding and interpretation of Scripture, and applied strict rules for novitiate and continuing membership (1QS 5-9). Most like the earliest Christian movement in its sense of divine grace (1QS 11; 1QH) and eschatological fulfilment and anticipation (e.g., 1QpHab, 1QSa, 1QM), it was furthest removed from the former in its strict application of purity rules and discipline.[84] If this too was Judaism it underlines the extent to which Torah and Temple were fundamental and defining characteristics of Judaism.

(4) Josephus also speaks of a *'fourth philosophy'* in *Ant.* 18.9, a reference which has caused considerable confusion, because it seems to indicate a coherent political body which existed from the time of Judas the Galilean (6 CE).[85] The confusion is increased if we identify the 'fourth philosophy' with the later Sicarii and Zealots. Certainly Josephus' description of the 'fourth philosophy'[86] implies a deliberate association with the tradition of 'zeal' stemming from Phinehas and the Maccabees, where resistance by force of arms to any dilution or infringement of Israel's distinctive relationship with Yahweh was the overmastering concern; a link with the 'Zealots', who saw Phinehas as their great hero, naturally follows. Moreover, Judas's sons were later crucified for anti-Roman activities in 47 or 48; and his descendants were also leaders in the revolt of 66-73.[87] On the other hand, Josephus does not use the term 'Zealot' until he gets to the revolt itself (first used

80. Sanders, *Judaism* 342, 347; Vanderkam, *Dead Sea Scrolls* 57.

81. Sanders, *Judaism* 352-64.

82. See, e.g., the texts from 1QS cited in Vermes, *Complete Dead Sea Scrolls* 97-117, and the 'Songs for the Holocaust of the Sabbath' on 321-30.

83. See below §13.3g and n. 124.

84. M. Newton, *The Concept of Purity at Qumran and in the Letters of Paul* (SNTSMS 53; Cambridge: Cambridge University, 1985).

85. So particularly M. Hengel, *The Zealots* (1961, ²1976; ET Edinburgh: Clark, 1989) here 89, followed by Witherington, *Christology* 81-88.

86. 'They have a passion for liberty that is almost unconquerable, since they are convinced that God alone is their leader and master. They think little of submitting to death in unusual forms and permitting vengeance to fall on kinsmen and friends if only they may avoid calling any man master' (*Ant.* 18.23).

87. Details in Schürer, *History* 2.600-601.

as a title in *War* 4.160-61).[88] And he uses the term earlier simply in the sense of 'someone who is zealous/ardent for a cause' — including himself as a youthful disciple of the hermit Bannus (*Life* 11);[89] here we should also recall that Paul could call himself a 'zealot' without indicating membership of a political party or resistance movement.[90] 'Sicarii' is the name Josephus uses for the assassins who emerged in the 50s and who used a short dagger *(sica)* concealed in their clothes to stab their enemies in a crowd (*War* 2.254-7); they were one of the factions in the final revolt, not to be identified simply with the 'Zealots'.

Taking all the data into account, we should almost certainly refrain from using the term 'Zealot' as a titular description of a political faction given to violence prior to the revolt beginning in 66.[91] The political situation in Palestine certainly deteriorated in the 50s, with increasing banditry building to the revolt itself. But prior to that the situation was much calmer. We should certainly not deduce from Luke's reference to Simon 'the zealot' (Luke 6.15; Acts 1.13) that Jesus had chosen a 'freedom fighter' or 'terrorist' as one of his disciples! At the same time, it is evident that the tradition of zealous and committed piety as exemplified by Phinehas was still widely prized through the first century. If this too was Judaism, its self-understanding as the elect people of God separated out from among the nations must also count as a fundamental defining characteristic.

b. The Evidence of Apocrypha and Pseudepigrapha

In addition to these particular groupings within Judaism (or forms of Judaism), we have to make room for other expressions of Judaism, most notably those found in the *pseudepigrapha*. For a grasp of first-century Palestinian Judaism there is an immediate problem here. All four of Josephus' 'sects' we know were operative in the land of Israel during the period with which we are principally concerned. But with the Apocrypha several of the items come from the diaspora, and the scope and datings of much of the Pseudepigrapha are so unclear that we are often uncertain as to which of the writings are of relevance to us.[92] At the

88. R. A. Horsley, 'The Zealots: Their Origin, Relationship and Importance in the Jewish Revolt', *NovT* 28 (1986) 159-92.

89. See also *Ap.* 1.162; in Philo, *Migr.* 62; *Som.* 1.124; 2.274; *Abr.* 22, 33, 60; *Mos.* 1.160-61; 2.55, 161, 256, etc. In the LXX Pentateuch it is God who is described as a 'zealot' (Exod. 20.5; 34.14; Deut. 4.24; 5.9; 6.15).

90. See above §9.2a.

91. See also D. R. Schwartz, 'On Christian Study of the Zealots', *Studies* 128-46; L. L. Grabbe, *Judaism from Cyrus to Hadrian* (2 vols.; Minneapolis: Fortress, 1992) 499-500; D. Rhoads, 'Zealots', *ABD* 6.1043-54.

92. The texts of the documents to be mentioned are most readily accessible in the OT

same time, however, many of the documents fall into groupings or reveal trends which must have been present within the land of Israel during the first century CE, so that a broad picture (which is all we need at this point) can be sketched.

(1) Most striking is the sequence of *apocalyptic writings,* particularly the *Enoch* corpus, *4 Ezra, 2 Baruch,* the *Apocalypse of Abraham,* and, we may add, the Apocalypse of John (Revelation).[93] These all grew out of the overmastering conviction that events on earth are determined by what happens in heaven, with the consequent desire to know more of these heavenly secrets. Prominent in them are angelic beings, both interpreter angels, but also glorious angels, the sight of whom is to assure the seer that he is close to the presence of the one God, but whose very glory can both enhance and threaten the exclusive majesty of the one God.[94] To be noted here also is the overlap between apocalyptic and mysticism.[95] This is a Judaism focused in the immediacy of spiritual (revelatory) experience, but in consequence also vulnerable to 'flights of fancy'.

(2) A *testamentary literature* also developed in this period (a patriarchal figure giving his last will and testament). Though only the precursors of the *Testaments of the Twelve Patriarchs* and the *Testament of Moses* fall for consideration within the period of our concern, the fact that the format was so widespread both in Israel and in diaspora Judaism is a further reminder that the interrelatedness between the two must have been considerable. The overlap with apocalyptic literature is substantial (warning us not to operate with too strict categories), but the most distinctive feature of the testaments is the desire to promote righteous living. In the *Testaments of the Twelve Patriarchs* the superiority of Levi over Judah (particularly *T. Jud.* 21.2-4; 25.1) indicates a Judaism where Temple and priest are still the central defining feature.[96]

Apocrypha and *OTP.* See further Introductions in *OTP;* Stone, ed., *Jewish Writings;* Kraft and Nickelsburg, *Early Judaism;* Schürer, *History* vol. 3.

93. In addition to those cited in n. 92, see also J. J. Collins, *The Apocalyptic Imagination: An Introduction to Jewish Apocalyptic Literature* (Grand Rapids: Eerdmans, 1984, [2]1998).

94. See particularly C. Rowland, *The Open Heaven: A Study of Apocalyptic in Judaism and Early Christianity* (London: SPCK, 1982); L. T. Stuckenbruck, *Angel Veneration and Christology: A Study in Early Judaism and in the Christology of the Apocalypse of John* (WUNT 2.70; Tübingen: Mohr Siebeck, 1995).

95. See particularly I. Gruenwald, *Apocalyptic and Merkavah Mysticism* (Leiden: Brill, 1980); see further below, vol. 3.

96. For a review of the ongoing debate, particularly regarding the *Testaments of the Twelve Patriarchs,* see J. J. Collins, 'Testaments', in Stone, ed., *Jewish Writings* 325-55; also 'The Testamentary Literature in Recent Scholarship', in Kraft and Nickelsburg, *Early Judaism* 268-85. The *Testament of Moses* is usually dated between 4 BCE and 30 CE (e.g., J. F. Priest, *ABD* 4.920-22) and so may be closer in origin to the period of Jesus' mission than any other extent writing of Second Temple Judaism. The *Testament of Job,* which cannot be dated more precisely than the first century BCE or CE, was composed in Greek.

(3) The difficulty of drawing firm lines between literary evidence from within the land of Israel and that from the diaspora is well illustrated by the *wisdom literature.* It is striking nonetheless that the only two which can be said to have originated in Hebrew (ben Sira and Baruch) both make a point of focusing universal divine wisdom explicitly in the Torah (Sir. 24.23; Bar. 4.1). Of the *stories of Jewish heroes and heroines* which must have fed popular piety wherever they were read, we might note how consistently they were portrayed as prospering precisely because of their loyalty to the food laws and refusal to eat the food of Gentiles.[97]

Of other relevant pseudepigrapha there are two which deserve special mention. The first is *Jubilees,* a reworking of Genesis and the early chapters of Exodus, and clearly designed to promote more rigorous obedience to the stipulations of the Torah. It probably comes from the early Maccabean-Hasmonean period, and is now generally regarded as a precursor of the Qumran Essenes. The second is the *Psalms of Solomon:* written in the aftermath of the Roman conquest of Jerusalem (63 BCE), it wrestles with the consequent problem of theodicy — how to square recent events with God's choice of Israel.

A major problem for us with all these documents is the question of how representative and influential they were. Although we know, for example, that portions of the *Enoch* corpus were evidently prized at Qumran and can see in CD 16.2-4 an allusion to *Jubilees,* we cannot deduce from this that they speak for significant groupings within first-century Judaism. After all, an apocalypse could have been the work of a single person and not speak for any party. At the opposite extreme it would be equally unwise to list them all as expressive of disparate Judaisms without any overlap or commonality. Just as it would be inadmissible as a procedure to identify each document with a single community, as though no sub-group could happily express the richness of its own communal self-perception through several different writings.[98] In particular, the breadth of the appeal of wisdom and heroic literature surely prevents us from seeing it as representative of disparate Judaisms. Frustrating though our lack of information may be here, then, we must be content to let these writings illuminate facets of Second Temple Judaism without imposing a systematised coherence or grand schema of our own.

---

97. Dan. 1.3-16; 10.3; Tob. 1.10-13; Jdt. 12.2, 6-9, 19; *Add. Esth.* 14.17; 1 Macc. 1.62-63; *Jos. Asen.* 7.1; 8.5.

98. We have already observed this as a fallacy to which several NT scholars commit themselves, e.g., in hypothesizing a distinctive (and distinctively) Q community (see above §§7.4b and 8.6d).

c. Other Judaisms

For the sake of completeness some mention ought to be made of other groupings known to us either in the land or in the period of our concern.

(1) Of those who exercised some degree of political power, along with the Sadducees, we should note the *'elders' (presbyteroi)*. 'The elders of the congregation' and 'the elders of the city' were a long established feature of Israel's life.[99] And 'elders' appear frequently in the NT, often with 'high priests' (17 times), 'rulers' (Acts 4.5, 8), or 'scribes' (12 times). As their name suggests, they were the older members of any community, revered for the wisdom they had gained through their long experience and accorded recognized status accordingly. Presumably they overlapped with 'the leading men *(prōtoi)* of the district' (Josephus, *Ant.* 7.230), 'the leading men *(prōtoi)* of the people' (*Ant.* 11.141; Luke 19.47). We are not thinking here of 'sects' or parties, of course, simply noting the kaleidoscope of groups and roles which constituted first-century Judaism.

(2) Similarly we should simply note the indispensable role of *priests* and *scribes* within the religio-social system of Second Temple Judaism. Here again, of course, there is no idea of 'parties'; these were simply the middle-ranking professional functionaries ('retainers') without whom the system would have broken down. The priests, by definition, existed to ensure the smooth running of the Temple cult, but that would require the presence of any particular priests in Jerusalem possibly only two or three weeks in the year. During the rest of the time they lived in the towns and villages of the land. There they were the resident legal (that is, also biblical) experts and teachers and evidently served as local magistrates and judges (Josephus, *Ap.* 2.187). No doubt some at least of the leadership in local communities was also provided by the elders.[100] The necessity for scribes is a reminder that the many transactions necessitated by daily living would require both legal experts and copyists, particularly where a low level of literacy must be assumed.[101] That there were scribes who attached themselves to priests or elders or Pharisees can probably be assumed, as the regular linkage of 'high priests and scribes', 'scribes and elders' and 'scribes and Pharisees' in the Gospels and Acts suggests.[102]

99. Lev. 4.15; Judg. 8.16; 21.16; Ruth 4.2; 1 Sam. 16.4; Jdt. 8.10; 10.6; 13.12.

100. Sanders, *Judaism* 170-82, emphasizing that this role persisted through our period; Pharisees had not superseded it. The older treatments by Jeremias, *Jerusalem* 198-207; Stern in Safrai and Stern, *Jewish People* ch. 11; and Schürer, *History* 2.238-50, are again too dependent on later rabbinic perspective.

101. See below at n. 277.

102. See further Saldarini, *Pharisees* ch. 11; Grabbe, *Judaism* 488-91; C. Schams, *Jewish Scribes in the Second-Temple Period* (JSOTS 291; Sheffield: Sheffield Academic, 1998). Schwartz argues that the NT's 'scribes *(grammateis)*' were Levites (*Studies* 89-101). Often referred to is ben Sira's idealisation of the scribal role (Sir. 38.24–39.11).

(3) Mention should probably be made here also of *'the people of the land'* (*'am ha'aretz,* or plural *'amme ha'aretz*). In its early use the phrase refers generally to the people living on the land, distinct from the country's leaders, priests, and prophets.[103] After the exile the phrase gained a pejorative sense by being used in reference to 'the people(s) of the land' with whom the Israelites not exiled had mingled in intermarriage.[104] This disparaging sense, of a population whose ritual purity was at best uncertain, was carried over into Mishnaic usage, particularly in the tractate *Demai,* on produce not certainly tithed, which includes strong discouragement against being a guest of an *'am-ha'aretz* (2.2-3). The phrase does not occur in the NT and it is doubtful whether it should be used to denote any similar disparagement of 'the common people' during the period of Jesus' mission.[105]

(4) The *Herodians* are probably also worthy of mention. This is the somewhat obscure group mentioned by Josephus in *War* 1.319 and in Mark 3.6 and 12.13/Matt. 22.16. Various identifications for the 'Herodians' have been offered.[106] But the term itself (*Hērōdianoi*) is a Latin formation (*Herodiani*) and suggests an analogy with party names like *Caesariani, Pompeiani,* and *Augustiani.* That could mean that the 'Herodians' were active partisans on behalf of Herod (in the Gospels references, Herod Antipas), though it could simply indicate known and presumably prominent supporters of Herod among leading families,[107] or possibly simply members of Herod's household. At any rate, if the term denotes a particular faction within first-century Judaism, it was a political faction which is in view, reminding us once again that the diversity of first-century Judaism was not simply religious in scope.

(5) Another possible group, or sequence of groups could be designated

103. 2 Kgs 11.20; Jer. 1.18; 34.19; 37.2; 44.21; Ezek. 22.24-29.

104. Ezra 9.1-2, 11; 10.2, 11; Neh. 9.30; 10.28-31. See further E. Lipinski, *'am', TDOT* 11.174-75.

105. Meier, *Marginal Jew* 38-39 n. 34; see further below §13.5.

106. H. H. Rowley, 'The Herodians in the Gospels', *JTS* 41 (1940) 14-27, reviewed eleven possibilities. The discovery of the Scrolls prompted a twelfth ('Herodians' = Essenes) (C. Daniel, 'Les "Hérodiens" du Nouveau Testament sont-ils des Esséniens?', *RevQ* 6 [1967] 31-53; also 'Nouveaux arguments en faveur de l'identification des Hérodiens et des Esséniens', *RevQ* 27 [1970] 397-402); though see also W. Braun, 'Were the New Testament Herodians Essenes?', *RevQ* 53 (1989) 75-88; Grabbe, *Judaism* 501-502. Further bibliography in Meier, *Marginal Jew* 3.610 n. 221.

107. Possibly overlapping with 'the leading men (*prōtoi*) of Galilee' (Mark 6.21). Mark 12.13/Matt. 22.16 indicates that they were active in Jerusalem, presumably not simply remnants of the faction most fully identified with Herod the Great, but on the lookout for opportunity to restore the full Herodian empire and rule. J. P. Meier, 'The Historical Jesus and the Historical Herodians', *JBL* 119 (2000) 740-46, doubts the historical value of the Gospel references.

'Hellenizers' or *'Hellenists'*. Some such term certainly can be used for those Judeans who supported the 'Hellenization' (2 Macc. 4.13) programme of Antiochus Epiphanes, which provoked the Maccabean revolt, as described in 1 Macc. 1–2. As already noted, the term 'Judaism' emerged to describe the opposition to 'Hellenization', understood as an attempt to dissolve the distinctives of Israel's covenant tradition (Torah, circumcision, food laws). Although the terms 'Hellenizers' and 'Hellenists' were not actually used, they can serve for those who supported a policy of rapprochement with what we might call 'international Hellenism', including in one degree or another the Hasmonean and Herodian aristocracy.[108] There would be considerable overlap between them, their retainers and those who settled in the Hellenistic cities on the Mediterranean coast (Caesarea Maritima and Ptolemais, Galilee's nearest port) and in Transjordan (the Decapolis, but including Scythopolis on the west bank), cities so characterised because they were thoroughly Greek in political and social structure. In Galilee itself the city of Sepphoris was rebuilt by Herod Antipas after its destruction in the unrest of 4 BCE, and served as Galilee's capital till 18 CE, before Antipas transferred his capital to the newly built Tiberias.[109] As we shall see below (§9.6b), these are not properly to be described as 'Hellenistic cities', but there was considerable hostility among ordinary Galileans towards these cities and their more Hellenised residents.

Nor should we forget the large amorphous body who are in fact identified simply as *'Hellenists'* in the NT (Acts 6.1; 9.29; 11.20). Broadly speaking, the term designates those influenced in significant degree by Greek language and culture. Of course, as is now acknowledged, all Judaism was influenced by Hellenistic culture in some measure; it was simply the international culture of the day.[110] But some were evidently so Greek-ized that they were known as 'Greek-speakers' = 'Hellenists' (that is, in an Aramaic context they probably could speak only Greek).[111] They were probably Jews returned from the Greek diaspora (in effect all Jews living in the western diaspora would have been 'Hellenists'). And in Jerusalem they seem to have had their own assemblies/synagogue(s), where, presumably, the language of communication was Greek (Acts 6.1, 9). These too have to be included within Palestinian Judaism in the first century.

(6) A survey of groups within the land of Israel in the first century cannot

---

108. The ambivalence of feelings towards Herod the Great in particular is illustrated by Josephus' designation of him as a 'half-Jew', because of his Idumean birth (*Ant.* 14.430).

109. See J. F. Strange, 'Sepphoris' *ABD* 5.1090-93 and 'Tiberias', *ABD* 6.547-49; also J. Murphy-O'Connor, *The Holy Land* (Oxford: Oxford University, ⁴1998) 412-18 and 455-60; on Sepphoris see also C. L. Meyers and E. M. Meyers, 'Sepphoris', *OEANE* 4.527-36.

110. See M. Hengel, *The 'Hellenization' of Judaea in the First Century after Christ* (London: SCM, 1989).

111. See further below, vol. 2.

ignore *the Samaritans*.[112] Unfortunately their history in this period is obscure beyond a few references,[113] and their own literature is too late to afford us much help. The fact that at various times they called themselves 'Judeans/Jews' (*Ant.* 11.340), 'Hebrews' (*Ant.* 11.344) and 'Israelites' (in a inscription of 150-50 BCE from Delos)[114] is a further reminder of how careful we have to be in our own use of such descriptive titles. It is sufficiently clear, however, that there was already a sharp breach between Samaria and the Judeans/Jews generally.[115] No doubt significant factors in the breach were folk memories of Samaria's hostility to Judea's reconstitution in the Persian era (Ezra 4–5; Nehemiah 4–6), and the sense that Samaritans were a people whose ethnic and religious identity had been gravely diluted.[116] But in the event, the breach came to focus much more sharply and decisively on the question of the Temple and the correct place to worship God (cf. John 4.20), with the Samaritan claim for Mount Gerizim backed up by their own version of the Pentateuch. The hostility between Judea and Samaria was inevitably deepened by John Hyrcanus's destruction of the Gerizim temple in 128 BCE.[117]

All this, of course, is of immediate relevance when we ask where Jesus fits into such a spectrum, and whether his first followers were also reckoned, at least initially, as belonging within Judaism. The fact that Luke could describe Jesus' followers as a 'sect' (Acts 24.14; 28.22), 'the sect of the Nazarenes' (Acts 24.5), just as he speaks of the 'sect' of the Sadducees (5.17) and the 'sect of the Pharisees' (15.5; 26.5), is certainly suggestive. Luke evidently wanted his readers to understand that the 'Christians' (11.26) were a 'sect' within Judaism, alongside the other Jewish 'sects'. There are larger questions here to which we will have to return in volume 2. For the moment, it is sufficient to reaffirm that Jesus himself should be regarded as standing foursquare within the diversity of the Judaism of his day. The tensions and hostilities which emerged during his mission should not be seen as tensions and hostility in regard to Judaism as

112. Schürer, *History* 2.16-20; R. T. Anderson, 'Samaritans', *ABD* 5.940-47; Grabbe, *Judaism* 502-507; S. Isser, 'The Samaritans and Their Sects', in Horbury et al., eds., *Judaism* 3.569-95; bibliography in Meier, *Marginal Jew* 3.594.

113. E.g., *Ant.* 17.319, 342; 18.85-89; 20.118-36; Acts 8.

114. A. T. Kraabel in *BA* 47 (1984) 44-46; and further L. M. White, 'The Delos Synagogue Revisited: Recent Fieldwork in the Graeco-Roman Diaspora', *HTR* 80 (1987) 133-60; *NDIEC* 8.148-51.

115. As implied in Matt. 10.5; Luke 9.52-54; 10.30-37; John 4.9; 8.48.

116. 'Apostates from the Jewish nation' (Josephus, *Ant.* 11.340; contrast Ezra 9–10); Sir. 50.25-26; *m. Sheb.* 8.10.

117. See further F. Dexinger, 'Limits of Tolerance in Judaism: The Samaritan Example', in E. P. Sanders et al., eds., *Jewish and Christian Self-Definition*. Vol. 2: *Aspects of Judaism in the Graeco-Roman Period* (London: SCM, 1981) 88-114; J. D. Purvis, 'The Samaritans and Judaism' in Kraft and Nickelsburg, *Early Judaism* 81-98.

such, but in regard to one or another (or more) of the groups or aspects of late Second Temple Judaism.[118]

d. Common Judaism

When all is said and done, however, the most relevant of the groups and tendencies so far mentioned represent a very small minority within the population of the land of Israel in the first century. Josephus indicates that the Pharisees were more than 6,000 strong (at the time of Herod the Great),[119] the Essenes more than 4,000, and the Sadducees a small wealthy elite (*Ant.* 17.42; 18.20; 13.298). We have no sure way of knowing how many or who the various apocryphal or pseudepigraphal writings spoke for, but that they represented distinctive groups of any significant number must be considered doubtful in view of Josephus' silence regarding them. The number of 'Hellenists' was no doubt a substantial minority of the population within the Hellenistic or Hellenized cities, but impossible to quantify, and they could not be said to have formed a coherent party. The Samaritans, on the other hand, were a significant political entity, but should probably be placed beyond the spectrum of what may properly be called 'Judaism' from a spectator perspective. All in all, then, the Judaisms so far described, about which we can speak with any confidence and whose distinctiveness gives at least a prima facie case for describing them as different 'Judaisms', probably constituted a relatively small minority of the Jews living in the land of first-century Israel.

It is at this point that Sanders' reminder is important, that in speaking of first-century Judaism we need to speak first and foremost of the practices and beliefs of the great mass of the people, what he calls *'common Judaism'*.[120] For these other forms of Judaism are simply luxuriant or exotic growths which, from a spectator's perspective, mark them out from what in comparison may seem the more commonplace but is in fact the much more extensive flower bed or garden. It is this common 'bedding' in the Judaism of the people at large which gives these diverse forms of Judaism their common denominator as 'Judaism'.[121] Or to

118. A more detailed study would have to consider also baptismal sects, not to mention groups of bandits! (see Grabbe, *Judaism* 501-502, 507-509 and 511-14). And the status of proselytes and 'God-fearers' in relation to Judaism will call for attention in vol. 2.

119. Hengel and Deines point out that *Ant.* 17.42 refers to over 6,000 Pharisees who refused to swear allegiance to Herod — implying that there may have been many more ('Sanders' Judaism' 33 n. 85).

120. Sanders, *Judaism* Part II.

121. Hengel's and Deines's criticism of the term 'common Judaism' ('Sanders' Judaism' 53) is not quite to the point (they suggest that 'complex Judaism' would be better), since it is the common identifying features of 'Judaism' which are in view at this point.

be more precise, it is because there is a Judaism more generally recognizable as constituting the life of the people (the Judeans/Jews) that we can go on to speak of different versions of Judaism practised by different groups of Jews. As we shall indicate shortly (§9.5), there was a common foundation of practice and belief which constituted the constant or recurring or common factors unifying all the different particular forms of first-century Judaism and on which they were built.

However, before we turn to describe this Judaism, or, again to be more precise, these common features of Second Temple Judaism, we have once again to remind ourselves that our phenomenological description of the diversity of first-century Judaism may not represent adequately the self-understanding and perspective of any of the particular forms of first-century Judaism. Before proceeding to 'common Judaism', therefore, we must try to step inside and see first-century Judaism in the land of Israel *'from within'*, what these groups claimed for themselves and thought of each other. Without taking some account of an insider's view, a spectator's view of first-century Judaism will always be inadequate. A spectator may be content to describe a Judaism which was richly diverse in character; but did the insiders share that recognition of diversity, and if not, how should that fact influence our perception of first-century 'Judaism'? Here too there is probably sufficient evidence in most cases, though in comparison with the first approach the issue here has rarely been addressed in modern discussions.

9.4. Jewish Factionalism — Judaism from Within

How do we get 'inside' the Judaism(s) of our period? Obviously by reading empathetically the documents which were written within Israel during our period, particularly those that were written from a self-consciously insider perspective and in defence of their self-perception, even if in the event they spoke for what may have been only small and relatively unrepresentative forms of Judaism. When we do so, at once a remarkable feature becomes apparent. For wherever we have such documents from within the Judaism(s) of the second half of the Second Temple or post-Maccabean period in the land of Israel we find a common theme regularly recurring — firm and unyielding claims to be the only legitimate heirs of Israel's inheritance, and sharp, hostile, often vituperative criticism of other Jews/Judaisms. The same is true whether it be the Dead Sea Scrolls, *1 Enoch,* the *Testament of Moses, Jubilees,* the *Psalms of Solomon,* or indeed Christian writings. The period was evidently marked by a degree of *intra-Jewish factionalism* remarkable for its sustained nature and quality of bitterness — a factionalism which included some at least of the other groups from whom we have no first-hand account from the period.[122] The point can be illustrated readily enough.[123]

The Qumran Essenes saw themselves as alone true to the covenant of the fathers, 'the sons of light', 'the house of perfection and truth in Israel', the chosen ones, and so on (1QS 2.9; 3.25; 8.9; 11.7). In contrast, the political and religious opponents of the sectarians are attacked as 'the men of the lot of Belial', 'traitors', 'the wicked', 'the sons of Belial' who have departed from the paths of righteousness, transgressed the covenant, and such like.[124] One of the chief sins for which these other Jews are condemned is the failure to recognize the Essene claim to have been given the correct insight into the Torah, and thus to be constituted as the people of the new covenant.[125] 'Those who seek smooth things', the 'deceivers',[126] are usually identified as the Pharisees, and the halakhic debates reflected in the recently published 4QMMT confirm that Pharisees were amongst the Qumran sect's disputants.[127]

The *Enoch* corpus gives evidence of a bitter calendrical dispute which racked Judaism probably during the second century BCE. 'The righteous', 'who walk in the ways of righteousness', clearly distinguished themselves from those who 'sin like the sinners' in wrongly computing the months and feasts and years (*1 En.* 82.4-7). The accusation in *1 Enoch* 1–5 is less specific, but again draws a clear line of distinction between the 'righteous/chosen' and the 'sinners/impious' (1.1, 7-9; 5.6-7), where the latter are clearly fellow Jews who practised their Judaism differently from the self-styled 'righteous' — 'You have not persevered, nor observed the law of the Lord' (5.4). Whether there were more specific targets remains obscure.

Similarly in *T. Mos.* 7 we find a forthright attack on 'godless men, who rep-

---

122. 'The heyday of Jewish sectarianism was from the middle of the second century BCE to the destruction of the temple in 70 CE' (Cohen, *Maccabees* 143); see also Saldarini, *Pharisees* 65, 210-11, and n. 56 above.

123. In what follows I draw particularly on my 'Pharisees, Sinners and Jesus' 73-76. See further the texts reviewed by M. A. Elliott, *The Survivors of Israel: A Reconsideration of the Theology of Pre-Christian Judaism* (Grand Rapids: Eerdmans, 2000) chs. 3-4. Cf. also P. F. Esler, 'Palestinian Judaism in the First Century', in D. Cohn-Sherbok and J. M. Court, eds., *Religious Diversity in the Graeco-Roman World: A Survey of Recent Scholarship* (Sheffield: Sheffield Academic, 2001) 21-46.

124. E.g., 1QS 2.4-10; CD 1.11-21; 1QH 10(=2).8-19; 1QpHab 5.3-8; 4QFlor[4Q174] 1.7-9.

125. E.g., 1QS 5.7-13; CD 4.7-8; 1QpHab 2.1-4.

126. 1QH 10(=2).14-16, 31-32; 12(=4).9-11; 4QpNah 1.2, 7; 2.2, 8; 3.3-7.

127. E.g., Vanderkam, *Dead Sea Scrolls* 60, 93, 107; J. A. Fitzmyer, 'The Qumran Community: Essene or Sadducean?', *The Dead Sea Scrolls and Christian Origins* (Grand Rapids: Eerdmans, 2000) 249-60 (here 251-52); others in Saldarini, *Pharisees* 279 n. 6. Schaper makes much of 4QMMT in his description of the early Pharisees ('Pharisees' 406-407).

resent themselves as being righteous' and who 'with hand and mind . . . touch unclean things', even though they themselves say, 'Do not touch me, lest you pollute me' (7.3, 9-10). Here too we may have to recognize an attack on Pharisees, by means of caricaturing Pharisaic concern to maintain purity,[128] although, if *Ep. Arist.* 139, 142, Josephus, *War* 2.150 and Col. 2.21 are of any relevance, the concern for purity and fear of defilement by touch was a good deal more widespread within first-century Judaism. The point here, however, is that a Jewish document characterizes such concern as the concern of 'godless men'!

Jubilees is directed to Israel as a whole, a plea for a more rigorous observance of the covenant,[129] but includes the conviction that many sons of Israel will leave the covenant and make themselves 'like the Gentiles' (15.33-34). Here too the calendar was a bone of contention: observance of the feast or ordinance, wrongly computed, counted as *non*-observance, as failure to maintain the covenant, as walking in the errors of the Gentiles (6.32-38).

Finally we may simply note how thoroughgoing is the polemic in the *Psalms of Solomon* on behalf of those who regarded themselves as 'the righteous', the 'devout', over against the 'sinners'.[130] It is clear enough that 'the righteous' were not Israel as a whole, but those who believed that they alone 'live in the righteousness of the commandments' (14.2). The 'sinners' were not only Gentiles or the blatantly wicked, but the Jewish opponents of the 'righteous', probably the Hasmonean Sadducees who had usurped the monarchy and (in the eyes of the devout) defiled the sanctuary (1.8; 2.3; 4.1-8; 7.2; 8.12-13, etc.).[131] When Messiah came such sinners would be driven out from the inheritance (17.23).

How serious was all this polemic? The range of opinion here is of some interest, particularly as it bears on the position of Christianity within the spectrum of first-century Judaism. At one end, for example, it may be argued that the disagreements are simply those of vigorous halakhic dispute, so that Jesus and the Pharisees of his day should be seen simply as friendly disputants.[132] At the other end, the polemic of Matthew 23 and John 8 would normally be regarded as indicating that a decisive breach with Judaism had already taken place.[133] In fact, however, the character of denunciation and quality of vituperation is remarkably

---

128. So, e.g., Flusser, *Jesus* 60; Jeremias, *Jerusalem* 250.

129. See, e.g., 2.17-33; 15.25-34; 22.10-24; 23.22-31; 30.7-23; 50.

130. E.g., 3.3-12; 4.1, 8; 13.6-12; 15.4-13.

131. So, e.g., R. B. Wright in *OTP* 2.642; Schürer, *History* 3.193-94; Sanders, *Judaism* 453. See further the analysis by M. Winninge, *Sinners and the Righteous: A Comparative Study of the Psalms of Solomon and Paul's Letters* (ConBNT 26; Stockholm: Almqvist and Wiksell, 1995) findings summarized 125-36.

132. This is the position of Sanders maintained in his writings since *Jesus and Judaism*.

133. See further below, vol. 3.

consistent across the range of literature surveyed above. We may consider, for example, the fearful curses called down on the men of Belial when the novice enters the Qumran community —

> Be cursed because of all your guilty wickedness!
> May he deliver you up for torture at the hands of the vengeful Avengers!
> May he visit you with destruction by the hand of all the wreakers of revenge!
> Be cursed without mercy because of the darkness of your deeds!
> Be damned in the shadowy place of everlasting fire! . . .

> (1QS 2.5-10 Vermes).

The curses against the deceitful and stubborn covenanter in 1QS 2.11-18 are no less fierce than those against the 'men of the lot of Belial'. Or in *Jub.* 15.34 'there is for them [those who have made themselves like the Gentiles] no forgiveness or pardon so that they might be pardoned and forgiven from all of the sins of this eternal error'. We might compare the warning against the 'eternal sin' in Mark 3.29, occasioned by refusal to recognize that Jesus' exorcisms were effected by the power of the Holy Spirit. And even the Johannine Jesus' castigation of 'the Jews' as sons of the devil (8.44) is readily echoed in *Jub.* 15.33-34, 4QFlor[4Q 174] 1.8 and *T. Dan* 5.6 (the last drawing on the Book of Enoch the Righteous). Perhaps most striking of all in its sustained character in the polemic reviewed above is the regular condemnation of *other Jews as 'sinners'*, given that the sinner in Jewish theology was excluded from participation in the world to come and condemned to eternal darkness.[134]

How much weight should we give to such considerations? Did the Jews who wrote 1QS or the *Psalms of Solomon* really believe that those thus cursed or called 'sinners' were as such indeed outside the covenant, beyond the saving righteousness of God? Did the Pharisees who are reported as criticising Jesus for eating with sinners (Mark 2.16; Luke 15.2) really think that these sinners would be condemned in the final judgment, and Jesus too? That is certainly the theological logic of their language. But did they always mean it?[135] Here we might note how incipient sectarianism forces an inevitable ambivalence on the key term of

---

134. E.g., Deut. 29.18; Ps. 92.7; *1 En.* 98.10-16; 102.3; *Jub.* 36.9-10; *T. Abr.* 11.11; *Pss. Sol.* 2.34; 3.11-12; see further J. D. G. Dunn, 'Jesus and Factionalism in Early Judaism', in Charlesworth and Johns, eds., *Hillel and Jesus* 156-75; Sanders, *Paul and Palestinian Judaism* index 'the Wicked'; D. A. Neale, *None but the Sinners: Religious Categories in the Gospel of Luke* (JSNTS 58; Sheffield: Sheffield Academic, 1991) 82-95.

135. The fact that some Jews were ready to kill other Jews over issues of Torah loyalty — Paul was one who attempted to 'destroy' the church of God out of Phinehas-like 'zeal' (Gal. 1.13-14; above at n. 25) — is a salutary reminder of how seriously at least some intended such language.

the insiders' self-understanding — 'Israel'. Are only those 'Israel' who have remained true to the covenant, as understood by the group in focus, or will God restore the wholeness of disobedient and exiled Israel in the end (in eschatological fulfilment of the pattern in Deut. 30)? We see the ambivalence, for example, in CD 3.12-4.12, where 'Israel' appears on both sides of the equation — God's covenant with Israel, Israel has strayed, the 'sure house in Israel', 'the converts of Israel'. Again in the tension in *Jubilees* between 15.34 and 22.23-30; or in the *Psalms of Solomon* between the sustained condemnation of Jewish 'sinners' and the final hope for Israel in 17.44-45 and 18.5.[136] Worth noting already is the same tension in Paul between the affirmation that 'not all who are from Israel are Israel' and the assurance that 'all Israel will be saved' (Rom. 9.6; 11.26). Nor should we forget that the debate on 'Who is a Jew?' is still with us, not least as a political question in the state of Israel.[137] Perhaps the imagery of 'focus' is helpful here in that so much of our literature operates with a 'close-up focus' for most of the time, and only occasionally with a 'long-range focus', and too little attention is given to the inconsistencies in detail which result from changing ('zooming') from one to the other.

What, we might ask alternatively, was the function of such abusive language? To condemn fellow Jews irretrievably? Or was it simply the language of self-legitimation, to confirm themselves in the rightness of their own beliefs/practices and in the crucial importance of these beliefs/practices? Or language of exhortation and evangelism, all the more condemnatory and fearful in order to frighten others into accepting their own beliefs and halakhoth? Here we may see the consequence of all sectarianism, or, alternatively expressed, the tendency to fundamentalism. The very affirmation of the fundamental importance of some key element of belief and practice carries with it the corollary that those who dispute or play down that key element are thereby damned. It is quite literally the curse of such incipient fundamentalism that it cannot recognize the legitimacy of alternative interpretations without denying its own. In this case, first-century Judaism is simply typical of the tensions between the ideals of 'the pure church' and comprehensiveness which have afflicted all religions and ideologies at one time or another.[138]

Here then is a tension constantly distorting the coherence of any descrip-

---

136. See further the sensitive discussion of Sanders, *Paul and Palestinian Judaism* 240-57; also 361, 367-74, 378 *(Jubilees)* and 398-406, 408 *(Psalms of Solomon)*.

137. Cf. particularly L. H. Schiffman, *Who Was a Jew? Rabbinic and Halakhic Perspectives on the Jewish-Christian Schism* (Hoboken: Ktav, 1985).

138. Moore perceptively observed that 'In all sects, and in every *ecclesiola in ecclesia,* it is the peculiarities in doctrine, observance, or piety, that are uppermost in the minds of the members; what they have in common with the great body is no doubt taken for granted, but, so to speak, lies in the sectarian subconsciousness' *(Judaism* 2.161). See also n. 56 above.

tion of Judaism in the land of Israel in the first century. The *spectator* perspective can observe the diversity of Judaism quite well, including the distinctive features of the different sub-groups, whether set against the broad sweep of common Judaism or not. But as soon as we get *inside* one of these Judaisms the picture changes, from a comfortable comprehensiveness, to a hostile jostling to remain 'in' by ensuring *inter alia* that others are defined as 'out'. The tension in part is between 'Judaism' perceived phenomenologically and 'Israel' perceived from within, but in part also between the insider's perception of an Israel of pure/purified form in the here and now and an Israel of eschatological completeness. Such tendency to sectarianism is probably inevitable, perhaps even desirable, wherever claims to ultimate truth are constitutive of identity, for it constantly recalls the larger body to its constitutive truth claim and underlines the inescapability of the tension between ideal and actual practice. Failure to recognize the presence of such tension in the case of first-century Judaism simply makes it harder to understand the dynamic of the group interactions, including the impact of Jesus and the emergence of his 'sect'. But where did Jesus stand within all this? — simply as further indicating the diversity, or as in effect reinforcing the factionalism, or as somehow representing the heart of Judaism, or as a false prophet, a rebellious son, an embryonic apostate, or what? We have already indicated several shafts of illumination which the tensions within the larger Judaism of the late Second Temple period seem to shed on features of the Jesus tradition, but the questions and issues are of course much greater. We will return to them in subsequent chapters.

At the same time, we need to recall once again that all this argument over who constitutes Israel, all this polemic, whether evangelistic or dismissive, was going on between relatively small groups within first-century Judaism. All the while 'common Judaism', the potentially restored comprehensive Israel, was still functioning as such. All the while that which fundamentally constituted Israel as Israel, Judaism as Judaism was still in effect. To this we therefore turn.

9.5. The Unity of First-Century Judaism

In some ways the most serious of the anachronisms with which modern research into Jewish and Christian origins labours is the very use of the term 'Judaism' in the plural (Judaisms). For nowhere in its early usage is 'Judaism' used in the plural; it occurs only in the singular. 'Judaism' was evidently perceived, from 'outside' as well, not as a multiplicity of forms but as a singular entity; there was a something called 'Judaism'. We may describe this as 'common Judaism', of which these other 'Judaisms' were particular expressions, remembering that Sanders' 'common Judaism' is derived principally from Josephus' spectator perspective. Or 'foundational Judaism', on which these more specific superstructures were erected. What matters is that there was a recognisable genus, 'Judaism', of which there were different species. It is this generic Judaism behind, below, within all these particular Judaisms with which we also need to be concerned.

In an earlier study I spoke of 'the four pillars of Second Temple Judaism',[139] and this categorisation still seems to me to provide a useful mode of description. It begins from the well-recognized fact that historically Judaism has always involved a combination of three principal factors — 'belief in God, God's revelation of the Torah to Israel, and Israel as the people who lives by the Torah in obedience to God'.[140] The only difference for first-century Judaism is that we could hardly fail to add a fourth factor — the Temple.

a. Temple

There can be no doubt that the Temple was the central focus of Israel's national and religious life prior to its destruction in 70 CE. Judea was a temple state. The Temple, its platform brilliantly designed and engineered by Herod's architects,[141] was the hub of political and economic power, the reason for Jerusalem's existence in the out-of-the-way Judean highlands. The power of the high priesthood was a major factor in Hasmoneans and Romans keeping it firmly under their control. The income generated through the sacrificial cult, the Temple tax and the pilgrim traffic must have been immense.[142] Above all, the Temple was the place where God had chosen to put his name, the focal point for the divine-human encounter and the sacrificial cult on which human well-being and salvation depended, a primary identity marker of Israel the covenant people.[143] In the

139. Dunn, *Partings* ch. 2.

140. *EncJud* 10.387. Cf. Schwartz's discussion of 'Who is a Jew?' — people, land, and law as the three defining elements in Jewish identity during the Second Temple period (*Studies* 5-15).

141. See, e.g., D. Bahat, 'The Herodian Temple', in Horbury, et al., eds., *Judaism* 3.38-58; Crossan and Reed, *Excavating Jesus* 191-99.

142. See also Jeremias, *Jerusalem,* particularly 21-30, 73-84 and 126-38; D. Mendels, *The Rise and Fall of Jewish Nationalism* (New York: Doubleday, 1992) ch. 10; E. Gabba, 'The Social, Economic and Political History of Palestine, 63 BCE–CE 70', in Horbury, et al., eds., *Judaism* 3.94-167 (here 123-25).

143. Holmén, *Jesus* 275-86. See also C. T. R. Hayward, *The Jewish Temple* (London: Routledge, 1996). Note the comments of A. Momigliano, 'Religion in Athens, Rome and Jerusalem in the First Century BC', in W. S. Green, ed., *Approaches to Ancient Judaism. Vol. 5: Studies in Judaism and Its Greco-Roman Context* (Atlanta: Scholars, 1985) 1-18: 'Jerusalem was also different from any other place because its Temple had long been the symbol of the

Roman period 'Jew' was as much a religious identifier as an ethnic identifier because it focused identity in Judea, the state whose continuing distinctive existence depended entirely on the status of Jerusalem as the location of the Temple. It should occasion no surprise, then, that Sanders devotes nearly one hundred pages of his description of 'common Judaism' in our period to an account of the Temple, its personnel, its cult, and the festivals which also focused on it.[144]

We saw also that the different sects highlighted the importance of the Temple — most obviously the Sadducees, but also the Qumran Essenes, and most likely also the Pharisees, who probably, in some measure like the Essenes, sought to extend or at least live out the holiness required for the Temple more widely in the holy land.[145] Here it is important to grasp the fact that the disputes and denunciations relating to the Temple, noted in the survey of the Judaisms above (§9.4), do not amount to a dispute regarding the fundamental importance of the Temple itself. On the contrary, it was precisely because the Temple was so important that disputes about its correct function were so important. It was not the Temple but its location (the Samaritans) and abuse (*Psalms of Solomon* and Qumran) which were denounced. This is particularly evident in the preoccupation with the Temple among the Qumranites (as in 11QT and the Songs of the Sabbath Sacrifice), even among a group who felt themselves distanced from its present operation.

How Jesus and his followers regarded the Jerusalem Temple will obviously be a key question for any historian of Christianity's beginnings (§§15.3; 17.3).

b. God

Belief in God as one and in God's un-image-ableness was certainly fundamental to the first-century Jew. The *Shema* was probably said by most Jews on a regular basis (Deut. 6.4, 7); Jesus was surely striking a familiar chord in the tradition attributed to him in Mark 12.28-31. And the twin commandment to acknowledge God alone and to make no images of God (Ex. 20.3-6; Deut. 5.7-10) was no doubt burnt into the heart and mind of the typical first-century Jew.

Little of this actually appears upon the surface of late Second Temple Juda-

---

unity of Judaism. I do not know of any other ancient god who had a sanctuary as exclusive as the Temple of Jerusalem. . . . Jerusalem was a place for pilgrims unmatched by Athens or Rome, with all their attractions' (14).

144. Sanders, *Judaism* chs. 5-8 (47-145); Hengel and Deines congratulate Sanders on producing what 'may well be the best presentation of the temple, its cult, and the priesthood which has appeared for a long while' ('Sanders' Judaism' 55).

145. This is one of the points at which Sanders criticises Neusner, but the weight of opinion, as represented by Vermes, Cohen, Saldarini, Segal, Stemberger, and Grabbe continues to be more supportive of Neusner; see, e.g., Dunn, *Partings* 41-42, and above §9.3a.

ism, for the simple reason that it was non-controversial and so could be taken for granted — an important reminder that the fundamental character of an item of belief and practice is not to be measured by the amount of verbiage it engenders, and that what belongs to the foundation may often be hidden from sight. But those who explained Judaism to the outsider found it necessary, as did Josephus, to point out that the acknowledgment of 'God as one is common to all the Hebrews' (*Ant.* 5.112).[146] And the abhorrence of idolatry was a common feature in all Judaism.[147] Within first-century Israel itself we need only recall Josephus' reports of the violent reaction from the people at large to misguided attempts by Pilate to bring standards perceived as idolatrous into Jerusalem (*Ant.* 18.55-59) and to the attempt of Caligula to have his own statue set up within the Temple (*Ant.* 18.261-72).[148]

Here again the issue of how Jesus, and subsequently the early Christians, regarded this fundamental affirmation of Jewish faith will inevitably be important for our own understanding of the emergence of Christianity from within its Jewish matrix (§§14.1-2).

c. Election

Equally fundamental was Israel's self-understanding of itself as the people of God specially chosen from among all the nations of the world to be his own. This conviction was already there in the pre-exilic period in such passages as Deut. 7.6-8 and 32.8-9. But it became a central category of self-definition in the post-exilic period from Ezra onwards (Ezra 9–10); it was the undergirding motivation behind the resistance to Hellenistic syncretism in the Maccabean crisis, and it constantly came to expression in the compulsive desire to maintain distinct and separate identity from the other nations (Gentiles).[149] The attitude is expressed in extreme form in *Jub.* 15.30-32 and 22.16. But it lies behind the everyday preoccupation with purity, which was so prominent in most of the Judaisms reviewed above and is attested also by the large numbers of ritual baths *(miqwaoth)* now uncovered by archaeology.[150] And it is closely related to the maintenance of

146. Similarly *Ep. Arist.* 132; Philo, *Decal.* 65.

147. Isa. 44.9-20; Wisd. Sol. 11–15; Ep. Jer.; *Sib. Or.* 3.8-45; 1 Corinthans 8–10; 1 John 5.21; *m. 'Abodah Zarah.* The theological rationale is nicely expressed by Josephus, *Ap.* 2.167, 190-91.

148. Further discussion in Sanders, *Judaism* 242-47; see also below §9.6a.

149. The prophecy of Balaam in Num. 23.9 was particularly significant for Jewish self-understanding — 'a people dwelling alone, and not reckoning itself among the nations'. 'Exclusivism was part and parcel of Judaism' (Sanders, *Judaism* 266).

150. See Sanders, *Jewish Law* 214-27; R. Reich, 'Ritual Baths', *OEANE* 4.430-1. More than three hundred ritual baths from the Roman period have been uncovered in Judea, Galilee,

strict laws of clean and unclean at the meal table, as both Lev. 20.24-26 and Acts 10.10-16, 28 remind us. The 'separation' of the Pharisees ('separated ones') and the Essenes within Second Temple Judaism was only an exaggerated expression of a conviction close to the heart of Israel's concept of election (to be separate from the [other] nations). This foundation pillar was thus closely linked to the others, since it expressed itself in fear of contamination by Gentile idolatry, and in the conviction that the holiness of Israel (land and people) was dependent on the holiness of the Temple (hence the prohibition which prevented Gentiles from passing beyond the court of the Gentiles in the Temple area).[151]

As already noted earlier, 'Judaism' was itself coined as an expression of ethnic and religious identity defined by opposition to the corruptive influences of the wider world. Thus the very term expresses, we may say, an understanding of Israel's election which in itself encouraged suspicion and exclusiveness. This is the attitude which came to the surface in the sectarian tendency of so many of the Judaisms reviewed above; the more thoroughgoing the definition and practice of the 'righteousness' by which Israel should be distinguished, the more 'the righteous' are required to distance themselves from and condemn others, not least other Jews, who fail to honour and observe that righteousness.[152] Ironically, however, it is the insider term 'Israel' itself which proves to be the more comprehensive, since, unlike 'Judaism', it does not begin as a term of opposition, is defined precisely not by race or status but only by electing grace (Deut. 7.6-8), and includes the task of bringing salvation to the end of the earth (Isa. 49.6). As we shall see later, this was a point on which Paul attempted to maintain his own understanding of himself as an 'Israelite' and of his mission as continuous with Israel's (Romans 9–11), though without much success.

---

and the Golan (see, e.g., Crossan and Reed, *Excavating Jesus* 168-70). There is some dispute as to whether all the stepped pools should be identified as *miqwaoth* (H. Eshel, 'A Note on "Miqvaot" at Sepphoris', in D. R. Edwards and C. T. McCollough, eds., *Archaeology and the Galilee* [University of South Florida; Atlanta: Scholars, 1997] 131-33; B. G. Wright, 'Jewish Ritual Baths — Interpreting the Digs and the Texts: Some Issues in the Social History of Second Temple Judaism', in N. A. Silberman and D. Small, eds., *The Archaeology of Israel: Constructing the Past, Interpreting the Present* [JSOTS 237; Sheffield: JSOT, 1997] 190-214 [I am grateful to Kathleen Corley for the latter reference]). But the objections would be valid only if mishnaic practice was already standard, something which cannot be assumed; and it is likely that the practice of *tebul yom* (immersion before sunset to reduce impurity) was already being enacted by this time, as is implied by the allusions in 4QMMT B15 and 4Q514, which would also suggest greater need for and use of *miqwaoth* (Kazen, *Jesus and Purity* Halakhah 76-81). That there were *miqwaoth* in Galilee, which testify to a concern to maintain purity even when attendance at the Temple was not immediately in view, is hardly to be disputed; see also my 'Jesus and Purity: An Ongoing Debate', *NTS* 48 (2002) 449-67 (§1c).

151. See, e.g., my *Partings* 38-42.

152. But see again the second half of §9.4.

d. Torah

Finally we must speak of the Torah (the five books of Moses, the Pentateuch), which is as fundamental to Israel's self-understanding as God, Temple, and election. It was the Torah which justified and explained the importance of the Temple and its cult, and which proved the more foundational and durable when rabbinic Judaism was able to transform itself from a religion of Temple and priest to one of Torah and rabbi in the centuries following the disasters of the two Jewish revolts. It was the Torah which had been given to Israel as a mark of the one God's favour to and choice of Israel, an integral part of his covenant with Israel, to show Israel how to live as the people of God (Deuteronomy), its significance classically expressed in the claim that universal divine Wisdom is now embodied therein.[153] And it was the Torah which served as boundary and bulwark separating Israel from the other nations by its insistence on their maintenance of the purity code.[154] Since the Torah was both school textbook and law of the land we may assume a substantial level of respect and observance of its principal regulations within common Judaism.[155] At any rate, it is important not to think of the Torah as exclusively religious documents and to recognize here not least the interlocking nature of Israel as a religio-national entity. The Torah, of course, was part of a larger concept of 'the Scriptures',[156] consisting of 'the Law and the Prophets',[157] or 'the Law, the Prophets and the Writings' (Tanak).[158] Josephus speaks of twenty-two books of sacred Scripture (*Ap.* 1.37-43). But the Torah was undoubtedly regarded as the definitive element, on which the rest was commentary.

Because of the Torah's centrality in determining what it meant to be the people of God in daily living, devotion to Torah was bound to be a feature in the divisions within Judaism. Again, not because the different groups disputed its importance, but for precisely the opposite reason. It was desire to meet the obli-

---

153. Sir. 24.23; Bar. 3.36–4.4.

154. E.g., Lev. 20.24-26; Dan. 1.8-16; *Ep. Arist.* 139, 142. See also n. 97 above, and further Dunn, *Partings* 23-31.

155. Following his treatment of the Temple and associated features Sanders devotes two chapters to the theme of 'observing the law of God' (*Judaism* 190-240).

156. The term is attributed to Jesus — Mark 12.10 pars.; 12.24 par.; 14.49 par.; Matt. 26.54; Luke 4.21.

157. Matt. 11.13/Luke 16.16; Matt. 5.17-18; 7.12; 22.40; John 1.45.

158. Luke 24.44. The threefold collection making up the Scriptures was already well established by the time of Jesus, as we see from the prologue of ben Sira and 4QMMT C 10, and from references to David as an inspired and authoritative writer (as in Mark 2.25 pars. and 12.36 pars.), though the third element (the writings) was not yet delimited. For discussion see, e.g., R. T. Beckwith, 'Formation of the Hebrew Bible', in M. J. Mulder, ed., *Mikra* (CRINT II.1; Assen: Van Gorcum, 1988) 39-86; and on the text(s) of Scripture current at the time of Jesus see M. J. Mulder, 'The Transmission of the Biblical Text', *Mikra* 88-104.

gations specified by the Torah for Israel as fully as possible which resulted in what was in effect a competitive dispute as to what that meant in practice (cf. not least Gal. 1.14). All would have agreed that they ought to live according to the principles of 'covenantal nomism',[159] but each group's claim that it (alone) was so living carried with it the effective denial that others were doing so. In these disputes circumcision played no role, since they were all disputes within Judaism; circumcision came into play as a boundary marker between Jew and Gentile, as the early Christian mission to Gentiles reminds us. But it is clear that other issues of calculating feast days and the right maintenance of purity (including Temple purity), food laws, and Sabbath were usually the flash points and make-or-break issues on which differences and divisions turned.[160] Here again we should recall the seriousness of these disputes as indicated by frequent use of the abusive epithet 'sinners' (§9.4), for a sinner was defined precisely as one who broke or disregarded the regulations of Torah. In such polemic the need for a group to find in the Torah its own self-affirmation had the inevitable corollary of making the Torah an instrument by means of which one group condemned another.

On this point too it may be important to reflect further on the distinction between Judaism and Israel. For it could be argued that it was an overemphasis on the Torah, and on such distinctives as circumcision and food laws, which gave the term 'Judaism' its national and anti-Gentile character. It was the Torah seen and emphasized in its function of separating Israel from the other nations which, we might even say, transformed Israel into Judaism. Not the Torah as such, but the Torah understood to define the Jew by his difference from the Gentile. Whether this was a factor within Jesus' mission is quite unclear, but it certainly became a factor in Paul's reconfiguration of his faith in the light of his conversion and sense of call to apostolic mission. Here again, a proper setting of the historical context, both for Jesus and for embryonic Christianity, will surely help us to a better grasp of how and why Jesus was remembered as he was and how and why Christianity developed as it did.

159. The term coined by Sanders and used by him to denote the obedience to the law which was generally understood to be the appropriate (and necessary) response to the grace of God given in the covenant (*Judaism* 262-78). 'Covenantal nomism' is Sanders's alternative to (rejection of) the older view of Jewish 'legalism' prevalent up to the 1970s in NT scholarship, and although some important qualification is required (see particularly F. Avemarie, *Torah und Leben: Untersuchungen zur Heilsbedeutung der Tora in der frühen rabbinischer Literatur* [Tübingen: Mohr Siebeck, 1996]), the basic balance which the phrase achieves between covenant-grace and law-requiring-obedience is still sound. See further below, vol. 2.

160. E.g., *1 En.* 82.4-7; 1QS 10.1-8; 4QpHos 2.14-17; *Pss. Sol.* 8.12, 22; *T. Mos.* 7.10; 1 Macc. 1.62-63; Gal. 2.11-14; *Jub.* 50.6-13; CD 10-11; Mark 2.23-3.5.

9.6. Galilean Judaism

In a treatment aimed at illuminating the character and impact of Jesus' mission, an analysis of 'Judaism' at that time may be insufficient to clarify the most immediate historical context of that mission. For, as already noted, 'Judaism' first appears as the national religion of those who lived in Judea; the 'Jews' were first 'Judeans'. But Jesus is remembered as a Galilean,[161] and no one disputes that most of his mission was centred in the Galilee.[162] But Galilee is not Judea. Does that mean that the Galileans were also not part of Judaism, that it is actually improper to call Jesus a 'Jew'? The issue has potentially far-reaching implications and cannot be avoided. There are two aspects to the issue: Was Galilee 'Jewish'? Was Galilee 'Hellenized'?

a. Was Galilee Jewish?

The first issue can be posed quite sharply in terms of early Judaism's own historical records. As part of the northern kingdom (Israel), Galilee had been separated from Judea since the division of the Davidic kingdom following Solomon's death (about 922 BCE). When finally overrun by the Assyrians (722 or 721) 'the Israelites' had been transported to Assyria (2 Kgs 17.6), 'exiled from their own land to Assyria until this day' (17.23), and replaced 'in the cities of Samaria' by settlers from Mesopotamia (17.24). According to 1 Maccabees, it was only in the course of the internecine warfare which marked the decline of the Syrian Empire that Samaria and Galilee were added/(offered?) to Judea (1 Macc. 10.30) in about 152 BCE.[163] But it was nearly another fifty years before the Hasmoneans, under Aristobulus I (104-103 BCE), regained full control of the area. Josephus' description of the forcible accession is noteworthy: Aristobulus 'compelled the inhabitants, if they wished to remain in the territory, to be circumcised and to live in accordance with the laws of the Jews/Judeans' (*Ant.* 13.318).[164] Then, after less than one hundred years of rule from Jerusalem, at the death of Herod the Great, Herod's kingdom was divided up and Galilee with Perea given to Herod Antipas (4 BCE–39 CE), while Judea was soon taken under direct imperial rule (6-41 CE). So the obvious question arises: Was Jesus brought up in an only superficially 'judaized' Galilee?

---

161. Mark 1.9; Matt. 2.22; 21.11; 26.69; 27.55; Luke 2.39; 23.6; John 7.41, 52.

162. E.g., Mark 1.14, 16, 28, 39; 3.7; Luke 4.14, 31; 23.5, 49, 55; Acts 10.37.

163. Schürer, *History* 1.141 and n. 9. In an earlier campaign, Simon, brother of Judas Maccabee, had rescued 'the Jews/Judeans of Galilee' and brought them back to Judea (1 Macc. 5.23); 'the early Maccabees by no means set out to Judaise those regions, but on the contrary, withdrew their Jewish population' (Schürer, *History* 1.142).

164. Schürer, *History* 1.217-18.

In the first thorough English language study of Galilee, Sean Freyne argued strongly that, despite the above data, Galileans retained a firmly Jewish identity.[165] Under the Ptolemies (Egypt) and Seleucids (Syria) the administrative region ('eparchy') of Samaria included both Galilee and Judea.[166] Josephus reports a decree of the Seleucid king Antiochus III that 'all the members of the nation (of the *Ioudaioi*) shall be governed in accordance with their ancestral laws' (*Ant.* 12.142), which Freyne thinks would have included Galilee.[167] Consequently, there was no need for a 'judaisation' of Galilee under the Hasmoneans.[168] Rather, 'Galilean Judaism was now politically reunited with what had always been its cultural and religious center'; 'the Jerusalem temple continued to exercise a powerful attraction for them'.[169] Richard Horsley, however, has protested that Galilee was not integrated into a culturally unified 'common Judaism'.[170] Rather we should recognize a cultural divide between Galilean peasants and imported aristocrats, initially Hasmonean 'Judeans' and subsequently the Hellenized appointees of the Herods.[171] The continuity was more at the level of ancient Israelite traditions stemming from the period of the northern kingdom.[172]

165. S. Freyne, *Galilee from Alexander the Great to Hadrian, 323 BCE to 135 CE: A Study of Second Temple Judaism* (Wilmington: Glazier, 1980). Freyne has consistently updated his views in the light particularly of fuller archaeological evidence; see his collected essays *Galilee and Gospel* (WUNT 125; Tübingen: Mohr Siebeck, 2000), especially 'Archaeology and the Historical Jesus' (160-82) and 'Jesus and the Urban Culture of Galilee' (183-207); also 'The Geography, Politics, and Economics of Galilee and the Quest for the Historical Jesus', in Chilton and Evans, eds., *Studying the Historical Jesus* 75-121; also 'The Geography of Restoration: Galilee-Jerusalem In Early Jewish and Christian Experience', *NTS* 47 (2001) 289-311.

166. Freyne, *Galilee* 33-35.

167. Freyne, *Galilee* 35-36.

168. The area taken over by Aristobulus is described as Iturea, and Freyne questions Schürer's conclusion that Iturea included any of lower Galilee (*Galilee* 43-44).

169. Freyne, *Galilee* 392-93 (quoting from his conclusions).

170. Horsley, *Galilee*. In light of the above (§§9.1-2), we should also note that 'Judaism' was not yet such an inclusive term as Freyne seemed to think. Like Freyne, Horsley has updated his views in the light of increasing archaeological data — particularly *Archaeology, History and Society in Galilee* — though Horsley's basic thesis has remained largely unchanged throughout.

171. Horsley argues that the requirement to live 'according to the laws of the Judeans' 'meant political-economic-religious subordination to the Hasmonean high priesthood in Jerusalem'; similarly (re-)circumcision was 'a sign of being joined to the "body-politic"'; but Galileans were not thereby 'integrated into the Judean *ethnos*' (*Galilee* 46-52). The disagreement between Freyne and Horsley is highlighted by the unresolved question of whether *Ioudaioi* in Josephus should be translated 'Jews' (Freyne) or 'Judeans' (Horsley).

172. Horsley here develops the earlier arguments of A. Alt, 'Zur Geschichte der Grenze zwischen Judäa und Samaria' and 'Galiläische Probleme', in *Kleine Schriften zur Geschichte des*

Recent archaeological findings, however, have transformed the debate, and when correlated with the literary data seem to settle the issue fairly conclusively.[173] Study of the settlement patterns of Galilean sites reveals two striking features. First, the data indicate an almost complete abandonment of the region, painting 'a picture of a totally devastated and depopulated Galilee in the wake of the Assyrian campaigns of 733/732 BCE'.[174] Second, the sudden burgeoning of data around the end of the second century BCE (architecture, pottery, and Hasmonean coins) indicates that there was a rapid rise in new settlements in the wake of the Hasmonean conquest, attesting also economic and political ties between Galilee and Jerusalem.[175] All these data refute Horsley's idea of a Hasmonean aristocracy imposing themselves over a continuing Israelite population and point clearly to a wave of Judean settlements spreading over a depopulated territory.

To this has to be added what Jonathan Reed calls four indicators of Jewish religious identity: stone vessels (chalk or soft limestone), attesting a concern for ritual purity;[176] plastered stepped pools, that is, Jewish ritual baths *(miqwaoth);* burial practices, reflecting Jewish views of the afterlife;[177] and bone profiles without pork, indicating conformity to Jewish dietary laws. Such finds have been made across Galilee, whereas they are lacking at sites outside the Galilee and the Golan.[178] In the light of such finds we can hardly do other than speak of the characteristically *Jewish* population of Galilee in the late Second Temple period.

Volkes Israel II (Munich: Beck, 1959) 346-62, 363-435. Horsley has further developed his case in finding 'Israelite traditions in Q' as reflecting popular tradition in Galilee (*Whoever* ch. 5).

173. I draw particularly on Reed, 'The Identity of the Galileans: Ethnic and Religious Considerations', in *Archaeology and the Galilean Jesus* 23-61. The discussion by M. Goodman, 'Galilean Judaism and Judaean Judaism', in Horbury, et al., eds., *Judaism* 3.596-617, is already somewhat dated.

174. Reed, *Archaeology* 28-35 (here 29); 'in the Galilean heartland . . . every single excavated site . . . was destroyed or abandoned at the end of the eighth century' (31); 'there is no archaeological evidence for an indigenous population in the centuries after 733/2 BCE' (33). Reed concludes: 'The position of Alt and its revival by Horsley must be abandoned' (34). Similarly Freyne, 'Archaeology' 177-81, who has also abandoned his earlier support of Alt ('Town and Country Once More: The Case of Roman Galilee', *Galilee and Gospel* 59-72 [here 67-68]; also 'Galilee', *OEANE* 2.371-72).

175. Reed, *Archaeology* 39-43. Reed also notes the (Hasmonean) destruction of Gentile sites between Judea and Galilee and on Galilee's periphery (42-43). The evidence also confirms Freyne's rejection of Schürer's hypothesis ('Archaeology' 177-79) that the Galileans were converted Itureans (Reed 34-39; n. 168 above). See again Freyne, 'Galilee', *OEANE* 2.372-73.

176. According to the Mishnah stone vessels are impervious to ritual impurity (*m. Kelim* 10.1; *Ohol.* 5.5; *Para.* 5.5).

177. 'Placing ossuaries inside so-called *kokhim* or loculi, horizontally shafted underground family tombs, was a distinctly Jewish phenomenon at the end of the Second Temple period' (Reed, *Archaeology* 47).

178. Reed, *Archaeology* 43-52.

The archaeological picture is confirmed by the literary data. Galilean regard for the Jerusalem Temple is fairly well attested. During the reign of Herod Antipas (which covers the adult life of Jesus), there are indications that Galileans were expected to pay tithes and other dues for the priests and Temple, even if in the event they were notably slack in doing so;[179] according to Mark 1.44 pars. there were priests in Galilee, who could expect to benefit from the tithes due to priests. Galilean participation is also attested in the great pilgrim festivals (in Jerusalem):[180] following the death of Herod the Great, Josephus speaks of 'a countless multitude' from Galilee and elsewhere who flocked into Jerusalem at Pentecost (*War* 2.43; *Ant.* 17.254); later on he notes 'the custom of the Galileans at the time of a festival to pass through the Samaritan territory on their way to the holy city' (*Ant.* 20.118; *War* 2.232); and the tradition of some Galilean participation in the pilgrim festivals echoed in Luke 2.41-43 and John 7.10 is no doubt soundly based. In addition, the reference to Pilate mingling the blood of Galileans with their sacrifices (Luke 13.1) suggests that at least some Galileans did participate in the Temple cult; and according to Mark 7.11 and Matt. 5.23-24, Jesus assumed similar participation for his hearers.

As for Galilean loyalty to the Torah, we need simply note here that Jesus' own knowledge and use of the Torah presumably imply that schooling in Torah was practised in Galilee. Some of the issues confronting Jesus were matters of Torah and Torah interpretation (including sabbath, purity laws, Temple offerings, and fasting)[181] and imply a similar breadth of concern regarding the law. As attested by Mark 1.44 pars., the local priests would be responsible for administering the law. Beyond the Gospel accounts, and over against later rabbinic disdain for 'the people of the land', we should note Josephus' account of Eleazar, 'who came from Galilee and who had a reputation for being extemely strict *(akribēs)* with regard to the ancestral laws' (*Ant.* 20.43-44). And we should certainly recall the striking episode occasioned by Caligula's order for a statue of himself to be erected in the Jerusalem Temple (39-40 CE). It evidently triggered just as vehement a response among the Galilean peasantry in Tiberias as would have been the case in Judea, the mass protest before the Roman legate Petronius declaring, 'We will die sooner than violate our laws' (*Ant.* 18.271-72).[182] The pillars of Temple, monotheism, and Torah (the second of the ten commandments) were evidently as deeply embedded in Galilean as in Judean soil.

Does all this mean that the Galileans can be described straightforwardly as

179. Freyne, *Galilee* 281-87, 294; Horsley, *Galilee* 142-44.

180. Freyne, *Galilee* 287-93; Horsley, *Galilee* 144-47.

181. See further below §14.4.

182. Josephus explicitly notes that the protesters 'neglected their fields, and that, too, though it was time to sow the seed'. Horsley agrees that this probably indicates a 'peasant strike' in Galilee (*Galilee* 71).

'Jews'? The implication that first-century CE Galileans were descendants of the Judean settlers a century earlier suggests a clear Yes answer. At the same time we need to recall the degree of ambivalence in the term (§9.2). Shaye Cohen's suggestion, that the shift in meaning of *Ioudaios* from (ethnic-geographical) 'Judean' to (religious) 'Jew' took place in the Hasmonean period (n. 28 above), correlates with the archaeological evidence regarding Galilee's Jewish character. But he also notes Josephus' readiness to regard 'Judea' as the name for the entire land of Israel, including Galilee,[183] and various occasions on which Josephus calls Galileans *Ioudaioi*,[184] while in other passages *Galilaioi* seem to be distinct from the *Ioudaioi*.[185] And if the earlier reflections were on target, and 'Jew/Judean' was more of an outsider's designation, the actual use of the term itself would depend more on how others viewed them and be less a matter of self-identity. Probably, then, the designation of Galilee as part of Judea was a matter of perspective, the dominant element in the state standing for the whole.[186] Ironically, in somewhat like manner, 'Israel', though applicable primarily to the northern kingdom in the period of the divided kingdoms, was too precious an expression of Jewish self-identity not to be used by all who claimed to stand in the line of inheritance from the patriarchs.[187]

The upshot is that we should have no qualms about calling Galileans in general 'Jews', including Jesus of Nazareth. And even if the propriety and overtones of the epithet are less clear-cut, the implication of the term itself, that the Galileans in general were practitioners of 'common Judaism', should be allowed to stand, whatever qualifications might be called for in particular instances.

---

183. Similarly Luke uses 'Judea' when he was probably thinking of Galilee (Luke 4.44), and he certainly seems to think of Judea as including Galilee (Luke 23.5; Acts 10.37). In Luke's Gospel Jesus does not leave Galilee till 17.11 and does not enter Judea proper till 18.35–19.10.

184. Particularly *War* 2.232; 3.229; *Ant.* 13.154; 20.43; *Life* 113. Cohen also observes that diaspora *Ioudaioi* continued to be regarded as citizens of Judea (*Beginnings of Jewishness* 72-76).

185. *Ant.* 20.120; *Life* 346, 349.

186. We may compare the use of 'Holland' for the Netherlands, of 'Russia' for a wider territory, including, e.g., the Ukraine, and of 'England' for the whole of the United Kingdom. Cohen speaks of *Ioudaioi* as either 'broadly defined' (including Galileans) or 'narrowly defined' (living in Judea) (*Beginnings of Jewishness* 73).

187. 'Israel implies the religious claim to be God's chosen people even when it is used in secular contexts, with no religious emphasis, as the accepted designation' (Kuhn, 'Israel' 362, with examples). Zeitlin, *Jews* 10, notes that the prophets of Judah (the southern kingdom) always delivered their messages in the name of the God of Israel, never of the God of Judah.

b. How Hellenized Was Galilee?

This is obviously the other side of the same coin. The question arises from the same data noted in posing the first question, summed up now in the ancient description of Galilee as 'Galilee of the nations/Gentiles'.[188] In the light of this description and the corollary of Galilean syncretism, Walter Grundmann could even and infamously argue: 'Galilee was Gentile' and 'Jesus was no Jew'.[189] The issue with regard to Jesus is reinforced by the presence of two cities in lower Galilee, Sepphoris and Tiberias, (re)established by Herod Antipas within Jesus' lifetime as administrative centres. From the model of the Hellenistic cities of the Decapolis and the Mediterranean coast it becomes possible to argue that the Galilean cities were themselves 'Hellenistic' in character and culture.[190] A further inference readily drawn is that Sepphoris would have attracted villagers from the locality for trade and social outings[191] and that the youthful Jesus would have (regularly?) visited Sepphoris, only two hours distant (5 km) from Nazareth by foot, perhaps even as a young carpenter assisting in the construction of its theatre.[192] Sepphoris was also a natural stopping place on the trade route from Tiberias to Ptolemais on the coast; so the potential for still wider influence on a young Galilean can readily be imagined.[193] A final layer of presupposition frequently added in the last decade or so is that the attitudes and principles of Cynic philosophy must have been familiar in such an urbanized culture,[194] no doubt in-

188. Isa. 9.1; 1 Macc. 5.15; Matt. 4.15.

189. W. Grundmann, *Jesus der Galiläer und das Judentum* (Leipzig: Wigand, 1941) 166-75.

190. 'Galilee was . . . an epitome of Hellenistic culture on the eve of the Roman era'; 'the Hellenistic ethos known to have prevailed in Galilee' (Mack, *Myth* 66, 73-74); 'a pervasive Hellenistic environment' ('Q and a Cynic-Like Jesus' 26 n. 9); 'semipagan Galilee . . . despised by the ethnically pure Judeans living to the south', 'a largely pagan environment' (Funk, *Honest to Jesus* 33, 189).

191. 'People from the surrounding area probably also flocked to Sepphoris on such occasions, either to attend the theater or to hawk their wares' (E. M. Meyers, 'Roman Sepphoris in Light of New Archeological Evidence and Recent Research', in L. I. Levine, ed., *The Galilee in Late Antiquity* [New York: Jewish Theological Seminary of America, 1992] 321-38 [here 333]).

192. R. A. Batey, *Jesus and the Forgotten City: New Light on Sepphoris and the Urban World of Jesus* (Grand Rapids: Baker, 1991): 'it requires no very daring flight of the imagination to picture the youthful Jesus seeking and finding employment in the neighboring city of Sepphoris' (70); 'The stage on which he acted out his ministry was cosmopolitan and sophisticated and his understanding of urban life more relevant than previously imagined' (103).

193. E. M. Meyers and J. F. Strange, *Archaeology, the Rabbis and Early Christianity* (Nashville: Abingdon, 1981) 43; Crossan, *Historical Jesus* 17-19.

194. Three Cynic teachers are associated with Transjordan Gadara: Menippus (third century BCE), but he learned and taught his Cynicism elsewhere; Meleager (first century BCE) who flourished in Tyre; and Oenomaus (early second century CE).

cluding Sepphoris,[195] and must have substantially shaped Jesus' own ideas, as evident particularly from the Q tradition of his teaching.[196]

Unfortunately, such hypotheses have failed to consider the historical evidence regarding lower Galilee, as Horsley has again been quick to point out. Sepphoris and Tiberias were not in fact like the Hellenistic cities of the Decapolis: they were built as administrative capitals, not as independent Hellenistic *poleis;* and unlike the latter, they had no territoral jurisdiction over the surrounding districts.[197] More to the point, they were not major Hellenistic cities (like Scythopolis or Caesarea Maritima) but minor provincial centres, quite lacking in the typical marks or wealth of Hellenistic cities.[198] The road running from Tiberias to Ptolemais through Sepphoris was not a major international trade route but carried only inter-regional traffic.[199] And the archaeological evidence for Sepphoris is as clear as for the rest of Galilee: no indications of large numbers of non-Jews and plenty of evidence of the same four indicators of Jewish religious identity (stone vessels, *miqwaoth,* absence of pork remains,

195. Downing's speculation on the point in *Cynics* becomes steadily more confident and far-reaching by dint of repetition: Cynic influence was possible (146, 148); 'the most likely explanation is that Jesus was formed in response to native Cynic . . . influences' (150, 153); 'a Cynic-influenced Galilean Jewish culture' (157); 'an existing Cynic influence among ordinary people in the Galilee of his own day' (161); 'Cynic tradition in some form had permeated ordinary Jewish society in southern Galilee' (164). Contrast Crossan, who notes that 'the Cynics avoided rural areas, preferring the greater audiences . . . found in larger cities' (*Historical Jesus* 340). But according to Mack, Jesus 'may have read some scriptures, just as he may have read Meleager' (*Myth* 64).

196. See above chapter 7 n. 70.

197. Horsley, *Galilee* 214-15 and n. 36, citing A. H. M. Jones, *The Greek City* (Oxford: Clarendon, 1966) 80 n.; Freyne, 'Jesus and Urban Culture' 195.

198. Freyne notes that, unlike the major Hellenistic cities, Sepphoris and Tiberias had no power to mint their own coins ('Jesus and Urban Culture' 193-94). Reed estimates the population of Scythopolis and Caesarea Maritima as between 20,000 and 40,000, in contrast to Sepphoris and Tiberias (8,000-12,000) (*Archaeology* 79-82, 89, 93-96, 117-24); 'no temple, no gymnasium, no hippodrome, no *odeon,* no *nymphaeum,* no euergistic inscriptions' (95); Sepphoris 'could not afford marble or imported columns' (124); its theatre, dating to the latter half of the first century, was one of the more modest theatres on the Eastern Mediterranean, with seating capacity of around 4,000 (108, 119-20); the inhabitants' private possessions do not appear to have been expensive (126); see also Crossan and Reed, *Excavating Jesus* 62-70; E. P. Sanders, 'Jesus' Galilee', in I. Dunderberg et al., eds., *Fair Play: Diversity and Conflicts in Early Christianity,* H. Räisänen FS (Leiden: Brill, 2002) 3-41 (here 29-34, 37-39). Acknowledging some dispute on the dating of the theatre in a private conversation at the SBL meeting in Denver, Colorado (November, 2001), Reed continued to maintain that it was probably not constructed till some decades after Jesus and Antipas. We should remember, however, that excavation of Sepphoris is incomplete and that it has been possible to excavate only a small part of Tiberias. On Jerusalem see Charlesworth, *Jesus* ch. 5.

199. Reed, *Archaeology* 146-48.

burial in *kochim* shafted tombs with ossuaries).[200] The conclusion that Sepphoris contained a predominantly Jewish and devout Jewish population is hard to avoid.[201]

All this tells against the Cynic hypothesis regarding Galilee and Sepphoris in particular. Sepphoris's 'thin veneer of cosmopolitan culture' was hardly conducive to Cynic philosophers:[202] and for their presence in Galilee there is no evidence whatsoever.[203] Of course the hypothesis that Jesus was influenced by Cynicism has been built primarily on the Q material.[204] But the attempt to restrict a Greek document like Q (even Q[1]) to Galilee ignores the evidence that Jesus' sayings were much more widely known.[205] And whether the Q teachings presuppose what Gerald Downing repeatedly insists is 'distinctively Cynic' influence,[206] rather than, say, a prophetic lifestyle which echoes that of Elijah and a prophetic critique of rich oppressors which echoes many oracles of the classical prophets, is a question to which we shall have to return.[207] For the present, however, it is important to observe that the historical context envisaged to explain Jesus' alleged indebtedness to Cynicism is poorly supported by what we know of that context.

The relationships predicated between Sepphoris and its surrounding villages (including Nazareth) are more difficult to assess. Horsley disputes with those who assume the traditional European pattern of market towns serving as

200. Reed, *Archaeology* 84, 127-28, 134; Crossan and Reed, *Excavating Jesus* 165-72; similarly Freyne, 'Jesus and Urban Culture' 191; M. Chancey, 'The Cultural Milieu of Ancient Sepphoris', *NTS* 47 (2001) 127-45.

201. Similarly Meyers, 'Roman Sepphoris': archaeological excavations 'point to a Torah-true population, judging by the number of ritual baths *(miqva'ot)* in houses and by the strict practice of burial outside the city precincts' (325). Reed adds that 'the coins and inscriptions from Sepphoris verify that Jews ranked in the highest civic circles in the first century' (*Archaeology* 134, referring back to the modest data on 121-22).

202. Horsley, *Archaeology* 59, 179-80; similarly Reed, *Archaeology* 218.

203. As Downing readily acknowledges (*Cynics* 146-47). Crossan's 'peasant Jewish Cynic' 'designates an unattested hybrid unlikely to be recognized as such in first-century Galilee or Judea' (J. W. Marshall, 'The Gospel of Thomas and the Cynic Jesus', in Arnal and Desjardins, eds., *Whose Historical Jesus?* 37-60 [here 60]). Further critique in D. E. Aune, 'Jesus and Cynics in First-Century Palestine: Some Critical Considerations', in Charlesworth and Johns, eds., *Hillel and Jesus* 176-92; and above chapter 7 n. 71.

204. Kloppenborg Verbin's attempt to reexpress the hypothesis in terms of a 'cynic-like' rather than Cynic Q (above chapter 7 n. 71) appears somewhat disingenuous, since the issue presumably is not simply one of analogy but of genealogy, that is, whether Cynic influence explains features of Q which otherwise would be less plausibly explained.

205. Koester, 'Sayings of Q' 138-40.

206. Downing, *Cynics* 143, 150, 152, 153, 160, 161.

207. Cf. Freyne, 'Jesus and Urban Culture' 197-98. Mack sees the Cynics 'as the Greek analogue to the Hebrew prophets' (*Lost Gospel* 114).

focal points for buying and selling rural produce.[208] On the contrary, he argues, the Galilean villages were basically self-sufficient; any surplus produce would go in taxes and tithes, which were paid/collected in kind from the threshing floors; the local economy was not heavily monetized.[209] And the picture of villagers flocking into Sepphoris ignores the hostility with which Sepphoris was viewed in the Galilean villages, as illustrated most dramatically by the devastation of Sepphoris in the revolt of 66 CE, 'the Galileans . . . venting their hatred on one of the cities which they detested' (Josephus, *Life* 375).[210] Perhaps the silence of the Jesus tradition as to any contact of Jesus with Sepphoris is eloquent after all!

On the other hand, Reed points out that Nazareth was bound to be oriented more to Sepphoris than to the south: Nazareth was one of the southernmost villages in Galilee; travel south would encounter the steep incline of the south side of the Nazareth ridge, and so would probably have been via Sepphoris and Tiberias, to skirt Samaria as far as possible; and the lines of trade did not run southward from the Nazareth ridge.[211] Moreover, the rebuilding of Sepphoris and maintenance of it as an administrative centre would presumably have required tax revenue and a shift in agricultural patterns in lower Galilee (to feed its population).[212] The wine installations, olive presses, threshing floors, and millstones found round and even inside Sepphoris indicate that it must have served as some kind of local centre.[213] And if the population as a whole was less Hellenized and more Jewish than has often been claimed, there would be less reason for devout Jewish villagers to bypass or avoid it.

In any case, the existence of some tension between city and village need not be doubted. One can readily surmise that there will always be a tendency towards friction between local bureaucrats and administrators on the one hand and the producers of agricultural and other material goods on the other. All the more so if much of the good land close by a city like Sepphoris (particularly the Beth

---

208. 'Villagers go to town to sell produce, both to buy goods and to acquire cash to pay taxes and tolls. Market gossip filters back' (Downing, *Cynics* 149); Horsley, *Galilee* 203 and n. 6, quotes similar assumptions of a European 'market' economy made by M. Goodman, *State and Society in Roman Galilee, AD 132-212* (Totowa: Rowman and Allanheld, 1983) 54-60; and Z. Safrai, *The Economy of Roman Palestine* (London: Routledge, 1994).

209. Horsley, *Galilee* 176-81, 202-207; also *Archaeology* 70-76, 83-85.

210. Horsley, *Archaeology* 118-30; in critique particularly of D. Edwards, 'The Socio-Economic and Cultural Ethos of the Lower Galilee in the First Century: Implications for the Nascent Jesus Movement', in Levine, ed., *Galilee* 53-73.

211. Reed, *Archaeology* 115-17; Freyne, 'Archaeology' 169-70, 171-73.

212. See also Freyne, 'Jesus and Urban Culture' 191-93. Both Freyne (191-92) and Reed (*Archaeology* 126) observe that Sepphoris's pottery and stone storage jars came from Galilean villages.

213. Reed, *Archaeology* 83-89.

Netofah valley) was being steadily acquired by Herod's elite.[214] That such tensions did indeed exist between Sepphoris and *inter alia* Nazareth is strongly suggested by the social situations reflected in many of Jesus' parables — wealthy estate owners, resentment against absentee landlords, exploitative stewards of estates, family feuds over inheritance, debt, day labourers (forced to sell off family patrimony because of debt?), and so on.[215]

How all this bears on Jesus and his own relationship with Sepphoris and Tiberias remains unclear. The silence of the Jesus tradition in regard to both is still surprising and somewhat ominous. It is another question to which we must return (§9.9e).

9.7. Synagogues and Pharisees in Galilee?

Two other topics which have occasioned much dispute and which are of direct relevance to our evaluation of the traditions regarding Jesus deserve some attention.

a. Galilean Synagogues/Assemblies

The Gospels refer a number of times to *synagōgai*,[216] and particularly speak of Jesus quite regularly teaching/preaching in Galilean *synagōgai*.[217] In every case the term is usually translated, not surprisingly, as 'synagogues'. But here again the translation rests on a number of unexamined assumptions: particularly that there were buildings ('synagogues') at the time of Jesus which were dedicated places of worship, for Torah reading and prayer. A common linked assumption is that the synagogue was a power base for Pharisees in some degree over against the Temple authorities.[218] The translation itself, 'synagogue', can thus constitute

214. Details briefly reviewed in G. Theissen, '"We Have Left Everything . . ." (Mark 10:28): Discipleship and Social Uprooting in the Jewish-Palestinian Society of the First Century', *Social Reality* 60-93 (here 89-91).

215. Freyne, 'Jesus and Urban Culture' 195-96, 205-206. See further Freyne's *Galilee, Jesus and the Gospels* (Dublin: Gill and Macmillan, 1988).

216. Note particularly reference to 'the best seats in the synagogues' (Mark 12.39 pars.; Luke 11.43) and being beaten/flogged in synagogues (Mark 13.9/Matt. 10.17).

217. Matt. 4.23/Mark 1.39/Luke 4.44; Matt. 9.35; Matt. 13.54/Mark 6.2/Luke 4.16; Luke 4.15; Luke 6.6; 13.10; John 6.59.

218. The common view of the time (mid-1970s) is voiced by Schillebeeckx ('the synagogues were certainly supervised by "the Scribes of the Pharisees"' — *Jesus* 232), and Goppelt ('Pharisaic-Rabbinic Judaism . . . had gained control of the synagogue in Jesus' day' — *Theology* 1.88).

evidence of Jesus' attachment to the synagogue as attesting his own Jewishness and initial willingness to work with the local religious authorities.

In the past twenty years, however, such assumptions have come under serious challenge.[219] The basic problem is that archaeology has failed to turn up clear evidence which would confirm the basis for such a historical reconstruction.[220] In consequence, a substantial body of opinion has emerged that *synagōgē* in the Gospels should be translated not as 'synagogue', precisely because of the (now traditional) implications of that term, but as 'assembly' or 'congregation' (the word's more literal meaning).[221] There is certainly something in this.

219. The most recent discussions on the subject are R. Hachlili, 'The Origin of the Synagogue: A Re-Assessment', *JSJ* 28 (1997) 34-47; H. C. Kee and L. H. Cohick, eds., *Evolution of the Synagogue: Problems and Progress* (Harrisburg: Trinity, 1999), particularly the essays by Kee, 'Defining the First-Century CE Synagogue' (7-26, reprinted from *NTS* 41 [1995] 481-500), in debate with J. F. Strange, 'Ancient Texts, Archaeology as Text, and the Problem of the First-Century Synagogue' (27-45), and R. H. Horsley, 'Synagogues in Galilee and the Gospels' (46-69, a reworking of ch. 10 of his *Galilee* and ch. 6 of his *Archaeology*); S. Fine, ed., *Jews, Christians, and Polytheists in the Ancient Synagogue: Cultural Interaction during the Greco-Roman Period* (London: Routledge, 1999), particularly the essays by E. P. Sanders, 'Common Judaism and the Synagogue in the First Century' (1-17), and P. W. van der Horst, 'Was the Synagogue a Place of Sabbath Worship before 70 CE?' (18-43). H. A. McKay, 'Ancient Synagogues: The Continuing Dialectic between Two Major Views', *Currents in Research: Biblical Studies* 6 (1998) 103-142 reviews the data and debate, with extensive bibliography.

220. 'Only three synagogue buildings within Israel/Palestine have been securely dated to the Second Temple period: Gamla, Masada, and Herodium' (E. M. Meyers, 'Synagogue', *ABD* 6.251-60 [here 255]; see further S. Fine and E. M. Meyers, 'Synagogues', *OEANE* 5.118-22). In addition, a structure at Magdala or Migdal (on the west shore of Galilee) is sometimes included, though with dimensions of less than sixty square metres it might at best be described as a 'mini-synagogue' (M. J. Chiat, 'First-Century Synagogue Architecture: Methodological Problems', in J. Gutmann, ed., *Ancient Synagogues: The State of Research* [BJS 22; Chico: Scholars, 1981] 49-60 [floor plans 112]; R. Hachlili, 'Early Jewish Art and Architecture', *ABD* 1.447-54 [here 449-50, floor plans 449]; Strange, 'Ancient Texts' 35-45; though on Magdala see M. Avian, 'Magdala', *OEANE* 3.399). Magdala would be the only example in Galilee, though Gamla, like Bethsaida technically in Herod Philip's territory, was evidently in close communication with Galilee proper. But see also Horsley, *Archaeology* ch. 6 and those cited by him on 221 nn. 2-3. On the synagogue in Capernaum, see below (n. 309). Kee has argued strenuously against a pre-70 date for the famous 'Theodotus inscription' from Jerusalem ('The Transformation of the Synagogue after 70 CE', *NTS* 36 [1990] 1-24; also 'Defining'); but see R. Riesner, 'Synagogues in Jerusalem', in R. Bauckham, ed., *The Book of Acts in Its Palestinian Setting* (Grand Rapids: Eerdmans, 1995) 179-210 (here 192-200); J. S. Kloppenborg Verbin, 'Dating Theodotus (*CIJ* II 1404)', *JJS* 51 (2000) 243-80.

221. Kee illustrates the (for him) false assumption which has hitherto been made regarding the meaning of *synagōgē* by reference to Josephus, *Ant.* 19.305, where the Greek actually speaks of the Jews prevented from 'being' *(einai)* a *synagōgē* and of 'the place of the *synagōgē*' *(en tō tēs synagōgēs topō)*, where the obvious sense of 'assembly' is obscured by the Loeb translation ('Defining' 13). It is worth noting that the equivalent word in Christian circles,

Synagōgē is a term which denotes in the first place the village gathering or town assembly, with the *archisynagōgos* more accurately described as 'leader of the assembly', the 'head-man', rather than 'ruler of the synagogue'.[222] One of the purposes of such gatherings would no doubt have been to hear Torah read and expounded,[223] usually by priest or elder but others could contribute,[224] on Sabbaths[225] and feast days, and presumably also to say prayers.[226] But no doubt assemblies would also be called to discuss the community's affairs, including the hammering out of disputes and local administration of justice.[227]

But where would such assemblies have met? Certainly we must accept the likelihood that in some places the gatherings would have taken place in a large

---

ekklēsia, had similar force, as is evident in 1 Cor. 11.18, 'when you come together in assembly' (*sunerchomenōn humōn en ekklēsia* — not 'in the church'). In the LXX *synagōgē* and *ekklēsia* are both used to translate the Hebrew *qahal,* denoting the 'assembly or congregation' of Israel (W. Schrage, *'synagōgē', TDNT* 7.798-852 [here 802]). See further Schürer, *History* 2.429-31 (nn. 12-14).

222. *Archisynagōgos* was a common name for the officer in charge of a Hellenistic association *(synagōgē);* see, e.g., R. E. Oster, 'Supposed Anachronism in Luke-Acts' Use of *synagōgē:* A Rejoinder to H. C. Kee', *NTS* 39 (1993) 178-208 (here 202-204); see also Horsley, *Galilee* 223-33; also *Archaeology* 145-51; also 'Synagogues' 48-61.

223. This is explicitly stated by Philo, *Som.* 2.127 ('will you sit in your assemblies [*synagōgiois*] . . . and read in security your sacred books, expounding any obscure point and in leisurely comfort discussing at length your ancestral philosophy?'); similarly *Mos.* 2.216; *Legat.* 156-57 (Kee, 'Defining' 13-14). See also *CIJ* 2.1404 (the Theodotus inscription — above n. 220); and further A. Runesson, *The Origins of the Synagogue: A Socio-Historical Study* (ConBNT 37; Stockholm: Almqvist and Wiksell, 2001) chs. 3-4.

224. Eusebius quotes Philo's otherwise lost *Hypothetica* 7.12-13: The Jews 'assemble in the same place on these seventh days . . . (and) some priest or one of the elders reads the holy laws to them and expounds them point by point' (*Praep. evang.* 8.7, 11-13). See also Sanders, *Jewish Law* 78-81; *Judaism* 199-202.

225. Moses 'appointed the Law to be the most excellent and necessary form of instruction, ordaining . . . that every week men should desert their other occupations and assemble to listen to the Law and to obtain a thorough and accurate knowledge of it' (Josephus, *Ap.* 2.175).

226. The obvious conclusion to draw from the use of *proseuchē* ('prayer') in the extended sense of 'prayer house' by Philo and Josephus. Thus Philo speaks of 'many' *proseuchas* 'in each section of the city' of Alexandria (*Legat.* 132, 134, 137-38) and regarded such places as 'all holy' *(panieros)* (*Legat.* 191); see further *Flacc.* 41-49. In Josephus see *Ant.* 14.258 and references in n. 230 below. For epigraphical references to 'prayer houses' see Schürer, *History* 2.425-26 n. 5, 439-40 n. 61; *NDIEC* 3.121-22. Gutmann is over-fussy in warning against the assumption that *proseuchē* is simply another word for 'synagogue' (*Ancient Synagogues* 3). See further van der Horst, 'Synagogue' 23-37, in critique of H. McKay, *Sabbath and Synagogue: The Question of Sabbath Worship in Ancient Judaism* (Leiden: Brill, 1994).

227. See also L. I. Levine, 'The Second Temple Synagogue: The Formative Years', in L. I. Levine, ed., *The Synagogue in Late Antiquity* (Philadelphia: Fortress, 1987) 7-31; and further *The Ancient Synagogue: The First Thousand Years* (New Haven: Yale University, 2000).

house,[228] as did the earliest Christian gatherings.[229] At the same time, there is no good reason to discount the literary evidence that there were buildings evidently set aside for communal gatherings, and called either 'synagogues' or 'prayer houses'.[230] And the floor plans of the buildings most securely identified as 'synagogues', with rows of benches along one or more of the walls, are hardly what we would expect for private dwellings.[231] These were no doubt buildings used for town assemblies, but probably also as a school room[232] and for social/festive events — in modern parlance not so much the village church as the village hall. This correlates well with what we envisaged earlier (§8.6a), and we can quite appropriately imagine the retelling of stories about and teaching of Jesus in such gatherings, whether in the village assembly itself or in gatherings of Jesus' own followers.[233] The difference, like the difference between 'church' = people and

228. The 'apparent contradiction', between the dearth of early Second Temple synagogue remains and the large number of references to synagogues in ancient literary sources, 'disappears if we assume that, in the first centuries, large private houses were used as places of worship alongside other buildings that came to be utilized for worship and other matters requiring public assembly' (Meyers, *ABD* 6.255); *m. Ned.* 9.2 talks of a house being made into a synagogue. Similarly Hachlili, 'Early Jewish Art', 449-50; Riesner, 'Synagogues in Jerusalem' 186. Crossan and Reed conclude: 'There certainly were *synagogues* . . . in the villages of Galilee at the time of Jesus, *gatherings* of Jews for communal and religious purposes, but who knows what their architectural form looked like?' (*Excavating Jesus* 26).

229. Acts 2.46; 12.12; 18.7; Rom. 16.5; 1 Cor. 16.19; Col. 4.15.

230. Philo, *Prob.* 81 ('sacred places which they call synagogues'); *Flacc.* 48 ('sacred buildings'); Luke 7.5 (the centurion 'built the synagogue for us'); Acts 18.7; Josephus, *War* 2.285, 289; 7.44. Josephus also recalls a general assembly *(sunagontai pantes)* in Tiberias in the prayer house *(proseuchē)*, a very large house or building *(megiston oikēma)* (*Life* 277; also 280, 293). A first-century CE inscription from Berenike (Libya) uses the term *synagōgē* twice, once in the sense 'congregation', the other in the sense 'building' (G. Lüdertz, *Corpus jüdischer Zeugnisse aus der Cyrenaika* [Wiesbaden: Reichert, 1983] no. 72; conveniently in Oster, 'Anachronism' 187-88; Oster 186 lists the range of terms used in inscriptions and papyri as well as Philo and Josephus). See also Schürer, *History* 2.439-40. Kee is much too resolute in his unwillingness to recognize that a building may be referred to in some of the NT texts other than Luke 7.5 ('Defining' 14-20); see particularly Oster's rejoinder to Kee ('Anachronism', here 194-97). Martin Hengel's argument is plausible that the term 'synagogue' came to be used for the place of assembly, not just the assembly itself, during the first century CE — 'Proseuche und Synagoge. Jüdische Gemeinde, Gotteshaus und Gottesdienst in der Diaspora und in Palästina' (1971), *Judaica et Hellenistica: Kleine Schriften I* 171-95.

231. See n. 220. Sanders is particularly critical of Kee's arguments (*Jewish Law* 77-78, 341-43 n. 29; *Judaism* 198-202; 'Common Judaism and the Synagogue'); also K. Atkinson, 'On Further Defining the First-Century CE Synagogue: Fact or Fiction? A Rejoinder to H. C. Kee', *NTS* 43 (1997) 491-502 (here particularly 499-501).

232. Philo calls the meeting house *didaskaleion,* that is, 'place of teaching' (*Mos.* 2.216; *Spec. Leg.* 2.62; also *Legat.* 312). See also Schürer, *History* 2.417-22.

233. Such gatherings are probably already indicated in the various references to the as-

'church' = building, may seem insubstantial, but it may also involve a significant shift in orientation for some and is another reminder of the need for historians of Jesus to jerk themselves consciously out of their contemporary perspective in order to gain a more soundly based historical perspective.

b. Pharisees in Galilee?

The dispute on whether Pharisees were resident or active in Galilee during this period also bears on the subject. It is true that the record of great Torah scholars in Galilee is minimal.[234] But there is a tradition which links Johanan ben Zakkai with the Galilean town of Arav (although Johanan is never referred to as a Pharisee).[235] And it is quite probable that some Pharisees at least accepted an obligation to live in the Galilee (which they would certainly have regarded as part of the land promised to Abraham) in order to make their central principles and halakhic rulings available throughout the holy land.[236]

This would certainly accord with the testimony of the Gospels, and though it is clear enough that a good number of references to Pharisees have been inserted into the recollections of Jesus' mission,[237] other evidence seems more substantial. In particular, the tradition of Mark 12.38-39 that the scribes (Pharisees in Matt. 23.6/Luke 11.43) had a reputation of expecting the best seats in the (village/local) assemblies, must reflect a pre-70 situation.[238] And the q/Q complaints

semblies of a region or locality ('their assemblies') in the Synoptics (Mark 1.39; Matt. 4.23; 9.35; 10.17; 12.9; 13.54; Luke 4.15), probably implying that the followers of Jesus had their own (separate) assemblies.

234. See my 'Pharisees, Sinners, and Jesus' 77-79.

235. Arav is not far from Sepphoris, and so also from Nazareth. Neusner dates Johanan's sojourn there between 20 and 40 CE (J. Neusner, *A Life of Rabban Yohanan ben Zakkai* [Leiden: Brill, ²1970] 47-53). See Freyne, *Galilee* 315-16.

236. Cf. the conclusions of Goodman, 'Galilean Judaism' 606. The otherwise surprising Matt. 23.15 suggests a history of some such sense of obligation on the part of some Pharisees to ensure an appropriate level of law observance on the part of those who claimed Israelite ancestry. Such an interpretation is certainly consistent with Josephus' account of Eleazar in *Ant.* 20.43-45 and with the 'Pharisaic tendency' (cf. Acts 15.5) within the earliest Judean churches, as attested in Gal. 2.4, 12-13 and in subsequent opposition to Paul's Gentile mission.

237. Details in my 'The Question of Antisemitism in the New Testament Writings of the Period', in J. D. G. Dunn, ed., *Jews and Christians: The Parting of the Ways AD 70 to 135* (Tübingen: Mohr Siebeck, 1992) 177-211 (tabulated 205).

238. Freyne, *Galilee* 319-22. Horsley observes that the much fuller role attributed to the Pharisees in the Gospels 'would have no credibility . . . unless they did, historically, on occasion at least, appear outside of their focus of operations in Jerusalem' and refers particularly to the tradition of Luke 11.43 and Mark 12.38-39 (*Galilee* 150).

against Pharisees and lawyers in reference to tithing and washing of cups (Matt. 23.23, 25/Luke 11.42, 39) presume local knowledge on the part of the (Galilean?) audiences of Pharisaic practices.[239] Luke's indication that there were those in Galilee who followed the Pharisees' way of life and who were friendly towards Jesus should not be wholly discounted (especially Luke 13.31). And, given the likelihood that the Pharisees were principally located in Judea, the testimony of Mark 7.1, that Pharisees and some scribes came down from Jerusalem to take stock of what Jesus was about, has a very plausible ring.[240] Nor should we forget that Paul's conversion while on some mission to Damascus as a Pharisee at least confirms that there were Pharisees in the 30s who saw themselves as responsible — or were authorized by the Jerusalem hierarchy, as Luke has it (Acts 9.1-2) — to monitor Torah fidelity even beyond the promised land (cf. Gal. 2.12).

None of this, however, bolsters the other assumption mentioned at the beginning of §9.7a, that Pharisees were actively involved in developing and ordering the synagogue.[241] There is no evidence for this assumption whatsoever.[242] The natural inference is rather that such gatherings were presided over by the local priest(s) or village elders, of whom one would have been chosen to serve as head/president *(archisynagōgos)*.[243] It was only subsequently, when rabbinic Judaism had become more established, that is, from the third century CE onwards, that rabbis became significantly involved in synagogue affairs and the traditional picture of Pharisees/rabbis controlling the synagogue even begins to become re-

239. Kloppenborg Verbin, *Excavating Q* 174.

240. It does not follow that such Pharisees acted for the priestly aristocracy in this, as Saldarini *(Pharisees* 296) and Horsley *(Galilee* 151-52) maintain. In their own view the Pharisees would presumably be representing the interests of Israel and Torah — not the same thing. Sanders's doubts on the question reflect his vigorous polemic against the view that the Pharisees 'ran' Judaism *(Jesus and Judaism* 265; *Jewish Law* 79-81; *Judaism* 388-402; see further below §17.2).

241. See, e.g., Gutmann: 'the synagogue, one of the unique Pharisaic institutions' *(Ancient Synagogues* 4); Hengel and Deines, 'Sanders' Judaism' 32-33; Horsley refers to Kee and Freyne *(Galilee* 340 n. 29). See also above, n. 218.

242. The traditions referred to above, that the Pharisees loved the *prōtokathedrias* ('places of honour, best seats') in the synagogue (Mark 12.38-39/Luke 20.46; Matt. 23.6/Luke 11.43), indicate desire for respect and honour, not recognized status in the organisation of the assembly. On 'Moses' seat' see S. J. D. Cohen, 'Were Pharisees and Rabbis the Leaders of Communal Prayer and Torah Study in Antiquity?', in Kee, ed., *Evolution of the Synagogue* 89-105 (here 93-96).

243. In citing the Theodotus inscription as proof that 'the synagogue was a thoroughly Pharisaic institution', Schaper ('Pharisees' 421-22), for example, ignores the fact that the one (Theodotus) who constructed the synagogue 'for the reading of the law and the teaching of the commandments' identifies himself as 'priest and *archisynagōgos*, son of an *archisynagōgos*, grandson of an *archisynagōgos*'.

alistic.[244] On the other hand, we have already noted that the attempt to de-politicise the Pharisees in the late Second Temple period pushes the evidence too far.[245] Given the observations in the preceding paragraph, the answer is probably that certain Pharisees periodically visited Galilean villages, that some at least were concerned by what they regarded as unacceptable slackness in Torah observance, and that they were generally well regarded by observant Jews,[246] though some at least engendered a degree of popular disdain by expecting undue recognition at sabbath assemblies and feast days and by a degree of overscrupulousness in their halakhoth. The relevance of such conclusions will become clear as we proceed.

9.8. The Political Context

In setting out the historical context we must remember, of course, that the land of Israel/Palestine was under Roman rule during the period of our interest. The Romans had conquered the territory under Pompey in 63 BCE, and established their rule most effectively through the client king Herod the Great (37-4 BCE). The united kingdom was then broken up among Herod's surviving sons, with Herod Antipas being given Galilee and Perea. Judea, after a spell under the unpopular Archelaus (4 BCE–6 CE), reverted to direct rule, which persisted from 6 CE till the outbreak of the revolt in 66 CE, apart from the brief interlude of Herod Agrippa (41-44).[247]

So long as taxes were paid and there was no undue unrest, the ruling hand of Rome was fairly light. It was most obvious in the capital, Jerusalem, where control was maintained over the national leadership of the High Priest, at least to the extent that the Romans retained the power to appoint and dismiss the one holding that office (Josephus, *Ant.* 18.34-35).[248] The Romans also retained in

244. S. J. D. Cohen, 'The Place of the Rabbi in Jewish Society of the Second Century', in Levine, ed., *Galilee* 157-73; also 'Were Pharisees and Rabbis the Leaders' 89-105; L. I. Levine, 'The Sages and the Synagogue in Late Antiquity: The Evidence of the Galilee', in Levine, ed., *Galilee* 201-22: 'throughout antiquity, and well into the Middle Ages, the rabbis never played an official role *per se* in the synagogue. They were not employees of the institution. . . . Moreover, the ancient synagogue was primarily a local institution. It was built by local donors, governed by a local body, and its practices and proclivities reflected local tastes' (212). Similarly Horsley, *Galilee* 233-35; also *Archaeology* 151-53; 'Synagogues' 61-64.

245. See above §9.3a.

246. Josephus no doubt overstates the regard in which the Pharisees were held (particularly *Ant.* 18.15), but overstatement is not *creatio ex nihilo*. See also Sanders, *Judaism* 402-404.

247. Full details in Schürer, *History* vol. 1. The fullest treatment of Herod Antipas is still H. W. Hoehner, *Herod Antipas* (SNTSMS 17; Cambridge: Cambridge University, 1972).

248. Schürer, *History* 1.377.

their own hands the power of capital punishment, though infringement of the Temple sanctuary was agreed to merit the death penalty.[249] During the years of direct rule there would have been a garrison stationed in Jerusalem (a cohort of perhaps only 500 men), and the prefect/procurator made a point of being present in person for major feasts, though he normally resided at Caesarea on the coast. But it is a striking fact that for most of the first half-century CE the governor of Judea may have had only some 3,000 auxiliary troops to uphold law and order, with small garrisons stationed in cities like Jericho and Ascalon, and the main body of the (three or four) legions retained in Syria (primarily for defence of the eastern frontier).[250] That hardly suggests a mounting 'spiral of violence' (Horsley) in the period of Jesus' mission.[251] These will be matters which we can clarify further later to the extent that it is necessary in discussing Jesus' final days, trial and execution in Jerusalem.[252]

For Galilee during the whole of Jesus' life there the fact of Roman rule would be, for the most part, even less obtrusive. As Sanders has repeatedly reminded us, the Romans were *not* an army of occupation. The typically ruthless Roman suppression of the uprising after Herod (the Great)'s death (4 BCE) would no doubt have formed a major scar on the local consciousness for the generation following. According to Josephus, the Galilean insurgents had been routed, Sepphoris captured and burnt, and its inhabitants enslaved (*War.* 2.56; *Ant.* 17.289).[253] And the fact that major cities were named in honour of the emperor and his family (Tiberias, Caesarea Maritima, Caesarea Philippi, Bethsaida Julias) would have been a constant reminder of the political realities. But otherwise,

---

249. Schürer, *History* 1.367-72; 2.219-23.

250. Schürer, *History* 1.361-67; E. M. Smallwood, *The Jews under Roman Rule from Pompey to Diocletian* (Leiden: Brill, 1976) 146-47. Helen Bond notes that during the first six years of Pilate's prefecture (26-32), that is, the period of Jesus' activity, there was no Syrian legate in residence to oversee affairs in Palestine (*Pontius Pilate in History and Interpretation* [SNTSMS 100; Cambridge: Cambridge University, 1998] 14).

251. The image is misleading; Horsley explicitly refutes the suggestion that Jewish society at the time of Jesus was a hotbed of violent revolution (*Jesus* 116; see also n. 264 below). Contrast the assumption of G. W. Buchanan, *Jesus: The King and His Kingdom* (Macon: Mercer University, 1984) that 'almost every year there was at least one guerrilla encounter with Rome in an attempt to evict the Romans from Jewish territory' (38-39, 142).

252. See further below §15.3a and §17.1e.

253. The excavations at Sepphoris have not so far unearthed any clear evidence of massive destruction in the early Roman period; Horsley therefore suggests that the Roman attack may have been directed against villages around Sepphoris (*Archaeology* 32). Either way it would have been a traumatic time for any young family. Does this provide a strengthening for the tradition that Jesus was born away from Nazareth, or, alternatively, some sort of historical basis for the tradition of Matt. 2.16?

during Antipas' rule all was relatively quiet.[254] Neither Sepphoris nor Tiberias was a garrison town.[255] This is the background reflected in the Gospels, with only religious and political figures of authority in view (priests, Pharisees, Herodians, 'leading men', Antipas 'that fox'). The centurion of Capernaum (Matt. 8.5-13/Luke 7.1-10) conceivably was in charge of a small garrison of Herod Antipas's forces (Capernaum being close to the border, the river Jordan, with Herod Philip's territory), though he may have been a mercenary or auxiliary, or could possibly even have retired to Capernaum.[256] And the saying about going the 'second mile' (Matt. 5.41) need imply only an occasional patrol or rotation or transfer of detachments through the territory.

The main political impact on the villages of Galilee, and on Jesus for most of his life, would have been in terms of taxes. That was why the Romans were in Palestine, and why rulers ruled territory — for the taxes they could levy on their subject peoples.[257] Galileans at the time of Jesus would have been subjected to two or three layers of taxation.[258] One was the tithes due to the priests (Neh. 10.35-39)[259] and the half-shekel temple tax,[260] probably amounting to at least fifteen percent of income.[261] The second was the levies (both land tax and custom tolls) instituted by Herod Antipas, not least to support his extensive build-

254. On this Freyne, *Galilee* ch. 6, Horsley, *Jesus* ch. 4 (also *Galilee* 259), and Reed, *Archaeology* 84, are agreed. See also U. Rappaport, 'How Anti-Roman Was the Galilee?', in Levine, ed., *Galilee* 95-102. Cf. Tacitus' report that 'under Tiberius (14-37 CE) all was quiet' (*Histories* 5.9). The incidents under Pilate were confined to Jerusalem (Josephus, *War* 2.169-77; *Ant.* 18.55-62); the episode mentioned in Luke 13.1-2 involving Galileans is impossible to evaluate satisfactorily as to either source or significance (Fitzmyer, *Luke* 1006-7); and Antipas's only military campaign, his unsuccessful war against the Nabateans under Aretas, took place in 36 CE. See also D. M. Rhoads, *Israel in Revolution, 6-74 CE* (Philadelphia: Fortress, 1976), conclusions 174-75; Sanders, *Judaism* 35-43; also 'Jesus' Galilee' particularly 6-13.

255. Contrast Chilton — a 'corrupt Roman outpost' (*Rabbi Jesus* 35).

256. It is quite unrealistic to envisage a Roman garrison stationed in Capernaum, that is, within the territory of a client ruler (Herod Antipas) (Reed, *Archaeology* 161-62); the legionary bathhouse excavated in the 1980s on the easternmost fringe of the town dates to the second century CE, when the territory was occupied by Roman forces (Reed 155-56; Crossan and Reed, *Excavating Jesus* 87-89). The border with Herod Philip's territory was insignificant in Roman eyes, the result of the subdivision of Herod the Great's kingdom on the latter's death.

257. Hence the census in Judea under Quirinius in 6 CE, to ascertain the taxation base. That it included Galilee is unlikely, since that was under the rule of Antipas; the revolt led by Judas 'the Galilean' in response to the census took place in Judea ('the Galilean' denoting region of origin not place of revolt). See further below chapter 11 n. 29.

258. See particularly Horsley, *Galilee* 139-44, 177-78, 217-19; Sanders, *Judaism* 146-69.

259. Referred to in Matt. 23.23/Luke 11.42; Luke 18.12.

260. Exod. 30.13; Matt. 17.24; Josephus, *Ant.* 18.312.

261. Sanders, *Judaism* 167; Horsley reckons over 20 percent (*Galilee* 217-18).

ing projects.[262] The third was the Roman tribute, reckoned at twelve and a half percent per year.[263] There is a dispute as to how heavy the tax burden was at the time of Jesus and whether it was increasing through the early decades of the first century.[264] Suffice it to say here that the total tax burden must have amounted in most years and in most cases to about one-third (or more) of all produce and income.[265] At such levels of taxation, subsistence farmers were always in danger of running into debt; smallholders would often have to sell out and become tenant farmers and day-labourers, or worse.[266] The pictures which the Gospels paint substantiate such probabilities,[267] but also indicate that the incidence of crushing poverty was not substantial.[268] Here again is valuable background for much of Jesus' teaching, to which we will return at various points.

In the light of all the data reviewed in this chapter we are now in a position to situate Jesus the Jew more clearly within his religious and local context.

262. The tolls collected at Capernaum (Mark 2.14 pars.), close to the frontier between Galilee and Herod Philip's territory across the Jordan, would have gone to Herod Antipas. According to Josephus the revenue from Galilee and Perea yielded an annual tribute of 200 talents (*Ant.* 17.318). See also Freyne, *Galilee* 191-92.

263. Sanders disputes that this was a separate tax: 'the produce tax *was* tribute' (*Judaism* 166). Perhaps more to the point, however, is the fact that some taxation (*kēnsos* — 'tax, poll-tax'/*phoros* — 'tribute') was perceived as paid to Caesar (Mark 12.14-17 pars.; Luke 23.2) and was probably thought of as distinct from tolls levied by Antipas for his own administration.

264. See particularly Sanders' debate in *Judaism* 157-69 with *inter alios* Horsley.

265. Sanders argues for under 28 percent in most years (*Judaism* 167); but does he give enough weight to the cost of Herod's building programmes (164-65) and to the fact that peasant productivity was the most sure and consistent basis for taxation? Much is guesswork, but a figure somewhere in the range from one-third to fifty percent is also canvassed (Hanson and Oakman, *Palestine* 113-16; Reed, *Archaeology* 86-87).

266. See also M. Goodman, *The Ruling Class of Judaea: The Origins of the Jewish Revolt against Rome, AD 66-70* (Cambridge: Cambridge University, 1987) ch. 3, particularly 55-68; and for the broader picture, Hanson and Oakman, *Palestine* 86-91 (on 'social banditry' during the period), 101-25, and for debate, G. Theissen, 'Jesus und die symbolpolitischen Konflikte seiner Zeit: Sozialgeschichtliche Aspekte der Jesusforschung', *EvT* 57 (1997) 378-400.

267. Particularly Matt. 20.1-7; but also Matt. 5.25-26/Luke 12.58-59; Matt. 5.42/Luke 6.30; Matt. 6.25-34/Luke 12.22-32; Matt. 6.12; 18.23-35; Luke 16.1-9. On the parable of the talents/pounds (Matt. 25.14-30/Luke 19.11-27) Kaylor remarks: 'The fate of the one-talent man mirrors the harshness of the system to those who do not fully participate in it according to the rules' (*Jesus* 162).

268. Mark 2.15-16 pars.; 12.39 pars.; Matt. 6.19-21; Luke 11.38; 12.16-21, 42; 14.12. Jesus was known for his good living (Matt. 11.19/Luke 7.34) and used the imagery of the banquet or feast quite often (Mark 2.19 pars.; Matt. 22.1-10/Luke 14.16-24; Matt. 25.1-12; Luke 12.36; 14.8).

9.9. An Outline of the Life and Mission of Jesus

It will be convenient to sketch an outline of Jesus' life and mission in the light of what we have learnt in chapter 9 before trying to fill in the outline in subsequent chapters.

a. The Chronological Framework

References in the Gospels to Herod the Great (37-4 BCE), to Herod Antipas (4 BCE–39 CE) and to the Roman prefect of Judea, Pilate (26-37 CE), enable us to locate Jesus and his mission with a fair degree of accuracy. Precision is not possible, but neither is it necessary. The key references are few, but consistent.

Jesus himself is generally reckoned to have been born some time before the death of Herod the Great in 4 BCE. A date between 6 BCE and 4 BCE would accord with such historical information as Matthew's birth narrative assumes (Matt. 2.16) and with the tradition of Luke 3.23 that Jesus was 'about thirty years of age' in the fifteenth year of Tiberius Caesar (Luke 3.1), reckoned as 27 or 28 CE. The date of his crucifixion is debated, with 14th Nisan 30 or 33 the chief alternatives, and the former gaining more support.[269] The former would also fit with the general impression that Jesus' mission must have extended over two or three years, given particularly the Fourth Gospel's mention of three Passovers (John 2.13; 6.4; 11.55).[270] Beyond that, the discussion quickly becomes bogged down, with the data affording no firm ground on which to advance.[271] We will have to be content with some degree of uncertainty, while recognizing that the range of uncertainty is unusually small for a historical figure from such a distant period.

b. Upbringing and Education

In the absence of firm evidence we can nevertheless make a number of valid generalisations.

---

269. The fullest summary review is by R. Riesner, *Paul's Early Period: Chronology, Mission Strategy, Theology* (Grand Rapids: Eerdmans, 1998) 3-10; add Meier, *Marginal Jew* 1.372-433; K. P. Donfried, 'Chronology, New Testament', *ABD* 1.1015-16; Theissen and Merz, *Historical Jesus* 151-61.

270. Chilton envisages a much longer period running in all to about fifteen years *(Rabbi Jesus)*.

271. The issue largely depends on whether we follow the Synoptic chronology for Jesus' death (the day after Passover) or the Johannine chronology (the day of Passover). But theological factors seem to be so much involved in both cases that it is difficult to make a clear choice. For a full discussion see Brown, *Death of the Messiah* 1350-78. See also below §9.9g; §17.1c.

Jesus' hometown is identified as a village in lower Galilee (Nazareth).[272] And Nazareth itself was probably a small and not very well-to-do village.[273] As a member of the family of a *tektōn* (Mark 6.3)[274] in a period of relative quiet we can envisage an upbringing which was not poverty-stricken but familiar with poverty.[275] The implication of Mark 6.3 is that Jesus was part of a large family (with four brothers and some sisters).[276]

Can we be more specific on Jesus' education? In particular, would he have been able to read and write? There is a strong presumption of widespread illiteracy among the lower social groups in the Roman Empire.[277] But as we

272. Mark 1.9; Matt. 21.11; John 1.45-46; Acts 10.38; he was known as 'Jesus the Nazarene' *(Nazarēnos),* that is, 'Jesus of/from Nazareth' (Mark 1.24/Luke 4.34; Mark 10.47; 14.67; 16.6; Luke 24.19). That *Nazōraios* was understood as a variant of *Nazarēnos* is clear (Matt. 26.71; Luke 18.37; John 18.5, 7; 19.19; Acts 2.22; 3.6; 4.10; 6.14; 22.8; 24.5; 26.9), despite the problems of deriving the form from *Nazaret(h)* (see, e.g., BAGD/BDAG, *Nazōraios;* H. Kuhli, *'Nazarēnos, Nazōraios', EDNT* 2.454-56). The suggestion that *Nazōraios* should be seen as an alternative form for *naziraios* (Nazirite) runs counter to the clear memory that Jesus' mission was not ascetic in character (Mark 2.19 pars.; Matt. 11.18-19/Luke 7.33-34) *(pace* K. Berger, 'Jesus als Nasoräer/Nasiräer', *NovT* 38 [1996] 323-35). Stegemann suggests that the Baptist's followers were called somewhat derisively, 'the Preservers' *(nasraya),* giving the Greek *nazarēnoi* or *nazōraioi,* indicating, therefore, that Jesus came from the circle of the Baptist *(Library* 219).

273. Reed reckons a population of less than 400 *(Archaeology* 131-32), even though, unlike Capernaum, later and modern building largely obscures the site. The absence of paved streets, public structures and inscriptions, and fine pottery, together with the discovery of few coins, suggests a poor or at best modest environment. Similarly Crossan and Reed, *Excavating Jesus* 31-36.

274. A term defined by Bauer as a 'carpenter, wood-worker, builder' (BAGD, *tektōn),* 'one who constructs, builder, carpenter' (BDAG); see particularly D. E. Oakman, *Jesus and the Economic Questions of His Day* (Lewiston: Edwin Mellen, 1986) 176-82; also Meier, *Marginal Jew* 1.280-81 ('woodworker'); Gnilka, *Jesus of Nazareth* 69.

275. See further Meier, *Marginal Jew* 1.278-85, who also observes that Jesus is never described as 'poor' (3.620); D. A. Fiensy, 'Jesus' Socioeconomic Background', in Charlesworth and Johns, eds., *Hillel and Jesus* 225-55. Contrast Buchanan, who thinks Jesus came from a wealthy family *(Jesus* 240); see also chapter 11 n. 62 below.

276. On Jesus' immediate family and the likelihood that Jesus' brothers and sisters were his true siblings see Meier, *Marginal Jew* 1.316-32; also 'On Retrojecting Later Questions from Later Texts: A Reply to Richard Bauckham', *CBQ* 59 (1997) 511-27. Further background information in S. Guijarro, 'The Family in First-Century Galilee', in H. Moxnes, ed., *Constructing Early Christian Families* (London: Routledge, 1997) 42-65.

277. E.g., both Horsley (in Horsley and Draper, *Whoever* 125-27) and Kloppenborg Verbin *(Excavating Q* 166-68) note recent estimates of less than 10% literacy in the Roman Empire under the principate, falling to perhaps as low as 3% literacy in Roman Palestine (citing particularly W. V. Harris, *Ancient Literacy* [Cambridge: Harvard University, 1989], and M. Bar-Ilan, 'Illiteracy in the Land of Israel in the First Centuries CE', in S. Fishbane and S. Schoenfeld, *Essays in the Social Scientific Study of Judaism and Jewish Society* [Hoboken: Ktav, 1992] 46-61). See also J. Dewey, 'Textuality in an Oral Culture: A Survey of the Pauline

have seen, Second Temple Judaism put a great emphasis on the study of Torah. The writing prophets could already assume a reading and writing public.[278] According to Josephus (*Ap.* 2.204), it was expected that children should be taught to read *(grammata paideuein)*.[279] And the *Testament of Levi* similarly sets forth the ideal of the father teaching his children their letters, so that they may 'unceasingly read the Law of God' (*T. Levi* 13.2). Consequently, even a Galilean villager (of some ability) might well have learned to read.[280] Jesus' quite widely attested challenge, 'Have you not read?',[281] probably presupposes his own reading ability.[282] And alongside the implication of considerable dependence on scribes,[283] we should note that the parable of the dishonest steward assumes a widespread if basic ability to write (Luke 16.6-7).[284] Moreover,

---

Traditions', in Dewey, ed., *Orality and Textuality* 37-65 (here 37-47). C. Hezser, *Jewish Literacy in Roman Palestine* (Tübingen: Mohr Siebeck, 2001) concludes that average Jewish literacy in the first century was more likely lower than the average Roman rate (496-97).

278. Riesner cites Isa. 8.1; 10.19; 29.11-12; 30.8; Hab. 2.2-3; Isa. 28.9-10 as reflecting the child's effort to learn letters by repeatedly speaking them out aloud (*Jesus als Lehrer* 112-15, 190-93); but too much should not be made of texts like *m. Yad.* 3.2-5 or of the evidence of widespread use, e.g., of phylacteries.

279. *Pace* Horsley (n. 277 above) more than 'public oral recitation' seems to be in view; see also A. Demsky, 'Literacy', *OEANE* 3.368. But Jacobson goes much too far in the opposite direction when he asserts that 'Palestine in Jesus' day was not an oral culture. It was in fact a remarkably literate society with a strong orientation to texts' (*First Gospel* 10).

280. Riesner marshalls what evidence there is in favour of an elementary/primary school functioning in Nazareth at the time of Jesus (*Jesus als Lehrer* 228-32). It is unclear how much weight can be put on Luke 4.16-21, since it appears to be an elaboration of the brief Markan account (6.1-6), which contains no reference to Jesus reading. Luke does tend to transpose his account into Hellenistic idiom, but it may still be significant that Luke could assume that Jesus was able to read. In John 7.15 surprise is expressed that Jesus does 'know letters' *(grammata oiden)* despite lack of formal education. But this may be no more than the ruling elite's contempt for the uncouth northerner. Similarly with the description of Peter and John in Acts 4.13 as *agrammatos,* 'unlettered' (see further in vol. 2). The portrayal of James, brother of Jesus, elsewhere in the NT implies a similar level of literacy (see again vol. 2). See also C. A. Evans, 'Context, Family and Formation', in Bockmuehl, ed., *Jesus* 15-21.

281. Mark 2.25 pars.; 12.10 pars.; 12.26 par.; Matt. 12.5; 19.4; 21.16; Luke 10.26. But Harris points out that the question is posed (in Matt. 12.3; 19.4; 21.42) to Pharisees or chief priests and scribes; '*they* presumably had read' (*Ancient Literacy* 281-82).

282. The great number and range of scrolls at Qumran presumably implies a substantial reading ability among its members.

283. See above §9.3c.

284. But we should observe Kloppenborg Verbin's caution: '"literacy" itself admits of various levels: signature-literacy; the ability to read simple contracts, invoices and receipts; full reading literacy; the ability to take dictation; and scribal literacy — the ability to compose' (*Excavating Q* 167). It is hardly clear that John 8.6, 8 indicates an ability to compose in writing; see, e.g., Meier, *Marginal Jew* 1.268-69.

the presence of Scripture scrolls is attested in Palestinian villages as early as 1 Macc. 1.56-57 and confirmed by Josephus for both Judea (*War* 2.229) and Galilee (*Life* 134).[285] So the picture painted in Luke 4.16-17 is in essence quite credible.[286]

Information on the languages spoken in Palestine at the time of Jesus steadily increases. There is no reason to question the very substantial consensus that Jesus gave at least the bulk of his teaching in Aramaic.[287] This is not to ignore the degree of penetration of the Greek language into first-century Palestine,[288] and the likelihood that Jesus knew at least some Greek and may indeed have spoken Greek on occasions.[289]

c. Jesus and Common Judaism

On the basis of earlier discussion, we can conclude meaningfully that a boy brought up in Nazareth in lower Galilee in the early years of the first century CE is properly described as a 'Jew'. That description would presumably have in-

285. See further M. Bar-Ilan, 'Scribes and Books in the Late Second Commonwealth and Rabbinic Period', in Mulder, ed., *Mikra* 21-38.

286. Meier as usual provides a balanced discussion (*Marginal Jew* 1.271-78, 303-309). He is followed by T. E. Boomershine, 'Jesus of Nazareth and the Watershed of Ancient Orality and Literacy', in Dewey, ed., *Orality and Textuality* 7-36: Jesus was probably literate but unable to write (22-23). Crossan has little doubt that Jesus was illiterate (*Birth* 235); similarly Chilton, *Rabbi Jesus* 99. In complete contrast Flusser assumes that 'Jesus' Jewish education was incomparably superior to that of St. Paul' (*Jesus* 30).

287. See particularly J. A. Fitzmyer, 'The Languages of Palestine in the First Century A.D.', *A Wandering Aramean: Collected Aramaic Essays* (Missoula: Scholars, 1979) 29-56; also 'Aramaic Background' 6-10. Meier's discussion of the subject is quite sufficient for our purposes (*Marginal Jew* 1.255-68, 287-300); see also L. T. Stuckenbruck, 'An Approach to the New Testament Through Aramaic Sources: The Recent Methodological Debate', *JSP* 8 (1991) 3-29; M. O. Wise, 'Languages of Palestine', *DJG* 434-44; Millard, *Reading and Writing* chs. 4 and 5 (especially 140-47). Flusser continues to maintain that Jesus taught in Hebrew (*Jesus* 128).

288. See especially Hengel, *'Hellenization';* S. E. Porter, 'Jesus and the Use of Greek in Galilee', in Chilton and Evans, eds., *Studying the Historical Jesus* 123-54. Particularly worthy of note is the presence of Greek manuscripts among the DSS and the predominance of Greek papyri in the Babatha archive written between 93 and 132 (Millard, *Reading and Writing* 113, 115).

289. Porter argues that possibly seven of Jesus' conversations took place in Greek — Matt. 8.5-13; John 4.4-26; Mark 2.13-14; 7.25-30; 12.13-17; 8.27-30; 15.2-5, each, apart from John 4, with parallels (*Criteria* 157-63). But even the plausibility of Matt. 8.5-13 is in question (was the centurion a Gentile? — see above §8.4b — and in Luke's version he used intermediaries). In Mark 15.2-5 the exchange is minimal.

cluded a pious upbringing by his parent(s)[290] and education in Torah at the local village (Nazareth) assembly/synagogue.[291] Whether he could read for himself or not, Jesus' knowledge of and familiarity with Scripture indicated in the Synoptic tradition[292] is entirely plausible, even for the son of an artisan.[293]

At least some pilgrimage to Jerusalem for the great feasts can be assumed. Luke's report that Jesus' parents 'went to Jerusalem every year *(kat' etos)* at the feast of the Passover' (Luke 2.41) may be exaggerated, but otherwise is entirely plausible.[294] The story of Luke 2.41-51 suggests that (preparation for) Jesus' transition to manhood would have been regarded as a particularly appropriate occasion for a pilgrimage.[295] At any rate, he would have been familiar with the Temple and its functionaries, priests who served locally as teachers and magistrates (Mark 1.44 pars.),[296] and the requirements of tithing (Matt. 23.23/Luke 11.42)[297] and purity.[298] He no doubt said the *Shema* (Deut. 6.4), probably as a daily obligation (cf. Mark 12.29-30 pars.), and prayed, probably two or three times a day (cf. Josephus, *Ant.* 4.212).[299] We can also assume that the adult Jesus observed the Sabbath, attended the synagogue, and 'gave every seventh day over to the study of our customs and law' (Josephus, *Ant.* 16.43), even though only Luke 4.16 indicates that synagogue attendance was his normal custom.[300] The

290. The piety of the parents can be deduced from the names they gave their children (Mark 6.3) — James/Jacob (the patriarch), Joses/Joseph, Judas/Judah, Simon/Simeon (three of Jacob's 12 children, and heads of the resultant tribes), not to mention Jesus/Joshua (Fredriksen, *Jesus* 240).

291. See above §9.7a. There is no archaeological evidence of a first-century synagogue at Nazareth, but again we note the difficulties confronting archaeologists on the site (above n. 273).

292. E.g., Mark 2.25-26; 7.6-8; 10.5-8; 12.26.

293. For the broad picture see, e.g., Schürer, *History* 2.417-22, but also further below.

294. Sanders estimates that between 300,000 and 500,000 would attend the Passover (Herod's temple could accommodate 400,000 pilgrims) out of a Palestinian Jewish population of between 500,000 and 1,000,000 (*Judaism* 127-28).

295. Mishnah tractate *Niddah* 5.6 implies that the thirteenth birthday marked a boy's transition to adult responsibility in legal and religious matters. *Hagiga* 1.1 may imply an older custom of taking boys on pilgrimage at a younger age to accustom them to the obligation (Fitzmyer, *Luke* 440-41).

296. Sanders, *Judaism* 177; see above §9.3c.

297. On tithing, see Sanders, *Judaism* 146-57; and further below §14.4g.

298. Mark 1.40-44 pars.; Mark 7.15-23/Matt. 15.11-20; Matt. 23.25-26/Luke 11.39-41. Noteworthy is the presence of a large ritual bath adjacent to the Gamla synagogue above the northeast corner of the Sea of Galilee (e.g., Oster, 'Supposed Anachronism' 195).

299. Jeremias, *Prayers* 66-81; 'It is hardly conceivable that the earliest community would have observed the hours of prayer had Jesus rejected them' (*Proclamation* 186-91); Sanders, *Judaism* 196-97, 202-208.

300. 'The shared convictions and practices that had nothing special about them, but

references to the 'tassels' of his garment suggest that he himself was a pious Jew who took his religious obligations seriously.[301] Almost certainly he would have encountered Pharisees and been familiar with their concerns to interpret the Torah for their own time. He probably at least knew of Essenes and would hardly be unaware of the history of tensions with the Samaritans.

d. Centre at Capernaum

That Jesus made Capernaum the hub of his mission is also clearly indicated in the records. He 'left Nazareth and made his home in Capernaum' (Matt. 4.13); he was 'at home' *(en oikō)* in Capernaum;[302] it was 'his own town' (Matt. 9.1); 'he used to teach' in the synagogue there (Mark 1.21/Luke 4.31).[303] The fact that the Q material contains fierce denunciations of Capernaum (Matt. 11.23/Luke 10.15), Chorazin, and Bethsaida (Matt. 11.21/Luke 10.13) is also relevant. It must mean that Jesus had concentrated his preaching efforts in these towns and had been rebuffed in greater or less measure.[304] Chorazin and Bethsaida are the two towns closest to Capernaum.[305]

---

which may also have characterized Jesus as an observant Galilean Jew, would have been taken for granted and so not mentioned because everybody knows that' (Keck, *Who Is Jesus?* 31).

301. Matt. 9.20/Luke 8.44; Mark 6.56/Matt. 14.36, with reference to the instructions of Num. 15.38-39 and Deut. 22.12 (note also Zech. 8.23).

302. Mark 2.1; 3.20; 9.33; Matt. 13.1, 36. If Mark 2.15 existed as a tradition separate from 2.13-14, then the 'house' mentioned there could conceivably have been Jesus' own (Jeremias, *Parables* 227 n. 92; cf. Taylor, *Mark* 204). But if the archaeological evidence regarding 'Peter's house' in first-century Capernaum is anything to go by (see, e.g., Charlesworth, *Jesus* 109-15; Murphy-O'Connor, *Holy Land* 218-19), one can certainly envisage the episode in Mark 2.2-12 taking place there, but hardly the hosting of a large meal.

303. See also Matt. 8.5/Luke 7.1/John 4.46; Matt. 17.24; Luke 4.23; John 2.12; 6.17, 24, 59. Crossan and Reed, *Excavating Jesus* 94-96, tendentiously dispute the data marshalled above on the basis of Mark 1.38 ('I came out [of Capernaum]') to support the alternative reconstruction of Jesus' mission as constantly itinerant ('this covenantal kingdom could not have a dominant place to which all must come, but only a moving center that went out alike to all').

304. Studies of Q deduce, with good form-critical logic, that the Q people must themselves have experienced rejection by these three Galilean towns (cf., e.g., Kloppenborg Verbin, *Excavating Q* 147-48, 171-74, 256). But even if the passages are designated as Q², it remains the case that they recall *Jesus* as making the denunciations. No activity of Jesus in Chorazin is reported in the Jesus tradition; but visits to Bethsaida are (Mark 8.22; Luke 9.10).

305. Chorazin was 'up the hill' behind Capernaum, some 3 or 4 km distant, and Bethsaida was about 13 km from Capernaum. Though technically in Herod Philip's territory (across the Jordan), Bethsaida was oriented to the towns and villages round the north and west of the lake (both Pliny, *Nat.Hist.* 5.21, and John 12.21 locate it in Galilee); see further J. F. Strange, 'Bethsaida', *ABD* 1.692-93. It is relevant that Peter and Andrew appear to have left

The size and importance of Capernaum have been much debated of late, with some rather wild figures circulated.[306] But Reed's account gives a much more sober estimate: a modest town of between 600 and 1,500 residents, that is, one of Galilee's larger villages.[307] According to Reed, there is no evidence of paved streets, colonnaded thoroughfares, or channels for running water or sewage; rather the streets were quite narrow, irregular (bent round house complexes), and made of packed earth and dirt.[308] Likewise lacking is evidence of public buildings (no theatre or administrative complex, no shops or storage facilities relating to the market place)[309] or public inscriptions denoting benefactions (a characteristic feature of Mediterranean cities of the period).[310] The construction of houses and domestic utensils was generally of low quality (no evidence of elite houses); there are no signs of wealth (no fine pottery or even simple glass, no mosaics, no frescoes, no marble).[311]

Capernaum's significance lay in its location. Situated on the northwest shore of the lake, it was probably the main fishing village of the area and supplied the hinterland, including Chorazin. More important, it was the last village

---

their home town (Bethsaida — John 1.44) and also settled in Capernaum (Mark 1.29 pars.). According to John, Philip had also come from Bethsaida (John 1.44; 12.21). Is it a coincidence that Andrew and Philip were the only members of Jesus' close disciples to have Greek names?

306. Meyers and Strange estimated a population of 12,000-15,000 (*Archaeology* 58); V. C. Corbo describes Capernaum as a 'city' laid out according to the normal urban plan, with a *cardo maximus* (principal street, north-south), with numerous *decumani* (intersecting streets, east-west) (*ABD* 1.866-69). See also Reed, *Archaeology* 143 and n. 15.

307. Reed, *Archaeology* 149-52; also Crossan and Reed, *Excavating Jesus* 81-87. Reed also notes that Capernaum is nowhere mentioned in literature prior to Jesus (*Archaeology* 140). S. Loffreda estimates a population of about 1,500 during the town's maximum expansion in the Byzantine period (*OEANE* 1.418).

308. Ibid 153.

309. The well-known synagogue in Capernaum most probably dates from the fourth or fifth century CE, though underneath there is evidence of walls of houses and stone pavements (S. Loffreda, 'The Late Chronology of the Synagogue of Capernaum', in L. I. Levine, ed., *Ancient Synagogues Revealed* [Jerusalem: Israel Exploration Society, 1981] 52-56; also Loffreda, 'Capernaum', *OEANE* 1.418). When these earlier structures are to be dated remains unclear. It is conceivable that a large house served for communal gatherings (Kee, 'Defining' 22). But it is also conceivable that there was an earlier synagogue, on the same site or elsewhere, and Luke's report that the centurion had 'built' (that is, presumably, paid for the building of) what must anyway have been a fairly unpretentious structure (Luke 7.5) cannot be dismissed out of hand. One could well imagine local personages trying to 'ape' the benefactions of more prestigious cities, like Tiberias round the lake. But see Crossan and Reed, *Excavating Jesus* 90-91.

310. Reed, *Archaeology* 154-56.

311. Ibid 159-60, 164-65; see also Murphy-O'Connor, *Holy Land* 217, 220-21. Chilton's imagination again takes off here: 'the decadence of Capernaum disgusted him (Jesus)'; 'the almost bacchanalian excesses that Capernaum offered' (*Rabbi Jesus* 82, 132).

in Herod Antipas's territory on the road running northeast, across the Jordan and through Herod Philip's territory (Gaulinitis) to Damascus. Hence it served also as a customs post. The Gospels name Matthew/Levi as (the) toll-collector at the time of Jesus (Mark 2.14 pars.). The presence of a military officer ('centurion'), presumably appointed by Herod Antipas, with some (personal?) staff (Matt. 8.9/ Luke 7.8), suggests also that Capernaum had some strategic importance.[312] Toll-collector and royal official require only a small revision of the picture emerging from the archaeological evidence to include a thin layer of provincial bureauocracy.[313]

Why did Jesus make his base there? It is quite possible that he was given room in a house there by one of his early followers.[314] Although on the border of Galilee, Capernaum gave ready access to the Jewish settlements in the Golan as well as the Galilean heartland. Worthy of consideration also is its proximity to Gentile areas to the north[315] and across the lake to the villages attached to the cities of the Decapolis.[316] This does not necessarily imply a concern on Jesus' part to include Gentile areas within his mission (see further below §9.9f). Reed speculates that Capernaum, so close to the edge of Herod Antipas's territory and on the lake, also allowed Jesus to slip out of Herod's jurisdiction when the need arose,[317] a factor worth bearing in mind in view of the short shrift given to Jesus' mentor John the Baptist by Antipas (Mark 6.14-29 pars.).

e. Relation with Sepphoris and Tiberias

As Nazareth was oriented to Sepphoris (§9.6b), so the villages on the northwestern quadrant of the lake would probably be in at least some degree oriented to

312. See above chapter 8 nn. 200-201 and chapter 9 n. 256.

313. Reed, *Archaeology* 165. But the Gospels do envisage Matthew's guests dining ('reclining') at a meal in Matthew/Levi's house (Mark 2.15 pars.), which implies a fairly substantial dwelling and Hellenistic etiquette. If Jairus was *archisynagōgos* of Capernaum (Mark 5.22-43 pars.), it could indicate that all three(?) of the most important local personages (chairman of the village assembly, toll-collector, and royal official/centurion) were attracted to or had favourable dealings with Jesus.

314. Does the *oikos* mentioned by Mark on several occasions (2.1; 3.20; cf. 7.17) refer to Jesus' own house or to Peter's house? See also n. 302 above.

315. 'Kedesh, a key Tyrian site on its border with Upper Galilee, was only 25 km north of Capernaum, and archaeological evidence of Syro-Phoenician settlements has been uncovered at several sites in the Huleh Valley . . .' (Reed, *Archaeology* 163).

316. Mark makes a point of recording Jesus' criss-crossing of the lake (Mark 4.35–5.43; 6.30-56; 8.1-26).

317. Reed, *Archaeology* 166 — 'the cat-and-mouse game with Antipas (Luke 13.31-33)'.

Antipas's other administrative centre at Tiberias. We have already noted the virtual silence of the Jesus tradition in relation to both cities.[318] Does it indicate that Jesus deliberately avoided these cities, whether for religious, social, or political reasons? The issue is made a little more complex when we consider references (notably in Q) which envisage mission to 'cities',[319] and others which warn against giving priority to the accumulation of wealth[320] — presumably with landowners and the social elite of the cities primarily in view.[321] The 'broad streets' *(plateiai)* referred to in some passages[322] were more likely to be found in cities, possibly implying some familiarity with the two Galilean cities.[323] Matt. 7.13-14 uses the imagery of a city gate *(pulē)*. Q tradition refers to law-courts and prisons (Matt. 5.25-26/Luke 12.57-59) and to deposits with bank(er)s *(trapezitēs/trapeza)* (Matt. 25.27/Luke 19.23), references rather more redolent of city than village life.[324] And Jesus was evidently accustomed to dining out[325] and familiar with the Greek practice of reclining at the meal table[326] and the custom of 'places of honour' at dinners.[327] Where, we might ask, did a relatively poor preacher learn such habits and learn of such customs?[328] We are not in a position to give a clear answer to such a question, but villages of the size of Nazareth, Capernaum, and Chorazin would hardly provide much opportunity,[329] and the

318. See above, §9.6b. Freyne also notes the absence of any 'Woes' pronounced against Sepphoris and Tiberias similar to those against Chorazin, Bethsaida, and Capernaum ('Jesus and Urban Culture' 190).

319. Matt. 10.11, 14-15/Luke 10.8-12; but given the indiscriminate use of *polis* in the Synoptics not too much should be made of these references.

320. Matt. 6.19-21/Luke 12.33-34; Matt. 6.24/Luke 16.13; Luke 12.13-21; 16.19-31.

321. In this section I am drawing on Reed, *Archaeology* particularly 192.

322. Matt. 6.5; Luke 10.10; 13.26; 14.21.

323. The 'marketplaces' alluded to in Mark 12.38/Luke 20.46 and Matt. 23.7/Luke 11.43 are probably the larger *agorai* of cities, but villages too would have had marketplaces (Mark 6.56) and other references are insufficiently specific (Matt. 11.16/Luke 7.32; Matt. 20.3; Mark 7.4).

324. But R. A. Piper notes 'the suspicion about the institutions of power' evident in such material ('The Language of Violence and the Aphoristic Sayings in Q', in J. S. Kloppenborg, ed., *Conflict and Invention: Literary, Rhetorical, and Social Studies on the Sayings Gospel Q* [Valley Forge: Trinity, 1995] 53-72 [here 63]).

325. Mark 2.15 pars.; Matt. 22.10-11; Luke 14.10; 22.27.

326. Mark 14.3/Matt. 26.7; Mark 14.18/Matt. 26.20; Luke 7.37, 49; 14.15.

327. Mark 12.39 pars.; Luke 14.7-8.

328. Cf. Buchanan, *Jesus* 180-83.

329. Though possibly Bethsaida might have afforded some opportunity, since it was Herod Philip's second city. According to Josephus, Philip raised Bethsaida from the status of a village *(kōmē)* to that of a city and renamed it Julia, after the Emperor's daughter *(Ant.* 18.28); Schürer, *History* 2.171-72, argues that this must have happened before 2 BCE, when Julia was banished by Augustus, but Murphy-O'Connor thinks that Julia the mother of the reigning em-

tradition of well-to-do figures adopting a patronal role in regard to a popular preacher was hardly new even then.[330]

The relative silence of the Jesus tradition with regard to Jesus' attitude to Herod Antipas is probably best correlated with its silence in regard to Antipas's two chief cities in Galilee (Sepphoris and Tiberias), suggesting a shared, and perhaps political, motive. Such possible allusions to Antipas as we find in Matt. 11.7-8/Luke 7.24-25[331] and Mark 10.42-45,[332] as well as the one explicit reference in Luke 13.31-33, imply a coded critique — coded no doubt in the light of what happened to the Baptist as a result of his outspoken criticism, but a critique nonetheless.[333] This strengthens the suspicion that the silence of the Jesus tradition as to any visit by Jesus to these cities is deliberate, and it suggests that Jesus may have deliberately avoided them as seats of Herodian power in Galilee.[334]

f. Mission through Galilee (and Beyond?)

The northwestern quadrant of the lake seems to have been the heartland of Jesus' mission. But he is also remembered as having travelled widely throughout Galilee.[335] Particular villages have become lodged in the Jesus tradition — a return to Nazareth (Mark 6.1-6 pars.) after he had already relocated at Capernaum (Luke 4.23) and miracles at Nain (Luke 7.11)[336] and Cana.[337] A commissioning of disciples to go about preaching 'from village to village' (*kata tas kōmas* —

---

peror Tiberius (14-37) is the more likely candidate (*Holy Land* 205). At any rate, the archaeological evidence suggests that it was still little more than a village (Reed, *Archaeology* 184; see also R. Arav, 'Bethsaida', *OEANE* 1.302-305).

330. Contrast Schottroff and Stegemann: 'The rich of Palestine were not among the disciples of Jesus' (*Hope of the Poor* 53); but are we in a position to draw such a sweeping conclusion?

331. See below chapter 11 n. 183.

332. Freyne, 'Jesus and Urban Culture' 199-200.

333. Note also the two references to the Herodians (see above §9.3c[4]) in Mark 3.6 and 12.13-17 par. (see below §15.3c).

334. Reed, *Archaeology* 137-38.

335. In summary statements: Mark 1.39/Matt. 4.23; Mark 6.6/Matt. 9.35; Luke 8.1. Josephus speaks of 204 villages in Galilee (including Upper Galilee) (*Life* 235). They would range in size from a few score inhabitants to relatively large towns of several thousand (Horsley, *Galilee* 190-93).

336. Traditionally identified with modern Nein, SSE of Nazareth, on the northern slope of the hill of Moreh, so properly in the plain of Jezreel (J. F. Strange, 'Nain', *ABD* 4.1000-1). This may indicate that it was not part of Lower Galilee proper (cf. Reed, *Archaeology* 116); but no clarity has been achieved regarding the southern border of Lower Galilee during this period.

337. John 2.1, 11; 4.46; Cana is indicated as Nathanael's hometown (John 21.2). It is usually identified with a site some 14 km north of Nazareth (J. F. Strange, 'Cana', *ABD* 1.827).

Luke 9.6) is also well-rooted in the tradition. As already noted, this is the basis of Theissen's portrayal of the earliest missionaries as itinerant charismatics (§4.6). But since most of Galilee, Upper as well as Lower, was within two days' journey from Capernaum, the amount of itinerancy involved should not be exaggerated.[338] In terms of their own means of living (food and shelter), Jesus and his team were evidently able to rely on village hospitality (Mark 6.10 pars.), and there is a firm tradition that a number of women acted as a support team, following him (Mark 15.40-41) and providing for him from their own means (Luke 8.2-3).[339]

In addition, there are also references to Jesus' fame reaching beyond Galilee, and indeed to outreach beyond Galilee. In typically hyperbolic fashion Mark reports crowds coming from Judea, Jerusalem, Idumea, and beyond the Jordan, and from Tyre and Sidon (Mark 3.8 pars.). More to the point, Jesus himself is recalled as travelling to the territory *(merē)*/borders *(horia)* of Tyre (and Sidon), in the far northwest (Mark 7.24/Matt. 15.21) where the boundary between Upper Galilee and Tyre is not clear, and where anyway the villages would be subject to Tyrian influence. Similarly, a trip north from the lake of Galilee would bring him into the territory *(merē)*/villages *(kōmas)* administered from Caesarea Philippi (Mark 8.27/Matt. 16.13), again heavily influenced by trade through Tyre.[340] And any trip across the lake meant an excursion into territories administered by cities of the Decapolis.[341] Jesus is never said to have visited any of the cities themselves. In these cases the Evangelists hint heavily that Jesus' own mission thus foreshadowed the subsequent Gentile mission.[342] But we should also recall that all these were territories which had at one time belonged to greater Israel and which could be regarded as Israel's heritage, part of the land promised to Abra-

338. 'Not itineracy but short day trips to the villages and towns of the region' (Arnal, *Jesus* 199-200). See also §14.3b below.

339. Including Joanna, wife of Chuza, Herod's steward *(epitropos)*. Chuza, we may imagine, managed (some of) Antipas's estates, possibly in the richly fertile plain of Gennesaret between Tiberias and Capernaum.

340. Freyne, 'Archaeology' 167-69; Reed, *Archaeology* 163-64.

341. Mark 5.1-20 pars.; 10.1 par. The wording of Mark 7.31 ('he returned from the territory of Tyre and went through Sidon to the Sea of Galilee through the territory of the Decapolis') has always remained a puzzle (Sidon being situated to the north of Tyre) — hence presumably the scribal modifications in p[45] etc. ('from the territory of Tyre and Sidon'). Conceivably it was Mark's (or the tradition's) way of signalling that Jesus went out of his way to avoid Upper Galilee (he circumvented its northern border); in which case, once again we should not exclude the possibility of a political motive — to stay out of reach of Antipas's authority (Gnilka, *Jesus* 190-91).

342. The sequence of Mark 7.1–8.10/9.1 is particularly noticeable — a mission outside Galilee (7.24–8.10), or including one brief unsatisfactory visit to the west shore of the lake (7.24–9.1), following Jesus' effective denunciation of the laws of clean and unclean (7.15-19).

ham.[343] In other words, we certainly cannot exclude the possibility that Jesus himself saw it as part of his task to extend his mission to the children of Israel still resident in these territories — hence the poignant episode with the Syrophoenician woman in Mark 7.24-30/Matt. 15.21-28.

g. Mission to Judea and Jerusalem?

The question whether Jesus visited Jerusalem during his mission, prior to its climax, is a thorny one. We have already noted the inherent probability of pilgrimage visits during Jesus' youth and young manhood (§9.9c), even though only Luke 2.41-51 offers any account of one. Assuming the usual location suggested for John's baptism, Jesus presumably must have travelled some three or four days south to be baptized (see below chapter 11 n. 52), though Jerusalem itself is not in view in this case. Apart from that, the fairly clear implication of the Synoptics is that Jesus never visited Jerusalem during his Galilean mission.[344] It is possible, of course, that they ignored any such visits in order to make the journey to Jerusalem climactic in its build-up to Jesus' final week in Jerusalem itself.[345] But so far as the Synoptics are concerned, Jesus' earlier mission was exclusively in the north.

The Fourth Evangelist, however, tells a different story. He narrates the 'cleansing of the Temple' in John 2.13-22. Jesus is portrayed as active in the south in a period of overlap with the Baptist's mission (John 3.22-26). John 5 is set in Jerusalem, and the action of the Gospel is set wholly in Jerusalem and its environs from 7.10 onwards. Some of this can readily be discounted: the Evangelist presumably set the cleansing of the Temple first as a headline under which or window through which to read the whole Gospel. And the play on what can properly be called Temple concerns is consistent throughout.[346] But other factors sug-

---

Luke compensates for his omission of the episode with the Syrophoenician woman by including a second mission of 70/72 disciples (Luke 10.1-12).

343. Freyne, 'Archaeology' 164-65; 'Jesus and Urban Culture' 189.

344. Does Matt. 23.37-39/Luke 13.34-35 ('O Jerusalem, Jerusalem . . . how often would I have gathered your children together . . .') imply actual visits to Jerusalem? Quite possibly, in the light of the Fourth Gospel's evidence below; though Gnilka notes that frequently in the Bible Jerusalem represents all Israel (*Jesus* 193).

345. The trip to the territory of Caesarea Philippi (Mark 8) marks the northernmost extent of Jesus' journeying; thereafter Mark gives the impression of a steady progression southwards to Jerusalem (Mark 9.30, 33; 10.1, 32-33; 11.1, 11, 15). By placing the turning point to Jerusalem earlier in his account (Luke 9.51) Luke gives added weight to the journey to Jerusalem. See further D. P. Moessner, *Lord of the Banquet: The Literary and Theological Significance of the Lukan Travel Narrative* (Minneapolis: Fortress, 1989).

346. E.g., rites of purification (2.6), true worship (4.21-24), and water and light ceremonies related to the Temple (7.37-39; 8.12). See further below, vol. 3.

gest that the Fourth Evangelist may be drawing on good tradition at least to some extent:

1. That there was an overlap between John's and Jesus' missions is very probable (see §11.2b).
2. If Jesus' mission was in any degree directed to the restoration of Israel, as seems most probable (§13.3), how could he fail to preach his message also within Judea and to the people of Jerusalem?
3. The Synoptics report followers from Judea and Jerusalem.[347] There seem to have been disciples in or around Jerusalem: Mary and Martha (Luke 10.38-41) are located in Bethany by John 11.1; the arrangements for the entry into Jerusalem and for the last supper suggest secret disciples in the city or its environs (Mark 11.1-6; 14.12-16); all four Gospels speak of Joseph of Arimathea (Mark 15.43 pars.);[348] and John's Gospel mentions also Nicodemus (3.1-15; 7.50; 19.39).
4. The Galilean mission in itself would not necessarily last for much beyond a year. Periodic visits to Jerusalem, to celebrate the pilgrim feasts there, can hardly be ruled out, and would help explain the longer period usually assumed for Jesus' mission. John 7.1-13 may retain an echo of uncertainty on Jesus' part as to the wisdom of such a visit, and coheres with the note of secrecy linked to at least some of his Jerusalem disciples.

In none of this can we hope to attain a high level of probability. As the early form critics realised, the tradents of the Synoptic tradition showed little concern in situating the great bulk of Jesus' teaching in specific times and places. They did structure their accounts round a turning point in the territory of Caesarea Philippi, but the degree of indiscrimination in including traditions before and after that turning point leaves the location of particular teachings quite uncertain. If there is an exception it is the account of Jesus' last week in Jerusalem and the disputes in which Jesus was embroiled at that time. Otherwise, it would be a mistake to attempt to pin down particular teachings to particular phases in Jesus' mission. In consequence, when we turn to a closer examination of the Jesus tradition itself I will usually make no attempt to build arguments on chronology or location of Jesus' teachings and doings.

However, some of the value of the above discussion on historical context can be encapsulated in a timeline and map.

---

347. Mark 3.8/Matt. 4.25; Luke 5.17; 6.17; 7.17.
348. On Joseph of Aramathea see further §17.1g(4), below.

Roman emperors	Jewish high priests	rulers of Judea	rulers of Galilee	
		Hasmonean high priests		
	Hyrcanus II 63-40 (d. 30)	Roman conquest by Pompey 63		
60 BCE				
50 BCE				
Assassination of Julius Caesar 44				
40 BCE	Antigonus 40-37			
Battle of Actium 31	Hananel 37-36, 36-30	Herod the Great 37-4 BCE		
30 BCE	House of Boethus 30 BCE–6 CE			
Augustus holds supreme power 27 BCE–14 CE				
20 BCE				
10 BCE				
		Archelaus 4 BCE–6 CE	Herod Antipas 4 BCE–39 CE	**Jesus** Birth 6-4 BCE
	House of Annas 6-41	Roman procurators: Coponius 6-9 Marcus Ambibulus 9-12 Annius Rufus 12-15		
10 CE	Tiberius 14–37			
	Caiaphas 18-37	Valerius Gratus 15-26		
20 CE		Pontius Pilate 26-37		
30 CE				Mission 28-30 Cruci-fixion 30

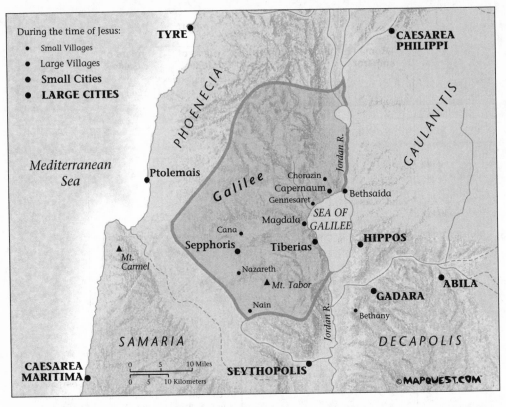

TYRE

**CAESAREA
PHILIPPI**

PHOENECIA

GAULANITIS

*Mediterranean
Sea*

Ptolemais

Galilee

Chorazin

Capernaum

Gennesaret

Bethsaida

Jordan R.

*SEA OF
GALILEE*

Magdala

Cana

Sepphoris

Tiberias

HIPPOS

Nazareth

Mt. Tabor

ABILA

GADARA

Bethany

Nain

Jordan R.

*Mt.
Carmel*

SAMARIA

DECAPOLIS

0   5   10 Miles

0   5   10 Kilometers

**CAESAREA
MARITIMA**

SEYTHOPOLIS

©MAPQUEST.COM

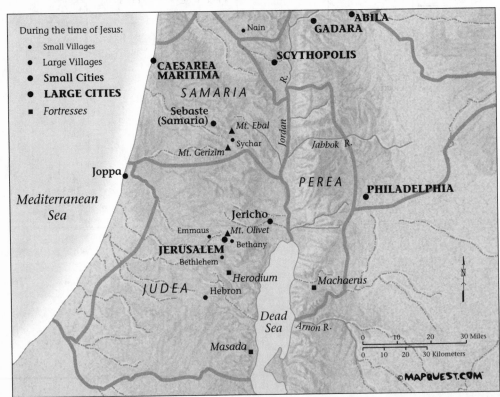

Nain

ABILA

GADARA

SCYTHOPOLIS

**CAESAREA
MARITIMA**

SAMARIA

R.

Sebaste
(Samaria)

Mt. Ebal

Sychar

Jabbok R.

Mt. Gerizim

Jordan

PEREA

PHILADELPHIA

Joppa

*Mediterranean
Sea*

Jericho

Emmaus

Mt. Olivet

Bethany

JERUSALEM

Bethlehem

■ *Herodium*

■ *Machaerus*

JUDEA

Hebron

*Dead
Sea*

Arnon R.

N

Masada ■

0   10   20   30 Miles

0   10   20   30 Kilometers

©MAPQUEST.COM

CHAPTER 10

Through the Gospels to Jesus

10.1. Can a Further Quest Hope to Succeed?

The question underlying most of what has preceded is whether any 'quest of the historical Jesus' can hope to succeed, given the quality of the data available to the quester and the character of the historical and hermeneutical tasks involved. It will be recalled that the original quest was counted a failure, its objectives (to uncover the 'inner life' of Jesus) deemed to be both illegitimate (faith must not be made to depend on the findings of historians) and impossible of achievement (in view of the theological character of the data).[1] We have been able to surmount the first obstacle by noting the importance for faith of the life and mission of Jesus and history's important role in informing, though not proving, faith. Moreover, it has become clear that to abstract faith from the historical task is to proceed unhistorically. For the first faith of those called by Jesus is itself part of the historical data to be considered. The task is to uncover historically the character of the impact Jesus made, of the effect he had on those who first formulated the traditions which have come down to us. Without taking account of their faith and the faith dimension integral to the Jesus tradition it will not be possible to provide a responsible historical account of the Jesus tradition.

In Part Two a fuller attempt has been made to answer the claim that a successful quest is impossible. Its findings point the way ahead.[2]

a. First, the study of the available sources (chapter 7) has reinforced the

1. See above chapter 5 nn. 46-47.
2. I have borrowed the title of the chapter from Keck's *Future* 26-35, and have taken account of his five provocative theses expounded there, but note that he continues to work with the imagery of 'layers' of tradition (29) and that he is characteristically 'new quest' in his focus on the 'intrinsic authenticity' of individual data (30).

conclusions already emerging in chapter 6. As we look at various aspects of the mission of Jesus our starting point will almost always be the Jesus tradition preserved in the Synoptic Gospels. We will certainly want to draw upon the traditions preserved by John at various points. And every so often we may expect a version of Jesus tradition in the *Gospel of Thomas,* in other Gospels, in Paul, or elsewhere, or in textual variants, to shed fresh light on elements within the broader sweep of tradition. But that broader sweep is much more likely to be provided by the Synoptic tradition than by any other source or combination of sources. The best test of the historical value of other versions (that is, as witnesses to what Jesus said and did) is almost always concord and coherence with the Synoptic tradition. Consequently, it is the Synoptic tradition which will be the main focus in what follows.

Within the Synoptic tradition the importance of Q steadily increased throughout the twentieth century. As very early testimony to the teaching of Jesus, the Q material will obviously have to be given close attention. There is a serious danger, however, of overconfidence in recent years on our ability to specify three aspects of Q in particular: (1) What is the relation of Q to the non-Markan material shared by Matthew and Luke (q) — that is, does all q = Q? (2) Do we know the length, order, and text of Q with sufficient detail to permit confident redactional analysis of Q itself and of its use by Matthew and Luke? (3) In compositional analysis of Q, is it possible to determine the character of the pre-Q material, whether a distinct layer (an earlier composition?) or simply different teachings of Jesus recalled individually or already grouped in coherent clusters for teaching purposes? The answers to these questions will vary from item to item as well as from scholar to scholar.

For my part the more important point to be observed is that the great bulk of the Q material is presented as teaching of Jesus himself. Even if we may not simply deduce from that that everything in Q 'goes back to Jesus', we are not thereby driven to the alternative conclusion that Q is only the teaching of early (Galilean?) communities and that we can say nothing more than that. *Tertium datur:* the Q material is remembered by such communities as *teaching given by Jesus,* and we should respect the claim implicit in that memory. If the Synoptic tradition does not give us direct access to Jesus himself, neither does it leave us simply in the faith of the first-century Christian churches stopped well short of that goal. What it gives us rather is *the remembered Jesus* — Jesus not simply as they chose to remember him, but also as the impact of his words and deeds shaped their memories and still reverberated in their gatherings.

b. Second, this line of argument is confirmed by our study of the oral phase of the Jesus tradition (chapter 8). This encouraged the conclusion that the impact of Jesus is still discernible in the stories and teachings which were performed in the earliest disciple/church gatherings and which gave these gatherings their identity and rationale. Such performances would have flexibility in detail and combination of elements and emphasis, but the main distinguishing features would have been constant, and core/key elements (usually involving words of Jesus) would have been relatively fixed. Both characteristics are still clearly evident in the Synoptic tradition. This finding probably applies only to the first fifty years or so, since John and subsequent Gospels show increasing 'editorial' freedom in what may be drawn from such episodes and teachings of Jesus' mission.

On the basis of these findings we can be more confident than the form-critical heritage has usually allowed in our assessments of what 'goes back to Jesus'. I emphasize again that I do not envisage 'getting back to Jesus' himself. All we have are the impressions which Jesus made, the remembered Jesus. Where my emphasis differs from that of other questers at this point is (1) my claim that we can get back to the earliest impact made by Jesus, made by events and teachings preserved in the Jesus tradition. This is because (2) the impact translated itself into community tradition from the first; the tradition not only bears witness to the impact made by Jesus but is *itself part of the effect Jesus had on those he called to discipleship*. And (3) the oral character of the traditioning (transmission) process means that in and through the performative variations of the tradition still evident in the Synoptic tradition we are still able to hear the stories first told about Jesus and the teachings of Jesus which first drew the tradents into discipleship and sustained the churches in the early years of their common life of discipleship. Where we find consistent features across a range of the performed tradition, then, we may conclude that they derive from the most formative influence on the tradition — that is, most likely, not from any one of the many performers of the tradition but from the creative impact of Jesus, as embodied in the tradition shared by and definitive for the communities which celebrated the tradition.

This will not prevent our recognition that in the retelling/performance of the tradition it was regularly given a fresh slant, that in the different versions we can see how the tradition was taken in different directions and often elaborated. The question will be whether that elaboration is consistent with the originating impulse, whether the elaboration clarifies an ambiguity or makes specific what was left unspecific, and so on. The implication of §8.2 is that jarring inconsistencies were unlikely to have been introduced or, if preferred by teacher or prophet, to have been accepted. But that implication will need to be further tested in what follows.

It will be characteristic of the examination of the Jesus tradition which follows, then, that the evidence is laid out synoptically for readers to see for themselves its character, both its diversities and its stabilities. Too many treatments of Jesus comment on pericopes without quoting them, or quote only one or another version. Details of variations have to be spelt out verbally, sometimes in mind-numbing detail. Since my earliest days in teaching, however, I have found that nothing brings home to students the reality of the Synoptic tradition so much as visual confrontation with a Synopsis, when the facts of divergence and the implausibilities of straightforward harmonization become immediately apparent. So now, it is my working conviction that nothing will make clearer the character of the traditioning process than visual exposure to the varying versions of the tradition as we still have them. An inevitable consequence is a longer book, with more space taken up with text, and for that I apologise. But the benefits, I believe, will outweigh the disadvantages, and the synoptic layout of the texts will offer opportunity for readers to make their own, fuller analysis than I can provide.

c. Third, study of the historical context of Jesus and his mission (chapter 9) has given us a number of further pointers in our quest. (1) We have been able to clarify what our terms often used so casually, particularly 'Jew' and 'Judaism', can properly signify with regard to the ancestral religion of Jesus in the first century. (2) A clearer grasp of the unity and diversity of Second Temple Judaism, of the factionalism and political realities of the period, enables us to recognize the multiplex context within which Jesus must have operated. (3) We can speak without reservation of Jesus as a 'Jew', a Jew from Nazareth in Lower Galilee, and in terms of fairly firm probabilities regarding his education and upbringing. (4) Archaeological data coherent with geographical notes culled from the Jesus tradition enable us to sketch in the broad social and political framework of Jesus' mission with some confidence, as well as raise some intriguing possibilities and unanswerable questions.

Having thus said what needs to be said and can be said regarding sources, methods, and context, we are ready to move on to a closer examination of the detail of the Jesus tradition itself.

10.2. How to Proceed?

How then to proceed? A review of predecessors, past and contemporary, confirms what might be expected anyway, that there are several dangers to be avoided. For example, we recall the criticism of the Liberal quest as too much predetermined by intellectual and cultural predispositions. In other cases the validity of the presentation has depended to an uncomfortable extent on the interpretation offered of a particular saying. For example, it is widely recognized that Schweitzer's reconstruction was largely based on Matt. 10.23;[3] and the influential German conviction that Jesus looked for vindication from the heavenly Son of Man has been overly dependent on Luke 12.8.[4] Form criticism encouraged an

---

3. Particularly *Quest*[2] 357-60.
4. Bornkamm, *Jesus* 176; Tödt, *Son of Man* 55-60; F. Hahn, *Christologische Hoheitstitel*

undue focus on the individual sayings within the Jesus tradition. Consequently the 'new' questers saw the way forward in terms of identifying criteria which would provide a 'critically assured' core of Jesus' teaching. The question whether Q (or Q[1]) gives immediate access to the historical Jesus (just as first questers were able to rely on Mark) has not been regularly asked (or not asked enough) in the current revival of interest in Q.[5] Of contemporary questers, Theissen has been overconfident that the primary level of Jesus tradition sought to inculcate the practice of charismatic vagrancy.[6] Funk is equally sure that the quest should begin with the parables of Jesus ('In the beginning was the parable') and that recognition of the authenticity of aphorisms should depend on whether they cohered with Jesus' own parable tradition.[7] Benedict Viviano works from the thirty-one overlapping sayings in Q and Mark to reconstruct a surprisingly complete picture.[8] In contrast, Sanders has stressed the methodological desirability of being able to build primarily on 'facts about Jesus' and not just on sayings, and much of his own study of Jesus depends on his entry point into the tradition at the 'cleansing' of the temple.[9] Crossan has no doubt that the conjunction of three vectors (a rather broadly conceived cross-cultural anthropology, Greco-Roman and Jewish history, and literary or textual analysis), plus his idiosyncratic stratification of the totality of Jesus tradition, gives him a sure way forward.[10] And Wright is equally convinced that by reading the elements of the Jesus tradi-

---

(Göttingen: Vandenhoeck und Ruprecht, 1963, [5]1995) 33-36, 455; ET *The Titles of Jesus in Christology* (London: Lutterworth, 1969) 28-34. Hahn accepted this observation in a private conversation in the late 1970s.

5. It is a/the key question posed repeatedly in the 49th Louvain Colloquium (2000) — Lindemann, ed., *The Sayings Source Q and the Historical Jesus*. For example, J. M. Robinson assumes the case for distinguishing Q[1] from Q[2] and confidently draws afresh the old Liberal picture of Jesus as a preacher of God's love, an insight soon lost from sight by the Q[2] redactor with his contrary emphasis on God as God of judgment (as a result of gruelling experiences during the Jewish war of 66-70) ('The Critical Edition of Q and the Study of Jesus', in Lindemann, *Sayings Source* 27-52 [here 39-47]), while Kloppenborg Verbin repeats earlier warnings against too quickly reading off the historical Jesus from Q[1] ('Discursive Practices' 149-90; see particularly his 'Sayings Gospel Q').

6. Theissen, *First Followers* ch. 2.

7. Funk, *Honest* 136, 165; Funk acknowledges his indebtedness to Patterson, *The Gospel of Thomas and Jesus*. Similarly *Acts of Jesus:* 'The parables and aphorisms form the bedrock of the tradition. They represent the point of view of Jesus himself' (9, 11).

8. B. T. Viviano, 'The Historical Jesus in the Doubly Attested Sayings: An Experiment', *RB* 103 (1996) 367-410.

9. Sanders, *Jesus* 4-5, and ch. 1, 'Jesus and the Temple' (61-76). Cf. already Roloff, *Kerygma,* who likewise emphasises that we must reckon not only with the tradition of Jesus' words but also with the narratives (271), and whose entry point into the tradition is the Sabbath conflict and the cleansing of the Temple (51-52).

10. Crossan, *Historical Jesus* xxxi-xxxii; also *Jesus* xi-xiii; also *Birth* 146-49.

tion against his meta-narrative of Israel in exile and restoration, he has the necessary 'large hypothesis', a serious historical hypothesis, within which all the details of the Jesus tradition find their place, a whole which illumines the parts most satisfactorily.[11]

My own conviction, arising from the considerations of the preceding chapters, is that it would be wise to look first at the broad picture,[12] or, drawing on Keck's term, to look for the 'characteristic Jesus' rather than the dissimilar Jesus.[13] Otherwise we are liable to become quickly bogged down and lost in a mire of details over individual disputed sayings.[14] It should be noted that the oral paradigm is equally susceptible to the same danger, since the variations of performance prevent any easy access to some 'original form' in individual cases.[15] If I am right, however, what we are looking at in the Jesus tradition, and what we are looking for through the Jesus tradition, is one whose mission was remembered for a number of features, each illustrated by stories and teaching and performed in the disciple circles and church gatherings, though not yet (properly speaking) 'documented' (the literary paradigm).[16]

11. Wright, *Jesus,* e.g., 79 (cited below in §12.6c at n. 416), 88, 225, 245, 517, 576-77 ('the controlling story: exile and restoration'). He has presumably been influenced by Meyer, who enunciates two principles of historical criticism: 'The technique of history is the hypothesis'; 'Hypotheses require verification' (*Aims* 90-91).

12. This is my variation of what Telford has categorized as the 'holistic' method and the tendency to ask 'broader questions' ('Major Trends' 50, 52, 57).

13. See above chapter 5 at n. 80. My proposal here echoes Dahl's suggestion that we should focus on 'cross sections' of the tradition: 'Cross sections of the tradition bring to the fore what was characteristic. . . . Words and reports of differing form and genre, transmitted within various layers of the tradition, mutually illumine each other and yield a total picture in which there appears something that is characteristic of Jesus. Whether the historicity of individual words or episodes remains uncertain is consequently of less importance. The fact that these words and occurrences found a place within the tradition about Jesus indicates that they agreed with the total picture as it existed within the circle of the disciples' ('Problem' 95). Cf. also Crossan's focus on 'complexes' rather than individual sayings (*Historical Jesus* xxxii-xxxiv); but Tuckett illustrates how arbitrary is his composition of these complexes ('Historical Jesus' 266-68, 270-72). Patterson uses Funk's term 'typifications' (*God of Jesus* 57-58, 271).

14. In Sanders' view, too much reliance on 'careful exegesis of the sayings material' has led too many NT scholars into a quagmire (*Jesus and Judaism* 131-33, 139), though his own method of correlating words with deeds allows him to be surprisingly confident in his own ability to reach a firm conclusion regarding what Jesus said about the Temple (71-76). But 'characteristic emphases' can be substantiated without necessarily being able to set each saying in a particular context.

15. See, e.g., the recent debate on whether Matt. 6.25-33/Luke 12.22-31 or *P.Oxy.* 655 is earlier (below, chapter 14 n. 45).

16. Reiser, 'Eschatology' 223, cites H. Strasburger, 'Die Bibel in der Sicht eines Althistorikers', *Studien zur Alten Geschichte* (Hildesheim: George Olms, 1990) 317-39: 'The very abundance of historical inconsistencies speaks in favor of an . . . untidy, but certainly de-

The same considerations also offer a broad-brush criterion for the would-be quester to which appeal should be made before turning to particular detail. The criterion is this: any feature which is *characteristic within the Jesus tradition and relatively distinctive of the Jesus tradition* is most likely to go back to Jesus,[17] that is, to reflect the original impact made by Jesus' teaching and actions on several at least of his first disciples. The logic is straightforward: if a feature is characteristic within and relatively distinctive of the Jesus tradition (in comparison with other Jewish traditions), then the most obvious explanation of its presence in the Jesus tradition is that it reflects the abiding impression which Jesus made on at least many of his first followers, which first drew them into and constituted their community with other disciples, and which was celebrated (together with the kerygmatic traditions of cross and resurrection) in the gatherings of the first churches through the first generation of Christianity.[18]

It should be noted once again that this approach to the Jesus tradition by no means excludes development within the tradition. It simply reconceives the processes of development. The oral paradigm acknowledges flexibility as well as stability; the Synoptic tradition demands no less by way of explanation of its lasting shape. All the Jesus tradition reflects the perspective of post-Easter faith, even though that developed faith has not left a material mark on many of the retellings. I have acknowledged that some sayings of early Christian prophets may be included within the present Jesus tradition, though not a lot, and only because they were consistent with the already received tradition. More to the point, in the retelling of various stories and sayings, as we have already observed, earlier tradition/performances have been supplemented or elaborated in different ways.[19] The tradition has been clarified in the light of events. Whether the Evangelists drew such elaborations from the churches' repertoire or felt free to develop a point in oral mode is impossible to say; I am open to both possibilities. What I am clearer on, however, is that such developments most likely were along the lines indicated or allowed by the tradition, rather than introducing wholly

---

veloped oral tradition whose honest basic effort at the beginnings of the formation of tradition was apparently to preserve as precise as possible a memory of Jesus, his teaching and proclamation, that is, to give a true and historical witness. And precisely this unique, unfalsifiable overall impression has undoubtedly been preserved in the canonical gospels . . . no matter how many details in the accounts may still, and perhaps forever, remain disputable' (336-37).

17. As Funk notes, 'distinctive' is a better historical category than 'dissimilar' (*Honest* 145).

18. The significance of these considerations for the resolution of classic disputes regarding the Son of Man and Jesus' preaching of the kingdom of God should be obvious; see below §§12.4-5 and 16.3-5. Schröter refers similarly to the Baptist and Son of Man traditions ('Markus, Q und der historische Jesus' 186-98).

19. Cf., e.g., Moule, *Birth* 111-12.

new features or elements which cut across or contradicted the earlier thrust of the tradition.

The reconceptualizing of the traditioning process which I thus offer can be summed up as a call to recognize the *living* character of the process, as against thinking in terms of literary relationships between static entities (texts). To adapt Schweitzer's famous metaphor,[20] the task of tracing the history of the Jesus tradition is not best conceptualized as an interminable journey through innumerable intermediate stations at which one must stop and change (the different layers of the tradition). The better image is a continuous run of performances of some classic, where performers and interpretation change but continue to perform the same classic. It is this postulate of *continuity through performance* which makes it realistic to identify an originating inspiration still audible in and through the diverse performances. That still audible impact of word and act is what gives 'the remembered Jesus' historical substance.

When we apply this initial criterion (what is characteristic and relatively distinct) to the Jesus tradition, a remarkably full portrayal quickly begins to take shape, as Sanders noted: a Galilean who emerged from the circle of John the Baptist and who operated for a lengthy period, most of his mission, in the small towns and villages of Galilee; a preacher whose main emphasis was the royal rule of God; a healer who was famous for his exorcisms in particular; a teacher who characteristically taught in aphorisms and parables, who successfully summoned many to follow him, and who had a close circle of twelve; a prophet who somehow challenged the Temple authorities and who was crucified outside the walls of Jerusalem by the Roman authorities on the charge of being a messianic pretender.[21] That already provides a solid platform on which to build, a substantial frame within which to fill in more detail.

Of course, all this needs to be worked out in a good deal more detail. But if such a broad picture can be sketched in with some confidence, then we are in a much better position to evaluate key particulars. The question again and again will be not simply 'Is this detail or that detail historically plausible/reliable?' but 'Does this particular story or teaching build into a coherent and consistent picture of the person who made the impact evident in the broader picture?' 'What was the impact of this person which resulted in this episode or saying being originally formulated?' Of course much of the detail will be hazy and disputed; debates over the

---

20. *Quest²* 299.

21. Sanders' several lists of 'almost indisputable facts', 'unassailable facts about Jesus' do not coincide, but the overall overlap with the data listed here is very substantial, though surprisingly he makes little of Jesus as teacher, simply that he preached the kingdom of God, or of Jesus as exorcist (*Jesus* 11, 17, 321, 326; also *The Historical Figure of Jesus* [London: Penguin, 1993] 10-11). C. A. Evans, 'Authenticating the Activities of Jesus', in Chilton and Evans, eds., *Authenticating the Activities of Jesus* 3-29, elaborates Sanders' 'facts'.

biographies of the great and the good have found it ever so. But the broad picture of Jesus can still be sound, even if much of the detail remains vague.[22] And the tradition will provide at least a number of specific features which illuminate the quality of personal encounter that caused them first to be recorded.

In short, there is a 'historical Jesus', or better, a historic Jesus, who is the legitimate and possible goal of further questing. Not a quasi-objective Jesus, Cynic or otherwise, who may or may not be significant for Christian faith. But the Jesus who historically speaking *was* significant for the first flowering of Christian faith. Such a quest, I believe, has good hope of success.

10.3. Thesis and Method

In sum, the basic argument of this book can be summed up in a number of propositions. (1) The only realistic objective for any 'quest of the historical Jesus' is Jesus remembered. (2) The Jesus tradition of the Gospels confirms that there was a concern within earliest Christianity to remember Jesus. (3) The Jesus tradition shows us *how* Jesus was remembered; its character strongly suggests again and again a tradition given its essential shape by regular use and reuse in oral mode. (4) This suggests in turn that that essential shape was given by the original and immediate impact made by Jesus as that was first put into words by and among those involved or eyewitnesses of what Jesus said and did. In that key sense, the Jesus tradition *is* Jesus remembered. And the Jesus thus remembered *is* Jesus, or as close as we will ever be able to reach back to him.

The consequences for my procedure in the following chapters should be noted. (1) I will focus attention on characteristic features/themes in the Jesus tradition and not linger long over particular sayings or episodes or make an emerging portrayal of an aspect of Jesus' mission overly dependent on one or two pericopes. At times the treatment will appear rather cursory, though I attempt to counter such an impression by fuller documentation in the footnotes. My hope is that those who want to see only the broader picture will find the main text sufficiently uncluttered as to speed them on their way. At the same time, the footnotes will go into some detail on particular points and provide sufficient (even if far from complete) indication of the scope of the debate on different specific questions.

(2) My concern is always with the Gospel (primarily Synoptic) tradition and what its enduring forms tell us about the tradition's history and its origins. For those long accustomed to studying the Synoptic problem and Synoptic parallels as a purely *literary* problem (one written document drawing from another), the procedure adopted in the following chapters may look no different from those

22. See again Dahl, 'Problem' 95 (cited above, n. 13).

which have been used before, where agreement denotes merely literary dependence and 'multiple attestation' of some features in a pericope reduces to the single attestation of the literarily prior version.

It is precisely this mindset that I wish to challenge.[23] My plea is that readers consciously change the 'default setting' of the literary paradigm, the 'pre-set preference' built into a centuries-old literary mindset, and allow the likelihood that such a paradigm is far too limited to explain the complexities of the Jesus tradition.[24] In particular, I wish to press the case: (a) that individual traditions and groups of traditions were almost certainly initially formulated and circulated in oral mode, (b) that most of them were given the shape which has endured into the Synoptic Gospels during that oral phase, and (c) that the Evangelists, including Matthew and Luke, would probably have known many of these oral traditions independently of their knowledge of written collections, including Mark and Q. Moreover, I believe (d) that in the stabilities and diversities of the tradition we can trace the continuities and variations in the performances/retellings of the tradition and not simply the literary dependence and redaction of the subsequent writers-down of the tradition. In the stabilities we see the identity of the tradition; in the diversities its vitality.

In thus throwing down the gauntlet I do not pretend that I can offer proof positive of my thesis. But in dealing with Synoptic traditions, who can realistically hope for proof positive of any thesis? I ask simply that the same judgment of plausibility which convinces most scholars of the priority of Mark and the existence of Q be exercised in relation to Synoptic texts where literary dependence is less obvious and is at least arguably less plausible. I ask simply that the spectacles of the literary mindset be removed and that over the following chapters the texts displayed synoptically be looked at afresh with the dynamics of oral performance and transmission in mind.

In short, my conviction remains that the shape and verbal variations of most of the Synoptic traditions are better explained by such an oral hypothesis than exclusively in terms of literary dependence. I suspect that the success or failure of this thesis will depend in large part on the degree to which readers have been able to change the default settings of their own personal 'onboard computers' from 'literary' to 'oral'.

23. I am grateful to Scot McKnight for bringing home to me the need to be more explicit on this point.

24. I develop the point in my 'Altering the Default Setting: Re-envisaging the Early Transmission of the Jesus Tradition', *NTS* 49 (2003).

PART THREE

THE MISSION OF JESUS

CHAPTER 11

Beginning from the Baptism of John

Two facts in the life of Jesus[1] command almost universal assent. They bracket the three years for which Jesus is most remembered, his life's work, his mission.[2] One is Jesus' baptism by John. The other is his death by crucifixion. Because they rank so high on the 'almost impossible to doubt or deny' scale of historical 'facts', they are obvious starting points for an attempt to clarify the what and why of Jesus' mission. It would be quite feasible, then, to begin with the crucifixion, as the event most amenable to historical study, and to work back from that.[3] But since Jesus' baptism by John is an equally strong fact, I prefer to begin at the beginning. An added advantage is that a study of John the Baptist in effect completes our review of the historical context from which Jesus emerged (chapter 9).

---

1. On the name 'Jesus' see Meier, *Marginal Jew* 1.205-208. Some modern translations use the Hebrew form 'Yeshua', which on first encounter has the useful effect of jerking readers out of their over-familiarity with the English form and reminding them that Jesus was a Jew.

2. I use the term 'mission' because it is the most accurate but also the most flexible term. 'Ministry', when used of someone's activity, has an almost unavoidable ecclesiastical overtone, despite its use also for high political office in the UK and elsewhere. 'Mission' was never quite so restricted in connotation. Not only does it refer to a religious enterprise ('missionary work'), but the term is also used of a body of people sent abroad to conduct negotiations, and recently it has become fashionable for businesses and higher education institutions to set out their goals in 'mission statements'. Its overtone of carefully conceived purpose, of responsibility to a sending authority, even of 'vocation', raises just the questions we will need to clarify as we proceed.

3. Thus Harvey, *Jesus;* Sanders, *Jesus,* follows similar logic in starting with the 'cleansing' of the temple.

11.1. Why Not 'Beginning from Bethlehem'?

If John's baptism of Jesus is a possible starting point, why not follow Matthew and Luke in pushing back to Jesus' birth? A 'life', whether conceived as a modern or an ancient biography, should at least say what is known of the subject's origins. There are several reasons why we do not follow that option.

a. Our whole procedure is based on the recognition that Jesus made an impact on those who became his disciples, an impact which is still evident in the traditions which have come down to us. We cannot say the same about the birth of Jesus or about the birth narratives. There is no hint, for example, that the shepherds of Luke 2.8-20 or the magi of Matt. 2.1-12 became disciples. Luke reports that Mary, Jesus' mother, 'kept all these things in her heart' (2.19; also 2.51). So 'impact' is certainly envisaged, but hardly in terms of a tradition told and retold in the thirty years before Jesus' mission began.

b. What about the birth narratives themselves? Do they not constitute the impact made on Mary? That is hardly likely.[4] It is not only that they are stories told about Mary (and others) rather than by Mary. More weighty is the evidence of the accounts themselves, that they have been in considerable measure contrived to bring out various significant allusions and theological emphases, not least by Matthew and Luke themselves.

I have in mind, in particular, in Matthew's case, the fulfilment quotations so characteristic of his Gospel,[5] the magis' star (2.2, 7-10) no doubt intended to evoke Num. 24.17 ('A star will come forth out of Jacob, and a sceptre shall arise out of Israel'),[6] the recognition of the significance of Jesus' birth by Gentiles (2.2, 11), and the evident parallelism between Jesus and Moses, Herod and Pharaoh, not least in the 'slaughter of the innocents' (2.16; Exodus 1–2).[7] This is not

---

4. *Pace* Riesner, who suggests that Luke 1–2 go back in part to Mary's reminiscences (*Jesus als Lehrer* 210); Byrskog, who in his assembly of eyewitnesses as the source of the Jesus tradition argues that Luke wants his hearers/readers to believe that 'Mary was his informant concerning certain episodes of Jesus' birth'; 'It is entirely plausible that the Jerusalem community entertained a certain interest in Mary's intimate memories concerning the birth of the risen Lord' (*Story as History* 89-90).

5. Matt. 1.22-23; 2.15, 17-18, 23; 4.14-16; 8.17; 12.17-21; 13.35; 21.4-5; 27.9-10. See further R. E. Brown, *The Birth of the Messiah: A Commentary on the Infancy Narratives in the Gospels of Matthew and Luke* (New York: Doubleday, 1977, ²1993) 96-104; Luz, *Matthäus* 1.134-41.

6. Num. 24.17 was a popular source of speculation and hope in Jewish thought of the time, not least at Qumran (CD 7.18-26 = 4QD^a frag. 3 3.7-10 = 4QD^d frag. 5 2-4; 4QTest [4Q175] 9-13; 1QM 11.6); note also *T. Levi* 18.3, and the change of Bar Kosiba's name to Bar Kokhba ('son of the star') (see further Davies and Allison, *Matthew* 1.233-35).

7. See again Brown, *Birth* 114-15; Davies and Allison, *Matthew* 1.192, 264-65. I have already speculated on memories of the destruction of Sepphoris (or of the surrounding villages)

to say that Matthew created all these motifs, though the fulfilment quotations are usually regarded as evidence of his own hand. Moreover, he clearly intends the theme of good news for Gentiles to bracket the whole Gospel (28.19),[8] and he has certainly developed the parallels between Moses and Jesus to his own purposes.[9] But, of course, he may well have been drawing on already well developed tradition.[10] My point here is simply that the tradition of Matthew's birth narrative is certainly developed tradition; by whom and how soon before (if not by) Matthew is less relevant.

With Luke the evidence is more difficult to evaluate. Above all we would like to know from where Luke derived the various songs/canticles which are such a feature of his account and which became such a staple element in Christian liturgy from the early Christian centuries.[11] It is hardly likely that they were sung at the time and were somehow recorded or remembered by Mary;[12] the births of those whose greatness is later recognized have always inspired poets and bards after the fact. But when did the songs emerge and where and in what circumstances? Their use if not their creation implies a recognition among those singing the songs of the significance already attributed to the events or people celebrated in the songs: John as fulfilling the prophecy of Elijah's return (1.17; Mal. 4.5), the emergence of a Davidic Messiah bringing salvation (1.69, 71, 77), and the opening of salvation to the Gentiles (2.30-32; echoing Isa. 42.6 and 49.6). In other words, the singing of these songs presupposes beliefs which did not begin to emerge till Jesus' mission and later.[13] Add to this the strong Lukan motifs evident in Luke 1-2 — the Spirit infilling,[14] the prominence given to

---

in consequence of the uprising which followed the death of Herod in 4 BCE, as a possible contributory factor to the Matthean episode (above chapter 9 n. 253).

8. 'Matthew is echoing the history of his own times, with the conversion of the Gentiles and persecutions before synagogues and sanhedrins and kings' (Brown, *Birth* 183).

9. Reference is usually made also to the fact that Matthew has grouped Jesus' teaching into five discourses, parallel in some degree to the Pentateuch. Further detail in Davies and Allison, *Matthew* 3.743 (Index 'Moses'); and further D. C. Allison, *The New Moses: A Matthean Typology* (Minneapolis: Augsburg Fortress, 1993) ch. 4.

10. See particularly Brown, *Birth* 104-19 and *passim*.

11. The Magnificat (Luke 1.46-55), Benedictus (1.68-79), Gloria in excelsis (2.14), and Nunc dimittis (2.29-32).

12. *Pace* particularly J. G. Machen, *The Virgin Birth of Christ* (London: Clarke, 1930) ch. 4.

13. Brown attributes them to a Jewish Christian community, composed possibly in Hebrew or Aramaic (*Birth* 346-55). But in the light of Fitzmyer's strong questioning of a semitic *Vorlage* (*Luke* 312, 359), Brown has qualified the opinion in his revised edition to talk only of canticles existing in semitized Greek (*Birth* 643-45).

14. The intensity of Spirit references in Luke 1–2, including talk of being 'filled with the Holy Spirit' (1.15, 41, 67; note also 1.17, 35, 47, 80; 2.25-27), is matched in the NT only by

women,[15] the 'option for the poor',[16] and the opening of the gospel to the Gentiles[17] — and it becomes difficult to avoid the conclusion that both content and form were heavily shaped in the early Christian communities, and thus are not independent of the impact which Jesus' mission had already made.

In short, we appear to be looking at traditions which stem from a period when Jesus' significance had already been recognized and which were intended in part to answer the question, How may we best acknowledge and celebrate his significance?

c. Can we be more precise? Raymond Brown's magisterial commentary on the infancy narratives observed that for all their differences, the two accounts (Matthew and Luke) agree on a common core: that Jesus was both son of David and son of God. Or to be more precise: the annunciation of Jesus as Davidic Messiah, but also (and more important) his begetting as God's son through the Holy Spirit.[18] Thus Matthew, for whom Jesus' Davidic sonship is central,[19] goes out of his way to affirm Jesus' legal descent from David through Joseph (1.1-17). In the crucial announcement, Joseph is addressed as 'son of David' (1.20): the child has been conceived 'from the Spirit' *(ek pneumatos);* in fulfilment of the Isaiah prophecy (Isa. 7.14), '"his name shall be called Emmanuel" . . . God with us' (1.23), another key Matthean motif.[20] That this Jesus is thus also God's son is held back till 2.15 — 'Out of Egypt have I called my son' (Hos. 11.1) — where it can also serve Matthew's purpose in presenting Jesus as the re-run of Israel's exodus and wilderness experience (Matt. 4.1-11).[21]

Luke's account of the earliest churches (Acts 2.4; 4.8, 31; 9.17; 13.9; note also 1.5, 8; 2.17-18, 38; etc.).

15. Elizabeth (Luke 1.5-13, 24-25, 40-45, 57-60), Mary (1.26-56; 2.5-7, 16-19, 34-35, 48-51), Anna (2.36-38). Elsewhere in Luke: the widow of Nain (7.11-17), the sinful woman (7.36-50), Galilean women followers (8.2-3), Martha and Mary (10.38-42), the crippled woman (13.10-17), the parable of the lost coin (15.8-10), the parable of the importunate widow (18.1-8), the widow's farthing (21.1-4), the daughters of Jerusalem (23.27-31).

16. The note struck in the Magnificat (Luke 1.51-53) is echoed in the prominence given to 'the poor' later in the Gospel (4.18; 6.20; 7.22; 14.13, 21; 16.19-31; 18.22; 21.1-4); the fact that Joseph and Mary's offering (2.24) was that permitted to the poor (Lev. 12.8) is often noted. See further Fitzmyer, *Luke* 247-51.

17. Foreshadowed in Luke's second mission of the seventy (Luke 10.1), probably indicating the second stage of mission in Acts, pioneered by Peter and the Hellenists (Acts 10.1–11.18; 11.19-26) and implemented most fully by Paul (9.15; 13.46-48; 18.6; etc.), as implied also by the two-stage 'mission' in Luke 14.21-22, 23-24.

18. Brown, *Birth* 158-63; also 133-38, 244-47 and n. 41, 307-16.

19. Matt. 9.27; 12.23; 15.22; 20.30-31; 21.9, 15; all but 20.30-31 are distinctive to Matthew.

20. See particularly D. D. Kupp, *Matthew's Emmanuel: Divine Presence and God's People in the First Gospel* (SNTSMS 90; Cambridge: Cambridge University, 1996).

21. See also below, n. 193.

On this point Luke is more straightforward. Jesus as 'son of David' is not a major theme for Luke's Gospel, which makes the prominence given to the theme in Luke's birth narrative all the more striking. As in Matthew, Joseph's descent from David is explicitly brought out in the run-up to the crucial announcement (1.27), as also that David is Jesus' royal father (1.32; also 1.69). Joseph's and Mary's move to Bethlehem is also testimony of Joseph's Davidic descent (2.4, 11). But the key factor is that Jesus is 'the Son of the Most High', 'the Son of God' (1.32, 35), because the Holy Spirit 'came upon' Mary and the power of the Most High 'overshadowed' her (1.35).

One of Brown's main points is that this assertion is not dependent on the language or 'conceptuality' of Isa. 7.14, which only Matthew cites.[22] The core tradition as such seems to be simply the double affirmation of Davidic and divine sonship. This conclusion integrates well with our earlier findings about tradition and the traditioning process. Here we have, in effect, a core tradition (Jesus is both son of David and son of God) which we find embedded in two much elaborated and diversely elaborated stories.[23] We can recognize quite a number of the distinctive emphases which both Matthew and Luke have put into their own performances of these stories. But the core of the diverse traditions seems to be constant and probably indicates the conviction and theme which was elaborated in and by the birth narratives.[24] In other words, so far as the tradition itself is concerned (the birth narratives), the earliest we can trace them (the tradition itself) is probably to that conviction — that is, the conviction that Jesus was not only David's son but also God's son. Here again, therefore, we are driven back to a starting point for the tradition as tradition to a conviction which probably took shape in these terms only after Easter. Of course, we are concerned to uncover how that conviction emerged and to what extent it was rooted in Jesus' own mission (see below, chapters 15 and 16). But so far as the tradition itself is concerned, at least as we have it in Matthew and Luke, it must be judged unlikely that the conviction emerged from the episodes recounted in Matthew 1–2 and Luke 1–2. The birth narratives seem to be the outworking of the conviction rather than vice-versa.

d. Are there, then, no historical facts concerning Jesus' birth to be gleaned from the birth narratives? The prospects are not good.

Matthew's moving star does not evoke a strong impression of historical

22. 'At most, reflection on Isa. 7.14 colored the expression of an already existing Christian belief in the virginal conception of Jesus' (Brown, *Birth* 149; also 523-24).

23. I regard it as unnecessary to counter in any detail the suggestion that Matthew or Luke derived his account from the other; on the usual arguments for literary dependence, such a suggestion is a non-starter. Matthew 1–2 and Luke 1–2 are much better explained as exotic examples of the oral paradigm (see chapter 8 above).

24. On Luke cf. particularly Fitzmyer, *Luke* 305-12, 340.

credibility.[25] If, instead, we attribute such detail to the symbolical imagination of the story-teller, how much of the story remains as a viable historical account? Likewise, the heavy typologizing particularly in regard to 2.13-18 (Herod as Pharaoh, Jesus as Israel in Egypt) leaves it very uncertain whether we can discern any historical events underlying the present story.[26] The 'slaughter of the innocents' is hardly out of character for Herod, but it is also unlikely to have escaped the notice of Josephus. And the whole Egyptian episode, including Joseph and Mary's return to settle in Nazareth, does seem somewhat contrived.[27]

More disturbing for those who have looked to the birth narratives for historical facts has been the probability that Luke got his facts wrong in the reason he gives for Jesus being born in Bethlehem of Judea.[28] The census under Quirinius took place in 6 CE, when Rome took direct control over Judea following the deposition of Herod's son Archelaus. That census would not have applied to Galilee, which was Antipas's territory. We know nothing of a universal census throughout the Roman Empire, then or earlier. And the idea of a census requiring individuals to move to the native town of long dead ancestors is hard to credit. It is difficult to avoid the conclusion that Luke was mistaken in dating the census so early (Luke 2.1-2), as he also was in his reference to Theudas in Acts 5.36-37.[29]

Most disturbing for Christian pilgrim piety is the outcome that Jesus' birth in Bethlehem has to be left in question.[30] Was the story to that effect contrived simply because of the Micah prophecy: 'And you Bethlehem, . . . from you shall come forth a ruler, who will shepherd my people Israel' (Mic. 5.2, cited by Matt.

25. The star 'went before *(proēgen)* them until it came and stopped *(elthōn estathē)* over the place where the child was' (Matt. 2.9). On attempts to link the star to a known comet or planetary conjunction see Brown, *Birth* 171-73, 610-13 — 'evidence of verisimilitude, not of history' (190).

26. Brown, *Birth* 214-16, 616; Davies and Allison have 'little doubt as to the origin of Matthew's infancy material. The haggadic legends surrounding the birth and early life of Moses (9 parallels are adduced) have determined the content of Matthew's source' (*Matthew* 1.192-93, 194).

27. 'A very artificial addition' (Davies and Allison, *Matthew* 1.190, referring to 2.22-23); see further Meier, *Marginal Jew* 1.211-13.

28. There was also a Bethlehem in Galilee (Josh. 19.15; Judg. 12.8, 10), usually identified with Beit Lahm, some seven miles from Nazareth (H. Cazalles, 'Bethlehem', *ABD* 1.714). Chilton confidently takes it to be the site of Jesus' birth (*Rabbi Jesus* 8-9, 294), though both Matthew and Luke have no doubt that the Davidic Bethlehem was in view (Matt. 2.1-6; Luke 2.4); note also the exchange in John 7.41-42.

29. See the full discussion in Schürer, *History* 1.399-427; Brown, *Birth* 547-56, 666-68; and Fitzmyer, *Luke* 1.400-405.

30. Brown, *Birth* 513-16; Meier, *Marginal Jew* 1.214-16; E. D. Freed, *The Stories of Jesus' Birth: A Critical Introduction* (Sheffield: Sheffield Academic, 2001) 75-86.

2.5-6)?[31] It is presumably significant that nothing more is made of Bethlehem outside the birth narratives. Elsewhere it is simply assumed that Jesus is 'from Nazareth',[32] that he is 'the Nazarene'.[33] The account of Jesus' visit to Nazareth presupposes that Nazareth and Galilee were his native place *(patris)* (Mark 6.1, 4; pars.). John indeed raises the double issue — 'Can anything good come from Nazareth?' (John 1.46; 7.52), and, according to Scripture, the Messiah 'comes from Bethlehem' (7.42) — without anywhere refuting the first or affirming that Jesus did in fact fulfil the prophecy (7.41). At the same time, there is never a hint that Jesus' descent from David was in question; it is simply taken for granted in what appear to be early creedal-type formulations.[34] So, once again, it is the core claim (Jesus as son of David) which seems least vulnerable to historical scepticism and of which the Bethlehem tradition may be an elaboration.[35]

What about the virgin birth, or more accurately, virginal conception? Were it the case that Mary remained a virgin and made this known, one might have expected Isa. 7.14 LXX to come into play earlier or elsewhere in the NT tradition as 'proof'. What we do have are two or three tantalising allusions or possible allusions to some popular knowledge or a rumour regarding an irregularity in Jesus' birth. (1) One comes in the account of Jesus' rejection in Nazareth. On hearing Jesus' teaching, the synagogue assembly asks:

Matt. 13.55	Mark 6.3
Is not this the son of the carpenter? Is not his mother called Mary and his brothers James, Joseph, Simon and Judas?	Is not this the carpenter, the son of Mary and brother of James, Joses, Judas and Simon?

31. The differences between Matthew's rendering of Micah 5.2 and the MT and LXX texts are of no consequence here.

32. Matt. 21.11; Mark 1.9; John 1.45, 46; Acts 10.38.

33. Mark 1.24; 10.47; 14.67; 16.6; Luke 24.19; John 18.5, 7; 19.19; Acts 2.22; 3.6; 4.10; 6.14; 22.8; 24.5; 26.9. See also above, chapter 9 n. 272.

34. Rom. 1.3; 2 Tim. 2.8; Ignatius, *Eph.* 18.2; 20.2; *Smyrn.* 1.1; also Rev. 5.5. See also O. Cullmann, *The Christology of the New Testament* (London: SCM, 1959) 128-30; 'the Davidic descent of Jesus cannot be disputed' (Hahn, *Hoheitstitel* 250 [*Titles* 245]).

35. See further Brown, *Birth* 505-12, who concludes that the evidence that Jesus was really a Davidide outweighs doubts to the contrary, but who also notes that 'there would be no irreparable theological damage to Christianity if Jesus were proved to have been of non-Davidic descent' (511). Similarly Meier, *Marginal Jew* 1.216-19, 237-42. An ossuary inscription from first century BCE indicates that the bones therein belonged to 'those who are from the house of David' (details in D. Flusser, 'Jesus, His Ancestry and the Commandment of Love', in Charlesworth, ed., *Jesus' Jewishness* 153-76 [here 158-59, illustration 150]). This confirms that lineal descent from David could and was being claimed at the time of Jesus. See further below §§15.2-4.

Here, as in other cases, the most obvious explanation for the difference between Matthew and Mark is that Matthew has modified Mark, while staying as closely as possible to Mark's wording. Why should Mark eliminate a reference to Jesus' father? But the awkwardness of the second question in Matthew points in the opposite direction. Much more intriguing: to call someone the son of his mother (Mark) would most probably strike many as implying some hint of illegitimacy (father unknown); otherwise he would be known as the son of his father (cf. Luke 4.23-38).[36] To avoid such an implication is surely the most obvious reason why Matthew thought it desirable to modify the tradition taken over from Mark.[37] In short, the Markan tradition may be evidence of some popular rumour regarding an irregularity in Jesus' birth.[38] (2) Does Matthew's inclusion in Jesus' genealogy of four women remembered for irregular sexual encounters, Tamar, Rahab, Ruth, and the wife of Uriah (Bathsheba) (Matt. 1.3, 5, 6),[39] imply an attempt on his part to absorb such rumours regarding Mary into his history of salvation?[40] (3) Does the jibe attributed to Jesus' opponents in John 8 have a similar implication — 'We were not born from *porneia*' (8.41) — since *porneia* covers a wide range of illicit sexual relations?

What are we to make of these data? Jane Schaberg confidently deduces that Jesus was indeed illegitimate and that this was known by Matthew and Luke.[41] Given the limited data available, a historical judgment cannot exclude the possibility of Jesus' illegitimacy. But the basis for the inference is exceedingly thin. Mark's language may have been judged too casual by those who sub-

36. E. Stauffer, 'Jesus, Geschichte und Verkündigung', *ANRW* II.25.1 (1982) 3-130 (here 23-25, 104 n. 835).

37. The variant reading for Mark 6.3 of p[45] and others ('Is not this the son of the carpenter and of Mary?') is probably to be explained along the same lines. Crossan suggests, less plausibly, that there was some embarrassment (cf. Luke 4.22; John 6.42) at calling Jesus a 'carpenter' (*Birth* 349-50). On *tektōn* ('carpenter') see above, chapter 9 n. 274.

38. The alternative explanation, that Joseph had been long dead (as in Brown, *Birth* 540-41), does not explain why p[45] and Matthew found it necessary to modify the original Markan text. In describing 'son of Mary' as a '"flip" comment', Meier probably does not give enough weight to what he earlier described as 'the derogatory tone of the Nazarenes' remarks' which caused Matthew and Luke to change Mark's text (*Marginal Jew* 1.225-27).

39. Tamar, who in effect seduced Judah (Genesis 38), Rahab the prostitute (Josh. 2.1-21; 6.22-25), Ruth who arguably may have seduced Boaz (Ruth 3.6-13), and Bathsheba, seduced by David (2 Sam. 11.2-27).

40. Brown, *Birth* 71-74. See the review of interpretations in Davies and Allison, *Matthew* 1.170-72; also W. J. C. Weren, 'The Five Women in Matthew's Genealogy', *CBQ* 59 (1997) 288-305; Freed, *Stories* ch. 2.

41. J. Schaberg, *The Illegitimacy of Jesus: A Feminist Theological Interpretation of the Infancy Narratives* (San Francisco: Harper and Row, 1987; paperback New York: Crossroad, 1990); followed by G. Lüdemann, *Virgin Birth? The Real Story of Mary and Her Son Jesus* (London: SCM, 1998).

sequently used his text; but it may be no more than that — too casual. If the implication was so obvious, would Mark himself not have attempted to avoid or correct it?[42] As for the women named in Matthew's genealogy, there is no hint of illegitimate births in the cases of Rahab and Ruth, and Solomon (son of David and Bathsheba) was not illegitimate;[43] and in Jewish tradition these women were well regarded.[44] As for John 8.41, sexual innuendo has always been a means of insult and denigration.[45] And the idea of illegitimacy has to be assumed behind the text of Matthew and Luke before it can be discerned there.[46]

What the core tradition affirms (Matthew and Luke) is that Jesus' birth was special — 'from the Holy Spirit' (Matt. 1.20), by the power of the Holy Spirit (Luke 1.35). That of itself need not imply a virginal conception,[47] but a virginal conception could well have been an elaboration of the basic affirmation,[48] especially when Isa. 7.14 was brought into play.[49] More to the point, the association

42. Schaberg, *Illegitimacy* 162-63, suggests that Mark 'met the charge not by dismissing it, but by, in a sense, dismissing the mother and brothers of Jesus' (3.31-35). But would dismissing Jesus' 'adoptive family' really 'meet the charge' of illegitimacy?

43. Brown, *Birth* 593-94.

44. Davies and Allison, *Matthew* 1.170, 173-75.

45. We need only think of the regular use of the term 'bastard' in street conversation today.

46. Brown, *Birth* 635-37, 707-708. Other, later texts cited by Schaberg are almost certainly dependent on and developed from the earlier hints. Chilton thinks Jesus would have been classified as a *mamzer*, an Israelite of suspect paternity; he had been conceived by Joseph and Mary 'soon after meeting and well before their marriage was publicly recognized' (that is, when they were not yet living together), and so was not illegitimate in the modern sense of the word (*Rabbi Jesus* 6-7, 12-13; also 'Jésus, le *mamzer* (Mt 1.18)', *NTS* 47 [2001] 222-27).

47. Both Brown and Fitzmyer point out that neither of the verbs used by Luke 1.35 — 'come upon' *(eperchesthai)* and 'overshadow' *(episkiazein)* — has a sexual overtone (*Birth* 290; *Luke* 337-38, 351).

48. See the discussion in Freed, *Stories* 59-69. Here we also need to be aware of the biological and theological corollaries of insisting that the virginal conception/birth was a historical fact. E.g. Arthur Peacocke concludes his brief study, 'DNA of Our DNA', in G. J. Brooke, ed., *The Birth of Jesus: Biblical and Theological Reflections* (Edinburgh: Clark, 2000) 59-67, with the blunt statement: 'For Jesus to be fully human he had, for both biological and theological reasons, to have a human father as well as a human mother and the weight of the historical evidence strongly indicates that this was so — and that it was probably Joseph. Any theology for a scientific age which is concerned with the significance of Jesus of Nazareth now has to start at this point' (66). Cf. Brown's sensitive handling of a sensitive subject (*Birth* 517-33, 697-708).

49. As is well known, the sense 'virgin' for Isa. 7.14 derives from the LXX term *parthenos* used for the less explicit Hebrew 'alma ('young girl'). It is unnecessary to hypothesize the influence of pagan parallels to explain the idea of virgin conception/birth (Schaberg, *Illegitimacy* 179-80; for data see, e.g., T. Boslooper, *The Virgin Birth* [Philadelphia: Westminster, 1962] 135-86), since stimulus from Jewish background and very early Christian reflection provide a much more obvious explanation for the distinctive features of the birth narratives (see particularly Davies and Allison, *Matthew* 1.200-202, 214-17).

of conception and birth from the Spirit with divine sonship (explicit in Luke, implicit in Matthew) strikes a chord which resonates with the beginning of Jesus' mission (see below §11.5) and with a fundamental motif in earliest Christianity.[50] The believers who experienced the Spirit bringing them such a vivid sense of sonship to God will hardly have thought that Jesus' sonship was of a lesser kind. On the contrary, the tradition of Rom. 8.15-17 and Gal. 4.6-7 presumes that these early experiences were understood as a sharing in Jesus' own sonship. This suggests in turn that the conviction that Jesus' own birth was 'from the Spirit' was arrived at very early in the disciple groups and first churches.

In other words, once again, as with Jesus' Davidic sonship, so also with Jesus' divine sonship, perhaps what we see most clearly in the birth narratives is diverse elaboration of the core conviction that Jesus was born of God's Spirit in a special way. If so, then once again the birth narratives provide a valuable index of how earliest Christian thinking developed. But they do not provide a good place from which to begin researching the history of Jesus' mission.

11.2. John the Baptizer

Despite the infancy narratives of Matthew and Luke, the Gospel tradition as a whole invites us to begin our study of the impact made by Jesus with John the Baptizer and with Jesus' baptism by John. Indeed, a historical study of Jesus has little choice but to attempt to 'locate' him in relation to John. For several reasons.

a. The Historical Stature of John

Initially at any rate, John seems to have had as great a claim to historical significance as Jesus, if not greater. He receives favourable mention by Josephus, who introduces him as 'John, the one called Baptist *(baptistēs)*' and goes on to speak of him at some length *(Ant.* 18.116-19), beginning thus:

> He was a good man and had exhorted the Jews to lead righteous lives, to practise justice towards their fellows and piety towards God, and so doing to join in baptism. In his view this was a necessary preliminary if baptism was to be acceptable to God. They must not employ it to gain pardon for whatever sins they committed, but as a consecration of the body implying that the soul was already thoroughly cleansed by right behaviour (18.117).

---

50. Particularly Rom. 8.14-17; Gal. 4.6-7; see also John 3.5-8, 34.

The account goes on to speak of the great enthusiasm aroused by John's preaching which caused Herod Antipas to fear a possible insurrection (18.118). We should note that Josephus introduces this brief description of John into his account of the dispute between Herod and Aretas, king of Petra (18.109-126), as the explanation for Aretas's victory. 'The verdict of the Jews was that the destruction of Herod's army was a vindication of John, since God saw fit to inflict such a blow on Herod' (18.119).[51]

The Gospel accounts likewise reflect the enthusiasm among the people engendered by John's preaching. The Evangelists' description of 'all Judea and all Jerusalemites' (Mark 1.5), 'all Judea and all the region round about' (Matt. 3.5), 'all the people' (Luke 3.21) flocking to be baptized is no doubt hyperbolic, but otherwise is consistent with Josephus' report.[52] The fact that John was known as 'the Baptist' attests a distinctive ritual act[53] which must have involved many. And the Q tradition in Matt. 11.7-9/Luke 7.24-26 likewise reflects a steady stream of people going out into the wilderness to see John. According to the same text he was generally reckoned a 'prophet', a fact of significance in itself, since the title had rarely been accorded or merited since Malachi.[54] Similarly the exchange in Mark 11.29-33 pars. implies that John was held in high popular esteem as a prophet.[55] Indeed, according to Luke, the people wondered whether John might be 'the Messiah' (Luke 3.15), a possibility echoed in John 1.20. Certainly he seems to have attracted a band of disciples,[56] which may have retained a recog-

51. 'To some of the Jews [it] seemed to be divine vengeance, and certainly a just vengeance, for his treatment of John' (18.116). The reference is to the defeat of Herod's army by the Nabatean king Aretas in 36 CE, about eight years after the probable date of John's execution (above, chapter 9 n. 254); see also below, §11.6.

52. Most agree that John must have operated mainly on the east side of the Jordan, in Perea, that is, the territory of Antipas, but close enough to the Dead Sea to be easily accessible from Jerusalem and Judea; see, e.g., discussion in J. Ernst, *Johannes der Täufer: Interpretation — Geschichte — Wirkungsgeschichte* (BZNW 53; Berlin: de Gruyter, 1989) 280-84; also 'Johannes der Täufer und Jesus von Nazareth in historischer Sicht', *NTS* 43 (1997) 161-83; Meier, *Marginal Jew* 1.43-46; Stegemann, *Library* 212-13. Flusser, however, locates the Baptist's activity in the vicinity of Bethsaida, north of the lake (*Jesus* 43-44, 258 n. 2).

53. See further below §11.3a.

54. Discussion, e.g., in R. L. Webb, *John the Baptizer and Prophet: A Socio-Historical Study* (JSNTS 62; Sheffield: Sheffield Academic, 1991) 307-78; J. E. Taylor, *The Immerser: John the Baptist within Second Temple Judaism* (Grand Rapids: Eerdmans, 1997) 213-34.

55. See also Matt. 14.5; Luke 1.76; and further M. Tilly, *Johannes der Täufer und die Biographie der Propheten. Die synoptische Täuferüberlieferung und das jüdische Prophetenbild zur Zeit des Täufers* (BZANT 137; Stuttgart: Kohlhammer, 1994).

56. Mark 2.18 pars.; 6.29 par.; Matt. 11.2/Luke 7.18; Luke 11.1; John 1.35-37; 3.25-30. Whether John himself intended to create a disciple band is much less clear, still less that he saw them as representative of Israel in any sense. Meier understates the evidence (*Marginal Jew* 2.92 n. 149). The argument that John's baptism was 'initiatory' (e.g., R. L. Webb, 'John the

nizable identity long after his death (cf. Acts 19.1-7). This thesis is probably confirmed by the clear polemical note in the Fourth Gospel against overestimating John's significance,[57] and is certainly strengthened by the testimony of the pseudo-Clementines.[58]

Would that we could shed more light on these scattered hints. At any rate, the fact that Jesus bulks so large in Christian retrospection should not be allowed to obscure the historical fact that for many in first-century Judaism John bulked larger.

b. Jesus, Disciple of John?

Still more to the point, it is highly probable that Jesus himself first emerged from the circle round John. Indeed, it is quite possible that Jesus began, properly speaking, as a disciple of John.[59]

The key fact here is that Jesus was baptized by John (Mark 1.9 pars). This is one of the most securely grounded facts in all the history of Jesus.[60] It is not something which his followers were likely to have made up; there was nothing about the impact made by Jesus which pushed them to attribute it to the influence of John on Jesus as Jesus' mentor. On the contrary, the fact of Jesus having been baptized by John seems to have been something of an embarrassment to them. For John's baptism is clearly signalled in the Synoptics as a 'baptism of repentance' (Mark 1.4 pars.), an emphasis which again accords with the report of

---

Baptist and His Relationship to Jesus', in B. Chilton and C. A. Evans, eds., *Studying the Historical Jesus* [Leiden: Brill, 1994] 179-229 [here 194-96, 205-206]) ignores the stronger indications that it was provisional and transitional in preparation for the more important baptism to come (see below §11.3c).

57. John 1.6-9, 19-23, 30-34; 3.28-30. The argument that the Fourth Evangelist was directed polemically against disciples of the Baptist has been taken seriously since it was first developed by W. Baldensperger, *Der Prolog des vierten Evangeliums, sein polemisch-apologetischer Zweck* (Tübingen: Mohr, 1898); see, e.g., R. Schnackenburg, *The Gospel according to St John,* vol. 1 (New York: Herder and Herder, 1968) 167-69.

58. Ps.-Clem., *Recog.* 1.54: 'Some even of the disciples of John, who seemed to be great men, have separated themselves from the people, and proclaimed their own master as the Christ' (also 1.60). The old suggestion that parts of Luke 1 were derived from a Baptist group (e.g., Bultmann, *History* 294-95) is too speculative to build on. More plausible is the suggestion of W. Wink, *John the Baptist in the Gospel Tradition* (SNTSMS 7; Cambridge: Cambridge University, 1968) 59-82, that 'the church possessed these traditions from the very beginning by virtue of the fact that it was itself an outgrowth of the Baptist movement' (71).

59. The point is widely recognized; see, e.g., Sanders, *Jesus and Judaism* 91; Webb, 'John the Baptist' 218-23, 226-29; Becker, *Jesus of Nazareth* 52.

60. For the historicity of Jesus' baptism by John see Meier, *Marginal Jew* 2.100-105; Webb, 'John the Baptist' 214-18. The Jesus Seminar confidently voted the event red, that is, genuine (Funk, *Acts of Jesus* 27-28, 54).

Josephus. That evidently proved an unsettling thought to many of Jesus' followers (had Jesus needed to repent?). Hence Matthew's added note that John himself
had urged the inappropriateness of his baptizing Jesus (Matt. 3.14-15).[61] Why Jesus submitted to baptism if it was not to express repentance on his own behalf has
been a thorny issue for Christian theology ever since.[62]

A second fairly firm fact is that Jesus' mission seems at first to have overlapped with John's. This is one of the points at which the Fourth Evangelist's testimony fills out what otherwise would have been a worrying historical gap.
Moreover, according to the Fourth Gospel, Jesus' first disciples came from the
circle of John's disciples (John 1.35-42). More striking still, Jesus may well have
modelled his own mission on John's. John's disciples seem to have seen Jesus as
a competitor proving to be too successful by half: Jesus was baptizing more people than John (3.26; 4.1)! This testimony is given more credibility by the Fourth
Evangelist's haste to deny it: 'it was not Jesus himself who baptized but his disciples' (4.2).[63] Even so, a mission in which Jesus' *disciples* baptized was not so
very different from John's, since 'baptism' was such a distinctive feature of the
mission of the one known as 'the Baptizer'!

Here we can detect the same sort of embarrassment as we found in Matt.
3.14-15. For the Synoptic Evangelists seem to go out of their way to draw a veil
over any period of overlap between Jesus and John. Mark 1.14 makes a point of
noting that Jesus began his own mission in Galilee only 'after John was arrested'
(followed by Matt. 4.12). And Luke marks out the distance between John and Jesus even more pointedly. He inserts the account of John's imprisonment by

61. Note also the Gospel of the Nazareans: 'Behold, the mother of the Lord and his
brothers said to him, "John the Baptist baptizes for the remission of sins; let us go and be baptized by him". But he said, "What have I committed, that I should be baptized of him, unless it
be that in saying this I am in ignorance?"' (Jerome, *contra Pelagianos* 3.2; text in Aland, *Synopsis* 27). In some ways, more striking still is the fact that the Fourth Evangelist does not even
mention Jesus' baptism by John in a description which focuses attention on John's witness of
the Spirit descending on Jesus (John 1.31-34). But the Fourth Evangelist does not even mention
'repentance' and since he also avoids mention of the last supper in John 13 there are presumably other theological motives at work.

62. See, e.g., the discussion by G. R. Beasley-Murray, *Baptism in the New Testament*
(London: Macmillan, 1963) 45-55; 'he identified personally with John's appeal for conversion'
(Schillebeeckx, *Jesus* 137); 'he has, by implication, confessed his sins' (Taylor, *Immerser* 272).
P. W. Hollenbach, 'The Conversion of Jesus: From Jesus the Baptizer to Jesus the Healer',
ANRW II.25.1 (1982) 196-219, argues rather fancifully that Jesus was 'a substantial member of
society'(!), who 'through John's preaching . . . discovered that he had participated directly or
indirectly in the oppression of the weak members of his society' (199-200). Cf. and contrast
Chilton: 'The Jordan's waters washed away his feelings of estrangement. He repented of the
anger he had felt, of his resentment against his own people in Nazareth' (*Rabbi Jesus* 49).

63. See further below §14.8b.

Herod Antipas right into the middle of his account of John (Luke 3.18-20). The effect is to have removed John from the scene *before* Jesus' baptism, the account of the baptism itself being then passed over in a single word (*baptisthentos,* 'having been baptized', 3.21).[64]

Once again, then, it is difficult to avoid the inference that there was an early period in Jesus' mission which the Synoptic Evangelists chose to ignore, presumably because the distinctive mission of Jesus began only after Jesus separated from the Baptist or was forced by John's arrest to strike out on his own in Galilee.[65] Whether on the basis of this finding we should speak of Jesus as John's 'disciple' may resolve simply into the question whether 'disciple' is the best term to use.[66] Whether it also means that in developing a distinctive mission Jesus also adopted a distinctive message is a question to which we will have to return.[67] For the time being, it is enough to note that John's baptism as marking the beginning of Jesus' mission is a historical fact of considerable substance.

c. The Beginning of the Gospel

The conclusion just reached is all the more striking in view of the fact that the Baptist is remembered in all strands of the Gospel tradition as 'the beginning of the gospel of Jesus Christ' (Mark 1.1). Mark is most explicit: 1.2-8 makes it clear that it is John who marks or even constitutes that 'beginning'; just as, later, John's martyr-like death prefigures that of Jesus (6.14-29). But the fact that Q, by general consent, begins with the preaching of John (Matt. 3.7-12/Luke 3.7-9, 16-17) carries the same implication.[68] Matthew, although beginning with the birth narratives, amazingly has John preaching precisely the same message as Jesus: 'Repent, for the kingdom of heaven has drawn near' (Matt. 3.2 = 4.17; cf. 10.7); the gospel of Jesus did indeed begin with John! Luke also prefaces his account of John's ministry with birth narratives, but they themselves begin with the account

64. 'By a literary *tour de force* John is imprisoned *before* he baptizes Jesus' (Wink, *John the Baptist* 46). But he pushes too hard in arguing that Luke understood Jesus to have baptized himself (83 and n. 1).

65. For further reflection on the overlap between John's and Jesus' missions see J. Murphy-O'Connor, 'John the Baptist and Jesus: History and Hypotheses', *NTS* 36 (1990) 359-74.

66. Chilton develops the fanciful thesis that Jesus spent his teenage years as a disciple *(talmid)* of John who inducted him into the practice of merkabah mysticism *(Rabbi Jesus* 32-63).

67. See below §12.4e. Even so, it may be significant that the same accusation is recalled as levelled against both John and Jesus ('he has Beelzebul/an unclean spirit' — Mark 3.22, 30; 'he has a demon' — Matt. 11.18/Luke 7.33) despite the differences of their lifestyle.

68. Schröter deduces that the beginning with John was already part of the oral tradition prior to Mark and Q *(Erinnerung* 448-49).

of the birth of John (Luke 1.5-25, 57-80); John appears to be the inescapable preface to Jesus.[69] And somewhat like Matthew, Luke describes John as 'preaching good news' (3.18 — *euangelizesthai*), the same verb used of Jesus' preaching (4.18, 43; etc.). The Fourth Evangelist likewise makes it clear that the story of Jesus cannot get under way without reference to John (John 1.6-8, 19-34), a point all the clearer if the prologue (John 1.1-18) was added after the Gospel had been drafted to begin with John the Baptist.[70]

In many ways most illuminating of all are the references in Acts. According to Acts 1.21-22 one of the key criteria in determining who could take Judas's place was whether that person had been in the company of the disciples 'during the whole time that the Lord Jesus came and went among us, beginning from the baptism of John . . .'. 'The baptism of John', *not* just Jesus' baptism by John, marked the beginning of Jesus' mission. Similarly, Peter's speech in Acts 10.37 sums up Jesus' mission in terms of 'what happened [or 'the word that was performed'] throughout the whole of Judea, beginning from Galilee after the baptism which John proclaimed'.[71]

The concern to 'locate' Jesus by reference to John is also evident in the Q traditions utilised by Matthew and Luke.[72] The particular claim that John should be recognized as Elijah returned (Matt. 11.14), forerunner of 'the great and terrible day of the Lord' (Mal. 4.5), is also implicit in Mark's use of Mal. 3.1 in his introduction to John (Mark 1.2, as also Matt. 11.10/Luke 7.27). The description of John as 'wearing camel's hair and a leather belt around his waist' may have been intended by Mark and Matthew to evoke the description of Elijah in 2 Kgs 1.8 (Mark 1.6/Matt. 3.4).[73] The identification is clearer in their conclusion to the account of Jesus' transfiguration (Mark 9.11-13/Matt. 17.10-12). Luke achieves the

---

69. Brown considers the possibility that Luke 3.1-2 formed the original opening of the Gospel and that the infancy narrative was prefixed after both Luke and Acts had been completed (*Birth* 239-41).

70. Discussion in Schnackenburg, *John* 1.221-24.

71. For the syntactical problems of Luke's Greek in both texts see Barrett, *Acts* 101, 522-24. For the likelihood that Acts 10.34-43 includes echoes of very early Christian preaching see below, vol. 2.

72. Matt. 11.2-11, 16-19/Luke 7.18-28, 31-35. The closeness of the parallel clearly indicates literary dependence, with editorial introductions, and Lukan elaboration at 7.20-21 and 29-30. But the link between Matt. 11.12-15 and Luke 16.16 is less easily explained in terms of literary dependence and may reflect oral transmission. The content of the passage is discussed more fully below (§12.5c).

73. But see also Meier, *Marginal Jew* 2.46-49. In contrast L. Vaage uses such data to sweep John also into the Cynic net ('More than a Prophet, and Demon-Possessed: Q and the "Historical" John', in J. S. Kloppenborg, ed., *Conflict and Invention* [Valley Forge: Trinity, 1995] 181-202 [here 190-91]). Cf. Josephus' description of Bannus, 'who dwelt in the wilderness, wearing only such clothing as trees provided, feeding on such things as grew of themselves' (*Life* 11).

equivalent objective in his birth narrative (Luke 1.16-17).[74] It was clearly important among the earliest Christian communities that John's widely recognized role as a prophet should be seen to accord with the significance attributed to Jesus. The tradition is related as from the perspective of Jesus and assumes his dominant role. But in apologetic terms an initial concern was probably that Jesus should benefit from the high regard in which John was more widely held in circles beyond that of Jesus' disciples.

The same concern is accentuated in the Fourth Gospel, where the subordination of John to Jesus is firmly marked: John was merely a witness, but a witness *par excellence* to Jesus.[75] If some polemic is also evident in the Fourth Evangelist's treatment of John, against continuing circles of Baptist disciples,[76] that simply confirms the weight of John's wider influence and the importance that must have been perceived from earliest days in Christian circles of being able to demonstrate how the relation between John and Jesus worked in favour of Jesus.

The point can be pressed a little more. In view of the later embarrassment regarding Jesus' relationship with John, it is impossible to think that the implied influence of John on Jesus entered the tradition at a late stage. That influence, at least in terms of Jesus' baptism by John and Jesus' emergence from the circle round John, must belong to bedrock historicity.

In contrast, we may note that the Jesus/John theme is almost wholly lacking in the *Gospel of Thomas*. The sole remnants are *GTh* 46 and 78:

Q 7.28	GTh 46
I tell you, <u>among those born of women</u> there has not arisen one <u>greater than John</u>; but he who is least in <u>the kingdom</u> of God is <u>greater than</u> he.	Jesus said, 'From Adam until John the Baptist, <u>among those born of women</u>, there is none <u>greater than John</u> the Baptist that his eyes should not be lowered (before him). But I have said, whoever among you becomes a child will know <u>the kingdom</u> and will be <u>greater than</u> John.

Q 7.24-25	GTh 78
Jesus began to speak to the crowds concerning John. 'What <u>did you go out into the</u> wilderness to look at? <u>A reed shaken by the wind?</u> What then did you go out to see? <u>A man clothed in soft clothing?</u> Behold those who are gorgeously apparelled and live in luxury are in royal palaces'.	Why <u>did you go out into the</u> countryside? To see <u>a reed shaken by the wind?</u> And to see <u>a man clothed in soft clothing</u> (like your) kings and great ones? They are clothed in soft clothing, and they are unable to discern the truth.

74. There is probably an allusion to Mal. 4.6 (cf. Sir. 48.10) in Luke 1.16.

75. John 1.6-9, 15, 19-36; 3.25-30; 5.33-36. Note the heavy emphasis on the 'witness' motif (1.7-8, 15, 19, 32, 34; 3.26, 28; 5.33-34, 36), particularly the triple confession of 1.20. As Wink observes, the Fourth Evangelist has narrowed the role of John to that of witness-bearer, but has also increased the focus on that role, 'the ideal witness to Christ' (*John the Baptist* 87-106, here 105).

76. As suggested above, n. 57.

In the latter (*GTh* 78), any allusion to John is absent (given only by the Q introduction). This is significant. For the distinguishing feature and frame of the 'gospel form' evident in all the canonical Gospels is provided not only by the Passion, but also by its beginning with John and his baptism, as attested also by Q. If the *Thomas* tradition is old, then those who made use of it can hardly have been unaware of this (as *GTh* 46 probably confirms). In which case it looks as though the *Thomas* tradents have deliberately abbreviated the Baptist motif. This suggests in turn a conscious elimination by the *Thomas* tradents of the strong note of imminent judgment, which characterizes the Q account of John's preaching (Q 3.7-9, 16-17), as part of a broader redactional diminution of the larger judgment motif in the Q/Synoptic tradition. This line of reasoning runs counter to the arguments of Koester and others that the theme of judgment in Q is a redactional development of Q (= Q²) unknown to *Thomas*.[77] On the contrary, it rather looks as though *Thomas* omits what was a clear recollection (in Q) of John's significance for the first disciples of Jesus and of (or despite) the judgmental character of John's preaching.[78] It will be well to bear in mind this initial finding since it will have bearing on our attempts to hear again the preaching of Jesus through the ears of his first disciples.

For the moment, however, the initial conclusion can be fully affirmed, that John was seen as the beginning of the good news of Jesus from the earliest days of discipleship to Jesus.

11.3. John's Baptism

The significance of John independently of Jesus and of his likely influence on Jesus makes it all the more important to understand as fully as possible this immediate antecedent to Jesus, the springboard, perhaps, from which Jesus launched his own career as a preacher.

a. 'The Baptist'

Of the little we know about John, the most outstanding feature was clearly his baptism. This is the point on which all accounts agree most closely. Mark introduces John as 'baptizing in the desert' (Mark 1.4), or as 'the baptizer' *(ho baptizōn)* (6.14, 24).[79] He sums up John's message as 'proclaiming a baptism of

---

77. Koester, *Ancient Christian Gospels* 86-99 (here 96-97). See further above §7.4c.

78. See A. Kirk, 'Upbraiding Wisdom: John's Speech and the Beginning of Q (Q 3:7-9, 16-17)', *NovT* 40 (1998) 1-16; and further below §12.4e.

79. The original text of Mark 1.4 may well have lacked the definite article: 'John came

repentance' (1.4), and reports others as referring to him as 'the Baptist' *(ho baptistēs)* (6.25; 8.28). In Matthew this is the title by which John is known by all — by the narrator, Jesus, Herod, and the disciples — John 'the Baptist';[80] similarly Luke[81] and, most interesting, Josephus — 'John, known as the Baptist *(baptistēs)' (Ant.* 18.116).[82] The term ('Baptist') is now so familiar to us that we forget its unusualness. The English word 'baptize' is, of course, a loan word taken directly into English from the Greek *baptizein.* Behind *baptizein* presumably lies the Hebrew/Aramaic *tabal.* And since we can hardly assume that the title 'the Baptist' was first coined in Greek, we must assume that John was known as *hattobel* (Hebrew) or *tabᵉla* (Aramaic). In both cases (Aramaic and Greek) we are talking about a term or title created *de novo.* So far as we can tell, no one prior to John had been designated 'the Baptist'; in Greek the term is unique to John. That presumably indicates the creation of a fresh usage: a foreign word is not usually drawn into another language unless it describes something for which there is no adequate native equivalent, and the direct translation (presumably) of *tabᵉla* into *ho baptistēs* probably signifies an equivalent recognition that an unusual or unique role required a fresh or unique formulation. The uniqueness of the designation carries over from Aramaic to Greek to English!

This immediately tells us that John was distinctive on this precise point. There have been various speculations about 'baptist movements' in the Jordan valley, with the implication that John's was or may have been one of a number of such practices.[83] But the fact that only John was picked out with this unusual formulation tells against such speculation.[84] Similarly the much-touted suggestion

---

baptizing in the desert' (Metzger, *Textual Commentary* 73). In 6.14 and 24, however, the tendency was to standardize an original *ho baptizōn* to *baptistēs.*

80. Matt. 3.1; 11.11-12; 14.2, 8; 16.14; 17.13.

81. Luke 7.20, 33; 9.19. The fact that the title is lacking in Matt. 11.18 (par. Luke 7.33) implies that Q did not use the title.

82. Vaage argues that John's baptism is marginalized in Q ('More than a Prophet' 188); but *The Critical Edition of Q* (Robinson, Hoffmann, and Kloppenborg) includes the opening reference of Q 3.7.

83. A particular manifestation 'of a much larger Jewish penitential and baptizing movement around the region of the Jordan in the 1st centuries BC and AD' (Meier, *Marginal Jew* 2.27), referring to J. Thomas, *Le mouvement baptiste en Palestine et Syrie (150 av. J.-C.–300 ap. J.-C.)* (Gembloux: Duculot, 1935). However, the only solid data we have for the period of John himself relate to the Essenes and Josephus' sometime 'guru' Bannus *(Life* 11-12). The data have been recently reviewed by K. Rudolph, 'The Baptist Sects', in Horbury, et al., *Judaism* 3.471-500.

84. The fact that Josephus also uses *baptismos* and *baptisis (Ant.* 18.117), as well as *baptistēs (Ant.* 18.116), only here in his writings also signals his own awareness of the singularity of what John was doing. In contrast, for his description of Bannus's 'frequent bathings' *(Life* 11) and the daily ritual washings at Qumran *(War* 2.129) Josephus does not use a *bapti-* form, but forms of *louō* ('bathe, wash').

that John derived the act which gave him his nickname from an already established practice of proselyte baptism[85] is seriously called into question.[86] If there was an already well recognized practice of 'baptism', why would John be picked out as 'the Baptist'? The more plausible alternative, that John was influenced in at least some measure by the emphasis placed on ritual bathing in Jewish piety, particularly 'down the road' at Qumran,[87] can still stand, but only if we recognize that the formulation of this specific designation must imply that John's ritual was distinctive, requiring a fresh formulation, 'baptism'.[88] Further confirmation is provided by the dialogue in Mark 11.28-33 pars., where the effectiveness of Jesus' reply depends on the high popular regard for what was a controversial innovation, John's *baptism* (11.30).

b. A Baptism of Repentance

What was so different about John's baptism? Two answers suggest themselves at once. First, it was probably a once-for-all immersion, as distinct from regular ritual baths. Although the text never says so explicitly, the inference is probably sound: otherwise we would expect John's baptising to be consistently described in continuous tenses;[89] there is nothing to suggest that Jesus was baptized by John more than once;[90] and a once-for-all baptism correlates with John's understanding of the imminent finality of the coming judgment (see below, §11.4b).[91] Second, the fact that John is distinguished as 'the baptizer' reminds us that in rit-

---

85. See, e.g., those cited by Beasley-Murray, *Baptism* 18 n. 2.

86. See further Beasley-Murray, *Baptism* 18-31; L. H. Schiffman, 'At the Crossroads: Tannaitic Perspectives on the Jewish-Christian Schism', in E. P. Sanders, ed., *Jewish and Christian Self-Definition,* Vol. 2 (Philadelphia: Fortress, 1981) 115-56 (here 127-31); Webb, *John the Baptizer* 122-28; S. J. D. Cohen, 'The Rabbinic Conversion Ceremony', in *Beginnings of Jewishness* 198-238 (here 222-25).

87. Beasley-Murray, *Baptism* 11-18; Davies and Allison, *Matthew* 1.299.

88. Cf. Webb, 'John the Baptist' 187-89; Stegemann lists eight points of difference (*Library* 221-22).

89. Imperfect (Mark 1.5/Matt. 3.6); present (Matt. 3.11/Luke 3.16/John 1.26); but also aorist (Mark 1.8; Luke 3.7, 21).

90. *Pace* Taylor who questions whether John's baptism was unrepeatable, but ignores the urgency of John's preaching (*Immerser* 70-71: 'it would be wrong to assume that only one of John's immersions was required per lifetime'). *Pace* also Chilton, who simply assumes that John's baptism was 'like Jewish baptism generally' and so could be repeated as necessity arose (*Rabbi Jesus* 48; earlier his 'John the Purifier', in Chilton and Evans, *Jesus in Context* 203-20); similarly Fredriksen, *Jesus* 190 ('multiple immersions').

91. Meier, *Marginal Jew* 2.51. The most obvious inference of Acts 19.3 is that a once-only baptism is envisaged.

357

ual immersion individuals immersed themselves. John was distinctive precisely because he immersed others.[92]

Worthy of more attention, however, is Mark's description of 'a baptism of repentance for the forgiveness of sins' *(baptisma metanoias eis aphesin hamartiōn)* (Mark 1.4/Luke 3.3). The people 'were coming out to him and were being baptized by him in the Jordan river, confessing their sins' (Mark 1.5/Matt. 3.5-6). This would differentiate John's baptism from the ritual purifications at Qumran even more. Immersion in a *miqweh* was for the removal of impurity, not removal of sin,[93] though in 1QS 3.6-9 the two cleansings seem to be closely related.[94] But John's baptism is to be distinguished from Qumran's ritual washings more because the ritual washings were clearly part of a larger complex in which commitment to and compliance with the ethos and rulings of the community were fundamental (as the context of 1QS 3 makes clear). In contrast, a baptism performed once, even with amendment of lifestyle, was rather different, both singular and innovative.[95]

It is the talk of 'forgiveness of sins' which should really catch the eye. This is not simply the testimony of Mark. Here again Josephus confirms what other-

---

92. Webb, *John the Baptizer* 180-81. This is the consistent picture of the Gospels (e.g., Mark 1.4, 5, 8, 9 pars.). Jeremias ignores most of the data in arguing that behind the Greek passive in Mark 1.9 lies Aramaic meaning 'immerse oneself' (*Proclamation* 51).

93. As Sanders has repeatedly pointed out, ritual impurity was not sin (particularly *Jesus* 182-83).

94. Webb, *John the Baptizer* 146-52. The rendering of 1QS 3.6-9 is important here: 'By a spirit of true counsel concerning the paths of man all his iniquities are atoned, so that he can look at the light of life. And by a spirit of holiness of the community, by its truth, he is cleansed of all his iniquities. And by a spirit of uprightness and humility his sin is atoned. And by the humility of his soul towards all the statutes of God his flesh is cleansed by being sprinkled with the waters of cleansing and sanctified with the waters of purification'. The act of atonement, normally linked to Temple sacrifice, is here attributed to the Spirit. The bath of purification cleanses the flesh. García Martinez wrongly translates the last phrase 'the waters of repentance'. J. Klawans, *Impurity and Sin in Ancient Judaism* (Oxford: Oxford University, 2000) concludes that 'the sectarian [Qumran] approach to purity was quite different from that articulated in the Hebrew Bible, where moral impurity and ritual impurity remained distinct: Sin did not produce ritual impurity, sinners were not ritually defiling, and sinners did not need to be purified. At Qumran, sin was considered to be ritually defiling, and sinners had to purify themselves' (90). Kazen is in basic agreement (*Jesus* 207). But M. Himmelfarb, 'Impurity and Sin in 4QD, 1QS and 4Q512', *DSD* 8 (2001) 9-37, questions whether the association of impurity and sin was characteristic of the Qumran sectarians.

95. It is Chilton's emphasis on John's baptism in terms of purification through ritual bathing which presumably leads him to the conclusion that John's baptism (ritual purifications) was regularly repeated (see his *Jesus' Baptism and Jesus' Healing* [Harrisburg: Trinity, 1998] 26-29; similarly Fredriksen, *Jesus* 190; above, n. 90). Kazen also overemphasizes the purificatory aspect of John's baptism (*Jesus* 231-39). But see Klawans, *Impurity* 140-42.

wise might be suspected. For though his description of John is obviously 'dressed up' for the benefit of his Roman readers, it is clear from his description that John was known as one who linked his baptism closely to the 'excusing' of the sins of those baptized (*epi tinōn hamartadōn paraitēsei, Ant.* 18.117).[96] In fact it is Josephus's language which points us to the really innovative feature in John's baptism. For the phrase just cited is cultic in character.[97] That is to say, it reminds us that the Torah made provision for sins to be dealt with through the sacrificial system. Of course, only God could forgive sin, but a priest was an indispensable intermediary in the offering of the sacrifice.[98] But John's preaching gives no indication that a sacrifice or act of atonement was necessary. In a sense, baptism took the place of the sin-offering.[99] That was the really distinctive feature of John's baptism: not that he rejected the Temple ritual on the grounds that repentance alone was sufficient, but that he offered his own ritual as an alternative to the Temple ritual.[100] Perhaps we should even say that John the Baptist in baptizing played the role of the priest.[101] How this went down with the Temple authorities we do not know. Possibly a one-off baptism would not be seen as much of a threat to the regular 'trade' in sin-offerings.[102] Nevertheless, John

---

96. Josephus uses *hamartas, hamartēma* and *hamartia* for 'sin' (the LXX uses only the last two of these three terms).

97. Josephus uses *hamartas* most often in his description of the sin-offering (*Ant.* 3.204, 230, 238-40, 249). And although *paraitēsis* can mean both 'request (that is, for pardon)' and 'excuse' (*Ant.* 2.43; *Ap.* 2.178), the closest parallels are in the same sequence in *Ant.* 3.238 — an offering 'in expiation of sins' *(epi paraitēsesin hamartadōn);* 3.221 — an offering 'to make intercession for sins' *(epi paraitēsei hamartēmatōn);* 3.241 — 'an expiation for sins' *(paraitēsis hyper hamartēmatōn);* see also 3.246, 247; 11.137, 233.

98. See, e.g., J. S. Kselman, 'Forgiveness', *ABD* 2.831-32.

99. At Qumran it was the community itself which atoned for sin 'by doing justice and undergoing trials' (1QS 8.1-7, here 4; also 9.3-6); note also Josephus, *Ant.* 18.19. It is worth recalling that Isa. 40.3 (the prophecy referred to John in Mark 1.3 pars.) is referred to the community in 1QS 8.12-14.

100. C. H. Kraeling, *John the Baptist* (New York: Scribner's, 1951); Webb, *John the Baptist* 203-205; 'John's baptism was a ritual of atonement' (Klawans, *Impurity* 139, 143). In the Diaspora the distance from the Temple would have encouraged the idea that sacrifices strictly speaking were unnecessary (cf. Philo, *Plant.* 108; *Mos.* 2.107-108), but those who came out to John lived within easy distance of the Temple.

101. The priestly connections of John are a fascinating sub-plot here, given the tradition of John's priestly descent (Luke 1) and the priestly self-identity of the Qumran community. Theissen and Merz, for example, think that the tradition of John's origin from a priestly family could be historical (*Historical Jesus* 198; see also 210). And P. Hollenbach, 'Social Aspects of John the Baptizer's Preaching Mission in the Context of Palestinian Judaism', *ANRW* II.19.1 (1979) 850-75, depicts John as an 'alienated rural priest' critical of the priestly aristocracy (especially 852-57).

102. 'An alternative to those sacrifices' (Webb, 'John the Baptist' 197); 'a clear alternative to the Temple' (Wright, *Jesus* 161); but would a once-only baptism constitute an attempt to

stood in a prophetic tradition which offered an effective encounter with the divine, an effective alternative to that focused in the Jerusalem Temple.

Josephus also gives a pointer to how the phrase used by Mark *(baptisma metanoias eis aphesin hamartiōn)* should best be understood. Was the *baptism* conceived as the effective agent in achieving the forgiveness or excusing the sins confessed?[103] That is less likely. It is more likely that the key factor was understood to be the repentance expressed by the baptisand. The phrase *metanoia eis aphesin hamartiōn* is almost a single concept — 'repentance-for-the-forgiveness-of-sins'. So at least Luke understood it (Luke 24.47; cf. Acts 5.31). According to Acts 13.24 John had preached 'a baptism of repentance'. Very striking, also, is the fact that Matthew drops the whole phrase. Instead, he describes John's baptism as 'for repentance' *(eis metanoian)* (Matt. 3.11), and leaves his only reference to 'forgiveness of sins' till his account of the last supper: the 'effective agent' 'for the forgiveness of sins' is the outpouring of Jesus' blood 'for many' (26.28). This theological ambivalence is echoed by Josephus' aesthetic unwillingness to regard John's baptism as a kind of (cultic) manipulation of God's acceptance: 'They must not employ it to gain pardon for whatever sins they committed, but as a consecration of the body implying that the soul was already thoroughly cleansed by right behaviour' *(Ant.* 18.117).[104] Josephus' emphasis obviously correlates well with Q's account of John's call for 'fruits worthy of repentance' (cf. Acts 26.20) and 'good fruit' (Q 3.8-9).[105] The best way to read Mark's phrase, therefore, is probably as 'a baptism which brought to expression the repentance-seeking-forgiveness of sins'.[106] This leaves open the ques-

---

'replace' the existing structures (160)? F. Avemarie, 'Ist die Johannestaufe ein Ausdruck von Tempelkritik', in B. Ego, et al., eds., *Gemeinde ohne Tempel/Community without Temple* (Tübingen: Mohr Siebeck, 1999) 395-410, concludes that not so much criticism as indifference is indicated in regard to the Temple.

103. For H. Thyen, *'Baptisma metanoias eis aphesin hamartiōn',* in J. M. Robinson, ed., *The Future of Our Religious Past,* R. Bultmann FS (1964; ET London: SCM, 1971) 131-68, the phrase 'characterizes John's baptism as an eschatological sacrament which effects both repentance and forgiveness' (132; similarly 135, 167); 'eschatological sacrament' was a popular description of John's baptism in the first half of the twentieth century (Schweitzer, *Quest*[2] 339-42; Bultmann, *Jesus and the Word* 23; Ernst, *Johannes der Täufer* 335 n. 219; still in Strecker, *Theology* 225, and Theissen and Merz, *Historical Jesus* 203-204, 210, 436).

104. Cf. again 1QS 3.8-9 cited in n. 94 above; contrast 1QS 3.3-6 and 5.13-14, which make clear that ritual purifications were of no avail without repentance (5.14) and membership in the community.

105. Luke adds some illustration of what would constitute 'good fruit' (Luke 3.10-14).

106. 'Repentance-baptism' (Taylor, *Mark* 154; R. A. Guelich, *Mark 1–8* [WBC 34A; Dallas: Word, 1989] 18-20; Webb, *John the Baptizer* 186-89, though he also accepts that 'in some way it *mediated* the forgiveness' [191]); similarly Webb, 'John the Baptist' 191-92; 'baptism of conversion' (Beasley-Murray, *Baptism* 34, 43); 'the seal on the declaration of willing-

tion whether John conceived of the forgiveness as immediate, as in the Temple cult, or future, that is, at the coming judgment.[107] But an answer depends also on how the coming one's own baptism is to be understood (see below §11.4c).

Given that the subsequent Christian use of both the term ('baptize') and the act (baptism) is derived from John's innovative practice, this conclusion may have more extensive theological corollaries. But there is another aspect of John's baptism which has been still more important for subsequent Christian belief.

c. A Baptism of Preparation

One of the most constant features in John's preaching is the promise of a future baptism which John contrasts with his own. The constant elements are common to all four Gospels, and probably also Q: 'I baptize you with water; he will baptize you with Holy Spirit'.[108] The implication is that reception of John's baptism was a way to prepare for the future baptism. Later Christian interpretation assumed that 'baptize' in both cases means 'baptize in water' and that the future baptism is (or proved to be) Christian baptism in 'water and Spirit' (cf. John 3.5).[109] But the first assumption hardly makes sense of John's contrast, in which his own baptism is clearly distinguished from the future baptism precisely in that John's baptism is 'in water', implying that the future baptism will have a different medium ('in Spirit'). As we shall see below (§11.4c), the metaphorical force of the imagery 'baptize' has been ignored. And identification of the future baptism with Christian baptism can be sustained only by taking John's contrast out of the immediate context of his preaching. Here again, since Christian usage is so

---

ness to repent' (Gnilka, *Jesus of Nazareth* 73); 'an expression of repentance' (Strecker, *Theology* 224); other bibliography in Webb 186 n. 79; earlier discussion in my *Baptism in the Holy Spirit* (London: SCM, 1970) 15-17. Taylor reacts against the phrase 'repentance-baptism', but confuses the discussion with the question whether John's baptism was 'initiatory', argues for a rather mechanical 'sequential relationship' (repentance before immersion), and fails to appreciate the power of the ritual moment in bringing a desire to repent to climactic and public expression (*Immerser* 88-98; note the tendentious rendering of 1QS 3.8-9 on p. 78). On 'repentance' see further below §13.2a.

107. Webb argues for the former (*John the Baptizer* 193); Ernst (*Johannes der Täufer* 334-36), Guelich (*Mark 1–8* 20) and Meier (*Marginal Jew* 2.54-55) for the latter, though Meier surprisingly does not bring Josephus into the discussion.

108. Mark 1.8; Q 3.16-17 (reconstructions of Q agree that it probably contained Matt. 3.11-12/Luke 3.16-17); John 1.26, 33.

109. E.g., O. Cullmann, *Baptism in the New Testament* (London: SCM, 1950) 10; K. McDonnell and G. T. Montague, *Christian Initiation and Baptism and the Holy Spirit* (Collegeville: Liturgical, 1991) 27, 30; earlier discussion in Dunn, *Baptism* 18-20.

derivative from John's we need at least to attempt to clarify John's talk of 'baptizing' by first setting it into the context of his message.

11.4. John's Message

The high evaluation of John by his contemporaries and in Christian tradition, as well as the likely influence of John on Jesus, also gives John's preaching an unexpected importance. It is unlikely that we will uncover and understand Jesus' preaching adequately unless we take the opportunity to grasp the content and character of what must have served in one degree or another as the foil for Jesus' mission.

a. Our Sources for John's Preaching

The tenor of John's message is probably clearest in the Q tradition of Matt. 3.7-12/Luke 3.7-9, 16-17.[110]

Matt. 3.7-12	Luke 3.7-9, 16-17
7 But when he saw many Pharisees and Sadducees coming for baptism, he said to them, 'You brood of vipers! Who warned you to flee from the wrath to come? 8 Bear fruit worthy of repentance. 9 Do not presume to say to yourselves, "We have Abraham as our ancestor"; for I tell you, God is able from these stones to raise up children to Abraham. 10 Even now the ax is lying at the root of the trees; every tree therefore that does not bear good fruit is cut down and thrown into the fire.	7 John said to the crowds that came out to be baptized by him, 'You brood of vipers! Who warned you to flee from the wrath to come? 8 Bear fruits worthy of repentance. Do not begin to say to yourselves, "We have Abraham as our ancestor"; for I tell you, God is able from these stones to raise up children to Abraham. 9 Even now the ax is lying at the root of the trees; every tree therefore that does not bear good fruit is cut down and thrown into the fire'.
11 I baptize you with water for repentance, but one who is more powerful than I is coming after me; I am not worthy to carry his sandals. He will baptize you with the Holy Spirit and fire. 12 His winnowing fork is in his hand, and he will clear his threshing floor and will gather his wheat into the granary; but the chaff he will burn with unquenchable fire'.	16 . . . 'I baptize you with water; but one who is more powerful than I is coming; I am not worthy to untie the thong of his sandals. He will baptize you with the Holy Spirit and fire. 17 His winnowing fork is in his hand, to clear his threshing floor and to gather the wheat into his granary; but the chaff he will burn with unquenchable fire'.

The fact that only Q contains this material and attests this emphasis is less of a problem than it might be. (1) There is an obvious reason why Christian tradition should ignore or discount the memory of John's preaching of judgment. Ac-

110. As already noted (chapter 4 n. 80, chapter 7 n. 29), this is one of the clearest evidences of literary interdependence between Matthew and Luke, best explained as each drawing on a common Greek source, Q.

cording to Q this was John's expectation for the one to come — that he would dispense judgment (Q 3.16-17).[111] But in the event, Jesus had not fulfilled this expectation — at least not this aspect of John's expectation. The fact that Mark lacks all note of judgment in John's preaching but knows the prediction of one who would 'baptize in Holy Spirit' (Mark 1.8) is significant: Mark's version appears to be an abbreviated or excerpted version of a fuller tradition which has been retained in Q.

(2) The silence of Josephus can be explained in not dissimilar terms. Josephus was evidently trying to present the Baptist in terms which would appeal to his readers: John was 'a good man who exhorted the Jews to cultivate virtue *(aretēn epaskousin)* and to practise justice to one another and piety towards God, joining in baptism' *(Ant.* 18.117). Tradition of John's preaching as preserved in Q would hardly enhance that appeal, as well as drawing on imagery unfamiliar to the typical readers of Josephus.

(3) More to the point, Q alludes back to the fierceness of John's expectation in the account of John's subsequent puzzlement: could Jesus indeed be 'the one to come' (Matt. 11.3/Luke 7.19)? And both Mark and Luke recall sayings of Jesus which use the imagery of 'baptism' for a fearful experience still to come.[112] Where did that imagery come from, if not from 'the Baptist' who coined the imagery in the first place? We should also recall that the imagery of being 'baptized in Holy Spirit', first coined by the Baptist, as all Evangelists (as well as Q) report, is retained into Christian usage.[113]

(4) Presumably this was one of the reasons why the Baptist's baptism made such a strong appeal. The implication is strong that it was no mere appeal to virtue and piety which drew so many out to John, but some threat of judgment which called for speedy and visible repentance.

(5) Above all, perhaps, we need to ask why early Jesus-disciple tradition should attribute such a fierce note of judgment to John if it was not what John had preached. There was nothing to gain from it, though no doubt any who wish to discount the Q tradition could find a reason or two.[114] In short, there seems to

---

111. There is no good reason to conclude that the two elements (Q 3.7-9, 16-17) originally circulated independently *(pace* Kloppenborg, *Formation* 102-107; W. Arnal, 'Redactional Fabrication and Group Legitimation: The Baptist's Preaching in Q 3:7-9, 16-17', in J. S. Kloppenborg, ed., *Conflict and Invention* [Valley Forge: Trinity, 1995] 170). The linking theme of 'fire' (Q 3.9,16-17) indicates rather a connected sequence already in the earliest tradition formation.

112. Mark 10.38-39; Luke 12.49-51. The influence of John's vivid language may be detected elsewhere: 'viper's brood' (Q 3.7; Matt. 12.34; 23.33); 'the coming wrath' (Q 3.7; 1 Thess. 1.10; Luke 21.23).

113. Acts 1.5; 11.16; 1 Cor. 12.13.

114. Arnal, 'Redactional Fabrication' 165-80, argues that Q's portrayal is wholly redactional (169-74).

be no good enough reason to leave the Q version of John's preaching out of the reckoning.

b. Judgment on Israel

The note of judgment is clear and unrelenting in Q's language and imagery: 'viper's brood',[115] 'the coming wrath' (Q 3.7),[116] 'the ax already laid at the root of the trees', 'every tree not bearing good fruit cut down and thrown into the fire' (Q 3.9),[117] 'the winnowing shovel to clear the threshing floor',[118] the chaff to be burned 'with unquenchable fire' (Q 3.17).[119]

That Israel is in view, whether individuals, Judea's leaders,[120] or Israel as such,[121] is evident from Q 3.8: 'Do not begin/presume to say to yourselves, "We have Abraham as our ancestor"; for I tell you, God is able from these stones to raise up children to Abraham'. The allusion is probably to another Isaiah passage — Isa. 51.1-2: 'Look to the rock from which you were hewn, and to the quarry from which you were dug. Look to Abraham your father'.[122] Also likely is a pun in the original — whether in Hebrew, *banim* ('sons')/*'abanim* ('stones'), or in Aramaic, *benayya* ('sons')/*'abnayya* ('stones').[123] The point, then, is that God's

---

115. The note of condemnation is clear (cf. Ps. 58.4; Matt. 12.34). *Echidna* ('viper') could be a variant of *aspis* ('asp') (Isa. 59.5 Aquila/LXX) and so conjures up such images as Deut. 32.33 and Ps. 140.3; the asp is also a figure for Satan at Qumran (as in 1QH 11[=3].17 and 13[=5].27).

116. John was no doubt influenced by the prophetic anticipation of God's judgment as a 'day of anger' (particularly Isa. 13.6-16; 34.8; Ezek. 7.19; Zeph. 1.15, 18; 2.2-3; 1QH 11[=3].28); as also Rom. 2.5 and Rev. 6.17. See further M. Reiser, *Jesus and Judgment* (Minneapolis: Fortress, 1997) 26-28, 171.

117. Again the imagery of judgment in these two phrases would be familiar to John's hearers (Isa. 10.33-34; Ezekiel 31; Daniel 4). Did Jesus echo and qualify this expectation in Luke 13.6-9 (Davies and Allison, *Matthew* 1.309-10)? See also Reiser, *Jesus and Judgment* 175-76.

118. Webb follows Schürmann, *Lukasevangelium* 1.177-78, in arguing that it is not the act of winnowing itself which is in view, but the next stage of cleaning the threshing floor by heaping the already winnowed grain into the barn and the chaff on to the fire (*John the Baptizer* 295-300; 'John the Baptist' 202-203); but see Reiser, *Jesus and Judgment* 177-78.

119. Threshing or winnowing as an image of judgment would be even more familiar (e.g., Ps. 1.4; Isa. 41.15-16; Jer. 15.7; 51.33; Mic. 4.12-13; Zeph. 2.2; 1Q17 [1QJubᵃ] 2-4).

120. The most obvious target would be the high priestly aristocracy (Webb, *John the Baptizer* 175-78). But Q does not seem to have specified the audience; Matthew's 'many of the Pharisees and Sadducees' (Matt. 3.7) is usually regarded as redactional.

121. 'All the people of Israel' (Acts 13.24).

122. As noted already by Chrysostom (Davies and Allison, *Matthew* 1.308).

123. Black, *Aramaic Approach* 145. But Casey remains unconvinced (*Aramaic Sources*

free choice of Abraham was no guarantee of the continuing security of his descendants, since God could choose again with the same freedom. John stood here in the tradition of prophetic rebuke to Israel for its presumption of God's favour in spite of sin.[124] In its own way his was a protest against the factionalism which disfigured Second Temple Judaism at this time (above §9.4). For the factions tended to meet the problem of Israel's continuing sin and disloyalty by narrowing the covenant to those loyal to each particular sect. John met it, however, by recalling his hearers to the fact that God's election in the first place was an act of sovereign freedom, and by calling them to repentance in the light of that sovereign choice. It does not follow that John had Gentiles in mind at this point, since the decisive category was still 'children of Abraham'. But the rebuke of Amos 9.7 is not so far removed, and later on Paul developed a not dissimilar argument in Rom. 9–11. At any rate, the fact that John was remembered as rebuking his hearers' presumption in their birth cannot be without significance when we go on to look at the Israel-orientation of Jesus' preaching.

Throughout the twentieth century, John's preaching of judgment has been described as 'eschatological'. In other words, it is deduced from the imagery used by John that John looked for the imminent coming of *final* judgment. That certainly seems to be the tenor of John's reference to 'the coming (day of) wrath', with the accompanying imagery of destruction by fire.[125] But as the echoes indicate,[126] the imagery utilized in Q 3.7-9, 17 regularly had in view future calamities on individuals or nations which were not necessarily seen as 'final'.[127] Moreover, the talk of raising up other children to Abraham hardly envisages the history of Abraham's descendants being brought to an abrupt end. And in the teaching attested only by Luke (3.10-14) the note of eschatological urgency is distinctly lacking.[128] So John's warning could equally have been to the current generation, with the implication that it was a final *warning* for them, rather than a warning of universal and temporal *finality*.

13-14). C. A. Evans, 'Authenticating the Activities of Jesus', in Chilton and Evans, eds., *Authenticating the Activities of Jesus* 3-29, wonders whether there is an echo of the Joshua tradition in Josh. 4.7 (8).

124. See particularly O. H. Steck, *Israel und das gewaltsame Geschick der Propheten* (WMANT 23; Neukirchen-Vluyn: Neukirchener, 1967).

125. The imagery of Q 3.17 may imply that wheat and chaff have already been separated by John's ministry; all that awaits is to shovel each heap into its appropriate final place (see n. 118 above).

126. Notes 116, 117, 119 above.

127. Cf. Webb, 'John the Baptist' 203-204.

128. Despite its sole attestation by Luke, the tradition of Luke 3.10-14 accords well enough with Q 3.8a, 9b and the testimony of Josephus, *Ant.* 18.117, not to be lightly dismissed; see particularly Ernst, *Johannes der Täufer* 93-98. A number of scholars include Luke 3.10-14 in Q (Kloppenborg, *Q Parallels* 10), but it is not included in *The Critical Edition of Q*.

c. He Will Baptize in Spirit and Fire

There can be little doubt that the same tone of judgment is present in the other image which intervenes between the image of ruthless pruning and the image of the threshing floor — 'he will baptize in Spirit and fire' (Q 3.16). It combines three powerful images. (1) The river or flood as a metaphor for being overwhelmed by calamity.[129] (2) The word-play behind *pneuma* (Hebrew/Aramaic *ruaḥ*), 'wind/spirit/Spirit', denoting judgment as well as blessing.[130] (3) Fire was the most obviously judgmental image,[131] as we can see from the way it was picked up at Qumran and in apocalyptic literature.[132] Particularly striking is the triple reference to fire in three successive verses of Q — most clear now in Matt. 3.10-12.

More powerful still was the combination of the images: fire and water as the medium of purification (Num. 31.23), Spirit imaged with water metaphors,[133] the spirit of burning as a means of cleansing,[134] but especially the river of fire that burns and destroys, probably in dependence on the vision of Dan. 7.10.[135] The most striking precedent combines all three images in a way which eerily foreshadows John's imagery and may even provide the source for it — Isa. 30.27-28:[136]

---

129. Pss. 18.4, 16; 32.6; 42.8; 69.2, 15; 88.7; 124.4-5; 144.7; Isa. 8.7-8; 43.2a; Jonah 2.5.

130. Isa. 4.4; Jer. 4.11-12; 1Q28b (1QSb) 5.24-25. The insertion of 'Holy' (Holy Spirit), in Q as well as Mark, presumably indicates the remembering of the Baptist's words within a Christian perspective. Webb, *John the Baptizer* 272-77, argues that 'Holy Spirit and fire' was original, but ignores the range of usage possible for *ruaḥ* and the significance of the composite image of 'immerse in . . .'. Meier, *Marginal Jew* 2.35-39 argues that Mark 1.8 is original (no 'and fire'), but ignores the background and imagery indicated in the following paragraphs (above) and fails to note the relevance of Mark 10.38-39/Luke 12.50. Becker is confident in the 'broad agreement' that the original spoke only of a baptism in fire (no 'Holy Spirit and'), since reference to the Spirit 'makes immediate sense only as a Christian expression' (*Jesus of Nazareth* 45 and n. 14; similarly Catchpole, *Quest* 7-12; Reiser, *Jesus and Judgment* 169-70, 185)! Theissen and Merz point out the paradox that a purely destructive baptism in fire would be *inferior* (in salvific effect) to the baptism of John (*Historical Jesus* 204). For earlier discussion see J. D. G. Dunn, 'Spirit-and-Fire Baptism', *NovT* 14 (1972) 81-92, reprinted in *The Christ and the Spirit*. Vol. 2: *Pneumatology* (Grand Rapids: Eerdmans, 1998) 93-102.

131. Isa. 10.17; 29.6; 47.14; 66.15-16; Jer. 21.12; Ezek. 22.31; 30.16; Joel 2.3; Amos 7.4; Obad. 18; Nah. 1.6; Zeph. 3.8; Mal. 4.1; *Pss. Sol.* 15.4. See further Reiser, *Jesus and Judgment* 172-73.

132. 1QS 4.13; 1QH 14(=6).18-19; *1 En.* 90.24-28; 100.9; 102.1; *Sib. Or.* 3.542-44; 4.176-78; *2 Bar.* 48.39, 43.

133. Isa. 32.15; 44.3; Ezek. 39.29; Joel 2.28-29; *Jub.* 1.23; 1QS 4.21.

134. Isa. 4.4; also 29.6; 66.15.

135. 1QH 11(=3).29-33; *1 En.* 14.19; 67.13; *Sib. Or.* 2.196-97, 203-205, 252-54; 3.54, 84-87; *4 Ezra* 13.10-11.

136. As indicated in my 'John the Baptist's Use of Scripture', in C. A. Evans and W. R. Stegner, eds., *The Gospels and the Scriptures of Israel* (JSNTS 104; Sheffield: Sheffield Aca-

Behold, the name of the Lord comes *(erchetai)* from far away,
burning with his anger, and in thick rising smoke,
and his lips are full of indignation (Greek different),
and his tongue is like a devouring fire *(kai hē orgē tou thymou hōs pyr
    edetai);*
his breath *(ruaḥ/pneuma)* is like an overflowing stream
that reaches to the neck;
to sift the nations with the sieve of destruction,
and to place on the jaws of the people a bridle that leads astray.

Whether John had this particular passage in mind is impossible to say, although the heavy dependence of his message on language which was characteristic of Isaiah has been apparent throughout this section. At the very least, however, we have to recognize that John placed himself in a tradition of prophetic and apocalyptic warning to Israel which drew on these powerful images.

Probably the most impressive feature at this point is the way John adapted this imagery in terms of the feature most distinctive of his mission as 'the Baptist'. The one to come would *baptize* in the river of God's fiery breath.

Here we need to remind ourselves of how the term 'baptize' was actually used before it became a technical term for the rite administered by the Baptist. In wider usage it meant simply 'dip, immerse, plunge, sink, drench or wash'.[137] In the LXX *baptizein* is used three times to denote a ritual washing or immersion.[138] And Josephus uses it characteristically of the sinking of a ship,[139] or of someone drowning or being drowned,[140] or of dipping something in water *(Ant.* 4.81).[141] More interesting still, the imagery of immersion obviously lent itself to metaphorical usage. So already the LXX of Isa. 21.4 uses the imagery of being overwhelmed by lawlessness *(anomia me baptizei).* Philo typically speaks of the river of the objects of sense 'drowning *(baptizonta)* the soul'.[142] Josephus uses *baptizein* of the act of plunging a sword into a throat *(War* 2.476), of a flood of people into a city drowning it *(War* 4.137), and of one 'sunken *(bebaptismenon)* into unconsciousness and drunken sleep' *(Ant.* 10.169).[143]

---

demic, 1994) 42-54, reprinted in my *Pneumatology* 118-29 (here 126-27), I remain surprised that so few have picked up this background imagery in their attempts to expound the Baptist's message.

137. LSJ, *baptizō.*

138. 4 Kgdms. 5.14 (translating *tabal* in 2 Kgs. 5.14); Jdt. 12.7; Sir. 34.25.

139. *War* 2.556; 3.368, 423, 525, 527; *Ant.* 9.212; *Life* 15.

140. *War* 1.437; *Ant.* 15.55.

141. See also Aquila's translation of Job 9.31 and Ps. 69.2.

142. *Leg.* 3.18; similarly *Det.* 176; *Migr.* 294; *Prov.* 2.67; cf. *Contempl.* 46.

143. *Sib. Or.* 5.478 speaks of the setting sun as 'plunged *(baptistheiē)* in the waters of the ocean'.

John appears to have been doing something similar. He envisaged the one to come as immersing people into the river of God's fiery breath as it (probably) flowed from heaven. As the imagery implied, this could be a destructive event. But as the imagery also implied, it could also be a purificatory, purgative event, burning away all impurities (as in Mal. 3.2-3).[144] According to Q, after all, he promised this further baptism not as a threat to those who refused his baptism, but as a prospect (promise?!) to those he himself baptized: 'I baptize you with water, but he will baptize you [the same 'you'!] with the Holy Spirit and fire' (Q 3.16). The parallel image was of wheat gathered into barns as well as of chaff burned (Q 3.17). And as noted earlier, Mark was not the only Evangelist to regard John as 'the beginning of the good news'.[145] John, in other words, took the imagery provided by his own distinctive act and drew on its powerful symbolism to give a new variation to an older prophetic/apocalyptic expectation. Or perhaps he baptized because he had already appreciated the power of the symbolism which it expressed. At any rate, we can assume that John saw his own distinctive practice of immersing the repentant in Jordan as somehow foreshadowing a much more fearful immersion to come. Presumably he expected that those who so repented would find the imminent immersion in the river of God's fiery breath to be purifying and cleansing rather than consuming and destructive.

We can probably go a little further. John's image of being baptized in the river of fire descending from heaven may have been John's own way of envisaging the final period of tribulation which in apocalyptic thought came to be seen as the necessary or inevitable precursor of the new age to come. This expectation was probably rooted in Daniel's prophecy that 'there shall be a time of anguish, such as has never occurred since nations first came into existence' before the people are delivered and the resurrection takes place (Dan. 12.1-2). It would be natural to link this prospect with the earlier imagery in Daniel's vision of the little horn prevailing over the saints of the Most High (Dan. 7.21).[146] Another powerful image was of a woman's labour pains ('birth-pangs') in giving birth, which was familiar from similar prophetic contexts[147] and evidently in current

144. Webb has some justification in criticising my 'Spirit-and-Fire Baptism' 84-86: to insist that the future event was envisaged as a 'single baptism' may press the language too strongly, particularly as I also accept that two outcomes are envisaged, destruction for the unrepentant, purification for the repentant (*John the Baptizer* 289-92; similarly Taylor, *Immerser* 139-43; the view is common — Ernst, *Johannes der Täufer* 53-54). But it still makes better sense of the imagery (a river of *ruah* and fire, not two rivers) to think of one baptism with two distinct outcomes rather than of two distinct baptisms.

145. Becker, however, insists that John prophesied only judgment: 'Nothing even approaching a promise of salvation crosses his lips . . .' (*Jesus of Nazareth* 38-39)!

146. Dan. 12.1 is echoed in *T. Mos.* 8.1; CD 19.7-10.

147. Isa. 13.8; 26.17-18; 66.7-9; Jer. 6.24; 13.21; 22.23; Hos. 13.13; Mic. 4.9.

use.[148] This is again properly described as 'eschatological'. But how 'final' was it? Resurrection and judgment on a cosmic scale sound final enough. But what lay beyond the purification and the birth pangs — both actually images of new beginnings? What was to happen to the trees that bore the fruit of repentance? What did the gathering of the wheat into the granary signify?

It is well that we pose such questions now, since they are a further reminder that the 'eschatological' character of John's preaching of judgment has been too much taken for granted without the meaning of 'eschatological' being adequately clarified. The matter is of prime importance for us, since the 'eschatological' character of Jesus' preaching has become so disputed of late, and since the question of influence from the Baptist at this point above all others cannot be escaped. Indicative of both the possibilities and the problems in this case is the fact that John's talk of one who would 'baptize in (Holy) Spirit and fire' was taken up in Christian tradition in an attenuated form ('baptize in Holy Spirit') and attributed to Jesus (Acts 1.5; 11.16)!

d. The One to Come

Least clear of all is the only other important feature of John's message — his expectation of who was to come. 'There comes after me one who is stronger than me. I am not worthy to untie the thongs of his sandals. . . . He will baptize you with Holy Spirit . . .'.[149] Whom did John expect? Of the main solutions offered,[150] none is wholly satisfactory.

(1) God is a possibility not to be lightly discarded.[151] In Mal. 3.1, a passage which is thoroughly bound up with the Baptist tradition (Mark 1.2; Matt. 11.10/ Luke 7.27), the messenger goes before the Lord. The Baptist tradition in the Lukan birth narrative reflects the same expectation (Luke 1.17, 76). And the exercise of (final) judgment is regularly attributed to God himself — as in Isa. 30.27-28. Probably decisive here, however, is the consideration that the talk of 'one stronger than me', and of being unworthy to untie his sandals (Mark 1.7 pars.), is really appropriate only to a comparison between two comparable figures. It is difficult to imagine John so trivializing the relation between God and a human being.[152]

---

148. 1QH 11(=3).7-12; *1 En.* 62.4; Mark 13.8; Rev. 12.2.

149. Mark 1.7-8 pars. Note the parallel to Mark 1.7 pars. in Acts 13.25.

150. See the brief review in Davies and Allison, *Matthew* 1.312-14; Webb's discussion is too schematic and indecisive (*John the Baptizer* 219-60, 282-88).

151. See particularly Ernst, *Johannes der Täufer* 50, 305, 309; Reiser, *Jesus and Judgment* 182-84; Chilton, *Jesus' Baptism* 47-48.

152. 'God does not wear sandals' (Stauffer, 'Jesus' 32). See further Meier, *Marginal Jew*

(2) Also possible is a heavenly figure, as exercise of such final judgment might seem to require. Most frequently suggested is the Son of Man,[153] on the assumption that the figure in Dan. 7.13-14 would already have been interpreted as a specific individual with a role in judgment.[154] The problem here, as we shall see later (§16.3b), is that it is very doubtful whether there was such a Son of Man concept and expectation at this time in Second Temple Judaism on which John could have drawn. And it is just as doubtful whether the sole occurrence of the verb 'coming' would be sufficient in itself to evoke the coming Son of Man, since the Jewish tradition, the *Similitudes of Enoch* and *4 Ezra* 13 (on which the suggestion depends), does not think of the Son of Man as 'coming'.[155]

(3) The suggestion that John would have thought of 'the one to come' as Elijah has more to commend it than is usually appreciated.[156] In Mal. 3.1 it is actually the messenger who 'is coming' (*erchetai*, as in Mark 1.7/Luke 3.16). It would have been natural to identify this messenger with Elijah spoken of in Mal. 4.5 (both are 'sent' by God), as Matt. 11.14 confirms ('Elijah who is to come'). Moreover, Elijah was remembered as a prophet of fire,[157] which fits both with the purificatory role attributed to the 'messenger of the covenant' in Mal. 3.2-3 and with the Baptist's expectation for the coming one. But did John see himself only as the forerunner of Elijah? The problem here is not that Christian tradition is convinced that John himself filled the role of Elijah,[158] for such reinterpretation of John's own expectation would be wholly understandable. The problem is rather that the role attributed to Elijah in Mal. 4.5 (cf. 3.2-5) seems to be essentially preparatory, 'before the great and terrible day of the Lord comes'. But, as

---

2.33-34; Webb, *John the Baptizer* 284-86 makes an effective response to J. H. Hughes, 'John the Baptist: The Forerunner of God Himself', *NovT* 14 (1972) 191-218; also 'John the Baptist' 198-202; brief discussion in Theissen and Merz, *Historical Jesus* 201-203.

153. Pesch, *Markusevangelium* 84, Stuhlmacher, *Biblische Theologie* 1.61-62, 110, 117, 124, Gnilka, *Jesus of Nazareth* 74-75, and Becker, *Jesus of Nazareth* 46-47, are typical of the continuing confidence among German scholarship that there was a recognized 'Son of Man' concept in the Judaism of the time (likewise Riches, *Jesus* 156, 176). Reiser mentions also the archangel Michael (Dan. 12.1; 1QM 17.6-7; *T. Mos.* 10.2; *T. Dan* 6.1-7) and Melchizedek (11QMelch) (*Jesus and Judgment* 182).

154. Note particularly that *4 Ezra* 13 draws both on the Danielic imagery (*4 Ezra* 13.3 — 'something like a figure of a man come up out of the heart of the sea') and on the imagery of Isa. 30.27-28 (*4 Ezra* 13.10-11).

155. As several have noted, 'coming' is not specific to any particular expected/hoped-for figure (see, e.g., Fitzmyer, *Luke* 666; Meier, *Marginal Jew* 2.199 n. 90).

156. Argued in a classic essay by J. A. T. Robinson, 'Elijah, John and Jesus', *Twelve New Testament Studies* (London: SCM, 1962) 28-52.

157. 1 Kgs. 18.38; 2 Kgs. 1.10, 12; Sir. 48.1; Luke 9.54. In Luke 9.54 the clear echo of 2 Kgs. 1.10, 12 was made explicit by the scribes who added 'as also Elijah did' (A C D W, etc.).

158. Luke 1.17; Matt. 11.14; Mark 9.11-13.

we have seen, the judgmental role attributed by John to the coming one seems to be much more 'final'.

(4) The traditional Christian interpretation of John's words is that he expected the Messiah.[159] The problem here, as again we shall see later (§15.2), is that there was no clear-cut or simple expectation of 'the Messiah' in Second Temple Judaism. Moreover, messianic expectation did not usually envisage a figure of fire, as we see in the most likely precedent (in the *Psalms of Solomon*) for such an expectation.[160] There is more obscurity here than the traditional Christian interpretation has allowed.

A question too seldom asked is whether John himself had a clear idea of who the coming one was to be. In fact the identification could hardly be less explicit — someone following John who would be stronger and greater than John. Subsequently John is remembered as sending disciples to ask Jesus, 'Are you the one coming, or should we expect someone else?' (Matt. 11.3/Luke 7.19). There is no good reason why this question should not reflect John's earlier expectation.[161] In which case it tells us that John had no clear idea as to who was to follow him. That the question could be posed in regard to Jesus presumably confirms the unlikelihood that John had in mind God or the Son of Man. The only clue John had himself was the judgmental role he attributed to the one to come. So we should probably not attempt to be more specific than John was himself. In historical terms, John may simply have had a conviction that someone much more significant was to follow, and that he had to baptize in preparation for a much more fearful baptism.[162] With that we will have to be content.

11.5. Jesus' Anointing at Jordan

This event is presumably to be regarded as the real beginning of Jesus' mission and therefore as deserving of particular attention. Would John's baptism and

---

159. So also C. H. Scobie, *John the Baptist* (London: SCM, 1964) 62-67; R. Leivestad, *Jesus in His Own Perspective* (Minneapolis: Augsburg, 1987) 36-37, 40. I have serious doubts as to whether a historical reminiscence of the Baptist's preaching can be detected behind the strongly theologized reworking of the Johannine tradition (with reference to John 1.29); but see Brown, *John* 1.58-63.

160. *Pss. Sol.* 17.21-43; 18.5-7. The imagery of 'cleansing' *(katharizein)* is stronger *(Pss. Sol.* 17.22, 30; 18.5). But R. Bauckham, 'The Messianic Interpretation of Isa. 10.34 in the Dead Sea Scrolls, 2 Baruch and the Preaching of John the Baptist', *DSD* 2 (1995) 202-16, sees evidence in 4QpIsa[a] [4Q16] 8-10.2-9 and 4Q285 5.1-6 that Isa. 10.34 had already been connected with 11.1-5 and given a messianic interpretation.

161. See below §12.5c.

162. Similarly Meier, *Marginal Jew* 2.35, 132.

preaching have been given such prominence otherwise? Possibly Yes, because John's preaching served at least as something of a foil for Jesus' preaching. And, as we have seen, the whole language and practice of 'baptism', which became so important in earliest Christianity, seems to have been derived from John. Even so, it is no doubt what happened to Jesus at or after his baptism by John which is the primary reason why John's baptism was regarded as the 'beginning' of the gospel.

a. 'Baptism by John' or 'Anointing with Spirit'?

It is hardly surprising that the episode in view is usually designated 'the baptism of Jesus by John'. But that is something of a misnomer. The fact is that in varying degrees the Evangelists all direct the hearer's/reader's attention beyond the baptism itself to what happened when Jesus emerged from the river — the descent of the Spirit and the heavenly voice.

Matt. 3.13-17	Mark 1.9-11	Luke 3.21-22
13 Then Jesus came from Galilee to John at the Jordan, to be baptized by him. . . . 16 And when Jesus had been baptized, immediately he came up from the water; and suddenly the heavens were opened and he saw the Spirit of God descending like a dove and alighting on him. 17 And a voice from heaven said, 'This is my Son, the Beloved, with whom I am well pleased'.	9 In those days Jesus came from Nazareth of Galilee and was baptized by John in the Jordan. 10 And immediately as he was coming up out of the water, he saw the heavens split open and the Spirit descending like a dove on him. 11 And a voice came from heaven, 'You are my Son, the Beloved; with you I am well pleased'.	21 Now when all the people were baptized, and when Jesus also had been baptized and was praying, the heaven was opened, 22 and the Holy Spirit descended upon him in bodily form like a dove. And a voice came from heaven, 'You are my Son, the Beloved; with you I am well pleased'.

All three Evangelists indicate that the baptism, that is, immersion *(baptisthēnai)* in the Jordan, *had been completed before the next events took place.* Mark links the baptism with its sequel by his regular *euthys* ('immediately') (Mark 1.10), by which he maintains the vigorous pace of his story-line elsewhere.[163] And Matthew, in following Mark somewhat awkwardly (Matt. 3.16a), presumably understood that the sequence of events followed in very close succession.[164] But Luke seems to be more concerned to link Jesus' baptism into the baptism of 'all the people'. Both baptisms precede the action which then takes place 'while Jesus

---

163. The baptism 'is quickly passed over and barely "narrated" in any real sense' (Meier, *Marginal Jew* 2.102). See also Ernst, *Johannes der Täufer* 17-19.

164. 'Matthew lays still less weight on the baptismal act than Mark' (Luz, *Matthäus* 1.155).

was praying' (Luke 3.21).[165] And John, as we have already noted, does not even mention the event of Jesus' baptism but focuses attention (by repetition) on John's witness of the Spirit's descending and remaining on Jesus (John 1.32-33). Equally significant is the fact that the early sermon in Acts 10.37-38 recalls how Jesus' mission 'began from Galilee after the baptism which John preached, how God anointed Jesus of Nazareth with the Holy Spirit and power'. In short, the story of Jesus' mission begins 'from the baptism of John' not so much because of Jesus' baptism by John, but because of what happened on that occasion.[166]

There were thus two key elements in the story as narrated in early Christian circles: the opening of the heavens as prelude to (1) the descent of the Spirit on (Mark says 'into') Jesus, and (2) the voice from heaven hailing Jesus as 'my son, the beloved, with whom I am well pleased'. The fact that the Fourth Evangelist has the same double emphasis, albeit in his own terms (1.32-34 — the Spirit descends and remains on Jesus; John testifies, 'This is the Son of God'), confirms that this is where the primary emphasis lay in the early traditions about the beginning of Jesus' mission.

(1) As Acts 10.37-38 makes explicit, the descent of the Spirit was obviously understood in early Christian reflection as Jesus' anointing by God for his mission. This was how the first followers of Jesus understood the prophecy of Isa. 61.1 to have been fulfilled in him: 'the Spirit of the Lord God is upon me, because he has anointed me . . .'. This 'anointing' (*mašah/echrisen* — Isa. 61.1; Acts 10.38) was presumably what constituted Jesus as 'the anointed one', 'Messiah/Christ' in their eyes.

---

165. On normal techniques for determining the content of Q it must be judged possible that Q contained an account of Jesus' baptism (the point being obscured by the primary dependence of Matthew and Luke on Mark's account) (so, e.g., Streeter, *Four Gospels* 291; Polag, *Fragmenta Q* 30; Catchpole, *Quest* 76; otherwise Kloppenborg, *Q Parallels* 16). The main reason for the conclusion is that the following Q account of Jesus' temptations (Matt. 4.1-11/Luke 4.1-13) seems to assume a report of Jesus being hailed as God's son (hence the temptation, 'If you are God's son . . .' — Q 4.3, 9) (Meier, *Marginal Jew* 2.103, with further bibliography n. 10). That would imply that the main focus in Q's account of the events at Jordan was on the heavenly voice hailing Jesus as God's son, though if the Q account also began with Jesus being led into the desert by the Spirit (Robinson/Hoffmann/ Kloppenborg, *Critical Edition of Q* 22-23), both Spirit and Son motifs would again be present as in the preceding episode and as in the core of the birth narratives.

166. The implications for Christian theology of baptism will have to be considered later, in vol. 2. For the moment, we may note that the subsequently popular idea that Jesus' baptism 'purified the water' for future Christian baptism first appears in Ignatius, *Smyrn.* 18.2 (see further Luz, *Matthäus* 1.152). McDonnell and Montague simply repeat Ignatius: 'the Spirit . . . in some way effected a sanctifying of the baptismal water through' Jesus (*Christian Initiation* 28). But in the NT itself Jesus' baptism is never presented as a model for Christian baptism (see further Dunn, *Baptism* 32-37). Equally unsatisfactory is it simply to identify Jesus' anointing as his baptism: 'his anointing was his baptism' (Harvey, *Jesus* 141).

(2) Equally as significant, the heavenly pronouncement was probably understood as a combination of Ps. 2.7 and Isa. 42.1.[167]

Ps. 2.7 'You are my son, today I have begotten you'.

Isa. 42.1 'Here is my servant, whom I uphold, my chosen, in whom my soul delights;
   I have put my spirit upon him . . .'.

The Isaiah passage looks somewhat remote from the Gospel account of the heavenly voice, but the quotation of Isa. 42.1 in Matt. 12.18 indicates that there was a version of Isa. 42.1 current in Christian circles which closely matches the second part of the heavenly pronouncement at Jordan.[168] Here is confirmation that the early story-tellers in the assemblies and churches of the Nazarene sect portrayed Jesus as the royal Messiah, son of God, in accordance with Ps. 2.7, and servant of Yahweh in accordance with Isa. 42.1. This was a status and function for Jesus which they saw to have been inaugurated by Jesus' anointing by the Spirit at Jordan.

b. But What Actually Happened?

It is all very well identifying the import of the tradition as it has come down to us. But how did the tradition reach its present form? In one degree or other, most specialists who have studied the passage have followed the line marked out by Strauss: here we have a classic example of the 'historical myth'.[169] That is to say, there is no reason to doubt that Jesus was actually baptized by John; but the account of the heaven(s) being opened, the Spirit descending as a dove, and the heavenly voice, are all evidence of mythical elaboration.[170] Such elaborations are obvious ways in which the first Christians sought to bring out the significance of that event for their evaluation of Jesus.

   Moreover, the Liberal attempts to read here an experience of Jesus, Jesus' own experience of being commissioned by God, are undermined by the character

   167. There is a large consensus on this point; see, e.g., Davies and Allison, *Matthew* 1.336-39.
   168. Matt. 12.18 cites Isa. 42.1 — 'Here is my servant, whom I have chosen, my beloved, with whom my soul is well-pleased . . .'. That the form of Matt. 12.18 is not simply due to influence from Matt. 3.17 is confirmed by the fact that the translation variants used by Matt. 12.18 are attested elsewhere (details in Davies and Allison, *Matthew* 1.337-38).
   169. Strauss, *Life* 87, 242-46.
   170. For the symbolism of the dove see, e.g., the brief review in Fitzmyer, *Luke* 483-84; fuller review in Davies and Allison, *Matthew* 1.331-34.

of the account itself. For as Dibelius pointed out, the disciples could have been made privy to such an intensely personal experience only if Jesus had told them about it. But in that case the story would presumably have been narrated in the words of Jesus and as teaching of Jesus (cf. Luke 10.18),[171] whereas what we have here is a story told from the viewpoint of the narrator. Whatever lies behind the tradition, it is less than likely that the tradition was first formulated by Jesus himself.[172]

This observation correlates with the further indications that the tradition has been developed in the course of transmission. In the history of the tradition, there seems to be a steady trend to make the whole event a more visible, more objective wonder. Our earliest version begins as a description of something seen and heard by Jesus alone: Jesus saw the heavens torn open and the Spirit descending; the heavenly voice is a personal communication, 'You are my son . . .' (Mark 1.10-11). In Matthew the opened heaven is not a vision of Jesus alone, and the heavenly address is more in the nature of a public announcement, 'This is my son . . .' (Matt. 3.16-17). In Luke, in accordance with his own predilection for tangible spiritual experiences,[173] the Spirit descends 'in bodily form' *(sōmatikō);* there really was a dove to be seen (Luke 3.22). In the Gospel of the Ebionites 'a great light shone around the place . . .'.[174] And in Justin, 'fire was kindled in the

---

171. Dibelius, *Tradition* 274 (cited above, chapter 5 n. 35). Those who think in terms of an actual experience of Jesus communicated to the disciples include Scobie, *John the Baptist* 146-47; Jeremias, *Proclamation* 49, 55-56; Leivestad, *Jesus* 39; Taylor, *Immerser* 264-77; Theissen and Merz, *Historical Jesus* 211-12; Funk, *Acts of Jesus* 54. Borg notes the heavenly voices in stories of 'other Jewish charismatic holy men' (see below, chapter 16 n. 19) and deduces that 'it is historically possible to imagine this as part of the experience of Jesus' (*New Vision* 41). Chilton takes the vision as a paradigmatic indicator that Jesus was becoming a skilled practitioner in merkabah mysticism, the technique of envisioning the divine Chariot as in the vision of Ezekiel 1 (*Rabbi Jesus* 50-53, 55, 58, *et passim*). M. Barker, *The Risen Lord: The Jesus of History as the Christ of Faith* (Edinburgh: Clark, 1996), pushes the same thesis much further: a merkabah experience at Jordan convinced Jesus that he had become the son of God, the Lord manifested on earth; 'he achieved at his baptism that sense of complete identification with God which the mystics so often call the resurrection life' (55, 107-10). S. L. Davies, *Jesus the Healer* (New York: Continuum, 1995) suggests that Jesus 'entered into a state of alter-persona consciousness, which he came to define as possession by God's spirit' and 'believed that . . . when the spirit was active in him he was transformed into the Son of God' (65, 61). Similarly, R. E. DeMaris, 'Possession, Good and Bad — Ritual, Effects and Side-Effects: The Baptism of Jesus and Mark 1.9-11 from a Cross-Cultural Perspective', *JSNT* 80 (2000) 3-30, sees indications of an altered state of consciousness (ASC) or possession trance, and suggests that the vision of Mark 1.10-11 has a greater claim to historicity than the account of Jesus' baptism (also Malina, *Social Gospel* 145).

172. Contrast Cullmann (*Christology* 283-84) and Witherington (*Christology* 148-55), who push directly from the present form of the tradition to Jesus' self-consciousness.

173. Dunn, *Unity and Diversity* 180-84.

Jordan' (*Dial.* 88.3).[175] The obvious question to be put is whether this trend was already under way before Mark penned the earliest written tradition that we know of. Or to put it bluntly, is the whole account a Christian romanticising of Jesus' baptism by John, in the light of the significance of Jesus as later recognized, reflected back on the acknowledged beginnings of his mission?

In fact, I do not think the basic thrust of this claim can be easily denied — but with one important qualification. It is the same qualification made earlier — that the perspective of faith evident in the tradition probably goes back to its first formulation. That is not the same as saying that the perspective goes back to the event itself. But no doubt the first disciple groups following Jesus reflected on the beginnings of his mission, and the relationship of his early mission with that of John. What would lead them to formulate the tradition in these terms?[176]

The most striking data related to that question are the indications that Jesus himself saw his mission in precisely the same terms. As we will see later, Jesus himself probably claimed to have been anointed with the Spirit (Isa. 61.1), and thought of his relationship to God as son to father. Not that Jesus made this self-understanding a subject of explicit teaching; but various things he did say were sufficient to give his disciples a sense of it;[177] their own impression of Jesus as Spirit-inspired and God's intimate would be part of the impact he made on them.[178] A key consideration, then, is that such distinctive and defining characteristics of Jesus' own sense of mission presumably crystallized at some point. The most obvious candidate for that 'point' was presumably the beginning of Jesus' mission, or at least the stage at which Jesus' mission assumed a character distinctive from that of the Baptist's. In the event, however, it was the baptism of Jesus which was early seen to mark both the beginning of Jesus' mission and the parting of the ways between Jesus and John. The natural corollary for those reflecting on the beginnings of Jesus' mission was to tell the story in such a way as to bring out these distinctive features of Jesus' mission. That is, they related Jesus' anointing by the Spirit and sonship to God to this beginning event. In just the same way, we noted above, when the Christian tradents came to reflect more fully on Jesus' birth they made his birth from the Spirit and sonship of God the central emphases (§11.1).[179]

It is worth noting that in neither case is there thought of Jesus *becoming*

174. Epiphanius, *Against Heresies* 30.13.7-8.

175. Both texts are in Aland, *Synopsis* 27.

176. In contrast there seems to have been no concern in the earliest tellings of the story (prior to Matt. 3.14-15) with the question why Jesus should submit to a baptism of repentance; it seems to have become a problem only later. For discussion see Meier, *Marginal Jew* 2.110-16.

177. See below, §§15.6c and 16.2.

178. Cf. again the claims made about rather than by Honi and Hanina (§16.2a at n. 19).

179. Meier, *Marginal Jew* 2.108-109 critiques my earlier suggestion in which, in a book

Messiah or son of God at that point.[180] In both cases the thought is of Jesus as Spirit-endowed and son of God from the beginning — whether the beginning of his mission, or the beginning of his life. But whether we can speak of Jesus himself experiencing the Spirit and sonship prior to his mission is quite obscure (despite Luke 2.49).[181] From the tradition itself we can deduce such a lively experience during his mission. Did he then experience a commissioning at Jordan? That is entirely possible, though the Fourth Evangelist's report of a period of overlap between the missions of John and Jesus leaves in question when it was that Jesus saw the need to strike out in distinction from John. All we can say is that in the formulation of the Jesus tradition, from the earliest days, so far as we can tell, the disciple story-tellers had no doubt that Jesus had been anointed by the Spirit at Jordan and was cherished by God as his son from that time or earlier.

11.6. The Death of John

Little more need be said about John at this point. Both the Synoptic tradition and Josephus speak of his execution by Herod Antipas after a period of imprisonment — in Herod's fortress at Machaerus, says Josephus (*Ant.* 18.119). The reasons given are at first glance quite different. In the Synoptics John arouses Herod's ire by condemning Herod's action in marrying his brother's wife (Herodias), but in Josephus John's preaching arouses such enthusiasm among his audiences to follow John's counsel 'in everything they did' that Herod actually fears serious unrest or even an uprising (*stasis,* 18.118). However, the two accounts may be closer than at first appears. For, as already noted, Josephus also thinks of John as a preacher of righteousness *(dikaiosynē),* commending his hearers 'to practise justice towards their fellows and piety towards God', and to cleanse their souls by right behaviour *(dikaiosynē,* 18.117). And the Synoptic tradition similarly recalls opinion of John as 'a righteous *(dikaios)* and holy man' (Mark 6.20), 'a prophet' (Matt. 14.5). The cause of Herod's action, then, was not that John posed

---

on religious experience, I speculated about an experience of Jesus significant for him in terms of his subsequently attested consciousness of sonship and Spirit (*Jesus and the Spirit* 63-65).

180. The full quotation from Ps. 2.7 (including 'Today I have begotten you') which appears in D and the old Latin witnesses is not original (see, e.g., Fitzmyer, *Luke* 485); but the reading was embraced by the Ebionites (Epiphanius, *adv. haer.* 30.13). In early tradition, however, Ps. 2.7 is referred to Jesus' resurrection (Acts 13.33; Heb. 1.5; 5.5; cf. Rom. 1.4).

181. Luke 2.41-51 smacks of hagiography. But we should recall the striking parallel from Josephus' own autobiography: 'While still a mere boy, about fourteen years old, I won universal applause for my love of letters; insomuch that the chief priests and the leading men of the city used constantly to come to me for precise information on some particular of our ordinances' (*Life* 9).

some kind of military or revolutionary threat.[182] John was rather a kind of Savonarola figure whose ascetic lifestyle and calls for moral reform cut too close to the bone and caused bitter resentment among the ruling elite.[183]

There are, however, several points worthy of comment here. First, we have a good example of the arbitrary power which rulers of the period were able to exercise. Both the Synoptics and Josephus agree that Herod was able to arrest and execute John without any obvious 'good cause' and without any formal procedure — 'on suspicion' *(hypopsia)*, says Josephus. We need to bear this in mind when we ask later whether Jesus foresaw his own death. Given the precedent of what had happened to his mentor, the Baptist, and given that Roman power in Judea would be, if anything, even more arbitrary and ruthless, it would be very odd indeed if Jesus did not reckon with the possibility of his life being abruptly cut short by quasi-judicial or other means.

Second, Mark 6.17-28 is probably the best example we have of a popular 'news-story' incorporated into the Synoptic tradition. John's popularity implies that there would have been considerable interest in what happened to him among the general populace. And popular interest was no doubt as much aroused about court gossip then as now. The story of John's execution, then, is probably the story which circulated in the village assemblies and market places of Herod's kingdom.[184] Since there is no distinctively Christian moral or emphasis, it is unlikely to have been constitutive tradition for the groups of Jesus' disciples,

182. Crossan, however, suggests that a call to the desert and baptism in Jordan would imply a re-entry into the Promised Land with obvious overtones of a new (military) conquest (*Historical Jesus* 231-32, 235); cf. Webb, *John the Baptizer* 364-65; Stegemann, *Library* 214, 218, 220-21, 224; Strecker, *Theology* 221-22 is quite sceptical. The suggestion would make more sense if the Baptist had required the baptisands to enter the river from the east side and to exit after baptism on the other, but the tradition contains no indication in that regard (*pace* S. McKnight, 'Jesus' New Vision within Judaism', in P. Copan and C. A. Evans, eds., *Who Was Jesus? A Jewish-Christian Dialogue* [Louisville: Westminster John Knox, 2001] 73-96 [here 80-81], citing C. Brown, 'What Was John the Baptist Doing?', *BBR* 7 [1997] 37-50).

183. More plausibly, Crossan also argues that the contrast between John and those 'in soft clothing', who are 'gorgeously appareled and live in luxury [and] are in royal palaces' (Matt. 11.8/Luke 7.25), intended a comparison between John and Herod Antipas (*Historical Jesus* 236-37). Theissen argues that the other contrast, 'a reed shaken by the wind' (Matt. 11.7/ Luke 7.24), likewise refers to Antipas ('The Beginnings of the Sayings Tradition in Palestine', *The Gospels in Context* 25-59 [here 26-42]; also *Lokalkolorit* 25-44); Crossan agrees (*Birth* 306-308).

184. Theissen regards it as 'popular folk tradition' and an example of the 'malicious gossip that pursued a number of the Herodian women in the first century' ('The Legend of the Baptizer's Death', *Gospels in Context* 81-97 [here 85, 94]; also *Lokalkolorit* 85-102). For the historical inaccuracies in the Markan report see Theissen, 'Legend' 86-89; Meier, *Marginal Jew* 2.172-73. Meier also notes the echoes of various OT stories, including Elijah's struggle with Ahab and his wife Jezebel (e.g., 1 Kgs 19.1-2; 21.17-26) and the book of Esther (173).

though they may have retold it in their own gatherings. And though Mark 6.29/
Matt. 14.12 may imply that John's own disciples were the source of the story for
the Jesus groups, the lack of more characteristic Baptist emphases probably
counts against that possibility too.[185] What matters then is not the accuracy or in-
accuracy of the detail, but that this was the general impression, a typically popular report. The Synoptic account records what was generally reported to be the
case. In other words, here we probably have a more extreme example of the fact
that tradition tells us not so much what happened as what was perceived to have
happened, not the event itself but the impact of the event.

11.7. Jesus Tempted

The Synoptic accounts follow Jesus' anointing at Jordan 'immediately' (Mark
1.12) with the account of his being tempted in the wilderness for forty days (Matt.
4.1/Luke 4.1). It can be judged quite likely that Jesus did spend some time in the
desert at the beginning of his mission.[186] Such a recoil for prayer and reflection is
entirely to be expected. The traditions of Moses and Elijah fasting forty days (in
connection with a direct revelation from God)[187] would not only have shaped the
later telling of the story but could also be expected to have shaped the motivation
of Jesus himself. After all, Jesus is remembered as retiring to deserted places at
other times for prayer.[188] Similar motivation probably lies behind Saul of Tarsus's
departure from Damascus into Arabia following the 'revelation' given to him on
the Damascus road (Gal. 1.12, 17). From the immediate context we might even
mention Josephus, recalling that as a young man he became the devoted disciple
of the ascetic Bannus in the wilderness for three years before settling to a more
traditional lifestyle (*Life* 11-12). Not least of interest is that Mark's description of
Jesus being 'driven out' into the wilderness by the Spirit (Mark 1.12) carries
strong echoes of the characteristic account of the shaman driven into the bush by
the inspiring Spirit to undergo a testing or purifying experience in preparation for
his future role.[189] That is to say, the Synoptic narrative may reflect typical reli-

---

185. Theissen, 'Legend' 84-85. In contrast, Josephus may be attempting to excuse
Herod in some degree by exaggerating the threat of insurrection posed by John's popularity.

186. Sanders, *Historical Figure* 112-17.

187. Exod. 34.28; Deut. 9.9, 18; 1 Kgs 19.8.

188. Mark 1.35/Luke 4.42; Mark 1.45/Luke 5.16; Mark 6.32/Matt. 14.13; Luke 6.12;
John 6.15; 11.54.

189. See, e.g., J. V. Taylor, cited in my *Jesus and the Spirit* 383 n. 105. Does this perhaps
explain why both Matthew and Luke soften the description of the Spirit's action — 'led up by
the Spirit' (Matt. 4.1), 'led by the Spirit' (Luke 4.1)?

gious experience and motivation before it reflects a story-teller's patterning of performance to conform to traditional accounts of such experiences.

At the same time, we recall the historical difficulty in locating such a wilderness period within the beginning of Jesus' mission (above §11.2b). If Jesus' mission did indeed initially model itself on John's (John 3.22-24) and assumed its distinctive shape only following John's imprisonment (Mark 1.14), we are left in some uncertainty as to the timing of any wilderness retreat, particularly as the Fourth Evangelist (our only source for the early overlap period) makes no reference to one. Did it happen 'immediately' after the initial encounter with John, or only after John had been removed from the scene? We are no longer in a position to answer such a question.

The question whether we can speak of 'the temptation of Jesus' as an experience of Jesus himself leaves us similarly non-plussed. (1) As with the question of Jesus' experience at Jordan (above §11.5), we need to take seriously the fact that what we have is a story *about* Jesus, not a story told by Jesus or teaching remembered as a personal communication from Jesus. Behind the story there are no doubt impressions left by Jesus, but how much more we can say remains unclear.[190] (2) Moreover, there can be little doubt that each of the Evangelists passes on a version which has been shaped in the various tellings. In Mark the interpretative element is modest: 'he was with the wild beasts', signifying, perhaps, Jesus being protected during the forty days (cf. Dan. 6.16-23), or possibly even an anticipation of paradise restored.[191] The Q version is much more elaborate, with its account of three specific temptations.[192] It is difficult to avoid the conclusion that the Q account has been shaped to bring out a parallel between Je-

---

190. Fitzmyer wonders whether 'Jesus recounted some form of these stories as figurative, parabolic résumés of the seduction latent in the diabolic opposition to him and his ministry' (*Luke* 509-10).

191. Cf. Gen. 2.19-20 with Isa. 11.6-9; 65.25; Hos. 2.18. See, e.g., Jeremias, *Proclamation* 69-70; Pesch, *Markusevangelium* 95-96; D. C. Allison, 'Behind the Temptations of Jesus: Q 4:1-13 and Mark 1.12-13', in Chilton and Evans, eds., *Authenticating the Activities of Jesus* 195-213 (here 196-99, though note also 202-203); various interpretations are reviewed by R. H. Gundry, *Mark* (Grand Rapids: Eerdmans, 1993) 54-59; J. W. van Henten, 'The First Testing of Jesus: A Rereading of Mark 1.12-13', *NTS* 45 (1999) 349-66.

192. As Kloppenborg notes, 'the temptation story in Q has often proved something of an embarrassment', which he partially resolves by treating it as 'a late addition to Q' (*Formation* ch. 6; here 246-47). The issue is bound up with the question of a link between the temptation narrative and what preceded (see above, n. 165). But it could equally be questioned whether the temptation narrative should not rather be attributed to oral tradition, picked up independently by Matthew and Luke (cf. Lührmann, *Redaktion* 56): the verbal agreements come precisely in the key exchanges of dialogue, as we would expect in oral tradition; and the variation in detail (tempted during or after forty days, the different order of the temptations) is quite what assemblies accustomed to the oral performance of tradition would expect.

sus' forty days in the wilderness and Israel's forty years in the wilderness.[193] But the idea of the 'testing'/'temptation' of the righteous is deeply rooted in Jewish tradition.[194] (3) Furthermore, there may be echoes of other episodes in Jesus' mission of which there were rather more witnesses: the expectation engendered by reports of a feeding miracle (cf. particularly John 6.26); the request for a miraculous sign, also represented as a 'testing', *peirazein* (Mark 8.11; Matt. 16.1/ Luke 11.16); and Jesus' affirmation that only God could demand total allegiance, again in response to a 'testing' *(peirazein)* question according to both Matthew (22.35) and Luke (10.25).[195] (4) Finally, the emphasis on temptation in regard to Jesus' sonship (Q 4.3, 9), as in the case of the heavenly voice at Jordan, suggests that the story of the temptation took its present shape only when the conviction regarding Jesus' divine sonship had taken firm and definite shape in the common faith of Jesus' disciples.[196]

The temptation tradition, therefore, can hardly be said to bear the marks of an impact made directly by Jesus, either 'there and then' or in his later teaching. The narrative attests an impact made, as it were, at one remove. An impression made by Jesus, perhaps through his whole mission, is dramatically represented in this story form.[197] That could mean that his disciples thought of Jesus as with-

193. Clearest in Matthew which is almost a midrash on Deuteronomy 6–8 (Jesus quotes from Deut. 8.3; 6.16; and 6.13); see particularly B. Gerhardsson, *The Testing of God's Son (Matt. 4.1-11 & Par.)* (ConBNT 2/1; Lund: Gleerup, 1966); 'a haggadic tale' (Davies and Allison, *Matthew* 1.352). The echoes of the manna miracle are strong (Exod. 16.4; Deut. 8.2-3; cf. John 6.25-34), and in the third temptation there may be an echo of Moses on top of Pisgah looking over the Promised Land (Deut. 3.27; 34.1-4); but other motifs are evidently at work too (see further Davies and Allison *ad loc.*). However, the allusion to the wilderness as a period of testing is clear (note the use of *peirazein/peirasmos* in Exod. 15.25; 16.4; 17.7; 20.20; Deut. 4.34; 8.2; 33.8; Ps. 95.9; Wisd. 11.9; 1 Cor. 10.13; Heb. 3.8-9). For a concise treatment see W. Popkes, *EDNT* 3.65-66.

194. Abraham (Gen. 22.1; Sir. 44.20; Jdt 8.26; 1 Macc. 2.52; *Jub.* 19.8), Job, David (Ps. 26.2), Hezekiah (2 Chron. 32.31), Daniel (1.12, 14), Tobit (Tobit 12.14S), Judith (Jdt 8.25), and the righteous (Wisd. 2.17; 3.5; Sir. 2.1; 4.17; 33.1).

195. Mark and Matthew also regard the question about tribute to Caesar as a 'test' *(peirazein)* question (Mark 12.15/Matt. 22.18), in answer to which Jesus sets in antithesis worldly power and the duty owed to God, as in the third temptation according to Matthew (4.8-10).

196. Cf. Luz, *Matthäus* 1.160.

197. Jeremias argues that the temptations all boil down to the same temptation: 'the emergence of Jesus as a political Messiah'. Since that issue has no *Sitz im Leben* in the early church, the nucleus of the temptation story probably goes back to a *pre-Easter* tradition (*Proclamation* 71-72). Wright argues that 'some kind of experience, early in his career, in which Jesus believed himself to have won an initial decisive victory over the "real enemy", must be postulated if we are to explain what was said during the Beelzebul controversy' (*Jesus* 457; similarly Allison, 'Behind the Temptations of Jesus' 207-13); on the latter see below §12.5d, particularly n. 371.

standing particular temptations at certain points — most notably when confronted with the likelihood of a fearful death (Mark 14.32-42 pars.).[198] But it could also mean that they saw Jesus' whole mission as characterized by a firm refusal to embrace the sort of alternative strategies for mission which the temptations represented.[199] Either way the temptation story does bear vivid witness to the impression made by Jesus on his disciples: that he was remembered as firmly rejecting populist or merely eye-catching options and as resolutely refusing to compromise on the whole-hearted devotion which God alone could demand.

This final thought on the sovereign demand of God, expressed so powerfully in the third temptation in Matthew's version, is a fitting preface to the principal emphasis of Jesus' own teaching.

198. The theme of temptation, *peirasmos* ('Pray that you might not enter into temptation'), is an integral part of the Gethsemane story (Mark 14.38/Matt. 26.41/Luke 22.46). Luke gives it particular emphasis (Luke 22.40), and two paragraphs earlier records Jesus as saying to his disciples, 'You are those who have continued with me in my temptations' (22.28). This correlates also with Luke's conclusion to the temptation narrative: 'When the devil had ended every temptation, he departed from him until an opportune time *(achri kairou)*' (Luke 4.13). In Luke's account Satan (presumably = 'the devil') does not re-enter the story till just before Gethsemane (Luke 22.3, 31).

199. Similarly Hebrews seems to think of Jesus enduring a fuller testing (4.15 — 'in every respect as we are'), but focused particularly in his Gethsemane ordeal (5.7-8). There is no indication that Hebrews has been directly influenced by the Synoptic tradition of Q 4.1-13.

CHAPTER 12

The Kingdom of God

12.1. The Centrality of the Kingdom of God

The centrality of the kingdom[1] of God *(basileia tou theou)* in Jesus' preaching is one of the least disputable, or disputed, facts about Jesus.[2] If we are looking for features which are characteristic of the Jesus tradition and relatively distinctive to the Jesus tradition, then the kingdom of God has to be one of the first to be considered.

In this we follow Mark's lead. In opening his account of Jesus' mission, Mark sets out a kind of summary statement or headline: 'After John had been handed over, Jesus came into Galilee proclaiming the gospel of God, and saying, "The time has been fulfilled, and the kingdom of God has drawn near; repent and believe in the gospel"' (Mark 1.14-15). The repetition of the term 'gospel' is distinctive of Mark's own perspective:[3] he sums up the whole of his presentation of Jesus as 'gospel' (1.1) and thus interlocks the Jesus tradition with the term ('gospel') which most characterized the post-Easter preaching of Paul in particular and which may have been coined by Paul for that purpose.[4] The point here is that

---

1. I will translate Greek *basileia* consistently as 'kingdom', its most obvious meaning. Whether the underlying Aramaic had a slightly different connotation is something to be discussed below (§12.2b).

2. See, e.g., those cited by Meier, *Marginal Jew* 2.237 and 273 nn. 4-5; Becker, *Jesus of Nazareth* 100-102; the *summa et compendium* of Jesus' message (H. Schürmann, *Gottes Reich — Jesu Geschick: Jesu ureigener Tod im Licht seiner Basileia-Verkündigung* [Freiburg: Herder, 1983] 23).

3. The redactional character of Mark's *euangelion* references (1.1, 14, 15; 8.35; 10.29; 13.10; 14.9) was first fully demonstrated by W. Marxsen, *Mark the Evangelist: Studies on the Redaction History of the Gospel* (1956, 1959; ET Nashville: Abingdon, 1969) 117-50.

4. See my *Theology of Paul* 164-69. Cf. Marxsen, *Mark* 138: 'The "gospel" which Mark

by headlining Jesus' preaching with just this term (1.14-15) Mark indicates his own understanding that the heart of that gospel is precisely Jesus' preaching of the kingdom of God.[5]

Matthew and Luke do not follow Mark in thus introducing Jesus' preaching as 'gospel'. But they both summarise Jesus' preaching subsequently in just the same terms: Jesus 'went about all Galilee . . . proclaiming the gospel of the kingdom' (Matt. 4.23; similarly 9.35); Jesus said to his disciples, 'I must preach the good news of the kingdom of God to the other towns as well' (Luke 4.43; also 8.1).[6] The Q tradition also recalls that Jesus sent out his disciples to proclaim the very same message as Jesus: 'The kingdom of God has drawn near' (Matt. 10.7/ Luke 10.9).

These summary statements reflect the weight of the Jesus tradition itself. The phrase 'kingdom of God'[7] occurs regularly in the Evangelists' recollection of Jesus' words — thirteen times in Mark, another nine times in the material shared by Matthew and Luke (q/Q), a further twenty-eight times in tradition distinctive of Matthew, and a further twelve times in tradition attested only by Luke.[8] It is hardly possible to explain such data other than on the assumption that Jesus was remembered as speaking often on the subject. No doubt a number of

---

writes is his commentary on the term "gospel" which Paul leaves (for the most part) unexplained'.

5. In parallel tradition Mark has 'for the sake of the gospel' (10.29), whereas Luke has 'for the sake of the kingdom of God' (18.29; 'for the sake of my name' in Matt. 19.29); or again, 'the gospel' (Mark 13.10) as compared with 'the gospel of the kingdom' (Matt. 24.14).

6. Luke does not use the noun *(euangelion)*, evidently preferring the verb *(euangelizesthai*, 4.18, 43; 7.22; 8.1; 9.6; 16.16; 20.1).

7. Matthew prefers 'the kingdom of heaven', though he does retain 'kingdom of God' in four passages (12.28; 19.24; 21.31, 43), probably reflecting earlier tradition. Why Matthew left some tradition unaltered is unclear. The usual explanation, that as a pious Jew he wished to avoid undue use of the divine name, makes sense, though, if so, it did not stop him from speaking of God frequently (though less frequently than Mark and Luke). At any rate the distinction does not amount to much (note 19.23 [kingdom of heaven] and 24 [kingdom of God]), though it is suggestive for the ambience of 'kingdom'. Cf. 1 Maccabees, which seems to have avoided use of 'God' altogether.

8. Mark 1.15; 4.11, 26, 30; 9.1, 47; 10.14, 15, 23, 24, 25; 12.34; 14.25; q/Q 6.20; 7.28; 10.9; 11.2, 20; 12.31; 13.20, 29; 16.16; Matt. 5.10, 19 (twice), 20; 7.21; 8.12; 13.19, 24, 38, 41, 43, 44, 45, 47, 52; 16.19; 18.3, 4, 23; 19.12; 20.1; 21.31, 43; 22.2; 23.13; 24.14; 25.1, 34; Luke 9.60, 62; 10.11; 12.32; 13.28; 17.20, 21; 18.29; 21.31; 22.16, 29, 30. It will be recalled (above, §7.7) that one of the most striking differences between the Synoptics and John's Gospel is that John has only five references to the kingdom of God (3.3, 5; 18.36 [thrice]), though 3.3 and 5 strongly echo Matt. 18.3. Twenty-two of *Thomas*'s one-hundred fourteen sayings refer to 'the kingdom (of God/heaven)'. See also P. Perkins, 'The Rejected Jesus and the Kingdom Sayings', in C. W. Hedrick, ed., *The Historical Jesus and the Rejected Gospels, Semeia* 44 (1988) 79-94.

the references just cited are redactional, added by the Evangelists when they composed their Gospels.[9] And we may be sure that others were introduced in the various retellings of the tradition which preceded the transition to written tradition.[10] But we may be equally confident that such retelling and redaction reflected an awareness, on the part of both the tradents and their audiences, that the kingdom had been a prominent theme of Jesus' preaching.

In the kingdom emphases of the Jesus tradition, indeed, we should probably see a prime example of the way the Jesus tradition was performed and handed on — by re-presenting a known and familiar theme with explanatory and other embellishments appropriate to the particular situation — rather as in musical performance 'grace notes' embellish a theme and bring out its highlights. An interesting case in point is probably the parable tradition. Jesus was evidently remembered as using parables to illustrate or illumine what he had in mind when he spoke of the kingdom. This is the testimony of both Mark (4.26, 30; cf. 4.11) and Q (Matt. 13.33/Luke 13.20). But Matthew's much more extensive use of the motif ('the kingdom of heaven is like . . .')[11] may indicate the technique of the story-teller retelling the parables as much as Jesus' own characteristic style. The point here is that it would make little difference either way: whether or not Jesus himself introduced all these parables (and others) with this formula, he was remembered as characteristically teaching about the kingdom by using parables.[12]

This consistency of the Jesus tradition and frequency within the Jesus tradition contrasts both with what we know of the early churches and with the traditions of Second Temple Judaism. In both cases, the imagery of God as king and of God's kingdom is familiar. But in neither case is it as prominent as in the Jesus tradition. In the Scriptures and post-biblical writings of Second Temple Judaism the phrase itself is hardly attested, and though reference is made to God's 'kingdom' or 'kingship', the theme is not particularly prominent.[13] As for usage among the early

---

9. E.g., Matt. 3.2; 13.19, 52; 16.19; 21.43.

10. Possible examples are Matt. 7.21; 8.12; 23.13; 24.14; Mark 9.47; 11.10; 12.34; Luke 18.29; 21.31; 22.16, 29-30.

11. Matt. 13.24, 31, 33, 44, 45, 47; 18.23; 20.1; 22.2; 25.1.

12. See also Jeremias, *Parables* 100-101.

13. 'The kingdom of God' (Wis. 10.10; *Pss. Sol.* 17.3). 'The kingdom (*malkut*) of Yahweh' (1 Chr. 28.5; 2 Chr. 13.8); 'my kingdom' (1 Chr. 17.14); 'his kingdom' (Ps. 103.19; Dan. 4.34; 6.26; Tob. 13.1; Wis. 6.4); 'your kingdom' (Ps. 145.11-13; *Pss. Sol.* 5.18). 'Kingship (*mamlaka, meluka*)' belongs to God (1 Chr. 29.11; Ps. 22.28; Obad. 21). Aramaic *malkuta'* (Dan. 3.33; 4.34). Latin *regnum* (*T. Mos.* 10.1). The fullest recent review is by O. Camponovo, *Königtum, Königsherrschaft und Reich Gottes in den frühjüdischen Schriften* (OBO 58; Freiburg: Universitätsverlag, 1984), concluding that the kingship of God is not a major theme in early Jewish literature and that it functions 'as a symbol, not as a precisely defined concept' (437-38). The sparse findings in regard to the DSS have to be qualified by the publication of C. Newsom, *Songs of the Sabbath Sacrifice: A Critical Edition* (Atlanta: Scholars, 1985). In

churches, it is true that Acts does continue the prominence of the motif[14] and indeed brackets its account of Christianity's beginnings with references to the kingdom (Acts 1.3, 6; 28.31). But most of these references are to Paul's preaching. And in Paul's own letters, the dominant voice still audible to us from first-generation Christianity, the theme is hardly prominent.[15] The strongest use of the theme is '(not) inheriting the kingdom',[16] which looks as though it is traditional (also Jas. 2.5) but is not found in the Gospels apart from the Matthean 25.34. Probably the formulation emerged in early Christian thought (Paul himself?) as Jesus' talk of the kingdom was blended with the much older imagery of inheriting the land of promise.[17] The point is that the overt overlap between Pauline usage and the Jesus tradition is minimal.[18] In other words, the prominence of the kingdom motif in the Jesus tradition cannot be explained as a reflection of a similar prominence of the motif within either the Judaism of Jesus' day or the teaching of the early churches. Once again, we have little choice but to attribute the prominence of the motif in the Jesus tradition to a memory of its prominence in Jesus' own teaching and preaching.

The point is all the stronger when we recall Jeremias's argument that the Jesus tradition has retained distinctive features of Jesus' teaching on the kingdom.[19] The imagery used in the tradition is indeed rather striking: the kingdom 'has drawn near',[20] it will 'come',[21] it 'has come upon' (Q 11.20), it is to be

---

her concordance to the often fragmentary texts (4Q400-407, 11Q17), Newsom lists over 50 references to God as 'king' *(mlk)* and 25 to God's 'kingdom' *(mlkut),* typically 'his glorious kingdom', or 'the glory of his kingdom' (424-26). The Qumran Songs can properly be described as 'the most important pre-Christian Jewish text on the theme of "God's kingship"' (A. M. Schwemer, 'Gott als König und seine Königsherrschaft in den Sabbatliedern aus Qumran', in M. Hengel and A. M. Schwemer, eds., *Königsherrschaft Gottes und himmlischer Kult im Judentum, Urchristentum und in der hellenistischen Welt* [WUNT 55; Tübingen: Mohr Siebeck, 1991] 45-118 [here 115]). See further below (§12.2).

14. Acts 1.3, 6; 8.12; 14.22; 19.8; 20.25; 28.23, 31.

15. 'Kingdom' appears eight times in the undisputed Paulines: Rom. 14.17; 1 Cor. 4.20; 6.9-10; 15.24, 50; Gal. 5.21; 1 Thess. 2.12; also Eph. 5.5; Col. 1.13; 4.11; 2 Thess. 1.5; 2 Tim. 4.1, 18.

16. 1 Cor. 6.9-10; 15.50; Gal. 5.21; Eph. 5.5.

17. The traditional idea of inheriting the land, which stemmed from the promise to Abraham (Gen. 15.7, 18, etc.), elsewhere in Judaism was transposed into the hope of inheriting eternal life *(Pss. Sol.* 14.10; *1 En.* 40.9; Mark 10.17 pars.; Matt. 19.29; Luke 10.25), the kingdom of God (Matt. 21.38, 43; see also 5.5), or the world to come *(2 Bar.* 14.13; 51.3). Cf. already Deut. 10.9: Levi has no inheritance in the land; the Lord is his inheritance. See also below, n. 73.

18. Rom. 14.17, not typical of Paul, may well reflect influence from the Jesus tradition (my *Theology of Paul* 191-92).

19. Jeremias, *Proclamation* 32-34.

20. Mark 1.15; Q 10.9; Luke 10.11.

21. Matt. 6.10/Luke 11.2; Luke 17.20; 22.18.

'sought',[22] people 'enter into' it,[23] and it is 'seized' and 'suffers violence' (Matt. 11.12/Luke 16.16). Such imagery is without parallel in early Jewish or early Christian literature. In the rest of the NT, only Acts 14.22 speaks similarly of people 'entering into the kingdom of God'. The Gospel motif is hardly to be explained from that isolated occurrence; rather, the latter is most obviously to be explained as an echo of the Jesus tradition.[24]

In short, the evidence we have points to one and only one clear conclusion: that Jesus was remembered as preaching about the kingdom of God and that this was central to his message and mission.[25] The impact of this preaching has been retained in the Jesus tradition, though less clearly elsewhere in earliest Christian writings.

12.2. How Should 'the Kingdom of God' Be Understood?

The conclusion just reached is clear and beyond dispute. But if talk of the kingdom was so distinctive of Jesus' preaching, how would it have been understood by his first hearers? In the case of a creative person such as Jesus evidently was we must always allow the possibility that distinctive emphases emerged from his own insight or inspiration. But even so we also must assume some context of meaning for his talk of 'the kingdom of God', since otherwise it would have been a meaningless term for his hearers, and the teaching of which it was the principal theme would have been more of a puzzle than anything else.[26] Nor will a narrative-critical approach be sufficient at this point: the term itself is used without definition, and the way what is said about the 'kingdom' actually illumines the term is at the heart of a long-running debate. Moreover, as we have just seen, the Evangelists themselves all assume that Jesus preached (the good news of) the kingdom of God from the first, as did also the disciples whom he sent out on mission. Alternatively expressed, the tradition shows Jesus and his mission disciples

---

22. Matt. 6.33/Luke 12.31; also Matt. 13.45. For possible Aramaic see Dalman, *Words of Jesus* 122.

23. Mark 9.47; 10.15, 23-25 pars.; Matt. 5.20; 7.21; 21.31; 23.13; John 3.5; *GTh* 22, 114. Note also Luke 13.24; 14.23; 16.16.

24. The 'entering into' the kingdom words are a good example of a Jesus tradition motif which on almost any reckoning has to be attributed to Jesus, even if individual cases may be best seen as elaboration of a motif remembered as having originated with Jesus. See, e.g., F. W. Horn, 'Die synoptischen Einlasssprüche', *ZNW* 87 (1996) 187-203 (here 193-97).

25. *Pace* Borg, *Jesus in Contemporary Scholarship* 87.

26. 'To say "the kingdom of God is at hand" makes sense only when the hearers know "the story so far" and are waiting for it to be completed' (Wright, *Jesus* 226); but note already the comments of G. B. Caird, *New Testament Theology* (Oxford: Clarendon, 1994) 367, and further below, §§12.3 and 12.6.

using the term (the kingdom of God) without explanation — as though its reference would have been self-evident to their hearers. So the question still arises: what meaning would the term have had in those circumstances?

a. The Connotation of *Basileia*

It has always been clear from lexicography that all the key terms had a breadth of meaning — Greek *(basileia),* early Hebrew *(mamlaka),* postexilic Hebrew and Aramaic *(malkut).* Without putting too fine a point on it, they all denoted 'kingship' in its various aspects, particularly the exercise of kingship, hence 'reign', and the territory ruled over, hence 'kingdom'.[27] This insight proved helpful to a European scholarship struggling to come to terms with late-nineteenth-century imperialism and helped broaden a sense which had been too narrowed by the German translation 'Reich' and the English translation 'kingdom'.[28] More to the point, the recognition that here was a term which was not monovalent but could express God's sovereignty (to use Dalman's term) in its different aspects helped make best sense of the usage attributed to Jesus. For on the one hand, talk of 'entering' the kingdom or 'reclining at table' in the kingdom, or of being 'great' in the kingdom[29] obviously evokes a spatial or territorial image.[30] But a more dynamic sense certainly seems to be implied in talk of the kingdom 'coming', having 'drawn near', and having 'come'.[31]

27. LSJ, *basileia;* BDB, *mamlaka, malkut;* Dalman, *Words of Jesus* 91-96; K. Seybold, *'melek', TDOT* 8 (1997) 359-60. Dalman preferred the term 'sovereignty'.

28. Dalman's observation — 'No doubt can be entertained that both in the Old Testament and in Jewish literature *malkuth,* when applied to God, means always the "kingly rule", never the "kingdom", as if it were meant to suggest the territory governed by him' (*Words of Jesus* 94) — had a major impact on twentieth-century study of Jesus' teaching. See, e.g., G. E. Ladd, *Jesus and the Kingdom: The Eschatology of Biblical Realism* (London: SPCK 1966) ch. 5: God's kingdom as 'a dynamic power at work among men in Jesus' person and mission' (135).

29. 'Enter' — see n. 23 above. 'Recline' — Matt. 8.11/Luke 13.29; Mark 14.18 pars.; Luke 14.15. 'Least/great' — Matt. 5.19; 11.11 par.; 18.1, 4; 20.21.

30. But J. Marcus defends the sense of 'Entering into the Kingly Power of God', *JBL* 107 (1988) 663-75.

31. In a sequence of contributions, Bruce Chilton, drawing especially on the Targum of Isaiah, has argued that the emphasis in the phrase is on 'the dynamic, personal presence of God', 'God in strength', 'the sovereign activity of God', 'the saving revelation of God Himself'; see particularly his *God in Strength: Jesus' Announcement of the Kingdom* (SNTU B1; Freistadt: Plöchl, 1979); also 'The Kingdom of God in Recent Discussion', in Chilton and Evans, *Studying the Historical Jesus* 255-80; also *Pure Kingdom: Jesus' Vision of God* (Grand Rapids: Eerdmans, 1996) 10-16. Earlier Goppelt: 'the coming of the kingdom was seen here [in the Beatitudes] first and foremost theocentrically as the personalized activity of God among his

At the beginning of the third quarter of the twentieth century, as harbinger of a forthright postmodern hermeneutic, Norman Perrin asked whether the term was not a good deal more flexible still. Scholars have been mistaken in regarding the kingdom of God as a *conception,* whereas it should rather be understood as a *symbol* intended to evoke the myth of God acting as king. To elucidate his point Perrin drew on a distinction proposed by Philip Wheelwright between a 'steno-symbol', a symbol with a one-to-one relationship to what it represents, and a 'tensive symbol', whose set of meanings can be neither exhausted nor adequately expressed by any one referent.[32] His conclusion was that 'Jesus used Kingdom of God as a tensive symbol, and that the literary forms and language he used were such as to mediate the reality evoked by that symbol'.[33] The potential of Perrin's observation has been most fully exploited by those who see the myth or story evoked by Jesus' kingdom talk in more specific terms as the restoration of Israel (Meyer, Sanders),[34] the 'metanarrative' of the return of Israel from exile and God's return to Zion (Wright).[35] Or should the reality evoked by the symbol be seen rather in terms of a radical prophetic protest against the social inequalities and oppression within first-century Palestine (Horsley)[36] or as a proclamation of radical egalitarianism, a 'brokerless kingdom', on behalf of Mediterranean peasantry as a whole (Crossan)?[37] Or should

---

people' (*Theology* 1.69). Such observations also call in question Riches's attempt to distinguish the term's 'core-meaning' from its 'conventional associations' (*Jesus* 18-19, 21-22, 42).

32. N. Perrin, *Jesus and the Language of the Kingdom: Symbol and Metaphor in New Testament Interpretation* (Philadelphia: Fortress/London: SCM, 1976) 5-6, 22-23, 29-32.

33. Perrin, *Language* 56.

34. Meyer, *Aims of Jesus* 125, 132-34 (index, 'Restoration'); Sanders, *Jesus* Part One (conclusion 116-19); also 'Jesus and the Kingdom: The Restoration of Israel and the New People of God', in E. P. Sanders, ed., *Jesus, the Gospels and the Church,* W. R. Farmer FS (Macon: Mercer University, 1987) 225-39. Sanders criticises the tendency to reduce the conceptual content of the phrase and to regard it as totally enigmatic: 'we know perfectly well what he meant in general terms: the ruling power of God' (*Jesus* 125-29, here 127; the criticism is directed against J. Breech, *The Silence of Jesus: The Authentic Voice of the Historical Man* [Philadelphia: Fortress, 1983], and B. B. Scott, *Jesus, Symbol-Maker for the Kingdom* [Philadelphia: Fortress, 1983]).

35. 'Exile and restoration: this is the central drama that Israel believed herself to be acting out' (*Jesus* 127); 'Jesus is reconstituting Israel around himself. This is the return from exile; this, in other words, is the kingdom of Israel's God' (131); Jesus' announcement of the reign of God 'cannot but have been heard as the announcement that the exile was at last drawing to a close, that Israel was about to be vindicated against her enemies, that her god was returning at last to deal with evil . . . "the reign of God" . . . spoke of covenant renewed, of creation restored, of Israel liberated, of YHWH returning' (172); see also 202-209, 227. Wright is followed by McKnight, *New Vision,* e.g., 70, though he also affirms that 'for Jesus the term "kingdom" was intentionally polyvalent' (80).

36. See above §4.6b.

37. Crossan, *Historical Jesus* 421-22.

we speak of the kingdom of God as a 'metaphor'[38] for the coming to power of God as 'the unconditional will for the good' (Theissen and Merz)?[39] At all events, we should heed well the warning not to treat Jesus' kingdom talk in isolation, far less in terms of individual sayings evaluated on their own. Is there not a larger story which his teaching was intended to evoke? If so, Jesus' kingdom teaching can be properly expounded only within that context, at least in the first instance. In other words, the context in view will be not merely the immediate context of the individual occurrences of the term within the Jesus tradition or even the context provided by each Gospel as a whole. It will have to be the context of Israel's memory of its own monarchic past, of Jewish current experience under the kingship of others, and of the hopes of the faithful regarding God's kingship for the future. Here again we find ourselves caught in the fascinating interplay between history and hermeneutics.

Such hypotheses as those just indicated cannot be dealt with satisfactorily at the theoretical level. They stand or fall by their success in making sense of the data. The obvious procedure, therefore, is to set out the 'context of meaning' more fully, that is, the context of usage and association which would have informed the hearing of Jesus' audiences, or, if you like, the context of meaning which Jesus could have been expected to assume for his audiences' understanding, however he may have attempted to tweak or challenge it. In which case, the first task is to clarify the more immediate context of meaning for talk of God's *malkut/basileia*.

b. God's Reign

Although talk of God's 'kingdom' is relatively scarce in the literature of Second Temple Judaism, the *content* of the phrase would have been familiar. The data have been reviewed several times recently, so all that is necessary here is to highlight the chief points of significance.[40]

38. Hengel and Schwemer think 'symbol' is 'zu unverbindlich, variabel und beliebig austauschbar', and prefer to talk of 'gewisse unveräusserliche Metaphern' (*Königsherrschaft Gottes* 6).

39. Theissen and Merz, *Historical Jesus* 246, 274-76.

40. M. Lattke, 'On the Jewish Background of the Synoptic Concept, "The Kingdom of God"' (1975), ET in B. Chilton, ed., *The Kingdom of God* (London: SPCK, 1984) 72-91; D. Patrick, 'The Kingdom of God in the Old Testament', in W. Willis, ed., *The Kingdom of God in 20th-Century Interpretation* (Peabody: Hendrickson, 1987) 67-79 (here 72-75); J. J. Collins, 'The Kingdom of God in the Apocrypha and Pseudepigrapha', in Willis, *Kingdom* 81-95; B. T. Viviano, 'The Kingdom of God in the Qumran Literature', in Willis, *Kingdom* 97-107; D. C. Duling, 'Kingdom of God, Kingdom of Heaven', *ABD* 4.49-56; G. Vermes, *The Religion of*

(1) A Jewish audience would, of course, be familiar with the idea of God as 'king *(melek)*' over all the earth, over all the nations, over all the gods. It was, after all, a familiar theme of worship in their psalm book.[41] Jewish worshippers would probably be accustomed to the chant, 'The Lord reigns *(malak)*';[42] 'The Lord has established his throne in the heavens, and his kingdom *(malkuto)* rules over all' (Ps. 103.19); 'Your kingdom *(malkut*e*ka)* is an everlasting kingdom, and your dominion endures throughout all generations' (Ps. 145.13).[43] In the Qumran *Songs of the Sabbath Sacrifice* God is regularly praised as 'king of the heavenly/godlike beings', 'king of glory', and so on.[44]

(2) Typically Jewish also is the conviction, already implied in several of the passages just mentioned, that only Israel has acknowledged God's kingship. Israel was chosen by God, so that God was Israel's king in a special sense, in a special relationship.[45] The Lord reigns on Zion.[46] He is the king of Israel.[47] Jesus and his contemporaries prayed, 'My King *(malki)* and my God'.[48] Worthy of particular note is the good news to be preached to Zion, even (or especially) in Israel's exile: 'Your God reigns *(malak)!*' (Isa. 52.7) — in echo of the earlier escape from bondage celebrated in the Song of Moses, 'The Lord will reign for ever and ever' (Exod. 15.18), which Qumran in turn referred to its hope of the Temple to be rebuilt 'in the last days' (4Q174 [4QFlor] 1.2-6). The early form of the Eighteen Benedictions accordingly prays, 'Restore our judges as in former times and our counsellors as in the beginning; and reign over us, thou alone' *(Shemoneh 'Esreh* 11).[49]

(3) But equally the hope/expectation was cherished that God's reign from Mount Zion, at present acknowledged only by Israel, would soon be manifested

---

Jesus the Jew (London: SCM, 1993) 121-35; Meier, *Marginal Jew* 2.243-88; K. Seybold and H.-J. Fabry, *'melek'*, *TDOT* 8 (1997) 365-75; Theissen and Merz, *Historical Jesus* 246-52; more discursively Becker, *Jesus of Nazareth* 86-100.

41. Pss. 10.16; 22.28; 29.10; 47.2-3, 7-8; 95.3; 103.19 *(malkut)*; 135.6 (as expanded at Qumran — *DSSB* 568). See further J. Jeremias, *Das Königtum Gottes in den Psalmen* (FRLANT 141; Göttingen: Vandenhoeck und Ruprecht, 1987); B. Janowski, 'Das Königtum Gottes in den Psalmen', *ZTK* 86 (1989) 389-454.

42. Pss. 93.1-2; 96.10; 97.1; 99.1.

43. See also Jer. 10.7, 10; Dan. 4.34; Mal. 1.14; *1 En.* 84.2; 1QH 18(= 10).8; 2 Macc. 1.24; *Pss. Sol.* 2.29-32; 17.3; Wis. 6.4; *T. Mos.* 4.2.

44. Newsom, *Songs of the Sabbath Sacrifice* 424-26.

45. The first and second usage are, of course, closely linked: 'He stands over against the nations and their gods explicitly as *melek* of Israel, proving himself in the divine trial as the superior, singular, and unique God' (Seybold, *TDOT* 8.370).

46. Pss. 24.7-10; 48.2; 149.2; Isa. 6.5; Jer. 8.19; *Jub.* 1.28.

47. Pss. 146.10; 149.2; Isa. 33.22; 41.21; 43.15; 44.6; Zeph. 3.15; *Pss. Sol.* 5.19; 17.1.

48. Pss. 5.2; 44.4; 68.24; 74.12; 84.3; 145.1.

49. Schürer, *History* 2.461.

over all the world and acknowledged by all (willingly or unwillingly).[50] Daniel's vision of the great statue representing four successive kingdoms climaxes in the vision of a stone 'cut from a mountain by no human hand' which would smash the statue and grow until it filled the whole earth (Dan. 2.35, 44-45). The theme became a favourite in post-biblical writing.[51] In particular, Qumran looked to God to display his kingship over Israel's enemies, and for the wealth of nations to flow into Zion (1QM 6.6; 12.7-16) in fulfilment of Isaiah 60. The third Sibyl predicts that 'the most great kingdom of the immortal king will become manifest over men' (*Sib. Or.* 3.47-48) and that God 'will raise up a kingdom for all ages among men' when 'from every land they will bring incense and gifts to the house of the great God' and 'there will be just wealth among men' (3.767-95).[52] The *Psalms of Solomon* 17 expects 'God's eschatological rule as king (to be) manifested and realized through the rule of the Son of David, the Lord Messiah'.[53] And the *Testament of Moses* envisages a climactic dénouement when God will rise from the throne of his kingdom, and 'his kingdom shall appear throughout all his creation' (10.1, 3).[54]

From this range of material we can gain a fairly clear idea of what reverberations talk of God's kingship would set off within the convictions of 'common Judaism'. Noticeable is the strength of the conviction regarding Yahweh as king. Whatever happened on earth, Israel comforted itself with the assurance that God's kingship, his kingly rule, is still in effect. Psalmist and prophet strengthened the faith conviction that whatever Israel's failure, and exile notwithstanding, Yahweh was still Israel's king. Reality as experienced in human perspective did not necessarily reflect reality seen from God's perspective. At the same time, the hope for the future, however symbolic in expression, evidently looked for a tangible effect in the life of Israel. Also to be noted is the fact that Israel's understanding of God's kingship embraced, as we might say, all three tenses (past, present, and future).[55] We may conclude at once that for Jesus to talk of 'the kingdom of God' would not have been strange to a typical Jewish audience in first-century Palestine and would certainly have evoked a range of faith convictions and hopes such as are illustrated above.

---

50. Isa. 24.21-23; Ezek. 20.33; Mic. 4.1-7; Zech. 14.9, 16-17.

51. S. Schreiber, *Gesalbter und König. Titel und Konzeptionen der königlichen Gesalbtenerwartung in frühjüdischen und urchristlichen Schriften* (BZNW 105; Berlin: de Gruyter, 2000) notes how the thought of God as king served as an antithetical image to hostile political domination and 'a depraved or hybrid kingship' (141).

52. *Sib. Or.* 3 is usually dated to the middle of the second century BCE with first-century BCE additions (Collins, 'Kingdom' 84-85).

53. Meier, *Marginal Jew* 2.258.

54. See above, chapter 9 n. 96.

55. Similarly Jeremias, *Proclamation* 98-100; cf. Caird, *New Testament Theology* ch. 4.

c. A Larger Story?

That a larger picture is in view in each of the range of usages just indicated is already implicit (in some cases explicit) in the passages cited. The understanding of Yahweh as king over all is obviously an expression of Israel's monotheistic faith and creation theology: to say that God is one is to recognize that he is the sole ruler of all creation. To say that God is 'our/my King' is an affirmation of God's election of Israel to be his people chosen from out of all the peoples on the earth. It will be recalled that monotheism and election are two of Israel's most fundamental convictions (§9.5). But the third aspect, that God's royal rule will be manifested to all, is a summary of a much more diffuse and diverse expectation. And since the future tense of God's kingdom is one of the most contested features of the Jesus tradition, it is well to say a little more about this expectation as part of the context within which Jesus' teaching would have been heard. Here too I make no attempt to provide a comprehensive survey or to offer new insights; my concern is simply to indicate the various clearly attested and most relevant motifs which suggest the sort of expectations that were cherished and may have been evoked by Jesus' kingdom talk among Jews living in the land of Israel in the first century CE.[56]

1. Based on Deut. 30.1-10, there was a widespread belief that after a period of dispersion among the nations, the outcasts/scattered of Israel would be gathered again and brought back to the promised land, the unity of the twelve tribes reestablished, and the relation of Israel as God's people, and Yahweh as Israel's God, restored.[57] Wright summarises it as the hope of *return from exile.*[58]

2. Bound up with this was the hope for a *renewed and abundant prosperity* (Deut. 30.5, 9),[59] the removal of disabilities and defects,[60] and/or in effect

56. I will focus on pre-70 Palestinian literature for the most part. Cf. Sanders, *Judaism* 289-303 for a similar survey.

57. Isa. 49.5-6, 22-26; 56.8; 60.4, 9; 66.20; Jer. 3.18; 31.10; Ezek. 34.12-16; 36.24-28; 37.21-23; 39.27; Zeph. 3.20; Zech. 8.7-8; Tob. 13.5; 14.5-6; Sir. 36.11-15; 48.10; Bar. 4.37; 5.5; 2 Macc. 1.27, 29; *1 En.* 90.33; *Jub.* 1.15-18; *Pss. Sol.* 11.1-9; 17.31, 44; 11Q19 [Temple] 59.9-13; *Shemoneh 'Esreh* 10. The theme of sin-exile-return is particularly prominent in *T. 12 Patr.* (*T. Levi* 14–16; *T. Jud.* 23; *T. Iss.* 6; *T. Zeb.* 9.5-9; *T. Dan* 5.4-9; *T. Naph.* 4; *T. Ash.* 7; *T. Ben.* 9.1-2); see H. W. Hollander and M. de Jonge, *The Testaments of the Twelve Patriarchs* (Leiden: Brill, 1985) 39-40, 53-56.

58. Wright, *The New Testament and the People of God* 268-71, 299-301; also *Jesus*, Index, 'Return from exile'. See also J. M. Scott, ed., *Exile: Old Testament, Jewish, and Christian Conceptions* (Brill: Leiden, 1997).

59. Isa. 32.14-20; 35.1-2; 44.3; Ezek. 34.25-29; 36.29-30, 33-36; Joel 2.18-26; 3.18; Amos 9.13-14; *1 En.* 10.19; *Sib. Or.* 3.744-54; most exuberant in *2 Bar.* 29.5-8.

60. Isa. 29.18; 35.5-6; 42.7, 18. Qumran saw the holiness of the community as depen-

a restoration of paradise[61] as variations.

3. Although this hope is often referred to as 'the messianic age',[62] the involvement of *a particular (messianic) figure* or divine agent seems to be more like another variation.[63] The imagery of a great feast is independent, though sometimes linked — hence (misleadingly) the description 'messianic banquet'.[64]

4. Some envisaged *a renewed covenant,* of a turning from transgression, a fresh outpouring of the Spirit, and a level of law-keeping and holiness not known before.[65]

5. A further variation brought to the fore by Sanders and deserving of special mention is the hope for the *building of a new temple.*[66]

6. Wright has drawn particular attention to another element within the various scenarios envisaged — *the return of Yahweh to Zion.*[67]

7. Within a widespread conviction of Israel's vindication and final triumph *the future of the other nations/Gentiles* was a matter of some speculation and disagreement.[68] A few could envisage only their destruction.[69] More commonly the expectation was for the Gentiles to come in pilgrimage to Zion to pay tribute[70] or to worship God there ('eschatological prose-

---

dent on the exclusion of those with such defects (1Q28a [1QSa] 2.3-10; 11Q19 [11QTemple] 45.12-14).

61. Isa. 11.6-8; 25.7-8; 51.3; Ezek. 36.35; *Jub.* 4.26; 23.26-29; *1 En.* 25.4-6; 1QH 16[= 8].4-11). See further D. S. Russell, *The Method and Message of Jewish Apocalyptic* (London: SCM, 1964) 283-84.

62. A popular description.

63. See, e.g., Theissen and Merz, *Historical Jesus* 531-37, and further below, §15.2.

64. Isa. 25.6; Ezek, 39.17-20; 1Q28a (1Qsa) 2; *1 En.* 62.14. See further D. Smith, 'Messianic Banquet', *ABD* 4.788-91. Even in the Jesus tradition the imagery is not strictly of a messianic banquet; see below, §12.4f.

65. Isa. 44.3-4; 59.20-21; Jer. 31.31-34; Ezek. 36.25-29; 39.28-29; Joel 2.28–3.1; Zech. 14.16-21; CD 8.21; 19.33-34; 1QpHab 2.3-4; 1Q34 2.5-6. See also H. Lichtenberger, 'Alter Bund und neuer Bund', *NTS* 41 (1995) 400-14, on the Qumran texts (401-406).

66. Tob. 14.5; *Jub.* 1.15-17, 29; *1 En.* 90.28-29; 91.13; 11Q19 (11QTemple) 29.2-10; *T. Ben.* 9.2; *Sib. Or.* 3.294. See Sanders, *Jesus and Judaism* 77-87; and further J. Ådna, *Jesu Stellung zum Tempel: Die Tempelaktion und das Tempelwort als Ausdruck seiner messianischen Sendung* (WUNT 2.119; Tübingen: Mohr Siebeck, 2000) 25-89.

67. Isa. 24.23; 25.9-10; 40.3-5, 9-10; 52.7-8; 59.20; Ezek. 43.2-7; Zech. 2.10-12; 8.3; 14.4; Mal. 3.1; *Jub.* 1.26-28; 11Q19 (11QTemple) 29.3-9; *Shemoneh 'Esreh* 16. See further Wright, *Jesus* 616-23.

68. Cf. the survey in Sanders, *Jesus and Judaism* 213-18.

69. Ps. 2.8-9; Zeph. 2.9-11; Sir. 36.1-9; Bar. 4.25, 31-35; *Jub.* 15.26; *1 En.* 90.19; 1QM; *Pss. Sol.* 17.24; and understandably in the aftermath of Jerusalem's destruction in 70 CE — *4 Ezra* 12.33; 13.38; *2 Bar.* 40.1; Rev. 19.17-21.

70. Isa. 18.7; 45.14; 60.3-16; 61.5-6; Hag. 2.7-9; 1QM 12.14; 4Q504 4.9-12; *Pss. Sol.* 17.30-31; *Sib. Or.* 3.772-76.

lytes').[71] This was often linked with the hope of the ingathering of the scattered tribes of Israel (1); but factions within Second Temple Judaism also included other Jews among the practitioners of evil to be defeated and judged.[72]

8. In some tension with the above sequence centred on the land of Israel (as in Isa. 60.21) was the broadening out of the concept of inheriting the land (promised to Abraham and his descendants) to embrace the whole earth.[73]

9. In analysing the message of John the Baptist we have already noted the expectation of *a climactic period of tribulation,* 'a time of anguish, such as has never occurred since nations first came into existence' (Dan. 12.1-2), of the transition to a new age likened to the 'birth-pangs' of a woman in labour.[74] Presumably that can be tied into the motif of the suffering and vindication of the righteous present in Daniel 7 but also elsewhere.[75]

10. Closely related are strands which seem to envisage *cosmic disturbances,*[76] even the destruction of creation,[77] and a new creation.[78]

11. Of a piece with much of the above was the hope for a (final) destruction of evil and *defeat of Satan.*[79]

12. Also included was the theme of *final judgment,*[80] which developed to in-

---

71. Pss. 22.27-28; 86.9; Isa. 2.2-4 = Mic. 4.1-3; Isa. 45.20-23; 56.6-8; 66.19-20, 23; Jer. 3.17; Zeph. 3.9-10; Zech. 2.11-12; 8.20-23; 14.16-19; Tob. 13.11; 14.6-7; *1 En.* 10.21; 90.30-36; *Sib. Or.* 3.715-19. See further J. Jeremias, *Jesus' Promise to the Nations* (London: SCM, 1958) 56-62; T. L. Donaldson, 'Proselytes or "Righteous Gentiles"? The Status of Gentiles in Eschatological Pilgrimage Patterns of Thought', *JSP* 7 (1990) 3-27.

72. See above, §9.4.

73. Sir. 44.21; *Jub.* 22.14; 32.19; *1 En.* 5.7; Rom. 4.13. See also n. 17 above.

74. See above, §11.4c. See further particularly D. C. Allison, *The End of the Ages Has Come: An Early Interpretation of the Passion and Resurrection of Jesus* (Philadelphia: Fortress, 1985) 5-25.

75. See below, chapter 17 n. 180.

76. Isa. 13.9-10, 13; 24.23; Jer. 4.23; Ezek. 32.7-8; Joel 2.10, 30-31; 3.15; Amos 8.9; Zeph. 1.15; Hag. 2.6, 21; *1 En.* 80.4; 1QH 11(= 3).35-36; *T. Mos.* 10.4-6; *Sib. Or.* 3.675-84.

77. Ps. 102.25-26; Isa. 34.4; 51.6; Zeph. 1.18; 3.8; *Jub.* 23.18; *1 En.* 10.2; 83; 91.16; 1QH 11[= 3].29-36; *Sib. Or.* 2.196-213; 3.80-92.

78. Isa. 65.17; 66.22; *Jub.* 1.29; 4.26; *1 En.* 72.1; 91.16-17; 1QS 4.25. See further Russell, *Method* 280-82.

79. Isa. 24.21-22; *Jub.* 5.6; 10.7-11; 23.29; *1 En.* 10.4, 11-13; 13.1-2; 14.5; 18.16; 21.3-6; 69.28; 90.23; 91.16; *2 En.* 7.1-2; *T. Mos.* 10.1; *T. Levi* 18.12; *T. Zeb.* 9.8; *T. Dan* 5.10-11; Jude 6; Rev. 20.2-3.

80. Isa. 66.15-16; Dan. 7.10; Zeph. 3.8; Mal. 4.1; Wis. 3.7, 18; 4.18-19; 5.17-23; *Jub.* 5.10-16; *1 En.* 1.7, 9; 10.13-14; 22.4, 11; 90.20-27; 91.7, 9, 14-15; 1QS 4.11-14; 5.12-13; 1QH 12(= 4).20, 26-27; CD 7.9/19.6; 8.1-3/19.13-16; 1QpHab 12.14; 13.2-3; *Pss. Sol.* 14.9; 15.10, 12; *4 Ezra* 7.33-43; see also the motif of the day of the Lord as a 'day of anger' (chapter 11 n. 116 above). The most thorough recent study is that of Reiser, *Jesus and Judgment* Part One

clude interesting sub-themes of heavenly books to be consulted on the day of judgment,[81] and the expectation that God will give judgment of the Gentiles into the hands of Israel.[82]

13. The related belief in *resurrection* evidently emerged in explicit thought only in the latter half of the Second Temple period.[83]

14. Sheol/Hades, from being understood as the abode generally of the dead, comes to be seen as a place of retribution for the wicked *(hell)*,[84] often equated with the fires of Gehenna (the valley of Hinnom).[85]

I repeat: the above outline is not intended to be complete or to include all relevant texts. The concern is simply to fill out what we might call 'the context of expectation' within which Jesus' preaching about the kingdom of God would have been heard. But even such a cursory review raises several important issues.

12.3. Three Key Questions

a. A Grand Narrative?

We have talked about a larger story. But should we be thinking of a *single* larger story? Can these different strands be combined into what historians have called a single 'grand narrative'? The historians' idea of a 'grand narrative' is rooted in the biblical conception of history as a linear and purposeful progression. So perhaps the collapse of that idea among contemporary historians (in reference to modernity)[86] should serve as a cue to biblical scholars to rethink the issue. The same warning has to be sounded if we assume that the different strands are parts of a coherent whole which we can now reconstruct; or, to change to the image of a jig-saw puzzle, if we assume that there must be a complete picture which we

(19-163); for the theme in *4 Ezra* see M. E. Stone, *Fourth Ezra* (Hermeneia: Minneapolis: Fortress, 1990) 149-51.

81. Exod. 32.32-33; Ps. 69.28; Dan. 7.10; 12.1; Mal. 3.16; *Jub.* 30.19-23; 36.10; 39.6; *1 En.* 89.61-64, 70-71; 98.7-8; 104.7; 108.7; CD 20.19; *Apoc. Zeph.* 7.1-8; *T. Abr.* (A) 12.7-18; 13.9-14.

82. Dan. 7.22 LXX; *Jub.* 32.19; Wis 3.8; 1QpHab 5.4; cf. *1 En.* 95.3; 1QS 5.6-7; 1QH 12[= 4].26; 1QM 6.6; 11.13f.; *T. Abr.*(A) 13.6; *Apoc. Ab.* 22.29. The thought is clearly echoed in 1 Cor. 6.2.

83. Isa. 26.19; Dan. 12.2-3; Hos. 6.2; 2 Macc. 7.10-11, 14, 23, 29; 1QH 19[= 11].12-14; *Shemoneh 'Esreh* 2. See further below §17.6b.

84. *Pss. Sol.* 14.6; 15.10; *1 En.* 22.10-13; 103.7-8; *2 En.* 10; 40.12–42.2.

85. *1 En.* 27.1-2; 54.6; 90.25; 91.14; 100.9; 103.7; *4 Ezra* 7.36-38; cf. already Isa. 66.24. See further J. Jeremias, *hades* and *geenna, TDNT* 1 (1964) 146-48, 657-58.

86. See above, §5.6.

can somehow hold in our minds apart from the pieces (the picture on the box) and which we can use to fit the pieces together to make up the whole. For the various attempts of twentieth-century scholars to construct other larger myths from what they took to be the extant parts do not inspire confidence.[87] What became apparent was that the resulting myths were the constructs of twentieth-century scholarship rather than of the ancients themselves. Should, then, alternatively, the various motifs be regarded simply as a sequence of disparate insights, hopes, and aspirations which were put forward without any pretence to completeness?

Probably so. In sequencing the above themes I have attempted to put them in an appropriate order. But how the themes are to be related to one another is hardly clear. For example, Ezekiel 34 envisages both Yahweh restoring and pastoring his sheep and David as shepherd (34.11-16, 23-24); the Messiah figure does not seem to play any part in the return of Israel from exile. Does the return of Yahweh to Zion depend on the Temple being rebuilt? How to square the different expectations regarding the Gentiles in regard to restored Israel? Are tribulation and judgment the same thing? Was the hope of new creation simply a more radical expression of hope for restored prosperity? Texts like Isaiah and *Jubilees* correlate some of the motifs, but leave others uncorrelated. The animal apocalypse of *1 Enoch* (chs. 85–90) is the nearest attempt at comprehensiveness, but not all of the above strands are woven in. *4 Ezra* also helps clarify some of the sequence probably most often in view: 'the day of judgment will be the end of this age and the beginning of the immortal age to come, in which corruption has passed away, sinful indulgence has come to an end, unbelief has been cut off, and righteousness has increased and truth has appeared' (7.113-14).

More important, we need to recall that many of the texts covered in the above review are sectarian in character. By no means can we assume that each text expressed a broad consensus view. The point is not simply that we need to allow, in effect, for different 'Judaisms' and thus for different 'stories' by which different Jews interpreted their lives and expressed their hopes. It is more the fact that other Jews, other Jewish sects, often fell under the condemnations or were excluded from the hopes expressed in these documents. In other words, the factionalism of Second Temple Judaism reinforces the fragmentary, and indeed disputed, character of many of these hopes in the detail with which they were spelled out.[88] None of this is to deny that those who spoke with hope for the future trusted implicitly that Yahweh is king and that he had a coherent purpose for Israel which he was in process of unfolding. It is simply to recognize the tensions

87. I refer to the 'Mandean fever' of the early decades of the century and the quest for the pre-Christian Gnostic redeemer myth and 'the divine man'.

88. See above, §9.4.

between the strands and the various expressions of that hope and to acknowledge not least the tensions between the different strands of Second Temple Judaism which expressed what may still have been a common hope rather differently.[89] One visionary's 'coherent story' is not easily synthesized with another's.

This should not occasion any surprise to those familiar with the Christian tradition. A study of early Christian expectation gives an equally fragmentary yield, a series of flashes of insight into what might be expected, which are equally difficult to synthesize.[90] And Christians of successive generations have been content to affirm a hope of heaven, even though the scope of that hope is hard to articulate beyond a sequence of glimpses afforded in Christian tradition — the parousia (return) of Christ, resurrection and judgment, no marriage or sexual relations, a heavenly banquet, participation in the worship of heaven, and so on — hardly a coherent story or grand narrative of life beyond death.

Insofar, then, as Jesus' kingdom talk 'plugs into' the Jewish expectation of the time, we have to bear in mind the same question as to whether he and his hearers operated with a single, comprehensive story. Or should we be prepared for an equivalent series of glimpses of the beyond and flashes of insight, rather than a coherent, complete story?

b. What Do We Mean by 'Eschatological'?

A second issue raised by this inventory of Second Temple Jewish expectation is the extent to which or sense in which we can speak of this expectation as 'eschatological'. This term has bewitched and befuddled the quest of the historical Jesus for a century. The Greek word *eschaton* clearly denotes 'end'. But end of what? The assumption since Schweitzer has been that what was in view was 'the end of time, the end of history, the end of the world'. That would be fine, if the expectation were clearly and consistently for a heavenly, eternal existence. But

89. T. F. Glasson with some justification criticized Schweitzer for claiming that there was a common 'late Jewish view' of eschatology which Jesus' preaching of the kingdom could assume, whereas he could briefly distinguish eight different types of teaching ('Schweitzer's Influence — Blessing or Bane?', *JTS* 28 [1977] 289-302, reprinted in B. Chilton, ed., *The Kingdom of God* [London: SPCK, 1984] 107-20 [here 108-12]). Chilton takes the point, but also observes that 'it would seem imprudent not to acknowledge that the range of apocalyptic literature, along with the Qumran scrolls, the earliest Targums and other intertestamental works, present a common expectation, variously expressed, that God was to act on behalf of his people in the foreseeable future' (Chilton's 'Introduction' 22).

90. I may refer to my *Theology of Paul* 314-15. Leivestad notes the consequences of accommodating a messianic kingdom within the eschatology in Revelation: two wars (Rev. 19.11-21; 20.7-10); two triumphs over Satan; two judgment scenes; two resurrections; two states of blessedness (*Jesus* 43-44).

much of the expectation reviewed in the fourteen-item list above was hope for a continued 'this-worldly' existence — the diaspora returned to the Promised Land, Israel triumphant over the nations, paradise restored, perhaps, but *on earth*.[91] So 'end' yes, certainly in the sense of the 'end' of a period of time, the end of an epoch. But 'the end of time, of history, of the world'? Yet at the same time there seem to be more radically 'final' elements within the strands of expectation — new creation, final judgment, and resurrection of the dead. What did 'life expectancy' beyond resurrection envisage?

The issue is not greatly clarified by the terminology used. The principal Hebrew terms of relevance are *qeṣ, 'aḥarit* and *'olam*.[92] The first normally denotes the 'end' of a period of time, sometimes with a final sense.[93] In Daniel, however, it is given a clear eschatological connotation — 'the time of the end' (*'eṯ qeṣ*, 8.17; 11.35, 40; 12.4, 9), 'the appointed time of the end' (*mo'ed qeṣ*, 8.19; 11.27), 'the end of days' (*qeṣ hayyamim*, 12.13).[94] *'Aḥarit* can also be used in the sense 'end' and accordingly is translated with Greek *eschaton*. Most relevant is the phrase 'end of days' (*'aḥarit hayyamim*);[95] what is noteworthy is that this phrase could be used both of a limited future time[96] or as envisaging the culmination of history.[97] In the DSS we find *qeṣ 'aḥarit* ('the final age', 'the last time', 'the end of days', 'time of the end' — García Martínez),[98] and elsewhere talk of the 'end of the age'.[99] But 1QpHab 7.7 also explicitly envisages that 'the

91. The same question arose in chapter 11 with regard to the Baptist's expectation (§11.4b).

92. See also J. Barr, *Biblical Words for Time* (London: SCM, [2]1969) 122-32.

93. Ezek. 21.30, 34 (21.25, 29); 35.5 (but see K. Koch, *'awon', TDOT* 10 [1999] 557); Hab. 2.3.

94. See also G. Delling, *telos, TDNT* 8 (1972) 53; LXX usually translates *qeṣ* by *synteleia* in these passages (65).

95. H. Seebass, *'aḥarit, TDOT* 1.210-12.

96. Most clearly Num. 24.14; but also Gen. 49.1; Deut. 4.30; 31.29; Jer. 48.47; 49.39. 'Jer. 23.20b = 30.24b stands on the borderline between future and eschaton' (Seebass, *TDOT* 1.211). NRSV translates the first four as 'in days/time to come', but the Jeremiah references as 'in the latter days'.

97. Isa. 2.2 = Mic. 4.1; Ezek. 38.16; Dan. 2.28; 10.14; Hos. 3.5. NRSV translates as 'in days to come' in Isaiah and Micah, 'in the latter days' in Hosea and Ezekiel, and 'at the end of days' in Daniel. This is clearly the sense in the regular use at Qumran (1QpHab 2.5-6; 9.6; 1Q28a [1QSa] 1.1; CD 4.4; 6.11; 4Q174 [4QFlor] 1.2, 12, 15, 19; 4Q178 3.3-4; 4Q182 [4QCat B] 1.1; 11Q13 [11QMelch] 2.4) and in 2 *Bar.* 25.1.

98. 1QpHab 7.7, 12; 1QS 4.16-17; 4QMMT C14; 5Q16. In *4 Ezra* note 6.7-10, 25; 7.112-13; 11.39-46; 14.9 (see Stone, *Fourth Ezra* 103-104).

99. 'The day of the end' (*1 En.* 10.12; 16.1; 22.4); 'the end of the ages (*synteleia tōn aiōnōn)' (T. Levi* 10.2; *T. Ben.* 11.3); 'the time of the end (*kairou synteleias)' (T. Zeb.* 9.9); 'the end of the age/world (*exitum saeculi)' (T. Mos.* 12.4); *4 Ezra* 7.113 (on 'the two ages' in *4 Ezra* see Stone, *Fourth Ezra* 92-93); 'the end of times' (*2 Bar.* 13.3; 19.5; 21.8; 27.15); cf. *1 En.* 16.1.

final age shall be prolonged';[100] and 11Q13 (11QMelch) 2.4-9 envisages 'the last days' as extending over the tenth jubilee.

'Olam is much more common and often used in the sense 'for ever' (le'olam, 'ad 'olam), or intensively 'for ever and ever' (le'olam wa'ed).[101] The problem in this case is what we might call the aspirational or hyperbolic overtone with which the phrase is uttered, or the fact that it evidently had a degree of conditionality. A slave was enslaved 'for ever', that is, for life.[102] The king was greeted formally, 'May the king live for ever'[103] — not a prayer for the king to be granted eternal life, but that he may reign for as long as possible. The promise of divine favour 'for ever' could be qualified or withdrawn, as the psalmist recognized only too clearly (Ps. 89.34-37, but also 38-45).[104] Even in judgment oracles, where the formula was obviously intended to indicate finality,[105] there could be hope of reverse,[106] though the concomitant promise of salvation for Israel 'for ever' presumably indicated a timespan stretching as far beyond the time horizon as it is possible to conceive.[107] Dan. 12.2-3 conceives of post-resurrection existence as either 'everlasting life (hayye 'olam)' or 'everlasting contempt (dir'on 'olam)'.

Are we then in danger of attributing a clarity of conviction to language and conceptions which were much less clearly conceptualized? Would it be more accurate (and fairer) to the hopes reviewed to speak in terms of periods of time without a predetermined closure in contrast to fixed spans of time, such as a Sabbath, a festival, a week, a year, a generation, or a reign? That the stereotyped

100. 2 Enoch seems to envisage the 'end' of the whole of creation, visible and invisible, when 'the times/time will perish, and there will be neither years nor months nor days nor hours . . . but there will be one age/eternity . . .' (65.7-8; cf. 33.2).

101. H. D. Preuss, ''olam', TDOT 10 (1999) 534-45; also E. Haag, ''ad', TDOT 10 (1999) 456-62.

102. Exod. 21.6; Deut. 15.17.

103. 1 Kgs. 1.31; Neh. 2.3; Dan. 2.4; 3.9; 5.10; 6.21.

104. Eli (1 Sam. 2.30-31); Saul (1 Sam. 13.13); notably the promise that David's throne would be established 'for ever' (2 Sam. 7.13; Ps. 89.29, 36-37; renewed in 11Q19 [11QTemple] 59.16-18), and that Yahweh (or his name) would dwell in Jerusalem 'for ever' (1 Kgs. 9.3; 1 Chron. 23.25; 2 Chron. 33.4, 7; but Lam. 2.1-9; renewed in Ezek. 43.7-9; 11Q19 [11QTemple] 47.3-4; 53.9-10).

105. Isa. 34.10; Jer. 17.4; 20.11; Ezek. 27.36; 28.19; 35.9; Zeph. 2.9; Mal. 1.4.

106. The 'desolation for ever' foreseen by Jeremiah (18.16; 25.9, 12; 49.33) is evidently countermanded by the promises of Isa. 58.12 and 61.4.

107. Isa. 9.7; 32.17; 34.17; 60.15, 19-21; Jer. 17.25; 31.40; Ezek. 37.26-28; Hos. 2.19; Joel 2.26-27; Mic. 4.7. In regard to kingdom texts, note especially Dan. 2.44; 3.33; 4.34; 6.26. Qumran saw itself as an 'everlasting community', an 'everlasting planting', an 'everlasting people' (1QS 2.25; 3.12; 8.5; 11.8; 1QH 11[= 3].21; 14[= 6].15; 16[= 8].6; 1QM 13.9). 11Q19 (11QTemple) repeatedly speaks of the ordinances relating to the temple as 'everlasting' (18.8; 19.9; 21.04; 25.8; 27.4; 35.9).

phrase *dor wador,* 'generation upon generation', could be used as equivalent to 'for ever'[108] should give us pause. But there is still a further potential confusion in language to be considered.

Throughout the twentieth century the issue has been obscured by a persistent confusion between the terms *'eschatology'* and *'apocalyptic'*. Two attempts were made in the 1980s to clarify the latter, though so far with uncertain success. One takes seriously the unsatisfactory use of 'apocalyptic' as a noun[109] and offers a threefold distinction: 'apocalypse' as a literary genre, 'apocalypticism' as a social ideology, and 'apocalyptic eschatology' as a set of ideas present in other genres and social settings.[110] The other has protested against treating the two terms as though they were synonyms:[111] 'apocalypse' (revelation) denotes the unveiling of heavenly mysteries; most of these 'revelations' concern 'final events', but by no means all.[112] If we are to observe such distinctions, then the items of Second Temple expectation can be called 'apocalyptic' insofar as they have been 'revealed' to the writers. The more popular use (also beyond theological circles) of 'apocalyptic' for a future scenario of supernatural interventions in human history involving unprecedented violence and horror should be resolutely avoided. 'Eschatological' is much the more appropriate term, even if it leaves us with the unclarity just discussed. Here again when we turn to the Jesus tradition we will need to scrutinise the hope expressed with care and use our own descriptive language circumspectly.

c. Literal, Symbol, Metaphor, or What?

The degree of fragmentation in the stories told and the lack of clarity in key terms (not least 'eschatology' itself) reinforce the question raised by Perrin. Is 'the kingdom of God' a concept or a symbol? Should kingdom talk and the content of eschatological expectation be unpacked in literal or symbolic terms? The issue is nicely posed by Wright's treatment. He sees apocalyptic language as 'an elaborate metaphor-system for investing historical events with theological signif-

108. Exod. 3.15; Deut. 23.2-3; Pss. 33.11; 61.6; 72.5; 79.13; 89.4; 100.5; 102.12; 106.31; 119.90; 135.13; 145.13; 146.10; Isa. 34.17; 51.8; Joel 3.20.

109. See, e.g., the objections of T. F. Glasson, 'What Is Apocalyptic?', *NTS* 27 (1980-81) 98-105.

110. See particularly Collins, *Apocalyptic Imagination* ch. 1 (1-42).

111. C. Rowland, *The Open Heaven: A Study of Apocalyptic in Judaism and Early Christianity* (London: SPCK, 1982); also *Christian Origins* 56-64.

112. We need only mention, for example, Paul's use of the term 'apocalypse' in Gal. 1.12 and 2.2, and 'The Astronomical Book' or 'Book of Heavenly Luminaries' which makes up *1 En.* 72-82.

icance'. Warnings of imminent judgment 'were intended to be taken as denoting ... socio-political events, seen as the climactic moment in Israel's history'.[113] To reduce the reality envisaged to the terms of the metaphor itself would be to mistake its character as metaphor. This is the mistake of those who interpret such apocalyptic language as predicting the actual end of the time-space complex. Its proper function, rather, is to invest current events with 'theological significance'. But Wright's treatment is less clear as to whether all the items listed in §12.2c are metaphorical in the same way (or to the same extent). He has the elements of apocalyptic eschatology primarily in view. But is the grand narrative of Israel's return from exile and Yahweh's return to Zion equally metaphorical ('the grand metaphor' perhaps)? Or in this case are we to expect a closer correlation between the terms of the metaphor and the reality in view?[114]

One way of tackling such an imponderable issue is to ask how Jews of Jesus' time would have understood the hopes indicated in §12.2c. Would they have looked for literal fulfilment or at least a close correlation between hope and reality, or might they have understood the hopes as 'metaphorical'? The beloved traditions of the exodus would certainly have encouraged many to look for visible divine intervention. We know, for example, that two of the would-be prophets of deliverance around Jesus' time acted on that assumption, seeking for a repetition of the miracles of crossing the Jordan dry shod and the fall of Jericho's walls (Joshua 3–4, 6).[115] And the memory of Samaria's deliverance from the Syrians (2 Kings 7) and Jerusalem's deliverance from Sennacherib's army (2 Kings 19) would hardly discourage such a realistic hope, as must have inspired many Zealots in the final days of the 66-70/74 revolt against Rome. So should a Christian expositor be comforted by the fact that the Baptist's expectation of judgment can find such a high degree of literal fulfilment in the catastrophe which engulfed Israel forty years after Jesus' mission?

On the other hand, the disappointingly ill-fulfilled hope of return from exile (as in Isaiah 43.1–44.8; 54–55) would surely have raised questions in the minds of others. And would there not be those who shared Philo's recognition that the Jews were so populous that no one country could hold them (*Flacc.* 46) so that hope for a wholesale return of the diaspora to the land of Israel would have been seen as unrealistic? Alternatively, one might have expected that in order to count as fulfilled, return from exile would have involved some measure of diaspora Jews returning to Palestine; and return of Yahweh to the Temple (as-

113. Wright, *Jesus* 96-97; see also above, §4.7 at n. 177. Similarly Kaylor, *Jesus* 77-78.

114. See also the questions raised by Allison, *Jesus of Nazareth* 153-64; also in his critique of Wright, 'Jesus and the Victory of Apocalyptic', in C. C. Newman, ed., *Jesus and the Restoration of Israel: A Critical Assessment of N. T. Wright's* Jesus and the Victory of God (Downers Grove: InterVarsity, 1999) 126-41, with response from Wright (261-68).

115. Josephus, *Ant.* 20.97-98, 167-70.

suming his absence) would presumably be signalled by at least a vision of divine glory settling again on the temple (cf. Ezek. 43.4-5). So we need to ask also whether the hope of (final) forgiveness of sins (rendering future sin offerings unnecessary?) and the hope of outpoured Spirit (rendering fresh teaching of the law unnecessary?) was as idyllic (symbolic) as the hope for abundant prosperity or paradise restored, and whether there was a realistic hope for the complete eradication of evil and transgression.

Here we need to be particularly careful with the term 'metaphor' itself. In literary criticism 'metaphor' is a type of trope, a 'trope' being a figure where the meaning of an individual word or phrase is altered or 'turned' from its conventional sense.[116] Thus metaphor is different from 'simile', for in a simile the words continue to bear their conventional sense, whereas 'metaphor is using a word to stand for something different from the literal referent, but connected to it through some similarity'.[117] Metaphor, Ricoeur has observed, is a semantic innovation which produces its meaning-effect by the impertinence of its attribution.[118] In his *Rule of Metaphor*,[119] he tells us, he 'risked speaking not just of a metaphorical sense but also of a metaphorical reference in talking about this power of the metaphorical utterance to redescribe a reality inaccessible to direct description'.[120] Similarly in her definitive study of metaphor, Janet Martin Soskice points out, inter alia, that physical objects are not metaphors, nor are metaphors merely decorative ways of saying something that could be said literally. Rather, metaphors are ways of saying that which cannot be said literally or which a literal description would be inadequate to describe. In religious language metaphors can be described as 'reality[-]depicting without pretending to be directly descriptive'.[121]

---

116. *Tropē* ('turn, turning'). The usage is classical; Quintilian defined 'trope' as the artistic alteration of a word or phrase from its proper meaning to another (*Institutes* 8.6.1).

117. S. Wright, *The Voice of Jesus: Studies in the Interpretation of Six Gospel Parables* (Carlisle: Paternoster, 2000) 8.

118. 'With metaphor, the innovation lies in the producing of a new semantic pertinence by means of an impertinent attribution: "Nature is a temple where living pillars . . .". The metaphor is alive as long as we can perceive, through the new semantic pertinence . . . the resistance of the words in their ordinary use and therefore their incompatibility at the level of a literal interpretation of the sentence' (*Time and Narrative* vol. 1 [Chicago: University of Chicago, 1984] ix).

119. *The Rule of Metaphor* (Toronto: University of Toronto, 1977).

120. *Time and Narrative* 1.xi.

121. J. M. Soskice, *Metaphor and Religious Language* (Oxford: Clarendon, 1985) here 145. Wright is familiar with this discussion (*New Testament and People of God* 63): 'metaphors are themselves mini-stories, suggesting ways of looking at a reality which cannot be reduced to terms of the metaphor itself' (129-30). Cf. Caird's rather looser discussion of metaphor in *Language* 152-59.

If there is something of historical as well as contemporary hermeneutical value here, we should be open to the possibility that Jesus' kingdom talk had a metaphorical character. That is, in speaking of the kingdom of God as he did he may have been 'turning' it from its conventional sense; God's kingship is not to be understood in the terms which 'kingship' normally evoked. Or again, it may have been 'reality[-]depicting without pretending to be directly descriptive', depicting that which could not be depicted otherwise. This is not quite the same as Perrin's understanding of the kingdom as a 'tensive symbol', one whose set of meanings can be neither exhausted nor adequately expressed by any one referent. But the point is similar, for the historian asking how the term would have been understood by Jesus' hearers as much as for the modern interpreter. If there is something in this, then we should beware of evaluating Jesus' kingdom talk by the extent to which it can be translated into something more literal. And fulfilment of eschatological hope is presumably not to be measured by the degree of correlation between language and event, even when a closer correspondence is in the event claimed. The suggestion here is that the language of vision (apocalypse) is not to be pressed for a literal cash value, that the correlation between such language and actual (literal) events is of less consequence than has usually been assumed, and that hope expressed in such language might well find satisfaction (fulfilment) in events quite different from those depicted.

Here again the vicissitudes of Christian hope may provide a helpful parallel. Christian hope is typically composed of images, principally drawn from the Apocalypse of John (Revelation), which include an immense walled city built of precious stones, a river and tree of life, and 'the marriage supper of the Lamb'. To take such symbolism literally is to misinterpret it. The metaphorical images are an attempt to indicate what cannot be described in literal terms. But for centuries Christians have been content to hope for heaven, without any real idea of what 'heaven' is and what 'actually' happens 'there', though some have indeed wanted to press the metaphors for some literal content. The question is whether it was any different for Second Temple Jewish expectation and hope.

d. How Then to Proceed?

It would be a mistake to think of these three key questions (§ 12.3a-c) as somehow secondary to the task of understanding the impact made by Jesus' kingdom preaching, as though we could first expound the kingdom texts and then go on to ask what his preaching evoked in the minds of his hearers. On the contrary, these questions go to the heart of the hermeneutical problem of perceiving how these texts were heard in the first century and of how we rehear that hearing today. So the typical way of tackling the problem — by focusing on one or two crucial texts, subjecting them to intensive analysis, drawing out immediate conclusions regarding their likely impact, and then pulling in other texts in support — is not the most obvious way to proceed. Questions about the larger picture, about the meaningfulness of describing individual passages as 'eschatological' (or 'apocalyptic') or about the symbolical or metaphorical force of any particular usage are unlikely to find a satisfactory answer by a process of atomistic exegesis.

Instead, in line with the methodological decision that we must look first for the broad picture (§10.2), it makes better sense to attempt to gain a broad overview of the full range of Jesus' kingdom teaching and its most closely related themes. In that way we can begin to appreciate the motifs and emphases which most characterized Jesus' kingdom preaching. And in the light of the full sweep of the Jesus tradition regarding the kingdom we will be in a better position to tackle the three key questions and to ask in a more informed and meaningful way what impact Jesus made at this point, what his preaching of the kingdom evoked in his hearers' minds. From what has been remembered and the way in which it has been remembered we will be in a better position to clarify (to the extent that that is possible) what response Jesus intended to evoke by his use of the phrase 'the kingdom of God'.

How best to order the material in such an overview? Various schemata have been offered at one time or another — theological and salvation-historical, ecclesiological and ethical, social and political. But the debate on the kingdom which exploded at the beginning of the twentieth century and reemerged in its last two decades with equal ferocity, has been triggered by one central feature — *the future/present tension within the Jesus tradition.* That is to say, the tradition represents Jesus as speaking of the kingdom as *yet to come* but also *already present.* I put the matter baldly in the first instance, though it is capable of almost infinite refinement, as we shall see. But there has never been any dispute among questers of the historical Jesus as to these bald facts (the kingdom both future and present in the Jesus tradition), not at least since the focus turned to the sayings of Jesus and John's Gospel was sidelined. Many find the continuing debate rather sterile, but talk of God's kingdom is too central to the Jesus tradition, so that we can hardly ignore either it or the debate about it. And since this twofold feature, this yet to come but already present, runs through the great bulk of the tradition and not just in kingdom passages, the future/present emphases continue to provide a useful means of structuring a review of the tradition. The immediate concern, of course, is to clarify how deeply rooted both 'tenses' (future/present) are in the Jesus tradition. But bearing in mind our three key questions, however, it will be important repeatedly to ask, In what sense 'future'? In what sense 'present'? In what sense 'eschatological'? In what sense 'symbol' or 'metaphor' or otherwise? And finally to ask whether some grand narrative emerges at the end of our analysis, whether the first memories of Jesus' preaching build into a coherent whole?

Given, then, that we want to be looking at the broad picture rather than attempting to draw large conclusions from individual texts (§10.2), I will focus primarily on characteristic emphases and themes in the Jesus tradition. The fact that the performers of the Jesus tradition evidently grouped similar thematic material (as we shall see) encourages the view that from earliest days in the traditioning process characteristic emphases in Jesus' teaching formed stable reference points round which other Jesus tradition could be gathered. In so saying I do not at all dispute that there is good evidence of compositional technique and redactional material in the present forms of the tradition and in the Q material evident behind Matthew and Luke.[122] My point is rather that *whole* themes are usually left largely unaffected by the redaction and are not best explained by being attributed holus-bolus to factional redaction. The consistency of such emphases across Mark, Q, Matthew, and Luke (and often *Thomas,* too) surely bears evidence of the impact made by the teaching of Jesus himself.

We have already gleaned a summary grasp of Jewish eschatological expectation regarding the exercise of God's kingship. And Jesus' mentor, the Baptist, certainly proclaimed a future and imminent judgment. So it makes sense to start with a review of the future emphasis in Jesus' preaching of the kingdom. And since it is the future emphasis of Jesus' own teaching which has once again become most controversial, it will require special attention. I will structure the review round the explicit kingdom references but include other elements of Jesus tradition with the same or related emphases.[123]

12.4. The Kingdom to Come

The future emphasis in Jesus' kingdom proclamation can be exposed to view fairly readily.

---

122. Well marshalled and discussed, e.g., by Schürmann, *Gottes Reich;* Kloppenborg, *Formation;* Catchpole, *Quest.*

123. But I leave aside the Son of Man material for the time being. In the neo-Liberal quest (Crossan, *Historical Jesus* 238-59; also Borg — see chapter 4 n. 173 above) and in discussions of Q (chapter 4 n. 175), the Son of Man motif has tended to determine the issue of eschatology (versus apocalyptic) in the Jesus tradition. It is important, therefore, to recognize the extent and character of the Jesus tradition's eschatology (including future eschatology) apart from the Son of Man issue (cf. Meier, *Marginal Jew* 2.350; Reiser, *Jesus and Judgment* 203-204). C. A. Evans, 'Daniel in the New Testament: Visions of God's Kingdom', in J. Collins and P. Flint, eds., *The Book of Daniel* (Leiden: Brill, 2001) 2.490-527, argues that much of Jesus' eschatology was influenced by themes and images derived from Daniel, including the kingdom of God, its imminence, and its mysteriousness (510-23).

a. The Kingdom Has Drawn Near

We have already indicated the headline and summary with which Mark introduces his account of Jesus' mission: 'the kingdom of God has drawn near *(ēngiken)*' (Mark 1.15). Matthew follows him (Matt. 4.17). We also observed that the parallel accounts of the sending out of the disciples on mission (Q) have them instructed by Jesus to deliver precisely the same message: 'The kingdom of God/heaven has drawn near' (Matt. 10.7/Luke 10.9; Luke 10.11).[124] This is a notable fact and one not to be lightly discounted, that Mark and the Q tradition agree in summarising the message of Jesus in precisely the same words. Arguments about whether the various elements of Mark 1.15 go back to Jesus or are redactional[125] continue to owe too much to a literary editing conception of the traditioning process. Here as elsewhere, it almost does not matter whether we can recover the precise words of Jesus. What matters is that this form of words had become fixed and established in the re-preaching of the earliest missionaries and churches as the central summary of Jesus' preaching of the kingdom.

The force of the verb is also clear: the perfect tense *(ēngiken)* here indicates an action already performed and resulting in a state or effect which continues into the present.[126] It is not a timeless nearness which is in mind; something had happened to bring the kingdom near.[127] The terminology is no doubt deliberate: the Evangelists would have known well enough the difference between 'near' and 'far' *(makran),*[128] and the Q tradents were certainly aware of the difference in saying that the kingdom had (already) come *(ephthasen)* (Matt. 12.28/Luke 11.20). C. H. Dodd famously blurred this difference by hypothesizing the same Aramaic term *(meta,* 'reach, arrive') behind both Mark's *ēngiken* and Q's

124. Luke's division of the mission material into two missions is of little consequence here: Luke 9.2 (the mission of the twelve) simply reports Jesus commissioning the twelve 'to proclaim the kingdom of God' (note also 9.11 and 9.60); Luke 10.9 (the mission of the seventy) adds 'to you' ('the kingdom of God has drawn near to you'). For a brief survey of the discussion see Meier, *Marginal Jew* 2.485 n. 155. *Thomas* has no parallel.

125. E.g., J. Schlosser, *Le Règne de Dieu dans les dits de Jésus* (EB; Paris: Gabalda, 1980) 96, 105-106; Crossan, *Fragments* 54-56; Lüdemann, *Jesus* 10-11; on Luke 10.9 similarly Schürmann, *Gottes Reich* 96-100. The reference to 'the gospel' is certainly Mark's formulation (see above, n. 3). The Jesus Seminar regard the whole of Mark 1.15 as late (apart from the reference to the kingdom of God, 'God's imperial rule') because 'Jesus' disciples remembered his public discourse as consisting primarily of aphorisms, parables, or a challenge followed by a verbal retort' (Funk, *Five Gospels* 40).

126. Good parallel illustrations of the usage are provided by Mark 14.42/Matt. 26.46; Luke 21.20; Rom. 13.12.

127. See particularly Merklein, *Jesu Botschaft* 51-53, 56-58.

128. Cf. particularly Mark 12.34; Acts 2.39.

ephthasen;[129] but a different Aramaic form is equally possible (*qereb,* 'approach'),[130] and Q's use of different Greek verbs presumably indicates an awareness early in the traditioning process of a significant difference between the two sayings. It is certainly difficult to give *engizein,* the verb used in both the relevant Markan and Q passages, any other sense than 'come near'.[131]

The sense, then, is of imminence rather than of presence.[132] Whatever underlying Aramaic may be detected, the Greek is clear enough. The Evangelists would presumably have had no doubt that the event which had thus brought the kingdom near was the mission of Jesus. But the fact that the emphasis was so fixed and so central in the tradition, for earliest missionaries and churches, strongly suggests that this was the emphasis behind the fixing and reuse of the tradition from the first. It was disciples who recalled Jesus as so preaching; it had been an important factor in their becoming disciples. It was as disciples who already saw in Jesus an event of final significance that they no doubt thus established and thus rehearsed the tradition.

What was it that had drawn near? God's kingdom, the exercise of God's kingship, the manifestation of God's sovereignty. The saying adds nothing to our understanding of 'the kingdom of God' *per se.* It focuses only on the nearness of the kingdom's appearing.

Under the same heading we should note also the parable of the budding fig tree, which all three Synoptic Evangelists have included in the apocalyptic discourse (Mark 13.28-29 pars.). The tradition uses the term *engys* ('near') twice:

> From the fig tree learn the parable: when already its branch has become tender and it puts forth its leaves, you know that the summer is near. So also when you have seen these things happening, you know that it is near, at the gates.

The reference to what is near is unclear in the Mark/Matthean form of the saying itself, though Luke identifies it as 'the kingdom of God'.[133] But the saying does

129. C. H. Dodd, *The Parables of the Kingdom* (London: Religious Book Club, 1935, ³1936) 44.

130. Dalman, *Words of Jesus* 106-107; Taylor, *Mark* 166-67; Black, *Aramaic Approach* 208-11; Chilton, *Pure Kingdom* 61-62; similar strictures in Casey, *Aramaic Sources* 27.

131. W. G. Kümmel, *Verheissung und Erfüllung* (³1956), ET *Promise and Fulfilment: The Eschatological Message of Jesus* (London: SCM, ²1961) 24; McKnight, *New Vision* 123; see further below, §12.5a.

132. Meier is less confident about the force of the saying and includes it in the 'already present' category (*Marginal Jew* 2.430-34); Crossan follows Kelber in reading 1.14-15 in conjunction with Mark 6.12, as 'the gospel of the Kingdom's hidden presence' (*Historical Jesus* 345); see also below, n. 280.

133. By sequencing the sayings in the apocalyptic discourse as he does, Mark, followed

seem to carry the same force as the *ēngiken* sayings: the coming of summer thus heralded cannot be long delayed.[134]

b. The Kingdom to Come

Equally worthy of note is the second petition of the Lord's Prayer: 'May your kingdom come' (Matt. 6.10/Luke 11.2). This is the prayer remembered as taught by Jesus to be his disciples' distinctive prayer, the prayer prayed probably from the first by the tradents in their lives of discipleship.[135] The fact that this prayer, which was probably firmly rooted in the spirituality of Jesus' disciples, prays for the kingdom to come, without any sense of it having already come, cannot but be important. One does not pray for something to come if it is already present.[136]

Moreover, the prayer looks as though it has been modelled on an early form of the Jewish Kaddish prayer:[137]

Exalted and hallowed be his great name
  in the world which he created according to his will.
May he let his kingdom rule
  in your lifetime and in your days and in the lifetime
  of the whole house of Israel, speedily and soon.

---

by Matthew and Luke, presumably refers the saying to the coming of the Son of Man (Mark 13.26 pars.). But apart from its present context it resonates more like a parable of the kingdom's sure coming (Taylor, *Mark* 520; Pesch, *Markusevangelium* 2.307-308, 311, who compares Luke 12.54-56; G. R. Beasley-Murray, *Jesus and the Kingdom of God* [Grand Rapids: Eerdmans, 1986] 333). Luke's addition of 'the kingdom of God' is probably redactional, but does the redaction carry with it an awareness of what the original reference was?

134. Cf. Jeremias, *Parables* 119-20.

135. See above, §8.5b. Of the five Q kingdom sayings which Schürmann traces back to Jesus with probability, this is the one of which he is most confident — a 'probability bordering on certainty' (*Gottes Reich* 135, 144; see also Schürmann's *Jesus* 18-30, 45-63). 'Jesus' understanding of God may best be seen from the Lord's Prayer, in which the essential content of Jesus' preaching is summarized' (Stuhlmacher, *Biblische Theologie* 1.84-85).

136. 'The meaning is not "may thy Kingdom grow", "may thy Kingdom be perfected", but rather, "may thy Kingdom *come*". *For the disciples,* the *basileia* is not yet here, not even in its beginnings. . . . Either the *basileia* is here, or it is not yet here. For the disciples and for the early church it is not yet here' (Weiss, *Proclamation* 73-74). Gnilka also observes that the aorist tense (in the Greek) refers to 'a single future coming' (*Jesus of Nazareth* 136).

137. Jeremias, *Proclamation* 198; Davies and Allison, *Matthew* 1.595; fuller details in C. A. Evans, 'Jesus and Rabbinic Parables, Proverbs, and Prayers', *Jesus and His Contemporaries* 251-97 (here 283-94).

It can hardly be accidental that the first two petitions of the Lord's Prayer are so similar to those of the Kaddish. This confirms the origin of Jesus' prayer within Jewish circles and probably implies that Jesus was himself influenced by an early form of the Kaddish[138] in modelling the prayer he taught.[139] The point is that both prayers look for an effective implementation of God's kingdom. As already noted, the Lord's Prayer's talk of the kingdom 'coming' is distinctive of the Jesus tradition; but bearing in mind the breadth of reference in the term (§12.2a above), the petition would probably have been understood, and prayed, as an expression of hope in God as king.[140] And the request would presumably be either that God would exercise his kingship more fully, or more likely, as in the typical hope reviewed above (§12.2b), that God intervene finally and decisively on behalf of his people — as perhaps in the other ancient Jewish prayer: 'Reign over us, you alone' (*Shemoneh 'Esreh* 11).[141] At any rate, both the Kaddish and the Lord's Prayer express a hope or expectation for the future — in the Kaddish for the near future ('in your lifetime and in your days . . . speedily and soon').[142]

Do the other petitions of the Lord's Prayer help in clarifying the issue? The question focuses chiefly on the last three requests. The fourth petition (in Matthew), which includes the difficult phrase 'our bread *ton epiousion*', may well be best rendered as 'Give us today our bread for the day ahead' (Matt. 6.11/Luke 11.3),[143] that is, as a prayer that can be prayed either morning or evening. In the context of Jesus' preaching and of Israel's history, it would thus invoke either

138. Since the attestation of the Kaddish is late the issue remains in some doubt; see J. Heinemann, 'The Background of Jesus' Prayer in the Jewish Liturgical Tradition', in J. J. Petuchowski and M. Brocke, eds., *The Lord's Prayer and Jewish Liturgy* (London: Burns and Oates, 1978) 81-89 (here 81); but there is no problem in hypothesizing a long period of oral use prior to transcription. Heinemann also has no doubt 'that the prayer of Jesus in Matt. 6:9 displays all the characteristics of Jewish private prayer' (88).

139. Perrin, *Language* 47; Schürmann, *Gottes Reich* 101. 'This way of creating prayers was and still is characteristic of most prayers. In order to make new prayers acceptable to a liturgical community, they must reflect the traditional language and form' (Betz, *Sermon on the Mount* 372-73).

140. While the first Christians looked for the coming of Jesus (cf. 1 Cor. 11.26; 16.22) (Lüdemann, *Jesus* 147).

141. Schlosser, *Règne* 258-59; Meier, *Marginal Jew* 2.298-300; 'In the final analysis, "Your kingdom come" is a prayer for God himself to come and achieve his end in creating a world' (Beasley-Murray, *Jesus and the Kingdom* 151).

142. Becker may be pushing too hard when he observes that 'Jesus reversed a traditional approach so that God's final demonstration of his rule as king came not at the end but at the beginning of the prayer and thus forced the present into a secondary position' (*Jesus* 269).

143. R. A. Guelich, *The Sermon on the Mount* (Waco: Word, 1982) 291-93; Davies and Allison, *Matthew* 1.607-609. But the matter is far from clear: see Fitzmyer, *Luke* 904-905; Beasley-Murray, *Jesus and the Kingdom* 153-54; Betz, *Sermon on the Mount* 397-99; 'the bread that is coming' — *lakma d'ateh* (Chilton, *Rabbi Jesus* 77).

thought of the heavenly banquet to come[144] or memory of the manna necessary to see the eater through to the Promised Land.[145] Either way, a forward look to a desired outcome equivalent to the coming of the kingdom may well be implicit, with the further implication that under God's rule sufficiency is assured. Likewise, the petition for forgiveness presumably has the final judgment at least partly in view:[146] the favourable judgment of God is depicted as dependent not on the petitioner's freedom from sin but on the petitioner's readiness to forgive others (Matt. 6.12/Luke 11.4a; see below §14.6).

Equally difficult to decide is whether the final petition has a similarly eschatological note: 'Do not bring us into *peirasmos*' (Matt. 6.13a/Luke 11.4b). The issue here is whether *peirasmos* signifies any 'test or trial' or looks particularly to the great tribulation widely expected to precede the age to come. In other words, is this a prayer for help in daily trial and tribulation[147] or a plea to be kept from the final and most testing trial of the present age?[148] The latter certainly chimes in with a characteristic fearful expectancy in Jewish apocalyptic writings of the period and in the preaching of Jesus' mentor, John the Baptist,[149] as indeed among the first Christians (see §12.4d below),[150] but the key term itself *(peirasmos)* is not specific enough to settle the issue.[151] The point here, however, is that the undisputed petition for the kingdom as still to come gives the prayer as a whole its eschatological note, and it is this note which echoes through the other petitions.

Other of the distinctive features observed by Jeremias above (§12.1) are also most naturally understood as implying a future kingdom. Most of the 'enter into' sayings clearly have that implication: the kingdom is to be entered into as into a future state or condition.[152] Similarly, the kingdom is to be 'sought' as something yet to be attained.[153] Presumably related is the contrast between 'the

---

144. Jeremias, *Proclamation* 199-201. See further below (§12.4f).

145. References in Davies and Allison, *Matthew* 1.609.

146. Davies and Allison, *Matthew* 1.612; Meier, *Marginal Jew* 2.301.

147. Betz, *Sermon on the Mount* 406-11.

148. Jeremias, *Prayers* 105-106; also *Proclamation* 202; 'the petition for protection from succumbing to the *peirasmos is* the desperate cry of faith on trial: preserve us from apostasy, keep us from going wrong' (*Proclamation* 129).

149. See above, §§11.4c and 12.2c.

150. Jeremias, *Proclamation* 129, 201-202; Davies and Allison, *Matthew* 1.613-14; Meier, *Marginal Jew* 2.301.

151. Guelich, *Sermon on the Mount* 294-96.

152. Of the passages cited in n. 23 above, only Matt. 21.31 and 23.13 are not clearly future-oriented, though Horn argues that the polemical thrust of these sayings marks them out as the earliest stratum of the 'entering the kingdom' motif ('synoptischen Einlasssprüche' 200-203).

153. See above, n. 22, and further Davies and Allison, *Matthew* 1.660.

(present) age and the age to come', where only in the latter can one enjoy 'eternal life' (Mark 10.30/Luke 18.30) and angelic existence (Luke 20.34-36).[154]

c. Eschatological Reversal

As many have observed, a persistent theme in the Jesus tradition is that of eschatological reversal. One of its most striking expressions appears in the collection of beatitudes. It cannot but be significant that both Matthew and Luke seem to have followed the compilers of the tradition in Q in putting the beatitudes at the head of the first collection of Jesus' teaching (the Sermon on Mount/Sermon on Plain, Matt. 5.3-12/Luke 6.20-23). As elsewhere in the Jesus tradition we see evidence of concern to group together like material, no doubt initially by teachers responsible for telling and being consulted about the tradition. Neither interest is shared by *Thomas*.

Matt. 5.3-6, 11-12	Luke 6.20-23	GTh 54, 69, 68
3 Blessed are the poor in spirit, for theirs is the kingdom of heaven. 4 Blessed are those who mourn, for they will be comforted. 5 Blessed are the meek, for they will inherit the earth. 6 Blessed are those who hunger and thirst for righteousness, for they will be filled.	20 Blessed are the poor, for yours is the kingdom of God. 21 Blessed are you who are hungry now, for you will be filled. Blessed are you who weep now, for you will laugh.	54 Blessed are the poor, for yours is the kingdom of heaven. 69 Blessed are they who are hungry, that the belly of him who desires may be satisfied.
11 Blessed are you when people revile you and persecute you and utter all kinds of evil against you falsely on my account. 12 Rejoice and be glad, for your reward is great in heaven, for in the same way they persecuted the prophets who were before you.	22 Blessed are you when people hate you, and when they exclude you, revile you, and defame you on account of the Son of Man. 23 Rejoice in that day and leap for joy, for surely your reward is great in heaven; for that is what their ancestors did to the prophets.	68 Blessed are you when you are hated and persecuted, and no place will be found where you have been persecuted.

Here once more there can be little doubt that Jesus is remembered as one who spoke in this form. In the retelling, the Evangelists have given the individual sayings their own slant, and the sequence may have been extended with fresh 'blesseds' (Matt. 5.7-10) and parallel 'woes' (Luke 6.24-26), added in the spirit

154. Note also Mark 3.29/Matt. 12.32. Matthew takes over the phrase 'the end of the age' from apocalyptic language (Matt. 13.39, 40, 49; 24.3; 28.20); see above, nn. 94-99. Dalman had already observed that if the ideas of 'this age' and 'the future age' were at all used by Jesus they 'were not of importance in His vocabulary' (*Words of Jesus* 148).

of those already part of the tradition.[155] The noteworthy feature at this point, however, is the agreement of Matthew and Luke with Q in placing the kingdom beatitude at the head.[156]

The common feature in the beatitudes is the theme of reversal, in which case the present tense of the first should probably be taken as a proleptic present: the kingdom is to be the poor's.[157] The poor are comforted in the present, not because their situation has already changed, but because they can be confident that God has not forgotten them and that their place in his kingdom is assured.[158] It does not necessarily follow that this was a hope of heaven. If Matthew's third beatitude (with no Lukan parallel) is any guide, the hope was for the meek[159] to inherit the land (Ps. 37.11), which Matthew later identifies with the kingdom (Matt. 21.43).[160] Here we find ourselves inextricably caught in the tension be-

155. For discussion see Davies and Allison, *Matthew ad loc.* and excursus, 1.431-42; Meier, *Marginal Jew* 2.323-36; Betz, *Sermon on the Mount* 105, 109-10. Note the sequence of (8 or 9?) beatitudes in 4Q525 2.1-8. For those who think the woes were part of Q, see Kloppenborg, *Q Parallels* 26, to which add particularly Catchpole, *Quest* 87-90. But we should avoid making the judgment of 'authenticity' dependent on our ability to recover 'the original form in its pristine purity' (Meier 2.320); performing and passing on the (oral) tradition was not conceived in such terms.

156. Schürmann suggests that in these beatitudes (cf. Mark 1.15) we hear Jesus' inaugural preaching in public (*Lukasevangelium* 1.332). In *Thomas* the first beatitude has no such prominence; but note also the tendency in *Thomas* (once again) to de-eschatologize the other two beatitudes.

157. Schürmann, *Gottes Reich* 87; Beasley-Murray, *Jesus and the Kingdom* 162-63; Luz, *Matthäus* 1.208; 'the line also anticipates an eschatological verdict' (Betz, *Sermon on the Mount* 118).

158. In Jewish writing the beatitude occurs both in wisdom writing as a moral exhortation and in eschatological contexts (particularly apocalypses) as promising future consolation (Guelich, *Sermon on the Mount* 64-65; Davies and Allison, *Matthew* 1.432-34; Meier, *Marginal Jew* 2.323-25; Betz, *Sermon on the Mount* 94, 97-105). Here the reversal theme makes clear the eschatological orientation: 'Strictly speaking, they should be pronounced by the divine judge in the afterlife, as verdicts at the eschatological judgment' (Betz 96). Kloppenborg Verbin plays down too much the eschatological thrust of Q 6.20b, as confirmed not least by its context in Q (6.20b-23)! ('Discursive Practices' 179-86). But see further below, §13.4.

159. The Hebrew terms 'poor' (*'aniyyim*) and 'meek' (*'anawim*) evidently overlapped in their range of meaning and are translated in the LXX by a variety of terms, including *ptōchoi* ('poor') and *praeis* ('meek'); see F. Hauck and S. Schulz, *praus, TDNT* 6 (1968) 647-48; E. Bammel, *ptōchos, TDNT* 6 (1968) 888-89; E. Gerstenberger, *'anâ, TDOT* 11.242, 244-45; and further below, chapter 13 n. 136. Betz demurs on the issue (*Sermon on the Mount* 125-26), but the Jewish provenance of the beatitude is not in question.

160. No Jew hearing the preceding parable (Matt. 21.33-42 pars.) would fail to identify the vineyard with Israel (Isa. 5.1-7; see further below, chapter 16 n. 68), and the Matthean addition identifies the vineyard with the kingdom of God. So (land of) Israel = vineyard = kingdom of God. Cf. Freyne, *Galilee, Jesus and the Gospels* 239-47.

tween different strands of eschatological expectation in Second Temple Judaism — between a hope for restoration of the dispersed to the land renewed in its bounty, a hope for social justice (righteousness),[161] a hope to 'inherit the earth' (world domination?), and a spiritualized hope for eternal life.[162]

Eschatological reversal is a theme repeated elsewhere in Jesus' kingdom teaching, particularly in Matthew. It is the child who typifies the kingdom participant; only such will enter (Mark 10.14-15 pars.; Matt. 18.3).[163] In contrast, the rich will find it exceedingly hard if not impossible to enter the kingdom (Mark 10.23-25 pars.).[164] Matthew also has a saying about toll-collectors and prostitutes 'preceding you into the kingdom of God' (Matt. 21.31).[165] Particularly prominent is the great(est)/least motif: the kingdom is like a mustard seed, smaller than all seeds, but when grown is greater than the other herbs (Mark 4.30-32 pars.);[166] the disciples argue about who is greatest (Mark 9.34 pars.), that is, no doubt, in the kingdom (Matt. 18.1, 4);[167] in Matthew's version (Matt.

161. 'The Beatitudes call for a renewal of those social values derived from covenant traditions' (Kaylor, *Jesus* 105).

162. See above, nn. 17 and 73.

163. The Jesus Seminar questioned whether talk of 'entering God's domain' could go back to Jesus on the grounds that the saying 'had been drawn into the context of baptism (note John 3) and thus had to do with the rites of initiation into the Christian community' (see below, chapter 14, n. 39). Even if the link to baptism could be justified, the confusion of *later use* with *origin* is obvious. It is worth noting that *Thomas* also speaks of those like children entering the kingdom without any evident allusion to baptism (*GTh* 22). See further above, n. 24.

164. Funk notes that the 'eye of a needle' saying 'became a point of reference for the Fellows [of the Jesus Seminar] in determining the authentic sayings of Jesus' — a graphic and humorous aphorism (*Five Gospels* 223, 371).

165. This is one of Matthew's few 'kingdom of *God*' sayings, which could indicate that he has drawn it from tradition and for some reason retained its traditional form. Its 'lack of fit' with the preceding parable also suggests that Matthew has drawn it from elsewhere in the tradition. See also Matt. 5.19.

166. Cited below (§12.5e). The Jesus Seminar concluded that the *Thomas* version is closest to the original, but in treating the saying as a parody of great empire (an allusion to Ezek. 31.2-9 and Dan. 4.9-12 is certainly possible, but in their retelling the Synoptics echo Ps. 104[103 LXX].12 more closely) the Seminar have missed the contrast between 'smallest seed' and 'great branch/plant' (eschatological reversal) which is fundamental for the saying (Funk, *Five Gospels* 59-60, 484-85; similarly Crossan, *Historical Jesus* 276-79); but see Bultmann, *Theology* 1.8; Jeremias, *Parables* 147-49; Kümmel, *Promise* 131-32; W. Schrage, *The Ethics of the New Testament* (Philadelphia: Fortress, 1988) 19-20; Scott, *Hear Then the Parable* 377-87; Meadors, *Jesus* 204-206; Davies and Allison, *Matthew* 2.417; Lüdemann, *Jesus* 32; A. J. Hultgren, *The Parables of Jesus* (Grand Rapids: Eerdmans, 2000) 395-96; Liebenberg, *Language* 289-91, 296, 312. Similarly the parable of the leaven — also a kingdom parable (Matt. 13.33/Luke 13.20-21/*GTh* 96); Liebenberg points out that leaven is not universally seen as a negative metaphor (*Language* 336-38).

167. Cited above, §8.4c.

20.21) the request by/for James and John is that they should be granted the seats on Jesus' right and left in his (obviously) future kingdom ('glory' — Mark 10.37);[168] it is the servant who is 'great';[169] the Baptist is greatest among those born of women, but the least in the kingdom is greater than he (Matt. 11.11/Luke 7.28).[170] Matthew also repeats 'the first will be last, and the last first' saying,[171] just as Luke repeats the Q(?) saying, 'Whoever exalts himself will be humbled, and whoever humbles himself will be exalted'.[172]

If the note of unexpected exaltation is prominent, so too is the note of unexpected judgment on those who might have assumed that their future status was secure. Notable is the prediction that many will come from east and west to recline in the kingdom, while Jesus' hearers ('the sons of the kingdom' in Matthew) will be thrown out (Matt. 8.11-12/Luke 13.28-29) — a striking variation on Israel's hopes for the return of the exiles with the eschatological pilgrims from the nations.[173] Other similar 'reversal parables' explicitly imaging the kingdom are the great supper (Matt. 22.3; Luke 14.15), where the expected guests refuse the invitation and the banquet is thrown open to all and sundry (Matt. 22.2-10/Luke 14.16-24),[174] Luke's parable of the rich man and Lazarus (Luke 16.19-

---

168. To attribute such a passage to factional rivalry within earliest Christianity (denigrating James and John) presupposes a degree of antagonism towards Jesus' most intimate circle of disciples and a cavalier handling of the Jesus tradition, which is almost entirely speculative and tendentious, *pace* the larger theses of T. J. Weeden, *Mark: Traditions in Conflict* (Philadelphia: Fortress, 1971); Kelber, *Oral*. Contrast Sanders: 'This cannot be a late invention. Later everyone recognized that Peter was the leading disciple, and the possible primacy of James and John would not have arisen' (*Historical Figure* 189).

169. Mark 10.41-45 pars.; Mark 9.35; Matt. 23.11; Luke 22.27.

170. See below, §12.5c.

171. Matt. 19.30; 20.16; Mark 10.31; Luke 13.30; *GTh* 4; on which see Crossan, *Fragments* 42-47.

172. Matt. 23.12; Luke 14.11; 18.14.

173. As Sanders observes, the hope of restoration generally included Gentiles (*Jesus and Judaism* 117). See also Becker, *Jesus of Nazareth* 66-68. The warning of Israel's rejection is hardly evidence of 'a secondary stage of the tradition' (Funk, *Five Gospels* 348) or of subsequent 'anti-Judaism' (Lüdemann, *Jesus* 156). Such warnings were hardly strange to Israel's prophetic tradition; we need only recall the Baptist (§11.4b; see also nn. 80, 105 above and §12.4e below). For detailed discussion see Beasley-Murray, *Jesus and the Kingdom* 169-74; Meier, *Marginal Jew* 2.309-17; 'this logion cannot come from primitive Christianity' (Theissen and Merz, *Historical Jesus* 254); older discussion in terms of the criterion of dissimilarity in Perrin, *Rediscovering* 161-63. See also Matt. 11.21-24/Luke 10.13-15 (§12.4e below), and cf. also Matthew's (redactional) conclusion to the parable of the wicked tenants: 'the kingdom of God will be taken away from you and given to a people that produces its fruit' (Matt. 21.43). On the possibility that the saying refers to the return of the scattered exiles rather than the incoming of Gentiles, see n. 442 below. Kaylor draws out the socio-political implications (*Jesus* 131-37).

174. This is the obvious reversal theme of the parable, and fits with the sustained empha-

31),[175] and Matthew's parable of the labourers in the vineyard, where the late-
comers receive the same payment as those who have laboured throughout the day
(Matt. 20.1-15).[176] The Queen of the South and the Ninevites will receive a more
favourable verdict at the last judgment than the present generation of Israel
(Matt. 12.41-42/Luke 11.31-32).[177] Finally we should note the exaltation promised to the twelve at the end of Q, that 'you will sit on thrones judging the twelve
tribes of Israel' (Matt. 19.28/Luke 22.30).[178]

In all this there is a present note: the very fact that the assurance is being
given in the here and now, and with such confidence, gives Jesus' message an immediacy of appeal. But the overall thrust is more forward-looking: the assurance
is that God is the God of different priorities and that this will become evident in

---

sis of Jesus' protest against the presumption of the righteous within Israel (see below §13.5).
Scott reads the parable as reversing and subverting the system of honour: 'The man who gives a
banquet loses his honor and joins the shameless poor' (*Hear Then the Parable* 173-74); but
does any version of the parable (including *GTh* 64) encourage that reading? See also n. 236.

175. See below, n. 213.

176. Despite its sole attestation in Matthew, the parable's subversive note (kingdom as
just reward) has generally impressed itself as characteristic of Jesus (Jeremias, *Parables* 33-38,
136-39; Scott, *Hear Then the Parable* 296-98; Funk, *Five Gospels* 224-25; Lüdemann, *Jesus*
213; Hultgren, *Parables* 41-42 nn. 38, 39). Gnilka treats it as paradigmatic of Jesus' message
(*Jesus of Nazareth* 82-93); also W. R. Herzog, *Parables as Subversive Speech: Jesus as Peda-
gogue of the Oppressed* (Louisville: Westminster John Knox, 1994).

177. Cited below (§12.5b). As with Matt. 8.11-12/Luke 13.28-29 (above, n. 173), the
assumption that warnings to Israel must be attributed to early Christian disappointment at the
failure of the mission to their fellow Jews (Funk, *Five Gospels* 188-89; Lüdemann, *Jesus*
339; see also above, §7.4c) is spurious. Jesus could well have seen the generation condemned
by Moses (Deut 1.35; 32.5, 20) as foreshadowing his own generation in the equivalent time
of eschatological expectancy (Moses spoke 'beyond the Jordan in the wilderness', Deut.
1.1). Manson drew attention to the strophic parallelism evident in the saying 'as the most distinctive characteristic of his (Jesus') poetry and his special contribution to the forms of poetry in general' (*Teaching* 56). See Davies and Allison, *Matthew* 2.357, Becker, *Jesus of Nazareth* 65-66, and further Reiser, *Jesus and Judgment* 230-41. Reiser takes up Manson's
neglected insight in concluding: 'In all probability, there is scarcely a word in the Jesus tradition that we can more confidently regard as authentic', referring *inter alia* to Semitic diction
and phraseology, the 'rabbinic' argumentation, and 'the strict form of symmetrically constructed double saying that has scarcely any parallels outside the Jesus tradition' (209, 211,
219-20).

178. The thought may be of the twelve 'ruling over' the twelve tribes (as did the judges
of old) (Horsley, *Jesus* 201-206 — he even translates *krinontes* as 'saving [effecting justice
for]'; C. A. Evans, 'The Twelve Thrones of Israel: Scripture and Politics in Luke 22:24-30', in
Chilton and Evans, *Jesus in Context* 455-79 [here 471-72]; Allison, *Jesus of Nazareth* 102, 141-
45; others in C. Tuckett, 'Q 22:28-30', in D. G. Horrell and C. M. Tuckett, eds., *Christology,
Controversy and Community,* D. R. Catchpole FS [NovTSup 99; Brill: Leiden, 2000] 99-116
[here 103 n. 20]; but see below, n. 205.

the near future.[179] There will be a reversal of status: those who expect high recognition will be disappointed and those held in low esteem will be shown to be highly esteemed by God.[180] The motif is by no means uniform. Nor is there much indication that this reversal might/will take place very soon; in these cases the future kingdom could well be conceived as a post-mortem state.[181] At the least, however, some final turning-of-the-tables is presumably in view, whether near or distant, whether at an individual or universal level. At all events, where we find such a consistent emphasis within the Jesus tradition we can scarcely doubt that it was an emphasis in Jesus' own preaching, leaving as it has such a mark in the tradition.[182]

d. Expectations of Suffering

The various strands of the reversal theme are evident apart from the theme itself. First the expectation of suffering. As we have already seen (§12.4b), the Lord's Prayer included a petition to escape the *peirasmos* (Matt. 6.13a/Luke 11.4b). And the final beatitude (Matt. 5.11-12/Luke 6.22-23) certainly assumes that disciples of Jesus should expect suffering. The latter was no doubt much pondered on and reused (as the many textual variants also indicate) and the divergent forms of the Matthean and Lukan forms probably reflect various situations of persecution in the early churches.[183] But Matthew's retention of the 'you' form (also *Thomas*) and the likelihood that Jesus knew well the tradition of prophet rejection and persecution (the Baptist had been executed)[184] strengthen the likelihood that he foresaw rejection and persecution for his disciples and uttered a blessing on them in anticipation.

These are part of a more widespread motif, which has provided a basic element for Mark's 'little apocalypse' (Mark 13.1-37) and Matthew's mission instructions (Matt. 10.16-39). The traditions drawn on in both have almost certainly

179. 'One does not envision a twelve-tribe "Israel" without the conviction that something stupendous is imminent' (Keck, *Who Is Jesus?* 51).

180. See also Allison, *Jesus of Nazareth* 131-34.

181. So Matthew seems to assume: following the final judgment, 'the righteous will shine like the sun in the kingdom of their Father' (Matt. 13.43).

182. Keck observes that the theme of 'eschatological reversal' 'shows just how far off-base is the portrayal of Jesus as a Cynic' since a life of poverty was a Cynic desideratum in itself (*Who Is Jesus?* 80).

183. See particularly Betz, *Sermon on the Mount* 147-53.

184. 2 Chron. 24.19; 36.15-16; Neh. 9.26; *Jub.* 1.12; 4Q166 (= 4QpHos^a) 2.3-5; *Mart. Isa.* 5; *Liv. Pro.;* Mark 12.2-5 pars.; Matt. 23.37/Luke 13.34; Matt. 23.29-31, 34-35/Luke 11.47-51; Luke 13.33. See again Steck, *Israel und das gewaltsame Geschick der Propheten.*

been much elaborated in the course of retelling and reflect the circumstances of the ongoing mission (notably Mark 13.9-13 pars.).[185] But it is still quite possible that the discourse began with or as a collection of Jesus' own forebodings regarding the future.[186] We shall see later the strong indications that he anticipated in some way the destruction of the Temple (§15.3a). It is also possible that Paul knew some early form of this collection.[187] Nor should we forget that Matthew and Luke knew other overlapping apocalyptic material[188] — evidence once again of concern to group remembrances of and traditions regarding Jesus.[189] And it is easy to see how several of the strands of Jewish expectation noted above (§12.2c) could have prompted such warnings, from Jesus as much as from his followers.[190]

Notable in the Markan sequence are the evocation of the image of eschatological birthpangs (Mark 13.8), the allusion to Dan. 12.1's anticipation of an unprecedented period of suffering to be endured (Mark 13.19-20), and the expectation of cosmic convulsions (13.24-25). The eschatological goal is clearly in sight: 'The one who endures to the end *(eis telos)* will be saved' (13.13).[191] Matthew retains all these elements in his own version of the 'little apocalypse' (Matt. 24.8, 13, 21-22, 29), but noticeably includes the last exhortation also in his mission instructions (Matt. 10.22). The expectation of suffering is less prominent in

185. The Jesus Seminar (Funk, *Five Gospels* 107-15) and Lüdemann (*Jesus* 88-93) dismiss the bulk of the material as reflecting the later situation of the early community and impossible to trace back to Jesus, thus reflecting the dominant consensus in current scholarship. Pesch, however, concludes that Mark 13 shows Mark to be, here as elsewhere, a 'conservator redactor' (*Markusevanglium* 2.267). G. R. Beasley-Murray, *Jesus and the Last Days: The Interpretation of the Olivet Discourse* (Peabody: Hendrickson, 1993), a major review of the debate, acknowledges Mark's hand throughout the discourse, but agrees with Pesch (363). Wright (*Jesus* 339-67) and McKnight (*New Vision* 135-37, 141-42, 145) are surprisingly uncritical in their use of Mark 13.

186. The 'parables of crisis' (see below §12.4g) are generally accounted among the oldest parts of the discourse.

187. Cf. Mark 13.5, 14 with 2 Thess. 2.3-4; Mark 13.6, 22 with 2 Thess. 2.9; Mark 13.26-27 with 1 Thess. 4.15-17 and 2 Thess. 2.1. The argument is pushed much further by D. Wenham, *The Rediscovery of Jesus' Eschatological Discourse* (Gospel Perspectives 4; Sheffield: JSOT, 1984).

188. Q? — Matt. 24.17-18, 27-28, 37-41/Luke 17.24-37.

189. 'It is beyond question that the theme of Luke 17.20-37 is a nucleus of the proclamation of Jesus, whereas Mark 13 is a theme that belongs to the early church' (Jeremias, *Proclamation* 124).

190. Lars Hartman earlier argued that the heart of Mark 13 was an original 'midrash' on Daniel which dealt with the great distress of the last days (*Prophecy Interpreted: The Formation of Some Jewish Apocalyptic Texts and of the Eschatological Discourse Mark 13 par.* [ConBNT 1; Lund: Gleerup, 1966] summary survey on 172-74); cf. Wright, *Jesus* 513-19.

191. The 'end' here presumably is eschatological, as in Daniel and *4 Ezra* (see above §12.3b).

the mission instructions in Mark and Luke, but Mark juxtaposes them with the story of the Baptist's fate (Mark 6.7-30) and Luke attaches the warnings of final judgment directed against the Galilean towns to his account of the mission of the seventy (Luke 10.1-16). In addition, we should recall that Matthew and Luke have retained at the heart of the disciples' preaching Jesus' own proclamation, 'The kingdom of God/heaven has come near' (Matt. 10.7/Luke 10.9).

Among other expectations of suffering we should note particularly what might be called the terms of discipleship. They involve willingness for hardship and total commitment (Matt. 8.18-22/Luke 9.57-62), the last two exhortations in Luke evoking the kingdom of God (9.60, 62). To 'enter life' (Mark has 'the kingdom') one must be willing to cut off offending hand or foot and to tear out offending eye (Mark 9.43, 45, 47/Matt. 18.8-9).[192] To be a disciple involves going the way of the humiliation and agony of crucifixion and readiness to lose one's life.[193] The disciple must be prepared to suffer contempt and abuse (Matt. 5.39/Luke 6.29).[194] To share Jesus' mission is to court danger.[195] And the contrast held out to disciples seeking advancement and honour in Jesus' final triumph is of drinking rather from Jesus' cup of suffering and sharing in some measure in Jesus' baptism of suffering (Mark 10.35-40/Matt. 20.20-28). As we shall see later, the latter imagery is probably best understood as an adaptation of the Baptist's own expectation of a baptism in the river of God's fiery breath.[196] A possibly overlapping collection in Q emphasizes that the effect of Jesus' mission is to provoke civil strife and family disruption (Matt. 10.34-36/Luke 12.49-53/*GTh* 16).[197]

Most of this clearly meshes into the traditions of the rejected prophet (n. 184 above), but also with the more typically apocalyptic expectation of sufferings prior to a final resolution in favour of the faithful sufferers.[198] Jesus is

192. Schlosser, *Règne* 632-33; Becker, *Jesus of Nazareth* 59-60. Allison argues that sexual sins are in view (*Jesus* 178-82); see further below, chapter 14 n. 251. Matthew has another version of the saying at Matt. 5.29-30.

193. The challenge is retained in both Mark 8.34-35 pars. and Q (Matt. 10.38/Luke 14.27; Matt. 10.39/Luke 17.33); see also §14.3e below. The image of crucifixion would not be unfamiliar to those who knew the ruthlessness of Roman rule (cf. M. Hengel, *The Charismatic Leader and His Followers* [1968; ET Edinburgh: Clark, 1981] 58; Gnilka, *Jesus* 166-67). See also chapter 14 n. 87 below.

194. 'A blow on the right cheek is a blow with the back of the hand, which even today in the East expresses the greatest possible contempt and extreme abuse' (Jeremias, *Proclamation* 239).

195. Matt. 10.16/Luke 10.3; Matt. 10.23 (see below §14.3b).

196. See above, §11.4c, and below, §§17.4d, 5c.

197. See also D. C. Allison, 'Q 12:51-53 and Mark 9:11-13 and the Messianic Woes', in Chilton and Evans, eds., *Authenticating the Words of Jesus* 289-310. The text is cited below (chapter 14 n. 242); and see further below, §14.7.

198. See above, n. 74.

thus remembered as sharing much of the Baptist's expectation.[199] The 'final resolution' can be conceived either as an individual's hope of heaven[200] or in terms of resurrection and final judgment following the eschatological tribulation introducing the age to come.

e. Judgment

The expectation of impending judgment can scarcely be excluded from the core memories of Jesus' preaching.[201] I have already noted it as a prominent feature of the theme of eschatological reversal (see §12.4c above): those who expect a place in the kingdom with Abraham, Isaac, and Jacob will be 'thrown out' (Matt. 8.11-12/Luke 13.28-29);[202] those who refuse the invitation to the great supper will have no place at it (Matt. 22.2-10/Luke 14.16-24);[203] there will be a final judgment when previous generations (including Gentiles) will condemn the generation of Jesus (Matt. 12.41-42/Luke 11.31-32);[204] the twelve will take part in that judgment (Matt. 19.28/Luke 22.28, 30).[205] To be noted is the fact that these are all Q passages.

199. We will examine how Jesus qualified John's message below (§§12. 5; 17.4d, 5c).

200. Wis. 5.1-5; Matt. 5.12/Luke 6.23; Luke 16.22.

201. Cf. Sanders, *Jesus and Judaism* 114-15. This is a theme to which Wright gives detailed attention (*Jesus* 182-86, 322-33). In what follows I draw particularly on Reiser, *Jesus and Judgment;* see also Becker, *Jesus of Nazareth* 49-80; Theissen and Merz, *Historical Jesus* 265-69; McKnight, *New Vision* 33-39.

202. See above, n. 177.

203. Reiser, *Jesus and Judgment* 241-45. For the Matthew/Luke parallel see §8.5e above. Theissen and Merz exaggerate when they describe this motif as occurring 'particularly frequently' within the preaching of the kingdom of God' (*Historical Jesus* 267). Note how *Thomas,* after narrating what looks like a performative variant of this tradition (four excuses given), concludes thus: 'Go out to the streets, bring those whom you will find, so that they may dine. The buyers and the merchants (shall?) not (come) into the place of my Father' (*GTh* 64).

204. See above, n. 177; for detailed discussion see Reiser, *Jesus and Judgment* 206-21.

205. Does the saying envisage final judgment or 'rule over' (n. 178 above)? But *krinein* is used nowhere else in the NT in the semitic sense of 'govern' (J. Dupont, 'Le Logion de douze trones [Mt 19,28; Lc 22,28-30]', *Biblica* 45 [1964] 355-92 [here 372]). And Q refers to final, though not necessarily condemnatory, judgment (Tuckett, 'Q 22:28-30' 103, 113; see further J. Verheyden, 'The Conclusion of Q: Eschatology in Q 22,28-30', in Lindemann, ed., *Sayings Source Q* 695-718; Meier, *Marginal Jew* 3.135-38). Matthew also clearly thinks of final judgment (cf. 25.31) and was evidently influenced by the portrayal of the Son of Man sitting on his glorious throne in judgment in the Similitudes of Enoch (see below, §16.4e) as Davies and Allison, *Matthew* 3.54-55 recognize. Luke prefaces the saying with Jesus as it were making his last will and testament *(diatithemai)* and assigning to the twelve a share in his kingdom (Luke 22.29-30a). But the thought of the twelve judging Israel is a reversal of Israel's hope of judging

In addition Matt. 5.25-26/Luke 12.58-59 warns about an impending judgment with overtones of finality.[206] And Matt. 11.21-24/Luke 10.12-15 speaks clearly of final (the last) judgment.

Matt. 11.21-24	Luke 10.12-15
21 <u>Woe to you, Chorazin! Woe to you, Bethsaida! For if the deeds of power done in you had</u> taken place <u>in Tyre and Sidon, they would have repented long ago in sackcloth and ashes.</u> 22 <u>But</u> I tell you, on the day of <u>judgment it will be more tolerable for Tyre and Sidon than for you.</u> 23 <u>And you, Capernaum, will you be exalted to heaven? No, you will be brought down to Hades.</u> For if the deeds of power done in you had been done in Sodom, it would have remained until this day. 24 But I tell you that on the day of judgment it will be more tolerable for the land of Sodom than for you.	12 I tell you, on that day it will be more tolerable for Sodom than for that town. 13 <u>Woe to you, Chorazin! Woe to you, Bethsaida! For if the deeds of power done in you had</u> been done <u>in Tyre and Sidon, they would have repented long ago</u>, sitting <u>in sackcloth and ashes.</u> 14 <u>But</u> at the <u>judgment it will be more tolerable for Tyre and Sidon than for you.</u> 15 <u>And you, Capernaum, will you be exalted to heaven? No, you will be brought down to Hades.</u>

As with Matt. 8.11-12/Luke 13.28-29 (n. 173), there is a widespread assumption that such an utterance must reflect the later frustration of (early Christian) mission failure.[207] But the only solid evidence of a Galilean mission is that of Jesus; only tendentious idealisation would refuse to accept that Jesus might have been more frustrated than his subsequent followers,[208] and the emphasis correlates well with the motif of eschatological reversal evident elsewhere in the remembered Jesus' preaching (above §12.4c).[209]

Other parables speak of a (final?) reckoning which the audiences need to anticipate now: the talents/pounds (Matt. 25.14-30/Luke 19.11-27),[210] the unmerciful

---

the nations (above, n. 82), which is hardly uncharacteristic of Jesus (see also Sanders, *Jesus and Judaism* 115; Lüdemann, *Jesus* 211-12). Not surprisingly, *Thomas* lacks any parallel.

206. Cited above, §8.5d. See again Reiser, *Jesus and Judgment* 281-90. Both the Jesus Seminar (Funk, *Five Gospels* 142, 344) and Lüdemann (*Jesus* 351) give a positive evaluation, though had the former sensed any eschatological overtone (rather than a critique of human courts) their judgment would, no doubt, have been more negative. But an allusion to final judgment seems inescapable (Davies and Allison, *Matthew* 1.519-21).

207. Sanders, *Jesus and Judaism* 114; Funk, *Five Gospels* 181; Lüdemann, *Jesus* 174.

208. Cf. Meadors, *Jesus* 215-20. 'The pronouncements could well have been made at the farewell from Galilee and the departure on the last journey to Jerusalem' (Gnilka, *Jesus* 195).

209. See further Davies and Allison, *Matthew* 2.270-71; Reiser, *Jesus and Judgment* 221-30. 'It is easier to assume that, since Jesus had condemned these places so harshly, there was no post-Easter mission at all in them than to argue the opposite position' (Becker, *Jesus of Nazareth* 64).

210. Another parable where variation between Matthew and Luke is best explained in terms of performance variation (whether by Jesus himself or his followers) rather than literary

servant handed over finally to the torturers/jailers *(basanistai)* until the unpayable debt is paid in full (Matt. 18.23-35),[211] the unjust steward (Luke 16.1-8),[212] and the uncaring rich man, whose fate to be tormented *(en basanois,* 16.23) in Hades ('the place of *basanos'*, 16.28) is simply taken for granted (Luke 16.19-31).[213] There is a similar note in the 'parables of crisis' reviewed below (§12.4g), as in the sayings which envisage a sudden disruption of everyday affairs (Matt. 24.37-41/Luke 17.26-35)[214] or a sudden calamity (flash flood) sweeping away a life's work (Matt.

---

dependence, and where the quest for an 'original' form is misguided; the *Gospel of the Nazareans,* in Eusebius, *Theophania* 4.22 (text in Aland, *Synopsis* 416; ET in Elliott, *Apocryphal New Testament* 11) shows how the retelling could vary, even in a version which acknowledges direct dependence on Matthew. Lüdemann speaks of 'an original version which can no longer be constructed' *(Jesus* 235); the Jesus Seminar give the bulk of the tradition a positive rating (Funk, *Five Gospels* 255-57, 373-75). Wright fairly asks, 'Was Jesus not a "popular story-teller"? Is there any popular story-teller on record who told stories only once, and then always in the least elaborate form possible?' *(Jesus* 633-34 n. 83). To be noted is the fact that the difficult conclusion (Matt. 25.29/Luke 19.26) is attested also by Mark 4.25 pars. and *GTh* 41. See also discussion in Beasley-Murray, *Jesus and the Kingdom* 215-18; Scott, *Hear Then the Parable* 217-35; C. A. Evans, 'Reconstructing Jesus' Teaching: Problems and Possibilities', in Charlesworth and Johns, eds., *Hillel and Jesus* 397-426 (here 414-25); Hultgren, *Parables* 271-91.

211. For the concept of the torments *(basanoi)* of hell, see *1 En.* 10.13; 22.11; Wis. 3.1; 2 Macc. 7.17; *4 Ezra* 7.36, 67, 86; 9.12-13; *T. Abr.* (A) 12.18; (B) 10.16. See further Reiser, *Jesus and Judgment* 273-81; Becker, *Jesus of Nazareth* 68-71. Despite its attestation only by Matthew and evidence of Matthean style in the retelling, most agree that the parable originated with Jesus (see, e.g., Hultgren, *Parables* 29 nn. 39, 40); contrast Lüdemann, who thinks that the parable's presence in the Jesus tradition is insufficient grounds for attributing it to Jesus *(Jesus* 208). Gnilka thinks that 'v.34 virtually turns the argument on its head' *(Jesus of Nazareth* 93). On the rhetoric of exaggeration ('impossible' elements) in the parable see Beasley-Murray, *Jesus and the Kingdom* 115-17.

212. Detailed discussion in Reiser, *Jesus and Judgment* 290-301. The picaresque (not to say offensive) character of the parable has usually been sufficient evidence that it must have come from Jesus, despite its sole attestation by Luke (e.g., D. O. Via, *The Parables* [Philadelphia: Fortress, 1967] 155-62; Funk, *Five Gospels* 358-59; Gnilka, *Jesus of Nazareth* 155-56)! Most agree that Jesus' version extended to 16.8a; to exclude 16.8a leaves an incomplete torso (Fitzmyer, *Luke* 1096-97; Scott, *Hear Then the Parable* 257-60; Hultgren, *Parables* 147-48). Cf. Becker: 'If the church had created the parable, the corrective explanations of vv. 8-13 would not have been necessary, and had the parable originated in Early Judaism, the church would have ignored it' *(Jesus of Nazareth* 57). Bailey demonstrates how much illumination falls on the parable when set into its historical context *(Poet and Peasant* 86-110).

213. When a parable is so Jewish in character (a 'Jewish legend' which 'breathes the rancorousness of Judaism'! — Bultmann, *History* 197, 203), the only ground for denying it to Jesus is antipathy to the theology of final punishment which it assumes (see further Fitzmyer, *Luke* 1125-27; Schottroff and Stegemann, *Hope of the Poor* 25-28; Funk, *Five Gospels* 361; Hultgren, *Parables* 115).

214. Theissen and Merz, *Historical Jesus* 269; Becker, *Jesus of Nazareth* 58-59; and

7.24-27/Luke 6.47-49).[215] Other parables strike the same note: the wheat and the tares, where the tares will be collected and burnt (Matt. 13.24-30/GTh 57),[216] with its strong echoes of the Baptist's preaching;[217] the fishnet, where the bad fish will be thrown out (Matt. 13.47-48);[218] the sheep and the goats, where the goats are condemned to 'eternal punishment *(kolasin)*' (Matt. 25.31-46);[219] and the rich fool

---

Lüdemann, *Jesus* 232 refer Matt. 24.40-41/Luke 17.34-35 back to Jesus; otherwise there would be a strong consensus that the tradition in both Matthew and Luke has been quite extensively developed.

215. Text cited in §8.5d, where it is argued that the differences between the two versions are better regarded as performance variants than editorial redaction (even if the two categories overlap). The Jesus Seminar (Funk, *Five Gospels* 158-59) attribute the parable to 'common Israelite, Judean, and rabbinic lore' (the fallacy of the criterion of dissimilarity again), and Lüdemann, *Jesus* 154, joins them in denying the parable to Jesus because it envisages final judgment. Otherwise Luz, *Matthäus* 1.412-13; Gnilka, *Jesus of Nazareth* 151-52.

216. Cited below (§12.5e). The parable reflects not only early Christian concern about mixed membership of the churches *(corpus mixtum)* (Funk, *Five Gospels* 194; Lüdemann, *Jesus* 183), but also Jesus' objection to attempts to achieve or maintain (by exclusion) a pure Judaism (see below, §13.5; E. Schweizer, *The Good News according to Matthew* [Atlanta: John Knox, 1975] 304; Davies and Allison, *Matthew* 2.409-10; Hultgren, *Parables* 299-301). Note also the parable of the seed growing secretly (Mark 4.26-29; also below §12.5e), with its echo (4.29) of Joel 3.13 — harvest as a symbol of universal judgment (cf. Rev. 14.15-16).

217. See above, §11.4b. The *Thomas* parallel is unusual in its retention of a note of future judgment (*GTh* 57); see also Reiser, *Jesus and Judgment* 256-58. A similar echo is in Luke's parable of the barren fig tree: if it does not produce fruit it should be cut down (Luke 13.6-9).

218.

Matt. 13.47-48	GTh 8
47 Again, the kingdom of heaven is like a net that was thrown into the sea and caught fish of every kind; 48 when it was full, they drew it ashore, sat down, and put the good into baskets but threw out the bad.	Man is like a wise fisherman who cast his net into the sea; he drew it out of the sea when it was full of little fishes. Among them the wise fisherman found a large good fish. The wise fisherman cast all the little fishes down into the sea (and) chose the large fish without difficulty.

The specific application to 'the end of the age' when the angels separate the evil from the righteous and cast the former 'into the furnace of fire' (Matt. 13.49-50) is probably Matthew's elaboration. But even so, *GTh* 8 does not have the note of judgment implicit in Matthew's version; *Thomas*'s parable is more like that of the hidden treasure or the valuable pearl (Matt. 13.44-46); the little fish are thrown back into the sea. The appropriateness of such a parable in a setting by the Sea of Galilee, accustomed to fishing by net, is obvious (Beasley-Murray, *Jesus and the Kingdom* 135-38; Hultgren, *Parables* 307-308).

219. The parable undoubtedly reflects Christian perspectives, but its moral emphasis is thoroughly Jewish in character (Bultmann, *History* 123-24; Davies and Allison, *Matthew* 3.425-28; Hultgren, *Parables* 323-26). The problem of discerning an earlier form is indicated by the opening reference to the Son of Man: is it integral to the parable? As with 19.28 (n. 205 above) the reference suggests later reflection on the role of the Son of Man; on the other hand, the 'coming' of the Son of Man here is to his 'throne of glory' (25.31); see further below, §16.4e.

who forgets that his soul/life may be required of him that very night (Luke 12.16-20/*GTh* 63).[220] Finally, we may recall that Luke 13.1-5 has Jesus warning that death may strike at any time and catch the unrepentant unprepared.[221]

Here again is a motif regarding future judgment which is widespread and thoroughly rooted in the different strands of Jesus tradition (in several cases where the tradition is attested in only one Synoptic Gospel we have noted that *Thomas* also attests the tradition). In such a case it must be considered most unlikely that the motif entered the tradition only in the early churches. That teachers and performers extended and elaborated the motif is certainly probable;[222] that Q reinforced the motif by its compositional structure is also probable,[223] as it is that the *Thomas* tradents omitted or softened the note of judgment (*GTh* 57 is an exception). But that such a distinctive motif should be introduced, despite its absence from the earliest recollections (that is, traditions) of Jesus' preaching, is much less likely.[224] That Jesus reacted against the Baptist's preaching of judgment and eschewed all such emphases is, of course, quite possible in principle.

220.

Luke 12.16-20	*GTh* 63
16 The land of a rich man produced abundantly. 17 And he thought to himself, 'What should I do, for I have no place to store my crops?' 18 Then he said, 'I will do this: I will pull down my barns and build larger ones, and there I will store all my grain and my goods. 19 And I will say to my soul, Soul, you have ample goods laid up for many years; relax, eat, drink, be merry'. 20 But God said to him, 'You fool! This very night your life is being demanded of you. And the things you have prepared, whose will they be?'	There was a rich man who had many possessions. He said, 'I will use my possessions that I may sow and reap and plant and fill my storehouses with fruit, so that I may lack nothing'. These were his thoughts in his heart. And in that night he died.

The parable is more a moralistic wisdom parable than distinctively eschatological in character (Fitzmyer, *Luke* 971-72; Funk, *Five Gospels* 338-39); the echo of Sir. 11.18-19 is particularly noticeable (see also Sir. 14.15 and 31.1-11) (Hultgren, *Parables* 105-108). Even so, the final question (Luke 12.20b) has more a note of judgment than its *Thomas* parallel.

221. Reiser, *Jesus and Judgment* 245-49; Gnilka, *Jesus* 205-206; Keck, *Who Is Jesus?* 86-87. Becker regards the passage as paradigmatic of Jesus' announcement of judgment (*Jesus of Nazareth* 53-54). On the issue of what historical episode Jesus/Luke may have had in mind, see Fitzmyer, *Luke* 1006-7; the episode narrated by Josephus, *Ant.* 18.58-59, is too remote from what Luke refers to here to justify Lüdemann's conclusion that 'Luke has confused things' (*Jesus* 352).

222. There is a strongly held view that the 'this generation' sayings reflect negative experiences in the later Christian mission; but see below, n. 397.

223. See, e.g., Kloppenborg Verbin, 'Discursive Practices' 164-69; and above, chapter 7 nn. 61-62.

224. See also Reiser, *Jesus and Judgment* 304; Theissen and Merz, *Historical Jesus* 268-69.

But that his disciples, knowing that he had done so, should nevertheless have imported such a thoroughgoing judgmental emphasis into the Jesus tradition is unrealistic. Such a development would imply both a disrespect for Jesus and a cavalier disregard in relation to their formative tradition, which does not square either with the character of oral tradition or with the esteem in which they held Jesus, as attested by the very fact of the Jesus tradition itself.[225]

In this case the judgment in view is consistently final in overtone, and frequently (though not always) has the last judgment explicitly in view. That Jesus spoke quite often of such judgment, and of its outcome in heaven[226] and hell,[227] must also be considered very likely. And since the kingdom of God seems to be a way of speaking of heaven, in at least some instances, hell for Jesus was presumably understood as exclusion from the kingdom, with its terrifying consequences.

f. Reward and Heavenly Banquet

Another strand of the eschatological reversal theme is the prospect of reward or vindication held out to those who responded to Jesus' message. This too is a feature of the beatitudes (Matt. 5.3-6, 10-12/Luke 6.20-23; see above §12.4c, d). The warning against being ashamed of Jesus (Mark 8.38 pars.) has a counterpart in the balanced antithesis, 'Those who confess me will be spoken for, those who deny me will be denied' (Matt. 10.32-33/Luke 12.8-9).[228] Faithful servants will be rewarded.[229] Triply attested is the promise that whoever loses his or her life (for Jesus' sake) will save it.[230] Jesus is remembered as promising to those who

---

225. 'Surely here is a theme that is so much a part of the tradition that, were one to deny it to Jesus, the very possibility of the modern quest would fall into disrepute for the reason that the sources are too untrustworthy' (Allison, *Jesus of Nazareth* 103).

226. Mark 10.21 pars.; Mark 12.25/Matt. 22.30; Matt. 5.12/Luke 6.23; Matt. 6.20/Luke 12.33; Matt. 5.16; Luke 10.20.

227. Hades in Matt. 11.23/Luke 10.15; Luke 16.23. Gehenna in Mark 9.43, 45, 47/Matt. 5.29-30/18.8-9; Matt. 10.28/Luke 12.5; Matt. 5.22; 23.15, 33. The (eternal) fire in Mark 9.43/Matt. 18.8-9; Mark 9.48; Matt. 5.22; 7.19; 13.40, 42, 50; 25.41; as already in the Baptist's preaching (Matt. 3.10-12/Luke 3.9, 16-17). Chilton maintains that the reference to Gehenna in Mark 9.47-48 is drawn from the closing words of the Targum of Isaiah (*Galilean Rabbi* 101-102, 107-108).

228. 'This calling of a person to account before the coming God . . . was the center of Jesus' expectation of judgment . . . not the pouring out of anonymous historical and cosmic catastrophes upon "this generation" . . .' (Goppelt, *Theology* 1.122). See further below, §16.4c(3).

229. Matt. 24.45-47/Luke 12.42-44; Matt. 25.20-23/Luke 19.16-19; Luke 6.35; Matt. 20.8; Luke 10.7. The language of (eschatological) reward *(misthos)* is also used in Mark 9.41/Matt. 10.42; Matt. 5.12/Luke 6.23; Matt. 6.1, (2, 5, 16). The theme is lacking in *Thomas*. See also below, §12.4g.

230. Mark 8.35 pars.; Matt. 10.39/Luke 17.33; John 12.25 (one of the Synoptic-like tra-

have left everything in discipleship 'much more in this life[231] and in the age to come eternal life' (Mark 10.29-30 pars.).[232] The disciples evidently anticipated high status in the kingdom (Mark 10.35-37), and Q apparently ends with the promise to the twelve that they will share in the judging of Israel (Matt. 19.27-28/Luke 22.28-30).[233] The prospect evidently included the assurance of resurrection in a heavenly mode of existence (Mark 12.24-27 pars.),[234] explicitly linked with the theme of reward in Luke 14.12-14. It would be surprising if Jesus had not encouraged his disciples with some such prospects of vindication and reward, as, once again, a well-rooted theme attests.[235] Most typical is the prospect of life after death, but also of reward following final judgment, with only one clear allusion to recompense in this life.

Here should also be mentioned the positive hope expressed in terms of hunger satisfied and the eschatological banquet. Those who hunger are blessed because they will be able to eat their fill and be satisfied (*chortazesthai,* Matt. 5.6/Luke 6.21a/*GTh* 69.2). The many coming from east and west will recline in

---

ditions round which John built his reflections). Missing the character of oral transmission, the Jesus Seminar conclude both that Luke 17.33 is 'the closest to what Jesus actually said', but also that 'Mark has Christianized a secular proverb' (Funk, *Five Gospels* 79, 367).

231. The surprising contrast with the expectations of §12.4d suggests the unlikelihood of the core saying (see the citation below, chapter 14 n. 240) being included subsequently within a tradition where Jesus' forebodings were so prominent. Reimarus took the saying seriously: the disciples had been induced by hopes of wealth and power, lands and worldly goods to follow Jesus, had grown out of the habit of working during their time with Jesus, and sought to maintain their position and hopes by inventing the resurrection of Jesus (Talbert, *Fragments* 145, 240-54).

232. 'Entry into life' is promised to those who make the necessary sacrifices (Mark 9.43, 45/Matt. 18.8-9; Matt. 7.14; 25.46), just as 'inheritance of eternal life' is promised to those sufficiently committed (Mark 10.17-21 pars.; Luke 10.25-28).

233. See above, nn. 178, 205.

234. The passage is usually regarded as an early church formulation, but Jesus is likely to have been closer to the Pharisees on such matters involving interpretation of Scripture, and the hope of resurrection expressed here does not appear to have been Christianized (see Taylor, *Mark* 480; Pesch, *Markusevangelium* 2.235; Davies and Allison, *Matthew* 3.222-23; J. P. Meier, 'The Debate on the Resurrection of the Dead: An Incident from the Ministry of the Historical Jesus?', *JSNT* 77 [2000] 3-24; full discussion in Meier, *Marginal Jew* 3.411-44, pointing out, *inter alia,* that the use of Exod. 3.6 is unique and idiosyncratic [3.435-37; bibliography in 3.468 n. 76]). Should *anastēsontai* (Matt. 12.41/Luke 11.32) be translated 'will be raised' (Allison, *Jesus of Nazareth* 136-39) or 'will rise up' as an accuser in court (BAGD, *anistēmi* 2b)?

235. Becker argues that the emphasis on God's graciousness (Matt. 20.1-15; Luke 15.11-32; 18.9-14) leaves no room for the idea of reward in Jesus' teaching (*Jesus* 241-47, 251). But when both themes are so well attested in the Jesus tradition, such playing off of one against the other smacks more of dictation to the tradition than of attentive listening to the tradition. At the same time we should recall the parable solely attested by Luke, 17.7-10; vv. 7-9 are usually attributed to Jesus (see Hultgren, *Parables* 250 and n. 16; also Lüdemann, *Jesus* 371).

the kingdom of heaven/God with Abraham, Isaac, and Jacob (Matt. 8.11/Luke 13.28-29). Here the kingdom seems to be equivalent to heaven or at least to the idealised future state following the final consummation. Or again, the kingdom is like a great (eschatological) banquet (Matt. 22.2-10/Luke 14.16-24),[236] or is the future note clearly struck only by Luke's introduction (Luke 14.15)?[237] Matthew would presumably agree, since he includes the parable of the maidens invited to the wedding feast (Matt. 25.1-13).[238] But the theme evidently had particular importance for Luke, since he adds to the parables encouraging watchfulness the note that the returning master will wait on his faithful servants at table (Luke 12.37), his parable of the prodigal son reaches its (initial) climax in a great banquet (15.24), and in his version of Jesus' promise that the twelve will be judges of Israel he includes the assurance that they will eat and drink at his table in the coming kingdom (22.30).[239]

It is at this point that we should probably include the verse attached to the other most prominent liturgical usage in the early tradition, the last supper. Mark recalls Jesus as saying, 'Truly I say to you, I will no longer drink of the fruit of the vine until that day when I drink it new in the kingdom of God' (Mark 14.25). As usual in the Passion narrative, Matt. 26.29 follows Mark closely. But as also is usual in the Passion narrative, Luke seems to have an independent tradition, which gives a closely similar rendering: 'Truly I say to you, from now on I will certainly not drink of the fruit of the vine until the kingdom of God has come' (Luke 22.18).[240] Here again the kingdom is understood as a future state, whether as one into which Jesus would be transposed (Mark) or as one to come (Luke). Jeremias describes the saying as a 'vow of abstinence' in view of the expected arrival of the kingdom,[241] though in the Mark/Matthew version it could be a hope for life beyond death (kingdom = heaven).[242] Marinus de Jonge has also ob-

236. The parable is generally traced back to Jesus; see, e.g., those cited by Hultgren, *Parables of Jesus* 339 n. 28; Lüdemann regards even the Lukan version as 'inauthentic'; 'the original parable . . . is represented most clearly by Thomas 64' (*Jesus* 360). See also above, nn. 174 and 203. On the appended Matt. 22.11-13 see Jeremias, *Parables* 187-89.

237. As Beasley-Murray in effect notes, if hearers locate themselves at the point where the summons is being given to the banquet, then the banquet is ready; take your seats! (*Jesus and the Kingdom* 120-21).

238. Cited below, §12.4g.

239. See also below, §14.8a.

240. See above, §8.5c. Here too the quest for an original form may be unnecessary, not to say misguided; cf. Meier's debate with Schlosser (*Marginal Jew* 2.303-306).

241. J. Jeremias, *The Eucharistic Words of Jesus* (³1960; London: SCM, 1966) 182-84; also *Proclamation* 137. In Luke 22.16-18 the 'vow of abstinence' includes food.

242. Cf. H. F. Bayer, *Jesus' Predictions of Vindication and Resurrection* (WUNT 2.20; Tübingen: Mohr Siebeck, 1986) 42-53; Casey, *Aramaic Sources* 242-47: 'We should not describe it as a vow of abstinence, but rather as a prediction. Jesus knew that this was to be his last

served that the expectation is independent of (and thus probably precedes) the more typical (Christian) expectation of Jesus' parousia.[243] Whatever the finer points of exegesis, we find another saying of Jesus closely related to another core tradition which envisages the kingdom as a future state.

g. The Parables of Crisis

In the material reviewed thus far, the emphasis on the kingdom as 'near' is a strong feature only of the first block. But the emphasis is strengthened by what Dodd called the 'parables of crisis'.[244] Only one is explicitly introduced as a kingdom parable, but since they are so similar in emphasis, that might be inconsequential; when the theme was so common, the reference to the kingdom might well have been taken for granted. Four parables are in view: the waiting slaves (Mark 13.34-36; similarly Luke 12.35-38), the thief in the night (Matt. 24.43-44/ Luke 12.39-40/*GTh* 21), the faithful and unfaithful servant (Matt. 24.45-51/Luke 12.42-46), and the wise and foolish maidens (Matt. 25.1-13).

Matt. 24.42	Mark 13.33-37	Luke 12.35-38
42 <u>Keep awake, therefore, for you do not know</u> on what day your <u>master is coming</u>.	33 Beware, keep alert; for you do not know when the time will come. 34 It is like a man going on a journey, when he leaves home and puts his slaves in charge, each with his work, and commands the doorkeeper to keep awake. 35 <u>Keep awake, therefore, for you do not know</u> when <u>the master</u> of the house <u>is coming</u>, in the evening, or at midnight, or at cockcrow, or at dawn, 36 or else he may find you asleep when he comes suddenly. 37 And what I say to you I say to all: Keep awake.	35 Be dressed for action and have your lamps lit; 36 be like those who are waiting for their master to return from the wedding banquet, so that they may open the door for him as soon as he comes and knocks. 37 Blessed are those slaves whom the master finds awake when he comes; truly I tell you, he will fasten his belt and have them sit down to eat, and he will come and serve them. 38 If he comes during the middle of the night, or near dawn, and finds them so, blessed are those slaves.

---

meal with his disciples . . .' (243). Chilton argues that the Aramaic form is a way of expressing confidence that the condition envisaged will endure (*Pure Kingdom* 86-90).

243. M. de Jonge, *Early Christology and Jesus' Own View of His Mission* (Grand Rapids: Eerdmans, 1998) ch. 5: 'Taken on its own, Mark 14.25 says no more than that Jesus expected to be resurrected/exalted and to be present at the eschatological meal at the final breakthrough of God's sovereign rule' (68). Meier notes other surprising absences in such a saying (*Marginal Jew* 2.308-309). 'In its essence it is an authentic saying of Jesus' (Becker, *Jesus* 341); similarly Lüdemann, *Jesus* 97.

244. Dodd, *Parables* 158-74.

Matt. 24.43-44	Luke 12.39-40	GTh 21.3
43 But know this: if the owner of the house had known in what watch the thief was coming, he would have stayed awake and would not have allowed his house to be broken into. 44 Therefore you also must be ready, for the Son of Man is coming at an unexpected hour.	39 But know this: if the owner of the house had known in what hour the thief was coming, he would not have let his house be broken into. 40 You also must be ready, for the Son of Man is coming at an unexpected hour.	Therefore I say: if the owner of a house knows that the thief is coming, he will be watching/on guard before he comes, and will not let him break into the house of his domain to carry away his goods. But you must keep watch/be on your guard against the world.

Matt. 24.45-51	Luke 12.42-46
45 Who then is the faithful and wise slave, whom his master has put in charge of his household, to give the others their food at the proper time? 46 Blessed is that slave whom his master will find so doing when he arrives. 47 Truly I tell you, he will put that one in charge of all his possessions. 48 But if that wicked slave says in his heart, 'My master is delayed', 49 and he begins to beat his fellow slaves, and eats and drinks with drunkards, 50 the master of that slave will come on a day when he does not expect him and at an hour that he does not know, 51 and will cut him in pieces and put him with the hypocrites, where there will be weeping and gnashing of teeth.	42 . . . Who then is the faithful and wise manager whom his master will put in charge of his service, to give them their rations at the proper time? 43 Blessed is that slave whom his master will find so doing when he arrives. 44 Of a truth I tell you, he will put that one in charge of all his possessions. 45 But if that slave says in his heart, 'My master is delayed in coming', and he begins to beat the other servants, men and women, and to eat and drink and get drunk, 46 the master of that slave will come on a day when he does not expect him and at an hour that he does not know, and will cut him in pieces, and put him with the unfaithful.

Matt. 25.1-13	Luke 13.25
1 Then the kingdom of heaven will be like this. Ten bridesmaids took their lamps and went to meet the bridegroom. 2 Five of them were foolish, and five were wise. 3 When the foolish took their lamps, they took no oil with them; 4 but the wise took flasks of oil with their lamps. 5 As the bridegroom was delayed, all of them became drowsy and slept. 6 But at midnight there was a shout, 'Look! Here is the bridegroom! Come out to meet him'. 7 Then all those bridesmaids got up and trimmed their lamps. 8 The foolish said to the wise, 'Give us some of your oil, for our lamps are going out'. 9 But the wise replied, 'No! there will not be enough for you and for us; you had better go to the dealers and buy some for yourselves'. 10 And while they went to buy it, the bridegroom came, and those who were ready went with him into the wedding banquet; and the door was shut. 11 Later the other bridesmaids came also, saying, 'Lord, lord, open to us'. 12 But in reply he said, 'Truly I tell you, I do not know you'. 13 Keep awake therefore, for you know neither the day nor the hour.	25 When once the owner of the house has got up and shut the door, and you begin to stand outside and to knock at the door, saying, 'Lord, open to us', then in reply he will say to you, 'I do not know you from where you come'.

Here we seem to have another of the tradition sequences noted above (§8.6b), in Q at least (the closeness of the parallel in the second and third examples implies a literary dependence); but the first example looks like independent oral tradition known also to Mark; and though only Matthew has the last, Luke knows its final scene. In other words, the traditioning process is reflected in the grouping sequences of Matt. 24.42–25.13 and Luke 12.35-46. Those responsible for performing the tradition on which Q in particular drew, but with similar emphases in other streams, were evidently concerned to recall that Jesus had spoken such parables.

There are two features common to the sequence of special note. One is the *certainty* of the coming of someone (master, thief, bridegroom) whose coming will be crucial for the future of the main characters of the parable (slaves, owner, bridesmaids), but also the *uncertainty* of the hour of that coming. The other is the resultant call to watchfulness, to stay awake *(grēgoreō),*[245] the variation indicating that the call did not hold a fixed place in the tradition, though performers of the tradition felt free to include it as they deemed appropriate. It should also be noted once again that the *Gospel of Thomas* has de-eschatologized the only element of this tradition which it has retained: 'you must keep watch/be on your guard against the world' *(GTh* 21.3; cf. 103).

Dodd justifiably argued that whereas the early churches in retelling these parables would have thought in terms of the coming (again) of Jesus, Jesus himself would have had a different perspective.[246] It is an issue, we might say, of where the hearers of the parable were intended to locate themselves within the time-frame of the parable. A natural tendency would be to locate oneself relative to the beginning of the parable — not long after the departure of the master, before the bridesmaids had fallen asleep, implying good opportunity to act responsibly in the time remaining. But what if the initial intention had been that hearers should locate themselves near the *end* of the parable, at the point when the mas-

245. Mark 13.34; Mark 13.35/Matt. 24.42; Mark 13.37; Matt. 24.43; 25.13; Luke 12.37.

246. Similarly Jeremias, *Parables* 48-58, 171-75. Dodd's and Jeremias's point is ignored by those who simply rule out the parables as 'inauthentic' because they reflect Christian concern over 'the delay of the parousia' (Lüdemann, *Jesus* 233-34, but he allows that Luke 12.39 'is probably authentic' [349]; others in Beasley-Murray, *Jesus and the Kingdom* 385 n. 53). The Jesus Seminar did not give enough weight to the likelihood that the 'thief in the night' motif elsewhere in earliest Christian writing (1 Thess. 5.2, 4; 2 Pet. 3.10; Rev. 3.3; 16.15) is an echo of Jesus' imagery (Funk, *Five Gospels* 252, 342; similarly Crossan, *Historical Jesus* 250-51; otherwise Crossan limits his discussion to the question of when the apocalyptic Son of Man entered the tradition [253-54]). The logic of the criterion of dissimilarity is that any parallel with Jesus tradition tells against the latter being traced back to Jesus; Jesus could have been neither conventional nor original! See also Beasley-Murray 213-14 and Davies and Allison, *Matthew* 3.392-94 [both on Matt. 25.1-13]; Scott, *Hear Then the Parable* 210-12; Hultgren, *Parables* 159-61, 176-77.

ter was about to return, the thief about to break in, the midnight shout was already heralding the bridegroom's coming?

Dodd pressed the point to support his thesis of 'realised eschatology', that is, that Jesus 'saw in his own ministry the supreme crisis in history', a crisis 'created by his own coming, rather than an expected crisis in the more or less distant future'.[247] But this pushes the point too far: true, the parables do not envisage a crisis 'in the distant future', but neither do they imply that the crisis has already happened or is already happening.[248] The repeated command to 'Keep awake' would be redundant if it referred only to a time (a coming) that was already past. It could function only as a figure of savage irony: 'Keep awake! But it's already too late!'. The more natural reading is to hear warning of a crisis indeed, a crisis whose coming is certain, and not only certain but imminent, though finally unknown as to date and time. Above all, *now* is the time to keep awake and watchful for what may happen at any minute.

What the expected crisis would be in real life is not indicated, but the imagery is consistently of being caught out unprepared, with the implication of great loss. So the coming of the kingdom here is consistent with failure in the final trial, being found wanting in the final judgment. At any rate the sequence of material confirms the strength of the strand of imminent expectation within the Jesus tradition.

h. The Kingdom as Imminent

One of the most influential of the earlier treatments of the subject has been that of W. G. Kümmel.[249] Kümmel drew particular attention to 'the pressing imminence of the end' in Jesus' preaching, that is, of the final consummation, which he identified with the coming of the kingdom. The imminence of the kingdom is clear enough in the *ēngiken, engys* material and 'parables of crisis' reviewed above.[250] And Kümmel throws in the parable of the unjust judge for good measure (Luke 18.2-8). Luke has presented it as an encouragement to persistent prayer (18.1). But Kümmel draws particular attention to the end of the parable —

247. Dodd, *Parables* 165; the parables 'were intended to enforce his appeal to men to recognize that the kingdom of God was present in all its momentous consequences, and that by their conduct in the presence of this tremendous crisis they would judge themselves as faithful or unfaithful, wise or foolish' (174).

248. Cf. Jeremias' modification of Dodd's position, summarized in *Proclamation* 138-39.

249. Kümmel, *Promise* ch. 1 (particularly 54-64); also 'Eschatological Expectation in the Proclamation of Jesus', in Robinson, ed., *The Future of Our Religious Past* 29-48.

250. Kümmel, *Promise* 19-25, 54-59; 'Eschatological Expectation' 32-35.

God's vindication will not be long delayed: 'I tell you, he (God) will see that justice is done them (his elect) *en tachei*' (18.8a), where *en tachei* must mean 'quickly, soon'.[251] What is in view so far as Luke was concerned is indicated by his final enigmatic sentence: 'Nevertheless, when the Son of man comes, will he find faith on the earth?' (18.8b) — nothing other than the final judgment, for only then can the elect hope to be vindicated. Luke probably draws the note of finality ironically from 18.5 *(eis telos)*.[252] 18.8a adds only the assurance that the vindication of those unjustly treated ('the elect')[253] will be imminent.

However, for Kümmel the clinching evidence comes in three much-disputed texts — Mark 9.1; 13.30; and Matt. 10.23.[254] The first of these, the only kingdom text of the three, signals a more confusing tradition history than most of what we have encountered thus far in chapter 12.

Matt. 16.28	Mark 9.1	Luke 9.27
Truly I tell you, there are some standing here who will not taste death before they see the Son of Man coming in his kingdom.	Truly I tell you, there are some standing here who will not taste death until they see that the kingdom of God has come with power.	But truly I tell you, there are some standing here who will not taste death before they see the kingdom of God.

The saying comes in the same sequence in all three Gospels, which may simply indicate the influence of Mark (the literary interdependence of the group of sayings is clear). And it does clearly indicate that some of the disciples will in some

251. Kümmel, *Promise* 59; 'Eschatological Expectation' 37. Since Jülicher, 18.6-8 have often been taken as an addition to the parable, the product of a Christian community facing persecution (Scott, *Hear Then the Parable* 176-77; others in Hultgren, *Parables* 257 n. 26; Lüdemann, *Jesus* 375). But 18.6-8a reads more as a continuation of the teaching than an interpretation superimposed (Hultgren 258-59). And the observations of Jeremias as to the Aramaic idiom employed and the shock of God's mercy being illustrated by an unfeeling judge (*Parables* 154-55) ought to be given more weight. See further Beasley-Murray, *Jesus and the Kingdom* 203-207.

252. 'Ironically', since 'the end' feared by the judge is the widow giving him a black eye *(hypōpiazō)*.

253. 'The elect' appears elsewhere in the Jesus tradition only in Mark 13.20, 22, 27 par. and Matt. 22.14; but it was a central feature of Jewish self-understanding (references in my *Romans* [WBC 38; Dallas: Word, 1988] 502).

254. But note Kümmel's qualification (*Promise* 149-51). Despite Kümmel, German scholarship usually discounts these texts as sayings of Jesus (see, e.g., Schürmann, *Gottes Reich* 38-41 and n. 65; Merklein, *Jesu Botschaft* 54-56; H. Merkel, 'Die Gottesherrschaft in der Verkündigung Jesu', in Hengel and Schwemer, eds., *Königsherrschaft Gottes* 119-61 [here 139-41]; Gnilka, *Jesus of Nazareth* 147-49; Becker, *Jesus of Nazareth* 121; Theissen and Merz, *Historical Jesus* 255). Similarly Perrin, *Rediscovering* 199-202. Allison suspects that they are three variants of one saying, with another variant in John 8.51-52 (*Jesus of Nazareth* 149-50). In contrast, McKnight follows Kümmel quite closely (*New Vision* 128-30, 133-37).

way experience the kingdom before they die.[255] By sequencing it as he does, Mark may well have intended his audiences to interpret that experience as the experience of the three inner core disciples (Peter, James, and John) in witnessing the transfiguration of Jesus (Mark 9.2-10 pars.).[256] That interpretation, however, is hardly plausible, since Mark himself reports that the transfiguration followed only six days later, but it may point to a certain degree of puzzlement on Mark's part regarding the prediction.[257]

What gives more cause for pause is that the key part of the saying for our purposes (the kingdom) appears to be so unstable. Of course, the variation is easily explained as the kind of variation which we could expect to find in the performance of oral tradition. But that is just the point: our findings thus far have suggested that the greater the variation, the less important the variable material was deemed to be within the traditioning groups and churches. Or should we be content to conclude simply that Jesus was remembered here as saying something about the kingdom as future? In which case, Kümmel's argument reemerges with some force: Jesus expected a public manifestation of God's kingdom within the lifetime of his disciples.[258]

The second of Kümmel's texts does not speak of the kingdom, but comes

255. Dodd argued that the perfect tense, *elēlythuian* ('has come'), refers to the awakening of the disciples to the fact that the kingdom had already come in his ministry (*Parables* 53-54); similarly some members of the Jesus Seminar think that the saying referred to the kingdom's (visible) arrival in Jesus' exorcisms (Funk, *Five Gospels* 81). But the perfect tense denotes rather completed arrival and ongoing presence, equivalent to 'until they see God's rule *established* in power' (Kümmel, *Promise* 26-27; Gundry, *Mark* 469).

256. The interpretation goes back to Clement of Alexandria. See, e.g., the brief review in Beasley-Murray, *Jesus and the Kingdom* 187-88.

257. Chilton argues that the Aramaic form of speech '*x* will not happen until *y*' is used to insist that both parts of the statement are valid, but combines the point with the claim that 'those who will not taste death' refers to people who never die (like Enoch and Elijah), leading to the thesis that the following story of the Transfiguration 'is a visionary representation of Jesus' promise' (*Pure Kingdom* 62-65); but it is unclear whether he thinks that the saying implies that some of Jesus' companions will never die. A more plausible interpretation would have been to link the prediction to the report of Pentecost, understood as an empowering display of God's rule by Luke (Acts 1.3-8); but no NT writer actually makes such a link. See further Gundry, *Mark* 467-69, and the helpful review of opinions in Davies and Allison, *Matthew* 2.677-81.

258. Kümmel, *Promise* 25-29; 'seeing' and 'coming in power' point 'too obviously to a publicly visible and tangible manifestation of the Reign of God to allow for evading the conclusion that this promise refers to the eschatological appearing of that Reign' ('Eschatological Expectation' 40-41); similarly Pesch, *Markusevangelium* 66-67; Fitzmyer, *Luke* 790. But most remain somewhat nonplussed by the saying. E.g., Meier (*Marginal Jew* 2.343-44) and Lüdemann (*Jesus* 59-60) think the more obvious setting for the emergence of the saying was after the first deaths within the first-generation churches.

in close association with the *engys* passage already reviewed (Mark 13.28-29): 'Truly I tell you, this generation will have by no means passed away before all these things happen' (13.30 pars.). In the context of Mark's Gospel 'these things' can only refer to the days of final tribulation, cosmic turbulence, the coming of the Son of Man and the final ingathering of the elect (13.19-27), which Mark seems to relate to the (anticipated) fall of Jerusalem (13.14-18). And, as Kümmel justifiably argues, 'it is beyond dispute *hē genea hautē* [this generation] can only mean the contemporaries of Jesus'.[259] The implication is again clear that Jesus expected a final catastrophe within the lifetime of his own generation. And even if the present context of 13.30 (and 13.30 itself) is the result of much reworking of tradition,[260] the readiness of the tradents of the Mark 13 traditions to attribute such a note of imminent expectation to Jesus presumably indicates their own and their community's conviction that the note was consistent with the longer established elements of the Jesus tradition.

The third of Kümmel's texts is what we might call Schweitzer's text, the text on which the latter's reconstruction of Jesus' mission largely turned[261] — Matt. 10.23: 'when they persecute you in one town, flee to the next; for truly I tell you, you will not have completed the towns of Israel before the Son of Man comes'.[262] The text is the most difficult of the three: only Matthew has it; he has attached it to a section drawn from Mark's apocalyptic discourse (Mark 13.9-13/ Matt. 10.17-22) generally regarded as the section of the 'little apocalypse' which reflects most clearly the circumstances of the later (Christian) mission; and the expectation of the Son of Man's (second) coming/return (to earth) may well also reflect a developed Son of Man christology.[263] So it is certainly possible to conceive of this saying emerging as a prophetic utterance within the earliest churches' mission,[264] that is, before a Gentile mission got underway or was fully accepted among the churches of Judea and Galilee.[265]

On the other hand, the Gentile mission did begin very early and was evi-

---

259. Kümmel, 'Eschatological Expectation' 38; also *Promise* 60-61; Davies and Allison, *Matthew 19–28* 367-68 concur.

260. As many conclude; see, e.g., Meier, *Marginal Jew* 2.344-47; Pesch argues that Mark 9.1 was the basis for 13.30 (*Markusevangelium* 308), whereas Beasley-Murray follows A. Vögtle in arguing that the influence was the other way round, with 13.30 closer to the Q saying Matt. 23.36/Luke 11.51 (*Jesus and the Kingdom* 190-93); but the difference between the latter and Mark 13.30 is too wide to provide much support for the hypothesis (Gundry, *Mark* 791).

261. See above, chapter 10 n. 3.

262. Kümmel, *Promise* 61-64; 'Eschatological Expectation' 44-45.

263. See below §16.4f.

264. Boring, *Sayings* 209-11; Meier, *Marginal Jew* 2.339-41; cf. Lüdemann, *Jesus* 168.

265. 'The towns of Israel' might include Samaria (though note Matt. 10.5), but no diaspora settlement would be so designated.

dently accepted, however hesitantly, by the Jerusalem leadership (Gal. 2.1-10). And it must be judged doubtful whether a prophetic utterance which in effect foreclosed on the option of a Gentile mission would have been accepted or retained within the circles influenced by the Jerusalem leadership. Uncomfortable as it may be, we ought to recognize the likelihood that Jesus the Jew's perspective on mission was more circumscribed than that of the leading exponents of mission after Easter; after all, the saying is of a piece with Matt. 10.5-6, which Matthew combines with the Q summary of the disciples' mission preaching: 'The kingdom of heaven has drawn near' (Matt. 10.7/Luke 10.9). It could be argued, therefore, that Jesus was indeed remembered as uttering something to this effect (but in terms of 'the Son of Man'?) and that both sayings (Matt. 10.5-6, 23) were preserved among believing Jews, despite their increasing irrelevance in the light of developments.[266] In short, the note of imminence cannot be easily escaped, but the value of the saying as a witness to Jesus' own expectation is unclear.

The other notable feature of Kümmel's contribution to the debate was his observation that the imminent expectation was qualified by recognition of an *interval* before the final consummation.[267] Here we may simply note the following aspects of the material already reviewed. 'Near' does not mean already 'here'; spring is not yet summer (Mark 13.28 pars.). The *peirasmos* has not yet engulfed the pray-er of the Lord's Prayer (Matt. 6.13/Luke 11.4). A period during which Jesus' followers will be persecuted and can expect suffering is anticipated. The 'vow of abstinence' implies a time before the fast will be broken (in the kingdom) (Mark 14.25 pars.). The parable of the unjust judge envisages a period of intercession (Luke 18.7). Some will not taste death before they see the kingdom (coming), but others (presumably) will not live to see it (Mark 9.1 pars.). 'This generation' could extend over more than one decade (Mark 13.30 pars.). A time of mission is envisaged (Matt. 10.23). Jeremias also notes that the parable of the barren fig tree envisages the possibility of God lengthening the period of grace before judgment is executed: 'Let it alone this year also' (Luke 13.6-9).[268]

In this range of material only one text envisages a considerable interval: 'but first the gospel must be preached to all the nations' (Mark 13.10/Matt. 24.14). However, this is one of the best examples of what appears to be an interpretative addition or qualification added to the tradition in the process of its being handed down.[269] In particular, (1) it hangs on the distinctively Markan, that

---

266. Beasley-Murray, *Jesus and the Kingdom* 289-90 (with review of earlier debate 283-89); Davies and Allison, *Matthew* 2.189-90. Meier, however, thinks that 10.5-6 'is more likely a product of some group within the first Christian generation that opposed widening the proclamation of the gospel to groups other than Jews' (*Marginal Jew* 3.542-44).

267. Kümmel, *Promise* particularly 75-82.

268. Jeremias, *Proclamation* 140.

269. Taylor, *Mark* 507-508; Kümmel, *Promise* 84-86.

is, redactional word 'gospel', (2) it interrupts the flow of the (anyway later) discourse in Mark 13.9-13 (as its omission by Matthew and Luke confirms), and (3) as we shall see, Jesus did not seem to envisage a mission as such to the Gentiles.[270] It certainly provides no sure basis for any view that Jesus anticipated a many-generation or century gap before the coming of the kingdom.

How the tradition just reviewed (§12.4h) related to the rest of the material in §12.4 is unclear. The common and consistent element, even with the qualification of some time elapse, is an expectation of an imminent event of climactic and crucial importance, the coming of God's kingdom, a crisis determinative of the future (final?) judgment.[271] Despite the diversity of imagery and detail it is difficult to imagine the communities which performed this tradition not seeing it as interrelated. The range and character of the traditions indicate rather a common theme much reflected on and rehearsed in the communities which treasured the Jesus tradition.

In sum, the kingdom references reviewed thus far cover an extensive range of the kingdom tradition. We have still to examine more fully the richer Son of Man tradition, including talk of his 'coming'; but that is more suitably dealt with later (see below §16.4), and it is important to appreciate just how extensive the future eschatological emphasis is within the Jesus tradition, apart from the Son of Man sayings.[272] Moreover, the teachings so far cited are worthy of particular attention since they were evidently seen to be important by those who performed the Jesus tradition and by the Evangelists in turn: they provided summaries of Jesus' preaching, they were linked to much cherished liturgical material, and they expressed major themes of eschatological reversal, impending judgment, and the sufferings and expected blessings of discipleship. Such traditions would have been central to the identity of the small groups of disciples from the first, and subsequently for the first churches founded in the 30s and 40s. They would have been treasured and rehearsed no doubt often in their gatherings, stirring hope of participation in the beatitude of God's future reign, stimulating repentance before the imminent judgment, stiffening resolve in the face of anticipated suffering, and encouraging prayer expectful of God.

What is striking about this material is the consistent emphasis within it on the kingdom of God as future or as yet to come or yet to impinge fully on those addressed. The imagery used varies substantially, but predominantly envisages a final intervention of God, usually with final judgment implied. To 'enter the

---

270. See below, §13.7; for alternative views on Mark 13.10 see chapter 13 n. 248 below.

271. The earlier confidence is well summarized by Schillebeeckx: 'That Jesus prophesied the imminent arrival of God's rule is beyond dispute' (*Jesus* 152).

272. Crossan, e.g., deals with the parables of crisis in a section headed 'the Apocalyptic Son of man' (*Historical Jesus* 250-51, 253-55).

kingdom' is equivalent to 'enter life'; the alternative is to be cast out into gehenna (again implying some sort of judgment). Sometimes the expectation may have been of the final divine intervention establishing things as they ought to be on earth,[273] that is, of the restoration of justice under God's rule.[274] But such variation is quite in character with the wider range of eschatological expectation within Second Temple Judaism summarised in §12.2. Undoubtedly the motifs were elaborated within the transmission of the Jesus tradition. But given the scope and extent of the motifs within the Jesus tradition, it is scarcely credible to conclude other than that Jesus was remembered from the first as proclaiming the kingdom as coming and as already drawn near.

12.5. The Kingdom Has Come

If the note of the kingdom still to come seems to be firmly struck in the Jesus tradition, the clashing note of the kingdom *already come* seems to be struck no less forcefully. It is clearly to be heard in all the strands of the Synoptic tradition, including parables, and particularly when Jesus speaks about his exorcisms and about the Baptist.

a. The Time Has Been Fulfilled

Mark's headline statement at the beginning of Mark's account of Jesus' mission, already quoted (§12.1), has a double emphasis. Not only does Jesus proclaim the kingdom's nearness; equally thematic is the note of fulfilment. The headline is introduced by the information that the Baptist had been removed from the scene (Mark 1.14a) and begins with the words, 'The time has been fulfilled *(peplērōtai*

273. Characteristic of the ambiguity is Matthew's use of *palingenesia* ('rebirth') in his version of the final judgment 'in the *palingenesia*' (Matt. 19.28 = 'in my kingdom' in Luke 22.30; = 'in the coming age' in Mark 10.30). *Palingenesia* had become a technical term in Stoic thought for the rebirth of the cosmos, but Cicero could describe return from banishment as *palingenesia* (*Att.* 6.6). Philo draws on the Stoic idea of cycles of cosmic conflagration and rebirth consistently in *Aet.* (9, 47, 76, 85, 93, 99, 103, 107), but also uses the term both for the reconstitution of the world after the flood (*Vit. Mos.* 2.65) and for life after death (*Cher.* 114). Similarly Josephus uses it for Israel's reestablishment in the land after the exile (*Ant.* 11.66), but also speaks of life after death as *palin genesthai* (*Ap.* 2.218) (F. Büchsel, *palingenesia, TDNT* 1 [1964] 686-88; Davies and Allison, *Matthew* 3.57).

274. See, e.g., Oakman, *Jesus* 207-16 ('the economic reign of God'); Herzog, *Parables as Subversive Speech;* also *Jesus, Justice and the Reign of God: A Ministry of Liberation* (Louisville: Westminster John Knox, 2000); Malina, *Social Gospel* 34-35 ('Jesus' proclamation of the kingdom of God was indeed his social gospel'); Crossan and Reed, *Excavating Jesus* 172-74.

ho kairos)' (1.15a). *Kairos* here obviously has its more weighty sense — the decisive time, the appointed time, the time of judgment.[275] The perfect tense of the verb indicates that the period prior to the expected 'time' has been completed (filled full); the expectation has been realised. The implication is clearly that some long-awaited climax has arrived; that time is now!

Of considerable interest is the fact that this headline summary encapsulates such a tension between 'already come' and 'yet to come': 'the time has been fulfilled; the kingdom of God has drawn near' (Mark 1.15). The verse proclaims that a crucial time has arrived,[276] an expected time has begun, the time of the 'about-to-come-ness' of the kingdom, the time during which the kingdom will come. In other words, *kairos* can be readily understood to indicate not simply an event, a date in time, but a period of time.[277] This accords with its usage and with the usage of the underlying Hebrew *('et)* and Aramaic *(z^eman),* denoting the beginning of a period of time, whether of blessing or of judgment.[278] In Ezek. 7.12 we find a striking parallel: 'the time has come, the day has drawn near *(ba' ha'et higgiya' hayom)'*.[279] In its time note, the message attributed to Jesus in Mark 1.15 is no different.[280] It is doubtful, therefore, whether any of Jesus' audiences hearing such a two-sided emphasis ('Your hopes are realised; soon, within your lifetime God will manifest his rule in a decisive manner') would have been as puzzled by it as have twentieth-century commentators.

275. As in 1 Sam. 18.19; 2 Sam. 24.15; Ezra 10.14; Ps. 102.13; Isa. 13.22; Jer. 10.15; 27.7; 46.21; Ezek. 7.7, 12; 21.25, 29; 30.2; Dan. 11.35, 40; 12.4, 9; Hab. 2.3. In the NT note, e.g., Mark 13.33; Matt. 26.18; Luke 19.44; 21.8, 24; John 7.6, 8; Rom. 3.26; 13.11; 1 Cor. 7.29; 2 Cor. 6.2.

276. Cf. Josephus, *Ant.* 6.49: 'when it (the time) came *(plērōthentos d' autou [tou kairou])'*.

277. See also the still salutary treatment by Barr, *Biblical Words for Time* 33-46, 51.

278. Cf. Ps. 102.13: 'You will arise and have pity on Zion, for it is time *('eth)* to favour her; the appointed time *(mo'ed)* has come'; Jer. 50.27, 31; Ezek. 30.3.

279. Very similar is Ezek. 7.7: 'The time has come, the day is near *(ba' ha'et qarob hayom)'*. And note how the formulation can vary: 'Our time has drawn near, our days have been fulfilled, our time has come (Hebrew *qarab qitsenu mal^e'u yamenu ki-ba' qitsenu;* Greek *ēngiken ho kairos hēmōn, eplērōthēsan hai hēmerai hēmōn, parestin ho kairos hēmōn)'*. The concept of time 'fulfilled' is common to both Hebrew and Greek thought (see, e.g., BAGD, *plēroō* 2; and further C. F. D. Moule, 'Fulfilment-Words in the New Testament: Use and Abuse', *NTS* 14 [1967-68] 293-320, reprinted in *Essays in New Testament Interpretation* [Cambridge: Cambridge University, 1982] 3-36; Chilton, *God in Strength* 80-86).

280. These points are missed by a number of scholars who press for a more consistently realized emphasis in the saying (Beasley-Murray, *Jesus and the Kingdom* 73-74; Guelich, *Mark* 43-44, who translates 'The kingdom of God has come in history'; Gundry, *Mark* 64-65; cf. Gnilka, *Jesus of Nazareth* 147 n. 156 — 'Mark 1:15 presupposes that the kingdom begins to be realized from this point on').

The other Synoptic Evangelists introduce the note of fulfilment in their own way. Luke gives headline significance to his account of Jesus preaching in the synagogue in Nazareth, where the note of fulfilment is struck by Jesus' reading from Isa. 61.1: 'The Spirit of the Lord is upon me, because he has anointed me to preach good news *(euangelisasthai)* to the poor . . .' (Luke 4.18).[281] According to the account, Jesus cut short the reading and announced: 'Today this scripture has been fulfilled *(peplērōtai)* in your hearing' (4.21). Now it is clear that Luke has brought the episode forward in his telling; Jesus' mission at Capernaum had been underway for some time (4.23). And much at least of the account is Luke's own retelling to bring out the importance of Jesus' message for the poor (the Sidonian widow) and the foreigner (Naaman the Syrian) (4.25-27).[282] Nevertheless, as with the Markan headline (Mark 1.15), so Luke has deemed it important that his audiences should hear the note of fulfilment loud and clear at the very beginning and should hear what follows in the light of this opening statement, providing, as it does, Jesus' own manifesto for his mission.

Matthew diminishes the difference between the Baptist and Jesus implicit in Mark's and Luke's accounts. He has John preaching the same message as Jesus: 'The kingdom of heaven has drawn near' (Matt. 3.2). And he omits Mark's opening clause; Jesus begins simply, 'Repent! The kingdom of heaven has drawn near' (4.17). But that can hardly be because Matthew denied a note of fulfilment to Jesus. On the contrary, it is precisely Matthew's objective to bring out just how much of Jewish expectation Jesus fulfilled,[283] and it is one of his fulfilment quotations which takes the place of the Markan fulfilment clause in Matthew's headline (4.14-16).

b. Expectation Realised

The Q material does not have the same fulfilment theme as the Synoptics, but the same note is struck even more clearly by two Q sayings — Matt. 13.16-17/Luke 10.23-24 and Matt. 12.41-42/Luke 11.31-32.

281. Luke no doubt regarded this *euangelisasthai* as 'preaching the good news of the kingdom' (Luke 4.43; 8.1). See also Beasley-Murray, *Jesus and the Kingdom* 88-89.

282. See, e.g., Fitzmyer, *Luke* 526-30. However, it is likely that Luke has drawn on older traditions: not only Mark 6.1-6a (including the proverb of Mark 6.4), but also those attesting awareness of the influence of Isa. 61.1-2 on Jesus (see below, §15.6c), and the references to Elijah and Elisha (4.25-27; Bultmann, *History* 32, 116; Becker, *Jesus of Nazareth* 62-63). See below, §§13.4, 7; Luke 4.25-27 fits with the eschatological reversal theme (§12.4c).

283. See above, chapter 11 n. 5.

Matt. 13.16-17	Luke 10.23-24
16 But blessed are your eyes, for they see, and your ears, for they hear. 17 For truly I tell you, that many prophets and righteous people longed to see what (you) see, but did not see it, and to hear what you hear, but did not hear it.	23 . . . Blessed are the eyes that see what you see! 24 For I tell you that many prophets and kings desired to see what you see, but did not see it, and to hear what you hear, but did not hear it.

Matt. 12.41-42	Luke 11.31-32
41 The people of Nineveh will rise up at the judgment with this generation and condemn it, because they repented at the proclamation of Jonah, and see, something greater than Jonah is here! 42 The queen of the South will rise up at the judgment with this generation and condemn it, because she came from the ends of the earth to listen to the wisdom of Solomon, and see, something greater than Solomon is here!	31 The queen of the South will rise at the judgment with the people of this generation and condemn them, because she came from the ends of the earth to listen to the wisdom of Solomon, and see, something greater than Solomon is here! 32 The people of Nineveh will rise up at the judgment with this generation and condemn it, because they repented at the proclamation of Jonah, and see, something greater than Jonah is here!

That these sayings belong to Q is clear enough from the degree of agreement, the second especially.[284] The note of fulfilled expectation could hardly be clearer. What was it that prophets and others longed for, if not the age to come, the age of restoration and salvation?[285] The claim is that in Jesus' mission that expectation has been fulfilled (Q 10.23-24): the blessings of the age to come are already evident.[286] Similarly with Q 11.31-32.[287] The episode in which the queen of the south expressed her wonder at Solomon's wisdom and success was the stuff of

284. Recognition of the dynamics of oral tradition renders the concern to strip away redaction less important (as in Meier, *Marginal Jew* 2.488-90 n. 166).

285. Jeremias, *Proclamation* 107-108; Jesus 'is the only Jew of ancient times known to us who preached not only that people were on the threshold of the end of time, but that the new age of salvation had already begun' (Flusser, *Jesus* 110). Comparison is regularly made with *Pss. Sol.* 17.44 (e.g., Manson, *Sayings* 80; Kümmel, *Promise* 112) and *Pss. Sol.* 18.6 (Beasley-Murray, *Jesus and the Kingdom* 84-85; Theissen and Merz, *Historical Jesus* 257); Lüdemann adds *1 En.* 58.2-6 (*Jesus* 331).

286. Typical of the Jesus Seminar's undue scepticism is the judgment of the majority that 'the saying could have been uttered by almost any (Christian) sage' and therefore cannot be attributed to Jesus; it 'could be taken to express the sectarian arrogance of early Christian leaders' (Funk, *Five Gospels* 193, 322). No concern is evident here to limit the insertion of material into the Jesus tradition to prophetic utterances understood as sayings of (the risen) Jesus — a possibility considered unlikely in this case by Boring, *Sayings* 152 ('the features of Christian prophecy manifest in it [Q 10.23-24] were also characteristic of Jesus' own speech'). Lüdemann also regards Q 10.23-24 as 'probably authentic', since no community situation is visible (*Jesus* 331).

287. Already discussed above (see nn. 177, 204).

legend (1 Kgs. 10.1-10), but in Jesus' ministry there was something greater! Jonah was famous for the success of his preaching in Nineveh (Jonah 3.5), but in Jesus' ministry something greater was happening! The implication is that the Galileans' failure to follow the lead given by the queen and the Ninevites made them the more culpable. We today may recoil at such a high self-esteem attributed to Jesus' mission. But it would be unwise to discount the tradition's testimony to Jesus' own remembered evaluation of his mission on that account alone.

The similar note of a markedly changed situation, of something new, which decisively relativizes previous or normal practice is also struck in another small collection of parabolic sayings preserved in Mark 2.18-22 pars.

Matt. 9.14-15	Mark 2.18-20	Luke 5.33-35

14 Then the disciples of John
 	
   came to him, saying, 'Why do we
 	
   and the Pharisees fast (often), but your disciples do not fast?' 15 And he said to them, 'The wedding guests cannot mourn as long as the bridegroom is with them, can they?
 	
   The days will come when the bridegroom is taken away from them, and then they will fast'.
	18 Now the disciples of John and the Pharisees were fasting; and people came and said to him, 'Why do the disciples of John and the disciples of the Pharisees fast, but your disciples do not fast?' 19 And he said to them, 'The wedding guests cannot fast while the bridegroom is with them, can they? As long as they have the bridegroom with them, they cannot fast. 20 The days will come when the bridegroom is taken away from them, and then they will fast on that day'.	33 Then they said to him, 'The disciples of John frequently fast and pray, like those of the Pharisees, but yours eat and drink'. 34 Jesus said to them, 'You cannot make wedding guests fast while the bridegroom is with them, can you?
		
		35 The days will come when the bridegroom is taken away from them, then they will fast in those days'.

Matt. 9.16-17	Mark 2.21-22	Luke 5.36-38
16 No one puts a piece of unshrunk cloth on an old cloak, for the patch pulls away from the cloak, and a worse tear is made. 17 Neither do they put new wine into old wineskins; otherwise, the wineskins burst, and the wine is spilled, and the wineskins are destroyed; but they put new wine into new wineskins, and so both are preserved.	21 No one sews a piece of unshrunk cloth on an old cloak; otherwise, the patch pulls away from it, the new from the old, and a worse tear is made. 22 And no one puts new wine into old wineskins; otherwise, the wine will burst the wineskins, and the wine is destroyed, and so are the wineskins; but new wine is for new wineskins.	36 He also told them a parable: 'No one tears a piece from a new cloak and puts it on an old cloak; otherwise the new will tear, and the piece from the new will not match the old. 37 And no one puts new wine into old wineskins; otherwise the new wine will burst the wineskins and will be spilled, and the wineskins destroyed. 38 But new wine must be put into new wineskins'.

Matthew and Luke appear to be dependent on Mark for their tradition, though we note in the case of all three characteristic features of oral retelling. That is to say, several of the pecularities of each make better sense as free retellings of the tradition which retain the main point in more or less the same words but vary the details, rather than as literary editing.[288] Marriage and the wedding banquet was obvious imagery for the restoration of Israel;[289] Jesus evidently used it on other occasions.[290] The imagery obviously gives voice to a sense of climax and fresh beginnings, evoking joy and celebration — a time for feasting, not for fasting.[291] Similarly, the mini-parables of unshrunk cloth and new wine indicate a new beginning which marks a sharp disjunction with what has gone before. The new cannot be contained with(in) the old without loss, though it is also noteworthy that both Mark and Matthew in their own retelling express a concern for the wineskins as well as the wine.[292]

A similar note is struck in two of Matthew's kingdom parables which have closer parallels in the *Gospel of Thomas:* the hidden treasure and the pearl of great value (Matt. 13.44-46).

Matt. 13.44-46	GTh 109, 76
44 The kingdom of heaven is like treasure hidden in a field, which someone found and hid; then in his joy he goes and sells all that he has and buys that field.	109 The kingdom is like a man who had a treasure (hidden) in his field without knowing it. And (after) he died, he left it to his (son. The) son knew nothing (about it). He accepted that field and sold (it). And he who bought it went ploughing (and found) the treasure. He began to lend money at interest to whomever he wished.

288. In the case of Mark 2.18-20, most regard 2.20 (or 2.19b-20) as an added gloss (in the light of Jesus' death) in order to explain and justify the resumption of fasting as a Christian discipline (cf. Acts 13.2-3; 14.23; 2 Cor. 6.5; 11.27; *Did.* 8.1); see, e.g., Perrin, *Rediscovering* 79-80; Pesch, *Markusevangelium* 174-76; Ebner, *Jesus* 188-91; and the careful analysis of Meier, *Marginal Jew* 2.439-50; Beasley-Murray, *Jesus and the Kingdom* 138-42 is more sympathetic to the view that the whole saying goes back to Jesus. Both the Jesus Seminar (Funk, *Five Gospels* 47, 49) and Lüdemann (*Jesus* 18) think it likely that 2.(18a-)19 and (21-)22 go back to Jesus in some form. On voluntary fasts in early Judaism see, e.g., Holmén, *Jesus* 128-34.

289. Isa. 49.18; 54.1-8; 62.4-6; Hos. 2.19-20. The possibility that the parable contains an implicit christological claim (Jesus as the bridegroom) is quite often canvassed (see, e.g., discussion in Beasley-Murray, *Jesus and the Kingdom* 140-41; Holmén, *Jesus* 153 n. 385); that is no doubt how it was retold in the early churches, but Jesus may simply have used the imagery of the kingdom present as a wedding banquet to justify his own 'feasting not fasting' attitude. See also below, chapter 15 n. 154.

290. See above, §12.4f. It is also worth noting that 'the wedding guests' (literally 'the sons of the bridechamber') is a semitism (Davies and Allison, *Matthew* 2.109).

291. *Thomas* retains an echo of the saying, but devoid of eschatological significance: 'When the bridegroom comes out of the bride-chamber, then let them fast and pray' (*GTh* 104).

292. Here again *Thomas* retains the echo, but as practical advice for good husbandry without any of the sense of something new at stake: 'No one drinks old wine and immediately desires to drink new wine. And new wine is not put into old wineskins, lest they burst; nor is old wine put into new wineskins, lest it spoil it. No one sews an old patch on a new garment, because a tear would result' (*GTh* 47.3-4).

45 Again, the kingdom of heaven is like a merchant in search of fine pearls; 46 on finding one pearl of great value, he went and sold all that he had and bought it.	76 The kingdom of the Father is like a merchant who had merchandise (and) who found a pearl. This merchant was prudent. He got rid of the merchandise and bought the one pearl for himself.

Here it is the kingdom which is explicitly in view: one stumbles upon it with surprise, the opportunity of a lifetime; it is of huge value; it is worth exchanging all that one possesses in order to attain it.[293] More to the immediate point, it is being discovered now; the transformation implied does not await some future consummation.[294] The fact that the parables are also attested by *Thomas* confirms that they were more widely known than just in Matthew's circle, though, as in other cases, the *Thomas* tradition seems to have been de-eschatologized.[295] In contrast, Matthew's version is wholly consistent with what we have already reviewed in §12.5.

These two parables contain the only explicit reference to the 'kingdom' so far in §12.5, though, of course, the two parts of Mark 1.15a should be taken together, and Luke no doubt understood the good news preached by Jesus as the good news of the kingdom. More explicitly to the point is a saying which only Luke attests, though *Thomas* provides further attestation (*GTh* 3, 113; cf. 51).[296] On being asked by Pharisees when the kingdom of God would come, Jesus answered: 'the kingdom of God is not coming with signs that can be observed (*paratērēseōs*),[297] nor will they say, "Look, here it is!" or "There it is!" For, look,

293. Jeremias, *Parables* 198-200. To make his point memorable Jesus was evidently prepared to cite an action of dubious morality (cf. Luke 16.1-8a) (Funk, *Five Gospels* 196-97; Lüdemann, *Jesus* 186); on the legality of the action (failure to inform the owner of the field) see Hultgren, *Parables* 411-12.

294. Becker, *Jesus* 239-40. Cf. J. D. Crossan, *In Parables: The Challenge of the Historical Jesus* (1973; New York: Harper and Row, 1985) 34-35, though Beasley-Murray fairly cautions against pressing the point as an attack on 'an idolatry of time' (*Jesus and the Kingdom* 112-13).

295. Note particularly the final sentence of *GTh* 109; on the Gnostic overtones see Hultgren, *Parables* 410-11. In *GTh* 76 the contrast is softer: the pearl is not exceptional, and the merchant parts only with his merchandise in order to buy it — a parable of prudent business practice rather than a life-changing decision.

296. The Jesus Seminar give a positive judgment on both Luke 17.20-21 and *GTh* 113.2-4 (Funk, *Five Gospels* 364-65, 531-32), though Lüdemann for some reason refrains from a judgment regarding the historicity of Luke 17.20-21 (*Jesus* 374). Merkel takes Luke 17.20-21 as one of two 'absolutely certain words' (the other is Matt. 12.28/Luke 11.20) as the firm core round which to gather traditions which cohere ('Gottesherrschaft' 142-47), and Keck thinks it is the only saying in which Jesus asserted the kingdom's presence (*Who Is Jesus?* 76-77). Sanders, however, in line with his conviction that the 'present' sayings are dubious, retains his opinion that Luke composed the verses 'unaided by a transmitted saying of Jesus' (*Historical Figure* 177).

297. 'In this Lucan context it [*paratērēsis*] refers neither to the [Pharisaic] "observance" of the Law nor to observance of cultic rites; it is to be understood instead in the Hellenistic sense, of watching for premonitory signs (e.g., from heaven) or of an apocalyptic allusion to

the kingdom of God is[298] among you *(entos hymōn)'* (Luke 17.20-21).[299] This was a key saying for the old Liberal questers. They took the final phrase as 'within you', a quite legitimate rendering, and as thus supporting the idea of the kingdom as a spiritual force within individuals, improving them morally and motivating them to do good.[300] But that would hardly be how Luke understood the phrase: he has Jesus making the pronouncement to Pharisees![301] 'Among you' is much the more favoured rendering today.[302] What is probably most significant about the saying for us is the tension it displays between the idea of the kingdom's coming and the idea of its presence: the kingdom's future coming is not a matter of calculation; the kingdom is already present. The future coming is not denied, only its calculability; but attention is directed rather to its presence.

Whatever we make of particular details and individual sayings, the same noteworthy fact emerges as in the previous case (§12.5a). We hear the same note of realised expectation, of something climactic of eschatological significance already happening, of something new breaking through old traditions, of God's kingdom as an unexpected discovery of life-changing import, of a present reality of God's rule

---

"times and seasons" (e.g., Wis 8:8; 1 Thess 5:1; cf. Mark 13.32; Matt 24.36), i.e. a sort of eschatological timetable' (Fitzmyer, *Luke* 1160; fuller discussion with similar conclusions in Beasley-Murray, *Jesus and the Kingdom* 99-100; Meier, *Marginal Jew* 2.424-26). Perrin extends the point: Jesus 'equally categorically rejected the treatment of the myth as allegory and its symbols as steno-symbols' (*Language* 45).

298. To translate the final clause with a future sense ('is to be'; 'will [suddenly] be', Jeremias, *Proclamation* 101) would lose the saying's more obvious antithesis, which can only be partially restored by inferring in addition something like 'is to be suddenly' (Beasley-Murray, *Jesus and the Kingdom* 102).

299. *GTh* 3: '. . . the kingdom is within you and outside you . . .'; *GTh* 113: 'His disciple(s) said to him: On what day does the kingdom come? (He said) It does not come when one expects (it). They will not say, Look, here! or Look, there! But the kingdom of the Father is spread out upon the earth, and men do not see it'.

300. E.g., Harnack, *What Is Christianity?* 55-57, 63; Dalman, *Words of Jesus* 145-47; J. Wellhausen, *Das Evangelium Lucae* (Berlin: Georg Reimer, 1904) 95; among current opinion note also C. C. Caragounis, 'Kingdom of God/Kingdom of Heaven', *DJG* 417-30 (here 423-24); T. Holmén, 'The Alternatives of the Kingdom: Encountering the Semantic Restrictions of Luke 17,20-21 *(entos hymōn)*', *ZNW* 87 (1996) 204-29. The interpretation is early and was shared by the rendering in *GTh* 3 and, it would appear, *Dial. Sav.* 16. See further Beasley-Murray, *Jesus and the Kingdom* 98-99, 100-101.

301. See further Meier, *Marginal Jew* 2.426-27 and n. 116.

302. See, e.g., Kümmel, *Promise* 33-35; Perrin, *Rediscovering* 73-74; Beasley-Murray, *Jesus and the Kingdom* 100-102, though Beasley-Murray and Fitzmyer are attracted by the sense 'within your grasp' (*Luke* 1161-62; also Wright, *Jesus* 469; McKnight, *New Vision* 102-103; cf. Theissen and Merz, *Historical Jesus* 260-61: 'The saying remains a riddle'). But that would also weaken the saying's contrast (Meier, *Marginal Jew* 2.427). Meier goes on to give good reasons for seeing in the saying a recollection of Jesus' teaching (428-30), including a possible reconstruction of the underlying Aramaic (483 n. 144).

which renders speculation as to its future irrelevant. This note, then, is clearly registered in all strands which go to make up the Synoptic (and *Thomas*) tradition, and all three Evangelists regarded it as particularly characteristic of Jesus' mission. It can hardly have been otherwise with the tradition on which they drew.

c. The Difference between the Baptist and Jesus

The 'already here' motif is nowhere more obvious than in the difference marked out in the tradition between John the Baptist and Jesus. John had predicted a coming judgment (§11.4). That note chimes in with some at least of the teaching attributed to Jesus (§12.4). But John had nothing of the 'already come' emphasis, whereas the Synoptic tradition regarded that too as central to Jesus' preaching. Here we find the chief difference between the preaching of John and that of Jesus. We have already hinted at it above (§12.5a), but the contrast is most obvious in the material which was gathered together on the subject by Q and expanded by both Matthew and Luke — another example of the tendency within the oral tradition to bring material on the same subject together in sequences.[303]

Jesus and John	Matthew	Luke	Q	GTh
1. Are you the one to come?	11.2-6	7.18-23	7.18-19, 22-23	
2. More than a prophet	11.7-10	7.24-27	7.24-27	78
3. The kingdom treated violently	11.11	7.28	7.28	46
4. The Law and the Prophets until John	11.12-13	16.16		
5. Wisdom's children	11.16-19	7.29-35	7.31-35	

1. Matt. 11.2-6	Luke 7.18-23
2 When John heard in prison the deeds of the Christ, he <u>sent</u> by means <u>of his disciples</u> 3 and said to him, '<u>Are you the one who is to come, or are we to wait for another?</u>' 4 <u>And</u> Jesus <u>answered them,</u> '<u>Go and tell John what you</u> <u>hear</u> <u>and see</u>: 5 <u>the blind receive their sight</u>, and <u>the lame walk, the lepers are cleansed, and the deaf hear,</u> and <u>the dead are raised</u>, and <u>the poor have good news brought to them. 6 And blessed is anyone who takes no offence at me</u>'.	18 The disciples of John reported all these things to him. So John summoned two <u>of his disciples</u> 19 and <u>sent</u> them to the Lord to ask, '<u>Are you the one who is to come, or are we to wait for another?</u>' . . . 22 <u>And</u> he <u>answered them,</u> '<u>Go and tell John what you</u> have <u>seen and heard</u>: <u>the blind receive their sight</u>, <u>the lame walk, the lepers are cleansed, and the deaf hear,</u> <u>the dead are raised</u>, <u>the poor have good news brought to them. 23 And blessed is anyone who takes no offence at me</u>'.

303. See above, §8.6b. For the *GTh* parallels see above, §11.2c. Q evidently had 7.24-28 as a single unit; the separation of two of its elements in *Thomas* can be explained as indicating either that the two sayings circulated separately, or that *Thomas*'s formation is the result of its abandoning/rejecting the Baptist tradition (see again §11.2c above).

2.	Matt. 11.7-10	Luke 7.24-27
	7 As they went away, Jesus began to speak to the crowds about John: 'What did you go out into the wilderness to look at? A reed shaken by the wind? 8 What then did you go out to see? A man dressed in soft (garments)? Look, those who wear soft (garments) are in the houses of kings. 9 What then did you go out to see? A prophet? Yes, I tell you, and more than a prophet. 10 This is the one about whom it is written, "See, I am sending my messenger ahead of you, who will prepare your way before you"'.	24 When John's messengers had gone, he began to speak to the crowds about John: 'What did you go out into the wilderness to look at? A reed shaken by the wind? 25 What then did you go out to see? A man dressed in soft garments? Look, those who are gorgeously apparelled and live in luxury are in royal palaces. 26 What then did you go out to see? A prophet? Yes, I tell you, and more than a prophet. 27 This is the one about whom it is written, "See, (I) am sending my messenger ahead of you, who will prepare your way before you"'.

3.	Matt. 11.11	Luke 7.28
	Truly I tell you, among those born of women there has not arisen one greater than John the Baptist; yet the least in the kingdom of heaven is greater than he,	I tell you, among those born of women no one is greater than John; yet the least in the kingdom of God is greater than he.

4.	Matt. 11.12-13	Luke 16.16
	12 From the days of John the Baptist until now the kingdom of heaven is being violently treated, and the violent take it by force. 13 For all the prophets and the law prophesied till John.	16 The law and the prophets were until John; since then the good news of the kingdom of God is preached, and everyone tries to enter it by force.

5.	Matt. 11.16-19	Luke 7.31-35
	16 But to what will I compare this generation? It is like children sitting in the marketplaces and calling to the others, 17 'We played the flute for you, and you did not dance; we wailed, and you did not mourn'. 18 For John came neither eating nor drinking, and they say, 'He has a demon'; 19 the Son of Man came eating and drinking, and they say, 'Look, a man, a glutton and a drunkard, a friend of tax collectors and sinners!' Nevertheless, wisdom is vindicated by her deeds.	31 To what then will I compare the people of this generation, and what are they like? 32 They are like children who sit in the marketplace and calling to one another, 'We played the flute for you, and you did not dance; we wailed, and you did not weep'. 33 For John the Baptist has come eating no bread and drinking no wine, and you say, 'He has a demon'; 34 the Son of Man has come eating and drinking, and you say, 'Look, a man, a glutton and a drunkard, a friend of tax collectors and sinners!' 35 Nevertheless, wisdom is vindicated by all her children.

Here we have what were recalled within the traditioning process as four or five different sayings or teachings of Jesus regarding John the Baptist. Sayings 1-3 and 5 are plausibly to be explained as a collection made or put into written form by Q, though we should note again the characteristic features of oral tradition, particularly in 1, where the key question and answer are firm, but the details of the retelling flexible. Saying 4 (Matt. 11.12-13/Luke 16.16) might well be better explained as drawn by Matthew and Luke independently from oral tradition, from the repertoire of the churches with which they were associated, with its characteristic oral features of different versions of a saying whose substance both versions preserve.

Such a sequence of tradition clearly attests a considerable interest among the early followers of Jesus in the question of the relation between Jesus and the Baptist. It is regularly assumed that the tradition is late, or at least later than the earliest recollections of Jesus' teaching.[304] But as we have seen, John was a figure of considerable repute (note again Matt. 11.7-9/Luke 7.24-26); and the fact that Jesus had emerged from the Baptist's circle would presumably have been widely known, especially if some of Jesus' closest disciples had also come from the Baptist circle.[305] Inevitably, then, questions would have arisen among the hearers of Jesus' preaching as to the relation between the two. Jesus' own disciples would have needed some instruction on the point. The more significant the claims made by Jesus regarding the kingdom of God, the more likely the issue was to arise. However the theme may have been elaborated, therefore, the tradition that Jesus in his teaching referred to the Baptist most likely began with Jesus' own attempt to explain the difference between his mission and that of the Baptist.

(1) Matt.11.2-6/Luke 7.18-23. That the Baptist himself put such a question to Jesus (Matt. 11.3/Luke 7.19) is entirely possible.[306] The Baptist's conception of the 'one coming/to come' may have been vague beyond the fact that the newcomer's mission would be one of judgment (§11.4d). That Jesus made such significant claims yet did not repeat the note of judgment, or at least give it such prominence, would presumably have raised questions for the Baptist. Had the question been contrived in subsequent Christian apologetic we might well have expected the episode to close with the report of the Baptist's acceptance of Jesus' answer. That at least would have accorded with the tendency in Christian tradition (noted in chapter 11) to depict the Baptist as a witness to Jesus. To depict Jesus' answer removing the Baptist's doubts would have been an attractive option (cf. Matt. 3.14-15). But the episode closes with the answer itself, which implies that that was as much as those who formulated the story knew. It is the saying of Jesus which formed the core of the tradition.[307] The tradents kept it

---

304. The Jesus Seminar is generally negative in its judgments, with the exception of Matt. 11.7b-8/Luke 7.24b-25 (Funk, *Five Gospels* 177-80, 301-303). Lüdemann regards sayings 1-3 as formulated from a post-Easter perspective, but reckons that saying 4 may go back to Jesus ('because of its offensive language') and saying 5 also as 'authentic' (*Jesus* 173, 306).

305. See above, §11.2c.

306. On the likelihood that the Baptist's prison conditions permitted at least some communication with his disciples see Meier, *Marginal Jew* 2.198-99 n. 89.

307. Jeremias sees here a good example of Aramaic rhythm: six two-beat lines (*Proclamation* 20-21).

so, even though the temptation among performers of the tradition to bring the story to a more satisfactory closure must have been strong (cf., e.g., Matt.8.13b/ Luke 7.10).[308]

The real interest focuses in Jesus' answer and deserves some attention. The language of the answer seems to be borrowed in large part from Isaiah.[309] Three features are worth noting. First, the striking echo of 4Q521, which came to light only with its publication in the early 1990s. Column 2 reads

> [1]. . . [the hea]vens and the earth will listen to his messiah . . . [5]For the Lord will consider the pious *(hasidim)* and call the righteous by name, [6]and over the poor his spirit will hover, and he will renew the faithful with his power. [7]For he will glorify the pious upon the throne of an eternal kingdom. [8]He who liberates the captives, restores sight to the blind, straightens the b[ent]. . . . [11]And the Lord will accomplish glorious things which have never been as [ ]. [12][For] he will heal the wounded, and revive the dead and preach good news to the poor.

The passage is remarkable. It talks of a future Messiah and an eternal kingdom in almost the same breath (2.1, 7), perhaps the latter in echo of 2 Sam. 7.13.[310] And in that connection it echoes the same range of passages in Isaiah — sight restored to the blind, cripples healed (2.8), the dead revived, and good news preached to

---

308. See also my earlier analysis in *Jesus and the Spirit* 55-60. Davies and Allison, *Matthew* 2.244-45, and Meier, *Marginal Jew* 2.132-36 argue similarly. Note Leivestad's hesitations at the use of the passage *(Jesus* 92-93); and contrast Gnilka who finds it 'advisable to attribute this text, which radiates scribal reflection, to a later context' *(Jesus of Nazareth* 131).

309.	Blind seeing	Isa. 29.18	('The eyes of the blind shall see');
		Isa. 35.5	('The eyes of the blind shall be opened');
		Isa. 42.7	('To open the eyes that are blind');
		Isa. 42.18	('you that are blind, look up and see').
	Lame walking	Isa. 35.6	('Then the lame shall leap like a deer');
	Deaf hearing	Isa. 29.18	('The deaf shall hear');
		Isa. 35.5	('and the ears of the deaf unstopped');
	Dead raised	Isa. 26.19	('Your dead shall live . . .');
	Good news preached to the poor	Isa. 61.1	('He has sent me to bring good news to the poor').

See further D. C. Allison, *The Intertextual Jesus: Scripture in Q* (Harrisburg: Trinity, 2000) 109-14, and further ch. 4.

310.	2 Sam. 7.13	God promises David a son: 'I will establish the throne of his kingdom for ever';
	4Q521 7	'He will glorify the pious upon the throne of an eternal kingdom'.

the poor (2.12).[311] Particularly noticeable is the inclusion of restoration of the dead to life, in direct echo of Isa. 26.19.[312] With such evidence it is no longer satisfactory to argue that the Q list was composed with hindsight in the light of resurrection faith.[313] On the contrary, we can deduce that an expectation was current at the time of Jesus to the effect that the coming of God's Messiah would be accompanied by such marvellous events, in fulfilment of Isaiah's prophecies.[314] It is this expectation which Matt. 11.5/Luke 7.22 takes up and claims to have been fulfilled in Jesus' mission.[315]

Second, another feature of the main Isaiah passages thus echoed in Matt. 11.5/Luke 7.22 is their close proximity to warnings of judgment.[316] Here we find a rather subtle response to the Baptist's question. The echo of these passages confirms that the Baptist was right to look to Isaiah's prophecies for an insight into what was to come.[317] But by omitting just the note of judgment on which the Baptist seems to have exclusively focused,[318] the response says in effect that John had neglected the other, more positive expectation of restoration, good

311. The strength of echo of Isa. 61.1c is muffled by the present MT Hebrew ('to proclaim liberty to the captives and release to the prisoners'). But Qumran had a variant reading: 'to proclaim liberty for the captives and opening of the eyes for the prisoners' (*DSSB* 372), reflected in LXX's *typhlois anablepsin* ('restoration of sight to the blind').

312. But possibly with an allusion also to the tradition of Elijah raising the dead (1 Kgs. 17.17-24; cf. 2 Kgs. 4.32-37). J. J. Collins concludes that the expected Messiah of 4Q521 is Elijah or a prophet like Elijah (*The Scepter and the Star: The Messiahs of the Dead Sea Scrolls and Other Ancient Literature* [New York: Doubleday, 1995] 119-21); similarly M. Becker, '4Q521 und die Gesalbten', *RevQ* 18 (1997) 73-96.

313. As still B. Kollmann. *Jesus und die Christen als Wundertäter* (FRLANT 170; Göttingen: Vandenhoeck und Ruprecht, 1996) 219-20.

314. The point is not essentially weakened if 4Q521 was only intended as a 'metaphoric' description of eschatological renewal, as argued by H. Kvalbein, 'The Wonders of the End-Time: Metaphoric Language in 4Q521 and the Interpretation of Matthew 11.5 par.', *JSP* 18 (1998) 87-110.

315. The note of fulfilment can hardly be disputed; see Beasley-Murray, *Jesus and the Kingdom* 82; P. Stuhlmacher, 'Der messianische Gottesknecht', *JBTh* 8, *Der Messias* (1993) 131-54 (here 142-43).

316. Isa. 26.21: 'The Lord comes out from his place to punish the inhabitants of the earth for their iniquity'; 29.20: 'The tyrant shall be no more, and the scoffer shall cease to be; all those alert to do evil shall be cut off'; 35.4: 'Here is your God. He will come with vengeance, with terrible recompense'; 61.2: 'the day of vengeance of our God'.

317. For the influence of Isaiah on the Baptist's preaching see above, §11.4c.

318. Luke brings this out less subtly by depicting Jesus as ending his reading from Isa. 61.1-2 just before the phrase 'and the day of vengeance of our God' (Luke 4.19-20). Contrast the other Qumran echo of Isa. 61.2 in 11QMelch 2.9-13, which in describing Melchizedek's role mentions both 'the year of favour' (2.9) and divine 'vengeance *(nqm)*' (2.13); cf. Allison, *Intertextual Jesus* 113.

news, and new life.[319] It is just such subtlety in using Scripture which is recalled as characteristic of Jesus' teaching elsewhere.[320]

Third, Matt. 11.5/Luke 7.22 is a remarkable confirmation from the sayings tradition that Jesus was well known as a successful healer: healings of blind, lame, and deaf are attributed to him, also restoration to life of people who had died. We will refer back to this mutual confirmation of narrative and sayings traditions later on.[321] Here we should note the insertion of an unexpected item in the Isaiah listings — 'lepers are cleansed'. There is nothing in Isaiah which might have inspired the inclusion of that item. Nor, it should be observed, is there any record of leprosy/skin diseases being healed in the records of the earliest churches. The item can be here only because it was generally believed (by Jesus too!) that he had also cleansed lepers.

In short, the most obvious explanation for the emergence of this tradition is that Jesus was remembered as giving just this answer to those who inquired on behalf of the Baptist. The final verse of the unit, 'Blessed is anyone who takes no offence at me' (Matt. 11.6/Luke 7.23), might also fall under the same favourable verdict.[322] For though the formulation no doubt resonated mightily in subsequent reflection on Jesus as a 'cause of offence', the *skandalon* in view here has nothing to do with the offence of the cross.[323] Moreover, the verb *(skandalizō,* Aramaic *tql)* is well attested in the Jesus tradition in a variety of contexts,[324] which together probably indicate Jesus' awareness of the 'scandalous' character of his mission (cf. Matt. 11.19a/Luke 7.34 above). So it should occasion no surprise if Jesus acknowledged the likelihood of the Baptist taking offence at one of his own circle striking out on his own and with an emphasis which cut across John's (cf. John 3.25-26).[325]

(2)/(3) The striking feature of sayings 2 and 3 (Matt. 11.7-11/Luke 7.24-28) is the remarkable combination of strong affirmation of the Baptist's role with

319. As so often, Wright brings the passage under the heading of 'return from exile' (*Jesus* 428-29) and thus obscures the richness and diversity of the prophetic images drawn upon; see further below, §12.6b.

320. As recalled, e.g., in the sequence Mark 12.24-27, 28-34, 35-37a pars. Contrast the Jesus Seminar, which assumes that use of Scripture is a clear sign of Christian apologetic (Funk, *Five Gospels* 177-78), as though Jesus could not have made such allusion to Scripture on his own account, unlike Qumran.

321. See below, §15.7.

322. Cf. Bultmann: 'What are the signs of the time? He himself! His presence, his deeds, his message!', citing Matt. 11.5 (*Theology* 1.7).

323. Cf. particularly 1 Cor. 1.23; Gal. 5.11.

324. Mark 9.43, 45, 47/Matt. 5.30, 29/Matt. 18.8-9; Mark 9.42/Matt. 18.6/Luke 17.2; Mark 14.27, 29/Matt. 26.31, 33; Matt. 17.27; 24.10; cf. Mark 6.3/Matt. 13.57; Matt. 15.12; John 6.61.

325. Similarly Meier, *Marginal Jew* 2.135.

the final 'put-down' of the last clause. That Jesus should have contrasted the Baptist so favourably with Herod Antipas (Matt. 11.7-8/Luke 7.24-25) is entirely plausible[326] and indicates that Jesus' teaching could have a sharp political edge. And the evaluation of the Baptist as 'more/greater *(perissoteron)* than a prophet' (Matt. 11.9/Luke 7.26) would be a surprising accolade for the followers of Jesus to have devised, since that was how they regarded Jesus himself (Matt. 12.41/ Luke 11.32). But it makes sense on the lips of one who owed the beginning of his own mission in some sense to the Baptist.[327]

It may even be that we can say the same of Matt. 11.10/Luke 7.27 — John as the messenger sent ahead to prepare the way of the Lord (Mal. 3.1). For such an identification need not imply either a developed christology or that Jesus saw himself fulfilling the role of the Lord. The Qumran community also saw itself as 'preparing the way of the Lord' (1QS 8.13-14; Isa. 40.3). And yet, at the same time, it looked for the coming of God's Messiahs.[328] All the same, the complexity of the allusion — to Exod. 23.20 and Mal. 3.1 (the allusion to Isa. 40.3 is less obvious) — probably does indicate fuller Christian reflection (cf. Mark 1.2-3).[329]

The more striking feature is the sharpness of the contrast in Matt. 11.11/ Luke 7.28 (attested also by *GTh* 46). The audaciousness of the antithesis attests a saying rhetorically structured to make a particular point.[330] The point is clear: something has happened between the mission of John and that of Jesus, something which has lifted possibilities onto a new plane; even the least on that new plane is superior to John. The explanatory word is, once again, 'kingdom'. It is the kingdom of God which marks the difference, which constitutes the new plane.[331] It was this emphasis which caused Bornkamm and other new questers to part company with Bultmann.[332] In the light of such a statement they could not remain content simply to locate Jesus under Judaism, with the implication that

326. See above, chapter 11 n. 183.

327. Meier notes 'the absence of any christological concern, the total focus on and praise of John without limitations . . . (and) the lack of any reference or allusion to Jesus at all' (*Marginal Jew* 2.139).

328. See below, §15.2a.

329. Meier, *Marginal Jew* 140-42.

330. 'A typically Semitic dialectical negation' again lacking christological content (Meier, *Marginal Jew* 2.142-44). Contrast Schürmann, *Gottes Reich:* a 'Zusatzwort' in which the original voice of Jesus can still hardly be heard (91).

331. Schlosser suggests that if John had already been executed the meaning is probably that any now alive and experiencing the kingdom are more blessed and privileged even than John (*Règne* 161-67). Leivestad denies any necessary implication that the Baptist is excluded from the kingdom. The import of the saying is simply that 'To be the greatest of prophets is less than to have a place in the kingdom to come' (*Jesus* 89). Compare Stuhlmacher in 'new quest' mode: 'a qualitative difference between him and the Baptist' (*Biblische Theologie* 1.64).

332. See above, §5.4.

the watershed between Judaism and the gospel came with (the message of) the death and resurrection of Jesus. Jesus' own mission and message already marked the dividing line. John represented the period of preparation, Jesus the period of fulfilment. In other words, between the missions of the Baptist and Jesus a decisive 'shift in the aeons' had taken place.[333] John could indeed be regarded as the greatest man ever born; but in comparison with the blessings of the kingdom, what John stood for was of much less importance.

Such language is striking indeed, though its rhetorical character should not be forgotten. It is of a piece with Jesus' concern for 'the little one', as attested elsewhere in the Jesus tradition.[334] More to the point here, it attests an amazing sense that something of final significance (the kingdom of God) was being unfolded through Jesus' mission.[335] As we have already noted, this was not the language used by the early Christians to articulate their equivalent sense of the final significance of Jesus' mission. The saying should probably be regarded, therefore, as one of Jesus' own remembered *bons mots*.

(4) Matt. 11.12-13/Luke 16.16 is one of those sayings which is so puzzling that it can have been retained only because it was remembered as a saying of Jesus.[336] What could it mean that the kingdom was being 'violently treated' or 'entered by force' *(biazetai)?* Who could the 'violent/men of violence *(biastai)*' be who were trying to seize it forceably? The best solution may be that 'men of violence' was a jibe used by those hostile to Jesus' mission: Jesus encourages the disreputable to think they can just push their way into the kingdom, can take it by storm![337] Jesus would then be remembered as teaching *ad hominem:* the king-

---

333. Bornkamm, *Jesus* 50-51, 56-57, 66-68; Robinson, *New Quest* 116-19. See also N. Perrin, *The Kingdom of God in the Teaching of Jesus* (London: SCM, 1963) 121-24. Of recent writers, Becker presses the point most consistently *(Jesus of Nazareth* 108-15); here 'the statement clearly excludes John from the Kingdom of God' (114).

334. Mark 9.42/Matt. 18.6; Matt. 10.42; 18.10, 14; Luke 9.48; 12.32; 17.2; cf. Mark 4.31/Matt. 13.32. On the unlikelihood that Jesus is to be identified with 'the least in the kingdom' see Meier, *Marginal Jew* 2.208-209 n. 132.

335. Sanders, *Jesus and Judaism* 92-93, 140. The already/not yet tension is sufficient explanation for the antithesis; it does not follow that 'there was already an anti-apocalyptic theology operative' *(pace* Crossan, *Birth* 310-11, 316).

336. On a possible Aramaic underlay see Dalman, *Words of Jesus* 139-43; Young argues for a Hebrew underlay, giving the translation, 'From the days of John the Baptist until now, the kingdom of heaven breaks forth and those breaking forth are pursuing [seeking] it' *(Jesus* 51-55).

337. F. W. Danker, 'Luke 16.16 — An Opposition Logion', *JBL* 77 (1958) 231-43; followed by Jeremias, *Proclamation* 111-12; Wink, *John the Baptist* 20-22; W. Stenger, *biazomai, biastēs, EDNT* 1.217; Theissen and Merz, *Historical Jesus* 271. It is the recognition that Jesus may have been turning a negative criticism to positive affirmation which resolves the problems posed, e.g., by Fitzmyer, *Luke* 1117-18 and Meier, *Marginal Jew* 2.216 n. 180. *Pace* Meier we

dom is indeed being 'taken by storm' by the 'men of violence'.[338] This again would be of a piece with Jesus' claims elsewhere that those who were regarded by the righteous as of no account to God were actually more likely to receive God's grace than were those who despised them.[339]

The point for us, however, is that here is another saying recalled in the (oral) tradition in which Jesus dated the presence of the kingdom (to be treated violently, or entered by force) from John the Baptist. In this case there is no sharp divide between John and Jesus. Both Matthew's 'from the days of John' and Luke's 'since then' are probably inclusive:[340] John's mission signalled the beginning of the period now most characterised by the preaching of Jesus and its effects. We need not be surprised at the contrast with the previous saying: the relation between John and Jesus could be put in different terms on different occasions.[341] Similarly Matt. 11.13/Luke 16.16a should not be pressed to imply that 'the Law and the Prophets' somehow ceased before or with the Baptist;[342] here too the rhetorical heightening of the contrast should be recognized. A new phase of God's kingly rule could be asserted, as here, without necessarily denigrating what had gone before.[343]

(5) The final member of the sequence of sayings on Jesus and the Baptist

---

should note that allusions to opponents' usage are not always signalled explicitly: cf., e.g., Paul's self-designation of himself as an 'abortion' (1 Cor. 15.8; see my *Theology of Paul* 331 n. 87) and Jesus' response to the designation 'Messiah' (see below, §15.4).

338. There may, however, also be an allusion to the eschatological trials which Jesus (and John) anticipated before the coming of the kingdom. Davies and Allison note the parallel with 1QH 10(= 2).10-11, 21-22, the 'violent ones' (*'rizim*) who oppress the author of the hymn (*Matthew* 2.256). For other attempts to make sense of an at best obscure saying see Beasley-Murray, *Jesus and the Kingdom* 91-96; Davies and Allison 254-56.

339. See below, §13.5.

340. Davies and Allison, *Matthew* 2.253-54.

341. Pedantic consistency which takes no account of difference of originating context should never be used as a criterion of 'authenticity'; Matthew evidently saw no problem in setting 11.11-13 in sequence. From his as usual careful analysis Schürmann concludes that behind the later kerygmatic transformations an *ipsissimum verbum Jesu* may after all be surmised (*Gottes Reich* 126-29, 134-35).

342. Luke 16.16 was a pivotal text in Conzelmann's analysis of the three periods in Luke's conception of salvation history: Israel/the law and the prophets, including the Baptist — Jesus — the church (*Theology of St Luke,* e.g., 16, 23, 112, 161). He is followed by Fitzmyer in modified form: for Luke the Baptist is a transition ending the period of Israel and inaugurating the period of Jesus (*Luke* 1115-16). See also Davies and Allison, *Matthew* 2.257-58. Meier is not sufficiently confident that he can discern the original intention of Jesus in the saying to make much of it (*Marginal Jew* 2.157-63). On Jesus' attitude to the law see below, §14.4.

343. The overstatement, e.g., of Kümmel, *Promise* 124, is indicative of the concern of the second questers to put a clear space between Jesus and his native Judaism; see also below, chapter 14 n. 98.

(Matt. 11.16-19/Luke 7.31-35) has several important features, and we will have to return to it more than once. Here we need merely note the difference implied between the mission styles of John and Jesus. John's had a notably ascetic character (Matt. 11.18/Luke 7.33); this certainly fits with the Baptist tradition in the Synoptics (Mark 1.6 par.) and may find an echo in Josephus's description.[344] But Jesus had a reputation for enjoying himself; this is attested not only by the controversial Matt. 11.19/Luke 7.34,[345] but also by the contrast drawn in the little parable which begins the unit (Matt. 11.16-17/Luke 7.31-32).[346] The parable itself can certainly be regarded as typical of Jesus' teaching style.[347] The contrast fits too with the expectation of Isa. 61.3 — 'a garland instead of ashes, the oil of gladness instead of mourning' — and with the other teaching tradition already referred to above (§12.5b). So there is no difficulty in recognizing here a memory of one of Jesus' more vivid attempts to signal his own understanding of the difference between his mission and that of John.[348]

The conclusion from this rather lengthy probe into the tradition of Jesus' own assessment of the Baptist and of the difference between them is clear. The earliest churches did not see the issue as one which had arisen only in their own time, but remembered it as a subject on which Jesus had spoken on several occasions. One can well imagine these teachings being grouped together even during the lifetime of Jesus, as his disciples, including former disciples of the Baptist, were themselves confronted by the question of how the relation of John and Jesus was to be understood. The point for us here is that the relation between the two was conceived in terms of a significant transition having taken place. There was a note of fulfilled expectation, of long-desired blessings now happening, of

344. John called for 'consecration *(hagneia)* of the body' (Josephus, *Ant.* 18.117); *hagneia* usually has the sense 'purity, chastity', 'strict observance of religious duties' (LSJ *hagneia;* BAGD *hagneia).*

345. See below, chapter 13 at nn. 183-84 and §16.4b(5).

346. Hultgren, *Parables* 204-206; 'It is difficult to imagine that the parable would have survived without an explanation' (205).

347. Contrasting pairs is one of the most characteristic features of Jesus' parables; e.g., shrunk or unshrunk cloth, new or old wineskins (Mark 2.21-22 pars.), two ways (Matt. 7.13-14/ Luke 13.23-24), wise and foolish builders (Matt. 7.24-27/Luke 6.47-49), two sons (Matt. 21.28-30), wise and foolish maidens (Matt. 25.1-13), the prodigal son and his brother (Luke 15.11-32), and a pharisee and tax-collector (Luke 18.9-14).

348. The portrayal of Jesus as 'a glutton and a drunkard' *(phagos kai oinopotēs),* both words *hapax legomena* in the NT but clearly pejorative (there may be an echo of Prov. 23.20-21), 'not likely to have been invented by his followers' (Funk, *Five Gospels* 180); the confusion (among commentators!) regarding the phrase 'the Son of Man' should not count against that logic (see below, §13.5 n. 184 and further §16.4). See also Meier's careful analysis (*Marginal Jew* 2.144-56), though he follows Sanders too uncritically in regard to the 'sinners' (Matt. 11.19/Luke 7.34) (149-50); see again below, chapter 15 n. 224.

the celebration that was consequently appropriate. Only one of the four sayings in the Q sequence expresses the point explicitly in kingdom terms, as does also the independent saying (4). But it would hardly distort the evidence to sum up the emphasis in terms of the kingdom being already active in and through Jesus' mission, in contrast to that of the Baptist.

Of particular importance theologically is the immediate corollary regarding the difference between the two eschatological views. The Baptist saw the present only as opportunity to flee from the wrath to come. Jesus saw the present as already manifesting the graciousness of God. He did not denounce or abandon John's expectation of judgment. But it was judgment preempted by grace.[349] This aspect of Jesus' mission will reemerge repeatedly in chapters 13 and 14 below.

In confirmation of what was deduced in §11.2b, then, it would appear that Jesus' teaching on and convictions regarding the kingdom were the crucial factor in his striking out independently of and with different emphasis from John. John's expectations had been too one-sided; the other dimension(s) of what the prophets had looked for could be experienced now already. That conviction and consequent emphases and practice marked some sort of parting of the ways between John and Jesus. The differing emphases of the traditions examined mean that we cannot conceptualise the relation between them as a neat dividing line, 'before' and 'after' some clearly defined eschatological turning point. And, so far as we can tell, there was never any question among Jesus' first followers of simply dismissing the Baptist or his message.[350] But the change of emphasis was nevertheless perceived by Jesus in earliest Christian memory as a change like the dawning of a new day following the darkest hour before dawn.

d. Jesus' Claims regarding His Exorcisms

Without doubt Jesus was known as a successful exorcist. This is a claim which is easily substantiated, as we shall see later (§15.7b, c). Here we need to take account of the tradition that Jesus spoke about that success and about its significance. And here again we find a collection, if not two collections, of Jesus' teaching on the subject. As with other such collections, the very fact of the collection

---

349. See particularly Becker, *Jesus of Nazareth* 74-78, referring to Matt. 20.1-16; Luke 15.11-32; and Luke 18.10-14: 'it is no longer the final moment of the old age before an imminent judgment; it is the beginning of the new age of salvation' (79). Similarly Merkel, 'Gottesherrschaft' 151-53; Gnilka, *Jesus of Nazareth* 96-101: the theme of 'incomprehensible, limitless goodness', 'incredible goodness', 'boundless goodness' (95, 101, 102).

350. *Pace* Hollenbach ('Conversion of Jesus' 203-17) and Crossan (*Historical Jesus* 237-38) who press for a radical transformation in Jesus' earlier attitude to John.

tells us two things. First that Jesus was remembered as speaking on the subject on several occasions. And second, that an early reflex among the groups of his followers and the early churches was to gather such sayings into an appropriate sequence, no doubt as an aid to more effective teaching and apologetic.[351]

Theme	Mark	Q	
1. Beelzebul	3.22-26	Matt. 12.24-26	Luke 11.15, 17-18
2. Finger/Spirit of God		Matt. 12.27-28	Luke 11.19-20
3. Strong man	3.27	Matt. 12.29	Luke 11.21-22
4. He who is not with me		Matt. 12.30	Luke 11.23
5. Unforgivable sin	3.28-29	Matt. 12.31-32	Luke 12.10
6. Return of the unclean spirit		Matt. 12.43-45	Luke 11.24-26

Here are two sets of sayings, one with three sayings (Mark), the other with six (Q/Luke), of which only two, (1) and (3), overlap in that sequence. Both the groupings and their diversity typify the process of oral transmission. In particular we might note that there was evidently a Q form of the first (1), as well as the Markan form; the two versions were evidently very close, though not identical. And Luke knows a version (Q?) of the strong man saying (3 — Luke 11.21-22) which has hardly any verbal contact with Mark 3.27 but makes the same point; if Luke 11.21-22 did indeed follow Q,[352] then Matthew chose to follow Mark.[353] At this stage we need consider only the first three items of the sequence (1-3).[354]

351. See also Schröter, *Erinnerung* 289-91. In arguing that Mark must have known and edited Q, H. T. Fleddermann, 'Mark's Use of Q: The Beelezebul Controversy and the Cross Saying', in M. Labahn and A. Schmidt, eds., *Jesus, Mark and Q: The Teaching of Jesus and Its Earliest Records* (JSNTS 214; Sheffield: Sheffield Academic, 2001), conceives the interrelations of the traditions in too narrowly literary terms

352. Kloppenborg, *Q Parallels* 92; Robinson/Hoffmann/Kloppenborg, *Critical Edition* 234-35, but with little confidence. Meier argues that Mark's form is 'more primitive' (*Marginal Jew* 2.417-18); the idea of 'binding' evil (Mark/Matthew) is certainly more traditionally Jewish (see above, n. 79) than Luke's less distinctively Jewish version, but Luke's version is perhaps modelled with allusion to Isa. 49.24-25; so here again we should probably be content to talk of performance variants where only the theme itself has been held constant.

353. It is worth noting that *Thomas* has a version of only the third (3) in the above collection and clearly reflects the Mark 3.27 version rather than Luke 11.21-22 (*GTh* 35).

354. On (5) see below, §16.4b(3).

Matt. 12.24-26	Mark 3.22-26	Luke 11.15-18
24 But when the Pharisees heard it, they said, 'It is only by Beelzebul, the ruler of the demons, that this man casts out the demons'.	22 And the scribes who came down from Jerusalem said, 'He has Beelzebul, and by the ruler of the demons he casts out the demons'. 23 And he called them to him, and spoke to them in parables, 'How can Satan cast out Satan? 24 And if a kingdom is divided against itself, that kingdom cannot stand. 25 And if a house is divided against itself, that house will not be able to stand. 26 And if Satan has risen up against himself and is divided, he cannot stand, but his end has come'.	15 But some of them said, 'By Beelzebul, the ruler of the demons, he casts out the demons'. 16 Others, to test him, kept demanding from him a sign from heaven. 17 But he knew their thoughts and said to them, 'Every kingdom divided against itself becomes a desert, and house falls on house. 18 If Satan also is divided against himself, how will his kingdom stand? for you say that I cast out the demons by Beelzebul'.
25 He knew their thinking and said to them, 'Every kingdom divided against itself is laid waste, and no city or house divided against itself will stand. 26 If Satan casts out Satan, he is divided against himself; how then will his kingdom stand?'		

Matt. 12.27-28	Luke 11.19-20
27 If I cast out the demons by Beelzebul, by whom do your sons cast them out? Therefore they will be your judges. 28 But if it is by the Spirit of God that I cast out the demons, then has the kingdom of God come upon you.	19 If I cast out the demons by Beelzebul, by whom do your sons cast them out? Therefore they will be your judges. 20 But if it is by the finger of God that I cast out the demons, then has the kingdom of God come upon you.

Matt. 12.29	Mark 3.27	Luke 11.21-22
29 Or how can one enter into a strong man's house and plunder his goods, without first tying up the strong man? Then indeed he will plunder the house.	27 But no one can enter into a strong man's house and plunder his goods without first tying up the strong man. Then indeed he will plunder the house.	21 When a strong man, fully armed, guards his manor, his property is safe. 22 But when one stronger than he attacks and overpowers him, he takes away his armour in which he trusted and divides the spoils.

All three are clearly linked by a common theme: Jesus' success as an exorcist signals the triumph of God's kingdom over Satan's. A large consensus of contemporary scholarship accepts that such an emphasis must have been a feature of Jesus' teaching. The consensus regarding (2) and (3) is particularly strong.[355]

355. The Jesus Seminar give a positive verdict with regard to the Q version of (1) (Luke 11.17-18), and also to (2) ('His remarks are witty and frustrate expectations') and (3) ('The analogy of the calculating and powerful robber suits Jesus' style: it is a surprising comparison and indulges in exaggeration') (Funk, *Five Gospels* 52, 185-86, 329-30, 493). Becker assumes the attack in (1) is historical, has no doubts on (2), but attributes (3) to the church (*Jesus* 108-10, 184-85). Lüdemann regards (2) and (3) as 'authentic' (*Jesus* 25, 337). On (1) Kollmann draws attention particularly to the lack of christological explication (*Jesus* 182). On (2): 'universally acknowledged' (Beasley-Murray, *Jesus and the Kingdom* 75); 'one of the assured re-

(1) The first (Mark 3.22-26 pars.) poses a nice conundrum to the charge of black magic or sorcery. Given the established view of demon possession as something sought by the demons, it would make no sense for the ruler of the demons to enable or assist in the ejection of demons.[356] We will reflect on the significance of the passage later on (§15.7b, h). Here we need simply note that the power of evil is depicted as a kingdom (explicitly in Matt. 12.26/Luke 11.18) with Satan[357] as ruler or prince *(archōn)*.[358] The implication is that Jesus' exorcisms are empowered not by that kingdom but by the kingdom of God.[359]

(2) This is made explicit in the second saying (Matt. 12.27-28/Luke 11.19-20): Jesus' exorcisms are effected by God's power and demonstrate that 'the kingdom of God has come upon *(ephthasen)* you'. This has been long regarded

---

sults of modern criticism' (Davies and Allison, *Matthew* 2.339). I attempted to address Sanders's doubts with regard to (2) *(Jesus and Judaism* 133-41) in my 'Matthew 12:28/Luke 11:20 — A Word of Jesus?' in W. H. Gloer, ed., *Eschatology and the New Testament,* G. R. Beasley-Murray FS (Peabody; Hendrickson 1988), reprinted in my *The Christ and the Spirit* vol. 2: *Pneumatology* (Grand Rapids: Eerdmans, 1998) 187-204. Sanders weakens his case by continuing to insist that what would have to be in view was the kingdom *'fully present'* in Jesus' actions (*Historical Figure* 177-78). On (3) Meier observes that the term *ischuros* ('strong') for Satan, 'the strong one', was not Christian usage and presumably, therefore, reflects a distinctive feature of Jesus' vocabulary recalled here (*Marginal Jew* 2.421).

356. J. Marcus, 'The Beelezebul Controversy and the Eschatologies of Jesus', in Chilton and Evans, eds., *Authenticating the Activities of Jesus* 247-77, argues that the logic of Mark 3.22-26 is that Satan's power is *not yet* broken, which therefore stands in contrast to the claim of 3.27. To meet the problem he hypothesizes that Jesus' eschatological thought underwent discernible change, 3.22-26 reflecting an earlier stage, 3.27 the later. The transition point was Jesus' baptism, the conclusion he drew from his baptismal vision (see below, n. 373). In other words, he hypothesizes a *pre-*baptismal exorcistic mission by Jesus — against all implications of the Gospel accounts. It makes better sense to see two metaphors/images used by Jesus at different times, one *ad hominem* (3.22-26), the other expressing his own conviction as to Satan's defeat in his exorcisms (3.27).

357. *'Beelzeboul'* was the name for an old Canaanite god, 'Baal, Lord of the heavens', so naturally seen as a/the rival to Yahweh, 'the Lord of heaven' (Dan. 5.23) (see further in Fitzmyer, *Luke* 2.920; Davies and Allison, *Matthew* 2.195-96). Since *b'l zbul* is a Hebrew (rather than Aramaic) formation, Casey speculates that the exchange between Jesus and the 'scribes who came down from Jerusalem' (Mark 3.22) was likely to have been in Hebrew (*Aramaic Sources* 88).

358. The conception of evil as a structured hierarchy with Satan (variously named; see, e.g., Fitzmyer, *Luke* 921) at the head was a fairly recent development in Jewish demonology (see *Jub.* 48.15; 1QS 3.20-25; 1QM 17.5-6; 18.1-3; 11QMelch 2.13; *T. Dan* 5.6).

359. Wright typically presses the parable into his master hypothesis: Jesus' mastery over the demons should lead to only one conclusion: 'Israel's god was at last becoming king' (*Jesus* 453-54). In contrast, by putting his discussion of the Beelzebul controversy into his chapter on 'Magic and Meal', Crossan ignores its relevance to the issue of the kingdom (*Historical Jesus* 318-20).

as one of the surest points of access to Jesus' own teaching,[360] not least because it is one of the clearest assertions of the kingdom's presence within and through Jesus' mission.[361] The structure of the saying should be noted: the two key phrases, at the beginning and end of the sentence (the places of emphasis), are 'Spirit/finger of God' and 'kingdom of God': 'but if it is by the *Spirit/finger of God* that I cast out demons, then has come upon you the *kingdom of God*'.[362] This indicates that the saying was thus formulated to emphasize the contrast with the preceding verse. The point is missed by those who argue that Jesus' logic would have meant attributing the same significance to the exorcisms of his Jewish compatriots.[363] What marked out Jesus' exorcisms was not just their success but the power by which he achieved that success.[364] That power is identified differently in the different retellings of the saying: either as 'the Spirit of God' (Matt. 12.28), that is, by implication, a plenitude of the (eschatological) Spirit which the other Jewish exorcists did not enjoy;[365] or as 'the finger of God' (Luke 11.20), that is, the (eschatological) equivalent to the power by which Moses overcame the Egyptian

---

360. E.g., Bultmann, *History* 162; Perrin, *Rediscovering* 63-67; Schlosser, *Règne* 137-39; Merkel, 'Gottesherrschaft' 142-44; Schürmann, *Gottes Reich* 106-108.

361. 'We also misunderstand the word if we understand it as saying that the Kingdom of God is present only proleptically' (Becker, *Jesus of Nazareth* 109); similarly Merklein, *Jesu Botschaft* 63-66; Gnilka, *Jesus of Nazareth* 129. Contrast R. H. Hiers, *The Historical Jesus and the Kingdom of God* (Gainesville: University of Florida, 1973): 'the defeat of the demons means . . . that the time for the establishment of God's Kingdom has come near' (63); similarly Buchanan, *Jesus* 31-33.

362. Davies and Allison miss the point by asserting a christological emphasis: '"If *I* cast out demons" . . . What matters is that *Jesus* cast out demons' (similarly Chilton, *Pure Kingdom* 68); and in asking 'How else but by God's power could Jewish exorcists cast out demons?' they ignore the strong note of realized eschatology (*Matthew* 2.339, 341). See also below, chapter 15 n. 384.

363. Bultmann, *History* 14; Kümmel, *Promise* 105-106; Perrin, *Rediscovering* 63; Sanders, *Jesus and Judaism* 134-35; Meier, *Marginal Jew* 2.410.

364. Dunn, *Jesus and the Spirit* 48. E. Grässer responds to the argument that there exists no qualitative difference between Jesus and other Jewish exorcists and that as an exorcist he is 'no unique phenomenon' quite sharply: '. . . as if the very fact that he brought the kingdom into play with his exorcisms did not make make him precisely that!' ('On Understanding the Kingdom of God' [1974], in Chilton, ed., *The Kingdom of God* 52-71 [here 56]).

365. It is almost universally agreed that Luke's 'finger' is more 'original' than Matthew's 'Spirit'; but a stronger case can be made for the latter than is usually appreciated (Dunn, *Jesus and the Spirit* 45-46; J.-M. Van Cangh, 'Par l'Esprit de Dieu — par le Doigt de Dieu', in Delobel, ed., *Logia* 337-42; further references in my 'Matthew 12:28/Luke 11:20' 196 n. 24; discussion in Meier, *Marginal Jew* 2.464 n. 51; see further P. W. van der Horst, '"Finger of God": Miscellaneous Notes on Luke 11:20 and Its Umwelt', in W. L. Petersen et al., eds., *Sayings of Jesus: Canonical and Non-Canonical,* T. Baarda FS [NovTSup 89; Leiden: Brill, 1997] 89-103). That the Spirit would be more fully poured out in the age to come was one strand in current Jewish expectation (see above, n. 65).

magicians.[366] But either way the point is the same: Jesus was remembered as claiming to be specially (eschatologically) empowered by God, and his consequent success as an exorcist was attributed to that fact. And this success was itself proof that the kingdom of God 'has come upon you *(ephthasen eph' hymas)*'.[367]

(3) The imagery of the third saying is also significant. Even without the context provided by both sequences (Mark and Q), it would be clear enough to a Jewish audience that the 'strong man' was an image for Satan and his possessions an image of the demoniacs.[368] Defeat of Satan, liberation of his captives, and specifically the 'binding' of Satan were looked forward to as part of the final climax of God's purpose, Satan bound and disabled for the ages (eternity?).[369] The point, then, is Jesus' claim, in effect, that this binding was already taking place,[370] indeed, that it had already taken place.[371] The strong man had been al-

366. An allusion to Exod. 8.19 (= 8.15 MT/LXX) would be self-evident: Pharaoh's magicians confess that Moses' miracles were wrought by 'the finger of God'. Indeed, the allusion may be more extensive: in CD 5.18-19 Jannes and Jambres, the names given to Pharaoh's magicians, are described as 'raised up' by Belial, that is, in effect, as effecting their miracles (in competition with Moses) by Belial's authority; the implication ties saying (2) much more closely to (1) and (3) than is at first apparent. See further my 'Matthew 12:28/Luke 11:20' 196. It is quite likely that such an exodus typology, with obvious eschatological overtones, was implicit in the saying from the first — 'a prelude to the liberation of Israel through the kingdom of God' (Theissen and Merz, *Historical Jesus* 258-60). On the originality of the saying as a saying of Jesus, see further Meier, *Marginal Jew* 2.413-17.

367. That the aorist of *phthanō* means 'has come/arrived/reached' cannot realistically be disputed (see particularly Kümmel, *Promise* 105-108; Beasley-Murray, *Jesus and the Kingdom* 75-80; Meier, *Marginal Jew* 2.412-13, 423 [with possible Aramaic reconstruction], 468 n. 70), though Caragounis insists that it denotes only imminence ('Kingdom of God' 423). See also above, §12.4a.

368. Contrast Buchanan, who consistently interprets Jesus' kingdom talk in political terms (see below, chapter 15 n. 35); here he suggests that the strong man was probably Rome and that binding him would require various kinds of sabotage (*Jesus* 215-16).

369. See above, n. 79. But we should recall that the length of time during which Satan is 'bound' varies in the texts cited; Tob. 3.17 and 8.3 remind us that there could be a temporary binding, for the purposes of a particular exorcism.

370. The Lukan version of the saying implies that Jesus is 'the stronger' (Luke 11.22), but in Mark the one who binds is not specified, and in Luke there is no particular christological emphasis given to the term (the equivalent fall of Satan in Luke 10.17-18 is occasioned by the disciples' success as exorcists, albeit in Jesus' name).

371. In Mark's layout it may be that he intended the 'when' of Satan's defeat to refer back to the temptation (particularly Jeremias, *Parables* 122-23; E. Best, *The Temptation and the Passion: The Markan Soteriology* [SNTSMS 2; Cambridge: Cambridge University, 1965] 15; Beasley-Murray, *Jesus and the Kingdom* 109-10; Wright, *Jesus* 457-59). But Mark 1.13 is not presented explicitly as a victory (Guelich, *Mark 1–8.26* 176-77). And we should beware of pressing the imagery of 3.27 as though it were allegorical in every detail; Tob. 3.17 and 8.3 also

ready disabled; that was why his possessions *(skeuē)* could be liberated from his control.[372]

Here it would be appropriate to mention also Luke 10.18. It is attested only by Luke, who gives it as Jesus' response to the return of the seventy(-two) disciples from their mission. They had witnessed the demons subjected to them in Jesus' name; that is, they too had enjoyed a successful ministry of exorcism. To which Jesus responds: 'I saw Satan fall like lightning from heaven'.[373] The implication is the same: exorcism by the power which Jesus commanded demonstrated the end of Satan's power.[374]

Even without this last poorly attested saying,[375] the thrust of the sequence of traditions is clear. Jesus was remembered not simply as a great exorcist, but also as claiming that his exorcisms demonstrated the fulfilment of hopes long cherished for a final release from the power of evil. If the manifestation of God's final reign was to be marked by the binding of Satan, then Jesus' exorcisms showed, to that extent at least, that the binding of Satan had already happened or was already happening, the final exercise of God's rule was already in effect.

e. Parables of Growth

One other group of texts deserve notice, although there is some dispute as to whether they are better considered with what I have covered above under §12.4.

---

remind us that exorcism and binding could be conceived as two sides of the one event. Ladd may be right in interpreting the sayings 'in terms of a spiritual defeat over Satan in the very fact of Jesus' ministry' (*Jesus and the Kingdom* 152-53).

372. *Skeuos* is used elsewhere of humans as 'vessels' of God (*Apoc. Mos.* 31.4; see also C. Maurer, *skeuos, TDNT* 7 [1971] 359-60), and in *T. Naph.* 8.6 for the wicked person as the devil's 'own peculiar instrument' or vessel. What is envisaged presumably is the sort of brigandage which, according to Josephus, became common in the decade before the Jewish revolt (*War.* 2.265); but the imagery would have been more widely familiar (Isa. 49.25; *Pss. Sol.* 5.3).

373. An actual vision of Jesus may but need not be implied (Bultmann, *History* 161 n. 2; Kümmel, *Promise* 113-14; Fitzmyer, *Luke* 860-62). J. Marcus dates the vision to Jesus' baptism ('Jesus' Baptismal Vision', *NTS* 41 [1995] 512-21). Similarly, Theissen and Merz wonder whether 'a reference to a vision of Jesus at his call has been preserved' (*Historical Jesus* 258). Becker, however, denies that a vision is in view (*Jesus of Nazareth* 108). At all events, there is far too little substance here to support Chilton's fanciful view of Jesus as an adept practitioner of merkabah mysticism (*Rabbi Jesus passim*).

374. Evans notes that the phrase used in Mark 3.26 (Satan 'has an end') echoes the expectation expressed in *T. Mos.* 10.1 ('Authenticating the Activities of Jesus' 15).

375. Note, e.g., Meier's reserve (*Marginal Jew* 2.492-93). In contrast, the Jesus Seminar give it a positive rating (Funk, *Five Gospels* 321), and Lüdemann is confident of its 'authenticity' (*Jesus* 329-30). Kollmann observes that it has been uninfluenced by post-Easter tradition formation (*Jesus* 194).

In his seminal work on the theme Dodd focused not only on 'parables of crisis' but also on 'parables of growth'.[376] They are important for us, since three of the 'parables of growth' are specifically designated kingdom parables (the last two also by *Thomas*) — the seed growing secretly (Mark 4.26-29), the wheat and the tares (Matt. 13.24-30/*GTh* 57), and the mustard seed (Mark 4.30-32 pars./*GTh* 20). There is also the parable of the sower to be considered, which is reproduced in all three Synoptics (Mark 4.2-9 pars.) and in *GTh* 9, with the same structure and point (three unfruitful soils contrasted with fruitful soil) and only minor storytelling variation.[377] And the parable of the leaven was also evidently reckoned as cut from the same cloth and also designated as a kingdom parable (Matt. 13.33/Luke 13.20-21/*GTh* 96).[378] The tendency to group material of similar theme is clearly evident, particularly in Mark and Matthew. The *Thomas* tradition suggests that the individual parables were also recalled separately, but the frequent repetition of the exhortation, 'Who has ears to hear, let him hear', attached to the end of *Thomas* parables, is an indication of widespread usage in the performance of Jesus' parables.[379] The memory of Jesus speaking on these themes is evidently well rooted in the tradition.

	Matthew	**Mark**	**Luke**	*GTh*
1. Sower	13.3-9	4.2-9	8.4b-8	9
2. Seed		4.26-29		21.4
3. Tares	13.24-30			57
4. Mustard Seed	13.31-32	4.30-32	13.18-19	20
5. Leaven	13.33		13.20-21	96

2. Mark 4.26-29	*GTh* 21.4
26 The kingdom of God is as if someone would scatter seed on the ground, 27 and would sleep and rise night and day, and the seed would sprout and grow, he does not know how. 28 The earth produces of itself, first the stalk, then the head, then the full grain in the head. 29 But when the grain is ripe, at once he goes in with his sickle, because the harvest has come.	. . . May there be a man of understanding among you. When the grain has ripened, he came quickly with his sickle in his hand (and) reaped it.

376. Dodd, *Parables* ch. 6.

377. See also Perrin, *Rediscovering* 155-59; Wright also gives particular attention to the parables of growth (*Jesus* 229-42).

378. On the details see Hultgren, *Parables* 406-407.

379. *GTh* 8.2; 21.5; 63.2; 65.2; 96.2 (also 24.2); cf. Mark 4.9 pars.; 4.23; Matt. 11.15; 13.43b; Luke 14.35b (also Rev. 13.9a).

3.	Matt. 13.24-30	GTh 57
	24 <u>The kingdom of</u> heaven may be compared to someone who sowed good <u>seed</u> in his field; 25 but while everybody was asleep, an <u>enemy</u> came and <u>sowed weeds among the</u> wheat, and then went away. 26 So when the plants came up and bore grain, then the weeds appeared as well. 27 And the slaves of the householder came and said to him, 'Master, did you not sow good seed in your field? Where, then, did these weeds come from?' 28 He answered, 'An enemy has done this'. The slaves said to him, 'Then do you want us to go and gather them?' 29 But he replied, 'No; for in gathering the weeds you would uproot the wheat along with them. 30 Let both of them grow together until the harvest; and at harvest time I will tell the reapers, Collect the weeds first and bind them in bundles to be burned, but gather the wheat into my barn'.	<u>The kingdom of</u> the Father is like a man who had (good) <u>seed</u>. His <u>enemy</u> came by night (and) <u>sowed</u> a <u>weed among the</u> good seed. The man did not allow them to pull up the weed. He said to them, 'Lest you go to pull up the weed, and you pull up the wheat along with it'. For on the day of the harvest the weed will appear; they will be pulled up and burned.

4. Matt. 13.31-32	Mark 4.30-32	Luke 13.18-19	GTh 20
31 He put before them another parable: '<u>The kingdom of</u> heaven <u>is like a mustard seed</u> that someone took and sowed in his field; 32 it is the smallest of all the seeds, but when it has grown it is the greatest of shrubs and becomes a tree, so that <u>the birds of the air</u> come and <u>make nests in its branches</u>'.	30 He also said, 'With what can we compare <u>the kingdom of</u> God, or what parable will we use for it? 31 It <u>is like a mustard seed</u>, which, when sown upon the ground, is the smallest of all the seeds on earth; 32 yet when it is sown it comes up and becomes the greatest of all shrubs, and puts forth large branches, so that <u>the birds of the air</u> can make nests in its shade'.	18 He said therefore, 'What is <u>the kingdom of</u> God like? And to what should I compare it? 19 It <u>is like a mustard seed</u> that someone took and sowed in his garden; it grew and became a tree, and <u>the birds of the air</u> made nests in its branches'.	The disciple(s) said to Jesus, 'Tell us what <u>the kingdom of</u> heaven is like'. He said to them, '<u>It is like a</u> grain of <u>mustard seed</u>, smaller than all seeds. But when it falls on the earth which has been cultivated, it puts forth a great branch (and) becomes a shelter for (the) <u>birds</u> of heaven'.

All three have been touched on already.[380] The point here is simply that such parables liken the kingdom to a process of growth or development, but also of climax. Dodd justifiably protested against the assumption that what is envisaged is a period of indeterminate (hidden) growth only now beginning to take place,[381]

380. (2) and (3) under judgment (§12.4e), and (4) under the theme of eschatological reversal (§12.4c) as an equally or more appropriate heading. That (2) goes back to Jesus in some form is agreed by the Jesus Seminar (Funk, *Five Gospels* 58-59) and Lüdemann, *Jesus* 31.

381. The older Liberal view, stressing the gradualness of the growth and so also the time intervening before the harvest (see, e.g., those listed by Ladd, *Jesus and the Kingdom* 185 n. 42), remains attractive to Gnilka, *Jesus* 139-44, Becker, *Jesus* 73, 122-24, and Theissen and Merz, *Historical Jesus* 261. Contrast Kümmel: 'it is not the growth of the crop, but the certain

and argued instead that the parables look back from the end of the process of growth, from the time of harvest.[382] In view of Matt. 9.37-38/Luke 10.2/*GTh* 73 the point cannot be ignored:[383] Jesus was recalled describing the harvest as here already, ready to be reaped; God's rule had already come to its expected fruition. On the other hand, both Matthew and Luke, in the mission instructions which follow, include the commission to preach, 'The kingdom of heaven/God has drawn near' (Matt. 10.7/Luke 10.9). So the point should not be pressed.[384] We should rather hesitate before setting these parables firmly into one or other of the alternative time-frames reviewed above.[385] They belong to the scatter of images on which Jesus probably drew in his preaching of God's kingdom, and he may have been a good deal less concerned about questions of timing than are modern questers. The parables of growth are worth noting at this point precisely because they express the tension and diversity within the Jesus tradition's talk of the kingdom's coming.[386]

In sum, it should now be clear that the Jesus tradition contains a second strong strand in the kingdom motif which emphasizes that in some sense the kingdom has come, is already present. As with the other (future) strand, the term 'kingdom' itself does not always feature. And again there are plenty of indications of the tradition being retold in a variety of performance variants. But the strand is held together by a common sense of fulfilment, of a new thing happening of supreme importance, of the blessings expected for the age to come already being experienced, of a complete change of tone from the Baptist's message, of

---

arrival of the harvest which nothing can influence, that is the point of the parable [Mark 4.26-29]' (*Promise* 128). The harvest would come 'only through the miracle worked by God: *automatē hē gē karpophorei*' (Hengel, *Charismatic Leader* 60), 'independent of every human act' (Bultmann, *Theology* 1.8), 'unfathomably, miraculously, without visible cause' (Schrage, *Ethics* 21).

382. Dodd, *Parables* 176-80, 185-86, 191, 193; Taylor, *Mark* 266, 268-69 (but recognizing that the idea of growth is integral to the parables in view).

383. Matt. 9.37-38/Luke 10.2 was the decisive factor for Dodd (*Parables* 178-79, 183, 187, 191).

384. Cf. R. Schnackenburg, *God's Rule and Kingdom* (Freiburg: Herder, 1963) 159. Hultgren represents the majority view in seeing the presentness of the kingdom mirrored more in the implication of patient waiting, of little beginnings, of a hidden but irresistible force (*Parables* 389, 398, 407).

385. As Perrin observes, 'The emphasis is upon God, upon what he is doing and what he will do, and the parable, like all the parables of this group, is an expression of the supreme confidence of Jesus in God and God's future. . . . Out of the experience of God in the present learn to have confidence in God's future' (*Rediscovering* 158-59). Oakman (*Jesus* 123-28) and Crossan (*Historical Jesus* 276-81) focus more on the ironic (or shocking) humour of using weeds (and leaven) to image the kingdom.

386. Cf. Beasley-Murray, *Jesus and the Kingdom* 124-25, 126-27.

Satan's power decisively (finally?) broken. It is difficult to think of a note of such persistence and variety having ever been absent from the memories of Jesus' preaching and teaching. On the contrary, this note of kingdom already come, of God's (eschatological) rule already active in the present, must have been characteristic of the Jesus tradition from the first. And that can only be because it was characteristic of Jesus' preaching and teaching.

12.6. Solving the Riddle

a. In Summary

The motif of 'the kingdom of God/heaven' spoke (and speaks) of at least two things fundamental to any quest of Jesus. (1) The Jesus tradition bears clear testimony to the centrality of the kingship of God in Jesus' preaching. That God was 'king', with all the implications of absolute sovereignty and power which the very title encapsulated, was also axiomatic in Jesus' framework of understanding and fundamental to his message. Jesus was evidently quite certain that what God does/has done/will do is of far greater importance than anything contrived on earth — a quantum leap of perspective to a different plane of motivation. For him it was all-important to align individual and societal goals by that reference point.

(2) Jesus was certain that God had a purpose for his creation which was unfolding, indeed, was reaching towards its climax, and that his own mission was an expression of that purpose and a vital agency towards its fulfilment. We have only begun to unpack these two dimensions of Jesus' kingdom talk, and the following chapters will continue the process, focusing particularly on the immediate implications for discipleship (How then should those who responded to his message of the kingdom henceforth live?) and for Jesus' own role in the kingdom and its coming.[387] In this chapter we have had to be content to outline the background to Jesus' usage, to sketch its most immediate features (leaving aside the often complementary talk of the Son of Man), and to focus attention on what has been the main question raised (the kingdom as present/future).

In sum, we can assume that the basic reference of what appears to have been his most characteristic phrase, 'the kingdom of God', was given by the traditional language of Jewish devotion. However, he is not remembered as talking about God as 'king' or worshipping God as 'king of the universe'. All his re-

---

387. A useful survey of recent debate may be found in D. C. Duling, 'Kingdom of God, Kingdom of Heaven', *ABD* 4.56-69 (here 62-65).

membered preaching of God's kingdom has to do in greater or less degree with what had previously been hopes and expectations for the future.[388]

Some of these hopes he claimed were already being fulfilled. Things were happening that earlier generations had longed to see. Something new, of life-changing value, was already before his hearers. Sight was being restored to the blind, the lame were walking, even the dead raised. Good news was being preached to the poor: the kingdom was theirs! The Baptist's message of imminent judgment had to be qualified in the light of what was already happening through Jesus' ministry. Satan's rule was already broken. There was an eschatological harvest already to be reaped.[389]

At other times Jesus spoke in still future terms. Of the kingdom of God pressingly close: it had drawn near (in his own ministry); it posed a crisis which had to be responded to at once. Of the kingdom of God as a sort of utopian ideal for the future on the earth: the last first, the humble exalted, the despised already able to press into it; some at least of the promised reward could be given in a further phase of history. Of the kingdom of God as a post-mortem state: to be 'entered into' after suffering and self-sacrifice. Of the kingdom of God as a final condition: following the unprecedented suffering anticipated in apocalyptic thought (and by the Baptist), following a final judgment involving other generations and nations, an angel-like existence.

Here then the Jesus quester is faced with a major problem. Both present and future strands of Jesus' preaching on the kingdom of God seem to be firmly rooted in the Jesus tradition and well established in all streams of the tradition. In the light of this evidence we have little choice other than to conclude that Jesus' teaching was remembered as being characterized by both emphases. Attempts to eliminate one or the other or to give one a weight which overwhelms the other have not generally been counted successful.[390] Individual items within the vari-

---

388. 'Jesus is not a "marginal Jew" in his eschatological preaching' (Theissen and Merz, *Historical Jesus* 276).

389. Riches argues, with reference to such data, that Jesus 'transformed' the traditional associations of the term 'kingdom' (*Jesus* ch. 5, particularly 103-104), but neglects the wider associations listed in §12.2c above, which suggest that 'transformation' is not the most appropriate term to use.

390. For example, Weiss's future emphasis is one-sidedly pressed by Hiers, *Historical Jesus;* Sanders is clear that in any choice between 'present' and 'future' the emphasis has to be put on the kingdom as 'immediately future' (*Jesus and Judaism* 152); Allison, *Jesus of Nazareth,* and Ehrman, *Jesus,* press the case more strongly. Caragounis finds no 'single kingdom of God saying which unequivocally demands to be taken in the present sense' ('Kingdom of God' 424). On the other side, Dodd argued that 'Jesus intended to proclaim the Kingdom of God not as something to come in the near future, but as a matter of present experience' (*Parables* 46); in turn Käsemann argued that the irreconcilable contradiction between the two emphases could be explained only by postulating that the 'already present' emphasis was authentic, and the 'still to

ous sequences may be detected as elaborations and developments of particular emphases or more specific themes. But it is impossible to root out sequences or either emphasis *in toto* without seriously distorting the tradition. Such would probably have been the scholarly consensus until the 1970s,[391] and most still find themselves driven to conclude that some sort of both-and, already–not yet description is unavoidable.[392]

b. Does Q Provide the Key?

The major developments since the 1970s consensus have been the stratification of Q and the greater significance accorded to the *Gospel of Thomas*. As already noted, Kloppenborg has disentangled a primary sapiential layer in Q composed of six 'wisdom speeches'(Q[1]) and concluded that a second apocalyptic layer, made up of five judgment speeches (Q[2]), was worked into the texture of Q[1].[393] The fact that Q[1] seems to accord so well with the non-apocalyptic character of *Thomas* strengthened Koester's conviction that *Thomas* not only contains early material but was itself composed very early. More to the point here, the mutual

---

come' emphasis reflected the teaching of the early communities ('The Beginnings of Christian Theology' [1960], *New Testament Questions of Today* [London: SCM, 1969] 82-107 [here 101-102]); and we have already noted the Jesus Seminar's antipathy to an 'eschatological Jesus' (chapter 4 n. 174 above). Koester, however, points out that the age of Augustus was an age of 'realized eschatology' ('Jesus the Victim' 10-13), thus undermining the principal argument for 'realized eschatology' as the most distinctive feature of Jesus' message on the criterion of dissimilarity.

391. Ladd's distinction between present 'fulfilment' and future 'consummation' well expressed the consensus position *(Jesus and the Kingdom)*. Typical of the existentialist perspective of the Bultmann school is H. Conzelmann, *An Outline of the Theology of the New Testament* (London: SCM, 1969): 'The contradiction between the "present" and the future sayings is only an apparent one. The two have the same significance for human existence: man's attitude of the moment towards the coming kingdom' (114). Manson's argument (*Teaching* 117-30) that the coming of the kingdom in Jesus' ministry is to be identified with one or other of the turning points in that ministry, most probably Peter's confession (Mark 8.27-30), is a variation of the older idea of two clear stages in Jesus' ministry, which Schweitzer developed in his own way (§4.5a above).

392. E.g., Schürmann, *Gottes Reich* 143; Stuhlmacher, *Biblische Theologie* 1.72; Gnilka, *Jesus of Nazareth* 135, 146, 149; Meier, *Marginal Jew* 2.450-54; Theissen and Merz, *Historical Jesus* 275. Crossan criticizes Meier for being 'honestly unable to combine what are not only divergent but even opposing strata of the Jesus tradition' (*Birth* 145-46), as though the interpreter's 'inabilities' should be a determinative factor in assessment of data. It is always a puzzle how commentators can be so sure of the irreconcilability of elements which Q and the Synoptic Evangelists were content to put side by side.

393. See above, chapter 4 n. 166.

confirmation afforded by Q¹ and *Thomas* to each other became the basis for the argument of the Jesus Seminar and Crossan that the earliest layer of the Jesus tradition was itself sapiential and non-apocalyptic. From which point it is but a step to conclude that Jesus' own preaching had the same character. That is to say, Jesus' preaching of the kingdom of God did not envisage any divine intervention into history, any 'apocalyptic' coming of the kingdom. The note particularly of judgment on 'this generation' entered the Jesus tradition, either through the influence of disciples of the Baptist joining the Jesus movement[394] or as a result of the failure of the early church's mission to Israel.[395]

This is an impressively coherent argument. But it contains several flaws. (1) As Kloppenborg has been the first to insist, the compositional history of Q does not determine the date or origin of the material drawn in to Q at the different stages in its composition.[396] Even if we are still able to distinguish later from earlier composition — and I remain unpersuaded that we have adequate criteria for such a task in a document whose text, content, and length remain so uncertain — it need only mean that Q¹ brought together one strand of the Jesus tradition.[397] Q¹, we might say, was simply an extension of the practice, of which we have seen numerous examples in §§12.4-5, of grouping together material of similar character and emphasis within the much more diverse range of the Jesus tradition.

(2) The argument trades uncomfortably on the 'one document per community' hypothesis — as though Q¹ constituted proof in itself that any community knowing and using it knew of and used no other Jesus tradition, or, alternatively, was opposed to another community which had (only) the other emphasis.[398]

(3) Despite Koester's best efforts, his argument that *Thomas* bears witness to an early non-eschatological stage in the Jesus tradition cannot escape the charge of *petitio principii* (question-begging).[399] We have noted above several

---

394. Funk, *Honest to Jesus* 168: the disciples of John who followed Jesus 'had not understood the subtleties of Jesus' position'.

395. See above, n. 222.

396. See particularly Kloppenborg, 'Sayings Gospel Q' 323 n. 70, 337.

397. In this case the widespread appearance of the motif of judgment on 'this generation' within the Synoptic tradition (Matt. 11.16/Luke 7.31; Matt. 12.41-42/Luke 11.31-32; Matt. 23.36/Luke 11.51; Mark 8.12, 38; Matt. 12.45; Luke 11.30, 50; 17.25; see also Meier, *Marginal Jew* 2.209 n. 134) and its relative absence elsewhere in the NT suggest a motif recalled as characteristic of Jesus' teaching and consequently included in retellings of the Jesus tradition (see also above, §§7.4c and 12.4e). 'It is characteristic of the "this *genea*" terminology in the New Testament that it is almost entirely to be found only in the Synoptic Gospels and there exclusively on the lips of Jesus. It is thus firmly established in the early Christian traditions as an expression used by Jesus and related to his preaching' (E. Lövestam, *Jesus and 'This Generation': A New Testament Study* [CBNT 25; Stockholm: Almquist and Wiksell, 1995] 102).

398. See above §7.4b.

399. See further the frequent references to Koester in §§7.6 and 8 above.

instances where it can be equally or more persuasively argued that *Thomas* has de-eschatologized the tradition which it has drawn upon.[400]

(4) The argument also trades, with equal discomfort, on the literary paradigm of tradition transmission, as though one could reach not only the earliest but even the original form by simple process of subtracting redaction from the later versions. But if my appeal to recognize the distinctive character of the oral traditioning process has any merit, we will have to acknowledge also both a continuity of tradition from the start and the unlikelihood of major new emphases being interjected which conflicted in serious measure with the established tradition.

(5) Too little weight has been given to the lack of support for the corollary hypotheses on which the coherence of the argument depends. The opposition between Jesus and John is overstated; the sequence discussed above (§12.5c), as well as the affirmation that the gospel began with John (§11.2c), indicate a more positive relation between them and that the break with John was not necessarily a denial of John's message.[401] The only disciples of John that we know to have joined Jesus did so at the very beginning (§11.2b); there is no other evidence of disciples of John joining the Jesus movement later and bringing in John's apocalyptic preaching as something different (if that was what distinguished the two, one would presumably join Jesus only in order to leave behind John's preaching!). And as noted above, it makes more sense to read the judgment pronounced on the Galilean towns in the context of Jesus' known Galilean ministry rather than in the context of an early church mission of which we have no other evidence.

All in all, the arguments based on the Q^1/*Thomas* conjunction are insufficient to break the earlier consensus. The weight, spread, and consistency of the twofold emphasis in Jesus' proclamation of the kingdom cannot so readily be nullified. Jesus was remembered as speaking of both the kingdom's future coming and its impact already in the present. The earlier tradents, no more than the Evangelists, evidently found no difficulty or inconsistency in recalling both emphases as integral to Jesus' message. That fact should be allowed to guide reconstructions of Jesus' preaching more fully than has usually been the case.

Can the issue be handled more sophisticatedly than by simply excising one or the other emphasis? For the presence of both emphases in the Jesus tradition does still pose something of a riddle to the modern interpreter. To us, if not to the first tradents, a claim that the kingdom is both yet to come and already active in the present does seem to pose difficulties of conceptualisation. How could Jesus have held and taught both emphases? What understanding of 'the kingdom of

---

400. See also Allison, *Jesus of Nazareth* 126-27, citing particularly *GTh* 35, 41 and 103, but referring also to *GTh* 10,16, and 91.

401. Crossan, e.g., argues that Jesus broke with John over the Baptist's apocalyptic message (*Historical Jesus* 259).

God' is involved? The most promising way to handle such questions is probably to pose again the three key questions outlined above (§12.3).

c. A Grand Narrative?

One solution to the riddle has been to read the Jesus tradition as a whole within an overarching hypothesis, a meta-narrative. Indeed, many would say that without such a grid into which to fit the data, the evidence is capable of too many divergent readings. Halvor Moxnes reminds us that Protestants were for a long time attracted by the master narrative of a decline from the age of spirit and freedom to the age of institutions and control ('early Catholicism' as a negative description).[402] And as noted earlier, the grand narrative of modernity actually provided the key for the old Liberal questers: a non-miracleworking, moral teacher affirmed a European optimistic individualism born of self-conscious cultural supremacy, industrial might, and imperialistic conquest. A century ago the paradigm shift occasioned by Weiss and Schweitzer made Jewish apocalyptic eschatology the story within which Jesus' kingdom proclamation was to be read. And though the apocalyptic paradigm was challenged at various points, for most of the twentieth century it retained its paradigmatic sway over Jesus questers, as it continues to do over a significant number.[403] But now that paradigm in turn has been undermined for many, and other hermeneutical keys are being sought.[404] Those Jesus questers unwilling to align themselves with postmodernism's pluralism and concomitant rejection of all grand narratives still look for the grand narrative which will provide the key to resolve the riddle of Jesus' kingdom preaching. Two such have been worked out most fully during the final decade of the twentieth century — by Dominic Crossan and Tom Wright.

(1) In his *Birth of Christianity,* in which he provides, as it were, the footnotes lacking in his *Historical Jesus,* Crossan makes clear that he operates with a grand narrative drawn from cross-cultural anthropology ('the Lenski-Kautsky model') — the grand narrative of 'peasant society', or egalitarian peasant society,[405] exploited by and resistant to the ruling classes.[406] On this broad template

---

402. H. Moxnes, 'The Historical Jesus: From Master Narrative to Cultural Context', *BTB* 28 (1998) 135-49 (here 138).

403. Sanders, *Jesus and Judaism* 10; also *Historical Figure* 183; Allison, *Jesus of Nazareth* 36-44; Lüdemann, *Jesus, passim.*

404. See also Moxnes's critique of other 'master narratives' on offer ('Historical Jesus' 138-48).

405. *Historical Jesus* 263-64.

406. *Birth* 151-59, 166-73; '*Peasant* is an interactive term for farmers who are exploited and oppressed' (216).

(not just peasant Judaism, but peasant society as such), Crossan stretches some of the particularities of Galilean archaeology[407] and finds confirmation of escalating peasant protest and turmoil at the time of Jesus in Horsley's thesis to that effect.[408] Together with his literary analysis by chronological stratification,[409] the result is one of the most impressive methodological *tours-de-force* since Strauss a century and a half earlier. When Jesus' kingdom preaching is located within this framework, Crossan argues that, while the kingdom could have been understood in apocalyptic terms at the time of Jesus, it was the *sapiential* kingdom which provides the best fit: 'The sapiential Kingdom looks to the present rather than the future. . . . One enters that Kingdom by wisdom or goodness, by virtue, justice, or freedom. It is a style of life for now rather than a hope of life for the future'.[410]

There are several problems with this grand narrative. For one thing, although Crossan protests that he does not wish simply to extrapolate from the Mediterranean world as though it was a single cultural unit, or to generalise too straightforwardly from the universals of peasant society, his treatment of Judaism is very limited and his analysis of the conditions in lower Galilee very restricted. But we really do need to have a clearer idea of what Judaism meant at the time of Jesus, of its distinctives, and how it shaped Jewish identity, in Galilee as well. There were national and religious factors operative in Jewish society and not simply social and economic factors, and arguably the former provided the dominant narrative by which even Jewish peasants made sense of their lives.[411] That narrative cannot simply be fitted into a larger economic narrative, *à la* Marx; the distinctives of Jewish tradition and identity actually form a counter-narrative, which for Jesus at least seems to have been determinative, and for his message of the kingdom not least.

For another, the half-dozen episodes of protest narrated by Josephus for the

---

407. *Birth* ch. 13.

408. *Birth* 148, 210, referring to R. A. Horsley and J. S. Hanson, *Bandits, Prophets, and Messiahs: Popular Movements in the Time of Jesus* (Minneapolis: Seabury, 1985); see also Crossan, *Historical Jesus* chs. 7, 9 (particularly 184-85), and 10 (particularly 218-19).

409. See above, chapter 4 n. 163.

410. *Historical Jesus* 284-92 (here 292); also *Jesus* 55-58.

411. See particularly the critique by S. Freyne, 'Galilean Questions to Crossan's Mediterranean Jesus', in Arnal and Desjardins, eds., *Whose Historical Jesus?* 63-91 ('If one were to follow Crossan's methodology to its logical conclusion . . . it would be difficult to locate Jesus anywhere, certainly not in Galilee', 64), and the warnings on this point by M. Sawacki, *Crossing Galilee: Architectures of Contact in the Occupied Land of Jesus* (Harrisburg: Trinity, 2000) 73-80; cf. J. A. Overman, 'Jesus of Galilee and the Historical Peasant', in Edwards and McCollough, eds., *Archaeology and the Galilee* 67-73 (here 69-72). M. Cserhati, *Methods and Models in the Third Quest of the Historical Jesus* (Durham PhD, 2000), also warns against the ideal construct of an egalitarian peasant society (as in Crossan, *Historical Jesus* 263).

period are too easily linked into a single trajectory of escalating unrest and violence. But with the exception of the turmoil after the death of Herod the Great
and the build-up to the first revolt in 66, all we have are a few isolated and idiosyncratic incidents, whose impact in Galilee during the 20s and early 30s was
probably minimal. For the rest, and during the ministry of Jesus, there is little indication of escalating unrest — injustice, oppression, and complaint no doubt,
but the impression of a moving escalator of heightening protest again owes more
to a larger generalisation read into the particularities of Jesus' historical situation
with too little care for the particularities themselves.[412]

Finally, it is rather surprising that Crossan draws his illustration and documentation for the sapiential kingdom entirely from diaspora Jewish (Philo, Wisdom of Solomon) and Greek literature *(Sentences of Sextus)*.[413] Quite how that
demonstrates an option open to Jesus is not clear, especially as the absence of
king/kingdom language in Jewish wisdom is so noticeable. In contrast the theme
is prominent in psalms, prophets, and apocalypses (§12.2b). All of which suggests
that Crossan is again extrapolating too quickly from a much wider hypothesis and
pushing unjustifiably hard for a non-apocalyptic sense for 'kingdom' as the context of meaning which would inform the hearing of Jesus' Galilean audiences.

(2) Wright is the most forthright in his assertion of the need for the quester
to work with a grand narrative.[414] He criticizes his predecessors for 'pseudo-
atomistic work on apparently isolated fragments' and argues instead that 'the real
task' is that of 'major hypothesis and serious verification'.[415] 'The scholar must
work with a large hypothesis, and must appeal, ultimately, to the large picture of
how everything fits together as the justification for smaller-scale decisions'.[416] In
other words, verification essentially consists in demonstrating how well individual details fit within the framework of the larger story. The point here is that the
phrase 'kingdom of God' evokes a story which may well be present even when
the phrase is absent, and individual sayings can be made sense of only in relation
to that story.[417] Wright's *Jesus and the Victory of God* is a massive exposition of

412. See above, §9.8.

413. *Historical Jesus* 287-91, simply reproduced in *Jesus* 56-58. The *Sentences of
Sextus* is 'a collection of Greek wisdom sayings assembled by a Christian redactor probably
near the end of the 2d century CE' (F. Wisse, *ABD* 5.1146-47).

414. Wright, *New Testament and People of God:* 'critical realism' as he understands it
'sees knowledge of particulars as taking place within the larger framework of the story or
worldview which forms the basis of the observer's way of being in relation to the world' (37);
'simplicity of outline, elegance in handling the details within it, the inclusion of all the parts of
the story, and the ability of the story to make sense beyond its immediate subject-matter: these
are what counts' (42); see further 98-109.

415. Wright, *Jesus* 33; see also 51, 87-89, 133.

416. *Jesus* 79.

417. *Jesus* 224-25.

Jesus on that basis, quite as impressive and enchanting as Crossan's, as one might have hoped for from two who take so seriously the medium of story in their work.

The problems with Wright's exposition begin with his identification of the grand narrative. He has no doubt that 'the controlling story' is that of 'exile and restoration':[418] that is, the conviction of most of Jesus' contemporaries that Israel was still in exile[419] and the preaching of Jesus to the effect that the exile was now over. The proclamation that 'the kingdom of God is at hand' summed up 'the entire narrative of Israel's new exodus, her final return from exile'.[420] There are three problems with this.

First, Wright exaggerates the importance of the theme of return from exile in Palestinian Judaism. The return of the scattered outcasts of Israel to the homeland in accordance with the original schema of Deuteronomy 30 was certainly a feature of Jewish eschatological hope.[421] But there is no real evidence that *those who actually were living in the land* thought of themselves as still in exile. Such a hypothesis hardly squares with the amazing hymn of praise to Simon the High Priest in ben Sira 50[422] or with the confidence that the purification of altar and temple attested the restoration of Israel's heritage (2 Macc. 2.17).[423] And the Sadducean priests responsible for the twice daily *Tamid* offering in the Temple presumably did not think of themselves as still in exile.[424] The hypothesis hardly

---

418. *Jesus* 245, 576-77. Sanders speaks more cautiously of 'a common hope for the restoration of Israel which could embrace a variety of themes' (*Jesus and Judaism* 124).

419. Particularly *New Testament and People of God* 268-72; *Jesus* xvii-xviii, 126-27, 203-204.

420. *Jesus* 244.

421. See above, §12.2c. Texts like Daniel, Tobit, and Baruch, of course, were written from the perspective of those still scattered among the nations (Dan. 9.3-19; Tob. 13.3-18; Bar. 2.11-15; 3.7-14). Such imaginative living again (as in liturgy) through epochal events of Israel's history — covenants with the patriarchs, passover and exodus, wilderness wanderings and entry into the promised land, Davidic kingdom and resilient faith under oppression, exile and return, Maccabean triumph, and loss of Temple (70 CE) — should not be treated woodenly or reduced to a single motif.

422. See Hayward, *Jewish Temple* chs. 3-4. The prayer in Sir. 36.13, 16 ('Gather all the tribes of Jacob, that they may inherit the land as in days of old') 'is for God to bring back to the Holy Land all the Jews who never returned after the Exile' (P. W. Skehan and A. A. Di Lella, *Ben Sira* [AB 39; New York: Doubleday, 1987] 422). The appeal for deliverance from oppression (36.1-22) is of a piece with the lamentation Psalms (Psalms 43, 54–57, 109, 140–41, and 143) and does not presuppose that the speaker believed himself or those who had already returned to the promised land to be still in exile.

423. I. H. Jones, 'Disputed Questions in Biblical Studies: 4. Exile and Eschatology', *ExpT* 112 (2000-1) 401-405, justifiably criticizes Wright for taking texts out of context, referring to Tob. 13.5-7; 2 Macc. 1.27-29; and Bar. 3.6-8 (402).

424. M. Casey, 'Where Wright Is Wrong', *JSNT* 69 (1998) 95-103 (here 99-100). R. P.

fits with the confidence of blamelessness on the part of a Pharisee like Saul (Phil. 3.6), and 'the righteous'/'sinners' antithesis in the *Psalms of Solomon* evidently worked with a frame of reference which was not dependent on the exile-restoration paradigm. The Qumran community certainly made use of the exile-restoration motif, but in different ways: a return from 'Damascus' already accomplished (CD 1.4-8),[425] an exile from Jerusalem in the wilderness (of Judea!),[426] and the threat of future exile to the wicked (repeating the pattern of Deut. 29.27-28).[427] The complexity of the use of the exile imagery is not adequately caught by concluding simply that the sect still considered itself in exile.[428] The same point about the complexity of the motif of restoration can be made with regard to *Jubilees*[429] and the 'sign prophets' in Josephus (*Ant.* 20.97-98, 167-72).[430] And generally it goes beyond the evidence to deduce that those

---

Carroll sees the absence of 'any sense of the permanence of the diaspora experience' in the prophetic literature as reflecting 'the point of view of the Jerusalem community' ('Deportation and Diasporic Discourses in the Prophetic Literature', in Scott, ed., *Exile* 63-85 [here 83]). 'The elite community regarded Jeremiah's prophecy as so entirely fulfilled, so thoroughly vindicated as to be no longer relevant . . .' (B. Halpern, 'The New Names of Isaiah 62:4: Jeremiah's Reception in the Restoration and Politics of "Third Isaiah"', *JBL* 117 [1998] 623-43 [here 630]).

425. 'CD does not mention the sixth century BCE return directly, because the writer considered the exile to have ceased only with the foundation of his own community' (J. G. Campbell, 'Essene-Qumran Origins in the Exile: A Scriptural Basis', *JJS* 46 [1995] 143-56 [here 148]).

426. M. G. Abegg, 'Exile and the Dead Sea Scrolls' in Scott, ed., *Exile* 111-27 (here 120-24), cites 1QpHab 11.4-8 (the 'exile' [*galot*] of the Teacher of Righteousness); 1QH 12.8-9 ('they drive me from my land'); 1QM 1.2-3 ('the exiles [*golâ*] of the desert'); 4Q171 2.26–3.1 ('the returnees/repentant from the desert'); 4Q177 8-10 ('exile'?); 4Q390 1 5-6 (the first to go up 'from the land of their captivity' [*m'rtz šbim,* an echo of Jer. 30.10; 46.27] in order to build the sanctuary, who will not join in the evil as of the pre-exilic period); cf. references to the community in the desert (1QS 8.13-14; 9.19-20). 4Q161 2.14, 'when they returned from the wilderness of the pe[ople]s', evidently echoes Ezek. 20.35, with its conception of the wilderness as a purgative intermediate stage between exodus from the lands of the diaspora and entry into the land itself (20.33-38).

427. 4Q169 3-4 4.1-4; Abegg fills out 4QMMT C21b-22 in the same terms ('Exile' 122-23).

428. As Abegg does ('Exile' 120 n. 38, 121).

429. B. Halpern-Amaru, 'Exile and Return in *Jubilees*', in Scott, ed., *Exile* 127-44, concludes: 'from the postexilic perspective of the author, restoration of a lost purity, not exile and return to the Land, is the signature of the imminent eschaton' (144).

430. C. A. Evans, 'Aspects of Exile and Restoration in the Proclamation of Jesus and the Gospels', in Scott, ed., *Exile* 299-328 (more or less equivalent to 'Jesus and the Continuing Exile of Israel', in Newman, ed., *Jesus and the Restoration of Israel* 77-100), is unwilling for the obvious imagery of reenacting the conquest of the promised land (the parting of the Jordan, the collapse of city walls) to stand without pressing the corollary that such movements must have 'regarded Israel as in a state of bondage, even exile' (305).

living in the land at the time of Jesus, who attended the Temple regularly or in pilgrimage, thought of themselves as still in exile.[431]

Second, it should be evident from the outline of Jewish expectation in §12.2c above that there was no single comprehensive grand narrative shaping the thought of Jesus' contemporaries. Return of the scattered outcasts to the land was certainly a prominent feature, but did not itself constitute the grand narrative of which all other elements of expectation were only a part. A major weakness of Wright's 'major hypothesis' therefore is his assumption that 'return from exile' (and Yahweh's return to Zion) were in effect the only 'controlling stories' which need to be considered as the framework for Jesus' kingdom preaching. But our analysis above (§§12.4-5) provided plenty evidence that other motifs of Jewish expectation were very much in play in Jesus' teaching as recalled by his disciples. I list them in the order of §12.2c:

2. the removal of disabilities and defects (§12.5c),
3. the imagery of a great feast (§12.4f, §12.5b),
7. probably an eschatological pilgrimage of the nations (§12.4c),
8. the meek inheriting the land (§12.4c),
9. suffering (§12.4d),
11. the defeat of Satan (§12.5d), and
12. (final) judgment (§12.4e).

Consequently, the question posed in §12.3a returns with renewed force: whether the evidence justifies the major hypothesis of a single, coherent grand narrative 'controlling' the range of Jewish expectation at the time of Jesus.[432]

Third, the most serious weakness of Wright's grand hypothesis is his inability to demonstrate that the narrative of return from exile was a controlling factor in Jesus' own teaching. It will not do simply to insert passages into the assumed narrative framework or to read tradition such as we have assembled above (§§12.4-5) through spectacles provided by the controlling story, as though by invocation of the mantra 'end of exile', 'return from exile' the interpretation of these traditions becomes clear.[433] 'Serious verification' requires demonstration of at least a fair number of plausible echoes and allusions to return from exile

---

431. See further F. G. Downing, 'Exile in Formative Judaism', *Making Sense in (and of) the First Christian Century* (JSNTS 197; Sheffield: Sheffield Academic, 2000) 148-68.

432. Cf. Borg's criticism of Sanders (using different imagery): 'the lens of "Jesus as prophet of restoration eschatology" enables us to see too limited a range of data and forces us to set aside too much data. Its explanatory power is inadequate' (*Jesus in Contemporary Scholarship* 81).

433. A disturbing feature of Wright's treatment is his willingness simply to cite texts without any supporting analysis (e.g., *Jesus* 166, 179-80).

within the Jesus tradition itself. The most plausible is the parable of the prodigal son, who repents and returns from 'a far country' (Luke 15.11-24).[434] But the grand narrative of return from exile proves inadequate to explain the second half of the parable, where the refusal of the elder brother to accept the younger clearly works with the different motif of contrasting pairs.[435] And Wright hardly strengthens his case by giving a pivotal place to the parable of the sower (Mark 4.2-8 pars.).[436] The problem is not that an allusion to the idea of the returnees from exile as seed being sown (again) in the land is farfetched.[437] It is rather that planting and fruitful growth are metaphors of much more diverse application[438] and that the parable's imagery of different soils and outcomes more naturally invites a different line of thought and application from that of return from exile.[439] The calling of twelve disciples certainly evokes thought of eschatological restoration or renewal of Israel (the twelve tribes),[440] but if 'return-from-exile theology' was a prominent feature of the rationale,[441] it is surprising that so little is made of it.[442] And the first petition of the Lord's Prayer ('May your name be

434. Wright, *Jesus* 125-31.

435. See above, n. 347, and further below, §13.5. As the corollary to his reading of the parable Wright (*Jesus* 127) infers that the elder brother would have been identified with the Samaritans (who objected to the return of the exiles to Judea), in complete disregard of the setting indicated by Luke (the parable was addressed to Pharisees' objection to Jesus eating with 'sinners', Luke 15.1-3).

436. Wright, *Jesus* 230-39.

437. Jer. 24.6; 32.41; Hos. 2.23; Amos 9.15 (cited by Wright, *Jesus* 232-33 n. 128).

438. Of the passages cited by Wright, consider Jer. 31.27 and *4 Ezra* 8.41; the parable could have evoked the classic reminder of God's part in the agricultural process (Isa. 28.23-26; for the imagery of fruitful growth see, e.g., BAGD, *karpos* 2, *karpophoreō* 2); at one point Wright himself assumes the identity of 'seed' and 'word', as the (later) explanation invites (*Jesus* 238), but he seems unconcerned that the explanation attached to the parable (which he includes with the parable itself) shows no awareness of Wright's 'controlling story' (Mark 4.13-20 pars). See further below, §13.1.

439. See also Liebenberg's criticism of G. Lohfink's somewhat similar interpretation that it is people who are sown, ignoring the basic structure of four groups of seeds (*Language* 363-68, referring to G. Lohfink, 'Die Gleichnis von Sämann [Mk 4:3-9]', *BZ* 30 [1988] 36-69; also 'Die Metaphorik der Aussaat im Gleichnis vom Sämann [Mk 4,3-9]', in *Studien zum Neuen Testament* [Stuttgart: KBW, 1989]).

440. Sanders, *Jesus and Judaism* 98-102; see further below, §13.3b.

441. Wright, *Jesus* 430-31; Evans, 'Exile' 317-18. Even so, the thought would be of the outcasts of Israel restored to the land and reunited with those already living there, not that the latter were still in exile.

442. On the imagery of 'the lost sheep of the house of Israel' and of Israel as a scattered flock (without a shepherd) see below, §13.3h. The dominant motif in Luke 13.28-29/ Matt. 8.11-12 is that of eschatological reversal (above, §12.4c) rather than of the return of the Jewish dispersion (*pace* Sanders, *Jesus and Judaism* 219-20; Allison, *Jesus Tradition in Q* 176-91).

sanctified') could evoke the prophecy of Ezek. 36.22-28.[443] For the most part, however, Wright is content to read the Jesus tradition through the lens of his grand narrative without further attempt at justification.[444] But in squeezing the diversity of Jesus' proclamation of the kingdom into conformity with that single controlling story[445] he misses much that is of central significance within that proclamation — not least Jesus' own critique of Israel's current leadership and concern for the 'poor' and 'sinners'.[446]

In short, we can be sure that Jesus the Jew shared in his people's confidence in God with regard to Israel and the future. But otherwise we should heed postmodernism's warning against uncritical dependence on grand narratives, against the superimposition of a unitary meta-narrative on much more complex data.[447]

443. *Jesus* 293; and particularly G. Lohfink, *Jesus and Community* (Philadelphia: Fortress, 1985) 15-17. McKnight also presses the implication of the first petition of the Lord's Prayer (*New Vision* 24-26), though the implications are broader than simply the restoration of Israel to the land (Fitzmyer, *Luke* 898-99). And it is hardly enough to respond to the question why Jesus did not use 'exile' terms by simply asserting 'Kingdom language is "end of exile" language; "end of exile" is the negative to the positive "kingdom"' (*New Vision* 83 n. 51).

444. Evans also comes to Wright's support by finding other indications of exile theology in Jesus' teaching ('Exile' 316-27): the 'sign from heaven', Mark 8.11-13 (dependent on Evans's assumption that the 'sign prophets' of Josephus were enacting return from exile; above, n. 430); the allusion to Isa. 56.7 in Mark 11.17 pars. (but an allusion to returning outcasts [Isa. 56.8] is twice removed; see further below, §§15.3d and 17.3); the gathering of the elect from the ends of the earth in Mark 13.27 (the allusion is to the LXX, not MT, of Zech 2.6 [LXX 10]; he assumes that 'the "elect" . . . include the exiles of Israel'); threat of exile implied in the woes uttered against Chorazin and Bethsaida (Matt. 11.21-23/Luke 10.13-15). When one has to strain so hard to find allusions to a 'controlling story' it must raise serious doubts as to whether 'return from exile' was indeed the 'controlling' story.

445. For example: Jesus' welcome of the poor was a sign of return from exile (*Jesus* 255); 'forgiveness of sins is another way of saying "return from exile"' (268-72); Mark 13 is 'the story of the real return from exile', and the anticipated destruction of Jerusalem marks the end of exile (340-43, 358-59, 364).

446. See below, §§13.5; 14.4, 8. On the other hand, simply to deny that Jesus made any use of the theme of the return of the exiles, as Becker does (*Jesus* 129), hardly does justice to the issues raised by Wright. For Becker, creation, not salvation history, is the focus of Jesus' kingdom message (125-35); but the distinction owes more to a debate within German scholarship than to the Jesus tradition, and the anti-Israel overtones of 136-37 are disturbing.

447. Cf. the critique of C. Marsh, 'Theological History? N. T. Wright's *Jesus and the Victory of God*', *JSNT* 69 (1998) 77-94 (here 87-88, 91-92).

d. What Kind of 'Eschatology'?

What kind of 'end' does the Jesus tradition envisage? The earlier discussion noted that the term ('end') was used more flexibly than discussions of Jesus' eschatology have usually allowed for. Since 'end' could denote the end of an epoch, and 'the end of days' did not necessarily envisage the end of time (§12.3b), the idea of Jesus claiming in some sense to have fulfilled expectations for the age to come in his mission is less problematic than might at first appear.[448] Similarly, the issues posed by the word 'apocalyptic' are a lot less clear than is often thought to be the case, since it can be used to indicate insight given by revelation and visions of heavenly realities now as well as in the (near) future. The features usually in view in the popular use of the term are hardly prominent in the Jesus tradition: cosmic convulsions are envisaged only in Mark 13.24-25; and 'divine intervention' is more implicit (particularly final judgment) than explicit, though, of course, we have still to discuss the tradition about the coming of the Son of Man. Even so, the issue remains: does the Jesus tradition not attribute to Jesus also a future and final eschatological expectation, including God's kingdom come in a way not experienced hitherto, God's final triumph over evil, final judgment of the nations, a state of affairs imaged as a great feast, and resurrection from the dead to angelic existence?[449]

A typical response has been to offer refinements of the key term 'eschatology' itself. Bultmann's transposition of chronological ultimacy into existential ultimacy was a classic example. But such a proposal goes well beyond any conception of 'end' drawn from language which Jews of Jesus' time would have recognized. Crossan wants to use 'eschatology' as 'the wider and generic term for world-negation',[450] and tries to mark out a middle ground between Q's 'apocalyptic eschatology' and *Thomas*'s 'ascetic eschatology' in Jesus' 'ethical eschatology'.[451] But does the replacement of an apocalyptic eschatology by some form of utopian ideal 'end' actually resolve the issue of Jesus' future eschatol-

448. Cf. Sanders's wrestling with the same sort of question (*Jesus and Judaism* 228-37). Becker tries to finesse the issue by stressing the continuity between 'the present reality and the coming perfection' in Jesus' mission, 'a continuous unity'; 'the point of Jesus' proclamation is that from now on God's kingdom will be a reality in this world'; 'the present is the beginning of God's final rule as king' (*Jesus* 104-107, 119-21). Similarly Merkel concludes that the presence of feasting and joy already during Jesus' mission means that the break integral to the two ages schema is lacking ('Gottesherrschaft' 159). But does this do more than reformulate the problem?

449. Goppelt, e.g., distances Jesus from 'apocalypticism', but has no doubt that Jesus announced the impending end of the world (*Theology* 1.55-61, 67-72).

450. *Historical Jesus* 238.

451. See now *Birth* chs. 15-16 (particularly 279-82); cf. Theissen's and Merz's reflection on the combination of present and future in the Lord's Prayer (*Historical Jesus* 261-64): 'the "kingly rule of God" is the expression of a powerful ethical energy' (264). See also Borg, *Jesus in Contemporary Scholarship* 70-73.

ogy? Here again the issue is nicely posed by Wright's treatment. He commits himself to Schweitzer's agenda of setting Jesus within the context of Jewish eschatology, but it is an eschatology whose apocalyptic features are simply cosmic sound effects.[452] This means that Wright is able to interpret the future elements of Jesus' expectation solely in terms of Jesus' own journey to Jerusalem and Jerusalem's destruction in 70 CE. That Jesus could have looked for anything more than that — judgment of the nations, resurrection to angelic existence, the heaven and hell of traditional Christian envisaging — Wright does not say.

The more common way forward has been the synthesis between the thesis of Schweitzer's 'thoroughgoing eschatology' and the antithesis of Dodd's 'realized eschatology' provided by Jeremias's inaugurated eschatology or 'eschatology that is in process of realization'.[453] Imagery such as a train drawing into a station, day beginning to dawn, the final stage of World War II begun with D-day and climaxing in V-day (appreciated by an earlier generation), has all been employed to illustrate the tension in Jesus' usage. My own pennyworth to the debate has been to note the parallel between early Christian eschatology and Jesus' own eschatology provided by reference to the Spirit in each.[454] In Paul's perspective certainly, the Spirit experienced by the early believers was to be understood as the 'first instalment' of the kingdom whose full inheritance was yet outstanding.[455] Jesus' own experience of anointing and ministry empowered by the same Spirit/power of God may in itself have convinced him that God's longed-for (final) manifestation of his royal rule was already in evidence[456] and that its full manifestation could therefore not be long delayed.

The point is that such treatments have found it impossible to deny that Jesus had expressed expectation for the *imminent* happening of events which did *not* happen. Jesus' kingdom preaching cannot be disentangled from imminent expectation, with or without 'apocalyptic' features. Which also means that Jesus had entertained hopes which were not fulfilled. There were 'final' elements in his expectation which were not realized. Putting it bluntly, Jesus was proved wrong by the course of events. The discomfort of the conclusion for scholars who were also believers was softened by the thought both that it made more 'real' the humanness of Jesus and that such a conclusion demonstrated their own dispassionate method and scrupulous honesty: this was not the 'historical Jesus' they would have wished to find!

452. *Jesus* 80-82, 96-97, 207-209. Wright is indebted to Caird, *Language* ch. 14.
453. Jeremias, *Parables* 230 ('sich realisierende Eschatologie').
454. J. D. G. Dunn, 'Spirit and Kingdom', *ExpT* 82 (1970-71) 36-40, reprinted in *The Christ and the Spirit* vol. 2: *Pneumatology* (Grand Rapids: Eerdmans, 1998) 133-41.
455. 2 Cor. 1.22; 5.5; similarly Rom. 8.23; cf. also Rom. 8.14-17; 1 Cor. 6.9-11; 15.44-50; Gal. 4.6-7, 29-30; Eph. 1.14. See further my *Theology of Paul* 421, 424, 469-70.
456. Cf. Borg, *Jesus* 198-99.

Nor is this a conclusion I would wish to resist on my own part. I do not think the conclusion can be easily escaped that Jesus expected the kingdom to come with final outcomes which have not appeared; some may want to say not *yet* appeared. But there is still more to be said.

Too little attention has been paid to the character of Jewish prophetic hope. The prophetic tradition learned to live with the failure of prophecy without denigrating the prophecies themselves.[457] We have already observed how Psalm 89 wrestles with the failure of the promises to maintain the Davidic line. Jeremiah's depiction of Judah's expected devastation as a return to chaos (Jer. 4.23) was not regarded as a false prophecy because the end of the world did not come.[458] Hab. 2.3 provided a cue for post-biblical Judaism's wrestling with the problem of delay.[459] In emphasizing that many Jews were still in exile, it is easy to pass over the fact that such beliefs could be held only because the earlier hopes for return from exile had not been fulfilled — or should we say not completely fulfilled? The resulting 'dissonance', according to Robert Carroll, 'gave rise to hermeneutics', including the transition from prophecy to apocalypse.[460] The hermeneutics included what he calls 'adaptive prediction' (citing Jeremiah and Ezekiel) and realized expectation (Ezra inspired by the preaching of Second Isaiah).[461]

More to the point, however, is the fact that the failed prophecies also gave rise to renewed prophecies.[462] For example, Jeremiah fully expected that after seventy years exile both Israel and Judah would be restored to the land and would prosper under a restored Davidic king.[463] That hope was only partially fulfilled, and the absence of complete fulfilment caused perplexity for Zechariah (Zech.

---

457. Schnackenburg, e.g., mentions texts which speak of a 'near expectation' — Isa. 13.6; 51.5; 56.1; Ezek. 7.1-13; 12.21-25; 30.3; Joel 2.1; Zeph. 1.7, 14-18 (*God's Rule* 201 n. 65). See also Meyer, *Aims* 245-49. 'The re-interpretation and adaptation of prophetic promises had always been a staple of Jewish religion, indeed a positive theological asset rather than a liability' (M. Bockmuehl, *This Jesus: Martyr, Lord, Messiah* [Edinburgh: Clark, 1994] 101).

458. Caird, *Language* 258-59.

459. A. Strobel, *Untersuchungen zum eschatologischen Verzögerungsproblem auf Grund der spätjüdisch-urchristlichen Geschichte von Habakuk 2,2ff.* (NovTSup 2; Leiden: Brill, 1961).

460. R. P. Carroll, *When Prophecy Failed: Reactions and Responses to Failure in the Old Testament Prophetic Traditions* (London: SCM, 1979) 124-28, 212. Carroll draws on L. Festinger, et al., *When Prophecy Fails: A Social and Psychological Study of a Modern Group That Predicted the Destruction of the World* (Minneapolis: University of Minnesota, 1956), and L. Festinger, *A Theory of Cognitive Dissonance* (Evanston: Row, Peterson, 1957). Texts indicative of the problem of delay include Isa. 10.25; Hab. 2.2, 3; Joel 1.15; 2.1 (168-72).

461. Carroll, *When Prophecy Failed* 172-77, 180-82.

462. In what follows I draw particularly on C. L. Holman, *Till Jesus Comes: Origins of Christian Apocalyptic Expectation* (Peabody: Hendrickson, 1996).

463. E.g., Jer. 25.12-13; 29.10-14; 30.3, 8-11; 31.1, 5-14; 32.36-41; 33.10-22.

1.12). But the hope was taken up again by Daniel, among others, in one of the most famous and lastingly influential prophecies, that of the seventy weeks of years (Dan. 9.24-27). It is generally accepted that the author was writing in the Maccabean period and saw himself as standing in the final week,[464] of which half (three-and-a-half 'times' = three-and-a-half years)[465] would be experienced under foreign subjection (7.25; 8.14; 9.27). So 'Daniel' fully expected that 'the end of days' was imminent (12.11-13). That hope again found only partial fulfilment in the establishment of the Hasmonean kingdom. But again it was taken up by Christians attempting to articulate a clear hope for the future.[466] The point is this: within Jewish prophetic/apocalyptic tradition there was some sort of recognition that the partial fulfilment of a hope did not nullify or falsify that hope. Instead the earlier hope became the basis and springboard for a fresh articulation of the same hope.

In somewhat similar reflections, Anthony Harvey observes that as a story needs an ending, so individuals looking to the future need some kind of closure or boundary to make time finite and comprehensible for them. When some crisis foreseen with the character of finality or the end comes and passes without the finality expected, it is not necessarily seen as invalidating the earlier warnings, which may simply be redirected to the next crisis.[467] When the end of a prophet's story of the future did not prove to be the end, it did not rob the prophetic message of its credibility in the eyes of those who cherished it.[468]

We could press the point by observing that any hope by its nature gives greater determinacy to what by its nature (the future) is indeterminate. For hope looks beyond the known present and past into the unknown future.[469] And in trying to speak of the future, hope (even inspired hope) can do no other than take the patterns and structures of the known and from them attempt to construct (or dis-

---

464. E.g., Collins, *Apocalyptic Imagination* 87-90, 109; Holman, *Till Jesus Comes* 50-51.

465. BDB, *mo'ed* 1b; *'ad* 2.

466. Rev. 11.2-3; 12.6, 14; cf. Luke 21.24. The prophecies were influential into the patristic period (e.g., Justin, *Dial.* 32.3-4; Irenaeus, *Adv. haer.* 5.25.3; 5.30.4). See also W. Adler, 'The Apocalyptic Survey of History Adapted by Christians: Daniel's Prophecy of 70 Weeks', in J. C. Vanderkam and W. Adler, *The Jewish Apocalyptic Heritage in Early Christianity* (CRINT 3.4; Assen: Van Gorcum, 1996) 201-38. Indeed Daniel's seventy weeks shaped Christian eschatology well into the eighteenth century.

467. Harvey was writing when the threat of nuclear war was at its height. It is interesting to note how the de-apocalypticisation of the threat of global confrontation marked by the end of the Cold War coincided with a de-apocalypticisation of the message of Jesus.

468. Harvey, *Jesus* ch. 4. 'Jesus and Time: the Constraint of an Ending', here 71-76, 89-90.

469. 'The future moves like a horizon . . . and always remains the same distance away' (Theissen and Merz, *Historical Jesus* 278).

cern) some sort of projection into the future.[470] That is the character of hope.[471] It gets things wrong, sometimes 'hopelessly' wrong, for the future is always unknown and can be known only when it has already become the present and the past. Yet we still hope, for hope is the only way we can cope with the future which might be crippling through the fear and dread which it otherwise inspires. More to the point here, prophetic hope was not hope in the future *per se,* but hope in *God* for the future, with concomitant concern for how that hope should determine living in the present.[472]

Now it would be impossible to enter into prophetic psychology at this point. But I cannot help wondering whether at the time of Jesus there was more conscious reflection on this feature of prophetic hope than has been allowed for.[473] The question is whether Jesus or his first followers took such considerations into account when they made their own forward-looking eschatological statements. Or rather, whether it is not the character of prophecy to make such firm predictions and the responsibility of the hearer, aware of the tradition, to recognize that its affirmation of old images and aspirations for the same ends should not be valued more highly than any element of prediction. Given my understanding of the fundamental role of hearing and receiving in the tradition process, the two-sidedness of oracles uttered-and-received and valued as prophecy means that no prophetic utterance, however clear and outspoken, should be considered on its own without any qualification which the hearing-receiving-retelling involves. Without anticipating subsequent discussion too much, this mediating but also qualifying role of the tradition was no doubt one of the reasons why the 'delay of the parousia' was evidently of relatively little significance for first-generation Christians.[474]

470. This is the element of validity in B. J. Malina's otherwise overpressed contrast, 'Christ and Time: Swiss or Mediterranean?', *The Social World of Jesus and the Gospels* (London: Routledge, 1996) 179-214. Note also Talman's observation cited below (chapter 15 n.24).

471. In contrast, apocalyptic eschatology is born more of despair for the present and can only depict the future in bizarre symbols, since little or nothing in the present gives substance to hope.

472. Cf. Bultmann: 'The essential thing about the eschatological message is the idea of God that operates in it and the idea of human existence that it contains — not the belief that the end of the world is just ahead' (*Theology* 1.23); Crossan and Reed: 'Like our contemporary "we shall overcome", the certainty of its *what* and *that* is not accompanied by an equal certainty of its *how* and *when*' (*Excavating Jesus* 75).

473. As there certainly was on the concomitant problem of false prophecy (see above, §8.2). Caird is confident that 'Luke and Paul did not expect their language about life after death to be taken with flat-footed literalness' (*Language* 248). 'It did not occur to the first Christians to repudiate the predictions of Jesus on the ground that they were not immediately fulfilled' (Meyer, *Aims* 248).

474. E.g., already in Mark's version of the apocalyptic discourse we hear the clarificatory qualifying note added: 'but the end is not yet' (13.7).

What emerges from this is the possibility that the understanding of time informing the eschatology of the Jesus tradition should not be conceived as simply linear. A tradition which could use the language of 'end' as flexibly as we have seen in writings of the time of Jesus should not be boxed into a mathematical image of a straight line between two points. Typology was evidently a hermeneutical device much used by teachers of Jesus' time — that is, the recognition of patterns discernible in God's past dealings with his people and thus enabling an informed expectation regarding God's dealings with his people in the future. To locate one's time and audience within the time-frame of an ancient narrative, as Hebrews does with the wilderness wanderings of Israel (Hebrews 4) and as preachers have done before and since, bespeaks an awareness that time need not be regarded simply as the unbroken onward sequence of events. Is it then simply the case that strong affirmations regarding the 'end' attest more the prophet's conviction and assurance in God and in the future as God's, as taught from the past, than any clarity of perception regarding the 'end' itself? The prophet expresses his or her trust in God for the future with an intensity of faith which makes her or him sure it will come tomorrow.[475] The prophet still 'gets it wrong' in temporal terms, but the tradition does not value the prophecy simply for its chronology.

What probably needs to be stressed in all this is that both Jesus' contemporaries and the first Christians could live with the disappointment of failed prophecy without that failure disturbing the core faith which found expression in the prophecy. Every so often, when the strain became too much, or in particular writings, they cried out, 'How long, O Lord?'. But for the most part they simply got on with living. The prophets turned from contemplating the future and in the same breath addressed the pressing issues of the present. Even writers of apocalypses, while writing and having written their apocalypses, no doubt continued to do Torah, to pray, and to live out lives of obedience as they saw it. The Qumran covenanters seem to have lived constructively out of a tension of prophecy fulfilled in their community and eschatological climaxes yet awaited.[476] If Paul is in any degree typical, the first Christians certainly lived in and from the tension between the already of eschatological hope fulfilled and the not yet of what was still worked for and awaited.[477]

Was it different for Jesus? It is worth noting that Matthew's tradition of the Lord's Prayer seems to have added the third petition ('May your will be done, as

---

475. Cf. McKnight, *New Vision* 12, 129-30, 138-39.

476. Schwemer notes that 'the juxtaposition of present and eschatological understanding of God's kingship receives fresh illumination through the Sabbath Songs: the eschatological expectation of God's kingship on earth has its basis in the present cultic celebration of the kingship of God in heaven' ('Gott als König in den Sabbatliedern' 117).

477. See, e.g., my *Theology of Paul* chapter 18.

in heaven, so on earth', Matt. 6.10b), presumably as an explanatory elaboration of the second petition ('May your kingdom come', 6.10a).[478] Does this indicate how the petition for the kingdom to come was understood early on? Either that the kingdom of God would be recognized (as present) when God's will was being done (on earth)[479] or that seeking for the kingdom would be unavailing without striving to do God's will? Matthew himself seems to draw that conclusion (Matt. 7.21).[480] Either way, Matthew's tradition does not treat the prayer for the kingdom's coming as an aspiration which can stand alone. As Luke's subsequent account was to put it: questions about the kingdom's future had their place (and sky-gazing was all very well), but what mattered now was the mission (Acts 1.5-11). Or as Lee Keck has more recently put it: 'The real question is not whether Jesus was right or wrong about the time of the kingdom but whether he was right about the God whom he imaged as king and father'.[481]

e. The Kingdom as Metaphor?

Before we paused to take stock, the preceding line of reflection was leading us into the problems of conceptuality, where the basic problem is that of language itself. Language as it were forces us into a linguistic/semiotic box, with words having to serve (inadequately) as both windows of insight and lines of communication. In doing both, they do neither very effectively. The basic issue, then, is how language deals with time, and in particular with the future.

Paul Ricoeur has observed that it is narrative which gives history its temporal flow, with the idea of beginning and end usually inherent in narrative.[482] Narrative draws on human experience and in evoking a response from the reader mediates between what has been and what is yet to be.[483] But if we cannot

---

478. As already noted (§8.5b), the most obvious explanation for such a difference in the two versions of the Prayer (Matthew's and Luke's) is liturgical elaboration. The alternative of taking the first two petitions in parallel (Gnilka, *Jesus of Nazareth* 137: '"name" is virtually synonymous with "kingdom"') is less illuminating. The possibility that the explanatory addition was 'authorized' by Jesus himself should not be excluded (see below, §16.2b).

479. See also Luz, *Matthäus* 1.344-45; Davies and Allison, *Matthew* 1.605-606.

480. Caird, *Theology* draws a similar conclusion with regard to Jesus: 'For Jesus, entering the Kingdom was synonymous with the life of discipleship — of submitting to the demands of the God who is King' (*Theology* 369).

481. *Who Is Jesus?* 112.

482. P. Ricoeur, *Time and Narrative* vol. 1 ch. 3.

483. This is my much too simplified attempt to draw out for my own purposes Ricoeur's 'threefold mimesis', that is, his distinction between mimesis$_1$, mimesis$_2$ and mimesis$_3$, in which I acknowledge my debt also to D. Pellauer's Foreword to M. Joy, ed., *Paul Ricoeur and Narrative* (Calgary: University of Calgary, 1997) xiv-xvi. In correlation with the reflections of the

understand the history of which Jesus was a part as a single (grand) narrative, what then? It is unsatisfactory to conclude that the only alternative option is to envisage a multiplicity of narratives for first-century Jews. For the undoubtedly different readings of God's hand in history which we find in the 'Judaisms' of the time were still perceived as different readings of the same narrative, as given in Israel's scriptures. The different readings were, in effect, variations on the common trust in God to work out his purpose for humankind and creation. What is lacking is a single *complete* narrative wholly agreed as to its details. What we have in the eschatology of §12.2c is a common basic outline of trust and hope elaborated and supplemented only by flashes of insight and inspiration. We have a narrative somewhat like a fragmentary Dead Sea scroll: we know that (most of) the fragments belong together (though some may come from an unknown document); but piecing them together is literally beyond us, because so much is missing or has been worn away. The incompleteness of the narrative means that the temporal flow breaks down, and we do not know how to relate episodes and visions to one another. An alternative image is that of a film full of flashbacks, where it is not always clear whether the scene portrayed at any moment is past or present. With the eschatology of the Jesus tradition we have as it were a film full of flash-forwards, but posing the same problem for the viewer. If we're not confused, then something is wrong: we are imposing our order on an intrinsically unordered narrative. The shattered mirror of prophecy gives a Picasso-esque image, and how the often jagged fragments fit into a whole is by no means clear.

Another term which has proved useful in such discussions is *'myth'* — myth understood not in the sense of *'un*historical', but in the sense of denoting that which is *beyond* history, that for which scenes drawn on the template of human history can function only pictorially or allusively.[484] Biblical scholars have become accustomed to using the term in relation to the 'time' of beginnings, the *Urzeit,* the opening chapters of Genesis. This is a 'time' which precedes history — historical time, by definition, being time which is in principle capable of being investigated by the normal tools of historical research. *Urzeit* is 'prehistory time', if we may put it so. What then about 'post-history time', *Endzeit?* One of the non-linear features of Jewish eschatology is the expectation that *Endzeit* will be as *Urzeit,* the 'end' will return to the beginning, heaven will be paradise restored. Which is also to say that post-history time will inevitably share the mythical character of prehistory time. Any attempt to speak about the final future will

---

previous section (§12.6d) one might note the inevitability of some 'slippage' between the three phases of the process.

484. My use of the term 'myth' is thus limited (see also 'Myth', *DJG* 566-69). I am aware of the debate regarding its much more extensive use; K. W. Bolle and P. Ricoeur, 'Myth', in M. Eliade, ed., *Encyclopedia of Religion* (New York: Macmillan, 1987) 10.261-82; R. A. Oden, 'Myth and Mythology', *ABD* 4.946-56.

have to use pictorial or allusive terms, unable to assert correlation between word and event with the same confidence as in dealing with historical time. To offer another analogy, history is somewhat like an autumn day — I view one from my window as I write these words — a day which begins with mists slowly clearing and ends with mist steadily gathering again. During the day, vision before and behind is clear enough. But in the beginning and ending periods, when it is far from clear when 'day' has really begun and really ended, no clear sense of position far less of direction is possible for one caught in the mists.

As an alternative mode of expression we have already mentioned Perrin's suggestion that the kingdom be seen as a 'tensive symbol' and Wright's rebuttal of Schweitzer for taking apocalyptic language literally. I prefer the term 'metaphor' precisely because, as I understand it, the metaphor is not readily translatable into something else. In the end Perrin wants to be able to unpack the tensive symbol of the kingdom into a variety of referents. And in the end Wright equally wants to translate the apocalyptic language of cosmic convulsion and 'end of the world' into the concrete event of Jerusalem's destruction.[485] But if we follow Ricoeur and Martin Soskice, metaphor is not a synonym or alternative for another linguistic mode of description. Metaphor says what cannot be said otherwise, at least not so effectively or so well, and possibly not at all. The metaphor not only expresses the hope, as though for something else. The metaphor *is* the hope. One can still ask what the metaphor refers to, but the appropriate correlative question is not, What does this *mean?* but What does this *evoke?*[486] We do not ask 'what it means' in regard to a piece of music like Beethoven's Eroica symphony or a piece of art like Picasso's 'Guernica' or a poem like William Blake's 'Jerusalem'; they appeal to heart more than to head. It is somewhat so with a metaphor. The troping effect 'turns' the metaphor from its logical referent and gives its appeal a non-rational, almost subliminal quality.

It should not occasion any surprise, therefore, when a sequence of metaphors 'describing' a particular subject do not gel with one another, for they are always aspectical and fragmentary by their very nature, mood-evoking more than meaning-communicative. The inherent polyvalency of the parables of the king-

---

485. Wright is indebted to Caird, *Language* 266 at this point. But in asserting that the biblical writers 'regularly used end-of-the-world language metaphorically to refer to that which they knew well was not the end of the world' (256), Caird is referring primarily to Dodd's realized eschatology (253). Keck warns of similar dangers in the currently more fashionable talk of Jesus' vocation to 'restore' Israel: 'Because "Israel" was a sacral, evocative symbol, he [Jesus] could use "twelve" to suggest the God-given future without describing it or organizing a movement to speed its coming or administer it when it arrived' (*Who Is Jesus?* 51).

486. Cf. Caird's understanding of 'expressive language': 'Whereas the object of referential language is to clarify and convey an idea, the object of expressive language is to capture and communicate or to respond to an experience' (*Language* 15-16).

dom subverts any attempt to draw a single uniform picture of the kingdom from them.[487] So scholars should not make too much of the crudities and inconsistencies in the hope expressed in the metaphor of the kingdom of God, as though it could be expressed otherwise and more adequately. But for centuries Jews hoped for the age to come and Christians have hoped for heaven without either having any clear idea of what they are hoping for beyond these terms and the most prominent images which fill out the core metaphor.

Again we ask, was it any different for Jesus and for those who first treasured and performed his words? Perhaps we should simply infer that 'the kingdom of God' for Jesus was an alternative way of speaking of the age to come, of heaven, and of the way heaven impacts on earth. It had reference, but no precision of 'meaning' — hence all the variegated, sometimes inconsistent images.[488] But its powerful symbolism evidently motivated Jesus as no other image or metaphor did.

All this discussion to clarify what Jesus may have meant or how he may have been heard when he spoke of 'the kingdom of God', and all to so modest an outcome! — or so it might seem to some. But if I am right in the final reflection above, it is more important to have clarified the evocativeness of the language before pressing it for more content of affirmation or practice. If the piano is to give out (a) coherent tune(s), it has first itself to be tuned. In this case I have said all that I can to fine-tune our hearing hermeneutically and can now begin to play tunes that should be more easily recognizable to devotees of the Quest.

487. Cf. the principal thesis of Liebenberg, *Language* (e.g., 46-47, 69, 158-59), though he also stresses the stability of 'generic-level structures' and that narrative contexts curtailed the parables' inherent polyvalency (58-59, 70-71, 156-57). 'Even when one reads them in isolation — in order to make sense of their stories — one has to assume a certain "Bedeutungshorizont" [horizon of meaning]' (58-59).

488. Leivestad, noting the great variety of eschatological expectations in early Judaism, adds the comment: 'Apparently Jesus did not feel the need to reduce them to any kind of order' (*Jesus* 167-68).

CHAPTER 13

For Whom Did Jesus Intend His Message?

We began by examining what was clearly the central single element in Jesus' preaching — the kingdom of God. That allowed us to survey and classify (in a provisional way) a very substantial amount of the tradition of Jesus' teaching. It will be necessary to return to much of that material to ask different questions of it as we proceed. In chapter 12 one issue proved sufficiently absorbing to require all our attention — the meaning of the term itself and what its use would have evoked for Jesus' hearers, particularly as regards their hopes for the future. Somewhat frustratingly it became apparent that the question 'What precisely did Jesus mean when he spoke of God's kingship as future?' was one to which no clear answer was forthcoming. Probably the more appropriate question was 'Did Jesus mean anything precisely (that is, which we today can turn into straightforward propositions) when he so spoke?' A firm confidence in God and in the future as God's, expressed in prophetic and, in some measure, apocalyptic language, is certainly evident. But to translate that language entirely into first- (or twenty-first) century prose is a self-defeating task, losing far more than it purports to gain. Language which speaks to the imagination and spirit can rarely be translated into factual description without substantive loss.

Fortunately, however, more light can be shed on the present aspect of the kingdom. As we ask different questions and focus attention on other aspects of Jesus' mission, the whole picture will become steadily clearer, not least as to the character of living appropriate to the kingdom. Over the next five chapters, therefore, we will ask in turn: To whom did Jesus direct his message of the kingdom? What did acceptance of it mean for those who responded? How did others see Jesus' role as regards the coming of the kingdom? How did he see his own role? And did he anticipate his death as part of that role? All these are subsets of the one overarching question which has haunted the 'quest of the historical Jesus' since Reimarus first posed it so sharply: What was Jesus' intention? What did he hope to accomplish by his mission?[1] However difficult it is to achieve an answer to that question, it simply will not go away. Human curiosity will demand an answer. A crucial test of any large-scale contribution to the quest is how well it handles that question and whether the answer offered makes good sense of the evidence available.

13.1. Hearing Jesus

The first of these subset questions (For whom did Jesus intend his message?), like the others, poses an immediate challenge. For our approach throughout has stressed the impossibility of our getting back to Jesus himself. All we have in the Jesus tradition is the deposit of how he was heard by those who responded positively to his message (Jesus remembered). Our opening question, therefore, is unavoidably transposed into: How was Jesus' intention heard by those who followed him? Which also means that this chapter could easily be retitled 'The call to discipleship', since that was how Jesus' preaching was in the event heard by those from whom the Jesus tradition stemmed.[2]

But to tackle the question that way, even if invited to do so by the tradition itself, leaves too many other issues untouched. Did Jesus address himself only to a small group within first-century Galilee? Did he intend or hope to call out only a remnant within Israel?[3] How was he heard by those who did not respond positively to his message? Was his mission successful in achieving its desired response? Or did Jesus fail in that he won so few disciples? These are less comfortable issues for faith to ask, but they are also issues which will not go away and cannot be ignored.

Such issues, in fact, are posed from within the Jesus tradition itself. The early tradents and compilers of the Jesus tradition were evidently exercised by similar questions, and their own retelling of the Jesus tradition attests similar concerns. These concerns come to clearest expression in an important motif in the Jesus tradition which is too often ignored. I refer to the emphasis on *hearing* what Jesus said, or, perhaps more accurately, on hearing appropriately, on right hearing.

Each of the Synoptic Evangelists independently has Jesus emphasizing the importance of hearing one of his parables.[4] In Q, Jesus highlights the privilege of

1. See above, §4.2. It has provided the main item on the agenda on the so-called 'third quest' since Meyer, *Aims of Jesus,* and whether acknowledged or not provides the principal motivation for more or less every attempt to reconstruct 'the historical Jesus'.

2. Hence my earlier, more popular treatment using that title — *Jesus' Call to Discipleship* (Cambridge: Cambridge University, 1992).

3. Jeremias, *Proclamation* 170-73.

4. Mark 4.3; Matt. 21.33; Luke 18.6.

his audiences seeing what they see and hearing what they hear (Matt. 13.16-17/ Luke 10.24).[5] The final parable of the Sermon on the Plain/Mount stresses the importance of hearing and doing Jesus' words (Matt. 7.24, 26/Luke 6.47, 49).[6] This last emphasis is characteristically Jewish, and, incidentally, reflects the teacher's urging within the context of oral performance and transmission. The emphasis is implicit in the Hebrew *shama'* ('hear'), with its overtone of 'attentive hearing, heedful hearing'.[7] Hence the *Shema* (Deut. 6.4-5: 'Hear, O Israel . . .'), which Mark has Jesus citing in full in Mark 12.29-30. And the emphasis was no doubt characteristic among the devout of Jesus' day.[8] Both Paul (Rom. 2.13) and James (Jas. 1.22-25) make the same point (hear and *do*), and it is more likely that each is reflecting an emphasis in the Jesus tradition than that either influenced the other or that they independently reiterated a traditional emphasis without awareness that or concern whether Jesus shared it.[9]

What is particularly striking is the way the Evangelists repeat the epigrammatic exhortation, 'He who has ears (to hear), let him hear'.[10] This is clearly a teaching device which the Evangelists (and presumably subsequent scribes) have felt free to include almost at random within the Jesus tradition.[11] The point is,

---

5. Cited above, §12.5b.

6. See above, chapter 12 n. 215. Luke brings out the same emphasis in his (or his tradition's) version of the episode of Jesus' rebuffing his mother and brothers (Mark 3.31-35 pars.):

Matt. 12.50	Mark 3.35	Luke 8.21b
Whoever <u>does the will of</u> my Father in heaven, <u>he is my brother and sister and mother.</u>	He <u>who does the will of God, he is my brother and sister and mother.</u>	My mother and my brothers are those who hear and do the word of God.

Similarly Luke 11.28: 'Blessed are those who hear the word of God and keep it'.

7. BDB, *šama'* 1.i-n. It is generally reckoned that in the Synoptic account of the transfiguration, the heavenly voice which concludes the most dramatic part of the scene ('This is my beloved son; hear him', Mark 9.7 pars.) has been framed to bring out an echo of the expectation of a Moses-like prophet (Deut. 18.15 — 'him you will hear/heed [*tišma'un*]').

8. In the Torah see particularly Num. 15.39; Deut. 4.1, 5-6, 13-14; 16.12; 30.8, 11-14. The Qumran covenanters saw themselves as 'the doers of the law' (1QpHab 7.11; 12.4-5; 4QpPs 37(4Q171) 2.15, 22-23). See also, e.g., Philo, *Cong.* 70; *Praem.* 79; Josephus, *Ant.* 20.44; *m. 'Abot* 1.17; 5.14; and further Str-B 3.84-88.

9. See also above, §8.1e. The Fourth Evangelist also emphasises the link between hearing and following (John 1.37, 40; 6.45; 10.3-5, 16, 27; cf. 1 John 1.1-5; 2.7, 24; 3.11; 4.6).

10. Mark 4.9 pars.; 4.23; 7.16 (some mss.); Matt. 11.15; 13.43; Luke 12.21 (a few mss.); 13.9 (very few mss.); 14.35; 21.4 (a few mss.); *GTh* 8.2; 21.5; 24.2; 63.2; 65.2; 96.2. The exhortation was taken up by the seer of Revelation (Rev. 2.7, 11, 17; 3.6, 13, 22; 13.9). The same concern is elsewhere expressed in equivalent formulations: 'Watch what/how you hear' (Mark 4.24/Luke 8.18); 'Hear me, all of you, and understand' (Mark 7.14/Matt. 15.10); 'I say to you who hear' (Luke 6.27).

11. 'It is almost pure performancial variation' (Crossan, *Fragments* 73).

however, that it was evidently considered to be typical of the Jesus tradition and therefore freely used in the retelling of that tradition. Such a feature could be attributed to the dominant influence of a very early teacher. But its wide dispersal through the tradition is better explained as a feature of Jesus' own teaching style, which was remembered as such from the first and which became not so much a fixed element in the tradition, but rather an established feature of the retelling of that tradition, somewhat in the manner of the formulaic phrases used by the folkloric singers of the great sagas.[12]

More to the point is the implication that what Jesus said may *not* be heard aright. The likelihood that Jesus' message would not be received or heeded is explicitly acknowledged (Mark 6.11/Q 10.10). Matthew and Luke retell the story of the rich young man as a case in point of someone who failed to hear/heed Jesus' word (Matt. 19.22/Luke 18.23). And the Evangelists do not hesitate to include other stories where Jesus' opponents are antagonized by what they hear him saying.[13] Especially striking is the way Mark and Matthew in particular use the parable of the sower as a kind of window into Jesus' parabolic teaching.[14] The significance is that all three Evangelists treat this as a parable of hearing, of different kinds of hearing.[15] For them, indeed, the emphasis of the parable is more on the different kinds of unfruitful hearing (Mark 4.4-7, 15-19 pars.), even though the parable itself ends by giving reassurance that there will be (much) fruitful hearing as well (Mark 4.8, 20 pars.). Evidently this was how the parable itself was heard in the typical performances of the earliest churches' tradition,[16]

---

12. See above, §8.3f.

13. Mark 11.18; Matt. 15.12; Luke 4.28; 16.14; John 6.60; 8.43.

14. Both set it at the head of their main parable collections (Mark 4; Matthew 13); Luke's collection is more modest (Luke 8.4-18). Because Matthew and Luke have followed Mark 4.2-20 so closely it is not possible to tell whether Q had any equivalent. Luke 8.16-18 has also followed Mark 4.21-25, but the Q/*Thomas* parallels are scattered (see above, chapter 8 n. 295). It would be curious if Q did not know a collection of parables. Perhaps this is a case where Q material is hidden from us because there is no q material!

15. Particularly Mark: he begins the parable with the call to 'Hear' (4.3); the verb 'hear' *(akouō)* occurs no less than 8 times in 4.9-20; the formulaic 'He who has ears to hear, let him hear' occurs twice in the sequence (4.9, 23), to be followed immediately by the caution, 'Take heed what you hear' (4.24), and the parable sequence ends by noting that Jesus 'spoke the word to them as they were able to hear' (4.33). That 'preaching is sowing' is what Liebenberg describes as 'a conventional conceptual metaphor' which provides the key to understanding the parable (*Language* 362, 370-76).

16. There should be little doubt that the explanation (Mark 4.13-20 pars.) has been added to the parable in the course of its transmission: particularly notable is the frequent reference to 'the word' in an absolute sense (7 times in Mark 4.14-20, its editorial character confirmed by 4.33), a feature far more reminiscent of later usage, especially Luke's account of the spread of 'the word' (Acts 4.4; 6.4; 8.4; 10.36; 11.19; 14.25; 15.7; 16.6; 17.11; 19.20; 20.7), than of anything Jesus is recalled as saying elsewhere (see further Hultgren, *Parables* 189-90).

and it probably had such an impact from the first.[17]

  Both Matthew and Luke also follow Mark in inserting between the parable and its explanation the somewhat puzzling, not to say disturbing comment, which purports to give the reason that Jesus spoke in parables.

Matt. 13.10-15	Mark 4.10-12	Luke 8.9-10

10 Then the disciples came and asked him, 'Why do you speak to them in parables?' 11 He answered, 'To you it has been given to know the mysteries of the kingdom of heaven, but to them
 it has not been given. . . .
13 Therefore I speak to them in parables,   that "seeing they do
not perceive,
and hearing they do not hear, nor do they understand".
 	
14 With them indeed is fulfilled the prophecy of Isaiah that says: "You will indeed hear, but never understand, and you will indeed see, but never perceive. 15 For the heart of this people has grown dull, and their ears are hard of hearing, lest they perceive with their eyes, and hear with their ears, and understand with their heart and turn, and I would heal them" ' (Isa. 6.9-10).
	10 When he was alone, those who were around him with the twelve asked him about the parables. 11 And he said to them, 'To you has been given the mystery of the kingdom of God, but for those outside,
	
	    everything comes in parables; 12 in order that "seeing they may see and not perceive,
	and hearing they may hear and not understand; lest they turn again and be forgiven"'.
		9 Then his disciples asked him what this parable meant.
		 10 He said,
		  'To you it has been given to know the mysteries of the kingdom of God; but to others
		
		   (I speak) in parables, in order that "seeing they may
		not perceive,
		and hearing they may not understand' ".

Liebenberg, however, justifiably questions whether the Evangelists necessarily intended their appended interpretation to be the only one possible (*Language* 351; further 376-414, especially 405-406). *GTh* 9 almost certainly reflects independent oral tradition (bibliography in Hultgren 185 n. 6): it lacks the Synoptists' explanation, and displays the sort of variations which would have been characteristic of oral performance.

  17. When we thus focus on the impact, the question of what Jesus may have intended (the 'meaning' of the parable) and whether the impacting imagery would have been the seed, the plants, or the different soils becomes inconsequential (see, e.g., the discussions referred to in Hultgren, *Parables* 185-88). That the parable most probably originated with Jesus is generally acknowledged (see, e.g., Perrin, *Rediscovering* 156; Funk, *Five Gospels* 54; Lüdemann, *Jesus* 28-29).

The clear use of Isa. 6.9-10 (Mark 4.12 pars.) certainly reflects the subsequent puzzlement at the failure of the disciples' post-Easter mission to their fellow Jews.[18] But that fact should not be allowed to exclude the possibility that Jesus himself was remembered as echoing Isaiah's own depressing commission when he spoke of his own.[19] The quotation here reflects distinctive features of the Aramaic Targum of Isa. 6.9-10,[20] indicating a retelling established within the Aramaic-speaking churches. We have also already observed that the traditions of both the Baptist's and Jesus' preaching seem to have been much influenced by reflection on Isaiah's prophecies, and there is no reason to doubt that both preachers were themselves influenced by their own knowledge of Isaiah.[21] So it would be rather surprising if Jesus, who must have been all too well aware of what had happened to the Baptist (the failure of his mission?), did not reflect on the sombre details of the great prophet's commission and on its implications for his own.

Here we are confronted with what might be called the paradox of the parable. Jesus would need no telling that the word he most probably used, *mašal*, had a range of meaning. Typically it denoted proverbial wisdom, as in ben Sira.[22] But in wider usage it often referred to an obscure or puzzling saying.[23] So the fact that *parabolē* became established as the Greek translation and gained its characteristic meaning in Christian tradition from the stories/parables of Jesus (rather than from his briefer metaphors and aphorisms), should not be allowed to obscure the original term's essential ambivalence. If Jesus referred to his teaching (in whole or part) as *mᵉshalim,* then the *double entendre* lay close to hand. He could hardly have been unaware that his teaching, while bringing light to some, came across to others as obscure and puzzling.

In this case contemporary reflection on the way parables function dovetails quite neatly into this older recognition of parabolic ambiguity. Parable even more than metaphor (§12.6e) depends for its effect on the hearer's hearing of it, on

18. John 12.40; Acts 28.26-27; also Rom. 11.8. See further J. Gnilka, *Die Verstockung Israels. Isaias 6,9-10 in der Theologie der Synoptiker* (SANT 3; Munich: Kösel, 1961); C. A. Evans, *To See and Not Perceive: Isaiah 6.9-10 in Early Jewish and Christian Interpretation* (JSOTS 64; Sheffield: Sheffield Academic, 1989).

19. Gnilka, *Verstockung* 198-205, and Evans, *To See* 103-106, both conclude that the logion derives from Jesus (further bibliography in Evans).

20. Manson, *Teaching* 77-78; Chilton, *Galilean Rabbi* 91-93.

21. See above, chapter 11 at nn. 122, 136 and nn. 115-17, 119, 129-31, 133-34, 147.

22. Sir. 1.25; 3.29; 13.26; 20.20, 27; 21.16; 38.33; 39.2; 47.17. Indicative is Josephus, *Ant.* 8.44, echoing 1 Kgs. 4.32.

23. The *mašal/parabolē* of Balaam (Num. 22.7, 18; 24.3, 15, 20, 21, 23); the proverb, 'Is Saul also among the prophets?' (1 Sam. 10.12); parallel to *šammâ/ainigma* (Deut. 28.37) or *ḥidâ/ainigma* (Prov. 1.6; Sir. 39.3; 47.15) or *ḥidâ/problēma* (Ps. 78.2), in the sense 'riddle or dark saying'.

how it impacts the hearer. The Synoptic tradition at Mark 4.10-12 pars. reflects the (later) confidence that the disciples had been the privileged recipients of special teaching: Jesus' teaching on the kingdom of God was a *mystērion,* a 'mystery or secret';[24] it had been revealed to them, but remained hidden from, obscure to, others.[25] Mark reinforces the point by using 'insider/outsider' language:[26] the mystery/secret of the kingdom has been revealed to the twelve, but to outsiders the parables are only riddles (Mark 4.11).[27] The language no doubt reflects the way Jesus' parables were recycled in some/many of the early communities, that is, to reinforce the sense of being a privileged minority 'let in on the secret' of God's kingship by Jesus.[28] In fact, however, the formulation simply reflected

24. There is general agreement that the term *mystērion* reflects the characteristic apocalyptic sense of divine secrets now revealed by divine agency (already in Dan. 2.18-19, 27-30; *1 En.* 103.2; 104.10, 12; 106.19; for Qumran see, e.g., 1QS 3.23; 4.18; 9.18; 11.19; 1QH 9[= 1].21; 10[= 2].13; 12[= 4].27-28; 15[= 7].27; 1QpHab 7.5, 8, 14; in the NT note Rom. 11.25; 1 Cor. 15.51; Eph. 1.9-10; 3.3-6; Col. 1.26-27; 2.2; 4.3; 2 Thess. 2.7; Rev. 1.20; 10.7). See further R. E. Brown's still valuable treatment, *The Semitic Background of the Term 'Mystery' in the New Testament* (FBBS 21; Philadelphia: Fortress, 1968).

25. *GTh* 62 is presumably making the same claim. The fact that there is a parallel in Q (Matt. 11.25-26/Luke 10.21) should be given more weight than is usually the case. Did Jesus, like the speaker in the 1QH psalms (the Teacher of Righteousness?), delight in the insight he had received and been able to impart to his closest disciples? The early (Q) communities remembered him as so exulting. And if Matt. 11.27/Luke 10.22 is seen as an interpretative addition (Kloppenborg, *Formation* 198), there is little reason to attribute the preceding verse(s) to early Christian exultation rather than to Jesus (see also Davies and Allison, *Matthew* 2.273-77).

26. The use of *hoi exō* ('those outside') in 4.11 is all the more pointed in Mark since he made the same contrast in the preceding episode: his mother and his brothers were 'outside' (3.31-32). Matthew and Luke omit or change the *hoi exō* in Mark 4.11. The characterisation of non-believers as 'outsiders' is already a feature of the Pauline churches (1 Cor. 5.12-13; Col. 4.5; 1 Thess. 4.12).

27. Josephus's description of the Qumran community contains a striking parallel: 'To those outside *(tois exōthen)* the silence of those within appears like some awful mystery *(mystērion)*' (*War* 2.133).

28. Hence the emphasis of Mark 4.33-34 (the conclusion to Mark's parable collection), followed by Matthew in his own way (Matt. 13.34-35). The issue here is obscured by the fact that the first Christians saw Jesus' resurrection as the principal key to unlock what had been still a puzzle for them regarding Jesus' teaching on the kingdom. Mark signals the contrast in 8.32: Jesus spoke 'plainly/openly' *(parrēsia,* no longer *en parabolē)* of his coming rejection, death, and resurrection (8.31). The tradition has been so elaborated here in the light of Easter faith that it is difficult to discern whether there was a pre-Easter form. It is worth noting, however, that the assertion of Mark 4.11, even when qualified by 4.33, cuts across the strong Markan theme of the dullness of the disciples (e.g., 6.52; 8.17-21); the passage hardly fits within the usual 'messianic secret' reading of Mark (cf. Pesch, *Markusevangelium* 1.240; H. Räisänen, *The 'Messianic Secret' in Mark's Gospel* [Edinburgh: Clark, 1990] 143). It should not occasion surprise that the Jesus tradition contains such clashing currents, which probably reflect the mix-

what had actually happened: many/most had been finally puzzled and antagonized by what Jesus had taught.

In the spirit of Isaiah (6.9-10) the outcome was understood as in line with God's intention, even as intended by God.[29] But the basic fact of widespread rejection must have been evident to Jesus himself well before the end of his mission: many heard and did not understand, many saw but did not perceive, many failed to turn and accept the healing offered by God through Jesus' mission.[30] The Jesus who denounced Capernaum, Chorazin, and Bethsaida for their failure to respond to his message (§12.4e) would hardly have been surprised to find that his parables were off-putting for so many. The fact that there is almost a predestinarian dogma of divine intention coming to expression at this point is not necessarily a signal of subsequent Christian reflection. Here again we need to ask with Schweitzer whether such a 'dogma' was not first given expression by Jesus himself.[31]

The likelihood that we are on the right trail here is strengthened by the related motif of hiddenness/openness. Mark, no doubt deliberately, includes the motif within his collection of parables (Mark 4.21-22) and is presumably followed by Luke 8.16-17. But Luke also knows similar versions of the same sayings, presumably from Q (Matt. 5.15/Luke 11.33; Matt. 10.26-27/Luke 12.2-3) and *Thomas* (*GTh* 6.4; 33.1-2).[32]

---

ture of fascination and bemusement with which many of Jesus' first disciples must have heard his teaching.

29. This conclusion is unavoidable in exegesis of Mark 4.12. The *hina* clause followed by the *mēpote* clause can hardly express other than purpose (Black, *Aramaic Approach* 212-14; Marcus, *Mark 1–8* 299-300; *pace* Manson, *Teaching* 78-79; Chilton, *Galilean Rabbi* 92-94). The fact that Matthew and Luke have both softened Mark's rigour (both omit the *mēpote* clause and Matthew reads *hoti* instead of *hina*) strongly suggests that they read Mark in the same way.

30. See also Beasley-Murray, *Jesus and the Kingdom* 105-107; Evans, *To See* 103-106.

31. See above, chapter 4 nn. 118-20. For further discussion on the detail of Mark 4.10-12 see particularly Guelich, *Mark 1–8* 199-212.

32. The Mark 4.22/Matt. 10.26/Luke 8.17/12.2 saying is also attested in *Oxy.Pap.* 654 5.2, 4 and *GTh* 5.2 — a rather impressive multiple attestation; it is consequently ranked highly by Crossan (*Historical Jesus* 350, 436). The Jesus Seminar agrees that Mark 4.21 pars. may well go back to Jesus in some form and that Jesus may well have said something like *GTh* 5.2, the earliest form of Mark 4.22 pars. (Funk, *Five Gospels* 56-57, 475-76); and Lüdemann concludes that both elements in Mark 4.21-22 'might very well go back to Jesus' (*Jesus* 30, 169). On Matt. 10.26-27/Luke 12.2-3 see S. McKnight, 'Public Declaration or Final Judgment? Matthew 10:26-27 = Luke 12.2-3 as a Case of Creative Redaction', in Chilton and Evans, eds., *Authenticating the Words of Jesus* 363-83, especially 378-81. See also Matt. 11.25/Luke 10.21; 13.35; Luke 18.34; 19.42.

Matt. 5.15	Mark 4.21	Luke 8.16	Luke 11.33	GTh 33.2
No one igniting a lamp puts it under a bushel, but on a lampstand, and it gives light to all in the house.	He said to them, 'Is a lamp brought in to be put under a bushel, or under the bed, and not on a lampstand?'	No one after lighting a lamp hides it under a jar, or puts it under a bed, but puts it on a lampstand, so that those who enter may see the light.	No one after lighting a lamp puts it in a cellar or under a bushel, but on a lampstand, so that those who enter may see the radiance.	No one lights a lamp and puts it under a bushel, nor does he put it in a hidden place, but rather he sets it on a lampstand so that all who enter and leave may see its light.

Matt. 10.26-27	Mark 4.22	Luke 8.17	Luke 12.2-3	GTh 6.4; 33.1
26 So have no fear of them; for nothing is covered up that will not be uncovered, and nothing secret that will not become known. 27 What I say to you in the dark, tell in the light; and what you hear whispered, proclaim on the housetops.	22 For there is nothing hidden, except to be disclosed; nor is anything secret, except to come to light.	17 For nothing is hidden that will not be disclosed, nor anything secret that will not become known and come to light.	2 Nothing is covered up that will not be uncovered, and nothing secret that will not become known. 3 Therefore whatever you have said in the dark will be heard in the light, and what you have whispered behind closed doors will be proclaimed on the housetops.	6.4 There is nothing hidden which shall not be made manifest, and there is nothing covered that shall remain without being revealed. 33.1 What you shall hear in your ear proclaim in the other ear upon your housetops.

Here again there seems to be a sense of contested truth, the disciples' sense of having been privileged with revelatory insights by Jesus, which they had a duty to make known and which would be vindicated in the end. Quite what it was that Jesus had said remains obscure(!), but the point is that he is recalled in these sayings as implying that his message was illuminating,[33] and that (presumably) his disciples had a responsibility to share it more widely before its truth is finally revealed to all. It is worth noting that the sayings have not been much developed or made the base for a more elaborate Christian claim to divinely given insights,[34]

33. The imagery of teaching, particularly Torah, as light giving guidance for life is firmly rooted in the Psalms and Wisdom literature of Israel (e.g., Pss. 43.3; 56.13; 119.105; Prov. 6.23; Eccl. 2.13; Sir. 32.16) (H. Conzelmann, *'phōs', TDNT* 9.322).

34. Notably, the material gathered in Mark 4.21-22, 24-25 remained scattered through Q, as also in *Thomas* (see above, chapter 8 n. 295). But Matt. 5.15/Luke 11.33 has been integrated into a similar 'light' cluster in Matt. 5.14-16), and combined differently in Q into a light/darkness cluster (Luke 11.34-35/Matt. 6.22-23).

which suggests that they remained somewhat obscure to the disciples but were retained because they were remembered as something said by Jesus.

Hearing Jesus, then, was not a straightforward business. The parable of the sower certainly suggested that there would inevitably be different hearings with different results. Those who heard and responded positively were, in the event, a relatively small group.[35] How much of this was foreseen by Jesus? Were his realistic aims quite modest? Did he count his preaching mission a success? It is dubious whether we can give any clear answers to such questions. What we can do, once again, is to focus on how he was heard by those who responded to his preaching and became his disciples.

13.2. The Call

We began the main review of Jesus' kingdom preaching where Mark began it — Mark 1.15 (§§12.4a, 5a). So it is appropriate to begin the next phase at the same point. For Mark completes his summary with an exhortation: 'The time has been fulfilled, and the kingdom of God has drawn near; repent and believe in the gospel'. According to Mark, Jesus called his hearers to repentance and faith.

a. 'Repent'

That this was a substantial theme in Jesus' preaching is a matter of some debate. It is true that Matthew follows Mark at this point, even though he modified Mark 1.15 itself (Matt. 4.17). Mark reports the mission of the twelve in similar terms: 'they went out and preached in order to bring their hearers to repentance *(hina metanoōsin)*' (Mark 6.12). On this point Jesus (and his disciples) are remembered as preaching with the same objective as the Baptist (Mark 1.4 pars.; Q 3.8).[36] But Mark 1.15 and 6.12 are both Markan summaries; Mark does not recall an actual word of Jesus himself on the theme. Q however does recall two sayings of Jesus already referred to more than once:[37] the woes against the Galilean towns who failed to repent (Matt. 11.21/Luke 10.13), and the similar commendation of the men of Nineveh who repented at the preaching of Jonah (Matt. 12.41/ Luke 11.32). And Luke includes further occasions when repentance was called for or spoken of.[38] But the total word count is not substantial.

35. Luke numbers only 120 in Acts 1.15.
36. See above, §11.3b.
37. See above, chapter 9 n. 304, chapter 12 n. 177, and §12.4e.
38. Luke 13.3, 5; 15.7, 10; 16.30; 17.3-4. The comment in 5.32 is certainly redaction-

However, as Jeremias pointed out, this is where a word count can be misleading.[39] He notes a number of parables and incidents in Jesus' ministry which in effect make clear what repentance involves: particularly the parables of the prodigal son (Luke 15.17) and the toll-collector (Luke 18.13) and the Q parable of the empty house (Matt. 12.43-45/Luke 11.24-26); and the incidents of the rich young man/ruler (Mark 10.17-31 pars.) and Zacchaeus (Luke 19.8).[40] We may conclude, then, with only a small degree of equivocation, that the memory of Jesus commending and calling for repentance is quite firmly rooted in the Jesus tradition as the tradition was rehearsed in the early communities of Jesus' disciples.

The meaning of the Greek, *metanoeō/metanoia* ('repent/repentance'), is not in dispute: 'to repent' is to change one's mind, often with an overtone of regret for the view previously held.[41] And something of this overtone is certainly detectable in the remorse shown by the prodigal son and the toll-collector.[42] But there is general agreement that behind the usage of the Baptist and Jesus lies the much more radical Hebrew/Aramaic term *šub/ṭub*, 'to go back again, return'.[43] This was more effectively translated in the LXX by the Greek *epistrephō*, with the same meaning. This enables us to recognize that the Baptist and Jesus were in effect calling for a 'return to the Lord', in echo of a constant refrain in their Scriptures, particularly the prophets.[44] The Essenes in turn understood themselves to have entered 'the covenant of conversion *(briṯ ṯᵉšubâ)*' (CD 19.16).[45] The call expressed in the Greek term *metanoeō*, therefore, would have initially been heard as a reiteration of the call of the prophets to turn back to God, that is, by implication, from a life in breach of God's commandments, from a social irresponsibility which should have been unacceptable in the people of Yahweh. Its radical quality is indicated quite

---

al. The theme was of some importance for Luke (Luke 24.47; Acts 5.31; 11.18; 20.21; 26.20). In Matthew note also Matt. 21.29, 32 *(metamelomai)*.

39. Jeremias, *Proclamation* 152-53; see also Goppelt, *Theology* 1.77-86; McKnight, *New Vision* 172-73; the point needs to be repeated to Becker, *Jesus* 236.

40. Wright also responds to Sanders's criticism of Jeremias on this point by pointing to the 'implicit narrative' (of Israel's restoration) *(Jesus* 247-48); see further below, §13.3a.

41. BAGD, *metanoeō, metanoia;* J. Behm, *metanoeō, TDNT* 4.978-79. Hence *metanoeō* is normally used in the LXX for Hebrew *niham* ('be sorry [for something]') (Behm 989-90).

42. Luke 15.17-19; 18.13. In Luke 17.4 we could quite properly translate, 'If your brother . . . says "I am sorry *(metanoeō)*", you should forgive him'.

43. See, e.g., E. Würthwein, *metanoeō, TDNT* 4.984; H. Merklein, *EDNT* 2.416. See further Jeremias, *Proclamation* 155. Behm notes that *metanoeō* is used to translate *šub* in later Greek translations of the OT *(TDNT* 4.990).

44. Deut. 4.30; 30.2, 10; Pss. 7.12; 22.27; 51.13; 78.34; 85.8; 90.3; Isa. 6.10; 19.22; 31.6; 44.22; 55.7; Jer. 3.10, 12, 14; 4.1; 5.3; 8.5; 24.7; Ezek. 18.30; Hos. 3.5; 6.1; 7.10; 14.2; Joel 2.12-13; Amos 4.6, 8-11; Zech. 1.3; Mal. 3.7.

45. See further R. Schnackenburg, *Die sittliche Botschaft des Neuen Testaments* (HTKNT Supp. 1; Freiburg: Herder, 1986) 1.43-44.

appropriately by rendering *metanoeō* as a call to 'convert', that is, for individuals to radically alter the manner and direction of their whole life, in its basic motivations, attitudes and objectives, for a society to radically reform its communal goals and values.[46] The prodigal son who literally turned round, abandoned his life-style and returned to his father (Luke 15.18-20a) is as good an illustration as one could want. Similarly the parable of the toll-collector illustrates that such a turn-round/repentance has to be unconditional (in contrast with the Pharisee's confidence in his acceptability to God, Luke 18.10-13).[47]

The only passage in the Synoptic tradition which expresses this sense of conversion by means of *strephō* ('turn') is Matt. 18.3 — 'Truly I say to you, unless you turn and become like children, you will never enter the kingdom of heaven' (Matt. 18.3). It seems to be Matthew's rendering of a less radical saying preserved in Mark 10.15/Luke 18.17.[48] But John 3.3, 5 probably indicates that the tendency to re-express Jesus' teaching at this point in more radical terms was common to more than one stream of the Jesus tradition: to enter the kingdom it was necessary not only to become like a little child *(paidion)*, but to become a newborn baby! And in *Thomas* it becomes the basis of a differently radical exposition *(GTh 22)*.[49]

b. 'Believe'

According to Mark Jesus called his hearers not simply to repent/convert, but also to believe — *pisteuete* (1.15). Mark has put the call in the language of later missionaries — to 'believe in the gospel'.[50] But talk of 'faith' is no stranger to the

46. Goppelt gives particular emphasis to the call for repentance (*Theology* chs. 3-4): 'Each of Jesus' demands was after nothing less than a transformation of the person from the very core, i.e., total repentance' (118).

47. Despite their sole attestation by Luke, it is widely agreed that these parables originated with Jesus (e.g., Fitzmyer, *Luke* 1083-86, 1183-85; Funk, *Five Gospels* 356-57, 369; Becker, *Jesus* 152, 76-77; E. Rau, 'Jesu Auseinandersetzung mit Pharisäern über seine Zuwendung zu Sünderinnen und Sündern. Lk 15,11-32 und Lk 18,10-14a als Worte des historischen Jesus', *ZNW* 89 [1998] 5-29; Hultgren, *Parables* 83-84, 125; Lüdemann, *Jesus* 365), though Lüdemann thinks Jesus did not speak the latter parable, because 'it is based on a fundamental hostility to the Pharisees which Jesus did not share' (376; contrast Becker 76).

48. Davies and Allison suggest that the Matthean form of the saying is more primitive than Mark 10.15, since 'receive the kingdom' is more likely a post-Easter expression (it occurs only here in the Synoptics) in contrast to Jesus' talk of 'entering the kingdom' *(Matthew* 2.757).

49. Note also *GTh* 46.2, which seems to have merged the thought here into the Q tradition, Matt. 11.11/Luke 7.28. See further below, §14.2.

50. 'Gospel' as a noun seems to have been coined by Paul or early missionaries, so there can be little doubt that 'in the gospel' is Mark's own gloss (see above, chapter 12 nn. 3-4).

Synoptic tradition of Jesus' words.[51] A striking feature is that the majority of the references to faith (or lack of faith) occur in relation to miracles: nearly two-thirds of those in the Synoptics, in Mark eight out of thirteen.[52] Typically the tradition recalls Jesus as saying things like, 'Do not fear, only believe' (Mark 5.36), 'All things are possible to him who believes' (Mark 9.23), and, most frequent, 'Your faith has saved you/made you well'.[53] The encounter with the centurion/ royal official at Capernaum is remembered as notable for the great impression which his faith made on Jesus (Matt. 8.10/Luke7.9; cf. John 4.48-50). And Matthew draws the same point from Jesus' other known encounter with a non-Jew (Matt. 15.28). It matters little whether all the episodes which report Jesus as speaking of belief/faith are accurate as memories on that point. For the tradition shows clearly that this was recalled as a regular theme, particularly in the miracle stories, and was drawn in (again as a recurrent formula) precisely because it held such a firm place in the retellings of the tradition from the first.

Notable also is the fact that the character of the faith envisaged is hardly distinctively Christian, as that took shape in the subsequent evangelistic mission — that is, faith in Jesus, particularly in his death and resurrection.[54] For the most part, in the Synoptic accounts the Evangelists do not even make the attempt to portray it as faith in Jesus.[55] What is envisaged is more trust, or reliance on the power of God to heal[56] or to answer prayer,[57] or generally trust in God's care and provision (Matt. 6.30/Luke 12.28),[58] though only Mark 11.22 explicitly speaks of

---

51. *Pisteuō* in Mark 5.36/Luke 8.50; 9.23; Mark 9.42/Matt. 18.6; Mark 11.23-24/Matt. 21.22; Matt. 8.13; 9.28; *pistis* in Mark 4.40/Luke 8.25; Mark 5.34/Matt. 9.22/Luke 8.48; Mark 10.52/Matt. 9.29/Luke 18.42; Mark 11.22/Matt. 21.21; Matt. 8.10/Luke 7.9; Matt. 17.20/Luke 17.6; Matt. 15.28; 23.23; Luke 7.50; 17.19; 18.8; 22.32. In John the usage has been considerably multiplied.

52. Cf. Jeremias, *Proclamation* 162-63; but see also chapter 15 n. 366 below.

53. Mark 5.34 pars.; 10.52 pars.; Luke 7.50; 17.19. See also C. L. Blomberg, '"Your Faith Has Made You Whole": The Evangelical Liberation Theology of Jesus', in J. B. Green and M. Turner, *Jesus of Nazareth: Lord and Christ*, I. H. Marshall FS (Grand Rapids: Eerdmans, 1994) 75-93 (76-83).

54. See, e.g., my *Theology of Paul* 174-77.

55. Roloff, *Kerygma* 173. The one exception is Mark 9.42 (A B L W, etc.)/Matt. 18.6: 'whoever causes one of these little ones who believes (in me) to stumble . . .'. But the absence of 'in me' from Mark's text is also well attested, and there is a strong possibility that Matthew added the phrase, which was then copied into Mark in later transcriptions (Metzger, *Textual Commentary* 101-102; Pesch, *Markusevangelium* 2.113). The position is clearer with the taunt of the crowd in Mark 15.32: 'let him now come down from the cross, that we might see and believe' (Mark 15.32), where it is evident that Matthew has added 'on him' and the Markan textual tradition indicates a variety of obviously later emendations to the same effect.

56. See, e.g., Mark 2.5 pars. and the passages cited in the preceding paragraph.

57. Mark 11.22-24/Matt. 21.21-22; Matt. 17.20/Luke 17.6.

58. *Oligopistos* ('little faith') seems to have been coined by Q (elsewhere only in Christ-

'faith in God'.[59] This strongly suggests that stories and teaching about the faith encouraged and commended by Jesus had already assumed a definitive shape before Easter. Equally striking is the complete absence of any reference to Jesus' own faith, or to Jesus as 'believing'.[60] Jesus is not the one who believes/trusts in God so much as the medium of God's healing power to those who trust in God.[61] In short, Jesus is presented neither as the example of one who believed, nor as the one in whom subsequent hearers should believe.

Behind the Greek *pisteuō* no doubt lies the hiphil of Hebrew *'mn* (*he'emin*, 'to trust, believe in, rely on, be confident in'), used of trust in God in passages scattered across the Hebrew Scriptures.[62] The noun equivalent to the Greek *pistis*, Hebrew *'emunâ* or *'emet*, had more the sense of 'firmness, reliability, faithfulness',[63] but it could embrace the sense of the hiphil verb, as seems to be implied by the usage attributed to Jesus. So if Jesus did indeed use the Aramaic equivalent of the noun *(hemanuta)*, in echo of the verb encouraging individuals to trust in God, it should be noted that the concept would be of 'firm faith', faith which is steady and committed in its reliance on God.[64] It was the firmness of the

ian literature); Matthew has made it one of his own motifs (Matt. 6.30; 8.26; 14.31; 16.8; 17.20). Since *oligopistos* 'lacks any real equivalent in the Semitic languages' Fitzmyer concludes that it can hardly be traced back to Jesus himself (*Luke* 979); but even if a direct translation equivalent is lacking, the thought itself could certainly be expressed by Jesus (cf. Str-B 1.438-39; Davies and Allison, *Matthew* 1.656).

59. Cf. Bornkamm, *Jesus* 129-37. Stegemann presses the point: 'Jesus appears simply as a *mediator* of heavenly, divine power' (*Library* 236).

60. Roloff, *Kerygma* 166-8, 172-3. Despite Fuchs (see above, chapter 5 n. 61) and the renewed emphasis on this point in Pauline studies consequent upon Richard Hays, *The Faith of Jesus Christ: An Investigation of the Narrative Substructure of Galatians iii.1–iv.11* (Chico: Scholars, 1983); further bibliography in my *Theology of Paul* 335. The one exception might be Mark 9.23: it is because Jesus has faith that 'all things are possible' to him; but the primary function of the reference is to encourage the father of the boy to believe (9.24) (brief discussion in Meier, *Marginal Jew* 2.655 with bibliography in notes).

61. In Matt. 9.28 Jesus encourages the two blind men to believe that he is able to help them; cf. Mark 11.31 pars. and Matt. 21.32, where the talk is of believing the Baptist. See further below, §15.7g(3).

62. Gen. 15.6; Exod. 14.31; Num. 14.11; 20.12; Deut. 1.32; 2 Kgs. 17.14; 2 Chron. 20.20; Ps. 78.22; Jonah 3.5 (BDB *'aman* hiphil 2c); plus Isa. 7.9; 28.16; 43.10 (A. Jepsen, *'aman*, TDOT 1.305-307); more consistently in the Apocrypha — Jdt. 14.10; Sir. 2.6, 8, 10; 11.21; Wis. 1.2; 12.2; 16.26; 18.6; 1 Macc. 2.59.

63. BDB *'emunah, 'emeth;* Jepsen, TDOT 1.310-13, 316-19.

64. The condemnation of a 'faithless *(apistos)* generation' (Mark 9.19) may echo Deut. 32.20 ('a perverse generation, sons in whom there is no faithfulness [*lo'-'emun*]'. Matt. 17.17/ Luke 9.41 ('a faithless and perverse generation') is usually reckoned a minor agreement against Mark, influenced more explicitly by Deuteronomy 32. Stuhlmacher, however, argues that Jesus presented 'a wholly novel view of faith' as a gift of God and as such faith in God (*Biblische Theologie* 1.91-92).

faith of the centurion (Matt. 8.10/Luke 7.9), the boldness of the faith of the friends of the paralyzed man and of the woman with a haemorrhage (Mark 2.5 pars.; 5.34 pars.), the persistence of the faith of Bartimaeus (Mark 10.52 pars.) which impressed Jesus. It was to an unyielding trust in God that Jesus gave assurance of answered prayer.[65]

c. 'Follow Me'

Unlike the Baptist, Jesus is remembered as calling on individuals to follow him — Simon and Andrew (Mark 1.17/Matt. 4.19), Levi/Matthew (Mark 2.14 pars.), Philip (John 1.43), those who were willing to deny themselves and take up their cross (Mark 8.34 pars.; Matt. 10.38/Luke 14.27), the rich young man (Mark 10.21 pars.), the would-be disciple (Matt. 8.22/Luke 9.59). Was this a selective invitation? Or was it coextensive with the call to repent and believe? The issue is obscured by the fact that not only are the immediate band of disciples described as 'following' Jesus,[66] but also individuals unbidden (Mark 10.52 pars.), women who supported him (Mark 15.41; Matt. 27.55), and even large crowds.[67] The most obvious answer to the question is that Jesus did issue a general call to repentance and faith (like the sower dispersing the seed widely?), but that he targeted specific individuals to be his disciples as such with a view to giving them more intensive teaching.[68] We will have to return to this subject below (§§13.3b and 14.3).

d. The Urgency of the Call

In view of the note of urgency which was a feature of Jesus' proclamation of God's reign (§12.4g-h), it is also worth observing the equivalent note of urgency

65. Cf. Mark 11.22-24 par. with Matt. 7.7-11/Luke 11.9-13.

66. Mark 1.18/Matt. 4.20; Mark 2.14 pars.; 6.1; 10.28 pars.; Matt. 8.10/Luke 7.9; Matt. 4.22; 19.28; 20.29; Luke 5.11; 22.39; John 1.37, 40; 10.4-5, 27. In one of the most influential contributions to the new redaction criticism Bornkamm observed that Matthew's setting of the sequence on 'following Jesus' (Matt. 8.18-22) immediately before the episode of the stilling of the storm (8.23-27), with the linking introduction, 'He embarked on the boat and his disciples followed him' (8.23), was Matthew's way of showing what discipleship/following Jesus would involve (G. Bornkamm, et al., *Tradition and Interpretation in Matthew* [London: SCM, 1963] 52-57).

67. Mark 2.15; Mark 3.7/Matt. 4.25/12.15; Matt. 8.1; 19.2; John 6.2. Alternatively we might ask whether the healed demoniac, who wanted to stay with Jesus but was sent home to tell his story there (Mark 5.18-20), was any less a follower of Jesus.

68. Cf. Hengel, *Charismatic Leader* 59-60; Schnackenburg, *Sittliche Botschaft* 59-66; see further above, §8.1b.

evident in some of Jesus' calls to discipleship, particularly the collection in Luke 9.57-62/Matt. 8.19-22.

Matt. 8.19-22	Luke 9.57-62
19 A scribe then approached and said, 'Teacher, <u>I will follow you wherever you go</u>'. 20 <u>And Jesus</u> says <u>to him, 'Foxes have holes, and birds of the air have nests; but the Son of Man has nowhere to lay his head'</u>. 21 Another of his disciples said to him, 'Lord, <u>first let me go and bury my father</u>'. 22 <u>But Jesus said to him, 'Follow me,</u> and <u>let the dead bury their own dead</u>'.	57 As they were going along the road, someone <u>said</u> to him, '<u>I will follow you wherever you go</u>'. 58 <u>And Jesus</u> said <u>to him, 'Foxes have holes, and birds of the air have nests; but the Son of Man has nowhere to lay his head'</u>. 59 To another he said, '<u>Follow me</u>'. But he said, '[Lord], <u>first let me go and bury my father</u>'. 60 <u>But Jesus said to him,</u> '<u>Let the dead bury their own dead</u>; but as for you, go and proclaim the kingdom of God'. 61 Another said, 'I will follow you, Lord; but let me first take leave of those at my home'. 62 Jesus said to him, 'No one who puts a hand to the plough and looks back is fit for the kingdom of God'.

One disciple (or potential disciple) is recalled as requesting, 'Let me first go and bury my father'. But Jesus told him, 'Leave the dead to bury their own dead' (Matt. 8.21-22/Luke 9.59-60).[69] The offensiveness of Jesus' reply has been much emphasized in recent years. To bury his father was one of the most elementary duties of a son; in Jewish custom (*m. Ber.* 3.1) it came before other fundamental religious duties like reciting the Shema.[70] Jeremias draws attention to the implicit urgency: 'In Palestine, burial took place on the day of death, but it was followed by six days of mourning on which the bereaved family received expressions of sympathy. Jesus cannot allow so long a delay'.[71] Bailey however suggests that an idiomatic usage has been misunderstood: 'the phrase "to bury one's father" is a traditional idiom that refers specifically to the duty of the son to remain at home and care for his parents until they are laid to rest respectfully': the delay might be considerable![72]

A similar urgency is evident in the third saying included by Luke (9.61-62): the would-be disciple is not even allowed to take leave of his family — in

---

69. The variation in detail between Matthew and Luke is what we might expect in oral retellings; contrast H. Fleddermann, 'The Demands of Discipleship Matt 8,19-22 par. Luke 9,57-60', in F. Van Segbroeck et al., eds., *The Four Gospels 1992: Festschrift Frans Neirynck* (Leuven: Leuven University, 1992) 541-61, who is unwilling to distinguish performance/retelling/editing from composition. For Matt. 8.20/Luke 9.58 see below, §16.4b(4).

70. See particularly Hengel, *Charismatic Leader* 8-15; Sanders, *Jesus and Judaism* 252-55. The offensiveness of the saying is a mark of its authenticity for both the Jesus Seminar (Funk, *Five Gospels* 161) and Lüdemann (*Jesus* 326).

71. Jeremias, *Proclamation* 132.

72. See further K. E. Bailey, *Through Peasant Eyes* (Grand Rapids: Eerdmans, 1980) 26-27; cf. Buchanan, *Jesus* 86; see also §14.4h below.

striking contrast to Elisha (1 Kgs 19.20-21).[73] Bailey again provides illumination from Middle Eastern culture: the request to 'take leave of' assumed the normal propriety of asking parental permission before responding to Jesus. In denying the request, Jesus was in effect claiming higher authority than the father — a shocking response.[74] An equivalent degree of commitment is called for in the saying which urges hearers (to strive) to enter through the narrow gate (into the kingdom/which leads to life) (Luke 13.24/Matt. 7.13-14).[75]

Jeremias also draws attention to the mission instruction, to 'exchange no greetings on the road' (Luke 10.4). 'This is a command which would be extremely offensive. In the East, greetings have a deeper significance than they do with us, because they have a religious meaning'. In Jesus' day it probably involved some ceremonial and consumed some time. The message of the kingdom cannot brook such delay (cf. 2 Kgs. 4.29).[76] A similar note is struck in another of Luke's singly attested sayings: the threat of unexpected calamity makes the call to repent all the more urgent (Luke 13.3, 5).[77] The weight which can be put on the latter sayings is not strong, but they are consistent with the urgency implicit in much of Jesus' kingdom teaching and in Matt. 8.21-22/Luke 9.59-60. And here as elsewhere there is no reason to set early church missionary enthusiasm against Jesus' imminent expectation as an either-or.

All four features, therefore, seem to have been characteristic of Jesus' mission call: to repent, to believe, and to follow, and to do so as a matter of urgent priority.

73. The reasons for the Jesus Seminar's rejection of Luke 9.62 as a word of Jesus are typical: 'Looking back (v. 62) suggests a social context in which group formation has already reached an advanced stage. . . . In addition, the image corresponds to themes in the Hebrew Bible: Lot's wife is destroyed when she looks back (Gen. 19.26). . . . (It) does not quite fit Jesus' exaggerated way of putting things' (Funk, *Five Gospels* 317). The first reason reads more in than out, the second makes the typically arbitrary assumption that Jesus' followers, but not Jesus, could have been influenced by a biblical story like that of Lot's wife, and the conclusion can only be described as odd (contrast Lüdemann, *Jesus* 326-27).

74. *Through Peasant Eyes* 27-31.

75. Cited above, §8.5d. That the saying goes back to Jesus in some form is agreed by Perrin, *Rediscovering* 144-45, and Funk, *Five Gospels* 347.

76. Jeremias, *Proclamation* 133; Fitzmyer notes that the instruction 'has also been interpreted not so much of haste as of dedication' (*Luke* 847), though evidently the effect would be the same. Despite its sole attestation by Luke, Robinson/Hoffmann/Kloppenborg have no hesitation in including Luke 10.4b in Q (*Critical Edition of Q* 164-65).

77. See above, chapter 12 n. 221. But urgency is not the same as rashness, as the Lukan parables on building a tower and going to war clearly indicate (Luke 14.28-33); on which see Hultgren, *Parables* 137-45.

13.3. To Israel

To whom was the call directed? To the people as a whole, to groups, to individuals, to individuals as Israelites, or what? We have already noted some distinction between a call to repentance and trust broadcast more widely and a call to discipleship directed to particular individuals, though the talk of 'following' Jesus made the distinction somewhat less clear.[78] But greater clarity is possible when we take seriously the recent recognition that Jesus entertained some hope for the restoration of Israel and directed his mission, in at least some measure, to that end.[79]

a. The Call to Return

If it is indeed the case that behind the Greek *metanoeō* is the Hebrew *šub* (§13.2a), then it should not escape notice that the call to 'repent' was a call to 'return'. This was a frequent appeal in the prophets,[80] including but by no means only the return necessary if the scattered of Israel were to be restored to the land.[81] Particularly poignant was the repeated call of Jeremiah 3: 'return, apostate Israel', 'return, apostate sons' (3.12, 14, 22).[82] In all cases the appeal was to Israel as a whole, to the covenant people failing as a whole to keep covenant with their God, though we should also note Ps. 22.27: 'All the ends of the earth shall remember and turn to the Lord; and all the families of the nations shall worship before you/him'. Similarly, the call to 'trust' (§13.2b) has covenantal overtones: to rely on Yahweh, on his commitment to his people.[83] The covenantal implications are evident in all the biblical passages cited above (n. 62) and Deut. 32.20, though, as with Ps. 22.27, we should again note the reminder to Israel that other nations could also trust in Israel's God (Jonah 3.5). We may conclude confidently, then, that any call of Jesus to 'repent and believe' would have been heard by his hearers as a reiteration of the prophetic call to the people of Israel to return to their God and to trust him afresh.

78. The same issue has been highlighted by Hengel, *Charismatic Leader* 59-63, and Sanders, *Jesus* 222-27.

79. See above, chapter 12 nn. 34, 35.

80. Isa. 44.22; 55.7; Ezek. 18.30; Hos. 3.5; 6.1; 14.2; Joel 2.12-13; Zech. 1.3; Mal. 3.7. But note again the enigmatic Isa. 6.10: '. . . lest . . . they turn and be healed' (see above, §13.1).

81. Deut. 30.2-5, 10; Jer. 24.5-7. Wright again focuses the motif too narrowly on return from exile (*Jesus* 246-58).

82. Jer. 3.12: *šubâ mᵉšubâ yisra'el* (literally 'turn back, turned-away Israel'); 3.14, 22: *šubu banim šubabim* (literally 'turn back, turned-away sons').

83. Cf. Wright, *Jesus* 258-64; McKnight, *New Vision* 164-66.

Does this also mean that Jesus hoped for a national return to God along the lines, perhaps, of the national revival of the time of Josiah (2 Chron. 34–35)? Did he share the later belief that if Israel would only repent, then the eschatological transition to the new age would take place and the full range of expectation for the age to come would be fulfilled?[84] The answers to these questions are less than clear.

b. The Choice of Twelve

Despite some counter-hypotheses (more idiosyncratic than persuasive), few questers have doubted that Jesus drew a circle of twelve disciples round him, a more intimate group than the larger ill-defined group of disciples. John Meier has recently reviewed the whole question thoroughly and little more needs to be added.[85] The key arguments are as they have always been.

(1) 'The twelve' as a description of a group of disciples close to Jesus is firmly rooted and widespread in the Jesus tradition.[86] The degree of variation[87] is typical of oral presentation. Notable is the fact that Paul recalls the summary of the gospel, which he received at his conversion (within two or three years of Jesus' crucifixion), as including a reference to a resurrection appearance to 'the twelve' (1 Cor. 15.5). It is hardly likely that this already traditional description of Jesus' closest disciples was established only as a result of the resurrection appearances[88] and much more likely that it reflects a core group already established round Jesus during his Galilean mission.

84. Str-B 1.162-65; but already implicit in Acts 3.19-21.

85. J. P. Meier, 'The Circle of the Twelve: Did It Exist during Jesus' Public Ministry?', *JBL* 116 (1997) 635-72, with full bibliographical details; also *Marginal Jew* 3.128-47; Meier also examines the data relating to each of the twelve (3.199-245). Of earlier treatments see particularly R. P. Meye, *Jesus and the Twelve* (Grand Rapids: Eerdmans, 1968) 192-209.

86. Mark 3.16/Matt. 10.2/Luke 6.13; Mark 4.10; Mark 6.7/Matt. 10.1/Luke 9.1; Mark 9.35; Mark 10.32/Matt. 20.17/Luke 18.31; Mark 11.11; Mark 14.10/Matt. 26.14/Luke 22.3; Mark 14.17/Matt. 26.20; Mark 14.20; Mark 14.43/Matt. 26.47/Luke 22.47; Matt. 19.28/Luke 22.30; Matt. 10.5; 11.1; Luke 8.1; 9.12; John 6.67, 70, 71; 20.24.

87. E.g., Matthew sometimes speaks of 'twelve disciples' (Matt. 10.1; 11.1; 20.17); Luke 9.12 reads 'the twelve' where Matthew and Mark have 'the disciples'; all three Synoptics refer to them as 'apostles' (Mark 6.30/Luke 9.10; Matt. 10.2/Luke 6.13; Luke 11.49; 17.5; 22.14; 24.10), partly in reflection of their role as Jesus' envoys (Mark 3.14; Matt. 10.2/Luke 6.13) and partly because of their subsequent status (hence the prominence of the term in Luke; cf. Acts *passim*).

88. The implication of the list of witnesses in 1 Cor. 15.3-8 is that the appearance to 'the twelve' was early. By then Judas had presumably disappeared from the scene, but 'the twelve' had already become fixed as a designation of Jesus' closest disciples. The Evangelists, how-

(2) There are several lists of 'the twelve':

Matt. 10.2-4	Mark 3.16-19	Luke 6.14-16	Acts 1.13
Simon Peter	Simon Peter	Simon Peter	Peter
Andrew his brother	James (son of	Andrew his	John
James (son of	Zebedee)	brother	James
Zebedee)	John brother of	James	Andrew
John brother of	James	John	
James	Andrew		
Philip	Philip	Philip	Philip
Bartholomew	Bartholomew	Bartholomew	Thomas
Thomas	Matthew	Matthew	Bartholomew
Matthew	Thomas	Thomas	Matthew
James (son of	James (son of	James (of	James (of
Alphaeus)	Alphaeus)	Alphaeus)	Alphaeus)
Thaddeus	Thaddeus	Simon the Zealot	Simon the Zealot
Simon the Cananean	Simon the Cananean	Jude (of) James	Jude (of) James
Judas Iscariot	Judas Iscariot	Judas Iscariot	

Again the variations are what we might expect in oral transmission: Simon Peter is as firmly rooted at the top as Judas Iscariot is at the end, though Philip and James (son of Alphaeus) also hold regular places at the head of the other two groups of four; otherwise the order varies (even between the two Lukan lists) for no obvious reason (beyond keeping Andrew with his brother). Most interesting is the discrepancy among the third groups of four: Thaddeus (Matthew/Mark) or Jude (of) James (Luke),[89] not to mention a certain degree of confusion as to who is 'the son of Alphaeus'.[90] This suggests that the degree of fixity in the oral transmission varied among the three groups of four, implying that the membership of the third group was deemed less important than that of the other two and so was

---

ever, do observe numerical propriety (Matt. 28.16; Luke 24.9, 33; Acts 1.26). How little of any of this can be attributed to Pauline influence is indicated by the total absence of any attempt to resolve or ease the dilemma that 'the apostle Paul' (a designation on which Paul himself was most insistent) was not one of the twelve apostles.

89. As is well known, John 14.22 attests a second Jude/(Judas). Pesch wonders whether Jude was introduced to the list in order to secure apostolic authority for the author of the letter of Jude (*Markusevangelium* 1.208). Meier ('Circle of Twelve' 648; *Marginal Jew* 3.131) and Casey (*Aramaic Sources* 196) air the possibility that one early member of the twelve left the group during Jesus' ministry and was replaced by another, though there is no hint of a replacement prior to Acts 1.21.

90. Levi (Mark 2.14; *Gos. Pet.* 14.60) = Matthew (Matt. 9.9) or James (Mark 3.18 pars.; Acts 1.13)?

recalled with less care.[91] Which suggests in turn that members of that group played a less prominent role in the earliest groups and churches, with the result that their identity (as members of Jesus' own inner circle) became somewhat confused in the corporate memory.[92] If this is indeed the case, then it is all the more striking that the fact of twelve core disciples was so firmly established in the tradition.

This line of reflection becomes stronger when we remember that the Jesus tradition records the actual calls of only five of the core disciples, the first four[93] and Levi/Matthew.[94] One might have expected that the tendency to glorify Jesus' twelve intimates evident from the second century[95] would already have resulted in their conversions/calls being regarded as a treasured item in repeated performances of the Jesus tradition during the first century.[96] But we hear nothing of how Thomas, Bartholomew and the last group of four came to follow Jesus. This presumably means that the early tradition was not much interested in them or their personalities.[97] Which presumably confirms that they made little impact on the corporate memory of the first Christian groups and churches. Several of those

91. It is perhaps significant in this regard that Papias mentions only the first seven (excluding Bartholomew) (Eusebius, *HE* 3.39.4).

92. 'So quickly did they fade from the scene that the majority of the names in the lists of the Twelve are just that — names and little more' (Meier, *Marginal Jew* 3.147). Cf. Casey, *Aramaic Sources* 195-96.

93. Peter and Andrew, James and John (Mark 1.16-20/Matt. 4.18-22 with Luke 5.1-11 and John 1.37-42). Note also Philip (John 1.43). Nathanael (John 1.45-51) has been identified with Simon the Cananean in the Greek liturgy, and with Bartholomew, but with insufficient reason (Brown, *John 1–12* 82); as we saw above (§13.2c) Jesus 'called' more than the twelve.

94. Levi/Matthew (Mark 2.14-15 pars.); but the puzzling disagreement between Mark/Luke (Levi) and Matthew (Matthew) raises the question whether the two were different persons and whether Mark 2.14-15 remembers the call of a toll-collector called 'Levi' but not the call of Matthew, one of the twelve, a question resolved by Matthew in renaming the toll-collector 'Matthew' (see discussion in Gnilka, *Matthäusevangelium* 1.330-31; Davies and Allison, *Matthew* 2.98-99).

95. See, e.g., W. A. Bienert in Schneemelcher and Wilson, *New Testament Apocrypha* 2.18-25.

96. Cf. §18.4c below. Undoubtedly the call of the two pairs of brothers (Mark 1.16-20 pars.) has been idealized, at least to some extent, presumably to give them paradigmatic status; the fact that the Synoptists have passed over any information regarding earlier contacts between Jesus and Andrew and Simon (John 1.40-42) gives the episodes added drama. But the performative flourish should not detract from the essential historicity of Jesus' call of the brothers (see particularly Pesch, *Markusevangelium* 112-14; Davies and Allison, *Matthew* 1.393-95; also below, chapter 14 n. 60).

97. In the Fourth Gospel, Andrew (John 1.40-42, 44; 6.8; 12.22), Thomas (11.16; 14.5; 20.24-28; 21.2), Philip (1.43-48; 6.5-7; 12.21-22; 14.8-9), and Judas, not Iscariot (John 14.22) all have larger roles.

whom Jesus chose literally left little or no mark.[98] Once again, then, it was the memory of twelve which stuck; the detail of who made up the twelve was of much less significance.

(3) Above all there is the presence of Judas the traitor in the list. That it was indeed 'one of the twelve',[99] 'who handed him (Jesus) over',[100] is again firmly rooted in the tradition of the first Christians. It must be judged very unlikely that the earliest tradents would have chosen on their own initiative to retroject such a choice back into the life of Jesus, raising questions as it did about Jesus' own insight into the character of his most intimate group of disciples.[101]

The point here is that the symbolism of 'twelve' is quite clear. The implication is that these disciples were thus chosen by Jesus for a role somewhat analogous to that of the twelve patriarchs of Israel.[102] That is, they were somehow to represent the restored people, the number twelve presumably indicating the reunification of the separated tribes, as in Ezek. 37.15-22.[103] That this deduction is on the right lines is strongly confirmed by the only Q passage which speaks of twelve: those thus specially chosen by Jesus will sit on (twelve) thrones judging

---

98. Even with James and John, the fact that they were nicknamed 'Boanerges, sons of thunder' (according to Mark 3.17) and the reason for the nickname are hardly to be explained by any traditions regarding them surviving from the period of the first churches (on the possible Galilean provenance of the nickname, see Dalman, *Words* 49). But there is always 'the beloved disciple' of the Fourth Gospel to be considered (see below, vol. 3).

99. Meier refers particularly to Mark 14.43 and John 6.71 as evidence of old tradition ('Circle of Twelve' 645).

100. Mark 3.19/Matt. 10.4/Luke 6.16; Matt. 26.25; 27.3; John 6.71; 18.2, 5. See also Mark 14.10, 43 pars.; Acts 1.16. See further below, §17.1b.

101. Meier naturally emphasises the criterion of embarrassment at this point ('Circle of Twelve' 663-70; *Marginal Jew* 3.143). 'It is harder to imagine how the promise of messianic dignity to the Twelve could have arisen only after Easter' (Theissen and Merz, *Historical Jesus* 216-17). Charlesworth relates how he changed his mind on the subject (*Jesus* 136-38). Because he cannot envisage the role played by such a betrayer, Funk judges 'Judas Iscariot the betrayer in all probability a gospel fiction' (*Honest* 234). Similarly Crossan, against the obvious trend of the evidence, argues that Judas was not one of the Twelve, since the institution 'did not exist until after Jesus' death' (*Who Killed Jesus?* [San Francisco: Harper, 1996] 81).

102. Cf. Jas. 1.1; Rev. 7.4-8; 22.2. 'The twelve are a visible symbol that the proclamation of the Kingdom of God is directed to all Israel' (Becker, *Jesus* 233).

103. Of the texts listed in chapter 12 n. 57, note also particularly Jer. 3.18 and Sir. 36.11. See also Horsley, *Jesus* 199-201; Gnilka, *Jesus* 183; Meier, *Marginal Jew* 3.148-54; S. McKnight, 'Jesus and the Twelve', *BBR* 11 (2001) 203-31. *Pace* Rowland, *Christian Origins* 152, 'twelve' implies restoration rather than remnant theology. Wright wonders whether the inner group of three (Peter, James, and John; see below, chapter 13 n. 250) was a Davidic symbol echoing the three who were David's closest bodyguards (2 Sam. 23.8-23; 1 Chron. 11.10-25) (*Jesus* 300).

the twelve tribes of Israel (Matt. 19.28/Luke 22.30).[104] At the same time, we should note that no attempt is made to choose each of the twelve from each of the twelve tribes, even symbolically; the symbolism was not dependent on any genealogy. And the note of restoration is also ambivalent, since the only role attributed to the twelve is that of dispensing judgment on Israel.[105] Nonetheless, the significance of the twelve as somehow symbolizing Israel in its (restored) wholeness is clear enough.[106]

c. The Flock of Yahweh

Notable also are the sheep and shepherd metaphors within the Jesus tradition — notable because they clearly evoked the popular image of Israel as Yahweh's flock.[107] The allusions are rather diverse and more weakly attested than most of the evidence reviewed thus far. But Jesus is remembered as drawing on this imagery on several occasions: the parable of the lost sheep, used differently by Matthew and Luke (Matt. 18.12/Luke 15.4),[108] the commission to go to 'the lost sheep of the house of Israel' (only in Matt. 10.6; 15.24),[109] and the quotation of Zech. 13.7 in Mark 14.27/Matt. 26.31.[110] Luke 12.32 also has Jesus encouraging

104. See also above, chapter 12 nn. 178, 205. W. Horbury, 'The Twelve and the Phylarchs', *NTS* 32 (1986) has reservations at this point.

105. See further above, chapter 12 n. 205. Again, as several have pointed out, it would be odd that a saying was subsequently attributed to Jesus which numbered Judas as one of Israel's judges (e.g., V. Hampel, *Menschensohn und historischer Jesus: Ein Rätselwort als Schlüssel zum messianischen Selbstverständnis Jesu* [Neukirchen-Vluyn: Neukirchener, 1990] 151; Meier, 'Circle of Twelve' 656).

106. Witherington justifiably warns against a simple identification of 'the twelve' with (all) 'the disciples'; 'Apparently the Twelve was formed not to be Israel, but rather to free Israel in light of what was to come' (*Christology* 127-28, 131).

107. Gen. 49.24; Pss. 28.9; 74.1; 77.20; 78.52; 79.13; 80.1; 100.3; Isa. 40.11; 49.9-10; Jer. 13.17, 20; Ezek. 34; Mic. 2.12; 5.4; 7.14; Zech. 10.2-3; 11.7, 15-17; Sir. 18.13; *Pss. Sol.* 17.40.

108. But also attested by *GTh* 107; *Gos. Truth* 31–32. For comparison of the four versions see Hultgren, *Parables* 49-52. The parable is regarded as probably going back to Jesus by both the Jesus Seminar (Funk, *Five Gospels* 214-15) and Lüdemann (*Jesus* 363), in both cases because such 'exaggerations' (leaving ninety-nine to look for one) are typical of Jesus; cf. also Becker, *Jesus* 139-40. The parable was also probably the basis for the Fourth Evangelist's more elaborate treatment of the theme (John 10.1-18). Note also Luke 19.10.

109. See above, chapter 12 n. 266.

110. On the text form see Davies and Allison, *Matthew* 3.485-86. As with most of the OT allusions in the Passion narrative, the reference to Zech. 13.7 here is usually seen as evidence of subsequent Christian reflection, though we can say that a Jesus who reflected on the sheep/shepherd imagery of Jewish thought might well have seen in Zech. 13.7 some foreshad-

his disciples: 'Do not be afraid, little flock; because your Father is pleased to give you the kingdom'[111] — where again the allusion is evidently to Israel as the flock protected by its divine shepherd.[112] Elsewhere the image of Israel like scattered sheep lacking direction, as in the wilderness (Num. 27.17) or under failing leadership,[113] is evoked by the depiction/(memory?) of people straggling round the shore of the lake to hear more from Jesus (Mark 6.34). Matthew has moved the allusion to introduce his version of the commission of the twelve (Matt. 9.36). Both are the work of the narrator, but the fact that Jesus' mission evoked such imagery can count as a strengthening of the likelihood that the imagery was prompted by what Jesus himself said and did.

In short, the imagery of Israel as Yahweh's flock had an irregular role within the Jesus tradition, but it is more likely that the extent to which the imagery is played upon was prompted by memory of Jesus' own usage than otherwise.

d. Inheriting the Land

In §12.4c we observed that Matthew's third beatitude ('Blessed are the meek, for they shall inherit the land/earth') clearly alludes to Ps. 37.11 ('The meek shall possess the land'). More to the point here, the allusion is clearly a play on the ancient covenant promise that Abraham's descendants would inherit the land.[114] Although Matthew probably took the beatitude's promise in a spiritual sense (§13.4b), we should at least be aware of the underlying strand of thought: in some sense 'the meek' would enjoy the fulfilment of the ancient covenant promise to Israel's patriarchs.

e. A New Covenant

As we saw above, it is likely that the last supper tradition recollects Jesus' final meal together with his disciples (§8.5c). Here we need simply observe that Jesus is recalled as describing it as a covenant meal, indeed, in the version common to Luke and Paul, as 'the new covenant in my (Jesus') blood' (Luke 22.20/1 Cor.

---

owing of his own fate. A similar understanding of Zech. 13.7 is reflected in CD 19.6-10 (see below, §17.5c).

111. Its isolated attestation puts Luke 12.32's status as a word of Jesus in question for most, though we can at least say that it is consistent with the rest of the motif (see also Beasley-Murray, *Jesus and the Kingdom* 185-87; Hampel, *Menschensohn* 39-40).

112. Is there also an allusion to Dan. 7.27 (Jeremias, *Proclamation* 181)?

113. 1 Kgs. 22.17; 2 Chron. 18.16; Jer. 50.6; Ezek. 34.5-6; Zech. 10.2; Jdt. 11.19.

114. Gen. 12.7; 13.15; 15.18; 17.8; 24.7; 26.3; 28.4, 13; 35.12; 48.4.

11.25). The implication, once again, is that as the Qumran community saw itself as participants in the 'new covenant',[115] so Jesus saw the group around him as anticipatory fulfilment of the new covenant (Jer. 31.31-34) which Yahweh was to make with his people.[116] As the twelve somehow represented restored Israel, so they represented Israel under the new covenant. No more need be said at this point, but we will return to the passage later (§17.5d[3]).

f. The Assembly of Yahweh

In two famous passages in Matthew, Jesus is reported as speaking of his *ekklēsia.* Matt. 16.18: 'You are Peter *(Petros)* and on this rock *(petra)* I will build my *ekklēsia,* and the gates of hell will not prevail over it'; Matt. 18.17: '. . . if he (your brother) refuses to listen to them (those who seek to reason with him), tell it to the *ekklēsia;* and if he refuses to listen even to the *ekklēsia,* let him be to you as a Gentile and a toll-collector'. Both passages are probably redactional and indicative of later developments. The former elaborates or cuts across Jesus' terser response to Peter in Mark 8.30, and the latter is part of what appears to be a developed rule of community discipline, reflecting the subsequent context where individual communities were called *ekklēsia* ('church').[117]

The only cause for pause is the fact that *ekklēsia* is regularly used in the LXX (about 100 times) to translate the Hebrew *qahal,* 'assembly'. Most notable are the phrases *qahal Yahweh* and *qahal Israel.*[118] In view of the evidence reviewed in this section (§13.3), the likelihood cannot be excluded that Jesus did speak on occasion of the assembly of Yahweh, and that he thereby intimated his hope to gather around himself the core of a reconstituted Israel. Perhaps even the thought would have been implicit that as those who gathered to hear Moses speak to them from God were his *qahal/ekklēsia,* so too those gathered to hear Jesus speak from God were a renewed *qahal/ekklēsia.* Any memory of Jesus on

---

115. CD 6.19; 8.21; 19.33-34; 20.12; 1QpHab 2.3-6; cf. 1QSb (1Q28b) 3.26; 5.21-23.

116. See further above, chapter 12 n. 65. Becker argues that since the (new) covenant idea is characteristic of the post-Easter church and not at home elsewhere in the preaching of Jesus, the conclusion is unavoidable that the covenant motif does not come from Jesus (*Jesus* 128-29). But the motif is wholly consistent with Jesus' more widely attested hopes for some sort of restoration of Israel.

117. See further below, vol. 3.

118. *Qahal Yahweh,* Num. 16.3; 20.4; Deut. 23.1-3, 8; 1 Chron. 28.8; Neh. 13.1; Mic. 2.5. *Qahal Israel* — Exod. 12.6; Lev. 16.17; Num. 14.5; Deut. 31.30; Josh. 8.35; 1 Kgs. 8.14, 22, 55; 12.3; 1 Chron. 13.2; 2 Chron. 6.3, 12-13. See further Davies and Allison, *Matthew* 2.613, 629. Jeremias notes 4QpPs 37(4Q171) 3.16: '(God) established him (the Teacher of Righteousness) . . . to build for himself a congregation *(lbnot lo 'dt) . . .'* (*Proclamation* 168). Still deserving of consideration is Cullmann, *Peter* 193-99.

the point has evidently been elaborated by Matthew. But whatever is to be made of the particular focus on Peter in 16.18 (see below, n. 251), the confidence that Yahweh's assembly would never be finally defeated by evil ('the gates of hell') would be very Jewish in character[119] and consistent with Jesus' eschatological assurance regarding the kingdom.[120]

g. A New Temple?

If I may draw on a conclusion to be argued for later, it is also likely that Jesus was remembered as saying something about the Jerusalem Temple being destroyed and rebuilt again (Mark 14.58).[121] Here again we recall that the building of a new temple was part of Jewish expectation.[122] The point to be noted here is the possibility that a renewed temple may have served as an image for a renewed/sanctified community.[123] We know that Qumran understood itself as a priestly community, functioning as an alternative to the corrupted cult in Jerusalem.[124] And it is possible that the first Christians understood themselves in a somewhat similar manner — as the beginning or base of a rebuilt house of God. (1) Paul's reference to James, Cephas, and John as 'pillars' (Gal. 2.9) evokes the picture of the Temple[125] and suggests that these three leading apostles were regarded as 'pillars in the (eschatological) temple' (as in Rev. 3.12).[126] (2) The idea of a group of believers as a 'temple or house of God' was evidently familiar within

119. Cf. Meyer, *Aims of Jesus* 192-95. Davies and Allison compare particularly Isa. 28.15-19 and 1QH 14[= 6].19-31 (*Matthew* 2.630, 632-34). See also above, chapter 12 n. 79.

120. K. Berger, *Formgeschichte des Neuen Testaments* (Heidelberg: Quelle und Meyer, 1984) 182-84, raises the question whether Jesus' talk of 'entering the kingdom' is a deliberate echo of the requirements for entry to the assembly (particularly Deut. 23.2-8); see also Horn, 'synoptischen Einlasssprüche' 197-200. Meier concludes that Matt. 16.16-19 first emerged in a post-Easter setting (*Marginal Jew* 3.226-35).

121. See below, §15.3a.

122. See above, chapter 12 n. 66.

123. Horsley, *Jesus* 292-96.

124. See particularly CD 3.12–4.12; 4QFlor. 1.1-7 and further B. Gärtner, *The Temple and the Community in Qumran and the New Testament* (SNTSMS 1; Cambridge: Cambridge University, 1965) chs. 2 and 3; G. Klinzing, *Die Umdeutung des Kultus in der Qumrangemeinde und im NT* (Göttingen: Vandenhoeck und Ruprecht, 1971) II. Teil; Newton, *Concept of Purity* ch. 2, especially 34-36.

125. 'Pillar' *(stylos)* is most frequently used in the LXX in reference to the supports of the tabernacle and pillars of the Temple. Particularly notable are the twin pillars set up in front of Solomon's temple (1 Kgs. 7.15-22; 2 Chron. 3.15-17), named Jachin and Boaz, which evidently had a covenant significance (2 Kgs. 23.3; 2 Chron. 34.31) now lost to us.

126. C. K. Barrett, 'Paul and the "Pillar" Apostles', in J. N. Sevenster, ed., *Studia Paulina*, J. de Zwaan FS (Haarlem: Bohn, 1953) 15-19.

earliest Christianity,[127] not to mention a sense somewhat similar to that at Qumran of being a priestly community.[128] (3) Jesus' talk of a new/rebuilt temple (Mark 14.58) is interpreted by the Fourth Evangelist as a reference to his own (resurrected) body (John 2.21), which conceivably may help explain Paul's ready assumption that the community of believers are in some sense 'the body of Christ' (Rom. 12.4-5; 1 Cor. 12.12-27). The data are rather sketchy and the connections convoluted, but they do at least suggest the intriguing hypothesis that Jesus saw the community of his disciples as in some sense the core of a renewed worshipping people of God.

h. The Diaspora?

With the hope of a restored Israel so prominently expressed in Jesus' mission, one might have expected some explicit reference to the return of the scattered exiles of Israel. Such an expectation could/would of course be included within the talk of repentance/return and the symbolism of the (restored) twelve (tribes). But it is surprising in that case that Jesus gave no clearer indications on the subject: the call to return is one which was repeated through Israel's history, not limited to a particular situation in that history; no attempt was made to include a diaspora Jew among the twelve. What about 'the lost sheep of the house of Israel'? But the commission of Matt. 10.6 hardly has the diaspora in view, since in the preceding sentence the disciples are forbidden to go 'on the way of/towards the Gentiles' (10.5).[129] And we have already noted the possibility that the similar allusion in the story of the Syrophoenician woman (Matt. 15.24) may at best suggest that Jesus extended his mission to greater Israel (§§9.9f). So too the imagery of the 'sheep without a shepherd' (Mark 6.34/Matt. 9.36) seems to be directed more against the failures of Jewish leadership[130] than to gathering in the scattered outcasts. It is true that Luke has set the parable of the lost sheep in parallel to the parable of the prodigal son (Luke 15.4-7, 11-32), with the latter's reference to the younger son's time in a 'far country' (15.13), but any equivalent inference has to be read into the former. All in all, once again, we have to conclude that little or no attempt has been made in the Jesus tradition to include the thought that Jesus' mission aimed to restore Israel by bringing exiled Israel to repentance as in Deut. 30.2.[131]

In sum, although the evidence becomes increasingly tenuous, the initial

---

127. 1 Cor. 3.9, 16; 6.19; 2 Cor. 6.16; Eph. 2.21; 1 Pet. 2.5.
128. Rom. 5.2; 12.1-2; 15.16; Phil. 2.25; 1 Pet. 2.5; Rev. 1.6; 5.10; 20.6.
129. See Jeremias, *Promise* 19-21; discussion in Davies and Allison, *Matthew* 2.168-69.
130. See above, n. 113.
131. See further above, §12.6c(2).

considerations are enough to establish the conclusion that Jesus was understood by his first disciples to have been engaged on a mission to and on behalf of Israel as a whole. His goal was the prophetic goal of recalling the people to return to their God. He chose twelve to be his inner group of disciples to represent Israel renewed (new covenant) and recalled to its destiny. He had a special concern for the sheep separated from the flock of Yahweh. The assumption, we can only infer, was that of the prophets: that Israel would flourish as a community only when as a people it genuinely turned to and trusted in God.

But would that ensure the coming of the kingdom, or would it be proof that the kingdom had come? We need to fill out the picture further.

13.4. To the Poor

Of all the prophecies which may have influenced Jesus, Isa. 61.1 stands out: 'The Spirit of the Lord God is upon me, because the Lord has anointed me; he has sent me to bring good news to the poor ('anawim/ptōchois)...'. Its influence is evident in the allusions to Isaianic prophecies in the reply to the Baptist's query (Matt. 11.5/Luke 7.22).[132] And the opening sequence of beatitudes (Matt. 5.3-6/Luke 6.20b-21) seems to have been framed with Isa. 61.1-3 (7) in mind.[133] So even if

132. See above, §12.5c(1).

133.

Isa. 61.1-3, (7)	Matt. 5.3-6	Luke 6.20b, 21b, 21a
(1) to preach good news to the poor	(3) Blessed are the poor . . .	(20) Blessed are the poor . . .
(2) to comfort all who mourn	(4) Blessed are those who mourn, for they shall be comforted	(21b) Blessed are you who weep now, for you shall laugh
(1) to preach good news to the poor	(5) Blessed are the meek,	
(7) they shall inherit the land (LXX)	for they shall inherit the land.	
	(6) Blessed are those who hunger and thirst for righteousness,	(21a) Blessed are those who hunger now,
(3) they will be called oaks of righteousness	for they shall be satisfied	for you shall be satisfied

The same tradition (Q?) probably lies behind both Matt. 5.4 and Luke 6.21b, and Luke modified it to heighten the parallel with Luke 6.25b. In which case Matthew has more likely preserved the earlier form, more closely echoing Isa. 61.2 (Fitzmyer, *Luke* 1.634; Robinson/Hoffmann/ Kloppenborg, *Critical Edition of Q* 48-49). In turn it becomes more likely that the echo of Isa. 61.1-2 evident in the sequence of Matthew's beatitudes was given in the tradition known to Matthew rather than being evidence of Matthean redaction (see further Davies and Allison, *Matthew* 1.436-39). On the overlap in meaning of 'poor' and 'meek' see above, chapter 12 n. 159.

Luke's portrayal of Jesus reading the passage and explicitly claiming its fulfilment (Luke 4.16-21) is an elaboration of the briefer tradition in Mark 6.1-6a, we can still be confident that his elaboration was based on a strong remembrance of Jesus making clear allusion to the passage on more than one occasion.[134]

The point here is that the proclamation of the good news to the poor evidently ranked at the forefront of Jesus' conception of his mission. The list of eschatological blessings already manifest in Jesus' mission climaxes not with the most striking (the raising of the dead), but with the fact that 'the poor have good news proclaimed to them' (Matt. 11.5/Luke 7.22). The first beatitude is a benediction on the poor: 'Blessed are the poor . . .' (Matt. 5.3/Luke 6.20). Here is a clear answer to our question: For whom did Jesus intend his message? At or near the top of any list which Jesus himself might have drawn up were clearly 'the poor'.

a. Who Were 'the Poor'?

Behind the Greek term *ptōchoi*[135] stands a number of Hebrew terms, particularly *'aniyyim*.[136] The Hebrew terms denote material poverty in its various aspects and consequences. Of these consequences the most important were the social responsibilities thereby laid upon the Israelite community (to relieve poverty) and what today would be called 'God's option for the poor'.[137]

(1) In the agricultural economies of the ancient Near East ownership of land was the basis of economic security. *Material poverty* might be the result of any one or more of a number of factors: bad harvests caused by natural disaster, enemy invasion and appropriation, indolence and bad management, malpractice by powerful neighbours, or entrapment in a vicious cycle of debt at extortionate interest. The poor, then, were those who lacked a secure economic base. Like widows, orphans, and aliens, they were in an especially vulnerable position, without any means of self-protection.

---

134. See also above, chapter 12 n. 282.

135. It is normally used in the plural; in the Gospels the only individuals described as 'poor' are the widow (Mark 12.42-43/Luke 21.3) and Lazarus in the parable of Luke 16.20, 22. The NT makes almost no use of the relatively lesser term, *penēs* (only in 2 Cor. 9.9's quotation from Ps. 112.9); in Greek usage *penēs* denotes one who has to work, but in the LXX any distinction is blurred (F. Hauck, *penēs, TDNT* 6.37-39; E. Bammel, *ptōchos, TDNT* 6.894-95).

136. In the LXX (HR) *ptōchos* is used to translate *'ani* (39), but also other terms, notably *dal* (22), *'ebyon* (11), *'anaw* (4), and in Proverbs *rosh* (9). BDB gives as the range of meaning in each case: *'ani* 'poor, afflicted, humble'; *dal* 'crushed, oppressed'; *'ebyon* 'in want, needy, poor'; *'anaw* 'poor, afflicted, humble, meek'; *rosh* 'in want, poor'. Isa. 61.1 uses *'anaw*. See further Bammel, *TDNT* 6.888-902.

137. In what follows see particularly Gerstenberger, *TDOT* 11.242-51.

The consequent responsibility laid upon the community is most clearly documented in Deut. 15.7-11 and 24.10-15, 19-22, where the harsh reality of poverty is well illustrated. The day labourer who owns no land of his own and must work for others must be paid the same day, otherwise he will have no means of buying food and will go to bed hungry (24.15). The individual who has to pawn his one and only cloak must have it back before the day ends, otherwise he will have no means of warding off the cold of the night (24.12-13). The poor have to depend on the generosity of the landowner for any share in the harvest (24.19-21).[138] The social stigma of poverty is mirrored in a sequence of proverbs, which no doubt echoes the common wisdom of the time.[139]

(2) Material poverty left the poor vulnerable to *economic exploitation.* Poverty was by no means always the result of individual fecklessness or slothfulness, of natural disaster or enemy action. It was also a social condition, with social causes, often the result of greed and manipulation on the part of others. The poor were vulnerable before those members of society who controlled economic and political power, and who were willing to use that power ruthlessly. Consequently, the poor were also the downtrodden and oppressed, often pushed by circumstances to the margin of society. Two episodes during the monarchy well illustrate the contrasting helplessness of the less powerful and the ruthlessness of avaricious power — the story told by Nathan the prophet to illustrate David's abuse of power (2 Sam. 12.1-6) and king Ahab's corruption of legal process to secure the property of Naboth (1 Kings 21). Where such reasonably well-to-do people as Uriah and Naboth proved so powerless before the powerful, what hope had the poor? Of the great prophets, Amos and Isaiah in particular become spokesmen for the poor in vitriolic denunciation of the acquisitiveness and exploitation of the poor on the part of the rich.[140]

(3) Since they were helpless and hopeless in the face of human oppression, the poor needed to rely all the more on God. And so the idea of 'the poor' came to include *those who recognized their vulnerability and looked to God for help,* since they could look nowhere else.[141] The psalmist in particular responds with the assurance that God is the champion of the poor.[142] Noteworthy is the degree

138. See also Exod. 23.6, 11; Lev. 19.10; 23.22; 25.25; Job. 29.12; Prov. 19.7; 22.9, 22; 28.8, 27; 29.7, 14; 31.20; Sir. 4.1, 4, 8; 7.32; 29.9.

139. Prov. 13.8; 14.20; 18.23; 19.4; 23.21; 28.19; 30.8-9.

140. Amos 2.6-7; 4.1; 5.11-12; 8.4-6; Isa. 3.14-15; 5.8; 10.1-2; 32.7; 58.3, 6-7; see also Job 24.3-4, 9, 14; Pss. 10.2, 9; 37.14; 94.5-6; 109.16; Prov. 30.14; Ezek. 16.49; 18.12, 17; 22.29; Mic. 2.2; Zech. 7.9-10; Sir. 13.19, 21, 23; CD 6.16.

141. E.g., Job 5.16; Pss. 10.12-14; 25.16; 34.6; 69.29, 32.

142. Pss. 9.18; 10.14, 17; 12.5; 14.6; 22.24-26; 35.10; 40.17; 41.1; 68.5, 10; 69.33; 70.5; 72.12-13; 102.17; 113.7; 132.15; see also 1 Sam. 2.8; 2 Sam. 22.28; Job 34.28; 36.6; Prov. 3.34; Isa. 11.4; 14.32; 29.19; 41.17; 49.13; 61.1; Jer. 20.13; Sir. 21.5; *Pss. Sol.* 5.11; 15.1.

to which the psalmist and his community identify themselves as the poor and needy.[143] Nearer the time of Jesus, this self-designation is echoed in the *Psalms of Solomon* and the Dead Sea Scrolls.[144]

The traditional Jewish understanding of poverty, therefore, was neither simplified nor idealized.[145] Starting from the harsh, often brutal reality of poverty, it recognized different dimensions of poverty — material, social, and spiritual. It was a concern which spread across all parts of the Jewish Scriptures — from Torah legislation for the caring society, through prophetic denunciation of the ruthlessness and heartlessness of the rich, to the psalmist's confidence in God as preeminently the God of the poor.

b. Jesus and the Poor

At various points in §9.9 we reflected on how social and political circumstances must have influenced or affected Jesus in his youth and young manhood in Galilee. As a member of the family of a *tektōn,* brought up in a small and not very well-to-do village, he would not have experienced destitution but would certainly have been familiar with poverty, as were also his immediate circle of disciples.[146] He would almost certainly have been aware of the tax burden which his fellow villagers bore, how many were caught in a tightening cycle of debt, and that some had been forced to sell off their generations-old patrimony to become tenant farmers or day-labourers.[147] His parables reflect awareness of tensions which probably existed in villages within the sphere of influence of Sepphoris and

143. 'I am poor and needy' (Pss. 40.17; 70.5; 86.1; 109.22); see also Pss. 18.27; 37.14; 68.10; 69.32; 72.2, 4; 74.19, 21; 140.12; Isa. 54.11. See further Gerstenberger, *TDOT* 11.246-47, 250.

144. *Pss. Sol.* 5.2, 11; 10.6; 15.1; 18.2; 1QpHab 12.3, 6, 10; 1QM 11.9, 13; 13.13-14; CD 19.9; 4QpPs 37(4Q171) 2.9-10; 1QH 10[= 2].32, 34; 13[= 5].13-18, 21; 23[= 18].14. See further Bammel, *TDNT* 6.896-99; L. E. Keck, '"The Poor among the Saints" in Jewish Christianity and Qumran', *ZNW* 57 (1966) 54-78 (here 66-77); Gerstenberger, *TDOT* 11.236.

145. Crossan generalizes too quickly from Lenski's model that not just poverty but destitution is in view: 'the unclean, degraded and expendable classes', 'the destitute, the beggars, and the vagrants' (*Historical Jesus* 273, 275). Similarly *Birth* 320-21, 344, but he includes within 'the destitute' (= 'the landless peasant') 'tenant farmers, sharecroppers, day-laborers, and beggars' (321).

146. E. W. Stegemann and W. Stegemann, *The Jesus Movement: A Social History of Its First Century* (Minneapolis: Fortress, 1999), locate them in the 'lower rural stratum'; during 'their nomadic existence' at least they would belong to the *ptōchoi* (203).

147. See above, §9.6b. Crossan argues that 'Jesus' primary focus was on peasants dispossessed by Roman commercialization and Herodian urbanization in the late 20s in Lower Galilee' (*Birth* 325).

Tiberias (including his home village, Nazareth, and his base, Capernaum) — wealthy estate owners, resentment against absentee landlords, exploitative stewards of estates, family feuds over inheritance, and so on. Likewise his teaching on anxiety (Matt. 6.25-33/Luke 12.22-31) reflects the day-to-day worries of the subsistence poor: 'what you will eat . . . what you will wear', where the next food and drink will come from.[148] Nor should it be forgotten that the Lord's Prayer, however much it transcends its originating context, is at heart a prayer of the poor:[149] for *God's* kingdom to come, for *God's* justice to prevail, for the bread needed now — today,[150] for debts to be cancelled,[151] for resoluteness in the face of temptation to give up and abandon responsibilities, or for rescue from potential prosecution in court (Matt. 6.9-13/Luke 11.2-4).[152] And behind the promise to the meek (*'anawim, praeis*) that they will inherit the land (Matt. 5.5), lies the ancient ideal that *every* member of Israel should continue to have a stake or part in the land of promise/inheritance, including the poor.[153]

Jesus' own attitude to the poor may well be best reflected in three episodes recorded by Mark. Most striking of all is the episode where the rich (young) man[154] is exhorted: 'Go sell what you possess and give to the poor, and you will have treasure in heaven' (Mark 10.21).[155] The exhortation clearly reflects the wel-

148. See also Schottroff and Stegemann, *Hope of the Poor* 16-17, 39-40. F. G. Downing, *Christ and the Cynics* (Sheffield: Sheffield Academic, 1988), notes parallels in Cynic teaching (19-20). See further below, chapter 14 n. 45.

149. Cf. particularly Oakman, 'The Lord's Prayer in Social Perspective' 155-82.

150. Becker suggests that the Lord's Prayer was 'a table prayer of Jesus' adherents' (*Jesus* 159, 161).

151. It has been long recognized that behind Matthew's *opheilēma* ('debt') lies the Aramaic *hobha* (Jeremias, *Prayers* 92; Black, *Aramaic Approach* 140; see also Casey, *Aramaic Sources* 59-60). The point is not that Matthew has failed to appreciate a possible sense of *hobha* to mean 'sin' (better reflected in Luke's *hamartia*) but that the underlying imagery is of financial debt, 'money owed' (Jeremias 92). Cf. Horsley, *Jesus* 253-54; Chilton, *Rabbi Jesus* 79-80 ('the burden of owing what could not be repaid became the principal metaphor of that alienation from God from which one prayed for release').

152. Jeremias cites K. H. Rengstorf's description of Matt. 7.7/Luke 11.9 as 'beggars' wisdom' (*Proclamation* 191).

153. Cf. again 4QpPs 37 (4Q171) 2.4-11. On the overlap between 'poor' and 'meek' see again Bammel, *TDNT* 6.904 and above, chapter 12 n. 159.

154. Note the typical performance variations: only Matthew has him as a 'young man' (*neaniskos*); only Luke calls him a 'ruler' (*archōn*). On Matthew's modification of Mark's opening see above (chapter 7 n. 20). Other variations do not affect the discussion here, and the closeness of the Synoptic parallels makes it unnecessary to cite the whole passage.

155. Most accept that an episode from Jesus' life is here recalled (see, e.g., the brief survey in Davies and Allison, *Matthew* 3.40; Lüdemann, *Jesus* 69-70). The Jesus Seminar regards the final clause ('treasure in heaven') as 'almost certainly a later modification' (Funk, *Five Gospels* 91); but as the only reference to 'treasure (*thēsauros*)' in Mark, it is better seen either

fare concerns of Jewish society. More to the point: implicit in the story is a warning against the danger of wealth: that it becomes something to be relied on, something which facilitates self-indulgence, and presumably, in the light of the social context recalled above, a means of social influence and economic power over others. In a word, the danger is that a person's wealth may become that person's god (Matt. 6.24/Luke 16.13).[156] It should not escape notice that the episode provides a vivid illustration of two other teachings of Jesus shared by Matthew and Luke. Matt. 6.21/Luke 12.34:[157] 'Where your treasure is there will your heart be also'.[158] And Matt. 6.24/Luke 16.13 (= Q): 'No one can serve two masters, for either he will hate the one and love the other, or be devoted to one and despise the other; you cannot serve God and Mammon'.[159] Precisely because wealth creates a false sense of security, a trust which should be placed only in God,[160] it all too quickly and too often becomes the most serious alternative to God.

This perception presumably explains the starkness of the warnings attached to the story: 'How hard it will be for those who have riches to enter the kingdom of God' (Mark 10.23); 'It is easier for a camel to go through the eye of a

---

as a root from which the fuller motif in Matthew and Luke grew or as an indication of a motif more deeply rooted elsewhere in the Jesus tradition (see further below, n. 161).

156. On Matt. 6.24/Luke 16.13 see further below.

157. Cited above, in §8.5d; Robinson/Hoffmann/Kloppenborg are surprisingly confident in their reconstruction of Q here (*Critical Edition of Q* 328-31).

158. It is also surprising that the sequence Matt. 6.19-21 commands so little confidence among Jesus questers on the ground, presumably, that it contains popular wisdom subsequently attributed to Jesus (cf. Funk, *Five Gospels* 150-51; Lüdemann, *Jesus* 148) or that there is no room for the concept of reward in Jesus' teaching (Breech, *Silence of Jesus* 46-49). But both *Thomas* and James seem to have known versions of 6.19-20 (*GTh* 76.3; Jas. 5.2-3), and the episode with the rich (young) man also attests that Jesus is recalled as speaking of having treasure in heaven (Mark 10.21 pars.; see also above, n. 155). There is no parallel to 6.21 in any ancient collection of proverbs (Betz, *Sermon on the Mount* 435), so where did it come from, if not from Jesus? And the refusal to recognize any concept of reward in Jesus' teaching is quite arbitrary (contrast above, §12.4f; see further Davies and Allison, *Matthew* 1.633-34). On the contrary, as the citation of Matt. 6.19-21/Luke 12.33-34 in §8.5d shows, it offers a good example of oral tradition performed differently in the versions known to Matthew and Luke and subsequently developed differently again (in a Platonizing way) by Justin Martyr (text in Aland, *Synopsis* 89) and others (details in Betz, *Sermon* 435-37, who then makes the implausible suggestion that 6.21 is a *de*-Platonized version of the saying).

159. In contrast to the preceding passage, there is a substantial measure of confidence on all sides that Matt. 6.24/Luke 16.13 (cf. *GTh* 47.2; *2 Clem.* 6.1; *Ps.-Clem. Rec.* 5.9.4) goes back to Jesus (Funk, *Five Gospels* 151; Lüdemann, *Jesus* 148); further details in Davies and Allison, *Matthew* 1.643-45; Betz, *Sermon on the Mount* 454-59.

160. 'Mammon' is usually explained as deriving from *'mn* ('to trust'), that is, something relied on (in contrast to God); 'the word signifies "resources", "money", "property", "possessions"' (Davies and Allison, *Matthew* 1.643; see also Meier, *Marginal Jew* 3.589 nn. 92, 93).

needle than for a rich man to enter the kingdom of God' (10.25/*Gos. Naz.* 16).[161] The hyperbole of the last sentence should not be treated woodenly; but neither should its offensiveness be diminished.[162] It was evidently appreciated by those performing the Jesus tradition that the warning against the dangers of wealth had to be stated in the starkest terms (cf. Mark 8.36 pars.), even if the last word lay with the power and generosity of God (10.27). And even should it be the case that the qualification was added in the course of transmission,[163] it reflects too closely Jesus' insistence that the kingdom is God's and that he alone determines who may enter, to be regarded as a corruption of some idealistic egalitarianism attributed to Jesus on the basis of the hyperbole (10.25) alone.

In a later episode, the poor widow is commended for giving to the Temple what she needed even for subsistence living (Mark 12.41-44).[164] Here we can see reflected the typical conviction of the psalmist that the poor are likely to be more open to God than are the rich and that the little they can do is more highly regarded by God than are the great doings of the powerful. The Jesus who is thus remembered within the tradition is a Jew in tune with the sentiments and values of his ancestral piety.

Somewhat cutting across the implications of the first two episodes is Mark's account of the anointing at Bethany (14.3-9). In terms of tradition history it is one of the most complex examples within the Gospels, and thus a good test-case for the model of oral tradition put forward in chapter 8.

Matt. 26.6-12	Mark 14.3-9	John 12.1-8
6 Now while Jesus was at Bethany in the house of Simon the leper,	3 While he was at Bethany in the house of Simon the leper, as he sat at the table,	1 Six days before the Passover Jesus came to Bethany, the home of Lazarus, whom he had raised from the dead. 2 There they gave a dinner for him. Martha served, and Lazarus was one of those at the table with him. 3 Mary took a pound of
7 a woman came to him with an alabaster jar of very expensive ointment, and she poured it on his head as he sat at the table. 8 But when the disciples saw it, they were angry and said,	a woman came with an alabaster jar of very costly ointment of nard, and she broke open the jar and poured the ointment on his head. 4 But some were there who said to one another in anger,	very costly ointment made of pure nard, anointed Jesus' feet, and wiped them with her hair. The house was filled with the fragrance of the ointment. 4 But Judas Iscariot, one of his

161. Few doubt that either or both were first uttered by Jesus in one form or another (Funk, *Five Gospels* 91-92; Lüdemann, *Jesus* 70). See also M. Hengel, *Property and Riches in the Early Church* (London: SCM, 1974) 23-30.

162. See again the brief review in Davies and Allison, *Matthew* 3.51-52; and further Bailey, *Through Peasant Eyes* 165-66; Meier, *Marginal Jew* 3.586 n. 80.

163. Pesch, *Markusevangelium* 2.144; Schottroff and Stegemann, *Hope of the Poor* 22-23.

164. Text cited above in §8.4c(5).

		disciples (the one who was about to betray him), said, 5
'Why this waste? 9 For <u>this</u> could have been <u>sold</u> for a large sum, and the money given to the poor'. 10 But <u>Jesus</u>, aware of this, <u>said</u> to them, 'Why do you trouble the woman? She has performed a good service for me. 11 For <u>you always have the poor with you,</u>	'Why was this waste of ointment? 5 For <u>this</u> ointment could have been <u>sold</u> for more than three hundred denarii, and <u>the money given to the poor'.</u> And they scolded her. 6 But <u>Jesus</u> <u>said,</u> 'Let her alone; why do you trouble her? She has performed a good service for me. 7 For <u>you always have the poor with you,</u> and you can show kindness to them whenever you wish;	'Why was <u>this</u> ointment not <u>sold</u> for three hundred denarii and <u>the money given to the poor?'</u> . . . 7 <u>Jesus</u> <u>said,</u> 'Leave her alone. She bought it so that she might keep it for the day of my <u>burial.</u> 8 <u>You always have the poor with you,</u>
<u>but you do not always have me.</u> 12 By pouring this ointment on my body she has prepared me for <u>burial.</u> 13 Truly I tell you, wherever this good news is proclaimed in the whole world, what she has done will be told in remembrance of her'.	<u>but you do not always have me.</u> 8 She has done what she could; she has anointed my body beforehand for its <u>burial.</u> 9 Truly I tell you, wherever the good news is proclaimed in the whole world, what she has done will be told in remembrance of her'.	<u>but you do not always have me'.</u>

This was evidently a much told story, whose fixed (and identifying) details are clear:[165] an event in Bethany, an embarrassing anointing of Jesus by a woman using very expensive ointment, a protest by some (disciples) at the seeming waste of something which could have been sold and the proceeds given to the poor; and, most noticeably, the story's climax in the seeming harshness of Jesus' response: 'You always have the poor with you; but you do not always have me',[166] possibly in echo of Deut 15.11.[167] What is of particular interest at this point is the way the story cuts across the sentiments of the two earlier Markan narratives: the protest echoes Jesus' exhortation to the rich (young) man! And it is Jesus who now demurs.[168] Evidently, then, the story circulated widely within the early groups of Jesus' followers as a warning not to idealize or absolutize Je-

---

165. I have not included Luke 7.36-50: the identifying details are almost wholly lacking (it seems to be a different story); but in the course of the transmission history details from the versions recorded here seem to have been drawn into the story told by Luke.

166. It is less clear how the other element in Jesus' response functioned (Mark 14.8-9 pars.) — as a supplementary climax (Mark/Matthew), or incorporated into the climax (John). See the discussion in Davies and Allison, *Matthew* 3.442-43 and further below, §17.4b.

167. Deut. 15.11: 'There will never cease to be poor (*'ebyon*) in the land; therefore I command you, "Open wide your hand to your neighbour, to the needy (*'ani*) and poor (*'ebyon*), in the land"'.

168. It is precisely the fact that the saying cuts across the earlier emphasis of 10.21 which should caution against dismissing it as a remembered teaching of Jesus (*pace* Funk, *Five Gospels* 116).

sus' attitude to the poor: high as the priority for the poor is, there may be particular situations where even higher priorities prevail.[169]

The inference that Jesus' call to and teaching on the poor are not reducible to some class-war dogma is strengthened by another interesting feature within the Jesus tradition on this theme. I refer to the fact that Jesus seems to have been heard differently by the two other main interpreters of his teaching — Matthew and Luke. Or perhaps we should say that Jesus' teaching in regard to the poor was heard across the spectrum of the meaning of poverty.

Luke had no doubt that Jesus spoke for the poor, the materially impoverished. His version of the first beatitude is abrupt and to the point: 'Blessed are you poor' (Luke 6.20b). It is followed by the equally stark, 'Blessed are you who hunger now, because you will be filled; blessed are you who weep now, because you will laugh' (6.21). And the sequence of beatitudes is followed by a parallel sequence of elsewhere unattested woes — on the rich, those who are full, those who laugh — warning of the corresponding eschatological reverse (6.24-25).[170] Here we need to recall also that it is Luke who has recorded the Magnificat, with the matching confidence, 'He (God) has filled the hungry (peinōntas) with good things, and the rich he has sent empty away' (Luke 1.53), with its echo of Hannah's song in 1 Sam. 2.7-8. It is Luke who alone records the minatory parables of the rich fool (12.16-21) and of the rich man and the beggar (ptōchos) Lazarus (16.19-31).[171] It is Luke who elaborates the shared tradition which urges the storing of treasure in heaven with the exhortation: 'Sell your possessions and give alms' (Luke 12.33-34/Matt. 6.20-21). It is in Luke too that Jesus urges his host to invite the poor to the feast and presses his point upon his host with a parable (14.13, 21).[172] It is Luke who has Jesus warning against 'every kind of greediness (pleonexia)' (12.15) and who accuses the Pharisees of being 'avaricious (philargyros)' (16.14). And it is Luke who tells of one (Zacchaeus, the rich toll-collector) who did what the rich (young) man refused to do (19.8). Who can doubt that this is a Lukan emphasis.[173] At the same time, bearing in mind the

169. Schrage may be right in pointing to the uniqueness of the situation, which 'forbids making the woman's action the norm of Christian conduct after . . . Good Friday' (citing R. Storch). He is on stronger ground when he adds, 'The story does not enshrine a timeless principle to be cited in downplaying social obligations in favor of emphasis on the cult' (*Ethics* 73).

170. See above, §12.4c.

171. See above, chapter 12 n. 213. Cf. Bammel, *TDNT* 6.906: 'The point of the story . . . is not the failure of the rich man in relation to the poor but the ineluctable alienation of his life, and that of all rich men, from the sphere of God. The hope of the poor man . . . is in the world to come, though not entirely'. The rich man 'thinks of life in complete isolation from the communal responsibilities that life in a covenant community entails' (Kaylor, *Jesus* 145).

172. See further below, §14.8.

173. See further, e.g., Fitzmyer, *Luke* 247-51; Schottroff and Stegemann, *Hope of the*

force of the Jewish tradition regarding the poor, the likely influence of Isa. 61.1-2 on Jesus' understanding of his mission, and the episode of the rich (young) man, who can doubt also that Luke has simply elaborated (perhaps with stories which he sought out for that purpose) what was already recalled as a deep-rooted concern of Jesus himself?

Matthew, on the other hand, seems to have focused more on the other end of the spectrum of the Jewish tradition regarding the poor — 'the poor' as those who, having nothing in their own possession on which to rely, trust only in God. Hence his version of the first beatitude renders it as 'Blessed are the poor *in spirit . . .*' (Matt. 5.3),[174] and the blessed hungry are those who 'hunger and thirst *for righteousness*' (5.6). Unlike Luke, Matthew has been content simply to reproduce without elaboration the other references to the poor which he found in Q (Matt. 11.5) and Mark (Matt. 19.21; 26.9, 11). And in his account of Jesus' resisting the temptation to turn stones into bread, it is Matthew who gives the full quotation of Deut. 8.3 — 'One does not live by bread alone, but by every word that comes from the mouth of God' (Matt. 4.4) — where Luke 4.4 quotes only the first clause. It seems likely, then, that Matthew or the tradition known to him celebrated the memory of Jesus reminding his hearers that material poverty was not the most serious condition in which individuals could find themselves. There were a different value system and a satisfaction offered which no bread made by human hands could supply. And, once again, bearing in mind the Jewish tradition regarding poverty and Matthew's and Luke's shared warnings that 'Where your treasure is there will your heart be also' (Matt. 6.21/Luke 12.34) and against trying to serve both God and Mammon (Matt. 6.24/Luke 16.13), it hardly seems justified to doubt that such warnings also reflected concerns and emphases of Jesus' teaching.

In short, Jesus' remembered attitude to the poor set him entirely within the traditional Jewish law and spirituality of poverty. He did not rail against the rich, as did Amos and *1 En.* 94.6-11 before him and Jas. 5.1-6 after him, though Luke's woes interpret his teaching in that direction (Luke 6.24-26). But he left the rich in no doubt as to the dangers of their position and their obligations under God's law. Zacchaeus heard the implied rebuke to an unjust system and responded in the spirit inculcated by Israel's poor law, just as later Anthony and

---

Poor ch. 3. L. T. Johnson, *The Literary Function of Possessions in Luke-Acts* (SBLDS 39; Missoula: Scholars, 1977) 132-40 overrides too much the social concerns expressed in Luke's presentation.

174. But note that the Qumran covenanters thought of themselves both as the poor (above, n. 144) and also as 'the poor in spirit' (1QH 6[= 14].3); see further D. Flusser, 'Blessed are the Poor in Spirit . . .', *Judaism and the Origins of Christianity* (Jerusalem: Magnes, 1988) 102-14, who refers particularly to 1QH 23[= 18].15; and Charlesworth, *Jesus* 68-70, referring particularly to the Righteous Teacher's self-designation in 1QH 13[= 5].13-15.

Francis of Assisi heard again Jesus' rebuke to the rich young man and call to leave all as God's word to themselves. Nor did Jesus idealize poverty or call for the abolition of private property or preach an absolute egalitarianism. He did indicate that the poor, who could trust in no possessions, were close to the heart of God. At the same time, however, it should not be forgotten that his teaching on the subject was predicated on the Deuteronomic assumption that the poor, as also part of the covenant people, had a rightful share in the nation's prosperity and that a just system should safeguard that right.[175] The new note he brought was the renewed assurance that God's kingdom is precisely for the poor, and not just as a future hope. The poor could even now experience the good news, could already experience a security before God, a comfort and satisfaction which was not dependent on their financial security. By implication, in the company of Jesus' followers, that security, comfort, and satisfaction were already being realized.[176]

13.5. To Sinners

The Synoptic tradition contains only a few sayings of Jesus in which he articulates a specific sense of personal commission. We have already noted two of these. One comes in Matthew's elaboration of Jesus' response to the Syrophoenician woman: 'I was sent (apestalēn) only to the lost sheep of the house of Israel' (§13.3).[177] Another in Luke's elaboration of Jesus' preaching in Nazareth: 'The Spirit of the Lord is upon me, because he has anointed me to preach good news to the poor . . .' (§13.4). But the saying with the strongest credibility — that is, remembered as said by Jesus, rather than an elaboration of his remembered attitude — is Mark 2.17 pars.: 'I came (ēlthon) not to call the righteous but sinners (hamartōloi)'.[178] The saying comes in response to criticism from Pharisees that Jesus ate with 'toll-collectors and sinners' (Mark 2.13-17 pars.) and as the climax to Jesus' call of Levi/Matthew, the toll-collector, follow-

175. Kaylor overstates his case when he argues that 'Jesus advocated the cause of the poor and powerless against the wealthy and powerful elites that governed under Roman rule', but he is on sounder ground in noting that 'the real choice is not between a timeless ethic or an ethic related to Jesus' contemporary situation, but between an ethic that engages the social world and one that does not' (Jesus 92-93).

176. Cf. Becker, Jesus 158.

177. To the same effect is Luke's conclusion to the Zacchaeus story: 'for the Son of Man came to seek and save the lost' (Luke 19.10). The saying has been added to some mss. at Matt. 18.11 and a similar saying by a few mss. at Luke 9.55.

178. For other ēlthon sayings attributed to Jesus in the Synoptic tradition (Matt. 5.17; 10.34-35) see below, chapter 15 nn. 224, 237. The motif is more extensive in the Fourth Gospel (John 5.43; 7.28; 8.42; 10.10).

ing which Levi/Matthew as we might say 'threw a party' to which 'many toll-collectors and sinners' (Mark/Matthew) came.

Matt. 9.12-13	Mark 2.17	Luke 5.31-32
Those who are in good health have no need of a doctor, only those who are ill. Go and learn what this means: 'I desire mercy and not sacrifice'. For I came not to call the righteous but sinners.	Those who are in good health have no need of a doctor, only those who are ill. I came not to call the righteous but sinners.	Those who are healthy have no need of a doctor, only those who are ill. I have come not to call the righteous but sinners to repentance.

The saying has the variations and elaborations typical of oral performance, and rounds off effectively Jesus' response to the criticism of consorting with 'sinners'.[179] There is an unwillingness on the part of many to allow that Jesus may have expressed his sense of mission in such a form.[180] But the saying is echoed in subsequent Christian literature, which suggests a lengthy history.[181] And we shall see below that the righteous-sinner antithesis fits closely with the factionalism of Jesus' time.[182] Moreover, the context indicated is strikingly echoed in the Q-reported jibe levelled against Jesus, that he was 'a glutton and a drunkard, a friend of tax-collectors and sinners' (Matt. 11.19/Luke 7.34).[183] It is scarcely credible that such a critique of Jesus was interjected into the Jesus tradition on the initiative of later disciples, and the likelihood that Jesus' practice of mission drew some such dismissive comment is generally acknowledged.[184]

In Luke the motif of Jesus' association with sinners is much elaborated: Pe-

179. Was the final clause added as a 'secondary explanation of the saying about the physician' (Bultmann, *History* 92)? But it would be equally appropriate to ask whether the whole passage (2.14/15-17), which makes such a neatly rounded teaching sequence, was ever performed in a truncated form. Pesch points out how unlikely it would be for the Christian community, who thought of themselves as accounted righteous *(dikaioi),* to develop a saying of Jesus which denied his concern for the *dikaioi (Markusevangelium* 167-68). For the association of restoration/healing and forgiveness in the Bible see Ebner, *Jesus* 152-54, 160.

180. Funk, *Five Gospels* 46-47 (but the first half of the saying 'sounded like Jesus'); Lüdemann, *Jesus* 17.

181. *Oxy.Pap.* 1224 (Elliott, *Apocryphal New Testament* 35-36) — but the fragment is broken off before the end of the first clause; 1 Tim. 1.15; *Barn.* 5.9.

182. See also Davies and Allison, *Matthew* 2.105-106.

183. Already cited above, §12.5c.

184. The Jesus Seminar's negative vote hung on the thread of disagreement regarding the use of the phrase 'Son of Man' (Funk, *Five Gospels* 180, 302-303), but the Seminar had little doubt that Jesus consorted with 'toll-collectors and sinners' and 'social outcasts' and that he was criticized for eating with them (*Acts of Jesus* 66-67); 'the outside testimony about John and Jesus is authentic' (Lüdemann, *Jesus* 173). See above, chapter 12 n. 348, and Holmén, *Jesus* 205-19.

ter urges him, 'Depart from me, for I am a sinful man' (Luke 5.8); the woman who is remembered as anointing Jesus' feet while he reclined at table is identified as a 'sinner' (7.37, 39); Luke introduces the three parables of lost things/people by reporting that 'toll-collectors and sinners were all drawing near to hear him', prompting the grumbling of some Pharisees and scribes that 'This man receives sinners and eats with them' (Luke 15.1-2); and Luke drives home the point by concluding the first two parables with the refrain, 'there is joy in heaven when one sinner repents' (15.7, 10); Luke also includes a parable contrasting a Pharisee and a toll-collector, where the latter prays, 'God be merciful to me, a sinner' (18.13); and it is Luke who notes the grumbles at Jesus going to be guest of Zacchaeus the rich toll-collector, 'a man who is a sinner' (19.7). We may conclude that even if Luke has elaborated the motif, there was a motif in the earliest memories of Jesus' mission to be elaborated.

Three features stand out in this catalogue, shared by Mark and Q, as also by the fuller material in Luke: (1) the term 'sinner (hamartōlos)' is remembered as regularly used in criticism against Jesus, (2) the term 'sinner' is regularly associated with 'toll-collector',[185] and (3) the criticism is most often levelled against Jesus for dining with such people. There is no reason to doubt that all three features are well rooted in the earliest memories of Jesus' mission, as is generally agreed. To clarify their significance it is necessary to clarify each feature: (a) who were the 'sinners'? (b) why the association of toll-collectors and sinners? (c) why was eating with sinners so offensive to some? The third question is best left till chapter 14, and the second can be dealt with briefly. But the first requires some attention.

a. Who Were the 'Sinners'?

One of the more spicey controversies of recent historical Jesus scholarship was occasioned by the swingeing criticism levelled by Sanders against Jeremias's answer to the question. Jeremias had confused the issue by defining 'sinners' as 'a specific term for those engaged in despised trades' and by lumping them together with 'the amme-ha-aretz (people of the land), the uneducated, the ignorant, whose religious ignorance and moral behaviour stood in the way of their access to salvation, according to the convictions of the time'.[186] Sanders responded that the term 'sinners' means 'the wicked', or as we might say, law-breakers, crimi-

---

185. Note also Matt. 21.31-32: 'Truly I tell you, toll-collectors and prostitutes are preceding you into the kingdom of God. . . . the toll-collectors and prostitutes believed him (the Baptist)'; see above, chapter 12 n. 165.
186. Jeremias, *Proclamation* 109-12.

nals, 'deliberate and unrepentant transgressors of the law'.[187] It was not used to refer to the ordinary or common people. 'The common people were not irreligious'.[188] Jeremias's treatment gave too much weight to the unacceptable view that Jesus brought a message of grace and forgiveness to an unfeeling or merely formalistic Judaism. Jesus' real offence, in Sanders's view, was that he consorted with law-breakers, those who disregarded their covenant obligations, and that he promised them the kingdom without requiring them to repent.[189]

Sanders, however, left himself equally vulnerable to criticism. If Jeremias had operated with a too undifferentiated definition of 'sinners' in Second Temple Judaism, Sanders was operating with an equally unnuanced view of why individuals might be described as 'sinners' within the Judaism of that day. It is true, of course, that 'sinner' *(raša')* means one who breaks or does not keep the law, as its regular use in the OT makes clear.[190] But the understanding of what the law required was by no means uniform or wholly agreed within Second Temple Judaism. Consequently there were many aspects of conduct where there would be dispute as to whether the action in question was in fact a breach of the law. The point is now nicely illustrated by the recently published 4QMMT. It itemises a range of issues where it is clear that the Qumran sect believed their halakhoth to be what the law required (B1-82). The letter seeks to persuade others that they should follow these rulings and thus be accounted righteous before God (C26-32), with the obvious corollary that failure to agree with and practise these rulings would leave them in breach of the law, that is, as sinners. Such is ever the way when points of doctrine or praxis become of such importance in a group that it finds it necessary to separate itself from others (C7) and to maintain a identity distinct from the others. The unavoidable conclusion for such a group is that others are 'sinners' because they fail to observe the doctrine or praxis which is of such self-definitional significance for the group.

In other words, 'sinners' was not an absolute term, such as could always be demonstrated in any law-court in the land. 'Sinner' also functioned as a *factional*

187. Sanders, *Jesus and Judaism* 385 n. 14 cites Jeremias approvingly here.

188. Sanders, *Jesus and Judaism* 177-80, 182; Sanders is followed by Meier, *Marginal Jew* 2.149, 211-12; 3.28-29; Crossan and Reed, *Excavating Jesus* 119 ('the deliberately, continuously, and obstinately wicked . . . those who are irrevocably evil').

189. Sanders, *Jesus and Judaism* 198-206; also *Historical Figure* 226-37; also with W. D. Davies, 'Jesus: from the Jewish Point of View', in Horbury et al., eds., *Judaism* 3.618-77 (here 636-43). Sanders' polemic against Jeremias drew vigorous protest from his former McMaster colleague Ben Meyer, 'A Caricature of Joachim Jeremias and His Work', *JBL* 110 (1991) 451-62, with response from Sanders, 'Defending the Indefensible', *JBL* 110 (1991) 463-77; and from Hengel and Deines, 'Sanders' Judaism' 68-69, speaking somewhat on behalf of German scholarship.

190. E.g., Exod. 23.1; Deut. 25.2; Pss. 1.1, 5; 10.3; 28.3; 37.32; 50.16-18; 71.4; 82.4; 119.53, 155; Prov. 17.23; Ezek. 33.8, 11, 19; Sir. 41.5-8.

term, a term of vituperative insult, a dismissive 'boo-word' to warn off members of the in-group against conduct outside the boundaries which defined the group.[191] This is precisely what we find in much of the literature of the Second Temple period. Already in Dan. 12.10 'the sinners' (*re ša'im*) who fail to understand Daniel's revelation are contrasted with 'the wise' (*maskkilim*) who do understand. In 1 Maccabees, the 'sinners and lawless men' certainly included those whom the Maccabees regarded as apostates, as Israelites who had abandoned the law (1 Macc. 1.34; 2.44, 48).[192] Similarly the 'sinners' in the various early Enochic writings are opponents of the self-styled 'righteous',[193] who 'sin like the sinners' in that they use what the Enochians regard as the wrong calendar and so fail to observe the feasts aright (*1 En.* 82.4-7). In just the same way, in the Dead Sea Scrolls *rš'm* refers to the sect's opponents,[194] where again it is the sect's interpretation of the law which determines that those who do not accept that interpretation are to be numbered among the wicked.[195] In some ways most striking of all are the *Psalms of Solomon,* where repeatedly the 'righteous', the 'devout',[196] inveigh against the 'sinners', where again it is clear that the latter often denotes the opponents of the righteous, that is, probably the Hasmonean Sadducees who controlled the Temple cult.[197] In all these cases the term 'sinners' does not denote non-practising, law-defiant Jews, those who would be generally regarded as law-breakers, but Jews who practised their Judaism *differently* from the writer's faction.[198] They were 'sinners', that is, law-breakers, but *only from a sectarian viewpoint* and only as judged by the sectarians' interpretation of the law.[199]

191. In what follows I again (as in §9.4) draw on my earlier 'Pharisees, Sinners and Jesus' 73-76; more briefly my *Partings* 103-105. On the factionalism of Second Temple Judaism see further above, §9.4, including n. 56. Crossan criticizes Sanders, with some justice, for treating sin only in individual terms and ignoring systematic evil and structural sin; but Crossan in turn, despite distinguishing between invective and portrayal, pays no attention to the way the term 'sinner' was actually used at the time (*Birth* 337-43).

192. J. A. Goldstein, *1 Maccabees* (AB 41; New York: Doubleday, 1976) 123-24.

193. *1 En.* 1.7-9; 5.4, 6-7; 22.9-13; and 94–104 *passim.*

194. 1QpHab 5.1-12; 1QH 10[= 2].10-12; 12[= 4].34; CD 2.3; 11.18-21; 19.20-21; 4QFlor (4Q174) 1.14.

195. E.g., 1QS 5.7-13; 1QH 15[= 7]12; CD 4.6-8. Note the citation of Dan. 12.10 in 4QFlor (4Q174) 2.3-4a, where the sect presumably identified itself with the *maskkilim* of Daniel.

196. E.g., *Pss. Sol.* 3.3-7; 4.1, 8; 9.5; 10.3, 6; 13.6-12; 15.6-7.

197. *Pss. Sol.* 1.8; 2.3; 7.2; 8.12-13; 17.5-8, 23. See again above, §9.4 at n. 131.

198. 'When viewed through the prism of the prevailing purity system, the dissident is seen clearly as outside the realm of what is holy and exclusive to the group' (Malina, *Social Gospel* 60); cf. Buchanan: 'outcasts from a liturgical point of view' (*Jesus* 132).

199. Sanders recognizes this aspect in talk of 'sinners' (*Jesus and Judaism* 210; and earlier in his *Paul and Palestinian Judaism,* index 'The Wicked'), but he fails to integrate it into his treatment of Jesus. On the seriousness of the charge see again above, §9.4.

A striking fact emerges from all this: that the language used in criticism of Jesus strongly reflects the polemical and factional use of the term elsewhere attested among Jesus' contemporaries. Most notable is the antithesis between 'righteous' and 'sinners' (Mark 2.17 pars.), reflected also in Luke's conclusion to the parable of the lost sheep (Luke 15.7) and in his parable of the Pharisee and the toll-collector (18.9, 14).[200] The conclusion lies close to hand that Jesus was criticised by some who regarded themselves as properly law-observant ('righteous') and that he was criticised for associating with *those whom 'the righteous' deemed to be 'sinners',* that is, those who disregarded or disputed interpretations of the Torah held dear by 'the righteous' *(ṣadikkim).* In other words, the sentiment of Mark 2.17c fits remarkably closely into a context typified by the Enochic corpus, the Dead Sea Scrolls, and the *Psalms of Solomon.* As we noted earlier (§9.4), the same literature also indicates the likelihood that Pharisees were heavily involved in such factional disputes. It must be judged very likely, then, that the critics of Jesus were indeed typically Pharisees (whose standpoint the *Psalms of Solomon* probably reflects most closely), and that it was indeed they who used the term 'sinners' in criticising Jesus' association with those deemed law-breakers by such Pharisees.[201]

In which case we should also note that in Mark 2.17 Jesus is not remembered as disputing the righteousness of the Pharisaic critics. As the saying stands, 'the righteous' in 2.17c correspond to 'those who are in good health' in 2.17b.[202] Even if at this point 'righteous' is as much a factional term as 'sinner', it is not the self-assertion of righteousness which Jesus here questions,[203] only the use of the pejorative 'sinner'. Nor does Jesus deny that the epithet is often justified: 'sinners' are equivalent to 'the sick'; he himself called for repentance (§13.2a); in the parable of the Pharisee and the toll-collector, the latter confesses that he is

200. Note also the use of *dikaioō* in Matt. 11.19/Luke 7.35; Luke 16.15; and cf. Matt. 21.32.

201. Even when *hamartōlos* is used in a non-factional context (Luke 5.8; 6.32-34; 7.37, 39; 13.2; 15.7, 10; 18.13) a dismissive (even self-dismissive) overtone is clear. 'Sinner' could sometimes be used to describe a prostitute, as implied in Matt. 21.31 (where 'prostitutes' replaces the more common 'sinners' in the association with toll-collectors) and Luke 7.37, 39. On Jesus' attitude to law-breaking see below, §14.4.

202. Cf. the affirmation given to the ninety-nine who do not need to repent in the parable of the lost sheep (Luke 15.7) and to the elder brother in the parable of the prodigal son (Luke 15.31). Elsewhere in the Jesus tradition the term 'righteous' *(dikaios)* is used positively, and not only by Matthew (Mark 6.20; Matt. 1.19; 10.41; 13.17, 43, 49; 23.29, 35; 25.46; Luke 1.6, 17; 2.25; 14.14; 23.47, 50), though it is noteworthy that not one of the instances is paralleled in a second Gospel. Given this feature of the data, McKnight is unwise to put as much weight on it as he does (*New Vision* 200-206).

203. We may ask whether Jesus criticizes the assertion of self-righteousness even in Luke 18.11-12, since a parallel like 1QH 15[= 7].26-35 suggests an attitude of gratitude more than of pride (Borg, *Conflict* 107-108).

'the sinner' (Luke 18.13). The point of Mark 2.17 is rather the implicit rejection of the use of 'sinner' by the self-perceived 'righteous' *as a term of dismissal.*[204] Jesus' protest was evidently directed against a factionalism which drew too narrow boundaries round what could be regarded as Torah-legitimate behaviour and which judged those outside these boundaries to be 'sinners', law-breakers, disowned by God.[205] He protested against a righteousness which could not recognize covenant loyalty unless it accorded with its own terms and definitions.[206]

So Jeremias was closer to the historical circumstances than Sanders allowed.[207] It was not that Jesus opened the door of the kingdom to criminals without repentance, as Sanders maintained,[208] or denied that there were 'sinners'. Rather Jesus objected against a boundary-drawing within Israel which treated some Israelites as outside the covenant and beyond the grace of God. Such attempts to erect internal boundaries within Israel, creating internal divisions within Israel, were contrary to the will of God. Jesus, in other words, was more critical of those who dismissively condemned 'sinners' than of the 'sinners' themselves. Just as the place of the poor within the people had to be reaffirmed (§13.4), so too the place of those regarded as 'sinners' by the narrow definitions and scruples of others had to be reaffirmed. Just as the poor were God's special concern, so the excluded and marginalized were of special concern for Jesus' mission.

b. Toll-Collectors

That Jesus was to be found in the company of toll-collectors *(telōnai)* is a consistent element in the criticism recalled against him.[209] Both Matthew and Luke re-

---

204. Cf. the elder brother's reference to his errant brother as 'this son of yours' rather than 'my brother', and the father's gentle rebuke 'this your brother' (Luke 15.30, 32).

205. Hence the title of the equivalent chapter in my *Jesus' Call to Discipleship* — ch. 4 'The Boundary Breaker'.

206. 'It is surprising how often the sayings of Jesus recur to this theme, of the folly and evil of self-righteousness and censoriousness' (Dodd, *Founder* 76). Surprisingly in view of his overall theme, Holmén, following Sanders, also misses the point (*Jesus* 200-205) and draws the questionable conclusion that Jesus 'was not trying to be faithful, but was, with purpose, unfaithful' (220).

207. Wright stays close to Jeremias on this (*Jesus* 264-68), but, strangely for one who focuses so much attention on the Israel dimension of Jesus' message, he ignores the factional overtones in the term, perhaps because it hardly fits with his dominant 'return from exile' scenario.

208. It was no doubt to avoid any such inference that Luke added 'to repentance' in Luke 5.32, as well as underlining the point in Luke 15.7, 10.

209. Mark 2.15-16 pars.; Matt. 11.19/Luke 7.34; Luke 15.1; 19.2 (*architelōnēs*, 'chief toll-collector').

cord teaching of Jesus which speaks favourably of toll-collectors.[210] One of his close disciples was a *telōnēs* (Matthew/Levi).[211] As is now generally agreed, in Palestine the term denoted collectors of indirect taxes, especially those levied on the transport of goods.[212] The title could be used both of supervisory officials like Zacchaeus and their employees who collected the taxes at toll booths or tax offices *(telōnion),* such as Matthew/Levi (Mark 2.14 pars.).[213]

Presumably toll-collectors are associated with 'sinners' in the Jesus tradition because they were regarded as typical 'sinners'. This partly reflects the general disapprobation of the tax-farmer in the ancient world.[214] Partly also the fact that such revenues would have been used to finance Herod Antipas's architectural ambitions or to reward his favourites or to contribute to the tribute owed to Rome (cf. Mark 12.14 pars.). A more important cause would be the widespread perception that tax-farmers used the opportunity to enrich themselves dishonestly at the cost of the tax-payers. Luke, alert to such aspects, indicates clearly both the suspicions (Luke 3.12-13; 18.11) and the reality (19.8). The more distinctively Jewish dismissal of unacceptable practice is reflected in two rather astonishing sayings recorded by Matthew: toll-collectors in effect put themselves alongside Gentiles, that is, outside the covenant people (Matt. 5.46-47; 18.17).[215]

Whatever the fuller facts of the matter, the situation recalled in the Jesus tradition is clear enough. Jesus in his dealings with toll-collectors laid himself open to the jibe 'a friend of toll-collectors and sinners' (Matt. 11.19/Luke 7.34).[216] Even they should not be regarded as 'beyond the pale': however unacceptable their means of livelihood might have been, they themselves were as

---

210. Matt. 21.31-32; Luke 18.10-14.

211. Mark 2.14 pars.; Matt. 10.3.

212. Hence some of Capernaum's importance (see above, §9.9d).

213. See especially J. R. Donahue, 'Tax Collectors and Sinners: An Attempt at Identification', *CBQ* 33 (1971) 39-61; also 'Tax Collector', *ABD* 6.337-38; Schottroff and Stegemann, *Hope of the Poor* 7-9; F. Herrenbruck, 'Wer waren die "Zöllner"?', *ZNW* 72 (1981) 178-94; also *Jesus und die Zöllner* (WUNT 2.41; Tübingen: Mohr Siebeck, 1990) 22-37.

214. O. Michel, *'telōnēs'*, *TDNT* 8.99-101; Schottroff and Stegemann, *Hope of the Poor* 10-13; Herrenbruck, *Jesus und die Zöllner* 89-94.

215. Luke 6.32-33 reads 'sinners' both times where Matt. 5.46-47 has 'toll-collectors' and 'Gentiles'. Matt. 18.17 ('let [the recalcitrant errant brother] be to you as a Gentile and a toll-collector') is without parallel. Possibly the earlier form of the first saying reflected the widespread dismissive attitude towards 'sinners' at the time of Jesus, while the performance tradition of Matthew's communities continued to express a Jewish attitude dismissive of Gentiles.

216. Horsley's attempt to rebut the evidence on this point is disappointingly tendentious (*Jesus* 212-23). Becker points out that relations with tax-collectors were neither of interest nor a problem for the post-Easter church (*Jesus* 163), so there are no grounds for postulating a later origin for the tradition.

much part of an Israel that needed to repent as others, more needful of the good news of God's kingdom than most others.

In short, within the wider summons to Israel to repent and trust afresh, Jesus seems to have made a special effort to reassure not just the poor but also those dismissed by the chief opinion-formers of the day as 'sinners' that God's kingdom was open to them too. That message was heard by many of the poor and sinners in the land of Israel, and the memory of that degree of success of Jesus' mission remains clear within the tradition.

13.6. Women

The tradition as a whole makes little effort to focus on the success or otherwise of Jesus' mission with women in particular. As was the case well into the twentieth century in western countries, there was no differentiation within the community as community between men and women. If the question had been posed, Christian women would not have felt themselves excluded even when the preacher addressed his (sic) congregation as 'brethren'. However, the newer sensitivities of the last generation have made students of all ancient texts more alert to the implicit patriarchalism more or less universal within them all.[217] And the continuing insistence of Catholic ecclesiology that Jesus' choice of an all-male twelve retains perennial significance for Christian understanding of ministry has made the issue of women as disciples inescapable.

Given that there is no real attempt within the Jesus tradition to highlight the role of women in relation to Jesus, the specific references to women disciples are all the more interesting.[218] Most noticeable is the fact that the woman who has been given most honour within Christian tradition, Mary the mother of Jesus, is nowhere included within the circle of discipleship round Jesus during his mission. She features only as recipient of a rebuke by Jesus (Mark 3.31-35 pars.).[219]

Within the Jesus tradition the much more prominent Mary is Mary Magdalene (Mary of Magdala/Migdal),[220] from whom, according to Luke 8.2, seven

217. See above, particularly Schüssler Fiorenza in chapter 4 n. 143.

218. For detailed review of the following material see B. Witherington, *Women in the Ministry of Jesus* (SNTSMS 51; Cambridge: Cambridge University, 1984) ch. 4. Jenkins dismisses attempts to draw further material from the apocryphal gospels (*Hidden Gospels* ch. 6): 'Feminist interpretations of the hidden gospels represent a triumph of hope over judgment' (146).

219. See further below, §14.7, and cf. John 2.4. Only John mentions her at the cross (John 19.25-27), though she appears already in Acts 1.14.

220. Mark 15.40, 47 pars.; 16.1 pars.; Luke 8.2; John 20.11-18; *GTh* 114.1. We recall that Magdala/Migdal lay on the shore of Galilee between Capernaum and Tiberias. On Mary of Magdala see also Funk, *Acts of Jesus* 476-78.

demons had been exorcised (presumably by Jesus). The tradition recalls her as the leader of a group of women[221] who observed Jesus' crucifixion 'from afar' (Mark 15.40 pars.) in contrast to the male disciples who had fled, who wished to anoint his body (Mark 15.47–16.1 pars.), who were first to see the empty tomb (Mark 16.2-8; Luke 24.22-23) and Jesus risen from the dead (Matt. 28.8-10),[222] and who informed the other disciples (Luke 24.10, 23).[223] Of particular interest is the report in Mark 15.41 that 'when he was in Galilee' these women 'used to follow *(ēkolouthoun)* and to take care of *(diēkonoun)* him'.[224] Mark adds that there were 'many other women who went up with him to Jerusalem'. Mary of Magdala is also mentioned first in another group of women (Luke 8.2), including Joanna, wife of Chuza, Herod's steward,[225] and (the otherwise unknown) Susanna, who with many others 'used to take care of *(diēkonoun)*' Jesus (and his disciples) 'out of their possessions/means *(hyparchonta)*' (8.3).[226] Such uncontrived detail indicates good tradition; Luke evidently had access here to first-hand recollections.[227] The implication that Jesus moved around Galilee on his preaching mission with quite a substantial entourage, including 'many women', need not be discounted; the larger the number of followers, the larger the network of family relations and contacts in the villages visited.

Another Mary,[228] with her sister Martha, of Bethany, is named by both Luke (10.38-42) and John (11.1–12.11), the double tradition again attesting its historical value. The account of Mary's attentiveness to Jesus' teaching evidently made a great impression on Luke, as, evidently, on Jesus himself (Luke 10.39, 42). In some contrast, in John it is Martha who is given the more impressive role (John 11.20-27). The Fourth Evangelist also emphasises that Mary and Martha (with their brother) were among Jesus' closest intimates (11.5, 11, 35).

Other women who leave a substantial mark in the tradition of Jesus' mission include the woman with the haemorrhage (Mark 5.21-43 pars.),[229] the Syro-

---

221. The other women mentioned are Mary the mother of James (the younger) and Joses/Joseph, Salome (Mark), and the mother of James and John (Matthew).

222. The Fourth Evangelist gives Mary of Magdala even more prominence as the sole recipient of the first resurrection appearance (John 20.11-18).

223. See further below, §18.3(1).

224. The Jesus Seminar had few doubts as to the historical value of these reminiscences (Funk, *Acts of Jesus* 158, 292-93).

225. See above, chapter 9 n. 339. Luke includes her in his list of women who went to the tomb (24.10).

226. The pattern of religious teachers being sponsored by well-to-do women, a repeated feature in Christianity's history, is thus given its dominical precedent.

227. Byrskog suggests that these women were eye-witnesses and informants in the formation and transmission of the Jesus tradition (*Story as History* 73-82).

228. For fuller details on the various Marys in the Gospel tradition see *ABD* 4.579-82.

229. The tradition recalls Jesus reacting to the woman's unexpected touch (Mark 5.30),

phoenician woman (Mark 7.24-30/Matt. 15.21-28), the woman who anointed Jesus' feet (Mark 14.3-9 pars.), probably another (a 'sinner') who anointed his head (Luke 7.36-50),[230] and in the Fourth Gospel the Samaritan woman at the well of Sychar (John 4.7-30, 39-42) and the woman caught in adultery (John 7.53–8.11). Matthew also recalls Jesus speaking of prostitutes going into the kingdom ahead of others (Matt. 21.31-32). Despite the lack of prominence given to women among Jesus' followers, then, the extent to which the Jesus tradition seems to have explicitly included women among Jesus' addressees and to have made womanly roles 'visible' is nonetheless unusual and should be noted.[231]

Once again, whatever the precise details, it would be impossible to remove these elements of the tradition without doing it unacceptable violence. The presence of women among Jesus' disciples and followers should not be doubted, and several seem to have been closer to him than even some of the twelve.[232] It is often said that there would have been something scandalous about Jesus' association with these women. But only the episode in Luke 7 evokes a response (7.39) like the jibe in Matt. 11.19/Luke 7.34. As part of a larger group of disciples and followers, their presence in Jesus' entourage would not necessarily have been offensive to good manners. And the teaching of Mary of Bethany was within the privacy of Martha's and Mary's home.

What then of the significance of the twelve being all men? The only difference between the situation just characterized and the function of the twelve, according to the tradition, is that Jesus not only directed teaching particularly to the twelve, but also that he commissioned them to engage in mission on their own (Mark 6.6b-13 pars.). Mark indicates that they were sent out 'two by two' (6.7), a

---

but not out of concern for the blood impurity which he would have contracted (Lev. 15.19-23), one of the most crippling series of rulings for a woman's place in society.

230. On the likelihood that Luke's version refers to a different episode see above, n. 165. In the Fourth Gospel the tradition has become so tangled that the woman is identified with Mary of Bethany (John 12.1-8).

231. In addition to those already mentioned, see also Mark 1.29-31 pars.; 3.35 pars.; Matt. 6.28/Luke 12.27; Matt. 13.33/Luke 13.20-21/*GTh* 96; Luke 7.11-17; 13.10-17; 15.8-10; 17.34-35; 18.2-5; 23.27-31. See further Schüssler Fiorenza, *In Memory of Her* 147, 152; Witherington, *Women* 35-52; L. Schottroff, *Lydia's Impatient Sisters: A Feminist Social History of Early Christianity* (Louisville: Westminster John Knox, 1995) 79-118; Theissen and Merz, *Historical Jesus* 219-25; and for background, T. Ilan, *Jewish Women in Greco-Roman Palestine: An Enquiry into Image and Status* (Tübingen: Mohr Siebeck,1995). 'In the cultural world of first-century Palestine, the very use of a woman in an illustration required a moral decision' (Bailey, *Poet and Peasant* 158, referring to Luke 15.8-10). Marshall notes that 'the strong presence of women among Jesus' followers has no Cynic precedent' ('Thomas and the Cynic Jesus' 60).

232. Meier notes that though the term 'disciple' is not used of any woman, the reality was otherwise (*Marginal Jew* 3.74-80).

practice which is inherently likely anyway and which is probably reflected in the structure of the list of the twelve (6 × 2, or 3 × 4).[233] It would not have been possible to conceive of women taking this role, preaching and expecting hospitality where they went — whether as two unaccompanied women, or each with a male companion.[234] Even if Jesus had wanted one or more women to function within the twelve, the role given to the twelve was simply unthinkable for a woman, for obvious social reasons. In other words, so far as our evidence takes us, the absence of women from the twelve was determined by social custom and cultural mores of the time, not by any theological rationale on the fitness or otherwise of women for mission/ministry.

In short, there is no hint in the Jesus tradition that Jesus thought of women as disadvantaged as a class in the way that the 'poor' and 'sinners' were. It was simply taken for granted that they were part of Israel and would share in the blessings promised to a renewedly repentant and trusting people. Hence the lack of specifically 'good news for women'. Even so, the prominence of women among Jesus' followers and his closeness to several, notably the two Marys, of Magdala and Bethany, must have raised a few eyebrows in 'polite society' at the time. And it surely indicates that Jesus saw no deficiency in their status as women or in their innate capacity for service and ministry.

13.7. Gentiles

Given the emphasis on the Israel-focus of Jesus' mission and the subsequent expansion of the Jesus movement into Gentile mission (Acts), we cannot fail to ask whether Jesus' aim in mission would have included Gentiles. For those anxious to demonstrate continuity between the mission of Jesus and that of the first Christians, the indications are not encouraging. We have already noted that Matthew has preserved mission instructions which forbad the missionaries going beyond Israel — 'Do not go on the way of/towards the Gentiles, and do not enter a Samaritan town . . .' (Matt. 10.5) — instructions which were probably given by Jesus himself.[235] Does that imply that Jesus may have seen no place for Gentiles

233. Jeremias argues that this practice was already customary in Judaism, partly for added protection and partly in echo of the legal requirement for two witnesses to establish a case (Deut. 17.6; 19.15) ('Paarweise Sendung im Neuen Testament', *Abba: Studien zur neutestamentlichen Theologie und Zeitgeschichte* [Göttingen: Vandenhoeck und Ruprecht, 1966] 132-39).

234. *Pace* Crossan, *Historical Jesus* 335; *Birth* 337; L. Schottroff, who finds hints in Q of itinerant prophetesses who followed Jesus ('Itinerant Prophetesses: A Feminist Analysis of the Sayings Source Q', in Piper, ed., *The Gospel behind the Gospels* 347-60).

235. See again above, §12.4h and n. 266; also §13.3c, h. Matthew has taken care to

in the kingdom of God? Not necessarily. For in the eschatological hopes of earlier prophets and seers, there was scarcely any thought of a mission to the Gentiles; Isa. 66.19 is a unique exception.[236] At the same time, however, we saw that a strong strand of Jewish expectation envisaged Gentiles coming in pilgrimage to Zion to pay tribute or to worship God there ('eschatological proselytes').[237] That Jesus may have shared this hope is suggested by a number of episodes and passages.[238]

For one thing, when Jesus did encounter Gentiles, he is remembered both as responding to their requests and as impressed by their faith.[239] Matthew incorporates into his version the Q saying which envisages many coming from east and west and reclining with the patriarchs in the kingdom (Matt. 8.11/Luke 13.29).[240] Jesus' warnings of eschatological reversal (§12.4c), that confidence based solely on descent from Abraham (not forgetting Matt. 3.9/Luke 3.8) was misplaced, carried with them the implication that Gentiles (including even Nineveh, Tyre, and Sidon)[241] might well be the beneficiaries of Israel's failure.[242] And Mark includes the full quotation from Isa. 56.7 in his account of the purging of the Temple — 'my house shall be called a house of prayer for all nations' (Mark 11.17) — one of the classic texts in Jewish expectation of a Gentile eschatological pilgrimage.[243] Nor should we forget that in telling the parable of the Good Samaritan Jesus must deliberately have intended to shock his hearers

counterbalance 10.5-6, 23 and 15.24 by adding references to the 'Gentiles' at other points in his tradition (10.18; 12.18-21 [Isa. 42.1-4]; 21.43; 24.9, 14; 25.32; and of course 28.19) to indicate that the restrictions imposed by Jesus were limited to the contexts where they occur.

236. Sanders, *Jesus and Judaism* 214.

237. See above, §12.2c(7).

238. Jeremias, *Jesus' Promise to the Nations* ch. 3; Lohfink, *Jesus and Community* 17-20; Rowland, *Christian Origins* 150-51.

239. Matt. 8.5-13/Luke 7.1-10; Mark 7.24-30/Matt. 15.21-28. According to Mark 7.27 Jesus, by implication, refers to Gentiles as 'dogs', presumably a traditional term of abuse (cf. Phil. 3.2). It is noteworthy that the Greek uses the word *kynarion,* 'little dog' (house dog or lapdog), rather than *kyōn,* a dog of the street (BDAG *kynarion*); whether such a distinction was possible in Aramaic is disputed (discussion in Davies and Allison, *Matthew* 2.554). And if Jesus referred to Gentiles as 'sinners' (Luke 6.34; cf. Matt. 5.47) he would simply be reflecting characteristic usage of the time (details, e.g., in my *Partings* 103). See also Keck, *Who Is Jesus?* 57-58.

240. See above, particularly chapter 12 nn. 173 and 442.

241. Matt. 11.22/Luke 10.14; Matt. 12.41/Luke 11.32.

242. McKnight suggests that reference to 'fish of every kind' in Matt. 13.47 'lends credence to the view that Jesus anticipated a universal kingdom' (*New Vision* 105; parable cited above, chapter 12 n. 218).

243. Matthew and Luke omit the key phrase 'for all nations' (Matt. 21.13/Luke 19.46), but the clear allusion to Isa. 56.7 remains and with it the evocation of the larger hope of eschatological pilgrimage.

by presenting a Samaritan as hero, when Samaritans were usually regarded as half-breeds and apostates (Luke 10.30-37).[244] At the very least, the parable suggests that Jesus' concern to break down boundaries within Israel (§13.5) may have extended beyond the bounds of Israel,[245] though we should beware of romanticizing Jesus' conscious intentions at this point.[246] Caution is even more necessary with the parable of the sheep and the goats, since it may be a further example of Matthew's own broader vision (see n. 235), but the possibility can hardly be excluded that Jesus did share an expectation of final judgment in which ethnic and religious identity was not a key factor but the universal responsibility to love the neighbour was.[247]

The picture which emerges is one in which Jesus did not envisage a mission to the Gentiles,[248] but took for granted the likelihood that Gentiles would be included in God's kingdom. He did not seek out Gentiles but responded positively to faith and commended unreservedly neighbour love wherever and by whomsoever it was expressed.

13.8. Circles of Discipleship

The ambiguity which we noted at the beginning of this chapter has reappeared again and again in the intervening discussions. Jesus seems to have preached with a view to reaching as many in Israel as would hear him, though probably he was well enough aware, or soon became so, that the commission of Isaiah was likely to be played out in his mission too. How he saw his call to particular individuals to follow him as fitting into the larger vision of an Israel returned to its Lord and trusting him afresh, and of both as fitting into his expectation of the

244. See above, §9.3c. The echoes of such hostility are plain in Luke 9.52-54; John 4.9; 8.48. See also M. Gourges, 'The Priest, the Levite, and the Samaritan Revisited: A Critical Note on Luke 10:31-35', *JBL* 117 (1998) 79-103. The Good Samaritan is one of relatively few passages attributed to Jesus which are given an unreserved vote of confidence by the Jesus Seminar (Funk, *Five Gospels* 323-24; similarly Lüdemann, *Jesus* 332; other bibliography in Hultgren, *Parables* 100 n. 40; Meier, *Marginal Jew* 3.602 n. 172, with critique of the Jesus Seminar's rationale in n. 173).

245. We may perhaps envisage a specific protest against limiting Lev. 19.18 in the way that Leviticus 19 implied (including 19.33-34).

246. Wright's claim that 'the story dramatically redefines the covenant boundary of Israel' (*Jesus* 307) overstates the implication.

247. Davies and Allison argue that Matthew was drawing the parable from tradition (*Matthew* 3.417-18); see further above, chapter 12 n. 219.

248. I have already discussed Mark 13.10/Matt. 24.14 in §12.4h above. The alternative case is made by E. J. Schnabel, 'Jesus and the Beginnings of the Mission to the Gentiles', in Green and Turner, eds., *Jesus of Nazareth* 37-58.

coming kingdom, remains unclear. As also whether we should recognize the distinction between 'disciples' and 'followers' as significant. Certainly Jesus seems to have been especially concerned to include those whom most others, or the main opinion-formers in particular, regarded and treated as outside the realm of covenant grace. Not just the poor, in line with the deeply rooted priorities of Torah and prophet, but also, surprisingly, 'sinners', who ought to be disapproved of by the faithful, until we remember that the 'righteous' were so stringent in their reading of the law that many practitioners of 'common Judaism' were in effect excluded in the perspective of the righteous. In all this the vision of a renewed Israel was little different from that of Jesus' prophetic predecessors. But Jesus did look for its fulfilment in the near future, and he did seek to anticipate it in the circle of discipleship which he drew around him.

The ambiguity suggests that we should speak of circles (plural) of discipleship, rather than of a single coherent circle.[249] The innermost circle seems to have been the twelve, with Peter and the brothers James and John at its heart,[250] and Peter as the chief spokesman.[251] But round the twelve we have seen a wider circle of followers, including women who followed (Mary of Magdala and others) and women who stayed at home (Mary of Bethany); the two Marys were evidently among Jesus' dearest companions. Should we characterize a further circle in terms of those who followed Jesus secretly, such as the owner of the upper room and Joseph of Arimathea? But then we have to mention also those who heard Jesus gladly (Mark 3.35) and sought to live out his teaching (Matt. 7.24-25), those whom he healed (Mark 10.52), those who turned and became as children (Matt. 18.3), the poor who trusted (Luke 6.20), the sinners who repented (Luke 18.13-14; 19.1-10), the Gentiles who displayed a faith which Jesus hardly met elsewhere (Matt. 8.10), and indeed, according to Luke, sympathetic Pharisees (Luke 7.36; 11.37; 14.1). What is striking about these circles of discipleship is the way they overlap and intertwine, forbidding us to make any hard and fast distinction between disciples and followers, or to designate different grades of

249. Cf. Ladd, *Jesus and the Kingdom* 248-54; Lohfink, *Jesus and Community* 31-35; Sanders, *Historical Figure* 123-27; Meier, *Marginal Jew* 3.627-30.

250. It makes better sense of the evidence to deduce that the prominence of the three in the earliest days of the new movement (Acts 1.13; 3–4; 12.2) is a reflection of an earlier pre-Easter prominence (Mark 1.29; 3.16-17; 5.37; 9.2; 13.3; 14.33) rather than the reverse. James the brother of John hardly features in the post-Easter story, and his early execution (Acts 12.2) leaves it unlikely that he made a deep enough impression in the traditioning process for that impression to be extended back into the tradition itself. Somewhat surprisingly, Meier concludes that 'the group of three may be a creation of Mark's redactional activity' (*Marginal Jew* 3.211-12).

251. Mark 8.29, 32 pars.; 9.5 pars.; 10.28 pars.; 11.21; 14.29 pars.; Matt. 15.15; 17.24-27; 18.21; Luke 8.45; 12.41; John 6.68; 13.6-9, 36-37; 21.3.

discipleship.[252] Mark recalls that those who tried to do so were rebuked by Jesus (Mark 9.38-41/Luke 9.49-50).[253]

In the light of all this, and still unable to resolve whether the response of discipleship was a condition of the kingdom's coming or the mode of its presence, we can at least attempt further clarification by asking: How should the discipleship for which Jesus called be characterized?

252. See particularly Schrage, *Ethics* 49-51.
253. See further Stauffer, 'Jesus' 61-63.

CHAPTER 14

The Character of Discipleship

At the beginning of chapter 13 a number of questions were posed with a view to gaining further clarification on the significance of Jesus' teaching on the kingdom of God. So far the Jesus tradition has provided quite an extensive answer to the first: For whom did Jesus intend his message of the kingdom? Uncertainty remains, however, as to whether Jesus realistically hoped for a national revival. Or did he simply seek out those who would respond, without necessarily having any clear idea on how the few who responded should be related to any wider hope for national restoration? Jesus would be neither the first and certainly not the last whose vision of what his vocation should expect to achieve was less than clear. Of course, the uncertainty may be simply that of the historian looking back, rather than of Jesus himself. But so far as the question initially posed is concerned, uncertainty remains regarding key elements of the answers as indicated by the Jesus tradition.

Further clarification is likely to be forthcoming from our second question, when we focus attention more closely on those who did respond to Jesus' preaching, rather than the unavoidably vaguer hopes for Israel as a whole. So we ask again: What did Jesus envisage his talk of the kingdom would mean for those who responded? How did he expect the kingdom to impact upon their lives? What did it involve to 'follow' Jesus? There is bound to be some overlap with material reviewed in chapter 13: not surprisingly, the first three characteristics correspond to the first three features of Jesus' call (§13.2); and we will be confronted with the same uncertainty in due course. But an overview of the character of the discipleship to which Jesus called is important in itself, and not least for those who in subsequent centuries have seen in that discipleship the precedent and in at least some measure the pattern for their own.

14.1. Subjects of the King

If the main emphasis of Jesus' preaching was 'the kingdom of God', then a major corollary of that emphasis is that God was being understood as King.[1] Rather surprisingly, however, this aspect of Jesus' message is little touched on.[2] The reason, no doubt, is that Jesus is almost never recalled as referring to God as 'king' in any of the streams of Gospel tradition.[3] In contrast, as we have already seen, in the worship of Jesus' time God would have been regularly addressed as 'king'.[4] Quite why Jesus is remembered as speaking so little of God as king is another quandary to which we will return in §14.2. Part of the answer may be that the fuller phrase 'the kingdom of God' was so dominant in Jesus' teaching that there was little need or occasion to speak *expressis verbis* of God as 'king'.[5] Be that as it may, the implication remains, and cannot have escaped Jesus' hearers, that in 'the kingdom of God' God is 'king'.

The ancient rationale of kingship is clear. Above all, the king was the pivotal and representative figure in ensuring the protection of his people against military threat from without and in administering justice within.[6] The 'down-side' of the system was already signalled in Samuel's response to Israel's request for a king in 1 Sam. 8.10-18 — the king's arbitrary power to requisition individuals and resources for his service. But the authority to command and the power to enforce compliance were no doubt accepted as the necessary corollary to the king's key functions as military leader and judge. Presumably it was the same logic which was at work in hailing Yahweh as

---

1. I follow Manson in giving first attention to Jesus' teaching on 'God as king' and 'God as Father' (*Teaching* chs. 4-8): 'the whole religion of Jesus centres round the twin conceptions of the heavenly Father and the heavenly King' (284).

2. Cf. McKnight, who notes how strange it is that so little has been written in scholarship about the God of Jesus, even though scholars like Manson have emphasized that 'in the teaching of Jesus his conception of God determines everything' (*New Vision* 15, citing Manson, *Teaching* 211).

3. Only in Matt. 5.35, where the Jesus tradition calls Jerusalem 'the city of the great king', in immediate echo of Ps. 48.2. Otherwise the nearest examples are two parables in Matthew which feature a king (Matt. 18.23-35; 22.1-14) and one in Luke (Luke 19.11-27). In contrast, the issue of the title's applicability to Jesus himself features quite regularly, particularly in the trial before Pilate (Mark 15.2, 26 pars.; Mark 15.9, 12; Mark 15.18/Matt. 27.29; Mark 15.32/Matt. 27.42; Luke 23.2, 37; John 18.33, 37, 39; 19.3, 12, 14, 15, 19, 21; also Matt. 2.2; 21.5; 25.34, 40; Luke 1.33; 19.38; John 1.49; 6.15; 12.13).

4. See above, §12.2b. The data are summarized in Seybold, *TDOT* 8.365-66.

5. We may note that Jesus is also recalled as assuming both the *Shema* and God's unique goodness as givens (Mark 12.29; 10.18).

6. See especially K. W. Whitelam, 'King and Kingship', *ABD* 4.40-48 (here 42-43, 44-45); also Seybold, *TDOT* 8.360-64.

king: within Yahweh's authority and power lay Israel's ultimate assurance of protection and justice.[7]

It is this confidence in God as protector and judge, that is, as the ultimate authority and power ensuring peace and justice, and as the one above all to whom submission and obedience is owed which is reflected in Jesus' talk of God's kingship. The subject owes unconditional obedience to the king; a double allegiance is impossible (Matt. 6.24/Luke 16.13/*GTh* 47.1-2).[8] Otherwise we need simply recall the strong emphasis in Jesus' kingdom preaching on eschatological reversal, judgment, and reward.[9] Those who cherished the Jesus tradition did not hesitate to emphasize both the 'up-side' and the 'down-side' of God as king. On the one hand, God would ensure justice for the poor. On the other hand, God could be portrayed as the master who would reward faithful servants and punish unfaithful servants[10] and as the king who would hand over his unmerciful servant to the torturers/jailers (Matt. 18.23-35). God was the one who would determine both the future bliss of the beggar Lazarus and the fate of the rich man to be tormented in Hades (Luke 16.19-31).

Particularly striking is the Q(?) saying Matt. 10.28/Luke 12.4-5:

Matt. 10.28	Luke 12.4-5
Do not be afraid of those who kill the body but are not able to kill the soul.　　　　　But <u>fear</u> rather <u>him who</u> is able to destroy soul and body in <u>hell</u>.	Do not be afraid of those who kill the body, and after that have no more that they can do.　But I will show you whom to fear: <u>fear him who</u>, after he has killed, has authority to cast into <u>hell</u>.

Luke's version appears to be both a typical oral variant and slight elaboration of something Jesus was remembered as saying.[11] The saying is an uncomfortable one and widely attributed to the situation of the later churches under persecution.[12] But fear of God is a deeply rooted theme within Israel's theology and worship, particularly in the Wisdom literature,[13] and the emphasis is hardly at odds with the portrayal of God as final judge elsewhere in the Jesus tradition. To exclude that portrayal from the 'authentic' Jesus tradition when it

---

7. See again Whitelam, *ABD* 4.43-44.

8. There is hardly any doubt that the warning against trying to serve two masters originated with Jesus (see above, chapter 13 n. 159). For the disciple likened to a 'slave, servant' *(doulos)* see Mark 10.44 pars.; 13.34; Matt. 24.45-51/Luke 12.42-46; Matt. 25.14-30/Luke 19.11-27; Matt. 10.24-25; 18.23-35; Luke 12.35-48; 17.7-10; John 13.16; 15.20.

9. See above, §12.4c, e, f.

10. Note particularly the 'parables of crisis', §12.4g.

11. Robinson/Hoffmann/Kloppenborg follow Matthew in reconstructing Q (*Critical Edition of Q* 296-99).

12. Funk, *Five Gospels* 173; Lüdemann, *Jesus* 169.

13. G. Wanke, *phobeō*, TDNT 9.201-203; H. F. Fuhs, *yare'*, TDOT 6.300-14.

is so much part of the Jesus tradition is certainly arbitrary, a judgment moti-vated, it would appear, more by the desire to find a comfortable and coherent Jesus, where coherence is determined by some later logic, than by consistency of scholarly method. At the same time, we should recall that the Hebrew con-cept of 'fear' includes the sense of 'be afraid of, stand in awe of, reverence, respect'.[14]

In the same vein the significance of the first petition of the Lord's Prayer should not escape notice. According to this prayer, the first priority for Jesus' fol-lowers is that God's name may be sanctified.[15] Integral to the petition are two an-cient concepts strange to contemporary ears. One is the 'name' as more than sim-ply an identifying label, but also as representing the person and embodying the authority of the one named.[16] In the Hebrew Bible the name *(shem)* of Yahweh 'so plainly denotes the personal rule and work of Yahweh that it may be used as an alternative name for Yahweh himself'.[17] In the first instance, then, the prayer is that God may be acknowledged as God, or, more specifically, in his role as Creator and God of Israel.[18]

The second strange concept is that of 'holiness'. Basic to it is the idea of otherness, set-apartness from everyday usage.[19] Used of God, it denotes the wholly otherness of God, constituting, as we might say, a fundamental rejection of any attempt to configure God as a projection of human ideals.[20] The point be-comes all the stronger when we realise that the petition is not for God's name to be rendered holy by others or even for its otherness to be recognized by human beings. The passive form of the verb ('be hallowed/sanctified') is a 'divine pas-sive', no doubt corresponding to the Hebrew *qadash* (Niphal), and echoing the OT thought that it is God himself who demonstrates his holiness and sanctifies his name.[21] There is of course also the thought that God should receive the

---

14. BDB, *yare'*; Wanke, *TDNT* 9.198-99. To be noted is the fact that fear of the Lord is understood as going hand in hand with loving the Lord with one's whole being (Deut. 6.2, 4-5; 10.12) (Fuhs, *TDOT* 6.307-308). In the Psalms the community that worships Yahweh is de-scribed as 'Yahweh-fearers' (308-309). But Fuhs also notes that fear of God as fear of the nu-minous is still clearly visible in several OT passages (300-303).

15. Text cited in §8.5b, and see further §12.4b.

16. H. Bietenhard, *onoma*, *TDNT* 5.242-83, especially 243, 250, 253-54. The nearest in contemporary usage is 'name' in the sense of 'reputation'.

17. Bietenhard, *TDNT* 5.255-58.

18. Becker consistently insists on setting these two features in antithesis — creation ver-sus 'salvation history' (*Jesus* here 270).

19. Cf. O. Procksch, *hagios*, *TDNT* 1.89-94.

20. This is the theological rationale for Israel's absolute refusal to make an image of God and its unyielding opposition to idolatry (itself to be regarded as just such a projection).

21. Lev. 10.3; 22.32; Num. 20.13; Isa. 5.16; Ezek. 20.41; 28.22, 25; 36.23; 38.16; 39.27.

proper reverence which is his due.[22] Here it is worth observing that the holiness of God is correlative to the fear of God, for it is the sense of the wholly/holy otherness of God which is at the root of the fear of God. But still it needs to be emphasized that the prayer is for God to take the necessary initiative. As in the Kaddish, the first two petitions of the Lord's Prayer correlate with each other: may God so manifest his holiness that his name may be fully honoured; may his kingdom come in order that his will may be done.

We should also note the further implication of Israel's Scriptures that God's name, God's reputation, is in substantial measure bound up with his people. It is generally recognized that 'to sanctify the name' is a traditional formula.[23] But it needs to be noticed also that what was envisaged is the honouring of God which will result from seeing God's work, particularly in his people. Just as, in contrast, it is Israel's transgression which profanes God's holy name,[24] and the catastrophes which ensue are what cause others to profane the name of Israel's God.[25] The point is classically underscored in the demand of the Holiness Code that Israel should be holy because Israel's God is holy (Lev. 19.2).[26]

So the first petition taught by Jesus was in no sense for God in himself, as it were, but precisely that God should demonstrate his authority and power and consequently should be properly feared. It is a prayer that God should bring about the hoped-for age to come when his name would no longer be desecrated by the way in which his people conduct themselves. And the implication is clear that those who so pray should themselves so live (in accordance with his will) as to document the reputation/name of the one they pray to. It is no accident that as this is the first petition in the disciples' prayer, so the first commandment for disciples is that they should love God with all their heart and soul and mind and strength (Mark 12.30 pars.). If fear of God is the correlate of the first petition, obedience is the correlate of the first commandment. No one can pray this prayer wholeheartedly who does not give God first place in all speaking and doing, and not as an exercise in heroic individualism but as a member of the people called to reflect the holy otherness of God in their daily living.[27]

22. Hence the emphasis also in Matthew that there is no place in discipleship for a frivolous attitude to God (Matt. 5.33-37; 23.16-22).

23. Lev. 22.32; Isa. 29.22-23; Ezek. 36.23; *1 En.* 9.4; 61.12; the Kaddish prayer (cited above, §12.4b).

24. Lev. 18.21; 19.12; 20.3; 21.6; 22.2, 32; Jer. 34.16; Ezek. 20.39; Amos 2.7; Mal. 1.12 (W. Dommershausen, *ḥll, TDOT* 4.410-12).

25. Isa. 48.11; 52.5 (cited by Paul in Rom. 2.24); Ezek. 20.9, 14, 22; 36.20-23; 39.7.

26. Similarly the implication of Deut. 7.6; 26.19.

27. McKnight concludes: 'Jesus' commands, then, are to be explained in an old-fashioned covenantal framework: the God of the Covenant, the Holy One of Israel, is calling his people for the final time to radical covenantal obedience. . . . the ethical demands of Jesus,

14.2. Children of the Father

Jesus' call for repentance corresponded to his kingdom preaching: to repent was to acknowledge previous failure to obey as a subject of the King should. In a similar way Jesus' teaching on God as Father corresponded to his call for belief and trust. This brings us to one of the most striking features of Jesus' teaching. For whereas Jesus is remembered as saying little or nothing explicitly about God as King, the memory of Jesus' teaching on God as Father is deeply embedded in the Jesus tradition.

The subject has been needlessly slanted in the history of its treatment, principally because successive scholars thought that they could find in it the most distinctive and most enduring (universal) element in Jesus' teaching, easily distinguished from the particularities of his native Judaism. The nineteenth-century Liberal treatments of Renan and Harnack were right to bring it to centre stage in their characterisations of Jesus' teaching, but they idealized and sentimentalized the theme (§4.3). Bultmann's recognition of the place of the emphasis was overshadowed by his stronger emphasis on Jesus' teaching on God as 'near' in contrast to the remoteness of God assumed to characterize Jewish thought of the time.[28] And Jeremias's characteristic treatment was too much dominated by his understanding of the term *abba* ('Father', as personal address) as a feature of Jesus' prayer life and teaching which marked an unprecedented intimacy with God in the Judaism of his time.[29]

We will return to the particular issue of Jesus' sonship below (§16.2). Here it needs to be stressed that the understanding of God as Father was nothing new to the Judaism of Jesus' time. The thought of God as Father of Israel, or of the king in particular, was long familiar in Jewish thought.[30] More recent in expression was the thought of individual Israelites, particularly the righteous, as sons of God.[31] Jeremias's claims need to be qualified by the recognition that the same 'righteous man' tradition was not unaccustomed to addressing God with a

---

in however radical a form, must be explained on the basis of Israel's covenant ethics, that is, on the basis of God's holiness' (*New Vision* 33).

28. Bultmann, *Jesus and the Word* ch. 4, particularly 137-41, 151.

29. Jeremias, *Prayers* ch. 1; *Proclamation* 178-84.

30. Israel in Exod. 4.22; Deut. 14.1; 32.6; Ps. 73.15; Isa. 1.2-3; 43.6; 45.11; 63.16; 64.8; Jer. 3.4, 19, 22; 31.9, 20; Hos. 1.10; 11.1; Mal. 2.10; Jub. 1.24-25; 19.29; *Pss. Sol.* 17.27. The king in 2 Sam. 7.14; 1 Chron. 17.13; 22.10; 28.6; Pss. 2.7; 89.26-27. See also R. Hamerton-Kelly, *God the Father: Theology and Patriarchy in the Teaching of Jesus* (Philadelphia: Fortress, 1979) 20-51; Vermes, *Religion* 173-80; M. M. Thompson, *The Promise of the Father: Jesus and God in the New Testament* (Louisville: Westminster John Knox, 2000) 35-55.

31. Pss. 68.5 ('father of the fatherless and protector of widows'); Ps. 103.13; Prov. 3.12; Sir. 4.10; 23.1; 51.10; Wis. 2.13, 16, 18; 5.5; 14.3; *Pss. Sol.* 13.9; 1QH 17[= 9].35-36 (see further G. Quell, *patēr, TDNT* 5.970-74; Jeremias, *Prayers* 11-29).

similar-sounding degree of intimacy.[32] And the suggestion that God was thought of as remote in the Judaism of Jesus' time speaks more of an earlier generation's tendency to denigrate 'late Judaism' as well as being contradicted by such evidence.[33] Nevertheless the fact that Jesus did encourage his disciples to trust in God as Father, while hardly unique within the Judaism of his day, may be said to be distinctive in its consistency and in the degree of childlike persistence which he encouraged his disciples to express in their prayers.

a. Child-Like Trust

The data are straightforward. Jesus is remembered as speaking of God quite regularly as 'your Father', the 'you' being his immediate disciples.[34] There can be little doubt that in the course of transmission the motif of God as Father has been extended within the Jesus tradition.[35] But the evidence is sufficient to suggest clearly that the extended motif was an elaboration of a well-remembered feature of Jesus' own teaching. In the Lord's Prayer the disciples are encouraged on their own part to address God as 'Father' (Luke 11.2/Matt. 6.9), which subsequent

32. Sir. 23.1, 4; 51.10 (Hebrew); Wis. 14.3; 3 Macc. 6.3, 8 (G. Schrenk, *patēr, TDNT* 5.981). Much has been made, by Vermes in particular, of the tradition of Honi the circle-drawer (first century BCE), who according to tradition prayed to God 'like a son of the house' (*m. Ta'an* 3.8) (*Jesus* ch. 3). Vermes, however, also notes the absence of such intimacy in the DSS prayers (*Religion* 180).

33. A basic misconception was that divine 'intermediaries' (Spirit, Wisdom, Word, Name, Glory, as well as angels) indicated thought of God's remoteness (Bousset-Gressmann 319, an often quoted passage; echoed by Bultmann in his *Jesus and the Word* 137-41; also *Primitive Christianity* 61), whereas they are better understood as ways of asserting God's immanence without compromising his transcendence (see my *Christology* 130, 150-51, 176, 219-20, 229, 252-53).

34. 'Your (singular) Father', Matt. 6.4, 6, 18. 'Your (plural) Father', Mark 11.25/Matt. 6.14-15; Matt. 5.48/Luke 6.36; Matt. 6.32/Luke 12.30; Matt. 7.11/(Luke 11.13); Matt. 5.16, 45; 6.1, 8, 26; 10.20, 29; 18.14; 23.9; Luke 12.32; John 20.17. I will discuss references to 'the Father' (Mark 13.32; Matt. 11.27/Luke 10.22) below (§16.2c).

35. Jeremias provided the following statistics for the use of the title 'Father' for God in the words of Jesus: three in Mark, four common to Matthew and Luke, four additional instances peculiar to Luke, thirty-one additional instances peculiar to Matthew, and one hundred in John (*Prayers* 30-32), to which may be added twenty in *GTh* (see below). Matthew's tendency to add references to God as Father is illustrated by Matt. 5.45/Luke 6.35; Matt. 6.26/Luke 12.24; and Matt. 10.29/Luke 12.6. Jeremias also notes a 'tendency of the later tradition to suppress "your Father" almost to vanishing point', a tendency attested not least by *Thomas*, which has only two instances of 'your Father' (*GTh* 15, 50.3, neither with parallels in the canonical tradition), as against twelve instances of 'the Father' (*GTh* 27, 40.1, *44.1, 57.1,* 69.1, *76.1,* 79.2, 83.1, *96.1, 97.1,* 98.1, and *113.1,* with italics in the list here indicating parallels where 'the Father' has been added).

Christian usage certainly regarded as distinctive.[36] The other side of the same coin is Jesus' characterisation of disciples as little children and his taking a little child as the model of discipleship.[37] As the complex of Mark 10.14-15 pars. shows, this tradition was rehearsed in different permutations,[38] but the one or more incidents during Jesus' mission thus recalled evidently made a deep and lasting impression on the Jesus tradition.[39]

From all this it should be clear that Jesus was remembered as conceiving of God's fatherhood not so much as a general corollary to his role as Creator — God as Father of inanimate creation and humankind generally.[40] Nor was he simply taking over the established Jewish motif of God as Father of Israel (n. 30). He was remembered as inviting his disciples into a new relation, new in quality or degree, to convert and 'become' as children (Matt. 18.3). At the same time, the call can again be understood as a call to reclaim the relationship with God intended for Israel, or better, to return to or realise afresh the relationship which God intended for his people (rather like the righteous individuals in the Wisdom literature). At any rate, whatever richer overtones may be audible, the tradition

36. Rom. 8.15-17; Gal. 4.6-7 (§16.2b at n. 48). Here I assume that Luke 11.2 is closer to what Jesus had himself taught (see above, §8.5b) and that behind the bare Greek *pater* stands the Aramaic *abba,* with its marked degree of intimacy (Jeremias, *Prayers* 90-91; see further below §16.2b), whereas the developed liturgical form in Matt. 6.9 is closer to more formal rabbinic usage (cf. Schrenk, *TDNT* 5.981-82; Jeremias, *Prayers* 22-23). At the same time it should be recalled that it is precisely Matthew who recalls Jesus encouraging prayer as a very personal and private communication with God as Father (Matt. 6.5-6, in a sequence of teaching perhaps echoed in *GTh* 6, 14).

37. *Paidion* (a very young child, infant) in Mark 9.36-37/Matt. 18.2, 5/Luke 9.47-48; Mark 10.14/Matt. 19.14/Luke 18.16; Mark 10.15/Matt. 18.3/Luke 18.17; John 21.5. *Nēpios* (a very young child, infant) in Matt. 11.25/Luke 10.21.

38. Was there a Q version of Matt. 18.5/Luke 9.48, obscured now by Matthew's and Luke's greater dependency on Mark? And we should not forget the development in John 3.3, 5 and the further echoes in *GTh* 22 and 46.2 (see also above, §13.2a).

39. Mark 10.15 'is perhaps the most memorable and pregnant of all the sayings of Jesus' (Perrin, *Rediscovering* 146). The Jesus Seminar agree that Jesus probably said something like Mark 10.14 pars., but consider it likely, from the way the saying has been drawn into the context of baptism in John 3.5, that rites of initiation are in view in all forms of Mark 10.15 and that therefore it is unlikely to have originated with Jesus (Funk, *Five Gospels* 89-90, 213, 486-87; the oddness of the rationale offered reflects a very divided vote). In contrast, Lüdemann regards Mark 10.14 as 'a community formation and therefore inauthentic', but finds that the criterion of coherence favours the authenticity of 10.15 (*Jesus* 68); Becker, *Jesus* 311-12. See further above, chapter 12 n. 163 and chapter 13 nn. 48 and 49.

40. Manson, *Teaching* 89-91; Schrenk, *TDNT* 5.978, 990-91 ('The word "father" is for those who accept the teaching of Jesus about "your Father"', 991); Jeremias, *Prayers* 38-43, who also emphasises that Jesus spoke thus only to his disciples (43 and n. 70), and critiques H. W. Montefiore's attempt to demonstrate that Jesus nevertheless taught the 'universal Fatherhood' of God ('God as Father in the Synoptic Gospels', *NTS* 3 [1956-57] 31-46).

clearly remembers Jesus' teaching as directed to his disciples and as encouraging them to live as children before God as Father.

The significance of the imagery is clear. 'To be a child is to be little, to need help, to be receptive to it'.[41] To become a disciple, then, is to become like a child, that is, to revert to a position of dependence.[42] The point is not that the would-be disciple should pretend to be a child or act in a childish manner. It is rather that disciples must recognize that before God they are in fact little children, not mature, not able to live a wholly independent life or to bear sole responsibility for themselves by themselves. The trust for which Jesus called ('Convert and trust') is the constant dependence and reliance of little children on their parent for their very existence and the ongoing significance of their lives. Here again the parable of the prodigal son, with its repeated reference to the father, illustrates what Mark 10.15 pars. asserted: that repentance/conversion is to return to the son's dependence on the father's extraordinary generosity (Luke 15.11-24).[43]

The childlike trust for which Jesus called is most vividly documented in the famous Q passage, Matt. 6.25-33/Luke 12.22-31.[44]

Matt. 6.25-33	Luke 12.22-31
25 Therefore I tell you, do not worry about your life, what you will eat or what you will drink, or about your body, what you will wear. Is not life more than food, and the body more than clothing? 26 Look at the birds of the air; they neither sow nor reap nor gather into barns, and yet your heavenly Father feeds them. Are you not of more value than they?	22 Therefore I tell you, do not worry about your life, what you will eat, or about your body, what you will wear. 23 For life is more than food, and the body more than clothing. 24 Consider the ravens: they neither sow nor reap, they have neither storehouse nor barn, and yet God feeds them. Of how much more value are you than the birds!
27 And can any of you by worrying add a single hour to your span of life? 28 And why do you worry about clothing? Consider the lilies of the field, how they grow; they neither toil nor spin, 29 yet I tell you, that even Solomon in all his glory was not clothed like one of these. 30 But if God so clothes the grass of the field, which is alive today and tomorrow is thrown into the oven, will he not much more clothe you, you of	25 And can any of you by worrying add a single hour to your span of life? 26 If then you are not able to do so small a thing as that, why do you worry about the rest? 27 Consider the lilies, how (they grow): they neither spin nor weave; yet I tell you, even Solomon in all his glory was not clothed like one of these. 28 But if God so clothes the grass in the field, which is alive today and tomorrow is thrown into the oven, how much more will he clothe you, you of

41. J. Behm, *metanoeō*, *TDNT* 4.1003.

42. 'The trust, the *emunah*, of a child is the *conditio sine qua non* for access to the Kingdom' (Vermes, *Religion* 144; and further 196-200).

43. Cf. Jeremias, *Proclamation* 155-56. Bailey brings out the extraordinary character of the father's love by setting the parable in its cultural context (*Poet and Peasant* 161, 165, 181-82, 186-87, 196-200). In arguing that children were 'nobodies' in the ancient world (*Historical Jesus* 269), Crossan once again ignores the positive imagery of childhood in Jewish biblical tradition (e.g., above, nn. 30-32). On the parable see also chapter 13 n. 147 above.

44. *GTh* 36 preserves a mere fragment of the teaching, but *P.Oxy.* 655 retains a fuller echo.

little faith? 31 Therefore do not worry, saying, 'What will we eat?' or 'What will we drink?' or 'What will we wear?' 32 For it is the nations that strive for all these things; and indeed your heavenly Father knows that you need all these things. 33 But seek first the kingdom of God and his righteousness, and all these things will be given to you as well. 34 So do not worry about tomorrow, for tomorrow will bring worries of its own. Today's trouble is enough for today.	little faith! 29 And do not keep striving for what you are to eat and what you are to drink, and do not keep worrying. 30 For it is the nations of the world that strive for all these things, and your Father knows that you need them. 31 Instead, seek his kingdom, and these things will be given to you as well. 32 Do not be afraid, little flock, for it is your Father's good pleasure to give you the kingdom.

It is impossible now to tell whether Jesus ever gave this as a single piece of teaching.[45] The Sermon on the Mount itself provides sufficient evidence of the tendency within church performances of the Jesus tradition to group material for teaching purposes; even here the final saying in the two sequences (Matt. 6.34/Luke 12.32) gives clear indication of performance/editorial freedom on such matters.[46] The more important point is that Jesus was remembered as encouraging a high degree of trust in the bounty of the Creator who is also the Father — as also in Matt. 10.29-31/Luke 12.6-7).[47] Faith excludes

45. The Jesus Seminar concluded that Matt. 6.31-34 and Luke 12.26, 29-31 are secondary accretions to the underlying tradition which can be traced back to Jesus (Funk, *Five Gospels* 151-53); Becker distances it from the 'itinerant radicalism' of the mission instructions, but concludes equally that it is authentic Jesus material (*Jesus* 131-32); Lüdemann regards Matt. 6.25-33 as authentic 'because they cannot be derived from the community' and fit the context of the disciples sent out by or accompanying Jesus from village to village (*Jesus* 149). There is an ongoing debate as to which of Q 12.22-31 and *P.Oxy.* 655 is the earlier, J. M. Robinson and C. Heil arguing in favour of the latter (*P.Oxy.* 655 is nearer to the simpler oral tradition), J. Schröter in favour of the former (*P.Oxy.* 655 is more likely post-Synoptic). For the latest rounds see Robinson and Heil, 'The Lilies of the Field: Saying 36 of the Gospel of Thomas and Secondary Accretions in Q 12.22b-31', *NTS* 47 (2001) 1-25; Schröter, 'Rezeptionsprozesse in der Jesusüberlieferung: Überlegungen zum historischen Charakter der neutestamentlichen Wissenschaft am Beispiel der Sorgensprüche', *NTS* 47 (2001) 442-68; and Robinson and Heil, 'Noch einmal: Der Schreibfehler in Q 12,27', *ZNW* 92 (2001) 113-22; Schröter, 'Verschrieben? Klärende Bemerkungen zu einem vermeintlichen Schreibfehler in Q und tatsächlichen Irrtümern', *ZNW* 92 (2001) 283-89. Earlier, Manson had observed that Matt. 6.26-30/Luke 12.24-28 provides a good example of poetic parallelism (*Teaching* 56).

46. The saying reflects popular wisdom (see particularly Davies and Allison, *Matthew 1–7* 662-63), drawn on either by Jesus or in subsequent performance.

47.

Matt. 10.29-31	Luke 12.6-7
29 Are not two sparrows sold for a penny? Yet not one of them will fall to the ground apart from your Father. 30 And even the hairs of your head are all counted. 31 So do not be afraid; you are of more value than many sparrows.	6 Are not five sparrows sold for two pennies? Yet not one of them is forgotten before God. 7 But even the hairs of your head have all been counted. Do not be afraid; you are of more value than many sparrows.

anxiety[48] about necessities; God is trustworthy. Uncertainty in face of the fragility of human existence (Isa. 40.6-7) need not cause anxiety. The child can be confident in the face even of crisis; the father will sustain through the crisis. The King is also Father, and his kingly rule can already be experienced in the trustworthiness with which he provides for their needs.[49]

Such teaching should not be discounted as unrealistic in the face of the experience of famine and political crises which many of Jesus' audiences would well remember and could expect to confront again. Jesus himself would hardly have been unaware of such harsh realities, and many of those who cherished his teaching will no doubt have had all too much experience of hard times and personal distress. The teaching was valued, then, presumably, not because it inculcated a careless disregard for harsh reality, but because it encouraged trust in the providence of a caring Creator,[50] the clarification of personal priorities (life itself [*nepeš, psychē*] as more important than food and clothing), and the calm acceptance of what cannot be changed.[51] Initially the imminence of the coming kingdom would have been the (or a) major factor in such a reordering of priorities. But the communities which cherished the teaching probably saw in it enduring encouragement to an unfretful faith for daily living (as Matt. 6.34 presumably implies), a tranquillity of trust even in the midst of stress and crisis. In neither case need (or should) an 'eschatological' (or apocalyptic) overtone be set in antithesis to a 'sapiential', as though the one excluded the other.

The Jesus Seminar were equally confident that this passage went back to Jesus (Funk, *Five Gospels* 172-73), whereas Lüdemann ignores the close parallel with Matt. 6.26/Luke 12.24 in dismissing the whole of Matt. 10.27-33 as 'inauthentic as they derive from a later situation of the community stamped by persecution' (*Jesus* 169), in striking contrast to his judgment on the earlier Matthean passage (above, n. 45).

48. The key word is *merimnaō*, 'be anxious, (unduly) concerned' (used five times: Matt. 6.25, 27, 28, 31, 34). In this case Bultmann's existentialist reading captures the thrust of the passage well: a warning against the illusion that life can be somehow secured by worrying about the means of life (*merimnaō, TDNT* 4.591-93).

49. Becker, *Jesus* 268.

50. The thought is hardly new in Jewish tradition; e.g., Job 12.10; 38.41; Pss. 104; 147.9; *Pss. Sol.* 5.9-10 (Davies and Allison, *Matthew* 1.650). Jeremias notes the disapproval voiced in *m. Ber.* 5.3 of prayer which refers to God's mercies extending 'to a bird's nest' (*Proclamation* 182). But Davies and Allison note also *m. Qidd.* 4.14 (649). A similar confidence was encouraged among Cynics (Downing, *Christ and the Cynics* 68-71).

51. 'You must see yourselves as human beings who stand in God's presence and are therefore more than the wretched needs that attack you' (Schottroff and Stegemann, *Hope of the Poor* 44).

b. Prayer

The other aspect of the childlike trust implicit in the above passage is given prominence elsewhere in Jesus' teaching and deserves separate comment — prayer. The
children of the Father know that they can take their concerns and requests to God
in confidence. This is clear already in the petitions of the Lord's Prayer, simple but
basic in the concerns they voice. It is to God as Father that Jesus encourages his
disciples to bring their requests for bread, for forgiveness, for deliverance from
temptation (Matt. 6.9-13/Luke 11.2-4).[52] Equally memorable is Jesus' assurance
that God hears and answers prayer — (Matt.7.7-11/Luke 11.9-13):

Matt. 7.7-11	Luke 11.9-13
7 <u>Ask, and it will be given you;</u> <u>seek, and you will find; knock, and the door will</u> <u>be opened for you.</u> 8 <u>For everyone who asks</u> <u>receives, and everyone who seeks finds, and for</u> <u>everyone who knocks, the door will be opened.</u> 9 Or <u>what</u> person <u>among you who, if</u> his <u>son</u> asks for bread, will give him a stone? 10 Or if he <u>asks</u> <u>for a fish, will give</u> him <u>a snake?</u> 11 <u>If you then, who are evil, know</u> <u>how to give good gifts to your children, how</u> <u>much more will</u> your <u>Father</u> who is in <u>heaven give</u> good things <u>to those who ask him.</u>	9 So I say to you, <u>Ask, and it will be given you;</u> <u>seek, and you will find; knock, and the door will</u> <u>be opened for you.</u> 10 <u>For everyone who asks</u> <u>receives, and everyone who seeks finds, and for</u> <u>everyone who knocks, the door will be opened.</u> 11 <u>What</u> father <u>among you who, if</u> your <u>son</u> <u>asks</u> <u>for a fish, will give</u> <u>a snake</u> instead of a fish? 12 Or if the child asks for an egg, will give a scorpion? 13 <u>If you then, who are evil, know</u> <u>how to give good gifts to your children, how</u> <u>much more will</u> the heavenly <u>Father give</u> the Holy Spirit <u>to those who ask him!</u>

Few question whether this teaching goes back to Jesus.[53] It is not just an encouragement to persistent prayer[54] but also an assurance of the eagerness of the Fa-

---

52. Note how by adding the assurance that 'your Father knows what you need before
you ask him' immediately before the Lord's Prayer (Matt. 6.8; the same assurance as in 6.32),
Matthew deliberately links the prayer to the subsequent teaching in 6.25-34.

53. Funk, *Five Gospels* 155; Lüdemann, *Jesus* 151. Note the typical performance variations (Matt. 7.9-10/Luke 11.11-12). It is presumably to Luke himself that we owe
crystallisation of the 'good things' promised (Matthew) into 'the Holy Spirit', since the Spirit
features more prominently in his Gospel (six appearances in Mark, twelve in Matthew, and seventeen in Luke). Partial echoes are retained in *P.Oxy.* 654 = *GTh* 2 and *GTh* 92, 94. Note also
John 16.23-24. Matt. 18.19 is probably an elaboration of the same motif as part of Matthew's
'community rule'. See also below, §15.7g (3).

54. Reinforced in the Greek by the present tenses: 'keep asking', 'keep seeking', 'keep
knocking' (though see also Davies and Allison, *Matthew* 1.679-80). Luke further reinforces the
point by appending the parable of the friend at midnight (Luke 11.5-8), another parable which,
despite its sole attestation by Luke, is usually referred back to Jesus without difficulty (Funk,
Five Gospels 327-28; Hultgren, *Parables* 233 n. 29; Lüdemann, *Jesus* 335); for discussion of
detail see Bailey, *Poet and Peasant* 119-33; Catchpole, *Quest* 201-11; Hultgren 226-33. It is
also Luke who records the parable of the unjust judge in Luke 18.2-8, making the same point
(see chapter 12 n. 251).

ther to give to his children.[55] At the same time any suggestion that Jesus naïvely encouraged his disciples to ask anything from God and assured them that God would give them whatever they requested would itself be naïve. The requests envisaged are of a piece with the Lord's Prayer petition for basic food needs (bread, fish, egg). And the assurance is not that God will give whatever is asked for but that whatever the Father gives will be good.

In short, the portrayal of discipleship in terms of childlike trust in and reliance on God as Father is consistent within the Jesus tradition. This emphasis should not be set in antithesis to the Jewish piety of the day, even if it can be regarded as an intensification of such piety. Nor should it be set in contrast to the understanding of God as king (§14.1), since the absolute authority of the father is always bound up in the term and in the relationship implied,[56] even if Jesus' teaching gave greatest emphasis to the aspect of fatherly care. Nor should it be lightly universalized, as though Jesus simply declared that all human beings were children of God, even if his stringent call for repentance and faith was in principle open to all. Granted these important qualifications, however, Jesus' teaching on the fatherhood of God remains one of the most distinctive and alluring features of the whole Jesus tradition.

14.3. Disciples of Jesus

A third feature of discipleship naturally follows from the third element of Jesus' call — the call to 'follow me' (§13.2c). 'Disciples' were those who responded to that call; they had become followers of Jesus. This is not to ignore again the likelihood that Jesus' call to repent and believe was addressed to all Israel (§13.3), nor to forget that there were many who 'followed' who should not be described as 'disciples' (§13.2c) or that 'circles of discipleship' (§13.8) which merge into 'the poor' and 'sinners' of/within Israel cannot be delimited with any precision. But neither should we underplay the clear recollection that Jesus called for a personal following.[57] He was at the centre of the circles of discipleship. Whatever

55. Hence the corresponding implication that the child of such a father can be bold in making requests known — as illustrated by Mark 5.27-28; 10.47-48; Matt. 8.8-9; 15.22-27.

56. Jeremias, *Prayers* 11; Schrenk stresses still more that 'the synthesis Father/Judge, Father/Lord makes any lack of respect impossible by imposing submission to his holy rule' (*TDNT* 5.985, and further 995-96); also worth noting is the authority and power of the Father assumed in the petitions of the Lord's Prayer.

57. That Jesus did gather around himself a group of committed disciples is one of the securest historical facts (Meier, *Marginal Jew* 3.41-47; bibliography 82-83 n. 1); *inter alia,* Meier points out that prior to Jesus no Palestinian Jewish author speaks of 'disciples' (44) and that the term is completely absent in a large number of the Apostolic Fathers (84-85 n. 6).

other relations were involved in that first discipleship, it was determined primarily by the relation of the disciple to Jesus. The discipleship for which Jesus called was discipleship of Jesus.

Martin Hengel, whose richly documented study on *The Charismatic Leader and His Followers* remains fundamental, has stressed that this was a feature which clearly distinguished the discipleship for which Jesus called from the other voluntary groupings of the time. There are no equivalent stories of 'calling' and 'following after' in rabbinic tradition.[58] And there is no hint that the recruits who joined the Qumran community were responding to some call. Both groups certainly attracted pupils and members, but the element of personal call to (as it would appear) targetted individuals was distinctive of the group round Jesus. Earlier on we hear of disciples of prophets ('sons of the prophets'),[59] but the only close parallel or precedent is Elijah's summons of Elisha to be his successor.[60]

However, there is some danger of exaggerating the distinctiveness of the immediate discipleship of Jesus, and Hengel discounts too quickly the idea of Jesus as 'example' or 'imitation' of Jesus in the Gospels.[61] Attention should also be given to the following features.

a. Learning

As disciples, the group round Jesus was a learning community. As disciples *(mathētēs),* they were learners (from *manthanō,* 'to learn'), with Jesus as their teacher *(didaskalos).*[62] Mark explicitly states that Jesus chose twelve 'in order

58. Hengel, *Charismatic Leader* 50-51; see also his response on this point (84-86) to H. D. Betz, *Nachfolge und Nachahmung Jesu Christi im Neuen Testament* (Tübingen: Mohr Siebeck, 1967) 27-43. But he also notes that the adherents of first-century 'prophets' reported by Josephus 'followed' them, to the Jordan (*Ant.* 20.97) or into the desert (20.167, 188) (*Charismatic Leader* 21 n. 19). See also Meier, *Marginal Jew* 3.50-54.

59. 2 Kgs. 2.3, 5, 15; 4.1; 5.22; 6.1; 9.1; Isa. 8.16; Jer. 36.4-10, 32; Amos 7.14.

60. See further Hengel, *Charismatic Leader* 16-18. Schrage, *Ethics* 46-49, Gnilka, *Jesus* 161-64, and Theissen and Merz, *Historical Jesus* 214-15, follow Hengel on the substance of this paragraph. See also Meier, *Marginal Jew* 3.91-92 nn. 25, 26.

61. Hengel, *Charismatic Leader* 1-2, 42-50, 53.

62. Data already in §8.1b. Occasionally in the Jesus tradition Jesus is even addressed as 'Rabbi'/'Rabbouni' (Mark 9.5; 10.51; 11.21; 14.45 par.; Matt. 26.25; John 1.38, 49; 3.2; 4.31; 6.25; 9.2; 11.8); indeed, the Baptist (John 3.26) and Jesus are the earliest Jewish teachers for whom such an address is attested (see also Theissen and Merz, *Historical Jesus* 354-55). Hengel makes too much of the relative absence of *manthanō* in the Synoptic tradition — only once in Mark 13.28/Matt. 24.32; he attributes the other two references (Matt. 9.13; 11.29) to redaction (*Charismatic Leader* 51). There is truth in his further assertion that Jesus' intention was not 'to create a new tradition, but to prepare for the service of the approaching rule of God'

that they might be with him' (Mark 3.14). This, of course, is part of Mark's emphasis on Jesus as 'teacher'.[63] But there can be little doubt that Jesus did give much teaching. And the fact that so much of it has been retained in the tradition is evidence enough that his disciples remembered the teaching, treasured it, and presumably attempted to live it out in their discipleship. To so argue is not to revert to Gerhardsson's portrayal of discipleship as a kind of proto-rabbinic school.[64] As has now been illustrated repeatedly, the present form of the Synoptic tradition is much more fully explained on the pattern of informally controlled community traditions. But that is wholly consistent with the characteristic portrayal of Jesus teaching, whether in synagogue and at table, or at lakeside, on hillside, or as they journeyed. What Jesus taught made a deep and abiding impression, still clearly evident in the Jesus tradition itself.[65] It requires no stretch of the imagination to deduce that Jesus himself intended his teaching to provide the structure of the discipleship to which he made summons. On this specific point the distance between Jesus and a Pharisaic or Wisdom teacher is not great, though much more still needs to be said (§14.4 below).

b. Mission

Mark also asserts that Jesus called Peter and Andrew to make them 'fishers of men' (Mark 1.17)[66] and that he chose twelve in order that he might send them out to preach and to exercise authority in the casting out of demons (Mark 3.14). He thus makes explicit what is implicit anyway in the tradition of Jesus sending out the twelve on mission (Mark 6.6-12 pars.).[67] That is, that Jesus chose an immedi-

---

(81), but there is a good deal more in the Jesus tradition than falls neatly under that heading. Crossan also protests that 'disciples' is probably not the best term, since it presumes a relation of master and students, with overtones of domination and control; he prefers to describe the kingdom of God as a 'companionship of empowerment' rather than Schüssler Fiorenza's 'discipleship of equals' (*Birth* 336-37), but at this point ideology is being allowed to trample over the language used in the Jesus tradition.

    63. See again above, chapter 8 nn. 22-23.

    64. See above, §8.3e. Note Hengel's critique of Gerhardsson at this point (*Charismatic Leader* 53, 80-81).

    65. We need only mention the end of the Sermon on the Mount/Plain (Matt. 7.24-27/ Luke 6.47-49) and the complex of remembered teaching in Mark 8.38/Luke 9.26 (cf. Matt. 10.32-33/Luke 12.8-9); see below, §15.8c(6).

    66. See particularly Hengel, who also offers a reconstruction of the Aramaic original (*Charismatic Leader* 76-78); Meier, *Marginal Jew* 3.159-61; see also above, chapter 13 n. 96.

    67. See above, chapter 8 n. 282. 'The Twelve were Jesus' *shaliḥim*' (Witherington, *Christology* 134); Witherington also thinks that they were sent out late in the Galilean ministry, perhaps just before the feeding of the five thousand (135).

ate group of disciples with a view to their assisting or sharing in his own mission. We have already noted that the Q tradition recalls Jesus sending out his disciples to proclaim the very same message that characterized Jesus' own preaching: 'The kingdom of God has drawn near' (Matt. 10.7/Luke 10.9).[68] Most striking is the saying preserved in Matt. 10.40/Luke 10.16 in teaching attached to the mission commission:

Matt. 10.40	Luke 10.16
He who receives you receives me, and he who receives me receives him who sent me.	He who hears you hears me, and he who rejects you rejects me; but he who rejects me rejects him who sent me.

The saying is usually taken to reflect the concerns of the subsequent communities in regard to their own authorisation,[69] and no doubt it does so. But the idea of Jesus' disciples as representing their master is recalled at various points in the ongoing tradition.[70] And the šaliaḥ principle (šaliaḥ = 'sent man'), that the one who is sent is as the one who sends (m. Ber. 5.5), is generally reckoned to be at the root of the concept of apostleship.[71] So the principle may be assumed to have been already familiar at the time of Jesus. In other words, here too the saying, in its different versions, simply makes explicit what was anyway implicit: that Jesus sent out his disciples to carry forward the mission to which he evidently believed himself to have been called.

To be a disciple, then, was to take part in Jesus' mission. Does this give sufficient ground for Theissen's description of Jesus' following as 'a movement of wandering charismatics'?[72] Not really. For all Theissen's concern to root his

68. It is doubtful whether the second commissioning of seventy(-two) in Luke 10.1-12 provides sufficient evidence of a second sending out by Jesus; it is more likely that Luke himself has compiled two commissionings from the differing Mark and Q traditions (e.g., Fitzmyer, *Luke* 842-43), possibly to foreshadow the double mission of earliest Christianity (to Jews and Gentiles), as in 14.21-23.

69. Funk, *Five Gospels* 175-76; Lüdemann, *Jesus* 329.

70. Mark 9.37 pars.; John 13.20; *Did.* 11.4; Ignatius, *Eph.* 6.1 (latter texts in Aland, *Synopsis* 149; see also Crossan, *Fragments* 104-19). The idea of acting 'in the name of' Jesus, that is, with his authority or authorisation, also carries the same overtones (Mark 9.37 pars.; 13.6 pars.; Mark 9.38-39/Luke 9.49; Matt. 7.22; 18.20; Luke 10.17).

71. See, e.g., Davies and Allison, *Matthew* 2.153-54 (bibliography in nn. 34-35), but see also chapter 15 n. 226 below.

72. Cited above, §4.6; for its influence see chapter 7 n. 96. Crossan regards this complex of sayings (*Mission and Message* — centring on *GTh* 14; Mark 6.7-13 pars.; Q 10.4-11) as 'the most important unit for understanding the historical Jesus . . .'. The itinerants in view are 'dispossessed and now landless laborers, close to but not yet beggars'. He envisages not a single sending, but 'a permanent process, with Jesus as the moving center of a changing group' and cites Patterson's argument (*Thomas and Jesus* 132) that 'originally the ideal of radical

analysis in the social conditions of the time, the description suggests that a hint of the old romantic idealism of a Renan still lingers. For one thing, it would appear that only a few who may properly be called Jesus' disciples actually went out on mission on Jesus' behalf.[73] And for another, a mission throughout Galilee need involve only a sequence of one or two days travel from a centre like Capernaum.[74] Indeed, apart from the references to the sending out of the twelve (Mark 6.7 pars.) and journeys to the region of Tyre and Sidon and perhaps the villages of Caesarea Philippi (7.24 par.; 8.27 par.), the Gospel accounts seem to envisage outreach mainly from a base in Capernaum, either across the lake, to villages/towns like Chorazin and Bethsaida, or less than a day's journey to places like Nain and Cana.[75]

Nevertheless, it could be fairly said that a sharing in Jesus' mission is another element in the distinctiveness of being a disciple of Jesus. For if Pharisees did not seek out disciples, neither did they send them out on mission. And there is no evidence of Essenes actually seeking to evangelize or proselytize in the name, say, of the Teacher of Righteousness. The nearness of the eschatological horizon was obviously an important factor in the case of Jesus' commission, but it is worth noting that the subsequent communities preserved and reused the mission instructions despite the horizon drawing no nearer. Worth noting also is the fact that the eschatological tension within the instructions between good news and healing offered on the one hand and judgment pronounced on the other[76] closely mirrors the same tension in Jesus' kingdom preaching (§§12.4-5).

---

itinerancy was not necessarily linked with early Christian "mission" at all but rather had more the quality of a permanent manner of living, a life-style advocated by the Jesus movement' (*Birth* 325-37, citing 325, 335, 337, 328). He further argues that a dialectic of dissent between itinerants and householders can be traced from the historical Jesus, through the Q material and into *Didache* (Part VIII): 'Behind Q Gospel 6:36-49 you must hear the criticisms made against the itinerants by the householders even as you read the itinerants countercriticizing the householders in defense of themselves' (357). That such Jesus tradition was used in many exhortations in early Christian communities is entirely probable (note particularly Luke 6.36), but Crossan grossly over-schematizes a complex of motifs.

73. Though also to be noted is the implication that disciples are to be 'salt' and 'light' (Matt. 5.13-16), Matthew's tradition drawing the implication from more general sayings in the tradition (Mark 9.49-50 and Luke 14.34-35; Mark 4.21 and Luke 8.16).

74. References to mission throughout Galilee (as in Mark 1.39; see above, §9.9f) have to be balanced against references to Capernaum as his settled base (see above, §9.9d).

75. See again §9.9f above, and on the likelihood that Jesus extended his mission to Judea and Jerusalem see §9.9g.

76. Mark 6.7 pars. (Matt. 10.8 heightens the parallel by including a foreshadowing of 11.5); Mark 6.11 pars.; Matt. 10.12-13, 15/Luke 10.5-6, 12.

c. Service

In the Gospel tradition Jesus is also presented as the model of service — Mark 10.41-45 pars.[77] In Mark, closely followed by Matt. 20.20-28, the teaching is Jesus' response to a request for/on behalf of James and John that they should be granted to sit on Jesus' right and left 'in your kingdom/glory' (Matt. 20.21/Mark 10.37). We need consider here only the closing section, where Matthew (20.24-28) follows Mark almost word for word:

Mark 10.41-45	Luke 22.24-27
41 When the ten heard this, they began to be angry with James and John. 42 So Jesus called them and said to them, 'You know that among the <u>Gentiles</u> those whom they recognize as their rulers <u>lord it over them</u>, and their great ones are tyrants over them. 43 <u>But</u> it is <u>not so</u> among <u>you</u>; but whoever wishes to become <u>great among you must</u> be your <u>servant</u>, 44 and whoever wishes to be first among you must be slave of all. 45 For the Son of Man came not to be served but to <u>serve</u>, and to give his life a ransom for many'.	24 A dispute also arose among them as to which one of them was to be regarded as the greatest. 25 But he said to them, 'The kings of the <u>Gentiles</u> <u>lord it over them</u>; and those in authority over them are called benefactors. 26 <u>But not so</u> with <u>you</u>; rather the <u>greatest among you must</u> become like the youngest, and the leader like one who <u>serves</u>. 27 For who is greater, the one who is at the table or the one who serves? Is it not the one at the table? But I am among you as one who <u>serves</u>'.

We have already noted how deeply rooted in the tradition is the great(est)/least motif,[78] and the variation between Mark and Luke is simply another indication of how the tradition of particular teaching could vary in the different retellings.[79] That Jesus' talk of the kingdom should have given rise to such ambition among his intimates is entirely credible, as also that the communities should cherish the memory of Jesus' rebuke as a stark reminder of where their own priorities should lie. What stands out here is that Jesus is remembered as putting forward his own sense of vocation and priorities as a model for his disciples. Whether Mark 10.45 is a much elaborated form of what Jesus said is something we will have to consider later.[80] Here the point is that the core memory is of Jesus depicting his role in servant terms and commending it as an example to his close circle.[81] It should be noted that Jesus apparently did not *dis*courage ambition (to be 'great'); but the greatness he commended was that of the *servant*.

77. Casey offers an Aramaic rendition of the whole episode (Mark 10.35-45) (*Aramaic Sources* ch. 5).

78. See above, §12.4c.

79. Luke has chosen to present the material as part of his account of the last supper (Luke 22.14-38).

80. See below, §17.5d(2).

81. The same memory no doubt lies behind John's account of Jesus' washing the disciples' feet (John 13.4-5, 12-17). Fuller discussion in Fitzmyer, *Luke* 1411-15; O. Wischmeyer, 'Herrschen als Dienen — Mark 10,41-45', *ZNW* 90 (1999) 28-44.

d. Prayer

For completeness we should recall two other features of the Jesus tradition. One is the degree to which Jesus provided a model to his disciples as a man of prayer. It is certainly true that Luke has extended the motif:[82] the obvious reason why he should record so often in his Gospel that Jesus prayed is that he wanted to present Jesus' own prayer practice as a pattern for his Christian readership.[83] But the pattern is already rooted in the memory that Jesus taught his disciples a prayer which evidently echoed his own style of addressing God as 'Abba' (Matt. 6.9/ Luke 11.2).[84] We may presume that the other instructions and encouragements he gave to his disciples in their praying (§14.2) similarly mirrored his own practice. To be a disciple of Jesus was to pray as Jesus prayed.

e. Suffering

Finally, we should note again how often the tradition recalls Jesus warning his disciples to be prepared for suffering. The motif has been sufficiently documented above (§12.4d), and little more need be said here. Persecution was part of the blessedness of sharing in the tradition of the prophets (Matt. 5.11-12/Luke 6.22-23). Most powerful is the cluster of sayings which Mark has appended to the confession of Peter and the first Passion prediction (Mark 8.27-33) — Mark 8.34-37.[85]

> 34He called the crowd with his disciples and said to them, 'If anyone wants to become my follower, let him deny himself and take up his cross and follow me. 35For he who wants to save his life will lose it, and he who loses his life for my sake and for the sake of the gospel will save it. 36For what will it profit someone to gain the whole world and forfeit his life? 37Indeed, what can a person give in return for his life?'

To follow Jesus necessarily involves following him to and through the humiliation and suffering of the cross;[86] disciples must be prepared to lose that which is

82. Luke 3.21; 5.16; 6.12; 9.18, 28-29; 11.1.

83. See, e.g., Fitzmyer, *Luke* 244-47.

84. See further Bockmuehl, *This Jesus* ch. 6; and below, §16.2b.

85. Matt. 16.24-26 and Luke 9.23-25 appear to be abbreviated versions of Mark and need not be cited here. See also above, chapter 12 n. 193.

86. The saying surely includes post-Easter reflection on Jesus' crucifixion (e.g., Pesch, *Markusevangelium* 2.61), but crucifixion as the extremest form of Roman contempt and humiliation would be familiar enough to Jesus and his audiences (chapter 12 n. 193 above), so a say-

of irreplaceable value to them — their very lives.[87] Suffering was to be the lot of the messenger, as a sheep among wolves (Matt. 10.16/Luke 10.3). Worth noting, however, is Matthew's addition to the mission instructions:

> A disciple is not above his teacher, nor a servant above his master. It is enough for the disciple to be like his teacher and the servant like his master. If they have called the master of the house Beelzebul, how much more will they malign those of his household (Matt. 10.24-25).

The saying undoubtedly reflects subsequent reflection on the lot of Jesus' disciples, but it is well enough grounded in Jesus' forebodings, elsewhere attested,[88] as to provide a fitting summary of this further aspect of discipleship. Disciples could not assume that the path of discipleship would be other than that trodden by Jesus himself.

Learning, missioning, serving, praying, and suffering hardly provide a complete description of discipleship and could hardly be regarded as a blueprint for all (though Jesus presumably expected all to both learn and pray). But they were evidently characteristics of the discipleship to which Jesus called, not least as following in his own footsteps. The common feature in each case is that they are marks of disciples *of Jesus*. If we revert to the image of 'circles of discipleship' (§13.8), the point needs to be made that they were 'circles' because Jesus was the centre.

---

ing which used crucifixion as illustration of the completeness of commitment called for is certainly possible to conceive (cf. *GTh* 55.2). Meier cites Epictetus 1.229-30 ('If you wish to be crucified, wait, and the cross will come') and Plato's *Republic* 1.124-25 (*Marginal Jew* 3.64-67, 108 n. 86).

87. Meier, *Marginal Jew* 3.56-64, affirms Taylor's remark: 'Few sayings of Jesus are so well attested as this' (*Mark* 382). Mark has elaborated the tradition he received (by adding at least 'and [for the sake of] the gospel'), but Jesus was evidently remembered as voicing the memorable sequence (8.35-37), perhaps in reflection on Ps. 49.7-8 (Pesch, *Markusevangelium* 2.62-64). See also E. Schweizer, *Erniedrigung und Erhöhung bei Jesus und seinen Nachfolgern* (Zürich: Zwingli, ²1962) 15-17 (ET of first edition, *Lordship and Discipleship* [London: SCM, 1960] 17-18), though he is dubious on the origin of 8.36-37; Crossan, *Fragments* 89-94. McKnight quotes Bonhoeffer with effect: 'When Christ calls a man, he bids him come and die' (*New Vision* 195; D. Bonhoeffer, *The Cost of Discipleship* [London: SCM, 1959] 99), though in private correspondence he points out that this is a dramatic over-translation of what Bonhoeffer actually wrote.

88. See below §17.4.

14.4. Hungering for What Is Right

The high evaluation accorded to the Torah in Jewish tradition has always been one of the distinguishing marks of Judaism (§9.5d) and one of the fundamental points of differentiation with Christianity. The attitude of Jesus to the law of Israel has therefore been one of the key issues for questers, not least with the question in view whether subsequent Christian rejection of the law can be traced back to Jesus himself, or can at least find validation in what he taught and in the way he conducted himself during his mission. The answers given have varied in accordance with the degree to which scholars were willing to locate Jesus within Judaism.

We have already recalled the sharp and wounding statements of Renan and Ritschl on the subject (§5.5). In the wake of the failed Liberal quest Bultmann provided an important new lead by insisting that Jesus must be viewed within Judaism: 'Jesus asserted the authority of the Law'.[89] The chief differentiating feature of Jesus' teaching was that he set one passage against another, rather than assuming that all passages are equally binding and that apparent contradictions are to be reconciled; he distinguished between essential and non-essential.[90] 'The divergence of Jesus from Judaism is in thinking out the idea of obedience radically to the end, not in setting it aside'.[91] It was in fact Bultmann's later characterisation of 'a sovereign attitude assumed by Jesus toward the Old Testament'[92] which became the springboard for his disciples and successors. As already noted, Käsemann was able to build a case for a new quest by identifying 'the distinctive element in the mission of Jesus' as the amazing authority which Jesus claimed for himself over against Moses and the Torah.[93] And Hengel takes the same position in asserting Jesus' 'sovereign liberty over against the letter of scripture, indeed over against the Mosaic Torah in general'.[94] Not untypical was Jeremias's

---

89. *Jesus and the Word* 64. 'Jesus actually lived as a Jewish rabbi' (58); 'Jesus agreed always with the scribes of his time in accepting without question the authority of the (Old Testament) Law' (61). 'The idea that Jesus had attacked the authority of the Law was wholly unknown to the Christian community' (63). It was against Bultmann's identification of Jesus as a rabbi that Hengel protested in *Charismatic Leader* 42.

90. *Jesus and the Word* 74-75.

91. *Jesus and the Word* 84. The point is then developed in more characteristic existentialist terms (84-98).

92. *Theology* 16.

93. Käsemann, 'Problem' 37-45, particularly 40; similarly Bornkamm, *Jesus* 58-60. Influenced by Käsemann, I also spoke of Jesus' 'sovereign freedom . . . with respect to sabbath and ceremonial law' in my earlier *Jesus and the Spirit* 43. Witherington speaks of Jesus' freedom 'not only to operate with a selective hermeneutic but also to add and subtract from Scripture' (*Christology* 65, 69).

94. Hengel, *Charismatic Leader* 47; 'Jesus stood outside any discoverable uniform teaching tradition of Judaism'; 'the fundamental point of distinction over against Phari-

presentation of a Jesus who 'criticized' the Torah, who abolished some of its precepts, and who 'rejected' the Halakhah 'in a radical way'.[95]

Unfortunately, the attempt to differentiate Jesus from Judaism precisely at this point has still too often succumbed to the temptation to depict Judaism as the darker foil against which the distinctiveness of Jesus could stand out more clearly. The shadow of anti-Judaism has distorted all parts of the resulting depiction. Bultmann could not avoid characterizing the Judaism of Jesus' time in terms of 'legalism': it was what Jesus protested against — the understanding that man's relation to God is a legal one; 'Jesus has wholly separated obedience from legalism'.[96] We have already referred to the typical Christian maligning of Pharisees as chief exponents of such legalism.[97] And it is not hard to find responsible twentieth-century commentators who saw no problem in talking of Jesus' negation or abrogation of the Law, or even of Jesus doing away with 'the law of the Jews — and with it Judaism itself as a religion'![98] It was against such tendencies and talk that Sanders uttered his major protest: Jesus was not anti-law or anti-Pharisee; rather he stood within the diversity of interpretation and debate which the Pharisees in particular already expressed.[99]

---

saism . . .' (49, 69-70). Similarly H. Merkel, 'The Opposition between Jesus and Judaism', in E. Bammel and C. F. D. Moule, *Jesus and the Politics of His Day* (Cambridge: Cambridge University, 1984) 129-44 (here 138-42).

95. Jeremias, *Proclamation* 204-11 (though he begins his treatment by affirming strongly that 'Jesus lived in the Old Testament', 205); similarly Goppelt, *Theology* 1.87-105, claiming that Jesus 'drew a sharp distinction between Torah and halakah' (89-90); Schrage, *Ethics* 56-68 ('Jesus' sovereign freedom', 62). On the older version of this view, that Jesus distinguished between the moral law and the ceremonial or ritual law, Sanders bluntly observes, 'We cannot find, in the Judaism of Jesus' day, any precedent for making [this] sort of distinction within the law' (*Jesus and Judaism* 248). D. J. Moo, 'Jesus and the Authority of the Mosaic Law', *JSNT* 20 (1984) 3-49, represents the more conservative concern to maintain that Jesus never abrogated the law (Scripture).

96. *Jesus and the Word* 65-98, 126 (here 92); *Theology* 1.13-14.

97. See above, chapter 9 n. 49.

98. See, e.g., W. Gutbrod, *nomos, TDNT* 1060-61, cited in my *Partings* 98, with further bibliography in 300 n. 2; the quotation is from Pannenberg, *Jesus* 255. For E. Stauffer, Jesus was 'the one who announces a morality without legalism, which in principle is free of any tie to the Mosaic Torah and Jewish obedience to the Torah' (cited by Theissen and Merz, *Historical Jesus* 347; see also 348-49, 359). C. E. B. Cranfield does not hesitate to draw the conclusion from Mark 7.15 that 'Jesus speaks as the one who is, and knows himself to be, *telos nomou* (Rom. 10.4)' (*St Mark* [Cambridge: Cambridge University, 1959] 244). Becker takes Luke 16.16 as authentic in saying 'that the Law and the Prophets lasted until John and that they belong to the time that . . . lies in the past' (*Jesus* 227); 'the Torah had to relinquish its soteriological function to the Kingdom of God' (284; similarly Gnilka, *Jesus* 209-10); see also above, chapter 12 n. 342.

99. 'I am one of a growing number of scholars who doubt that there were any substantial

The shift in the terms of discussion from a gospel versus law confrontation[100] to an inner-Jewish debate is welcome, but the issues require further clarification — on two points in particular. First, we need to remind ourselves of the important link between law-keeping and covenant identity: certain obligations were perceived as fundamental to Israel's identity as God's covenant people (including Sabbath and food laws); they functioned in effect as test cases of covenant loyalty; to be observant on these matters was to keep the covenant.[101] We have already noted Jesus' awareness of the divisive 'down-side' of such concerns in the corollary so often drawn, that those who failed such tests were disloyal to the covenant, were 'sinners'.[102] And since Jesus himself was evidently criticised for the way he (and/or his disciples) conducted himself on two of these test cases (Sabbath and eating), the relevance of this dimension to what was at stake in these controversies is obvious.

Second, we also need to recall that the law was the standard of right and wrong, the measure of righteousness, of justice. What was at stake in Jesus' controversies regarding the law was not matters of scholastic definition and dispute but the right relations between God and his people, and among his people. We have already noted the importance of this dimension in Jesus' kingdom preaching, particularly in the theme of eschatological reversal (§12.4c). It was even clearer in the priority he gave in his mission to preaching good news to the poor and warnings he gave to the unconcerned wealthy (§13.4). That is why I have entitled this section 'Hungering for what is right', rather than 'Jesus and the law'. The title is obviously drawn from Matthew's fourth beatitude (Matt. 5.6), not because I am particularly confident that Matthew's form can be traced back to Jesus himself,[103] but because Matthew's version probably captures well Jesus' own priorities on the subject.

The importance of both these further dimensions to the traditional terms of

---

points of opposition between Jesus and the Pharisees' (Sanders, *Jesus* 264); similarly Rowland, *Christian Origins* 156-59. The point is pushed still harder by Vermes, *Religion* 11-45; Flusser likewise argues that 'Jesus is never shown in conflict with current practice of the law' (*Jesus* 58-66). Several Jewish scholars have described Jesus as a Pharisee; see Hagner, *Jewish Reclamation* 231-32; see also H. Falk, *Jesus the Pharisee: A New Look at the Jewishness of Jesus* (New York: Paulist, 1979). For the debate on possible parallels between or even influences from Hillel to Jesus see Charlesworth and Johns, eds., *Hillel and Jesus* Part One.

100. Or what Strecker denotes as 'the Pauline-Lutheran model' (*Theology* 246-47).

101. See above, §9.5d. It is Holmén, *Jesus* (referred to above, chapter 9 n. 56) who puts the issue in terms of covenant loyalty; by bringing the covenant into view he revitalizes the tired debate as to whether Jesus radicalized or relaxed Torah observance (*Torahverschärfung* vs. *Torahentschärfung*) (*Jesus* 338-39).

102. See above, §13.5.

103. The passage is cited above in §12.4c.

the discussion of Jesus and the law will, I hope, become clear as we proceed. For convenience I will begin by following the sequence provided by Mark.[104]

a. The Sabbath

The Jesus tradition retains at least two vivid episodes in which Jesus or his disciples were criticized for failure to observe the Sabbath by plucking grain on the Sabbath (Mark 2.23-28 pars.) and healing a man with a withered hand on the Sabbath (Mark 3.1-5 pars.).[105]

Matt. 12.1-8	Mark 2.23-28	Luke 6.1-5
1 At that time Jesus went through the grainfields on the sabbath; his disciples were hungry, and they began to pluck heads of grain and to eat. 2 When the Pharisees saw it, they said to him, 'Look, your disciples are doing what is not lawful to do on the sabbath'. 3 He said to them, 'Have you not read what David did when he and his companions were hungry? 4 How he entered the house of God and ate the bread of the Presence, which it was not lawful for him or his companions to eat, but only for the priests. 5 Or have you not read in the law that on the sabbath the priests in the temple break the sabbath and yet are guiltless? 6 I tell you, something greater than the temple is here. 7 But if you had known what this means, "I desire mercy and not sacrifice", you would not have condemned the guiltless.	23 One sabbath he was going through the grainfields; and as they made their way his disciples began to pluck heads of grain. 24 The Pharisees said to him, 'Look, why are they doing what is not lawful on the sabbath?' 25 And he said to them, 'Have you never read what David did when he and his companions were hungry and in need of food? 26 How he entered the house of God, when Abiathar was high priest, and ate the bread of the Presence, which it is not lawful for any but the priests to eat, and he gave some to his companions'.	1 One sabbath while Jesus was going through the grainfields, his disciples plucked some heads of grain, rubbed them in their hands, and ate them. 2 But some of the Pharisees said, 'Why are you doing what is not lawful on the sabbath?' 3 Jesus answered them, 'Have you not read this, what David did when he and his companions were hungry? 4 That he entered the house of God and took and ate the bread of the Presence, which it is not lawful for any but only the priests to eat, and gave some to his companions?'
8 For the Son of Man is lord of the sabbath'.	27 Then he said to them, 'The sabbath was made for man, and not man for the sabbath; 28 so the Son of Man is lord even of the sabbath'.	5 Then he said to them, 'The Son of Man is lord of the sabbath'.

---

104. I will delay discussion of Jesus' attitude to the Temple (whose rites, of course, were entirely based on the Torah) till later (§§15.3a, d and 17.3).

105. Luke recalls two other or variant episodes (Luke 13.10-17 and 14.1-6), and the memory of criticisms made of Jesus for failure to observe the Sabbath is retained in John 5 and 9.

Matt. 12.9-14	Mark 3.1-6	Luke 6.6-11
9 He left that place and entered their synagogue; 10 a man was there with a withered hand,	1 Again he entered the synagogue, and a man was there who had a withered hand. 2 They watched him to see	6 On another sabbath he entered the synagogue and taught, and there was a man there whose right hand was withered. 7 The scribes and the Pharisees watched him to see
and they asked him, 'Is it lawful to cure on the sabbath?' in order that they might accuse him. 11 He said to them, 'Suppose one of you has only one sheep and it falls into a pit on the sabbath; will you not lay hold of it and lift it out? 12 How much more valuable is a human being than a sheep!	whether he would cure him on the sabbath, in order that they might accuse him.	whether he would cure on the sabbath, in order that they might find an accusation against him. 8 Even though he knew what they were thinking,
So it is lawful on the sabbath to do good'.	3 And he said to the man who had the withered hand, 'Come here'. 4 Then he said to them, 'Is it lawful on the sabbath to do good or to do harm, to save life or to kill?' But they were silent.	he said to the man who had the withered hand, 'Come and stand here'. He got up and stood there. 9 Then Jesus said to them, 'I ask you, is it lawful on the sabbath to do good or to do harm, to save life or to destroy it?'
13 Then he said to the man, 'Stretch out your hand'. He stretched it out, and it was restored, as sound as the other. 14 But the Pharisees went out and conspired against him, how to destroy him.	5 He looked around at them with anger; he was grieved at their hardness of heart and said to the man, 'Stretch out your hand'. He stretched it out, and his hand was restored. 6 The Pharisees went out and immediately conspired with the Herodians against him, how to destroy him.	10 After looking around at all of them, he said to him, 'Stretch out your hand'. He did so, and his hand was restored. 11 But they were filled with fury and discussed with one another what they might do to Jesus.

The signs of stories retold to improve the telling are clear enough, particularly the transition from a generic 'son of man' to the titular 'Son of Man' (Mark 2.28 pars.),[106] Matthew's addition of pertinent precedents to strengthen the case (Matt. 12.5-7, 11-12), and both Matthew's and Luke's omission of Mark's misleading reference to Abiathar (Mark 2.26). But it is equally clear that the same two episodes are in view in each retelling, probably linked together at an early stage in a teaching sequence of controversy stories, on which Mark was able to draw (Mark 2.1–3.6).[107] Of course it is likely that the early groups and communities of Jesus' disciples used the stories to explain and defend their own attitude to the Sabbath. But the claim of the stories is that Jesus himself defended and validated actions on the Sabbath which others regarded as unlawful. And the likelihood must be re-

106. See further below, §16.4b(2).

107. See further my 'Mark 2.1–3.6: A Bridge between Jesus and Paul on the Question of the Law', *NTS* 30 (1984) 395-415, reprinted in my *Jesus, Paul and the Law* 10-31; see also above, chapter 8 at n. 300.

garded as strong that Jesus did indeed treat the Sabbath more freely than a more rigorous halakhah approved in at least two incidents, which left a deep impression on his disciples' memories.[108] Sanders caricatures the scenes thus narrated,[109] but the tradition is clearly pre-Markan, and thus pre-70, and so demonstrates that pre-70 Pharisees already had a reputation for scrupulous Sabbath observance. It can also be demonstrated that such levels of scrupulosity were current at the time of Jesus.[110] And the likelihood of some Pharisees, down from Jerusalem to gain a first-hand impression of the teacher from Nazareth, expressing criticism of his and his disciples' lack of respect for the Sabbath is entirely plausible.[111]

The point which these remembered episodes enshrine is twofold. (1) First, that Jesus had a high regard for the Sabbath as a gift from God. To be noted is that neither episode even suggests the abolition or abandonment of the Sabbath. The question under debate is not *whether* the Sabbath should be observed,[112] but

108. See particularly Pesch, *Markusevangelium* 1.183, 195-96. There is something strange in an argument which accepts that Jesus said something like Mark 2.27 and that he 'sometimes deliberately transgressed the sabbath commandment', but denies that the only explicit examples of him so acting in regard to the Sabbath ever took place during Jesus' mission (Funk, *Five Gospels* 49-50, 350; *Acts of Jesus* 68; Lüdemann, *Jesus* 19-21). Casey argues that 2.23–3.6 is a literal translation of an Aramaic source (*Aramaic Sources* 138-92).

109. 'Pharisees did not organize themselves into groups to spend their Sabbaths in Galilean cornfields in the hope of catching someone transgressing' (*Jesus* 265-66; not much softened in *Historical Figure* 214; followed by Fredriksen, *From Jesus to Christ* 106).

110. *Jub.* 2.17-33; 50.8-12; CD 10.14–11.18. E.g., *Jub.* 2 includes the instructions: 'that they should not prepare thereon anything which will be eaten or drunk, which they have not prepared for themselves on the sixth day' nor 'draw water or bring in or take out any work within their dwellings . . .'. CD 11.12-17 include the rulings: 'No one should help an animal give birth on the sabbath. And if [it falls] into a cistern or a pit, he should not take it out on the sabbath. . . . And any living man who falls into a place of water or into a [reservoir?], no one should take him out with a ladder or a rope or a utensil' (similarly 4Q265 frag. 7 1.5-9). If Luke 14.1-6 is a variant version of Mark 3.1-5 pars. (NB Matt. 12.11), then Luke 14.5/Matt. 12.11 can be taken as indication that Pharisaic Sabbath halakhah was not so strict on this point as Essene or Qumran halakhah (cf. *m. Yoma* 8.6); see also S. Westerholm, *Jesus and Scribal Authority* (CBNTS 10; Lund: Gleerup, 1978) 95-96. The importance of the Sabbath elsewhere in Jewish tradition is clear; see particularly Gen. 2.2-3; Exod. 20.8-11; 31.16-17; Deut. 5.12-15; Neh. 9.13-14; Isa. 56.6; Ezek. 20.16; 1 Macc. 1.43; Josephus, *Ant.* 11.346; 14.241-6, 258, 263-64; Philo, *Abr.* 28-30; *Decal.* 102; *Spec. Leg.* 2.59, 70; *Legat.* 155-58; Eusebius, *Praep. Evang.* 13.12.9-16; see further E. Lohse, *sabbaton, TDNT* 7.2-14.

111. See further above, §9.3a(1). Theissen naturally points out how well the episodes fit with the situation of itinerant charismatics, *in via,* here today and gone tomorrow (Theissen and Merz, *Historical Jesus* 369). See also W. R. G. Loader, *Jesus' Attitude to the Law* (WUNT 2.97; Tübingen: Mohr Siebeck, 1997) 51-53.

112. *Pace* Goppelt: 'He suspended the sabbath commandment as such and by doing so suspended the Law, the very foundation of Judaism' (*Theology* 1.93-94, though note also 105) — one of those now embarrassing over-interpretations which was never justified.

how it should be observed.[113] This in itself is a decisive indication that the stories took their present shape in a firmly Jewish context.[114] (2) At the same time, in both episodes Jesus refuses to make the Sabbath a test case of obedience to God, a distinctive mark of God's people. He shows no interest in treating the Sabbath as an indicator of covenant loyalty.[115] Rather he presses beyond such concerns to more fundamental issues of fundamental rights and responsibilities: that the Sabbath was made for human beings, not human beings for the Sabbath,[116] and that at no time, however sacred, can it be wrong to do good or save life. It is on the basis of these 'first principles' that Jesus is remembered as supporting a less fussy observance of the Sabbath, in contrast to halakhoth which sought to defend the Sabbath law by elaborating it.[117] To thus focus too much attention on 'the fence round the Torah' was itself to endanger what the fence was intended to protect.[118] The outworking of this deeper sense of what is right was not merely exceptional (neither the disciples nor the man was in immediate danger); it indicated rather how the Sabbath should be observed.

b. Qorban

Mark records a further point of dispute with 'tradition' *(paradosis)* in 7.9-13 (retained by Matt. 15.3-6 in abbreviated form):

> 9(Jesus) said to them, 'You have a fine way of rejecting the commandment of God in order to keep your tradition. 10For Moses said, "Honour your father

113. Pre-rabbinic as well as rabbinic Judaism was well aware that there were circumstances in which the particular commandments regarding the Sabbath would have to be suspended (1 Macc. 2.41; CD 50.11; further Lohse, *TDNT* 7.14-15). But can one deduce from the closest parallel sayings — R. Simeon ben Menasya (ca. 180 CE), 'The Sabbath is given over to you and not you to the Sabbath'; R. Mattithiah ben Heresh, 'whenever there is doubt whether life is in danger, this overrides the Sabbath' (*m. Yoma* 8.6) — that such rulings were current at the time of Jesus, as Vermes argues *(Religion* 24)?

114. Had Jesus disowned the Sabbath it is unlikely that the Jewish Christian missionaries opposed to Paul in Galatia would have been able to insist on it quite so strongly; cf. M. J. Cook, 'Jewish Reflections on Jesus', in LeBeau et al., eds., *Historical Jesus* 95-111 (here 101-102).

115. Holmén, *Jesus* 100-106.

116. Is there also an eschatological note and/or echo of the Genesis provision of the Sabbath for creation (as well as God), for humankind at the end of the age as for Adam at the beginning? If so, it is not obvious.

117. Cf. R. Banks, *Jesus and the Law in the Synoptic Tradition* (SNTSMS 28; Cambridge: Cambridge University, 1975) 122-23; see also Westerholm, *Jesus* 92, 96-103.

118. Similarly to read Jesus' words 'as seeking to define what the Sabbath law itself allows' (Moo, 'Jesus' 9, 16) is to continue to regard the Sabbath as law rather than as gift.

and your mother" (Exod. 20.12; Deut. 5.16), and, "He who speaks evil of father or mother, let him surely die" (Exod 21.17; Lev. 20.9). [11]But you say, "If someone tells his father or mother, What you would have gained from me is Qorban (that is gift [to God])", [12]then you no longer allow him to do anything for his father or mother, [13]thus making void the word of God through your tradition which you hand on'.

The passage seems to indicate that it was possible for a son to avoid all obligations to parents by fictitiously dedicating to the Temple all the support he owed them, even if the vow was made out of spite or anger.[119] Such a ruling would presumably have been based on the law regarding vows (Num. 30.2).[120] Num. 30.3-15 gives various precedents for circumstances where the command of 30.2 could be disregarded. And the Mishnah tractate *Nedarim* ('Vows') shows similar concern to alleviate the strict principle enunciated in 30.2 (*m. Ned.* 9.1 bears directly on the present case). But from Mark 7.9-13 it would appear that at the time the Jesus tradition took its shape on this point, a harsh ruling[121] was in force for some at least (Shammaites?) to the effect that a vow made in the circumstances indicated could *not* be retracted.[122]

Here again, then, Jesus is remembered as pressing behind the detail of debate on the law of vows and building his own ruling regarding the matter on the basis of what he evidently regarded as the more fundamental concern — particularly the Decalogue's commandment that children should honour their parents.

c. Hand-Washing

Mark (or already the earlier tradition) has inserted the Corban issue into a more extensive discussion on purity halakhah — Mark 7.1-8, 14-23. For the first part it

---

119. Jeremias, *Proclamation* 210. On the term *'qorban'* see Meier, *Marginal Jew* 3.582-83 n. 69.

120. 'When a man vows a vow to the Lord, or swears an oath to bind himself by a pledge, he shall not break his word; he shall do according to all that proceeds out of his mouth'.

121. Note the language of tradition and formal transmission — *paradosis* (7.8, 13), *paradidōmi* (7.8).

122. Note again the debate implied in *m. Ned.* 9.1. See A. I. Baumgarten, 'Korban and the Pharisaic Paradosis', *JANES* 16 (1984) 5-17, cited by Davies and Allison, *Matthew* 2.524; M. Bockmuehl, *Jewish Law in Gentile Churches: Halakhah and the Beginning of Christian Public Ethics* (Edinburgh: Clark, 2000) 5-6; Meier, *Marginal Jew* 3.583-84 n. 70. 'Many old halakhot are based on the understanding that a vow could not be dissolved' (Westerholm, *Jesus* 77-78). Sanders, *Jewish Law* 56-57, is dubious (though less confident on the point) that such a ruling was current among Pharisees of the time, but notes a similar ruling in Philo, *Hypothetica* 7.5.

is necessary only to cite Mark 7.1-8, again followed by Matthew in an abbreviated version (Matt. 15.1-3):

> ¹The Pharisees gathered together to him and some of the scribes come from Jerusalem. ²They saw that some of his (Jesus') disciples ate with hands defiled *(koinais),* that is, unwashed. ³For the Pharisees, and all the Jews, do not eat unless they wash their hands, observing the tradition of the elders; ⁴and when they come from the marketplace, they do not eat unless they purify themselves; and there are many other (traditions) which they have received to observe, washings of cups and pots and bronze vessels. ⁵And the Pharisees and the scribes asked him: 'Why do your disciples not conduct themselves in accordance with the tradition of the elders, but eat bread with hands defiled *(koinais)?'* ⁶But he said, 'Well did Isaiah prophesy of you hypocrites, as it is written, "This people honours me with their lips, but their heart is far from me; ⁷in vain do they worship me, teaching as doctrines the precepts of men" (Isa. 29.13 LXX). ⁸You leave the commandment of God, and observe the tradition of men'.

Mark has obviously inherited an account which captures much authentic detail from the period: it speaks of hands as 'defiled', where the word in Greek *(koinos* = 'common') reflects the uniquely Jewish sense of 'profane, unclean, defiled';[123] and again the account reflects the importance in Pharisaic circles of 'the tradition *(paradosis)* of the elders', faithfully handed down *(paralambanō)* to be observed by succeeding generations. For his part Mark, or already the version which came to him, has made efforts to clarify the potential confusion of *koinos,* by translating it to give the Greek its Jewish sense ('that is, "unwashed"'), and by adding the exaggerated ('all the Jews'?) explanation of vv. 3-4.[124] Here again Sanders doubts whether Pharisaic concern for purity of hands had developed so far before 70 CE and thus questions the historical veracity of the report.[125] But once again

---

123. The special sense is given because *koinos* was used as equivalent to the biblical *tame'* (e.g., Lev. 11.4-8; Deut. 14.7-10; Judg. 13.4; Hos. 9.3) or *ḥol* (Lev. 10.10; Ezek. 22.26; 44.23). The step was taken subsequent to the LXX rendering of the Hebrew Bible but was established in the Maccabean crisis (1 Macc. 1.47, 62; note also Josephus, *Ant.* 11.346) and is well attested in relation to eating food by the mid-first century CE by Rom. 14.14 and Acts 10.14; 11.8, as well as by Mark 7.2, 5.

124. The fact that Mark cites the LXX of Isa. 29.13 need not mean that the episode was first created in the Greek but only that when the episode was put into Greek the story-teller (not unnaturally) used the LXX version of the quotation. The last line of the Hebrew ('their fear of me is a commandment of men learned by rote') would have made Jesus' point equally well (see also Pesch, *Markusevangelium* 1.372-73). Col. 2.22 looks like an echo of Mark 7.7/Matt. 15.9 (see my *Colossians and Philemon* 193).

125. *Jesus and Judaism* 185-86, 264-65. The argument is again weakened by Sanders's resort to sarcasm: 'nor is it credible that scribes and Pharisees made a special trip to Galilee

the pre-Markan tradition clearly attests a pre-70 Pharisaic concern on the subject; and if pre-70, why not at the time of Jesus? The sensitivities on impurity contracted by *touching* are clear from of old.[126] And the fact that a whole Mishnah tractate is devoted to the subject, *Yadaim* ('Hands'), indicates a long tradition history of halakhic concern. So there is no real reason to dispute the testimony (for that is what it is) of Mark 7 that the concern was already active in Pharisaic halakhoth at the time of Jesus.[127]

Of interest here is the picture of Jesus in effect debating halakhah with Pharisees and/or scribes who identified themselves with Pharisaic tradition, and who, we note again, are recalled in this instance as having come down from Jerusalem (v. 1). The accusation of v. 5 can be read also as an invitation to debate, to explain practice brought into question by evolving halakhah. In this case Jesus is not remembered as setting a more fundamental principle in opposition to a traditional ruling. Rather he takes the warning of Isa. 29.13, a warning of the danger of superficiality in worship[128] and of treating human formulations too unquestioningly, and indicates his view that 'the tradition of the elders' is succumbing to that danger in the case in point.[129]

---

from Jerusalem to inspect Jesus' disciples' hands' (265). Luke knows a similar tradition and criticism in a different context (Luke 11.38).

126. E.g., Lev. 5.2-3; 7.19, 21; 11.8, 24-28; Isa. 52.11; 65.5; *T. Mos.* 7.9-10; cf. Col. 2.21. Ebner draws particular attention to Hag. 2.11-14 (*Jesus* 237-38).

127. In *Jewish Law* 31, 39-40, 90-91, 228-31, Sanders observes that Pharisees practised hand-washing at their own Sabbath and festival meals, but again notes that there is no evidence in rabbinic literature that Pharisees washed their hands before eating ordinary meals. But how well grounded is such a clear distinction in Pharisaic purity concerns between 'Sabbath and festival meals' and 'ordinary meals'? At least we can say that hand-washing prior to eating communally would have been consistent with the concerns regarding the susceptibility of hands to uncleanness already evident in traditions attributed to the period (particularly *m. Ber.* 8.2, 4; *m. Mik.* 1.5-6; further documentation in Sanders 228-31); see further especially Kazen, *Jesus* 62-72, 81-85; also Westerholm, *Jesus* 73; R. P. Booth, *Jesus and the Laws of Purity: Tradition History and Legal History in Mark 7* (JSNTS 13; Sheffield: JSOT, 1986) 194-202; J. C. Poirier, 'Why Did the Pharisees Wash Their Hands?' *JJS* 47 (1996) 217-33; Funk, *Acts of Jesus* 94-95. Flusser follows G. Alon in concluding that prior to the destruction of the Temple washing hands before a meal was regarded as advisable but not obligatory and was not accepted by all the sages (*Jesus* 59-60).

128. One of the more polemical terms attributed to Jesus by both Mark (7.6) and Q (Matt. 7.5/Luke 6.42) is *hypokritēs* ('play-actor, pretender, dissembler'), which could have the Hebrew *hanep* behind it (K. Seybold, *hanep, TDOT* 5.38-39), but the Greek should not be taken as indication of possible influence on the young Jesus from the theatre in Sepphoris (*pace* R. A. Batey, 'Jesus and the Theatre', *NTS* 30 [1984] 563-74), since the theatre was probably not built till the second half of the first century (chapter 9 n. 198). Marcus notes the similar condemnation of the Pharisees in Josephus, *Ant.* 17.41 and Qumran (1QH 12[= 4].13) (*Mark* 1.444).

129. Here again is to be noted the similar criticism of Pharisees made at Qumran: they

d. Purity

In the second half of the same sequence the subject returns to the issue of purity — Mark 7.14-23/Matt. 15.10-20:[130]

Matt. 15.10-20	Mark 7.14-23
10 Then he called the crowd to him and said to them, 'Listen and understand: 11 it is not what goes into the mouth that defiles a person, but it is what comes out of the mouth that defiles a person'. 12 Then the disciples approached and said to him, 'Do you know that the Pharisees took offence when they heard what you said?' 13 He answered, 'Every plant that my heavenly Father has not planted will be uprooted. 14 Let them alone; they are blind guides of the blind. And if one blind person guides another, both will fall into a pit'. 15 But Peter said to him, 'Explain this parable to us'. 16 Then he said, 'Do you also still fail to understand? 17 Do you not see that whatever goes into the mouth enters the stomach, and is expelled into the sewer? 18 But what comes out of the mouth proceeds from the heart, and this is what defiles. 19 For it is from the heart come evil intentions, murder, adultery, fornication, theft, false witness, slander. 20 These are what defile a person, but to eat with unwashed hands does not defile'.	14 Then he called the crowd again and said to them, 'Listen to me, all of you, and understand: 15 there is **nothing from outside** a person that by going into him **can** defile him, but the things that come out from a person are what defile a person'. 17 When he had left the crowd and entered the house, his disciples asked him about the parable. 18 He said to them, 'Then do you also fail to understand? Do you not see that whatever goes into a person **from outside cannot** defile him, 19 since it enters, not into the heart but into the stomach, and goes out into the sewer?' (**Thus he declared all foods clean**.) 20 And he said, 'It is what comes out of a person that defiles the person. 21 For it is **from within**, from the human heart, that intentions come: fornication, theft, murder, 22 adultery, avarice, wickedness, deceit, licentiousness, envy, slander, pride, folly. 23 All these evil things come **from within**, and they defile a person'.

Freedom in handling the tradition is clear enough in Matthew's insertion of some Q (and other) material (Matt. 15.13-14/Luke 6.39), and the free use of vice catalogues in Mark 7.21-22/Matt. 15.19.[131] But the greatest interest for us here is the subtle way Matthew has edited the key point of the pericope. For he restates the teaching by omitting key words and phrases in Mark's account (7.15, 18-19, 21, 23 — in bold above). These are precisely the points which make it clear that

change the law for the 'smooth things' *(bhlqot)* which they teach (1QH 12[= 4].10-11) (Westerholm, *Jesus* 18-19).

130. Matthew makes a point of tying the whole sequence together by adding at the end: 'but to eat with unwashed hands does not defile a person' (15.20). In what follows I draw on my earlier study 'Jesus and Ritual Purity: A Study of the Tradition-History of Mark 7.15', *A cause de l'évangile,* J. Dupont FS (LD 123; Saint-André: Cerf, 1985) 251-76, reprinted in my *Jesus, Paul and the Law* (London: SPCK, 1990) 37-60.

131. For documentation and bibliography on vice-lists see my *Theology of Paul* 662-63.

Mark's version posed the issue of food purity (and by implication ritual purity generally) in terms of outright antithesis[132] ('it is *not* possible for *anything* from outside to defile'; 'thus he declared the end of the law distinguishing unclean from clean foods').[133] In Matthew's version, however, the outright antithesis has become more like a sharply drawn comparison, indicating priority of importance without denying validity to what is deemed of lesser importance.[134]

How to explain this divergence? In the history of modern interpretation there has been an amazingly strong conviction that it is Mark, the earlier Gospel, who has retained Jesus' own teaching at 7.15.[135] In contrast, it can be easily argued that Matthew, writing in a context where Jewish law was still highly regarded, should have wished to soften Jesus' teaching accordingly.[136] The former, however, is a difficult position to maintain. For if Jesus had spoken so clearly and decisively on the subject it becomes difficult to see how Peter could ever have been recorded as saying subsequently, 'I have never eaten anything common or unclean' (Acts 10.14; 11.8), or why the issue of food laws could have become so divisive in earliest Christianity.[137] We should also observe that

132. The implication of antithesis is heightened by the double use of *exōthen,* 'from outside' (7.15, 18) and *esōthen,* 'from inside' (7.21, 23), terms which appear only here in Mark's Gospel; but we already observed Mark's careful use of *exō* ('outside') in Mark 3.31-32 and 4.11 (above, chapter 13 n. 26).

133. The laws on clean and unclean foods seem to be in particularly in view: Lev. 11.1-23; Deut. 14.3-21. For the wider ramifications of purity law see above, chapter 9, e.g., §9.5c.

134. Sanders appositely cites as parallel *Ep. Arist.* 234: Jews honour God 'not with gifts or sacrifices, but with purity of heart and of devout disposition' (*Historical Figure* 219).

135. Bultmann, *History* 105; Taylor, *Mark* 342-43; Bornkamm, *Jesus* 98; Perrin, *Rediscovering* 150; Goppelt, *Theology* 1.91; Pesch, *Markusevangelium* 383; Riches, *Jesus* 136-44 ('Jesus simply discarded it [the notion of impurity] as unusable' [144]); Stauffer, 'Jesus' 49; Schrage, *Ethics* 66-67; Gnilka, *Jesus* 215-16; J. L. Houlden, *JSNT* 18 (1983) 58-67 (here 63); Becker, *Jesus* 304-308; Theissen and Merz, *Historical Jesus* 365-67; others in my 'Jesus and Ritual Purity' 54 n. 12. Schnackenburg, *sittliche Botschaft* 74-75 is more cautious. Funk, *Five Gospels* 69 and Lüdemann, *Jesus* 49 accept the probable authenticity of the saying without discussing the priority of Matthew or Mark.

136. See, e.g., B. Lindars, 'All Foods Clean: Thoughts on Jesus and the Law', in B. Lindars, ed., *Law and Religion: Essays on the Place of the Law in Israel and Early Christianity* (Cambridge: Clarke, 1988) 61-71. H. Hübner's discussion (*Das Gesetz in der synoptischen Tradition* [Witten: Luther, 1973]) is framed by talk of Matthew's '(re-)Qumranizing' and '(re-)Judaizing' of the Gospel tradition (9-10, 237-39).

137. Gal. 2.11-14; Rom. 14.1–15.6; cf. 1 Corinthians 8 and 10.20-30. The point has been made most forcefully by Sanders: 'the point of the saying [Mark 7.15] is so clear that the positions of the "false brethren" Peter and James [referring to Gal. 2.11-14] becomes impossible to understand if the saying be considered authentic' (*Jesus* 266-68). Similarly H. Räisänen, 'Zur Herkunft von Markus 7.15', in J. Delobel, ed., *Logia: les paroles de Jésus* (Leuven: Leuven University, 1982) 477-84 (here 479-82); Vermes, *Religion* 25-26; Fredriksen, *Jesus* 108; cf. Harvey, *Jesus* 39-41; further in my 'Jesus and Ritual Purity' 55 nn. 16-17.

there is no memory of Jesus eating pork or non-kosher food preserved in any Jesus tradition.

Would it not make more sense of the larger picture, and of the likely oral traditioning processes already documented, to consider the possibility that Matthew's and Mark's treatments are varied accounts of the same teaching? Need we assume that Mark's was the only version known to Matthew of Jesus' teaching on this point?[138] It is more likely, rather, that Mark represents a performance trend, presumably in Gentile or mixed churches,[139] in which this tradition was heard as validating an antithesis between inward and ritual purity; Mark, or already his source, underlines the trend by adding the interpretative note in 7.19. Matthew, on the other hand, represents the way the tradition was being retold in churches where continuity with Jewish tradition was more important.[140] It is not necessary, in other words, to make an either-or decision in explaining Matthew's form — either early tradition or Matthean redaction of Mark. Both could have been the case: Matthew knew a different version[141] and either drew directly on it or used it to make an edited version of what Mark had written.[142]

---

138. Cf. Banks, *Jesus and the Law* 139-41. The attempt of Davies and Allison to clarify the early understanding of Mark 7.15 without calling on the Matthean form, because it 'is simply a redactional version of Mk 7.15', thus ignores the help which the Matthean form of the saying can provide (*Matthew* 2.527-31). Similarly Westerholm, *Jesus* 80-84; Booth, *Jesus and the Laws of Purity* 221-23 (conclusion); Merklein, *Jesu Botschaft* 96-100 and n. 16; Bockmuehl, *Jewish Law* 11; Holmén, *Jesus* 239-49. All reach conclusions similar to my own as to the point of Jesus' teaching. I indicate my disagreements with Booth in 'Jesus and Ritual Purity' 58-59. See also Loader, *Jesus' Attitude* 74-76.

139. Rom. 14.14 must provide some indication of the way the saying was being understood among Gentile churches. It is generally regarded as one of the clearest echoes of Jesus tradition in Paul (my 'Jesus and Ritual Purity' 50, with bibliography in 58 n. 73; also above, chapter 8 n. 48).

140. Does *Thomas* attest an independent version of the saying or dependence on Matthew: 'For what will go into your mouth will not defile you, but what comes out of your mouth, that is what will defile you' (*GTh* 14.5). See further my 'Jesus and Ritual Purity' 43-44.

141. In my 'Jesus and Ritual Purity' I note that the saying, particularly the Matthean form, goes back into an Aramaic *mašal* quite readily (41-42). It is of relevance to note that both W. Paschen, *Rein und Unrein* (München: Kösel, 1970) 173-77, and Hübner, *Gesetz* 165-68, argue that Mark 7.18b and 20b preserve elements closer to the underlying Aramaic than 7.15. Kazen favours my solution (*Jesus* 66-67).

142. I have suggested elsewhere that Matthew's omission of Markan features may often best be explained by his awareness that these features had been added by Mark (or by the stream of tradition known to Mark) — 'Matthew's Awareness of Markan Redaction', in F. van Segbroeck, et al., eds., *The Four Gospels 1992*, F. Neirynck FS (Leuven: Leuven University, 1992) 1349-59.

The conclusion that follows is threefold. (1) Jesus was recalled as speaking on the subject of purity and as insisting that purity of heart is more important than ritual purity.[143] Here again when confronted with an issue of the law, Jesus is remembered as focusing on a deeper, more important issue, quite in the spirit of the older calls to circumcise the heart (not just the flesh):[144] that which defiles a person most grievously comes from the heart.[145] (2) Jesus' teaching was heard differently. Some heard Jesus as not content to debate issues of ritual purity solely at the level of ritual but pressing home the concerns behind such law and halakhoth to the more fundamental level of purity of motive and intention.[146] Others heard Jesus, when the teaching was rehearsed within wider circles of discipleship, as validating or commending a more radical conclusion, to the effect that Israel's purity law no longer applied to the followers of Jesus. (3) Either way, it is again evident that Jesus had no interest in making ritual purity a test case of covenant

143. Note also the sixth beatitude, 'Blessed are the pure in heart' (Matt. 5.8), and the Q saying, Matt. 23.25/Luke 11.39/*GTh* 89:

Matt. 23.25	Luke 11.39	*GTh* 89
Woe to you, scribes and Pharisees, hypocrites, for you cleanse the outside of the cup and of the plate, but inside you are full of extortion and rapacity.	Now you Pharisees cleanse the outside of the cup and of the dish, but inside you are full of extortion and wickedness.	Jesus said, 'Why do you wash the outside of the cup? Do you not understand that he who made the inside is also he who made the outside?'

Despite the variations a common point is maintained: a contrast between inside and outside, between inward (im)purity and outward purity, which indicates the latter to be of lesser importance. The Jesus Seminar think the *Thomas* version reflects most closely something Jesus said (Funk, *Five Gospels* 89). See also Westerholm, *Jesus* 89-90. On the question of historical context reflected, see the debate between J. Neusner, '"First Cleanse the Inside"', *NTS* 22 (1976) 486-95; and H. Maccoby, 'The Washing of Cups', *JSNT* 14 (1982) 3-15; moderated by Davies and Allison, *Matthew* 3.296-98. Note also *P.Oxy.* 840 (text in Aland, *Synopsis* 393-94; Elliott, *Apocryphal New Testament* 33-34); Kazen finds in it 'the memory of Jesus as displaying a controversial attitude to purity, which was motivated by giving more weight to inner purity than to outer purification' (*Jesus* 256-60).

144. Deut. 10.16; Jer. 4.4; 9.25-26; Ezek. 44.9; 1QpHab 11.13; 1QS 5.5.

145. Chilton maintains that 'purity was Jesus' fundamental commitment, the lens through which he viewed the world' (*Rabbi Jesus* 90). But astonishingly, he argues that for Jesus purity (not impurity) came from within ('the innate purity of Israelites' — 92; 'Israelites were already pure and did not need to be cleansed by elaborate ritual observances' — 140), even quoting Mark 7.15 in support (87), and that that purity activated became the agent of the kingdom (136); similarly 'A Generative Exegesis of Mark 7:1-23', in Chilton and Evans, *Jesus in Context* 297-319 (here 305-306). Similarly *Temple:* 'bathing does not make one pure, but celebrates the fact of purity' (123-25, 142). Hence the subsequent attempt to 'cleanse' the Temple by celebrating that purity in right sacrifice (see below §17.3c).

146. Cf. Klawans, *Impurity* 146-50: 'Jesus nowhere defends ritual purity as a symbol of moral purity' (149).

loyalty.[147] The emphasis on matters of purity, so characteristic of the factional rivalries of the time (§§9.3-4), was for Jesus an overemphasis. Such concern to keep oneself separate from the impure, as a way of professing Israel's set-apartness (Lev. 20.24-26), found no echo in Jesus' conduct and association with fellow Jews, with 'sinners', or with the Gentiles he occasionally encountered.

e. Divorce

The other episode in Mark of direct relevance to us at this point is Jesus' teaching on divorce — Mark 10.2-12/Matt. 19.3-9:

Matt. 19.3-9	Mark 10.2-12
3 <u>Some Pharisees came</u> to him, and to test him they said, '<u>Is it lawful for a man to divorce his wife</u> for any cause?' 4 <u>He answered,</u>	2 <u>Some Pharisees came,</u> and asked him, '<u>Is it lawful for a man to divorce his wife</u>?', thus testing him. 3 <u>He answered</u> them, 'What did Moses command you?' 4 They said, 'Moses allowed a man to write a certificate of dismissal and to divorce her'. 5 But Jesus said to them, 'Because of your hard-heartedness he wrote this commandment for you.
'Have you not read that the one who made them at <u>the beginning "made them male and female"</u>, 5 and said, "<u>For this reason a man shall leave his father and mother and be joined to his wife, and the two shall become one flesh</u>"? 6 <u>So they are no longer two, but one flesh. Therefore what God has joined together, let no one separate</u>'. 7 They said to him, 'Why then did Moses command us to give a certificate of dismissal and to divorce her?' 8 He said to them, 'It was because of your hard-heartedness that Moses allowed you to divorce your wives, but from the beginning it was not so.	6 But from <u>the beginning</u> of creation, "God <u>made them male and female</u>". 7 "<u>For this reason a man shall leave his father and mother</u> [<u>and be joined to his wife</u>], 8 <u>and the two shall become one flesh</u>". <u>So they are no longer two, but one flesh.</u> 9 <u>Therefore what God has joined together, let no one separate</u>'. 10 Then in the house the disciples asked him again about this matter.
9 And I say to you, <u>whoever divorces his wife</u>, except for unchastity, <u>and marries another commits adultery</u>'.	11 He said to them, '<u>Whoever divorces his wife and marries another commits adultery</u> against her; 12 and if she divorces her husband and marries another, she commits adultery'.

In terms of how the Jesus tradition was heard and passed down, the subject of this pericope is one of the most interesting. For the memory that Jesus taught on the subject of divorce is well attested, not only here but also in Q (Matt. 5.32/Luke 16.18) and by Paul (1 Cor. 7.10-11). Here as elsewhere, the diversity of the tradition should not be counted against its origin in Jesus' own teaching,[148] but

147. Holmén, *Jesus* 236-37: 'he clearly questioned the significance of the purity paradigm in the view of the Jews as the people of God' (251).

148. As in Funk, *Five Gospels* 88-89, 142-43.

simply attests how that teaching was handled and developed as it was retaught in the differing circumstances of the various early communities.[149]

The memory is of Jesus in debate with Pharisees with regard to the disputed ruling in Deut. 24.1.[150] What distinguishes Jesus' stand on the question is the way, once again, he cuts behind the Deuteronomic ruling to the more fundamental characterisation of marriage in Gen. 2.24. The creation of humankind as man and woman (1.27; 2.21-23) points to the conclusion, 'Therefore a man leaves his father and his mother and clings to his wife, and they become one flesh' (2.24).[151] Divorce is thus to be understood as a falling short of that ideal,[152] and Jesus probably pressed the logic of the ideal by turning his face against divorce and remarriage in principle[153] — without thought, be it noted, of allowing divorce as a way of maintaining covenant purity (as in Ezra 9–10). This was also the version which Q (Q 16.18) and Paul (1 Cor. 7.10-11) knew, but it is noticeable that both Matthew and Paul in their reteaching of the tradition qualify it, no doubt as a result of being confronted by situations of marriage breakdown, and in

149. 'Jesus' rejection of divorce and remarriage is attested in the three earliest Christian sources known to us, Q, Paul, and Mark' (Holmén, *Jesus* 167); 'unanimously acknowledged' (162 and n. 433).

150. Matthew makes this still clearer by adding 'for any cause', thus indicating that the debate was about the interpretation of the second clause of Deut. 24.1 — 'if then she finds no favour in his eyes because he has found some indecency *('erwâ)* in her'. In effect he retells the episode as a contribution to the debate between the schools of Hillel and Shammai on how rigorously Deut. 24.1 should be interpreted. In adding 'except for unchastity *(porneia)'*, Matthew shows Jesus supporting what was remembered as Shammai's more rigorous interpretation (see my *Unity and Diversity* 247 and those cited in n. 31; further bibliography in Loader, *Jesus' Attitude* 175 n. 93; see further Bockmuehl, *Jewish Law* 17-21). But in so doing, he changes a point of ideal principle back into one of practical law.

151. Cf. CD 4.14–5.11, where remarriage is ruled out since 'the principle of creation is "male and female he created them"' (Gen. 1.27); Sanders deduces from this parallel the overwhelming probability that Jesus' original ruling also cited Scripture and that Jesus' teaching sprang immediately from his eschatological sense of living in the last days (*Jesus* 257-60).

152. 'Jesus appears to assume that any appeal to exceptional circumstances is an attempt to evade a completely unambiguous resolve to do the absolute will of God' (Keck, *Who Is Jesus?* 155). Wright deduces that the renewal envisaged by Jesus would contain a 'cure' for the 'hardness of heart' (which had been the reason for Moses' divorce ruling) (*Jesus* 284-87).

153. Mark 10.12 looks like an elaboration of the tradition, envisaging as it does the possibility of a woman initiating divorce, something not permitted in the Judaism of Jesus' day (Josephus, *Ant.* 15.259); discussion in Taylor, *Mark* 419-21; Westerholm, *Jesus* 117-18; and further Schrage, *Ethics* 94-97. It should also be noted that in a society where only the husband could initiate divorce and where the *'erwâ* of Deut. 24.1 could be interpreted liberally ('even if she spoiled a dish for him' — *m. Git.* 9.10), an absolute prohibition of divorce was a way of protecting the wife. See further J. L. Nolland, 'The Gospel Prohibition of Divorce: Tradition History and Meaning', *JSNT* 58 (1995) 19-35; A.-J. Levine, 'Jesus, Divorce, and Sexuality: A Jewish Critique', in LeBeau et al., eds., *Historical Jesus* 113-29 (here 116-21).

effect reinstate the Mosaic ameliorating ruling: 'except for sexual immorality *(porneia)*' (Matt. 5.32/19.9);[154] the believing partner is not bound (1 Cor. 7.15). In each case the principled assertion of Jesus is retained, even when continuing human 'hard-heartedness' once again causes the ideal practice to be hedged around with qualification.

Outside the Markan tradition special mention should also be made of three other passages.[155]

f. Antitheses

We need not enter into the debate as to the sources of Matthew's sequence of six antitheses (Matt. 5.21-48). It is quite likely that the introductory formula ('You have heard that it was said . . .') is the mark of the teacher who made this collection of Jesus' teaching (Matthew himself?), since it appears nowhere else within the Jesus tradition. It is equally likely that Jesus was remembered as setting his own teaching on various subjects in some measure over against previous rulings or as giving radical interpretations of particular Scriptures, even if not in such a formulaic manner.[156] The point is that the antitheses are best understood as pressing home or pressing behind some specific law to the more fundamental issue within or behind the law.[157] Over all, they call for a more fundamental reorientation of human and social relationships than can be achieved or maintained by legislation.[158] Not just murder is condemned, but unjustified anger, insult, or

154. On the meaning of *porneia* here see discussion in Davies and Allison, *Matthew* 1.529-31.

155. Since the paucity of Q sayings that have to do with the Torah is often commented on (e.g., Kloppenborg, 'Sayings Gospel Q' 332-34), we should note that all three of the following examples include Q material: Matt. 5.32/Luke 16.18; Matt. 5.39-41/Luke 6.29-30; Matt. 5.44-47/Luke 6.27, 32-34; Matt. 23.23/Luke 11.42; Matt. 8.21-22/Luke 9.59-60; as well as Matt. 23.25/Luke 11.39, cited above (n. 143).

156. Bultmann's argument that 5.21-22, 27-28, 33-37 have been drawn from pre-Matthean tradition and 'have given rise to analogous formulations, in which unattached dominical sayings have found a home' (*History* 134-36) has proved influential. See, e.g., Guelich's brief survey of opinion (*Sermon on the Mount* 178; also 265-71); Schrage, *Ethics* 59-60; Merklein, *Jesu Botschaft* 105-10; Luz, *Matthäus* 1.245-46; Stuhlmacher, *Biblische Theologie* 1.103; Becker, *Jesus* 288-91; Allison, *Jesus* 185-86.

157. 'Jesus radicalized rather than abrogated the law . . . it is not against the law to be stricter than the law requires' (Sanders, *Jesus* 260). In contrast, is it really justified by the text to conclude that 'Jesus combats legalistic behavior patterns' (Gnilka, *Jesus* 213)? Vermes cites other overstatements (*Religion* 30-32).

158. See further Guelich, *Sermon on the Mount* 237-55. On the divorce antithesis (Matt. 5.31-32/Luke 16.18) see above (§14.4e); and on the love of enemy antithesis (Matt. 5.43-48/Luke 6.27-28, 32-36) see below, §14.5.

sneering dismissal of another (Matt. 5.21-22); not just adultery, but lust (5.27-28); not just false oaths, but casual oath-taking and calculating equivocation (5.33-37).[159] Doing what is right cannot be reduced to outward acts and set formulae. The one antithesis which seems to 'abolish' a law,[160] the one on retaliation (5.38-42),[161] is again better heard as pressing behind a law specifically intended to limit retaliation and prevent blood-feuds to a more fundamental sense of right and responsibility as expressed in a practice of non-retaliation and positive response when personally threatened.[162]

g. Tithing

Tithing was also important within Judaism[163] and became a matter of significant concern for the later rabbis (see especially *m. Demai*). The shared Matthew/Luke tradition on the subject (Matt. 23.23/Luke 11.42) suggests that there was debate already current in the pre-70 period concerning certain herbs.[164] The saying is notable in that Jesus is remembered not as denouncing such concerns as over-trivial or wrong, but, once again, as reminding his hearers that there are more important things to be concerned about — notably 'justice and mercy' — wholly in the spirit of and with a probably intended echo of Mic. 6.8. The saying corresponds to Jesus' attitude implied in the parable of the Pharisee and the toll-collector (Luke 18.9-14): tithing is not criticized any more than prayer, but it does not form a basis or reason for acceptability to God;[165] nor does it serve as a test case of faithfulness to covenant law.[166]

159. Note the strong echo of this last antithesis in Jas. 5.12, another instance of how the Jesus tradition functioned and was heard within the early communities (see further above, §8.1e). Josephus reports a similar attitude regarding oaths among the Essenes (*War* 2.135; cf. CD 9.9-12; 16.7-12; see further B. Kollmann, 'Erwägungen zur Reichweite des Schwurverbots Jesu (Mt 5,34)', *ZNW* 92 [2001] 20-32). Becker observes: 'Of course, they did not understand this practice as contrary to the Torah. Refusing to do something that the Torah permits is not a violation of the Torah' (*Jesus* 296). See also Westerholm, *Jesus* 104-13; Holmén, *Jesus* 176-86.

160. Jeremias, *Proclamation* 207; Schrage, *Ethics* 64-65. The law in question, *lex talionis,* is Exod. 21.24; Lev. 24.20; Deut. 19.21.

161. Text cited above, §8.5d, with Lukan parallel (Luke 6.29-30) and reference to *Did.* 1.4-5 and *GTh* 95. See also above, chapter 12 n. 194, and fuller discussion in Davies and Allison, *Matthew* 1.539-48.

162. See the full and excellent discussion by Betz, *Sermon on the Mount* 277-84.

163. Lev. 27.30-33; Num. 18.24-32; Deut. 14.22-29; 26.12-15; see further Sanders, *Judaism* 146-57; a major marker of covenant obedience (Holmén, *Jesus* 106-11).

164. For further details see Davies and Allison, *Matthew* 3.293-94.

165. See further Westerholm, *Jesus* 55-61.

166. Holmén, *Jesus* 127-28.

h. Filial Duty

The one passage where Sanders is willing to recognize that Jesus 'superseded the requirements of piety and the Torah' is Jesus' command to the would-be disciple, 'Leave the dead to bury their own dead' (Matt. 8.21-22/Luke 9.59-60).[167] 'Disobedience of the requirement to care for one's dead parents is actually disobedience to God'.[168] But if an idiomatic usage is involved, then Sanders here is overreacting as much as those he criticizes in other instances.[169] Even so, we can properly speak of Jesus grasping the opportunity of some situation, whose particularities were not deemed important enough to retain in the tradition, to emphasize the absolute priority of God's work. We now may look askance at such uncompromising commitment, but it should be recognized and honoured for what it was.

All this is wholly consistent with the observations already made in §9.9c regarding what might be called Jesus' own Torah piety. He is also recalled as observing the law on leprosy[170] and as directing the rich young man who enquired regarding eternal life to the second table of the ten commandments (Mark 10.19 pars.).[171] The tradition reviewed above and elsewhere depicts him as basing his own teaching foursquare on the Torah.[172] Matthew records a saying in which Jesus assumes continued participation in the Temple sacrifices (Matt. 5.23-24).[173] Another passage has him being consulted on an issue of in-

---

167. Sanders, *Jesus* 252-55: 'the most revealing passage in the synoptics for penetrating to Jesus' view of the law', where he pays tribute to and follows Hengel's treatment (252).

168. *Jesus* 253; 'a blatant offense against Torah and Halacha' (Becker, *Jesus* 285); 'a direct affront . . . to the dominant created orders of classical antiquity. . . . Burial was the moment par excellence to demonstrate expected and applauded filial loyalty. To ignore it, as Jesus proposed, could only reveal great indecency. Jesus was being simply shameless' (Vaage, *Galilean Upstarts* 90, 93). See also §13.2d.

169. Was the father already dead? Bailey cites the mediaeval commentator Ibn al-Salibi (ca. 1050, written in Syriac): '"Let me go and bury" means: let me go and serve my father while he is alive and after he dies I will bury him and come' (*Through Peasant Eyes* 26); see again above, §13.2d. Bockmuehl protests against Hengel and Sanders that 'the notion of a special religious duty transcending even basic family obligations is one that would have been culturally familiar to Jesus' audience' and suggests less plausibly a possible Nazirite setting for the saying (*Jewish Law* 23-48); but if Bailey is right the resolution is to be found more in terms of idiom than of halakhah.

170. Mark 1.44 pars.; Luke 17.14; Lev. 13.4-9.

171. Though it should also be remembered that one of the key points of the story is that keeping all these commandments 'from my youth' proved insufficient; the young man fell short in regard to a more demanding principle (Goppelt, *Theology* 1.98). Cf. also Rom. 13.8-10.

172. Mark 7.10; 10.6-7; 12.26; 12.29-31 (see below, §14.5).

173. *Pace* Goppelt: The saying 'did not presuppose that Jesus' disciples continued to offer gifts in the temple; it had purely metaphorical quality' (*Theology* 1.96). Note also Mark

heritance law (Luke 12.13). And over all, the Jesus tradition's many echoes of Scripture, Isaiah and the Psalms in particular, attest the extent to which 'Jesus lived in the Old Testament'.[174] Matthew can even portray Jesus as claiming to have come not to abolish but to fulfil the law and as calling for a strict observation of its commandments (Matt. 5.17-20). There is little doubt that Matthew here impresses his own priorities on the tradition, but had his presentation been totally unfounded and at odds with Jesus' elsewhere remembered teaching,[175] it is unlikely that his attempt to redraw the Jesus tradition so radically on this point would have been so successful.[176] Here not least we need to remember that the Jesus tradition consists of what Jesus was *heard* as teaching, and to recall that what is heard and remembered depends as much on the hearer as on the speaker.

Even so, we may conclude that the richer tradition of Jesus in debate with scribes and Pharisees regarding points of law and disputed issues of halakhah stands up well to scrutiny. Whether 'sovereign freedom' in regard to the law and tradition is an appropriate description of Jesus' attitude to the law is less clear. The description may be better applied to Jesus' teaching and debating technique, as one confident in the importance of the fundamental concerns which motivated his own mission. At any rate, the Jesus who is thus remembered as teaching and debating evidently did not set himself antithetically over against the law. Rather his teaching in this area can be characterized in terms of pressing behind the immediate issue to the deeper questions of motive and right(eousness), refusing to take the easy way out in testing cases of applying the most immediately obvious ruling, and digging deep into the law to discern the divine rationale (justice) in its particular *miṣwot*.[177] To do the will of God

---

12.41-44 par. (cited above, §8.4c). Contrast Meier's conclusion that 'Jesus clearly accepted the Jerusalem temple *as part of the present order of things*' (*Marginal Jew* 3.500, his emphasis).

174. Jeremias, *Proclamation* 205-206, with full documentation; see also R. T. France, *Jesus and the Old Testament* (London: Tyndale, 1972); Vermes, *Religion* 50-70; Theissen and Merz, *Historical Jesus* 357-58; contrast Becker: 'Jesus makes no use of the authority of the Torah when he speaks' (*Jesus* 254-55; also 278-79, 281).

175. Matt. 5.18, after all, is drawn from tradition common to Luke 16.17 (Q?).

176. On the issue of how much in Matt. 5.17-20 may be referred back to Jesus see especially Banks, *Jesus and the Law* 204-26; Davies and Allison, *Matthew* 1.482-503. By 'fulfil' Matthew may have meant 'complete', that is, 'reveal the true meaning of the law and demonstrate it in action', as documented in what follows (see further Guelich, *Sermon on the Mount* 139-41).

177. Cf. Banks, *Jesus and the Law* (though his consistent christological focus reflects more the emphasis of the developed interest of the Evangelists themselves); Westerholm, *Jesus* 130; Becker, *Jesus* 229-30; Theissen and Merz, *Historical Jesus* 381, 394-95 ('at its centre it [Jesus' ethical preaching] is oriented on the Torah; however, it is oriented on a Torah read in the prophetic spirit'); Bockmuehl, *Jewish Law* 6, 14.

was still the primary goal,[178] even if that will could not be discerned simply by reference to the Torah.[179]

Moreover, it would appear that on issues of law and halakhah which had become test cases of obedience and loyalty to the covenant, Jesus declined to go down that road. His standing before God did not depend on particular interpretations and applications of Torah. His Jewishness did not require a pattern of observance which marked him off as separate from the dissident or the disobedient. We should not be surprised, then, that the fundamental concerns Jesus enunciated and defended gave stimulus and scope to his subsequent followers to press still further at various points into a rationale for conduct which no longer remained within the boundaries clearly marked out by the law.

Finally, if it remains likely that Jesus' own emphases were determined in large part by his eschatological perspective,[180] we should also note that this factor has not left many distinctive marks on the tradition at this point. What is commended in all this is not a pattern of conduct necessary for entry into the kingdom, nor an 'interim ethic' (Schweitzer) required only for the interval before the coming of the kingdom, but (by implication) a quality of kingdom life, the character of living appropriate for those who look for the kingdom's coming and who seek to live already in its light.

14.5. Love as Motivation

Bound up with the emphases just documented is a particular feature whose importance deserves separate mention. It is the fact that Jesus was remembered as giving particular prominence to the Torah injunction to 'love your neighbour as yourself' and as pressing home its full implications. The tradition at this point is clear.

---

178. Mark 3.35/Matt. 12.50; Mark 14.36 pars.; Matt. 6.10; 7.21; 21.31; Luke 12.47. See Schnackenburg, *Sittliche Botschaft* 77-79.

179. In *Jesus' Call to Discipleship* I suggested a distinction between *principles* that are applied in the light of circumstances and *rules* that are to be obeyed whatever the circumstances (84). But the shift in kingdom perspective implied in Matt. 11.11-12/Luke 16.16 is not reducible to neat epigrams, even if the rhetorical character of the latter text also needs to be recalled (§12.5c[4]).

180. Merklein, e.g., summarizes Jesus' moral teaching as 'eschatologically qualified instruction *(Weisung)*' rather than as 'intensified' or 'radicalized' Torah teaching (*Jesu Botschaft* 101-102).

a. Mark 12.28-31 pars.

Matt. 22.35-40	Mark 12.28-31	Luke 10.25-28

35 . . . one of them [Pharisees], a lawyer,
 	
 asked him a question to test him. 36 'Teacher, which commandment in the law is the greatest?' 37 He said to him,
 	
 '"You shall love the Lord your God with all your heart, and with all your soul, and with all your mind".
        38 This is the greatest and first commandment. 39 The second is like it: "You shall love your neighbour as yourself". 40 On these two commandments hang all the law and the prophets'.
	28 One of the scribes came near and heard them disputing with one another, and seeing that he answered them well, he asked him,
	        'Which commandment is the first of all?' 29 Jesus answered, 'The first is, "Hear, O Israel: the Lord our God, the Lord is one; 30 and you shall love the Lord your God with all your heart, and with all your soul, and with all your mind, and with all your strength".
	
	 31 The second is this, "You shall love your neighbour as yourself". There is no other commandment greater than these'.
		25 Just then a lawyer stood up to test him, saying,
		
		        'Teacher, what must I do to inherit eternal life?' 26 He said to him, 'What is written in the law? What do you read there?' 27 He answered, '"You shall love the Lord your God with all your heart, and with all your soul, and with all your strength, and with all your mind;
		
		       and your neighbour as yourself"'. 28 And he said to him, 'You have given the right answer; do this, and you will live'.

There is no doubt that the injunction to 'Love your neighbour as you love yourself' was a central principle and key motivation in earliest Christian paraenesis; the attestation puts that beyond question.[181] Such a consistent singling out of just this commandment (Lev. 19.18) can hardly be coincidental. Nor is it likely that the emphasis was due to some unknown teacher or that it arose spontaneously at the same time in several Christian circles.[182] When the Jesus tradition contains such a clear memory that Jesus had elevated Lev. 19.18 to such prominence, the most obvious explanation must be that it was the impact of just that teaching which ensured its continuing importance among those who named Jesus as

---

181. Rom. 13.8-10; Gal. 5.14; Jas. 2.8; *Did.* 1.2; 2.7; *Barn.* 19.5; *GTh* 25; cf. John 15.12. In the same spirit is the consistent Pauline exhortation to consideration for others (as in Rom. 12.9-10; 15.1-2; Phil. 2.1-5).

182. Explicit references to Lev. 19.18 are lacking in Jewish literature prior to Jesus, and such allusions as there are give it no particular prominence, though subsequently the opinion is attributed to Rabbi Akiba (early second century) that Lev. 19.18 is 'the greatest general principle in the Torah' (*Sipra* on Lev. 19.18); see my *Romans* 778-80, referring particularly to A. Nissen, *Gott und der Nächste im antiken Judentum. Untersuchungen zum Doppelgebot der Liebe* (WUNT 15: Tübingen: Mohr Siebeck, 1974), and K. Berger, *Die Gesetzauslegung Jesu* I (WMANT 40; Neukirchen-Vluyn: Neukirchener, 1972) 50-55, 80-136; data also in Davies and Allison, *Matthew* 3.237-38; Theissen and Merz, *Historical Jesus* 384-90; M. Reiser, 'Love of Enemies in the Context of Antiquity', *NTS* 47 (2001) 411-27.

Lord.[183] The Jesus tradition itself comes to us in different performance variations: Matthew and Mark sum up the significance of the teaching in regard to the law in different but complementary words (Matt. 22.40; Mark 12.31b); somewhat surprisingly it is Mark (rather than Matthew) who takes the opportunity to include the beginning of the *Shema* (Mark 12.29);[184] and Luke has given the teaching an intriguing twist by having the key commands uttered by a lawyer *(nomikos),* with Jesus approving (Luke 10.27-28). It is also to Luke that we owe one of Jesus' most vivid and enduring parables, spoken to illustrate the love command, the parable of the Good Samaritan (Luke 10.29-37), with its final punchline, 'Go and do likewise' (10.37).[185] But once again we find that the key teaching remains stable throughout, however presented.

We can therefore be confident that it was indeed Jesus' teaching which resulted in the importance accorded to 'loving the neighbour' in the Jesus tradition and in earliest Christianity.[186] Two features are particularly worth noting. First, that the command to love one's neighbour is put second to the primary command, to love God with all one's being (Mark 12.30 pars.; §14.1 above).[187] The implication is that the two go together,[188] perhaps also that the second is possible in long-term reality only as the corollary to the first.[189] Perhaps too that each is both a deeply rooted emotion and an act of resolute will ('with all your heart . . . with all your might'). Second, worth noting also is the realism in the way the command is formulated. It does not call for the disciple to love everyone, as

183. 'The centre of his ethos and the culmination of his moral instructions' (Schnackenburg, *Sittliche Botschaft* 89). Becker has no doubt that 'this theme' (the love command) was part of Jesus' message, but is surprisingly dogmatic in his insistence that 'Of course, Jesus does not directly quote the Torah' (*Jesus* 249, 254).

184. But the citation of Deut. 6.5 in all three versions (Mark 12.30 pars.) shows that Mark's elaboration simply makes explicit what was already implicit.

185. See above, chapter 13 n. 244.

186. The Jesus Seminar shows a strange unwillingness to allow that Jesus could himself have been creative in his use of Lev. 19.18; the most some were willing to allow is that 'Jesus might have affirmed the interpretation of the law given by Hillel', referring to Hillel's teaching the negative form of the Golden Rule (*b. Sabb.* 31a) (Funk, *Five Gospels* 104-105). Lüdemann judges 'the historical yield of the tradition' at this point as 'nil, since it is firmly rooted in the community and is to be derived from its needs' (*Jesus* 86), thus evoking some unknown creative genius in disregard of the tradition itself and confusing use made of and importance attributed to a tradition with origin of the tradition.

187. 'A wholly original conjunction of Deut. 6.4-5 and Lev. 19.18' (Stuhlmacher, *Biblische Theologie* 1.100-101). Note also that Luke's version of the saying on tithing (Matt. 23.23/Luke 11.42) includes 'love of God' as part of the higher obligation.

188. See particularly V. P. Furnish, *The Love Command in the New Testament* (Nashville: Abingdon, 1972) 27-28, 33, 37.

189. See further Schrage, *Ethics* 81-85. Cf. Moo: 'For Jesus, it is not a question of the "priority of love over law" but of the priority of love *within* the law' ('Jesus' 11).

though that might be possible.[190] Only the neighbour — that is, as the Good Samaritan illustrates, whoever God gives as neighbour on the road of everyday life.[191] And it does not call for a love beyond human capacity or a love which requires hatred of the self as a corollary, only (!) for the care which one naturally bestows on oneself to be the measure of the love shown to the neighbour.[192]

b. Matt. 5.43-48/Luke 6.27-28, 32-36

More striking still is the passage preserved in the Sermon on the Mount/Plain:

Matt. 5.43-48	Luke 6.27-28, 32-36
43 You have heard that it was said, 'You shall love your neighbour and hate your enemy'. 44 But I say to you, <u>Love your enemies</u> and <u>pray for those who</u> persecute <u>you</u>, 45 so that you may be sons of your Father in heaven; for he makes his sun rise on the evil and on the good, and sends rain on the righteous and on the unrighteous. 46 For <u>if you love those who love you</u>, what reward do you have? Do not even the tax collectors do the same? 47 And if you greet only your brothers, what more are you doing than others? Do not <u>even</u> the Gentiles <u>do the same?</u>	27 But I say to you that listen, <u>Love your enemies</u>, do good to those who hate you, 28 bless those who curse you, <u>pray for those who</u> abuse <u>you</u>. . . . . 32 And <u>if you love those who love you</u>, what credit is that to you? For even sinners love those who love them. 33 And if you do good to those who do good to you, what credit is that to you? For <u>even</u> sinners <u>do the same</u>. 34 If you lend to those from whom you hope to receive, what credit is that to you? Even sinners lend to sinners, to receive as much again. 35 But love your enemies, do good, and lend, expecting nothing in return. Your reward will be great, and you will be children of the Most High; for he is kind to the ungrateful and the wicked. 36 Be merciful, just as your Father is merciful.
48 Therefore, be perfect, as your heavenly Father is perfect.	

Here again there is good evidence that the teaching was heard and recycled in subsequent paraenesis: Rom. 12.14 and *Did.* 1.3 both clearly echo the Lukan

190. 'Jesus' concern is not a vague love for the whole world, which can so easily become sentimental illusion' (Schrage, *Ethics* 79).

191. Bornkamm points out that Jesus changes the question, 'Who is my neighbour?' (Luke 10.29) to another: 'To whom am I neighbour?' (10.36) (*Jesus of Nazareth* 113); Furnish, *Love Command* 40. 'One cannot define one's neighbour; one can only be a neighbour' (H. Greeven, *plēsion, TDNT* 6.317).

192. Note also Bultmann's observations: 'the neighbour is not a sort of tool by means of which I practise the love of God'; 'only if love is thought of as an emotion is it meaningless to command love; the *command* of love shows that love is understood as an attitude of the will' (*Jesus and the Word* 115, 118); 'the example of the merciful Samaritan shows that a man can know and must know what he has to do when he sees his neighbour in need of his help' (*Theology* 1.19; similarly 24).

form of the saying, and the same teaching seems to have influenced the formulation of 1 Cor. 4.12 and 1 Pet. 3.9.[193] It is Jesus, then, who is recalled in the tradition (Q?), drawn on and elaborated by Matthew and Luke, as extending the love command to a hitherto unheard-of application.[194] No more here than before is there any cause to attribute such teaching to some unknown disciple of immense influence.[195] It is because it was Jesus who is remembered as so teaching, and probably only because it was him, that the teaching has been preserved.[196] In this instance above all we catch a glimpse of how radically Jesus was prepared to press a different motivation and ideal for community and for discipleship under pressure. And not just as an individualistic ethic,[197] but as a breaking through of a concept of neighbour love determined primarily by covenant faithfulness.[198] Love should be the first and the final criterion for conduct

193. Details in my *Romans* 745. Note also *P.Oxy.* 1224 (Aland, *Synopsis* 84). Further echoes and allusions, as well as OT anticipations, are suggested by Davies and Allison, *Matthew* 1.551-53, though they have no doubt that 'Love your enemies' was 'undoubtedly the invention of Jesus' own mind' (552). See also J. Piper, *'Love your Enemies': Jesus' Love Command in the Synoptic Gospels and the Early Christian Paraenesis* (SNTSMS 38; Cambridge: Cambridge University, 1979) 19-65; Fitzmyer, *Luke* 637-38; Guelich, *Sermon on the Mount* 224-29, 252-55; McKnight, *New Vision* 206-10, 218-24.

194. It is frequently noted that the Qumran covenanters were bidden to 'hate all the sons of darkness' (1QS 1.10-11) (e.g., Furnish, *Love Command* 46-47; Charlesworth, *Jesus* 74; further details in Davies and Allison, *Matthew* 1.549-50). But W. Klassen suggests that the double counsel, 'Be good to (or love) your friends and hate your enemies', was widespread in the ancient world, so that it is unnecessary to look for a specific reference ('"Love Your Enemies": Some Reflections on the Current Status of Research', in W. M. Swartley, ed., *The Love of Enemy and Nonretaliation in the New Testament* [Louisville: Westminster, 1992] 1-31 [here 12]). See further Betz, *Sermon on the Mount* 301-13.

195. The Jesus Seminar had no doubts that 'Love your enemies' is close to the heart of Jesus' teaching (as also Bultmann, *History* 105) and were positive in their judgment regarding Matt. 5.45b-46/Luke 6.32, but returned a negative verdict on Matt. 5.44b/Luke 6.28, despite the parallels in Romans and *Didache* (Funk, *Five Gospels* 145-47, 291-97). Lüdemann is even more robust in his affirmation of the authenticity of Matt. 5.44a, since 'it was evaded in primitive Christianity' (*Jesus* 144). See also Holmén, *Jesus* 258-72. The nearest parallel outside Jewish tradition is Epictetus 3.22.53-54: the Cynic 'must needs be flogged like an ass, and while he is being flogged he must love those who flog him . . .'; less close parallels in Downing, *Christ and the Cynics* 23-25; Vaage, *Galilean Upstarts* 47-50.

196. 'It is Jesus' commandment to *love* the enemy which most of all sets his ethic of love apart from other "love ethics" of antiquity' (Furnish, *Love Command* 66).

197. 'Love of enemies is not the high point of universal love of humanity, but the high point of overcoming of self, the surrender of one's own claim' (Bultmann, *Jesus and the Word* 112).

198. Jesus 'brings together the terms love and enemy not to expand the circle of those whom one is to love, but to move away from that kind of thinking to a totally new orientation of love' — so Becker, *Jesus* 255, but he presses this over-dialectically (and sermonically) into a

and for all social relationships. The teaching which Matthew has put immediately prior to this under the preceding antithesis illustrates the outworking of such an attitude and priority (Matt. 5.38-42/Luke 6.29-30).[199] For it urges not simply non-retaliation, but a positive outgoing generosity ('let him have your cloak also; go with him a second [mile])'.[200] This is how love responds to provocation.[201]

c. Matt. 7.12/Luke 6.31

Matt. 7.12	Luke 6.31
Everything, therefore, whatever you wish that people should do for you, so also do for them; for this is the law and the prophets.	And as you wish that people should do for you, do for them likewise.

The aptly named 'Golden Rule' was well known in its essential principle in many forms, both within Second Temple Judaism and beyond.[202] This is regularly

---

contrast with love of neighbour (255-57). Merklein emphasizes the eschatological context — love of enemy as the actualization of God's kingship (*Jesu Botschaft* 116-28).

199. Cited above, §8.5d. '"Love your enemy" would have meant "Love the Romans"' (Borg, *Conflict,* 130); not the Romans, but the local adversary (Horsley, *Jesus* 150, 261-73); Matt. 5.39-41 'a strategy of coping with soldiers who took what they needed, by violence if necessary' (Chilton, *Rabbi Jesus* 46). Perrin points out that the 'coat/cloak' saying is, literally taken, ridiculous ('A man acting in that manner would soon be back before the court on a charge of indecent exposure!') and concludes that it was never meant to be taken literally: 'What we have here are illustrations of a principle. The illustrations are extreme . . . but that is deliberate. They are intended to be vivid examples of a radical demand, and it is as such that we must regard them' (*Rediscovering* 147-48). 'So drastic and wellnigh intolerable a demand must almost certainly derive from the historical Jesus' (Catchpole, *Quest* 111). Cynic parallels in Downing, *Christ and the Cynics* 25-26.

200. Cf. G. Theissen, 'Nonviolence and Love of Our Enemies (Matthew 5:38-44; Luke 6:27-38)', *Social Reality* 115-56, who argues that 'experiences of the Jewish War and the post-war era are reflected in the way traditions about loving our enemies are formulated in Matthew' (132-37 [here 136]) and, once again, that those in view are 'wandering charismatics' (144-46); but Theissen also draws attention to the two classic examples of effective nonviolent resistance by Jews in Palestine during the 20s and 30s (Josephus, *War* 2.174; *Ant.* 18.271-72) to demonstrate that such teaching by Jesus would have offered a real and realistic political option (149-54). Cf. and contrast Becker, *Jesus* 252-53.

201. 'The credibility of these radical demands is to be found in Jesus alone. He himself fully lived in accordance with these instructions. . . . These words are conceivable only as his own' (Gnilka, *Jesus* 230). See also Schrage, *Ethics* 76-79.

202. Davies and Allison, *Matthew* 1.686-88 again provide a convenient summary of the data, usually in the negative form ('Don't do to others what you would not want others to do to you'), including Tob. 4.15; *Ep. Arist.* 207; Philo, *Hypothetica* in Eusebius, *Praep. evang.* 8.7.6;

taken to indicate the likelihood that the principle has been drawn into the Jesus tradition and did not originate for that tradition in a particular articulation of Jesus.[203] The inadequacy of such an argument should be obvious: if the principle was so common, Jesus himself may well have signalled his agreement with it. But in this case one of the curiosities of the tradition is that the echoes in *P.Oxy.* 654 6.2 and *GTh* 6.2 are closer to the form in Tob. 4.15,[204] which does indeed suggest that in these cases the tradition has indeed been drawn from sources other than Jesus. So the possibility certainly cannot be excluded that the Golden Rule was drawn into the Jesus tradition as a way of summing up Jesus' teaching on love as the motivating force for disciples' relations with others. Since it makes the same point as the law summed up in the call for neighbour love (§14.5a above), nothing is lost either way.

14.6. Forgiving as Forgiven

A further mark of the love for which Jesus called is the readiness to forgive. Characteristic of the discipleship to which Jesus called was the two-sided theme of forgiven as forgiving, forgiven therefore forgiving. The importance of this two-sidedness of forgiveness is already clear in the Lord's Prayer: 'Forgive (*aphes*) us our debts, as we also have forgiven our debtors' (Matt. 6.12); 'Forgive (*aphes*) us our sins, for we ourselves also forgive everyone indebted to us' (Luke 11.4).[205] And Matthew underlines the point by adding and elaborating an emphasis also found in Mark:[206]

T. Naph. 1.6; and the famous response of Hillel, *b. Sabb.* 31a. A more positive form is not unique to the Christian tradition (cf. Sir. 31.15; *2 En.* 61.1-2; Sextus, *Sent.* 89); see particularly the survey by A. Dihle, *Die goldene Regel. Eine Einführung in die Geschichte der antiken und frühchristlichen Vulgärethik* (Göttingen: Vandenhoeck und Ruprecht, 1962) 80-108; also P. S. Alexander, 'Jesus and the Golden Rule', in Charlesworth and Johns, eds., *Hillel and Jesus* 363-88.

203. Bultmann, *History* 102-103; Funk, *Five Gospels* 156, 296; Lüdemann, *Jesus* 152; but also Davies and Allison, *Matthew* 1.688. On the other hand, Vermes's point should be given weight: 'the very fact that the distinctive positive wording is used rather than the common negative formulation, must . . . count as a definite argument in favour of Jesus having actually framed it' (*Religion* 41).

204. Tob. 4.15: 'What you hate, do not do to anyone'; *P.Oxy.* 654 6.2 = *GTh* 6.2: 'Do not do what you hate'. Note also that in Christian tradition (*Did.* 1.2; Acts 15.20, 29a D) it is the negative form of the rule which is quoted.

205. Such differences of wording and tense are a further reminder that the concern in reteaching the Jesus tradition was for substance and present relevance, not for a more pedantic verbatim memorization. The different words used for 'forgive' in the following material make the same point.

206. Cf. also Matt. 5.23-24 — reconciliation as both forgiving and being forgiven; and

Matt. 6.14-15	Mark 11.25
14 For if you forgive people their transgressions, your heavenly Father will also forgive you. 15 But if you do not forgive people, neither will your Father forgive your transgressions.	When you stand praying, if you have anything against someone, forgive, in order that your heavenly Father may forgive you your transgressions.

Luke makes a similar point in another saying: 'Forgive *(apoluete)* and you shall be forgiven *(apolythēsesthe)*' (Luke 6.37).[207] The same point is implicit in the saying which urges generous and repeated forgiveness, which Matthew shares with Luke (Matt. 18.15, 21-22/Luke 17.3-4)[208] and to which he has appended the parable of the unforgiving servant in order to drive home the point (Matt. 18.23-35).[209] And it is presumably this model of 'forgive as forgiven' which is followed in the subsequent Christian exhortation to be 'forgiving *(charizomenoi)* of each other, if anyone has a cause for complaint against another; as the Lord also forgave *(echarisato)* you, so must you' (Col. 3.13).[210] Matthew has also made 18.15, 21-22 the frame for his 'community rule' on dealing with sins within the *ekklēsia* (18.15-20), where a procedure to reclaim the errant brother is regularized and the authority of the community on the matter of forgiveness (cf. John 20.23) is stressed, by virtue of Jesus' presence in the midst. This tradition certainly reflects later situations in the life of the churches known to Matthew. The point here is simply to note that forgiveness continued to be a major concern in relationships within the churches and that its importance was rooted in Jesus'

---

the counsel to 'be at peace with one another' (only in Mark 9.50, but probably known to Paul: Rom. 12.18; cf. Matt. 5.9; Matt. 10.13/Luke 10.6).

207. Note the clear echoes in *1 Clem.* 13.2 and Pol., *Phil.* 2.3 and 6.2. Perrin is particularly enthusiastic over Matt. 6.14-15: 'No saying in the tradition has a higher claim to authenticity than this petition, nor is any saying more important to an understanding of the teaching of Jesus *(Rediscovering* 150-52). The Jesus Seminar conclude that Jesus said something like Luke 6.37, although they are less confident regarding Mark 11.25 (Funk, *Five Gospels* 99-100, 297). Despite complete lack of support from the textual tradition, Lüdemann argues that the Markan text is dependent on Matthew (only here in Mark do we find reference to 'your heavenly Father') and is therefore probably a gloss *(Jesus* 79).

208. Cited above, §8.5e; 'the reply of Jesus is a *reductio ad absurdum* of any quantitative treatment of the question. There are no limits' (Dodd, *Founder* 67-68). As Becker notes, the warning 'Do not judge, and you will not be judged' (Matt. 7.1/Luke 6.37) and the warning against unjustified anger (Matt. 5.21-22) are the opposite side of the same coin *(Jesus* 249-52). We can add the further Q saying regarding the speck and the log (Matt. 7.3-5/Luke 6.41-42/ *GTh* 26), whose 'authenticity' is differently evaluated by Funk, *Five Gospels* 153-54, 298, 488 (all versions 'awarded pink status'), and Lüdemann, *Jesus* 150 ('these verses have their context in the community and therefore [*sic*] do not go back to Jesus').

209. The parable is usually attributed to Jesus (see above, chapter 12 n. 211).

210. The use of *charizomai* to denote 'forgive' echoes its use in the little parable in Luke 7.42-43.

teaching on the subject.[211] Here too we should recall Luke's saying on forgiveness (Luke 6.37), which follows immediately on his version of the saying which brings Jesus' teaching on love of enemy (§14.5) to an end: 'Be merciful just as your Father is merciful' (6.36). What Matthew's version heard as the Father's *'perfection',*[212] Luke's version heard as the Father's *mercy,* no doubt with the paradigmatic theologoumenon of Exod. 34.6-7 very much in the background.[213]

At this point it is futile to debate as to whether Jesus envisaged divine forgiveness as conditional on human forgiveness or saw human forgiveness as the consequence of divine forgiveness.[214] The teaching was no doubt heard with both emphases. Unforgiving disciples need to be warned of what it is they actually pray in the Lord's Prayer: to refuse forgiveness is to invite judgment.[215] But it is equally, if not more important to realize that the motivation to forgive depends on the awareness of having needed forgiveness oneself and of having been so generously forgiven. The will to forgive springs from the experience of forgiveness, the generosity of forgiveness offered from gratitude at forgiveness received.[216] The alternative is a sequence of relationships eroded from within by

211. Wright, *Jesus* 294-95, and McKnight, *New Vision* 224-27, refer specifically to the jubilee tradition (cancellation of debts, Lev. 25.10; Isa. 61.1; cf. Luke 4.16-30), connected with both the return from exile and forgiveness (Isa. 40.1-2; Jer. 33.7-8; Ezek. 36.24): 'Jesus expected his followers to live by the Jubilee principle among themselves . . . that they should forgive one another not only "sins" but also debts' (Wright 295). See more fully S. H. Ringe, *Jesus, Liberation, and the Biblical Jubilee* (Philadelphia: Fortress, 1985) 65-80; M. Barker, 'The Time Is Fulfilled: Jesus and Jubilee', *SJT* 53 (2000) 22-32.

212. But Matthew has already stressed the importance of the disciple being merciful (Matt. 5.7); *oiktirmones* (Luke 6.36) forms a hendiadys with *eleēmones* (Matt. 5.7), as Exod. 34.6 shows (see further e.g., R. Bultmann, *oiktirō, TDNT* 5.160). And by God's 'perfection' Matthew evidently understood God's generosity (5.45-47); NEB/REB translate, 'There must be no limit to your goodness, as your heavenly Father's goodness knows no bounds'; see further particularly Betz, *Sermon on Mount* 321-25. On 'imitating God' see also Schnackenburg, *Sittliche Botschaft* 85-86.

213. *Did.* 1.4-5, with the same sequence of teaching, shows that the concept of being 'perfect' *(teleios)* was being understood by the tradents of the Jesus tradition in terms of generosity. Contrast the 'perfection' of complete obedience required at Qumran (1QS 1.7-15).

214. The same unclarity is present in the conclusion to Luke 7.36-50: Jesus says of the woman that 'her sins, which are many, are forgiven, for she loved much; but he who is forgiven little, loves little' (7.47). Cf. NEB/REB's translation: 'I tell you, her great love proves that her many sins have been forgiven; where little has been forgiven, little love is shown'; Schrage, *Ethics* 39; and see further C. F. D. Moule, '". . . As we forgive . . .": a note on the distinction between desserts and capacity in the understanding of forgiveness', *Essays in New Testament Interpretation* 278-86.

215. Note already Sir. 28.2: 'Forgive your neighbour the wrong he has done, and then your sins will be pardoned when you pray'.

216. 'Forgiveness has been truly received only when it makes the heart forgiving'

the cancer of mistrust and the poison of unhealed sores. Jesus evidently saw clearly that a community can be healthy and outgoing only when forgiveness is regularly both given and received among its members. So it should be in the community of the kingdom of God.

14.7. A New Family?

In recent years much attention has been given to those passages in the Jesus tradition where Jesus seems to encourage his disciples to disown their families and to offer discipleship itself as a quasi-familial structure in which God is father and fellow disciples are brothers and sisters to whom primary loyalty should be given. The two most important texts are (a) Matt. 10.37/Luke 14.26/*GTh* 55, 101 and (b) Mark 3.20-21, 31-35 pars./*GTh* 99.

a. Luke 14.26

Matt. 10.37	Luke 14.26	*GTh* 55	*GTh* 101
He who loves father or mother more than me is not worthy of me; and he who loves son or daughter more than me <u>is not worthy of me.</u>	If anyone comes to me and <u>does not hate his father and mother,</u> wife and children, brothers and sisters, yes, and even life itself, he <u>cannot be my disciple.</u>	He who <u>does not hate his father and his mother will not be able to be my disciple;</u> and (he who does not) hate his brothers and his sisters and does not bear his cross as I have, will <u>not be worthy of me.</u>	He who <u>does not hate his fa[ther] and his mother</u> as (I do), <u>will not be able to be my</u> [disciple]. And he who does [not] love his [father and] his mother as I (do), will not be able to be my [disciple], for [my mother] . . . but in truth she gave me life.

There can be little doubt that Jesus said something like Luke 14.26: the shocking nature of the wording ('hate' — *miseō*) is confirmed by the *Thomas* parallels.[217] It is also likely that Matthew has softened a harsher-sounding saying (Q).[218] To

(Bultmann, *Theology* 1.24); 'One cannot be a recipient of forgiveness unless and until one is an agent of forgiveness. It's as simple as that and as difficult as that' (Funk, *Honest to Jesus* 213).

217. Perrin, *Rediscovering* 141; Funk, *Five Gospels* 174-75, 353; Becker, *Jesus* 309-10; Lüdemann, *Jesus* 362; 'all but universally credited to Jesus' (Davies and Allison, *Matthew* 2.221). Further detail in Fitzmyer, *Luke* 1060-64; Charlesworth, *Jesus* 84-89.

218. It looks as though Matthew has added the phrase 'is not worthy of me' to 10.37, to increase the parallel with Matt.10.38 (*axios* is a thematic term for Matthew in this chapter —

be noted also are the reports that those called by Jesus 'left' their occupations and father — the fishermen brothers (Mark 1.18, 20 pars.) and Levi/Matthew (Mark 2.14 pars.) — and the equally shocking (?) nature of the call to follow in Luke 9.57-62/Matt. 8.19-22.[219] These can then be juxtaposed with a set of mission instructions which send out the missionaries with minimal personal supplies and dependent on hospitality (Mark 6.8-10 pars.).[220] From all these ingredients a potent brew can be quickly mixed to conjure up a picture of discipleship as renunciation of normal life (work and relations) for a kind of charismatic or Cynic vagabondry.[221]

But there are too many elements omitted from the recipe for the brew to be acceptable, at least in such stark terms: (1) We have already noted that Jesus made his 'home' at Capernaum (§9.9d),[222] which he evidently used as a base for mission outreach, not least to places like Chorazin and Bethsaida. (2) We have also observed that in practical terms, mission 'throughout all Galilee' need not have meant more than a sequence of one or two days travel from a centre like

---

note also 10.10-13) (*GTh* 55.2 agrees with Matt. 10.38 at this point, rather than Luke 14.27); he has also set out 10.38 in parallel clauses in a way which matches 10.39/Luke 17.33. Only Luke has the saying: 'So, therefore, whoever of you does not renounce all that he has cannot be my disciple' (14.33), consistent with his emphasis elsewhere (see above, §13.4b).

219. But how shocking were they? See above, §§13.2c-d and 14.4h.

220. It is difficult to tell how much these instructions have been 'worked over' as they were used and reused in many missionary commissionings in the early churches in different territories and social settings (see above, chapter 7 n. 96). But they certainly fit the context of mission in the Galilee, and there need be no doubt that they took their initial shape in that context.

221. 'Total lack of security' (Hengel, *Charismatic Leader* 5); 'an existence on the fringes of normal life . . . homeless charismatics' (Theissen, 'Wandering Radicals' 40; similarly 'We Have Left Everything' 62, 83-85); 'itinerant radicalism' (Crossan, *Historical Jesus* 346); 'itinerant, en route, without a home' (Gnilka, *Jesus* 169). In more modest terms by S. C. Barton, *Discipleship and Family Ties in Mark and Matthew* (SNTSMS 80; Cambridge: Cambridge University, 1994) 63-64; C. Osiek and D. L. Balch, *Families in the New Testament World: Households and House Churches* (Louisville: Westminster John Knox, 1997) 126. A. D. Jacobson, 'Jesus against the Family: The Dissolution of Family Ties in the Gospel Tradition', in J. M. Asgeirsson, et al., eds., *From Quest to Q*, J. M. Robinson FS (BETL 146; Leuven: Leuven University, 2000) 189-218, protests against the prevailing 'radical therefore authentic' assumption and argues that the key sayings (Q 14.26; 12.51-53; 16.18 and perhaps 9.57b-60a) are inauthentic, probably creations of the early Jesus movement (191-99). He further hypothesises that the wandering preachers 'probably had begun to form fictive families in village settings' (199), functioning 'in much the same way as other families' (208, referring to Mark 10.29-30); this is 'mirror-reading' taken to extreme.

222. 'Mark 10.28, "We have left everything" . . . means primarily "we have placed everything in the service of the Jesus movement", not "we have given everything away"' (Schrage, *Ethics* 104-107; here 104-105).

Capernaum (§14.3b). The minimalist equipment in the mission instructions is much more appropriate for the length of journeys typical in Galilee than, say, for Paul's weeks-long journeyings across Asia Minor and round the Aegean.[223] Certainly any suggestion that Jesus and his disciples were constantly on the move, never settled anywhere for any length of time, is greatly exaggerated.[224] (3) And here again, as with Matt. 8.21-22/Luke 9.59-62 (§14.4h), we need to ask about Jesus' rhetoric.[225] Jesus was evidently not above using shock tactics to bring home to would-be disciples that such resolve required unqualified commitment, not least in the face of the eschatological crisis. Matthew's rendition may convey the principal point adequately, even if it loses the shock value of the 'hate' language.[226]

b. Mark 3.20-21, 31-35[227]

20And he came home; and the crowd came together again, so that they could not even eat. 21When those connected with him heard it, they went out to restrain him, for people were saying, 'He has gone out of his mind'. . . . 31Then his mother and his brothers came; and standing outside, they sent to him and called him. 32A crowd was sitting around him; and they said to him, 'Your

223. That the mission instructions agree (Mark 6.8 pars.) in forbidding those sent out to take a 'knapsack' *(pēra)* is noteworthy, since the *pēra* was so typical of the Cynic (e.g., Crossan, *Historical Jesus* 338-39; *Birth* 333-35).

224. Cf. the travel arrangements made by Essenes, at least according to Josephus, as they moved about among their various community centres (*War* 2.124-27).

225. Crossan speaks of the 'virulence' of the language, a 'rather savage attack on the family', but goes on to argue that Jesus would not have been attacking traditional peasant society; Jesus was 'speaking especially to those whose family had failed' (*Birth* 323-25). Barton notes the precedents in biblical and Jewish sources where 'allegiance to God and devotion to the will of God transcend family ties and legitimate their subordination' (*Discipleship* ch. 2). Arnal sees the language as hyperbolic, rhetorical statements designed to stress that the commitment called for must be unconditional (*Jesus* 174-77).

226. Manson agrees that Luke 14.26 is closer to the original words of Jesus ('a literal rendering'), but notes that in idiomatic use 'hate' could have the force of 'love less' (*Sayings* 131); similarly Hamerton-Kelly, *God the Father* 66; Flusser, *Jesus* 35 (referring to Gen. 29.30-33).

227. It looks as though Matthew and Luke have derived their accounts (Matt. 12.46-50; Luke 8.19-21) from Mark. But apart from the fact that both Matthew and Luke omit Mark 3.20-21, for obvious reasons, the variations introduced are not sufficiently significant to warrant including all three versions. *GTh* 99 abbreviates the teaching almost as much as Luke: 'The disciples said to him, "Your brothers and your mother are standing outside". He said to them: "Those here who do the will of my Father are my brothers and my mother; these are they who will enter the kingdom of my Father"'.

mother and your brothers and sisters are outside, looking for you'. [33]And he replied, 'Who are my mother and my brothers?' [34]And looking around at those who sat in a circle round him, he said, 'Here are my mother and my brothers! [35]Whoever does the will of God, that one is my brother and sister and mother'.

It is clear that Mark has deliberately heightened the contrast between those sitting round Jesus and his family. He opens the story with the account of 'those connected with him *(hoi par' autou)*'[228] concerned at Jesus' mental stability (3.20-21).[229] At that point he inserts his sequence of Jesus in controversy regarding his exorcisms (3.22-30),[230] thus associating the concerns of Jesus' family with the outright opposition of the scribes down from Jerusalem (3.22). The implication is that his family's fear concerning Jesus' mental stability is similar to the accusation that Jesus is an agent of Beelzebul (3.22) and causes them to seek to withdraw him from the public.[231] As already observed earlier, Mark also heightens the contrast by repeating the description of his family as 'outside *(exō)*' (3.31-32). Matthew and Luke both soften the contrast by omitting 3.20-21, abandoning the Markan sandwich, and omitting one of the *exōs*.[232]

Even when Mark's colouring of the episode has been discounted, however, a disturbing scene remains. But does it amount to Jesus' disowning his family? If Mark is right, their motivating concern was lest he was mentally disturbed, possibly acting as a deranged false prophet.[233] In that situation, Jesus' implied re-

228. *Hoi para tinos* denotes those closely connected with a person and so can mean 'family, relatives' (BAGD/BDAG *para* A3b; Taylor, *Mark* 236; Marcus, *Mark* 1.270); the problem is that no suitable single word for 'family' was available to Mark. That Mark intended to refer to Jesus' family is put beyond reasonable doubt by the sequel in 3.31-35.

229. Hamerton-Kelly argues for the translation 'And when those who were with him heard this [i.e., that the crowd was so thick that he had no chance to eat] they went out to restrain it [the crowd], for they said, it is out of control' (*God the Father* 64-65); but while that reading works with *krateō* ('restrain'), it is hardly plausible to refer *exestē* to the crowd ('it is out of its mind'); 'out of control' is a highly tendentious rendering.

230. This is an example of the well-known feature of the Markan sandwich, where other material is inserted between the two halves of the one story (as in Mark 5.21-43 and 11.12-25).

231. Barton, *Discipleship* 75.

232. Osiek and Balch think Luke has the most radical critique of marriage, though the suggestion that the tax collectors at Levi's feast are 'potentially a new fictive family' pushes too hard (*Families* 136-37), since Luke goes out of his way to portray Jesus dining with various people, including Pharisees (n. 256 below). But the beatitude of Luke 11.27-28/*GTh* 79 closely parallels Mark 3.33-35.

233. *Existēmi* usually denotes extreme mental perturbation (e.g., Gen. 27.33; 42.28; Exod. 19.18; 1 Sam. 13.7; Isa. 7.2; 13.8; 33.3; Ezek. 26.16, the LXX translating various Hebrew terms; see HR). But Isa. 28.7 uses it to describe priest and prophet reeling from strong

buke to them need not indicate a total breakdown of relationships with his family.[234] Mark 6.3-4 also indicates local disillusion with Jesus in his home village,[235] and in the final reference to his family includes them within the unbelieving response: Jesus 'marvelled because of their unbelief' (6.6).[236] But the fact that Mary his mother and his brothers are numbered with the disciples in Acts 1.14 hardly suggests a severe rupture.[237] Equally Mark 3.34-35 certainly seems to invite talk of Jesus' relations with his own family being replaced by relationships with his disciples.[238] But is there not a danger of making a theological mountain (the community of disciples as fictive family replacing all loyalty to birth family) out of the molehill of a vivid repartee on a particular occasion?[239] It is also true that Jesus elsewhere is recorded as promising to those who have left family and possessions to follow him, that the compensations of being part of a community of disciples will outweigh the loss (Mark 10.29-30

---

drink; Philo similarly uses it to describe the drunken-like effects of God-possession (*Ebr.* 146; cf. Acts 2.4, 13; Eph. 5.18); and *T. Job* 35.4; 36.6; and 39.13 use it for suspected derangement (probably on the basis of Job 36.28). Note also the parallel in John 10.20: 'he has a demon and is mad *(mainetai)*'.

234. Even when Mark's tendentious presentation is recognized (Barton, *Discipleship* 69-81) — though I am dubious about reading 'house' in Mark (7.17; 9.28, 33; 10.10) as implying new community in place of family dwelling (as distinct from place of private teaching) — Barton rightly warns against using the episode to press for more extreme conclusions (82-85). To acknowledge Markan redaction is to recognize that the *Sitz im Leben Jesu* was almost certainly less sharply confrontational. Lüdemann is convinced of the historicity of 3.21, but thinks that 3.35 reflects the later situation of converts who had been thrown out by their families and judges it to be not historical (*Jesus* 24-25).

235. Cited below (§15.6c).

236. Both Matthew and Luke again soften the sharpness, here by omitting 'among his relatives' and Luke also by omitting 'and in his house' (Matt. 13.57; Luke 4.24; also John 4.44). Barton concludes that both phrases were added by Mark (*Discipleship* 90); against Pesch, *Markusevangelium* 1.320-21. What this tells us about Mark's attitude to Jesus' family (Mark uses it 'to skewer the family of Jesus', Jacobson, 'Jesus against the Family' 206) is a subject to which we will have to return in vols. 2 and 3.

237. Note also John 7.3-10; 19.26-27.

238. Jesus 'called people away from the bondage of natural family relationships to a new family joined by faith in God freely given'; 'liberation must start as release from the cord of birth' (Hamerton-Kelly, *God the Father* 101-102, reading the tradition through the Oedipus complex); Osiek and Balch, *Families* 127-28; Funk, *Five Gospels* 53 (Matt. 12.48-50 is accorded greater credence than Mark's version — 190); 'Blood relationships are devalued in Jesus' idea of the family; his real family is the family of God' (Funk, *Honest* 197-99); 'Jesus speaks almost virulently against the family' (Crossan, *Historical Jesus* 299); 'the shocking demands for family disloyalty that he (Jesus) made on his followers' (Wright, *Jesus* 149; also 401-403, 430-32); Jacobson, 'Jesus against the Family' 203-204.

239. If we treated such sayings as Mark 10.15 pars. in the same way, we could conclude that the kingdom consists only of little children.

pars.).[240] But again we need to ask whether this amounts to saying that there can be no discipleship without renunciation of family and possessions.[241] Or is it simply an encouragement to those for whom discipleship did involve such a breach[242]

240.

Matt. 19.29	Mark 10.29-30	Luke 18.29-30
29 And everyone <u>who has left houses</u> <u>or brothers</u> or sisters or father or mother <u>or children</u> or fields, <u>for</u> my name's <u>sake,</u> will receive a hundredfold, and will inherit <u>eternal life.</u>	29 Truly I tell you, there is no one <u>who has left house</u> <u>or brothers</u> or sisters or mother or father <u>or children</u> or fields, <u>for</u> my <u>sake</u> and for the sake of the gospel, 30 who will not receive a hundredfold now in this time — houses, brothers and sisters, mothers and children, and fields, with persecutions — and in the age to come <u>eternal life.</u>	29 Truly I tell you, there is no one <u>who has left house</u> or wife <u>or brothers</u> or parents <u>or children,</u> <u>for</u> the <u>sake</u> of the kingdom of God, 30 who will not get back very much more in this time, and in the age to come <u>eternal life.</u>

Note the typical performance variations. The saying is regularly regarded as a reflection of the aspirations of the later communities (Funk, *Five Gospels* 93; Lüdemann, *Jesus* 70), though it should be noted that Jesus himself provided the obvious template for the realisation of such aspirations. See also Jacobson, 'Jesus against the Family' 208 (above, n. 221).

241. Hengel consistently presses Matt. 8.21-22/Luke 9.59-60 in this direction: 'requires a break even with the strongest of human links, the family'; 'demands complete freedom from all family ties for the disciple'; 'breaking with one's own family' (*Charismatic Leader* 5, 13, 29-30, 33-35). But he also notes two prophetic precedents, Ezek. 24.15-24 and Jer. 16.1-4 (11-12; also 16-17). See further McKnight, *New Vision* 179-87, 193. And note again Bailey's cautionary observations (chapter 13 at n. 72 and chapter 14 n. 169).

242. Similarly with the Q(?) saying Matt. 10.34-36/Luke 12.51-53/*GTh* 16:

Matt. 10.34-36	Luke 12.51-53
34 Do not think that I came to cast <u>peace</u> on <u>the earth</u>; I came to cast not peace but a sword.

35 For I came to turn a person <u>against</u> his <u>father,</u> and a <u>daughter against</u> her <u>mother,</u>   and a <u>daughter-in-law against</u> her <u>mother-in-law</u>; 36 and a person's enemies will be the members of his household. | 51 Do you consider that I have come to bring <u>peace</u> in <u>the earth</u>? No, I tell you, but rather division! 52 For from now on five in one household will be divided, three against two and two against three; 53 they will be divided: father against son and son <u>against father,</u> mother against daughter and <u>daughter against mother,</u> mother-in-law   against   her   daughter-in-law   <u>and</u> <u>daughter-in-law against mother-in-law.</u> |

Note again the typical performance variations. If the tradition goes back to Jesus (it is soundly dismissed by Funk, *Five Gospels* 173-74 as contradicting Jesus' commendation of unqualified love, and by Lüdemann, *Jesus* 350 as reflecting later experience; but see further below, §17.4d), it simply draws on the eschatological expectation of severe and disruptive tribulation (references in Meier, *Marginal Jew* 3.111 n. 96), modelled no doubt by corporate memory of many family betrayals in the history of Israel's not infrequent crises, and particularly Mic. 7.6 (C. Heil, 'Die Rezeption von Micha 7,6 LXX in Q und Lukas', *ZNW* 88 [1997] 211-22; other references in Davies and Allison, *Matthew* 2.219-20). Such family disruption is thought of as an unavoidable consequence of the coming eschatological crisis (Mark 13.12-13 pars.), not as a necessary concomitant to discipleship (Allison, *End of the Ages* 118-20).

that there would be abundant compensation in the fellowship of 'the new eschatological family'?[243]

After all, it is Mark who also makes a point of including the story of Peter at home with his mother-in-law after he and Andrew had 'left their nets' to follow Jesus (Mark 1.29-31);[244] and we should perhaps recall that later on Peter would apparently go on mission accompanied by his wife (1 Cor. 9.4)! The mother of James and John is included among the women at the cross, as also the mother of (the other) James (Mark 15.40/Matt. 27.56).[245] Mark and Matthew recall Jesus as giving high priority to the commandment to honour one's parents (Mark 7.9-13/Matt. 15.3-6).[246] It is the Markan version of Jesus' teaching on divorce which teaches the indissolubility of the marriage bond (Mark 10.7-9).[247] All three Synoptists include the same commandment in Jesus' reply to the rich young man (Mark 10.19 pars.).[248] They also make a point of including stories where Jesus responds to the appeals of distraught parents on behalf of their children, thus in effect affirming the importance of the parental role and bond.[249] And we should perhaps also recall that the most vivid portrayal of conversion in the Jesus tradition, the parable of the prodigal son, depicts the son as returning to his father and to his family household (Luke 15.17-24).[250] Powerful though the imagery of discipleship as new family is, therefore, it should not be pressed into too sharp a contrast with responsibility to birth-

243. Note particularly Barton's cautioning remarks (*Discipleship* 106-107). To be noted also is the element of eschatological hyperbole: 'hundredfold . . . houses, mothers . . .'.

244. Barton observes that 'there is no sign of antipathy toward familial and occupational ties *per se* . . . (and) no indication that the leaving is to be a permanent state of affairs' (*Discipleship* 66). 'The centurion in Capernaum does not give up his property or profession' (Matt. 8.5-13) (Osiek and Balch, *Families* 133). J. Painter, 'When Is a House Not Home? Disciples and Family in Mark 3.13-35', *NTS* 45 (1999) 498-513, notes that the mission of Jesus depended on the hospitality of the households of his followers. See also Lohfink, *Jesus and Community* 39-44.

245. Was 'Salome' (Mark 15.40) 'the mother of the sons of Zebedee' (Matt. 27.56)?

246. See above, §14.4b.

247. Jesus' vision of a quite different post-resurrection existence, where no marriage is necessary (or possible?) (Mark 12.25 pars.), should not be set against the teaching here or counted as evidence for an anti-family attitude in the present.

248. Note that in the final exchange with the young man, the one thing lacking (to sell his possessions, give to the poor and follow Jesus, 10.21 pars.) is called for in addition ('one thing you lack') to the commandments of the second table of the decalogue (10.19 pars.), not in place of them.

249. Mark 5.21-24, 35-43 pars.; 7.25-30 par.; 9.14-29 pars.; see further J. Francis, 'Children and Childhood in the New Testament', in S. C. Barton, ed., *The Family in Theological Perspective* (Edinburgh: Clark, 1996) 65-85, particularly 72-75.

250. *Pace* Funk, who suggests that 'the prodigal mirrors the journey of Jesus; it has autobiographical overtones' (*Honest* 189).

family.[251] The Jesus tradition certainly resonates very positively with the imagery, but none of the stages of the Jesus tradition reflected in the Gospels (not even Mark) would validate pressing it to a necessary or unavoidable antithesis.

14.8. Open Fellowship

I have left this characteristic of discipleship to the last, not because it is of lesser importance than the rest, but because it sums up much that was both characteristic and distinctive of the social self-understanding that Jesus encouraged in his disciples. Two features in particular stand out: table-fellowship and absence of boundaries. They overlap, but it is worth attempting to give them separate treatment.

a. Table Fellowship

Jesus' practice of eating in company was clearly a regular and important feature of his mission. We have already noted that Jesus had a reputation for eating and drinking too much — 'a glutton and a drunkard' (Matt. 11.19/Luke 7.34).[252] We should hardly take such an accusation literally.[253] But presumably Jesus did spend a fair amount of time at the meal table, no doubt in conversation and teach-

---

251. It is unclear what Matt. 19.12 ('. . . there are eunuchs who have made themselves eunuchs for the sake of the kingdom of heaven') contributes to the discussion. It can certainly be attributed to Jesus (see particularly Davies and Allison, *Matthew* 3.22-25; Allison, *Jesus* 182-85) and could be taken as a piece of autobiography (without implication of literal self-castration) in partial explanation of why Jesus himself did not marry (e.g., Schrage, *Ethics* 93; Gnilka, *Jesus* 172-73), quite possibly as a jibe directed against Jesus by his critics (J. Blinzler, '*Eisin eunouchoi*. Zur Auslegung von Mt 19,12', *ZNW* 48 [1957] 254-70; F. J. Moloney, 'Matthew 19.3-12 and Celibacy', *JSNT* 2 [1979] 42-60 [here 50-52]; Meier, *Marginal Jew* 3.504-505, 507-508). But if so, is it more than a vivid expression of complete commitment to his mission (cf. Paul: 1 Cor. 7.32-35; 9.5, 12)? And is there any real indication that Jesus expected quite such an extreme expression of dedication from all his disciples (contrast 1 Cor. 9.5)? Allison pushes the evidence too hard (Matt. 19.10-12; 5.27-28; Mark 9.42-48 [chapter 12 n. 192]; 12.18-27) in arguing that Jesus can be understood as a 'millenarian ascetic' some of whose teaching 'reveals a deep alienation from the world as it is' (*Jesus* 172-216, quotation from 205). Nor should Matt. 23.9 ('Call no man your father on earth') be cited here (*pace* Gnilka, *Jesus* 201-202; cf. Barton, *Discipleship* 130). As Barton notes (215 n. 294), what is in view is not household authority but teaching authority (see also Davies and Allison, *Matthew* 3.276-77).

252. Cited above, §12.5c; and see also §13.5.

253. 'An urban partygoer', 'the proverbial party animal' (Funk, *Honest* 192, 208). Jeremias argues that the denigration of Jesus is derived from Deut. 21.20 and 'stigmatizes him on the strength of this connection as a "refractory and rebellious son", who deserved to be

ing.[254] A particular criticism was that 'he ate with tax-collectors and sinners'.[255] It is also worth noting that of the several criticisms attributed to Pharisees, four have to do with matters of table-fellowship or eating practices: eating with the religiously unacceptable (n. 255), feasting rather than fasting (Mark 2.18 pars.), plucking grain (Mark 2.23-24 pars.), and eating with defiled (= unwashed) hands (Mark 7.5/Matt. 15.2). In contrast, Luke in particular makes a point of recalling how often Jesus accepted invitations to 'dine out'.[256]

Luke also implies that Jesus' action as host, in blessing the bread and breaking it, had become a familiar act by which he could be recognized.[257] The same feature may indeed be at the heart of the event recalled in the tradition as the feeding of the five thousand (Mark 6.32-44 pars.): Jesus 'took the five loaves . . . blessed them, broke them, and gave them to his disciples . . .' (Mark 6.41 pars.).[258] However much the memory has been elaborated in the retelling, the story as it has reached us was most probably based on the memory of a meal in a barren area seen to have symbolic significance from the first.[259] It is significant for the same reason that all Evangelists agree that Jesus' final time with his disciples was spent in fellowship at the meal table — the last supper (Mark 14.22-25 pars.). That shared meals were a feature of the earliest Jerusalem community from the first (according to Luke) presumably implies that this practice was a carry-over from their time with Jesus.[260]

Here we need simply to recall also how Jesus used the already familiar im-

---

stoned' (*Parables* 160). Fitzmyer points out that the Greek used here *(phagos kai oinopotēs)* scarcely reflects the LXX *(symbolokopōn oinophlygei) (Luke* 681), though H. C. Kee, 'Jesus: A Glutton and a Drunkard', *NTS* 42 (1996) 374-93, questions the importance of the observation (390-91). The phrase more likely echoes Prov. 23.20-21 ('the drunkard [*methusos*] and the glutton [*pornokopos*] will become poor'), where the same Hebrew is used as in Deut. 21.20 *(zolel w^esobe'),* 'the point being that Jesus is considered a fool' (BDAG, *oinopotēs*).

254. Some teaching is specifically related to the context of the meal table (Mark 2.15-17 pars.; 6.30-44 pars.; 14.3-9 pars.; 14.17-25 pars.; Luke 7.36-50; 10.38-41; 11.37-52; 14.1-24; 24.36-49). But it is highly probable that much more teaching whose particular context of first delivery has not been attached to the tradition was delivered in that context. Trocmé believes that 'most of the parables were part of the conversation at meals in the houses where Jesus had been invited' *(Jesus* 91).

255. Mark 2.15-16 pars.; Matt. 11.19/Luke 7.34; Luke 15.1-2; 19.10. See again above, §13.5.

256. Mark 2.15-16; 14.3; Luke 5.29; 7.36; 10.38; 11.37; 13.26; 14.1, 12; 19.5-7.

257. Luke 9.16; 24.30-31, 35. Was this a detail which Luke gleaned from his eye-witnesses (Luke 1.2)?

258. The actions are, of course, typical at the beginning of a Jewish meal, but the Lukan references alluded to in the preceding note suggest a cherished memory.

259. See further below, §15.7f.

260. Acts 1.4; 2.46; note also 20.7, 11; 1 Cor. 10.14-22; 11.17-34; Jude 12. Perrin argues similarly *(Rediscovering* 104-105).

agery of the banquet or wedding feast as an image for life in the coming king-dom.[261] Once again, even if the motif has been elaborated in the (re)telling, there should be little doubt that Jesus' own teaching had provided his disciples with the motif in the first place. And equally there need be little doubt that Jesus' own practice had been of a piece with that teaching.[262]

In a day when much of Western society seems to have lost the sense of the importance of family and communal meals, it is important to remind ourselves of the importance of the principle and practice of hospitality in the ancient world, and particularly of the religious and social significance of the meal table in the Ancient Near East. The ideal had long since been characterized in the Greek leg-end of Philemon and Baucis.[263] In Jewish thought Abraham and Job were ex-tolled as the models of hospitality, where again it was precisely the sharing of food which was the expression of that hospitality.[264] And the same social eti-quette is assumed in Jesus' mission instructions (particularly Luke 10.7/*GTh* 14.2).[265] Jeremias has expressed this significance of the meal table well:[266]

> . . . to invite a man to a meal was an honour. It was an offer of peace, trust, brotherhood and forgiveness; in short, sharing a table meant sharing life. . . . In Judaism in particular, table-fellowship means fellowship before God, for the eating of a piece of broken bread by everyone who shares in the meal brings out the fact that they all share in the blessing which the master of the house has spoken over the unbroken bread.[267]

261. See above, §12.4f.; also M. Trautmann, *Zeichenhafte Handlungen Jesu* (FB 37; Würzburg: Echter, 1980) 161-62 (with bibliography).

262. Becker insists that Jesus' table-fellowship should not be regarded as merely antici-patory of what has not yet happened; it was 'the realization of the coming Kingdom of God' (*Jesus* 160-61).

263. Ovid, *Metamorphoses* 8.613-70.

264. Abraham in Genesis 18; Philo, *Abr.* 107-14; Josephus, *Ant.* 1.196; *1 Clem.* 10.7; probably Heb. 13.2. Job in *T. Job* 10.1-3; 25.5; 53.3. See further those cited in my *Romans* 744.

265. It is primarily on the basis of these texts (plus Mark 6.10) that Crossan bases his very strong judgment that 'the heart of the original Jesus movement (was) a shared egalitarian-ism of spiritual and material resources', 'open commensality' (*Historical Jesus* 341-44, 261-64).

266. Jeremias, *Proclamation* 115. He cites appositely 2 Kgs. 25.27-30 (par. Jer. 52.31-34) and Josephus, *Ant.* 19.321.

267. Barrett, *Jesus* 50, appositely cites W. R. Smith, *The Religion of the Semites* (1901): 'Every stranger whom one meets in the desert is a natural enemy, and has no protection against violence except his own strong hand or the fear that his tribe will avenge him if his blood be spilt. But if I have eaten the smallest morsel of food with a man, I have nothing further to fear from him; "there is salt between us", and he is bound not only to do me no harm, but to help and defend me as if I were his brother . . .' (269-70). See also Bailey, *Through Peasant Eyes* 14-15;

It is this significance of the meal table which explains why table-fellowship was such a sensitive issue at the time of Jesus and thereafter. To eat with another was a mark of acceptance of that other. To eat regularly with another was to forge and express a special bond of fellowship. By the same token, to refuse table-fellowship was to deny the acceptability of the other. Table-fellowship functioned as a social boundary, indicating both who was inside the boundary and who was outside.[268] This significance is particularly clear in the cases of two of the principal sects/brotherhoods at the time of Jesus — the Pharisees and Essenes.

The importance of table-fellowship for the Pharisees is one of the issues between Neusner and Sanders referred to in §9.3a above. Neusner observed early on how many of the pre-70 rabbinic traditions attributed to the houses of Hillel and Shammai deal directly or indirectly with the purity of food, its preparation and preservation.[269] Sanders protested at what he regards as a complete over-statement.[270] But the supporting evidence is too strong for Neusner's claim to be discounted entirely. We have already noted the consensus that the Pharisees were a purity sect (§9.3a), and purity concerns came to focus no more sharply than at the meal table.[271] And we also noted above how many of the criticisms of Jesus attributed to Pharisees in the Jesus tradition relate to common meals. There is a question which we may never be able to resolve completely as to whether such concerns were shared only by a sub-group within the larger body of Pharisees — the *haberim* ('associates'). But it is very difficult to distinguish Pharisees and *haberim*,[272] and it may be that the latter term indicates simply the characteristic praxis of Pharisees.[273]

---

and further J. Bolyki, *Jesu Tischgemeinschaften* (WUNT 2.96; Tübingen: Mohr Siebeck, 1998) 177-204.

268. Cf. especially Saldarini, *Pharisees,* particularly 212-16. Jews today would be among the first to observe that it is precisely at the meal table that the current different forms of Judaism come to clearest expression. The rules one follows in regard to the meal table show what kind of Jew one is.

269. Neusner, *Politics* 86, referring to his more detailed study *Rabbinic Traditions.*

270. Sanders, *Jewish Law* 166-236; here Hengel and Deines agree with Sanders's criticism of Neusner's overstatement, but warn in turn against overreaction ('Sanders' Judaism' 43).

271. It should cause no surprise that the popular literature of the period emphasized the hero's/heroine's faithfulness in the matter of the meal table (Dan. 1.13-16; 10.3; Tob. 1.10-12; Jdt. 12.2, 19; Add. Esth. 14.17; *Jos. Asen.* 7.1; 8.5).

272. Sanders, *Jesus and Judaism* 187; *Jewish Law* 154-55, 250. See also Schürer, *History* 2.398-400; Westerholm 13-15; the careful discussion in Saldarini, *Pharisees* 216-20; and Hengel and Deines's critique of Sanders ('Sanders' Judaism' 38-39 n. 96).

273. See further my *Partings* 109-11; also 'Jesus, Table-Fellowship, and Qumran', in J. H. Charlesworth, ed., *Jesus and the Dead Sea Scrolls* (New York: Doubleday, 1992) 254-72 (here 257-60).

Whatever the precise details, it would appear that Jesus' practice of table-fellowship was a bone of contention between Jesus and his chief critics. The issue highlights what was evidently a marked difference in attitude on the point. Many Pharisees saw their practice of table-fellowship as characterizing Israel set apart to Yahweh,[274] as therefore requiring separation from anything which would threaten that holiness, and as therefore requiring separation from the impure, the non-observant, the sinner, precisely at and by means of the meal table.[275] Jesus in contrast enacted an *open* table-fellowship:[276] he himself was open to invitations from a wide range of people; he was notorious for eating with tax-collectors and sinners. Holiness for Jesus, we might say, was not a negative, excluding force, but a positive, including force.[277] According to Mark 2.17 in context, Jesus likened his practice of eating with sinners to the doctor's activity in healing the sick. And in so acting out this conviction he inducted his disciples into the practice as part of their discipleship.

Our evidence indicates that the Qumran Essenes were even more strict in their maintenance of the purity of the meal table. The daily meal required purification beforehand; it began and ended with prayer and was eaten in reverential silence; the garments worn at the meal were like 'holy vestments'; only after a rigorous novitiate was the would-be covenanter permitted to touch 'the common food'.[278] In striking parallel with the Jesus tradition reviewed above, the Qumran covenanters evidently saw their daily meal to be a foretaste of the eschatological banquet in the presence of the royal Messiah.[279]

In striking contrast with Jesus, however, the Qumran community, even more rigorously than the Pharisaic *haberim,* saw it to be imperative that all who

274. See above, §9.3a.

275. Ps. 1.1 itself would be sufficient warrant for such a policy.

276. 'Table-fellowship is putting into practice the openness of which the parables speak' (Becker, *Jesus* 150).

277. Borg, *Conflict* 134-36, but more widely applicable in his thesis (particularly 82-99); independently K. Berger, 'Jesus als Pharisäer und frühe Christen als Pharisäer', *NovT* 30 (1988) 231-62, suggested that 'the concept of offensive holiness/purity is an essential building block for understanding the conflict of Jesus with the Pharisees' (246-47); Chilton in turn speaks of Jesus' 'contagious purity/holiness' (*Jesus' Baptism* 58-71); similarly S. McKnight, 'A Parting within the Way: Jesus and James on Israel and Purity', in B. Chilton and C. A. Evans, *James the Just and Christian Origins* (Leiden: Brill, 1999) 83-129 (here 94-98).

278. Josephus, *War* 2.129-33, 138-39; now confirmed by the Rule of the Community (1QS 6). Josephus also notes that even the expelled member of the community was still bound by his oath; he was 'not at liberty to partake of other men's food', and so often died of starvation (*War* 2.143).

279. This is indicated by the parallels between the rules for the daily meal (1QS 6) and the description of the eschatological meal in which the Messiah of Israel was expected to participate (1Q28a [1QSa] 2).

were unclean should be excluded from their assembly. The matter is referred to several times in the extant DSS and was obviously crucial for them.[280] Particularly specified is anyone 'paralysed in his feet or hands, or lame *(psh)*, or blind *('wr)*, or deaf, or dumb, or smitten in his flesh with a visible blemish *(mwm)'*. Such are to be excluded because the angels of holiness are present in the congregation (1Q28a [1QSa] 2.3-10). The list evidently echoes Lev. 21.17-24, the list of categories excluded from the priesthood,[281] and reminds us that Qumran saw itself as a priestly or cultic community.[282] The point of interest here is that Luke has preserved a tradition where Jesus stresses the importance of hosts inviting to their meals 'the poor, the maimed *(anapeirous)*, the lame *(chōlous)*, and the blind *(typhlous)'* (Luke 14.13, 21). In context the implication is that such behaviour would be surprising to contemporary etiquette and quite possibly offensive to certain religious sensibilities. In fact, the closeness of Luke's terminology to that used at Qumran[283] suggests quite strongly that Jesus gave his exhortation with Qumran in view.[284] At any rate, the tradition which came down to Luke appears to have been formulated with that contrast in mind. Either way, Jesus was remembered as deliberately posing his vision of open table-fellowship in direct antithesis to the ideal practised at Qumran.[285]

Here then is a further point of clear distinctiveness distinguishing the dis-

280. 1Q28a [1QSa] 2.3-10; 1QM 7.4-6; 4QCD[b] (cited by J. T. Milik, *Ten Years of Discovery in the Wilderness of Judaea* [SBT 26; London: SCM, 1959] 114); 11QT 45.12-14.

281. Say to Aaron, 'None of your descendants throughout their generations who has a blemish *(mwm)* may approach to offer the bread of his God. For no one who has a blemish shall draw near, a man blind *('wr)* or lame *(psh)*, . . . or a man who has an injured foot or an injured hand . . .' (Lev. 21.17-21).

282. See further above, chapter 13 n. 124.

283. The Greek *chōlos* is the unvarying LXX translation for the Hebrew *psh*, and *typhlos* likewise of *'wr*. *Anapeiros* is a variant form of *anapēros*, which denotes physical disability of an unspecified kind. Whoever put Luke 14 into its present form, therefore, may well have intended *anapeiros* to serve as an appropriate equivalent to *hgr*, 'crippled, maimed' (1QM 7.4; 4QCD[b]), or possibly *mwm*, 'blemish' (Lev. 21.17-18; 1Q28a/1QSa 2.5; 1QM 7.4), since physical impairment is clearly in view in the DSS texts at least. See further my 'Jesus, Table-Fellowship, and Qumran' 265-67.

284. Other possible allusions to Essene self-understanding and practice are the reference to 'the sons of light' in Luke 16.8 (Flusser, *Jesus* 94) and the Sabbath dispute referred to in n. 110 above (Charlesworth, *Jesus* 65-67); see also above, n. 194, and the review of the discussion of possible points of contact between Jesus and the Dead Seas Scrolls by J. H. Charlesworth, 'The Dead Sea Scrolls and the Historical Jesus', in Charlesworth, ed., *Jesus and the Dead Sea Scrolls* 1-74; W. O. McCready, 'The Historical Jesus and the Dead Sea Scrolls', in Arnal and Desjardins, eds., *Whose Historical Jesus?* 190-211; H. Lichtenberger, 'Jesus and the Dead Sea Scrolls', in Charlesworth and Johns, eds., *Hillel and Jesus* 389-96.

285. 'In the Judaism of that day one can hardly imagine a more obvious contrast to the table-fellowship of Jesus' (Becker, *Jesus* 161).

cipleship to which Jesus called from the other patterns of Israel's restoration theology. Pharisees and Essenes both pursued, with differing degrees of strictness, an ideal which required that those concerned for Israel's holiness and restoration should not only maintain a high level of purity themselves but should also, as a necessary corollary, hold themselves apart from others whom they regarded as impure. The rigour with which they practised this ideal is admirable in its devotion and self-discipline. Jesus, however, is consistently remembered as seeing things differently. The ideal of the kingdom which he promoted was one more motivated by concern for others in their various disabilities, a community marked more by such mutual concern than by the law strictly interpreted and rigorously enforced. What for many Pharisees and Essenes was a sinful disregard for covenant ideals was for Jesus an expression of the good news of the kingdom.

b. Absence of Boundaries

The point emerging above highlights a remarkable feature of the discipleship to which Jesus called. As with his initial call to 'the poor' (§13.4) and to 'sinners' (§13.5), so with the character of discipleship for which his own practice provided the template. Whereas others sought to protect Israel's special status before Yahweh by drawing tighter boundaries round the people of promise, Jesus sought to break down these boundaries and to create a fellowship which was essentially open rather than closed. His open table-fellowship, so much both constituting and characterizing the community which practised it, made the point more clearly than any other aspect of his mission. How far the point can be pressed is less clear. Presumably Jesus had meals alone with his disciples which were of a private nature and not obviously open,[286] and presumably also the last supper (Mark 14.22-25 pars.) was not an isolated occasion.[287] But otherwise the fact that the Synoptic Evangelists have made so little attempt to depict Jesus using shared meals as opportunities to give his disciples private instruction[288] both indicates that the predominant memory in the Jesus tradition was of the openness of Jesus' table-fellowship and implies that even by the time of the Synoptic Evangelists there was no great wish to contradict that im-

286. Are such meals hinted at in Mark's references to Jesus and his disciples having no time to eat (3.20; 6.31)?

287. Note again, however, that the 'houses' into which Jesus was able to slip every so often were for private teaching (n. 234 above); no mention is made of eating together in such houses.

288. The tradition of Mark 14.3-9 is confused at just this point. Other than the occasions listed above (n. 254) only the last supper (much elaborated in the Fourth Gospel) and Luke 24.36-49 could be so classified.

pression. Unlike both Pharisees and Qumranites, table-fellowship was not fenced around to mark off the insiders from the outsiders. There was no purity barrier to be surmounted before one could enjoy Jesus' company and listen to him.

This inference and its implications become all the stronger when we recall the even more 'thunderous silence' in the Gospels regarding any practice of *baptism* by Jesus. As we saw earlier (§11.3a), baptism was a practice initiated by John the Baptist. And in his hands it formed a preparatory gateway which by passing through one prepared for the baptism of the one to come. It formed a rite of passage, analogous in function, despite its once-only administration, to the purificatory baths necessary for membership of the Qumran community and prior to members' participation in the common meal. At the other end of Jesus' mission, at the very beginning of the post-Easter community, baptism reemerges — and again as an indispensable rite of passage for those committing themselves to the new community.[289] But in between, we hear absolutely nothing about any baptismal rite being administered by Jesus. And even if Jesus, or at least his disciples, did maintain John's baptismal practice for the period of overlap with the Baptist's mission (§11.2b), the clear implication is that he or they ceased the practice when Jesus began his own distinctive Galilean mission (which is where the Synoptics pick up the story).

Some have recently argued that Jesus himself did baptize and in fact continued to baptize throughout his mission.[290] But on this hypothesis, the complete silence of the Synoptic tradition regarding Jesus' continued baptismal practice is quite simply baffling. There are many episodes in which some reference could have been inserted — as in Jesus' reply to the rich young man (Mark 10.21 pars.). And one might well assume that those performing the tradition in the company of the baptized would have been happy to insert several such references in order to underline the continuity between their own practice and that of Jesus. In fact, the only reason given for the post-Easter groups' subsequent baptismal practice is that it was received as a command from the risen Lord, and that is how the authorisation of Christian baptism is remembered.[291] Since the first Christians trace their practice to a post-Easter revelation and since the only hint that Jesus may have continued John's practice for a time (John 4.2) is quickly refuted, we have little choice but to conclude that Jesus himself did not baptize during the bulk of his mission, that is, the mission recorded by the Synoptic Evangelists.

289. Acts 2.38, 41; 8.12-13, 16, 36; etc. 1 Cor. 12.13; Heb. 6.2; 1 Pet. 3.21.
290. R. T. France, 'Jesus the Baptist?' in Green and Turner, eds., *Jesus of Nazareth* 94-111 (here 105-107); Meier, *Marginal Jew* 2.126-29, 166-67; Taylor, *Immerser* 294-99.
291. Matt. 28.19; otherwise the longer ending added to Mark (16.16). See further vol. 2.

But if that is so, then the question Why did Jesus *not* baptize? becomes of pressing relevance. Jesus' mission fits neatly between two missions marked out by the practice of baptism (the Baptist's and the post-Easter Jerusalem community of his followers), with lines of influence and continuity linking all three. But on this point Jesus' mission is distinct. Why? In the light of our findings regarding Jesus' table-fellowship, one answer obviously commends itself. That Jesus did not baptize for the same reason that he did not fence his table-fellowship with purity restrictions. Even baptism could form too much of a ritual barrier, excluding those not (yet) prepared to undergo it for whatever reason. No less than the Baptist, Jesus called for repentance (§13.2a). But the repentance he looked for expressed itself not in terms of baptism, but in acts of loving concern (Mark 10.21 pars.) and restitution for wrong-doing (Luke 19.8).

The point need not and should not be pressed too much, to argue, for instance, that Jesus was anti-ritualistic. The tradition of the last supper is sufficient counter on that issue (Mark 14.12-25 pars.). And if Jesus did indeed call for the highest loyalty from his disciples (as implied above all by Luke 14.26), then it can scarcely be denied that such loyalty has an exclusive side to it. Nevertheless a circle of discipleship which acknowledged its centre in Jesus could be said characteristically to look *outward* rather than *inward*. Any dispute regarding questions of status and hierarchy was roundly rebuked by Jesus: the model of discipleship is precisely *not* the stratified hierarchy of typical social organisations and national structures.[292] Conversely, any attempt to control access to Jesus[293] or to withhold recognition from another 'because he was not one of us' (Mark 9.38-39/Luke 9.49-50) seems to have met with Jesus' equally strong rebuke. Such a persistent note of a fellowship which is characteristically open and never simply preoccupied with its own affairs is hard to escape and should be given more weight than has usually been the case in Christian questing for Jesus.

14.9. Living in the Light of the Coming Kingdom

The tradition reviewed in the last two chapters could be sliced, tweaked, and expanded in many ways. But enough has been said to give us a fair idea of the

292. Mark 9.33-37 pars.; 10.35-45 pars. 'There is no suggestion of the twelve functioning as "priests" to others' "laity"' (Dunn, *Jesus' Call to Discipleship* 106). In Matthew the authority given to Peter to 'bind and loose' in Matt. 16.19 is given to 'the disciples'/'the church' (18.18). Matthew also includes an explicit warning against any attempts within the community to claim an authoritative status which infringes the authority exclusive to God and Christ (23.8-12).

293. Mark 10.13-14 pars.; Luke 7.39-50.

strong impression left by Jesus on his disciples in regard to what he expected from them.

a. His message of the kingdom oriented discipleship firmly by reference to God, God as both king and Father. Life was to be lived out of reverence for, fear before, trust in, and whole-hearted love for God. The generosity of God as Creator in bountiful provision, as the Lord who forgives unpayable debts, and as the Father who responds unfailingly to his children was also to be the pattern for Jesus' disciples. To give God first place would require a reorientation of any ambitions for social advance and wealth accumulation, a willingness to endure rejection and suffering, and, for some at least, disruption and renunciation of family life. In all this the eschatological note (chapter 12 above), while not always clearly evident, can usually be assumed as a reverberating echo-chamber in which the teaching was first heard. There are no real grounds for playing off 'sapiential' against 'eschatological' as motives for Jesus' ethical teaching.[294] The Creator is also the king, and the coming kingdom is always there as an integral presupposition. It would be merely playing games to oppose the 'first' of Matt. 6.33 ('Seek first the kingdom of God') to the 'first' (and 'second') of the love command(s) in Mark 12.28-31.

b. Jesus' message was directed to Israel. He called, as the prophets of old called, for his people to return to their Lord, but *now,* in view of the kingdom to come. The social values he preached were those long ago laid down in Torah and urged by prophet, particularly God's priority for the poor.[295] But he also protested against those whose claim to righteousness was divisive and dismissive of those who interpreted Torah righteousness in different terms. Characteristic of his fellowship was its openness to those normally regarded as unsuitable table companions. Not that he had much realistic hope of his message winning a widespread hearing. But neither did he speak in terms of a remnant, erect boundaries round his group, or turn his back on Israel, despite repeated frustration. His call was rather for his followers to *be* Israel, to live as Israel should before God.

c. The evidence gives little support for any suggestion that Jesus set out to renew local community[296] or to rebuild peasant community.[297] His teaching

---

294. Cf. Schrage, *Ethics* 30-37.

295. There are Cynic parallels, some close (chapter 13 n. 148; as elsewhere chapter 14 nn. 50, 195, 199), but they are better seen as parallel responses to equivalent situations in the Greco-Roman world rather than lines of influence. The Jewishness of Jesus is as clear here as anywhere.

296. Horsley, *Jesus* chs. 8-9 (above, §4.6b), though he is justified in characterizing Jesus' strategy in terms more of local community than of Theissen's wandering charismatics (228-40); similarly Herzog, *Jesus* 208-16.

297. Crossan, *Historical Jesus* 344; *Birth* 330-31; Crossan and Reed, *Excavating Jesus* 126.

amounts to no blueprint for a complete social order, such as one might construct from the Dead Sea Scrolls. The social divisions and economic hardship of the time are regularly reflected in the Jesus tradition. The rich are strongly counselled to beware of the dangers their wealth brings and to give willingly to the poor. But Jesus is not recalled as putting forward economic policies to reconstruct society and make it more just. Conversely, however, Jesus himself neither withdrew from 'society' nor encouraged his disciples to do so. We have noticed more than once that Jesus' teaching and conduct indicate considerable involvement in society.[298] Nor are there any grounds in Jesus' teaching for a clear distinction between private and public morality. On the contrary, principles are clearly enunciated 'across the board' — on societal topics like the importance of providing for the poor, Sabbath, purity, and divorce, on the primary importance of inward integrity and motivation from love of neighbour, on the dangers of rules being allowed to stifle such love, on service of others as the true measure of greatness — principles which certainly have an idealistic quality, but which can nevertheless serve as a yardstick by which both social policy and private morality might be measured.[299] Conversely, the warnings against taking the values of acquisitive society as any kind of pattern or norm for the community of discipleship are clear. Does all this qualify him for the epithet 'subversive sage', 'transformative sage'?[300] Why not? The prophetic protest has rarely unsettled too comfortable, too selfish society for very long. But Jesus' protest 'remains on the table' for any society willing to acknowledge that its ethos has been shaped by the Jesus tradition in any measure. The political edge of Jesus' teaching at this point should not be blunted.

d. Neither will we find a complete system of ethics in Jesus' teaching. Claims that he ignored or abrogated the law are at best exaggerated, at worst anti-Jewish. The principles he advocated were no less drawn from Torah than were the rules to which he objected. But his own ethical responses were more instinctual than systematic, taking account of the human element in the particular situation.[301] Like his vision of the kingdom to come (chapter 12 above), the ethos which he documented by word and action is episodic and illustrative. Nor, we should perhaps stress again, can his teachings be neatly allocated under the heading of personal ethics rather than social ethics. True, he spoke to and dealt with

298. A major weakness of Vermes's *Religion* is the failure to set Jesus' teaching in its sociopolitical context.

299. Cf. Theissen and Merz, *Historical Jesus* 370-72.

300. Borg, *Jesus* 116 (see also above, §4.7). Borg also accepts Horsley's description of Jesus as 'a social prophet', but distances himself from Horsley's elaboration, as in n. 296 above (*Jesus in Contemporary Scholarship* 105 and n. 24).

301. Cf. Keck: 'Jesus had a purpose, but he did not have a program' (*Who Is Jesus?* 156; see also 157-59).

people as individuals, but not as isolated individuals, and not as individuals without responsibilities to others in society, the poor as well as the neighbour, the socially and religiously marginalized as well as the individual sinner. Nor, finally, should we try to distinguish a 'disciple ethos' from a 'general ethos'.[302] As it proved impractical to distinguish 'disciples' from 'followers' (§§13.2-3) and to draw clear boundaries between different circles of discipleship (§13.8), so there are no grounds for arguing that Jesus looked for different levels of actualization of their discipleship. Not all might have to leave family and abandon possessions, but principled living, love of neighbour, and forgiving the fellow-disciple knew no such distinctions.

e. Did Jesus seek to establish a church? The question has such an anachronistic ring as to be almost not worth asking. But if by 'church' we mean the 'assembly' gathered before the Lord God, then it could be said that Jesus envisaged his disciples so functioning. Should we rather speak of a new family, that is of discipleship as a fictive family with God as Father and Jesus as eldest brother? Not if by that we mean a new social grouping by definition set over against and in antithesis with birth-families and other common social groupings. But if we mean by that a community bonded by 'brotherly love', distinguished by its openness to the marginalized, characterized by members putting themselves out for one another as one would for a beloved sister or brother and not by hierarchy, priestly craft, or power-play, then the concept would not be so far adrift from what Jesus seems to have hinted at.

In short, we could sum up Jesus' vision for the present as 'living in the light of the coming kingdom'. Not as an 'interim ethic', in Schweitzer's terms,[303] that is, as a radically idealistic ethic for the extraordinary conditions of the in-between time before the kingdom comes, nor as a means of bringing in the kingdom.[304] Nor as though the kingdom was already consummated and there was nothing more to look forward to: Jesus' disciples still have to pray, 'May your kingdom come'; the resurrection as envisaged in Mark 12.18-27 pars. has still to take place! But rather as the character of kingdom life, lived already here and now in anticipation of God's ordering of society when his will is done on earth as it is in heaven.[305] Not as living in a spiritual world, whether 'beyond time and space' or beyond the 'world's' reach; but as living in a sacramental universe, where the signs of God's providential care are everywhere to be recognized, learned from, and received with thankfulness. Not as a closed society, deter-

302. Merklein, *Jesu Botschaft* 128-31.

303. Schweitzer, *Mystery* 97; *Quest*[1] 352; *Quest*[2] 323, 454-56.

304. Schrage, *Ethics* 26-30.

305. Cf. A. E. Harvey, *Strenuous Commands: The Ethic of Jesus* (London: SCM, 1990) ch. 9, 'Living "As If"' (the kingdom were already a reality).

mined by rules and excluding boundaries, but as a community which seeks above all else God's priorities, in which forgiveness is experienced, which is often surprised by grace, and which knows well how to celebrate God's goodness in the openness of table-fellowship and love of neighbour.

PART FOUR

THE QUESTION OF JESUS' SELF-UNDERSTANDING

CHAPTER 15

Who Did They Think Jesus Was?

There is an undeniably controversial, even outrageous element in much of Jesus' mission, both his teaching and his conduct. We have been able to indicate something of the character of that element and to catch echoes of its offensiveness at several points in the last two chapters. In such a case it is impossible to concentrate exclusively on the teaching and the conduct itself and not to ask also about the man who so taught and who so lived.

15.1. Who Was Jesus?

Such a simple question. And yet with more potential to mislead a quester than any other. For one thing, the question plays on the assumption which has bedevilled so much talk of 'the historical Jesus' — that there is an entity 'back there' who is somehow independent of his disciples' response to him, but who is nevertheless recoverable by historical inquiry.[1] For another, the question quickly becomes entangled in definitions of identity, in confusion between being and doing, role and relationship. *Is* a person what he *does,* what he thinks and feels and hopes, or what he achieves? She is a daughter to one, sister to another, colleague to another, wife to another, mother to yet another. Which role defines *her* most accurately? Is *she* simply the sum of the roles she fills, of the relationships of which she is part?[2] I mention such issues only to underline the fact that simple questions may not be able to produce simple answers. Rather, by oversimplifying, simple questions can prevent rather than facilitate any quest for truth.

1. See above, §6.5.
2. I allude, of course, to the long-running debate regarding personhood and identity in the social sciences.

To re-pose the issue in terms of Jesus' self-understanding might seem to cut through some of these confusions. It is who *Jesus* thought he was that counts, surely. This is the assumption which has dominated for most of Christianity's history, even though the point is frequently made that personal identity does not necessarily depend on personal awareness of that identity. The pauper could be a prince without knowing it; to *be* who he was did not depend on Jesus *knowing* who he was. Even so, to this day such questions as whether Jesus was conscious of divine identity and personal pre-existence continue to be the subject of lively debate in many Christian circles.[3]

Within the quest such issues were more the concern of the nineteenth-century Liberals, as characterized by Schleiermacher's conception of Jesus' 'God-consciousness' and by the preoccupation with Jesus' 'messianic consciousness'.[4] The reaction, lasting through most of the twentieth century, has been to deny the possibility of gaining access to the self-consciousness of a historical person. And my own emphasis that the only historical Jesus accessible to us is the remembered Jesus would seem to strengthen that viewpoint. At the same time, however, the issue of Jesus' self-awareness has not gone away. For example, the issue was finessed by Robinson's attempt to define a new concept of history and the self,[5] and by the renewed interest in 'the aims of Jesus' sparked off by Meyer. The characterisations of Jesus in such terms as a 'charismatic vagrant' (Theissen), as a 'Mediterranean Jewish peasant' (Crossan), or as 'Rabbi Jesus' (Chilton) all carry implications for Jesus' own ideas of what he was about, even when the implications are not pursued. And Wright's bold thesis that Jesus 'saw his journey to Jerusalem as the symbol and embodiment of YHWH's return to Zion' poses the issue as sharply as ever.[6] My own emphasis on the impact made by Jesus also does not necessarily close off the road to Jesus' self-understanding. For the clearer the impression made, the clearer the object making the impression. And even were it the case that only a few sayings of Jesus had been transmitted as initially heard, particular sayings might well be taken to express a self-claim or self-understanding which still resonates in these sayings as handed down.[7] How far we can press down that line will become clearer as we proceed.

Initially, however, it makes best sense to ask the prior question: 'Who did *others* think Jesus was?' Not because we have clear testimony on the point from other than Jesus' own disciples; we have already observed more than once that

3. See, e.g., G. O'Collins, *Christology: A Biblical, Historical and Systematic Study of Jesus* (Oxford: Oxford University, 1995) ch. 10, particularly 234-49.

4. See above, chapter 4 at n. 49.

5. 'Jesus' understanding of his existence, his selfhood, and thus in the higher sense his life, is a possible subject of historical research' (*New Quest* 72).

6. Wright, *Jesus* 639.

7. See further my *Christology* 25-26.

the only testimony we have comes from or through those who responded positively to Jesus' mission. But Jesus' mission as so far described was bound to provoke those who heard his preaching and witnessed what he did to ask 'Who is this?' Who was this Galilean Jew who proclaimed the kingship of God soon to be fully realized, who called to committed discipleship, and who debated so effectively with Pharisees from Jerusalem? The question is recalled sufficiently often within the Jesus tradition for us to be confident that it was posed in one form or another at least at various junctures during his mission.[8] More to the point, there were several role models or categorizations which his audiences could use to make sense of what they heard and saw, depending on how they understood the categorizations and on how they 'heard' Jesus. Again, as we shall see, the Jesus tradition echoes with some of these categorizations at various points; so here too we can claim to be tracing and filling in the contours of the impact made by Jesus. Not least it will be of importance to ask how Jesus himself reacted to these possible role models and to any attempts to identify him with them.

15.2. Royal Messiah

We begin with the term most closely identified with Jesus at least from the time of Paul: Messiah = *Messias* = *Christos*. It is a familiar fact to any student of NT literature that *Christos* had become so attached to the name Jesus within about twenty years of his death that it functioned more or less as a personal name: Jesus Christ.[9] Nor can there be any doubt that behind this usage is the Christian claim that Jesus was 'the Christ', the Messiah. That claim had already become so familiar, so taken-for-granted among the first Christians that the titular sense was fast disappearing; Jesus as Messiah no longer functioned as a claim to be argued but simply as a fact to be assumed. That must mean that for the first Christians the claim that Jesus was indeed Messiah had been established from the first; they were distinguished precisely by the claim; they were 'Christ-ians', Messiah-ists. But when did the claim become established? Was it made already during Jesus' mission? And, not least, did Jesus himself make the claim, did he embrace a/the role which would have been recognized as 'messianic'? These are the issues which need to be resolved in what follows.[10]

8. Mark 1.27/Luke 4.36; Mark 6.2-3 pars.; 6.14-16 pars.; 8.27-28 pars.; 14.61 pars.; John 7.40-52; 9.16-17, 29-30; 10.19-21.

9. See my *Theology of Paul* 197-99. See also M. Hengel, 'Jesus, the Messiah of Israel', *Studies in Early Christology* (Edinburgh: Clark, 1995) 1-72 (here 1-15).

10. In what follows I will be drawing on my 'Messianic Ideas and Their Influence on the Jesus of History', in J. H. Charlesworth, ed., *The Messiah: Developments in Earliest Judaism and Christianity* (Minneapolis: Fortress, 1992) 365-81.

First, however, we need to pause and to remind ourselves that the confidence of an older generation which assumed a single, coherent, widespread Jewish hope for the coming of 'the Messiah' has long since been abandoned.[11] Talk of 'the messianic age', as of Jesus' 'messianic self-consciousness', traded on that assumption. But the discovery of the Dead Sea Scrolls and more careful analysis of the texts of the period have highlighted several important features. (1) Anointing was traditionally associated with three principal roles — king, priest, and prophet;[12] as we shall see, all three figures featured in Israel's eschatological expectation. (2) However, the term itself, 'Messiah' *(mašiaḥ),* 'anointed one', while variously used in the OT, predominantly in terms of a continuing Davidic line,[13] nowhere appears as the title for an eschatological figure.[14] (3) We have already noted (§12.2c) that a messianic figure was not integral to Israel's eschatological expectation, which was often expressed without reference or allusion to such a figure. (4) Where a messianic hope is articulated it is not always the same figure/role which is in view.[15] As we shall see, the hope of a royal Messiah was one of a more diverse hope, which featured also, or alternatively, a priestly and prophetic figures. Nevertheless, as we attempt to clarify the categories which Jesus' audience might have been expected to attempt to fit him into, it is the role of royal Messiah which calls for first attention.

11. E.g., O. Cullmann, *The Christology of the New Testament* (London: SCM, 1959) 111-12; Neusner, et al., eds., *Judaisms and Their Messiahs;* J. H. Charlesworth, 'From Messianology to Christology: Problems and Prospects', in Charlesworth, ed., *The Messiah* 3-35 (here 14). 'It was Primitive Christianity's exclusive concentration on Christ that first reduced this tradition to a single person' (Becker, *Jesus of Nazareth* 191-92). See also Schreiber's review of recent literature (*Gesalbter und König* 5-19).

12. (1) Predominantly the king (e.g., 1 Sam. 16.13; 2 Sam. 2.4, 7; 5.3, 17; Ps. 89.20): 'the Lord's anointed' (1 Sam. 24.6, 10; 26.9, 11, 16, 23; 2 Sam. 19.21; Pss. 2.2; 89.38, 51; 132.10); (2) the (high) priest (Exod. 28.41; 30.30; Lev. 4.3, 5, 16; 6.22; Dan. 9.25-26; note also 2 Macc. 1.10 and *T. Levi* 17.2-3); (3) occasionally a/the prophet (1 Kgs. 19.16; 1 Chron. 16.22; Ps. 105.15; Isa. 61.1-3); details in F. Hesse, *TDNT* 9.497-509; the concept of prophets anointed by the Spirit may have been more prominent at Qumran (CD 2.12; 6.1; 1QM 11.7; 4Q270 2.14).

13. S. Talmon, 'The Concepts of *Mašiaḥ* and Messianism in Early Judaism', in Charlesworth, ed., *The Messiah* 79-115: 'It must be emphasized that in practically all its occurrences, the noun *mašiaḥ* serves as a royal title' (87-93); similarly A. S. van der Woude, *TDNT* 9.509: in post-biblical Judaism as in the OT, '"the Lord's anointed" or "my, his anointed" is used only for a royal figure'.

14. J. J. M. Roberts, 'The Old Testament's Contribution to Messianic Expectations', in Charlesworth, ed., *The Messiah* 39-51 (here 51).

15. G. S. Oegema, *The Anointed and His People: Messianic Expectations from the Maccabees to Bar Kochba* (JSPSupp 27; Sheffield: Sheffield Academic, 1998) concludes that it is not possible to speak of a messianic 'idea' in Judaism or of a history of ideas in the development of messianic expectations. 'We can only locate its historical realizations, but not the idea itself' (306).

a. Jewish Expectation of a Royal Messiah

The roots of the expectation are clear. David had been promised a son who would secure his kingdom and throne for ever (2 Sam. 7.12-13, 16). This promise was picked up and echoed in the confidence that God would raise up a shoot from the stump of Jesse (Isa. 11.1-2), a royal 'branch' (Jer. 23.5; 33.15), a Davidic 'prince' (Ezek. 34.24; 37.25). How far the hope so expressed was eschatological or simply confidence for the continuation of the Davidic line is less clear.[16] The hope is still being voiced in the difficult times of the post-exilic period (Hag. 2.23; Zech. 3.8; 6.12), but thereafter fades, presumably with the disappearance of the Davidic line. John Collins, in one of the most recent assessments of the evidence, concludes that there is very little evidence of messianism in Judaism in the period 500-200 BCE.[17]

Equally, however, it is clear that the hope of a royal Messiah revived, presumably in conjunction with the reemergence of the reality of kingship in the Hasmonean period and its failure to realize the old hopes.[18] The most striking expression of the hope is in *Pss. Sol.* 17.21-24:

> See, Lord, and raise up for them their king, the son of David, to rule over your servant Israel in the time known to you, O God. Undergird him with the strength to destroy the unrighteous rulers, to purge Jerusalem from gentiles who trample her to destruction; in wisdom and in righteousness to drive out the sinners from the inheritance; to smash the arrogance of sinners like a potter's jar; to shatter their substance with an iron rod; to destroy the unlawful nations with the word of his mouth . . . *(OTP)*.

Very interesting is the further reference to this figure as 'their king . . . the Lord Messiah' (17.32; similarly 18.5-7).[19]

16. So also with 1 Sam. 2.10; Pss. 2.2, 6-9; 89.49-51; 132.10-18.

17. Collins, *Scepter and Star* 22-48, where the many exegetical issues are indicated in regard to the texts cited. W. Horbury, *Jewish Messianism and the Cult of Christ* (London: SCM, 1998) 13-31, 36-63 heavily qualifies the conclusion by arguing that 'Messianism [was] a deep-rooted and long-standing influence in the community at the beginning of the Second-Temple period' (25) and throughout the Second Temple period (63).

18. It is unclear whether the Dan. 9.25 reference to an 'anointed leader *(mašiaḥ nagid)*' refers to Zerubbabel or Joshua the high priest; the reference in 9.26 to the 'anointed one' being 'cut off' is probably to the murder of the high priest Onias III (2 Macc. 4.33-38); similarly Dan. 11.22; see further J. J. Collins, *Daniel* (Hermeneia; Minneapolis: Fortress, 1993) 355-56; Horbury, *Messianism* 7-12.

19. For the translation ('Lord Messiah') see R. B. Wright's footnote in *OTP* 2.667-68; otherwise M. de Jonge, *TDNT* 9.513-14 n. 107. Brock (in Sparks, *AOT* 679, 681) translates 'the anointed Lord' for 17.32, but 'the Lord's anointed' for 18.7, although accepting the consistency of the phrase *christos kyrios/christou kyriou.*

More striking still is the way the older hopes have been revived in the DSS. The promise of 2 Sam. 7.14 is taken up, probably in association with Ps. 2.7, in 4Q174 (4QFlor) 1.10-12.[20] The 'branch of David' and the Davidic 'prince' from Isaiah, Jeremiah, and Ezekiel reappear in a number of scrolls.[21] Equally striking is Qumran's expectation of two messianic figures, the messiahs of Aaron and Israel, that is, a priestly Messiah and a royal Messiah,[22] with the 'Messiah of Israel'[23] almost certainly to be identified as the royal Messiah.[24]

Moreover, if indeed the Psalter was given its canonical shape by about this time, then it is important to note that the royal messianic psalms (Psalms 2, 72, and 89) had been given key structural positions, thereby indicating that they were seen in some degree as a key to the psalter and its significance (a 'messianic Psalter').[25] And not least of interest is the prayer for 'the kingship of the house of David, thy righteous Messiah' in *Shemoneh 'Esreh* (the Eighteen Benedictions) 14.[26]

To be noted here is the common assumption that the royal Messiah would be a powerful ruler executing justice for all.[27] A frequent motif is his warlike character in rooting out evil and destroying Israel's enemies. 'You shall break

20. The scroll breaks off at what was probably the beginning of an interpretative reading of Psalm 2. See further W. M. Schniedewind, *Society and the Promise to David: The Reception History of 2 Samuel 7:1-17* (New York: Oxford, 1999), here 157-65.

21. 1QSb (1Q28b) 5.20; 1QM 5.1; 4Q161 (4QpIsa^a) 3.18; 4Q174 (4QFlor) 1.11; 4Q252 5.3-4; CD 7.19-20; 4Q285; see detail and further in Collins, *Scepter and Star* 57-73. Elsewhere note Sir. 47.22 (picking up Isa. 11.1) and 1 Macc. 2.57 (picking up 2 Sam. 7.13, 16).

22. 1QS 9.11; cf. CD 12.23–13.1; 14.19; 19.10-11; 20.1. On the likelihood that CD's phrase ('Messiah of Aaron and Israel') refers to two Messiahs, see again Collins, *Scepter and Star* 74-83.

23. 1QSa (1Q28a) 2.12, 14, 20.

24. See further C. A. Evans, 'Jesus and the Messianic Texts from Qumran', *Jesus and His Contemporaries* 83-154; Schreiber, *Gesalbter und König* 199-245 (conclusion 240, 245). I responded to L. Schiffman, 'Messianic Figures and Ideas in the Qumran Scrolls', in Charlesworth, ed., *The Messiah* 116-29, in my 'Messianic Ideas' 367 n. 2. Note also Talmon's observation that in the configurations of messianism which he examines, 'the conception of the "Age to Come" is intrinsically conceived as the memory of the past projected into the future' (87; in reference to Qumran, 104). M. O. Wise, *The First Messiah* (San Francisco: Harper, 1999) pushes too hard to draw out from 1QH a picture of the Teacher of Righteousness as a claimant to messianic status.

25. B. Janowski, 'Zur Bedeutung der Psalmen für eine Theologie des Alten Testaments', in E. Zenger, ed., *Der Psalter in Judentum und Christentum* (Freiburg: Herder, 1998) 381-420 (here 404).

26. Schürer, *History* 2.461; this may have been part of the prayer at the time of Jesus; in the more elaborate Babylonian recension, the prayer is for the throne of David to be raised up quickly and the shoot of David to shoot forth quickly (14-15; Schürer 458, 461-62).

27. Cf. particularly F. Hahn, *Christologische Hoheitstitel* 133-58 (*Titles of Jesus* 136-48, 242-43).

them with a rod of iron and dash them in pieces like a potter's vessel' (Ps. 2.9). 'He shall smite the earth with the rod of his mouth, and with the breath of his mouth shall slay the wicked' (Isa. 11.4). *Pss. Sol.* 17 has already been cited.[28] 'With your sceptre may you lay waste the earth. With the breath of your lips may you kill the wicked' (1QSb [1Q28b] 5.24-25). The Prince of the whole congregation will lead in battle (1QM 5.1); 'when he rises he will destroy all the sons of Seth' (CD 20-21). Collins notes that the main features of this picture persist in the apocalypses of *4 Ezra* and *2 Baruch,* which are independent of the Dead Sea sect.[29] Josephus reports that the military revolt in 62 was incited by 'an ambiguous oracle' in the sacred Scriptures to the effect that one of their own countrymen 'would become ruler of the world' (*War* 6.312). And it is worth recalling that the military leader bar Kochba was hailed as Messiah in the second Jewish revolt (132-35 CE).

So the twofold conclusion looks to be well founded that in various strands of Judaism before and after Jesus there was a lively hope for the restoration of the Davidic line and that the Davidic Messiah was widely thought of as a warrior king who would destroy the enemies of Israel.[30] To this we should add the evidence marshalled by Horsley that there were several aspirants to kingship at the death of Herod (the Great) and in the first Jewish revolt (66-74).[31] The term 'Messiah' does not appear, but the episodes indicate that the idea of kingship continued to have a strong appeal among the Jewish populace, and a close correlation with the more specific idea of Davidic kingship/messiahship can probably be assumed — as again Bar Kochba confirms. So we can extend Collins's conclusion with some confidence that the hope of a royal Messiah was widespread

---

28. Charlesworth argues that the picture here is 'nonmilitary': he conquers with 'the word of his mouth' ('Messianology to Christology' 20-21; similarly Sanders, *Historical Figure* 240-41). But the emphasis is on the *destruction* wrought by the Messiah; the distinction between military or nonmilitary is rather fine and somewhat pointless (cf. Isa. 11.4 and 1QSb [1Q28b] 5.24-25 [cited here]; Matt. 3.12/Luke 3.17 [§11.4]; 2 Thess. 2.8; Rev. 1.16; 19.15, 21). See further Schreiber, *Gesalbter und König* 171-72, 541-42.

29. Collins, *Scepter and Star* 67-68.

30. To the same effect, Collins, *Scepter and Star* 68, 95; Schreiber, *Gesalbter und König* 245, 541-42.

31. Initially and most fully expressed in Horsley and Hanson, *Bandits* ch. 3; also Horsley, *Jesus* 52-54. At the death of Herod the references are to Judas the Galilean (Josephus, *War* 2.56; *Ant.* 17.271-72), Simon (*War* 2.57-59; *Ant.* 17.271-76), and Athronges (*War* 2.60-65; *Ant.* 17.278-85); Horsley and Hanson note that Josephus summarizes these various movements under the heading of 'kingship' (*War* 2.55) and desire to be 'king' (*Ant.* 17.285). In the first revolt the clearest reference is to Menahem, son of Judas the Galilean (*War* 2.434), and Horsley and Hanson argue that the key leader, Simon bar Giora, acted and was treated as king (citing *War* 7.29-31, 36, 153-54). See also C. A. Evans, 'Messianic Claimants of the First and Second Centuries', *Jesus and his Contemporaries* 53-81.

also among the unlettered masses. It should be observed that this finding reverses the trend noted above, consequent upon the new appreciation of the diversity of eschatological hope. For most of the second half of the twentieth century the general assumption has been that the royal Messiah was only one among several messianic figures who featured in some expressions of that hope, and that royal messianism was therefore not particularly prominent in the eschatological expectation of the period. The sounder conclusion now appears to be: one expression of a more diversely expressed hope, yes; but the most prominent and widespread of the various expressions of that hope.[32]

In the light of the above we can go on to ask whether Jesus would have been reckoned a credible contender for such a role. Was Jesus regarded as royal Messiah during his life? Contemporary scholarship is more split on this question than ever. The spectrum stretches from a confident Yes! to an equally confident No!

b. Jesus the Revolutionary

One end of the spectrum is confident that Jesus intended to lead a revolution against Rome's overlordship. Starting with Reimarus this thesis has been offered at various times during the past two hundred years.[33] Particularly in the 1960s, the portrayal of Jesus as equivalent to the modern freedom fighter proved to be very influential in Liberation theology.[34] But the most scholarly statement of the thesis has been that of S. G. F. Brandon.[35]

Brandon's argument is basically that the Gospels' presentation of Jesus is a

32. R. A. Horsley's conclusion 'that there was little interest in a Messiah, Davidic or otherwise, let alone a standard messianic expectation, in the diverse Palestinian Jewish literature of late Second Temple times' is much too strong ('"Messianic" Figures and Movements in First-Century Palestine', in Charlesworth, ed., *The Messiah* 276-95 [here 295]).

33. For a thorough review see E. Bammel, 'The Revolution Theory from Reimarus to Brandon', in E. Bammel and C. F. D. Moule, eds., *Jesus and the Politics of His Day* (Cambridge: Cambridge University, 1984) 11-68.

34. Illustrations in J. P. M. Sweet, 'The Zealots and Jesus', in Bammel and Moule, *Jesus and Politics* 1-9 (here 1-2).

35. S. G. F. Brandon, *The Fall of Jerusalem and the Christian Church* (London: SPCK, [2]1957); also *Jesus and the Zealots* (Manchester: Manchester University, 1967); also *The Trial of Jesus of Nazareth* (London: Batsford, 1968; Paladin, 1971). See also Buchanan, *Jesus,* who argues consistently for a political sense for the kingdom of God: 'Jesus was convinced that God was prepared to give the Kingdom of Heaven to the Jews of his time with him as the new Messiah to sit on David's throne at Jerusalem . . . he was at that very time recruiting followers and raising funds to undertake a movement that would evict the Romans from power' (200; see also, e.g., 84, 123, 127, 154, and particularly 200-22, 240-52).

political whitewash. Their accounts have been toned down to eliminate all features of Jesus' attempt to foment revolution, but the political whitewash has not entirely succeeded. Enough elements were so firmly rooted in the tradition that they could not be excised completely. The key data are as follows:[36] one of Jesus' close disciples was Simon the zealot, that is one of those committed to violent resistance to Roman rule; Jesus' entry into Jerusalem (Mark 11.1-10 pars.) was 'virtually a proclamation of rebellion';[37] the 'cleansing of the Temple' (Mark 11.15-17 pars.) was an attempt to seize the Temple by force, a messianic *coup d'état,* probably part of a wider uprising in which Barabbas took part (Mark 15.7); Jesus' response to the question about paying tribute (Mark 12.13-17 pars.) was to rule decisively against it — the Holy Land and its resources belonged emphatically to God, not to Caesar (hence Luke 23.2); Luke 22.36-38 indicates that Jesus urged the acquisition of weapons, and there was armed resistance when Jesus was arrested (Mark 14.47 pars.); and Jesus was crucified as a royal messianic pretender (Mark 15.26 pars.) and on a charge of subversion and revolt (Luke 23.2).

Brandon's thesis has won little scholarly support.[38] We will examine the most overtly 'messianic' episodes within Jesus' mission in some detail below. But we can draw immediately on our earlier findings on at least two points. First, it is highly unlikely that Simon's nickname of 'zealot' (Luke 6.15) had any of the connotations of 'freedom-fighter' at the time of Jesus.[39] Mark, writing round about the time of the first revolt, may have chosen to disguise the fact by calling Simon 'the Cananean', from the Aramaic word for 'zealot' or 'enthusiast' *(qan'an);* that is, he transliterated rather than translated the Aramaic. Even so, however, the connotation at the time of Jesus was of a zealous person, not of an advocate of revolutionary violence.[40] Second, if Jesus did indeed teach that love

36. Already in *Fall of Jerusalem* 101-107; *Zealots* ch. 7; *Trial* (Paladin) 78-81, 99-101, 122-23, 174-76.

37. Brandon, *Trial* (Paladin) 175.

38. Bammel and Moule, *Jesus and Politics* was intended primarily as a response to Brandon. See also M. Hengel, *Was Jesus a Revolutionist?* (Philadelphia: Fortress, 1971).

39. See above, §9.3a (4).

40. Even less plausible are the suggestions that Peter's surname Barjona meant 'terrorist' and that the surname Iscariot indicated Judas to be one of the Sicarii (as still maintained by O. Cullmann, *Jesus and the Revolutionaries* [New York: Harper and Row, 1970] 8-9, 63 n. 13; Buchanan, *Jesus* 247), both anachronistic for the time of Jesus: like the Zealots, the Sicarii did not emerge for another twenty or so years (see again above, §9.3a[4]; also Davies and Allison, *Matthew* 2.156-57). On the 'two swords' passage see Hahn, *Hoheitstitel* 167-70 (*Titles* 153-55); Cullmann, *Revolutionaries* 47-49 ('This is no summons to a holy war'); Hengel, *Was Jesus a Revolutionist?* 21-23; G. W. H. Lampe, 'The Two Swords (Luke 22:35-38)', in Bammel and Moule, *Politics* 335-51; 'Luke understood the acquisition of two swords in Luke 22.38 not as a preparation for revolt but as a repeal of the rules for mission and of the renunciation of any pos-

of neighbour included love of enemies (§14.5b), as most agree, then that alone knocks a large hole in any thesis that Jesus sought a military solution.[41] And in more general terms we have already noted how quiet Palestine was at this period, with Roman detachments in Judea more for police duty, as we might say, than as an oppressive military garrison.[42] Apart from the serious troubles at the death of Herod (4 BCE) and subsequently in the first revolt (66-74 CE), what we hear of in the intervening period amounts to little more than relatively minor (for the era as a whole) civil disturbances and crowd control.[43]

Even so, the other data listed above do raise serious questions which will require fuller discussion, and we should recall the possibility that Jesus' movements in Galilee were determined by political considerations.[44] So even if it is the case that Brandon has greatly overstated his thesis, it remains an open question as to whether Jesus was a focus of political agitation or was unaware of the political overtones of his actions. It would be a mistake to treat the issue of Jesus as royal Messiah too narrowly, as though only that role carried political overtones.

c. Jesus' Messiahship as a Post-Easter Affirmation

Other scholars are equally convinced that the issue of royal messiahship did not arise during Jesus' mission; he was first designated as Messiah after Easter, in consequence of his resurrection — as Acts 2.36 and 13.33 imply. Messiahship was then read back into the life of Jesus; but wherever it arises in the Gospels, the motif of messiahship is redactional.

This view emerged only with Wrede's thesis of 'the messianic secret' at the beginning of the twentieth century (see above §4.5b). Prior to that the more or less universal assumption had been that Jesus' messiahship was a central feature of his mission, both in his own consciousness and as the reason for his death. Hengel notes that Wrede himself was not so confident as to deny the older consensus outright.[45] But it was Wrede's argument that the messianic secret was a Markan motif, not a historical motif, which opened the eyes of the subsequent

---

sibility of defence on journeys which they called for' (Theissen and Merz, *Historical Jesus* 460).

41. McKnight also draws attention to the (lightly attested) theme of peace-making in Jesus' teaching (Matt. 5.9; Matt. 10.12-13/Luke 10.6; Luke 19.42) (*New Vision* 229-32); though note also Matt. 10.34/Luke 12.51 (see above, chapter 14 n. 242).

42. See above, §9.8.

43. Including the episodes during Pilate's prefecture (see above, chapter 9 n. 254).

44. See again §9.9a-f.

45. Hengel, 'Jesus, the Messiah of Israel' 16.

generation to the fact of redaction and swung the pendulum of critical opinion away from the older view of Mark as earliest source and therefore most historical source for a life of Jesus.[46]

The nub of Wrede's argument[47] is that Jesus' repeated commands that demoniacs and those healed by Jesus keep silence[48] are historically incomprehensible (Jesus' reputation was already widespread); only as a unified theological concept do they become understandable in Mark's Gospel.[49] The secret in view is that Jesus is a supernatural being, the Son of God;[50] that is why the secret is revealed only by spiritual beings (demons) and by heavenly revelation (baptism and transfiguration),[51] episodes whose historical value was generally discounted by historical scholarship. But that he was such a being is Christian and post-resurrection belief,[52] it being initially believed that Jesus only became Messiah at and as a result of his resurrection.[53] Wrede's explanation, then, is that the idea of Jesus' messiahship first emerged in the early community, not with Jesus himself. Had Jesus proclaimed himself as Messiah, the messianic secret could never have arisen.[54] The clue is given by Mark 9.9: Jesus' messianic sonship should not, could not be known more widely until after his resurrection; 'the phrase "until he should have arisen from the dead" tells us plainly enough that we are dealing here with a "viewpoint" and not with history'.[55]

This conclusion, that the messianic secret is a theological (and therefore unhistorical) construction, quickly became an established result of twentieth-century critical scholarship, particularly in Germany. The consequence is that at

---

46. Both Charlesworth ('Messianology to Christology' 34-35) and Wright (*Jesus* 28) cite Norman Perrin's 'The *Wredestrasse* Becomes the *Hauptstrasse:* Reflections on the Reprinting of the Dodd Festschrift', *JR* 46 (1966) 296-300.

47. One of the best summaries of Wrede's argument is in H. Räisänen, *The 'Messianic Secret' in Mark's Gospel* (Edinburgh: Clark, 1990) 38-48. The book is a revision of his *Das 'Messiasgeheimnis' im Markusevangelium. Ein redaktionskritischer Versuch* (Helsinki, 1976) incorporating the substance of his earlier *Die Parabeltheorie im Markusevangelium* (Helsinki, 1973). See also Christopher Tuckett's 'Introduction' to his edited volume, *The Messianic Secret* (London: SPCK, 1983) 1-28 (3-7 on Wrede).

48. Mark 1.23-25, 34, 43-45; 3.11-12; 5.43; 7.36; 8.26.

49. Wrede, *Messianic Secret* 48-53, 67-68. Wrede was fully aware of the implausibilities of some of the commands (49-52, 125-28); Räisänen justifiably criticizes my earlier study at this point (*Messianic Secret* 44 n. 22; referring to my 'The Messianic Secret in Mark', *TynB* 21 [1970] 92-117, as abbreviated in Tuckett, ed., *Messianic Secret* 116-31).

50. Wrede, *Messianic Secret* 72-80.

51. Mark 1.11; 9.7.

52. Wrede, *Messianic Secret* 218-20.

53. The texts in view are Acts 2.36; Rom. 1.4; Phil. 2.6-11 (*Messianic Secret* 215-16).

54. Wrede, *Messianic Secret* 220, 227-28.

55. Wrede, *Messianic Secret* 68-69.

the end of the twentieth century the consensus is almost the exact reverse of the consensus at the end of the nineteenth. As Hengel notes, 'Today the unmessianic Jesus has almost become a dogma among many New Testament scholars'.[56]

Let it be said at once that Wrede identified a distinctive feature of Mark's Gospel — what might indeed be characterized as a 'secrecy' motif. The presence of the motif in the obviously Markan summaries (1.34 and 3.11-12) puts that issue beyond doubt. But three questions begin to unravel Wrede's case to an extent too little appreciated.

(1) Is the 'secret' a single, coherent motif? Wrede so argued. But subsequent analysis has been more impressed by the complexities and diverse strands in the Markan material surveyed by Wrede. They do not all readily cohere under the single heading 'messianic' secret. The admirably clear exposition of Heikki Räisänen puts that issue equally beyond dispute.[57]

(2) Do the tensions within and between these strands simply reflect different layers of tradition, tensions not resolved by the redaction process?[58] On the normal understanding of redactorial freedom and creativity, one would have expected inconsistencies to be more fully ironed out. The presence of unresolved tensions suggests rather a respect for the tradition being utilized. Which raises in turn the question whether the stubborn elements in the tradition are stubborn because they were primary tradition, that is, they embodied very early memories of Jesus. In other words, are we witnessing the tensions and inconsistencies of real life situations rather than the compositional 'flaws' of the redaction?[59] I have already suggested the possibility that even the 'parable theory' of Mark 4.11-12 may have roots in memories of Jesus' own reaction to his lack of success at least in some villages (§13.1). And a similar question will have to be posed in regard to the 'confessions' of demoniacs and the command to silence in Jesus' exorcisms (§15.7d(5)).

(3) Above all, there is the challenge to Wrede's argument that the decisive basis for Jesus' messiahship was the resurrection, first posed by Schweitzer and regularly repeated thereafter.[60] Belief that Jesus had been raised was not enough

---

56. Hengel, 'Jesus, the Messiah of Israel' 16.

57. Räisänen, *Messianic Secret,* e.g., 16-21, 71-75, ch. 4, 232, 242-43.

58. Contrary to a common perception, Wrede recognized traditional material; he did not regard the secret as a Markan creation (e.g., *Messianic Secret* 145); it was Bultmann who took scholarship down that road (*History* 348-50); but see, e.g., G. Strecker, 'The Theory of the Messianic Secret in Mark's Gospel' (1964), in Tuckett, ed., *Messianic Secret* 49-64 (here 51-54).

59. As Räisänen, *Messianic Secret,* exemplifies, the dominant alternative to Bultmann's reworking of Wrede has been to conclude the latter: still 'theological, and therefore unhistorical'. For the traditional material utilized by Mark see Räisänen 101-102, 144-49, 168-70, 195-96, 222-23, 232, with summary 244-48.

60. See, e.g., Tuckett, *Messianic Secret* 7-9.

of itself to give rise to belief that Jesus was/had become Messiah; messiahship was not an obvious, far less necessary, corollary of resurrection. The thought that the Baptist had been raised did not carry that corollary (Mark 6.14).[61] Others were thought to have been exalted to heaven (Moses, Elijah, Isaiah) with never any thought of their consequent messiahship obtruding; 'exaltation does not imply Messiahship'.[62] The messiahship of the crucified Jesus is the *presupposition* of the scriptural apologetic mounted by the first Christians, not its achievement; 'the title "Messiah" was inseparably connected with the name of Jesus because Jesus was condemned and crucified as a messianic pretender'.[63] In short, the only obvious reason why the risen Jesus was hailed as Messiah was that resurrection was seen as a vindication of a claim which had been in play *before* Jesus' crucifixion and resurrection. But if the question of Jesus as Messiah was an issue during his lifetime, then the whole logic underpinning Wrede's central thesis begins to go into reverse.

One of the major problems in the discussion on this subject has been that the issue of Jesus as Messiah has been made to depend too much on the messianic secret theory and has been too much skewed into a discussion of the latter, whereas 'the messianic secret' is primarily an issue of Markan theology (Wrede's chief point). What we need to do here, then, is to step back from the diverting and narrowing subject of the messianic secret and to ask again the *historical* question: Was the issue of messiahship raised during Jesus' mission, if so, to what extent, and are we able to tell from the tradition how he reacted to it?

15.3. An Issue during Jesus' Mission

It is *a priori* likely that an individual who spoke memorably of God's kingdom, who gathered disciples around him, and who created something of a stir would have raised in many minds the equivalent to the modern question 'Who does he think he is?' It should now be clear that 'claimant to royal messiahship' was one possible answer to be considered. If Simon, one of Herod's slaves, and Athronges the shepherd could aspire to kingship (Josephus, *Ant.* 17.273-74, 278), we can hardly assume that Jesus' lowly birth would have ruled him out as a potential candidate. He may well have been known to be a descendant of David,

61. Schweitzer, *Quest*[1] 343 = *Quest*[2] 309.

62. Weiss, *Earliest Christianity* 1.31.

63. N. A. Dahl, 'The Crucified Messiah' (1960), most easily accessible in his *Jesus the Christ: The Historical Origins of Christological Doctrine* (ed. D. H. Juel; Minneapolis: Fortress, 1991) 27-47 (here 39-40).

as our sources indicate; at least no hint is given that any such claim was disputed.[64] And the reports that the Baptist was considered a possible candidate to messiahship[65] need not be wholly discounted. In fact, there are several incidents involving Jesus, whose historicity *in toto* is very hard to dismiss and in which the issue of messiahship (or the equivalent religio-political claim) is central.[66] We will begin with the climax of Jesus' 'career', his trial and condemnation, since the case is almost indisputable there,[67] and work backwards.

a. Jesus' Trial and Condemnation (Mark 15.1-39 pars.)[68]

One of the clearest and most striking facts regarding Jesus is that he was executed as a messianic pretender. (1) He was condemned for claiming to be 'the king of the Jews', as all four canonical Gospels agree (Mark 15.26 pars.). 'King of the Jews' was never a Christian title, so the only reason for its appearance in the account of Jesus' execution is that it summed up the charge on which he was executed.[69] That is, he could be credibly (or mockingly) treated as an aspirant to the throne of Herod and therefore a challenge to Rome's rule.[70] (2) He died by crucifixion; he was executed (15.15, 20, 24, 37 pars.). The point is deeply rooted in the earliest Christian traditions[71] and has never been seriously questioned. Crucifixion was a Roman punishment; it could have been ordered only by Pilate

64. See above, §11.1.

65. Luke 3.15; John 1.19-20.

66. The issue is clearest in the following (Markan) texts; but E. P. Meadors argues for 'The "Messianic" Implications of the Q Material', *JBL* 118 (1999) 253-77, referring to Q 4.1-13; 6.20; 7.22; 10.22; 11.20, 31b; 13.34-35; 22.29-30.

67. I follow the same logic as Harvey, *Jesus* ch. 2.

68. To analyse the full account synoptically would be too space-consuming; we will focus on the key elements here and take up other questions in §17.1 below.

69. 'Could the formulation really represent the historicization of a dogmatic motif? This is highly implausible' (Dahl, 'Crucified Messiah' 37). 'It was precisely the suggestion that Jesus represented some kind of political threat to the Roman authorities that Christians of the early centuries had most strenuously to deny' (Harvey, *Jesus* 13). Similarly Hengel, 'Jesus, the Messiah of Israel' 45-47, 58; Wright, *Jesus* 486-89; Theissen and Merz, *Historical Jesus* 458-59; Becker, *Jesus* 353-54. Surprisingly, D. R. Catchpole ('The "Triumphal" Entry', in Bammel and Moule, *Jesus and Politics* 319-34) concludes from a sequence of inconsequential arguments that 'the historicity of the *titulus* has to be doubted' (329-30), in agreement with Bultmann, *History* 284. Contrast Hengel 47-50 and Lüdemann, *Jesus* 108. Other bibliography in Evans, 'Authenticating the Activities of Jesus' 24 n. 52.

70. Note R. A. Horsley, 'The Death of Jesus', in Chilton and Evans, eds., *Studying the Historical Jesus* 395-422 (here particularly 413-14).

71. 1 Cor. 1.17-18, 23; 2.2, 8; 2 Cor 13.4; Gal. 3.1; 6.12, 14; Phil. 2.8; 3.18; Col. 1.20; 2.14; Heb. 12.2; Rev. 11.8.

the Prefect;[72] this memory too is deeply burned into the Christian tradition.[73] This was the way Rome treated rebels against its rule.[74] (3) It follows in turn that there must have been some trial or hearing before Pilate (15.2-5 pars.).[75] There are various problematic features about the fuller accounts at this point,[76] but no doubt that the key issue before Pilate was whether Jesus had claimed to be 'the king of the Jews' (15.2 pars.).[77] Whether or not Pilate regarded Jesus as a serious threat to Rome's power need hardly be decided; at the very least the charge provided sufficient reason (or excuse) to dispatch a potential troublemaker.[78] The representative of Rome's ruthless *imperium* required no further reason.[79]

Moving backwards, we need not become involved in the old question of

72. Theissen and Merz, *Historical Jesus* 455-58, provide a good summary of the legal powers and procedures involved. Further detail in Gnilka, *Jesus* 298-302.

73. Mark 15.1-15 pars.; Acts 3.13; 4.27; 13.28; 1 Tim. 6.13; Ignatius, *Magn.* 11; *Trall.* 9.1; *Smyrn.* 1.2; but also Josephus, *Ant.* 18.64; Tacitus, *Annals* 15.44. The point is frequently made that Pontius Pilate is the only person other than Jesus named in the classic creeds: *passus sub Pontio Pilato;* see further below §17.1 introduction and §17.1e.

74. See M. Hengel, *Crucifixion* (London: SCM, 1977) 46-50; H.-W. Kuhn, 'Die Kreuzesstrafe während der frühen Kaiserzeit. Ihre Wirklichkeit und Wertung in der Umwelt des Urchristentums', *ANRW* II.25.1 (1982) 648-793 (here 706-18). E.g., Josephus reports the crucifixion of 2,000 rebels by the Roman legate Varus after he put down the revolt following the death of Herod the Great (*Ant.* 17.295). 'There can be no reasonable doubt that Jesus met a death which was reserved for those whom the Roman governor regarded as a threat to the peace and security of the state' (Harvey, *Jesus* 12-13); see also Becker, *Jesus* 350-51.

75. Probably at Herod's palace, where he usually resided, rather than at the fortress Antonia (see, e.g., Charlesworth, *Jesus* 120-22; Gnilka, *Jesus* 299-300; S. Légasse, *The Trial of Jesus* [London: SCM, 1997] 60-62; Murphy-O'Connor, *Holy Land* 22, 34).

76. Particularly the practice of releasing a prisoner at Passover (Mark 15.6-14 pars.; see below chapter 17 n. 67) and whether Herod Antipas was at all involved (Luke 23.6-12), as is quite possible — the note about renewed friendship (23.12) may well be more than a novellistic touch (discussion in Fitzmyer, *Luke* 2.1478-79). For Pilate's own role and character see Bond, *Pontius Pilate* and below §17.1e.

77. Evans points out that the Jesus Seminar's rejection of the historicity of the trial scene (Funk, *Acts of Jesus* 152) leaves it unable to provide a convincing explanation of what led to Jesus' death ('Authenticating the Activities of Jesus' 26-28).

78. Kuhn, 'Kreuzesstrafe' 732-33. According to Josephus, Herod Antipas had decided to get rid of John the Baptist as a precautionary measure (*Ant.* 18.118). But there is no good reason to doubt the tradition that Pilate took the opportunity afforded him to follow a (quasi-)judicial procedure (*pace* Crossan, *Who Killed Jesus?* 117).

79. 'From the viewpoint of the rulers the crucifixion of Jesus was not a mistake' (Horsley, *Jesus* 320; see further Horsley's 'The Death of Jesus' 395-422). Fredriksen's study of Jesus is motivated by the question Why was Jesus executed by the Romans as an insurrectionist but not his followers? (*Jesus* 8-11). Her answer is that Jesus was crucified because *others* thought he was Messiah. Pilate knew Jesus was harmless, but potential trouble could be easily dealt with by eliminating the focus of the messianic enthusiasm (234-35, 240-41; see further below, n. 163).

whether Mark 14.55-64 is the account of a proper trial before a properly convened body properly described as 'the Sanhedrin'.[80] All that the account itself indicates is a hearing before an *ad hoc* council convened by Caiaphas to advise him.[81] To pursue questions of legality (in reference to the subsequent constitution and procedure of the Sanhedrin)[82] is therefore largely a waste of time, with so many probable anachronisms in play as to render the question itself almost meaningless. This is not to deny that some sort of legal process took place. The fact that Jesus was 'handed over' is well rooted in the tradition. It is true that the term has been characteristically elaborated in terms of Judas as the 'betrayer',[83] and theologized in terms of Jesus being 'handed over' for our sins/us.[84] But the more basic technical sense of 'handed over into the custody of' is still evident,[85] including the Semitic construction 'delivered into the hand(s) of'.[86] So there is a strong likelihood that behind Mark 14.55-64 lies the historical fact that Jesus was 'handed over' to the Roman authorities as the outcome of a hearing before an *ad hoc* council convened by the High Priest Caiaphas.[87]

As to the account of the hearing before Caiaphas itself, there can be little doubt that Mark 14.55-59 is at best a partisan account of what happened (the testimony against Jesus is regarded as 'false'). But the account could well have been based on nonpartisan reports. We can be sure that the first followers of Jesus would have been curious about what had transpired before Caiaphas's council. And at least some information may well have been gleaned from one or two of those present — whether from attendants, or guards, or even a member of the

80. Here again, to analyse the full account synoptically would be too space-consuming; we will focus on key elements (below and §16.4c[2]).

81. See particularly Sanders, *Jesus* 296-301; also *Judaism* 475-90: 'The trial of Jesus agrees very well with his [Josephus's] stories of how things happened' (487).

82. Cf. especially P. Winter, *On the Trial of Jesus* (Berlin: de Gruyter, 1961). On the legal issues see particularly J. Blinzler, *Der Prozess Jesu* (Regensburg: Pustet, [4]1969); Brown, *Death* 357-72. Theissen and Merz summarize the contrasts between the Markan/Matthean 'trial' and the rules relating to trials in the Mishnah (*Historical Jesus* 460-62). See further P. Egger, *"Crucifixus sub Pontio Pilato". Das "Crimen" Jesu von Nazareth im Spannungsfeld römischer und jüdischer Verwaltungs- und Rechtsstrukturen* (Münster: Aschendorff, 1997).

83. Mark 3.19/Matt. 10.4/Luke 6.16; Mark 14.10-11, 18, 21, 42, 44/Matt. 26.15-16, 21, 23, 24-25, 46, 48/Luke 22.4, 6, 21-22; Matt. 27.3-4; Luke 22.48; 24.20.

84. Rom. 4.25; 8.32; Gal. 2.20; Eph. 5.2, 25.

85. Mark 10.33/Matt. 20.19/Luke 18.32; Mark 15.1, 10/Matt. 27.2, 18; Mark 15.15/ Matt. 27.26/Luke 23.25; Matt. 26.2; Luke 20.20; John 18.30, 35; Acts 3.13; cf. 1 Cor. 11.23.

86. Mark 9.31/Matt. 17.22/Luke 9.44; Mark 14.41/Matt. 26.45; Luke 24.7; further details in BDAG, *paradidōmi* 1b; Davies and Allison, *Matthew* 2.734 and n. 16.

87. Cf. Josephus, *Ant.* 18.64: 'when Pilate, because of an accusation made by the leading men among us *(tōn prōtōn andrōn par' hēmin),* condemned him to the cross . . .'. Of contemporary discussions see particularly Harvey, *Jesus* 23-31.

council, and whether by direct information or through the popular account circulated in the marketplace and Temple courts is of less moment.[88]

According to the tradition, the key charge brought against Jesus was that he had threatened to destroy the Temple (Mark 14.58 pars.):

Matt. 26.61	Mark 14.58	John 2.19	*GTh* 71	Acts 6.14
I am able to destroy the temple of God and to build it in three days.	I will destroy this temple that is made with hands, and in three days I will build another, not made with hands.	Destroy this temple, and in three days I will raise it up.	I will destroy [this] house, and no one will be able to [re]build it . . .	We have heard him say that this man Jesus of Nazareth will destroy this place and will change the customs that Moses handed to us.

The core of the tradition is clear, as also its diverse elaboration in the different versions: Jesus' talk of destroying *(katalysai)* the Temple.[89] The case for recognizing a historical memory enshrined here is surprisingly strong. Jesus is recalled elsewhere as predicting the destruction of the Temple,[90] a possibility which no one with any political sensitivity could easily discount.[91] Matthew and Mark also record that the accusation was echoed by the crowd later (Mark 15.29/Matt. 27.39-40). And though Luke omits the charge at this point in his Gospel, it reappears in the testimony brought against Stephen in Acts 6.14.[92]

88. The often repeated comment that there were no later Christian witnesses present (as in Becker, *Jesus of Nazareth* 197) is rather facile: were all present sworn to secrecy? were no inquiries made of any of those present by curious outsiders?

89. 'Made with hands/made without hands *(cheiropoiētos/acheiropoiētos)*' probably reflects the transposition of the tradition into Hellenistic Jewish categories (cf. Acts 7.48); similarly Pesch, *Markusevangelium* 2.434; R. E. Brown, *The Death of the Messiah: From Gethsemane to the Grave. A Commentary on the Passion Narratives in the Four Gospels* (2 vols.; New York: Doubleday, 1994) 439; though O. Betz, 'Probleme des Prozesses Jesu', *ANRW* II.25.1 (1982) notes that *acheiropoiētos* ('made without hands') is derived from Aramaic (631 n. 184) and draws attention particularly to 4Q174 (4QFlor) 1.2-3, 6 (631-32); and Ådna argues for the significance of Exod. 15.17 to conclude that the contrast was probably an original element of the Temple word (*Jesu Stellung* 90-153).

90. Both in Mark (Mark 13.2/Matt. 24.2/Luke 21.6) and in Q material (Matt. 23.38/Luke 13.35). Holmén notes the possible allusion to Hag. 2.15 (*Jesus* 295-96, 302-303).

91. C. A. Evans summarizes the various premonitions and prophecies of the destruction of the Temple in 'Jesus and Predictions of the Destruction of the Herodian Temple', *Jesus and His Contemporaries: Comparative Studies* (Leiden: Brill, 1995) 367-80.

92. This is in line with Luke's tendency to delay important sayings and developments till his second volume (cf. particularly Mark 7 with Acts 10; also Mark 6.17-29 with Acts 24.24-26, and Mark 4.12 with Acts 28.25-27).

Most striking is the fact that both John and *Thomas* record it as a saying of Jesus himself.[93]

On the basis of this evidence, it has to be judged likely both that Jesus did in fact say something about the destruction (and rebuilding) of the Temple, and that reports of this saying constituted the principal and most effective testimony against him at the hearing before Caiaphas.[94] That other testimony was offered is indicated by Mark and Matthew (Mark 14.55-56/Matt. 26.59-60), but no indication is given of what it amounted to.[95] And all the testimony against Jesus, including the testimony on his Temple saying, is branded by Mark and Matthew as 'false'.[96] Yet the fact that John (and *Thomas*) have no hesitation in attributing more or less the same saying to Jesus himself confirms the less explicit testimony of Mark 13.2, that Jesus did indeed say something politically sensitive about the Temple. However accurate the report of what Jesus actually said, then, we can be confident that something Jesus had said about the destruction (and restoration)[97]

93. Crossan regards *GTh* 71 as the most original version we have (*Historical Jesus* 356; cf. his earlier *Fragments* 302-12); whereas Becker regards John 2.19 as original (*Jesus* 329).

94. See also G. Theissen, 'Jesus' Temple Prophecy', *Social Reality and the Early Christians* (Minneapolis: Augsburg Fortress, 1992) 94-114 (especially 94-97); 'a prophecy which demonstrably caused so much perplexity and difficulty was not attributed to Jesus only at a later stage' (Theissen and Merz, *Historical Jesus* 433); Holmén, *Jesus* 296-301. Full discussion in K. Paesler, *Das Tempelwort Jesu. Die Traditionen von Tempelzerstörung und Tempelerneuerung im Neuen Testament* (FRLANT 184; Göttingen: Vandenhoeck und Ruprecht, 1999).

95. Several have argued that Jesus was charged with leading the people astray and false prophecy (A. Strobel, *Die Stunde der Wahrheit* [WUNT 21; Tübingen: Mohr Siebeck, 1980] 81-92; Betz, 'Probleme' 570-96; Stuhlmacher, *Biblische Theologie* 1.147-48; Wright, *Jesus* 439-42, 548-51; Becker, *Jesus* 336). But although this became a later accusation (see below, §15.7g), the Gospels do not mention it as part of the accusation at the trial. Jesus is once called a *planos* ('deceiver'), echoing Deut. 13.1-5 (Matt. 27.63; also John 7.12, 47), but Mark knows nothing of this, and Luke talks in terms of political agitation (Luke 23.2). See also G. N. Stanton, 'Jesus of Nazareth: A Magician and a False Prophet Who Deceived God's People?' in Green and Turner, eds., *Jesus of Nazareth* 164-80 (here 175-80).

96. There could be several reasons why the first followers of Jesus regarded the testimony at the hearing as 'false'. In particular, did Jesus claim that he himself would destroy the Temple (Mark 14.58, but cf. Matt. 26.61; Acts 6.14, but cf. John 2.19)? And the second half of the saying ('I will build another in three days') may have proved embarrassing for some of Jesus' followers (cf. Acts 6.14 and John 2.21); but see above, §13.3g. See further the full discussion in J. Schlosser, 'La parole de Jésus sur la fin du Temple', *NTS* 36 (1990) 398-414; Brown, *Death of the Messiah* 444-60; and my '"Are You the Messiah?": Is the Crux of Mark 14.61-62 Resolvable?', in D. G. Horrell and C. M. Tuckett, eds., *Christology, Controversy and Community*, D. R. Catchpole FS (NovTSup 99; Leiden: Brill, 2000) 1-22 (here 5-6).

97. The considerations which follow depend only on the talk of building the Temple being part of the accusation against Jesus, but it is quite likely that Jesus did say something to this effect (see n. 96); cf. Fredriksen, *Jesus* 226-28; Lüdemann, *Jesus* 438; contrast Becker, who removes the key elements in the account as Markan redaction (*Jesus* 330, 347-48).

of the Temple provided the chief ground or excuse for bringing him before Caiaphas's council. The charge was not without substance![98]

The point of more immediate relevance here is that the charge (regarding the Temple's destruction and rebuilding) and Jesus' failure to respond to it are reported as having provoked the question of the High Priest, 'Are you the Messiah, the Son of the Blessed One?' (Mark 14.60-61).[99] Whether there was any connection between the charge and the question has rarely been discussed, but in fact the link between the Temple charge and the Messiah question gives a greater credibility to the question than most seem to have realized. The link was recognized by Otto Betz nearly four decades ago, but his insight has been rarely acknowedged.[100]

The link is provided by the ancient promise of 2 Sam. 7.12-14, the primary root of Israel's ideology of Davidic kingship. For the promise of Nathan to David was threefold: that he would have a son (son of David), who would build 'a house for my name' (the Temple), and whom God would regard as his son (God's son). It was Betz who first noticed that 4Q174 (4QFlor) 1.10-13 interpreted 2 Sam. 7.12-14 of the royal Messiah, the 'branch of David', and the relevance of the text to the trial scene. For if a messianic reading of Nathan's prophecy was 'in the air' at the time of Jesus, that would provide all the explanation necessary for Caiaphas's question. In effect Caiaphas asks: 'You are charged with promising to build the Temple. Do you then claim to fulfil Nathan's prophecy? Are you the royal Messiah, God's son?' The prophecy of Nathan and its interpretation at Qumran provide the missing link between charge and question.[101]

The probability is strong, therefore, strong beyond plausible rebuttal, that

---

98. Horsley, *Jesus* 160-64.

99. On the issue whether the High Priest could/would have used the phrase 'the son of the Blessed' see Brown, *Death* 469-70, and my 'Are You the Messiah?' 9-10, where I point out that it is as difficult to explain the emergence of the phrase in the middle of the first century (when Mark did use it) as in the year 30.

100. O. Betz, 'Die Frage nach dem messianischen Bewusstsein Jesu', *NovT* 6 (1963) 24-37; also 'Probleme' 625-28, 633-34. Exceptions are Meyer, *Aims of Jesus* 179-80; Hampel, *Menschensohn* 174-75; and Witherington, *Christology* 258. Even Brown does not refer to it in his exhaustive treatment of the passage in *Death* (though he does refer in his bibliography to Betz's 'Probleme'), presumably because he himself does not pursue the question of the linkage of thought between 14.58 and 14.61. In reference to Mark 14.53-65, our regular samples of sceptical historicism, Funk, *Five Gospels* 121-22 ('mostly fabrication of the Christian imagination'), and Lüdemann, *Jesus* 101-102 ('the historical value of the pericope is nil, apart from v. 58') totally ignore the link indicated by Betz; similarly Légasse, *Trial of Jesus* 40-41; Fredriksen, *Jesus* 222, 255.

101. Cf. also Zech. 6:12-13 — 'the man whose name is the Branch . . . shall build the Temple of the Lord . . . and shall sit and rule upon his throne'. For other 'Branch' expectation see above, §15.2a.

the issue of messiahship was raised at the hearing before Caiaphas and that the outcome of the hearing turned on that issue.[102] Moreover, since royal Messiah translated readily enough as 'king of the Jews', the obvious deduction is that Jesus was 'handed over' to Pilate's jurisdiction on the charge of claiming to be David's royal successor, in the full knowledge that one who claimed to be a king was likely to receive short shrift from the prefect. And so it proved. There are other questions to which we must return in regard to Jesus' trial and execution. But for the moment it is sufficient to have demonstrated the high historical probability that the issue of Jesus' messiahship was the decisive (legal) factor in (or, should we say, excuse for) Jesus' execution.

b. The Question about David's Son

Mark 12.35-37a pars. is one of the most difficult Synoptic passages to evaluate in historical terms. But its relevance is so clear that it cannot be ignored.

Matt. 22.41-45	Mark 12.35-37a	Luke 20.41-44
41 Now while the Pharisees were gathered together, Jesus asked them a question, 42 saying, 'What do you think of the Christ? Whose son is he?' They said to him, 'The son of David'. 43 He said to them, 'How is it then that David, inspired by the Spirit, calls him Lord, saying, 44 "The Lord said to my Lord, Sit at my right hand, till I put your enemies under your feet"? 45 If David thus calls him Lord, how is he his son?'	35 And as Jesus taught in the temple, he said, 'How can the scribes say that the Christ is the son of David? 36 David himself, inspired by the Holy Spirit, declared, "The Lord said to my Lord, Sit at my right hand, till I put your enemies under your feet." 37 David himself speaks of him as Lord; so how is he his son?'	41 But he said to them, 'How can they say that the Christ is David's son? 42 For David himself says in the Book of Psalms, "The Lord said to my Lord, Sit at my right hand, 43 till I put your enemies a stool for your feet." 44 David thus calls him Lord; so how is he his son?'

The central feature is Jesus' quotation of Ps. 110.1, and the assumption that the text was generally taken to be messianic. However, there is no clear evidence that Ps. 110.1 was interpreted messianically in pre-Christian Judaism,[103] whereas the evidence that Ps. 110.1 played a key role in the development of earliest christological understanding is beyond dispute.[104] The passage is therefore usually

---

102. Wright argues more directly: 'If Jesus has been doing and saying things against the Temple, the natural implication is that he thinks he is the anointed one, the Messiah' (*Jesus* 523). See also Stuhlmacher, *Biblische Theologie* 1.115-17.

103. Texts cited by Davies and Allison, *Matthew* 3.254 n. 23.

104. See particularly M. Hengel, '"Sit at My Right Hand!" The Enthronement of Christ at the Right Hand of God and Psalm 110:1', *Studies* 119-225.

taken to be a retrojection of the christological use of Ps. 110.1 back into Jesus' mission.[105]

On the other hand, Ps. 110.1 probably originated as a royal psalm (like Psalms 2, 72, and 89), so that a messianic interpretation lay close to hand.[106] And the possibility cannot be excluded that Jesus himself was the first to suggest a messianic interpretation.[107] Moreover, the format does not read much as a bold affirmation of either Jesus' Davidic sonship or of his lordship.[108] It has more the character of a riddle, the sort of riddle which was once the delight of oral societies. In this case the riddle obviously plays on the presupposition of a patriarchal society that the son was by definition subservient to the father. So how could the anointed king be both David's son and David's lord? Perhaps, then, the tradition originated with the memory of Jesus posing the conundrum in a day when the possible messianic significance of Ps. 110.1 was beginning to be discussed.[109] That he was in the event (shortly after this) denounced to Pilate and then crucified as a messianic claimant makes it rather more credible that the issue of messiahship was in the air prior to Jesus' arrest.[110]

c. Paying Tribute to Caesar (Mark 12.13-17 pars.)

Since Matthew and Luke appear to be variants of Mark we need take note only of Mark as representative of the Synoptic tradition, though the versions in *Thomas* 100 and *Pap. Eg.* 2 (fragment 2 recto) are also worth noting.

---

105. The conclusions of Funk, *Five Gospels* 105, and Lüdemann, *Jesus* 87, are not untypical.

106. See D. M. Hay, *Glory at the Right Hand: Psalm 110 in Early Christianity* (SBLMS 18: Nashville: Abingdon, 1973) 19-33.

107. Fitzmyer, *Luke* 2.1311; cf. Stuhlmacher, *Biblische Theologie* 1.124; Wright, *Jesus* 507-10. The fact that it is the LXX of Ps. 110.1 which is quoted is hardly determinative otherwise (*pace* Becker, *Jesus* 196); of course the Greek-speaking churches used the LXX in their version of the tradition, but the pun ('The Lord said to my lord') works as well in Aramaic (Fitzmyer, *Luke* 2.1322).

108. 'The allusive character of the saying favours the view that it is an original utterance; . . . It is difficult to think that the doctrinal beliefs of a community could be expressed in this allusive manner' (Taylor, *Mark* 493). Contrast C. Burger, *Jesus als Davidssohn* (FRLANT 98; Göttingen: Vandenhoeck, 1970), who argues that the idea of Jesus as David's son was rejected in the pre-Markan pericope (52-59); but supporting evidence that Jesus' Davidic sonship was questioned within early Christianity is lacking (see above, chapter 11 n. 34).

109. Cf. D. Daube, *The New Testament and Rabbinic Judaism* (London: Athlone, 1956) 160-63 (a haggadic question on two texts which seem to conflict). Cf. also the enigmatic quality of 4Q491, discussed by Hengel, 'Sit at My Right Hand' 201-203, and Collins, *Scepter and Star* 147-49.

110. 'The Messiah question runs through the Passion story of all the gospels like a red thread' (Hengel, 'Jesus, Messiah of Israel' 45, 58).

Mark 12.13-17	GTh 100	Pap. Eg. 2
13 And they sent to him some of the Pharisees and some of the Herodians, to entrap him in his talk. 14 And they came and said to him, 'Teacher, we know that you are true, and care for no man; for you do not regard the position of men, but truly teach the way of God. Is it lawful to pay taxes to Caesar, or not? 15 Should we pay them, or should we not?' But knowing their hypocrisy, he said to them, 'Why put me to the test? Bring me a coin, that I may see it'. 16 And they brought one. And he said to them, 'Whose likeness and inscription is this?' They said to him, 'Caesar's'. 17 Jesus said to them, 'Render to Caesar the things that are Caesar's, and to God the things that are God's'. And they were amazed at him.	They showed Jesus a gold (coin) and said to him, 'Caesar's agents demand taxes from us'. He said to them, 'Give to Caesar what belongs to Caesar; give to God what belongs to God; and give to me what is mine'.	. . . came to him to tempt him, saying, 'Teacher Jesus, we know that you have come from God, for the things which you do bear witness beyond all the prophets. Tell us then: Is it lawful to render to kings what pertains to their rule? Shall we render it to them or not?' But Jesus, knowing their mind, said to them in indignation, 'Why do you call me teacher with your mouth, when you do not do what I say? Well did Isaiah prophesy of you when he said: This people honour me with its lips, but their heart is far from me; in vain do they worship me, (teaching as doctrines merely human) commandments'. . . .

Few if any doubts are entertained as to the authenticity of this episode;[111] *GTh* 100 looks like an abbreviated oral variation, climaxing with the key core saying slightly elaborated; and *Pap. Eg.* 2 may attest either further independent oral variation or perhaps oral knowledge of Mark (7.6-8 as well as 12.13-17). The exchange occasioned by a question put by some Pharisees and Herodians is not overtly messianic, but was certainly of inescapable political significance.[112] Why would such a question be put to Jesus, unless it was considered that his opinion might be regarded as significant or at least that his answer might provide opportunity to denounce him as a political threat? Potential messianic claims and tensions lurk only a little way below the surface.

d. 'Cleansing the Temple' (Mark 11.15-17 pars.)

The likelihood that Jesus' dictum regarding the Temple's future provided the grounds for his arrest naturally draws attention to the event which the Synoptics report as having taken place a few days earlier — traditionally known as 'the cleansing of the Temple' (Mark 11.15-17 pars.).[113]

111. Funk, *Five Gospels* 102; *Acts of Jesus* 125-26; Lüdemann, *Jesus* 83.

112. See also W. Horbury, 'The Temple Tax', in Bammel and Moule, *Jesus and Politics* 265-86. The specific mention of Herodians (only here in Matthew, but also in Mark 3.6, never in Luke) heightens the political overtone (see above, §9.3c[4]).

113. There is a broad consensus that John has set the account at the beginning of his

Matt. 21.12-13	Mark 11.15-17	Luke 19.45-46	John 2.13-16
12 And Jesus entered the temple and drove out all who sold and bought in the temple, and he overturned the tables of the money-changers and the seats of those who sold pigeons. 13 He said to them, 'It is written, "My house shall be called a house of prayer"; but you make it a den of robbers'.	15 And they came to Jerusalem. And he entered the temple and began to drive out those who sold and those who bought in the temple, and he overturned the tables of the money-changers and the seats of those who sold pigeons; 16 and he would not allow any one to carry anything through the temple. 17 And he taught, and said to them, 'Is it not written, "My house shall be called a house of prayer for all the nations"? But you have made it a den of robbers'.	45 And he entered the temple and began to drive out those who sold, 46 saying to them, 'It is written, "My house shall be a house of prayer"; but you have made it a den of robbers'.	13 The Passover of the Jews was at hand, and Jesus went up to Jerusalem. 14 In the temple he found those who were selling oxen and sheep and pigeons, and the money-changers at their business. 15 And making a whip of cords, he drove them all, with the sheep and oxen, out of the temple; and he poured out the coins of the money-changers and overturned their tables. 16 And he told those who sold the pigeons, 'Take these things away; you shall not make my Father's house a house of trade'.

There is a wide consensus that Jesus did indeed engage in a symbolic act in the Temple.[114] The tradition is clear that the action itself involved the upsetting of some tables of money-changers[115] and pigeon-sellers[116] and the prevention of the trading involved.[117] Whatever Jesus may have intended (and we should be-

---

Gospel to serve as a window through which the rest of his Gospel should be read. J. Murphy-O'Connor, 'Jesus and the Money Changers (Mark 11:15-17; John 2:13-17)', *RB* 107 (2000) 42-55, represents the minority opinion when he argues that Jesus' action in the Temple must have taken place very early in his career, when he was still under the influence of the Baptist.

114. Most recently M. D. Hooker, *The Signs of a Prophet: The Prophetic Actions of Jesus* (London: SCM, 1997) 44-48; and below, n. 231. Becker is a fairly lone voice when he concludes 'that Jesus did not engage in the action in the temple and that it cannot have been the cause of his final fate' (*Jesus* 333, 345).

115. The Temple tax was paid in Tyrian half-shekels and shekels, not Greek or Roman coinage (which carried pagan mottoes). So it would be natural for pilgrims to delay payment till they actually reached the Temple.

116. *Peristera* can be rendered either 'pigeon' or 'dove' (BDAG). Doves were the offering of the poor (Lev. 5.7; 12.8; 14.22; Luke 2.24).

117. Sanders accepts the basic scenario: the trading was conducted in Solomon's portico. But he dismisses the possibility that there was trade in animals (cattle and sheep, John 2.14-15) given the amount of fodder, manure, and noise inevitably involved (the queue of lambs at Passover was presumably exceptional); that trade was presumably conducted outside the Temple precincts (*Judaism* 68, 86-90; cf. Gnilka, *Jesus* 276). Charlesworth notes that access was possible from the so-called Solomon's stables beneath the southern end of the Temple platform, where larger animals could be stalled, to the area within the double Hulda Gate in the

ware of the easy assumption that he was following out a clearly thought-through strategy),[118] the act could hardly have been understood by the priestly authorities as other than critical of the Temple in its present form or operation.[119] Here we need to bear in mind that the Temple was the principal focus for economic and political power as well as for religious power.[120] An act seen as critically or pro-

---

southern wall of the Temple (*Jesus* 117-18). But J. Ådna, *Jerusalemer Tempel und Tempelmarkt im 1. Jahrhundert n. Chr.* (Wiesbaden: Harrassowitz, 1999) dismisses the suggestion: there was storage space there for materials used in sacrifice, but not for living sacrificial beasts (126-28). V. Eppstein, 'The Historicity of the Gospel Account of the Cleansing of the Temple', *ZNW* 55 (1964) 42-57, has raised the possibility that shortly before Passover Caiaphas had permitted a more extensive market to be set up in the court of the Gentiles (55); but the sources appealed to are late (see further critique in Ådna, *Jesu Stellung* 328-30).

118. Chilton (*Temple of Jesus* 100-11) in particular has developed an elaborate theory to explain why Jesus 'occupied' the Temple: the 'occupation' was designed to prevent the sacrifice of animals acquired on the site; money-changing was not an issue (110-11) — that feature is likely fictional (130); Jesus was seeking to realize the Targum of Zechariah's prophecy of the kingdom coming when offerings were directly presented in the Temple (without the intervention of middlemen) by both Israelites and non-Jews (*Rabbi Jesus* 197-200). Chilton notes a halakhah attributed to Hillel that offerings should be brought to the Temple by the owners for sacrifice, against the Shammaites' insistence that an animal might be handed over directly without the owner laying hands on it (*Temple* 101-102), and deduces that Jesus similarly regarded the offerer's actual ownership of what was offered as a vital aspect of sacrifice (109, 128). Following Eppstein (n. 117 above), Chilton suggests that Jesus was protesting against a recent innovation of Caiaphas to permit such trade within the precincts of the Temple (107-109). Similarly his *Pure Kingdom* 115-23.

119. In the debate about the significance of Jesus' act occasioned by Sanders, *Jesus* 61-71 (followed by Fredriksen, *Jesus* 207-12), see R. Bauckham, 'Jesus' Demonstration in the Temple', in *Law and Religion: Essays on the Place of the Law in Israel and Early Christianity,* ed. B. Lindars (Cambridge: Clarke, 1988) 72-89; C. A. Evans, 'Jesus' Action in the Temple: Cleansing or Portent of Destruction?' *CBQ* 51 (1989) 237-70, revised in Chilton and Evans, *Jesus in Context* 395-439; also 'Jesus' Action in the Temple and Evidence of Corruption in the First-Century Temple', *Jesus and His Contemporaries* 319-44; Bockmuehl, *This Jesus* ch. 3, particularly 197-99 n. 27; H. D. Betz, 'Jesus and the Purity of the Temple (Mark 11:15-18): A Comparative Religion Approach', *JBL* 116 (1997) 455-72; P. M. Casey, 'Culture and Historicity: The Cleansing of the Temple', *CBQ* 59 (1997) 306-32; K. H. Tan, *The Zion Traditions and the Aims of Jesus* (SNTSMS 91; Cambridge: Cambridge University, 1997) 166-81; Ådna, *Jesu Stellung* 335-76 (on the historicity of the episode 300-33). In contrast, D. Seeley, 'Jesus' Temple Act', *CBQ* 55 (1993) 263-83, cannot find sufficient explanation at the historical level and deduces from the way Mark has integrated it into his Gospel that the episode is better seen as a Markan composition. The Jesus Seminar agreed on the likelihood that 'Jesus precipitated some kind of temple incident by his aggressive criticism of the commercialization of the temple cult' (Funk, *Acts of Jesus* 122). Holmén sees the decisive clue in the allusion to Jer. 7.11 in Mark 11.17 ('a den of robbers'), but observes that not just the sellers but also the buyers were expelled according to Mark 11.15 (*Jesus* 310, 317, 323-26).

120. See above, §9.5a.

phetically subversive of the priestly power, upon which Israel's stability under Roman rule was thought to depend, would provide sufficient excuse for a policy of *realpolitik* to dictate Jesus' removal from the scene.[121] Whether Jesus' saying about the Temple was uttered by him on that occasion (as in John 2.19) or not, it seems to have provided the excuse needed.

To what extent Jesus' Temple demonstration can be described as 'messianic' is less clear. The essential ambiguity of the scene means that its significance would be more in the eye of the beholder than in the intention of Jesus, and most of the options would have at least some messianic overtones.[122] Despite Brandon, we can be confident that it was not a military action or a serious attempt to capture the Temple platform. Any such threat would certainly have met with a prompt response from the Antonia fortress overlooking the Temple mount.[123] But any disturbance in an area so sensitive both strategically and religiously might well have raised messianic questions in the minds of many. That the symbolism of Jesus' action spoke of the Temple's destruction[124] is certainly possible, though the point is hardly as clear-cut as Sanders assumed. Alternatively, if the symbolism spoke to some of condemnation of the present procedures for sacrifice (the principal purpose of the Temple),[125] then the coherence of that symbolism with Jesus' dictum on the Temple's future would no doubt raise the same questions about Jesus' messianic pretensions. Alternatively again, the action may well have appeared to others as some sort of symbolic purification (cleansing) of the Temple.[126] After all, the thought of such purification as necessary if Zion was to fulfil its eschatological function is clearly present in several

121. See, e.g., Crossan and Reed, *Excavating Jesus* 220-22, and further below, §17.1e.

122. See also my *Partings* 47-49.

123. The point is vividly illustrated by the episode in Acts 21.30-35 (see further Schürer, *History* 1.366). *Pace* Horsley, *Jesus* 297-98, the numbers involved in the events of 4 BCE and 66 CE made for quite different and much more serious situations (Josephus, *War* 2.10-13, 409-32); see further Catchpole, '"Triumphal" Entry' 332-33. Chilton envisages a religious protest (rather than a military attack), involving 'an army of zealots' (150-200 men) intent on purifying the Temple, but completed with such speed that the Temple police were outmanoeuvred and the Roman garrison were unable to act before the protesters melted into the crowds (*Rabbi Jesus* 228-29).

124. Sanders, *Jesus* 61-71; also *Historical Figure* 253-62; Horsley, *Jesus* 299-300; Crossan, *Historical Jesus* 357-59; Lüdemann, *Jesus* 77-78.

125. The action against the money-changers and pigeon-sellers could be read as an attack on the Temple tax itself, necessary to maintain the daily sacrifices, and on the cult itself, but equally as a protest against corruption and abuse of the system — perhaps even as an expression of country-boy outrage at the massive institution and bureaucracy involved! See further below, §17.3.

126. M. D. Hooker, 'Traditions about the Temple in the Sayings of Jesus', *BJRL* 70 (1988) 7-19 (here 17-18); Stuhlmacher, *Biblische Theologie* 1.150-51; cf. the earlier 'cleansings' *(katharizein)* of Nehemiah (Neh. 13.4-9) and Judas (1 Macc. 4.36-58).

strands of Jewish expectation.[127] And the Jesus tradition's echo of two or more important expressions of eschatological expectation[128] indicates that earliest Christian interpretation of the symbolic act went along the same lines. Although such expectations did not necessarily feature a royal Messiah (but note *Pss. Sol.* 17.30), it is likely that the one who enacted them in symbolic fashion would prompt speculation regarding his own eschatological and messianic (anointed) status.

Here too, therefore, it is hard to doubt that among the reverberations set off by Jesus' action in the Temple would be the question, 'Could this be the expected Davidic messiah?'

e. The Entry into Jerusalem (Mark 11.1-11 pars.)

The famous account of Jesus setting in train arrangements for his entry into Jerusalem on an ass *(pōlos)*[129] climaxes in the acclamation he received:

Matt. 21.9-11	Mark 11.9-11	Luke 19.37-40	John 12.13-19
9 And the crowds that went before him and that followed cried out, 'Hosanna to the Son of David! Blessed is he who comes in the name of the Lord!	9 And those who went before and those who followed cried out, 'Hosanna! Blessed is he who comes in the name of the Lord! 10 Blessed is the kingdom of our father David that	37 . . . the whole multitude of the disciples began to rejoice and praise God with a loud voice for all the mighty works that they had seen, 38 saying, 'Blessed is the King who comes in the name of the Lord! Peace	13 So they took branches of palm trees and went out to meet him, crying, 'Hosanna! Blessed is he who comes in the name of the Lord, even the King of Israel!'

127. Isa. 4.4; Mal. 3.1-4; *Jub.* 4.26; 11QT 29.8-10; *Pss. Sol.* 17.30. Tan points out that *Pss. Sol.* 17.30 has in view the purging of Jerusalem; the Temple is not mentioned (*Zion Traditions* 172-73). But he ignores the severe condemnation of Temple profanation earlier (*Pss. Sol.* 1.8; 2.3; 7.2; 8.11-13, 22). Cf. Wright: 'Jesus was performing Maccabean actions' (*Jesus* 493).

128. Mark 11.17 pars. cite or clearly echo both Isa. 56.7 and Jer. 7.11; possibly also Zech. 14.21, on which Catchpole places particular weight ('"Triumphal" Entry' 333-34); see earlier C. Roth, 'The Cleansing of the Temple and Zechariah xiv.21', *NovT* 4 (1960) 174-81. On expectation of an eschatological pilgrimage of Gentiles to participate in the Temple service see above, chapter 12 n. 71. Caird suggests that the thought is of the court of the Gentiles being filled (all of it?!) with a market, so as to deprive the Gentiles of a place to sacrifice and worship (*Theology* 397). In contrast, Crossan and Reed observe that with its huge court of Gentiles, the Temple was already 'a house of prayer for all nations' (*Excavating Jesus* 198, 200); but would Gentile access to this outermost court have been seen as fulfilment of Isaiah's eschatological vision (Isa. 56.3-8)?

129. See Davies and Allison, *Matthew* 3.116.

Hosanna in the highest!' 10 And when he entered Jerusalem, all the city was stirred, saying, 'Who is this?' 11 And the crowds said, 'This is the prophet Jesus from Nazareth of Galilee'.	is coming! Hosanna in the highest!' 11 And he entered Jerusalem, and went into the temple; and when he had looked round at everything, as it was already late, he went out to Bethany with the twelve.	in heaven and glory in the highest!' 39 And some of the Pharisees in the multitude said to him, 'Teacher, rebuke your disciples'. 40 He answered, 'I tell you, if these were silent, the very stones would cry out'.	. . . . 19 The Pharisees then said to one another, 'You see that you can do nothing; look, the world has gone after him'.

Despite various doubts to the contrary, it is likely that the episode is rooted in disciples' memories of Jesus' entry into Jerusalem. (1) Noteworthy are the local details at the beginning (Bethphage, Bethany, and the Mount of Olives in Mark 11.1).[130] (2) The acclamation itself evidences the characteristics of oral transmission: the core is constant in all four Gospels ('Blessed is he who comes in the name of the Lord'), but in each individual performance the core has been elaborated differently. (3) 'Hosanna' *(hosa'-na)* is firmly embedded (in John too), but appears nowhere else in the NT.[131] (4) Mark's account is surprisingly low-key: it is unclear how many beyond the immediate disciples were involved;[132] the acclamation is restrained (the other three Evangelists make it an acclamation of 'the son of David', 'the king'); the details are consistent with Zech. 9.9 but do not seem to have been derived from it;[133] and the story ends somewhat lamely, without any implication of a momentous event (as in Matthew) or hostile reaction (as in Luke and John).[134]

So most of the messianic implications in the story belong to the elaborated

130. Taylor characteristically points to these and other features as typical of 'the eyewitness rather than the artist' (*Mark* 452); see also Pesch, *Markusevangelium* 2.187-88.

131. *Hosa'-na* was a liturgical shout, probably derived from the Hebrew of *hosi'a-na* = 'save now' (Ps. 118.25); but probably the Aramaic had developed the sense of 'praise', as suggested by Matthew's usage, echoed also in *Did.* 10.6 ('Hosanna to the Son of David'), and by Luke's talk of the disciples' 'praise' while omitting the 'Hosanna' (see further E. Lohse, 'Hosianna', *Die Einheit des Neuen Testaments* [Göttingen: Vandenhoeck und Ruprecht, 1973] 104-10; Davies and Allison, *Matthew* 3.124-25).

132. Contrast Matthew — 'the crowds'; John 12.12 — 'the great crowd coming for the feast'.

133. Contrast Matt. 21.5-7; John 12.14-15.

134. The absence of a formal welcome in contrast to the parallel stories cited by Catchpole ('"Triumphal" Entry' 319-21; Catchpole's treatment is warmly applauded by Räisänen, *Messianic Secret* 232-34) calls in question his conclusion that the story has been determined from the first by later christology set in the shape of such 'triumphal entry' stories. See further B. Kinman, *Jesus' Entry into Jerusalem in the Context of Lukan Theology and the Politics of His Day* (Leiden: Brill, 1995), conclusions on 173-75. Cf. Witherington: 'it can be argued that Jesus is simply being accompanied by various pilgrims who are singing the pilgrim songs, one of which is based on Ps. 118:26ff.' (*Christology* 104-105).

retellings of the later Evangelists. But even so, a constant element in the tradition is Jesus' approach to or entry into Jerusalem on an ass. And since pilgrims would normally enter on foot, Jesus' choice (as it would appear) to ride an ass must have been intended as a statement of some significance — presumably as another enacted parable, for those who had ears to hear.[135] That some, of the disciples at least, caught an echo of Zech. 9.9 would hardly be surprising.[136] And we should recall that the entry was followed shortly by the more dramatic symbolic act in the Temple. But the core tradition leaves it unclear as to what Jesus' fuller intentions were at this point and whether his enacted parable was meant to be instructive or merely provocative.

f. The Healing of the Blind Man

As with the question about David's son (§15.3b), it is impossible to ignore the episode narrated in Mark 10.46-52 pars. The key element for us is that the blind beggar (Bartimaeus, according to Mark) repeatedly called on Jesus as 'son of David' (Mark 10.47-48 pars.).

Matt. 20.29-34	Mark 10.46-52	Luke 18.35-43
29 As they were leaving Jericho, a large crowd followed him. 30 There were two blind men sitting by the roadside. When they heard	46 They came to Jericho. As he and his disciples and a large crowd were leaving Jericho, Bartimaeus son of Timaeus, a blind beggar, was sitting by the roadside. 47 When he heard	35 As he approached Jericho, a blind man was sitting by the roadside begging. 36 When he heard a crowd going by, he asked what was happening. 37
that Jesus was passing by, they shouted, 'Lord, have mercy on us, Son of David!' 31 The crowd sternly ordered them to be quiet; but they shouted all the more, 'Lord, have mercy on us, Son of David!' 32 Jesus stood and called them, saying,	that it was Jesus of Nazareth, he began to shout and say, 'Jesus, Son of David, have mercy on me!' 48 Many sternly ordered him to be quiet, but he shouted even more loudly, 'Son of David, have mercy on me!' 49 Jesus stood and said, 'Call him here'. And they called the blind man, saying to him, 'Take heart; get up, he is calling you'. 50 So	They told him, 'Jesus of Nazareth is passing by'. 38 Then he called out, 'Jesus, Son of David, have mercy on me!' 39 Those who were in front sternly ordered him to be quiet; but he shouted even more loudly, 'Son of David, have mercy on me!' 40 Jesus stood still and ordered the man to be brought to him;

135. The point is stressed by Harvey, *Jesus* 121-29.

136. See also Tan, *Zion Traditions* 138-48. C. A. Evans, 'Jesus and Zechariah's Messianic Hope', in Chilton and Evans, *Authenticating the Activities of Jesus* 373-88, draws attention to the number of allusions to Zechariah in Jesus' final week in Jerusalem (particularly Zech. 9.9; 13.7; 14.20-21; see also below, chapter 17 n. 73) and suggests that 'the theology of the prophet Zechariah may have informed Jesus' understanding of his mission to Jerusalem' (386).

	throwing off his cloak, he sprang up and came to Jesus. 51 Then Jesus said to him, 'What do you want me to do for you?' The blind man said to him, 'Rabbouni, let me see again'. 52 Jesus said to him, 'Go; your faith has saved you.' Immediately he regained his sight and followed him on the way.	and when he came near, he asked him, 41 'What do you want me to do for you?' He said, 'Lord, let me see again'. 42 Jesus said to him, 'Receive your sight; your faith has saved you.' 43 At once he regained his sight and followed him, glorifying God.
'What do you want me to do for you?' 33 They said to him, 'Lord, let our eyes be opened'. 34 Moved with compassion, Jesus touched their eyes. Immediately they regained their sight and followed him.		

As to the historical value of the detail we should note the following. (1) Here again the episode is located: on the outskirts of Jericho.[137] (2) It is more likely that the name 'Bartimaeus' (Aramaic *bar timai*)[138] was omitted in the retellings of the story than that Mark gratuitously added it. (3) The term 'Son of David' is hardly characteristic of the miracle stories in the Jesus tradition (though Matthew adds in a number).[139] (4) The Aramaic 'Rabbouni' *(rabboni* or *rabbuni),*[140] appearing only here (10.51) and John 20.16 in the NT, is surely a sign of primitive formulation. (5) The variation in the silence motif (10.48) is unique in Mark, and the absence of a final command to silence is somewhat at odds with Mark's 'secrecy' motif.[141] (6) The concluding note ('he followed him') indicates that Bartimaeus became a disciple, and suggests that within the disciple circles it may well have been Bartimaeus's own testimony which provided the initial and enduring form of the tradition.[142]

The point then, is that the very early Jesus tradition recalled an occasion when Jesus was addressed as 'son of David'. This certainly suggests that Jesus' reputation had given rise to popular speculation about his messiahship. That a beggar's boldness should give voice to and attempt to trade on the speculation would be hardly surprising.

---

137. Meier, *Marginal Jew* 2.688. See also H.-J. Eckstein, 'Markus 10,46-52 als Schlüsseltext des Markusevangeliums', *ZNW* 87 (1996) 33-50.

138. Str-B 2.25; Meier, *Marginal Jew* 2.687-88; Kollmann, *Jesus* 238-39.

139. Meier, *Marginal Jew* 2.688-89 and 738 n. 50. In the historical situation, its use presupposes (a) that Jesus' Davidic descent was well enough known, and (b) that his reputation as a healer was sufficient to evoke the popular(?) expectation of a Davidide with healing power (see below, 15.7a) (similarly Funk, *Acts of Jesus* 118).

140. Str-B 2.25.

141. Only 'somewhat', since there are several other stories in Mark which do not fit within that motif (1.29-31; 2.1-12; 3.1-6; 5.25-34; 7.24-30; 9.14-27).

142. P. J. Achtemeier, '"And He Followed Him": Miracles and Discipleship in Mark 10:46-52', in R. W. Funk, ed., *Early Christian Miracle Stories, Semeia* 11 (Missoula: Scholars, 1978) 115-45.

g. Peter's Confession

The question whether Jesus was considered to be the royal Messiah during his mission can hardly avoid Mark 8.27-30 pars.

Matt. 16.13-20	Mark 8.27-30	Luke 9.18-21	John 6.66-69
13 Now when Jesus came into the district of Caesarea Philippi, he asked his disciples, 'Who do people say that the Son of man is?' 14 And they said, 'Some say John the Baptist, others Elijah, and others Jeremiah or one of the prophets'. 15 He said to them, 'But who do you say that I am?' 16 Simon Peter answered, 'You are the Christ, the Son of the living God'. . . . . 20 Then he charged the disciples to tell no one that he was the Christ.	27 And Jesus went on with his disciples, to the villages of Caesarea Philippi; and on the way he asked his disciples, 'Who do people say that I am?' 28 And they said to him, 'John the Baptist; and others Elijah; and others one of the prophets'. 29 And he asked them, 'But who do you say that I am?' Peter answered him, 'You are the Christ'. 30 And he charged them to tell no one about him.	18 Now it happened that as he was praying alone the disciples were with him; and he asked them, 'Who do the crowds say that I am?' 19 And they answered, 'John the Baptist; but others Elijah; and others, that one of the old prophets has risen'. 20 So he said to them, 'But who do you say that I am?' And Peter answered, 'The Christ of God'. 21 But he charged and commanded them to tell no one this . . .	66 After this many of his disciples drew back and no longer went about with him. 67 Jesus said to the twelve, 'Do you also wish to go away?' 68 Simon Peter answered him, 'Lord, to whom shall we go? You have the words of eternal life; 69 and we have believed, and have come to know, that you are the Holy One of God'.

The passage obviously plays a pivotal role in Mark's Gospel: there is a clear before-and-after-Caesarea-Philippi structure to Mark's plot.[143] And consequently the episode is frequently regarded as the product of early Christian, or specifically Markan, theology, with the Wredean Markan secret (Mark 8.30) seen as a decisive pointer in that direction.[144] Characteristic embellishments by Matthew (16.16b-19 — the famous commission of Peter)[145] and Luke (9.18 — Jesus praying)[146] do not affect this conclusion.

Nevertheless, there are several indications that Mark has been able to draw on a well-rooted memory, with the variations between the Synoptists characteristic of performance flexibility. (1) Again we note the unusual feature that Mark's version has recalled the locale where the teaching took place[147] and the still more

143. See further below in vol. 3.
144. See particularly Räisänen, *Messianic Secret* 176; Funk, *Acts of Jesus* 103-104.
145. See above, §13.3f.
146. See above, chapter 14 n. 82.
147. Bultmann thought the whole narrative was an Easter story carried back into the

unusual feature that it happened 'on the way'.[148] (2) John's account also recalls a turning point (in Galilee) which drew a confession from Peter (John 6.69). Since there is no literary interdependence between the two versions, the probability is that both attest a memory of some such event and the diversity of the ways it was handled in different streams of oral performances. (3) If the question whether Jesus was Messiah arose at all during Jesus' mission, as it almost certainly did at its end, then almost certainly among the first to ask the question would be his close disciples. They, after all, had sacrificed families and livelihood to follow Jesus. It would be very surprising if the impact he made on them and the relative success of their mission had not prompted them to ask just this question. And that Peter should be the one to blurt out their common hope and expectation (cf. again Mark 9.34; 10.37 pars.) would be entirely in keeping with other indications of his character. (4) Finally, we should note that in the sequel, joined firmly to the confession in the Synoptics, Peter is called 'Satan' by Jesus.[149] Whatever the tensions between apostles in the decades following,[150] it is hard to credit that such a rebuke of the one regarded on all sides as the first disciple of Jesus emerged in that period, and still harder to believe that such a rebuke would have gained a place in the Jesus tradition and acceptance as part of it.[151]

Over all the probability must be deemed quite high that in Mark 8.27-30 pars. we see recalled an episode within the mission of Jesus in which the issue of Jesus' messiahship was raised.

h. The Feeding of the 5000 (Mark 6.32-44 pars.)

When we return to this episode below, we will find grounds sufficient to conclude that behind it, very likely, lies the shared memory of a large communal meal, probably near the (north-)eastern edge of the Sea of Galilee (§15.7f). But if indeed such an event took place, including some sort of shared meal in a desolate

---

ministry of Jesus (*History* 259), but no other resurrection appearance to any of the twelve is recorded as taking place so far north or outside Judea or Galilee. Too little asked are the questions: Why would the disciples have been in that territory following Jesus' crucifixion? Alternatively, why would a resurrection appearance be attributed to that region?

148. The only other occasion in the Gospels where Jesus is envisaged as teaching 'on the way' are the close parallel Matt. 20.17 and the post-resurrection Luke 24.32.

149. Mark 8.33/Matt. 16.23; cf. John 6.70. Others have suggested that if the command to silence and the Passion prediction are removed as redactional, then Jesus rebukes Peter for confessing him as Messiah (e.g., Hahn, *Hoheitstitel* 174-75, 226-30 [*Titles* 157-58, 223-28]; Fuller, *Foundations* 109; Theissen and Merz, *Historical Jesus* 539). But see Stuhlmacher, *Biblische Theologie* 1.114-15.

150. Cf. Galatians 1–2; 2 Corinthians 10–13.

151. Similarly Meier, *Marginal Jew* 3.236-38, citing the criterion of embarrassment.

place (*erēmos*, 6.32), then it would probably carry strong messianic overtones for those with even half an ear. Such an event might well recall the manna miracle of Israel's wilderness wanderings or evoke the prophetic hope of a fruitful desert in the age to come (Isa. 32.15; 35.1-2), the expectation of another David who would feed the flock of Israel (Ezek. 34.23), or the same association as we find in the wilderness community of Qumran between the communal meals they were enjoying at that very time and the messianic meals awaited in the future (1QSa).[152]

Most striking is the note in John 6.15 that the episode ended with the crowd threatening to 'take Jesus by force to make him king', causing him to withdraw from the scene. Had John's note stood alone it could well have been discounted, even though it is not particularly characteristic of John's own plot-line. But it seems to be matched by a curious feature at the same point in Mark's version: at the end of the meal Jesus 'compelled (*ēnankasen*) his disciples to embark on the boat and to go ahead to the other side' (6.45). Mark leaves the word without explanation: why should Jesus have chosen to force his disciples to leave, and to do so before he 'dismissed the crowd' (6.45)? The link with John 6.15, for which there is no evidence of collusion on either side, suggests an obvious answer. Part of the crowd had indeed seen a messianic significance in the event; the disciples had been caught up in a mounting wave of enthusiasm; Jesus responded first by forcing the disciples to embark on the lake; and then, perhaps only then, could he successfully dismiss the crowd.[153] Mark also reports that Jesus himself then withdrew into the hills to pray (6.46), and since he reports only three such occasions during Jesus' mission, perhaps he intended to imply that a critical juncture in Jesus' mission had been reached (cf. 1.35, 38; 14.35-36).

To sum up, we have been able to identify a number of incidents during Jesus' mission which, in terms of tradition formation, all seem to be more or less firmly rooted in earliest memories and which all raised in one way or another the question whether Jesus was to be regarded as the expected royal Messiah.[154] It would be simply unrealistic and (historically speaking) irresponsible to consign all these traditions to the post-Easter faith of Jesus' disciples. The question posed by Pilate, providing him with the legal justification for Jesus' execution, was surely posed by others at earlier stages in Jesus' mission.[155] We can be

152. J. C. O'Neill, 'The Silence of Jesus', *NTS* 15 (1968-69) 153-67 (here 163-64).

153. Dodd, *Historical Tradition* 212-17.

154. Although Mark undoubtedly saw christological significance in Jesus' talk of the bridegroom in 2.19-20 and the reference to David in 2.25-26, it is quite another question as to what Jesus may have intended by these references (see, e.g., Roloff, *Kerygma* 58; Davies and Allison, *Matthew* 2.110; Guelich, *Mark* 1.123). See also above, chapter 12 n. 289.

155. 'It is inconceivable, in the light of the eschatological character of Jesus' message, that the messianic issue would not have come up either for Jesus or his contemporaries' (Rowland, *Christian Origins* 182).

fairly confident, therefore, that one of the central props of Wrede's thesis is unsound. If the 'messianic secret' is indeed part of Mark's secrecy motif, then it is not because the secret was intended to cloak the fact that the idea of Jesus as Messiah had been conceived and achieved only as a result of Easter. Could this be the Messiah, the son of David? If the tradition reviewed above has any historical value, that question must have occurred to many who witnessed or heard of Jesus as his mission moved towards its climax before it became the formal ground for his execution.

15.4. A Role Declined

The conclusion just reached obviously poses the follow-up question: How did Jesus respond to such speculation? If the issue of Jesus as Messiah was indeed raised during at least the latter part of his mission, as seems most likely, then it can hardly have escaped Jesus himself. He must have been confronted with the issue. In which case it is inconceivable that his disciples did not recall and reflect on his reaction to it. Did he share that speculation? Did he regard himself as Messiah, son of David? The same episodes offer an interesting answer to these questions too. It will make better sense on this occasion to follow the sequence in most likely chronological order.

a. The Feeding of the 5000

The episode highlights two findings. (1) There was abroad, at least in the region of Lake Galilee itself, a popular conception of the royal Messiah, who would echo the great events of Israel's first liberation of Canaan[156] and fulfil the prophetic hope of a prosperous new age under a new Davidic king. Such a king, we might note, Pilate would certainly want to crucify for obvious political and military reasons. Jesus was probably seen by many in Galilee as at least potentially such a Messiah. (2) More interesting, however, is the clear implication that Jesus reacted against this role. The reaction presumably implies that he saw the role as a misleading or false characterisation of his mission.[157] And even if the role had

156. We recall the two figures who attempted to repeat the miracles of the initial conquest of the Promised Land — the crossing of the Jordan and the fall of the walls of Jericho (Josephus, *Ant.* 20.97, 169-70).

157. Cf. Witherington, *Christology* 98-101, who also suggests that the feeding of the five thousand was the last act of Jesus' Galilean ministry (117). This suggestion would meet Fredriksen's argument that a messianic claim could not have been voiced in Galilee (she places the feeding on the lake's western shore) without provoking Antipas to suppress it (*Jesus* 215-18).

any attraction to him,[158] a wise man would recognize the inflammability of the Galilean crowd and its potential fickleness. The lesson learned or confirmed here would go a long way to explain Jesus' reticence in other situations.

b. Peter's Confession

Here the focus turns to the enigmatic command to silence, which, according to Mark, was Jesus' response to Peter's confession of Jesus as Messiah (Mark 8.30). In the tradition itself there is no indication that Jesus denied the confession. But neither is there any indication that he accepted or welcomed it (Matt. 16.17 fills in this lacuna). In Mark's version, 8.30 is a word neither of rebuke nor of congratulation. It is a command to silence (on the issue of messiahship), followed immediately by explicit and pointed teaching expressing Jesus' conviction that his mission would end in rejection and suffering (8.31). Now the command certainly functions in Mark's Gospel as part of his secrecy motif. But a historical reading is entirely plausible: Peter's confession was of Jesus as royal Messiah in accordance with the popular understanding of the Davidic Messiah as a mighty warrior (§15.2a), and Peter's conception of the royal Messiah was close to that of the crowd at the feeding miracle and on the same lines as that of the Zebedee brothers when they asked for seats on the right and left of Jesus in his kingdom (Mark 10.35-37 par.).[159] If Jesus did not see his role in such terms, how might he have responded? One alternative was to damp down such expectation and to attempt to indicate (or construct) a role model closer to what he saw for himself. That is what Jesus did, implies Mark,[160] and we have already seen that expectation of suffering

158. Does the account of Jesus' first temptation (Matt. 4.3/Luke 4.3) contain an echo of this episode?

159. Cullmann, *Christology* 122-26; Taylor, *Mark* 377; Pesch, *Markusevangelium* 2.34; cf. Leivestad, *Jesus* 93-95. Despite Räisänen's firm judgment — 'Nothing points to the alleged Jewish nationalist meaning' (*Messianic Secret* 179) — the plausibility remains: if the question of Jesus as royal Messiah did arise for the disciples (as seems inherently likely), the only obvious category of 'Messiah' into which they could fit their hopes was that of the kingly, military leader (§15.2a).

160. Catchpole, '"Triumphal" Entry' 326, and Räisänen, *Messianic Secret* 179-81, are right to point out that the command to silence does not function in the narrative as a correction; Mark certainly did not want to dispute that Jesus was Messiah. The tendency to link Jesus' rebuke of Peter (Mark 8.33) directly to Peter's confession (8.29), as summarized in Charlesworth, 'Messianology to Christology' 12 (Jesus 'apparently rejected Peter's confession, that he [Jesus] was the Christ, as satanic'), should also be resisted. At the same time, Hengel not unfairly turns the question round: 'Is it not an indication of the relative trustworthiness of the gospel tradition that the . . . "community" never produced an unambiguous scene in which Jesus announces his claim *coram publico* with a clear "I am the Christ"?' ('Jesus, Messiah of Israel' 59).

strongly featured in Jesus' teaching.[161] In which case, the command to silence functions more to indicate a messianic misunderstanding than a messianic secret.

c. The Healing of the Blind Man

What is most striking in this case is the fact that nothing is made of the messianic significance of the title ('son of David'). The story shows Jesus responding to a beggar's persistence, but neither as rebuking nor as acknowledging the title. That suggests, again, that the story is framed from the perspective of the one who benefited from the event; it was his healing that was most important. It is not told with christological intent and tells us little or nothing about Jesus' own attitude to the title.

d. The Entry into Jerusalem

Three features should be noted here. (1) Mark carefully avoids portraying the episode as an overt messianic claim. The Zechariah prophecy is not referred to. The ovation seems to come more from the disciples than the crowd. And the cries of welcome fall short of complete messianic recognition and homage. (2) If the image of Jerusalem's king is deliberately evoked (Zech. 9.9), then the choice of an ass to ride on picks out the one image of humility within the fuller portrayal of Zion's triumphant king.[162] (3) It must be significant that the authorities made no move to arrest Jesus as a result of his entry. Nor is any hint given that reference to it was part of the testimony against Jesus at his trial (though the notes on the hearing before Caiaphas are exceedingly brief). Presumably, then, no clear political significance could be or was read into the event. Was this, then, a kind of parable of the claims implicit in Jesus' mission? For those with ears attuned to catch political overtones, there was nothing beyond the boisterous procession of a bunch of pilgrims to be reported. But for those who looked for the coming of God's reign the event carried clear overtones of eschatological import.[163]

161. See above, §12.4d, and further below, §17.4c.

162. 'Rejoice greatly, O daughter of Zion! Shout aloud, O daughter of Jerusalem! Lo, your king comes to you; triumphant and victorious is he, humble *('ani)* and riding on an ass, on a colt the foal of an ass. I will cut off the chariot from Ephraim and the war horse from Jerusalem; and the battle bow shall be cut off, and he shall command peace to the nations . . .' (Zech. 9.9-10). *'Ani,* of course, evokes the same range of meaning (poverty, affliction, humility) as we observed in §13.4.

163. Others draw stronger conclusions: 'the entry was probably deliberately managed by Jesus to symbolize the coming kingdom and his role in it' (Sanders, *Jesus* 308); 'a conscious, deliberate demonstration and provocation' (Leivestad, *Jesus* 140); 'there can be little

e. The Cleansing of the Temple

The cleansing of the Temple points in a similar direction. We can rule out the suggestion that Jesus attempted a military coup, intended presumably to seize the vacant throne of Herod the Great. That leaves us with a prophetic protest which acknowledged the centrality of the Temple for God's dealings with Israel, but also enacted some kind of aspirations for the Temple (or a new temple) to fulfil its eschatological role. Again the lack of reference to the episode in Jesus' trial (unless it is implicit in the testimony about Jesus' Temple word) may indicate that it was not reckoned as particularly serious, either politically or prophetically. And that is about as much as we can say with confidence. How the episode contributes to the question of whether Jesus saw his role in messianic terms is hard to say.[164] But he acted presumably in the light of the eschatological expectations for the Temple (renewed Temple), and possibly as a self-conscious actor in the eschatological drama already beginning to unfold.

f. Tribute to Caesar

Our question is not much further clarified by Jesus' response to the question about tribute to Caesar. For it has always been recognized as a classic example of diplomatic ambiguity. Brandon's argument that it would have been heard as forbidding tribute, since the land and all its produce belongs to God, has an echo in the accusation attested only in Luke 23.2 ('We found this man perverting our nation, and forbidding us to give tribute to Caesar').[165] But the clearer inference, given that the saying was uttered with reference to a denarius bearing the head of Tiberius (Mark 12.16 pars.),[166] is that Jesus acknowledged the right of the Em-

doubt that Jesus associated himself with Zech. 9:9' (Witherington, *Christology* 106); 'clearly messianic' (Wright, *Jesus* 491); Jesus deliberately evoked and enacted the kingly role indicated in Zech. 9.9 — Israel's 'divinely appointed king who was to lay claim to his city to inaugurate the eschatological restoration' (Tan, *Zion Traditions* 149-56). In some contrast, Fredriksen, though dubious of most of the detail in the Gospels' accounts, argues that it was the crowd, not the disciples, and not Jesus himself, who first identified and proclaimed Jesus as Messiah (*Jesus* 241-58).

164. Bolder again is Witherington: 'Only royalty would dare to interfere as Jesus did'; '. . . he saw himself as the messianic figure of Zechariah' (Zech. 14.21) (*Christology* 113-15). See further below, §17.3.

165. The phrase is the same in Luke 20.22 (*Kaisari phoron dounai*) and 23.2 (*phorous Kaisari didonai*), although Mark 12.14/Matt. 22.17 use the Latin loan word *kēnsos* (census) rather than *phoros* (see further BDAG *ad loc.*).

166. On the identity of the coin see H. St. John Hart, 'The Coin of "Render unto Caesar . . ."', in Bammel and Moule, *Jesus and Politics* 241-48.

peror to levy tribute from his subject peoples.[167] Here again, the fact that the charge features so little in the trials of Jesus (Luke 23.2 apart) suggests that no case of any weight could be built on it.[168] That the saying contributes anything towards an answer to our question, therefore, is at best uncertain. But it certainly bears witness to Jesus' own political astuteness.

g. The Question about David's Son

As well as being of disputed historicity, the passage's riddling quality puts the onus on the hearer to draw out its significance. Does it reveal anything of Jesus' own self-understanding?[169] Was he playing 'cat and mouse' with his interlocutors, or simply engaging in a stimulating intellectual exchange?

h. The Trial of Jesus

The trial of Jesus, however, provides more answers. The interest again centres on Jesus' response to the questions put to him by both Caiaphas and Pilate. What is of particular interest is the ambivalence of the reply in all but one version.

Matt. 26.63-64	Mark 14.61-62	Luke 22.67-68
63 And the High Priest said to him, 'I adjure you by the living God that you tell us <u>if you are the Christ</u>, the son of God. 64 Jesus says to him, 'You say'.	61 Again the High Priest asked him and says to him, 'Are you <u>the Christ</u>, the son of the Blessed?' 62 But Jesus said, '<u>I am</u>'.	67 . . . saying, '<u>If you are the Christ</u>, tell us'. But he said to them, 'If I tell you, you will not believe; 68 and if I ask, you will not answer'.

167. This was presumably how the saying was taken by Paul, if it is indeed the case that Rom. 13.7 contains an echo of it (Rowland, *Christian Origins* 144-45). See also Cullmann, *Revolutionaries* 45-47; F. F. Bruce, 'Render to Caesar', in Bammel and Moule, *Jesus and Politics* 249-63, who points out, *inter alia,* that if the issue became more sharply confrontational subsequently for the Zealots, leading to the first revolt in 66, it is also true that Christians also subsequently concluded that it was necessary to say No to Caesar; Witherington, *Christology* 101-104, 117; Crossan and Reed observe that in asking for a coin, Jesus shows that he did not even carry Caesar's coin (*Excavating Jesus* 181).

168. This tells against the argument, e.g., of Horsley, *Jesus* 306-17, that it would have been almost impossible to hear the saying as somehow legitimating 'the things of Caesar'. That some chose to hear it as a challenge to Caesar's authority is certainly implied by Luke 23.2; but the saying itself would hardly give sufficient substance to the charge itself. Wright's treatment (*Jesus* 502-507) also raises the question whether all the 'layers of meaning' which might be detected in Jesus' answer were thereby intended by Jesus.

169. 'This text, when coupled with others, strongly suggests that Jesus did see himself in more than ordinary human categories' (Witherington, *Christology* 191).

Matt. 27.11	Mark 15.2	Luke 23.3
And the ruler asked him, saying, 'Are you the king of the Jews?' Jesus replied, 'You say'.	And Pilate asked him, 'Are you the king of the Jews?' But he answered him and says, 'You say'.	And Pilate asked him, saying, 'Are you the king of the Jews?' But he answered him and said, 'You say'.

Apart from Mark 14.62 all the replies are at best ambivalent: 'You say *(su eipas, su legeis)*'. There is some doubt about the Markan exception.[170] But even if we conclude that the original text of Mark was indeed the unambivalent 'I am *(ego eimi)*', it is more likely that Mark has modified an ambiguous 'You say' (or equivalent) by making Jesus' response a resounding affirmation, than that Matthew has transformed such an unequivocal 'Yes' to the unsatisfactory 'You say so' = 'That's your way of putting it'.[171]

The point, then, is that the reply Jesus is recalled as giving both to Caiaphas and to Pilate was probably the same: 'You say so'. What was being thus signified? At least an unwillingness to accept the title of Messiah/king, or, to be more precise, an unwillingness to accept the role which the title indicated to the questioner. Is the implication, then, that Jesus accepted the title in a different sense? All apart from Mark, and only in the answer to Caiaphas, indicate that 'Messiah' was a term Jesus preferred *not* to use for his own role.[172] These exchanges are important. For they exemplify a dilemma which must frequently have confronted Jesus: could he accept or use a title which implied a role he was unwilling to embrace?

To sum up this probe into one of the most sensitive titular claims made for Jesus, sensitive to both Jews and Christians: Was Jesus remembered as claiming to be the royal Messiah of prophetic and eschatological expectation? And can we deduce from the evidence reviewed whether Jesus regarded himself as the royal Messiah? Despite the doubts of those who focus more on the stage of tradition re-presented by Mark and the other Synoptic Evangelists, it is certainly possible to offer a historically responsible answer to the former question. Indeed, it is almost impossible to escape the conclusion that the issue of Jesus' messiahship was raised during the latter stages of his mission and that he was remembered as reacting to the issue on his own account. So how did he react? Did he claim to be the long-hoped-for David's royal son? In the light of our findings above, the answer has to be a qualified No![173]

170. I had previously followed Taylor, *Mark* 568, in suggesting that the very weakly attested longer reading ('You say that I am') is original ('Messianic Ideas' 375-76).

171. 'There is no sufficient evidence that this was an accepted form of affirmation, either in Greek, or in Hebrew or Aramaic' (Dodd, *Founder* 101); though Dodd also points out that 'a title which he would not deny to save his life cannot have been without significance for him' (103). See also my 'Are You the Messiah?' 11-12.

172. Similarly Cullmann, *Christology* 118-21; Vermes, *Jesus the Jew* 148-49.

173. Cf. Bornkamm's conclusion: 'We should not speak about Jesus' non-Messianic history before his death, but rather of a movement of shattered Messianic hopes . . .' (*Jesus* 172).

The answer is No because Jesus is never once recalled as using the title 'Messiah' of himself or as unequivocally welcoming its application to him by others (Mark 14.62 is the sole exception).[174] It is also sufficiently clear from several, though not all, of the episodes reviewed above, that Jesus ignored or refused or rejected the dominant current understanding of the royal Messiah as a royal and military power like Herod the Great. This answer is consistent also with Jesus' remembered response to his disciples' ambition to share in royal power and privilege: that should not be the model for discipleship (Mark 10.35-45 pars.).[175]

The qualification is necessary, however, because there is a legitimate query as to whether the then current understanding of the royal Messiah's role was the only one possible from Israel's prophetic texts. The fact that the first Christians took over the title 'Messiah' so speedily and so completely (§15.2) suggests that there were other strands of Israel's expectation which had what might be called 'messianic potential'.[176] It is certainly striking that the first disciples did not abandon the title in the light of Jesus' failure to realize any of their own hopes for a share in royal power. And we ruled out of play at an early stage the alternative suggestion that they had never entertained the thought of Jesus' messiahship prior to their Easter experience. The only plausible option remaining is that they had in fact been convinced that Jesus was Messiah, son of David, during his mission, but that their conception of his messiahship was radically transformed by the events of Good Friday. In that light they in effect emptied the title of its traditional content and filled it with new content provided by the law and the prophets and the psalms; Luke 24.25-27, 44-46 is one version of that process and strongly suggests the abruptness with which the transformation took place. In so doing, we could say that they were taking up the pointers Jesus had provided in his talk of eschatological reversal and suffering (§12.4c-d), but that does not quite validate the corollary that Jesus believed and taught his role to be that of a suffering royal Messiah.

Fascinating as the debate on Jesus' royal messiahship is, therefore, the term itself, royal Messiah, is too contested to allow a satisfactory conclusion. Either

174. The term 'Christ' does not even appear in the Q material.

175. Cf. Barrett: 'I do not see how the gospel material, critically evaluated, can lead to the conclusion that Jesus publicly stated the claim, "I am the Messiah"; or even that he thought privately in these terms' (*Jesus* 23); Theissen and Merz: 'Jesus had a messianic consciousness, but did not use the title Messiah'; he reshaped messianic expectations into a 'group messianism' — referring to Matt. 19.28/Luke 22.28-30 (*Historical Jesus* 538-40).

176. This was one of my main points in 'Messianic Ideas' (particularly 366, 369-70). Reading the Jesus tradition in the echo chamber of his controlling story, Wright concludes confidently that Jesus thought he was 'Israel-in-person, Israel's representative . . . the Messiah' (*Jesus* 538).

its reference was too clear, in which case Jesus seems to have declined it. Or its reference was unclear, in which case the debate as to whether Jesus laid claim to it does not advance the discussion very far. And though the first Christians certainly did use it, they did so only by transforming its reference in the light of Jesus' teaching and death. But if our concern is to know what Jesus thought on the matter as the best explanation for the impact which he made as attested by the Jesus tradition, it is as well to focus our attention elsewhere.

15.5. Priestly Messiah

For the sake of completeness we need at least to mention this further strand of Jewish expectation at the time of Jesus. For from various sources it is evident that some of Jesus' contemporaries invested considerable hope in the other most prominent anointed figure in the life of ancient Israel — the anointed priest. The development is usually traced back to Zechariah 4, where two anointeds are envisaged, not only Zerubbabel, the royal figure, but also Joshua the high priest.[177] The influence of Zechariah's vision is already evident in ben Sira 45–50,[178] but comes to full flower in the *Testaments of the 12 Patriarchs,* where Levi (the priest) is superior to Judah (the king),[179] and in the Qumran scrolls, where the priestly Messiah (the Messiah of Aaron) takes precedence over the Messiah of Israel.[180]

From the perspective of the present study, the most striking feature of this messianic expectation is that it was apparently never seen as an option for Jesus. Presumably this was because it was well enough known that Jesus was not of the appropriate tribe; he was not descended from Levi. Equally notable is the fact that when the possibility of presenting Jesus as (high) priest is followed up, the author to the Hebrews has to develop a unique argument: Jesus does not belong to the priestly order of Aaron, but to that of the mysterious Melchizedek (Heb. 4.14–5.10; 7).

177. Hesse, *TDNT* 9.500-501, 507-508.
178. 49.11-12; Aaron is extolled at greater length (45.6-22) than David (47.2-11).
179. Most clearly *T. Jud.* 21.2-4: the Lord 'set the kingship beneath the priesthood. . . . As heaven is higher than the earth, so is the priesthood of God higher than the kingship on the earth'; full detail in Hollander and de Jonge, *Testaments* 56-61, 222. A small fragment of *T. Levi* reads 'the kingdom of priesthood is greater than the kingdom . . .' (1Q21 [1QTLevi ar] Fragment 1).
180. 'The Messiah of Aaron': 1QS 9.11. In 1QSa (1Q28a) 2.17-21 the Messiah of Aaron stretches out his hand to the bread before the Messiah of Israel; in 1QSb (1Q28b) the blessing of the high priest precedes that of the prince of the congregation (see further Collins, *Scepter and Star* 74-77, 83-95).

It is worth noting these details, if only for two reasons. (1) There was evidently sufficient knowledge regarding Jesus' descent for it to be obvious to all concerned that he did not have a priestly lineage. (2) Those who made evaluations of Jesus, whether his disciples or others, did not feel free to create facts regarding his lineage or to fit him better into some expected role. This in turn suggests, by way of contrast, that the knowledge regarding Jesus' fitness to be considered for other roles was well grounded also.

15.6. The Prophet

Much the more interesting possibility was that Jesus might be considered a prophet. For in terms of eschatological expectation, the role of prophet was almost as prominent as that of royal Messiah and more widespread than the hope of an anointed priest.

a. Jewish Expectation

Three prophetic figures feature in Jewish eschatological expectation.

(1) Mal. 4.5-6 evidently aroused considerable speculation regarding the *return of Elijah:* 'Lo, I will send you the prophet Elijah before the great and terrible day of the Lord comes. And he will turn the hearts of the fathers to their children and the hearts of children to their fathers, lest I come and strike the land with a curse'. This expectation was echoed in Sir. 48.9-10: 'you who are ready at the appointed time, it is written, to calm the wrath of God before it breaks out in fury,[181] to turn the heart of the father to the son, and to restore the tribes of Jacob'. The expectation does not seem to have left much trace in the pseudepigrapha,[182] though it is alluded to in the DSS.[183] But the expectation obviously lies behind various formulations in the Gospels,[184] as also the opinions voiced in Mark 6.15 par. and 8.28 pars. concerning who Jesus might be.[185] One of the most interesting features of Jewish expectation is the associ-

---

181. The Syriac reads, 'before the day of the Lord'; the Hebrew is missing.

182. But see *Sib. Or.* 2.187-90.

183. 4Q521 fragment 2 3.2: 'The fathers will return to the sons' (echoing Mal. 4.5; Sir. 48.10); 4Q558: 'to you I will send Elijah, before. . . .'

184. Luke 1.17: John the Baptist 'will go before him in the spirit and power of Elijah, to turn the hearts of the fathers to the children . . .'; Mark 9.11-12/Matt. 17.10-11: 'Elijah comes (first) to restore all things'; Matt. 11.14: 'Elijah who is to come'; John 1.21: 'Are you Elijah?'.

185. More detail in J. Jeremias, *El(e)ias, TDNT* 2.931-34. Note also Justin, *Dial.* 8.4; 49.1.

ation of Elijah with Enoch,[186] since both did not die but were translated to heaven.[187]

(2) Deut. 18.15, 18 was an obvious basis for speculation regarding a *prophet like Moses:* Moses promises, 'The Lord your God will raise up for you a prophet like me from among you . . .', of whom the Lord promises, 'I will put my words in his mouth, and he shall speak to them all that I command him'. Surprisingly, however, little seems to have been made of this prophecy in Jewish expectation by the time of Jesus,[188] though it features in one of Qumran's testimony collections[189] and was picked up and referred to Jesus in earliest Christianity (Acts 3.22-23; 7.37). We will pursue the significance of a possible echo in the transfiguration narrative below (Mark 9.3-5 pars.).

(3) There also seems to have been less definable and probably overlapping expectation regarding an unnamed *prophet,* or should we say, an *eschatological prophet.* This is usually focused on Isa. 61.1-3: 'the Spirit of the Lord is upon me, because the Lord has anointed me to preach good tidings to the afflicted . . .'. The allusion to this passage and to Isa. 52.7 in two of the most interesting of the Qumran scrolls indicates the attraction exerted by talk of the one who 'preaches good tidings' on those looking for eschatological clues in the prophets.[190] Also well known is the somewhat surprising fact that 1QS 9.11 awaits the coming of 'the prophet' as well as the Messiahs of Aaron and Israel. Of particular interest for us is the range of options canvassed in Mark 6.15 pars. and 8.28 pars. — not just John the Baptist or Elijah, but also 'a prophet like one of the prophets' (Mark 6.15; 8.28), 'one of the old prophets has arisen' (Luke 9.8, 19), and 'Jeremiah' (Matt. 16.14). And John's Gospel refers to speculation regarding 'the prophet'.[191]

Of course, the separation of the above strands is simply for analytical purposes. There is no suggestion that these various prophetic hopes were distinguished in the expectations and speculations of the time of Jesus. On the con-

186. *1 En.* 90.31 (cf. 89.52); *Apoc. Elij.* 5.32; this expectation may well lie behind the vision of the two witnesses in Rev. 11.3.

187. Gen. 5.24; 2 Kgs. 2.11-12; Sir. 48.9.

188. The Samaritans and the later rabbis did take up the hope to some extent; see, e.g., my *Christology* 277 n. 63 and 304 n. 141. Leivestad suggests that animosity to everything Samaritan explains why Deuteronomy 18 was not more exploited in Jewish texts (*Jesus* 64).

189. 4Q175 (4QTest), which cites Deut. 5.28-29; 18.18-19; Num. 24.15-17; and Deut. 33.8-11 in sequence.

190. 4Q521 (already cited above, §12.5c); 11QMelch 2.15-16: 'This [. . .] is the day of [peace about whi]ch he said [. . . through Isa]iah the prophet, who said ["How] beautiful upon the mountains are the feet [of] the messen[ger who] announces peace, the mess[enger of good who announces salvati]on, [sa]ying to Zion: your God [reigns]' (Isa. 52.7); 'the messenger' is interpreted as 'the anointed of the Spirit *(mašiaḥ haruaḥ)*' and correlated with the talk in Dan. 9.25 of 'an anointed, a *nagid*' (on the reference of *nagid* see above, n. 18).

191. John 6.14; 7.40, 52; in 7.52 'the prophet' is the reading of p[66] and p[75].

trary, the indications are that the different strands of expectation were often woven together as various prophecies provided fresh insights or confirmation.[192] At the same time, the range of the material should serve as a useful reminder of how amorphous the eschatological hopes for (an) anointed one(s) actually were.

b. An Option Canvassed in regard to Jesus

Little doubt need be entertained that Jesus was seen in the role of a prophet during his mission. The testimony of the Jesus tradition is both quite widespread and consistent across its breadth.

(1) We have already noted Mark 6.15 pars. and 8.28 pars., which report the rumours/speculation that Jesus was John the Baptist, Elijah, or a prophet. Such reports are certainly part of the developed form in which these stories were told: in the one case they are attributed to Herod Antipas; in the other such inadequate rumours serve as a foil for Peter's confession of Jesus as 'the Messiah' (8.29). But the variations noted above (a prophet, one of the old prophets, Jeremiah) more likely attest the range of rumours which circulated (and continued to circulate) within Palestine regarding Jesus, rather than some subtle christological exercise whose point is now lost to us.[193]

(2) That the question was voiced whether Jesus was a, or even the, prophet is attested more widely.[194] The references in John's Gospel, though drawn fully into John's dramatic presentation, confirm that Jesus as (the) prophet was a possibility debated among those intrigued by the reports of Jesus' mission (see above, n. 191). That various miracles reported of Jesus seemed to parallel those attributed of old to Elijah and Elisha[195] would presumably not have escaped notice. The account of Jesus being mocked as a failed prophet (Mark 14.65 pars.) should also be given some weight.[196]

(3) Not irrelevant here is the fact that the Baptist was also seen as a prophet. According to John 1.21 he was asked whether he was 'the prophet'. The overtones of John as an Elijah-type figure may well have deeper roots than Christian apologetic (§11.2c). The report of John's popularity in Q (Matt. 11.7-9/Luke 7.24-26)[197] and the argument about Jesus' authority (Mark 11.27-33

192. For an earlier review see Cullmann, *Christology* 14-23; more recent Collins, *Scepter and Star* 74-75, 112-22.

193. See also Cullmann, *Christology* 31-35.

194. Matt. 21.11: 'Who is this? The crowds said, 'This is the prophet, Jesus from Nazareth of Galilee'; 21.46; Luke 7.16, 39; 24.19.

195. See below, nn. 244, 288, and 315.

196. Detailed discussion in Brown, *Death of the Messiah* 568-86; see also above, n. 95.

197. See above, §11.2a, including Matt. 14.5.

pars.)[198] both assume that John was widely seen as a prophet.[199] If John was thought to be a prophet, then it would be natural for the same speculation to be voiced in regard to Jesus.

(4) Also not irrelevant is the fact that Josephus speaks of prophets active during the decades leading up to the Jewish revolt and the destruction of Jerusalem. The two for whom he uses the term 'prophet' both intended to reenact miracles of the entry into the Promised Land: Theudas, to part the river Jordan and provide his followers[200] an easy passage (presumably back into the land) (*Ant.* 20.97); and 'the Egyptian', 'who had gained for himself the reputation of a prophet' (*War* 2.261) and who predicted that at his command the walls of Jerusalem would fall down to provide his followers[201] entry into the city (*Ant.* 20.169-70). Josephus also refers to others who promised 'signs of deliverance',[202] and though he does not describe them all as prophets, the recent practice of classifying them all as 'sign prophets' is quite justified.[203] This, together with the relating to the Baptist, provides sufficient evidence that the category of 'prophet' was still a viable one at the time of Jesus.[204] It would have been surprising had there had been no attempt to 'fit' Jesus to it.

(5) There is a firm if confusing tradition that Jesus was asked for a 'sign'.

Matt. 12.38-42	Matt. 16.1-2, 4	Mark 8.11-12	Luke 11.16, 29-32
38 Then some of the scribes and Pharisees said to him, 'Teacher, we wish to see a <u>sign</u> from you'.	1 And the Pharisees and Sadducees came, and <u>to test</u> him they asked him to show them <u>a sign from heaven</u>.	11 The Pharisees came and began to argue with him, seeking from him <u>a sign from heaven, to test</u> him.	. . . 16 while others, <u>to test</u> him, sought from him <u>a sign from heaven</u>. . . . .
39 But he answered them,	2 He answered them, . . .	12 And he sighed deeply in his spirit, and	29 When the crowds were increasing, he began to say,

198. But opinion is divided on the historical value of the passage; see, e.g., Bultmann, *History* 189; Perrin, *Rediscovering* 75; Fitzmyer, *Luke* 2.1272-73; Funk, *Five Gospels* 100; Davies and Allison, *Matthew* 3.157-58; Lüdemann, *Jesus* 80.

199. Josephus does not call the Baptist a 'prophet', but that may well be because he regarded the category as dubious ('sign prophets'), whereas he respected John (§11.2a).

200. Josephus speaks of 'the very great crowd', or 'the greatest part of the crowd' (as in Matt. 21.8; cf. Mark 4.1); but Acts 5.36 numbers Theudas's followers at only about 400.

201. *War* 2.261 puts the figure at 30,000; Acts 21.38 at 4,000.

202. *War* 2.258-60 = *Ant.* 20.168; *Ant.* 20.188; *War* 6.285-87 ('many prophets'); 7.437-41.

203. Particularly P. W. Barnett, 'The Jewish Sign Prophets — AD 40-70 — Their Intentions and Origin', *NTS* 27 (1981) 679-97; and Gray, *Prophetic Figures* 112-44.

204. It is now generally recognized that the idea of the prophetic Spirit having been withdrawn (with reference to the very variegated evidence of Ps. 74.9; Zech. 13.2-3; 1 Macc. 4.45-46; 9.27; *2 Bar.* 85.1-13) has been much exaggerated; see particularly J. Levison, 'Did the Spirit Withdraw from Israel? An Evaluation of the Earliest Jewish Data', *NTS* 43 (1997) 35-57.

| 'An evil and adulterous generation seeks for a sign; but no sign shall be given to it except the sign of the prophet Jonah. 40 For as Jonah was three days and three nights in the belly of the whale, so will the Son of man be three days and three nights in the heart of the earth'. . . . | 4 'An evil and adulterous generation seeks for a sign, but no sign shall be given to it except the sign of Jonah'. So he left them and departed. | said, 'Why does this generation seek a sign? Truly, I say to you, no sign shall be given to this generation'. | 'This generation is an evil generation; it seeks a sign, but no sign shall be given to it except the sign of Jonah. 30 For as Jonah became a sign to the men of Nineveh, so will the Son of man be to this generation'. . . . . . . |

Very likely Jesus was challenged on this point one or more times during his mission; John 6.30 echoes the same or a similar recollection. The challenge is of a piece with Josephus's reports of 'sign prophets' (above). Their signs were what would have validated their claims.[205] So we can deduce without straining the evidence that any such request would be an invitation to Jesus to prove the claims being made in his preaching (similarly Mark 11.27-33 pars.). The tendency in the transmission of the tradition was to label the request a temptation (*peirazein*) and/or to recall it as put by those remembered as Jesus' chief questioners elsewhere (Pharisees and ?). The core of the tradition in its various forms is Jesus' denunciation of the 'generation' which 'seeks a sign' and the strong affirmation[206] that 'no sign shall be given to it'.[207]

From this point on the picture becomes much less clear. Mark recalls only the abrupt refusal: the request itself was a blatant denial of the significance of the miracles already performed (Mark 6.30-44; 8.1-10); hence the elaboration in 8.14-21, building up to Peter's confession at Caesarea Philippi (8.22-33). But did Jesus offer Jonah as a sign on one of the occasions when the request was made? That is quite possible,[208] since Q continues the sequence with Jesus' reference to Jonah's success in winning the Ninevites to repentance (Matt. 12.4/Luke 11.32).[209] And

205. See further D. Flusser, 'Jesus and the Sign of the Son of Man', *Judaism* 526-34.

206. In Mark 8.12c the *ei* (Hebrew *'im*) indicates an abbreviated version of a strong Hebraic imprecation: '(May I be cursed) if . . .' (e.g., 2 Kgs. 6.31; Ps. 7.3-5).

207. The refusal of a sign is generally reckoned to be original, either in the form of Mark 8.12 (e.g., R. A. Edwards, *The Sign of Jonah* [London: SCM, 1971] 75-77; Pesch, *Markusevangelium* 1.409; Lüdemann, *Jesus* 54) or of Q (below, n. 208). The decisive consideration in the Jesus Seminar's negative judgment is the currently common view that 'this generation' is a mark of later perspective (*Five Gospels* 73); but see above, §§7.4c and 12.4e.

208. The possibility that Mark omitted the reference to Jonah is regularly canvassed (e.g., Bultmann, *History* 117-18; Perrin, *Rediscovering* 192-93; Davies and Allison, *Matthew* 2.352; Hooker, *Signs* 18-23; J. L. Reed, 'The Sign of Jonah: Q 11:29-32 in Its Galilean Setting', *Archaeology* 197-211 [here 203, with further bibliography in n. 21]).

209. Cited above, §12.5b. Note also the 'eschatological or prophetic correlative' in Q

though one of Matthew's versions elaborates the sign of Jonah in terms of the Son of Man's burial for three days (Matt. 12.40), that is assuredly to be regarded as elaboration in hindsight.[210] The 'sign', as elaborated in terms of Jonah's successful preaching, presumably suggested to others simply that God would honour repentance in response to the preaching of judgment — as in the case of Jonah's preaching to the Ninevites, so also in the case of the preaching of (the Baptist and) Jesus.[211]

What do we learn from this confused tradition? First, we have a further example of the way tradition was used and reused, and of the stability of its core elements. Although there are clear indications of elaboration and of editorial structuring on the part of all the Evangelists, it would still betray a misunderstanding of the oral traditioning process to inquire which of the versions was more 'original'. Quite likely there were variant versions from the beginning. Second, a clear memory has been preserved that Jesus was asked for a sign. His mission was evidently of such a character as to invite the sceptical to make such a request; he was a likely candidate for the role of 'sign prophet'. Third, a less clear, or elaborated, memory of his response has also been preserved: that he resisted the implication that he was that sort of prophet and may have referred enigmatically to Jonah and (probably) Jonah's success in his preaching to the notoriously wicked city of Nineveh.

c. What of Jesus Himself?

If then Jesus was seen to fit the category 'prophet', how did he see the matter himself? Was he remembered as claiming to fulfil the expectations regarding a prophet, or the prophet, or as acting as a prophet? The evidence here is rather

---

11.30 ('just as . . . so . . .'), probably a Hebraic construction (D. Schmidt, 'The LXX Gattung "Prophetic Correlative"', *JBL* 96 [1977] 517-22); Kloppenborg refers also to 1Q27 1.6 and 4Q246 2.1-2 (*Formation* 130 n. 127). But 11.30 is generally regarded as a 'redactional clasp' linking the two early traditions 11.29 and 11.31-32 (Reed, 'Sign of Jonah' 202, bibliography in n. 17).

210. There is little dissent among commentators at this point (see also below, chapter 16 n. 163 and chapter 17 n. 185).

211. Similarly Manson, *Sayings* 89 ('The preaching of Jonah is the sign'); Edwards, *Sign of Jonah* 95; Fitzmyer, *Luke* 2.933-34; Reed, 'Sign of Jonah' 208-11 (with 'a barb aimed at Jerusalem'). Hooker suggests that the Baptist's preaching of judgment is in view (Hooker, *Signs* 24-31, with further bibliography), but if the earliest form of the saying included a reference to 'the Son of Man', that is less likely. Others have argued that the sign refers to the divine vindication of the messenger — Jonah miraculously delivered from death (Beasley-Murray, *Jesus and the Kingdom* 254-57; Bayer, *Jesus' Predictions* 141-42, and those cited by him, n. 210).

patchy but builds up to a more positive answer than in the case of the royal Messiah.[212]

To be noted at once is the proverb recalled as Jesus' response to the negative reaction he received at Nazareth: 'a prophet is not without honour except in his home village *(patris)*' (Mark 6.4/Matt. 13.57); 'no prophet is acceptable in his home village' (Luke 4.24/*GTh* 31); 'a prophet has no honour in his own home village' (John 4.44); 'a prophet is not acceptable in his home village' (*P.Oxy.* 1 lines 30-35). Evidently the memory of Jesus saying something along these lines was well rooted in Christian tradition.[213] As the non-Synoptic versions indicate, the proverbial character of the saying meant that it could be retold apart from the Nazareth context of the Synoptics. The evidence certainly strongly suggests that Jesus saw the negative responses he received as of a piece with the tradition of rejected prophets.[214] At the same time, the talk is of 'a prophet'; there is no suggestion that Jesus saw himself as 'the prophet'. Since the post-Easter believers certainly regarded him as more than a prophet, it is not without significance that they have retained this more lowly self-estimate in the tradition.

The same considerations weigh in favour of the solely attested Luke 13.31-33:

> At that very hour some Pharisees came and said to him, 'Get away from here, for Herod wants to kill you'. And he said to them, 'Go and tell that fox, "Behold, I cast out demons and perform cures today and tomorrow, and the third day I finish my course. Nevertheless I must *(dei me)* go on my way today and tomorrow and the day following; for it cannot be that a prophet should perish away from Jerusalem'.

Although the saying is certainly in service to Luke's christology,[215] the introduction to it has some unique features: the warning from friendly Pharisees, the news that Herod intended to act against Jesus as he had against his mentor John, and the highly political dismissal of Herod ('that fox').[216] Why would Luke at-

---

212. In what follows I again draw on and revise the fuller discussion in my *Jesus and the Spirit* 82-84.

213. There is a general willingness to recognize a saying of Jesus (see, e.g., Funk, *Five Gospels* 63; J. R. Michaels, 'The Itinerant Jesus and His Home Town', in Chilton and Evans, *Authenticating the Activities* of Jesus 177-93). Here as elsewhere, the presence of a proverbial saying need not imply that it was drawn from Jewish wisdom; an inspirational teacher like Jesus presumably coined his own epigrams as well as his own versions of similar sayings (Bultmann, *History* 31 n. 2 cites an Arabic proverb: 'The piper has no friends in his own town').

214. See above, chapter 12 n. 184.

215. See, e.g., Fitzmyer, *Luke* 1.213-15.

216. The term 'fox' *(alōpēx)* is presumably a metaphor for craftiness (BDAG, *alōpēx;* Fitzmyer, *Luke* 2.1031).

tribute such a politically sensitive saying to Jesus, had it not come to him in tradition (from some eyewitness? — Luke 1.2). The reference to Jesus' impending death naturally raises suspicions that the saying has been formulated with hindsight ('third day', perish in Jerusalem).[217] But here too it is very distinctive. The reference is to Jesus' characteristic healing ministry,[218] not to the most striking miracles also attributed to him in the Gospels. And though the language is Lukan,[219] it would be unwise to ignore Schweitzer's old argument that the dogmatic note *(dei)* echoes Jesus' own sense of the divine necessity determining his course.[220] In any case, here again the thought is of Jesus (only) as 'a prophet', in the line of rejected prophets.[221]

More striking, however, are the indications that Jesus very likely drew on the programmatic prophecy of Isa. 61.1-3 to inform his own mission. We have already given details of the several allusions and need only recall them here. He probably referred disciples of the Baptist to this passage in Matt. 11.5/Luke 7.22 (§12.5c[1]) and framed two or three beatitudes with Isa. 61.1-3 in mind (§13.4). Whether it is justified to deduce from such remembered sayings that Jesus thereby intended his disciples to think of him as 'the (eschatological) prophet' may well be another question.[222] But that he, like Qumran, found the Isaiah prophecy instructive and inspirational for his mission is very likely.[223]

Beyond this the evidence is less explicit but worth reviewing briefly in that it fills out the picture quite appreciably. Can we, for example, speak of a sense of prophetic commissioning on the part of Jesus, since Jesus is recalled as occasionally saying 'I came', or that he 'was sent' (that is, by God)? The most important examples of the former are 'I came to call sinners' (Mark 2.17 pars.); 'I came to cast . . .' (Matt. 10.34; Luke 12.49); 'the Son of Man came to serve' (Mark 10.45 par.).[224] The most important of the latter cases are Mark 9.37/Luke 9.48: 'Who-

217. See further below, §17.4c(2).

218. See below, §15.7b-e.

219. See again Fitzmyer, *Luke* 1.168-69, 179-80.

220. See above, §4.5b.

221. On Matt. 23.29-36/Luke 11.47-51 see below, §15.8 n. 427, and on Matt. 23.37-39/Luke 13.34-35 see below, §17.3a.

222. 'An implicit messianic claim'; 'some sort of transcendent claim, whether or not we call it messianic' (Witherington, *Christology* 165-66); 'Jesus saw himself called to be the "Coming One" as the messianic evangelist and helper *(Nothelfer)* of the "poor" (Isa. 61.1-2)' (Stuhlmacher, *Biblische Theologie* 1.66).

223. For earlier discussion see my *Jesus and the Spirit* 53-62.

224. See also Mark 1.38/(Luke 4.43: 'I was sent'); Matt. 11.18-19/Luke 7.33-34; Matt. 5.17; Luke 19.10. 'There are no possible grounds for objecting to the idea that Jesus could have spoken in the first person about himself and his coming; that need be no more than what befits his prophetic self-consciousness' (Bultmann, *History* 153); O. Michel, '"Ich komme" (Jos. Bell. III.400)', *TZ* 24 (1968) 123-24, already pointed to the parallel in Josephus, *War* 3.400,

ever receives me, receives . . . him who sent me'; Matt. 10.40: 'He who receives me receives him who sent me'; and Luke 10.16: 'he who rejects me rejects him who sent me'.[225] The thought is the familiar one of the prophet as speaking for God, God's *šaliaḥ*.[226] Has Matthew taken up the thought in his version of the healing of the Syrophoenician's daughter: 'I was sent only to the lost sheep of the house of Israel' (Matt. 15.24)?[227] A more weighty consideration is that the Fourth Evangelist also knew the tradition (particularly John 13.20) and that it probably provided the basis for that Evangelist's presentation of the Son as 'sent' by the Father,[228] itself a development from the idea of prophetic commissioning.[229] How did the motif first enter the Jesus tradition? Almost certainly as a memory of Jesus' own words. The alternative of presupposing its origin in prophetic utterance within early church assemblies is much less persuasive. A typical prophetic 'I'-saying might well express the confidence of (the risen) Jesus' presence and action (as Matt. 18.20). But a prophet expressing someone else's (Jesus') *self*-affirmation of divine commissioning ('I came/was sent') would be unprecedented.

Finally we should note the possibility that Jesus may have shaped his mission self-consciously in terms of classic prophetic priorities, particularly in championing the cause of the poor and sinner in the face of establishment priorities and unconcern (§§13.4-5).[230] Several recent studies have drawn fresh atten-

---

where Josephus says to Vespasian, 'I have come to you as a messenger of the greatness that awaits you'; Theissen and Merz similarly note that '"I have come" is not an expression from post-Easter christology' and conclude that 'Jesus will have spoken of himself in this way' (*Historical Jesus* 525). Full discussion in E. Arens, *The ELTHON-Sayings in the Synoptic Tradition: A Historico-Critical Investigation* (OBO 10; Freiburg: Universitätsverlag, 1976), who concludes that only Luke 12.49 can be confidently traced back to Jesus *(ipsissima verba Iesu),* though Mark 2.17b par. and Matt. 10.34b may retain the *ipsissima vox Iesu,* and that the evidence attests more a vocation-consciousness *(Sendungsbewusstsein)* than a self-consciousness *(Selbstbewusstsein)* (337-39).

225. See also Meier, *Marginal Jew* 3.157, 190 n. 105.

226. Cf. Jer. 1.7; 7.25; Ezek. 2.3; 3.5-6; Obadiah 1; Hag. 1.12. The point is strongly pressed by Witherington, *Christology* 136, 142-43; see also above, chapter 14 n. 71. But Meier properly cautions by pointing out that the *šaliaḥ* institution is not documented before the time of Jesus *(Marginal Jew* 3.166 n. 9 and 189 n. 102).

227. We find an equivalent elaboration in Luke 4.43: to preach the kingdom of God is a divine necessity *(dei)* driving Jesus' mission.

228. John 3.17, 34; 5.36, 38; 6.29, 57; 7.29; 8.42; 11.42; 17.3, 8, 21, 23, 25; 20.21.

229. See particularly J. A. Bühner, *Der Gesandte und sein Weg im 4. Evangelium* (Tübingen: Mohr Siebeck, 1977).

230. D. C. Allison finds several allusions to Exodus and Moses at several points in traditions that can be traced back to Jesus, suggesting that Jesus may have taken himself to be a Mosaic prophet (e.g., Q 11.3 — manna; 11.20 — 'finger of God' — cf. Exod. 8.19; 'Q's New Exodus and the Historical Jesus', in Lindemann, ed., *Sayings Source Q* 395-428 [here 423-28]).

tion to the various 'prophetic actions' attributed to Jesus:[231] particularly the choice of twelve, his eating with toll-collectors and sinners, his healings and exorcisms, the entry into Jerusalem, the symbolic action in the Temple, and the last supper. That Jesus every so often acted, not like the sign-prophets of whom Josephus speaks, but in the mode of the great prophets[232] must be judged very likely. And there are various suggestions in the Jesus tradition that Jesus was remembered as exercising both prophetic insight (notably Luke 7.39)[233] and prophetic foresight.[234] No doubt much of all this was elaborated in the many retellings of such episodes, and much that was remembered began in the eye of the beholder. But that there were some such memories remains likely, and that in itself is significant.

d. More than a Prophet?

There are several hints that Jesus may have seen his mission in terms transcending the category of prophet. It is difficult to gain a firm handle on the point, since the Evangelists themselves evidently did not regard the category of prophet as adequate for Jesus, as we see most clearly in Luke 24.19-27 and John 6.30-33, 49-51. But possibly they were building on hints within the tradition itself.

The most obvious of these are as follows: (1) Use of Isa. 61.1-3 may imply a claim to be not just another prophet, but the (eschatological) prophet.[235] (2) The parable of the vineyard tenants (Mark 12.1-9 pars.) evidently trades on

Wright *(Jesus, passim)* and McKnight *(New Vision* 229-32) argue that Jesus took up the prophetic hope for Israel's restoration as the end of exile.

231. Trautmann, *Zeichenhafte Handlungen;* Sanders, *Historical Figure* 253-54; Schürmann, *Jesus* 136-56; Theissen and Merz, *Historical Jesus* 431-36; Hooker, *Signs* 38-54; S. McKnight, 'Jesus and Prophetic Actions', *BBR* 10 (2000) 197-232.

232. Hooker, for example, instances Isaiah walking around naked (Isaiah 20), Jeremiah publicly smashing a pot (Jeremiah 19), and Ezekiel eating a scroll or lying on his side for many days (Ezek. 2.9–3.3; 4.4-6).

233. See also Mark 2.5 pars.; 2.8 pars.; 3.4 pars.; 3.16 pars.; 9.33-35; 10.21 pars.; 12.15 pars.; 12.43-44 par.; 14.18, 20 pars.; Matt. 12.15/Luke 11.17; Luke 19.5; John 1.47-48; 2.24-25; 4.17-19.

234. Mark 10.39 par.; 13.2 pars.; 14.8 par.; 14.25 par.; 14.30 pars.; cf. Mark 5.36, 39 pars. On the 'Passion predictions' see below, §17.4c.

235. M. Hengel, 'Jesus as Messianic Teacher of Wisdom and the Beginnings of Christology', in *Studies* 73-117 (here 109-12): 'As messianic teacher and prophet he was the Spirit-bearer *par excellence*' (114); Witherington, *Christology* 45-46. See also Koester, cited above in chapter 7 n. 60. Contrast Cullmann's confident conclusion that 'Jesus did not identify himself in this way' (that is, as 'the Prophet') *(Christology* 37); similarly Flusser, *Jesus* 125.

the tradition of rejected prophets (12.2-5), but the climax features not the owner's chief steward, but his son (12.6-7), a suggestive graduation in category.[236] (3) In a famous article Dodd also observed that Jesus is recalled as saying not only 'I was sent', but 'I came',[237] and suggested that the latter indicated something more than prophetic commission, in the same way that 'I say to you' transcends the typically prophetic 'Thus says the Lord'.[238] (4) This chimes in with the sense of eschatological newness which comes through in several of Jesus' sayings: something greater was happening than the repetition of prophetic hope; something greater than the prophet Jonah,[239] whom Jesus may have offered as a sign (§15.6b above). Which in turn strengthens the implication of Matt. 11.6/Luke 7.23 (§12.5c[1]) that Jesus saw himself, at least as proclaimer of the kingdom, to be part of the eschatological newness which he proclaimed — and its offensiveness.[240]

(5) This is probably the place where we should mention the tradition of Jesus' transfiguration (Mark 9.2-10 pars.), where Jesus is transformed *(metamorphousthai)* and discourses with Moses and Elijah. Particularly worthy of note is the fact that the two men who appear in his company are both prophets (no royal figure is involved). The point is strengthened by the echo of Deut. 18.15 generally detected in the heavenly voice's command to 'Hear him' (9.7): Jesus is the 'prophet like Moses'. Not only so, but Jesus on his mountain undergoes a greater transformation than did two of Israel's greatest heroes most famous for their mountain-top revelatory experiences:[241] the brightness of his whole appearance more than matches that of Moses (Exod. 34.29-30), and Elijah heard only the 'sound of sheer silence' (1 Kgs. 19.12 NRSV).

What more can be said in regard to our present concerns? As Strauss long ago observed, this is a case where the theological significance of what is being

236. See further below, §16.2c.

237. Mark 2.17 pars. (§13.5); Matt. 11.19/Luke 7.34 (§12.5c); Luke 12.49 (§17.4d); see also Mark 1.38 par.; 10.45 par. (§17.5d[2]); Matt. 10.34-36/(Luke 12.51-53); Matt. 5.17; Hampel finds in 'the Son of Man came' in Luke 19.10 Jesus' own self-designation (*Menschensohn* 205-208).

238. C. H. Dodd, 'Jesus as Teacher and Prophet', in G. K. A. Bell and A. Deissmann, eds., *Mysterium Christi* (London: Longmans, 1930) 53-66 (here 63).

239. Matt. 13.16-17/Luke 10.23-24 and Matt. 12.41-42/Luke 11.31-32 (both cited in §12.5b). That Jonah came from Gath-Hepher (2 Kgs. 14.25), which can be located near Sepphoris and where his tomb is popularly located (see particularly Reed, 'Sign of Jonah' 204-208), may be significant: Jesus is compared favourably with two of the greatest northern prophets — Elijah and Jonah.

240. Taking 'symbol' in its 'thick' sense, Meier concludes, 'All these symbolic-prophetic acts of Jesus were understood by him to unleash the powers of the kingdom which they foreshadowed' (*Marginal Jew* 3.624).

241. Exodus 33–34; 1 Kings 19.

narrated dominates the pericope.[242] Whether some historical reminiscence lies behind it is a question which can be posed but hardly answered with any confidence.[243] The tradition is certainly a further affirmation of the theme 'more than a prophet', even than the greatest prophets. And as we have seen, it can be strongly maintained that the theme itself originated in very early perceptions of Jesus' mission, including comments that Jesus was recalled as himself making. But if anything, it was more likely these perceptions which gave rise to the story than vice-versa.

In short, there need be little doubt that Jesus was regarded as a prophet by many, that he saw himself in the tradition of the prophets, and probably also that he claimed a(n eschatological) significance for his mission (and thus himself) which transcended the older prophetic categories.[244]

242. Strauss, *Life* 540-46. The Jesus Seminar follow a well-trod path in suggesting that the transfiguration 'may have been a resurrection story relocated by Mark' (Funk, *Acts of Jesus* 464). See also J. P. Heil, *The Transfiguration of Jesus: Narrative Meaning and Function of Mark 9:2-8, Matt 17:1-8 and Luke 9:28-36* (AB 144; Rome: Pontifical Biblical Institute, 2000).

243. B. E. Reid, *The Transfiguration: A Source- and Redaction-Critical Study of Luke 9:28-36* (Paris: Gabalda, 1993) concludes that 'the most that can be said with certainty[!] about the historicity of the transfiguration event . . . is that the disciples had a revelation concerning Jesus' identity and mission, in which Jesus' passion, death, and resurrection were understood as mandated by God in accord with the divine plan of salvation' (147). In line with his thesis of Jesus as an adept practitioner of mysticism, the transfiguration for Chilton 'represents the mature development of Rabbi Jesus' *kabbalah*' (*Rabbi Jesus* 192-93). Cf. E. Fossum, 'Ascensio, Metamorphosis', *The Image of the Invisible God* (NTOA 30; Göttingen: Vandenhoeck und Ruprecht, 1995) 71-94, and the critique by D. Zeller, 'Bedeutung und religionsgeschichtlicher Hintergrund der Verwandlung Jesu (Markus 9:2-8)', in Chilton and Evans, eds., *Authenticating the Activities of Jesus* 303-21 (with bibliography 303 n. 1). J. J. Pilch, 'The Transfiguration of Jesus: An Experience of Alternate Reality', in P. F. Esler, ed., *Modelling Early Christianity: Social Scientific Studies of the New Testament in Its Context* (London: Routledge, 1995) 47-64, suggests that the episode may be understood in terms of the model of 'altered states of consciousness' drawn from psychological anthropology.

244. Sanders sums up a fair consensus when he notes: 'Many scholars have agreed that, of various roles which we can identify, Jesus best fits that of "prophet"' (*Jesus* 239); 'a charismatic and autonomous prophet' (*Historical Figure* 238); cf., e.g., C. G. Montefiore, described by Hagner as 'the champion of Jesus the prophet' (*Jewish Reclamation* 238); Becker, *Jesus* 212-16, 227; the subtitles of Allison, *Jesus of Nazareth: Millenarian Prophet,* and Ehrman, *Jesus: Apocalyptic Prophet;* B. Witherington, *Jesus the Seer* (Peabody: Hendrickson, 1999) 277-90. The basic proposition of Schillebeeckx's *Jesus* was that 'in his life on earth Jesus acts . . . as the eschatological prophet from God' (245; see also particularly 185-88, 441-49, 475-80, 486-99). Similarly Meier finds that his three volumes investigating the Jesus tradition support the self-chosen portrait of Jesus as 'the Elijah-like, miracle-working, eschatological prophet' ('From Elijah-Like Prophet to the Royal Davidic Messiah', in D. Donnelly, ed., *Jesus: A Colloquium in the Holy Land* [New York: Continuum, 2001] 45-83).

15.7. 'A Doer of Extraordinary Deeds'

Where do the traditions regarding Jesus' miracles fit into all this? They form a major part of the Jesus tradition, and prior to the Enlightenment's problematizing the very category of 'miracle' they constituted weighty proof that Jesus was from (or of) God (§4.2). Since then the probative value (and therefore the market value) of these traditions has fallen through the floor, and it has not recovered much in recent years. But the records of Jesus 'mighty works' are too important a feature of the Jesus tradition for us to ignore. In proceeding, however, it may be better to avoid the still problematic category 'miracle', still usually understood in terms of divine intervention in the normal workings of nature. For the time being it will be preferable to use the less loaded definition 'remarkable occurrences' *(COD)*, the common NT term 'deeds of power' *(dynameis),* or Josephus's description of Jesus as 'a doer of extraordinary deeds *(paradoxōn ergōn poiētēs)'* *(Ant.* 18.63).[245] It will not be possible, however, to avoid some discussion of the equally problematic term 'magic'. I will follow the same procedure as in the other sections of these two chapters.

a. Jewish Expectation

There is surprisingly little indication that either the royal or the priestly Messiah was expected to work deeds of power.[246] It should be noted, however, that both David and Solomon had reputations as exorcists. David is described in early Israelite history as one who was able by his music to make Saul well when the latter was tormented by an 'evil spirit from God' and to cause the evil spirit to depart (1 Sam. 16.14-16, 23). Not surprisingly Josephus explains the effect of David's harp-playing in terms of 'charming away, singing away by means of a spell' *(exadō, Ant.* 6.166-8),[247] and *Pseudo-Philo* 60 actually records the song that Da-

---

245. *Paradoxos* has the basic sense of 'contrary to expectation, incredible' (LSJ), 'contrary to opinion or exceeding expectation' (BDAG). See also Meier's discussion 'What Is a Miracle?' *(Marginal Jew* 2.512-15 and 524-25 n. 5), with good bibliography (522-24 n. 4). Crossan defines a miracle as 'a marvel [that is, 'not a trick or a deceit but a marvel or a wonder — something that staggers current explanation'] that someone interprets as a transcendental action or manifestation'; 'to claim a miracle is to make an interpretation of faith, not just a statement of fact' *(Birth* 303-304); but why did he insert 'just' in the second quotation?

246. This was taken to warrant the blanket assertion 'that miraculous healing was not associated in Judaism with the Davidic Messiah' (Fuller, *Foundations* 111); similarly Hahn: 'working miracles and proclaiming glad tidings is not the task of the royal Messiah' (Hahn, *Hoheitstitel* 393 [*Titles* 380]).

247. LSJ, *exadō,* cites Lucian, *Philops.* 16; *Trag.* 173.

vid played 'in order that the evil spirit might depart from him'. 11Q5 (11QPs[a])
27 describes the various psalms which David composed, including 'songs to be
sung over the afflicted *(hpgo'im)'* (27.9-10).[248]

Solomon too had a reputation as a maker of spells, deduced, presumably,
from his knowledge of plants described in 1 Kgs. 4.33. The Wisdom of Solomon
develops the thought: Solomon knew 'the powers of spirits *(pneumatōn bias)'*
and 'the varieties of plants and the virtues of roots' (Wis. 7.20). And Josephus
takes up the same tradition: 'God granted him knowledge of the art used against
demons for the benefit and healing of men. He also composed incantations
(epōdas) by which illnesses are relieved, and left behind forms of exorcisms
(tropous exorkōseōn) with which those possessed by demons drive them out,
never to return' *(Ant.* 8.45). Dennis Duling notes a recension of Psalm 91
(11QPs[a]) which contains Solomon's name just before the term 'demons' in column 1.[249] Such legends are greatly elaborated in the later *Testament of Solomon*,[250] but the evidence that Solomon's reputation had already grown in this direction at the time of Jesus is clear enough.[251]

The point of course is that such a development may have influenced the expectation regarding the royal Messiah. That the eschatological 'son of David'
might have power over evil spirits, like the first son of David,[252] would probably
not cause too much surprise for many of Jesus' contemporaries.

During the second half of the twentieth century scholars placed more emphasis on the miracle-working power of the expected *prophet*. The history of Is-

248. *Pgo'im* is better translated 'afflicted or stricken' (i.e., by evil spirits) than by 'possessed' (García Martinez). My colleague Loren Stuckenbruck notes that several of the instances
of 'possession' in Second Temple literature are more accurately defined as 'affliction' (referring to *Jub.* 10.7-14; *ps.-Philo* 60.1; 1QapGen 20.16-17; cf. *1 En.* 15.12).

249. *OTP* 1.945.

250. See further D. C. Duling, 'Solomon, Exorcism, and the Son of David', *HTR* 68
(1975) 235-52; also his Introduction to 'Testament of Solomon', *OTP* 1.944-51; also 'The
Eleazar Miracle and Solomon's Magical Wisdom in Flavius Josephus's *Antiquitates Judaicae*
8.42-49', *HTR* 78 (1985) 1-25. The *Testament* claims to be written by Solomon 'to the sons of
Israel . . . that they might know the powers of the demons and their forms, as well as the name
of the angels by which they are thwarted' (15.14). The *Testament* is not usually dated before the
third century, but probably contains earlier material (Duling, *ABD* 6.118).

251. See also K. Berger, 'Die königlichen Messiastraditionen des Neuen Testaments',
NTS 20 (1973-74) 1-44 (here 3-9). Meier, *Marginal Jew* 2.737 n. 46, justly criticizes C. Burger,
Jesus als Davidssohn (Göttingen: Vandenhoeck und Ruprecht, 1970) for failing to take up the
question of Solomon and Jewish traditions about him as an exorcist and healer in his examination of the Jewish background of the 'son of David' title.

252. There is a debate as to whether Solomon was known at the time of Jesus as 'son of
David' (as in Prov. 1.1; Eccl. 1.1; *T. Sol.* title; 1.7; 5.10; 20.1). This may be relevant, since no-
where in the Jesus tradition is the name 'son of David' associated with an exorcism (contrast
Mark 10.47-48/Matt. 20.31-32; Matt. 9.27; 12.23; 15.22).

rael celebrated two principal periods of wondrous happenings: the period of wilderness and conquest and the period of Elijah and Elisha (1 Kings 17–19; 2 Kings 4–8). So any hope for a prophet like Moses or for Elijah's return might well have included expectation of great natural wonders or amazing healings. The former is certainly borne out by Josephus's account of the various 'sign prophets', where two of the cases cited evidently expected a repeat of the miraculous crossing of the Jordan and of the amazing collapse of Jericho's walls (§15.6b).

In all this we should particularly note again 4Q521 with its expectation of an 'anointed one' who would give sight to the blind, straighten the bent, heal the wounded, and revive the dead (2.1, 8, 12). But we should also recall (§12.2c[3]) that the expectation of a supernatural new age characterized by healing and defeat of evil could also be expressed without reference to any messianic figure.

It should not be forgotten that healings were often attributed to gods in the ancient world (particularly Asclepius)[253] and that belief in the powerful effect of amulets and spells was widespread. Within Judaism we may think especially of exorcisms, of which the best known are the expulsion of a demon from Tobias's bride (Tobit 6–8), Abraham's exorcism of Pharaoh (1QapGen 20.16-29), and Josephus's report of the exorcism of a demon by one Eleazar in the presence of Vespasian (*Ant.* 8.46-48).[254] We can probably assume that many of the spells and incantations collected later go back to the first century,[255] not least because the key formula, 'I adjure you by . . .'[256] is quite well attested for the period.[257] Within the NT itself we may note references to the activity of a number of exorcists.[258]

In such a context it would hardly be surprising if exorcisms and other mighty works were included in the 'checklist' by which many people in Galilee and Judea attempted to assess Jesus' mission.

253. See, e.g., H. C. Kee, *Miracle in the Early Christian World* (New Haven: Yale University, 1983) ch. 3; W. Cotter, *Miracles in Greco-Roman Antiquity* (London: Routledge, 1999) 11-34; H.-J. Klauck, *The Religious Context of Early Christianity* (Edinburgh: Clark, 2000) 154-68.

254. Texts for these and other miracle stories from Jewish sources are provided by C. A. Evans, 'Jesus and Jewish Miracle Stories', *Jesus and His Contemporaries* 213-43 (here 227-43). The Qumran community knew the Tobit story well (4Q196-200).

255. H. D. Betz, *The Greek Magical Papyri in Translation* (Chicago: University of Chicago, ²1992).

256. *PGM,* e.g., 3.10, 119; 4.1239, 3080.

257. Including the fragmentary text in 4Q560 2.5-6 ('I, O spirit, adjure . . . I enchant you, O spirit . . .'); Acts 19.13; Josephus, *Ant.* 8.47; *PGM* 3.36-37; 4.289, 3019-20, 3046; 7.242; and note *T. Sol.* 5.9; 6.8; 11.6 (14.8); 15.7; 18.20, 31, 33; 25.8 (BDAG *horkizō;* G. H. Twelftree, *Jesus the Exorcist* [WUNT 2.54; Tübingen: Mohr Siebeck, 1993] 82-83). Note also the data in §15.6a.

258. Matt. 12.27/Luke 11.19; Mark 9.38-39; Acts 19.13-19.

b. Jesus' Reputation

One of the most compelling features of the whole sweep of ancient opinion regarding Jesus is his reputation as an exorcist and healer. It is no exaggeration to claim that it is one of the most widely attested and firmly established of the historical facts with which we have to deal.[259] The outlines can be sketched in fairly briefly.

(1) In the Gospels, healing stories are frequently told about Jesus. For example, in Mark there are thirteen such stories,[260] with exorcisms the largest single category.[261] The latter are prominent also in summary statements.[262] Unusually in the sermons in Acts, Jesus is proclaimed as 'a man attested to you by God with mighty works and wonders and signs which God did through him' (Acts 2.22); 'he went about doing good *(euergetōn)* and healing all that were oppressed by the devil, for God was with him' (10.38).[263]

(2) Jesus' reputation as a powerful exorcist is attested for his own time; his name was evidently prized as one to call on, no doubt precisely because he himself had been so successful in casting out demons. According to Luke, Jesus' own disciples invoked his name with success.[264] And others apparently attempted to do the same.[265] Origen boasts proudly: 'The name of our Lord Jesus has already expelled innumerable demons out of soul and body — there are *de visu* witnesses' *(contra Celsum* 1.25). Jesus' lasting fame is probably indicated by the appearance of his name in some incantations preserved among the magical papyri[266] and in several references in the *Testament of Solomon.*[267]

(3) Witness to Jesus' fame as healer and exorcist is preserved outside Christian tradition more explicitly. Josephus, as already noted, describes Jesus as 'a doer of extraordinary deeds' *(Ant.* 18.63). Later Celsus, Origen's *bête noire,* attributed to Jesus 'certain magical powers' (Origen, *contra Celsum* 1.28, 68).

---

259. See, e.g., B. L. Blackburn, 'The Miracles of Jesus', in Chilton and Evans, *Studying the Historical Jesus* 353-94, particularly 354-62; those cited by Evans, 'Authenticating the Activities of Jesus' 12-13 nn. 19 and 22; and the firm conclusion of Kollmann, *Jesus* 306-307.

260. Mark. 1.29-31, 40-45; 2.1-12; 3.1-5; 5.21-24a and 35-43, 24b-34; 7.31-37; 8.22-26; 10.46-52; see also Matt. 8.5-13/Luke 7.1-10; Luke 13.10-17; 14.1-6; 17.11-19; 22.49-51; John 5.1-9; 9.1-41. *P. Eg.* 2 fragment 1 recto contains a version of Mark 1.40-45 (text in Aland, *Synopsis* 60).

261. Mark 1.21-28; 5.1-20; 7.24-30; 9.14-29; also Matt. 12.22-23/Luke 11.14; Matt. 9.32-33; Luke 8.2. The absence of exorcisms in John's Gospel is noteworthy.

262. Mark 1.32-34, 39; 3.10-11; 6.5, 7, 13, 56; Luke 7.21; 13.32.

263. On the traditional material used by Luke in the Acts sermons see below, vol. 2.

264. Luke 10.17; Acts 16.18.

265. Mark 9.38; Acts 19.13.

266. *PGM* 4.1233, 3020; 12.190, 390.

267. *T. Sol.* 6.8 (see *OTP* 1.968 nn.); 11.6; 17.4; 22.20.

And the accusation of sorcery in rabbinic tradition (*b. Sanh.* 43a)[268] may well be an echo of the charge levelled against Jesus in Mark 3.22 pars. that he 'expelled demons by the (power of) the ruler of demons'.[269] What is interesting in this testimony, hardly partisan on behalf of Christian claims, is that the accounts of Jesus' healing and exorcistic success are nowhere disputed, only the reasons for that success.

(4) Not least of importance is the fact that Jesus' success as healer and exorcist is attested also in the sayings tradition. That is, he is recalled as referring to that success and drawing deductions from it. We have already laid out the key data:[270] the Baptist's disciples are referred to Jesus' success in bringing about the healings that Isaiah had anticipated in the age to come (Matt. 11.5/Luke 7.22),[271] and both Mark and Q made collections of the lessons Jesus drew from his success as an exorcist (Mark 3.22-29 pars.). We need no more doubt that Jesus believed that he had been a successful healer and exorcist than we should doubt that Paul had the same conviction regarding his own 'signs and wonders' (Rom. 15.19). Jesus was presumably referring to various episodes during his mission when people had indeed been healed, demoniacs released, lepers 'cleansed', and even the dead raised/revived, the sort of episodes which are recorded in the narrative Jesus tradition and which were the basis of his more widely attested reputation.

c. The Root of Jesus' Reputation

It will not be necessary to review the tradition of Jesus' 'extraordinary deeds' in detail. John Meier has recently provided a thorough and scrupulously careful historical analysis,[272] and I have little to add at that level. From the perspective of an oral traditioning process we are also disadvantaged in comparison with the traditions of Jesus' teaching, both because the q/Q (and other Gospels) material contains so little of the miracle tradition and because in most cases Matthew and

---

268. See Van Voorst, *Jesus* 114, 117-19, and above, §7.1.

269. Fuller discussion in Stanton, 'Jesus of Nazareth: Magician and False Prophet?' 164-80. Stanton refers particularly to Justin, *Dial.* 69.7, 108; *Apol.* 1.30; Origen, *contra Celsum* 1.6, 28, 68, 71; 2.32, 48-49; *b. Sanh.* 43a; 107b; *Acts of Thomas* 96, 102, 106-107; and note already John 8.48 and 10.20.

270. See above, §12.5c-d.

271. As already noted, the only item of the six-item list which would not be prompted by Isaianic prophecies is 'lepers cleansed'. The inclusion of that item makes sense only if Jesus was remembered not simply as healing 'lepers' but as regarding these healings in the same light as he regarded his Isaianic healings.

272. Meier, *Marginal Jew* 2, Part Three (509-1038). An earlier, less critical survey is provided by H. van der Loos, *The Miracles of Jesus* (NovTSup 9; Leiden: Brill, 1965).

Luke seem to have drawn directly on Mark.[273] That is, the comparison of versions which has enabled us to detect the core and thematic stability of particular traditions is less obvious in the traditions of Jesus' powerful deeds.

We should however disabuse ourselves of any suggestion that simply because a story narrates a miracle it must be a late addition to the tradition. Strauss's objection to the rationalist attempts to explain away the miracles remains valid: the stories are *intended* to be accounts of *miracles*.[274] But that does not necessarily mean that the stories are wholly the product of later reflection. If we have learned anything from our analyses of Jesus tradition thus far it is that traditions characteristically were elaborated in the retelling without affecting the stability of subject matter and core. The point here, then, is that the element of miracle must in at least some cases belong to the core. *The stories were being told as miracles from the first.*[275] Only so could Jesus' reputation as exorcist and healer have become so firm and so widespread so quickly.[276] At the same time, we should not lapse into talk of 'the original report' of a miracle,[277] as though there was one single 'original' from which all subsequent accounts derived. Even in the disciple circles there would have been a variety of tellings and retellings round the stable core of miracle.

Here too we need to recall the lessons learned above in §6.3. In the study of history there are no objective facts, only interpreted data. There is no objective Jesus, no artefact ('the historical Jesus') at the bottom of the literary tell to be uncovered by clearing away all the layers of tradition. All we have is the remembered Jesus, Jesus seen through the eyes of those who followed him, Jesus enshrined in the memories they shared and the stories they told and retold among

---

273. The possibility of detecting 'miracle sources' behind Mark and John (§7.8f) is best left to vol. 2; the overlap between Synoptic and Johannine miracle tradition is confined to the healing of the centurion's/royal official's servant (John 4.46-54; discussed in §8.4b) and the linked feeding and walking on the water miracles (John 6; see below §15.7f); otherwise the lack of overlap hinders the sort of tradition-historical analysis which we assay in this volume.

274. See above, §4.2.

275. This would include stories of (apparently) bringing back individuals to life (as in Mark 5.35-43 pars.; and Luke 7.11-17; as also in Acts 9.36-43 and 20.9-10). See Meier's very thorough discussion of the stories of Jesus raising Jairus' daughter, the widow of Nain's son, and Lazarus and the reference in Matt. 11.5/Luke 7.22 (*Marginal Jew* 2.773-873).

276. Goppelt also observes that the customary assumption that miraculous motifs would have been transferred to Jesus is not well founded: 'No one ascribed miraculous healings to comparable figures in his surroundings, e.g., John the Baptist or the Teacher of Righteousness at Qumran' (*Theology* 1.144). 'The tradition of Jesus' miracles has too many unusual features to be conveniently ascribed to conventional legend-mongering' (Harvey, *Jesus* 99-110 [here 100]).

277. G. H. Twelftree, *Jesus the Miracle Worker* (Downers Grove: InterVarsity, 1999) tends to fall into this trap (e.g., 285). Meier's warning at this point is also apposite (*Marginal Jew* 2.735 n. 38).

themselves. So too there are no objective events of people being healed, no non-miracles to be uncovered by clearing away layers of interpretation. All we have in at least many cases is the shared memory of a miracle which was recounted as such more or less from the first day. What the witnesses saw was a miracle, not an 'ordinary' event which they interpreted subsequently as a miracle. There must have been many who experienced Jesus' ministrations to them as miracles, individuals who were genuinely healed and delivered, and these successes were attributed there and then to the power of God flowing through Jesus. Only so could Jesus' reputation as exorcist and healer have become so firm and so widespread so quickly. In such cases, we may say, the first 'historical fact' was a miracle, because that was how the event was experienced, as a miracle, by the followers of Jesus who witnessed it.

d. Jesus the Exorcist

Two of the exorcism narratives are of particular interest — the demoniac in the synagogue at Capernaum (Mark 1.23-28/Luke 4.33-37) and the Gerasene demoniac (Mark 5.1-20 pars.). It will suffice to cite only Mark in both cases, since Luke follows Mark closely in the first case, and despite the improvements introduced by the others in the second.[278]

> 1.23And immediately there was in their synagogue a man with an unclean spirit; 24and he cried out, 'What have you to do with us, Jesus of Nazareth? Have you come to destroy us? I know who you are, the Holy One of God'. 25But Jesus rebuked him, saying, 'Be silent, and come out of him!' 26And the unclean spirit, convulsing him and crying with a loud voice, came out of him. 27And they were all amazed, so that they questioned among themselves, saying, 'What is this? A new teaching! With authority he commands even the unclean spirits, and they obey him'. 28And at once his fame spread everywhere throughout all the surrounding region of Galilee.

> 5.1They came to the other side of the sea, to the country of the Gerasenes. 2And when he had come out of the boat, there met him out of the tombs a man

---

278. The account of the possessed boy (Mark 9.14-27 pars.) has already been cited above (§8.4c). Matthew describes the boy in Mark 9.14-29/Matt. 17.14-21/Luke 9.37-43 as 'moonstruck' (*selēniazetai,* Matt. 17.15), indicating that he suffered from what we would now describe as epileptic seizures, which in the ancient world were thought to be caused by the moon (BDAG, *selēniazomai;* E. Yamauchi, 'Magic or Miracle? Diseases, Demons and Exorcisms', in D. Wenham and C. Blomberg, eds., *Gospel Perspectives.* Vol. 6: *The Miracles of Jesus* [Sheffield: JSOT, 1986] 89-183 [here 129-30]; see also Kollmann, *Jesus* 211-12). Pesch notes that it is hardly a typical exorcism story (*Markusevangelium* 2.95).

with an unclean spirit, 3who lived among the tombs; and no one could bind him any more, even with a chain; 4for he had often been bound with fetters and chains, but the chains he wrenched apart, and the fetters he broke in pieces; and no one had the strength to subdue him. 5Night and day among the tombs and on the mountains he was always crying out, and bruising himself with stones. 6And when he saw Jesus from afar, he ran and worshiped him; 7and crying out with a loud voice, he said, 'What have you to do with me, Jesus, Son of the Most High God? I adjure you by God, do not torment me'. 8For he had said to him, 'Come out of the man, you unclean spirit!' 9And Jesus asked him, 'What is your name?' He replied, 'My name is Legion; for we are many'. 10And he begged him eagerly not to send them out of the country. 11Now a great herd of swine was feeding there on the hillside; 12and they begged him, 'Send us to the swine, let us enter them'. 13So he gave them leave. And the unclean spirits came out, and entered the swine; and the herd, numbering about two thousand, rushed down the steep bank into the sea, and were drowned in the sea. 14The herdsmen fled, and told it in the city and in the country. And people came to see what it was that had happened. 15And they came to Jesus, and saw the demoniac sitting there, clothed and in his right mind, the man who had had the legion; and they were afraid. 16And those who had seen it told what had happened to the demoniac and to the swine. 17And they began to beg Jesus to depart from their neighbourhood. 18And as he was getting into the boat, the man who had been possessed with demons begged him that he might be with him. 19But he refused, and said to him, 'Go home to your friends, and tell them how much the Lord has done for you, and how he has had mercy on you'. 20And he went away and began to proclaim in the Decapolis how much Jesus had done for him; and all men marvelled.

In both cases the indications of retelling are clear enough.[279] But most of the key features could actually be attributed to eyewitness accounts without difficulty.

279. E.g., Mark's typical 'immediately' (1.23); 'their synagogue' (1.23); and the 'choral' ending (1.27). Luke's performance of 'the Gerasene demoniac' is much more polished (Luke 8.26-39), and Matthew's abbreviates Mark's prolix version by some two-thirds (Matt. 8.28-34), but the cry of the demoniac (Mark 5.7) and the climax of the exorcism (5.11-14, 17) remain constant in all three performances. It is certainly possible that Isa. 65.4 was in mind at some stage in the early shaping of the story. One should be cautious, however, about reading too much into the name of the Gerasene demoniac ('Legion'): that the image of the Roman military structure is evoked is hardly to be doubted; but given the relatively light hand of Rome on Galilee (§9.8) and that as a Greek city Gerasa would have been friendly towards Rome (Schürer, *History* 2.150), it is unwise to build too much from parallels with modern colonialism (as does Crossan, *Historical Jesus* 313-18; cf. Theissen, *Miracle Stories* 255; Horsley, *Jesus* 154-57, 184-90; Cotter, *Miracles* 121-22); Meier's cautionary comments are timely (*Marginal Jew* 2.666-67 n. 25).

1. Mention of the locale can probably be attributed to the recollections and initial tellings of some of those involved. In 1.23 'synagogue' should not be taken to imply a sanctified sanctuary; *synagōgē* may refer simply to the regular village assembly.[280] And there is no good reason why the second exorcism should have been located in the territory of Gerasa, had a memory to that effect not been part of the tradition from the first.[281]

2. It was apparently not uncommon for demoniacs to engage the would-be exorcist in a verbal duel.[282] 'What have you to do with us/me?' (1.24; 5.7) is a Semitic idiom probably meaning 'Why are you bothering us/me?'[283]

3. In particular, success was thought to depend on the authority attaching to a powerful name which the exorcist might call upon or command ('I adjure you by . . .').[284] So the demoniac, or one who believed himself so possessed, might well hope to gain protection from or even advantage over the exorcist by claiming to know the name of the exorcist.[285] A striking feature of the

---

280. See above, §9.7a.

281. Mark makes a lot, by implication for those alert to the signals, of impurity (tombs, unclean spirit[s], pigs); but these still would not explain why the territory of Gerasa (?) was chosen for the location. Pesch detects three distinct stages in the growth of the story prior to Mark, the earliest the account of an exorcism in the territory of Gerasa (like that in 1.21-28) (*Markusevangelium* 1.282, 292-93). But as with his earlier *Der Besessene von Gerasa: Entstehung und Überlieferung einer Wundergeschichte* (SBS 56; Stuttgart: KBW, 1972), Pesch's discussion still falls too much into the old form-critical trap of assuming an original pure form *(reine Form)* and discernible stages in a transmission process. See also Meier, *Marginal Jew* 2.653; J. Ådna, 'The Encounter of Jesus with the Gerasene Demoniac', in Chilton and Evans, ed., *Authenticating the Activities of Jesus* 279-301, in dialogue particularly with F. Annen, *Heil für die Heiden. Zur Bedeutung und Geschichte der Tradition vom besessenen Gerasener (Mk 5,1-20 parr.)* (Frankfurt am Main: Knecht, 1976). Most commentators discuss what location was intended — Gerasa being some 50 km southeast of Lake Galilee; Matthew altered the reference to Gadara, which had a harbour on the southeastern corner of the lake; the text of Mark was probably altered by some to read Gergesa = modern Kursi? (see, e.g., Metzger, *Textual Commentary* 23-24, 84).

282. Mark 5.7; Acts 19.15; according to Lucian, 'the patient himself is silent, but the spirit answers in Greek or in a language of whatever country he comes from' (*Philops.* 16); Philostratus, *Life* 3.38; 4.20.

283. Twelftree, *Jesus the Exorcist* 63-64. An interesting feature in both episodes is the variation from singular to plural ('What have you to do with *us?* . . . the spirit came out of *him*' in 1.24-26; '*My* name is Legion, for *we* are many' in 5.9), which suggests that the conceptualisation of the force(s) which caused possession was unclear; see further my interaction with G. H. Twelftree, 'Demon-Possession and Exorcism in the New Testament', in my *Pneumatology* 170-86 (here 176-81).

284. See above, nn. 256 and 257.

285. Still important are the observations of O. Bauernfeind, *Die Worte der Dämonen im Markusevangelium* (Stuttgart: Kohlhammer, 1927) 13-18. The evidence persuaded Bultmann that the motif could not be attributed solely to the 'messianic secret' (*History* 209 n. 1). See further Twelftree, *Jesus the Exorcist* 61-68.

second case, for those familiar with the battles of exorcism, is the apparent attempt by the *demoniac* to put a spell on *Jesus* by calling on the power of God (5.7). It would occasion no surprise to those familiar with exorcistic technique that Jesus responded by asking for the demon's name (5.9).[286]

4. 'The Holy One of God' (1.24) is hardly a common title for Christ,[287] so attribution to later Christian faith is less obvious. And conceivably the exorcistic power of one reputed to be a holy man might have occasioned such an address.[288] Not so very different is the case with the phrase 'son of God Most High' (5.7).[289] *Theos hypsistos* was a title which stretched across cultural lines,[290] so one might wonder whether its unique appearance in the Jesus tradition at this point is to be attributed to retellers of the Jesus tradition recognizing its appropriateness for a setting in the mixed culture of the Decapolis territory.[291] At the same time, the appearance of the phrase in 4Q246 indicates that it was quite 'at home' in a Jewish Palestinian milieu.[292]

5. The command to silence (1.25) also functions less as the expression of a 'messianic secret' and more as part of the verbal duel.[293] The silencing of the demoniac/demon[294] is a necessary preliminary to the successful exorcism.

286. *PGM* 1.160-62; 4.3037-39. Typically in the *Testament of Solomon,* Solomon asks the demon's name (to gain a 'handle on' the demon — 2.1, 4; 4.3; 6.3, 5-7; 8; 9.2; 11.3-4, etc.) and also ascertains the name of one who is stronger (title: 'what their authorities are against men, and by what angels these demons are thwarted'; 2.4; 4.10, 12; 5.9, 13; 6.8; 8.5-10; 11.6; 13.3-7; 14.7; 15.3, 6; 16.6, etc.).

287. Apart from Mark 1.24/Luke 4.34, only John 6.69 and Acts 3.14.

288. The point depends more on a history-of-religions perspective, although we should recall that Elijah was similarly challenged ('What have you against me, O man of God?' 1 Kgs. 17.18), Elisha is described as 'a holy man of God' (2 Kgs. 4.9) (see also Kollmann, *Jesus* 203-204), and one of the two charismatic rabbis to whom Vermes has drawn particular attention, Hanina ben Dosa, had something of a reputation for exercising authority over demons (Vermes, *Jesus the Jew* 65-80, 208-209). Presumably 'the seven sons of the Sceva' traded on the sanctity of Sceva's high priestly status to induce the same sense of the numinous in their role as itinerant exorcists (Acts 19.13-14). Of the exorcists referred to in Matt. 12.27/Luke 11.19 and Mark 9.38 we know nothing.

289. Cf. Vermes, *Jesus the Jew* 202-203, 206-10. Since Solomon was the one to whom the promise of 2 Sam. 7.14 originally applied, it is conceivable that a son of David who cast out demons might be addressed as 'son of God'; but supporting evidence is lacking.

290. BDAG, *hypsistos* 2.

291. The only other two NT occurrences are Acts 16.17 (again on the lips of a demoniac shortly to be exorcised) and Heb. 7.1.

292. See below, chapter 16 n. 15.

293. *PGM* 3.204; 5.321-29 (Theissen, *Miracle Stories* 140-41).

294. Literally 'be muzzled'. Examples of its use in the magical papyri in Twelftree, *Jesus the Exorcist* 69-70.

6. The actual exorcism, 'Come out of him' (1.25; 5.8), is used in other exorcism formulae.[295] Similarly, in 9.25 the phrase 'I command you' is familiar in magical incantations seeking to control demons and gods;[296] and the phrase 'Never enter him again' (9.25) can be paralleled in the literature relating to exorcisms.[297]

When confronted with such parallels we can never escape this conundrum: Do we have here stories which have been conformed to the standard pattern of such stories, or should we rather see here the sort of episodes which gave rise to the pattern? More tantalising still, if such were indeed characteristic features of exorcism practice/stories: Would the degree of conditioning implied actually shape the way the exorcist (and demoniac!) acted or the way the exorcism was 'seen' (and then narrated) by the onlookers? Either way, we have to assume that such events were witnessed, put into oral form, and circulated among Jesus' followers (and more widely); otherwise the strength and extent of Jesus' reputation as an exorcist are hardly possible to explain.[298]

e. Jesus the Healer

Mark again provides a good range of examples of the range of healings which were credited to Jesus during his mission, no doubt in marketplace gossip as well as disciple gatherings. To draw from them the conclusion that stories *like* these must have circulated during his mission is to toy again with the idea that we should try to uncover a historical Jesus who was similar to but somehow different from the Jesus of the Synoptics. *These* were the stories which were being circulated during his mission. Nor, once again, should we allow ourselves to slip into the comfortable hypothesis that they were put into miracle-story form only at

295. Philostratus, *Life* 4.20; Lucian, *Philops.* 11, 16; *PGM* 4.3013; see also D. E. Aune, 'Magic in Early Christianity', *ANRW* 2.23.2 (1980) 1507-57 (here 1531-32); Kollmann, *Jesus* 202-203.

296. E.g., *PGM* 1.253, 324; 2.43-55; 4.3080; 7.331; 12.171.

297. Josephus, *Ant.* 8.47; Philostratus, *Life* 4.20. See further Twelftree, *Jesus the Exorcist* 95-96.

298. Meier concludes that Mark 1.23-28 serves as 'a global representation of "the sort of thing" Jesus did during his ministry in Capernaum', that 'an exorcism performed by Jesus near Gerasa lies at the basis of the Gospel narrative in Mark 5.1-20' (similarly Ådna, 'Encounter' 298-99), and follows Pesch (*Markusevangelium* 2.95) in discerning 'some historical remembrance' behind Mark 9.14-29 (*Marginal Jew* 2.650, 653, 656). The Jesus Seminar 'agreed that Jesus healed people and drove away what were thought to be demons' (Funk, *Acts of Jesus* 60). Lüdemann even concludes that 'the activity of Jesus in driving out demons is one of the most certain historical facts about his life' (*Jesus* 13).

some later stage, when memory had been suffused (and transformed) by the Easter experience.[299] Some at least of the Gospel healing stories were almost certainly given verbal expression in the immediate aftermath of the events described, as the disciples who had witnessed the event talked of it among themselves, gave the story its basic shape, and agreed on its central point.

Since Matthew and Luke, where they have the same story, seem to be more or less dependent on Mark, here again we need cite only Mark's version.[300] I cite several in order to give the flavour of at least one retelling of the tales (Mark's).[301]

1.29And immediately he left the synagogue, and entered the house of Simon and Andrew, with James and John. 30Now Simon's mother-in-law lay sick with a fever, and immediately they told him of her. 31And he came and took her by the hand and lifted her up, and the fever left her; and she served them.

40And a leper came to him beseeching him, and kneeling said to him, 'If you will, you can make me clean'. 41Moved with pity, he stretched out his hand and touched him, and said to him, 'I will; be clean'. 42And immediately the leprosy left him, and he was made clean. 43And he sternly charged him, and sent him away at once, 44and said to him, 'See that you say nothing to any one; but go, show yourself to the priest, and offer for your cleansing what Moses commanded, for a proof to the people'. 45But he went out and began to talk freely about it, and to spread the news, so that Jesus could no longer openly enter a town, but was out in the country; and people came to him from every quarter.

299. Note the widespread reaction against Bultmann's judgment that the miracle stories were of 'Hellenistic origin' (*History* 240-41). E.g., C. H. Holladay, Theios Aner *in Hellenistic Judaism: A Critique of the Use of This Category in New Testament Christology* (SBLDS 40; Missoula: Scholars, 1977): 'To account . . . for the presence of miracles and miracle traditions within the Gospels on the basis of a Hellenistic *Sitz im Leben,* particularly that of missionary preaching, as the earlier form critics did, seems to be a highly dubious exercise' (239); H. C. Kee, *Medicine, Miracle and Magic in New Testament Times* (SNTSMS 55; Cambridge: Cambridge University, 1986): 'the phenomenon of healing in the gospels . . . is a central factor in primitive Christianity, and was so from the beginning of the movement. It is not a later addendum to the tradition, introduced in order to make Jesus more appealing to the Hellenistic world, but was a major feature of the Jesus tradition from the outset' (124).

300. Crossan, however, argues that *P.Eg.* 2 fragment 1 recto is an independent variant of Mark 1.40-45, that John 5.1-7, 14 is a variant tradition of Mark 2.1-12, and that Mark 8.22-26 and John 9.1-7 go back to the same source (Crossan, *Historical Jesus* 321-26).

301. For treatment of the other miracle stories within the Jesus tradition, see Meier, *Marginal Jew* 2 chs. 21-22, and Twelftree, *Jesus* chs. 12-15. On the sole miracle story attributed to Q (Matt. 8.5-13/Luke 7.1-10) see above, §8.4b.

2.1And when he returned to Capernaum after some days, it was reported that he was at home. 2And many were gathered together, so that there was no longer room for them, not even about the door; and he was preaching the word to them. 3And they came, bringing to him a paralytic carried by four men. 4And when they could not get near him because of the crowd, they removed the roof above him; and when they had made an opening, they let down the pallet on which the paralytic lay. 5And when Jesus saw their faith, he said to the paralytic, 'My son, your sins are forgiven'. 6Now some of the scribes were sitting there, questioning in their hearts, 7'Why does this man speak thus? It is blasphemy! Who can forgive sins but God alone?' 8And immediately Jesus, perceiving in his spirit that they thus questioned within themselves, said to them, 'Why do you question thus in your hearts? 9Which is easier, to say to the paralytic, "Your sins are forgiven", or to say, "Rise, take up your pallet and walk"? 10But that you may know that the Son of man has authority on earth to forgive sins' — he said to the paralytic — 11'I say to you, rise, take up your pallet and go home'. 12And he rose, and immediately took up the pallet and went out before them all; so that they were all amazed and glorified God, saying, 'We never saw anything like this!'

5.21And when Jesus had crossed again in the boat to the other side, a great crowd gathered about him; and he was beside the sea. 22Then came one of the rulers of the synagogue, Jairus by name; and seeing him, he fell at his feet, 23and besought him, saying, 'My little daughter is at the point of death. Come and lay your hands on her, so that she may be made well, and live'. 24And he went with him. And a great crowd followed him and thronged about him. 25And there was a woman who had had a flow of blood for twelve years, 26and who had suffered much under many physicians, and had spent all that she had, and was no better but rather grew worse. 27She had heard the reports about Jesus, and came up behind him in the crowd and touched his garment. 28For she said, 'If I touch even his garments, I shall be made well'. 29And immediately the hemorrhage ceased; and she felt in her body that she was healed of her disease. 30And Jesus, perceiving in himself that power had gone forth from him, immediately turned about in the crowd, and said, 'Who touched my garments?' 31And his disciples said to him, 'You see the crowd pressing around you, and yet you say, "Who touched me?"' 32And he looked around to see who had done it. 33But the woman, knowing what had been done to her, came in fear and trembling and fell down before him, and told him the whole truth. 34And he said to her, 'Daughter, your faith has made you well; go in peace, and be healed of your disease'. 35While he was still speaking, there came from the ruler's house some who said, 'Your daughter is dead. Why trouble the Teacher any further?' 36But ignoring what they said, Jesus said to the ruler of the synagogue, 'Do not fear, only believe'. 37And he allowed no one to follow him except Peter and James and John the brother of James. ³⁸When they came to the house of the ruler of the synagogue, he saw a tumult, and people weeping and wailing loudly. ³⁹And when he had entered, he said to them, 'Why do you make a tumult and weep? The child is not dead but sleeping'. ⁴⁰And they laughed at him. But he put them all outside, and took the child's father and mother and those who were with him, and went in where the child was. ⁴¹Taking her by the hand he said to her, *'Talitha cumi';* which means, 'Little girl, I say to you, arise'. ⁴²And immediately the girl got up and walked (she was twelve years of age), and they were immediately overcome with amazement. ⁴³And he strictly charged them that no one should know this, and told them to give her something to eat.

7.³¹Then he returned from the region of Tyre, and went through Sidon to the Sea of Galilee, through the region of the Decapolis. ³²And they brought to him a man who was deaf and had an impediment in his speech; and they besought him to lay his hand upon him. ³³And taking him aside from the multitude privately, he put his fingers into his ears, and he spat and touched his tongue; ³⁴and looking up to heaven, he sighed, and said to him, *'Ephphatha'*, that is, 'Be opened'. ³⁵And his ears were opened, his tongue was released, and he spoke plainly. ³⁶And he charged them to tell no one; but the more he charged them, the more zealously they proclaimed it. ³⁷And they were astonished beyond measure, saying, 'He has done all things well; he even makes the deaf hear and the dumb speak'.

8.²²And they came to Bethsaida. And some people brought to him a blind man, and begged him to touch him. ²³And he took the blind man by the hand, and led him out of the village; and when he had spit on his eyes and laid his hands upon him, he asked him, 'Do you see anything?' ²⁴And he looked up and said, 'I see men; but they look like trees, walking'. ²⁵Then again he laid his hands upon his eyes; and he looked intently and was restored, and saw everything clearly. ²⁶And he sent him away to his home, saying, 'Do not even enter the village'.

The evidence of Mark's retelling is clearly visible — particularly the typical 'immediately'³⁰² and the endings with their choral effect (2.12; 7.37) or interplay of silence and publicity (1.44-45; 5.42-43; 7.36). Nor is it hard to hear the voice of the story-teller adding the sarcastic comment about doctors (5.26), a not unfamiliar motif,³⁰³ but no doubt borne out by the hard experience of several in

302. Mark 1.29, 30, 42, 43; 2.8, 12; 5.29, 30, 42.
303. 2 Chron. 16.12; Sir. 10.10; 38.15; Tob. 2.10; 1QapGen. 20.20; Philo, *Sac.* 70; *m. Qidd.* 4.14.

most audiences.[304] And personally I have no doubt that Mark has used the account of the two-stage healing (8.22-26) to indicate the painfully slow transition of Jesus' own disciples from their blindness (8.18) to the partial sight of Peter's confession (8.29) and beyond (9.9).[305]

At the same time, the fact that most of the stories have a firm location is hardly to be attributed to subsequent adornment.[306] The simple intimacy and unadorned character of what is only the second healing in Mark's account (1.29-31) is remarkable, even by Mark's standard — nothing worthy of special note here![307] Equally remarkable is the description of Jesus' emotional state when confronted with leprosy:[308] not only was he 'deeply moved' (1.41 — *splanchnistheis*),[309] but Mark describes him as 'snorting' (1.43 — *embrimēsamenos*)[310] at the leper.[311] Somewhat surprising too, given Mark's attitude to the law of clean and unclean elsewhere (7.19), Jesus commands the man to 'go show yourself to the priest, and

304. Was it Mark who created the 'Markan sandwich' in 5.21-43 (cf. 3.20-35; 11.12-25; 14.53-72), or did a twin episode thus interwoven already in the tradition (and in memory) give him the idea of using the same technique elsewhere? Here is a good example of the difficulty of discerning Markan redaction (cf. above, §7.4c at n. 75). For the discussion on the point see particularly Guelich, *Mark* 292-93.

305. Similarly, e.g., Guelich, *Mark* 430; Meier, *Marginal Jew* 2.691-92.

306. The house of Simon and Andrew (1.29); 'at home' in Capernaum (2.1); Bethsaida (8.22); on Capernaum and Bethsaida see above, §9.9d and nn. 305 and 329 respectively; here note also Meier, *Marginal Jew* 2.692-93 and his response to Guelich's conclusion that 'Bethsaida' is redactional in n. 71.

307. Peter's mother-in-law is never mentioned again. 'This brief vignette comes as close as any to qualifying as a report of an actual happening' (Funk, *Acts of Jesus* 59); similarly Lüdemann, *Jesus* 13. See also Pesch, *Markusevangelium* 1.131-32. Meier, however, almost falls over backwards in his desire not to claim too much for this story (*Marginal Jew* 2.707-708). Luke treats the healing as a quasi-exorcism: Jesus 'commanded the fever' (Luke 4.39; cf. 4.35).

308. On what the description *lepros/lepra* (1.40, 42) might have denoted see D. P. Wright and R. N. Jones, 'Leprosy' *ABD* 4.277-82.

309. For the debate on whether the more weakly attested *orgistheis* ('angered') should be regarded as the earlier reading see Meier, *Marginal Jew* 2.748 n. 106.

310. LSJ, *embrimaomai;* see Taylor, *Mark* 188-89; 'growling' (Marcus, *Mark* 1.206). See also S. Eitrem, *Some Notes on the Demonology in the New Testament* (Uppsala: Almquist and Wiksells, ²1966) 51-55.

311. Opinion is divided on this episode. Lüdemann thinks the tradition has no historical value (*Jesus* 14). But the Jesus Seminar 'agreed by a narrow margin that Jesus cured the "leper" of some form of dermatitis' (*Acts of Jesus* 62). The usually more conservative Pesch, however, is much less impressed (*Markusevangelium* 1.147); Meier declines to make any claims about the details of the story, though he is more confident than Pesch 'that during his ministry Jesus claimed to heal lepers and was thought by other people to have done so' (*Marginal Jew* 2.706); and Kollmann thinks that the 'obviously christological adaptation and outbidding of 2 Kgs 5'(!) allows no certain clue to the leprosy healings of Jesus (*Jesus* 225).

offer for your cleansing what Moses commanded' (1.44).[312] It is also hard to doubt a vivid memory behind the description of the paralysed man's four friends as they 'removed the roof where Jesus was, and digging through *(exoryxantes)*[313] let down the pallet' (2.4).[314] The fact that one of those involved is remembered by name ('Jairus') is hardly surprising, since he was leader of the village assembly (5.22); an episode involving such a prominent local figure would inevitably create a stir.[315] In the interwoven episode, the seriousness of the woman's condition in a society where blood and a woman's bleeding was so defiling[316] is simply assumed rather than stated; the story took its shape in a Palestinian context where an explanation was unnecessary.[317] Not to be missed are the Aramaic words of Jesus preserved in 5.41 *('talitha koum')* and 7.34 *('ephphatha').*[318] It may well be the case that later tradents retained the words in Aramaic because they gave an appropriate sense of magic and mystery in a Greek-speaking context.[319] But these are not non-

312. Guelich pushes too hard the suggestion that the phrase *eis martyrion autois* should be translated 'as evidence against them' (*Mark* 76-77), since what is more obviously in view is compliance with the law as laid down in Leviticus 13–14 (though cf. 6.11). Matthew and Luke took over the phrase unchanged.

313. 'Probably in reference to making an opening by digging through the clay of which the roof was made . . . and putting the debris to one side . . . , so that it does not fall on the heads of those in the house' (BDAG, *exorysso* b). Luke's retelling assumes the tiled roofs of more substantial houses familiar to his Greek-speaking readers (Luke 5.19).

314. See also Pesch, *Markusevangelium* 1.157-58, and further below, §17.2b. 'The story reflects an incident in the public life of Jesus' (Funk, *Acts of Jesus* 64); contrast Lüdemann, *Jesus* 15.

315. See also Meier, *Marginal Jew* 2.784-88; Twelftree, *Jesus* 305-307. Meier (782-84) justifiably criticizes Pesch (*Markusevangelium* 1.312-13) for pressing too hard the possible symbolical significance of the name Jairus ('he will enlighten or awaken'?). And although the parallels with Elijah (1 Kgs. 17.17-24) and Elisha (2 Kgs. 4.18-37) naturally attract attention, it is clear that no attempt has been made to frame the story of Jairus's daughter on the template they provide; they hardly provide a 'model' (Lüdemann, *Jesus* 37; contrast the stilling of the storm and the feeding of the 5,000 below, §15.7f).

316. The restrictions on a woman with a discharge of blood were severe (Lev. 15.19-27; see also *m. Zabim*); with a continuous flow of blood she would have been socially crippled, may indeed have been quarantined (Marcus, *Mark* 1.357-58). In which case, her boldness in breaching a serious taboo was all the more striking.

317. See also Pesch, *Markusevangelium* 1.305-306; Twelftree, *Jesus* 317-18. The Jesus Seminar suggest that the gist of the story 'in its earliest form must have been something like this: "There was a woman who suffered from vaginal hemorrhaging. She touched Jesus' cloak and the bleeding stopped instantly"' (Funk, *Acts of Jesus* 80). Kollmann can see only the interests of Hellenistic Jewish Christian missionary propaganda (*Jesus* 229-31).

318. On the Aramaic involved see M. Wilcox, 'Semitisms in the New Testament', *ANRW* 2.25.2 (1984) 998-99, 1000-1002 ('Talitha' is possibly a personal name = Greek *Thaleththi*); Marcus, *Mark* 1.474-75.

319. 'The magic word' (Bultmann, *History* 213-14). According to Lucian, healers

sense words, such as we find in the magical papyri.[320] On the contrary, they probably belonged to the tradition from the first, as the words which the first Aramaic-
speaking tradents recalled Jesus as speaking.[321] Finally, we should note that, although Mark has made good use of the story of the two-stage healing, the story itself hardly does Jesus much credit as a healer.[322] The embarrassment of his relative failure and the crudity of his technique is probably sufficient indication that
the story goes back to a tradition of Jesus' mission, recalled despite (or because
of) its problematic character.[323]

Whatever we now may think of the events which might have occasioned
these stories, the most obvious conclusion to draw is that there were various incidents during Jesus' mission which were experienced/witnessed as miracles, understood as healings brought about by divine power flowing through Jesus.
These first impressions would almost certainly have been embodied in the remembrances of these episodes as they were first circulated among Jesus' followers. Strauss was right: remove the element of miracle and you eliminate the very
reason why the story was told in the first place.

f. The Nature Miracles

The most 'extraordinary deeds' attributed to Jesus are usually designated 'nature miracles', most notably the stilling of the storm (Mark 4.35-41 pars.), the
feeding of the 5,000 (6.32-44 pars.), and the walking on the water (6.45-52

---

tended to use *rhēsis barbarikē*, 'foreign language' (*Philops.* 9); see also Theissen, *Miracle
Stories* 64-65.

320. See Meier's robust response to F. L. Horton, 'Nochmals *ephphatha* in Mk 7:34',
ZNW 77 (1986) 101-108 (*Marginal Jew* 2.759 n. 159); contrast Kollmann, *Jesus* 233-34.

321. 'These [Aramaic healing] formulas were probably preserved for the purpose of
guiding Christian thaumaturges in exorcistic and healing activities' (Aune, 'Magic in Early
Christianity' 1534-35).

322. Is this part of the reason that Matthew and Luke both omit it?

323. The criterion of embarrassment is emphasized by Meier: 'having Jesus spit in a
person's face does not seem to fit any stream of christology in the early church' (*Marginal Jew*
2.693); he also notes the number of *hapax legomena* in 8.23-25 (741-42 n. 76). Similarly in regard to Mark 7.31-37: embarrassment (713-14) and *hapax legomena* (758 n. 154). Meier is followed by Twelftree, *Jesus* 300-301, 322-23. Lüdemann agrees: 'because of the specific details
[Mark 7.31-37] may have a high claim to authenticity' (*Jesus* 52; contrast Pesch,
Markusevangelium 1.399). Similarly on Mark 8.22-26: 'such an abstruse story as this can
hardly be derived from the community' (*Jesus* 55) — the sort of over-confident comment which
invites a pencilled 'Oh!' in the margin. The Jesus Seminar (Funk, *Acts of Jesus*) was more confident regarding Mark 8.22-23: 'The Fellows by a narrow majority concluded that Jesus cured
at least one blind person' (103), but more ambivalent on 7.32-35 (98-99).

THE QUESTION OF JESUS' SELF-UNDERSTANDING §15.7

pars.).[324] I have already cited the first of these above (§8.4c), so need quote only the other two here. In the first case there is a faint possibility that Matthew and Luke knew another version close to that of Mark (Matt. 14:13-21/Luke 9.10-17), but for present purposes it will suffice to quote only Mark. The greater interest lies in the fact that in both cases there is a Johannine parallel to the Synoptic version.

Mark 6.32-44	John 6.1-14
32 And they went away in the boat to a lonely place by themselves. 33 Now many saw them going, and knew them, and they ran there on foot from all the towns, and got there ahead of them. 34 As he went ashore he saw a great crowd, and he had compassion on them, because they were like sheep without a shepherd; and he began to teach them many things. 35 And when it grew late, his disciples came to him and said, 'This is a lonely place, and the hour is now late; 36 send them away, to go into the country and villages round about and buy themselves something to eat'. 37 But he answered them, 'You give them something to eat'. And they said to him, 'Shall we go and buy two hundred denarii worth of bread, and give it to them to eat?' 38 And he said to them, 'How many loaves have you? Go and see'. And when they had found out, they said, 'Five, and two fish'. 39 Then he commanded them all to sit down by companies upon the green grass. 40 So they sat down in groups, by hundreds and by fifties. 41 And taking the five loaves and the two fish he looked up to heaven, and blessed, and broke the loaves, and gave them to the disciples to set before the people; and he divided the two fish among them all. 42 And they all ate and were satisfied. 43 And they took up twelve baskets full of broken pieces and of the fish. 44 And those who ate the loaves were five thousand men.	1 After this Jesus went to the other side of the Sea of Galilee, which is the Sea of Tiberias. 2 And a great crowd followed him, because they saw the signs which he did on those who were diseased. 3 Jesus went up on the mountain, and there sat down with his disciples. 4 Now the Passover, the feast of the Jews, was at hand. 5 Lifting up his eyes, then, and seeing that a great crowd was coming to him, Jesus said to Philip, 'How are we to buy bread, so that these people may eat?' 6 This he said to test him, for he himself knew what he would do. 7 Philip answered him, 'Two hundred denarii would not buy enough bread for each of them to get a little'. 8 One of his disciples, Andrew, Simon Peter's brother, said to him, 9 'There is a lad here who has five barley loaves and two fish; but what are they among so many?' 10 Jesus said, 'Make the people sit down'. Now there was much grass in the place; so the men sat down, in number about five thousand. 11 Jesus then took the loaves, and when he had given thanks, he distributed them to those who were seated; so also the fish, as much as they wanted. 12 And when they had eaten their fill, he told his disciples, 'Gather up the fragments left over, that nothing may be lost'. 13 So they gathered them up and filled twelve baskets with broken pieces from the five barley loaves, left by those who had eaten. 14 When the people saw the sign which he had done, they said, 'This is indeed the prophet who is to come into the world!'

324. On the others usually included in this category — the coin in the fish's mouth (Matt. 17.27), the cursing of the fig tree (Mark 11.12-14, 20-21 par.), the miraculous catch of fishes (Luke 5.1-11/John 21.1-14?), and the changing of water into wine (John 2.1-11) — see Meier, *Marginal Jew* 2.880-904, 934-50, whose conclusions seem eminently sensible. On the first, see also R. Bauckham, 'The Coin in the Fish's Mouth', in Wenham and Blomberg, eds., *Miracles of Jesus* 219-52.

Mark 6.45-52	John 6.15-21
45 Immediately he compelled <u>his disciples</u> to <u>get into the boat</u>, and go before him to the other side, to Bethsaida, while he dismissed the crowd. 46 And after he had taken leave of them, he went up on the mountain to pray. 47 And when evening came, the boat was out on the sea, and he was alone on the land. 48 And he saw that they were making headway painfully, for the <u>wind</u> was against them. And about the fourth watch of the night he came to them, <u>walking on the sea</u>. He meant to pass by them, 49 but when they saw him <u>walking on the sea</u> they thought it was a ghost, and cried out; 50 for they all saw him, and were terrified. But immediately he spoke to them and said, 'Take heart, <u>it is I; do not be afraid</u>'. 51 And he got <u>into the boat</u> with them and the wind ceased. And they were utterly astounded, 52 for they did not understand about the loaves, but their hearts were hardened.	15 Perceiving then that they were about to come and take him by force to make him king, Jesus withdrew again to the mountain by himself. 16 When evening came, <u>his disciples</u> went down to the sea, 17 got into a <u>boat</u>, and started across the sea to Capernaum. It was now dark, and Jesus had not yet come to them. 18 The sea rose because a strong <u>wind</u> was blowing. 19 When they had rowed about three or four miles, they saw Jesus <u>walking on the sea</u> and drawing near to the boat. They were frightened, but he said to them, '<u>It is I; do not be afraid</u>'. 21 Then they wanted to take him <u>into the boat</u>, and immediately the boat was at the land to which they were going.

This is one of the more interesting instances of the traditioning process within the earliest Christian groups. Clearly we have two versions of the same tradition. Equally clearly, one has not been derived from the other at a literary level. The only obvious explanation is two oral versions of the same episodes which came to Mark and John independently.[325] As oral tradition, the core detail in each case is fairly modest. Intriguingly, in the first almost the only verbal agreement is limited to the numbers (200 denarii, 5 loaves, 2 fishes, 12 baskets, 5,000 participants); presumably a key factor here was the lack of core saying of Jesus.[326] In the latter, the most significant constant is the words of Jesus: 'It is I *(egō eimi); do not be afraid'.*

What is most striking, however, is the fact that the two stories had evidently become so firmly attached to each other. Their attachment was so firm that the Fourth Evangelist retained the second miracle story even though it interrupted the pattern of miracle followed by discourse which he otherwise followed throughout the 'book of signs' (John 2–12); in this case the addition of the sequel required a somewhat awkward bridge passage (6.22-25) back to the discourse

325. It should also be noted that the feeding of the 5,000 is the only miracle to be recorded in all four Gospels (Matt. 14.13-21/Mark 6.32-44/Luke 9.10b-17/John 6.1-15), though for some reason not at all clear Luke omits the walking on the water sequel (simply to note that this marks the beginning of Luke's 'great omission' [of Markan material — Mark 6.45–8.26] explains nothing).

326. I am uncertain what to make of the second feeding miracle in Mark — the feeding of the 4,000 (Mark 8.1-10/Matt. 15.32-39). I suspect Mark has picked up what was a variant version where it was not the numbers that were held constant but the eucharistic motif — 'took bread, gave thanks, broke and gave' (cf. particularly Luke 22.19); see also Meier, *Marginal Jew* 2.961-64, 1030-31 n. 301.

consequent upon the feeding miracle (6.26-59). The most obvious conclusion to draw from this is that the two stories were united in oral tradition more or less from the beginning, so that in oral performance it had become itself traditional to tell the two together.[327] This is all the more striking, given the indications of the diversity in detail, and thus flexibility in performance, which the parallel accounts above indicate. Could the explanation be that the twin tradition started life as twins because it embodied a twin memory?

In terms of the tradition as it now stands, the possibility can arouse only qualified enthusiasm. A feature of all three 'nature miracles' (including the stilling of the storm) is the degree to which they have been shaped to bring out biblical echoes and parallels. In the telling of the stilling of the storm (Mark 4.35-41) there are clear echoes of the Jonah story[328] and possibly also of the famous sea storm passage in Ps. 107.23-30.[329] In the feeding of the 5,000 (Mark 6.32-44) the echo of 2 Kgs. 4.42-44 seems to have shaped the account of the miracle itself.[330] And in the walking on the water (Mark 6.45-52) it is hard to doubt that the scriptural talk of God (or divine Wisdom) walking on the sea has played some part in

---

327. See also Meier, *Marginal Jew* 2.905-906, 908-12, 951-56, 993-94 n. 110.

328. Jonah 1.4: Jonah boards a boat *(ploion)*, it is caught up in a great *(megas)* storm, which puts the boat in grave peril. 1.5: the mariners are afraid, but Jonah had gone down into the bowels of the boat and sleeps *(katheudōn)*. 1.6: the captain rebukes Jonah for showing no concern lest 'we perish' *(apolōmetha)*. 1.9-10: when Jonah confesses his faith, his companions are 'exceedingly afraid' *(ephobēthēsan phobon megan)*. 1.15: when Jonah is thrown into the sea, it ceases from its raging. 1.16: the mariners are again 'exceedingly afraid'. See also Pesch, *Markusevangelium* 1.270-73; Meier, *Marginal Jew* 2.931, 1008 n. 184.

329. Particularly 107.28-29: 'They cried to the Lord in their trouble, and he delivered them from their distress; he made the storm be still, and the waves of the sea were hushed'. See also Marcus, *Mark* 1.336-39.

330.

2 Kgs 4.42-44		Mark 6.37-44	
42-43	20 loaves of barley; 100 men.	38, 44	5 loaves; 5000 men.
42	Elisha said, 'Give it to the men that they might eat'.	37	He answered them, 'You give them something to eat'.
43	But his servant said, 'How am I to set this before a hundred men?'	37	They said to him, 'Shall we go and buy 200 denarii worth of bread and give it to them to eat?'
44	So he set it before them.	41	. . . to set before them.
44	And they ate and had some left.	42-43	They all ate and were satisfied; and they took up 12 baskets full of broken pieces . . .

See, e.g., Pesch, *Markusevangelium* 1.355-56; Meier, *Marginal Jew* 2.960-61; and the fuller discussion in Davies and Allison, *Matthew* 2.480-85.

forming the story.[331] Whatever the memories enshrined in these traditions, there-fore, it would appear that a theological agenda has given them their enduring shape: Jesus as greater than Jonah, as greater than Elisha, as enacting or embody-ing the Creator's mastery over the elements.

At the same time, there are incidental details in each case which suggest that some historical reminiscences have been incorporated in these stories. In the stilling of the storm, that 'other boats were with them' (Mark 4.36) is not an inte-gral part of the story; it is left hanging there, without completion.[332] Is this part of the tradition present because an eyewitness recollection of what must have been a rather vivid scene became lodged in the retellings? The unusual note that the disciples took the initiative ('they took Jesus with them, just as he was', 4.36) and the 'cushion' in 4.38 raise the same question.[333]

Similarly in the feeding miracle, we should note what look like flashes of eyewitness reminiscence: the crowd straggling round the shore evoking the old picture of Israel as sheep without a shepherd (6.34; §13.3c), the numbers (five and two), which do not seem to bear any obvious symbolism (6.38), the 'green' grass (6.39),[334] and the various groups arranged like 'beds of leeks' (*prasiai, prasiai,* 6.40). In addition, we have already noted the intriguing and uncontrived link between Mark's and John's transitions between the two stories (§15.3h). Taking these factors into consideration, Meier's conclusion seems to be emi-nently fair: 'it is more likely than not that behind our Gospel stories of Jesus feeding the multitude lies some especially memorable communal meal of bread and fish, a meal with eschatological overtones celebrated by Jesus and his disci-ples with a large crowd by the Sea of Galilee'.[335]

In the case of the walking on the water there are a number of curious fea-tures which do not fit well with the overall epiphanic effect. 'He *wanted* to pass

---

331. He comes from the mountain (cf. Deut. 33.2; Hab. 3.3); he walks on the water (Job 9.8b; Hab. 3.15; Ps. 77.19; Isa. 43.16; also Wis. 14.3; Sir. 24.5-6); he passes by (cf. Exod. 33.19, 22; 34.5-6; 1 Kgs. 19.11); *egō eimi* (cf. Exod. 3.14; Isa. 43.1-3, 10-11); see more fully Meier, *Marginal Jew* 2.914-9. The account of Peter also walking on the water (Matt. 14.28-31) appears to be a Matthean elaboration highlighting the leading role of Peter (as in 16.16-19), but as an example of 'little faith' and a foil to his later commendation (16.17-19). P. J. Madden, *Je-sus' Walking on the Sea: An Investigation of the Origin of the Narrative Account* (BZNW 81; Berlin: de Gruyter, 1997) concludes that the episode is best understood as a displaced resurrec-tion appearance narrative (138-39).

332. A 'splinter of tradition' (Pesch, *Markusevangelium* 1.270).

333. Murphy-O'Connor also notes that fishermen 'have still to watch for sudden gusts from the surrounding wadis which can whip the normally tranquil surface to turmoil in a matter of minutes' (*Holy Land* 410).

334. An echo of Ps. 23.2 is at best distant; even so, Twelftree warns against putting any weight on it (*Jesus* 319).

335. Meier, *Marginal Jew* 2.965-66.

them by' (6.48); the statement of intention makes for an awkward moment, not least since he then did not pass them by.[336] The statement that 'they thought they saw a ghost *(phantasma)'*[337] also can hardly be explained from the OT background and fits awkwardly. Of course, the repeated description of their fear ('cried out', 'were terrified', 6.49-50) heightens the drama and prepares the way dramatically for the subsequent resolution (cf. Luke 24.37; Acts 12.9). But if truth be told, the story at this point reads more like a straight ghost story than anything else. Noticeable here is *pantes* — 'they *all* saw him' (6.50) — a characteristic feature in ghost stories. Finally there is the curious discordance between the two endings: according to John's version, 'they wanted to take him into the boat', and John leaves it unclear whether the wish was realized (contrast Mark 6.51); instead those in the boat find that they 'were suddenly at the shore' (John 6.21). All in all the impression is given of a dream-like state, of movement and encounter impressionistic rather than clearly recalled.[338]

Consequently, I find myself wondering whether behind even the two sea-miracles we can detect some half-remembered experience which provided the basis and stimulus for the theological elaboration which gave the traditions their definitive character.[339] As with the feeding of the large crowd, were there those of the disciples who experienced one or more dangerous journeys across the lake as a miracle of rescue or revelation? Here again, we should not assume originally non-miraculous accounts which were only later reworked as miracles. Strauss's point carries weight here too. And despite the theological overlay being impenetrable at most points, some reminiscences do still seem to poke through.[340] Possibly then here too we have to envisage traditions given the shape which still de-

---

336. Matthew omits the phrase; perhaps the statement of intention worked too much against the epiphany theme, which otherwise we would expect him to have found congenial.

337. See BDAG, *phantasma*.

338. In *Jesus and the Spirit* 73 and 380 n. 27 I note the parallel of *operatio in distans* brought forward by Rudolf Otto. B. J. Malina, 'Assessing the Historicity of Jesus' Walking on the Sea: Insights from Cross-Cultural Social Psychology', in Chilton and Evans, eds., *Authenticating the Activities of Jesus* 351-71, warns against limiting discussion to *literary* parallels, evaluates the episode as an example of altered states of consciousness, and concludes: 'As reported in the Gospels, the incident has all the hallmarks of historical verisimilitude and should be ranked as a historically authentic episode' (369).

339. I see no grounds for taking the two sea-miracles as variants of each other (see Meier, *Marginal Jew* 2.996-97 n. 110).

340. However, Meier concludes firmly: 'the walking on the water is most likely from start to finish a creation of the early church, a christological confession in narrative form'; 'the stilling of the storm is a product of early Christian theology' (*Marginal Jew* 2.921, 933). Similarly Pesch, *Markusevangelium* 1.276, 362-63. Twelftree, *Jesus,* is content to leave the question of the origin of the stilling of the storm 'open' (317), though he presses a little more for a more positive conclusion in regard to the walking on the water (321-22).

termines them more or less from the first telling, and by those reflecting on experiences which they interpreted in and by the telling. But even granted the possibility I doubt whether much weight can be placed on it.

g. Was Jesus a Magician?

The question has been hotly debated since Morton Smith proposed a straightforward Yes answer.[341] But the debate remains confused and not really capable of delivering a satisfactory answer. A key problem is the definition of 'magic' and the range of practices covered by the term;[342] in particular, is the attempt to manipulate and coerce spiritual powers a defining feature of magic? A correlated problem is that the overlap of religion, ritual, and magic[343] means that any attempt to interact with the spiritual realm unavoidably leaves itself vulnerable to a charge of magic or sorcery. 'Magic' is a social classification, and where the term is regarded as negative, as is usually the case,[344] its use indicates the polemical attitude of the opponent more than a factual description.[345]

Two points can be made with reasonable clarity. First, if magic is defined in terms of rituals and practices used to coerce the gods and spirit powers, then we can certainly say that it was 'omnipresent in classical antiquity'.[346] This would be true of Palestinian as well as diaspora Judaism.[347] Second, as already

341. M. Smith, *Jesus the Magician* (San Francisco: Harper and Row, 1978); similarly Crossan, *Historical Jesus* 305 (but with qualifications); good bibliographies in Meier, *Marginal Jew* 2.553-56; and Klauck, *Religious Context* 209-31.

342. Meier proposes a sliding scale, a spectrum or continuum of characteristics, running from the 'ideal type' of miracle at one end to the 'ideal type' of magic at the other (*Marginal Jew* 2.537-52). His discussion includes a useful review of other studies (560-61 n. 26).

343. Cf., e.g., the Introduction to M. Meyer and R. Smith, *Ancient Christian Magic: Coptic Texts of Ritual Power* (San Francisco: HarperSanFrancisco, 1994) 1-6; 'Books written by sociologists tend to have "religion" in their titles, while books written by anthropologists are often about "magic"' (3). Similar to Meier, Klauck proposes magic and religion as 'antithetical poles within a continuum, two end points joined by a common line'; in simplified slogan terms, 'coercion is typical of magic, and petition typical of religion' (*Religious Context* 217-18).

344. E.g., Theissen, *Miracle Stories* 233, 238-43; Aune, 'Magic in Early Christianity' 1518-19; H. D. Betz, 'Magic in Greco-Roman Antiquity', *ER* 9 (1995) 93; Crossan, *Historical Jesus* 304-10 ('magic as religious banditry'); other bibliography in Meier, *Marginal Jew* 2.558-59 n. 19.

345. The point is illustrated by the accusation levelled against Jesus that he used sorcery to expel demons (Mark 3.22 pars.). Despite recognizing that the accusations are 'polemical name-calling, not neutral character description', Crossan nevertheless unjustifiably draws from the accusation the suggestion 'that perhaps Jesus healed in ecstatic trance' (*Birth* 341).

346. F. Graf, *Magic in the Ancient World* (Cambridge: Harvard University, 1997) 1.

347. See P. S. Alexander, 'Incantations and Books of Magic', in Schürer, *History* 3.342-

noted, one of the most consistent attacks directed against Jesus by the early opponents of Christianity was the charge of sorcery.[348] What were the grounds for such a charge? Four features of Jesus' technique call for comment.

(1) At the time of Jesus it was evidently typical for healers and exorcists to use *material aids,* particularly in exorcisms. In Tobit's exorcism, success is achieved through burning a fish's liver and heart (Tob. 8.3). In Josephus's report, the smell of a root drew out the demon through the demoniac's nostrils (*Ant.* 8.45-49). According to Justin, fumigations and magic knots were used (*Dial.* 85.3). In the *Testament of Solomon,* Solomon seals the demons with a ring given him by the Lord Sabaoth through the archangel Michael.[349] A further motif sometimes to be found is the demon manifesting its departure by knocking over something *en route.*[350] This latter raises the intriguing possibility that the stampede of the pigs in Mark 5.13 pars. originally had the same function of demonstrating that the 'legion' of unclean spirits/demons had truly departed from the man.[351] That episode apart, the accounts of Jesus' exorcisms are remarkably free of reference to material aids. Jesus apparently made no use of any such aid in his exorcisms. Did Jesus deliberately eschew what appears to have been regular features of typical exorcistic practice?

(2) In the reports of his healings, however, we read of Jesus regularly taking by the hand,[352] or stretching out his hand and *touching* the leper (Mark 1.41 pars.). In Mark's account *'laying on of hands'* is regarded as Jesus' normal mode of ministering to the sick.[353] Was this distinctive? It is frequently noted that the

---

79; C. E. Arnold, *Ephesians: Power and Magic: The Concept of Power in Ephesians in Light of Its Historical Setting* (SNTSMS 63; Cambridge: Cambridge University, 1989) 29-34; and the data indicated above (§15.7a); for OT references see the summary in Betz, 'Magic' 96.

348. See again Stanton, 'Jesus of Nazareth: Magician and False Prophet?' (above, n. 95). For an earlier review see Smith, *Jesus the Magician* ch. 4. Smith cites the accusation against Jesus of being a 'doer of evil' (John 18.30), which he takes on the basis of later Roman legislation to be the equivalent of 'magician' (41, 174). He even sketches the life of 'Jesus the magician' as it was pictured by those who did not become his disciples (67) — rather like trying to reconstruct the picture of a 1,000-piece jigsaw puzzle out of the 20 pieces still preserved.

349. *T. Sol.* 1.6; 2.5; 5.11; 7.3, 8, etc.; interesting variations in 18.15-16, 28, 32-35, 38, etc.

350. Josephus, *Ant.* 8.48 (a bowl of water spilled); Philostratus, *Life* 4.20 (a statue knocked over). See also Theissen, *Miracle Stories* 66-67.

351. Alternatively, the thought may be of the demon being sent into some other object which could then be disposed of (Twelftree, *Jesus the Exorcist* 75).

352. Mark 1.31/Matt. 8.15 ('touched her hand'); Mark 5.41 pars. It is to be noted, however, that Jesus is never recorded as touching demoniacs (Aune, 'Magic in Early Christianity' 1529); the only near exception is Mark 9.27, when the exorcism has already succeeded.

353. Mark 5.23 (hands)/Matt. 9.18 (hand); Mark 6.2 ('through his hands'); 6.5; 7.32; 8.23; Luke 4.40; 13.13. Perhaps also in blessing (Matt. 19.13, but Mark 10.13/Luke 18.15 read

practice is unknown in biblical and post-biblical Judaism, though now attested in 1QapGen 20.28-29, where the exorcism is achieved by prayer and the laying on of hands.[354] Perhaps, then, a spontaneous gesture of Jesus (of sympathy and personal rapport?), when confronted with sickness, is recalled here. More to the point, his success in healing is attributed to it (n. 353). We may deduce further that the remembrance of this characteristic gesture influenced earliest Christian practice.[355]

More striking are the reports of Jesus using *spittle* in his healings. In the case of the deaf-mute, Jesus 'put his fingers into his ears, and he spat and touched his tongue' (Mark 7.33); and in the case of the blind man at Bethsaida, 'he spat into his eyes, laid hands on him', and then 'again laid his hands on his eyes' (8.23, 25). The Fourth Evangelist also records Jesus as spitting on the ground, making clay of the spittle, and anointing the eyes of a blind man (John 9.6). These reports easily lend themselves to the classification of 'magic'.[356] But as Joel Marcus reminds us, spittle was a popular folk remedy in the ancient world and was highly regarded by professional physicians like Galen.[357] The spittle of famous personalities was highly prized.[358] And it was also thought to be effective in Jewish circles.[359] It would be hardly surprising, then, if Jesus used such means, either because he himself (or those whom he treated) shared the common belief. The 'magic' may be only in the eye of the beholder.[360]

In terms of *physical* contact the other striking case is the episode of the

---

'touch'; Mark 10.16/Matt. 19.15). See also *epilabomenos*, 'took hold of' (Mark 8.23; Luke 9.47; 14.4).

354. See, e.g., E. Lohse, *cheir, TDNT* 9.428, who also notes that the LXX translates *epithēsei tēn cheira* in 2 Kgs. 5.11 (n. 23). Aune notes that in Hellenistic traditions touch as a healing rite is only rarely used by human miracle workers ('Magic in Early Christianity' 1533). Apollonius, however, is described as 'touching' a girl seemingly dead (Philostratus, *Life* 4.45). See also Eitrem, *Notes* 41-46; Theissen, *Miracle Stories* 62, 92-93; Yamauchi, 'Magic or Miracle?' 135-36.

355. Acts 3.7; (5.12); 9.12, 17, 41; (14.3; 19.11); 28.8; Mark 16.18.

356. Smith, *Jesus the Magician* 92, 118; Aune, 'Magic in Early Christianity' 1537-38; some discussion in Meier, *Marginal Jew* 2.567-68 n. 54.

357. Marcus, *Mark* 1.473-74, citing Galen, *Natural Faculties* 3.7. Pliny the Elder also commends the potency of saliva, the 'physic of the tongue' (*Natural History* 28.7.35-39; texts in Cotter, *Miracles* 187-89). See also Eitrem, *Notes* 56-60, who observes that Jesus never made use of the popular method of blowing a sickness away (47-49); Theissen, *Miracle Stories* 63; Yamauchi, 'Magic or Miracle?' 137-41.

358. Tacitus (*Histories* 4.81) and Suetonius (*Vespasian* 7) both record a blind man begging Vespasian to heal him with his spittle.

359. Marcus cites *b. B. Bat.* 126b, where R. Hanina sends people in need to his son, 'for he is a first-born, and his saliva heals' (*Mark* 1.473).

360. A concern of this sort may have been a factor in Matthew's and Luke's decision to omit the two Markan episodes.

woman being healed by the power which flowed from/through Jesus' garment (Mark 5.27-30). Here again it is easy to detect magical overtones or a magical conception of miracle.[361] At the same time, however, we should recall that Luke saw no difficulty in attributing cures to the power of Peter's shadow and the power of handkerchiefs touched by Paul (Acts 5.15; 19.12), while at the same time depicting Peter and Paul as both distancing themselves from and as triumphing over magical practices.[362] The history of canonizations and relics is too full of reports of such healings, equally open to alternative critical interpretation,[363] for Mark's account to be lightly dismissed in its description of the healing itself.

(3) Deserving of separate mention is the point observed earlier that the majority of the references to faith (or lack of faith) in the Synoptics occur in relation to miracles.[364] Some sort of synergism is clearly envisaged between Jesus' healing power and the trust (in God) of those healed. Indeed, according to Mark 6.5, Jesus' power to work miracles was dependent on or limited by the faith of those he might otherwise have helped.[365] This too is a distinctive feature of the Jesus tradition[366] and is almost certainly rooted in memories of Jesus' work as a healer.[367] That Jesus encouraged an expectant trust is also well enough attested, not only in regard to the disciples' prayer generally (§14.2b),

361. Meier, *Marginal Jew* 2.709.

362. Acts 8.18-24 (Simon practised magic [*mageuō*], 8.9); 13.4-12 (Elymas was a *magos*, 13.6, 8); 16.16-18 (the girl had 'a spirit of divination' [*pneuma pythōna*], 16.16); 19.13-20 (those who practised magic [*ta perierga prassein*], 19.19).

363. Smith begins with such a report culled from the *New York Times* (*Jesus the Magician* 10); see also Crossan, *Birth* 297-98, and illustrations in my *Jesus and the Spirit* 379 nn. 19, 21.

364. Mark 2.5 pars.; 5.34, 36 pars.; 9.23-24; 10.52 pars.; Matt. 8.10/Luke 7.9; Matt. 8.13; 9.28; 15.28; Luke 17.19; see further above, §13.2b. Presumably one reason Jesus refused the request for a 'sign' (§15.6b) was that the request demonstrated the absence of faith; the sign he gives is the call for repentance (and faith)!

365. Matt. 13.58 softens what might otherwise be considered a demeaning admission by Mark; Luke ignores the Markan passage altogether.

366. Perrin maintains that such a use of 'faith' is completely absent from Hellenistic healing stories and is 'without parallel anywhere in the Hellenistic literature' (*Rediscovering* 134-36; see also Jeremias, *Proclamation* 162-63; Goppelt, *Theology* 1.149-51); but Aune questions this, referring to A. Oepke's brief note in *TDNT* 3.210 and observing that credibility and trust were inevitably features of any magician's success ('Magic in Early Christianity' 1535-36). See further Theissen, *Miracle Stories* 130-33, who concludes that 'the faith associated with New Testament miracles is based on traditional motifs, but articulates (*sic*) them in a new way'.

367. '"Your faith has saved you", which presumably goes back to Jesus, shows an awareness which is opposed to trust in magical manipulation' (Theissen and Merz, *Historical Jesus* 306-307).

but also in the hyperbolic reference to asking for the impossible (faith to move a mountain).[368]

(4) As indicated in the discussion of Jesus' exorcisms (§15.7d), the exorcist's *authority* or *power source* was a key factor, as signalled particularly by the formula, 'I adjure you by X'. By this formula the exorcist appealed to, or called upon, or even commanded another power (X) greater than that of the demon to expel the demon. It was precisely by following this logic that the first Christians sought to heal others 'in the name of Jesus'.[369] Presumably, then, it is significant that Jesus himself is never recalled as using such a formula, but only (once) the bare order, 'I command you' (Mark 9.25).[370] Is the implication that Jesus did not need to call on some other authority, that his healing and exorcistic ministry was effective through his own power?[371]

There is a further corollary to be followed up here. But if we first sum up the issue of Jesus as a magician, the results are fairly clear. Jesus did not 'come across' as a typical magician. Josephus may have characterized Jesus as 'a doer of extraordinary deeds', but he avoided terms like *magos* ('magician') and *goēs* ('sorcerer, cheat'), which he did not hesitate to use of the sign-prophets and others of the period.[372] On the evidence reviewed above, Josephus probably reflected the most common view that Jesus could not be dismissed simply as a magician and cheat. The avoidance of material aids and absence of incantations in the reports of his miracles simply reinforce the point. At the same time, his occasional use of spittle, and one or two strange episodes (the woman being healed by touching his garments, the pigs?), gave scope to those who wished to denigrate Jesus, and 'magician' or 'sorcerer' was a convenient slur which evidently appealed to the opponents of the movement which he inaugurated.[373] At this point

368. Known both to Mark (Mark 11.22-24/Matt. 21.21-22) and, with performance variation, in q/Q (Matt. 17.20/Luke 17.6), also *GTh* 48, and echoed in 1 Cor. 13.2. With such a range of attestation it is hard to doubt that Jesus said something to this effect (e.g., Jeremias, *Proclamation* 161; Davies and Allison, *Matthew* 2.727-28; Theissen and Merz, *Historical Jesus* 293; Becker, *Jesus of Nazareth* 182; Lüdemann, *Jesus* 79, 202).

369. Acts 3.6, 16; 4.7, 10, 12, 30; 16.18; Jas. 5.14.

370. See also Eitrem, *Notes* 30-34.

371. Chilton deduces from the conjunction of Mark 3.20-21 with 3.22-29 that Jesus practised exorcism and healing by going into a trance meditating on the divine chariot (*Rabbi Jesus* 93-95, 245).

372. Josephus, *War* 2.261 (the Egyptian); 2.264; 4.85; *Ant.* 20.97 (Theudas); 20.142, 160, 167, 188.

373. Smith's own reconstruction is of the same character. For example, he deduces from Mark 6.14 that Jesus was accused of necromancy (he had raised the Baptist from the dead); the story of Jesus' anointing at Jordan 'resembles nothing so much as an account of a magical rite of deification'; Jesus' pronouncement that he had come to bring family strife (Matt. 10.35-36) echoes the practice of casting spells to cause hatred and use of incantations in family quarrels;

the argument is not so different from the argument about Jesus as a Cynic. In both cases there are parallels which can be pressed to affirm Jesus as magician, Jesus as Cynic.[374] But is either case a good example of sober historical evaluation? I think not.

h. Eschatological Significance

If we are looking for the most distinctive feature of Jesus' exorcisms and healings, it is most obviously to be found in the eschatological significance which he is recollected as attributing to them. Here we need simply refer to the same two passages already mentioned above and discussed in §12.5c-d, Matt. 11.5/Luke 7.22 and Mark 3.22-29 pars. Most striking is the fact that Jesus seems to have regarded his successful exorcisms as the defeat (or evidence of the defeat) of Satan, as the plundering of his Satan's possessions (§12.5d[3]). This must have seemed an extraordinary claim to those who expected the destruction of evil and the defeat of Satan as the climax to God's purpose and the presupposition for a new age of restored paradise (chapter 12 n. 79). But it is a claim of that order which Jesus' disciples recalled him as making.

The significance of the key saying, Matt.12.27-28/Luke 11.19-20, has already been noted (§12.5d[2]). It was the fact that Jesus achieved his success by the *Spirit/finger of God* which demonstrated or proved that the *kingdom of God* had come to them.[375] It was this which distinguished Jesus' exorcistic success from the success of his Jewish contemporaries (Matt. 12.27/Luke 11.19):[376] he laid claim to a plenitude of power which, by implication, these other exorcists did not experience.[377]

Thus to recognize that tradition's testimony that Jesus was laying claim to a special anointing by the Spirit (Isa. 61.1) helps explain the puzzling saying with which Mark climaxes his collection of exorcism sayings (Mark 3.29) and

---

'the clearest evidence of Jesus' knowledge and use of magic is the eucharist, a magical rite of a familiar sort' (*Jesus the Magician* 34, 104, 111, 152); Twelftree has an extended review of Smith (*Jesus the Exorcist* 190-207). Meier (*Marginal Jew* 2.558 n. 16) cites A. F. Segal, 'Hellenistic Magic: Some Questions of Definition', in R. van den Broek and M. J. Vermaseren, eds., *Studies in Gnosticism and Hellenistic Religions,* G. Quispel FS (Leiden: Brill, 1981) 349-75: 'The early charge of magic against Jesus is not so much clear proof that Jesus was a magician as a clear example of the social manipulation of the charge of magic' (369).

374. Crossan does not hesitate to use both terms for Jesus (*Historical Jesus* 305, 421).

375. On the echo of Moses' triumph over the Egyptian magicians in talk of 'the finger of God', see above, chapter 12 n. 366.

376. Twelftree was unable to find any evidence to suggest that the 'Spirit' was appealed to as a source of power-authority for exorcism (*Jesus the Exorcist* 109 n. 50).

377. See further my *Jesus and the Spirit* 46-49, 60-62.

which Q presumably preserved elsewhere (Luke 12.10): the saying concerning the danger of blaspheming against the Holy Spirit.[378] It is sometimes attributed to early enthusiastic groups of disciples or Christians as an expression of their confidence that they were themselves inspired by the Spirit — and (in their own eyes) inspired to such a manifest degree that opposition to them should be regarded as opposition to the Spirit.[379] The point here, however, is that Matt. 12.28/ Luke 11.20 attests that very confidence on the part of Jesus himself.[380] It may be more comfortable for critics to attribute such (overweening?) self-assertion to unknown enthusiastic Christians from the next few decades. But it was Jesus who was explicitly recalled as making the former assertion (Matt. 12.28/Luke 11.20), so that his own expression of confidence in his exorcistic ministry as manifestly of God would hardly be surprising or out of character.[381] Just the same confidence comes to clear expression in Jesus' condemnation of the Galilean villages and 'this generation':[382] his mission was so manifestly of God that their rejection of it was all the more culpable.

The fact that Matt. 11.5-6 concludes the reference to the eschatological blessings evident in Jesus' mission with the benediction 'Blessed is the one who takes no offence at me' (Matt. 11.6/Luke 7.23) reinforces this line of thought.[383] Did Jesus see himself simply as the channel of eschatological blessing? It sounds more as though he saw his mission as embodying these blessings, himself as the decisive agent in the realisation of eschatological hopes.[384] In terms of the debate sparked by Bultmann, it was not simply that the proclaimer became the proclaimed (that is, after Easter). Rather, the proclaimer was integral to the proclamation. Here too we can include the 'something greater than Solomon', 'some-

---

378. Cited below §16.4b(3).

379. E.g., Tödt, *Son of Man* 119; but see above, chapter 8 n. 104.

380. The point is not dependent on 'Spirit' being the earlier version (see above, §12.5d[2]).

381. Davies presses the point to argue that Jesus as a spirit-possessed healer understood himself as 'the embodiment of the spirit of God' (*Jesus the Healer,* here 21).

382. Matt. 11.21-23/Luke 10.13-15, linked by Matthew to the testimony regarding the Baptist and by Luke to the mission of the seventy; Matt. 12.41-42/Luke 11.31-32, linked quite closely by both Matthew and Luke to the sequence of exorcism sayings. See also §12.4e above.

383. See above, §12.5c(1).

384. I do not think the point can be pressed so hard in Matt. 12.28/Luke 11.20: it is unclear whether *egō* was part of the original Q text (the mss. evidence is very mixed as regards Luke 11.20); more to the point, however, the text (in its Greek form at least) is constructed so as to set 'Spirit/finger of God' in the place of emphasis, not the 'I'. The point is missed and the christological corollary pressed too hard by Twelftree, *Jesus the Exorcist* 108-109, and H. K. Nielsen, *Heiligung und Verkündigung. Das Verständnis der Heiligung und ihres Verhältnisses zur Verkündigung bei Jesus und in der ältesten Kirche* (Leiden: Brill, 1987) 45; see also above, chapter 12 n. 362.

thing greater than Jonah' motif. For now we have observed its presence not only in the sayings tradition (Matt. 12.41-42/Luke 11.31-32) but also implied in Jesus' success as an exorcist and in talk of Jonah('s preaching) as a sign and integral to the story of the stilling of the storm, probably from its first telling. What should we take from this for Jesus' own evaluation of the category of 'healer, exorcist' as descriptions of his mission?

In all this we are touching on what Bultmann described as 'the immediacy of [Jesus'] eschatological consciousness' coming to expression in such material,[385] somewhat surprisingly given Bultmann's overall reaction to Liberal attempts to penetrate into Jesus' self-consciousness. Today, when eschatology is being reinterpreted in more social and political terms, Bultmann's description has been largely left behind. But if self-awareness can legitimately be detected behind certain assertions (and ways of acting),[386] then Bultmann's observation remains valid. We are unlikely to appreciate Jesus' kingdom teaching and his mission as a whole unless we are willing to recognize that Jesus claimed (was remembered as claiming) a distinctive, and distinctively eschatological, empowering for his mission, as evidenced particularly in his healings and exorcisms.

15.8. Teacher

In many ways this was the most obvious category for audience and onlookers to 'fit' Jesus into.[387] At the same time, it was the least overtly messianic and eschatological of the categories so far reviewed. To bring out the point we may as well follow the same procedure as before.

a. Jewish Expectation

Can we even speak of an expectation of an eschatological teacher? There certainly seems to have been an explicit expectation in these terms cherished at

385. Bultmann, *History* 126.

386. J. H. Charlesworth notes that 1QH 16(= 8).4-11 reflects the self-understanding of the Teacher of Righteousness ('The Righteous Teacher and the Historical Jesus', in W. P. Weaver and J. H. Charlesworth, *Earthing Christologies: From Jesus' Parables to Jesus the Parable* [Valley Forge: Trinity, 1995] 46-61 [here 48-50]; cf. also Wise, *First Messiah*).

387. 'The earliest sources portray Jesus as a teacher of wisdom, a sage' (Funk, *Honest* 143). On the relation between Jesus' healings and his mission Keck comments: 'he was not a healer who found he had something to say but a teacher who found it necessary to heal' (*Who Is Jesus?* 83).

Qumran — 'the interpreter of the law'[388] — perhaps stimulated by hope of a Moses-like prophet. The further fact that the founder (?) of the Qumran community was known as 'the teacher of righteousness *(morh hsdq)*'[389] is also significant. We do not know whether the name was accorded to him because he fulfilled some expectation or simply because he proved to be such an influential teacher and interpreter of Scripture. But the fact that a figure making such eschatological claims was known simply by that title is a clear indication that the title itself (teacher) was not lacking in weight in Jewish circles.[390]

Here too it is relevant to recall that Solomon was remembered as especially wise (1 Kgs. 3.12). The thought was channeled into the idea of Solomon as exorcist (§15.7a), but the alternative deduction of the son of David as a teacher of wisdom (Proverbs, Koheleth) lay close to hand.[391]

We should also note that some of the eschatological expectation seems to have envisaged an immediacy of teaching by God: 'all your sons shall be taught by the Lord' (Isa. 54.13); 'no longer shall each man teach his neighbour and each his brother, "Know the Lord", for they shall all know me, from the least to the greatest, says the Lord' (Jer. 31.34). Where God was expected to teach directly to the individual heart, there would seem to be little scope for a teacher as intermediary. Given the diversity of eschatological expectation, the point can hardly be pressed, but the evidence available hardly suggests that 'teacher' was a prime messianic or eschatological title at the time of Jesus.

b. Jesus' Reputation

All the more striking, then, is the fact that 'teacher' is the most common title used for Jesus in the Jesus tradition.[392] The parallel between Jesus and his disciples on the one hand and rabbis and their pupils on the other is deficient, but it cannot be emptied of all significance.[393] Nor should we forget that Josephus also characterized Jesus as 'a teacher of people' (*Ant.* 18.63).[394]

The most striking evidence, however, is the content of the Jesus tradition

---

388. 4Q174 (4QFlor) 1.11 (different from the 'branch of David'); CD 6.7; 7.18 (identified with the star).

389. See particularly 1QpHab 1.13; 2.2; 5.10; 7.4; 11.5; CD 1.11; 20.1, 28, 32. But there was no thought of the Torah being replaced (see, e.g., Schürer, *History* 2.535-36).

390. How these two figures were related in Qumran thought remains unclear (see Collins, *Scepter and Star* 102-104, 111-12).

391. Matt. 12.42/Luke 11.31 is relevant here.

392. Data in chapter 8 nn. 22-23 and chapter 14 n. 62 above.

393. See above, §14.3a.

394. See above, §7.1. Lucian referred to him as 'that crucified sophist' (*Peregrinus* 13).

itself. Jesus was remembered as a teacher because his teaching was so memorable, in its style as well as its content. We need only recall the teaching of Jesus reviewed above in chapters 12 and 14. In particular, we need have no hesitation in recognizing the high incidence of wisdom sayings, aphorisms, and maxims, which are such a feature of the Q material, so well exemplified in the Sermon on the Mount (Matthew 5–7).[395] And it is beyond dispute that Jesus told many parables. Indeed, although he hardly invented the parable form, it can be affirmed with full confidence that the parable was a distinctive feature of his teaching, both in the extended use he made of it and in its character as an extended metaphor.[396] So much so that a more accurate title for Jesus than 'teacher' would have been *mošel* ('parabolist'), one who characteristically spoke in parables and pithy sayings *(me̱salim)*.[397] Here, as in the case of Jesus the exorcist, the criterion of 'characteristic and relatively distinctive' (§10.2) proves its effectiveness, and there should be little doubt that we are in direct touch with the enduring impact left by Jesus.

It follows also that Jesus must have seen himself as fulfilling the role of teacher in at least some measure. He is always remembered as responding positively to the address 'Teacher'.[398] And he may have deliberately spoken of himself in such terms (Matt. 10.24-25/Luke 6.40). There is nothing controversial so far.

c. The Surprising Authority with Which Jesus Taught

This feature is picked out more explicitly in the Jesus tradition. He is remembered as one who provoked surprise and questioning at the authority with which he taught.[399] For example, Mark characteristically links Jesus' teaching with his exorcisms and mighty works: 'What is this? A new teaching with authority *(kat'*

395. D. E. Aune, 'Oral Tradition and the Aphorisms of Jesus', in Wansbrough, ed., *Jesus* 211-65, has catalogued 147 aphorisms in the Synoptic tradition plus 8 in John, 4 in *Thomas,* 8 in other Gospels (242-58). See further Ebner, *Jesus* 393-412, who contests the 'Cynic Jesus' and 'subversive wisdom' hypotheses by pointing out that Jesus did not set himself against the law (cf. §14.4 above).

396. See, e.g., Hultgren, *Parables* 5-11, and further above, §§12.6e and 13.1.

397. Gerhardsson, *Origins* 70; see also Vermes, *Religion* ch. 4. For a useful review of recent literature on the parables and an indication of outstanding issues in current parable interpretation, see C. L. Blomberg, 'The Parables of Jesus: Current Trends and Needs in Research', in B. Chilton and C. A. Evans, eds., *Studying the Historical Jesus* (Leiden: Brill, 1994) 231-54.

398. The only seeming exception is Mark 10.17-18/Luke 18.18-19; but the reaction there is to the epithet '*good* teacher'.

399. Mark 1.22/Matt. 7.28-29/Luke 4.32; Mark 1.27/Luke 4.36; Mark 11.27-33/Matt. 21.23-27/Luke 20.1-8; Matt. 8.9/Luke 7.8; see also Mark 2.10 pars.; 3.15 par.; 6.7 pars.; Luke 10.19.

exousian)! He commands even the unclean spirits and they obey him' (Mark
1.27); 'Where does he get all this? What wisdom has been given to him! Such
mighty works take place through his hands!' (6.2). The centurion at Capernaum
is recalled as likening Jesus' authority to his own: 'I too am someone under authority, having soldiers under me; and I say to one "Go", and he goes, and to another "Come", and he comes, and to my slave "Do this", and he does it' (Matt.
8.9/Luke 7.8). As a final example we should note the tradition that a high-
powered delegation[400] asked Jesus, 'By what authority do you so act? Who gave
you this authority?' (Mark 11.28 pars.). The considerations of Taylor and Pesch
in favour of the historicity of the encounter[401] have not won very much support.[402] But such an encounter would have been memorable, and it is less plausible to explain the origin of the exchange in the subsequent history of the early Jerusalem community (contrast Acts 3–5), as Bultmann suggested.[403]

In short, the motif of surprise at the authority implicitly claimed by Jesus
has undoubtedly been made much of in the telling and retelling of the Jesus tradition — understandably so. But it would be even more surprising if the motif was
not well rooted in memories of the reactions which Jesus' teaching evoked. The
character of so much of the teaching still raises eyebrows today. How much more
then! The quest for an uncontroversial Jesus whose mission created no furore
must be about the most futile of all the quests.

What was it about the authority implicit in Jesus' teaching which caused
surprise and offence? Several answers have established themselves with a fair
measure of consensus and can be rehearsed quite briefly.

(1) He lacked formal training. He came from a very modest background;
his level of literacy may not have been very high (§9.9b). The only teacher he
was known to have associated with was John the Baptist, who evidently also
lacked formal training.

(2) His teaching did not appeal to past tradition or earlier authorities. Such
appeal certainly became the standard form for subsequent rabbinic teaching, but

---

400. This is the only occasion in which 'chief priests and elders' are recalled as engaging Jesus in dialogue.

401. Taylor, *Mark* 468-69; Pesch, *Markusevangelium* 2.212; see also Dunn, *Jesus and
the Spirit* 77; Fitzmyer, *Luke* 2.1272-74; Davies and Allison, *Matthew* 3.157-58.

402. Funk, *Five Gospels* 100; Lüdemann, *Jesus* 80.

403. *History,* 19-20. The Jesus Seminar voted strongly against the historical value of the
episode, because Jesus' words 'did not take the form of a parable or an aphorism, which means
that it is difficult to imagine how they could have been transmitted during the oral period, except as part of this story' (*Five Gospels* 100); this concept of oral tradition suffers from acute
anorexia. Dodd notes that the implication of Jesus' reply 'is that there is a kind of authority
which is self-authenticating; either you recognize it or you don't, and if you don't there is nothing more to be said' (*Founder* 148).

already in the Jesus tradition we find reference to 'the tradition of the elders'.[404] And the implication of Jesus' debates with other teachers regarding various matters of halakhah is that present conduct was based on the developing halakhah being passed down. Jesus is recalled as resisting that trend in one degree or other.[405]

(3) The main thrust of Jesus' teaching was not directed to the exposition of Torah. As already noted, claims that he set himself against the Torah are seriously overstated; on the contrary, we can certainly say that his teaching was thoroughly rooted in Scripture.[406] At the same time, however, the main category in his teaching (the kingdom of God) and the principal mode of his teaching (parables) were more innovative than traditional in character.

(4) Two features of Jesus' teaching style have attracted considerable attention. First, his use of 'Amen' to introduce a particular utterance. The term is familiar in both Hebrew and Aramaic ('amen) as marking a strong solemn affirmation of what has been said, most typically in a formal liturgical context.[407] The Jesus tradition gives clear testimony that Jesus used the term consistently in his own teaching.[408] And that he did so in a quite distinctive way. For whereas in regular usage 'Amen' affirmed or endorsed the words of someone else, in the Jesus tradition the term is used without exception to introduce and endorse Jesus' *own* words.[409] This quite unique use can hardly be attributed to the early Christians; their own use of 'Amen' was in accord with the traditional pattern.[410] Of course, we can hardly exclude the likelihood that in performing the tradition the tradents/teachers extended the motif within the tradition. But neither can it be seriously doubted that the usage began with Jesus and was a distinctive feature of his own teaching style. Why else

404. Mark 7.5, 8-9, 13/Matt. 15.2-3, 6.

405. See above, particularly §14.4.

406. See the conclusion to §14.4 above.

407. Num. 5.22; Deut. 27.15-26; 1 Kgs. 1.36; 1 Chron. 16.36; Neh. 5.13; 8.6; Pss. 41.13; 72.19; 89.52; 106.48; Jer. 11.5; 28.6; in Isa. 65.16 Yahweh is twice described as 'the God of truth (*ᵉlohe-'amen)'*. In the DSS the formula is usually the double 'Amen, Amen' (1QS 1.20; 2.10, 18; 4Q286 fragment 5 line 8; fragment 7 4.1, 5, 10; 4Q287 fragment 1 line 4; fragment 4 line 3; fragment 5 line 11; 4Q289 fragment 2 line 4; 4Q504 fragment 4 line 15; fragment 17 2.5; fragment 3 2.3; frags. 1-2 1.7; 7[recto].2, 9; 4Q507 fragment 3 line 2; 4Q511 fragments 63-64 4.3).

408. See below, n. 418. Parentheses in the list there indicate where the Synoptic parallel lacks 'Amen'. The list shows that the formula ('Amen, I say to you') was favoured by Matthew, but not by Luke; if Matthew extended the motif, equally Luke may have reduced it.

409. Jeremias, *Prayers* 112-15: 'It has been pointed out almost *ad nauseam* [referring to Dalman, *et al.*] that a new use of the word *amen* emerged in the four gospels *which is without analogy in the whole of Jewish literature and in the rest of the New Testament*' (112). See also Fitzmyer, *Luke* 536-37; Keck, *Who Is Jesus?* 101-102.

410. Of some thirty other examples in the NT, 1 Cor. 14.16 is the most interesting; otherwise it is characteristically attached to the end of a doxology.

would it have been retained throughout the Jesus tradition, and in transliterated form?[411] That must be one of the most secure conclusions capable of being derived from a serious engagement with the tradition history of Jesus' teaching. And an obvious corollary lies close to hand: Jesus used this formula to call attention to what he was about to say and to give it added weight.[412]

(5) The second striking feature of Jesus' teaching style is the 'I say to you *(legō hymin/soi)*' formula. This was a feature which attracted Käsemann, and in effect he launched the new quest on it. But he focused too narrowly on the adversative form — 'but I say to you *(egō de legō)*' — and on its use in the antitheses of Matthew's Sermon on the Mount. He saw there an authority claim which rivalled that of Moses and even set Jesus over Moses.[413] That was unfortunate, since it put the motif in service to the older Jesus versus the law debate and laid too much weight on the antitheses of Matt. 5.21-48. We have already noted that that line of argument has been pushed too far (§14.4), and the strong likelihood that the repetition of the motif is the work of the teacher (Matthew?) who laid out the antitheses of the Sermon (§14.4f). And the absence of *egō* in most cases[414] rather blunts the description of the feature as 'the emphatic *egō*'.[415] However, the motif itself is too firmly rooted within the Jesus tradition to be dismissed entirely, both in affirmative[416] and adversative[417] form (between which there is often not much difference).

411. Note that Luke uses the alternative forms: 'Of a truth *(ep' alētheias)* I say to you' (Luke 4.25; parallel to *amēn legō hymin* in 4.24); 'Truly *(alēthōs)* I say to you' (9.27/[Mark 9.1]; 12.44/[Matt. 24.47]; 21.3/[Mark 12.43]). Since it is unlikely that Luke knew or translated Aramaic himself, the distinctive Lukan formulation must mean that his (oral) source had been put into Greek by someone who knew that the *'amen* came from the verb *'aman* ('confirm, support'; niphal 5: 'reliable, faithful'; hiphil 2: 'trust, believe', BDB) and who therefore translated rather than transliterated the *'amen*.

412. See also Theissen and Merz, *Historical Jesus* 523-24.

413. Käsemann: 'the words *egō de legō* embody a claim to an authority which rivals and challenges that of Moses' ('Problem' 37). Similarly Jeremias: 'the one who utters the *egō de legō hymin* in the antitheses not only claims to be the legitimate interpreter of the Torah . . . but also has the unparalleled and revolutionary boldness to set himself up in opposition to the Torah' (*Proclamation* 253).

414. *Egō* appears in the formula only in the antitheses (Matt. 5.22, 28, 32, 34, 39, 44); the only well attested exception is Luke 16.9 (cf. Mark 11.33/Matt. 21.27).

415. Jeremias, *Proclamation* 250; 'the remarkable accumulation of the emphatic *egō* in his sayings' (251)!

416. Mark 2.11/Luke 5.24; Mark 11.24; Matt. 6.25/Luke 12.22; Matt. 11.9/Luke 7.26; Matt. 23.39/Luke 13.35; Matt. 5.20; 12.31; 16.18; 18.10; 19.24; 21.43; Luke 7.9, 28, 47; 10.12, 24; 11.8, 9, 51; 12.5, 51, 59; 13.24; 14.24; 15.7, 10; 16.9; 17.34; 18.8, 14; 19.26, 40; 22.16, 34, 37 (the overlap with Lukan items in n. 418 indicates how frequently Luke, or his tradition, omitted 'Amen').

417. Mark 9.13/Matt. 17.12; Mark 13.37; Matt. 5.44/Luke 6.27; Matt. 6.29/Luke

More striking still, in the light of the previous observation (4), is the regular appearance of the form, 'Amen, I say to you',[418] elaborated in the Johannine tradition to the double, 'Amen, amen, I say to you'.[419] Here again the corollary lies close to hand: Jesus was remembered as regularly speaking with an assertion of personal authority, not appealing to another authority but giving his own view on some point in a tone of confidence as to the importance of what he was saying.[420]

(6) This last observation can be extended a little further. For other features of Jesus' teaching already noted seem to indicate that he placed a tremendous weight of significance on his teaching and expected his disciples to do so too. I think here particularly of the high priority he expected his followers to give to his call to discipleship[421] and the implication of the (more contested) tradition that response to his words could make the decisive difference between success and disaster, between favourable and unfavourable judgment.[422] Whatever we make of particular instances of this emphasis in the Jesus tradition, the motif resonates too closely with what we have noted above for it to be wholly dismissed.

d. Something Greater Than a Teacher?

Perhaps we need to take one step still further. At first sight, there is nothing distinctively eschatological resonating in Jesus' claim to a direct and immediate authority, that is, from God. But consider the following strands already drawn out a little way: (1) Presumably the implicit claim of direct authority is

---

12.27; Matt. 5.22, 28, 32, 34, 39; 8.11; 11.22, 24; 12.6, 36; 19.9; 26.29, 64; Luke 12.4, 8; 13.3, 5.

418. Mark 3.28/(Matt. 12.31); Mark 8.12; Mark 9.1/Matt. 16.28/Luke 9.27; Mark 9.41/Matt. 10.42; Mark 10.15/Matt. 18.3/Luke 18.17; Mark 10.29/Matt. 19.28/Luke 18.29; Mark 11.23; Mark 12.43/Luke 21.3; Mark 13.30/Matt. 24.34/Luke 21.32; Mark 14.9/Matt. 26.13; Mark 14.18/Matt. 26.21; Mark 14.25/(Matt. 26.29); Mark 14.30/Matt. 26.34/(Luke 22.34); Matt. 5.26/(Luke 12.59); Matt. 8.10/(Luke 7.9); Matt. 11.11/(Luke 7.28); Matt. 13.17/(Luke 10.24); Matt. 23.36/(Luke 11.51); Matt. 24.47/Luke 12.44; Matt. 5.18; 6.2, 5, 16; 10.15, 23; 17.20; 18.13, 18, 19; 19.23; 21.21, 31; 24.2; 25.12, 40, 45; Luke 4.24, 25; 12.37; 23.43. Parentheses signify an 'I say to you form' without 'Amen'.

419. John 1.51; 3.3, 5, 11; 5.19, 24, 25; 6.26, 32, 47, 53; 8.34, 51, 58; 10.1, 7; 12.24; 13.16, 20, 21, 38; 14.12; 16.20, 23; 21.18.

420. I echo here H. K. McArthur, *Understanding the Sermon on the Mount* (London: Epworth, 1961) 56.

421. Mark 3.31-35 pars.; Matt. 10.37/Luke 14.26; see above, §14.7.

422. Matt. 7.24-27/Luke 6.47-49; Matt. 10.32-33/Luke 12.8-9; see further above, §12.4e-f.

of a piece with Jesus' proclamation of God's rule. He spoke with the authority of one who proclaimed its imminence and whose mission already enacted God's reign in the present. (2) We should also recall Dodd's observation that the 'I say to you' seems to transcend the typically prophetic 'Thus says the Lord', just as, possibly, the 'I came' transcends the prophetic 'I was sent'.[423] The 'Amen, I say to you' points in the same direction.[424] (3) The same inference may be drawn from the fact that Jesus' exorcistic practice seems to have embodied a similar claim to an immediacy of authority: 'I command', rather than, 'I adjure you by . . .'.[425] (4) We also noted the possibility which the tradition enshrines that Jesus made explicit claim to be the *šaliaḥ* of God, God's eschatological emissary and representative.[426] (5) Is there a similar implication that Jesus saw himself as the emissary of divine Wisdom[427] — that is, not just as teacher of wisdom, but as the eschatological spokesman for Wisdom, acting in God's stead?[428]

It may be that such a line of exposition pushes the data too hard. As with the accounts of the transfiguration and the 'nature miracles', the voices of post-Easter reflection may well have begun to drown out the pre-Easter reminiscences

423. See above, §15.6d. Davies argues that when Jesus spoke possessed by the Spirit of God it was his alternate persona that spoke (as in demon possession) explaining who it was — the spirit/Son of God — and deduces from this that some of the 'Johannine style' sayings attributed to Jesus can therefore be regarded as 'historically authentic' (*Jesus the Healer* ch. 11).

424. Cf. Jeremias: 'Here is a consciousness of rank which lays claim to divine authority' (*Prayers* 115); the '*egō* is associated with *amēn* and thus claims to speak with divine authority'; 'the emphatic *egō* indicates that the person who uses it is God's representative' (*Proclamation* 253-54). 'Here speaks a prophet — indeed perhaps more than a prophet!' (Theissen and Merz, *Historical Jesus* 524).

425. See above, §15.7g-h.

426. Mark 9.37/Luke 9.48; Matt. 10.40; Luke 10.16 (see above, §15.6c); Witherington, *Christology* 142-43.

427. Luke 7.35/(Matt. 11.19): Jesus and John as children of Wisdom (Matthew's 'deeds' is probably redactional, to form an inclusio with 11.2); Matt. 11.25-27/Luke 10.21-22: a uniqueness of knowledge and authority (see below §16.2c[1]); Luke 11.49-51/(Matt. 23.34-36): Jesus as one of those sent by Wisdom? In each case, Matthew has developed the motif to identify Jesus with divine Wisdom (see my *Christology* 197-204), but that step does not seem to have been yet taken in the q/Q form of the tradition (*pace* Witherington, *Christology* 49-53, who jumps too quickly to the possibility that Jesus saw himself as divine Wisdom incarnate; similarly *Jesus the Sage: The Pilgrimage of Wisdom* [Minneapolis: Augsburg Fortress, 1994] 201-208). See further J. Schlosser, 'Q et la christologie implicite', in Lindemann, ed., *Sayings Source Q* 289-316. See also Schüssler Fiorenza, *In Memory of Her* 132-35; also *Jesus: Miriam's Child, Sophia's Prophet* (New York: Continuum, 1995) 141-43.

428. See further Hengel, 'Jesus as Messianic Teacher' 75-87, noting *inter alia,* the close tie-in between Wisdom and Spirit — the gift of supernatural wisdom and prophetic inspiration are interchangeable (93-104).

and voice of Jesus himself at precisely the points being explored here.[429] Nevertheless, as we move on to the remaining categories which Jesus rather than others may have used in speaking of his mission, we are left with two powerful impressions. One is that Jesus' mission seems to have broken through all the most obvious categories by which his mission could be evaluated; he evidently did not fit with any degree of comfort into any of the pigeon-holes by which observers might have wished to label him. The other is the tantalising possibility that Jesus deliberately claimed a degree of distinctiveness for his mission, for all its thoroughly Jewish character, which left both hearers and disciples struggling for words to express the significance of what they were seeing and hearing — and remembering.

But if we want to follow up the possibility of probing into Jesus' own self-understanding, there is more directly relevant data to examine.

---

429. Even so, Sanders does not hesitate to affirm that 'Jesus claimed to be spokesman for God' (*Jesus* 271, 281); 'He regarded himself as having full authority to speak and act on behalf of God'; 'not only spokesman for, but viceroy of, God' (*Historical Figure* 238, 242, 248). I. H. Marshall, *The Origins of New Testament Christology* (Leicester: IVP, 1976) pushed the point still harder (45-51).

How Did Jesus See His Own Role?

We have already begun to explore this question in asking how Jesus is remembered as responding to the categories his contemporaries would most likely have fitted him into; the division between chapters 15 and 16 is as much a matter of convenience as of substance. Two further categories are suggested by the Jesus tradition itself, son of God and son of man, and these will be the principal focus of this chapter. But it also makes sense to begin by drawing together the threads of chapter 15 insofar as they provide an answer to the question posed in chapter 16.

In all this it remains important to bear in mind my primary focus on the *impact* made by Jesus. But in this case it is necessary to hazard the next step, the difficult task of attempting to trace out, by reference to the 'shape' of the impact made by Jesus, the 'shape' of what made that impact (§15.1) — that is, what Jesus may have said or indicated about his own perception regarding his own role which has resulted in such features of the Jesus tradition.

16.1. Eschatological Agent

It is probably necessary to describe what we can discern of Jesus' own assessment of his role in some such vague terms ('eschatological agent'), because none of the categories just reviewed seems to have been entirely acceptable to him. To recap briefly and baldly.

Royal Messiah/Son of David (§§15.2-4) was a category full of eschatological significance. But was it a significance Jesus could embrace for his own mission? Evidently not. The tradition indicates that, as a role-description, it was more trouble than it was worth, liable to cause more misunderstanding than to bring clarification. As a messianic title it could not be ignored: it was too fundamental to Jewish hope and expectation. But as a role-description it pointed in the

705

wrong direction. No wonder, then, that when the first Christians used it of Jesus, as use it they must, they did so by transforming its current significance completely. But for Jesus himself, the pre–Good Friday Jesus, the title was evidently more of a hindrance than a help.

Priestly Messiah (§15.5) was a title or role which was never thought to be appropriate by anyone involved in or spectator of Jesus' mission, Jesus included.

The other three categories, *prophet, healer,* and *teacher* (§§15.6-8), were more acceptable, because even when eschatological in character, the roles they described were not so clearly or fully defined. They could be acknowledged by Jesus, then, without causing his mission to be misunderstood. They provided some description and illuminated important aspects of his work, but otherwise, the implication is clear, their function was subsidiary to his main kingdom objectives. And no single one of them provided a complete or sufficient description of his mission.[1]

At the same time, the bound-togetherness of Jesus and his proclamation of God's kingship, the fact that the kingdom was present precisely in and through Jesus' mission, a fact so clearly attested in the memory of his teaching, bespeaks an eschatological significance for Jesus of which, however self-deprecating, he can hardly have been unaware.[2] In the Jesus tradition bearing on each of the three roles just mentioned, we found what we might call 'the eschatological plus' or 'the eschatological extra'. It was not simply as prophet that Jesus seems to have seen himself, but as the eschatological prophet who had been given the role indicated in Isa. 61.1-3. It was not simply as a healer or exorcist that he acted, but with a still perceptible sense of a plenitude of eschatological power evidenced in both his exorcisms and his healings. His disciples recalled an exclusiveness in his claim to eschatological anointing by the Spirit of God, which, in his own words, marked him off from other exorcists and healers and from the prophets who preceded him, including even his own mentor, the Baptist. So too, he taught, but evidently did not see himself simply as a teacher. More than that, he is remembered as claiming an immediacy of apprehension of God's will, and by his very words and manner of teaching he is remembered as claiming an authority for his teaching which outstripped that of the most obvious contemporary parallels.

Elsewhere in the world of his time there were, of course, examples of individuals who in ecstasy spoke in the person of the god who was thought to possess them. There were kings who claimed to be epiphanies of deity. But there was

---

1. The same applies to the term 'charismatic' as description of Jesus (Vermes, *Jesus* ch. 3 [79]; Dunn, *Jesus* ch. 4; Borg, *Jesus: A New Vision* ch. 3; Theissen and Merz, *Historical Jesus* ch. 8) — appropriate, but insufficient.

2. Merklein, *Jesu Botschaft* 149-52.

nothing quite like this son of an artisan, from the most modest of backgrounds, who in sober and wholly rational speech claimed to speak for God as his representative at the end of the present age, nothing quite like the unpretentious arrogance of his regular introductory formula, 'Amen, I say to you'.

How far the logic of this line of exposition can be pushed is not at all clear. The Jesus tradition strongly suggests that at the very least Jesus claimed for his mission an extraordinary significance, of eschatological fulfilment in the present and of final import for his hearers. At the very least we overhear in the words of the remembered Jesus a claim for the divine significance of his mission, as the (not just an) eschatological emissary of God. How much more can be said is much less clear. In particular, how much the claim for the significance of his *mission* was also a claim for the significance of *himself* remains an open question. Can we draw a neat line between a mission which somehow embodied the kingdom and Jesus himself as the embodiment of that mission?[3] The very fact that the Jesus tradition itself poses the issue (the issue of implied christology), and not just in its later embellishments, is a factor not to be ignored or underestimated.

The problem can be posed thus. Since Jesus seems to have broken through all the available categories to the extent that he did, it becomes almost impossible to find suitable terms to describe his role or define his significance.[4] If the available word-pictures and metaphors proved inadequate, what to do? In such a case an obvious answer is to coin a new word-picture or metaphor or to take a different one and fill it with new meaning. Did Jesus follow the same line of reasoning?

A final caution before we proceed. In all this I have spoken as though Jesus had a clear idea of what his role was or should be. But that is an assumption which cannot and should not be taken as given. Apart from anything else, I have already concluded that Jesus' own conception of the kingdom of God, the principal element in his preaching, was far from clear (§12.6). Why should it be any different with the still less tangible topic of Jesus' self-assertion or self-evaluation? We cannot even be sure that Jesus asked a question like 'Who am I?' let alone that he thought it important to articulate some particular answer. So in

---

3. Stuhlmacher presses the case: 'Jesus' person, his conduct, and his word, are to be understood as embodiment of God *(Verleiblichung Gottes)*. Jesus was not only an eschatological prophet sent by God, but he has borne witness to God's rule as the parable of God in person (E. Jüngel and E. Schweizer)' *(Biblische Theologie* 1.74, 110). Cf. McKnight's heading: 'The Kingdom Operative Only through Jesus' *(New Vision* 89).

4. Cf. M. de Jonge, *Jesus, The Servant-Messiah* (New Haven: Yale University, 1991) 66-67, 80, who appositely cites Eduard Schweizer's description of Jesus as 'the man who fits no formula' ('der Mann, der alle Schemen sprengt'), citing E. Schweizer, *Jesus* (London: SCM, 1971) 21-22. 'What must not be overlooked is the likelihood that Jesus himself is responsible for the scholars' failure to classify him precisely' (Keck, *Who Is Jesus?* 52).

what follows we must be even more cautious lest the echoes we hear from the elements of the Jesus tradition now to be examined are audible only as the reverberations from the echo-chamber of subsequent Christian faith.

16.2. God's Son

The caution just voiced is of particular relevance on this subject. For in Christian tradition, Jesus is no less than 'the Son of God, begotten from the Father, only begotten, that is, from the substance of the Father . . . begotten not made . . .'.[5] It was by thus affirming and defining his divine sonship ('begotten') that Christ's deity and status in relation to God the Father were clarified and catholic orthodoxy distanced itself from the lesser christologies of Gnostic and Arian.[6] With the Council of Nicaea, in other words, 'Son of God' became the key title for Christ.[7] For Christianity thereafter, 'the Son of God' had only one referent — Jesus Christ.

But the Nicene Creed represents the crystallization of a process stretching over nearly three centuries. Our concern here is with the *beginning* of that process. Already within the NT itself we see that process under way, with the sonship of Jesus to God as Father becoming more prominent. Whereas in Mark and Q Jesus speaks of God as Father only three or four times, in Matthew we find more than thirty such references, and in the Fourth Gospel about one hundred instances.[8] Evidently, then, there was a growing tendency to introduce such references into the Jesus tradition, thus indicating that the concept of Jesus as God's Son was already becoming more important in the first century. Why so, and when did the process begin?

As with so much of christology, the decisive stimulus is frequently traced to the resurrection. Indeed, a neat line of development can readily be drawn, tracing the origin of Jesus' divine sonship, the moment of his begetting, steadily further back in time: from resurrection (Acts 13.33; Heb. 5.5), to baptism/Jordan (Mark 1.11 pars.), to conception/birth (Matt. 1.20/Luke 1.35), to pre-existence (John 1.14, 18).[9] That looks to be more analytically pleasing than natural. But it certainly poses the issue as to whether there is anything in the pre-Easter Jesus

5. The creed of Nicea (AD 325), following J. N. D. Kelly, *Early Christian Creeds* (London: Longmans, [2]1960) 215-16.

6. See further Kelly, *Early Christian Creeds* 231-42.

7. In what follows I will be drawing on my *Jesus and the Spirit* ch. 2, and *Christology* ch. 2. At this point note the exchange with Maurice Wiles in the Foreword to the second edition of the latter (xxviii-xxxi).

8. Jeremias, *Prayers* 29-30; details above, chapter 14 n. 35.

9. As I suggested in *Christology* 61.

tradition which might have given foothold or stimulus to what certainly appears to be a substantial development of one form or another.

Here as before it is wise to set the context in which any such language used of or by Jesus would have been heard.

a. The First-Century 'Context of Meaning'

It is important to grasp at once that, in contrast to later Christian usage, 'son of God' was not such an exclusive title or distinctive designation in the thinking of the time. The usage has been reviewed frequently in the last three decades of the twentieth century so that no more than a brief summary is necessary here.[10]

Within the wider circles of Hellenistic culture 'son of God' was used of legendary heroes like Dionysus and Heracles, of oriental, especially Egyptian, rulers, and of famous philosophers like Pythagoras and Plato; in Stoic philosophy Zeus was popularly thought of as the father of all men.[11] Within Jewish tradition the term had been used collectively for Israel[12] or in the plural for angels/the heavenly council[13] or the king.[14] The Qumran scrolls have made clear that the expected royal Messiah was also thought of as God's son.[15] Equally interest-

10. E.g. P. W. von Martitz, G. Fohrer, E. Schweizer, and E. Lohse, *huios, TDNT* 8.335-62; Vermes, *Jesus the Jew* 194-200; M. Hengel, *The Son of God: The Origin of Christology and the History of Jewish-Hellenistic Religion* (London: SCM, 1976) 21-56; J. Fossum, 'Son of God', *ABD* 6.128-33. Fuller detail also in my *Christology* 14-16.

11. Details in von Martitz, *TDNT* 8.336-40; Hengel, *Son of God* 24; Fossum, *ABD* 6.132-33.

12. Exod. 4.22; Jer. 31.9, 20; Hos. 11.1; see also, e.g., Deut. 14.1; 32.6, 18; Isa. 43.6; Jer. 3.4, 19; Hos. 1.10; Wis. 9.7; 18.13; *Jub.* 1.24-25; *Pss. Sol.* 17.27.

13. Gen. 6.2, 4; Deut. 32.8; Job 1.6-12; 2.1-6; 38.7; Pss. 29.1; 89.6; Dan. 3.25; cf. *1 En.* 13.8; 106.5.

14. 2 Sam. 7.14; 1 Chron. 17.13; 22.10; Pss. 2.7; 89.26-27. See further Fohrer, *TDNT* 8.347-53; Fossum, *ABD* 6.128-29.

15. 1QSa (1Q28b) 2.11-12 ('when [God] begets the Messiah'); 4Q174 (4QFlor) 1.10-12 (2 Sam. 7.12-14 refers to 'the "branch of David" who will arise with the Interpreter of the law'). C. A. Evans, 'A Note on the "First-Born Son" of 4Q369', *DSD* 2 (1995) 185-201, thinks the 'first-born son' of 4Q369 1 2.6 is a Davidic and messianic figure. On 4Q246 ('He will be called son of God, and they will call him son of the Most High') see the discussion in Collins, *Scepter and Star* 154-64; J. D. G. Dunn, '"Son of God" as "Son of Man" in the Dead Sea Scrolls? A Response to John Collins on 4Q246', in S. E. Porter and C. A. Evans, eds., *The Scrolls and the Scriptures: Qumran Fifty Years After* (Sheffield: Sheffield Academic, 1997) 198-210 (with further bibliography). See also *1 En.* 105.2; *4 Ezra* 7.28-29; 13.32, 37, 52; 14.9. The Qumran evidence should have killed stone dead the old view that 'son of God' was not a messianic title in Second Temple Judaism (e.g., W. Bousset, *Kyrios Christos* [1913; ET Nashville: Abingdon, 1970] 93; Kümmel, *Promise* 83); even so Fuller was only willing to conclude

ing is the fact that particularly within the Wisdom literature the righteous thought of themselves as 'sons of God'[16] and prayed to God as 'Father'.[17] And Vermes has drawn special attention to the two 'charismatic rabbis', Honi the circle-drawer (first century BCE), who according to tradition prayed to God 'like a son of the house' (*m. Ta'an.* 3.8),[18] and Hanina ben Dosa, from the generation following Jesus, who was addressed by a heavenly voice as 'my son'.[19] Also relevant is the Semitic idiom whereby the family or hereditary relationship of son to father ('son of') is extended to denote a variety of relations, including professional groups[20] or those who share particular characteristics.[21]

It is possible, then, that 'son of God' provided another category into which Jesus might have been fitted. This would have been seen as an appropriate corollary to any identification of Jesus as royal Messiah, son of David. We have al-

---

that 'son of God was just coming into use as a Messianic title in pre-Christian Judaism' (*Foundations* 32); and Sanders can find no evidence outside the Christian movement for the combination of 'Messiah' and 'Son of God' (*Jesus* 298).

16. Wis. 2.13, 16, 18; 5.5; Sir. 4.10; 51.10; a recurrent feature in Jewish thought is that God's discipline is like that of a father disciplining his son (Deut. 8.5; 2 Sam. 7.14; Prov. 3.11-12; Wis. 11.10; *Pss. Sol.* 13.9; 18.4; Heb. 12.5-6). See further Charlesworth, *Jesus* 149-52.

17. Wis. 14.3 (*pater*); Sir. 23.1, 4 (*pater*); 51.10; *3 Macc.* 6.3, 8 (*pater*); 4Q372 fragment 1 line 16 (*'abi*); 4Q460 frag. 5 1.5 (*'abi*).

18. Witherington draws attention to S. Safrai, 'The Teaching of the Pietists in Mishnaic Literature', *JJS* 16 (1965) 15-33), who shows that the phrase 'refers to a royal slave, the term "house born" or "son of a house" referring to a domestic slave' (*Christology* 183).

19. *b. Ta'an.* 24b; *Ber.* 17b; *Hul.* 86a. See further Vermes, *Jesus the Jew* 206-207; Flusser, *Jesus* 113-18; Fossum, *ABD* 6.130-31.

20. The documentation in the following notes is drawn from H. Haag, *'ben' TDOT* 2.149-53, 160-61 (here 152): 'son of perfumer' = perfumer (Neh. 3.8), 'sons of singers' = singers (Neh. 12.28), 'sons of Korah' (superscription to Pss. 42.1; 44.1; 46.1; 47.1; 49.1; 84.1; 87.1; 88.1), 'sons of Asaph (2 Chron. 35.15), priests = 'sons of priests' (Ezra 2.61; 10.18; Neh. 12.35; 1 Chron. 9.30), 'sons of Aaron' (Lev. 1.5, 11; 2.2-3, 10; 13.2; 21.1; Num. 10.8; 2 Chron. 35.14), 'sons of Levi' (Deut. 21.5; Ezra 8.15), 'sons of Zadok' (Ezek. 40.46; 44.15; 48.11; 1QS 5.2; 9.14; 1QSa [1Q28a] 1.24; 2.3; 1QSb [1Q28b] 3.22), prophets = 'sons of the prophets' (1 Kgs. 20.35; 2 Kgs. 2.3, 5, 7, 15; 4.1, 38; 5.22; 6.1; 9.1; singular Amos 7.14), a wise man = 'son of wise men' (Isa. 19.11); see also BDB, *'ben'* 7a.

21. The valiant = 'sons of strength' (Deut. 3.18; Judg. 18.2; 21.10; 1 Sam. 14.52; 18.17; 2 Sam. 2.7; 1 Kgs. 1.52; 2 Kgs. 2.16; 2 Chron. 17.7), 'sons of daintiness' (Mic. 1.16), 'sons of pride' (Job 28.8; 41.26[34]), 'sons of rebellion' (Num. 17.25[10]), 'sons of Belial' (Deut. 13.14[13]; Judg. 19.22; 1 Sam. 2.12; 10.27; 25.17; 1 Kgs. 21.10, 13; 2 Chron. 13.7), etc. (Haag 153, 161; BDB, *'ben'* 8); 'sons of light' (1QS 1.9; 2.16; 3.13, 24-25; 1QM 1.1, 3, 9, 11, 13; etc.), 'sons of the covenant' (1QM 17.8; 4Q501 line 2; 4Q503 fragments 7-9 line 3), 'sons of justice' (1QS 3.20, 22; 4Q503 fragments 48-50 line 8). Similarly in the NT, e.g., 'sons of the kingdom' (Matt. 8.12; 13.38), 'sons of light' (Luke 16.8; John 12.36; 1 Thess. 5.5), 'son of peace' (Luke 10.6), 'sons of the bridal chamber' (Mark 2.19 pars.), 'sons of this age' (Luke 16.8; 20.34), 'sons of the evil one' (Matt. 13.38); see further F. Hahn, *'huios'*, *EDNT* 3.383.

ready noted that such an eschatological reading of 2 Sam. 7.12-14 provides a plausible rationale for the High Priest's question in Mark 14.61.[22] Alternatively, had Jesus been linked to the Wisdom tradition of the suffering righteous, the term might equally have been regarded as appropriate. A point of some significance, however, is that in the Wisdom tradition the term seems to have been more self-chosen by the righteous, expressive of his or her own confidence in God, than a description applied by others. Is this a pointer towards what we might expect?

The common denominator in all these cases is that 'son of God' denoted someone specially related to or favoured by God. With the king, the status was more formal; he represented God to his people. But in its broader reference the phrase seems to have denoted someone who was intimate with God, who closely reflected God's character, who fully did God's will. The theological logic is clear from Sir. 4.10 and Matt. 5.45/Luke 6.35:[23] to be compassionate to the orphan and widow is to be like a son of God; to act with uncalculating generosity and love even to the enemy is to model oneself on God, is to be(come) a son of God. Is this the context of meaning which would have informed any initial usage of the phrase in reference to Jesus? If so, we should simply note that initially to call Jesus God's son was a far cry from the subsequent Christian usage — Christ as the 'only-begotten'. It is true that in the earliest post-Easter phase, Christians were thought to share in Christ's sonship.[24] But even then, the divine sonship of Jesus was seen to be quite distinct and unique, with Christian sonship dependent on and derivative from Christ's. So the question still remains when this sense of Jesus' sonship as something quite distinctive first emerged and whether it has pre-Easter roots.

As usual we must look to the Jesus tradition for any answers that might be forthcoming. And as with 'Messiah', the task is difficult, since the term is not bandied about (like 'teacher') or repeatedly evoked (like 'prophet'). But one feature of the tradition has captivated questers and provided amazingly positive results.

b. Jesus' *Abba* Prayer

The Jesus tradition is quite clear that Jesus addressed God as 'Father' in his prayers. Jeremias pointed out that all five strata of the Gospel material are unanimous on the point.[25] But the case hangs primarily on two instances — Matt. 11.25-26/Luke 10.21 and Mark 14.36 pars.

22. See above, §15.3a.

23. Sir. 4.10: 'Be a father to orphans, and be like a husband to their mother; you will then be like a son of the Most High, and he will love you more than does your mother'; Matt. 5.45/Luke 6.35 has already been cited in §14.5b.

24. Rom. 8.14-17, 29; Gal. 4.6-7.

25. Mark 14.36/Matt. 26.39/Luke 22.42; Matt. 11.25-26/Luke 10.21; Matt. 26.42; Luke 23.34, 46; John 11.41; 12.27-28; 17.1, 5, 11, 21, 24-25 (Jeremias, *Proclamation* 62).

Matt. 11.25-26	Luke 10.21
25 At that time Jesus said, 'I thank you, Father, Lord of heaven and earth, because you have hidden these things from the wise and the intelligent and have revealed them to infants; 26 yes, Father, for such was your gracious will'.	21 At that same hour Jesus rejoiced in the Holy Spirit and said, 'I thank you, Father, Lord of heaven and earth, because you have hidden these things from the wise and the intelligent and have revealed them to infants; yes, Father, for such was your gracious will'.

If we confine comment for the moment to the first half of the saying (the prayer proper),[26] even here opinion is greatly divided.[27] Nevertheless, it is clear that the Q tradition retains a vivid memory of Jesus praying to God as Father. The prayer itself is thoroughly Jewish and was probably first uttered in Aramaic.[28] The note of exultation at revelation received is consistent with the strong sense of eschatological hope realized which is so deeply rooted in the Jesus tradition.[29] As also the delight at the privilege granted to those usually regarded as incapable or ineligible to receive such insight and favour.[30] The thought of God giving wisdom and insight to infants and of the wise lacking discernment is also a familiar motif in Jewish wisdom and apocalyptic writing,[31] which may well suggest what prompted this particular formulation.[32] But why should such an exultation be attributed to Jesus in the early communities? If it was taken to refer to Jesus himself, who would have called him *nēpios* ('infant')? If it was exultation in their own sense of having been granted revelation, there is no reason why it should have been formulated as a prayer of Jesus (contrast 1 Cor. 1.18–2.13). And if the newly minted prayer needed to be qualified by adding Matt. 11.27/Luke 10.22, why retain the former — unless it was part of the tradition from the first?[33] In contrast, it is entirely likely that such an exultation, uttered with disciples gath-

26. On Matt. 11.27/Luke 10.22 see below §16.2c(1).

27. Davies and Allison note that the majority of scholars pronounce in favour of authenticity (*Matthew* 2.278). But the Jesus Seminar voted against it (Funk, *Five Gospels* 182), and Lüdemann judges it inauthentic, 'as the "Risen One" is speaking' (*Jesus* 331).

28. Davies and Allison, *Matthew* 2.273-78.

29. See above, §12.5. In biblical usage, *exomologeō* in the sense 'confess, profess' gives rise to the further meaning 'praise', as often in the LXX (BDAG, *exomologeō* 4; O. Hofius, *exomologeō*, *EDNT* 2.8-9). Not dissimilar are the eschatological exultations characteristic of 1QH 10[2].20, 31; 11[3].19, 37; 12[4].5; 13[5].5, 20; 15[7].6, 26, 34; 16[8].4; 19[11].3, 15.

30. See above, §§13.4-5.

31. Pss. 19.7; 119.130; Dan. 1.17 (youths); Wis. 10.21; Sir. 3.19 (v.l.). Funk refers to Ps. 8.2 ('out of the mouths of babes and infants') (*Five Gospels* 182), which Matthew inserts into the cleansing of the Temple pericope (Matt. 21.16); and Davies and Allison refer particularly to Isa. 29.14, which Paul takes up in 1 Cor. 1.19 (*Matthew* 2.275-77).

32. The Qumran Teacher likewise rejoices that he has been 'prudence to the simple' (*petayyim* = *nēpioi*) (1QH 10[2].9).

33. So, e.g., Boring, *Sayings* 150-52.

ered round,[34] made a huge impression on them and was from the first part of the remembered tradition shared and reflected on in disciple groups.

Matt. 26.39	Mark 14.35-36	Luke 22.41-42	John 12.27	Heb. 5.7-8
And going forward a little way he fell on his face and prayed saying,	And going forward a little way he fell to the ground and prayed that if it was possible the hour would pass from him. And he said, 'Abba, Father, all things are possible to you. Let this cup pass from me. Yet not what I wish, but what you wish'.	And he withdrew from them about a stone's throw, and knelt and prayed saying,		In the days of his flesh, Jesus offered up prayers and supplications, with loud cries and tears, to the one who was able to save him from death, and he was heard because of his reverent submission.
'My Father, if it is possible, let this cup pass from me. Nevertheless, not as I wish but as you wish'.		'Father, if you are willing, let this cup pass from me. Nevertheless, not my will be done but yours'.	Now is my soul troubled, and what am I to say? 'Father, save me from this hour'? But for this purpose I came to this hour.	Although he was a son, he learned obedience through what he suffered.

The tradition here is of particular interest. The point is regularly made that the tradition itself indicates that Jesus was too far from the (sleeping!) disciples to be overheard.[35] It is also clear that Matthew's second 'Father' reference (Matt. 26.42) is an elaboration of Mark's less explicit account (Mark 14.39); is this true of all the references? And the Hebrews passage is obviously influenced by the Wisdom motif of the son disciplined by the father (n. 16 above). On the other hand, the wide attestation of the tradition is impressive,[36] and the unmartyr-like description of Jesus in the garden (Mark 14.33: 'greatly distressed [*ektham-beisthai*] and troubled') is hardly likely to be a Christian composition.[37]

34. Prayer, like reading, was not usually a silent activity in the ancient world (pseudo-Philo 50.5; P. W. van der Horst, 'Silent Prayer in Antiquity', *Numen* 41 [1994] 1-25).

35. 'Since there were no witnesses, Mark (or the tradition before him) must have imagined what Jesus said' (Funk, *Five Gospels* 120). Funk again betrays unawareness of the character of oral tradition when he adds: The 'variations and additions illustrate how loosely the evangelists treated even written discourse, to say nothing of the oral tradition they may have received' (120).

36. Dodd, *Historical Tradition* 67-72.

37. 'Loud cries and tears' (Heb. 5.7). See further my *Jesus and the Spirit* 17-20, with earlier bibliography, where I note *inter alia* that *ekthambeisthai* seems to denote shuddering horror — 'to be moved to a relatively intense emotional state because of something causing great surprise or perplexity' (BDAG) — hence the softening of Matt. 26.37 *(lypeisthai)*. It is important to note (*pace* Lüdemann, *Jesus* 98-99) that the intensity of this description is not derived from the Psalms. 'The temptation of Jesus in the garden completely went against any ancient ideal of martyrdom' (M. Hengel, *The Atonement: The Origins of the Doctrine in the New Testament* [London: SCM, 1981] 71). Becker contrasts Luke's portrayal of the martyr Paul (*Jesus* 345).

A possible tradition history may be suggested by the echo of the Lord's Prayer in Mark,[38] surprising since Mark does not contain the Lord's Prayer. The parallel suggests that the Gethsemane story was put into this form by someone aware of the Lord's Prayer, presumably to underscore the seriousness of the circumstances envisaged in the Prayer,[39] and to present Jesus' own prayer as an exemplary model. This in turn suggests that the memory of Jesus' distraught state in Gethsemane had burnt itself deep into the remembrance of those who had been closest to him.[40] On the other hand, since the Lord's Prayer could itself have provided the template on which the story was formed,[41] we cannot draw the further corollary with any confidence that they heard the prayer itself. Yet at the same time, we have to ask what would have prompted the first tradents to present Jesus as praying in the manner he taught them other than the knowledge/memory that he did so pray?[42]

Is there then evidence of sufficient weight that Jesus did indeed address God as 'Father'? On examination, Jeremias's five strata (n. 25 above) prove to be less substantial than initially appeared. We have already noted that the 'special Matthew' reference (Matt. 26.42) is more likely to be attributed to Matthew's redaction than to his source. With John it is hard to distinguish the vocative 'Father' from John's much developed Father/Son motif. And we shall see that similar questions hang over the unique Lukan references (§17.1f). But once again we have to ask where the motif itself originated. And once again the greater likelihood is that the motif began in the earliest memories of Jesus' prayers than that a whole new way of praying is to be attributed to an unknown spiritual leader from whence it was

38.

Lord's Prayer	Mark 14.36, 38	Matt. 26.39, 41	Luke 22.42, 46
pater *genēthētō to thelēma sou*	*abba, ho patēr* *ou ti egō thelō alla ti su*	*pater mou* *ouch hōs egō thelō, all' hōs su*	*pater* *mē to thelēma mou alla to son ginesthō*
mē eisenenkēs hēmas eis peirasmon	*hina mē elthēte eis peirasmon*	*hina mē eiselthēte eis peirasmon*	*hina mē eiselthēte eis peirasmon*

Although Matthew and Luke have strengthened the allusion, they have not created it. Notable is the fact that the allusion includes the third petition, that is, the elaboration of the second petition which only Matthew includes (the allusion is strongest in Luke!). Also curious (coincidental?) is the fact that the Johannine parallel follows the initial *pater* address with 'Father, glorify your name' (John 12.28), possibly a further echo of the Lord's Prayer (first petition)?

39. See the discussion above, §12.4b. The text is cited above, §8.5b.

40. They could have been aware of such distress before they fell asleep, though the sleep motif is a more likely indication of redactional (hortatory) interest than the prayer (Dunn, *Jesus and the Spirit* 19-20; Davies and Allison, *Matthew* 3.493 n. 13).

41. The cup motif is certainly to be related to Mark 10.39/Matt. 20.23 in some way (see below §17.4d).

42. Further discussion on tradition history and bibliography in Bayer, *Jesus' Predictions* 63-70.

retrojected into the Jesus tradition. This likelihood is strengthened by three factors. (1) In only one of his recorded prayers does Jesus fail to call on God as 'Father', and that is the cry on the cross: 'My God, my God, why have you forsaken me?' (Mark 15.34 par.).[43] The tradition in effect acknowledges an exception here. Even the redactional history of the unanimous tradition points to a motif elaborated rather than invented. (2) The prayer Jesus taught his disciples encourages them also to address God as 'Father'. The obvious implication is that this manner of address was seen from the beginning as an echo of Jesus' own manner of praying. So far as the Gethsemane prayer is concerned it would hardly be sufficient to conclude simply that it was derived from the Lord's Prayer. More likely both elements are rooted in a common memory of Jesus' own prayer and teaching on prayer. (3) We will return to the testimony of early Christian prayer (Rom. 8.15; Gal. 4.6) below.

There are also good grounds for the further conclusion that Jesus used the Aramaic address *Abba*.[44] The use of this term is attested in the Jesus tradition only in Mark 14.36. But since Matthew and Luke read the Greek vocative *pater* at that point, the probability is that underlying the vocative *pater* in the other prayers of Jesus (including the Lord's Prayer) was Aramaic *abba*.[45] The most striking evidence here is given by Paul's evocation of what seems to have been a (or the) common prayer form within his churches:

> Rom. 8.15-17: You have received the spirit of adoption by whom we cry, "Abba, Father". The Spirit itself bears witness with our spirit that we are children of God. And if children, also heirs — heirs of God and heirs together with Christ.

> Gal. 4.6-7: God sent the Spirit of his Son into our hearts crying, "Abba, Father". Consequently you are no longer a slave, but a son. And if a son, then also an heir through God.

The notable features here are threefold. First, Paul reminds his readers of what he knew (Galatians) and could assume (Romans) was an experience shared by Gen-

---

43. 'If one accepts literally that anguish at the opening moment (Gethsemane) when Jesus could still call God "*Abba*, Father", one should accept equally literally this screamed protest against abandonment wrenched from the utterly forlorn Jesus who now is so isolated and estranged that he no longer uses "Father" language but speaks as the humblest servant' (Brown, *Death of the Messiah* 1051).

44. Despite the sparsity of evidence, the support for this conclusion is amazingly strong; e.g., Hahn, *Hoheitstitel* 320 (*Titles* 307); Perrin, *Rediscovering* 40-41; Funk, *Honest* 208.

45. It is evident from the parallel forms in Matt. 11.25-26/Luke 10.21, one with vocative *pater,* the other with *ho patēr,* that *ho patēr* also functioned as a form of address, hence the translation, '*Abba* (that is) *ho patēr*' = '*Abba*, Father'. As Mark 14.36 also indicates, the latter quickly established itself in the Jesus tradition and in Christian prayer.

tile Christians ('*we* cry', '*our* hearts'). Second, these Gentile (Greek-speaking) churches continued to use an Aramaic prayer-form. This must be because it had become such a firmly established form in the earliest (Aramaic-speaking) churches that the first Greek-speakers were simply inducted to it as new converts, and thus it became a regular expression and mark of Christian devotion. Third, in both passages the prayer is seen to express the Christians' own sonship, which is obviously seen as a reflection of Christ's sonship. The Spirit who cries '*Abba*' is the Spirit of the Son; the cry is proof that those who so pray share in his sonship and inheritance.

The most obvious conclusion to draw from all this is that the *Abba* prayer was so cherished among the first believers *precisely because it was Jesus' own prayer form*. It was precisely because it was his way of praying that their use of it served as assurance that they shared in his sonship. I have made this argument several times, but still the importance to the case (that the *Abba* prayer was taken over in Christian circles from, and in imitation of Jesus' own distinctive way of praying) seems not to be adequately appreciated. In my judgment, the case for arguing that Jesus regularly addressed God as '*Abba*' in his prayers, a case which is but weakly founded within the Jesus tradition itself, is in the end dependent for its persuasiveness on the testimony of the two Pauline texts.[46]

Was the *Abba* prayer a distinctive feature of Jesus' prayer? In giving an affirmative answer, this was one of the places where Jeremias overreached the data.[47] We have already noted that the same address to God *(pater, 'abi)* is attested elsewhere for the time of Jesus (above, n. 17). Nevertheless, the tradition of Christian usage attested in Rom. 8.15 and Gal. 4.6 clearly assumes that the *Abba* prayer was *a mark of Christian worship,* and therefore, presumably, *distinctive* of Christians. And by the same logic as above, it follows that they must have regarded Jesus' *Abba* address as distinctive of *Jesus*' prayer. It also follows that the first disciples, who in their own praying in Aramaic established the *Abba* prayer as Christian, cannot have been aware of *abba* as a regular address in the prayers of fellow Jews.[48] The obvious qualification thus called for to Jeremias's

---

46. Cf. J. A. Fitzmyer, 'Abba and Jesus' Relation to God', in *À Cause de L'Évangile,* J. Dupont FS (LD 123; Paris: Cerf, 1985) 15-38 (here 31-32). The point is made independently by Thompson, *Promise* 67-68 (citing particularly Meier, *Marginal Jew* 1.266).

47. Jeremias, *Proclamation* 63-68; but we should note that Jeremias's findings and arguments are largely supported by Fitzmyer ('Abba and Jesus' Relation to God'). For sympathetic restatements of Jeremias's argument see Witherington, *Christology* 216-21, and Thompson, *Promise* 21-34.

48. It will not do simply to reply that 'Abba' may have been in more regular usage by one or more sections of Second Temple Judaism. Deductions should be drawn from the evidence available, though, of course, always remaining open to correction from further evidence. *Pace* M. R. D'Angelo, 'Abba and "Father": Imperial Theology and the Jesus Traditions', *JBL*

claim is that it was not so much Jesus' *use* of *abba* in his prayer which was distinctive, but the fact that *abba* was his *consistent* and almost *unvarying* form of address to God.

The significance of Jesus' use of *abba* in address to God is not much doubted, though it has also been exaggerated. By common consent, *abba* was a family word, expressive of a family relationship of some intimacy. This is presumably why it was so little used in contemporary Jewish prayer: it was regarded as too familiar, bordering on presumption.[49] In contrast, it is hard to avoid the opposite deduction, that Jesus used this prayer form because he regarded it as appropriate; that is, his prayer was expressive of his sense of his own relationship towards God. Like Hanina, he prayed to God 'like a son of the house'. We can even begin to deduce that Jesus could have prayed so consistently only if he had experienced his relationship with God as an intimate family relationship.[50] And to that extent we can begin to see how this broader category (God's son) began to be filled with a new significance which Christians subsequently took further.

One other point. The implication of Luke's version of the Lord's Prayer is that Jesus taught his disciples also to say *abba* to God as a distinguishing badge of their discipleship (Luke 11.1-2). This, however, does not constitute a weakening of the conclusion regarding the distinctiveness of Jesus' *Abba* prayer. For, as with Rom. 8.15 and Gal. 4.6, it is precisely disciples of Jesus who are encouraged so to pray, and as a mark of their discipleship. There is a clear sense on each occasion, then, that the disciple's sonship expressed in the *Abba* prayer is not somehow independent of Jesus' sonship but is precisely *derivative* from Jesus' sonship. The point is of a piece with the observation that Jesus chose twelve disciples (to represent Israel). He did not choose another eleven so that he with them might represent Israel, he being one of the twelve. He set himself in some measure over against the twelve, distinct from them, as the one who called them. This observation fits too with the older point that Jesus is often remembered as saying 'my Father' and 'your Father', but never as joining with his dis-

---

111 (1992) 611-30 (particularly 614-16). See also my earlier response to Morton Smith on this point in *Christology* 27-28.

49. In *m. Ta'an.* 3.8 Simeon ben Shetah seems to criticize Honi for such presumption. But the point should not be overstated: J. Barr, 'Abba Isn't Daddy!', *JTS* 39 (1988) 28-47; Vermes, *Religion* 180-82.

50. 'Jesus was aware, in a peculiarly intense and intimate way, that God was his father' (Barrett, *Jesus* 29); 'Jesus' uniqueness in his relation to God undoubtedly lies in its unaffected simplicity' (Schillebeeckx, *Jesus* 260, also 268); 'an unusual directness' (Stuhlmacher, *Biblische Theologie* 1.85-87); 'He regarded his relationship with God as especially intimate' (Sanders, *Historical Figure* 239); Caird, *Theology* 403; Goshen-Gottstein, 'Hillel and Jesus' 50-53; see also and further McKnight, *New Vision* 49-65; with proper hesitation, Thompson, *Promise* 30-32, 69-70, 78-82. Witherington notes that Barr does not dispute that *abba* is the language of intimacy (*Christology* 218).

ciples in saying 'our Father'.[51] And we recall also the conclusion of Jesus' reply to the Baptist: 'Blessed is anyone who takes no offence at me' (Matt. 11.6/Luke 7.23). All this strengthens the likelihood both that Jesus thought of himself as God's son and that he sensed his sonship to be something distinctive in its intimacy and immediacy.[52] Such certainly seems to be the most obvious conclusion to draw from the impact which he left on, in and through the Jesus tradition at this point.

c. Did Jesus Teach That He Was God's Son?

Leaving aside the much developed Johannine tradition,[53] there are three passages which cannot be ignored: Matt. 11.27/Luke 10.22; Mark 12.6; and 13.32. I have dealt with them in some detail in *Jesus and the Spirit,* with indecisive results.[54] Does a more explicitly tradition-historical approach add anything new?

(1) Only the Son (Matt. 11.27/Luke 10.22):

Matt. 11.27	Luke 10.22
All things have been handed over to me by my Father; and no one knows the Son except the Father, and no one knows the Father except the Son and anyone to whom the Son chooses to reveal him'.	All things have been handed over to me by my Father; and no one knows who the Son is except the Father, or who the Father is except the Son and anyone to whom the Son chooses to reveal him'.

Matt. 11.27/Luke 10.22 is the continuation of the fuller Q passage Matt. 11.25-27/Luke 10.21-22 (§16.2b), whose language, style, and structure clearly indicate an Aramaic origin.[55] The variations between Matt. 11.27 and Luke 10.22 are no more than performance variants.[56] The problem for questers is that both forms look like developed tradition. Two considerations are of greatest weight. First, the saying is untypical of the Synoptic tradition and has a distinctively Johannine

51. Dalman, *Words* 190; Bornkamm, *Jesus of Nazareth* 128-29; Goppelt, *Theology* 1.203; Theissen and Merz, *Historical Jesus* 526.

52. See again my earlier discussions in *Jesus and the Spirit* 23-26 (where the discussion focuses on the question of Jesus' own experience), and in *Christology* 28-33 (where the discussion focuses more on whether Jesus had a consciousness of pre-existence).

53. See again my *Christology* 29-32.

54. *Jesus and the Spirit* 26-36. I omit consideration of Luke 22.29-30 ('my Father's kingdom') here, since it is attested only by Luke and cannot be attributed to Q; but see *Jesus and the Spirit* 36.

55. Burney, *Poetry* 133, 171-72; Manson, *Sayings* 79; Jeremias, *Prayers* 46-47; also *Proclamation* 57-58. There is disagreement on whether the two sayings originally belonged together; for contrasting views see Fitzmyer, *Luke* 2.866; Davies and Allison *Matthew* 2.279.

56. See also discussion in Davies and Allison, *Matthew* 2.280-81 and n. 206.

ring.[57] This Q passage may thus indicate one of the shoots which grew into the full Johannine bloom. But it also may indicate that the development was already well under way in Q. If, for example, John 10.15 ('the Father knows me and I know my Father') attests awareness of an early tradition somewhat along these lines,[58] then Matt. 11.27/Luke 10.22 already attests a heightened exclusivity in the christological claims of Q.

Second, the claim to unrestricted authority and the absoluteness and exclusiveness of the relation postulated between 'the Father' and 'the Son' are unprecedented in the pre-Easter Synoptic tradition.[59] Again it is possible to argue for an earlier, less exclusive, form of the tradition. Jeremias suggested that the chiastic parallelism of the two lines 'is simply an oriental periphrasis for a mutual relationship: only father and son really know each other'.[60] And the Wisdom literature throws up several parallels of not so dissimilar claims to knowledge of God,[61] particularly Wis. 2.10-20, where it is said of the righteous man: 'He claims to have knowledge of God, and calls himself a child *(paida)* of the Lord . . . and boasts that God is his father' (vv. 13, 16).[62] However, the more we think we can see a less controversial father-son saying behind Matt. 11.27/Luke 10.22, the more controversial the present form of the Q passage seems to be.[63]

Here it is wise to acknowledge that such a discussion is unavoidably caught in the inadequacies of the historical method.[64] For its natural recourse is to search out precedents and parallels to help explain particular and distinctive data. And the tendency or temptation is to conform the data to the precedents, to explain by explaining away the less obviously explicable elements.

57. Cf. John 1.18; 3.35; 5.20; 7.29; 10.15; 13.3; 14.7, 9; 17.25. This is the decisive consideration for Funk, *Five Gospels* 182, and Lüdemann, *Jesus* 330-31, in deciding for the saying's inauthenticity. Note also *Dial. Sav.* 134.14-15: 'How will someone who does [not] know [the Son] know the [Father]?'

58. Dodd, *Historical Tradition* 359-61.

59. The closest parallel to Matt. 11.27a in the Synoptic tradition is (the post-resurrection saying) Matt. 28.18: 'All authority in heaven and on earth has been given to me'.

60. Jeremias, *Prayers* 47-48; taking up a suggestion of Dalman, *Words* 193-94.

61. F. Christ, *Jesus Sophia. Die Sophia-Christologie bei den Synoptikern* (Zürich: Zwingli, 1970) 89 refers to Job 28.1-28; Sir. 1.6, 8; Bar. 3.15–4.4; cf. 1 Cor. 2.11. M. J. Suggs, *Wisdom, Christology and Law in Matthew's Gospel* (Cambridge: Harvard University, 1970) 89-95 refers particularly to Wis. 2.17-18 and 4.10, 13-15. For the DSS, see W. D. Davies, '"Knowledge" in the Dead Sea Scrolls and Matt. 11.25-30', *HTR* 46 (1953), reprinted in *Christian Origins and Judaism* (London: DLT, 1962) 119-44. E. Schweizer refers particularly to 1QS 4.22; 9.17-18; 11.3, 15-18; 1QSb (1Q28b) 4.25-28; 1QH 10[2].13; 18[10].27-28 (*TDNT* 8.373 n. 281).

62. Cf. Schillebeeckx, *Jesus* 265.

63. Contrast I. H. Marshall, 'The Divine Sonship of Jesus', *Interpretation* 21 (1967) 87-103, reprinted in *Jesus the Saviour: Studies in New Testament Theology* (London: SPCK, 1990) 134-49 (here 137-39); Witherington, *Christology* 221-28.

64. See above, §6.3c.

So here we have to ask whether it could have been Jesus himself who expressed himself so exultantly, perhaps only once, in terms which went beyond those used by the righteous man in Wisdom or the Teacher of Righteousness at Qumran.[65] In other words, do we at this point hear with and through Jesus' first disciples another example of the eschatological plus (§16.1) — a boasting in the plenitude of authority bestowed on him, an exultation at the closeness of his relation with God as Father, and a sense that the climax of eschatological revelation depended on his imparting it to others? All these elements link into implicit claims already documented. The question, then, would be whether it was Jesus himself, who on one occasion at least, crystallized them in the form preserved here. Or should the saying proper be attributed rather to those responsible for the early formation of the Jesus tradition, aware as we may suppose them to have been of such implicit eschatological claims and concerned to formulate them more explicitly and memorably for teaching and liturgical purposes?[66] I can see nothing in the text which points decisively in favour of one alternative rather than the other.

(2) The parable of the wicked tenants (Mark 12.1-9 pars.):

Matt. 21.33-41	Mark 12.1-9	Luke 20.9-16	GTh 65
33 'Listen to another parable. There was a landowner who planted a vineyard, put a fence around it, dug a wine press in it, and built a watchtower. Then he leased it to tenants and went to another country. 34 When the harvest time had come, he sent his slaves to the tenants to collect his produce. 35 But the tenants seized his slaves and	1 Then he began to speak to them in parables. 'A man planted a vineyard, put up a fence, dug a wine trough, and built a watchtower; then he leased it to tenants and went to another country. 2 At the appropriate time, he sent a slave to the tenants to collect from them his share of the produce of the vineyard. 3 But they seized him, and	9 He began to tell the people this parable: 'A man planted a vineyard, and leased it to tenants, and went to another country for a long time. 10 When the season came, he sent a slave to the tenants in order that they might give him his share of the produce of the vineyard; but the tenants	He said: A good man had a vineyard. He gave it to tenants that they might cultivate it and he might receive its produce from them. He sent his servant so that the tenants might give him the produce of the vineyard. They seized his servant (and)

65. See above, n. 29. Particularly worthy of note is 1QH 12[4].27: 'through me you have enlightened the face of the many'.

66. Cf. Fuller: 'Matt. 11:27 is not a "christological contraction", but an explicit expression of the implicit Christology of Jesus' own use of Abba' (*Foundations* 133 n. 20), in critique of Hahn, *Hoheitstitel* 327 (*Titles* 312); Fitzmyer: 'Although I am inclined to regard the substance of these sayings (Luke 10.21-22) as authentic, that substance should more likely be traced to an implicit christology expressed in Jesus' words and deeds in his earthly ministry' (*Luke* 2.870). Davies and Allison, however, 'fail to detect any truly telling signs of an origin with Jesus', but go on to argue for the influence of Exod. 33.12-13, with the implication that the Moses-like prophet (Deut. 18.15) would have the same exceptional face-to-face knowledge of God (Deut. 34.10) (*Matthew* 2.283-86). For earlier discussion see my *Jesus and the Spirit* 27-34.

beat one, killed another, and stoned another. 36 Again he sent other slaves, more than the first; and they treated them in the same way.	beat him, and sent him away empty-handed. 4 And again he sent another slave to them; this one they beat over the head and insulted. 5 Then he sent another, and that one they killed. And so it was with many others; some they beat, and others they killed. 6 He had still one other, a beloved son. Finally he sent him to them, saying, "They will respect my son". 7 But those tenants	beat him and sent him away empty-handed. 11 Next he sent another slave; that one also they beat and insulted and sent away empty-handed. 12 And he sent still a third; this one also they wounded and threw out. 13 Then the owner of the vineyard said, "What shall I do? I will send my beloved son; perhaps they will respect him". 14 But when the tenants saw him, they discussed it among themselves and said,	beat him; a little more and they would have killed him. The servant came and told it to his master. His master said, 'Perhaps he did not know them'. He sent another servant; the tenants beat him as well.
37 Finally he sent his son to them,			Then the owner sent his son. He said,
saying, "They will respect my son". 38 But when the tenants saw the son,			'Perhaps they will respect my son'.
they said to themselves, "This is the heir; come, let us kill him and get his inheritance". 39 So they seized him, threw him out of the vineyard, and killed him. 40 Now when the owner of the vineyard comes, what will he do to those tenants?' 41 They said to him, 'He will put those wretches to a miserable death, and lease the vineyard to other tenants who will give him the produce at the harvest time'.	said to one another, "This is the heir; come, let us kill him, and the inheritance will be ours". 8 So they seized him, killed him, and threw him out of the vineyard. 9 What then will the owner of the vineyard do? He will come and destroy the tenants and give the vineyard to others'.	"This is the heir; let us kill him so that the inheritance may be ours". 15 So they threw him out of the vineyard and killed him. What then will the owner of the vineyard do to them? 16 He will come and destroy those tenants and give the vineyard to others'.	Since those tenants knew that he was the heir of the vineyard, they seized him (and) killed him. He who has ears, let him hear.

It is worth recording the full parable, even though our interest is more narrowly focused on Mark 12.6 pars., since it so well illustrates the variations typical of repeated performances. To be noted is the fact that the framework and structure are stable, but the details, particularly those of the vineyard's construction, the sequence of servants sent, and their treatment, vary, probably according to the whim of the performer (or Evangelist). The simpler *Thomas* version certainly gives substance to the view that the Synoptic versions have been elaborated to bring out the allusions to the vineyard of Israel in Isa. 5.1-7 (Mark/Matthew), to Jesus' death 'outside' (Jerusalem), and to the subsequent turn away from Israel in the Gentile mission.[67] But the Synoptic version also retains the basic structure

67. E.g., Fitzmyer, *Luke* 2.1278-81; Scott, *Hear Then the Parable* 245-51; Witherington, *Christology* 213; Funk, *Five Gospels* 101, 510-11. Further bibliography in K. Snodgrass, *The*

and sequence. And it would be surprising if a Jewish audience did not hear an allusion to Israel as God's vineyard[68] and to the prophets as God's rejected messengers, even in the shorter version.[69] Moreover, the basic parable accords well with central thrusts in Jesus' preaching elsewhere, particularly the evocation of the well-established theme of prophet rejection and the expectation of judgment on Israel (§12.4c-e).

The point of immediate interest is that the sending of the owner's son is the climax of the parable. Indeed, if anything forms the core of the parable it is the father's 'sending' of his son in the hope that the tenants 'will respect' him (Mark 12.6 pars.). This feature cannot simply be dismissed as christological colouring[70] since the contrast between servants and son is integral to the dramatic climax of the parable.[71] By the same token, however, one should not read too much christological weight into Jesus' possible use of the motif. Even so, it cannot but be significant that Jesus was remembered as likening his mission to that of a son, and both in continuity with and in distinction from the earlier missions of the prophets as servants. The same sense of eschatological climax is evident, and its expression in son imagery is consistent with our findings thus far.[72] The impor-

---

Parable of the Wicked Tenants (WUNT 27; Tübingen: Mohr-Siebeck, 1983) 3-11; Hultgren, *Parables* 361 n. 30, 365 n. 44. Hultgren's own discussion of the relation of the different versions assumes that only literary dependence is at issue (365-66). Lüdemann, *Jesus* 81-82, pays too little attention to *Thomas*'s version and its relevance for evaluating the parable's performance-/tradition-history. It is much more plausible that the sequel to the parable, the 'stone' testimony from Ps. 118.22-23 (Mark 12.10-12 pars., including *GTh* 66), was an addition to the parable as its christological potential became clear in the light of Jesus' crucifixion (see e.g., Hultgren 363-64, with further bibliography n. 34; otherwise Wright, *Jesus* 497-501, stretching the interpretative thread to near breaking point [501]).

68. 'A Jew could not tell a story about a vineyard without embarking upon allegory (cf. Isa. 5.7)' (Barrett, *Jesus* 27). See further G. J. Brooke, '4Q500 1 and the Use of Scripture in the Parable of the Vineyard', *DSD* 2 (1995) 268-94; J. C. de Moor, 'The Targumic Background of Mark 12:1-12: The Parable of the Wicked Tenants', *JSJ* 29 (1998) 63-80; W. J. C. Weren, 'The Use of Isaiah 5,1-7 in the Parable of the Tenants (Mark 12,1-12; Matthew 21,33-46)', *Biblica* 79 (1998) 1-26.

69. As many have observed, the parable may also reflect the harsh realities of absentee landlords and dissatisfied tenant-farmers of Jesus' own time (e.g., Dodd, *Parables* 125-26; Charlesworth, *Jesus* 145-47; Funk, *Five Gospels* 101); see also M. Hengel, 'Das Gleichnis von den Weingärtnern: Mc 12:1-12 im Licht der Zenonpapyri und der rabbinischen Gleichnisse', *ZNW* 59 (1968) 1-39; C. A. Evans, 'Jesus' Parable of the Tenant Farmers in Light of Lease Agreements in Antiquity', *JSP* 14 (1996) 65-83.

70. But the description of the son as 'beloved' may well have been added by Mark (followed by Luke) to enhance the christological reference (cf. Mark 1.11; 9.7).

71. 'It is the logic of the story, and not any theological motive, that has introduced this figure' (Dodd, *Parables* 130); see also those cited by Bayer, *Jesus' Predictions* 94 n. 24.

72. Earlier discussion in *Jesus and the Spirit* 35-36; see also Charlesworth, *Jesus* 147-53.

tant corollary that the parable may have expressed Jesus' own conviction, that he would be treated no differently from the prophets rejected by previous generations, and now John the Baptist, is one to which we will have to return (§17.4a).

(3) Nor the Son (Mark 13.32):

Matt. 24.36	Mark 13.32
But about that day and hour no one knows, neither the angels of heaven, nor the Son, but only the Father.	But about that day or hour no one knows, neither the angels in heaven, nor the Son, but only the Father.

This is clearly of a piece with Jesus' expectation of the kingdom's coming. It could be either an isolated saying attached to the apocalyptic discourse at some stage in the traditioning process or part of a larger block of Jesus' teaching which formed the basis of the discourse from the beginning. Either way, it is less likely to have been derived entirely from an early christological elaboration of the early tradition; apart from anything else, it runs too strongly against the sort of christological affirmation already attested in Matt. 11.25-27/Luke 10.21-22.[73] It is the reference to 'the Son' which seems to be the principal indication of later christological perspective.[74] But as C. K. Barrett pointed out, 'The description of Jesus by the most honorific title available would be precisely the sort of compensation that tradition would introduce'.[75] In effect this observation removes Mark 13.32 from the catalogue of firm evidence that Jesus spoke of himself as God's son ('the Son') in his teaching.[76]

In the event, then, the possible examples of Jesus referring to himself as God's son in the course of teaching his disciples do not provide very strong grounds for the conclusion that he did so. At most we can say, with a certain degree of confidence, that the sense of sonship which comes to expression in Jesus' remembered *Abba* prayer is evident also in the tradition of his teachings in one or two references to his relationship with God using father-son imagery.

73. 'Jewish tradition maintained that Abraham and Moses and others had foreseen all of history and the end of the world. Would Jesus' followers have made him out to be less than they?' (Davies and Allison, *Matthew* 3.378).

74. Funk, *Five Gospels* 114; Lüdemann, *Jesus* 93.

75. Barrett, *Jesus* 25-26; cf. Schweizer, *TDNT* 8.372; Kümmel, *Theology* 75; Leivestad, *Jesus* 112. Witherington again presses the argument that 'Jesus saw himself as fulfilling the role of Wisdom on earth' (*Christology* 228-33). But one might ask whether it would have occurred to Jesus to exclude himself from the 'no one', whereas it would certainly have occurred to the tradents.

76. Similarly, and with earlier bibliography, *Jesus and the Spirit* 35 and nn. 124-25.

d. Conclusion

In short, there are grounds, not substantial but probably sufficient, to support these conclusions regarding the remembered Jesus: (1) that Jesus' *Abba* prayer was both a characteristic and as such a distinctive feature of his praying, (2) that this prayer was properly heard to express a profound sense of and confidence in his relationship with God as his Father, and (3) that Jesus was also recalled as alluding to this relationship on a few occasions during his mission. We can deduce further, without strain, that this sense of sonship must have been (4) crucial, even central, to Jesus' own self-understanding and (5) the source of the immediacy of authority with which he proclaimed the kingdom of God, in both its eschatological immanence and imminence.[77] Only if this were the case would the Fourth Gospel's massive expansion and elaboration of the Father-Son theme have been as justifiable in tradition-historical terms; and only so would the other elaborations and developments of the Son-christology have been as acceptable as in the event they proved to be.

As for what Jesus' sonship meant for his disciples, the tradition does not encourage us to infer that Jesus made his relationship with God, as son to father, a subject of explicit instruction, still less that he required his disciples to assent to such a belief regarding himself. Nor that this sense of relationship was a secret mystery which he taught only to an inner group, a higher stage of initiation, a goal to be achieved along the path of discipleship. What the Jesus tradition does indicate is that Jesus sought to induct his disciples into that same sense of sonship, not least by teaching them to pray as he did, and that he encouraged them all to live out of their own relationship to God as Father, as he did. And what seems also to have been the case, he saw his disciples' relationship to God as Father as in some sense a sharing in his own sonship to the Father.

From the little evidence we have on the subject these are surprisingly large, but also surprisingly strong conclusions.

16.3. Son of Man: The Issues

After 'the kingdom of God/heaven' there is no phrase so common in the Jesus tradition as 'the son of man'. Its importance within the Jesus tradition, and possibly as a key to that tradition, therefore, can hardly be exaggerated. More to the immediate point, it seems to be the nearest thing in the Jesus tradition to a self-chosen self-designation. For example, in the healing of the paralysed man Jesus

---

77. Keck presses the point more strongly: 'Jesus probably saw himself as God's obedient son, replicating the Father's way' (*Who Is Jesus?* 97-100; see also 140-44).

says 'that you may know that the Son of Man has authority on earth to forgive sins' and then to the paralytic 'I say to you, rise, take up your pallet and go home' (Mark 2.10-11). Later on Jesus teaches that 'the Son of Man must suffer many things . . . and be put to death and rise after three days' (8.31). And in the hearing before High Priest Caiaphas he says, 'You will see the Son of Man sitting at the right hand of power and coming with the clouds of heaven' (14.62). No one for whom the Gospel of Mark was intended would fail to recognize 'the Son of Man' as a reference to Jesus himself. So, is this the key for which we have been looking? Did Jesus speak of himself as the son of man/Son of Man?

Would that it were so straightforward. These initial simple observations cloak a controversy which has raged (the term is not inappropriate) for more than a century and shows no sign of abating. Indeed, the ongoing 'Son of Man' debate is one of the great embarrassments for modern historical scholarship, since it has been unable to produce any major consensus.[78] Does, then, the fragmentation of scholarly judgment on this topic simply illustrate the truth of the postmodern critique of historical method? Given the extent of the motif in the Jesus tradition, that would be an important conclusion with considerable ramifications.

Broadly speaking, for the last 150 years, the controversy has been between two principal interpretations — what might be characterized as the *human* son of man and the *heavenly* Son of Man. Traditionally 'the Son of Man' was understood as an expression of Jesus' humanity and so as a counterpoise to his status as 'the Son of God', stressing his divinity. But the reference to 'one like a son of man' coming with the clouds of heaven in Dan. 7.13 was always a problem for that view, and the publication of *1 Enoch* in the first half of the nineteenth century gave a lasting boost to the heavenly Son of Man interpretation.[79] As linguistic resources and analytical technique improved through the twentieth century, these two views have continued to provide the main options, but each with several variations.[80]

The heart of the issue is disagreement on the root of the usage, on the source of the phrase in the Jesus tradition. There are two main possibilities. The difficulty has been to see how the two relate to each other within the Jesus tradition.

---

78. E.g., D. Burkett, *The Son of Man Debate: A History and Evaluation* (SNTSMS 107; Cambridge: Cambridge University, 1999) quotes the pessimistic sentiments of A. J. B. Higgins, R. H. Fuller, and F. H. Borsch (2, 121).

79. Burkett, *Son of Man Debate* particularly 13-31.

80. W. Horbury, 'The Messianic Association of "The Son of Man"', *JTS* 36 (1985) 34-55, gives a nicely concise review of the twentieth-century discussion (34-36).

a. A Philological Root

No one disagrees that *ho huios tou anthrōpou* is inelegant Greek, without parallel elsewhere in Greek of the time. Few if any now dispute that the phrase must have entered Greek as a literal translation of the Hebrew *ben 'adam* or the Aramaic *bar* *ᵉnaša*[81] or that the Hebrew/Aramaic phrase denotes simply 'man'. In Hebrew 'sons of men' is a familiar phrase to denote (a) human community,[82] with 'son of man' (singular) used on a number of occasions of an individual or typical individual within that community.[83] The last case gives the classic examples, Ps. 8.4 ('what is man that you are mindful of him, and the son of man that you care for him?') and the regular address to Ezekiel as 'son of man'.[84] Significant is the fact that 'sons of men/son of man' often has the connotation of frailty, in contrast to God.[85] This range of usage, no doubt as familiar as the Scriptures were for most devout Jews, is bound to form an important part of the context of meaning within which the Aramaic phrase in the Jesus tradition would have first been heard. So how would the phrase *bar* *ᵉnaša* have been heard at the time of Jesus?

When Geza Vermes reinvigorated the moribund discussion in the 1960s, it was by arguing from later rabbinic usage that *bar naša* (lacking the initial aleph) was used not only for 'a human being' and as an indefinite pronoun, but also, and most important for Vermes, as a circumlocution for 'I'.[86] Maurice Casey, who has established himself as the most authoritative voice among the present generation of NT specialists on the Aramaic behind the Jesus tradition, took up from Vermes but disagreed with him regarding this crucial third category: the Aramaic idiom

81. 'The writers of the gospels must have had some particular reason for translating it with an almost wooden literalness' (Dodd, *Founder* 111). Discussion in D. R. A. Hare, *The Son of Man Tradition* (Minneapolis: Fortress, 1990) 231-35.

82. *bᵉne 'adam* in Deut. 32.8; Pss. 11.4; 12.2, 9 [1, 8]; 14.2; 31.20[19]; 36.8[7]; 45.3[2]; 49.3[2]; 53.3[2]; 57.5[4]; 58.2[1]; 62.10[9]; 66.5; 89.48[47]; 107.8, 15, 21, 31; 115.16; Prov. 15.11; Eccl. 1.13; Jer. 32.19; Ezek. 31.14; Dan. 10.16; Joel 1.12; 1QS 11.6, 15; 1QH 10[2].24-25; 12[4].32; 14[6].11; 19[11].6; 4Q181 1.1; CD 12.4, etc.; *bᵉne 'iš* in Pss. 4.3[2]; 49.3[2]; 62.10[9]; Lam. 3.33; 1QS 3.13; 4.15, 20, 26; 1QM 11.14; 4Q184 1.17; *bᵉne* *ᵉnaša'* in Dan. 2.38; 5.21 (Haag, *TDOT* 2.151, 161).

83. Num. 23.19; Job. 25.6; 35.8; Pss. 80.18[17]; 146.3; Isa. 51.12; 56.2; Jer. 49.18, 33; 50.40; 51.43; 1QS 11.20; 1QH 12[4].30.

84. 93 occurrences, starting at 2.1; also Dan. 8.17; *1 En.* 60.10. One is tempted to parallel the still current form of address 'Hey man', or even the more common 'Hey you!'.

85. See, e.g., Job 25.6; Pss. 8.4; 36.7; 53.2; 62.9; 89.47; Prov. 15.11; Eccl. 1.13; Isa. 51.12; Lam. 3.33; Ezek. 31.14; Dan. 5.21; Joel 1.12; 1QS 11.20; in Ezekiel its usage gives 'an increased emphasis on the distance separating God and man' (Haag, *TDOT* 2.163); see also C. C. Caragounis, *The Son of Man* (WUNT 38; Tübingen: Mohr Siebeck, 1986) 55-57.

86. G. Vermes, 'The Use of *bar nash/bar nasha* in Jewish Aramaic', in Black, *Aramaic Approach* 310-28; also in abridged version in *Jesus the Jew* 163-68, 188-91.

was used to make statements about a group of people, rather than all people, among whom the speaker was included, but never in reference to the speaker exclusively.[87] Both views, however, have been vigorously challenged on the ground that the Aramaic we know from the time of Jesus does not attest such usage.[88]

Four observations are appropriate at this point. First, there is some danger of holding the categories — generic (everyone), indefinite (someone), personal (everyone/a group including me, someone like me, a man [like me]) — too rigidly distinct so far as informal speech is concerned.[89] Second, even though Qumran has transformed our knowledge of Aramaic during the Second Temple period, the stock of Aramaic from this period is still very small, so that all judgments on what was possible within first-century CE Aramaic speech have to be hedged about with that qualification.

Third, there was presumably some continuity of usage from Hebrew into early Aramaic and on into later Aramaic.[90] In the instances of *ben 'adam* noted above (n. 83), there are some interesting examples: Job. 35.8 puts in parallel 'a

87. M. Casey, *Son of Man: The Interpretation and Influence of Daniel 7* (London: SPCK, 1979) 224-27; also particularly 'General, Generic and Indefinite: The Use of the Term "Son of Man" in Aramaic Sources and in the Teaching of Jesus', *JSNT* 29 (1987) 21-56. Casey was followed in turn by B. Lindars, who argued somewhat similarly for an intermediate sense between the generic (a human being) and personal reference — an idiomatic generic sense ('a man in my position') (*Jesus Son of Man: A Fresh Examination of the Son of Man Sayings in the Gospels* (London: SPCK, 1983) 23-24.

88. Dalman already responded to H. Lietzmann's assertion that the term 'son of man' 'does not exist in Aramaic' (*Words* 239); for a fuller review see Caragounis, *Son of Man* 16-19. J. A. Fitzmyer, 'The New Testament Title "Son of Man" Philologically Considered' (1974), *A Wandering Aramean: Collected Aramaic Essays* (Missoula: Scholars, 1979) 143-60 responded to Vermes (particularly 152-53); and again 'Another View of the "Son of Man" Debate', *JSNT* 4 (1979) 58-68, in response to G. Vermes, '"The Son of Man" Debate', *JSNT* 1 (1978) 19-32. See now Becker, *Jesus of Nazareth* 201, citing A. Vögtle, *Die 'Gretchenfrage' des Menschensohnproblems* (QD 152; Freiburg: Herder, 1994) 31-64. Most recently P. Owen and D. Shepherd have reexamined the data and conclude that '"son of man" as a means of idiomatic self-reference, whether exclusively (Vermes), or inclusively as part of a generic statement (Lindars, Casey), is not attested . . . in any phase of Aramaic pre-dating the time of Jesus' — 'Speaking Up for Qumran, Dalman and the Son of Man: Was *Bar Enasha* a Common Term for "Man" in the Time of Jesus?' *JSNT* 81 (2001) 81-121 (here conclusion 121), with fuller bibliography of Casey and Lindars (82 n. 7) and further references at this point (84-88).

89. Cf. R. Bauckham, 'The Son of Man: "A Man in My Position" or "Someone"?', *JSNT* 23 (1985) 23-33, particularly 29 (the possibility of an indefinite sense used as a 'deliberately oblique or ambiguous self-reference'); Davies and Allison, *Matthew* 2.46-47. Lindars' treatment left him vulnerable to Caragounis's critique (*Son of Man* 28-33). The discussion of Casey and Lindars by Hare, *Son of Man* also illustrates the danger of working with too distinct categories (246-50).

90. Cf. particularly M. Casey, 'The Use of the Term *br (')nsh(')* in the Aramaic Translations of the Hebrew Bible', *JSNT* 54 (1994) 87-118.

man like yourself' and 'a son of man'; similarly Ps. 80.17 explains 'the man of your right hand' as 'the son of man whom you made strong for yourself'; and in 1QH 12[4].27-37 the speaker uses 'son of man' and 'sons of man' when clearly thinking of his own weakness and imperfection. For Aramaic usage, an ancient (eighth century BCE) inscription uses *bar 'nš* to refer to the speaker and his descendants (*Sefire* 3.14-17).[91] And 1QapGen 21.13 instances a case where *br 'nš* is used of an individual, very similar to Dan. 7.13's 'one like *br 'nš*'.[92] These suggest that *bar ʿnaš* would have been quite capable of being used with reference to an individual at the time of Jesus.

Fourth, and not least of importance, the Gospels themselves surely have to count as evidence for first-century usage: the Synoptics were certainly written within the first century and certainly draw on earlier tradition; and, as already noted, the Greek phrase is certainly a translation of the Aramaic idiom. So the question falls back into one of exegesis of the Jesus tradition itself. Should there be sayings using the phrase which most obviously implied some kind of self-reference or were understood as self-references, then that may constitute sufficient evidence in itself that the phrase could have been so used by Jesus and understood accordingly. Stated like that, of course, the argument is in danger of circularity. All will depend on the credibility of any cases adduced.

One other feature cannot be ignored. It is the fact that the double articular form (literally 'the son of the man') is absolutely consistent in the Jesus tradition, whereas we lack examples of the articular form *ben ha'dam* and of the definite *bar ʿnaša*. The former is attested only in 1QS 10.20, where the definite article appears to have been added (supralinear); the latter appears to be totally absent in the Aramaic of the period.[93] There may however be no problem here. Casey maintains that the articular Greek could be an appropriate translation of the indefinite *bar ʿnaš* as much as for the definite *bar ʿnaša*.[94] Alternatively, it may equally be possible that the definite usage *bar ʿnaša* was a peculiarity of Jesus' own style, a way of particularizing the more generic/general or indefinite sense (in effect, 'that son of man').[95]

---

91. Casey, 'General, Generic and Indefinite' 22-23.

92. See further Casey, *Aramaic Sources* 36-38; Owen and Shepherd attempt to minimize the sense and significance of these Aramaic examples ('Son of Man' 114-20).

93. Dalman, *Words* 238; Owen and Shepherd, 'Son of Man' 121.

94. Casey, 'General, Generic and Indefinite' 27-36; ; also 'Idiom and Translation: Some Aspects of the Son of Man Problem', *NTS* 41 (1995) 164-82 (here 170-78); also *Aramaic Sources* 118-21 (responding to D. Burkett, 'The Nontitular Son of Man: A History and Critique', *NTS* 40 [1994] 504-21, slightly modified in his *Son of Man Debate* ch. 8).

95. In partial response to C. F. D. Moule, 'Neglected Features in the Problem of "the Son of Man"', in J. Gnilka, ed., *Neues Testament und Kirche,* R. Schnackenburg FS (Freiburg: Herder, 1974) 413-28; also *The Origin of Christology* (Cambridge: Cambridge University,

b. An Apocalyptic Root

One of the very few instances of the Aramaic singular *bar* ʿ*naš* (without the final -*a* which is equivalent to the definite article) prior to the time of Jesus is Dan. 7.13. It is part of one (or two) of Daniel's great visions (7.9-14):

> [9]As I watched, thrones were set in place, and one that was Ancient of Days took his seat; his clothing was white as snow, and the hair of his head like pure wool; his throne was fiery flames, and its wheels were burning fire. [10]A stream of fire issued and came forth from before him; a thousand thousand served him, and ten thousand times ten thousand stood before him; the court sat in judgment, and the books were opened. . . . [13]As I watched in the night visions, behold, with the clouds of heaven there came one like a son of man, and he came to the Ancient of Days and was presented before him. [14]To him was given dominion and glory and kingdom, that all peoples, nations and languages should serve him; his dominion is an everlasting dominion, which shall not pass away, and his kingdom one that shall not be destroyed.

The second (part of the) vision seems to be a continuation of an adapted creation myth. In the original myth the beasts of sea, air, and land are created, and then man (human being) as the climax of creation (Gen. 1.20-27); man's supremacy is indicated by his being given dominion over the beasts (1.28), and the power to name them (2.19-20). In Daniel 7 the sequence is the same: four beast-like creatures appear from the sea (7.2-8), and finally a man-like figure appears (7.13);[96] dominion is taken from them and given to him (7.12, 14). In the interpretation of the vision(s) the beasts are identified as four kings or kingdoms, and the manlike figure is identified with 'the saints of the Most High' (7.17-18, 23-27). The implication is clear: that as 'man' = the human being was climax to creation and given dominion over the rest of creation, so Israel was the climax of God's universal purpose and would be given dominion over all other nations.[97]

1977) 11-22; also '"The Son of Man": Some of the Facts', *NTS* 41 (1995) 277-79 ('the [well-known, Danielic] Son of Man'). Cf. Lindars, *Jesus Son of Man* 24-27.

96. The preposition *k*- ('like') is used for various elements of the visions to denote not the reality (the beasts are all bizarre), but something like the reality of a lion, human stance, a leopard, human eyes, a man (Hampel, *Menschensohn* 29). T. B. Slater, 'One like a Son of Man in First-Century CE Judaism', *NTS* 41 (1995) 183-98, mistakes the function of the *k-:* it does not denote 'another type of being'; it simply indicates the unclarity/ambiguity of what is seen in the vision.

97. This aspect of the passage is strangely neglected by discussions of the religio-historical background of the Daniel 7 imagery, though it does not preempt these discussions, otherwise well reviewed by J. J. Collins, *Daniel* (Hermeneia; Minneapolis: Fortress, 1993) 280-94; but cf. A. Lacocque, 'Allusions to Creation in Daniel 7', in J. J. Collins and P. W. Flint, eds., *The Book of Daniel: Composition and Reception* (2 vols.; Leiden: Brill, 2001) 1.114-31.

The long-running debate on who the 'one like a son of man' was intended to refer to in the original text continues to rumble on. The current main alternatives are a heavenly (angelic) representative of Israel ('the saints of the Most High') or simply a symbolic representation of Israel.[98] Either way the overall point seems to be clear enough: Daniel 7 is a piece of propaganda on Israel's behalf in the context of Judea's oppression by its Syrian overlords.[99]

As is well known, this vision became very influential in Jewish apocalyptic thinking. Its influence is most evident in the *Similitudes of Enoch,* a section of what is now known as *1 Enoch* (*1 En.* 37–71),[100] and in *4 Ezra* 13.[101] In these, Daniel's manlike figure is clearly identified as a particular individual, 'the Elect One' in the *Similitudes,*[102] a particular 'man' in *4 Ezra.*[103] In this case the issue is whether the *Similitudes* and *4 Ezra* provide evidence of the way Daniel's vision had *already* been interpreted at the time of Jesus. Alternatively expressed, the issue is whether there was by the beginning of the first century CE a clear concept of and belief regarding the Son of Man, a heavenly figure, expected to exercise final judgment in favour of Israel over Israel's enemies. Particularly in dispute is the dating of the *Similitudes.* The assumption behind much German scholarship on the subject has been that they were written during the decades before Jesus.[104]

---

98. See again the review in Collins, *Daniel* 304-10 (particularly 309-10). But is it really implicit in Daniel's vision that the 'one like a son of man' was also God's Son (as argued particularly by Moule, *Origin* 25-26; and S. Kim, *"The 'Son of Man' " as the Son of God* [WUNT 30; Tübingen: Mohr-Siebeck, 1983])? Kim argues on the unprecedented ground that the representative/head of the saints of the Most High (= the sons of God) would be the Son of God (but see nn. 12-13 above), and can cite only the rather obscure 4Q246 in support (see above, n. 15), though with support now from Collins (see further below, n. 109).

99. There is a large-scale consensus that Daniel is a product of the Maccabean period and that Daniel 7 reflects the crisis occasioned by the persecution of Antiochus Epiphanes in the period 175-167 BCE.

100. *1 En.* 46.1-3: 'And there I saw one who had a head of days, and his head was white like wool; and with him there was another, whose face had the appearance of a man, and his face was full of grace, like one of the holy angels. And I asked one of the holy angels . . . about that Son of Man, who he was, and whence he was, and why he went with the Head of Days. And he answered me and said to me, This is the Son of Man who has righteousness . . .' (Knibb).

101. *4 Ezra* 13.1-3: 'After seven days I dreamed a dream in the night: and behold, a wind arose from the sea and stirred up all its waves. And I looked, and behold, this wind made something like the figure of a man come up out of the heart of the sea. And I looked, and behold, that man flew with the clouds of heaven . . .' (*OTP*).

102. For detail see Caragounis, *Son of Man* 101-10.

103. See further J. J. Collins, 'The Son of Man in First-Century Judaism', *NTS* 38 (1992) 448-66; also *Daniel* 79-84; K. Koch, 'Messias und Menschensohn. Die zweistufige Messianologie der jüngeren Apokalyptik', *JBTh* 8, *Der Messias* (1993) 73-102.

104. See below, §16.3c(2). With the allusion to the Parthians and Medes in 56.5 suggest-

But the absence of the *Similitudes* from the Dead Sea Scrolls despite the popularity of the Enoch corpus at Qumran[105] leaves a question mark over the existence of the *Similitudes* much before the destruction of Qumran in 68 CE.[106] So there is a substantial possibility that both the *Similitudes* and *4 Ezra* postdate Jesus' mission by some decades.[107]

Of course the ideas in both documents could predate the publication of these documents by some decades.[108] In a study focused to such a degree on the oral tradition prior to the written Gospels and their written sources, that possibility is hardly to be excluded. However, both documents introduce their interpretation of Daniel 7 as though they are offering a new interpretation and not referring to something already familiar.[109] And the way they make use of Daniel's vision

---

ing a date sometime after 40-38 BCE, the Synoptic usage itself was taken as alluding to a belief regarding the Son of Man like that in the Similitudes, and thus closed the circle of reasoning; Caragounis continues round the same circle (*Son of Man* 89-93).

105. The point is ignored by Collins in his 'Son of Man' 451-52.

106. For discussion of the data see my *Christology* 76-77 with notes. The debate on the dating of the *Similitudes* was summarized by J. H. Charlesworth, *The Old Testament Pseudepigrapha and the New Testament* (SNTSMS 54; Cambridge: Cambridge University, 1985) 108-10; see also Burkett, *Son of Man Debate* 70-73. More recent discussion has brought no advances to the debate. Both Hengel, *Studies* 105, and Hampel, *Menschensohn* 41 n. 2, reflect the indeterminacy of the data.

107. There is no dispute that *4 Ezra* was written after the destruction of Jerusalem (70 CE).

108. This is the argument developed most fully in recent years by Horbury, 'Messianic Association'; see also his *Messianism* 64-108.

109. See the quotations in nn. 100 and 101 above. So also Perrin, *Rediscovering* 165-66, 172-73. *Pace* Horbury, 'Messianic Association' 41, it is a tendentious interpretation to claim that in these sources 'the messianic interpretation is assumed without argument'. Slater, 'One like a Son of Man' 197-98, draws an equally confident conclusion (critiqued by Burkett, *Son of Man Debate* 111-14). Collins expresses himself more carefully: 'The manner in which he is introduced [in the *Similitudes*] does not presuppose that Son of Man is a well-known title'; 'they offer no reason to think that this figure was known independently of Daniel'; 'the vision [of *4 Ezra*] cannot be taken as evidence for a "Son of Man" concept independent of Daniel 7'; but Collins finally concludes that the correspondences between *4 Ezra* and the *Similitudes* 'point to common assumptions about the interpretation of Daniel 7 in first century Judaism' ('Son of Man' 452, 459, 462, 465-66; similarly *Scepter and Star* 177 and 185, contrasted with conclusions on 182, 188). So both texts show that an allusion to Daniel's vision would have been readily recognized; there is no evidence that Daniel's vision had already generated something like a 'Son of Man' theology independent of the three texts in view; and yet we can deduce 'common assumptions about the interpretation of Daniel 7' prior to and independent of the *Similitudes* and *4 Ezra*. Hmmm! In *Daniel* 77-79 and *Scepter and Star* 154-72, Collins draws in 4Q246 (see above, n. 15) and suggests that 'the "Son of God" figure may well represent the earliest interpretation, or reinterpretation, of the enigmatic "one like a son of man" in Daniel 7' (*Daniel* 78; similarly *Scepter and Star* 167; cf. Kim above, n. 98); but it is hardly clear that 'the son of God' in 4Q246 is a messianic figure (see again my response to Collins in n. 15 above).

hardly suggests taking over or reference to an established title.[110] So we cannot deduce from the *Similitudes* and *4 Ezra* themselves that *their* interpretation of Daniel's manlike figure was an already established one or even drew upon an established tradition of interpreting Daniel's vision.[111] In fact, there is a third apocalypse which interprets Dan. 7.13 and which does so as though for the first time, namely the Apocalypse of John (Revelation).[112] This suggests an alternative scenario, where, *inter alia,* the crisis building to the first Jewish revolt (very like the circumstances which produced Daniel 7) and the trauma of its catastrophic failure excited renewed apocalyptic fervour in which Daniel's vision became a focus and stimulus for fresh speculation, producing in turn the distinctive but not dis-

110. In the *Similtudes,* following the initial identification of the one who 'had the appearance of a man', the reference is characteristically to 'that Son of Man' — that is, a reference back to the figure identified in 46.1-3, not any indication of an established title (Casey, *Son of Man* 99-102). Moreover, the fact that three different Ethiopic expressions are used for 'son of man' in the *Similitudes* suggests attempts at an innovative allusion to Daniel's vision (by using translation variants) rather than the evocation of an established title (Casey 101-102). Hare notes U. B. Müller's observation (*Messias und Menschensohn in jüdischen Apokalypsen und in der Offenbarung des Johannes* [Gütersloh: Mohn, 1972] 41, that 'when "the Son of man" is introduced by way of allusion to Dan. 7:13, it is not a known figure who is merged with the Elect One previously depicted; "the Son of man" is a cipher requiring interpretation' (*Son of Man* 13). 'The writer of the Similitudes did not just borrow; he transformed' (J. Vanderkam, 'Righteous One, Messiah, Chosen One, and the Son of Man in 1 Enoch 37–71', in Charlesworth, ed., *Messiah* 169-91, here 188). Likewise, the fact that *4 Ezra* simply speaks of a 'man' (rather than 'son of man') strongly implies that the Aramaic idiom was still well known at the time of writing, and that Dan. 7.13 was recognized as a case in point (cf. Casey 124-26). Cf. also Stone, *Fourth Ezra:* 'It is important to observe that even if "the man" in the dream was the traditional "Son of man", the figure seems to have needed interpretation for the author or his readers. Moreover, the author of *4 Ezra* has shorn this figure of all of its particular characteristics in the interpretation and treated it as a symbol. This would be inconceivable if the "Son of man" concept was readily recognizable to him and his readers' (211).

111. Equally with Akiba's reported opinion regarding the second throne of Dan. 7.9 (see below, n. 190): it is more likely that it is remembered as the first time this view was expressed within rabbinic Judaism rather than providing an indication of an earlier well established view. Nor should we assume that the vision of Moses' heavenly enthronement, as in *Ezekiel the Tragedian* 68-89, necessarily evoked or alluded to Daniel 7 (where the enthronement of the manlike figure is at best implied), when other texts envisage the enthronement of great heroes of the past — e.g., Adam and Abel (*T. Abr.* 11), Job (*T. Job* 33.3), the righteous (*Apoc. El.* 1.8) — without any dependence on Daniel 7 (*pace* Horbury, 'Messianic Association' 38, 42-43, 45-47); Collins makes no suggestion of a link between *Ezekiel the Tragedian* and Daniel 7 (*Scepter and Star* 144-45). In further texts where Horbury argues that 'man' was already a recognized messianic title (48-52), 'man' is a referent, not a title.

112. Rev. 1.7, 13; 14.14. These allusions ('a son of man') are notably different from the consistent Gospel usage ('the Son of Man') and hardly to be explained as due to the direct influence of the latter.

similar interpretations of Daniel's vision. In each case the hope which the man-like figure of Dan. 7.13 embodied was crystallized in a particular individual — the Son of Man, the Man, Jesus exalted. Here too no clear consensus has emerged. But the range of possibilities should certainly make one cautious about building a thesis which depends on a pre-Jesus dating for the *Similitudes* and the use the *Similitudes* make of Dan. 7.13.[113]

A third issue is when the influence from Daniel's vision first entered the Jesus tradition. That there was such influence is not a matter of dispute. We have already noted the likely influence of the first part of the vision on John the Baptist.[114] More to the point here, there is no doubt that the vision of one like a son of man coming on the clouds influenced the tradition of Jesus' words. The clearest cases are Mark 13.26 pars. and 14.62 pars.:[115]

> Mark 13.26: 'and then they shall see the son of man coming on clouds with much power and glory'.

> Mark 14.62: 'you will see the son of man sitting on the right hand of power and coming on the clouds of heaven'.

These examples certainly indicate an awareness of Daniel's vision on the part of the tradents. But do they indicate an awareness of a Jewish Son of Man expectation such as we find in the *Similitudes of Enoch?* And was the influence of the language of Dan. 7.13 part of the Jesus tradition from the first? Opinions are as varied here as with the other issues and, of course, they criss-cross across the range of issues, so that the total picture becomes very complex and confusing.

In terms of issues posed, not least troublesome is the question of how the two possible roots, philological and apocalyptic, relate to each other. They are so different, as different as human and heavenly! Could it be that both were equally important as roots of the son of man usage in the Jesus tradition? Does either or both go back to Jesus? If only one, which came first? And if both go back to Jesus, are there any indications of how they hung together in his own thinking? Such questions continue to fill not just articles but whole monographs.

---

113. Leivestad believes it to be 'methodologically inexcusable to use . . . the Similitudes as a source for Jewish conceptions at the time of Jesus' (*Jesus* 19-20; see further 153-55).

114. See above, chapter 11 at n. 135.

115. Other references speak of 'the Son of Man coming' (Matt. 10.23; Matt. 24.44/Luke 12.40; Luke 18.8), coming in glory (Mark 8.38 pars.; Matt. 16.28), or coming in glory to judge (Matt. 19.28; 25.31; similarly John 5.22, 27). See further my 'The Danielic Son of Man in the New Testament', in Collins and Flint, eds., *The Book of Daniel* 2.528-49.

c. The Major Options

The possibility of different roots for the son of man usage of the Jesus tradition and the interweaving of the various issues have inevitably given rise to a variety of interpretations of the confusing data.[116]

(1) One line of interpretation goes like this. The philological root is the primary source of Jesus' own usage: Jesus did speak of himself as the 'son of man', equivalent to 'a man like me', 'one'. The influence of Dan. 7.13 is secondary: it entered the Jesus tradition after Easter. The clearest evidence of this is Mark 14.62, where Dan. 7.13 has been amalgamated with Ps. 110.1, since the latter was one of the primary proof-texts in early Christian apologetic.[117] As the first Christians scoured the Scriptures to make sense (in terms of their own sacred writings) of what had happened to Jesus, they lighted on Ps. 110.1; and subsequently Dan. 7.13 was drawn in. In so doing they gave *bar ᵉnaša* a titular sense ('the Son of Man'); and in due course this resulted in the non-titular usage ('the son of man') being transformed likewise into a title.

This view was overwhelmed during the first two-thirds of the twentieth century by the influence of Weiss and Schweitzer. Only with the restatement of Vermes has it regained prominence,[118] winning substantial support among English-speaking scholars.[119] It is also the view strongly promoted within the Jesus Seminar, including Borg and Crossan.[120]

(2) A second line of interpretation goes like this. The eschatological root is primary. Jesus was dependent on already current apocalyptic reflections on Dan. 7.13, in which the 'one like a son of man' was already understood as a heavenly figure. Jesus referred to this figure in expressing his confidence that God would vindicate his mission and his words — 'the Son of Man' as a heavenly A. N.

---

116. For a similar analysis and much fuller documentation see Burkett, *Son of Man Debate* 43-56.

117. Influential has been N. Perrin, 'Mark 14.62: The End Product of a Christian Pesher Tradition?', *NTS* 12 (1965-66) 150-55, reprinted with a postscript in *A Modern Pilgrimage in New Testament Christology* (Philadelphia: Fortress, 1974) 1-22; also *Rediscovering* 175-81.

118. Vermes, *Jesus the Jew* ch. 7.

119. Apart from Casey and Lindars, already documented, note particularly R. Leivestad, 'Exit the Apocalyptic Son of Man', *NTS* 18 (1971-72) 243-67; D. Juel, *Messianic Exegesis: Christological Interpretation of the Old Testament in Early Christianity* (Philadelphia: Fortress, 1988) 151-70; Hare, *Son of Man* (though see above, n. 89). In German scholarship note particularly H. Bietenhard, '"Der Menschensohn" — *ho huios tou anthrōpou*. Sprachliche und religionsgeschichtliche Untersuchungen zu einem Begriff der synoptischen Evangelien', *ANRW* II.25.1 (1982) 265-350 (here 266-313).

120. Borg, *Conflict* 221-27; also *Jesus* 51-53, 84-86; Crossan, *Historical Jesus* 238-59; Funk, *Five Gospels* 4; but Funk is confusing: 'an oblique reference to himself'; 'undoubtedly referred to any human being' (Funk, *Honest* 91, 210).

Other. The key text here is Luke 12.8, where a distinction between Jesus and the Son of Man seems to be clearly implied. Such a distinction would not have been introduced after Easter. On the contrary, it was Easter which convinced the first Christians that the Son of Man to whom Jesus looked was none other than Jesus himself.[121] So this eschatological reference must be primary, with the other Son of Man sayings a reflection of this basic faith assertion as the first Christians meditated on Jesus' mission and death.

This was the dominant view in the first two-thirds of the twentieth century, when German scholarship still set the agenda for NT scholarship at large,[122] and it retains strong support in German-speaking scholarship.[123]

(3) A third option of looking for some accommodation between the first two options has naturally attracted attention. In particular, coming more from the side of the first option, it has been observed that 'son of man' has the connotation of frailty and weakness. So Jesus could have been referring to himself in conscious awareness of his weakness — 'son of man' denoting 'I as a man', with implications of suffering and ignominy to follow. Add to this the tradition of the suffering righteous, as in Wisdom, who nevertheless held out the hope of being vindicated — a tradition which in fact includes Dan. 7.13-14![124] And suddenly we find that all components of the Son of Man Jesus tradition are present: Jesus used the phrase precisely to indicate both his expectation of suffering and his confidence in vindication. Here the Passion predictions come immediately to the fore.[125] The line of interpretation proved very attractive to English-speaking scholarship as the main alternative to the dominant German view.[126]

---

121. The exegesis of Tödt, *Son of Man* 42, 55-60, and Hahn, *Hoheitstitel* 24-26, 32-42, 457-58 (*Titles* 22-23, 28-34) was particularly influential, but Bultmann had already made the point (*History* 112).

122. See also Bornkamm, *Jesus of Nazareth* 176-77, 229-31; Fuller, *Foundations* 34-43, 122-25; Riches, *Jesus* 176-78; in modified form by A. Yarbro Collins, 'The Influence of Daniel on the New Testament', in Collins, *Daniel* 90-112.

123. Merklein, *Jesu Botschaft* 155-65; Gnilka, *Jesus* 249-50, 258-62; Becker, *Jesus* 200-201, 210-11; Vögtle, *Gretchenfrage,* regards Luke 12.8-9 as the key to clarifying the Son of Man problem; Strecker, *Theology* 257-58; also Schillebeeckx, *Jesus* 459-72. But note Bietenhard's robust response ('Der Menschensohn' 313-46); O. Hofius also vigorously disputes that 'the Son of Man' was already a messianic title ('Ist Jesus der Messias? Thesen', *JBTh* 8, *Der Messias* [1993] 103-29 [here 110-11, 113, 118-19); cf. also Hengel's criticism at this point ('Jesus as Messianic Teacher' 105). 'The point of Luke 12.8-9 . . . lies not in the distinction between Jesus and the coming Son of Man, but precisely in their belonging-togetherness (*Zusammengehörigkeit*)' (Stuhlmacher, *Biblische Theologie* 1.122).

124. This line of interpretation is particularly associated with E. Schweizer, 'Der Menschensohn (Zur eschatologischen Erwartung Jesu)', *ZNW* 50 (1959) 185-209, reprinted in *Neotestamentica* (Zürich: Zwingli, 1963) 56-84; also *Erniedrigung* 33-52 (= *Lordship* 44-45).

125. Mark 8.31 pars.; 9.31 pars.; 10.33-34 pars.; I delay discussion of them till §17.4c.

126. I. H. Marshall, 'The Synoptic Son of Man Sayings in Recent Discussion', *NTS* 12

Coming more from the side of the second option, a mediating middle interpretation has suggested that 'the Son of Man' was not someone other than Jesus but Jesus' way of indicating what he expected his future role to be. To put the point in oversimplified terms, 'the Son of Man' was what Jesus expected to become![127]

(4) Not entirely unexpectedly, a fourth option has been strongly canvassed. If the third option argues in effect that *both* usages (philological and apocalyptic) go back to Jesus, the fourth argues that *neither* goes back to Jesus; none of the son of man/Son of Man sayings are authentic. Here the observation initially made by Philipp Vielhauer has been especially influential.[128] Vielhauer noted that in the earliest strata of the Jesus tradition 'kingdom of God' and 'Son of Man' belong to *separate* strands. Since, then, the kingdom motif is indisputably authentic Jesus' usage, the Son of Man motif must have been drawn in later. The basic development in the tradition postulated by the second line of interpretation is accepted (the whole motif began with the influence of Dan. 7.13), with the difference that the development is thought to have begun only after Easter. This was an earlier flight from apocalyptic,[129] equivalent to that which now characterizes the neo-Liberal questers.[130] The argument is much the same: the Jesus who proclaimed the presentness of God's reign could not also have proclaimed a future coming; all future-imminent eschatology is the work of the earliest Christians' eschatological enthusiasm, and that includes the influence of Dan. 7.13.[131]

(1965-66) 327-51, reprinted in *Jesus the Saviour* 73-99; M. D. Hooker, *The Son of Man in Mark* (London: SPCK, 1967) 182-95; Moule, *Origin* 11-22; J. Bowker, 'The Son of Man', *JTS* 28 (1977) 19-48; Witherington, *Christology* 233-61 (particularly 243). Also Cullmann, *Christology* particularly 158-64; de Jonge, *Jesus* 51-54; Stuhlmacher, *Biblische Theologie* 1.122-23. Caragounis reviews the whole Synoptic tradition under the heading 'The Influence of Daniel's "SM" upon the SM in the Teaching of Jesus' (*Son of Man* 168-243).

127. So already Weiss, *Proclamation* 115 n. 83, 119-21; Schweitzer, *Quest*[2] 230-32. Subsequently R. H. Fuller, *The Mission and Achievement of Jesus* (London: SCM, 1954) 102-103, 107-108 (but Fuller revised his views — see above, n. 122); A. J. B. Higgins, *Jesus and the Son of Man* (London: Lutterworth, 1964) 185-95; also *The Son of Man in the Teaching of Jesus* (SNTSMS 39; Cambridge: Cambridge University, 1980) particularly 80-84; Jeremias, *Proclamation* 272-76; Rowland, *Christian Origins* 185-86; a further variation in Hampel, *Menschensohn* (bar ᵉnaša as 'cipher for his function as *Messias designatus*', 164); Flusser, *Jesus* 131; Theissen and Merz, *Historical Jesus* 551-52; C. M. Tuckett, 'The Son of Man and Daniel 7: Q and Jesus', in Lindemann, ed., *Sayings Source Q* 371-94 (here 389-94).

128. P. Vielhauer, 'Gottesreich und Menschensohn in der Verkündigung Jesu' (1957), *Aufsätze zum Neuen Testament* (München: Kaiser, 1965) 51-79.

129. Pointed out by K. Koch, *Ratlos vor der Apokalyptik,* the note of bewilderment *(ratlos)* being lost in the ET *The Rediscovery of Apocalyptic* (London: SCM, 1972).

130. See above, §4.7.

131. Influential here also was the argument of E. Käsemann, 'The Beginnings of Christian Theology' (1960), *New Testament Questions of Today* (London: SCM, 1969) 82-107 (here

With issues so complex and so tangled can there be much hope for a consensus of any breadth?

16.4. Son of Man: The Evidence

In terms of a tradition-historical analysis a number of observations can be made with varying degrees of confidence, but all substantial.

a. A Phrase Used by Jesus

The phrase occurs 86 times in the NT: 69 in the Synoptic Gospels, 13 in John's Gospel, and only 4 times elsewhere. Of these four, three are quotations from or allusions to OT passages,[132] each of them referring to 'a son of man' and showing no awareness of the consistent articular usage of the Gospels ('the Son of Man'). Only one titular usage ('the Son of Man') appears outside the Gospels — in Stephen's vision in Acts 7.56. This is a striking fact: the phrase belongs almost exclusively to the Gospels.

Even more striking is the fact that in all four Gospels the phrase appears in effect *only* on the lips of Jesus.[133] Jesus is never addressed as 'Son of Man' or confessed as 'the Son of Man' in the narratives, nor is he subsequently worshipped as 'the Son of Man' in the churches' worship.[134] The contrast at this point with other titles for Jesus is marked.[135]

101-105); see also Conzelmann, *Outline* 131-37; Perrin, *Rediscovering* 173-99; *Modern Pilgrimage* 45; Becker, *Jesus* 201 n. 122 cites P. Hoffmann, 'Jesus versus Menschensohn', in L. Oberlinner and P. Fiedler, eds., *Salz der Erde — Licht der Welt*, A. Vögtle FS (Stuttgart: KBW, 1991) 165-202, and Vögtle's own *Gretchenfrage*, as providing an impressive defence of the view.

132. Heb. 2.6 = Ps. 8.4; Rev. 1.13 and 14.14 alluding to Dan. 7.13.

133. John 12.34 is only an apparent exception.

134. It is doubtful whether we can identify a Son of Man christology anywhere in Paul (see my *Christology* 90-91): the claim that Paul 'was clearly acquainted with the title but refrained from using it' (Caragounis, *Son of Man* 164) confuses Adam christology with Son of Man christology. Becker simply assumes that any talk of Jesus coming from heaven (1 Cor. 16.22; 1 Thess. 1.9-10; 4.13-18) is a Son of Man christology which thus 'clearly can be documented' as 'widespread in the earliest post-Easter christological development' (*Jesus of Nazareth* 200).

135. 'We know that the identification of Jesus with other eschatological figures was canvassed and queried (Mark 6.15 pars.; 8.28 pars.; Matt. 11.3 par.), and we have clear credal or evangelistic affirmations identifying Jesus as the Messiah, the prophet like Moses, the Son of God (e.g., Mark 8.29; Acts 3.22-23; 9.20) — just as we have in 1 Enoch 71.14 precisely the sort

In short, we are confronted with two clear features. First, 'the Son of Man' hardly appears in early christology as a feature independent of the Gospel usage. Second, the phrase is thoroughly integrated into the Jesus tradition. It is very hard to credit, therefore, that the phrase might have originated outside the Jesus tradition and been introduced to the Jesus tradition only after Easter. To hypothesize that a way of thinking about Jesus was *so significant* that it could be intruded thoroughly into the Jesus tradition, and yet have been *so insignificant* as to leave virtually no other trace is to push against the manifest weight of the evidence.[136] Much the most obvious deduction is that the usage within the Jesus tradition originated there. Moreover, the tradition remembers the usage as peculiar to Jesus, 'the son of man' as a characteristic Jesus usage. Here again the deduction is obvious: *it was remembered as a speech usage distinctive of Jesus because that is precisely what it was.*[137] It was Jesus who, if we may put it so, introduced 'the son of man' phrase into the Jesus tradition. The evidence could hardly point more plainly to that conclusion.

What of Vielhauer's famous argument: that the failure of the two principal motifs of the Jesus tradition (kingdom of God, son of man) to intertwine suggests that one (Son of Man) was inserted later (above, n. 128)? The argument is hardly so persuasive as first appears. For the feature is just as puzzling on the hypothesis that 'the Son of Man' was introduced to the tradition some time after it had been in circulation. Performers/tradents who felt free to introduce 'the Son of Man' as thoroughly as they did would hardly have been so inhibited as to fail to intertwine the new motif with the tradition's core motif (kingdom of God). A simpler explanation is that the two motifs did not naturally lie together: where 'the son of man' implied only weakness and suffering, kingdom was hardly an obvious companion; and where 'the son of man' contained any allusion to Dan. 7.13 it also thereby included an allusion to dominion and kingship, making further reference to the kingdom of God redundant.[138] Some such explanation must be offered, whatever the son of man's entry-point into the Jesus tradition.

This is not to say that all son of man sayings can forthwith be traced back to Jesus. For there are also clear indications of the tradition being reworked, of interpretative elaboration, of performative variation, of editorial insertion, where the son of man reference is strictly speaking to be attributed to the tradent rather

---

of identification that presupposes a recognized Son of Man concept ("You are the Son of Man . . .") which we do *not* find in the Christian tradition' (Dunn, *Christology* 85).

136. Hare, e.g., notes the illogicality of postulating a Greek-speaking church which developed the son of man traditions so thoroughly, yet 'found the title of no value whatsoever for liturgy and confession' (*Son of Man* 234).

137. Similarly, e.g., Jeremias, *Proclamation* 266.

138. Cf. Marshall, *Jesus* 81-83.

than to Jesus.[139] But all the more significant in these cases is the fact that this reworking was *confined* within the Jesus tradition and was *conformed* to the pattern of a phrase found only on Jesus' lips. This surely suggests that the pattern itself was already so firmly fixed within the tradition, from the first, and was from the first so massively consistent, that tradents and Evangelists naturally maintained the form in their own performance and editing.

b. A Man Like Me

In the light of this first conclusion, the key question ceases to be whether it was linguistically possible for Jesus to have spoken of 'the Son of Man'. Rather, given that he *did* so speak, the question is how he would have been understood. The evidence already reviewed indicates that such a usage would have been meaningful in terms of the traditional Semitic idiom, including the possibility of an individual or implied self-reference.[140] Here we must recall just how common the idiom was and how it could be used in the singular with the implication that the 'man' indicated shared the typical weaknesses of the human species; the polite English idiom 'one' is sufficiently close to carry the connotation which we observed earlier in the use of *ben 'adam*.[141] This also means that we need to disabuse ourselves of any assumption that the phrase itself inevitably carried an allusion to Dan. 7.13. The Daniel reference was itself a specific use of the idiom and hardly 'took over' the whole idiom. Notwithstanding Dan. 7.13, the idiomatic 'son of man' still denoted humankind as a whole or in its individual typicality.

The key data within the Jesus tradition are the two early references to 'the son of man' in Mark (Mark 2.10, 28), the intriguing Mark/Q saying on the unforgiveable sin (Mark 3.28-29/Matt. 12.31-32/Luke 12.10/*GTh* 44), the Q 'nowhere to lay his head' saying (Matt. 8.20/Luke 9.58/*GTh* 86), the 'friend of sinners' saying (Matt. 11.18-19/Luke 7.33-34),[142] and the several cases where 'the son of man' is equivalent to 'I' in the parallel tradition. For convenience I repeat elements of previous fuller citations.

(1) Mark 2.10 pars.[143]

---

139. Matt. 16.28; see also Matt. 26.2/Mark 14.1; Matt. 24.30a added to Mark 13.26.

140. It is worth asking how Paul would have expressed himself had he written 2 Cor. 12.2 in Aramaic — 'I knew a man *(anthrōpos = bar ʿnaš?)* in Christ . . .' — since the large consensus is that Paul was speaking of himself.

141. See above, nn. 83-85.

142. These passages were already identified by Bultmann as resulting from a misunderstanding of the Aramaic idiom (*Theology* 1.30).

143. Mark 2.1-12 is cited in full in §15.7e.

Matt. 9.6-8	Mark 2.10-12	Luke 5.24-26

6 'But that you may know that the Son of Man has authority on earth to forgive sins' — he then said to the paralytic,
     'Rise, take up your bed and go to your home'. 7 And he rose
 	
 and went to his home.
 8 When the crowds saw it, they were filled with awe, and they glorified God, who had given such authority to men.
	10 'But that you may know that the Son of Man has authority on earth to forgive sins'—he said to the paralytic— 11 'I say to you, rise, take up your pallet and go to your home'. 12 And he rose, and immediately took up the pallet
	     and went out before them all; so that they were all amazed and glorified God,
	     saying, 'We never saw anything like this!'
		24 'But that you may know that the Son of Man has authority on earth to forgive sins'—he said to the one who was paralyzed— 'I say to you, rise and take up your bed and go to your home'. 25 Immediately he stood up before them, took what he had been lying on, and went to his home, glorifying God. 26 Amazement seized all of them, and they glorified God and were filled with awe, saying, 'We have seen strange things today'.

Of interest here is the fact that the Son of Man saying belongs to the core of the story, together with the following command to the paralytic. Quite possibly it was the stability of the core, encasing the awkwardness of the turn to the paralytic,[144] which ensured that that awkward element was retained in the retellings of the story. In the form as thus 'fixed' and maintained, 'the Son of Man' has titular force, presumably in part at least because in context the self-reference to Jesus himself is so clear. At the same time it should be noted that the auditors in the narrative express no surprise and take no offence at the usage; this presumably counts at least somewhat against the thesis that 'the (heavenly) Son of Man' was a well-known figure in first-century Jewish expectation.[145] Nor can we assume, to repeat the point, that the phrase in and of itself carried an allusion to the Danielic manlike figure.[146] It may also be significant that Matthew's conclusion (ignoring Mark's typical choral ending) has the crowd glorifying God (so also Mark/Luke) that he 'had given such authority to men *(tois anthrōpois)*' (Matt. 9.8). Does this reflect awareness (by the most Jewish of the Synoptic Evangelists) that the strange Greek *ho huios tou anthrōpou* (9.6) originally referred to man (humankind)? In which case, Matthew's tradition preserves awareness of an earlier sense of 'the son of man', even though it had been lost in the Markan ver-

---

144. See Guelich, *Mark* 81-83 and Hampel, *Menschensohn* 189-97 for discussion of the integrity of the narrative. Caragounis robustly disputes the suggestion of awkwardness in the Greek (*Son of Man* 180-87).

145. Cf. Casey, *Son of Man* 159-61, who offers an Aramaic reconstruction (160).

146. Hooker, *Son of Man* 89-93, further 178-82, 190-95 (taking up from Tödt, *Son of Man* 126-30), focuses on the Danielic overtones of the one like a son of man being given 'authority' (also Caragounis, *Son of Man* 188-90; Witherington, *Christology* 246-47); but in the pericope the surprise is only at the authority claimed, not at any claim to be the authorized Son of Man (see further Hare, *Son of Man* 185-90). Here as elsewhere, Hampel simply applies his thesis — *bar* ᵉ*naša* as a cipher bringing to light 'the exclusive and unique consciousness of mission and so messianic self-understanding of Jesus' (*Menschensohn* 199).

sion of the saying itself (possibly when the Aramaic was put into Greek).[147] Something similar is clearer in the second example. In short, we may tentatively conclude that Jesus was initially remembered as drawing attention to the surprising fact that 'that son of man', 'someone like me' had authority *(exousia)* to pronounce sins forgiven.[148]

(2) Mark 2.28 pars.

Matt. 12.8	Mark 2.27-28	Luke 6.5
8 For <u>the Son of Man is lord of the Sabbath</u>.	27 Then he said to them, 'The Sabbath was made for man, and not man for the Sabbath; 28 so <u>the Son of Man is lord</u> even <u>of the Sabbath</u>'.	5 Then he said to them, '<u>The Son of Man is lord of the Sabbath</u>'.

Here the point of interest is the climax of Mark's account of the Sabbath controversy over plucking the grain (Mark 2.23-28).[149] If we assume for the moment that underlying 'the Son of Man' (2.28) lies the Aramaic *bar ᵉnaša,* 'the son of man', then we are confronted with a variation on the regular parallelism in Jewish writing between 'man' and 'son of man' (2.27-28).[150] This suggests that the saying would have been heard initially in these terms: the Sabbath was made for man; therefore the son of man is lord of the Sabbath. In other words, in response to criticism of his disciples, Jesus was remembered as defending their action as appropriate to the lordship which God had given to humankind (or Israel) over all his creation.[151] It would appear that by the time the tradition reached Mark the more generic 'son of man' had been taken as a more exclusively personal reference and given titular significance ('the Son of Man').[152] In turn, Matthew and Luke, confronted with Mark's now not quite so coherent sequence (2.27-28), presumably chose (independently?) to omit the now redundant 2.27 and left the

147. Cf. also Lindars, *Jesus Son of Man* 44-47, though he doubts Matthew's awareness of the idiom since he normally understands the Son of Man as an exclusive self-reference on Jesus' part (46).

148. Colpe, *TDNT* 8.430-31 defends Wellhausen's often criticized view at this point (n. 236). See further below §17.2b.

149. Cited above, §14.4a.

150. As in Ps. 8.4, cited above at n. 83.

151. See particularly Casey, *Aramaic Sources* 158-66. The case here is regularly seen as much stronger than with Mark 2.10; see, e.g., Pesch, *Markusevangelium* 1.185-86; Guelich, *Mark* 125-27 (with earlier bibliography and debate); Hampel, *Menschensohn* 202-203; Crossan, *Historical Jesus* 257. But to push too strongly for an exclusively generic sense (as Hampel and Crossan do) ignores the significance of the articular form — 'that son of man'.

152. Hooker is justified in recognizing that 'the Son of man is again portrayed as one who possesses authority . . . beyond that exercised by any ordinary individual' (*Son of Man* 99) — at the level/stage of Mark's performance of the tradition.

climactic apophthegm with an exclusively christological focus.[153] But this was in effect only an extension of the original, that what was true of (eschatological?) humankind in general was especially true of Jesus (and his disciples).[154] Here again we can well envisage that the translation of the tradition into Greek, where the Aramaic idiom would have been lost to view, was a major factor.

(3) Mark 3.28-29 pars.

Matt. 12.31-32	Mark 3.28-29	Luke 12.10	GTh 44
31 Therefore I tell you, every sin and blasphemy will be forgiven to men,	28 Truly I tell you, everything will be forgiven to the sons of men, whatever their sins and blasphemies whatever they blaspheme;		Jesus said: He who blasphemes against the Father will be forgiven,
but blasphemy against the Spirit will not be forgiven.			
32 And whoever speaks a word against the Son of Man it will be forgiven to him, but whoever speaks against the Holy Spirit, it will not be forgiven to him, either in this age or in the age to come.	29 but whoever blasphemes against the Holy Spirit has no forgiveness for ever, but is guilty of an eternal sin.	10 And everyone who speaks a word against the Son of Man it will be forgiven to him; but to the one who blasphemes against the Holy Spirit will not be forgiven.	and he who blasphemes against the Son will be forgiven, but he who blasphemes against the Holy Spirit will not be forgiven, either on earth or in heaven.

In terms of tradition history this is one of the most interesting examples in the Gospels. In all four cases a saying is recalled which contrasts two kinds of sins/blasphemies: those which may be forgiven and blasphemy/speaking against the Holy Spirit, which will not be forgiven. The interest begins with the fact that the first half of the saying seems to have been preserved in at least two different versions: Mark speaks of unspecified sins/blasphemies, Matthew/ Luke (= Q) in contrast envisages speaking against the Son of Man, and *Thomas* has a further variation — blasphemies against (the Father and) the Son. The interest quickens when we note that in Mark the first half speaks of sins/blasphemies being forgiven to 'the sons of men', a usage ('sons of men') unparalleled in the Gospels.

It could be, of course, that Jesus was remembered as saying two different

153. Becker, *Jesus* 299; Ebner, *Jesus* 176-79; cf. Funk, *Five Gospels* 49; in contrast, Lüdemann, *Jesus* 19-20, shows little awareness of the ambiguities of the Aramaic idiom.

154. In this case Lindars fails to show sufficient sensitivity to the possible tradition history behind Mark's version (*Jesus Son of Man* 102-106).

things on different occasions, and in the tradition the two versions have become somewhat assimilated. But the more straightforward explanation of the divergent forms is that underlying each is the same Aramaic saying, using *bar ᵉnaša,* which was taken different ways in reference, probably before translation into Greek, but with the difference consolidated in the transition to Greek. It is not too difficult to envisage such a saying, possibly in the somewhat cryptic form 'All that blasphemes to the *bar ᵉnaša* will be forgiven'.[155] The 'all', *bar ᵉnaša,* and the syntax are ambiguous. The saying could be taken to refer to all (everything) being forgiven to *bar ᵉnaša* (man/men/sons of men/humankind). Or it could be taken to refer to all (everyone) blaspheming against *bar ᵉnaša* being forgiven. In which case it rather looks as though

- Mark has inherited a version of the former possibility (Mark 3.28),[156]
- Q has inherited a form where *bar ᵉnaša* has been taken as a titular self-reference, as in the two cases already considered,
- Matthew, aware of both versions, and of the Aramaic idiom, has simply conflated both to make a double saying, and
- *Thomas* has lost the Son of Man reference altogether but has retained the Q version's basic antithesis.

If then Jesus did utter a *bar ᵉnaša* saying of this form, what did he mean by it? A good question, to which no firm answer is possible. For if I am right, the tradition in its original form was a classic *mašal,* a riddle, as dependent for its meaning on how it was heard as on how it was uttered. And, if I am right, it was heard in two distinctively different ways, whether immediately or in the course of its early re-expression and transmission. I have already suggested that the saying provides a good clue to Jesus' own self-conscious claims to inspiration by the Spirit (§15.7h). Here the point is rather the further indication that Jesus is likely to have used the *bar ᵉnaša* phrase in a more general way (as in Mark 2.28), or perhaps in a deliberately ambiguous way to include a self-reference (as in Mark 2.10). In both the Markan and Q collections of exorcism sayings, of course,[157] the context is one of Jesus' responding to personal attack. And if I am right, the second half of the saying (blasphemy against the Holy Spirit) also had a personal reference, since Jesus' exorcisms as demonstration of

155. For more carefully laid out Aramaic reconstructions see R. Schippers, 'The Son of Man in Matt. 12.32 = Luke 12.10 Compared with Mark 3.28', *Studia Evangelica* IV (1968) 231-35; Colpe, *TDNT* 8.442-43 (followed by Higgins, *Son of Man* 116-17); Lindars, *Jesus Son of Man* 35-37; Marcus, *Mark* 1.275 (modifying Lindars slightly); Davies and Allison, *Matthew* 2.345-46 also think Lindars is close to the truth; cf. Hare, *Son of Man* 264-67.

156. In the same way Ps. 145.3 LXX renders Ps. 146.3's *ben 'adam* as *huioi anthrōpoi.*

157. See above, §12.5d.

the Spirit's power were immediately in view (§15.7h). So a personal reference within a more ambiguous reference is quite likely, but we can hardly be more positive than that.

(4) Matt. 8.20/Luke 9.58/*GTh* 86.[158]

Matt. 8.20	Luke 9.58	GTh 86
And Jesus says to him, 'Foxes have holes, and birds of the air have nests; but the Son of Man has nowhere to lay his head'.	And Jesus said to him, 'Foxes have holes, and birds of the air have nests; but the Son of Man has nowhere to lay his head'.	Jesus said, [Foxes have their holes] and birds have [their] nests, but the Son of Man has nowhere to lay his head (and) to rest.

Thomas clearly knows this tradition; it is the only Son of Man saying in *Thomas*. The contrast indicated is quite conceivable as a general son of man = humankind *mašal:* nature provides an appropriate habitat for creatures like foxes and birds, but human beings *(bar 'ᵉnaša)* require more before they can sleep comfortably.[159] But in the context within which the saying was remembered and circulated (Matt. 8.19-22/Luke 9.57-62), *bar 'ᵉnaša* was obviously taken as a self-reference, that is, as a warning to less than wholly committed would-be disciples.[160] Either way the saying is not untypical of Jesus' use of exaggeration for effect: human beings can live in caves and Jesus could usually expect hospitality during his mission. But, as with Matt. 6.25-34/Luke 12.22-32, he evidently wanted to press home the need for greater, more radical trust in God.[161]

(5) In one other case already cited the most obvious explanation is that an underlying *bar 'ᵉnaša* was used with more directly personal reference: Matt. 11.18-19/Luke 7.33-34.

158. For the context in Q see above, §13.2d.

159. Bultmann, *History* 28. M. Casey, 'The Jackals and the Son of Man (Matt. 8.20/ Luke 9.58)', *JSNT* 23 (1985) 3-22 observes that an underlying Aramaic form would probably have referred to 'places to roost' rather than 'nests', which would make the contrast clearer — and meet the usual response that birds have to build their nests as much as humans their homes (as in Burkett, *Son of Man Debate* 94).

160. See also Colpe, *TDNT* 8.432-33; Lindars, *Jesus Son of Man* 29-31; Hare, *Son of Man* 272-73. The Jesus Seminar found the saying congenial, taking the implication to be that Jesus was a homeless wanderer ('human vagabonds of Jesus' type') (Funk, *Five Gospels* 160-61); cf. Lüdemann, *Jesus* 326.

161. *Pace* Hahn, *Hoheitstitel* 44-45 (*Titles* 36), the saying is perfectly intelligible without postulating a post-Easter christological heightening; similarly Schürmann, *Gottes Reich* 163. Caragounis strains to find allusions to Daniel (*Son of Man* 175-79). Hengel wonders whether behind the saying lies a Wisdom reference — 'the motif of Wisdom homeless upon the earth' (*1 En.* 42.2) — ('Jesus as Messianic Teacher' 92-93).

Matt. 11.18-19	Luke 7.33-34
18 <u>For John</u> came neither <u>eating</u> nor <u>drinking,</u> and they <u>say, 'He has a demon';</u> 19 <u>the Son of Man</u> came <u>eating and drinking, and</u> they say, '<u>Look, a man, a glutton and a drunkard, a friend of tax collectors and sinners!'</u>	33 <u>For John</u> the Baptist has come <u>eating</u> no bread and <u>drinking</u> no wine, <u>and</u> you <u>say, 'He has a demon';</u> 34 <u>the Son of Man</u> has come <u>eating and drinking, and</u> you say, '<u>Look, a man, a glutton and a drunkard, a friend of tax collectors and sinners!'</u>

The presence of 'the son of man' does not constitute an argument against the origin of the saying in Jesus' teaching.[162] On the contrary it strengthens the likelihood that Jesus was remembered as referring to himself in this allusive fashion.[163]

(6) 'The Son of Man' = 'I'. Finally we should note a number of cases where one side of a Synoptic parallel reads 'the son of man', while the other reads 'I'. The most striking examples are Matt. 5.11/Luke 6.22;[164] Matt. 10.32-33/Luke 12.8-9; Mark 8.27/Matt. 16.13; and Mark 10.45/Luke 22.27.

Matt. 5.11	Luke 6.22
<u>Blessed are you when</u> people <u>revile</u> you and persecute you and utter all kinds of evil against you falsely on account of **me**.	<u>Blessed are you when</u> people hate you, and when they exclude you, <u>revile</u> you, and defame you on account of **the Son of Man**.

Matt. 10.32-33	Luke 12.8-9	Rev. 3.5
32 <u>Everyone</u> therefore <u>who acknowledges me before men,</u> **I** also will <u>acknowledge</u> before my Father in heaven; 33 but whoever <u>denies me before men,</u> I also will <u>deny</u> before my Father in heaven.	8 And I tell you, <u>everyone who acknowledges me before men,</u> **the Son of Man** also will acknowledge before the <u>angels</u> of God; 9 but he who <u>denies me before men</u> will be <u>denied</u> before the <u>angels</u> of God.	And **I** will acknowledge his name <u>before my Father</u> and before his angels.

Matt. 16.13	Mark 8.27
Now when <u>Jesus came</u> into the district of Caesarea Philippi, <u>he asked his disciples, saying, 'Who do men say that</u> **the Son of Man** is?'	<u>Jesus came</u> out with his disciples into the villages of Caesarea Philippi; and on the way <u>he asked his disciples, saying</u> to them, '<u>Who do men say that</u> **I** am?'

162. See above, §§12.5c and 13.5 and chapter 15 n. 224.

163. Note the play again on 'son of man', 'man'; Black observes that *anthrōpos* followed by a substantive ('a man, a glutton') is a Semitic idiom (*Aramaic Approach* 106-107). See further Colpe, *TDNT* 8.431-32; Lindars, *Jesus Son of Man* 31-34; Casey, 'General, Generic and Indefinite' 39-40; Hare, *Son of Man* 259-64. Matt. 12.40/Luke 11.30 could serve as another example (Lindars 38-44), but it is not so clear that 'the son of man' was part of the saying as originally recalled (see above, §15.6b[5]).

164. Fuller citation above, §12.4c.

Matt. 20.28	Mark 10.45	Luke 22.27
28 Just as the **Son of Man** came not to be served but to serve.	45 For the **Son of Man** came not to be served but to serve.	But **I** am among you as one who serves.

In each case the most obvious explanation is that an original *bar 'enaša* saying has given rise to the variant versions in Greek.[165] Either each saying was put into Greek by different individuals — one was content to translate literally *(ho huios tou anthrōpou),* and the other recognized the Aramaic idiom and translated the phrase as a personal reference *(emou, egō, me)*[166] — or Matthew, confronted with a *ho huios tou anthrōpou* reference in the first two cases and recognizing the Aramaic idiom, chose to bring out the personal reference implicit in the Aramaic idiom in context, but in the third either knew a variant *bar 'enaša* form or assumed its presence from the implied 'men'/'son of man' play and elected to use the Greek *ho huios tou anthrōpou.*[167] Either way, these 'Son of Man'/'I' parallels provide a strong indication of an awareness somewhere in the transmission of these sayings that the two phrases could be synonymous, and thus also a remembrance of Jesus using *bar 'enaša* as a way of referring to himself.

There is more that needs to be said, especially on the Matt. 10.32-33/Luke 12.8-9 complex.[168] But for the moment we can conclude that there is substantial evidence that Jesus was remembered as using the phrase *bar 'enaša* in an ambiguous or *mašal*-like way. The transition from Aramaic to Greek seems to have occasioned a double development. On the one hand, some translated literally *(ho huios tou anthrōpou)* and thus lost the idiom, while others attempted to translate idiomatically and produced a more explicit self-reference and thus lost the ambiguity. On the other hand, some maintained the sense of a more generic reference to man/men (humankind), although the dominant tendency was to give the phrase a more weighty titular force in reference to Jesus ('the Son of Man'). As for Jesus himself, the implication is that Jesus did indeed use *bar 'enaša* in an ambiguous or *mašal*-like way, including a somewhat modest self-reference, but not as a title. Tradition-historical analysis indicates that this usage was recognized so long as the tradition remained within an Aramaic milieu.

165. Contrast Schürmann, *Gottes Reich* 160-61, who can see only the titular form in post-Easter colours; Hampel, *Menschensohn* 152-58, 212-13, whose grasp of the scope of the *bar 'enaša* idiom is too limited and tendentious (159-64).

166. On the parallel between Rev. 3.5c and Matt. 10.32/Luke 12.8, see A. Yarbro Collins, 'The "Son of Man" Tradition and the Book of Revelation', in Charlesworth, ed., *Messiah* 536-68 (here 559-62).

167. Cf. Davies and Allison, *Matthew* 1.462; 2.216, 617.

168. See below §16.4c(3).

c. Influence of Dan. 7.13

The view that Jesus' use of the phrase would have evoked a current belief regarding the (messianic) Son of Man already developed from the Dan. 7.13 usage has to surmount a huge obstacle from the outset. For within the Jesus tradition the phrase is used again and again without provoking surprise or outrage at an implied evocation of or challenge to a contemporary belief regarding 'the Son of Man'. The one occasion within the Gospel tradition when the phrase appears on other than Jesus' lips is John 12.34, where Jesus' teaching provokes the crowd to ask, 'Who is this "the Son of Man"?' The phrase is evidently thought of as obscure; it did not 'connect' with current beliefs.[169]

What then of the texts where the influence of Dan. 7.13 is most obvious (Mark 13.26 pars. and 14.62 pars.) and of Mark 8.38 pars./Matt.10.32-33/Luke 12.8-9, where an allusion to a contemporary Son of Man expectation is often heard?

(1) Mark 13.26 pars.

Matt. 24.29-31	Mark 13.24-27	Luke 21.25-28
29 Immediately <u>after the suffering</u> of <u>those days</u> <u>the sun will be darkened, and the moon will not give its light,</u>	24 But in <u>those days, after</u> that <u>suffering,</u> <u>the sun will be darkened, and the moon will not give its light,</u>	25 There will be signs in the <u>sun,</u> the <u>moon,</u> and the <u>stars,</u> and on the earth distress among nations confused by the roaring of the sea and the waves. 26 Men will faint from fear and
<u>and the stars will</u> <u>fall from heaven, and the powers of heaven will be shaken.</u> 30 Then the sign of the Son of Man will appear in heaven, and then all the tribes of the earth will mourn, and <u>they will see the Son of Man coming</u> on the <u>clouds</u> of heaven <u>with power and</u> great <u>glory.</u> 31 And <u>he will send out</u> his <u>angels</u> with a loud trumpet call, and they will <u>gather his elect from the four winds,</u> <u>from</u> one <u>end of heaven</u> to the other.	25 <u>and the stars will</u> be <u>falling from heaven, and the powers</u> in the <u>heavens will be shaken.</u> 26 Then <u>they will see the</u> Son of Man coming in clouds <u>with</u> great <u>power and glory.</u> 27 Then <u>he will send out</u> the <u>angels,</u> and <u>gather his elect from the four winds,</u> <u>from</u> the <u>end</u> of the earth to the <u>end of heaven.</u>	foreboding of what is coming upon the world, for <u>the powers</u> of the <u>heavens will be shaken.</u> 27 Then <u>they will see the Son of Man coming</u> in a cloud <u>with power and</u> great <u>glory.</u> 28 Now when these things begin to take place, stand up and raise your heads, because your redemption is drawing near.

Of interest here is the fact that the Son of Man reference, with its clear allusion to Dan. 7.13, seems, once again, to be part of the core tradition. Of course, the core could already express a developed Son of Man christology.[170] But the issue of

---

169. The question is 'Who is this Son of Man?', not simply 'How can you say that the Son of Man must suffer?' (*pace* Horbury, 'Messianic Association' 37).

170. Cf. Lindars, *Jesus Son of Man* 108-10; Hampel, *Menschensohn* 165-67; Funk, *Five Gospels* 112-13; Lüdemann, *Jesus* 91.

whether *Jesus* could or could not have so spoken usually depends more on a prior judgment as to whether Jesus would have used apocalyptic imagery, and as to whether there was a Son of Man expectation to which Jesus could have referred. But the possibility can hardly be excluded that the saying reflects Jesus' own expressed hope for the future, drawing on the imagery of Daniel's vision.[171]

Two other features call for comment. One is that the action envisaged seems to be in heaven, where the cosmic events take place (all three Synoptics), where the sign of the Son of Man appears (Matthew), and from which the Son of Man sends angels (Matthew/Mark). The implication is that the 'coming' is, as in Dan. 7.13, a coming in heaven,[172] though it could also be understood as a coming *from* heaven.[173]

The other is that Matthew's version seems to have added another Son of Man reference (Matt. 24.30) and in so doing blended an echo of Zech. 12.10-14[174] into the Dan. 7.13 allusion.[175] This seems to accord with a particular Matthean interest in the Son of Man. Of the nine Matthean references,[176] two were probably drawn from Mark,[177] the two most explicit allusions to Dan. 7.13 itself. Two seem deliberately to have strengthened the Danielic allusion, by adding a 'Son of Man' reference.[178] And three more are unique to Matthew, without

171. A. Yarbro Collins criticizes Perrin for narrowing the options to either a clearly defined preexisting conception of the Son of Man or a post-Easter Christian construction; 'he failed to consider the possibility that Jesus interpreted Dan 7:13 in an innovative way in his teaching' ('Influence of Daniel' 92). M. Stowasser, 'Mk 13,26f und die urchristliche Rezeption des Menschensohns. Eine Anfrage an Anton Vögtle', *BZ* 39 (1995) 246-52, regards Mark 13.26-27 as the earliest Son of Man saying in the NT. Casey is scrupulously fair in not closing off options on indecisive data (*Son of Man* 165-77; Aramaic reconstruction 165).

172. Wright presses the point: 'The "son of man" figure "comes" to the Ancient of Days. He comes *from* earth *to* heaven, vindicated after suffering' (*Jesus* 361).

173. See the discussion in Hooker, *Son of Man* 158-59; Beasley-Murray, *Jesus and the Last Days* 429-30. Perrin assumes only a parousia reference (*Rediscovering* 173-76). Sanders sees an expectation of Jesus (of a heavenly figure who comes with angels) reflected also in 1 Thess. 4.15-17 (*Jesus* 144-45; *Historical Figure* 246-47).

174. Zech. 12.10, 12, 14: '. . . when they look on him whom they have pierced, they shall mourn, . . . each tribe by itself . . . and all the tribes that are left . . .'

175. The fact that Zech. 12.10 is also conflated with Dan. 7.13-14 in Rev. 1.7, and without obvious dependence on Matt. 24.30, suggests that Matthew's tradition was not the only one to develop a Christian apologetic along these lines (cf. Crossan, *Historical Jesus* 244-46). See further Davies and Allison, *Matthew* 3.360-61.

176. Matt. 10.23; 16.27-28; 19.28; 24.30 (twice), 44; 25.31; 26.64. 28.18 may also contain an allusion to the dominion granted to the manlike figure/saints of the Most High in Daniel 7. For detail see my 'Danielic Son of Man' 529-32.

177. Mark 13.26/Matt. 24.30b; Mark 14.62/Matt. 26.64; see further below §16.4c(2).

178. Mark 9.1/Matt. 16.28 (cited above, in §12.4h); Matt. 19.28/Luke 22.30 are cited below in §16.4e.

Synoptic or Johannine parallel.[179] The obvious inference is that Matthew's own portrayal of the Son of Man is itself evidence of a development within the Synoptic tradition, and, almost certainly, of Matthew's own hand in that development, a development which reflects the continuing influence of Daniel 7 at the time of Matthew's writing.

(2) Mark 14.62 pars.

Matt. 26.63-66	Mark 14.61-64	Luke 22.67-71
Then the high priest said to him, 'I put you under oath before the living God, tell us if you are the Messiah, the Son of God'. 64 Jesus said to him, 'You have said so. But I tell you, From now on <u>you will see the Son of Man</u> <u>seated at the right hand of the Power</u> <u>and coming on</u> <u>the clouds of heaven</u>'.	Again the high priest asked him, 'Are you the Messiah, the Son of the Blessed One?' 62 Jesus said, 'I am; and <u>you will see the Son of Man</u> <u>seated at the right hand of the Power, and coming</u> with <u>the clouds of heaven</u>.'	67 They said, 'If you are the Messiah, tell us'. He replied, 'If I tell you, you will not believe; 68 and if I question you, you will not answer. 69 But from now on <u>the Son of Man</u> will be <u>seated at the right hand of the power</u> of God'. 70 All of them asked, 'Are you, then, the Son of God?' He said to them, 'You say that I am'. 71 Then they said, 'What further testimony do we need? We have heard it ourselves from his own lips!'
65 <u>Then the high priest tore his garments</u>, saying, 'He has blasphemed! <u>Why do we still need witnesses?</u> <u>You have now heard his blasphemy</u>. 66 <u>What is your</u> verdict?' They answered, 'He <u>deserves death</u>'.	63 <u>Then the high priest tore his clothes</u> and said, 'Why <u>do we still need witnesses?</u> 64 <u>You have heard his blasphemy!</u> <u>What is your</u> decision?' All of them condemned him as <u>deserving death</u>.	

We have already examined the build-up to this climactic exchange in the hearing of Jesus before the High Priest Caiaphas (§15.3a). What strikes one now is that Jesus' reply, referring to the Son of Man seated at the right hand of power, belongs to the core of the narrative, as attested also by Luke's retold version. This was how Jesus was remembered as supplementing his ambiguous (?) answer to Caiaphas's question. Here again there are two features of the episode which deserve attention at this point.

The first is the double intertextual allusion in the Mark/Matthew version, both to Dan. 7.13 ('the Son of Man coming on the clouds of heaven'), and to Ps. 110.1 ('seated at the right hand' of God).[180] An observation of potential signifi-

179. Matt. 10.23 (cited in §12.4h above); 24.30a; 25.31 (cited below in §16.4e); also 28.18.

180. Why the Markan/Matthean tradition speaks of God as 'the Power' is unclear. Brown notes the lack of contemporary parallel (*Death* 496), though C. A. Evans, 'In What Sense "Blasphemy"? Jesus before Caiaphas in Mark 14.61-64', *Jesus and His Contemporaries* 407-34, provides parallels in later rabbinic usage (422). But note also D. Flusser, 'At the Right Hand of Power', *Judaism* 301-305; as with 'the Blessed' (above, chapter 15 n. 99), the occur-

cance is that the Dan. 7.13 reference seems to be primary and the Ps. 110.1 reference to have been inserted into it.[181] For one thing, the Psalm reference has had to be adapted to the syntax of the clause 'Son of Man coming on the clouds'.[182] And for another, the effect of the insertion is to postpone the 'coming on the clouds' until after the enthronement; that is, the inserted allusion seems to turn the coming from a coming *to* the Ancient of Days into a coming *from* the heavenly throne room.[183] It is quite likely that Luke's version lacks (has omitted?) the 'coming on the clouds' for this reason, that is, to remove the resulting awkwardness; by giving the Ps. 110.1 allusion primary weight, Luke leaves the Son of Man seated in heaven (cf. Acts 7.56).[184] This suggests that the saying was not first uttered/formed as a composite[185] but only became composite in the course

---

rence is as difficult to explain for Mark in the 60s as it is for Jesus in 30 (Dunn, 'Are You the Messiah?' 15).

181. This weakens the often observed parallel provided by the Midrash on Ps. 2.7, where in a sequence of testimonia Dan. 7.13-14 follows Ps. 110.1 in sequence (see, e.g., Beasley-Murray, *Jesus and the Kingdom* 299-300). In any case, it hardly provides good evidence that the two texts had already been associated in Jewish thinking prior to Jesus.

182.

Dan. 7.13	Mark 14.62	Ps. 110.1
Behold one like a <u>son of man</u> came (*ērcheto*) on <u>the clouds of heaven</u>	You will see the <u>son of man</u> seated <u>at</u> the <u>right hand</u> of the Power and *coming* (*erchomenon*) with <u>the clouds of heaven</u>	The Lord said to my lord, Sit <u>at my right hand</u>

183. That exaltation rather than return was envisaged has been strongly maintained by T. F. Glasson, 'The Reply to Caiaphas (Mark xiv.62)', *NTS* 7 (1960-61) 88-93; also *The Second Advent: The Origin of the New Testament Doctrine* (London: Epworth, 1945, [3]1963) 64-65; similarly J. A. T. Robinson, *Jesus and His Coming* (London: SCM, 1957) ch. 2; Barrett, *Jesus* 81-82. The argument has been influential. Hooker takes up from Glasson and suggests that the sitting and coming should not be seen as chronologically sequential but as equally expressive of a hope of vindication (*Son of Man* 166-71). Moule attempts to finesse the issue by suggesting that 'The *"coming"* of the Son of Man, precisely because it is his coming to God for *vindication, is* also his coming to earth in judgment and . . . for *"visitation"*' (*Origin* 18). Wright seems to want to include the destruction of the temple (AD 70) in the vindication which Caiaphas will see (*Jesus* 525-26); and, confusingly, 'the "Son of Man" will come — using the Roman armies — to crush rebel Jerusalem' (638). See also de Jonge, *Early Christology* 92-93.

184. Evans offers an alternative in arguing that if the throne was conceived as the chariot throne (Ezekiel 1), then the 'coming' could indeed follow the 'sitting', since the chariot throne was moving ('In What Sense?' 419-20; Davies and Allison, *Matthew* 3.530 also refer to *LAE* 22.3). In which case Luke's version presumably missed the allusion. However, Evans produces no parallel to the idea of the chariot throne 'coming with the clouds'.

185. *Pace* Tödt, *Son of Man* 37-40; Lindars, *Jesus Son of Man* 110-12; Stuhlmacher, 'Messianische Gottesknecht' 147-50; Casey, *Son of Man* 178-83, does not consider this possibility (though cf. Ezek. 1.4).

of transmission, most likely with the Dan. 7.13 allusion primary, then supplemented by the Ps. 110.1 allusion,[186] and the resulting awkwardness causing Luke's version to resimplify the imagery.

The second notable feature is the report that Jesus' reply was accounted 'blasphemy' by the High Priest. This has created puzzlement similar to that caused by talk of God as 'the Blessed' and 'the Power' (n. 180). For on a strict definition of 'blasphemy' it is very doubtful whether there is any blasphemous content, even in the full answer of Mark 14.62. 'Blasphemy' strictly speaking referred only to naming the name of Yahweh,[187] and 'Son of the Blessed' does not fall under that definition.[188] How, then, could the High Priest have condemned Jesus for blasphemy? One possible answer is that the term 'blasphemy' could have been used in a looser sense (of any serious threat to Israel's conviction regarding Israel's God), and polemical rhetoric could presumably have made exaggerated claims then as now.[189]

An intriguing alternative is that a saying understood as a self-referential allusion to Daniel's vision might have been taken as a claim to be the one who fulfilled the manlike figure's role in taking the second throne beside the Ancient of Days in heaven. We know that a century later even the great rabbi Akiba was accused of profaning the Shekinah for a similar speculation — that the second throne (of Dan. 7.9) was for the Messiah.[190] Also that Akiba was linked with the fascinating tradition of four who shared a mystical experience in which they entered paradise (*t. Hag.* 2.3-4). Another of the four is reported to have hailed the second enthroned figure as a second power in heaven, and for this he is condemned in rabbinic tradition as an archheretic, because he denied the Jewish axiom of the unity/oneness of God.[191] Some have suggested that this association of

---

186. See further my 'Are You the Messiah?' 14-18. Others maintain that Ps. 110.1 was the primary reference, supplemented by Dan. 7.13 (Perrin, *Rediscovering* 179; J. R. Donahue, *Are You the Christ? The Trial Narrative in the Gospel of Mark* [SBLDS 10; Missoula: SBL, 1973] 172-75; Hampel, *Menschensohn* 179-85; B. F. Meyer, 'Appointed Deed, Appointed Doer: Jesus and the Scriptures', in Chilton and Evans, *Authenticating the Activities of Jesus* 155-76 [here 172-73]).

187. Lev. 24.16 LXX; *m. Sanh.* 7.5.

188. See Brown, *Death* 521-22; *pace* J. Marcus, 'Mark 14:61: "Are You the Messiah-Son-of-God?"', *NovT* 31 (1989) 125-41.

189. See again Brown, *Death* 522-26; also Evans, 'In What Sense?' 409-11. For the breadth of use of *blasphēmeō* and *blasphēmia*, see BDAG *ad loc;* D. L. Bock, *Blasphemy and Exaltation in Judaism and the Final Examination of Jesus* (WUNT 2.106; Tübingen: Mohr, 1998) 30-112; and note Mark 3.28-29 pars. above (§16.4b[3]).

190. *b. Hag.* 14a; *b. Sanh.* 38b.

191. *b. Hag.* 15a; *3 En.* 16. There is a direct line of thought between Daniel 7's 'one like a son of man', Enoch's identification with the Son of Man (*1 En.* 71.14), and Metatron in *3 En.* 3–16 (note particularly 4.2 and 16).

ideas explains the blasphemy charge in Mark 14.64.[192] And though the lateness of these other traditions urges caution, we do know that a form of mysticism was practised within late Second Temple Judaism focused particularly on the chariot throne of God (Ezekiel 1).[193]

Taken together, these two features suggest a possible rationale underlying the reported exchange between Jesus and the High Priest as it was crystallized in the Jesus tradition, almost certainly from a very early date. The tradition was of Jesus using Daniel's vision of the manlike representation of the saints of the Most High to express his own hopes for vindication.[194] This was heard as a claim that Jesus himself would be enthroned in heaven.[195] In the *realpolitik* situation of a leadership determined to be rid of Jesus, any self-referencing allusion to the Danielic son of man could be cynically exploited to present Jesus as a threat to one of the core principles of Second Temple religion (the wholly otherness of the one God). In terms of ruling-class propaganda, such a charge would help ensure the support of the people, just as the charge of messiahship could be transposed into a threat to Caesar's kingship to ensure Pilate's support.

(3) Mark 8.38 pars./Matt.10.32-33/Luke 12.8-9:

192. Rowland, *Christian Origins* 170-71; J. Schaberg, 'Mark 14:62: Early Christian Merkabah Imagery?', in J. Marcus and M. L. Soards, eds., *Apocalyptic and the New Testament*, J. L. Martyn FS (JSNTS 24; Sheffield: JSOT, 1989) 69-94; Evans, 'In What Sense?' 419-21; Wright, *Jesus* 642-44; Davies and Allison, *Matthew* 3.534; Bock, *Blasphemy* 113-237. As D. R. Catchpole, *The Trial of Jesus* (Leiden: Brill, 1971) shows, the suggestion is not new (140-41). Cf. C. F. D. Moule, 'The Gravamen against Jesus', in E. P. Sanders, ed., *Jesus, the Gospels and the Church*, W. R. Farmer FS (Macon: Mercer University, 1987) 177-95; and Hofius who presses still further in seeing here 'the claim to a status and a function which could only be grounded in an *essential* unity with God' ('Ist Jesus der Messias?' 121).

193. There are already hints to that effect in Sir. 49.8 and *1 En.* 14.18-20. The Qumran Songs of the Sabbath Sacrifice imply something to the same effect being practised in the worship of Qumran. Paul himself may have been a practitioner of such mysticism (2 Cor. 12:2-4) (J. W. Bowker, '"Merkabah" Visions and the Visions of Paul', *JSS* 16 [1971] 157-73; see also Segal, *Paul the Convert*). The great rabbi Yohannan ben Zakkai, founder of the rabbinic school at Yavneh following the disaster of 70, is also attested to have been a practitioner (*t. Hag.* 2.1).

194. This is not the same as saying Jesus thought he would *become* the Son of Man (denied, e.g., by Hooker, *Son of Man* 188), which presupposes concepts and categories ('the Son of Man') already more firmly delineated than we have seen to be likely for the time of Jesus. Chilton, however, assumes that the angelic figure of Daniel's vision ('one like a person') was a key element in Jesus' visionary practice (*Rabbi Jesus* 157-61), an intimacy bordering on identification (171-72); cf. his earlier '(The) Son of (the) Man, and Jesus', in Chilton and Evans, eds., *Authenticating the Words of Jesus* 259-87, especially 274-86.

195. If this is a plausible way to interpret the tradition at the time of the Synoptists, then it is no less plausible for the situation of Jesus, 40-50 years earlier, since the data regarding mystical practice and misgivings about such practice (n. 193 above) are no stronger for the one than for the other.

Matt. 16.27	Mark 8.38	Luke 9.26
For the Son of Man is about to <u>come</u> <u>in the glory of his Father</u> <u>with</u> his angels, and then he will repay to each in accordance with his way of acting.	For whoever is ashamed of me and of my words in this adulterous and sinful generation, the Son of Man will also be ashamed of him when he <u>comes</u> <u>in the glory of his Father</u> <u>with</u> the holy angels.	For whoever is ashamed of me and of my words, of him <u>the Son of Man</u> will be ashamed when he <u>comes</u> in his glory and <u>the glory of</u> the <u>Father</u> and of <u>the holy angels.</u>

Matt. 10.32-33	Luke 12.8-9
32 <u>Everyone</u> therefore <u>who acknowledges me</u> <u>before men,</u> I <u>also will</u> <u>acknowledge before</u> my Father in heaven; 33 <u>but</u> <u>whoever denies me before men,</u> I also will deny before my Father in heaven.	8 And I tell you, <u>everyone</u> <u>who acknowledges me</u> <u>before men,</u> the Son of Man <u>also will</u> <u>acknowledge before</u> the angels of God; 9 <u>but</u> <u>whoever denies me before men</u> will be denied before the angels of God.

Here the influence of Dan. 7.13 is less clear, but still probable. It is impossible to tell now whether different teachings of Jesus are recalled in these passages. The first three of the five cited passages are linked clearly by the common theme of 'the Son of Man coming in judgment', which has probably been elaborated in the Matt. 16.27 tradition to bring out the judgment theme more prominently (cf. Matt. 25.31). The last four are linked by the common theme of denial/shame (on earth) being reciprocated by denial/shame at the final judgment (in heaven), which is complemented in Q by a reciprocal acknowledgment theme, whether from the store of remembered Jesus' teaching, or as an elaboration of the more threatening version. Evidently there were several versions of the saying(s) being circulated — Q, Mark, and possibly Matt. 16.27.[196]

Two observations are pertinent. First, Luke 12.8-9 has been the lynchpin of the dominant German view that Jesus saw the Son of Man as a heavenly figure to whom he looked for vindication of himself and his teaching, if only at the final judgment. But that view assumes that Jesus would be referring to a well-known heavenly figure (as attested in the *Similitudes of Enoch*), and we have seen good reason to question such an assumption.[197] We have also already observed that 'the Son of Man' version has an 'I' parallel in Matt. 10.32, so quite possibly an original *bar* *ᵉnaša* saying (with a play on 'men', 'son of man') is in view.[198] The

196. Further discussion in Beasley-Murray, *Jesus and the Kingdom* 291-96.

197. See above, §16.3b; also, e.g., Hare, *Son of Man* 221-24.

198. As Leivestad notes, 'It is a basic poetic device in Semitic poetry to interchange synonymous terms in parallel lines' (*Jesus* 117). Casey offers an Aramaic reconstruction of Mark 8.38 (*Son of Man* 161-62). See further Lindars, *Jesus Son of Man* 48-58, who suggests an original saying something like this: 'All who confess me before men will have a man to speak for them (i.e, an advocate) before the judgment seat of God; but all those who deny me before men

problem (the decisive factor?) for many has evidently been the difficulty of conceiving that Jesus spoke of such a role for someone like himself in the final judgment.[199] But is that so inconceivable?[200] Alternatively, if the identity of Jesus
with the Son of Man is not entirely clear, does that not make the saying's origin
as an assertion of that identity less plausible?[201]

Second, there is some ambiguity in regard to the location of the final judgment. The Q version is clear that it will happen *in* heaven, before the angels or
God himself. But the Mark 8.38 version allows the possibility that the coming of
the Son of Man is *from* heaven, parallel to the coming of the kingdom (Mark 9.1
pars.). Should we then see here a transition from the heavenly scene depicted in
Daniel, of the one like a son of man 'coming' with the clouds (Dan 7.13) to be
enthroned and to share in God's judgment (7.9-10, 14)? That is, if Jesus did
speak of the Danielic manlike figure, did he speak in terms of a coming to heaven
or from heaven? Or is the coming from heaven a subsequent development in the
Son of Man tradition, perhaps of a piece with the development from 'the son of
man' to 'the Son of Man'?

d. The Day(s) of the Son of Man

One of the most intriguing sequences of Son of Man sayings comes in Luke
17.22-30/Matt. 24.23, 27, 37-39.

Matt. 24.23, 27, 37-39	Luke 17.22-30
23 Then if anyone <u>says to you</u>, 'Look! Here is the Messiah!' or 'There he is!'—<u>do not</u> believe it.	22 Then he said to the disciples, '*The days* are coming when you will long to see **one of the days of the Son of Man**, and you will not see it. 23 They will <u>say to you</u>, "Look there" or "<u>Look here!</u>" Do not go, <u>do not</u> set off in pursuit.
27 <u>For as the lightning</u> comes from the east and flashes as far as the west, <u>so will be</u> **the coming** of <u>the Son of Man</u>.	24 <u>For as the lightning</u> flashes and lights up the sky from one side to the other, <u>so will</u> **the Son of Man be** in his day. 25 But first he must endure

will find that they have an accuser before the judgment seat of God' (54). It needs to be stressed
again that the issue is *not* how an original 'I' saying was replaced by the 'Son of Man' title or
vice-versa (*pace* Schürmann, *Gottes Reich* 166-67; Crossan, *Historical Jesus* 248-49;
P. Hoffmann, 'Der Menschensohn in Lukas 12.8', *NTS* 44 [1998] 357-79).

199. Funk, *Five Gospels* 80; Lüdemann, *Jesus* 343-44.

200. Jeremias pointed out that nowhere else is Jesus recalled as looking for a saving figure other than himself (*Proclamation* 276; similarly Lohse, 'Frage' 42-44; Marshall, *Jesus* 83-
85; Hampel, *Menschensohn* 159-60); we should also recall that the language of confessing and
denying is more appropriate to a witness than a judge (Hare, *Son of Man* 222; also 269-71; disputed by Becker, *Jesus* 208-209).

201. See particularly Beasley-Murray, *Jesus and the Kingdom* 225-27.

. . . . 37 For as the days of Noah were, <u>so will be</u> **the coming** of <u>the Son of Man</u>. 38 For as in those days before the flood <u>they were eating and drinking, marrying and</u> giving <u>in marriage, until the day Noah entered the ark,</u> 39 and they knew nothing until <u>the flood came and</u> swept them <u>all</u> away, so too <u>will be</u> **the coming** of <u>the Son of Man</u>.	much suffering and be rejected by this generation. 26 Just as it was in *the days of Noah,* <u>so too it</u> <u>will be</u> in **the days <u>of the Son of Man</u>**. 27 <u>They</u> were eating and drinking, and <u>marrying and</u> being given <u>in marriage, until</u> *the day* Noah entered the ark, and <u>the flood came and</u> destroyed <u>all</u> of them. 28 Likewise, just as it was in *the days of Lot*: they were eating and drinking, buying and selling, planting and building, 29 but on *the day* that Lot left Sodom, it rained fire and sulphur from heaven and destroyed all of them 30—it will be like that on **the day that** <u>the Son of Man</u> is revealed'.

Clearly Matthew and Luke are drawing on common material. But each has so integrated the material to his own schema that it is difficult to gain a clear impression of the tradition history involved.[202] In particular, it is unclear whether Luke has introduced talk of the day(s) of the Son of Man, a phrase unique to this section, and unclear quite what was in view with the phrase.[203] It seems to envisage a period (days) during which life continues in its normal round, only to be disrupted by sudden catastrophic judgment (day). That fits well enough with Jesus' warnings of impending judgment elsewhere.[204] But is the implication that the son of man is a figure like Noah and Lot, warning of impending judgment, and/or that the son of man will be the major figure in the impending judgment? In the former case we would then have a parallel to the sign of Jonah (§15.6b) and could probably infer that an indefinite/self-referential *bar* ᵉ*naša* lies behind it.[205] The latter however gives only weak support for the suggestion that Dan. 7.13 is being alluded to, or that the phrase would be heard by Jesus' audience 'as a well-known term for the eschatological agent of judgment'.[206] Unfortunately, the possibility of drawing confident conclusions as to Jesus' own usage is not strong.[207]

202. See further below, §16.4f.

203. See further Fitzmyer, *Luke* 2.1168-69.

204. See above, §12.4e. Cf. *Pss. Sol.* 18.5: 'the appointed day at the raising up *(anaxei?)* of his Messiah'.

205. Cf. Hampel, *Menschensohn* 59-70, 79-98.

206. *Pace* Becker, *Jesus* 206; the judgment in favour of authenticity by Bultmann (*History* 122) and Tödt (*Son of Man* 48-52) depends on the assumption that reference was to a well-known figure (challenged by Perrin, *Rediscovering* 195-97).

207. Higgins argued for the more complex case that Luke 17.24, 26, 30 are the only genuine utterances of Jesus (apart from Luke 11.29-32 and 12.8-9), partly on the ground that they did not speak of his 'coming' (whether in exaltation or to earth), but only warned of the imminence of the (judgment) day (*Son of Man* 56-72, 79, 124). See also Lindars, *Jesus Son of Man* 94-97.

e. Influence of the *Similitudes of Enoch*

Since the possibility of Jesus having been influenced by the *Similitudes* is so crucial, any firm evidence of influence from the *Similitudes* on the Jesus tradition is bound to be significant. And indeed there is such evidence — again, noticeably, in Matthew (Matt. 19.28 and 25.31).

Matt. 19.28	Luke 22.28-30
28 Jesus said to them, 'Truly I tell you, at the renewal of all things, when **the Son of Man is seated on the throne of his glory,** you who have followed me also <u>will sit on</u> twelve <u>thrones, judging the twelve tribes of Israel</u>'.	28 You are those who have stood by me in my trials; 29 and I confer on you, just as my Father has conferred on me, a kingdom, 30 so that you may eat and drink at my table in my kingdom, and you <u>will sit on</u> <u>thrones judging the twelve tribes of Israel</u>.

Matt. 25.31 — When **the Son of Man** comes in his glory, and all the angels with him, then he will **sit on the throne of his glory** (the beginning of the parable of the final judgment of the sheep and the goats).

The case for hearing an echo of Daniel's vision here is the triple theme in the double vision of Dan. 7.9-10 and 13-14: the implication of the plural 'thrones' (7.9) is that the 'one like a son of man' (7.13) took his place on the second throne (or one of the other thrones) in order to share in the judgment (7.10) presided over by the Ancient of Days (7.9). Equally persuasive, however, is the case for seeing some influence creeping into these verses from the elaboration of the Danielic vision in the *Similitudes of Enoch*. For it is only there that the implication of Daniel's vision is made explicit. In the *Similitudes* the Elect One is repeatedly said to sit down 'on the throne of his glory' to judge,[208] and the Elect One is clearly identified in the *Similitudes* with 'that Son of Man' (*1 En.* 69.27).[209] It is probable, then, that the two Matthean passages have been influenced, at least in their final form, by the repeated imagery of the *Similitudes of Enoch,* as well as by the double vision of Daniel 7, which certainly lies behind the *Similitudes*.[210]

Furthermore, these two references in Matthew, together possibly with John

208. Particularly *1 En.* 55.4; 61.8; 62.3; 69.27.

209. See further above, chapter 16 n. 102.

210. Similarly John 5.27:

1 En. 69.27: the whole judgment was given to the Son of Man;

John 5.27: the Father has given the Son authority to execute judgment, because he is the Son of Man.

See further J. Theisohn, *Der auserwählte Richter. Untersuchungen zum traditionsgeschicht-lichen Ort der Menschensohngestalt der Bilderreden des äthiopischen Henoch* (Göttingen: Vandenhoeck, 1969) Kap. 6. Hare questions the significance of any influence from the *Similitudes* (*Son of Man* 162-65, 175-78); but see also Burkett, *Son of Man Debate* 78 n. 20.

5.27, are the only indications within the Gospels of knowledge of *1 Enoch*'s developed Son of Man tradition. Matthew and John are usually dated to the last two decades of the first century. There is no indication of any similar influence from the *Similitudes*' portrayal of the Son of Man in the Jesus tradition, either in Mark or in Q.[211] This strongly suggests that the influence of the *Similitudes* began to impact on the Jesus tradition only in the last two decades of the first century. And it may also strengthen the suggestion that the *Similitudes* were not known (not written?) before, say, the third quarter of the first century.[212]

f. Direction of Travel

A further intriguing feature which emerges from the data is the ambiguity over what might be called 'the direction of travel' envisaged in the Son of Man's coming.

In Dan. 7.13 the Son of Man clearly comes to the Ancient of Days: 'with the clouds of heaven there came one like a son of man, and he came to the Ancient of Days and was presented before him'. The action all takes place *in heaven;* implied is the enthronement of the manlike figure, interpreted in the following verses as the triumph of the saints of the Most High.[213] Wherever the allusion to Dan. 7.13 is strong, therefore, it is likely that the 'coming (on clouds)' was understood as a coming in heaven.[214] At the same time, we have already observed that as they *now* stand, the two most obvious allusions (also?) suggest a coming *from* heaven.[215]

The Q material has a similar ambiguity. The Q version of the Mark 8.38 complex clearly implies the Son of Man acting in heaven (Matt. 10.32-33/Luke 12.8-9), although the Mark 8.38 pars. could again be understood as a coming from heaven (§16.4c[3]). The likening of the Son of Man to a flash of lightning (Matt. 24.27/Luke 17.24) has overtones of divine theophany (in/from heaven) and of judgment (coming from heaven).[216] On the other hand, the sequence Matt. 24.43-44/Luke 12.39-40[217] raises the possibility that early in the retelling of Je-

---

211. As repeatedly assumed, e.g., by Tödt, *Son of Man* 33-67; Witherington, *Christology* 235, 260-61.

212. See further my discussion *Christology* 75-78, and above, n. 106.

213. *Pace* Casey, *Son of Man* 22, 24-29, who thinks that Daniel may have envisaged a judgment taking place on earth; but in Jewish apocalyptic the throneroom(s) are consistently located in heaven.

214. Robinson, *Jesus and His Coming* 45 and n. 2.

215. Mark 13.26 pars.; 14.62 pars. (above, §16.4c).

216. Cf. Davies and Allison, *Matthew* 3.354.

217. Cited above, §12.4g.

sus' parable the Son of Man imagery replaced that of the master of the household returning unexpectedly.[218] And Luke's addition to the parable of the widow and the unjust judge (Luke 18.8) also implies a coming to earth: 'when the Son of Man comes *(elthōn),* will he find faith on the earth?'

Matthew's elaboration of the Jesus tradition simply adds further confusion. A coming to be enthroned (in heaven) in glory is clearly envisaged in the two passages most likely to have been influenced by the *Similitudes of Enoch* (Matt. 19.28; 25.31). But Matthew also elaborates the thought of the Son of Man's coming by reference to Jesus' *parousia,*[219] the regular term for Christ's (second) coming/advent in the NT letters.[220] A coming to earth is probably implied also in Matt. 10.23 and 24.44 *(erchesthai).*[221] These all seem to be a development from the coming *(erchomenon)* in Matt. 24.30 (= Mark 13.26), one of the explicit quotations of Dan. 7.13,[222] where the transition of thought (from a coming to heaven to a coming to earth) may still be evident.[223]

The obvious possibility emerging from all these cases is that there has been a tendency to reverse the direction of travel in the course of transmission of the Jesus tradition. What began as a straightforward evocation of Daniel's vision, of an exaltation and implied enthronement in heaven, has been steadily developed into the more complex thought of enthronement followed by a redescent to earth.[224] The indications of such a development are most clear in four cases: the transition of thought still evident in Mark 13.26-27 pars. and in the Mark 8.38 complex; the probable insertion of Ps. 110.1 into the Dan. 7.13 allusion in Mark 14.62 pars.; and the coalescence of the idea of the Son of Man's coming with the return of the master/householder/bridegroom in various parables.

218. Similarly Lindars, *Jesus Son of Man* 97-98.

219. Matt. 24.27, 37, 39, answering the disciples' query in 24.3; *parousia* appears nowhere else in the Jesus tradition. Matthew is the only Evangelist to use the term. Is this Matthew's redaction of an original reference to 'the day(s)' of the Son of Man (Luke 17.24, 26, 30), or are both redactional, and a preredactional form is unrecoverable (see above, §16.4d)?

220. 1 Cor. 15.23; 1 Thess. 2.19; 3.13; 4.15; 5.23; 2 Thess. 2.1, 8; Jas. 5.7-8; 2 Pet. 1.16; 3.4; 1 John 2.28.

221. Cited above, §§12.4h and 12.4g respectively.

222. Cited above, §16.4c(1).

223. Matt. 24.30-31: 'the sign of the Son of Man will appear in heaven, and then all the tribes of earth will mourn, and they will see the Son of Man coming on the clouds of heaven with power and great glory. And he will send out his angels with a loud trumpet call (cf. 1 Thess. 4.16), and they will gather his elect from the four winds, from one end of heaven to the other'.

224. Cf. Robinson, *Jesus and His Coming* chs. 3-4.

16.5. Son of Man: A Hypothesis

It is no wonder that the Son of Man material in the Jesus tradition has proved so intractable for those seeking some significant measure of consensus for the results of the quest. The degree of complexity of the data is unparalleled in the Jesus tradition. The parallels on which historical research so much depends, both in linguistic and apocalyptic usage, are so disputed as to dating and relevance as to leave any historical hypothesis vulnerable to attack from more than one angle. Moreover, the data have manifestly been developed. That is to say, the tradition has not simply been performed and transmitted. In the course of the transmission the understanding of the material has developed. The core elements have probably changed in meaning while remaining the same in words ('the son of man' has become 'the Son of Man'). An event in heaven (seen in vision, or in some final climactic revelation) has possibly been developed to express hope for Jesus' return from heaven.

How then did Jesus see his own role? The difficulty of hearing Jesus and of gaining a perception of his self-understanding in relation to 'the son of man' is more severe than in any other case within the Synoptic tradition. Not because 'the son of man' motif was wholly retrojected into the Jesus tradition at a later stage of the traditioning process. Nor even because the motif has been greatly modified. But simply because what was initially heard by the first disciples in Jesus' use of the phrase 'the son of man' grew in significance during that earliest traditioning period. It is precisely here, the nearest Jesus came to a self-referential role-description, that the impact of Good Friday and Easter quickly caused these disciples to perceive (recognize?) a greater significance in that phrase and to express that greater significance in their early performances of the tradition, without making much (if any!) alteration to the actual words used.

If all that is so, can any firm hypothesis, let alone conclusion, be drawn? I believe so.

a. At least we can be confident regarding the starting point, that is, that *Jesus himself used the phrase 'the son of man'* (§16.4a). In terms of tradition-historical analysis the case could hardly be clearer or stronger.[225] When so many issues in the Jesus tradition are difficult to resolve because the evidence is so confusing, students should be relieved to find one instance at least where the weight of evidence tips the balance so heavily in one direction. It is disappointing that so many have allowed less clear-cut data or less weighty considerations to undermine one of the firmest findings available to us. If we cannot be confident that Jesus used the phrase 'the son of man' in his speech, and quite regularly,

---

225. 'It is certain that Jesus used the expression "son of man"' (Theissen and Merz, *Historical Jesus* 548).

then there is almost no feature of the Jesus tradition of which we can confidently assert that Jesus spoke in this way.

b. Beyond that confidence quickly diminishes. As to the possibility of identifying an Aramaic phrase behind the Gospels' Greek, the negative results of searches for Aramaic parallels are undeniably a major problem. Nevertheless, I think the evidence is strong enough to support the conclusion that *Jesus did use Aramaic* bar 'enaša *in a general and self-referential way,* probably best indicated by a translation such as 'a man like me', equivalent to the English 'one'. Jesus the *mošel* would presumably have been attracted by the phrase's ambiguity between general reference and self-reference and by the play it made possible between 'men', 'man', 'a man like me'. At any rate such an ambiguous word-play is evident at various points in the Jesus tradition. That is to say, Jesus was remembered as using the phrase in that way. It is hardly credible that the ambiguity and word-play were introduced once the tradition had been put into Greek. It must have been a feature of the tradition in its Aramaic phase. This usage should therefore count as evidence for Aramaic usage in pre-70 Palestine and not be dismissed because clear parallels are lacking elsewhere in our deposit of first-century Aramaic. In which case there seems little cause to deny the usage to Jesus himself, as the Jesus tradition attests.

c. It can be judged also likely that Jesus' word-play on *bar 'enaša* included at least some reference to 'one like *bar 'naš*' in Dan. 7.13. With the possible exception of Luke 12.8, there is no evidence to speak of supporting the view that Son of Man was an already established title of or way of referring to a hoped-for heavenly redeemer figure. Nor is there evidence (apart from Mark 14.62-64 par. where the Dan. 7.13 allusion is clear) that *bar 'enaša* would have caused offence to Jesus' hearers. A plausible thesis, then, is that it was Jesus himself who saw in the Danielic *bar 'naš* both a further play on the Aramaic idiom and a signal which give him hope of vindication, whatever happened to him.[226] Because of the ambiguity of the Aramaic phrase itself, and because Dan. 7.13 was an example of the idiom ('one like a human being'), such an allusion need not have been heard as a claim to *be* the manlike figure, but could be taken simply as an allusion to the vindication-following-suffering role which the figure represented for the faithful of Israel. We shall have to return to this possibility in §17.4 below.

d. This last conclusion correlates well with what we can learn in regard to the *Similitudes of Enoch.* The likelihood that the *Similitudes* were introducing a fresh interpretation of Daniel's vision undermines the counter-argument that they presuppose a prior interpretation of Dan. 7.13 as referring to a heavenly angelic judge able to act on Israel's behalf. And the fact that clear indications of influence from the *Similitudes* appear only late in the development of the Jesus tradi-

---

226. Cf. particularly Bietenhard, 'Der Menschensohn' 345-46.

tion (Matthew, John) strengthens the suspicion that the *Similitudes* did not appear on the scene anyway until some time after Jesus' mission was ended.

e. As to the development clearly evident within the Jesus tradition at this point. It seems to have started with Jesus' own use of the Aramaic idiom *(bar ᵉnaša)* into which he himself drew the particular *bar ᵉnaš* allusion to Dan. 7.13. In the course of transmission the self-reference in 'the son of man' became more pronounced, and the transition to Greek established the phrase as a formal title ('the Son of Man'). In the same process the initial allusion to Dan. 7.13 was made more complex by a succession of elaborations: by incorporation of an allusion to Ps. 110.1 (Mark 14.62), by reversal of the direction of travel to include the thought of Jesus' return *(parousia)* from heaven (particularly Matthew), and by development of an allusion to the also-developed use of Daniel's vision in the *Similitudes of Enoch* (Matthew and John).

This hypothesis is quite strong in tradition-historical terms, even though supporting evidence from outside the Jesus tradition is confusing and indecisive. Its strength is that it takes seriously the Jesus tradition both as the attempt to remember what Jesus said and as the attempt to interpret that tradition in the light of developing faith-insight (christology) and changing circumstances. Its greatest value is in demonstrating the likelihood that Jesus himself was influenced by both of the roots (more often set in antithesis by contemporary questers), that he thought of himself as very much bound up with the frailties of humankind, and that the Danielic vision may have encouraged him in hope of being welcomed by the Most High on the completion of his mission. Its greatest deficit for traditional Christian faith is the corollary that the tradition of Jesus *coming* (*again* to earth) may have originated from a post-Easter merging of the Son of Man coming motif with the return motif of the crisis parables.

16.6. Conclusion

Our examination of the relevant evidence is not yet complete. There are other aspects of the matter still to be discussed, but better dealt with in the next chapter. Even so, however, some appropriate conclusions can already be drawn.

In one sense our findings thus far are disappointing. We have to conclude as likely that Jesus made no attempt to lay claim to any title as such; also that he rejected at least one which others tried to fit him to. We can sharpen the point a little. It would appear that Jesus saw it as no part of his mission to make specific claims for his own status. The nearest we have to such a claim is his use of the non-title *bar ᵉnaša,* too ambiguous to be a demand for explicit faith in himself, more an expression of his own hope for vindication. Allusion to his own role comes out more as a by-product of his proclamation of God's kingdom; his role was a role in relation to that, rather than an assertion of his own status as such. Evidently, it was his proclamation of the kingdom which was important; the identity of the proclaimer was a secondary matter.[227] To push further down that line would raise the interesting question as to whether Jesus saw faith regarding God's kingly rule as dependent on faith in him, whether the discipleship to which he called required a particular belief in Jesus. Or did it simply involve a sharing in Jesus' *abba* faith in God as Father and in his mission to live in the light of the coming kingdom?

On the other hand, our review of the data has underlined the unwisdom of pitching the discussion in terms of clear-cut titles (the Messiah, the Son of Man, etc.). Should the discussion not be pitched rather in terms of more amorphous concepts, of embryonic insights, of roles taken on rather than titles claimed? Are the indications not more of a man who read/heard his Scripture with eschatological overtones and who saw there possibilities and patterns which broke through the more established and traditional categories? In which case, we can begin to speak more firmly of the man who was remembered as one who above all took on the role of eschatological spokesman for God. And from that we can deduce, without strain, something of Jesus' own self-understanding regarding that role — his conviction of being God's eschatological agent at the climax of God's purposes for Israel, his sense of intimate sonship before God and of the dependence of his disciples on him, and his probably strong hope for final acknowledgment as the man who was playing the decisive role in bringing the kingdom to fulfilment and consummation.

At a responsibly historical level, can we say more?

227. Cf. Harvey, *Jesus* 145.

PART FIVE

THE CLIMAX OF JESUS' MISSION

CHAPTER 17

Crucifixus sub Pontio Pilato

From very early days the Apostles' Creed jumped at once from Jesus' birth to his suffering and death — *natus ex Maria virgine, passus sub Pontio Pilato, crucifixus, mortuus et sepultus* ('born from the Virgin Mary, suffered under Pontius Pilate, was crucified, dead, and buried'). Whatever the richer theological reasoning behind the huge gap between Jesus' birth and death, the gap itself reflected the difficulty of pinning down hard historical data to times and places within that gap. The same difficulty has meant that the last five chapters have been little concerned to locate and sequence Jesus' doings and teachings. For the same reason I had to leave open the question whether Jesus visited Jerusalem during the years of his Galilean mission, and if so how often (§9.9g).

But with the last few days of Jesus' mission we begin to feel firmer ground under foot. For the sources which deal with the subject are in complete agreement: the climax of Jesus' mission was a (final) visit to Jerusalem, and he was executed there, probably at Passover 30 CE.[1]

17.1. The Tradition of Jesus' Last Week

A glance at a Synopsis is sufficient to show that the Gospels all work with a common framework for that final period, starting with the entry into Jerusalem (Mark 11.1-10 pars.) and building through various teachings and a final meal together, to Jesus' arrest, trial, and execution (Mark 14–15 pars.). The most obvious explanation of this feature is that the framework was early on fixed within the traditioning process and remained so throughout the transition to written Gos-

---

1. On the chronology of Jesus' mission see above, §9.9a.

pels. This suggests in turn a tradition rooted in the memory of the participants and put into that framework by them.

That this was likely to have been the case has been long recognized in the case of 'the Passion narrative' (Mark 14–15).[2] It is inherently probable that its two principal features (the 'last supper' and the story of Jesus' arrest, condemnation, execution, and burial) would have been important for the identity of each new group or church from the day of its establishment.[3] The *a priori* probability is borne out by the already traditional formulations cited or alluded to by Paul. The Lord's Supper was clearly a central identifying and bonding feature of his churches (1 Cor. 10.14-22; 11.17-22) and was based entirely on the memory of the last supper and what happened there as already sacred tradition (11.23-26).[4] Various formulae had quickly become established and are often echoed: that he had been 'handed over *(paradidōmi)*'[5] and 'died'.[6] 'The cross' and the memory of Jesus' shameful death by crucifixion are already established features in early preaching.[7] The memory of his suffering quickly became a powerful factor in Christian spirituality.[8] And the Apostles' Creed's commemoration of Pontius Pilate is already foreshadowed in 1 Tim. 6.13. In other words, here we have an extended example of the pattern of oral tradition in its stability of structure and theme and in the focus on core elements.[9]

2. Scholarship on this subject is heavily in debt to the massive and magisterial treatment of Raymond Brown, *The Death of the Messiah,* here on the interrelation of the Gospel narratives 36-93, with full bibliographies 94-106. See also particularly J. B. Green, *The Death of Jesus: Tradition and Interpretation in the Passion Narrative* (WUNT 2.23; Tübingen: Mohr Siebeck, 1988); W. Reinbold, *Der älteste Bericht über den Tod Jesu. Literarische Analyse und historische Kritik der Passionsdarstellungen der Evangelien* (BZNW 69; Berlin: de Gruyter, 1994). Pesch, *Markusevangelium* 2.1-27, argued for a much more extended pre-Markan Passion narrative, running from Mark 8.27, which he hypothesizes emerged in the Aramaic-speaking Jerusalem community before 37 CE (21); but a firmer 'starting point' across the Gospels is the entry into Jerusalem. See also A. Yarbro Collins, *The Beginning of the Gospel: Problems of Mark in Context* (Minneapolis: Fortress, 1992).

3. Put like that it becomes immediately obvious why Q does not have a Passion narrative, since Q itself is not structured as a narrative but as a collection of Jesus' teaching, and why also it is unlikely that Q was the only teaching or liturgical material possessed by most churches.

4. See above, §8.5c.

5. Rom. 4.25; 8.32; 1 Cor. 11.23; Gal. 1.4; 2.20; Eph. 5.2, 25; 1 Tim. 2.6; Tit. 2.14; *1 Clem.* 16.7.

6. Rom. 5.6, 8; 14.15; 1 Cor. 8.11; 15.3; 2 Cor. 5.14-15; 1 Thess. 5.10; Ign. *Trall.* 2.1; see further my *Theology of Paul* 175.

7. Particularly 1 Cor. 1.17-18, 23; 2.2, 8; 2 Cor. 13.4; Gal. 3.1; 5.11; 6.12, 14; Heb. 12.2.

8. Rom. 8.17; 2 Cor. 1.5; Phil. 3.10; Heb. 5.7-8; 1 Pet. 2.19-23.

9. Typical is the variability of the episode of Peter's denials within the structure (tabulated by Brown, *Death* 418-19).

Within the larger framework (Mark 11–15 pars.) there was plenty of room for significant performance variants. The likelihood that the eschatological discourse in Mark 13 is the product of significant elaboration has already been noted.[10] Matthew includes several parables, some of which Luke has in his much longer journey to Jerusalem.[11] And John ventures substantial variation, not least in adding a whole raft of teaching to the sequence, the 'farewell discourses' (John 14–17).

As usual, the attempt to explain the more detailed variations has focused on the possibility of detectable (written) sources. The debate has centred particularly on the questions of a pre-Markan Passion narrative and a Lukan special source.[12] But no consensus has been achieved, or is achievable, since the criteria for distinguishing Markan and Lukan redaction from putative literary sources are at best indecisive.[13] The hypotheses both of recoverable written sources and of a narrative wholly created by Mark[14] are incapable of substantive demonstration.[15] Here again we need to be more open to the reality of oral tradition, including the use of written sources in oral mode.[16] That is to say, the reality of Mark 11–15

10. See above, §12.4d.

11. Particularly Matt. 22.1-14/Luke 14.15-24; Matt. 24.45-51/Luke 12.41-46; Matt. 25.14-30/Luke 19.11-27; also Matt. 23.37-39/Luke 13.34-35; Matt. 24.37-42/Luke 17.26-35. Had there been a more extensive pre-Markan Passion narrative (n. 2 above), then Luke's extended journey to Jerusalem (Luke 9.51-18.14) has cut right across it.

12. Discussion in Brown, *Death* 53-57, 64-75. Other bibliography in J. T. Carroll and J. B. Green, 'The Gospels and the Death of Jesus in Recent Study', *The Death of Jesus in Early Christianity* (Peabody: Hendrickson, 1995) 5-9, 17-19, who reflect also the recent trend to concentrate more on the function of the Passion narrative within each Gospel (7-16 and chs. 2-5).

13. M. L. Soards has provided a thorough analysis of the attempts to reconstruct a pre-Markan Passion narrative (in Brown, *Death* 1492-1524, tabulation 1502-17); Brown notes in reference to the thirty-four scholars' views surveyed, that 'there is scarcely one verse that all would assign to the same kind of source or tradition' (55). On the question of a special Lukan source, scholars are more or less equally divided (*Death* 66-67 nn. 70, 72); Brown notes that he, like Hawkins and G. Schneider, began with the hypothesis of a special Lukan Passion narrative, but subsequently abandoned the hypothesis (67).

14. The case that Mark edited and unified individual traditions, composed new material and thus created the Passion narrative sequence as a narrative has been argued particularly by the contributors to W. H. Kelber, ed., *The Passion in Mark* (Philadelphia: Fortress, 1976); see also Funk, *Acts of Jesus* 23.

15. Brown observes that some of the episodes in Mark's narrative 'cannot have circulated independently without a connection to the passion' (*Death* 54) and goes on to summarize the inadequacy of the criteria for discerning redaction in a case like the Markan Passion narrative (55-57).

16. Crossan (*Birth* 562-63) notes that Koester has moved from the assumption of a single written source for the Passion narrative to the recognition of 'different versions of the passion narrative . . . owing to the *oral performances* of the story in ritual celebrations, ever enriched by new references to the scriptures of Israel' (citing 'The Historical Jesus and the Cult of

pars. is of a story, stable in overall structure, with closer agreement at specific points signalling the core elements for the tradents.[17] That each performer of the tradition, including the Evangelists, should be free with less consequential details or should elaborate matters of greater consequence, is no surprise.[18] Their respect for the tradition, which is also evident, was manifestly not expressed in slavish 'copying'. Even with the most sacred tradition, the degree of fixity was still only relative and subject to individual elaboration — as the traditions of the last supper clearly indicate.[19]

Of course, with this body of tradition in particular, we can have no doubt that it was first formulated after the events of Good Friday and Easter. So, more clearly than with most of the tradition of Jesus' earlier doings and teachings, we can be sure that its initial telling was from a post-Easter perspective. That perspective is apparent at various places, as we shall see. But even so, there is little cause to doubt the historical character of the broad structure and sequence of the narrative or of its principal elements as initially formulated, presumably, by eyewitness participants. Without such continuity it would be difficult to explain how the 'gospel', which focused on the significance of the events narrated, became so quickly established as the foundation of all the churches known to Paul.

Turning to that detail, we have already covered most of the key elements and can refer simply to the earlier discussion[20] — particularly the entry into Jerusalem (Mark 11.1-10 pars.), the symbolical protest in the Temple (Mark 11.15-17 pars.), the various disputations thereafter (Mark 11.27–12.37),[21] the eschatological discourse and parables (Mark 13 pars.),[22] the Gethsemane prayer (Mark

---

the Kyrios Christos', *Harvard Divinity Bulletin* 24 [1995] 13-18 [here 18]). Funk disagrees: the Passion narrative 'cannot be based on the oral transmission of discrete scenes loosely connected. . . . It was probably a written narrative from its inception' whose 'full development . . . may not have begun until after the fall of Jerusalem' (*Honest* 238). But his inability to envisage how Koester's 'hypothetical [oral] narrative was transmitted during the oral period' (239) simply attests how limited is his own conception of the oral Jesus tradition.

17. Brown's own conclusion is that at the pre-Gospel level 'there existed at least a sequence of the principal stages in the death of Jesus, along with some stories about episodes or figures in that death. There may have been one or more preGospel narratives of the passion composed from this material, but neither the fact nor the wording of the contents of such a narrative can be established persuasively' (*Death* 92). The conclusion still works too much with the model of a literary narrative.

18. See further Dschulnigg's discussion of Pesch's argument for an extended pre-Markan Passion narrative (*Sprache* 323-31) and Brown's discussion of the special features of Matthew's and John's Passion narratives (*Death* 59-63, 75-92).

19. See again §8.5c above.

20. Apart from those indicated, reference is all to §15.3a.

21. See above, §15.3b-e.

22. See above, §12.4d.

14.36),[23] the hearing before the high priest and the trial before Pilate (Mark 14.53-65; 15.1-5), and the crucifixion *titulus* (Mark 15.26 pars.). But there are a number of other issues of some significance which require at least brief discussion: John's attribution of the primary trigger for Jesus' arrest to Jesus' raising of Lazarus (John 11.45-53), Judas's motivation in 'handing over' Jesus (Mark 14.10-11 pars.), the character of the 'last supper' (14.22-25 pars.), the arrest of Jesus and flight of the disciples (14.43-52 pars.), the role of Pilate (15.1-15 pars.), the influence of the OT on the description of Jesus' death (15.22-38 pars.), and Jesus' burial (15.42-47 pars.).

a. What Triggered Jesus' Arrest?

The historical value of the Fourth Evangelist's account of Lazarus has always been problematical. Not simply because it narrates a very striking raising from the dead. Jesus had a reputation as one who had raised the (prematurely reckoned?) dead (Matt. 11.5/Luke 7.22),[24] and the memory of an event which gave rise to this reputation may be discerned behind the Johannine account.[25] Nor simply because John has made the narrative the basis for one of his characteristic christological elaborations (John 11.25: 'I am the resurrection and the life'). It is John's style to weave such meditations round typical 'signs' that Jesus did and traditional epigrams that epitomized his teaching.[26] The historical question arises rather and precisely from the clash between the Synoptics and John on the events leading up to Jesus' arrest.

The implication of the Synoptics is pretty clear that if there was any single incident which triggered the move to arrest Jesus it was his 'prophetic sign' in the Temple. That is at best an implication, but the inference does lie close to the surface. Mark indicates that what Jesus said in regard to the Temple provoked the high priests and scribes to seek his destruction (Mark 11.17-18), though the connection is looser in Luke (Luke 19.46-47) and lacking in Matthew. But all three agree that a direct challenge to the authority claimed by Jesus soon followed (Mark 11.27-33 pars.) and indicate a steady deepening of antagonism between Jesus and the scribes (12.1-40 pars.) prior to Judas's decision to hand Jesus over to the high priests (14.10-11 pars.). The sense of a situation sliding towards tragic climax is clear and probably did not need to be much elaborated in the telling. The Temple incident marked the beginning of the slide.

---

23. See above, §16.2b.

24. See above, §12.5c and chapter 15 n. 275.

25. So Meier concluded: 'I think it likely that John 11:1-45 goes back ultimately to some event involving Lazarus, a disciple of Jesus, and that this event was believed by Jesus' disciples even during his lifetime to be a miracle of raising the dead' (*Marginal Jew* 2.831).

26. See above, §7.7.

The Fourth Evangelist, however, evidently chose to move the Temple incident to serve as the frontispiece of his account of Jesus' Jerusalem ministry (John 2.13-22).[27] Though, perhaps mindful of the episode's actual historical role, John is the only one to include Jesus' word about the destruction of the Temple (John 2.19), the word which seems to have formed the primary accusation against Jesus (Mark 14.58).[28] But having removed the 'trigger' event from the last week of Jesus' mission, he had to provide another plausible 'trigger'. On a Johannine schema, the choice of the raising of Lazarus, with its message of life-giving power overcoming death, made it a similarly suitable frontispiece to the Johannine account of the final days.[29] Given John's freedom in rescheduling important episodes and in elaborating earlier tradition, his version of a 'trigger' event has much less claim on the attention of those engaged in 'the quest of the historical Jesus' than do the Synoptics.

b. The Motivation of Judas

As already noted (§13.3b), the role of Judas as the one who 'betrayed' Jesus is too deeply rooted in the tradition to be doubted as to its historicity. Whatever the precedents,[30] it is hardly likely that they provided a sufficient template on which some tradent with dramatic flair cut the cloth of his imagination to create Judas *ex nihilo*.[31] The embarrassment of Jesus having personally selected Judas and promised him one of the thrones to judge the twelve tribes (Matt. 19.28/Luke 22.30) would surely have created more tension in the Jesus tradition than is evident were the Judas traditions of later contrivance.

But if Judas did 'betray' Jesus, the question Why cannot easily be silenced — or answered. The question has been of endless fascination, just because Christian hindsight regarded the act as so heinous, the very pinnacle of evil, the most unforgivable of all sins.[32] But equally others have been drawn to a more

---

27. See above, chapter 15 n. 113.

28. See above, §15.3a.

29. See Brown's earlier discussion in *John* 1.428-30.

30. The story of Ahitophel, David's trusted counsellor who deserted him, is the most obvious example: the story includes David's crossing of the Kidron and ascent of the mount of Olives (2 Sam. 15.23, 30), and Ahitophel's subsequent suicide by hanging (17.23); further detail in Brown, *Death* 125-26, 643; Davies and Allison, *Matthew* 3.565-66.

31. Brown concludes that the Ahitophel story probably generated Matthew's account of Judas's suicide by hanging (*Death* 656-57).

32. 'It would have been better for that man if he had not been born' (Mark 14.21c/ Matt. 26.24c). His death is depicted in Acts 1.18 in the classic terms of the death of an evil man (cf. 2 Sam. 20.10; Wis. 4.19; 2 Macc. 9.9), and he 'went to his own place' (Acts 1.25) —

sympathetic portrayal of the man who, in Christian faith, was an essential pawn (both indispensable and dispensable) in the sacred drama to achieve Christ's atoning death for the sins of the world. Who could not feel for the man elected to be so despised and rejected, the all-time hate figure for subsequent centuries of Christianity?[33] The trouble is that we have so little to go on. The Evangelists hint that he did it for greed (Mark 14.11 pars.).[34] And John reinforces the suggestion by naming him thief (John 12.6). But otherwise they show little interest in him beyond the fact that he 'handed Jesus over'. And the reports of Judas's death (Matt. 27.3-10/Acts 1.16-20), which gave an opportunity to exculpate Judas in at least some measure,[35] were hardly counted as core tradition, come to us in scarcely reconcilable versions, and scarcely provide sufficient basis for speculation as to his motivation, either for his suicide or his earlier action.[36] Judas remains an enigma.

c. The Last Supper

We need have no doubt that Jesus did meet with his disciples for what proved to be their final meal together 'on the night when he was handed over' (1 Cor. 11.23).[37] Paul confirms that the timing was part of the core and foundation tradition which he received as part of his personal Christian formation, and which he in turn passed on when he established the church in Corinth. Such a meal would have been in character anyway for a mission in which table-fellowship was such a marked feature (§14.8a). And though as a meal shared only with his closest disciples it is actually unique within the Gospel tradition, the implication of the ear-

---

presumably hell! In Dante's *Divine Comedy* Judas the arch-traitor is forever being devoured by Lucifer (along with Brutus and Cassius!) in the deepest depths of hell (*Hell,* Canto 34.55-69). See also H. Maccoby, *Judas Iscariot and the Myth of Jewish Evil* (London: Halban, 1992).

33. Note, e.g., the portrayal of Judas in the 'hit' musicals of the 1960s and 1970s 'Jesus Christ Superstar' and 'Godspell' and in Scorcese's *The Last Temptation of Christ.* The most recent attempt to rehabilitate Judas is by W. Klassen, *Judas: Betrayer or Friend of Jesus?* (Minneapolis: Augsburg, 1996), who makes much of the fact that *paradidōmi* means 'hand over' rather than 'betray' (47-58); also 'The Authenticity of Judas' Participation in the Arrest of Jesus', in Chilton and Evans, eds., *Authenticating the Activities of Jesus* 389-410.

34. But only Matthew counts the sum as 'thirty pieces of silver' (Matt. 26.15), and there is a suspicion that he derived the figure from Zech. 11.12-13, which he quotes in 27.9.

35. Matthew's account includes report of Judas' remorse: 'I have sinned by betraying innocent blood' (27.4).

36. Further discussion in Brown, *Death* 637-60 (bibliography 566-67); Davies and Allison, *Matthew* 3.559-60 (bibliography 572-73); also Klassen, *Judas* 160-76.

37. See above, §8.5c.

lier narrative is probably that much of Jesus' teaching directed to his inner circle of disciples took place in the context of meals.[38]

There is, however, a major and tantalising question difficult to resolve: Was the last meal a Passover? That is clearly how the Synoptic Evangelists wanted it to be understood (Mark 14.1-2, 12-17 pars.). And in his classic study Jeremias finds grounds for an affirmative answer in the facts that the meal was eaten in Jerusalem (not Bethany), and at night, and that wine was drunk, and in the words of interpretation (Mark 14.22-24 pars.).[39] On the other hand, there is no allusion to the normal elements in the Passover meal,[40] the last supper tradition itself does not speak of it as a Passover, and the execution of Jesus was unlikely to take place on the day of Passover itself. The Fourth Evangelist strengthens the last observation by reporting that Jesus was crucified on the day of preparation *(paraskeuē)* for the Passover (John 19.14), that is *prior* to the Passover meal (18.28).[41] One can hardly avoid the suspicion that John is making a theological point here: Jesus, the lamb of God (1.29, 36), was crucified at the time the Passover lambs were being slaughtered,[42] that is, along with the *other* Passover lambs.[43] Even so, as the evidence stands, in this case it is as likely as not that John has been able to draw his theological point from the actual historical sequence. And as likely as not also that the Synoptic version re-

38. Given the Fourth Evangelist's handling of Jesus' 'signs', I am less confident than R. A. Bauckham that a positive answer can be given to his question 'Did Jesus Wash His Disciples' Feet?' (in Chilton and Evans, *Authenticating the Activities of Jesus* 411-29), in reference to the last supper in particular.

39. Jeremias, *Eucharistic Words* ch. 1, particularly 41-62; similarly Pesch, *Markusevangelium* 2.362; I. H. Marshall, *Last Supper and Lord's Supper* (Exeter: Paternoster, 1980) 57-75; Stuhlmacher, *Biblische Theologie* 1.133-35 (pressing also the symbolism of the twelve); Gnilka, *Jesus* 280-81; Wright, *Jesus* 555-59; Casey, *Aramaic Sources* 236-38.

40. Arguably Jesus himself would not have taken a lamb to the Temple to be slaughtered, given the disturbance he had caused a few days earlier. But someone must have attended to such an indispensable part of the Passover ritual. Sanders speculates: 'Perhaps "they [the disciples] prepared" means "they bought a lamb, had it slaughtered at the Temple and put it on a spit to roast"' (*Historical Figure* 251). Casey, however, has no trouble in envisioning Jesus himself taking the responsibility (*Aramaic Sources* 222-23). For the ritual itself see Sanders, *Judaism* 132-38.

41. Also *Gos. Pet.* 2.5. See Brown, *Death* 845-46. It should be recalled that the Jewish day ended with nightfall, so an evening meal (after nightfall) would take place on the next day; on Jewish time-keeping Jesus was crucified on the same day that he ate his last meal with his disciples.

42. The time of day when the slaughtering began is not clear; most valuable is Brown's note (*Death* 847 n. 47).

43. That John intended Jesus' death to be understood as that of the Passover lamb is implied in 19.29 (the mention of hyssop — cf. Exod. 12.22) and clear in 19.36 (citing the Passover regulation — Exod. 12.46).

flects an early alternative interpretation of the core last supper tradition as a Passover meal.[44]

When arguments are so finely balanced it is wise not to press for one alternative as against another. Both interpretations indicate that the link between Jesus and the Passover was early on seen as important and instructive (cf. 1 Cor. 5.7). Each elaborated the link in his own way. But as for the meal itself we are hardly encouraged by the data to conclude more than that Jesus gave a heightened significance to what he may already have sensed was likely to be their last meal together.[45] What that heightened significance was is a subject to which we will have to return below (§§17.3c, 4e, 5d).

d. The Arrest of Jesus and Flight of the Disciples

That Jesus was arrested is not in doubt, and it is hardly likely that the tradition was recalled independently of the fuller story of Jesus' final hours. The tradition is firm on a number of features:[46] that the event took place across the Kidron/on the Mount of Olives (Mark 14.26 pars.),[47] that Judas led/came with the arresting party (14.43 pars.), that one of those with Jesus offered resistance to the extent of cutting off the ear of a member of the arresting party (14.47 pars.),[48] and that Jesus remonstrated briefly (14.48-49 pars.). Round that core several performance elaborations are evident: perhaps the betrayal with a kiss (Mark 14.44-45), Jesus' rebuke to the one who resisted (Matt. 26.52-54) and healing of the wound (Luke 22.51),[49] and the mysterious young man in Mark 14.51-52.[50]

The character of the arresting party is confused in the various tellings: a 'crowd' from the chief priests (and scribes) and elders (Mark 14.43/Matt. 26.47);

44. See further Brown, *Death* particularly 1364-73: 'we have here a theologoumenon, i.e., the presentation of the Last Supper as a paschal meal is a dramatization of the preGospel proclamation of Jesus as the paschal lamb' (1370).

45. Nicely concise discussions in E. Schweizer, *The Lord's Supper according to the New Testament* (1956; ET Philadelphia: Fortress, 1967) 29-32; O'Toole, 'Last Supper, *ABD* 4.235-37; Theissen and Merz, *Historical Jesus* 423-27.

46. Cf. Pesch, *Markusevangelium* 2.403; see further Légasse, *Trial of Jesus* 14-22.

47. S. Safrai maintains that there was a tradition current at the time of Jesus of a specific location on the Mount of Olives where King David used to pray which became a focal point of prayer (Flusser, *Jesus* 144 n. 26).

48. The fact that the anonymity of the one who resisted is retained in the Synoptic tradition (otherwise John 18.10) suggests that the story was framed early on when it would still be necessary to safeguard the individual concerned ('protective anonymity') from possible reprisals (Theissen and Merz, *Historical Jesus* 447).

49. Meier is fairly certain that the story is a Lukan creation (*Marginal Jew* 2.714-18).

50. Often taken to be Mark himself; see, e.g., discussion in Taylor, *Mark* 561-62.

chief priests and 'temple officers' *(stratēgoi)* and elders (Luke 22.52); a 'cohort *(speira)*' and 'attendants *(hypēretai)*' (John 18.3). But beyond some story-telling flourish,[51] the various accounts hold together well enough. There is no reason to conclude that there was Roman involvement,[52] since all agree that the arresting party came from the chief priests, who could use Temple police for the purpose *(stratēgoi?).*[53]

The flight of the disciples is recalled only by Mark and Matthew (Mark 14.50/Matt. 26.56). But together with the subsequent denial of Peter, dramatically retold in all four Gospels (Mark 14.66-72 pars.),[54] and the (almost) total absence of the male disciples from the crucifixion scene,[55] they are too shameful to have been contrived. Here not least the suggestion that such stories emerged as malicious, factional rumours against Peter and the others[56] can be dismissed as fanciful; the likelihood of such material being accepted and becoming established within this core tradition is very small indeed. It is much more plausible that those penitent over their failure should have sought to make some amends by including recollection of it within the core tradition for whose basic shape they were no doubt primarily responsible.[57]

e. The Role of Pilate

Pilate is almost as enigmatic a figure as Judas. This is no doubt the result of a notable tension between the Gospel accounts and our knowledge of Pilate from Josephus and Philo.[58] For in the latter, Pilate comes across as a ruthless governor,

51. A cohort would normally consist of 600 soldiers!

52. *Speira* is the normal Greek term for the Roman cohort, but Roman military terms were used for non-Roman troops (Brown, *Death* 248 n. 11; see also above, chapter 8 nn. 200, 201).

53. See Brown, *Death* 1430-31; fuller discussion on 246-52.

54. The description of place (courtyard), participants (servant woman and others), and details (fire, accusation, Galilean dialect) certainly smacks of eyewitness recall (Taylor, *Mark* 572; Pesch, *Markusevangelium* 2.451-52; Meier, *Marginal Jew* 3.242-45). The differing tellings as to detail and setting within the larger story (tabulated in Brown, *Death* 418-19, 590-91) are typical of performance variation.

55. The one exception might be the mysterious 'beloved disciple' (John 19.26-27). Possibly we should add Simon of Cyrene, evidently known to Mark's circle as 'father of Alexander and Rufus' (Mark 15.21; see further Brown, *Death* 913-17; Légasse, *Trial of Jesus* 80-81; Davies and Allison, *Matthew* 3.610-11); did he become a disciple as a result, and also a source for some of the details recounted by Mark (thus providing an answer to Lüdemann's dismissive question, 'Who would have had a correct recollection of that?' — *Jesus* 107)?

56. E.g., K. E. Dewey in Kelber, ed., *Passion in Mark* 106.

57. See further Schillebeeckx, *Jesus* 320-27; Brown, *Death* 614-26.

58. Philo, *Legat.* 299-305 (set up shields in Herod's palace in Jerusalem); Josephus, *War*

determined to impose his will, and only moved otherwise by the possibility of unfavourable reports being sent back to Emperor Tiberius[59] — in other words, a fairly typical middle-ranking official[60] representing the awesome power of the empire in a tiresome but sensitive part of its eastern territories. The fact that he held office as long as he did (26-37)[61] indicates both his astuteness and his ability to survive most of the crises he engendered, apart from the last.[62] There can be little doubt that he would have had no qualms about arbitrarily executing someone who could be plausibly accused of trouble-making or worse.[63] Crucifixion, we may recall, was a Roman form of punishment for recalcitrant slaves and political rebels.[64] That Jesus was crucified on the direct authority of Pilate himself need not be doubted for a minute.[65]

The only reason for hesitation before drawing such a straightforwardly firm conclusion is what we might call the counter-evidence of the Gospels themselves. For they clearly evidence a strong tendency to shift responsibility for the execution of Jesus away from the Roman to the Jewish authorities.[66] Pilate 'perceived that it was out of envy that the chief priests had handed him over' (Mark 15.10). He gave the crowd the option of saving Jesus or Barabbas (Mark 15.6-15).[67] Luke emphasizes that Pilate sent Jesus to Herod (Luke 23.6-

---

2.169-77; *Ant.* 18.55-89 (introduced standards with effigies of Caesar into Jerusalem by night, used Temple treasury money to build an aqueduct, ruthlessly suppressed a Samaritan 'uprising').

59. See particularly Bond, *Pontius Pilate* chs. 2-3.

60. The Roman governors of the few third-class imperial provinces, of which Judea was one, were drawn from the equestrian order and commanded only auxiliary troops (Bond, *Pontius Pilate* 5, 9-11).

61. The usual dates for Pilate's term of office, though D. R. Schwartz argues for a starting date in 19 ('Pontius Pilate', *ABD* 5.396-97).

62. The accusation of needless slaughter of the Samaritans is the reason given by Josephus for Pilate's dismissal in 36/37 (*Ant.* 18.85-89); see further n. 70 below.

63. One of Philo's virulent accusations against Pilate is that he was responsible for 'frequent executions of untried prisoners' (*Legat.* 302); though see Bond, *Pontius Pilate* 31-33.

64. See particularly Hengel, *Crucifixion* 33-63; Kuhn, 'Kreuzesstrafe' 706-32.

65. We recall that both Josephus (*Ant.* 18.63-64) and Tacitus (*Annals* 15.44) attribute Jesus' execution to Pilate (above, §7.1). That the death penalty was a power *(ius gladii)* reserved to the Roman authorities is now generally accepted; see, e.g., Légasse, *Trial of Jesus* 51-56.

66. See also Carroll and Green, *Death of Jesus* 182-204.

67. It is frustratingly difficult to assess the historical value of the Barabbas episode, not least since the name is uncannily akin to that of Jesus (Jesus Barabbas; 'Do you want me to release Jesus Barabbas or Jesus called Messiah?' — Matt. 27.17), and the custom of releasing a prisoner at Passover (Mark 15.6/Matt. 27.15; in Luke 23.17 only as v.l.) is otherwise unknown (hence the dismissive treatment of Lüdemann, *Jesus* 105-106; 'parable, not history' — Crossan and Reed, *Excavating Jesus* 225). But see full discussion in Brown, *Death* 793-803, 811-20; briefly in Pesch, *Markusevangelium* 2.467; Légasse, *Trial of Jesus* 67-69; Davies and Allison, *Matthew* 3.583, 585; Theissen and Merz, *Historical Jesus* 465-66.

12).[68] He declared Jesus innocent and wanted to let him off (Luke 23.14-15, 20, 22). Matthew has the story, grist to many a subsequent novellist's imagination, of Pilate's wife warning him to 'have nothing to do with that just man' (Matt. 27.19), as also the account of Pilate washing his hands and declaring himself 'innocent of this man's blood' (27.24);[69] it was the chief priests and elders who wanted to 'destroy' Jesus (27.20), 'all the people' who accepted the blood guilt (27.25). And John imagines a debate between Jesus and Pilate, in which Pilate is impressed by Jesus' answers and repeatedly insists, 'I find no case against him' (John 18.38; 19.4, 6); he is dissuaded from releasing Jesus only by the threat of complaint made against him to the Emperor (19.12).

Roman history shows from many examples that provincial governors were vulnerable to complaints of unjust government; so there are certainly plausible elements in the basic scenario.[70] Even so, the depiction of Pilate being in effect bullied by the high priest and his counsellors, to execute a man of whose innocence he was convinced, almost certainly owes more to political motivation than to historical recollection.[71] Of course, the policy of excusing Roman injustice is understandable for a movement which soon sought to win converts through the eastern territories of the Roman Empire. And in subsequent Christian fiction it was pushed still further to a ridiculous extent.[72] But the startling contrast here with the treatment of Judas is a reminder of some very unsavoury undercurrents within early Christianity.

The outcome of these tensions is to leave the role of Pilate in Jesus' execution tantalisingly obscure at various points. After all, the more negative portrayal of Pilate by Josephus and particularly Philo was probably as biased against Pilate as the more exonerating portrayal of the Gospels is biased in his favour. At the very least, however, the primary responsibility for Jesus' execution should be

68. The fact that only Luke has this episode raises the question of its historical value more sharply, but there is nothing intrinsically implausible in the basic account; see, e.g., Fitzmyer, *Luke* 2.1478-79; Brown, *Death* 783-86; Flusser, *Jesus* 163-64.

69. These certainly read like novellistic embellishment — based, perhaps, on Deut. 21.6-8 and Ps. 26.5-6 (Koester, *Ancient Christian Gospels* 221). Neither Brown (*Death* 803-807, 831-36) nor Davies and Allison (*Matthew* 3.587-88, 590-91) think it necessary to make a case for their historicity.

70. It was a complaint by Samaritans against Pilate's overreaction to a 'disturbance' *(thorybos)* in Samaria which occasioned his downfall a few years later (Josephus, *Ant.* 18.88-89); see further n. 62 above.

71. Note, however, Josephus's confirmation that Pilate condemned Jesus to be crucified on the accusation of 'men of the highest standing amongst us' (*Ant.* 18.64). Bond points out that the Gospels are by no means uniform in their portrayal of Pilate. It is only Luke who presents him as weak, whereas Mark presents him as a skilful politician and John as manipulative, derisive, and sure of his authority (*Pontius Pilate* 117-18, 159-60, 192-93, 205-206).

72. See the Pilate cycle collected in Elliott, *Apocryphal New Testament* 164-225; in the Coptic church Pilate has even been canonized.

firmly pinned to Pilate's record, and the first hints of an anti-Jewish tendency in the Gospels on this point should be clearly recognized and disowned.

f. The Account of Jesus' Death

It has long been recognized that OT echoes, particularly of the Psalms, and particularly Psalm 22, have been influential in shaping the tradition of Jesus' crucifixion. The most notable are as follows:[73]

Gospels		Psalms 22, 31, 69
1. Mt 27.35 Mk 15.24 Jn 19.24	They divided his clothes by casting lots for them	22.18 They divide my clothes among them, and for my clothing they cast lots.
2. Mt 27.39 Mk 15.29	Those who passed by derided him, shaking their heads . . .	22.7 All who see me mock at me; they make mouths at me, they shake their heads.
3. Mt 27.43	He trusts in God; let God deliver him now, if he wants to . . .	22.8 He hoped in the Lord; let him deliver him; let him save him because he wants to (LXX).
4. Mt 27.46 Mk 15.34	My God, my God, why have you forsaken me?	22.1 My God, my God, why have you forsaken me?
5. Mt 27.48 Mk 15.36 Jn 19.29 (Mt. 27.34 Mk 15.23)	Someone ran, filled a sponge with sour wine, put it on a stick, and he drank it.	69.21 For my thirst they gave me sour wine to drink.
6. Lk 23.46	Father, into your hands I place my spirit	31.6 Into your hands I shall place my spirit.

In the face of such evidence it is difficult to avoid the conclusion that the narrative has been shaped to bring out these echoes.[74] The point is most obvious in the particular elaborations of Matthew (27.43) and Luke (23.46), where the specific quotation of the psalm is obviously an addition to a more sparsely told tradition.[75] But even so, it is hard to escape the conclusion that the tradition itself was formulated from the beginning in the light of the psalms in both verses.[76] This

73. For fuller documentation and discussion see D. J. Moo, *The Old Testament in the Gospel Passion Narratives* (Sheffield: Almond, 1983) ch. 4 (tabulated 285-86); Brown, *Death* 1445-67; J. Marcus, 'The Old Testament and the Death of Jesus: The Role of Scripture in the Gospel Passion Narratives', in Carroll and Green, *Death of Jesus* 205-33 (tabulation 207-209); Davies and Allison, *Matthew* 3.608-609. Moo also documents references to the Servant songs and the use of Zech. 9–14 in the Passion narratives (chs. 2-3; tabulation 163-64, 222); similarly Marcus 214-15, 219.

74. Bultmann, *History* 280-81; Bornkamm, *Jesus* 156-57; B. Lindars, *New Testament Apologetic* (London: SCM, 1961) ch. 3: 'passion apologetic' (particularly 88-110); Juel, *Messianic Exegesis* 89-117; Koester, *Ancient Christian Gospels* 220-30.

75. Discussion in Brown, *Death* 994-96, 1066-69.

76. 'If there is a pre-Markan passion tradition that can be isolated, the psalms surely

does not mean that the details in question were created in the light of the scriptural allusions:[77] the crucifixion with two others (Mark 15.27 pars.) is hardly derived from Isa. 53.12;[78] the mocking (Mark 15.29-32 pars.), like its earlier counterpart,[79] is determined more from within the tradition (echoing the earlier accusation and trial verdict) than by the scriptural echoes ('shaking their heads'); it is not implausible that the attendant soldiers should have offered some of their own vinegary wine *(oxos)* to drink,[80] whether out of malice *(Gos. Pet.* 5.16-17) or compassion; and some memory of Jesus crying out in the words of Ps. 22.1 (problematic as narrated for subsequent christology) may have prompted the search for other echoes of the psalm (see below).[81] But it does mean that from the first, the shape of the tradition may have obscured as well as enhanced various details of the event.[82] Was it ever otherwise with partisan accounts?[83]

---

form the basis of the tradition. It is unlikely that Jesus' story was ever told as a recitation of facts' (Juel, *Messianic Exegesis* 113). The *Gospel of Peter* attests a variant (not necessarily a more original) instance of the procedure (cf. Koester, *Ancient Christian Gospels* 220-30); but Koester's conclusion — 'No question *(sic),* the Gospel of Peter has preserved the most original narrative version of the tradition of scriptural interpretation' (230) — is hardly justified. See further above, chapter 7 n. 154.

77. As already pointed out by Dibelius, *Tradition* 188-89. Moo, *Old Testament,* notes indications that the scriptural texts were themselves emended in order to fit more closely to the events as they were remembered. A good example is the use of Zech. 11.13 in Matt. 27.9-10 (Lindars, *New Testament Apologetic* 116-22; Dunn, *Unity and Diversity* 92-93, 95-96). Juel concludes on the use of Psalm 89 in the tradition (echoing Dahl, cited above in chapter 15 n. 63): 'The psalm was cited not to prove Jesus was the Christ but to make sense of that confession' *(Messianic Exegesis* 117).

78. 'He was numbered with the transgressors' (Isa. 53.12).

79. The purple robe, the crown of thorns, the mock homage (Mark 15.16-20 pars.); cf. Isa. 50.6: 'I gave my back to those who struck me and my cheeks to those who pulled out the beard; I did not hide my face from insult and spitting'. Flusser notes also the mockery of Karabas described by Philo in *Flacc.* 36-39 *(Jesus* 169-70, 210-12) and suggests that Pilate's 'Behold the man' (John 19.5) was a mocking acclamation echoing the soldiers' mockery (207-20); in reference to Matt. 26.68/Luke 22.64 Flusser also suggests that Jesus was made the butt of an ancient game, 'Who is it that struck You?' (187-94).

80. See MM *oxos,* BDAG, *oxos.*

81. A case could also be made for quotation of Zech. 13.7 in Mark 14.27/Matt. 26.31 in view of the strong shepherd/sheep motif in Jesus' teaching (Wright, *Jesus* 533-34; see §13.3c n.110 above); see also Marcus, 'Old Testament' 220.

82. The point should not be exaggerated; the restraint of the tradition should also be noted. As Keck observes, 'no gospel reports that the Voice spoke where one might expect it most of all — at the crucifixion. . . . At Golgotha the silence of God was deafening' *(Who Is Jesus?* 128; see also the powerful meditation on the holiness of God in regard to Jesus' crucifixion which follows [134-40]).

83. In a paper delivered at the SBL annual meeting in Denver, Colorado (November 2001), Mark Goodacre noted how many details of the accounts cannot be derived from Scrip-

In terms of the traditioning process, if I am right, the evidence points to two important corollaries. One is the implication that (one of) the earliest disciple responses to the shock of Jesus' execution was to turn to Scripture to see what sense could be made of it. For a people to whom Scripture was life and light, the reaction is wholly understandable. It would be equally understandable that the great 'suffering psalms', including, not least, Psalms 22 and 69, should have become luminous at that time. No wonder, then, that the first attempts to speak about the event in a tradition-forming way drew on just these psalms to incorporate the disciples' perspective on what had happened.[84]

If the account was based even partially on eyewitness memory, then it is not unimportant to recall that the only eyewitnesses that all the Evangelists agree on were women disciples (Mark 15.40 pars.).[85] There is a strong possibility, therefore, that these women played a significant role in forming the tradition of Jesus' death.

At least one other point should be raised — that is, regarding Jesus' last words from the cross, which have provided the basis for generations of Christian meditation. In the light of which, and given the character of the tradition just adduced, it is somewhat disturbing to have to acknowledge how weakly rooted these last words are in the tradition.

	Matthew	Mark	Luke	John
1. Father forgive them, for they don't know what they're doing.			23.34 (v.l.)	
2. Woman, here is your son.				19.26
Here is your mother.				19.27
3. Truly I say to you, today you will be with me in paradise.			23.43	
4. Eloi, Eloi lama sabachthani.	27.46	15.34		
5. I thirst.				19.28
6. It is finished.				19.30
7. Father, into your hands I place my spirit.			23.46	

A stunning feature immediately becomes apparent: that only one of the 'last words' is attested by more than one author. And since Matthew's Passion

---

ture — the women watching 'afar off', Simon of Cyrene, the name 'Golgotha', the time (the third hour), the title 'king of the Jews'. He suggests that between the polarized alternatives of 'history remembered' and 'prophecy historicized' (as posed by Crossan, *Who Killed Jesus?* x-xi, 1-13, against Brown, *Death*) a third is more plausible: 'history scripturized'. Crossan confuses rather than clarifies this particular issue by tying it so closely to the issue of anti-Semitism in the accounts of Jesus' death.

84. See also A. Yarbro Collins, 'From Noble Death to Crucified Messiah', *NTS* 40 (1994) 481-503. See again Koester's claim that 'the different versions of the passion narrative in the gospel literature' derive from 'the oral performances of the story in the ritual celebrations, ever enriched by new references to the scriptures of Israel' (above, n. 16).

85. But see also n. 55 above.

narrative is heavily dependent on Mark, it means in effect that each of the 'last words' is dependent on single attestation. Moreover, only one is attested by Mark (15.34). Luke's first word has weak support in the textual tradition (23.34),[86] his second is part of the unsupported account of a conversation between the three crucified,[87] and his third looks like one of the psalm elaborations already noted (where Mark 15.37 has only that 'Jesus let out a great cry'). John's first word is bound up with his otherwise unattested 'beloved disciple' tradition (19.26), his second seems to be a somewhat contrived way of introducing the allusion to Ps. 69.21 (he said it 'in order to fulfil the Scripture' — 19.28), and his third sounds a more triumphant note than any of the other Gospels (19.30).

The uncomfortable conclusion probably has to be that most of the words from the cross are part of the elaboration in the diverse retellings of Jesus' final hours. Had there been words more clearly recalled, experience of the Jesus tradition elsewhere suggests that they would have become a core within the fuller story of Jesus' death and so would have remained stable within the varying retellings of the story. Without such attestation we are pushed by the evidence to the alternative conclusion: that the stable element was the scene itself and the broad structure (attested by Mark/Matthew, variantly by Luke, and still more variantly by John), and that beyond that much of the detail belongs to the category of performance variation.

Of the seven 'last words', the one with strongest historical claim is certainly the only one attested by Mark/Matthew — 'My God, my God, why have you forsaken me?' (Mark 15.34/Matt. 27.46). The citation of Ps. 22.1 certainly raises suspicions.[88] On the other hand, the Greek is clearly an attempted transliteration of Aramaic.[89] The potential embarrassment for Christian apologetics ('the cry of desolation') would surely have been obvious from the first and could have been easily countered by somehow extending the allusion to the confident climax of the psalm.[90] And the likelihood that Jesus fell back on familiar words of worship when *in extremis* (heard by the faithful few who waited near him till

86. It is omitted by p[75] B D* W Θ and early Latin, Syriac, and Coptic versions, but the echo in Acts 7.60 suggests that Luke was aware of the Luke 23.34 tradition, so the textual tradition is puzzling.

87. Brown suggests that Luke has taken the 'Amen' saying from another context and used it here (*Death* 1001-2).

88. E.g., Bultmann, *History* 313; Funk, *Five Gospels* 125-26; Lüdemann, *Jesus* 108 (a community product and therefore inauthentic; 'This follows conclusively [*sic*] from the contradiction between the different cries on the cross and the lack of an appropriate eye-witness or tradent').

89. See Pesch, *Markusevangelium* 2.495, 501; Davies and Allison, *Matthew* 3.624; and further Brown, *Death* 1051-58.

90. 'He did not despise or abhor the affliction of the afflicted; he did not hide his face from him (MT)/me (LXX), but heard when he (MT)/I (LXX) cried to him' (Ps. 22.24).

the end) is hardly to be dismissed out of hand. Nor the likelihood that the words were allowed to fall out in other performance traditions precisely because of their potential embarrassment.[91]

All in all then, the results are more meagre than we might have hoped for.[92] The tradition of Jesus' crucifixion and death, as attested by those who witnessed it, is firm enough in outline.[93] But the tradition was evidently formed from the first to bring out scriptural allusions and to give the whole a spiritually edifying character. That was how Jesus' death was remembered from the beginning — as fulfilling scriptural types and as providing a good model of martyr-like piety and concern for others.

g. The Burial of Jesus

Some assume that Jesus' body would have been routinely disposed of by the authorities.[94] But the tradition is firm that Jesus was given a proper burial (Mark 15.42-47 pars.), and there are good reasons why its testimony should be respected.[95] (1) The tradition of Jesus' burial is one of the oldest pieces of tradition we have (1 Cor. 15.4 — *hoti etaphē*),[96] and, unlike the preceding narrative, no de-

---

91. Cf. Brown, *Death* 1086-88. J. B. Green, 'Death of Jesus', *DJG* 146-63, makes a good case for arguing that Luke is not responsible for the quotation of Ps. 31.6 (Luke 23.46) (151-52).

92. The accounts of three hours of darkness (Mark 15.33 pars.), the veil of the sanctuary being rent (Mark 15.38 pars.), the centurion's 'confession' (Mark 15.39; but note Luke 23.47), the earthquake (Matt. 27.51; *Gos. Pet.* 6.21), and the dead saints being raised (Matt. 27.52-53) are best attributed to dramatic recital and theological elaboration (discussion in Brown, *Death* 1034-43, 1098-1140, 1143-52, 1160-67, 1192-93).

93. The accounts hardly give an adequate indication of the horror and agony of death by crucifixion, but we can fill out at least some of the details from what we know of crucifixion elsewhere — 'that most cruel and most horrible of punishments' (Cicero) (see, e.g., Hengel, *Crucifixion* 24-32; G. S. Sloyan, *The Crucifixion of Jesus* [Minneapolis: Fortress, 1995] 14-18; Légasse, *Trial of Jesus* 88-91). John's account of the final phase (John 19.31-37) is refracted through a theological prism (19.36-37), though attributed to an eyewitness (19.35), but both the practice of breaking the legs of a crucified man (to hasten his death) and that of a spear thrust to ensure death are attested for the period (see, e.g., Légasse 161 nn. 112, 113).

94. Crossan is confident that 'Nobody knew what had happened to Jesus' body' (*Historical Jesus* 394). Behind the Gospel narratives 'lies, at worst, the horror of a body left on the cross as carrion or, at best, a body consigned like others to a "limed pit"' (*Birth* 555).

95. Nicely summarized in Davies and Allison, *Matthew* 3.647-48.

96. A point especially emphasized by M. Hengel, 'Das Begräbnis Jesu bei Paulus', in F. Avemarie and H. Lichtenberger, eds., *Auferstehung — Resurrection* (WUNT 135; Tübingen: Mohr Siebeck, 2001) 119-83 (here 121, 129-38, 175-76).

tail is drawn from Scripture.[97] (2) Jewish law required that the body of an executed criminal should be taken down before nightfall (Deut. 21.22-23); Josephus
confirms that this was current practice (*War* 4.317). Although the Romans might
have preferred to leave the corpse on the cross as a warning to others,[98] it is unlikely that they would have disregarded Jewish religious law and custom at such a
sensitive time (Passover). (3) There are some reports of permission being given
for a crucified victim to be taken down ahead of normal practice;[99] and the skele-
tal remains of a crucified man discovered at Giv'at ha-Mivtar were buried in a
family tomb.[100] It is not irrelevant to recall that, according to Mark 6.29, the Baptist's disciples were given permission to take his body after execution and buried it
in a tomb. (4) Joseph of Arimathea is a very plausible historical character: he is attested in all four Gospels (Mark 15.43 pars.) and in the *Gospel of Peter* (2.3-5);
when the tendency of the tradition was to shift blame to the Jewish council, the
creation *ex nihilo* of a sympathiser from among their number would be surprising;[101] and 'Arimathea', 'a town very difficult to identify and reminiscent of no
scriptural symbolism, makes a thesis of invention even more implausible'.[102] It
would be surprising if Jesus had not won some such support within the higher ech-
elons of Jewish society.[103] (5) Similarly the presence of the women at the cross

97. Of the three clauses describing Jesus' death and resurrection in 1 Cor. 15.3-4, only
the reference to Jesus' burial *(hoti etaphē)* lacks the accompanying phrase 'according to the
Scriptures'.

98. Hengel, *Crucifixion* 87-88.

99. Philo, *Flacc.* 83: 'I have known cases when on the eve of a holiday of this kind, people who have been crucified have been taken down and their bodies delivered to their kinsfolk,
because it was thought well to give them burial and allow them the ordinary rites'; Josephus,
Life 420: '. . . on my return I saw many prisoners who had been crucified, and recognized three
of my acquaintances among them. . . . Titus gave orders immediately that they should be taken
down and receive the most careful treatment. Two of them died in the physicians' hands; the
third survived'. Brown is not confident on this point (*Death* 1207-9).

100. See particularly J. Zias and E. Sekeles, 'The Crucified Man from Giv'at ha-Mivtar:
A Reappraisal', *IEJ* 35 (1985) 22-27.

101. *Pace* Funk: 'probably a Markan creation' (*Honest* 234). Contrast M. Myllykoski,
'What Happened to the Body of Jesus?' in I. Dunderberg, et al., eds., *Fair Play: Diversity and
Conflicts in Early Christianity,* H. Räisänen FS (Leiden: Brill, 2002) 43-82, who concludes that
'the oral tradition emphasized that Jesus was buried by a respected member of the Sanhedrin,
and that his burial was simple but honourable' (82; critique of Crossan 76-81; further bibliography 44 n. 3). John 19.39 also names Nicodemus. Flusser finds that the rabbinic records regarding Nicodemus complement John's picture (*Jesus* 148-49). But the amount of spices indicated
(about 75 lbs.) is extraordinary (cf. John 2.6).

102. Brown, *Death* 1240.

103. Crossan (*Birth* 554-55) makes too much of minor differences (typical of varied performance, whether oral or literary) regarding Joseph's status as a member of the council which
condemned Jesus (see further above, §15.3a and n. 81). Lüdemann (*Jesus* 111) is similarly

and their involvement in Jesus' burial can be attributed more plausibly to early oral memory than to creative story-telling.[104] I see no reason, therefore, to dissent from Brown's overall conclusion: 'there is nothing in the basic preGospel account of Jesus' burial by Joseph that could not plausibly be deemed historical'.[105]

In short, we can be fairly confident that the tradition of Jesus' final days was already being recalled and reflected on from the very earliest days of communal gatherings of Jesus' followers after Easter 30 CE. The tradition was probably held within a broad structure, but there was evidently flexibility in what might be included within the structure, the performances were subject to the usual variation, and individual episodes were variously elaborated as occasion allowed. The Evangelists' accounts are in effect frozen examples of such performances. In particular, the tradition of Jesus' trial, execution, and burial (the Passion narrative) seems to have been more thoroughly integrated into a single narrative more or less from the first, possibly for sacred recitation within the early followers' worship (at Passover?). It often reflects the scriptural passages drawn in to illuminate the earliest recollections of the events, and gives evidence of the devotional meditation which the retellings both evoked and came to embody. But in character, otherwise, it is similar to the oral tradition identifiable throughout the Gospel tradition and reflects the same traditioning processes. If in the variations of the tradition we can detect the particular interests of individual churches or Evangelists, we can also confidently detect in the stabilities of structure and structural elements the character of the tradition as it was being retold from the beginning.

What then still needs to be clarified are a number of more specific questions: can we gain a clearer insight into why Jesus was executed? and can we say more regarding Jesus' own perception and motivation in the events that transpired?

---

sceptical but accepts the likelihood that Joseph was the one who undertook the burial, without following through the corollaries (that the place of Jesus' burial would have been known). Acts 13.29 hardly provides adequate basis for an alternative scenario — that Jesus was laid in a tomb by unnamed Jews (G. Lüdemann, *The Resurrection of Jesus: History, Experience, Theology* [London: SCM, 1994] 43-44); more realistic is E. Haenchen's comment, 'In reality Luke has only shortened the account as much as possible' (*Acts of the Apostles* [Oxford: Blackwell, 1971] 410).

104. Cf. K. E. Corley, 'Women and the Crucifixion and Burial of Jesus. "He was Buried: On the Third Day He Was Raised"', *Forum* 1 (1998) 181-225; see further below, §18.2a.

105. *Death* 1241. The archaeological evidence pointing to the traditional site for Jesus' tomb is surprisingly strong — within the present church of the Holy Sepulchre in Jerusalem, a site not brought within the walls of the city till they were extended in 41-43 CE (see further Charlesworth, *Jesus* 123-25; Légasse, *Trial of Jesus* 82-87, 102; Murphy-O'Connor, *Holy Land* 45-48; M. Broshi in Flusser, *Jesus* 251-57; J. E. Taylor, 'Golgotha: A Reconsideration of the Evidence for the Sites of Jesus' Crucifixion and Burial', *NTS* 44 [1998] 180-203).

17.2. Why Was Jesus Executed?

One of the flaws of the most characteristic Liberal portrayal of Jesus was the unlike-lihood that anyone would have wanted to crucify such an attractive moral teacher.[106] In recent questing it has been more widely recognized that a test of any hypothesis' viability is whether it provides a satisfactory answer to the question, Why was Jesus crucified? To be 'historical' the historical Jesus must have been crucifiable.[107] There is also no doubt that primary responsibility for Jesus' execution must be laid at the door of the Roman authorities, Pilate in particular (§17.1e), and that Jesus was executed as a threat (messianic pretender) to Rome's hold over Israel (§15.3a). But the Jesus tradition also records that the move to have Jesus executed was initiated from the Jewish side of the uneasy alliance between the Jewish authorities and the Roman governor. And although the Jewish responsibility has been exaggerated in the course of transmission (§17.1e), there is no good reason to doubt the basic facts of Jesus' arrest by Jewish Temple police (§17.1d) and subsequent hearing before a council convened by the high priest Caiaphas for the purpose (§15.2a).[108] So our question still stands, Why was Jesus arrested and 'handed over' to Pilate?

Typical of older attempts to answer this question was the assumption that Jesus' challenge to the *law* was the crucial break-point between Jesus and the Jewish authorities.[109] The corollary was that the authorities in question were principally the Pharisees — a deduction which followed naturally from Mark 3.6,[110] and which could easily be bolstered by reports of other hostile encounters with the Pharisees (particularly the diatribe of Matthew 23). That whole hypothe-sis has largely crumbled away as a result of Sanders's onslaught. Although he overstates his case, he has so undermined the two principal supports that they can hardly bear much if any of the weight formerly placed on them: the Pharisees were not in a position of power to determine Jesus' fate;[111] and Jesus' disputa-tions regarding the Torah and current halakhah were unlikely to have been as rad-ical or as offensive as later Christian opinion has assumed.[112]

---

106. We may recall the famous William Temple quotation (chapter 4 above, at n. 110).

107. A point variously emphasized by Sanders, Horsley, and Wright (see, e.g., above, chapter 8 n. 7).

108. On Caiaphas, including the discovery of an ossuary inscribed with the name 'Jo-seph bar Caiapha', see Flusser, *Jesus* 195-206; Crossan and Reed, *Excavating Jesus* 240-42.

109. Theissen and Merz cite J. Roloff as typical of traditional Protestant exegesis: 'Jesus died because of the convictions of his Jewish opponents, because in all his behaviour he had re-belled against the will of God in the law which they had advocated . . .' (*Historical Jesus* 464). Becker seems still to want to go down this path (*Jesus* 335).

110. Cited above, §14.4a.

111. *Pace* Chilton: 'The Sanhedrin, dominated by the pesky Pharisees' (*Rabbi Jesus* 220); but see again Sanders, *Jesus* 312-17; also *Judaism* 458-90.

112. See above, §§9.3a(1) and 14.4.

More important is the fact that Pharisees hardly feature at all in the Passion narratives of the Gospels. In Mark no mention is made of Pharisees after 12.13 (early in the final week). In Matthew Pharisees appear only at 27.62 subsequent to the polemic of ch. 23. In Luke no mention is made of Pharisees after 19.39 (the entry into Jerusalem). And in John the only mention made of the Pharisees after ch. 12 is 18.3. 'Scribes'[113] and 'elders'[114] are included among the Jewish authorities who initiate the key events, but no attempt is made to identify the former as 'scribes of the Pharisees' (Mark 2.16/Luke 5.30).[115] Given the frequency of reference to Pharisees elsewhere in the Jesus tradition, it is evident that no real attempt has been made to attribute responsibility to them for the legal moves against Jesus. On the contrary, the Jesus tradition preserves virtually no memory of Pharisaic involvement in Jesus' execution.[116]

In contrast, the chief priests *(archiereis)* feature regularly.[117] So far as the passion narratives themselves are concerned, then, on the Jewish side the chief actors in the unfolding drama of Jesus' arrest and condemnation were the chief priests. This in turn clearly implies that the crucial factors behind Jesus' arrest and condemnation were issues of Temple and high-priestly authority, and otherwise not the Torah. Can we be more specific?

a. Temple Protest and Temple Saying

Little more need be said on this point. The prominence of the chief priests in the move to silence Jesus fits well with the earlier observations: that the Temple was not only the centre of Israel's religion but also the very substantial economic base for the political power of the high priestly families (§9.3a) and that Jesus' symbolical act in the Temple and talk of the Temple's destruction provided the final reason/(excuse?) for Jesus' arrest and the primary accusations levelled against

---

113. Mark 14.1/Luke 22.2; Mark 14.43; Mark 14.53/Matt. 26.57; Mark 15.1/Luke 22.66; Luke 23.10; Mark 15.31/Matt. 27.41; note also the Passion predictions (Mark 8.31; 10.33) and Mark 11.18.

114. Matt. 26.3; Mark 14.43, 53/Matt. 26.47, 57; Luke 22.52; Mark 15.1/Matt. 27.1; Matt. 27.3, 12, 20, 41.

115. 'Scribes' are regularly mentioned with Pharisees, but as a separate group (Mark 7.1/Matt. 15.1; Matt. 5.20; 12.38; 23.2, 13, 15, 23, 25, 27, 29; Luke 5.21; 6.7; 11.53; 15.2; John 8.3). See above, §9.3c(2).

116. Cf. Légasse, *Trial of Jesus* 35-38. I have already noted the unlikelihood that the charge against Jesus was that of being a false prophet or a magician (above, chapter 15 n. 95).

117. Sixteen occurrences in Mark 14–15, nineteen in Matthew 26–28, thirteen in Luke 19–24, and fourteen in John 18–19. Sanders sets out the data synoptically (*Jesus* 310-11); see the fuller analysis of the various parties involved in opposition to Jesus in Brown, *Death* 1424-34.

him (§15.3a). Most likely it was because Jesus was seen as a threat to the status quo, a threat to the power brokers within Israel's social-religious-political system, that they decided to move decisively against him.[118] In the event it would seem that they were able to portray the decision to hand Jesus over to Pilate for summary execution as a purely religious one (Jesus guilty of 'blasphemy' — Mark 14.63-64 pars.). In the event too Pilate took not very much persuasion to condemn Jesus as a political challenge to Roman power (§17.1e).[119] But it is unlikely that Pilate would have taken steps to remove Jesus without that persuasion. Jesus was executed, in the final analysis, because he had become too much of a thorn in the side of the religious-political establishment.

But how much of a thorn? Was it only when he went to Jerusalem that he became so perceived? Or had there been smouldering resentment earlier which burst into flame only on Jesus' (final) trip to Jerusalem? Here the boot is more on the other foot, in that in the Gospels (even John), the chief priests hardly feature before Jesus' entry into Jerusalem;[120] earlier the chief protagonists are consistently described as scribes and Pharisees. At the same time there are hints that Jesus' words and actions would probably have been seen as an irritation (or worse) to priestly prerogatives.

b. Forgiveness — Bypassing the Cult?

We have already observed the relative prominence of the prospect of forgiveness held out to repentance by both the Baptist and Jesus.[121] The point should not be exaggerated, as though either of them offered a forgiveness nowhere else available within Second Temple Judaism.[122] For Israel delighted in their God as a

118. Sanders, *Jesus* 287-90, 301-305; also *Historical Figure* 265-69, 272-73. Cf. particularly E. Rivkin, *What Crucified Jesus?* (Nashville: Abingdon, 1984); Horsley, *Jesus* 323-26. On the sensitivity with which criticism of the Temple would be received by the Jerusalem leadership see further Theissen, 'Jesus' Temple Prophecy'. Becker urges caution: 'Relating Jesus' temple action to his death may be a popular thing to do today, but that connection is nowhere indicated by the sources' (*Jesus* 332; he is aware of Mark 11.18). But the link between the Temple saying and the action against Jesus (Mark 14.58) is firm (see above, §15.3a), and some association between Temple action and Temple saying can be safely assumed.

119. 'A man who spoke of a kingdom, spoke against the temple, and had a following was one marked for execution' (Sanders, *Jesus* 295).

120. Apart from the Passion predictions (Mark 8.31 pars.; Mark 10.33/Matt. 20.18), only John 7.32, 45 call for consideration; the other Johannine references all follow on John's trigger event, the raising of Lazarus (John 11.47, 49, 51, 57; 12.10).

121. See above, §§11.3b, 13.2a.

122. So Perrin, *Rediscovering* 97, 107; rebuked by Sanders, *Jesus* 200-204 (both cited in my *Partings* 44-45).

God of forgiveness, a merciful and gracious God 'forgiving iniquity and transgression and sin' (Exod. 34.6-7).[123] Prayer for forgiveness was part of Israel's liturgy.[124] And the sacrificial system, particularly the sin offering and the Day of Atonement, was designed to provide forgiveness.[125] So talk of forgiveness now and the reality of forgiveness experienced now would hardly have been strange to the devout Jew of Jesus' time.

Jesus, however, is recalled as causing surprise or offence by saying 'Your sins are forgiven' both to the paralyzed man, (Mark 2.5, 9 pars.),[126] and to the 'sinner' who anointed his feet in Luke 7.48-49.[127] In the former case the story now attests the Son of Man's authority to forgive sins (2.10), and that affirmation answers the querulous response of the scribes, 'Who can forgive sins but God alone?' (2.7). But the statement, 'Your sins are forgiven', is simply a pronouncement of forgiveness, and the passive form of the verb[128] indicates that it is God who forgives (as when a Christian priest pronounces absolution in a present-day Christian congregation).[129] Presumably this was the implication too when the Baptist pronounced sins forgiven (as implied by Mark 1.4/Luke 3.3),[130] or when in the Prayer of Nabonidus from Qumran, Nabonidus says 'an exorcist forgave my sin' (4QprNab 4).[131] In neither case is there any thought of the individual in question usurping a divine prerogative, only of human *mediation* of divine forgiveness.[132]

A more likely cause of protest in the incident itself was that Jesus pro-

---

123. Exod. 34.6-7 is regularly echoed in Jewish Scripture (Num. 14.18; Neh. 9.17; Pss. 86.15; 130.4; 145.8; Dan. 9.9; Joel 2.13; Jon. 4.2; Mic. 7.18; Nah. 1.3).

124. E.g., 1 Kgs. 8.30-50; 2 Kgs. 5.18; 2 Chron. 6.21-39; Pss. 25.11; 32; 51; 79.9; *Prayer of Manasseh.* As Ps. 51.16-19 reminds us, while sacrifice without such prayer was recognized to be vain, effective prayer which could dispense with sacrifice was not contemplated. Note also, of course, Matt. 6.12/Luke 11.4; Mark 11.25/Matt. 6.14-15.

125. In the legislation governing sin offerings and guilt offerings (Leviticus 4–5) we find the repeated phrase, 'so the priest shall make atonement for him for his sins, and he shall be forgiven' (4.26, 31, 35; 5.10, 16, 18). Note also the range of sins against God and the neighbour covered by such provision (Lev. 6.1-7). Eschatological forgiveness (Jer. 31.34) was presumably not thought of as a first-time forgiveness but as a complete or final (?) forgiveness.

126. Cited above, §15.7e.

127. But otherwise the Jesus tradition is silent on the subject, apart from John 20.23.

128. The 'divine passive' (Jeremias, *Proclamation* 11).

129. Already in John 20.23 that is regarded as 'authority to forgive sins' (to echo Mark 2.10 pars.).

130. In a similar way the Qumran sect bypassed the Temple by claiming that atonement could be experienced independently of the Temple cult (see above, chapter 11 nn. 94, 99).

131. García Martínez reconstructs the preceding phrase (missing) as 'I prayed to the God Most High and an exorcist forgave my sin' (3-4) — a plausible suggestion, since Nabonidus goes on to testify (presumably) to the ineffectiveness of the prayers he had made previously to the gods of silver and gold . . . (7).

132. Sanders, *Jesus* 273; Leivestad, *Jesus* 137-38.

nounced sins forgiven both *outside* the cult and *without reference* (even by implication) to the cult. Sins were (apparently) forgiven there and then; there is no suggestion in the tradition that a sacrificial offering would be necessary. In other words, it was not so much that Jesus usurped the exclusive prerogative of God to forgive sins which caused offence, as that he usurped the role which God had assigned to the priest and the cult in the established religion of the people.[133] John's baptism of repentance for the forgiveness of sins raised similar questions (§11.3b).

There is certainly a danger of drawing too much from a single incident, and the sparseness of the theme within the Jesus tradition forbids any attempt to make much of the theme (Jesus and forgiveness). The point is simply that if Jesus' (occasional) pronouncing of sins forgiven caused any upset, the upset would most likely have been to those who valued the religious proprieties embodied and safeguarded in the Temple system. The chief proprietors (guardians and beneficiaries) of the system were the high priestly families. Possibly, then, news of another, like the Baptist, seeming to bypass the cult, would have been a factor already causing irritation to the Temple authorities well before Jesus (finally) entered Jerusalem.

c. Purity — Dispensing with the Cult?

A more likely cause of irritation to the religious authorities were reports of Jesus' disregard for purity ritual. We have already noted how central to Second Temple Judaism were concerns for purity, and how these concerns were heightened by the factionalism of the period; indeed, such concerns were one of the major factors making for that factionalism (§§9.4, 5c-d). Borg in particular has consistently highlighted the 'politics of holiness/purity': 'the purity system was the ideology of the ruling elites'.[134] The Temple lay at the centre of these concerns: the purity required was to enable participation in the Temple cult;[135] the Temple stood in effect at the centre of a sequence of concentric circles of holiness (holy land, holy city, holy Temple, Holy of Holies).[136] Which also means, of course, that holiness/purity was a particularly priestly concern (Leviticus 21–22). The

133. If they so chose, those who heard such a pronouncement in a critical spirit could regard it as 'blasphemy' (Mark 2.7 pars.), as challenging God's ordering of how sins should be forgiven. Cf. Sanders, *Jewish Law* 61-63; and see the discussion above, §16.4c(2).

134. Borg, *Conflict passim; Jesus: A New Vision* index 'politics of holiness'; *Jesus in Contemporary Scholarship* ch. 5 (here 110-12).

135. Sanders, *Jesus* 182-83; *Judaism* 70-72 ('The ideas of holiness and separation, which allowed only what was most pure to come near, informed the entire arrangement of the temple and its rites').

136. Jeremias, *Jerusalem* 79. *M. Kel.* 1.6-9 (cited in my *Partings* 39) simply elaborates the logic already implicit in Lev. 15.31 and Num. 35.34 and explained by Josephus, *Ap.* 102-109.

concern of Pharisees and Qumranites for purity (§9.3a) does not constitute counter-evidence; it simply affirms their own recognition of the importance placed on the purity of the Temple cult by the Torah.[137]

Over against such concerns we have the striking sequence of episodes set out by Mark. Jesus touches a man with skin disease (leprosy — Mark 1.40-45), in evident disregard for the seriousness of the man's impure condition, and declares him clean prior to any examination by a priest or offering of sacrifice (Lev. 13–14). Jesus casts out 'unclean spirits' (Mark 1.23, 26-27; 3.11) and is accused of having 'an unclean spirit' (3.30). He eats with 'sinners', in defiance of law and propriety (2.16). He cites as precedent the disregard shown by David and his followers for the sanctity of the tabernacle and the bread of the presence (2.25-26). Jesus exorcizes a man with a legion of unclean spirits, living among tombs (subject to corpse impurity, the most virulent of defilements), outside the holy land, and sends the spirits into pigs (unclean animals) (5.1-17).[138] He is touched by and heals a woman with a haemorrhage (5.24-34), and thus in a state of perpetual impurity (Lev. 15.25-27), and grasps by the hand the little girl already pronounced dead (Mark 5.41). His mission instructions counsel acceptance of hospitality offered, without thought of impurity which might thereby be contracted (6.10). He disregards purity concerns (washing hands) and disputes the validity of purity logic (Mark 7.1-8, 14-23). In short, even if Mark has highlighted the theme by his structuring of the narrative and sharpening of the issue,[139] the theme itself is clearly and firmly rooted in the tradition. It is not a matter of much doubt that Jesus was remembered as casual in regard to purity ritual.[140] That in itself

---

137. Here we may draw attention once again to the importance of 4QMMT as evidence of disputes between Qumran and Pharisees on halakhoth regarding sacrifices and purity.

138. See further above, §15.7d.

139. See particularly on Mark 7.1-23 (above, §14.4c-d). But note also the purity concerns in the Q passage Matt. 23.25/Luke 11.39 (above, chapter 14 n. 143), and the purity overtones in the parable of the Good Samaritan, which no Jew would miss — the man might well be dead (see, e.g., J. D. M. Derrett, *Law in the New Testament* [London: DLT, 1970] 211-17; Rowland, *Christian Origins* 142; Kazen, *Jesus* 189-96).

140. Cf. particularly the central thesis of Kazen, that Jesus was 'indifferent' to various purity concerns, referring to Jesus' several encounters with three major kinds of impurity, skin disease, menstrual bleeding, and corpses (*Jesus* ch. 4). This is not the same as saying that Jesus was casual about purity; what was at stake was a different concept of purity, how it was maintained and how impurity was avoided (see again above, §14.4c-d). On the other hand, we should probably assume that Jesus and his disciples performed the usual rites of purification during the week of preparation for the Passover (Sanders, *Historical Figure* 250-52; Fredriksen, *Jesus* 205-206; Kazen, *Jesus* 248-50, 255). See further my 'Jesus and Purity'. See also W. Loader, 'Challenged at the Boundaries: A Conservative Jesus in Mark's Tradition', *JSNT* 63 (1996) 45-61.

would make his mission a cause of irritation to the Temple authorities and make Jesus himself a target for their hostility.

In short, there are sufficient indications that the emphases of Jesus' teaching and the manner in which he prosecuted his mission were likely to have roused increasing anger and hostility towards him from the high priestly families and Temple authorities. The symbolic action in the Temple and statement about its destruction were likely only to confirm long germinating suspicions and to persuade the policy-makers that Jesus should be silenced as soon as possible.

If then we can deduce a reasonable explanation for the events leading up to Jesus' execution, what of Jesus' own intentions in all this? The question raises complex and much disputed issues and is best broken down to a sequence of questions. The discussion just completed immediately raises the first of these. For if it is indeed the case that Jesus had already aroused priestly opposition and that to go up to Jerusalem was to put himself within the grasp of his most powerful opponents, we can hardly avoid asking why he went.

17.3. Why Did Jesus Go Up to Jerusalem?

Within the framework of the Gospels the answer is clear. The Evangelists, telling the story in the light of the fuller insight which Easter brought, have no doubt that the whole sequence was foreordained. Luke especially emphasizes the 'plan' predetermined by God,[141] the divine necessity of what had happened,[142] and begins his account of the journey to Jerusalem with the ominous words: 'When the days drew near for him to be taken up *(analēmpseōs),* he set his face to go to Jerusalem' (Luke 9.51).[143] As before,[144] we need not infer that the whole motif is the creation of a post-Easter perspective. We can hardly exclude the likelihood that Jesus himself may have been driven by some sense of destiny.[145] But how well rooted within the Jesus tradition is an answer along these lines? Those who

141. *Boulē* ('plan') in Luke 7.30; Acts 2.23; 13.36; 20.27; *horizō* ('determine') in Luke 22.22; Acts 2.23; 10.42; 17.31.

142. *Dei* ('it is necessary that . . .'), eleven occurrences in Luke (particularly 9.22; 13.33; 17.25; 22.37; 24.7, 26, 44) and seventeen in Acts; much less frequent in Mark and Matthew, but most significantly in Mark 8.31/Matt. 16.21 (on the Passion predictions see below, §17.4c). See further Fitzmyer, *Luke* 1.179-80; J. T. Squires, *The Plan of God in Luke-Acts* (SNTSMS 76; Cambridge: Cambridge University, 1993).

143. See again Fitzmyer, *Luke* 1.827-28.

144. See above, chapter 13 at n. 31.

145. 'When the details are bracketed out, what remains is the rudimentary sense of destiny' (Keck, *Who Is Jesus?* 117-18). Contrast Becker: 'Jesus and his followers went to the city of Zion simply to take part in the festival' (*Jesus* 345).

have sought the answer from within the Jesus tradition have generally looked for other (or additional) reasons.

In the absence of undisputed indications of Jesus' own intention, it is most natural to look for an answer in relation to the chief emphasis of Jesus' mission. In brief, how did a journey to Jerusalem relate to Jesus' preaching of the kingdom (chapter 12)? If indeed he entertained hope for the restoration of Israel — and some such hope seems clearly evident[146] — then it would follow ineluctably that Jerusalem as Israel's spiritual centre must play a key role in the realisation of that hope.[147] K. H. Tan has recently reviewed the chief answers given by earlier questers,[148] which indicate that, analytically speaking, answers usually embrace one or more of three options. (1) Was it simply that Jesus, convinced of the importance and urgency of his message, wanted to deliver it in the capital? Perhaps he cherished the hope, however forlorn, that his call for return in view of the coming kingdom would reach the hearts of Israel's leaders and win a positive response from them.[149] (2) Or was it rather that he was determined to confront and outface a recalcitrant leadership? I have already examined one version of this (Jesus as leader of a militant rebellion) and found it wanting (§§15.2b, 4). But could the intention have been rather to call for (or even set up) an alternative religious rather than political system?[150] (3) Most radical of all, if the kingdom was to come, then Jerusalem was the most likely place where 'it' (whatever 'it' was to be) would happen. Perhaps, then, Jesus entertained the idea of somehow triggering the kingdom's coming by his preaching or activity in Jerusalem?[151] Schweitzer's portrayal (§4.5a) was the most famous and disturbing answer along these lines. But his is by no means the only answer possible.[152]

a. To Restore Jerusalem to Yahweh's Kingship?

In seeking to illuminate Jesus' motivation in going up to Jerusalem, Tan himself has focused attention on the substantial Zion traditions within Israel's Scrip-

---

146. See above, §§12.4c and 13.3.

147. I number the following options for analytic purposes; answers actually offered usually overlap.

148. Tan, *Zion Traditions* 11-21.

149. Cf., e.g., Bornkamm, *Jesus* 155; Schillebeeckx, *Jesus* 296-98.

150. Cf. Merklein, *Jesu Botschaft* 135-37, 140-42; see further below, §17.3c.

151. Cf. Evans, who suggests that 'Jesus did anticipate setting up a messianic administration that would displace the religious establishment of Jerusalem' (*Jesus and His Contemporaries* 454).

152. Tan naturally cites Meyer here (*Aims* 202-22); he was unable to take account of Wright, *Jesus* (see below).

tures and early postbiblical writings. He notes that in Jewish Scripture there is a fundamental conviction regarding Zion as the dwelling-place and throne of God. From this twin concept, Zion theology emerges: Zion as the place of refuge, security, and blessing[153] and particularly Zion as the destination for the eschatological pilgrimage of the nations, Zion as the centre for Yahweh's universal dominion.[154]

That Jesus shared this Zion theology is suggested for Tan by three passages.[155] (1) In Matt. 5.34-35 Jesus calls Jerusalem 'the city of the great king' (Ps. 48.1). Despite its sole attestation in Matthew, this may well contain a recollection of Jesus' teaching.[156] (2) In Luke 13.32-33 Jesus speaks of reaching his goal *(teleioō),* by implication, in Jerusalem. This is more problematic, since *teleioō* occurs in the Synoptics only in Luke (2.43; 13.32), and 13.33 is one of Luke's *dei* passages; in other words, there is more than a hint of suspicion that the note of divinely intended outcome may owe more to Luke's retelling than the earlier tradition.[157]

(3) Luke attaches 13.31-33 to the Q lament over Jerusalem:

Matt. 23.37-39	Luke 13.34-35
37 Jerusalem, Jerusalem, the city that kills the prophets and stones those who are sent to it! How often have I desired to gather your children together as a hen gathers her brood under her wings, and you were not willing! 38 See, your house is left to you, desolate. 39 For I tell you, you will not see me again until you say, 'Blessed is the one who comes in the name of the Lord'.	34 Jerusalem, Jerusalem, the city that kills the prophets and stones those who are sent to it! How often have I desired to gather your children together as a hen (gathers) her brood under her wings, and you were not willing! 35 See, your house is left to you. And I tell you, you will not see me until the time comes when you say, 'Blessed is the one who comes in the name of the Lord'.

The saying is regularly discounted as a word of Jesus precisely because of the strength of the self-affirmed role claimed by Jesus and the suggestion of a prophecy after the event.[158] But the later insertion of such a saying into a tradition which gave no account of earlier visits by Jesus to Jerusalem is somewhat difficult to credit. The implication that death by stoning was the likely outcome for Jesus is hardly a creation *ex eventu.* A saying within Q almost certainly predates the destruction of Jerusalem (not till 70 CE), and so is a gloomy foreboding on ei-

---

153. E.g., Pss. 9.12-13; 20.2-3; 46.6; Isa. 7.1-17; 30.1-5; 31.1-3. See also J. D. Levenson, 'Zion Traditions', *ABD* 6.1098-1102.

154. See above, chapter 12 nn. 70, 71; Tan, *Zion Traditions* 29 n. 33, 31-42.

155. Tan, *Zion Traditions* Part II.

156. See above, chapter 14 n. 159.

157. See above, §15.6c. But Becker builds his answer to the question about Jesus' own view of the future from Luke 13.32 *(Jesus* 338-39).

158. Steck, *Israel* 53-55; Funk, *Five Gospels* 245; Lüdemann, *Jesus* 357.

ther count.[159] And the question whether Jesus was motivated by a sense of destiny in regard to his own role vis-à-vis Jerusalem cannot be answered simply by dismissing the clearest evidence in favour of a positive answer.[160]

Tan concludes from the language that Jesus' goal was 'the restoration' of Jerusalem to be the city of Yahweh's kingship. And he goes on to bolster this conclusion by examining Jesus' entry into Jerusalem, the incident in the Temple, and the last supper.[161] From these episodes he concludes that Jesus enacted the entrance of the promised messianic king, that in the Temple he sought to set in motion the restoration of Zion, expecting the Temple to fulfil its anticipated eschatological role as the goal of the eschatological pilgrimage of the Gentiles, and that in the last supper he intended to ratify a covenant and thus to constitute his disciples as the restored people of God *in nuce*.[162] Even if Tan pushes his thesis rather hard, particularly with regard to the entrance into Jerusalem,[163] the overall case is well argued and has more substance than most of its competitors.[164]

b. To Enact Yahweh's Return to Zion?

Already before Tan, Wright developed a still bolder Zion thesis: that a central feature of Second Temple Jewish hope was for *Yahweh's* return to Zion[165] and that Jesus 'intended to enact, symbolize and personify that climactic event'.[166] Wright develops his case by means of two lines of interpretation.

159. Even without *erēmos* ('desolate'), the verb *aphietai* ('left') still has the sense of 'abandoned' (BDAG, *aphiēmi* 3a).

160. The issue largely turns on whether the imagery of protective shelter would inevitably conjure up the thought of Yahweh's protection of Israel. No doubt it did, but then we have to consider whether the choice of a *hen's* wings (nowhere else attested in Jewish literature) was a playful parody on the more typical imagery of a powerful eagle's wings (Exod. 19.4; Deut. 32.11; cf. Pss. 36.7; 57.1; Isa. 31.5) — not quite such a vainglorious image! On the other hand, the concluding quotation from Ps. 118.26 may be an elaboration in echo of the same passage as quoted in the account of the entry into Jerusalem (Mark 11.10 pars.). See also Tan, *Zion Traditions* 104-13; for others who recognize here a saying of Jesus see Davies and Allison, *Matthew* 3.314 n. 20.

161. Tan, *Zion Traditions* chs. 6-8.

162. I draw the language used here from Tan's conclusions (*Zion Traditions* 230-33). So already Dodd: 'he was formally installing them as foundation members of the new people of God' (*Founder* 96).

163. Tan, *Zion Traditions* 140-41, 149-53.

164. See the discussions elsewhere on each passage — §§15.3d-e, 15.4d-e, and, below, 17.3c, 4e and 5d(3).

165. He documents the theme fully in *Jesus* 616-23; see above, chapter 12 n. 67.

166. *Jesus* 615, 631, 639.

(1) Jesus spoke of himself as the Son of Man who would 'come' to the Ancient of Days to take the other throne with Yahweh (Dan. 7.9-14). I have already speculated along the lines of such a possibility on my own account (Mark 14.62; §16.4c), but remain unclear how such a future vindication/coming in or to heaven (as Wright insists) relates to Jesus' earlier coming to Jerusalem on Wright's thesis.

(2) Jesus' parable of the talents/pounds comes to us in its two forms (Matt. 25.14-30/Luke 19.12-27).[167] Matthew's version envisages a 'man' who, 'going on a journey' *(apodēmōn),* entrusted his property to his servants (as in Mark 13.34), and who returned 'after a long time' to settle accounts (Matt. 25.19). Luke's version has a nobleman *(eugenēs)* who goes to a distant country 'to receive a kingdom for himself and return', likewise expecting his servants to trade profitably with the money he entrusted to them. Although only Luke talks in kingly terms,[168] Wright deduces that the king/master in such teaching of Jesus (as in other Jewish parables) would normally be taken to refer to Israel's God.[169] He likewise dismisses an interpretation of the master's/king's return in terms of the 'second coming', and argues that it is better read as referring to Yahweh's return to Zion 'and to the devastating results that this will produce'.[170]

On this point too I have already indicated sympathy with the view that talk of 'second coming' belongs more to the perspective of the subsequent retelling of the parables of 'return' and other 'coming' sayings, than to the perspective of first utterance.[171] And talk of a returning master/owner/bridegroom as symbol of impending crisis and judgment is firmly enough rooted in the Jesus tradition (§12.4g). But it is far from clear from these data that Jesus saw himself in this role or his journey to Jerusalem as an enacting or embodiment of Yahweh's return to Zion.

Here as before we must be careful not to impose an order or clarity of our own creation on data that are characteristically parabolic/metaphorical. Talk of 'Yahweh's return to Zion' was certainly one important strand in the multiplex strands of Jewish expectation, and it is quite likely that it influenced Jesus' own formulation when he spoke of the mounting crisis confronting Israel and its lead-

---

167. See above, chapter 12 n. 210.

168. The echo of Archelaus' attempt to secure the full inheritance of his father's (Herod the Great's) kingdom in 4 BCE is generally acknowledged (Josephus, *War* 2.1-38, 80-100; *Ant.* 17.219-49, 299-320); whether or not Jesus told the story in this form, the fact that an almost explicit political comment was circulated among early Christian groups is itself noteworthy.

169. *Jesus* 634, citing e.g. Luke 16.1-13; Mark 12.1-12 pars; *m. Abot* 1.3; 2.14-16; 3.1, 17; 4.22; and quoting Dodd, *Parables* 151; Wright goes on to cite the parables of crisis and other material surveyed above under §12.4e, g (*Jesus* 640-2).

170. *Jesus* 636.

171. See above, §§12.4g and 16.4f.

ers. But as with the other main part of Wright's 'controlling story' (return from exile), the thesis that Yahweh's return to Zion was a major factor in persuading Jesus to go up to Jerusalem would be more persuasive if the echoes were stronger, clearer, and more persistent. And the further suggestion that Jesus saw his own journey to Jerusalem as itself enacting Yahweh's return to Zion has no single firm point of support within the Jesus tradition. Wright's hypothesis is a fascinating retelling of that tradition, quite in character with subsequent varied retellings, but it can hardly be attributed to the core tradition as that was formulated in the beginning.

c. To Replace the Jerusalem Cult?

The hypothesis that Jesus intended to make a fundamental challenge to the Jerusalem leadership has been extended further by correlating Jesus' word and action in regard to the Temple with his words and actions which we call the last supper. Theissen and Merz argue that Jesus intended the latter (the last supper) to replace the former (the Temple). He intended a showdown not just with the leaders of Israel, but with the whole Temple and cult as such. His word and action in the Temple declared the end of the Temple.[172] His words and actions in the upper room declared the beginning of the Temple cult's replacement, bread instead of a sacrificial animal, a new covenant without sacrifice.[173]

Rather similar is Chilton's extension of his thesis about the fundamental importance of purity for Jesus. Chilton focuses on Jesus' meals with his disciples, but argues that they saw a distinctive shift in the ideology of the meal fol-

---

172. Similarly Crossan: Jesus' action '"destroys" the Temple by "stopping" its fiscal, sacrificial, and liturgical operations' (*Historical Jesus* 357-58); Légasse, *Trial of Jesus* 27-35; and the earlier argument of F. Hahn, *The Worship of the Early Church* (1970; ET Philadelphia: Fortress, 1973) 23-30.

173. Theissen and Merz, *Historical Jesus* 432-36; similarly Ådna concludes that the death of Jesus 'replaces and supersedes the sacrificial cult in the Temple once for all as the atoning death for the many' (*Jesu Stellung* 419-30 [here 429]; see also his 'Jesus' Symbolic Act in the Temple (Mark 11:15-17): The Replacement of the Sacrificial Cult by His Atoning Death', in Ego et al., eds., *Gemeinde ohne Tempel* 461-75); cf. Tan, *Zion Traditions* 218-19. Holmén follows suit: 'Jesus' action was directed against the cult itself' (*Jesus* 319-23, 328-29), though he confuses prophetic criticism of insincerely offered sacrifices with criticism of the cult *per se* (321-23); but he is right in noting that one of Israel's fundamental identity markers was being put in question in some degree, so that the reappearance of the accusation (that Jesus would 'destroy this place') in the charge against Stephen (Acts 6.14) becomes that much more understandable. However, Casey's argument seems overdrawn, that Jesus' life and teaching embodied Judaism as a religion; 'Jesus offered people the spiritual centre of Judaism' (*From Jewish Prophet to Gentile God* [Cambridge: Clarke, 1991] 72-74).

lowing his 'occupation' of the Temple. It was then that his meals became so of-fensive as to warrant action against him. For 'body' and 'blood' are sacrificial terminology and indicate that the meals themselves were being understood as sacrifices, indeed as better sacrifices than those offered in Caiaphas's corrupt Temple. In other words, Jesus was setting up an alternative cult; wine and bread replaced sacrifice in the Temple.[174]

Such theses have the value for Christian scholarship of tracing back to Jesus' own intention a new cult (eucharist) to replace the Temple. But they suffer from the major drawback that the first Christians, who evidently continued to attend the Temple, and to participate in the sacrificial system,[175] must then have wholly mis-understood Jesus' intention in the matter.[176] And Chilton's version in particular has to transpose talk of 'my body' and 'my blood' into the idea of bread as Jesus' (re-placement for the) flesh of sacrifice and wine as Jesus' (replacement for the) blood of sacrifice. But the firmer link between the last supper and Jesus' Temple protest (occupation) is thus gained at the expense of the link between the last supper and Jesus' death. Since the latter is so clear already in the earliest forms of the tradition the result is, once again, a hypothesis forced upon the tradition rather than one which grows out of the tradition. We are not likely to gain adequate answers to why Jesus went up to Jerusalem without clarifying how Jesus understood his death.

17.4. Did Jesus Anticipate His Death?

A second question regarding Jesus' own motivation is simply an extension of the first. If Jesus' mission in Galilee was causing increasing irritation among the Jeru-salem authorities, it is not very likely that Jesus was unaware of this fact, and more than likely that he was aware of the possibility of arrest — and worse. Did he then go up to Jerusalem knowing that he might well pay for the action with his life?[177]

---

174. Chilton's much repeated thesis (e.g., *Temple* 150-54; *Pure Kingdom* 124-26; *Rabbi Jesus* 253-55).

175. Acts 3.1 (the ninth hour was when the evening sacrifice was offered: Josephus, *Ant.* 14.65); 21.26; Matt. 5.23-24.

176. Bockmuehl, *This Jesus* 75 and 201-202 n. 50; Klawans, 'Interpreting the Last Sup-per' 9-10. Cf. Becker: 'If Jesus had predicted the destruction of the temple or had pronounced God's judgment on Jerusalem, the earliest post-Easter church would probably have established itself in Galilee rather than in Jerusalem' (*Jesus* 334).

177. J. Gnilka, 'Wie urteilte Jesus über seinen Tod?' in K. Kertelge, ed., *Der Tod Jesu. Deutungen im Neuen Testament* (QD 74; Freiburg: Herder, 1976) 13-50, seeks to avoid misun-derstanding by distinguishing between 'Todesbereitschaft' (readiness for death) and 'Todes-gewissheit' (certainty of death) (58). L. Oberlinner, *Todeserwartung und Todesgewissheit Jesu. Zum Problem einer historischen Begründung* (SBB 10; Stuttgart: KBW, 1980) develops the point (conclusions 165-67).

Most of the relevant data has been reviewed well enough in earlier studies[178] and requires little fresh discussion.

a. The Fate of the Prophets

The likelihood that Jesus saw himself as at least standing in the tradition of Israel's prophets, perhaps even as the climax of that tradition, has already been indicated (§§15.6, 16.2c[2]). Also that Jesus' expectation of suffering probably grew out of a full awareness of the proverbial fate of Israel's prophets (§12.4d). It is more than likely, then, that Jesus expected to suffer a prophet's rejection, 'martyrdom in Jerusalem as part of the prophetic office'.[179] Given also the tradition that the righteous could expect to suffer, anyone who put doing God's will before everything else must have expected to suffer for it, even to die for it.[180] Above all, Jesus would hardly have been unaware of what had happened to his mentor, John the Baptist; and though John had suffered at the hands of Antipas, Jesus would hardly assume that things might be different in Judea.

b. Mounting Hostility

If §17.3 is on the right track, then, again, Jesus must have been aware that his continued mission and liberty were likely to come under increasing threat. Earlier on I aired the possibility that Jesus' movements in Galilee were motivated in part at least by the need to keep clear of Antipas's clutches (Luke 13.31).[181] His political antennae seem to have been sufficiently sensitive on that front.

178. Particularly Jeremias, *Proclamation* 277-86; V. Howard, 'Did Jesus Speak about His Own Death?' *CBQ* 39 (1977) 515-27; Ådna, *Jesu Stellung* 412-19; P. Balla, 'What Did Jesus Think about His Approaching Death?' in Labahn and Schmidt, eds., *Jesus, Mark and Q* 239-58; S. McKnight, 'Jesus and His Death: Some Recent Scholarship', *CR:BS* 9 (2001) 185-228.

179. Jeremias, *Proclamation* 280; Stuhlmacher, *Biblische Theologie* 1.127-8; Theissen and Merz, *Historical Jesus* 429-30; see above, chapter 12 n. 184; on Mark 12.1-9, see §16.2c(2).

180. The psalms often voice complaints on the theme, including Psalms 22 and 69; note particularly Ps. 34.19 (e.g., Davies and Allison, *Matthew* 2.656-57); Pesch lists the extensive Psalm allusions forming the OT substructure of the pre-Markan Passion narrative (*Markusevangelium* 2.13-14). The motif is taken up in Wisdom literature, notably Job and Wis. 3.1-10 and 5.1-5 (cited below, §17.6a). And it is obvious in apocalyptic expectation of a final tribulation (§11.4c). See further particularly L. Ruppert, *Jesus als der leidende Gerechte* (SBS 59; Stuttgart: KBW, 1972); G. W. E. Nickelsburg, *Resurrection, Immortality and Eternal Life in Intertestamental Judaism* (Cambridge: Harvard University, 1972) chs. 2-4; K. T. Kleinknecht, *Der leidende Gerechtfertigte. Die alttestamentlich-jüdische Tradition vom "leidenden Gerechten" und ihre Rezeption bei Paulus* (WUNT 2.13; Tübingen: Mohr Siebeck, 1984) I. Hauptteil.

181. See above, §9.9e-f.

In addition, serious charges had probably been levelled against him: of sorcery, of sabbath violation, possibly of being a rebellious son[182] — all of which, according to the later transcribed ruling of *m. Sanh.* 7.4, were punishable by stoning. According to Matt. 23.37/Luke 13.34 (§17.3a) Jesus may have reckoned with the possibility of being stoned. And according to Mark 14.8 pars. (§13.4b n. 166) Jesus may have anticipated the likelihood of burial without anointing, that is, a criminal's burial. Arguably, the fact that such premonitions were not realized (he was not stoned, he probably was given a proper burial) indicates that Jesus was remembered as so surmising, despite the fact that a different outcome transpired.[183]

Whatever had gone before, Jesus could hardly have undertaken the symbolic action in the Temple (whatever it was) without being fully aware that he was throwing down a gauntlet to the Temple authorities (§15.3d), especially if he had also spoken provocatively about the Temple's destruction and replacement (§15.3a).[184] Nor is it likely that he was at all surprised by his subsequent arrest or by the accusations brought against him. Jesus would have been extraordinarily naïve had he not seen where such actions and opposition were likely to end.

c. The Passion Predictions

The most controversial evidence to be considered is the three statements attributed to Jesus — in many ways the most interesting of the Son of Man sayings, left aside earlier as most appropriately considered at this point.

Matt. 16.21	Mark 8.31	Luke 9.22
21 From that time on, Jesus began to show his disciples that he must go to Jerusalem and undergo great suffering at the hands of the elders and chief priests and scribes, and be killed, and on the third day be raised.	31 Then he began to teach them that the Son of Man must undergo great suffering, and be rejected by the elders, and the chief priests, and the scribes, and be killed, and after three days rise again.	22 . . . saying that 'The Son of Man must undergo great suffering, and be rejected by the elders, and chief priests, and scribes, and be killed, and on the third day be raised'.

182. See above, §§12.5d, 15.7b, and 14.4a and chapter 14 n. 253.

183. Jeremias, *Proclamation* 284. On the other hand, Mark 2.20 (or 2.19b-20) looks as though it is an elaboration of 2.19a in the light of Jesus' death, expressive of the sense within the early groups of disciples that after all, in the changed circumstances, fasting was again appropriate (see, e.g., Pesch, *Markusevangelium* 1.175-76; Guelich, *Mark* 1.111).

184. C. A. Evans is of the opinion that Jesus did not specifically talk of his own death until after entering Jerusalem and concludes that the Passion predictions should be dated to the Passion week itself ('Did Jesus Predict His Death and Resurrection?' in S. E. Porter, et al., eds., *Resurrection* [JSNTS 186; Sheffield: Sheffield Academic, 1999] 82-97 [here 86-91]).

Matt. 17.22-23	Mark 9.31	Luke 9.43b-44
22 As they were gathering in Galilee, Jesus said to them, 'The Son of Man is about to be handed over into the hands of men, 23 and they will kill him, and on the third day he will be raised'.	31 for he was teaching his disciples, saying to them, 'The Son of Man is to be handed over into the hands of men, and they will kill him, and having been killed, after three days he will rise again'.	. . . he said to his disciples, 44 'Let these words sink into your ears: The Son of Man is about to be handed over into the hands of men'.

Matt. 20.18-19	Mark 10.33-34	Luke 18.31-33
18 See, we are going up to Jerusalem, and the Son of Man will be handed over to the chief priests and scribes, and they will condemn him to death, 19 and will hand him over to the Gentiles to be mocked and flogged and crucified; and on the third day he will be raised.	33 See, we are going up to Jerusalem, and the Son of Man will be handed over to the chief priests and the scribes, and they will condemn him to death, and will hand him over to the Gentiles; 34 they will mock him, and spit upon him, and flog him, and kill him; and after three days he will rise again.	31 See, we are going up to Jerusalem, and everything that is written about the Son of Man by the prophets will be accomplished. 32 For he will be handed over to the Gentiles; and he will be mocked and insulted and spat upon; 33 and after they have flogged him, they will kill him, and on the third day he will rise again.

Clearly the tradition intends to recall that Jesus predicted his death, including the 'handing over' and the attendant suffering. Equally clear are the indications of (a) saying(s) much repeated and manifesting typical performance variations.

(1) Here is one of the instances (§16.4b) where Matthew's version shows awareness of a self-referential *bar* ʿ*naša* (Matt. 16.21).

(2) More striking are the variations in the final clause: Mark consistently says 'after three days', whereas Matthew and Luke say 'on the third day'; Mark consistently puts the verb in active voice ('he will rise again' — *anastēnai, anastēsetai*), while Matthew consistently prefers a passive form ('he will be raised' — *egerthēnai, egerthēsetai*), and Luke uses both forms. It is hard to avoid the obvious deduction, that in the version of Matthew/Luke the less precise 'after three days' has been made more precise in the light of the resurrection tradition ('on the third day').[185] And Matthew's 'he will be raised' may also reflect a more theologically careful affirmation that Jesus was raised by God — reflecting the regular confessional formula of the early years of expansion.[186]

(3) The range of variation is extensive, from the brevity of Luke's version

185. See, e.g., Evans, 'Did Jesus Predict?' 85-86, 95, with further bibliography in 86 n. 9; see also below, §18.4b(5). The fact that Matt. 12.40 quotes Jonah 2.1 'three days and nights' without qualification may suggest that the extension of 'the sign of Jonah' to the parallel between Jonah's time in the whale with Jesus' time in the earth took place at an early stage in the development of the sign of Jonah saying (§15.6b[5]).

186. See again my *Theology of Paul* 175 nn. 69 and 72.

of the second prediction, to the fulness of all three versions of the third prediction (handed over to Gentiles to be mocked, spat upon, flogged, and killed). Here again it very much looks as though the third prediction has been elaborated in the light of events, so that the greater precision of its telling might reflect (predict) more accurately what was recalled as actually to have happened.[187] Matthew takes the process one step further by specifying the method of execution as crucifixion (Matt. 20.19).[188]

This evidence of tradition history of substance held firm but with differing introductions, variations in detail, and clarification and elaboration to bring out particular points is wholly in line with a transmission process repeatedly documented in the earlier chapters. These were much recalled and reflected-on elements of the Jesus tradition.

But are they performance versions of something Jesus himself was remembered as saying?[189] Again previous experience would indicate the likelihood that such a firmly recalled tradition was originally derived from those who heard Jesus saying something memorable. It is no longer possible to tell from the traditions whether Jesus spoke on the subject more than once: the threefold sequence looks as though it is part of a much fuller story of Jesus, as the shadow of the cross begins to loom ever larger for the story-teller.[190] And the elaboration in the light of events seems to be more extensive than with most of the Jesus tradition reviewed in earlier chapters. But it is quite possible to detect within the tradition variations a core saying which has been thus elaborated.[191]

187. Handed over to Gentiles — Mark 15.1 pars.; mocked, spat upon — 15.19-20, 31 pars.; flogged (mastigoō) — John 19.1 (Mark 15.15/Matt. 27.26 use the Latin loanword flagello = Greek phragelloō; Davies and Allison, Matthew 3.593, note how savage such a flogging could be, referring to Josephus, War 6.304; BDAG, phragelloō — 'a punishment inflicted on slaves and provincials after sentence of death had been pronounced on them'). The alternative suggestion — that the Passion narrative has been based on the third Passion prediction (as in Bayer, Jesus' Predictions 172-74) — is less plausible.

188. For similar considerations see, e.g., Davies and Allison, Matthew 2.659.

189. The possibility is regularly dismissed out of hand: 'secondary constructions of the Church' (Bultmann, History 152); Perrin, Modern Pilgrimage 75, 90; Funk, Five Gospels 75-78; Theissen and Merz, Historical Jesus 550, 552; Lüdemann, Jesus 56, 63, 71. The absence of these traditions from Q is regularly cited as a principal reason for giving a negative answer. But this would be decisive only if Q had been intended to provide a complete inventory of Jesus' teaching or was the only Jesus tradition known to those who used it. The Q material shows awareness of Jesus' death (chapter 7 n. 52 above), but such allusions would hardly be sufficient on their own to satisfy Christian curiosity and liturgy. More likely, traditions like the Passion predictions were linked with the story of Jesus' death, perhaps in an extended Passion narrative, as Pesch has suggested.

190. The threefold sequence which talks of the Son of Man being 'lifted up' in the Fourth Gospel (John 3.14; 8.28; 12.32-34) may reflect the same sequencing and indicate that the structure of the longer story was established very early (cf. Brown, Death 1483-87).

191. Bayer strongly resists the attempt to trace the different sayings to 'one primitive

The second prediction (Mark 9.31 pars.) appears to be the least developed of all the versions: 'The son of man is (about) to be handed over into the hands of men'.[192] Particularly to be noted are the characteristic play of words ('son of man', 'men'), which presupposes an original Hebrew/Aramaic formulation,[193] the 'divine passive', and the fact that 'handed over into the hands of' is a Semitic construction.[194] The form of the verb expresses a foreboding of imminent destiny or fate (whether with the *mellei*, 'about to be', or not).[195] In other words, we have an Aramaic *mašal,* expressing in bare, proverbial terms the prospect of Jesus' arrest: 'the man is to be handed over to the men'.[196] The basic structure has been held firm in subsequent retellings, but tradents and story-tellers evidently could not resist elaborating both the 'handing over' and the 'men' in the light of what actually happened. Conversely, precisely the bare, aphoristic character of the core *mašal,* so evidently untouched by such elaborations, points to the probability that it was Jesus himself who formulated the *mašal,* most likely in explaining to his disciples why he must go up to Jerusalem.

Several conclusions follow at once. (1) We have one (or more) further instance(s) where Jesus was remembered as using the form *bar ᵉnaša,* and precisely

---

form' (*Jesus' Predictions* ch. 7, as concluded on 200); but in oral tradition analysis the concept of 'one primitive form' is inappropriate.

192. Goppelt, *Theology* 1.189: 'This unmistakable riddle went back in all probability to Jesus himself'. This version was also recalled elsewhere within the Passion narrative (Mark 14.41/Matt. 26.45). Hahn suggests that Mark 14.21 indicates a different type of Passion saying, motivated by the need to demonstrate scriptural fulfilment ('the son of man goes as it is written concerning him'), and traces both 9.31/14.41 and 14.21 back to Palestinian community tradition (*Hoheitstitel* 46-53; *Titles* 37-42; cf. Tödt, *Son of Man* 201). Lindars (*Jesus* 74-76) and Casey ('General, Generic and Indefinite' 40-49) also draw particular attention to Mark 14.21, but Casey argues that 8.31 brings us closer to what Jesus actually said. For the division of opinion as to whether 8.31 or 9.31 is 'original' see Beasley-Murray, *Jesus and the Kingdom* 392-93 n. 84, who favours the view that each passage contains 'independent traditions of instruction given on more than one occasion' (238-40 and n. 85).

193. See above, §16.4b.

194. See above, chapter 15 n. 86.

195. Jeremias suggests an underlying Aramaic participle to denote the near future (*Proclamation* 281 and n. 2). Several have pointed out (e.g., Tödt, *Son of Man* 188) that the simple future tense of Dan. 2.28 ('what will be in the latter days') is rendered in the LXX with a *dei* formulation ('what must happen at the end of days') — as in the first Passion prediction (Mark 8.31 pars.). Beasley-Murray adds Lev. 5.17 and Isa. 30.29 (*Jesus and the Kingdom* 238-39).

196. Jeremias, *Proclamation* 281-82 (suggesting Aramaic *mitmᵉsar bar ᵉnasa lide bᵉne ᵉnasa*); Hampel, *Menschensohn* 296-302, who notes the parallel form in *T. Abr.* A 13.3 ('Every man is judged by man', *pas anthrōpos ex anthrōpou krinetai*). Lindars argues for the form 'a man may be delivered up . . .' (*Jesus* 63, 68-69); criticized by Casey, 'General, Generic and Indefinite' 40, but Casey in turns strives unnecessarily to give the 'son of man' a general reference (43-46). See also Bayer, *Jesus' Predictions* 169-71, 178-81. Pursuant to his main thesis, Caragounis argues that the elements of the fuller sayings can be derived directly from Daniel (*Son of Man* 197-200).

in a word-play which indicates the flexibility of the phrase in Jesus' use — both as 'a man' (human person), but also with evident self-reference ('someone, one'). (2) More to the immediate point, Jesus evidently did indeed anticipate that his mission would not be accepted in Jerusalem; he would be arrested and given over to the power of human authorities (with all that that would probably entail). (3) Nevertheless, he seems to have embraced that outcome as divinely intended, whether as destiny or dogma. Whether we can say more will become evident in §§17.5, 6.

d. Other Metaphors

Jesus is recalled as using other metaphors speaking of suffering which he expected to endure — metaphors of cup, baptism, and fire.

Matt. 20.22-23	Mark 10.38-39	Luke 12.49-50
20 Then the mother of the sons of Zebedee came to him with her sons, and kneeling before him, she asked a favour of him. 21 And he said to her, 'What do you want?'	35 James and John, the sons of Zebedee, came forward to him and said to him, 'Teacher, we want you to do for us whatever we ask of you'. 36 And he said to them, 'What do you want me to do for you?' 37 And they said to him, 'Grant us	
She said to him, 'Declare that these two sons of mine will sit, one at your right hand and one at your left, in your kingdom'. 22 But Jesus said, 'You do not know what you are asking. Are you able to drink the cup that I am about to drink?'	to sit, one at your right hand and one at your left, in your glory'. 38 But Jesus said to them, 'You do not know what you are asking. Are you able to drink the cup that I drink, or be baptized with the baptism that I am baptized with?' 39 They replied,	49 I came to cast fire on the earth, and how I wish it were already kindled! 50 I have a baptism to be baptized with, and how distressed I am until it is completed!
They said to him, 'We are able'. 23 He said to them, 'My cup you will indeed drink,	'We are able'. Then Jesus said to them, 'The cup that I drink you will drink; and with the baptism with which I am baptized, you will be baptized;	
but to sit at my right hand and at my left, this is not mine to grant, but it is for those for whom it has been prepared by my Father'.	40 but to sit at my right hand or at my left is not mine to grant, but it is for those for whom it has been prepared'.	

Matthew may well have derived his version directly from Mark, though why in that case he should have omitted the 'baptism' saying (Mark 10.38b, 39b) is unclear. Luke 12.50 has a different form of the same saying and indicates that the saying was retold independently of the context in which it has been retained by Mark. Did Matthew then know a form of the story from which the baptism saying had been extracted for separate use? Either way, the double attestation of Mark and Luke indicates that Jesus was remembered as using the imagery of baptism to describe the suffering he expected to have to endure.[197]

In the Markan/Matthean context, the cup saying (Mark 10.38a/Matt. 20.22) also denotes expectation of suffering.[198] What is striking is the prediction that James and John would have to drink from the same cup (Mark 10.39a/Matt. 20.23 — and endure the same baptism: Mark 10.39b). Such a prediction can hardly have been first articulated in the early years of Christianity.[199] It must go back to Jesus and have been retained within the Jesus tradition, despite lack of fulfilment thus far, because it was remembered as a prediction of Jesus and treasured as such.[200]

Here we should recall also that the cup imagery reappears in all forms of the Gethsemane tradition (Mark 14.36 pars.).[201] Jesus in his great distress and anguish asks to be exempted from the suffering implied in the image: 'let this cup pass from me'. As already noted,[202] the not at all flattering portrayal of Jesus in the garden is probably a fair representation of his state of mind. By then, Jesus must have been all too well aware of what likely lay ahead, and was recalled as blanching at the prospect.

More intriguing is the double fire/baptism saying in Luke 12.49-50. (1) It is highly enigmatic. To what did the early churches refer it? From what fulfilment could they have derived it? (2) The sayings are obviously parallel in form ('fire I came to cast . . . ; baptism I have to be baptized with . . .'), suggesting a Semitic structure and origin.[203] (3) *Thomas* has an interesting parallel to Luke 12.49: 'Jesus said, 'I have cast fire upon the world, and see, I am guarding it until it is ablaze' (*GTh* 10). Both Luke and *Thomas* recall Jesus as talking about casting fire on the earth/world.

197. On baptism as a metaphor for suffering see below (n. 206 and §17.5c).

198. The 'cup' to be drunk from was a familiar metaphor for suffering divine judgment (e.g., Pss. 11.6; 75.7-8; Isa. 51.17, 22; Jer. 25.15-17, 27-29; Ezek. 23.31-34; Hab. 2.16; Zech. 12.2; 1QpHab 11.14-15; *Pss. Sol.* 8.14). Casey draws attention also to *Mart. Isa.* 5.13, and *Targ. Neof.* on Deut. 32.1: 'people (sons of men) who die and taste the cup of death'. See further Bayer, *Jesus' Predictions* 70-77.

199. James was martyred about 44 CE (Acts 12.2), but Irenaeus reports that John lived to the time of Trajan (98-117 CE; *Adv. haer.* 2.22.5; 3.3.4); the data are briefly reviewed in Davies and Allison, *Matthew* 3.90-92, including n. 39 on the much less reliable tradition that John was killed at the same time as James.

200. See also Bayer, *Jesus' Predictions* 59-61.

201. Although John has totally transformed the tradition of Jesus' prayer in Gethsemane, he has taken care to include reference to the cup of suffering: 'the cup which my Father has given me, shall I not drink it?' (John 18.11).

202. §16.2b.

203. Burney, *Poetry* 63, 90; see also Black, *Aramaic Approach* 123. Characteristic Lukan style *(echō, synechomai)* demonstrates no more than performance variation (cf. Beasley-Murray, *Jesus and the Kingdom* 248-49).

(4) More striking still are the indications in the Jesus tradition that Jesus was remembered as saying something else similar.

Matt. 10.34	Luke 12.51	GTh 16
Do not think that I came to cast peace on the earth; I came to cast not peace but a sword.	Do you consider that I have come to bring peace in the earth? No, I tell you, but rather division!	Jesus said, Men perhaps think that I have come to cast peace upon the world, and they do not know that I have come to cast divisions upon the earth, fire, sword, war.

The gloomy saying is of a piece with other anticipations of eschatological tribulation in the Jesus tradition and can hardly be discounted simply because it is articulated as a commission accepted by Jesus.[204] What is noticeable here is that GTh 16 includes talk of Jesus casting fire on the earth, as in Luke 12.49.[205]

(5) Most striking of all is the echo of the distinctive metaphor coined by the Baptist: 'He will baptize you with the Holy Spirit and fire' (Matt. 3.11/Luke 3.16). It was the Baptist, we may recall, who brought the metaphor of baptism into play as an image for the great tribulation to come, in which he expected his hearers to be immersed.[206] That two of the three key images in the Baptist's prediction (baptism, fire) should reappear here with similar effect and in a not dissimilar combination (both predictive of intense tribulation) can hardly be dismissed as merely coincidental.[207] More likely, Jesus was remembered as taking up and echoing (deliberately) the Baptist's metaphor. That Jesus also transformed the metaphor we shall go on to consider below (§17.5). For the moment, however, it is sufficient to note the likelihood that Jesus applied the Baptist's metaphor to his own mission and that he saw in it further indication that he himself must undergo an intense experience (baptism) of suffering.

e. The Last Supper

Even if the proposals of Theissen and Merz and Chilton (§17.3c) go beyond the evidence, the tradition is firm that Jesus spoke words which signalled his sense of

204. See above, chapter 14 n. 242 plus other tribulation predictions, §§11.4c, 12.4d; and further U. B. Müller, *Die Entstehung des Glaubens an die Auferstehung Jesu* (SBS 172; Stuttgart: KBW, 1998) 39-42.

205. Robinson/Hoffmann/Kloppenborg include Luke 12.49, 51 in their critical reconstruction of Q: [[Fire have I come to hurl on the earth, and how I wish it had already blazed up!]] [[Do you]] think that I have come to hurl peace on earth? I did not come to hurl peace, but a sword! (*Critical Edition of Q* 376-81).

206. See above, §11.4c; Allison, *End of the Ages* 124-28.

207. Casey's difficulties in envisioning the Aramaic form of Mark 10.38c would be eased if he recognized the link back to the words of the Baptist (*Aramaic Sources* 203-205).

imminent death.[208] We have already noted the indications of liturgical development in each version of the tradition (§8.5c), but also of a core memory of what Jesus said. A simplified reminder of the words actually attributed to Jesus is sufficient to make the point.

Matt. 26.26-29	Mark 14.22-25	Luke 22.17-20	1 Cor. 11.23-26
26 'Take, eat; <u>this is my body</u>'. 27 'Drink from it, all of you; 28 for <u>this is my blood of the covenant,</u> which is poured out for many for the forgiveness of sins'.	22 'Take; <u>this is my body</u>'. 24 '<u>This is my blood of the covenant,</u> which is poured out on behalf of many'.	19 '<u>This is my body,</u> which is given for you. Do this in remembrance of me'. 20 'This cup <u>is the new covenant</u> in <u>my blood</u> which is poured out for you'.	24 '<u>This is my body</u> which is for you. Do this in remembrance of me'. 25 '<u>This</u> cup <u>is the new covenant</u> in <u>my blood.</u> Do this, as often as you drink it, in remembrance of me'.

Two characteristic acts of prophetic symbolism, one at the beginning and one 'after supper' (according to the Luke/Paul tradition) evidently made a lasting impression on those who met with him. Jesus invited those round the table to see in the bread broken and shared among them a symbol of himself; likewise the wine poured into the common cup. The symbolism of death is clear even without the varied interpretations of the core which no doubt began from the first recall of Jesus' words in sacred commemoration of his death after Easter.

There need be little doubt, then, that Jesus did anticipate rejection for his message in Jerusalem, to share the fate of the prophets, to suffer as a man in the hands of men, to drink the cup of suffering and be fully caught up in the final tribulation. Can we say still more? The last line of reflection suggests a deeper resonance in Jesus' own expectation for himself.

17.5. Did Jesus Give Meaning to His Anticipated Death?

The traditional material already examined offers up several possible positive answers to this further question.

---

208. The words at the last supper, together with the so-called 'vow of abstinence' (Mark 14.25), can probably be said to imply 'a consciousness of imminent death' on the part of Jesus (Theissen and Merz, *Historical Jesus* 430-31); 'the saying makes it highly probable that Jesus knew he was a marked man' (Sanders, *Historical Figure* 264).

a. The Righteous Martyr?

The thought that the unjust suffering and death of a righteous man might mark the end of the people's suffering and even contribute somehow to its ending had already been expressed in regard to the Maccabean martyrs.[209] If Jesus was at all influenced by the strong tradition within Jewish wisdom and apocalyptic thought regarding the suffering righteous, as seems likely (§17.4a-b), then it is entirely possible that he spoke of his own anticipated suffering and death in the same terms.[210]

b. The Suffering Son of Man

I have already pressed the likelihood that Jesus used the vision of Daniel's 'one like a son of man' to inform his own expectations (§16.5). We can now add the observations of Jane Schaberg that the core saying (Mark 9.31) also shows evidence of influence from Daniel: 'son of man' (Dan. 7.13); 'handed over' (7.25); not to mention 'raised' (12.2).[211] It is also by no means clear that Daniel's $k^e bar$ *$na\check{s}$ ('one like a son of man') was yet perceived as a use of *bar* *$na\check{s}$ any different from the normal Hebrew/Aramaic idiom ('a son of man'). In other words, it remains likely that this way of describing the figure in the vision (whether symbol or angelic representative) was chosen precisely because

209. 2 Macc. 7.33-38, but also anticipated in 1 Macc. 2.50 and 6.44 (Casey, *Aramaic Sources* 214-16). The early Maccabean literature (1 and 2 Maccabees) probably emerged in the first half of the first century BCE (J. A. Goldstein, *2 Maccabees* [AB; New York: Doubleday, 1983] 71-84). Goldstein points out that in 2 Maccabees 7 'the mother and her sons do not substitute for the rest of suffering Israel. They are part of suffering Israel and hope that their deaths will mark the turning point prophesied by Moses, which is in any case sure to come' (315-16). Casey also mentions Dan. 11.35 (but see Collins, *Daniel* 386). And Witherington, *Christology* 252, mentions 1QS 5.6, 8.3-10 and 9.4, and *T. Ben.* 3.8; but the latter clearly reflects Christian influence, and the 1QS texts hardly refer to the death of the righteous as having atoning value (note the brief discussion in R. A. Kugler, 'Rewriting Rubrics: Sacrifice and the Religion of Qumran', in J. J. Collins and R. A. Kugler, eds., *Religion in the Dead Sea Scrolls* [Grand Rapids: Eerdmans, 2000] 90-112 [here 90-92]). See also E. Lohse, *Märtyrer und Gottesknecht. Untersuchungen zur urchristlichen Verkündigung vom Sühntod Jesu Christi* (Göttingen: Vandenhoeck, 1955, ²1963); Hengel, *Atonement* 1-32, 65-75.

210. See also Schürmann, *Gottes Reich* 225-45. Although the distinctive martyr theology emerged within Hellenistic Judaism, the roots of the theology are deep in Second Temple Judaism, and the ideal of sacrificing one's life for a friend is much more widely attested, being taken up e.g. in *T. Ash.* 2.3 and Paul (Rom. 5.7); see further G. Stählin, *'philos'*, *TDNT* 9.153-54.

211. J. Schaberg, 'Daniel 7.12 and the New Testament Passion-Resurrection Predictions', *NTS* 31 (1985) 208-22 (here 209-13).

'a son of man' typically denoted the human condition in all its frailty (§16.3a n. 85). Since, in the appended interpretation, the manlike figure represents 'the saints of the Most High' in their vindication following the terrible suffering inflicted on them by the fourth kingdom (Dan. 7.19-23, 25), the 'one like a son of man' is a fitting symbol of Judah's frailty before the onslaught of Antiochus Epiphanes.[212]

In other words, we should not let the subsequent interpretation of Daniel's vision, where a specific heavenly being is envisaged (but 'son of man' is not yet a firm title), deflect us from recognizing the likelihood that a use of the idiomatic 'son of man' would quite naturally see Dan. 7.13 as an example of the same idiom. That is to say, as soon as we recognize that an implication of suffering frailty was part of Daniel's 'one like a son of man', it becomes equally easy to see that a *mašal* like that embedded in the second Passion prediction could quite readily evoke also Daniel's vision.

Neither should we allow the traditional classification of the Son of Man sayings in the Gospels into three categories (present activity, suffering, coming)[213] to confuse us into assuming that these were different usages requiring different explanations. If Jesus did draw on Daniel's vision on at least some occasions (§16.4c), then it was not simply to inform his hope of vindication (§16.5c), but to instruct his sense that suffering prior to that vindication was unavoidable. Here thought of the frailty of *bar ᵉnaš* meshes into the thought of the suffering righteous. Daniel's vision is itself part of that substantial tradition in Jewish thought: that the righteous of Israel ('the saints of the Most High') must expect to suffer for their devotion to Yahweh.

Daniel's use of *kᵉbar ᵉnaš* as a way of speaking of the (suffering) righteous of Israel raises one further possibility: that Jesus saw in Daniel's vision a prediction of the sufferings he (Jesus) must suffer as representative of, on behalf of, Israel. The thought does not come to expression in Daniel's vision, any more than the martyr theology of 2 Maccabees 7 expressed thought of vicarious suffering. But however inchoate, the thought is not far from the surface in Jesus' use of *bar ᵉnaša,* and not just when that usage contained an allusion to Dan. 7.13. For if Jesus did indeed refer to himself as 'the (son of) man', then in some degree he was focusing what was generally true of humankind in his own condition. And if he did find in Dan. 7.13 an image to inspire his own mission, then that inspiration may well have included some sense that the 'one like a son of man' represented Israel.

212. Cf. particularly Hooker, *Son of Man* 108-109.
213. Bultmann continues to be widely followed (*Theology* 1.30); e.g., Merklein, *Jesu Botschaft* 153; Flusser, *Jesus* 126; Theissen and Merz, *Historical Jesus* 546-48; Strecker, *Theology* 257; Becker, *Jesus* 204.

For many this line of reflection will have become much too speculative. But it interweaves with and is strengthened by the strand which emerged from the other metaphors used by Jesus (§17.4d).

c. Other Metaphors

One point which I did not follow up in the analysis of the metaphors of baptism and fire above (§17.4d) was that Jesus applied these metaphors to his *own* expected suffering. This in fact is the most striking feature of Jesus' usage: he evidently took up the Baptist's metaphor (baptism and fire) and applied it to himself. The Baptist had predicted one to come who would baptize *others* in fire (or fiery spirit) (§11.4c). Jesus affirmed the Baptist's expectation — where else could just this metaphor have come from? — but indicated that he *himself,* rather than dispensing the judgment, would himself have to endure it.[214]

Here we can see the likelihood that Jesus did not disown the Baptist's expectation of judgment entirely. It was not the primary emphasis of his own kingdom preaching (§12.5c), but he did not reject it altogether. What we hear, rather, is Jesus taking up the Baptist's distinctive metaphor and transforming it by treating it as a prescription of his *own* destiny.[215] The parallelism of the Lukan version probably allows the expansion of each member of the twin saying to embrace the thought of the other:

I have a baptism (with which to baptize but have first) to be baptized with (it).

I came to cast fire on the earth and how I wish it was already kindled (on myself).

In other words, we are not actually so very far from Schweitzer's infamous scenario: that Jesus not only expected the final tribulation to happen imminently, but by the time he reached (set off for?) Jerusalem had also concluded that he himself would have to endure the same tribulation.[216] On his own behalf only? Or in solidarity with others? Or somehow on their behalf? Here unfortunately the previous clarity of the line of reflection fades, and we are left with the possible

214. Cf. Meyer, *Aims* 213; Allison, *End of the Ages* 128; Beasley-Murray, *Jesus and the Kingdom* 250-52; Leivestad, *Jesus* 103 ('the death of Jesus would, as it were, become the flame that ignites the world conflagration'); Witherington, *Christology* 123-24.

215. I take up here my earlier suggestion argued in 'The Birth of a Metaphor — Baptized in Spirit', *ExpT* 89 (1977-78) 134-38, 173-75, reprinted in my *The Christ and the Spirit.* Vol. 2: *Pneumatology* (Grand Rapids: Eerdmans, 1998) 103-17 (here 107-12). Cf. particularly A. Vögtle, 'Todesankündigungen und Todesverständnis Jesu', in K. Kertelge, ed., *Der Tod Jesu. Deutungen im Neuen Testament* (QD 74; Freiburg: Herder, 1976) 80-88.

216. *Quest*[2] 347-49. Wright argues similarly (*Jesus* 577-84, 609-10).

implications of the imagery and its transformed usage — as with the unclarity of the implication of the righteous martyr (§17.5a) and the suffering Danielic son of man (§17.5b).

One possibility is that Paul's own further development of the baptismal metaphor in Rom. 6.3-4 ('baptized into Jesus' death') reflects Jesus' own adaptation of the metaphor. For if Jesus did use the Baptist's metaphor as an image of his own anticipated death, then that could easily have provided the inspiration for Paul's unprecedented use of the same metaphor. Paul could speak of a *baptism* into *Christ's death,* only because he was aware of the tradition that Jesus had spoken of his *death* as a *baptism.*[217] In which case the same question arises: whether the representative significance which Paul saw in Jesus' death, as expressed not least in this metaphor, was already anticipated in at least some measure in Jesus' own references to his imminent death.

Before turning to the last and most contested material, we should also mention Zech. 13.7, cited in Mark 14.27/Matt. 26.31 ('I will strike the shepherd and the sheep will be scattered'). The point is that the use of the same prophetic text in CD 19.7-10[218] seems to have in view the same expectation of eschatological tribulation (the final 'visitation') and raises similar questions as to whether the smiting of the shepherd had vicarious overtones.

d. The Suffering Servant

One motif more than any other, if it could be attributed to Jesus, would enable us to give a positive answer to the question of this section (§17.5). Did Jesus also speak of the destined outcome of his mission in terms of the Servant of Yahweh in (deutero-)Isaiah? In particular, can we supplement the portrayal of Jesus influenced by Daniel's vision with the portrayal of him influenced by the *suffering* Servant of Isaiah 53? Can we fairly deduce that Jesus saw his death as a *vicarious* suffering, a suffering on behalf of others? Strongly affirmative answers were characteristic of earlier generations of scholarship,[219] but in the second half of

217. See further my 'Birth of a Metaphor' 114-16; also *Theology of Paul* 451-52.
218. On the textual problems see Collins, *Scepter* 80-82.
219. In the twentieth century the case was argued afresh particularly by H. W. Wolff, *Jesaja 53 im Urchristentum* (Berlin: Evangelische, [2]1950); J. Jeremias, *pais theou, TDNT* 5.712-17 = with W. Zimmerli, *The Servant of God* (London: SCM, 1957, revised 1965) 99-106; Cullmann, *Christology* 60-69; Caird, *Theology* 404-408. M. D. Hooker, *Jesus and the Servant* (London: SPCK, 1959) describes this as 'the traditional view'; the assumption was widespread that Jesus fused the Danielic Son of Man with the suffering Servant of Isaiah. The case has been strongly restated by Stuhlmacher, 'Messianische Gottesknecht' 144-50; also *Biblische Theologie* 1.124, 127-30. For further bibliography see Burkett, *Son of Man* 47-48 nn. 9-12.

the twentieth century a more negative answer quickly became dominant over a wide spectrum of scholarship.[220] The difficulty in returning an affirmative answer lies in the character of the evidence.

First the text of what modern scholarship knows as the fourth servant song of Second Isaiah — Isa 52.13–53.12.

52.13See, my servant shall prosper; he shall be exalted and lifted up, and shall be very high. 14Just as there were many who were astonished at him — so marred was his appearance, beyond human semblance, and his form beyond that of mortals — 15so he shall startle many nations; kings shall shut their mouths because of him; for that which had not been told them they shall see, and that which they had not heard they shall contemplate. 53.1Who has believed what we have heard? And to whom has the arm of the LORD been revealed? 2For he grew up before him like a young plant, and like a root out of dry ground; he had no form or majesty that we should look at him, nothing in his appearance that we should desire him. 3He was despised and rejected by others; a man of suffering and acquainted with infirmity; and as one from whom others hide their faces he was despised, and we held him of no account. 4Surely he has borne our infirmities and carried our diseases; yet we accounted him stricken, struck down by God, and afflicted. 5But he was wounded for our transgressions, crushed for our iniquities; upon him was the punishment that made us whole, and by his bruises we are healed. 6All we like sheep have gone astray; we have all turned to our own way, and the LORD has laid on him the iniquity of us all. 7He was oppressed, and he was afflicted, yet he did not open his mouth; like a lamb that is led to the slaughter, and like a sheep that before its shearers is silent, so he did not open his mouth. 8By a perversion of justice he was taken away. Who could have imagined his future? For he was cut off from the land of the living, stricken for the transgression of my people. 9They made his grave with the wicked and his tomb with the rich, although he had done no violence, and there was no deceit in his mouth. 10Yet it was the will of the LORD to crush him with pain.

220. In English-speaking scholarship Hooker's *Jesus and the Servant* marked a turning of the tide (her research was completed in 1956); quickly supported by C. K. Barrett, 'The Background of Mark 10:45', in A. J. B. Higgins, ed., *New Testament Essays: Studies in Memory of T. W. Manson* (Manchester: Manchester University, 1959) 1-18 (Barrett had examined Hooker's thesis); also *Jesus* 39-45, but foreshadowed by C. F. D. Moule, 'From Defendant to Judge — and Deliverer' (1952), *The Phenomenon of the New Testament* (London: SCM, 1967) 82-99. In German scholarship the influence of Tödt, *Son of Man* 158-61, 167-69, 202-11, and Hahn, *Hoheitstitel* 54-66 (*Titles* 54-67), proved decisive for the following generation. Fuller represented the swing in opinion, from his earlier *Mission* 86-95, to *Foundations* 115-19; and de Jonge, despite the deliberate echo of T. W. Manson's title, pronounces himself still convinced by Barrett and Hooker (*Jesus, The Servant-Messiah* 48-50).

When you make his life an offering for sin, he shall see his offspring, and shall prolong his days; through him the will of the Lord shall prosper. [11]Out of his anguish he shall see light; he shall find satisfaction through his knowledge. The righteous one, my servant, shall make many righteous, and he shall bear their iniquities. [12]Therefore I will allot him a portion with the great, and he shall divide the spoil with the strong; because he poured out himself to death, and was numbered with the transgressors; yet he bore the sin of many, and made intercession for the transgressors.

Its relevance at this point is obvious: it envisages one (Yahweh's servant) who would suffer and be held of no account (53.2-3), whose sufferings would be vicarious, on behalf of others (vv. 4-6), who would be killed (vv. 7-9), and whose vicarious suffering would be willed and accepted by God (vv. 10-12).[221]

There is little dispute that the passage became very influential in earliest Christian reflection on Jesus' death. But what evidence is there that Jesus himself was influenced by this passage?[222]

(1) Luke 22.37. The tradition of Jesus' teaching contains only one direct quotation from Isaiah 53[223] — in Luke 22.37, a tradition attested solely by Luke:

[35]He said to them, 'When I sent you out without a purse, bag, or sandals, did you lack anything?' They said, 'No, not a thing'. [36]He said to them, 'But now, the one who has a purse must take it, and likewise a bag. And the one who has no sword must sell his cloak and buy one. [37]For I tell you, this

221. How the Servant was intended to be understood remains disputed, the two chief options still being Israel or some particular individual. See discussion, e.g., in W. Zimmerli, *pais theou*, *TDNT* 5.666-73; H. G. Reventlow, 'Basic Issues in the Interpretation of Isaiah 53', in W. H. Bellinger and W. R. Farmer, eds., *Jesus and the Suffering Servant: Isaiah 53 and Christian Origins* (Harrisburg: Trinity, 1998) 23-38. 'There is still no evidence for a Jewish interpretation of Isaiah 53 in terms of a suffering messiah' (Collins, *Scepter* 123-26 [here 124]). M. Hengel, 'Zur wirkungsgeschichte von Jes 53 in vorchristlicher Zeit', in B. Janowski and P. Stuhlmacher, eds., *Der leidende Gottesknecht. Jesaja 53 und seine Wirkungsgeschichte* (Tübingen: Mohr Siebeck, 1996) 49-91, notes that 4Q491 and 4Q540-41 lack the motif of a representative death for sin (69-75, 88-90), but nevertheless concludes that the supposition is not altogether unfounded that 'there were already in pre-Christian time traditions of suffering and atoning eschatological-messianic figures in Palestinian Judaism' which Jesus could have known and been influenced by (91).

222. Especially noticeable are the quotations in Matt. 8.17 (Isa. 53.4); Acts 8.32-33 (Isa. 53.7-8); and the multiple allusions in 1 Pet. 2.22-25 (Isa. 53.4, 6, 9, 12); Hooker now accepts that Rom. 4.25 contains a clear echo of Isaiah 53, but remains convinced that a negative answer has to be given to the question, 'Did the Use of Isaiah 53 to Interpret His Mission Begin with Jesus?' in Bellinger and Farmer, *Jesus and the Suffering Servant* 88-103.

223. John 12.38 (Isa. 53.1) and Matt. 8.17 (Isa. 53.4) are not presented as words of Jesus.

Scripture must be fulfilled *(telesthēnai)* in me, "And he was counted among the lawless" (Isa. 53.12); and indeed what is written about me is being fulfilled *(telos echei)'*. 38They said, 'Lord, look, here are two swords'. He replied, 'It is enough'.

The quotation[224] belongs to an obviously ancient context: the mysterious 'two swords' saying would probably be embarrassing in many circles (hence its absence from Mark and Matthew?); here we probably have another case where the criterion of embarrassment is decisive.[225] But the quotation itself is framed by characteristic Lukan language.[226] The verse does seem to disrupt the context, where v. 38 follows directly from v. 36.[227] And it fits with Luke's use elsewhere of the Servant motif as part of a 'humiliation-exaltation' motif (rather than in terms of vicarious suffering).[228] So the question arises whether the quotation of Isa. 53.12 is part of the early proof-from-prophecy apologetic prominent elsewhere in the Passion narrative (§17.1f), though why it should have been inserted here remains unclear. A tradition-historical analysis cannot trace it back to Jesus with any confidence.

(2) Mark 10.45. The fuller passage has already been cited in §14.3c; here we need recall only the final verse.

Matt. 20.28	Mark 10.45	Luke 22.27
28 Just as the Son of Man came not to be served but to serve and to give his life a ransom for many.	45 For the Son of Man came not to be served but to serve, and to give his life a ransom for many.	27 For who is greater, the one who reclines [at the table] or the one who serves? Is it not the one who reclines? But I am among you as one who serves.

224. So far as the text itself is concerned *(kai meta anomōn elogisthē),* a direct derivation from the Hebrew can certainly be argued for *(wᵉ 'eṭ-pošᵉ'im nimnā)* (Jeremias, *Proclamation* 294 n. 4), though the transmission was possibly influenced by knowledge of the LXX *(kai en tois anomois elogisthē),* where *logizō* is not the usual rendering of *manā.*

225. See also above, chapter 15 n. 40.

226. Nolland refers particularly to 'what is written' and 'must be fulfilled in me' *(Luke* 3.1076-77).

227. Lindars, *New Testament Apologetic* 85. *Pace* Jeremias: 'The reason given in v. 37 for this announcement — that, because Jesus will be driven out of the community of Israel as an *anomos,* so his disciples, too, will be treated as *anomoi* and refused food and their lives threatened — is indispensable to the whole context' *(Servant* 105; followed by Marshall, *Luke* 826). But the rationale of 22.37 is fulfilment/completion *(telesthēnai, telos)*; as an explanation of 22.36, 38 it is rather contrived with so much having to be read in and still leaving the intent of 22.36 unclear.

228. Fitzmyer, *Luke* 1432; see Acts 2.23-24; 3.14-15; 4.10; 5.30; 8.32-33; 10.39-40; 13.28-30; also below on Luke 22.27.

Jeremias claims that Mark's text shows strong influence from Isa. 53.10-11:[229]

Mark 10.45	Isa. 53.10, 11
to give his life *(dounai tēn psychēn autou)* a ransom *(lytron)* for many *(anti pollōn)*	10 you make his life *(tasim napšo)* a sin offering *('ašam)* 11 shall make many (*larabbim*) righteous

The links are certainly striking, though somewhat diffuse; the allusion is not obvious and has to be worked at before it becomes clear.[230] More significant from a tradition-historical perspective is the fact that Luke seems to know a different version of the teaching which climaxed in the saying, including a version of the conclusion which lacks any of the elements on which the allusion to Isa. 53 depends.[231] John 13.3-17 was probably developed out of another version of the teaching, climaxing with similar teaching of Jesus on service.[232] If it is appropriate to talk in terms of core tradition at this point,[233] the core is the image of Jesus as one who serves/came to serve.[234] It is quite likely, then, that the final clause of the Markan/Matthean version (assuming an allusion to the Isaianic Servant) is an elaboration, presumably at an early stage, of the core

229. Jeremias, *Servant* 99-100; *Proclamation* 292-93 n. 3.

230. The challenge of Hooker, *Servant* 74-79, and Barrett, 'Mark 10:45', in particular, was against the claim that linguistic connections could be demonstrated between Mark 10.45 and Isaiah 53; see now also Hampel, *Menschensohn* 317-25, and Casey, *Aramaic Sources* 211-13 (particularly on *lytron*). The case for dependence on Isaiah 53 has been restated by Davies and Allison, *Matthew* 3.95-96, who conclude: 'We do not claim that Mt 20.28 par. is a *translation* of any portion of Isaiah 53, LXX, MT or targum. Rather, it is a summary which describes the *'ebed* who gives his life as a sin offering for many' (96). Also by R. E. Watts, 'Jesus' Death, Isaiah 53, and Mark 10:45', in Bellinger and Farmer, *Jesus and the Suffering Servant* 125-51 (particularly 136-47).

231. It is less likely that Luke omitted Mark 10.45b for soteriological reasons; he does not avoid 'ransom' language elsewhere — Luke 1.68; 2.38; 24.21; Acts 7.35 (Fitzmyer, *Luke* 1212). More likely he knew the variant tradition and used/reworked it in preference to Mark 10.35-45. Cf. Gnilka, 'Wie urteilte Jesus?' 41-49; 'dying for' as 'the oldest interpretation of Jesus' death' (50).

232. Lindars, *Jesus* 77.

233. Pesch argues that Luke 22.27 is derived by redaction from Mark (*Markusevangelium* 2.164-65; followed by Hampel, *Menschensohn* 310-12), and Marshall suggests an original saying composed of two parts (Luke 22.27 + Mark 10.45) abbreviated by each Evangelist (*Luke* 813-14, followed by Kim, *Son of Man* 43-45), but a variant oral tradition makes better sense of the data than does a process conceived in terms of literary editing; the choice to follow an alternative version is more readily conceivable than arbitrary abbreviation of a unified tradition.

234. This saying in itself would be sufficient basis for a central thrust of Schürmann's *Gottes Reich:* 'as in life, so in death' (205-208), Jesus' 'pro-existence' death (e.g., 243-45).

tradition, in the light of the developing use of Isaiah 53, to illuminate the significance of Jesus' death.[235]

A complementary solution has built on the striking linguistic parallels between Mark 10.45 and Isa. 43.3-4: '. . . I *give* Egypt as your *ransom (kopr^eka)*, Ethiopia and Egypt *in exchange for* you *(taḥteka)*. . . . I give men *('adam[ot]* LXX *anthrōpous pollous) in return for* you, and nations for your life'.[236] But the thought behind the language is quite remote.[237] A more plausible source for the ransom imagery can be found in Ps. 49.7-8:[238] 'Truly, no man can ransom himself or give to God the price of his life, for the ransom of his life is costly and can never suffice', bearing in mind that Jesus may have alluded to the same passage elsewhere (Mark 8.37/Matt. 16.26).[239] But the parallel equally explains why a teacher might have elaborated the servant motif by adding the allusion.

A further or alternative possibility is that the core saying was originally formulated with *bar ^enaša*: Mark/Matthew's *bar ^enaša* = Luke's 'I'; and note the parallel between 'the one who serves' and 'I' in Luke.[240] Several have observed that the key term, 'serve' (differently rendered in Greek), appears in Daniel's vision of 'one like a son of man', who 'was given dominion and glory and kingdom, that all peoples, nations, and languages should serve him' (Dan. 7.14). It is possible, then, that Jesus deliberately contrasted his role as *bar ^enaša* who serves, with the lordship and authority given to the 'one like a son of man' = 'the saints of the Most High' in Daniel 7.[241] In which case, Jesus would have drawn on Daniel's vision not only to confirm his role as *bar ^enaša* but also to contrast

---

235. Cf. Bultmann, *History* 144; Lohse, *Märtyrer* 117-22; Tödt, *Son of Man* 203-207; Hahn, *Hoheitstitel* 57-59 (*Titles* 56-57); Lindars, *Jesus* 78-80; Pesch concludes that Mark 10.45 is a unified but secondary composition of the Greek-speaking Jewish Christian community (*Markusevangelium* 2.162-64).

236. The parallel was first noted by W. Grimm, *Die Verkündigung Jesu und Deuterojesaja* (Frankfurt, ²1981) 239-68, and has proved influential (see Hampel, *Menschensohn* 326-33 and those cited by him in n. 453; also Stuhlmacher, *Biblische Theologie* 1.121).

237. See further D. Vieweger and A. Böckler, '"Ich gebe Ägypten als Lösegeld für dich". Mk 10,45 und die jüdische Tradition zu Jes 43,3b, 4', *ZAW* 108 (1996) 594-607.

238. Hampel, *Menschensohn* 328-31.

239. See above, §14.3e.

240. It is widely acknowledged that 1 Tim 2.5-6 is an echo of Mark 10.45. It makes confession of 'the *man (anthrōpos)* Christ Jesus, who gave himself a ransom *(antilytron)* on behalf of many'. Perrin suggests an original I-saying 'transformed' into a Son of Man saying (*Modern Pilgrimage* 102), but that is much more arbitrary than presupposing a *bar ^enaša* saying which could be taken either way.

241. Barrett, 'Mark 10:45' 8-9; and particularly P. Stuhlmacher, 'Vicariously Giving His Life for Many, Mark 10:45 (Matt. 20:28)', *Reconciliation, Law and Righteousness: Essays in Biblical Theology* (Philadelphia: Fortress, 1986) 16-29 (here 21); followed by Kim, *Son of Man* 39-40.

it: Daniel focused on the theme of vindication; Jesus characterized the mission of *bar 'enaša* more as one of service.[242]

There is a clear danger that both sets of suggested allusions (Isaiah 53; Daniel 7) are more in the eye of the beholder than contrived or intended by the initial tradents. But at least the latter has the support of a more extensive motif, including other clear allusions, whereas the case for seeing here evidence that Jesus himself was influenced by Isaiah 53 is not much strengthened.

(3) Mark 14.24. Jeremias finds a further allusion to the suffering Servant in the words of institution at the last supper.[243]

Matt.26.28/Mark 14.24	Luke 22.20	1 Cor. 11.25
This is my blood of the covenant, which is poured out on behalf of many.	This cup is the new covenant in my blood which is poured out for you.	This cup is the new covenant in my blood.

The suggested allusion in this case is to Isa. 53.12: 'he poured out his life to death' *(he'erā lammawet napšo);*[244] but the imagery is not sacrificial.[245] Equally significant, Jeremias claims, is once again the reference to '(the) many' (Mark/Matthew), since a fivefold reference to '(the) many, *(ha)rabbim'*, is a striking feature of Isa. 52.13–53.12.[246] Here too it is hard to escape the sense of a commentator striving to find allusions, rather than of an allusion which most biblically familiar hearers would quickly recognize.[247]

More to the point, any allusion is arguable only for the Mark/Matthew version of the cup word. The imagery of blood poured out is not present in Paul's version. And the present Lukan formulation, whose core version is the Pauline one, may well reflect a secondary adaptation of the Pauline formula to its Markan/Matthean parallel — though, even so, lacking reference to 'the many'. I have already noted that the parallel body/blood formulation (Mark/Matthew)

242. Cf. Schillebeeckx, *Jesus* 303-306.

243. Cited above, §8.5c.

244. *'Ara* is used in the sense 'pour out', with *nepeš* as its object in Ps. 141.8 ('pour out a person's life'); here with the hiphil in the same sense. 'Pour out' is appropriate imagery since the *nepeš* is closely associated with the blood (Gen. 9.4-5; Lev. 17.11; Deut. 12.23) (H. Niehr, *TDOT* 11.345).

245. For which the usual term would be *šapak* (as in Lev. 4.7, 18, 25, 30, 34). It is true that the LXX uses *ekcheō* (as here in the Synoptics: *ekchynnomenon*), but at this point Jeremias ignores the underlying Hebrew (*Proclamation* 290). 'The established usage *haima ekchein* contains no direct allusion to Isa. 53.12' (Pesch, *Markusevangelium* 2.359).

246. J. Jeremias, *'polloi'*, *TDNT* 6.537-38: 53.11c, 12a (with article), 52.14, 53.12e (without article), one as an adjective (52.15). Jeremias presses the point too hard: for Jesus 'the many' here are 'the peoples of the world' (*Eucharistic Words* 226-31).

247. Similarly Hooker, *Jesus and the Servant* 82-83; Schürmann, *Gottes Reich* 220-21.

more than likely reflects a developed celebration where the two elements (bread and wine) were taken in close succession, and thus also the likelihood that the Paul/Luke version (body and cup) is closer to the original formulation.[248] All told, then, the case for seeing an allusion to the Servant of Isaiah in what Jesus originally said is not very strong.

The alternative (if that is the best way to put it), strongly suggested in both versions, is that Jesus spoke of his anticipated death in terms of a *covenant sacrifice* rather than a sin offering.[249] The precedent here would be Exod. 24.8: 'Moses took the blood and dashed it on the people, and said, "See the blood of the covenant that the Lord has made with you . . ."'.[250] This meshes well with the earlier possibility indicated above in §13.3e, that Jesus (somewhat like the Qumran covenanters) saw the group around him as somehow constituting the renewal of God's covenant with Israel,[251] or spoke with a view to the establishment of the new covenant promised in Jer. 31.31-34.[252] Jesus may well have gone the more willingly to his death because he saw it as the sacrifice which would bring into effect that long-promised covenant.[253]

If this suggestion is on the right lines, then we have another powerful motif on which Jesus is remembered as drawing to make sense of what was about to happen to him: the suffering righteous/(martyr), the son of man frail to death, destined to drain the cup and be baptized with the fiery baptism predicted by the Baptist, and now also covenant sacrifice. What we cannot say with any of the confidence expressed in regard to the other images is that the suffering Servant of Isaiah 53 was one of the powerful images that Jesus was recalled as drawing on.[254] Moreover, the concern on the part of commentators to draw on its moving

248. See above, §8.5c. The same logic applies to Luke's 'poured out for you', which parallels the body 'given for you' (Luke 22.19).

249. But Stuhlmacher would question strongly whether there is any justification for posing these as alternatives (*Biblische Theologie* 1.136-42); see also below n. 253.

250. 'The blood of the covenant' (Exod. 24.8; cf. Zech. 9.11) is echoed in 'my blood of the covenant' (Matt. 26.28/Mark 14.24), but the Paul/Luke version 'is scarcely any less of an allusion to the covenantal sacrifice of Exod 24:3-8 than the Marcan formula' (Fitzmyer, *Luke* 1391).

251. The 'for you' of Luke 22.20 would presumably have in view particularly the twelve as representatives of (eschatological) Israel (Vögtle, 'Todesankündigungen' 94-96).

252. The point does not hang on the presence of the word 'new' ('new covenant', only in the Paul/Luke version), though if early tradents did introduce it they would no doubt have claimed that they were simply making explicit what was implicit. See also Tan, *Zion Traditions* 204-16.

253. We should not play off covenant sacrifice and atoning sacrifice against each other, since there was a tendency to run the two together, evident in the Targums (Pesch, *Markusevangelium* 2.359), as also in description of the Passover lamb as a sacrifice (1 Cor. 5.7).

254. Contrast Wright, who suggests that 'Isaiah 40–55 as a whole was thematic for Jesus' kingdom-announcement' (*Jesus* 603).

portrayal of vicarious suffering to elucidate Jesus' own self-understanding may
have distracted attention from and even obscured the other images in regard to
which a better case can be made.

There are no other references within the Jesus tradition which are likely to
change that conclusion.[255] The upshot is that a convincing case cannot be made
that Jesus saw himself as the suffering Servant. That is not to deny that he might
have reflected on the Servant passages, as he evidently did on other Scriptures.
Indeed, the more Isaiah 53 was already seen to be part of the more extensive motif of the suffering righteous, the more likely it is that Jesus did reflect on what
the Servant passages might contribute to his understanding of his own role. The
point, however, is that the Jesus tradition does not allow us to draw that as a firm
conclusion. That may simply be a reminder of the inadequacy of our critical
tools. But the Jesus tradition itself has to be determinative for us, and even a
modest tradition-historical analysis of the key passages raises substantive doubts.

So, what meaning did Jesus give to the death which he evidently anticipated with increasing certainty (and angst) as his mission neared its climax? The
tradition indicates a number of positive answers. (1) He would suffer as part of
God's will, as others, the faithful and righteous, had before him. Perhaps he cherished the hope, like the Maccabean martyrs, that his death would mark the final
end to Israel's suffering. (2) As 'the one' chosen to call Israel to return and to
somehow reconstitute Israel in the mounting eschatological crisis he probably
expected to suffer as the saints of the Most High suffered at the time of the
Maccabees. Possibly, in contrast to Daniel's 'one like a son of man' he saw his
destiny characterized more in terms of service than of being served. (3) Sooner
or later, he probably concluded that he himself would have to endure the eschatological tribulation (the cup of suffering, the fiery baptism) predicted by the Baptist — perhaps on behalf of his disciples/renewed Israel.[256] (4) If God was indeed

---

255. Other suggested references in Jeremias, *Proclamation* 286-87, and review in
Hooker, *Jesus and the Servant* 62-102. The use of *paradidonai* ('hand over') in the LXX of Isa.
53.6, 12 has naturally attracted attention in view of the prominence of the term in the Passion
predictions (Mark 9.31 pars.; 10.33 pars.) and the Passion narratives (Mark 14.10-11, 18, 21,
41-42, 44; 15.1, 10, 15). Given the probable allusion to Isa. 42.1 in the words from heaven at
the Jordan (Mark 1.11 pars.), Cullmann claims boldly that Jesus 'became conscious at the moment of his baptism that he had to take upon himself the *ebed Yahweh* role' (*Christology* 66-
67), but the words are not remembered as a saying of Jesus and cannot be taken as a direct indication of Jesus' own self-understanding (see above, §11.5b). On the other hand, Jesus seems to
have drawn on Isa. 61.1-2 to express the priorities of his mission (§15.6c), but there are no indications that the eschatological prophet of Isaiah 61 was identified with the Servant of Isaiah 53.

256. But we should recall that Jesus also expected his disciples to experience great suffering (the eschatological tribulation, §14.3e). The difficulty we have in correlating these expectations is no reason for doubting that Jesus could have held both (see §12.6e above).

to make a fresh covenant with his people, then presumably a covenant sacrifice was also required; Jesus' death would serve as that sacrifice.[257]

Much of this is speculative. How could it not be when we are trying to do the impossible — to 'get inside' the head of a historical figure? But the speculation is rooted in and grows directly from the data of the Jesus tradition itself, from how Jesus was remembered in the earliest formulated memories of his mission. And it makes sense of what otherwise must seem a foolhardy policy pursued by Jesus during his last days.

But there is yet more to be said and one further question which needs to be asked.

17.6. Did Jesus Hope for Vindication after Death?

I have already indicated my conclusion that a positive answer can be given to this final question. The answer will certainly have to be qualified by the character of the Jesus tradition and by indications of post-Easter reflection. Here more than anywhere else the tradition was likely to be formulated more or less from the first in the light of what the first disciples believed happened on Easter morning. Even so, however, there remains a strong possibility of discerning a hope initially formulated prior to that Easter morning.[258]

a. Hope of Vindication

We have previously noted the already strong conviction within Second Temple Judaism that the righteous should not despair that their righteousness was in vain. The same motif which holds out the expectation of suffering and death for the righteous looks beyond that death to vindication beyond.

(1) Most clear is Wis. 3.1-9 and 5.1-5:

> 3.1But the souls of the righteous are in the hand of God, and no torment will ever touch them. 2In the eyes of the foolish they seemed to have died, and their departure was thought to be a disaster, 3and their going from us to be their destruction; but they are at peace. 4For though in the sight of others they were punished, their hope is full of immortality. 5Having been disciplined a little, they will receive great good, because God tested them and found them

257. Vögtle suggests that it was only at the last supper that Jesus came to conceive of his death as not only a suffering of God's judgment *(Gerichtstod)* but as necessary for the salvation of others ('Todesankündigungen' 111-12).

258. *Pace* Keck, *Who Is Jesus?* 110.

worthy of himself; 6like gold in the furnace he tried them, and like a sacrificial burnt offering he accepted them. 7In the time of their visitation they will shine forth, and will run like sparks through the stubble. 8They will govern nations and rule over peoples, and the Lord will reign over them forever. 9Those who trust in him will understand truth, and the faithful will abide with him in love, because grace and mercy are upon his holy ones, and he watches over his elect.

5.1Then the righteous will stand with great confidence in the presence of those who have oppressed them and those who make light of their labours. 2When the unrighteous see them, they will be shaken with dreadful fear, and they will be amazed at the unexpected salvation of the righteous. 3They will speak to one another in repentance, and in anguish of spirit they will groan, and say, 4'These are persons whom we once held in derision and made a by-word of reproach — fools that we were! We thought that their lives were madness and that their end was without honour. 5Why have they been numbered among the children of God? And why is their lot among the saints?'

Nor should we be surprised that early Christian reflection seized upon Ps. 16.8-11 (Acts 2.25-28; 13.35), since the confidence in God expressed there seems to extend beyond death to a continuing life and 'pleasures for ever-more':[259]

16.1Protect me, O God, for in you I take refuge. 2I say to the LORD, 'You are my Lord; I have no good apart from you.' . . . 9Therefore my heart is glad, and my soul rejoices; my body also rests secure. 10For you do not give me up to Sheol, or let your faithful one see the Pit. 11You show me the path of life. In your presence there is fullness of joy; in your right hand are pleasures for-evermore.

(2) If Jesus did indeed draw on Daniel's vision of the 'one like a son of man', then we need simply to recall the capacity of that vision to encourage hope of vindication following suffering.[260] As the manlike figure represented the saints of the Most High in their vindication following horrendous suffering, so he provided a further expression of the suffering-vindication hope. That Jesus may have been influenced by this vision is further suggested by the fact that it talks of the kingdom being given to that son of man (Dan. 7.14), to the saints of the Most High (7.18, 22, 27). The possibility is thus provided of a direct link between Jesus' ex-

---

259. Lindars, *New Testament Apologetic* 38-45; but see also B. Janowski, 'Die Toten loben JHWH nicht. Psalm 88 und das alttestamentliche Todesverständnis', in Avemarie and Lichtenberger, *Auferstehung — Resurrection* 3-45 (here 41-44).

260. See above, §§16.3b, 4c, and 17.4c.

pectation of the kingdom to come and his own destiny in future vindication. That Jesus could have hinted at such a prospect is also confirmed by the expectation of some of the twelve that they would share in that kingdom (Mark 10.36 par.) and by Luke 22.29-30.[261] Both passages indicate in different ways that such a sharing in kingly rule will be consequent on shared suffering,[262] and take us back into the same circle of thought as the suffering-vindicated son of man.

(3) If Mark 14.24 recalls Jesus' talk of his death as covenant sacrifice (§17.5d[3]), then we should also recall that 14.24 is attached to 14.25, the 'vow of abstinence' in prospect of celebration in the kingdom of God (cf. Luke 22.18, 20).[263] Jesus may have seen his death as the sacrifice which renewed the covenant or brought into effect the new covenant. But if so, he expected also to share in its benefits, presumably in a post-mortem existence.

(4) Should it be the case that Isa. 53 also influenced Jesus (though the Jesus tradition does not enable us to make a positive affirmation on the point), then we need simply recall that Isa. 53 too holds out the prospect of vindication after death for the suffering Servant. I need refer only to 53.10-11 cited above (§17.5d). Here too we should recall that according to the Acts record of the earliest Christian preaching, the earliest apologetic use of Isa. 53 in Christian circles was in elucidation of the suffering-exaltation theme.[264]

(5) Finally, there is the broader consideration that Jesus presumably correlated in some way his proclamation of the good news of God's soon-coming kingdom with his anticipated death. It is hardly likely that he saw his death as marking the failure of God's predetermined purpose, much more likely as the acting out of that purpose or embraced within that purpose. However daunting the prospect, Jesus surely did not see his death as defeat and disaster; would he have set his face to go to Jerusalem so resolutely in that case? Much more likely, he saw his expected death as a prelude to the consummation of God's purpose, the birth-pangs of the age to come, perhaps even the means by which the kingdom would come. And if so, presumably he expected to be vindicated after death and to share the continued joys of that kingdom.

Eduard Schweizer put the point well, even if in terms of his own thesis regarding the Son of Man:

261. See above, chapter 12 n. 205 and §14.3c.
262. Mark 10.38-39; Luke 22.28. The fact that Luke has appended 22.28-30 to his version of the rebuke to the disciples' overweening ambition (Luke 22.24-27/Mark 10.41-45) implies his recognition of the same circle of thought.
263. See above, §12.4f; similarly Gnilka, 'Wie urteilte Jesus?' 33-35; also *Jesus* 282-83; Schürmann, *Gottes Reich* 210-13, 219-20; Becker, *Jesus* 341-42; Müller, *Entstehung* 42-46. 14.25 'indicates that Jesus viewed his death as part and parcel of the process whereby the kingdom comes' (Beasley-Murray, *Jesus and the Kingdom* 269).
264. See further Juel, *Messianic Exegesis* 119-33, and above, n. 228.

If Jesus did foresee suffering and rejection for himself and his disciples, then, of course, he saw it not as catastrophe but as a gateway to the glory of the coming kingdom. If he did call himself the Son of Man and connected the title *(sic)* with his lowly state on earth as well as the glory to come, then he must have expected something like his exaltation to the glory of God.[265]

b. Hope of Resurrection?

Could it be that Jesus expressed his hope of vindication in terms of resurrection? The Passion predictions certainly indicate so: 'and after three days/on the third day he will rise again/be raised'. But we have already seen that their present form shows clear signs of elaboration: the vaguer 'after three days' has become 'on the third day'; the less explicit 'killed' has become 'crucified' (§17.4c). Moreover, behind the sayings clarified in hindsight there may well be discerned a simpler *mašal:* 'the man is to be handed over to the men'. In this form there is no expression of vindication hope, of resurrection. Is then the expectation of resurrection part of the post-Easter elaboration of the *mashal?*

The only reason for hesitating on the point is the fact that resurrection was one form of vindication hope which had become prominent in late Second Temple Judaism. It is most clearly indicated in what is usually reckoned a late (fourth or third century BCE) addition to Isaiah (Isa. 24–27) and in Dan. 12.1-3.[266]

> Isa. 26.19Your dead shall live, their corpses shall rise. O dwellers in the dust, awake and sing for joy! For your dew is a radiant dew, and the earth will give birth to those long dead.

> Dan. 12.1-3At that time Michael, the great prince, the protector of your people, shall arise. There shall be a time of anguish, such as has never occurred since nations first came into existence. But at that time your people shall be delivered, everyone who is found written in the book. 2Many of those who sleep in the dust of the earth shall awake, some to everlasting life, and some to shame and everlasting contempt. 3Those who are wise shall shine like the

---

265. Schweizer, *Lordship and Discipleship* 36 (see further *Erniedrigung* 26-28, 31-33, 46-52); similarly Barrett, *Jesus* 76; Schillebeeckx, *Jesus* 284-91, 311 ('Jesus' whole life is the hermeneusis of his death'); Beasley-Murray, *Jesus and the Kingdom* 245-46, 269-70.

266. For fuller review and discussion see H. C. C. Cavallin, *Life after Death: Paul's Argument for the Resurrection of the Dead in 1 Cor 15.* Part I: *An Enquiry into the Jewish Background* (Lund: Gleerup, 1974); Collins, *Daniel* 394-98; A. Chester, 'Resurrection and Transformation', in Avemarie and Lichtenberger, *Auferstehung* 47-77 (here 48-70), and Hengel, 'Begräbnis' in the same volume 150-72.

brightness of the sky, and those who lead many to righteousness, like the stars forever and ever.

The earliest expressions of martyr-theology already express hope of vindication in terms of resurrection (2 Macc. 7.9, 14). There is also a consistent hope of resurrection expressed in the *Testaments of the Twelve Patriarchs,* though the extent of Christian redaction there is unclear,[267] and probably also in *1 Enoch.*[268] We also know that the belief in resurrection was firmly embraced by the Pharisees,[269] as indeed by Jesus himself.[270] So it would hardly be surprising if Jesus had entertained hope of vindication in terms of resurrection.

What this hope would refer to, however, is almost certainly what might best be described as the general and final resurrection — resurrection prior to final judgment (as implied in Dan. 12.2) and disposition of eternal destiny ('some to everlasting life, and some to shame and everlasting contempt'). *If Jesus hoped for resurrection it was presumably to share in the general and final resurrection of the dead.*

There are some indications of 'resurrection' language being used in service of a prophet *redivivus* concept: Jesus as John the Baptist 'raised from the dead' (Mark 6.14 pars.), 'Jeremiah' (Matt. 16.14), 'one of the old prophets has risen' (Luke 9.8).[271] But these are presented as expressions of troubled or puzzled minds trying to make sense of disquieting phenomena — Jesus acting like one of the old prophets, disturbingly like the Baptist. The hopes regarding the return of Enoch and Elijah are only partly parallel, since neither was thought to have died (§15.6a); but pseudo-Philo identified Elijah with Phinehas (Num. 25), preserved in secret ('in Danaben') by God until his return as Elijah (*LAB* 48.1).[272] And the

267. *T. Sim.* 6.7; *T. Jud.* 25.1, 4; *T. Zeb.* 10.2; *T. Ben.* 10.6-8; cf. *T. Levi* 18.13-14; *T. Dan* 5.12; with clear echoes of Isa. 26.19; see further Hollander and de Jonge, *Testaments* 61-63, 125.

268. *1 En.* 22.13; 90.33; 92.3; 91.10, (17b); cf. 46.6; 51.1; 61.5; 62.15; 92.3; 104.2. See M. Black, *The Book of Enoch or 1 Enoch* (Leiden: Brill, 1985) *ad loc.* On whether the Qumran community shared belief in a future resurrection (only 1QH 14[= 6].32-34 and 19[= 11].12 call for serious consideration) see H. Lichtenberger, 'Auferstehung in den Qumranfunden', in Avemarie and Lichtenberger, *Auferstehung* 79-91.

269. The testimony of Acts 23.6-8 and Mark 12.18 pars. agrees with the Hellenistically slanted description of Josephus (*War* 2.163, 165; *Ant.* 18.14, 16); in *m. Sanh.* 10.1 resurrection has become an article of faith for the rabbis.

270. Explicitly Mark 12.24-27 pars., but presumably implied also in Matt. 8.11-12/Luke 13.28-29; and note Luke 16.19-31. See further above, chapter 12 n. 234.

271. K. Berger, *Die Auferstehung des Propheten und die Erhöhung des Menschensohnes* (Göttingen: Vandenhoeck und Ruprecht, 1976) draws attention to this text as an example of 'individual, non-eschatological resurrection of prophets' (15-22).

272. R. Hayward, 'Phinehas — the Same Is Elijah: The Origin of a Rabbinic Tradition', *JJS* 29 (1978) 22-38.

Nero *redux* or Nero *redivivus* (Nero returned, Nero living again) rumours which circulated after his death[273] well exemplify the fears or hopes that might be entertained regarding some famous or controversial person after he has disappeared from the scene.[274] Such confused speculations, however, do not amount to a coherent theology such as was already current in Second Temple Judaism regarding the final resurrection.[275] The distinguishing feature here is that the hope of resurrection is attributed to someone prior to his death, not as speculation regarding the earlier but unexpected or poorly attested death of someone else.[276]

Could it be, then, that Jesus on one or more occasions elaborated the simpler *mašal* predicting the (son of) man's handing over to men by adding the hope for vindication in terms explicitly of resurrection?[277] The earliest versions of the tradition attributed to Jesus envisage being raised 'after three days'.[278] The phrase almost certainly means 'soon', 'shortly' (in a short time), as in the equivalent time interval envisaged in Luke 13.32-33 and Mark 14.58.[279] That would certainly tie in with Jesus' expectation of imminent denouement (§12.4g-h) and with his recalled expectation of a period of abstinence prior to his participation in the feasting of the kingdom (Mark 14.25 pars.).[280] In the ambiguities of a hope capable of expression only in metaphor and symbol (§12.6e), the image of rising up to a new day, of being raised with others into a final form of existence qualitatively different from life which ended in death, provided a sharper articulation of

273. For details see D. E. Aune, *Revelation* (WBC 52, 2 vols.; Dallas: Word, 1998) 2.737-40.

274. Cf. Mark 6.14, in reference to the Baptist, even though Herod had been responsible for his execution! In Heb. 11.35 'resurrection' is probably used typologically: the restoration of life of dead children (1 Kgs. 17.17-24; 2 Kgs. 4.18-37) foreshadows the 'better resurrection' (that is, final resurrection), just as the various elements of the old covenant foreshadow the 'better hope' of the new (Heb. 7.19, 22; 8.6; 9.23; 10.34; 11.16, 35, 40; 12.24). Alternatively, the thought is of the mother of the seven martyred brothers (2 Maccabees 7) receiving them back in confident hope of resurrection, in the same spirit displayed by Abraham who received back the about-to-be-sacrificed Isaac 'figuratively *(en parabolē)*' (Heb. 11.17-19; cf. 9.9).

275. It is equally unclear whether the blessing of God as the one 'who makes the dead alive' (*Shemoneh 'Esreh* 2) has in mind resurrection or simply restoration to mortal life (cf. Ps. 71.20; Tob. 13.2; Wis. 16.13; *Jos. As.* 20.7; *T. Gad* 4.6).

276. It should also be noted that the (probably first-century CE) work *The Lives of the Prophets* thinks in terms only of final resurrection (2.15; 3.12).

277. As, e.g., Casey argues (above, n. 192).

278. Schaberg argues that the 'after three days' may be an interpretation and shortening of Daniel's 'a time, two times and half a time' (Dan. 7.25; cf. Rev. 11.2-12) ('Daniel 7, 12' 210-11; see above at n. 211).

279. See further Jeremias, *Proclamation* 285; Meyer, *Aims of Jesus* 182; Davies and Allison, *Matthew* 2.661; Bayer, *Jesus' Predictions* 205-208; cf. Lindars, *Jesus* 71-73; Beasley-Murray, *Jesus and the Kingdom* 246-47.

280. Cf. particularly Bayer, *Jesus' Predictions* 224-29, 249-53.

that hope than did most other images. It is entirely possible that Jesus articulated his own hope of vindication in such terms.

The probability remains, however, that any hope of resurrection entertained by Jesus for himself was hope to share in the final resurrection.[281] If we tie that possibility also into the bundle of kingdom and tribulation beliefs already discussed, then the possibility is quite strong that Jesus saw the climax to his mission as the climax to God's eschatological purpose. Jesus (and his disciples) would suffer the final tribulation through which God's kingly purpose would achieve its goal; the kingdom would come. His death would introduce that final climactic period, to be followed shortly ('after three days'?) by the general resurrection, the implementation of the new covenant, and the coming of the kingdom. That still leaves us with the same ambiguities of disparate metaphors and diverse imagery as confronted us at the end of chapter 12. But to be able to say even as much is to say more than historical questers have usually allowed.

---

281. See also Evans, 'Did Jesus Predict?' 91-96.

CHAPTER 18

Et Resurrexit

18.1. Why Not Stop Here?

In Bach's B Minor Mass the solemn, slow-moving chorus 'Crucifixus' is followed at once by the joyous allegro, 'Et Resurrexit'. Which is what one might expect in Christian worship. But in a historical study of Jesus should we follow suit? After all, on pretty well any definition, 'resurrection' moves beyond history, at least in the sense of 'that which can be observed by historical method'.[1] Death is, almost by definition, departure from the time-space continuum, the only arena in which any historical method can operate. No one regards post-mortem existence as a viable subject of historical study. So why not end the quest of the historical Jesus at his death? If 'the flight from history' (chapter 5) can be justified anywhere, it can surely be justified here.[2] Many questers accept the logic and write accordingly, even if they add some reference to Christian belief in Jesus' resurrection as an epilogue.[3]

In this case, however, I will not follow that logic but will bring this volume to a close with a chapter on Jesus' resurrection. I do so for several reasons. First, in what is projected as a three-volume study of *Christianity in the Making*, it

---

1. The limitations of the historical method and the problems of speaking about the resurrection as a 'historical event' are familiar to students of the subject. The recent study by A. J. M. Wedderburn, *Beyond Resurrection* (London: SCM, 1999) is a model of scrupulous care in this respect (see here 9-19).

2. For a review and critique of Barth and Bultmann on the subject see Carnley, *Structure* ch. 3, especially 127-30.

3. E.g., Sanders limits himself to a tantalising half-page in *Jesus* 320, but includes a five-page Epilogue in *Historical Figure* 276-80; Gnilka — 'Easter Epilogue' (*Jesus* 319-20); Becker adds only a brief consideration of how the Easter faith influenced the reception of the Jesus material (*Jesus* 361-64).

makes better sense to round off the first volume, on Jesus, with a treatment of what Christians have always (from the first) believed was the most remarkable thing about Jesus — his resurrection from the dead. That belief seems to have been not only fundamental for Christianity as far back as we can trace, but also presuppositional and foundational.[4] Any claims to disentangle a Jesus movement or form of Christianity which did not celebrate Jesus' resurrection inevitably have to assume what they are trying to prove *(petitio principii),* since all the data available (including Q) were retained by churches which did celebrate his resurrection.[5] As a historical statement we can say quite firmly: no Christianity without the resurrection of Jesus. As Jesus is the single great 'presupposition' of Christianity, so also is the resurrection of Jesus. To stop short of the resurrection would have been to stop short.

Second, the Gospels themselves obviously regarded the resurrection of Jesus as the climax of their accounts of the remembered Jesus. The story of Jesus would be incomplete without including the story of his resurrection.[6] Even Mark, who records no appearance of Jesus, clearly affirms the resurrection and points forward to such appearances (Mark 16.6-7).[7] We should respect that perspective and be prepared to investigate what that conviction was based on.[8] Of course the

4. 'God raised him from the dead' is probably the earliest distinctively Christian affirmation and confession. It is presupposed again and again in the earliest Christian writings (Rom. 4.24-25; 7.4; 8.11; 1 Cor. 6.14; 15.4, 12, 20; 2 Cor. 4.14; Gal. 1.1; Col. 2.12; 1 Thes. 1.10; Eph. 1.20; 2 Tim. 2.8; Heb. 13.20; 1 Pet. 1.21; Acts 3.15; 4.10; 5.30; 10.40; 13.30, 37). It was the faith to which Paul was converted, probably within two to three years of Jesus' death (1 Cor. 15.3-8).

5. On Q see above, §7.4. J. S. Kloppenborg does not dispute the influence of 'Easter faith' on Q ('"Easter Faith" and the Sayings Gospel Q', in R. Cameron, ed., *The Apocryphal Jesus and Christian Origins, Semeia* 49 [1990] 71-99 [here 83]; for Q 'Jesus arose in his words' [92]), but still assumes, without sufficient warrant, that had the Easter 'events' been significant for the Q community/ies they would have been included within Q's 'narrative world'. But we will have to revisit the whole question in vol. 2.

6. I use the last phrase 'the story of his resurrection' loosely. The story is of empty tomb and sightings of Jesus after his death; the nearest we have to a description of 'the resurrection' itself is the manifestly imaginative *Gos. Pet.* 10.39-42. So care has to be taken lest language used predispose the quester towards a particular reading of the data. We shall return to this issue in §18.5.

7. There is a very broad consensus that Mark's Gospel ended at 16.8 (textual data and evaluation in Metzger, *Textual Commentary* 122-26); the longer ending (16.9-20) shows knowledge of Luke 8.2; Luke 24.10/John 20.11-18; Luke 24.13-39 and episodes from Acts; it was probably added to Mark 16 to round off the Gospel more satisfactorily in the second century. On the possibility of a book ending with the conjunction *gar* ('for') see P. van der Horst, 'Can a Book End with *gar*? A Note on Mark xvi.8', *JTS* 23 (1972) 121-24.

8. By the same logic we might have included discussion of Jesus' 'ascension' (Luke 24.51). But it is unclear how the concept 'ascension' relates to the concept 'resurrection' (cf.

Evangelists' inclusion of Jesus' resurrection as part of their accounts of Jesus' mission is a reminder to us that they viewed the whole life of Jesus in the light of that climax. But we have seen sufficient indication of the impact made by Jesus even before his death, so we can hardly avoid asking here too what it was that was being remembered.

Third, I have emphasized from the beginning that there can be no real hope, historically speaking, of getting back to an 'objective' Jesus (as though it was possible somehow to strip away the 'subjective' elements of the responses to him). All we have is the impact Jesus made on those who responded to him, the impact crystallized in the tradition — the remembered Jesus. To that extent, the final chapters of the Gospels are no different from the earlier chapters. They too embody the impact made by Jesus; 'resurrection' is the crystallization of that impact. As with the earlier chapters, we have to attempt to discern the outline of the impacting body from the impression left by the impact. It also follows that as with 'the historical Jesus' generally there is an unavoidable intangibility about that which made the impact. If we cannot grasp 'the historical Jesus' in our own hands, as it were, still less can we grasp the 'resurrection' of this Jesus. But the challenge in terms of discerning and analysing the beginning of the tradition process is essentially no different.[9]

Here as before we can proceed only by scrutinizing the tradition itself. Again and again we have found good reason to conclude that the core of the various traditions so far examined was probably formed more or less by the impact which Jesus made through his teaching and actions; the traditions themselves were part of the impression made. That is, the very sharing of experience among Jesus' followers gave lasting shape to these formative impressions. Traditions were being formulated right away, and not only at several removes from the occasions which they recalled, and were performed with diversity of emphasis and

---

Luke 24.26; John 20.17!); contrary to a common assumption, Matthew does not end with an 'ascension' (Matt. 28.16-20), and only Luke, and only in his second volume, clearly distinguishes the two (Acts 1.9-11). The subject is better dealt with in vol. 2.

9. Bultmann's famous dictum remains true: 'If the event of Easter Day is in any sense an historical event additional to the event of the cross, it is nothing else than the rise of faith in the risen Lord. . . . All that historical criticism can establish is the fact that the first disciples came to believe in the resurrection' ('New Testament and Mythology' 42). Similarly Bornkamm: 'The last historical fact available to it [historical scholarship] is the Easter faith of the first disciples' (*Jesus* 180). The thrust of my inquiry, however, is slightly differently directed: not How can we explain the rise of Easter *faith?* but How can we explain the rise of the Easter *tradition?* To some extent that circumvents the impasse posed by Wedderburn's formulation of the problem: '"Jesus is risen" is not a historical statement and is not open or accessible to the historian's investigation' (*Beyond Resurrection* 9). The assertion is misleading: 'Jesus is risen' as a statement *is* historical and accessible to historical investigation; the problem lies with what the statement affirms.

detail from the start. Is the same true for what we may conveniently call simply 'the resurrection traditions'? They fall obviously into two groups — the traditions regarding Jesus' tomb, and the 'resurrection appearances'.

18.2. The Empty Tomb Tradition

We have already noted the likelihood that Jesus' body was given a proper, if hasty, burial.[10] The tradition that this tomb was found empty 'on the first day of the week' is very similar to the traditions already examined: the Synoptics have parallel versions, while the Fourth Gospel has its own distinctive account.

Matt. 28.1-8	Mark 16.1-8	Luke 24.1-12
	1 When the sabbath was over, Mary Magdalene, and Mary the mother of James, and Salome bought spices, so that they	
1 After the sabbath, as the first day of the week was dawning, Mary Magdalene and the other Mary went to see the grave. 2 And suddenly there was a great earthquake; for an angel of the Lord, descending from heaven, came and	might go and anoint him. 2 And very early on the first day of the week, when the sun had risen, they went to the tomb.	1 But on the first day of the week, at early dawn, they went to the tomb, taking the spices that they had prepared.
rolled away the stone and sat on it. 3 His appearance was like lightning, and his clothing white as snow. 4 For fear of him the guards shook and became like dead men.	3 They had been saying to one another, 'Who will roll away the stone for us from the entrance to the tomb?' 4 When they looked up, they saw that the stone, which was very large, had already been rolled back. 5 As they entered the tomb, they saw a young man, dressed in a white robe, sitting on the right side; and they were alarmed.	2 They found the stone rolled away from the tomb, 3 but when they entered, they did not find the body. 4 While they were perplexed about this, suddenly two men in dazzling clothes stood beside them. 5 The women were terrified and bowed their faces to the ground,
5 But the angel said to the women, 'Do not be afraid; I know that you are looking for Jesus who was crucified. 6 He is not here; for he has been raised, as he said. Come, see the place where he lay. 7 Then go quickly and tell his disciples, "He has been raised from the dead, and indeed he is going ahead of you to Galilee; there you will see him". This is my message for you'.	6 But he said to them, 'Do not be alarmed; you are looking for Jesus of Nazareth, who was crucified. He has been raised; he is not here. Look, there is the place they laid him. 7 But go, tell his disciples and Peter that he is going ahead of you to Galilee; there you will see him, just as he told you'.	but the men said to them, 'Why do you look for the living among the dead? He is not here, but has risen. 6 Remember how he told you, while he was still in Galilee, 7 that the Son of Man must be handed over to sinners, and be crucified, and on the third day

10. See above, §17.1g.

		rise again'. 8 Then they remembered his words, 9 and returning from the tomb,
8 So they left the tomb quickly with fear	8 So they went out and fled from the tomb, for terror and amazement had seized them; and they said nothing to anyone, for they were afraid.	
and great joy, and ran to tell his disciples.		they told all this to the eleven and to all the rest. 10 Now it was <u>Mary Magdalene</u>, Joanna, <u>Mary the mother of James</u>, and the other women with them who told this to the apostles. 11 But these words seemed to them an idle tale, and they did not believe them.

Mk 16.2; Lk 24.12	John 20.1-10
Mk 16.2 And very early <u>on the first day of the week</u>, when the sun had risen, <u>they went to the tomb.</u> Luke 24.12 But <u>Peter</u> got up and ran to the tomb; stooping and looking in, <u>he saw the linen wrappings</u> by themselves; then he <u>returned</u> home, amazed at what had happened.	<u>Early on the first day of the week</u>, while it was still dark, <u>Mary Magdalene</u> <u>went to the tomb</u> and saw that <u>the stone</u> had been removed from the tomb. 2 So she ran and went to Simon Peter and the other disciple, the one whom Jesus loved, and said to them, 'They have taken the Lord out of the tomb, and we do not know where they have laid him'.
	3 Then <u>Peter</u> and the other disciple set out and went toward the tomb. 4 The two were running together, but the other disciple outran Peter and reached the tomb first. 5 He bent down to look in and saw the linen wrappings lying there, but he did not go in. 6 Then Simon Peter came, following him, and went into the tomb. <u>He saw the linen wrappings</u> lying there, 7 and the cloth that had been on Jesus' head, not lying with the linen wrappings but rolled up in a place by itself. 8 Then the other disciple, who reached the tomb first, also went in, and he saw and believed; 9 for as yet they did not understand the scripture, that he must rise from the dead. 10 Then the disciples <u>returned</u> to their homes.

Here we have quite a good example of the traditioning processes. A stable core is clear, as also in *Gos. Pet.* 12.50-57: Mary Magdalene and others(?)[11] went to the tomb early on the first day of the week; they found the stone rolled away; according to the Synoptic versions, they saw (an) angel(s),[12] who informed them, 'He is not here; he has been raised';[13] at some point they (in John's Gospel, ini-

11. Does John use the device of 'silent companions' (cf. John with Peter and Silas with Paul in Acts 3–4, 16–18)? This may well be indicated by the 'we' of 20.2.

12. Mark almost certainly intended the 'young man' *(neaniskos)* to be understood as an angel (Mark 16.5). The appearance of an angel is quite typically described as a *neaniskos, neanias* (Tob. 5.5, 7 [LXX S]; 2 Macc. 3.26, 33; Josephus, *Ant.* 5.213, 277; Hermas, *Vis.* 2.4.1; 3.1.6; 3.2.5; 3.4.1; 3.10.1, 7; Lucian, *Philops.* 25). It was equally typical to describe heavenly beings as clothed in white (Dan. 7.9 — God as well; 2 Macc. 11.8; *T. Levi* 8.2; Acts 1.10; Rev. 4.4; 7.9, 13-14; 19.14; cf. *1 En.* 87.2; 90.21; Mark 9.3). The other Evangelists were in no doubt that the tradition referred to angels (Matt. 28.3-5; Luke 24.4, 23; John 20.12). Cf., e.g., Taylor, *Mark* 606-607.

13. Should we include 16.7 in the core? The omission of such a note by both Luke and John is understandable since they go on to tell of appearances in Jerusalem. But even if the

tially Peter and the other disciple) entered the tomb and saw for themselves. Round this relatively stable core the story is retold with marked diversity. Some of that variation is the result, no doubt, of the Evangelists' own interests: Mark has left his auditors in suspense, with the women saying nothing to anyone (Mark 16.8);[14] Matthew worked in (somewhat awkwardly) the story of the guard[15] and assumed it appropriate to include another earthquake (28.2);[16] Luke has changed the promise of an appearance in Galilee (16.7) to the reminiscence of something said in Galilee (Luke 24.6-7);[17] John focuses on Mary of Magdala,

---

verse is to be regarded as a Markan insertion (e.g., Bultmann, *History* 285; C. F. Evans, *Resurrection and the New Testament* [London: SCM, 1970] 78-79; R. H. Fuller, *The Formation of the Resurrection Narratives* [London: SPCK, 1972] 53, 60-61) it clearly draws on very early tradition attested by 1 Cor. 15.5-7 and the appearances in Galilee (§18.3[8] below; Pesch, *Markusevangelium* 2.538-39).

14. The silence of the women is of a piece with the secrecy motif in Mark (1.44; 5.43; 7.36; 8.30) and even to the last reinforces the instruction of 9.9: only after the appearances themselves (signalled in 16.7) can the story properly be told (cf. Räisänen, *Messianic Secret* 207-11). The effect is also to relativize the role of the women and to reinforce the role of the disciples as the primary witnesses of and for the resurrection (Pesch, *Markusevangelium* 2.536; D. R. Catchpole, *Resurrection People: Studies in the Resurrection Narratives of the Gospels* [London: Darton, Longman and Todd, 2000] 20-8); see further below, n. 26. The motif is modified by Luke 24.11 (it is the disciples who respond negatively to the reports of the women; similarly Mark 16.11), but with the similar effect of making Peter the primary witness (24.12, 34). J. D. Hester, 'Dramatic Inconclusion: Irony and the Narrative Rhetoric of the Ending of Mark', *JSNT* 57 (1995) 61-86, argues that Mark's 'rhetorical irony' forces readers to find an interpretation which rescues the story from failure.

15. Matt. 27.62-66; 28.4, 11-15. The story of the guard is generally regarded as an apologetic addition: the silence of the other Evangelists is hard to explain otherwise; the difficulty of integrating their presence with the earlier account of the women coming to the tomb is obvious in the sequence 28.2-5 (what were the guard doing during 28.5-10?); and the reason given for setting the guard (knowledge of Jesus' resurrection prediction and anticipation of the disciples' resurrection proclamation: 27.63-64) speaks more of later apologetic concern — perhaps to counter the alternative explanation (the disciples stole the body) already in circulation and still in play at the time of Matthew (28.15). See, e.g., Davies and Allison, *Matthew* 3.652-53.

16. Again the silence of the other Evangelists probably indicates a Matthean storytelling flourish — as in 27.51-54. It is a way of indicating the eschatological significance of the event (cf. Matt. 24.7 pars.; Zech. 14.4-5). Readers of the time would be familiar with the device (used also in Scripture) of signalling epochal events by referring to such perturbations in heaven or on earth (see, e.g., Brown, *Death* 1113-16, 1121-23).

17. It is hardly possible to evade the conclusion that Luke 24.6 ('Remember how he told you, while he was still *in* Galilee') has modified Mark 16.7 ('he is going ahead of you *to* Galilee'), especially when it is recalled that Luke omitted Mark 14.28 ('But after I have been raised I will go before you into Galilee'), to which 16.7 obviously refers back. The reason is clear too: Luke has chosen to omit any reference to or account of resurrection appearances in Galilee (note particularly Luke 24.49; Acts 1.4); see further vol. 2.

in preparation for the appearance to Mary (John 20.11-18) and makes a point of including the eyewitness testimony of Peter and the other disciple to the emptiness of the tomb (20.3-10);[18] the *Gospel of Peter* enhances an anti-Jewish motif and decorates the retelling with a fuller conversation among the women (*Gos. Pet.* 12.52-54).

As in other examples of the Jesus tradition it makes far too little sense to explain the differences by the hypothesis that Matthew and Luke knew only the version provided by Mark.[19] They could, of course, have adapted Mark's account, but to conceptualize the traditioning process in terms of literary editing hardly explains, for example, the diverse descriptions of the time of day (Mark 16.2 pars.). And overall it makes far greater sense to assume that there were various versions of the story of the empty tomb in circulation, retellings of the core tradition with variation of detail and embellishments of emphasis such as we would expect in an oral traditioning process. Matthew and Luke had access to Mark's version, but in their churches the story of the empty tomb had no doubt been part of their common tradition, probably for as long as their churches had been in existence.[20] We might well ask whether there were ever churches in the circles from which the Evangelists came which did not know and retell with appropriate dramatic intensity the story of the empty tomb?[21] The further alternative, that the story of the empty tomb first emerged as part of the liturgical celebration of the early Jerusalem community at the site of the tomb,[22] is still less

---

18. Is it so clear that 'he believed' in 20.8 denotes the 'transference of the rise of Easter faith from the Christophanies to the empty tomb', as Fuller maintains (*Formation* 136)? The note certainly emphasizes the priority of the beloved disciple's believing, but John at once adds 'for they did not yet know the Scripture that he must rise from the dead' (20.9) and goes on to describe two transitions to Easter faith with Mary (20.15-16) and Thomas (20.25-28), where the motif of seeing (Jesus) is emphasized (20.29).

19. Crossan assumes that all versions of the story of the empty tomb (including John 20) derived from Mark's account (*Birth* 556); similarly Bultmann, *History* 287; L. Geering, *Resurrection — a Symbol of Hope* (London: Hodder, 1971) 51; Funk, *Honest* 221; *Acts of Jesus* 23-24, 465-66. Contrast Koester's conclusion that all three writings (Mark, John, *Gos. Pet.*), 'independently of each other, used an older passion narrative . . .' (*Ancient Christian Gospels* 240).

20. The likelihood is that the pre-Markan Passion narrative included/ended with 16.1-8; see particularly Pesch, *Markusevangelium* 2.519-20; U. Wilckens, *Resurrection* (Edinburgh: St. Andrew, 1977) 29, 39-44; P. Perkins, *Resurrection: New Testament Witness and Contemporary Reflection* (London: Chapman, 1984) 115-24; Becker, *Jesus* 344.

21. H. von Campenhausen, 'The Events of Easter and the Empty Tomb', *Tradition and Life in the Church* (London: Collins, 1968) 42-89, gives particular weight to the reliability of the tradition regarding the burial by Joseph of Arimathea (76; see above, §17.1g).

22. Notably L. Schenke, *Auferstehungsverkündigung und leeres Grab. Eine traditionsgeschichtliche Untersuchung von Mk 16,1-8* (SBS 33; Stuttgart: KBW, ²1969), and Schillebeeckx, *Jesus* 331-37. Pesch observes that the central motif, 'He is not here', tells against an interest in the empty tomb as postulated (by Schenke, *Markusevangelium* 2.537).

credible. Such a liturgical tradition, *ex hypothesi,* would have been stable in form and content; it is hardly likely that an established liturgy would have given rise to such diverse retellings.

From where then did the tradition emerge? What gave it the degree of stability evident within the diverse retellings?[23] As with the other traditions reviewed earlier, the most obvious answer is: Those who were involved in the episode, those who experienced the impact of the event, those who in speaking of what they had thus seen and heard gave the tradition its definitive and lasting shape.[24] In terms of the story as told, that must mean either the women who visited the tomb, or those who also saw the empty tomb, or those to whom the story was first told, or the initial group among whom the story was first celebrated. Of course it would not be told on its own. It was part of the celebration of Jesus' resurrection. But can we indeed conclude that it was part of that celebration from the first? There are various indications which point firmly to a positive answer.[25]

a. The Preeminent Role Attributed to Mary of Magdala and Other Women

This is one of the firmest features of the tradition in all its variation. It is they who first tell of the empty tomb;[26] Mary has the honour of reporting the empty

23. In contrast to their evaluation of the appearance to the eleven, Theissen and Merz in their evaluation of the empty tomb tradition ignore this feature of the tradition (*Historical Jesus* 499-503).

24. Evans, *Resurrection* 75-79 questions whether 'an historical kernel of the empty tomb story' can be established (76); but a kernel/core of *tradition* is not the same thing. In view of Pesch's discussion (*Markusevangelium* 2.537-38) I should also stress the difference in my form of tradition-historical analysis from what he describes as a 'subtraction process' *(Subtraktionsverfahrens),* whereby a 'historical core' is thought to be uncovered by stripping away all legendary embellishments. My concern (like his) is always to explain how the tradition reached its present shape. My hypothesis (in distinction from his) is that the stable elements in a tradition indicate the shape and core (not historical core) which gave the tradition its identity, which maintained the tradition's identity through diverse retellings, and which therefore were probably constitutive of the tradition from the first.

25. Cf. particularly E. L. Bode, *The First Easter Morning: The Gospel Accounts of the Women's Visit to the Tomb of Jesus* (AB 45; Rome: Biblical Institute, 1970) 151-75. W. L. Craig, *Assessing the New Testament Evidence for the Historicity of the Resurrection of Jesus* (Lewiston: Mellen, 1989) marshalls the arguments and presses the case most strongly (352-73). Cf. also the even-handed review in J. M. G. Barclay, 'The Resurrection in Contemporary New Testament Scholarship', in G. D'Costa, ed., *Resurrection Reconsidered* (Oxford: Oneworld, 1996) 13-30 (here 18-23).

26. Matt. 28.8/Luke 24.9; Luke 24.22-23. On the silence of the women (Mark 16.8) see above, n. 14. Of course Mark did not intend to suggest that the story died with the women. One

tomb to the other disciples — *apostola apostolorum*.[27] Yet, as is well known, in
Middle Eastern society of the time women were not regarded as reliable witnesses: a woman's testimony in court was heavily discounted.[28] And any report
that Mary had formerly been demon-possessed (Luke 8.2) would hardly add
credibility to any story attributed to her in particular.[29] Why then attribute such
testimony to women — unless that was what was remembered as being the
case?[30] In contrast, can it be seriously argued that such a story would be contrived in the cities and/or village communities of first-century Palestine, a story
which would have to stand up before public incredulity and prejudice? This consideration alone may be sufficient to explain why the tradition cited by Paul does
not include the testimony of women in its list of witnesses (1 Cor. 15.4-8).[31]

It is a little surprising that Mark and Matthew say nothing about any other
witnesses to an empty tomb, since we have other testimony within the tradition.
John's account of Peter and the other disciple seeing for themselves (John 20.3-
10) is hardly intended to replace Mary's testimony,[32] since John immediately
proceeds to give Mary the honour of the first resurrection appearance as well

---

way or another it got out; Mark knows it! It is part of Mark's genius that he leaves his story
open at the end, open for the congregations who hear it being read to carry it on from what they
know happened thereafter and what they know from personal experience is still happening. As
Pesch (*Markusevangelium* 2.535-36) and Wedderburn (*Beyond Resurrection* 281 n. 320) remind us, the closing note of 'fear' should not necessarily be regarded as a negative feature.

27. Schüssler Fiorenza, *In Memory of Her* 332.

28. Josephus indicates what was probably the typical prejudice of the time: 'From
women let no evidence be accepted, because of the levity and temerity of their sex' (*Ant.*
4.219). Luke shares the same scepticism (Luke 24.11)! Subsequently it was specified in the
Mishnah that the law about 'an oath of testimony' (Lev. 5.1) applied only to men and not to
women (*m. Shebu.* 4.1); the ineligibility of women as witnesses was a benchmark of what was
to be counted as ineligible (*m. Rosh Hash.* 1.8). Even today in Islamic states a woman's testimony is regarded as worth only half the value of a man's. See also M. Hengel, 'Maria
Magdalena und die Frauen als Zeugen', in O. Betz et al., eds., *Abraham unser Vater*, O. Michel
FS (Leiden: Brill, 1963) 243-56.

29. Celsus speaks dismissively of the testimony of 'a half-frantic woman' (Origen,
c. Cels. 2.59).

30. That the story as initially told included seeings of angels neither adds to nor detracts
from the testimony regarding the empty tomb; visions of angels were part of the 'mechanics' of
revelatory experiences (data, e.g., in C. A. Newsom, 'Angels', *ABD* 1.252). Whether that fact
conditioned the *seeing* process as much as the *narrating* process is a moot point.

31. See also Wedderburn, *Beyond Resurrection* 59-61: 'It is far likelier that a prominent
role of women, particularly of Mary of Magdala, was later suppressed, than that such a tradition was a later accretion' (60); Catchpole, *Resurrection People* 199-201.

32. H. Grass argues, however, that John 20.2-10 is a secondary addition to John 20.1,
11-18 (*Ostergeschehen und Osterberichte* [Göttingen: Vandenhoeck und Ruprecht, ²1961] 54-
57).

(20.11-18). The report here may rest on the independent testimony of 'the one whom Jesus loved' (20.2), who seems to have been a source for some at least of John's Gospel.[33] What gives it more weight is the confirmatory testimony in Luke 24: not simply 24.12, cited above,[34] but also the reference back in 24.24: 'Some of those who were with us went to the tomb, and found it just as the women had said; but him they did not see'.[35] If there was, then, further testimony to the emptiness of the tomb, the fact that Mark and Matthew were evidently content with the story of the women alone presumably indicates how much weight was attributed to the women's testimony, and from the first.[36]

b. Archaeological Evidence

Archaeological evidence from Jerusalem in particular provides some interesting circumstantial support. The evidence indicates that during the Herodian period there developed the practice of secondary burial. The initial burial, typically in a rock-hewn chamber, allowed the flesh to decay from the bones. Probably a year after initial burial the bones were collected and put in an ossuary (bone box), which was retained inside the loculi tomb.[37] Of special interest is the fact that this practice seems to have been distinctively or uniquely Jewish.[38] Also that

33. On the significance of 'the beloved disciple' here see Brown, *John* 1004-7, and note particularly 19.35 and 21.24 (Brown 936-37, 1127-29). We will have to return to the question of the beloved disciple's identity in vol. 3. For the present, see particularly Brown xcii-xcviii.

34. In the second block of text at the beginning of §18.2. Given the strength of textual attestation of Luke 24.12, it is surprising that it was omitted by RSV and was given such a modest ranking by UBS[3] (see Metzger, *Textual Commentary* 184, 191-93; Fitzmyer, *Luke* 131, 1547; Lüdemann, *Resurrection* 138-39).

35. Lüdemann's argument, that Luke 24.12 is 'a development of the tomb tradition of Mark 16.1-8, working in the tradition of the first appearance to Peter' (*Resurrection* 139), hardly explains why both 24.12 and 24 exclude any reference to the appearance to Peter. If 24.34 was sufficient to safeguard the priority of the appearance to Peter, then 24.12 was unnecessary.

36. Carnley suggests that the women were the only ones to whom the witness of the empty tomb could be attributed since the disciples had fled to Galilee (*Structure* 59-60). But this ignores the possibilities which Luke and John attest, and equally the possibility that not all the disciples, not even all the eleven, had returned to Galilee (Luke 24.13-32; John 21.2: only seven of the eleven).

37. Theissen and Merz miss this point when they suggest the possibility that the ossuary rather than the tomb would have become the focal point of such a 'cult of relics' (*Historical Jesus* 500). Funk seems unaware of the practice (*Honest* 235).

38. Details, diagrams, and technical bibliography in R. Hachlili, 'Burials' *ABD* 1.789-94 (here 789-91); Reed, *Archaeology* 47-48 (quoted above, chapter 9 n. 177); see also Meyers and Strange, *Archaeology* 94-100. The practice is referred to, e.g., in *m. B. Bat.* 6.8; *m. Mo'ed Qat.* 1.5-6.

such loculi *(kokim)* tombs have been found within yards of the traditional site of Jesus' tomb, confirming that the original site was a quarry which facilitated such burial practice.[39]

Why did Jews of the Herodian period develop this distinctive burial practice? The answer is probably to be found in their beliefs about the prospects for those who had died. It will hardly be accidental, then, that the belief in future resurrection of the dead had been developing in the decades before the Herodian period, particularly in reflection on the Maccabean martyrs.[40] Also that the belief was shaped very much in terms of physical restoration of the body which had perished.[41] The obvious deduction, then, is that the practice of secondary burial was developed with a view to the hoped-for resurrection.[42] Since resurrection would mean restoration of the physical body, the bones should not be allowed to disperse and be lost. Rather they should be kept together, so that God would have them as the framework on which to reconstruct the body. The process had already been signalled in Ezekiel's great vision: bones coming together, bone to bone, to be covered by sinews and flesh, and awaiting the breath *(ruah/pneuma)* of recreated life (Ezek. 37.7-10).[43] The subsequent rabbinic opinion that in the reconstruction of the bodies of the dead all that was needed was one small bone which did not decay (the *luz,* the tip of the coccyx),[44] presupposes the earlier assumption that all the bones would be required and the questioning which arose because many bodies were almost destroyed or buried incomplete.

---

39. Details and photograph in Murphy-O'Connor, *The Holy Land* 54-55.

40. See above, §17.6b.

41. According to 2 Maccabees 7 it is precisely the physical torture and mutilation of the seven brothers which stimulated the hope of physical restoration: 'an eternal revivification of life' (7.9), the confidence of the third brother that he would receive back body parts cut off in torture (7.11), the life and breath *(pneuma)* received at birth would be given back by the Creator (7.22-23), the mother is confident that she will 'get back' her sons (7.29). Similarly, in completing his gory suicide, Razis 'tore out his entrails, took them with both hands and hurled them at the crowd, calling upon the Lord of life and spirit to give them back to him again' (14.46). *2 Bar.* 50.2 gives the assurance that the form of the resurrected will be as when they died; *Sib. Or.* 4.181-82: 'God himself will again fashion the bones and ashes of men and he will raise up mortals again as they were before'.

42. *Pace* S. Fine, 'A Note on Ossuary Burial and the Resurrection of the Dead in First-Century Jerusalem', *JJS* 51 (2000) 69-76. Crossan and Reed also demur on the point, pointing out that the Caiaphas ossuary is that of a Sadducee, who would not have believed in resurrection (*Excavating Jesus* 237-41, 244). Confronted by the irrevocability of death, however, some may qualify previously firmly held beliefs.

43. 'The wonder of the dead bones' in Ezekiel 37 provides hope for the coming age in Sir. 49.10; 4Q385 fragment 2 = 4Q386 fragment 1 = 4Q388 fragment 8; *Liv. Pro.* 3.12; *Sib. Or.* 2.221-24.

44. Moore, *Judaism* 2.385.

c. The Absence of Any Hint of an Undisturbed Tomb

The relevance of the archaeological evidence is obvious. In Jerusalem (and elsewhere in the land of Israel) any claim that a body had been raised would most likely be understood in terms of restoration or reconstitution of the dead body. The corollary would have been that the (old) body had disappeared: physical resurrection necessarily implied empty tomb.[45]

It is notable, then, that there is no hint at any point in the material available to us of questions being posed to early Christian claims regarding the resurrection of Jesus by reference to an undisturbed burial location.[46] The subsequent rabbinic polemic against Christian claims has not taken up the point or suggested, for example, that the disciples had forgotten where Jesus' tomb was. Matthew tells us that in his day the story was still being circulated that the disciples had stolen the body (Matt. 28.15).[47] If that is indeed the case, then the opponents of the Christian interpretation of events apparently did not deny that the tomb was empty. They followed the same logic: empty tomb could imply resurrection, unless there was another explanation for the tomb being empty.[48]

This silence is all the more impressive, since the story of the empty tomb was probably being told in Jerusalem shortly after the event. As we shall see later, the indications are strong that the Jesus movement 'took off' within Jerusalem within a short time after Jesus' death.[49] Whatever the precise details and dates, *the resurrection of Jesus, and not just a re-preaching of Jesus' earlier message,* seems to have been the heart of infant Christianity's distinctive message from the first.[50] Acts indicates that such preaching drew hostile fire from those

45. Against the thesis that Mark created the narrative of the empty tomb (J. D. Crossan, 'Empty Tomb and Absent Lord [Mark 16:1-8]', in Kelber, ed., *Passion in Mark* 135-52; also *Birth* 556-59; A. Yarbro Collins, 'The Empty Tomb and Resurrection According to Mark', *Beginnings of the Gospel* 119-48), it has to be asked whether an empty tomb tradition in support of a belief in *resurrection* would have emerged anywhere outside Palestine.

46. The same would apply if it had been known, or was assumed, that Jesus' body had been casually discarded; but there is no hint of that either (§17.1g). Of the possibility that the place of burial/disposal was unknown (still being recycled by Carnley, *Structure* 55-57, and Wedderburn, *Beyond Resurrection* 65) there is not the slightest hint in early anti-Christian polemic.

47. G. Stanton, 'Early Objections to the Resurrection of Jesus', in S. Barton and G. Stanton, eds., *Resurrection,* L. Houlden FS (London: SPCK, 1994) 79-94, notes that the same explanation was current at the time of Justin's *Dialogue with Trypho* 108 (84-86).

48. 'The rise of the Jewish polemic is of considerable importance, for it shows that "resurrection" to the Jewish mind naturally suggested resurrection *from the grave*' (Fuller, *Formation* 73).

49. See vol. 2.

50. Luke's use of primitive material in the sermons in Acts is notable here; see particularly 2.22-32; 3.13-15, 19-21; 10.36-41 (see also n. 4 above and further below, vol. 2).

responsible for 'handing over' Jesus, the Temple authorities in Jerusalem (Acts 4–5), and there is no reason to doubt it.[51] The point is, obviously, that nothing would have so punctured the claims made by Peter and the others than a counter-testimony as to what had happened to Jesus' body — whether undisturbed after proper burial, decomposed beyond recognition, or otherwise disposed of. The priestly Sadducees, of course, did not believe in resurrection. All the more reason for them to provide an alternative explanation of what had happened to Jesus' body to squash the doctrine itself the more effectively. An empty tomb gave their opponents, Pharisees as well as Christians, too much scope for their belief in resurrection (Acts 23.6-9).

d. The Absence of Any Tomb Veneration

One of the most striking factors to be considered is that we have no record in the early decades of Christianity of any tomb being venerated as the place where Jesus had been laid to rest. Despite theories to the contrary,[52] Luke, who shared the very physical understanding of Jesus' resurrection body (Luke 24.39), never gives the slightest hint of worship or prayer on the site of Jesus' burial in his account of Christianity's beginnings in Jerusalem (Acts 2–5). Nor does Paul ever as much as hint that one of the reasons he visited Jerusalem was to join in veneration on the site of Jesus' final resting place. This is indeed striking, because within contemporary Judaism, as in other religions, the desire to honour the memory of the revered dead by constructing appropriate tombs and (by implication) by veneration of the site is well attested.[53] To this day in Israel such sites of famous prophets and rabbis of old can be pointed to; and even if particular traditions are much later in origin,[54] the traditions themselves attest a characteristic instinct and ethos whose roots no doubt penetrate into the dim past well before the time of Jesus. Both Matthew and Luke recall Jesus as referring to this instinct to honour the tombs of prophets (and the righteous, adds Matthew) (Matt. 23.29/

---

51. Paul's role as 'the persecutor' ('he who persecutes us') (Gal. 1.23; also 13) obviously predated his conversion (possibly even within eighteen months of Jesus' crucifixion) by some months at least, which confirms the fact of 'persecution' within months (one or two years) of Jesus' death. See again vol. 2.

52. See again Schenke (n. 22 above).

53. 1 Macc. 13.27-30; Josephus, *War* 4.531-32; 5.506; *Ant.* 7.392; 13.249 (the tomb left undisturbed for centuries); 16.179-83 (note the comments); 18.108; 20.95; Acts 2.29; 'those who are God's faithful pray at the place [the tomb of Jeremiah] to this very day' (*Liv. Pro.* 2.4); see further J. Jeremias, *Heiligengräber in Jesu Umwelt* (Göttingen: Vandenhoeck, 1958).

54. See, e.g., Murphy-O'Connor, *The Holy Land* 116-18, 124, 126-27, 137-39, 370, 397, 456.

Luke 11.47), and there is no reason to doubt what we may describe as a valid sociological observation.

Why would the first Christians not act out this pious instinct and tradition? The only obvious answer, in the light of the evidence thus far reviewed, is that they did not believe any tomb contained his body. They could not venerate his remains because they did not think there were any remains to be venerated.[55] The same point has to be made against the oldest alternative explanation for the empty tomb: that the disciples had stolen the body (Matt. 28.13-15).[56] For if the disciples had indeed removed the body, it is inconceivable that they would not have laid it reverently to rest in some other fitting location. In which case, it is almost as inconceivable that a surreptitious practice of veneration would not have been maintained by those in the know and that some hint of it would not have reached a wider circle of disciples. The consideration would remain relevant however many or however few were involved in the deception. The story enshrined in the tradition of the Gospels remains the stronger alternative: the first Christians knew where Jesus' body had been laid (the memory may have lasted through to the time of Constantine),[57] but they paid it little attention, because so far as they were concerned, his grave was empty. He had not remained in the tomb.

55. I first put forward this argument in *Jesus and the Spirit* 120. In critique, Wedderburn (*Beyond Resurrection* 63-65) thinks a likelier explanation is that they had difficulty in identifying the body in a common grave (though he recognizes that the practice of collecting the bones and putting them in an ossuary presupposes some way of identifying remains in such cases — citing Brown, *Death* 1210) or that they would hardly wish to venerate a site where several bodies had been casually disposed of — Crossan's 'limed pit' (chapter 17 n. 94 above); similarly, B. R. McCane, '"Where No One Had Yet Been Laid": The Shame of Jesus' Burial', in Chilton and Evans, eds., *Authenticating the Activities of Jesus* 431-52. But does that follow? Christians soon venerated a cross, of all things! A tradition with such a firm core (that the tomb was empty) is more likely to embody originating memory. Wedderburn also cites Carnley's dismissal of the argument in view of 'the pious interest in the alleged site of the Holy Sepulchre in our own day' (*Structure* 58; cf. Barclay, 'Resurrection' 23); but Carnley ignores the manifest heightening of such 'pious interest' in the period following the Constantinian establishment. The fact remains that evidence for such interest in a tomb (whether empty or undisturbed) in the earliest decades of Christianity is wholly lacking. If anything, the puzzling end of Mark 16.1-8 attests the early problematic character of the earliest accounts of the tomb being empty, whereas confidence in a martyr's exaltation readily went hand-in-hand with veneration of his tomb (Stuhlmacher, *Biblische Theologie* 1.177-78). Lüdemann argues in somewhat contradictory directions, both that Joseph of Arimathea attended to the burial of Jesus and that it was known to be an ignominious burial, but also that the early Christians would have venerated it had Jesus' tomb been known (*Resurrection* 45).

56. This was also the solution of Reimarus, *Fragments* 161-64, 212, and, somewhat surprisingly, Jeremias, *Proclamation* 304-305.

57. See above, chapter 17 n. 105.

e. What of Paul's Testimony?

An important cross-current in all this is indicated by the question whether Paul knew of the empty tomb tradition. For it is noteworthy that the clearest account of resurrection tradition outside the Gospels (1 Cor. 15.3-8) testifies only to resurrection appearances and does not include any account of an empty tomb. Still more noteworthy is the fact that Paul offers a different conceptualization of the resurrection body (including that of Jesus — 15.13-16, 20-23) from the physical restoration conceptualization thus far assumed. The resurrection body is a different body from that put into the ground at death (15.37-38), a 'spiritual body' in contrast to the 'soulish body' of earthly existence (15.44-50).[58] Does that mean, then, that Paul denied the physical restoration understanding of Jesus' resurrection and thus that he knew nothing of, could dispense with, or even refute any tradition of the empty tomb?

An affirmative answer is unlikely. The tradition which Paul received at his conversion spoke not only of Jesus' death but also of his burial: 'what I received [as already established tradition was] that Christ died for our sins in accordance with the Scriptures, and that he was buried, and that he appeared . . .' (15.3-4). Why the second clause ('that he was buried')? Why not the immediate transition from death to resurrection, as in other accounts?[59] The most obvious answer is that the disposal of the body in burial was an important point in the earliest confessional statements.[60] Which probably reflects the place of the tomb narratives — burial but also empty tomb — in the earliest traditions of Easter.[61] At this point the argument can probably go into reverse. For the interesting fact emerges that Paul retains reference to what happened to Jesus' body, even though in his conceptualization the resurrection body was (may) not (have been) so tightly cor-

---

58. See further below, §18.5b and vol. 2.

59. E.g., Acts 3.15; 10.39-40.

60. See above, chapter 17 n. 96. Even if the point of 1 Cor. 15.4 is to confirm the reality of death (Wedderburn, *Beyond Resurrection* 87), the confirmation was precisely by burying the body (in a tomb). While Paul himself may have been uninterested in the emptiness (or otherwise) of Jesus' tomb (Grass, *Ostergeschehen* 173; Lüdemann, *Resurrection* 46), it does not at all follow that the tradition he received was similarly uninterested (K. Lehmann, *Auferweckt am dritten Tag nach der Schrift* [QD 38; Freiburg: Herder, 1968] 78-86). On the other hand, Craig's confidence outstrips the evidence: 'Paul certainly believed that the grave was empty' (*Assessing* 113).

61. Fitzmyer draws attention to the similar formulation in Acts 13.28-31 — crucified, laid in a tomb, raised and appeared (*Luke* 1534); as in Acts 2.29, 'buried' probably implies 'grave/tomb'. As again Luke's two accounts suggest (Luke 23.52–24.7 and Acts 13.28-31), a reference to burial probably implied a now vacant burial location. The suggestion that the *affirmation* of the empty tomb preceded any *narrative* account of its discovery fails to appreciate that such affirmation would almost certainly have taken narrative form from the first.

related with the dead body as we have supposed for the Jerusalem conceptualization of resurrection.[62]

The likely explanation for the divergent conceptualizations is that Paul was operating in a much more characteristically Hellenistic milieu, which took for granted a greater discontinuity between flesh and spirit than the Jewish conception of the body. I will follow that point through later.[63] For the moment, its relevance is twofold. First, Paul's understanding appears to be a second-stage conceptualization, occasioned by the spread of the Christian gospel into the wider Hellenistic world beyond Palestine. Which also implies that it was in some degree a reaction to or moving on from an older conceptualization (still summarily recalled in the burial clause of the confession received by Paul). Which in turn brings us back to the empty tomb tradition.[64] Second, to some extent the two streams of tradition (empty tomb, resurrection appearances) were independent from each other:[65] Paul could virtually ignore the former; and the earliest accounts of the empty tomb make no mention of any appearance at the tomb itself. This restraint makes it hard to argue that one stream of tradition gave rise to the other.[66] On the contrary, though interdependent in terms of the earliest conceptualization of Jesus' resurrection, the traditions themselves seem to have emerged from and to have kept alive independent memories.

Here then we find a tradition (Mark 16.1-8 pars.) which, like most of the

62. But the argument of M. Goulder, 'Did Jesus of Nazareth Rise from the Dead?' in Barton and Stanton, eds., *Resurrection* 58-68, that Mark's empty tomb story was created to supply 'the exact need of a Pauline church that believed in a physical resurrection' (64-65) is odd: where is the evidence that a *Pauline* church believed in a *physical* resurrection?

63. See below, §18.5b.

64. It should be noted that I am reversing the common argument that the earliest traditions were only of appearances and that the empty tomb tradition is a later, legendary embellishment to provide proof for an already existing belief in Jesus' resurrection and indicative of a growing materialistic conception of the resurrection (particularly Grass, *Ostergeschehen* 88-90, 173-86). Paul's treatment of the subject cannot serve as an example of earlier conceptualization of Jesus' 'resurrection' within Palestine. See further below, §18.5b.

65. Cf. the main thrust of von Campenhausen's argument: the two 'essential and reliable pieces of data' which emerge from his analysis are 'a series of indubitable appearances of Christ, which must be placed in Galilee, and the discovery of the empty tomb in Jerusalem' ('Events of Easter' 77). Similarly U. Wilckens, 'The Tradition-History of the Resurrection of Jesus', in C. F. D. Moule, ed., *The Significance of the Message of the Resurrection for Faith in Jesus Christ* (London: SCM, 1968) 51-76 (here 71-72); J. E. Alsup, *The Post-Resurrection Appearance Stories of the Gospel-Tradition* (Stuttgart: Calwer, 1975) 85-116. The same observation is the beginning point for Pannenberg's discussion of 'Jesus' Resurrection as a Historical Problem' (*Jesus* 88-89). See also I. U. Dalferth, 'Volles Grab, leerer Glaube? Zum Streit um die Auferweckung des Gekreuzigten', *ZTK* 95 (1998) 379-409.

66. Cf. Lüdemann, *Resurrection* 171-72; but contrast also his earlier conclusion that 'The story [Mark 16.1-8] is first inferred from the "dogma"' (121), referring to 1 Cor. 15.3-5.

others examined earlier, seems to have begun as the expression of eyewitness testimony, quickly prized because of its potential import and soon told and told again in the circles of first disciples as a basic component of their conviction that God had raised Jesus from the grave.

18.3. Appearance Traditions

The second sequence of traditions is much more extensive, but also much more diverse. Indeed, there is nothing quite like them in the Jesus tradition and an effective synoptic analysis is almost impossible. In the following table I set out the data in as close to a putative chronological order as the data permit, without putting any weight on the chronological relationships at this stage.

To whom	Where	When	Matthew	Mark	Luke	John	1 Cor.
1. Mary	At tomb	Sun. a.m.		(16.9)		20.11-18	
2. Women	Near tomb	Sun a.m.	28.8-10				
3. Peter	?	Sunday			24.34		15.5
4. Cleopas	Emmaus	Sun p.m.		(16.12-13)	24.13-35		
5. Eleven	upper room	Sun. eve.			24.36-49	20.19-23	15.5
6. Eleven	upper room	+ 7 days				20.26-29	
7. 120?	Jerusalem	40 days			Ac. 1.3-11		
8. Eleven	Galilee	?	28.16-20	16.7		21.1-23	
9. 500+	?	?					15.6
10. James	?	?					15.7
11. Apostles	?	?					15.7
12. Paul	Damascus	+ 2 years?			Ac. 9 etc.		15.8

(1) and (2) *The appearance(s) to the women* — Matt. 28.8-10; John 20.11-18.

Matt. 28.8-10	John 20.11-18
8 So they (the women) left the tomb quickly with fear and great joy, and ran to tell his disciples. 9 And look, Jesus met them and said, 'Greetings!' And they came to him, took hold of his feet, and worshiped him. 10	11 But Mary stood weeping outside the tomb. As she wept, she bent over to look into the tomb; 12 and she saw two angels in white, sitting where the body of Jesus had been lying, one at the head and the other at the feet. 13 They said to her, 'Woman, why are you weeping?' She said to them, 'They have taken away my Lord, and I do not know where they have laid him'. 14 When she had said this, she turned around and saw Jesus standing there, but she did not know that it was Jesus. 15 Jesus said to her, 'Woman, why are you weeping? Whom are you looking for?' Supposing him to be the gardener, she said to him, 'Sir, if you have carried him away, tell me where you have laid him, and I will take him away'. 16 Jesus said to her, 'Mary!'

Then Jesus said to them, 'Do not be afraid; go and tell my brothers to go to Galilee; there they will see me'.	She turned and said to him in Hebrew, 'Rabbouni!' (which means Teacher). 17 Jesus said to her, 'Do not hold on to me, because I have not yet ascended to the Father. But go to my brothers and say to them, "I am ascending to my Father and your Father, to my God and your God"'. 18 Mary Magdalene went and announced to the disciples, 'I have seen the Lord'; and she told them that he had said these things to her.

Are these variant versions of the same tradition? On the face of it the obvious answer is No. They are different as to participants, locale, and content; they lack a common core. Not only so, but there is the glaring contrast between the vague and rather unsatisfying account of Matthew, and the first of a sequence of aesthetically (both artistically and emotionally) appealing encounters now concluding John's Gospel (Mary, Thomas, Peter).[67] Moreover, John's account has the characteristically Johannine motifs of Jesus speaking of his Father and of his ascension,[68] the latter intriguingly located, it would appear, between his first and subsequent appearances.[69] On the other hand, there are several points of connection: the first appearance, Mary of Magdala's involvement, close relation to the empty tomb, the motif of grasping (*kratein* — Matthew) or touching (*haptesthai* — John) Jesus, and the command to tell the other disciples ('my brothers').[70] The variations in fact are no greater than in other cases where John seems to have been able to draw on a version similar to what we find in the Synoptics.[71] Is this then simply a case of a tradition of the same event (or claim) which has become quite diverse in the retellings?

Whatever the tradition history behind the two accounts, the key question for

67. It is easy to understand why the Johannine account has stimulated far more artists than the Matthean.

68. Note particularly John 1.51 and 3.13 and cf. John's use of the motifs of Jesus being 'lifted up' (3.14; 8.28; 12.32, 34) and glorified (7.39; 12.16, 23; 13.31; 17.1, 5).

69. See particularly discussion in Brown, *John* 992-93, 1011-17.

70. Davies and Allison, *Matthew* 3.668-69. *Pace* those who maintain that Matt. 28.9-10 was constructed out of Mark 16.1-8; so, e.g., Grass, *Ostergeschehen* 111 ('a mere doublet of the angelophany'); Fuller, *Formation* 78 (again 137), who concludes that the earlier tradition of an angelophany has been converted into a christophany (but Matthew *retained* the angelophany!); Alsup, *Post-Resurrection Appearance Stories* 111-14.

71. Notably John 4.46-54 par.; Matt. 8.5-13/Luke 7.1-10 (above, §8.4b); John 6.1-14 par.; Mark 6.32-44 pars. (above, §15.7f). As in these cases, it is less likely that John derived his account from the Synoptic parallel as such (*pace* Crossan, *Birth* 560-61); Crossan's test of 'redactional peculiarities of one writer discovered in another' (565), in this case that John knows Matthew's redactional 'my brothers' (561), depends on the view that Matt. 28.9-10 has been derived redactionally from Mark 16.1-8 (560), which is implausible because it assumes that all diversities in gospel tradition are to be explained in terms of literary dependence. Contrast Koester: 'Each of the authors of the extant gospels and of their secondary endings drew these epiphany stories from their own particular tradition, not from a common source' (*Ancient Christian Gospels* 220).

us is the one previously posed in relation to the empty tomb traditions: Why did these Evangelists accord the role of first witnesses to women? As already observed, it was hardly a tactic designed to inspire confidence in future hearers of the claim that God has raised Jesus (§18.2a). Why did Matthew bother to include the account at all, since its primary purpose seems to have been to reinforce the message already given by the angels that the disciples would see the risen Jesus in Galilee? 28.9-10 could easily have been omitted by Matthew without loss, leaving the transition to the Galilee appearance (28.16-20) more straightforward.[72] The only obvious answer is that there was a persistent report within the communal memory of the earliest churches that the first witnesses had been women, a report which Matthew could not ignore, however less than satisfying his telling of it.

Likewise, why did John give such prominence to Mary of Magdala at this late stage in his narrative? Unlike the other characters who feature prominently in John's appearance stories,[73] she was not one of the array of characters to whom John gives speaking parts earlier in his narrative. John makes no attempt to identify her as the woman taken in adultery (8.2-11 — if that was part of John's original narrative) or as the Mary who anointed Jesus' feet (12.1-8).[74] Mary of Magdala first appears as witness of the crucifixion (19.25) before taking solo centre stage in the drama of 20.1-18. Here again the most obvious explanation for this is that John (the Johaninne tradition) was in touch with an early memory (beloved disciple?) that Mary of Magdala had indeed been the first to see Jesus.[75]

(3) *The appearance to Peter* — Luke 24.34; 1 Cor. 15.5.

Luke 24.34	1 Cor. 15.5
The Lord has risen indeed and has appeared (*ōphthē*) to Simon.	and that he appeared (*ōphthē*) to Cephas,

72. It is unclear in what way 28.9-10 provides 'a better transition between the story about the tomb and the concluding christophany' (Lüdemann, *Resurrection* 131).

73. Thomas in 11.16; 14.5; Simon Peter in, e.g., 1.42; 6.68; 13.6-11, 36-38; 18.15-18, 25-27.

74. The popular tradition of later centuries that Mary had been a prostitute is based (without justification) on identifying her as the woman in John 8.2-11 and/or the 'sinner' in the Lukan anointing story (Luke 7.36-38) parallel to John 12.1-8 (there is a striking overlap at Luke 7.38/John 12.3); see, e.g., R. F. Collins, 'Mary', *ABD* 4.580, 581-82.

75. Theissen and Merz, *Historical Jesus* 496-99; Funk, *Acts of Jesus* 478-79 ('Mary was among the early witnesses to the resurrection of Jesus'). Lüdemann's discussion is rather confused (*Resurrection* 157-60). Byrskog justifiably asks concerning the women's witness, Mary's in particular, 'How else but through their influence in the early community would the account of their presence have endured the androcentric force of transmission and redaction?' (*Story as History* 78-82 [here 81]). 'The tradition was too resilient to be effaced' (J. Lieu, 'The Women's Resurrection Testimony', in Barton and Stanton, eds., *Resurrection* 34-44 [here 42]). See further C. Setzer, 'Excellent Women: Female Witness to the Resurrection', *JBL* 116 (1997) 259-72.

There is a formulaic ring to both assertions: this is the language of church confession more than of personal testimony. Its effect here is to give the appearance to Peter[76] first place in importance. In Paul's list of witnesses, Peter is first (1 Cor. 15.5). In Luke's account, the drama of the appearance to Cleopas and his companion is allowed to unfold completely (Luke 24.13-32), but on their return to Jerusalem the confession of the eleven is given pride of place (24.34) before Cleopas and his companion tell their story (24.35). Since neither Luke nor Paul mentions appearance(s) to women disciples, we can hardly avoid asking whether they knew but chose to ignore or even to suppress such reports. That must certainly be judged very possible. The alternative that they did not know such reports is less likely, given the traditions which impressed both Matthew and John. Once again the motivation would be understandable, given the low esteem for women as reliable witnesses.

At the same time it is worth also noting that Luke has not forced the priority of the appearance to Peter to the front of the queue by, for example, placing it at the tomb (to replace the report on which John 20.11-18 was based?). On the contrary, he makes explicitly clear that the male disciples who went to the tomb did not see Jesus there (24.24). The priority of the appearance to Peter is not signalled with drums and trumpets. There is a reticence at this point which could possibly reflect Peter's own reticence on the subject.[77]

Should we include John 21.15-24 at this point?

> [15]When they had finished breakfast, Jesus said to Simon Peter, 'Simon son of John, do you love me more than these?' He said to him, 'Yes, Lord; you know that I love you'. Jesus said to him, 'Feed my lambs'. [16]A second time he said to him, 'Simon son of John, do you love me?' He said to him, 'Yes, Lord; you know that I love you'. Jesus said to him, 'Tend my sheep'. [17]He

---

76. In Paul's letters Peter is usually referred to as Cephas (*Kēphas,* 1 Cor. 1.12; 3.22; 9.5; 15.5; Gal. 1.18; 2.9, 11, 14), that is, the name which according to tradition was given to Peter by Jesus (John 1.42; Matt. 16.18); see further J. A. Fitzmyer, 'Aramaic *Kepha*' and Peter's Name in the New Testament', *To Advance the Gospel: New Testament Studies* (Grand Rapids: Eerdmans, 1981, [2]1998) 112-24.

77. This observation undermines the argument of W. Marxsen, *The Resurrection of Jesus of Nazareth* (London: SCM, 1970) 89-96, that the resurrection faith of all the other disciples derived from Peter's ('Only the appearance to Peter was constitutive', 93); to make his case for the priority of Peter's faith he has to argue that John 20.8 certainly implies that Peter also believed and that the beloved disciple was 'second to believe' (58-59)! Similarly Lüdemann: 'all the other Easter experiences rest on the earliest Christian creed' — 'that Jesus has arisen and appeared to Simon'; 'The first vision to Peter proved formally "infectious"' (*Resurrection* 143, 174). The earlier confidence on the subject is well illustrated by Weiss's quotation from Weizsäcker: 'The fact that Peter was the first to see the risen Lord is the most certain historical fact in this whole obscure history' (*Earliest Christianity* 24).

said to him the third time, 'Simon son of John, do you love me?' Peter felt hurt because he said to him the third time, 'Do you love me?' And he said to him, 'Lord, you know everything; you know that I love you'. Jesus said to him, 'Feed my sheep. 18Truly truly, I tell you, when you were younger, you used to fasten your own belt and to go wherever you wished. But when you grow old, you will stretch out your hands, and someone else will fasten a belt around you and take you where you do not wish to go'. 19(He said this to indicate the kind of death by which he would glorify God.) After this he said to him, 'Follow me'. 20Peter turned and saw the disciple whom Jesus loved following them; he was the one who had reclined next to Jesus at the supper and had said, 'Lord, who is it that is going to betray you?' 21When Peter saw him, he said to Jesus, 'Lord, what about him?' 22Jesus said to him, 'If it is my will that he remain until I come, what is that to you? Follow me!' 23So the rumour spread in the community that this disciple would not die. Yet Jesus did not say to him that he would not die, but, 'If it is my will that he remain until I come, what is that to you?' 24This is the disciple who is testifying to these things and has written them, and we know that his testimony is true.

Although set in context of an appearance to seven disciples (21.1-14), the Johannine account[78] has a very personal, even intimate character. The thrice repeated 'Do you love me?' is obviously framed to echo Peter's threefold denial of Jesus (18.17-18, 25-27). The note about the beloved disciple (21.20) relates back into the earlier account of the last supper (13.23-25). And the perspective is clearly that of the later story-teller (21.19a, 23). But apart from the 'Amen, amen' of 21.18 the language of the principal exchange (21.15-19) is not particularly Johannine.[79] And once again we are confronted with a testimony linked to the beloved disciple, who is then identified as the source of the tradition, including a saying of the risen Christ which had occasioned a rumour which the final redactors[80] thought it necessary to quash (21.23-24).

What are we to make of this? Is this the missing appearance to Peter? The fact that it is located in Galilee cuts across the clear assertion of Luke that the appearance took place in Jerusalem on the first Sunday (Luke 24.34). On the other hand, we have already noted Luke's seeming determination to restrict the post-resurrection appearances to Jerusalem.[81] And the parallels between John 21.1-8

78. Or more precisely, the final redactor's account. John 21 is generally regarded as an addition to a Gospel which concluded with 20.30-31 (see, e.g., Brown, *John* xxxii-xxxix, 1077-82).

79. The point would be disputed, not least in relation to the issue whether the author of John 21 is the same as the Evangelist (details in Brown, *John* 1080).

80. Or, should we say, 'final final redactors' (see again Brown, *John* 1124-25)?

81. Luke 24.49; Acts 1.4.

and Luke's unique account of Peter's call (Luke 5.1-11) suggest to some that Luke did know of a post-Easter appearance to Peter at the lake in Galilee.[82] More to the point, the report of Mark 16.7 ('He is going ahead of you to Galilee; there you will see him') seems to preclude appearances in Jerusalem! Could it be, then, as many conclude, that the communal memory was of initial appearances *in Galilee,* and that the whole tradition of initial appearances in (and around Jerusalem) was developed for public consumption by the Jerusalem church? The plot thickens; or is it simply that there is confusion on this point now impossible to resolve?

The key question for us is whether we can take the claim of the Johannine tradition seriously, that is, in effect, that the beloved disciple preserved an otherwise untapped source of testimony from the dawn of the new movement. If so, then one possible pointer towards a solution to the problem of such divergent versions is that throughout Peter's life the appearance to Peter was retained as personal testimony and never allowed to become church tradition as such. In which case, it was only after Peter's death that the testimony could be retold, and only then from a Johannine (beloved disciple) perspective, a perspective, it would appear, for which the issue of both Petrine and Jerusalem priority was not an important factor.[83]

(4) *The appearance on the road to Emmaus* — Luke 24.13-35.

[13]Now on that same day two of them were going to a village called Emmaus, about seven miles from Jerusalem, [14]and talking with each other about all these things that had happened. [15]While they were talking and discussing, Jesus himself came near and went with them, [16]but their eyes were kept from recognizing him. [17]And he said to them, 'What are you discussing with each other while you walk along?' They stood still, looking sad. [18]Then one of them, whose name was Cleopas, answered him, 'Are you the only stranger in Jerusalem who does not know the things that have taken place there in these days?' [19]He asked them, 'What things?' They replied, 'The things about Jesus of Nazareth, who was a prophet mighty in deed and word before God and

82. John 21 takes for granted that (some of) the disciples were fishermen, a fact not previously mentioned in the Gospel; see also, e.g., Grass, *Ostergeschehen* 79-81; Lüdemann, *Resurrection* 86-87; Funk, *Acts of Jesus* 278-80. The points of parallel are similar in scope to those which relate Q 7.1-10/John 4.46-54 and Matt. 28.9-10/John 20.11-18 to each other; see discussion in Brown, *John* 1089-92. Crossan suggests that all the 'nature' miracles of Jesus have Jesus' 'resurrectional victory over death' as their background (*Historical Jesus* 396-410). Barker turns such logic on its head by arguing that the original 'raising' of Jesus was at his baptism (*The Risen Lord* 26).

83. By appending the encounter with Peter to the explicitly numbered 'third' appearance (21.14) the redactor in effect ignored (or surrendered) any claim that this was the first appearance.

all the people, 20and how our chief priests and leaders handed him over to be condemned to death and crucified him. 21But we had hoped that he was the one to redeem Israel. Yes, and besides all this, it is now the third day since these things took place. 22Moreover, some women of our group astounded us. They were at the tomb early this morning, 23and when they did not find his body there, they came back and told us that they had indeed seen a vision of angels who said that he was alive. 24Some of those who were with us went to the tomb and found it just as the women had said; but they did not see him'. 25Then he said to them, 'Oh, how foolish you are, and how slow of heart to believe all that the prophets have declared! 26Was it not necessary that the Messiah should suffer these things and then enter into his glory?' 27Then beginning with Moses and all the prophets, he interpreted to them the things about himself in all the Scriptures. 28As they came near the village to which they were going, he walked ahead as if he were going on. 29But they urged him strongly, saying, 'Stay with us, because it is almost evening and the day is now nearly over'. So he went in to stay with them. 30When he was at the table with them, he took bread, blessed and broke it, and gave it to them. 31Then their eyes were opened, and they recognized him; and he vanished from their sight. 32They said to each other, 'Were not our hearts burning within us while he was talking to us on the road, while he was opening the Scriptures to us?' 33That same hour they got up and returned to Jerusalem; and they found the eleven and their companions gathered together. 34They were saying, 'The Lord has risen indeed, and he has appeared to Simon!' 35Then they told what had happened on the road, and how he had been made known to them in the breaking of the bread.

Here is another unsupported account. It is clearly a Lukan version: the marks of Luke's style[84] and his skill as a story-teller are evident.[85] In particular, the theme of Jesus as prophet is characteristic of Luke (24.19),[86] as is the attribution of Jesus' crucifixion directly to the Jewish leadership (24.20).[87] The motif of

---

84. The stylistic features are listed by Fitzmyer, *Luke* 1555-56.

85. See further Fitzmyer, *Luke* 1557-60; Catchpole, *Resurrection People* ch. 3, who draws particular attention to the parallel with the story of Tobit and the angel Raphael (94-98). Luke 24 is such a wonderful story that it positively invites an approach like that of J. I. H. McDonald, *The Resurrection: Narrative and Belief* (London: SPCK, 1989) here 103-109 (criticism by Wedderburn, *Beyond Resurrection* 33). But it is still a necessary and valid exercise to inquire into the tradition which Luke has retold so superbly.

86. Note particularly Luke 4.24; 7.16, 39; 9.8, 19; 13.33-34; Acts 3.22-23; 7.37; see further R. J. Dillon, *From Eye-Witnesses to Ministers of the Word: Tradition and Composition in Luke 24* (Rome: Biblical Institute, 1978) 114-27; D. P. Moessner, *Lord of the Banquet* (Minneapolis: Fortress, 1989).

87. Acts 2.23, 36; 3.14-15, 17; 4.10; 5.30; 10.39; 13.28.

Scripture proving the necessity that the Messiah should suffer is also an important theme for Luke-Acts (24.26).[88] And above all, the way the appearance climaxes in the revelation at the breaking of the bread (24.30-31, 35) provides Luke the link he evidently wanted between the table-fellowship characteristic of Jesus' mission and the breaking of bread characteristic of the earliest church (Acts 2.42, 46).[89]

At the same time, the signs of older tradition retold by Luke are also clear: the identification of one of the participants (Cleopas)[90] and of their destination (Emmaus),[91] the sort of expectations which Jesus' mission must have engendered for many of his followers (24.19, 21),[92] and the note that some of the male disciples also saw the empty tomb, despite the silence on the point in the rest of the Synoptic tradition (24.24).[93] In addition, the account of Jesus' exposition of Scripture (24.27) probably reflects an early sense within the first post-Easter disciple groups that only in the light of the resurrection were they enabled to see prophecies in Scripture to which they had hitherto been blind.[94] Likewise the episode may reflect that it was precisely in the breaking of bread that the first disciples became aware of Jesus' continuing presence, not simply as a recollection of Jesus' earlier table-fellowship, but in celebration of Jesus' presence with them in a new way.[95] It is a feature of the resurrection appearances which not only Luke emphasizes,[96] but also John (John 21.12-13).

Is it an answer, then, that Luke came across the Emmaus story in his search

88. Luke 24.26-27, 45-46; Acts 26.23.

89. See above, §14.8a.

90. Had the name been added later (a tendency in story-telling) it is likely that both disciples would have been named. Was the other his wife? Cf. John 19.25 — the wife of Clopas (not Cleopas) (cf. BDAG, *Kleopas;* Fitzmyer, *Luke* 1563). According to Hegesippus, there was a Clopas who was the brother of Joseph, so uncle of Jesus (Eusebius, *HE* III.11). Lüdemann, *Jesus* 412, is confused here: it was Symeon, Clopas's son, who was therefore 'cousin *(anepsios)*' of Jesus (*HE* IV.22.4). See further A. M. Schwemer, 'Der Auferstandene und die Emmausjünger', in Avemarie and Lichtenberger, *Auferstehung* 95-117 (here 105-106).

91. For the confusion regarding the location of Emmaus see J. F. Strange, 'Emmaus', *ABD* 2.497-98; Schwemer, 'Auferstandene' 100-101.

92. See above §15.3e-h.

93. Fitzmyer also thinks that Mark 16.12-13 is a snippet of pre-Lukan tradition, which Luke built up into his dramatic story, rather than a late summary of the Lukan account (*Luke* 1554-55).

94. From as early as we can trace, Scriptures like Psalms 16 and 110 and Isaiah 53 were seen to have prophesied Jesus' suffering and resurrection. Would any of the first Christians have disagreed with Luke's attribution of that interpretation to the risen Christ? Schwemer notes the link both to the Isa. 6.9-10 motif (see above, §13.1) and to the experience referred to in 2 Cor. 3.13-16 ('Auferstandene' 113-15).

95. Paul presupposes as a generally recognized given that the Lord's Supper was celebrated under Christ as host (1 Cor. 10.21; see my *Theology of Paul* 620-21).

96. Luke 24.41-43; Acts 1.4; 10.41. On Acts 1.4 see further below (7).

for eyewitness testimony (Luke 1.2)?[97] Why otherwise would he attribute the first fully narrated appearance of the risen Jesus to two otherwise unknown and relatively obscure disciples, only one of whom is named (Cleopas)? The story cuts across the priority otherwise given to the appearances to Peter (despite 24.34) and to the twelve. So probably Luke took up the basic tradition simply because it was there, however awkwardly it fitted in with the overall schema.

(5) *Appearances to the eleven in Jerusalem* — Luke 24.36-49; John 20.19-23; 1 Cor. 15.5.

Luke 24.36-49	John 20.19-23
36 While they were talking about this, (Jesus) himself <u>stood among them and said</u> to them, '<u>Peace be with you</u>'. 37 They were startled and terrified, and thought that they were seeing a spirit. 38 He said to them, 'Why are you frightened, and why do doubts arise in your hearts? 39 Look at my hands and my feet, that it is I myself. Touch me and see; for a spirit does not have flesh and bones as you see that I have'. 40 <u>And having said this, he showed them his hands and his</u> feet. 41 While in their <u>joy</u> they were disbelieving and still wondering, he said to them, 'Have you anything here to eat?' 42 They gave him a piece of broiled fish, 43 and he took it and ate in their presence. 44 Then he said to them, 'These are my words that I spoke to you while I was still with you — that everything written about me in the law of Moses, the prophets, and the psalms must be fulfilled'. 45 Then he opened their minds to understand the scriptures, 46 and he said to them, 'Thus it is written, that the Messiah is to suffer and to rise from the dead on the third day, 47 and that repentance and forgiveness of sins is to be proclaimed in his name to all nations, beginning from Jerusalem. 48 You are witnesses of these things. 49 And see, I am sending upon you what my Father promised; so stay here in the city until you have been clothed with power from on high'.	19 When it was evening on that day, the first day of the week, and the doors of the house where the disciples had met were locked for fear of the Jews, <u>Jesus</u> came and <u>stood among them</u> and said, '<u>Peace be with you</u>'. 20 <u>And having said this, he showed them his hands and his</u> side. Then the disciples <u>rejoiced</u> when they saw the Lord. 21 Jesus said to them again, 'Peace be with you. As the Father has sent me, so I send you'. 22 When he had said this, he breathed on them and said to them, 'Receive the Holy Spirit. 23 If you forgive the sins of any, they are forgiven them; if you retain the sins of any, they are retained'.

This is the closest we have in the resurrection appearance traditions to the traditioning pattern so familiar in earlier chapters. We seem to have a common core: 'Jesus stood among them and said "Peace be with you", and having said this he showed them his hands and his feet/side',[98] followed by a note of the disciples' joy. The fact that the core is evident in a Luke-John parallel rather than the

---

97. Byrskog, *Story as History,* surprisingly makes nothing of this possibility.

98. Luke 24.36b, 40 belong to the phenomenon known as 'Western non-interpolations'. That is, they are *absent* from Western witnesses of the textual tradition, witnesses which more commonly *add* to the traditional text. This raises the possibility that the references here have been interpolated into Luke, presumably from the Johannine parallel. However, the theory of Western non-interpolation has been undermined by the publication (1961) of the early (third-century) p[75], which contains the passages in question, and the majority opinion now concludes that they were all part of Luke's text. See again Metzger, *Textual Commentary* 186-87 (observing that an interpolation would probably have read 'his side' rather than 'his feet'), 191-93; Aland and Aland, *Text of the New Testament* 33, 37.

more typical Synoptic parallel is also significant, since the Synoptic and Johannine traditions come so close only rarely.

The core has been elaborated by each Evangelist in their typical ways. Luke stresses the materiality of Jesus' risen body (24.39, 43);[99] he continues the fulfilled prophecy motif (24.44-46);[100] he foreshadows the theme of a witness 'beginning from Jerusalem' (24.47-48);[101] and he gives the first clear indication that, so far as he was concerned, the disciples never stirred from Jerusalem (24.49).[102] John continues his negative portrayal of 'the Jews' (20.19);[103] he strengthens the 'peace' motif (20.19, 21);[104] and he compresses into this first appearance to the chief disciples his own equivalent both of the Pentecostal commissioning (20.21-22)[105] and of ecclesiastical authorization (20.23).[106]

Here then we probably can speak of a tradition told and retold in the early Christian communities; we have it only in two well-developed versions and one credal formula (1 Cor. 15.5). The fact that what was thereby recalled was a group experience rather than that of an individual is presumably significant. This was church tradition from the first, having been given its still visible spine, presumably, from the participants' talking about it among themselves.[107]

99. Luke makes a point of stressing the tangibility of divine action within the everyday world: the dove at Jordan 'in bodily form' (Luke 3.22), the witness of the transfiguration not a dream (9.32), the 'many convincing proofs' of the resurrection (Acts 1.3), the angel who released Peter from prison real and not a vision (12.9), the Spirit's coming evidenced by visible and audible phenomena (2.4, 6, 33; 4.31; 8.17-18; 10.45-46; 19.6), and so on (see further my *Unity and Diversity* 180-84).

100. See above, n. 88.

101. See above, §8.1c.

102. For the centrality of Jerusalem as the point of continuity with Israel's history and fountainhead of the Christian mission, see below, vol. 2.

103. The negative role attributed to 'the Jews' is a feature of the Fourth Gospel; see, e.g., several essays in R. Bieringer, et al., eds., *Anti-Judaism and the Fourth Gospel: Papers of the Leuven Colloquium, 2000* (Assen: Van Gorcum, 2001), and further below, vol. 3.

104. The triple greeting 'Peace be with you' in the resurrection narratives (20.19, 21, 26), is clearly intended to hark back to the farewell bestowal of peace in 14.27 (also 16.33).

105. John 20.22 is traditionally called 'the Johannine Pentecost', and can indeed be regarded as John's theological compression of the Pentecost tradition (Acts 2) into the single complex of Jesus' death and resurrection/ascension (cf. 19.30). Note also the deliberate use of *emphysaō* ('breathe'), in obvious echo of the LXX Gen. 2.7 (already echoed in Ezek. 37.9 and Wis. 15.11); this is new creation. See further my *Baptism* 173-82.

106. John 20.23 is closer to Matt. 16.19 and 18.18 than to Luke 24.47 (see further Brown, *John* 1039-45).

107. I press the point against those who argue too glibly from the fact that the earliest tradition is *confession* of resurrection appearances (1 Cor. 15.5-8) and conclude that there were no *narratives* of resurrection appearances in the beginning (e.g., Wilckens, 'Tradition-History' 73-75). One form (kerygmatic confession) does not exclude another (narrative). It is much

It was as an expression of shared experience that such tradition was first formulated.[108]

(6) *Appearance to Thomas* — John 20.24-29.

> [24]But Thomas (who was called the Twin), one of the twelve, was not with
> them when Jesus came. [25]So the other disciples told him, 'We have seen the
> Lord'. But he said to them, 'Unless I see the mark of the nails in his hands,
> and put my finger in the mark of the nails and my hand in his side, I will not
> believe'. [26]A week later his disciples were again in the house, and Thomas
> was with them. Although the doors were shut, Jesus came and *stood among
> them and said, 'Peace be with you'*. [27]Then he said to Thomas, 'Put your fin-
> ger here and see my hands. Reach out your hand and put it in my side. Do not
> doubt but believe'. [28]Thomas answered him, 'My Lord and my God!' [29]Jesus
> said to him, 'Have you believed because you have seen me? Blessed are
> those who have not seen and yet have come to believe'.

This should probably just be regarded as a further variation on the basic appearance to the eleven tradition. It has the same core features: Jesus (again) stood
among them and said, 'Peace be with you' (20.26), and having said this he
(again) showed them (Thomas) his hands and his side (20.27). The pericope's
function in John's Gospel is presumably to provide an answer to those who (like
Thomas, one of the twelve!) doubted the testimony to Jesus' resurrection
(20.25).[109] Significant is the fact that John does not actually describe Thomas as
putting finger or hand in Jesus' wounds. The seeing alone is sufficient for
Thomas to make a confession far beyond anything attested for the first disciples
at that stage (20.27-28).[110] And the final blessing is for those who believe simply
on the basis of the apostolic testimony without having even seen (let alone physically checked) for themselves (20.29).

(7) *Appearances in Jerusalem* — Acts 1.3-11. The opening of the Acts account is so much oriented to the plot of Acts that it is more appropriately considered in volume 2 (as also Luke's ending of his Gospel — Luke 24.50-52). Here

---

more plausible that the *initial* talk of a group experience among those who participated in it
took a *narrative* form.

108. Cf. Theissen and Merz: 'The agreements are clear enough for it [to be] possible for
us to infer a real event behind the accounts. . . . in our view there is no doubt that it really happened' (*Historical Jesus* 496). What 'it'?

109. See particularly Brown, *John* 1031-33. 'The story of "doubting Thomas" deals
with the problems of the second Christian generation, which has the Easter testimony only in
the form of the Gospel of John' (Theissen and Merz, *Historical Jesus* 495).

110. The confession 'My Lord and my God' is the climax not only of John's high christology (cf. particularly 1.1, 18; 5.18; and 10.33) but of the second Christian generation's growing perception of who Jesus really was (see my *Partings of the Ways* ch. 11).

however we should note the way Luke describes Jesus' involvement with 'the apostles' in the days following his resurrection.

> 3After his suffering he presented himself alive *(zōnta)* to them by many convincing proofs *(tekmēriois)*, appearing *(optanomenos)* to them during forty days and speaking about the kingdom of God. 4While eating *(synalizomenos)* with them, he ordered them not to leave Jerusalem, but to wait there for the promise of the Father.

Three features deserve comment here. (1) Luke describes Jesus simply as 'alive', rather than 'risen'. This is no doubt a variation of the 'raised' formula (Luke 24.7, 46), but it is a distinctively Lukan emphasis (Luke 24.5, 23) and probably reflects one of the earliest reactions of all: that Jesus (who had died) was alive (again)! (2) By speaking of *tekmēria*,[111] Luke is pressing his belief in the tangibility of the resurrection appearances (Luke 24.39),[112] but the term presumably indicates his own response to those who questioned the Christian claims regarding Jesus' resurrection (cf. Acts 17.32). (3) Most intriguing is the use of *synalizō* in 1.4. It means literally to 'eat salt *(hals)* with', and so to 'eat at the same table with, share table-fellowship with'.[113] Luke here extends his table-fellowship motif,[114] possibly again as part of the 'convincing proofs' (again Luke 24.39). In context the implication is almost of a continuous period — a forty-day-long resurrection appearance![115] Would Luke have denied this? Probably so, in view of Luke 24.31. But he has made no effort to avoid giving that impression. There is a confusing mix here of far-reaching claim and imprecise formulation, rather as in Matthew's two resurrection appearances (Matt. 28.9-10, 16-17), which probably reflects the vagueness of traditional memory rather than the writers' deliberate choice.

(8) *Appearances in Galilee* — Mark 16.7; Matt. 28.16-20; John 21.1-23.

Matt. 28.16-20	John 21.1-14
16 Now the eleven disciples went to Galilee, to the mountain to which Jesus had directed them. 17 When they saw him, they worshiped him;	1 After these things Jesus showed himself again to the disciples by the Sea of Tiberias; and he showed himself in this way. 2 Gathered there together were Simon Peter, Thomas called the Twin, Nathanael of Cana in Galilee, the sons of Zebedee, and two others of his disciples. 3 Simon Peter said to them, 'I am going fishing'. They said to him, 'We will go with you'. They went out and got into the boat, but that night they caught nothing. 4 Just after daybreak, Jesus stood on the shore; but the disciples did not know that

111. *Tekmērion:* 'that which causes something to be known in a convincing and decisive manner' (BDAG, *tekmērion*); '*necessary* proofs . . . leading to certain conclusions' (Barrett, *Acts* 1.70).

112. See above, n. 99.

113. BDAG, *synalizō* 1; the text makes sense enough, so there is no need to hypothesize a variant spelling of *synaulizō* ('stay with'), as in NRSV (see Barrett, *Acts* 1.71-72).

114. See again above, §14.8a.

115. Grass, *Ostergeschehen* 48-49.

| but some doubted. 18 And Jesus came and said to them, 'All authority in heaven and on earth has been given to me. 19 Go therefore and make disciples of all nations, baptizing them in the name of the Father and of the Son and of the Holy Spirit, 20 and teaching them to observe everything that I have commanded you. And remember, I am with you always, to the end of the age'. | it was Jesus. 5 Jesus said to them, 'Children, you have no fish, have you?' They answered him, 'No'. 6 He said to them, 'Cast the net to the right side of the boat, and you will find some'. So they cast it, and now they were not able to haul it in because there were so many fish. 7 That disciple whom Jesus loved said to Peter, 'It is the Lord!' When Simon Peter heard that it was the Lord, he put on some clothes, for he was naked, and jumped into the sea. 8 But the other disciples came in the boat, dragging the net full of fish, for they were not far from the land, only about a hundred yards off. 9 When they had gone ashore, they saw a charcoal fire there, with fish on it, and bread. 10 Jesus said to them, 'Bring some of the fish that you have just caught'. 11 So Simon Peter went aboard and hauled the net ashore, full of large fish, a hundred and fifty-three of them; and though there were so many, the net was not torn. 12 Jesus said to them, 'Come and have breakfast'. Now none of the disciples dared to ask him, 'Who are you?', because they knew it was the Lord. 13 Jesus came and took the bread and gave it to them, and did the same with the fish. 14 This was now the third time that Jesus appeared to the disciples after he was raised from the dead. |

In contrast to the accounts of the appearances to the eleven in Jerusalem, the accounts of the appearances in Galilee have no point of contact whatsoever. Even the common locale is not so much agreed, since in Matthew they encounter Jesus on a mountain,[116] whereas in John the meeting takes place on the shore of the lake.

It is obvious that Matthew has used whatever tradition was available to him[117] to bring his Gospel to a climax with the affirmation of Jesus' divine authority, the great commission, and the conclusion to his 'God with us' theme.[118] This in itself marks out the appearance from the other more 'earthbound' appearances, giving it a more 'heavenly' character.[119] Another interesting feature is the close of 28.17: 'they worshipped *(prosekynēsan)* him, but some doubted

116. Matthew evidently intended the 'mountain' to be understood as the place where divine revelation is given (Matt. 5.1; 15.29; 17.1; 24.3; 28.16); see particularly T. L. Donaldson, *Jesus on the Mountain: A Study in Matthean Theology* (JSNTS 8; Sheffield: JSOT, 1985).

117. B. J. Hubbard, *The Matthean Redaction of a Primitive Apostolic Commissioning* (SBLDS 19: Missoula: Scholars, 1974) reconstructs a primitive commissioning narrative behind the several appearances to the eleven: 'Jesus appeared to the eleven. When they saw him they were glad, though some disbelieved. Then he said: preach (the gospel) to all nations, (baptize) in my name for the forgiveness of sins. (And behold), I will send the Holy Spirit upon you' (131).

118. Since O. Michel, 'The Conclusion of Matthew's Gospel' (1950), ET in G. N. Stanton, ed., *The Interpretation of Matthew* (London: SPCK, 1983) 30-41, it has been common to regard 28.18-20 as the climax, if not the key, to Matthew's Gospel. On the 'God with us' motif (Matt. 1.23; 18.20; 28.20) see above, chapter 11 n. 20. Notable is the absence of any account of an ascension.

119. See my *Jesus and the Spirit* 124, and the distinction suggested by J. Lindblom, *Gesichte und Offenbarungen* (Lund: Gleerup, 1968) 104-105, 108-109, 111-12, between appearances on earth (what he calls 'christepiphanies') and appearances from heaven ('christophanies').

(edistasan)'.[120] The first verb is quite a favourite of Matthew;[121] but only Matthew of the NT writers uses the second (14.31; 28.17). Even at the end there are those of 'little faith *(oligopistos)*' (14.31), to whom Jesus appears (14.31), and even commissions despite their doubts! Unlike both Luke and John, who show how the doubts were resolved,[122] Matthew leaves the note of doubt unresolved (as in 14.31).[123] Is this a subtle pastoral tactic of Matthew or a reminiscence that in the shared experiences we call 'resurrection appearances' not all were so persuaded of what they saw and experienced?

Somewhat surprisingly, the distinctive notes of Johannine reuse of tradition are lacking in John 21.1-14, apart from the identification of the beloved disciple as one of the seven involved (21.7). Perhaps John saw the episode simply as setting the scene for the conversation with Peter (21.15-23). In fact, however, it is the indications of an early reminiscence, largely uncomplicated by later perspective, which catch the attention. At the heart of the story is a memory linked explicitly to seven disciples, the identity of two of them no longer clear to the memory (21.2).[124] It is a memory of disciples who had lost any sense of direction or motivation (21.3). The scene itself has an earthy homeliness: tired and frustrated fishermen (21.3-5), Peter stripped naked for the task at hand (21.7), the details of distance from the shore and the number of fish (21.8, 11),[125] and the breakfast of fish and bread, presumably on the shore (21.9, 12-13). Is this another memory that John attributes to the beloved disciple — hence the numbering of the account as Jesus' *third* appearance (21.14)?

(9)-(12) *Further appearances* — 1 Cor. 15.6-8.

> 6Then he appeared to more than five hundred brothers at one time, most of whom are still alive, though some have died; 7then he appeared to James, then to all the apostles. 8Last of all, as to an 'abortion', he appeared to me also.

120. In context the 'some' can only mean 'some of the eleven' (Davies and Allison, *Matthew* 3.681-62).

121. Matt. 2.2, 8, 11; 4.9-10 (= Luke 4.7-8); 8.2; 9.18; 14.33; 15.25; 18.26; 20.20; 28.9, 17 (cf. Luke 24.52).

122. Luke 24.41-43; John 20.24-29. The motif is extended in the (second-century?) *Epistula Apostolorum* 10-12.

123. See further my *Jesus and the Spirit* 123-25.

124. The *Gospel of Peter* breaks off in the middle of what was presumably a longer list: Peter, Andrew, Levi, the son of Alphaeus, whom the Lord . . .' (*Gos. Pet.* 14.60); why would Andrew not be mentioned by John? It is not inappropriate to recall the Jesus tradition's confusion over the identity of the less well-known members of the twelve (see above, §13.3b[2]).

125. No explanation for one hundred fifty-three as a symbol has succeeded in winning much support (see, e.g., Brown, *John* 1074-76).

Despite uncertainties about the extent of tradition which Paul received,[126] there is no reason to doubt that this information was communicated to Paul as part of his introductory catechesis (15.3).[127] He would have needed to be informed of precedents in order to make sense of what had happened to him. When he says, 'I handed on *(paredōka)* to you as of first importance *(en prōtois)* what I also received *(parelabon)*' (15.3), he assuredly does not imply that the tradition became important to him only at some subsequent date. More likely he indicates the importance of the tradition to himself from the start; that was why he made sure to pass it on to the Corinthians when they first believed (15.1-2).[128] This tradition, we can be entirely confident, was *formulated as tradition within months of Jesus' death.*[129]

It is disappointing, then, that we have no further record of the appearances listed by Paul as third, fourth, and fifth, probably in chronological order.[130] The intriguing question they raise is how lengthy was the period over which these appearances stretched. The appearance claimed by Paul could have been no earlier than about eighteen months after Jesus' death.[131] Had there been no appearances beyond a few weeks after the resurrection — Luke says forty days (Acts 1.3) — the claim made by Saul/Paul would surely have been regarded with considerable

126. See, e.g., the debates and bibliography cited in my *Jesus and the Spirit* 98, 385 nn. 6-7, and the more recent discussion in Craig, *Assessing* 1-49; Schrage, *1 Korinther* 4.19-24. On the question whether the formula originated in Aramaic, see the review of the discussion in Lehmann, *Auferweckt* 87-115; if formulated in Greek, the credal formula must still go back to the Greek-speaking Hellenists of whom Acts speaks (Acts 6.1; 8.1-3; 9.1-2; 11.19). In any case, there is no question that the tradition included resurrection appearances, at least those to Peter and the Twelve: Paul uses the Aramaic *Kēphas,* and 'the twelve' *(hoi dōdeka)* is *hapax* in Paul; the *hoti* at the beginning of v. 5 includes at least these appearances within the tradition received; and it is precisely for this appearance tradition that Paul introduced his discussion of the resurrection with it.

127. The language of tradition transmission *(paradidōmi, paralambanō)* is unmistakable (BDAG, *paradidōmi* 3).

128. Hence also the frequent echoes of formulae confessing the resurrection in Paul's letters (above, n. 4); that Paul considered the resurrection of Jesus crucial for Christian faith as a whole is clear from 1 Cor. 15.12-19. See also the review of the discussion on 1 Cor 15.3-8 in Theissen and Merz, *Historical Jesus* 487-90.

129. 'We can assume that all the elements in the tradition [15.3b-5, 6a, 7] are to be dated to the first two years after the crucifixion of Jesus' (Lüdemann, *Resurrection* 38). Contrast Funk's 'suspicion that the lists and reports were compiled long after the fact' (*Honest* 267).

130. The sequence of 'then . . . then . . . then *(epeita/eita)*' which links the second to fifth appearances could denote simply an ordered account. But usage elsewhere suggests a list set out in chronological order (BDAG, *eita, epeita*). And the fact that Paul introduces the final item (the appearance to himself) with 'last of all *(eschaton de pantōn)*' confirms that he is thinking of a sequence which spanned a period of time (Dunn, *Jesus and the Spirit* 101, and those cited on 385-86 nn. 13-15; Schrage, *1 Korinther* 4.51-52). But the argument of the following paragraph does not depend on the six appearances listed having followed a strict chronological sequence.

131. On the date of Paul's conversion, see again below, vol. 2.

suspicion. That he was able to press the claim so emphatically[132] and that it was accepted by the Jerusalem leadership[133] presumably indicates that the span of appearances reached to nearer the time of Paul's conversion.[134] This deduction is consistent with the numbers and personnel mentioned. For an appearance to 'more than five hundred' is most likely dated to a period when the new movement had begun to win converts and adherents.[135] And 'all the apostles' probably indicates a time when the movement was becoming more missionary-minded.[136] Where Luke and Paul agree is in signalling that the period of resurrection appearances came to an end: after forty days, says Luke; 'last of all to me', says Paul.[137]

The other striking tension introduced by the inclusion of the appearance to Paul within the listed resurrection appearances is that, according to the Acts accounts, the appearance was from heaven,[138] whereas all the other appearances are recorded as appearances on *terra firma*. This adds a further dimension to the questions raised by the accounts to which we shall have to return (below §18.5c). The compensation, if that is the appropriate word, is that with the appearance to Paul we have the closest thing to a firsthand personal testimony to a resurrection appearance. Not that we can attribute the Acts accounts without question to Paul

132. By including the appearance to himself with the same formula ('he appeared' — *ōphthē*) Paul implies that the appearance to himself was of the same order as that to those earlier in the list; the question asked in 1 Cor. 9.1 ('Have I not seen Jesus our Lord?') assumes that no responsible person would have replied negatively.

133. No other conclusion can be drawn from the albeit defensive Gal. 1.1–2.10.

134. Craig wishes to hold to Luke's timetable (no appearances after Pentecost), but he does not answer the question of whether and why in that case a claim to a much later appearance would have been accepted (*Assessing* 72-73 n. 31).

135. Cf. Grass, *Ostergeschehen* 101, 109-10; Fuller, *Formation* 36. Crossan cuts across the obvious implication of 1 Cor. 15.5-8 by pushing the suggestion of 'a trajectory of revelatory apparition moving the emphasis slowly but steadily from *community* to *group* to *leader*' (*Historical Jesus* 397-98). Lüdemann, *Resurrection* 100-108, follows the well-worn line that the appearance to the 500-plus is a variant tradition to Pentecost (Acts 2.1-13) (similarly Funk, *Acts of Jesus* 455); but see already my *Jesus and the Spirit* 142-46.

136. Cf. again Fuller, *Formation* 40-42, and my *Jesus and the Spirit* 98, where it is pointed out that 'the apostles', for Paul at least, was not simply another name for the twelve, but included people like Andronicus and Junia (Rom. 16.7) and Barnabas (Gal. 2.9; 1 Cor. 9.5-6); see further vol. 2. Probably irrelevant here, but worth noting nonetheless, is that Luke seems to count Cleopas and his unnamed companion as apostles (Luke 24.10, 13).

137. The force of Paul's self-description as 'an abortion' is often missed. An 'abortion' properly speaking is a premature birth. The implication is that Paul's conversion had to be forced ahead of due time in order that he might be included within the circle of apostle-making resurrection appearances before the circle closed (see my *Jesus and the Spirit* 101-102; *Theology of Paul* 331 n. 87; and further below, vol. 2).

138. 'A light from heaven' (Acts 9.3; 22.6: light and voice presumably from the same source; 26.13, 19: 'the heavenly vision').

himself. It is rather that Paul seems to refer or allude to the appearance on the Damascus road on other occasions as well as 1 Cor. 15.8. 'Have I not seen Jesus our Lord?' he asks in 1 Cor. 9.1. His talk of 'seeing the light of the gospel of the glory of Christ', and of 'the light of the knowledge of the glory of God in the face of Jesus Christ' (2 Cor. 4.4, 6) probably alludes to his great light experience on the Damascus road (n. 138).[139] And in Gal. 1.16 he expresses his conviction and gratitude that God has been pleased 'to reveal his Son in me' in a context where he is evidently thinking of his conversion and commissioning as an apostle.[140]

18.4. The Tradition within the Traditions

a. The Diversity of the Traditions

Can we penetrate through these various traditions to their origin? In comparison with the Synoptic tradition of Jesus' mission, the prospects are not bright.[141] There are too many idiosyncratic and puzzling curious features about the data.[142]

(1) So many of the appearances have only single attestation: to Cleopas and his unidentified companion, to the 500-plus, to James, and to 'all the apostles' — four of the twelve appearances listed above. In addition, the appearance to Peter is referred to twice, but as a bare mention each time, unless we include John 21.15-19.

(2) Where there is some overlap it is almost tangential — particularly in the case of the appearances to Mary/women at/near the tomb, and the appearance to the eleven in Galilee. The only substantively overlapping traditions are the varied accounts of appearances to the rest of the twelve in Jerusalem. There a core is evident, more substantial as a core, indeed, than any other shared Synoptic/Johannine pericope.

(3) On the other hand, it is precisely the appearances to the eleven which pose the question 'Where?' most sharply — Jerusalem or Galilee? Some divergence in location is to be expected in the diversity of performance. But overall

---

139. See, e.g., M. E. Thrall, *2 Corinthians* (ICC; Edinburgh: Clark, 1994, 2000) 1.316-20 (bibliography in n. 878).

140. See, e.g., my *Theology of Paul* 177-79.

141. 'It is quite remarkable that an almost hour-by-hour remembrance prevailed for the death and burial of Jesus but an almost total discrepancy prevailed for what was, I would presume, even more important, namely, the extraordinary return of Jesus from beyond the grave . . .' (Crossan, *Historical Jesus* 395).

142. As noted above (chapter 4 n. 23), Reimarus's treatment still constitutes the classic enumeration of the contradictions within the resurrection narratives; for a summary see Wedderburn, *Beyond Resurrection* 24-25.

the diversity is beyond anything we have so far encountered — except in the two accounts of Judas's death (Matt. 27.3-10/Acts 1.16-19), where the lack of agreement signals, if anything, the relative *lack* of importance of the tradition for the early Christian communities! In contrast, I started by noting that the several accounts of the appearance to Paul, which all occur in the same writing (Acts), provide a good example of what has proved to be the typical traditioning process for the Jesus tradition (§8.4a). But they strictly speaking are not part of the Jesus tradition. Whereas the appearances to the twelve/eleven are the conclusion to the Jesus tradition according to the unanimous voice of the canonical Gospels. Should we then conclude that they too were unimportant for the early communities of Jesus' disciples?!

(4) Equally baffling is the tension between appearances on earth and appearances from heaven. How could the appearance to Paul have proved so acceptable to the Jerusalem leadership if what was clearly perceived as an appearance from heaven was exceptional? Or does the ambiguity of the Matt. 28.16-20 indicate some confused perception on the point?[143] And we do not know what 'category' other appearances (to the 500-plus, to 'all the apostles') fell into. Is there room, therefore, for an argument such as that of Peter Carnley, that all the early appearances were actually 'from heaven'?[144]

There is no question, then, as to the diversity of the traditions at this point. The more important question, however, is whether the differences are out of character with a traditioning process which took for granted variability among performances.[145] Which raises the further question whether the obvious conclusion that the traditions in their present forms are unharmonizable has paid sufficient attention to the character of the tradition and of the traditioning process.[146]

b. A Core Tradition?

In point of fact, however, a number of common elements are readily discernible in the appearance traditions which span a considerable portion of their diversity.

143. See above at n. 120.

144. Carnley, *Structure* 236-41: 'the entire thrust of the evidence is towards the view that whatever was "seen" appeared "from heaven"' (242-43).

145. When Evans observes that 'It is hardly the same Lord who speaks. In Matthew it is evidently a Matthean Lord who speaks, in Luke a Lukan Lord and in John a Johannine Lord' (*Resurrection* 67), is he doing more than simply observing the characteristic features of performative variation?

146. It is equally unsatisfactory for Craig simply to argue that 'the controlling presence of living eyewitnesses would retard significant accrual of legend' (*Assessing* 387). What is required, and what I try to provide, is a cogent account of the traditioning process itself.

(1) A key element is that they '*saw*' Jesus: Mary saw Jesus (John 20.14); he appeared *(ōphthē)* to Peter (Luke 24.34/1 Cor. 15.5) and the others listed in 1 Cor. 5.5-8;[147] Cleopas recognized Jesus at the last (Luke 24.31); Jesus showed his wounds (Luke 24.40/John 20.20); they tell Thomas, 'We have seen the Lord' (John 20.25), and Thomas believes because he saw (20.29); the eleven see Jesus in Galilee (Matt. 28.17) and he shows himself to them (John 21.1); Paul 'saw' Jesus on the road to Damascus.[148] This 'seeing' was evidently regarded as of first importance, as both Luke (Acts 1.22) and Paul (1 Cor. 9.1) attest. No one could be recognized as an 'apostle' who had not seen the Lord.

(2) Somewhat paradoxically, an almost equally attested motif is *failure to recognize* Jesus. This failure is signalled in several of the most elaborate accounts of appearances: to Mary (John 20.14-15), to Cleopas (Luke 24.16), and to the seven on the lake (John 21.4). It is matched by the note of doubt and disbelief: notably in the appearances to the eleven in Jerusalem (Luke 24.41), to Thomas (John 20.24-29), and to the eleven in Galilee (Matt. 28.17). Whereas the failure to recognize is remedied within the account and the doubt of Thomas is carefully met, Matthew makes no attempt to indicate that the doubt of the eleven in Galilee was removed.[149]

(3) Another common motif is that of *commission:* the women (Mary) are to tell the brothers (Matt. 28.10/John 20.17), Peter is to feed the sheep (John 21.15-19), the commission to tell is implicit in Cleopas' haste to return to Jerusalem when it was already evening (Luke 24.31-35), the eleven are explicitly commissioned both in Jerusalem[150] and in Galilee (Matt. 28.19-20), and the appearance to 'all the apostles' prior to the appearance to Paul was presumably what made them apostles (1 Cor. 15.7).[151] As with the 'seeing', this element was evidently crucial if one who 'saw the Lord' was to be recognized as an apostle.[152]

(4) Less common, but a motif in several accounts is an appearance in the

147. It is important to observe, as Carnley reminds us (*Structure* 139-43), that the documentation in 1 Cor. 15.5-7 is presented as evidence.

148. Acts 9.17, 27; 22.14-15; 26.16.

149. Cf. Jeremias: 'The characteristic feature of the earliest stratum of tradition is that it still preserves a recollection of the overpowering, puzzling and mysterious nature of the events . . . the same mysterious chiaroscuro . . .' (*Proclamation* 303).

150. Luke 24.47/John 20.21; Acts 1.8.

151. The seeing alone did not constitute apostleship, as the implied distinction between the appearances to the 500-plus and to 'all the apostles' indicates; even so, the former are cited as witnesses, most of whom were still alive (1 Cor. 15.6) and so (it is also implied) available to be consulted as witnesses.

152. Acts 1.22; 1 Cor. 9.1-2; 15.8-11. This is the strength of U. Wilckens's categorisation of these clauses as 'legitimation formulae' ('Tradition-History' 59-60; *Resurrection* 12-13, 114), even if he overdoes the point ('Tradition-History' 66). See further my *Jesus and the Spirit* 110-14, 128-32; Perkins, *Resurrection* 195-214.

context of or involving a *meal* in Luke,[153] in John 21.12-13, in the longer Markan ending (Mark 16.14), and in Ignatius, *Smyrn.* 3.3.[154]

(5) Not least of relevance is the tradition that Jesus first appeared *'on the first day of the week'* (Sunday) following his crucifixion and burial, explicit or implicit in the first five of the appearances listed in §18.3. Here we should add that 'on the first day of the week' was clearly part of the core tradition of the discovery that the tomb was empty (§18.2). Furthermore it clearly accords with the 'third day' tradition which was already firmly attached to the confessional formula received by Paul after his conversion: 'that he was raised on the third day in accordance with the Scriptures' (1 Cor. 15.4). Nor should we forget the striking but often neglected fact that from as early as we can trace, Sunday had become a day of special significance for Christians,[155] 'the Lord's day',[156] precisely because it was the day on which they celebrated the resurrection of the Lord.

The emergence of this tradition could be explained as one of the fruits of the search for proof from prophecy,[157] or even from the memory of something Jesus had said. The only problem in the first case is that the one plausible Scripture candidate is Hos. 6.2,[158] but no NT writer ever cites it as such a proof — a remarkable fact, given the extensive use of Scripture consistently evident in NT treatment of Jesus' death and resurrection.[159] And in the second, the earliest

---

153. Luke 24.30-31, 35, 41-43; Acts 1.4; 10.41.

154. Crossan adds in the earlier feeding miracles (Mark 6 and John 6), suggesting that 'Those bread and fish Eucharists and their institutionalization stories went back before anyone ever thought of writing a biographical narrative of Jesus and hence of having to decide what happened "before" and what "after" his death' (*Historical Jesus* 399). In contrast, Roloff observes a tension between the meal traditions and the thrust of the resurrection kerygma (*Kerygma* 263).

155. Acts 20.7; 1 Cor. 16.2.

156. Rev. 1.10; *Did.* 14.1; Ignatius, *Magn.* 9.1; *Gos. Pet.* 9.35; 12.50. For full discussion see W. Rordorf, *Sunday: The History of the Day of Rest and Worship in the Earliest Centuries of the Christian Church* (London: SCM, 1968).

157. Grass, *Ostergeschehen* 127-38; Evans, *Resurrection* 47-50, 75-76: 'not intended as a chronological but as a theological statement' (48); Fuller, *Formation* 23-27; Lüdemann, *Resurrection* 47.

158. Hos. 6.1-2: 'Come, let us return to the Lord; for he has torn, that he may heal us; he has stricken, and he will bind us up. After two days he will revive us; on the third day he will raise us up, that we may live before him.' So most recently Evans, 'Did Jesus Predict?' 94-96. The earlier attempts by Lehmann, *Auferweckt* 262-90, and H. K. McArthur, 'On the Third Day', *NTS* 18 (1971-72) 81-86, to explain the reference from rabbinic interpretation of this (and other) 'third day' passages do not carry much weight for such an early Christian credal formula; but cf. Schrage, *1 Korinther* 4.39-43.

159. Jeremias observes that Tertullian, *Adv. Judaeos* 13, is the first to cite Hos. 6.2 in connection with the resurrection (*Proclamation* 304). It could be, of course, that the 'in accor-

memories of what Jesus may have said[160] are not so precise as 'on the third day' ('after three days') and in the Passion predictions were amended to 'on the third day' — presumably because what was remembered as having happened was remembered as happening 'on the third day'.[161]

If we are looking for 'core' elements in the traditions, then the first, third, and fifth of those just listed could be fairly regarded as such. And as with the core elements of the Jesus tradition proper we can be confident that these were part of the tradition from the first, indeed, that the tradition first emerged as expression of the impact made by the experiences enshrined in the core.[162] No one who has studied the data can doubt that the Christian witness on this theme began from a number of experiences understood as seeings of Jesus alive after he had been dead.[163] It was not that some conviction regarding Jesus was subsequently cast in the form of a resurrection experience story. The stories were remembered as visual or visionary experiences, because that is how they were experienced; that was the impact crystallized in the core tradition. They not only *believed* they had seen the Lord, they had *experienced* a seeing of the Lord alive from the dead.

Moreover, the formative experiences were evidently also experiences of personal encounter and communication. It came to them as a personal commissioning. That was evidently how Paul experienced the appearance to him.[164] And presumably it was the degree of conformity between his related experience and the earlier appearance-experiences which persuaded the first disciples that their former archenemy had indeed been converted, and not only so, but commissioned to join their ranks as a proclaimer of the resurrection. How we interpret these experiences may be another question.[165] *What we should recognize as beyond reasonable doubt is that the first believers experienced 'resurrection appearances' and that those expe-*

---

dance with the Scriptures' refers to the 'he was raised . . .', rather than specifically to 'on the third day'. See further Wedderburn, *Beyond Resurrection* 48-53.

160. Mark 8.31; 9.31; 10.34; 14.58.

161. See above, §17.4c(2).

162. Cf. Alsup's analysis in *Post-Resurrection Appearance Stories* ch. 3, which he summarizes thus: 'although the appearance stories of the gospel tradition show an almost unprecedented fluidity and proclivity to redactional freedom and variation a pre-redactional form with constants of motif and theme is discernible behind that fluidity, a form fixed enough . . . [to be called] a NT *Gattung*.' 'It would seem that the farthest point in the origins of the tradition to which we may reach back is to the *Gattung* itself which declared that the risen Lord encountered and re-established fellowship with his own and sent them out in his service' (213, 274).

163. E.g., Pannenberg cites J. Leipoldt: 'One cannot doubt that the disciples were convinced that they had seen the resurrected Lord. Otherwise the origin of the community in Jerusalem and with it of the church becomes an enigma' (*Jesus* 91).

164. It is for this reason that Paul's conversion may equally be described as a commissioning; see again my *Theology of Paul* 177-79.

165. See further below, §18.6.

riences are enshrined, as with the earlier impact made by Jesus' teaching and actions, in the traditions which have come down to us.

The 'third day' tradition is more problematic. For if it was initially formulated in relation to the resurrection appearances,[166] that runs quite counter to the strong tradition of resurrection appearances first in Galilee (Mark), or first at least to the male disciples (Matthew). To reach Galilee from Jerusalem took far longer than three days. Perhaps, then, it emerged from the memory of appearances in and around Jerusalem on the evening of the first Sunday (Luke, John). Or should we give more weight to the fact that it is the empty tomb tradition which consistently includes in its core the time note, 'on the first day of the week', whereas the Jerusalem appearance traditions simply take up from the stories of the empty tomb, or speak of '(the evening of) the same day'?[167] The empty tomb traditions also include proclamation of Jesus' resurrection, so the conclusion, 'raised on the third day', could have been early drawn and become part of the first confessional affirmation from the first.

In short, although the enduring forms of the resurrection appearance traditions give minimal evidence of a core spine elaborated in the subsequent performances still available to us, we can nevertheless speak of a core tradition evident within and through the diversity of these traditions.

c. The Silences of the Tradition

But we have still to take account of what in many ways is the most striking and astonishing feature of all — that is, the absence of accounts of appearances to Peter and to James (brother of Jesus). On almost any reckoning, these must have been regarded as the most significant of the appearances for the initial band of disciples. Peter evidently soon began to function as the initial leader of the Jerusalem church (Acts 3–5), to be succeeded by James (brother of Jesus)[168] when Peter probably began to embark on a wider outreach.[169] The appearance to Peter

---

166. Hahn, *Hoheitstitel* 205-206 (*Titles* 180). But this common deduction is usually predicated on the prior assumption that it was the appearances alone which gave rise to the conviction that Jesus had been raised from the dead (e.g., Bultmann, *Theology* 1.45; Grass, *Ostergeschehen* 184).

167. Bode deduces from the absence of a more explicit 'third day' motif in the empty tomb traditions that they were formulated early, before the motif became influential (*First Easter Morning* 124-26, 161-62); similarly Wilckens, *Resurrection* 10-11; Hengel, 'Begräbnis' 132-33 n. 51.

168. No one doubts that the James of 1 Cor. 15.7 is the James of Gal. 1.19 and 2.9, 12.

169. See particularly Gal. 2.7-9. Acts 12.1-17 suggests that Peter also had to leave Jerusalem for his own safety. The subject is another to which we shall have to return in vol. 2.

is given pride of place in the tradition received by Paul (1 Cor. 15.5), and its priority is echoed in Luke 24.34. If there was any appearance for which an account might have been expected, it is this one. And yet, such an account is completely lacking (apart from/prior to John 21.15-23).[170] Why? The same question can be asked regarding the appearance to James.[171]

The deduction cannot surely be that such stories would have been unimportant for the first believers. The confession of 1 Cor. 15.5 gives almost as much prominence to the appearance to the twelve as to the appearance to Peter, and we have seen that stories of the appearance to the twelve abound. So why not stories which spell out in narrative form the claim that the first appearance was to Peter — and that it was an appearance which (presumably) brought James into the movement?[172]

The hypothesis developed in this volume points to a different answer. According to the hypothesis, the Jesus tradition has taken the shape still evident in the Synoptic Gospels by virtue of being community tradition, tradition told and retold again and again and again in the first and spreading communities of believers in Jesus. The more likely conclusion to draw from the character of the appearance traditions, therefore, is that the appearance traditions did *not* function in that way in the early churches. They were *not* church tradition. Rather, they were regarded more as *personal testimony,* and they functioned in that way. The appearances could be confessed by the churches and their teachers. But they were not (could not be) elaborated as stories by elders and teachers, because as stories they belonged first and foremost to the one(s) who witnessed the appearance.

This suggestion seems to be borne out by the very personal character of so many of the appearance stories: to Mary, to Cleopas, to Thomas, to Peter (John 21), to Paul. Paul seems to imply as much when he notes that most of the 500-plus were still alive (1 Cor. 15.6), with the implied invitation that his auditors

170. Of all the Gospels, the absence of such an appearance to Peter story is most surprising in Matthew, given Matthew's distinctive interest in Peter (especially Matt. 14.28-32; 16.16-19).

171. *Gospel of the Hebrews* 7 contains an account of the appearance to James (which may well be based on 1 Cor. 15.7). The account adds: 'He took bread and blessed and broke it and gave to James the Just and said to him, "My brother, eat your bread, for the Son of Man is risen from those who sleep"' (Elliott, *Apocryphal New Testament* 9-10, who numbers the fragment as 4).

172. Jeremias suggests that 'the radical groups in Palestinian Jewish Christianity . . . took offence at the universalism of Peter (Gal. 2.12b; Acts 11.2) and therefore displaced him from the role of having been first to experience an appearance of the Risen Lord' (*Proclamation* 307); but even so, that would still leave unexplained the silence of the tradition which has come down to us. Equally implausible is the older view of Harnack, that the appearance to Peter was suppressed (outlined and approved by Lüdemann, *Resurrection* 85); Marxsen is more plausible at this point (see n. 77 above).

could ask them for themselves. Their story could be told only by the witnesses themselves. In contrast, the stories of the appearances to the women and to the eleven in Galilee (Matthew) are vague and lacking in personal character.[173] Only as such, lacking the force of personal testimony, could they be told as tradition. And is this the reason that the stories of the appearances to Peter and James are not told in the earliest accounts? Because Peter and James did not tell them: they were too private and personal? The possibilities are intriguing, but at this stage remain no more than that.

d. In Sum

In sum, what we have, then, are two distinct sets of traditions (empty tomb and appearances) whose correlation in terms of resurrection rationale is evident, but whose tradition history correlation is less clear. In tradition-historical terms the probability is strong that the tradition of the empty tomb, including its discovery 'on the first day of the week', goes back to claims made by women. Despite some uncertainty as to whether and how this information should be used, it was in the event accepted, as signalled by the confirmatory report of some disciples (Luke 24.24), identified by John as Peter and the beloved disciple (John 20.3-10), though disregarded in the Pauline tradition (1 Cor. 15.3-5). This tradition-historical conclusion is strengthened by the historical probabilities regarding the emptiness of the tomb (§18.2).

In the case of the resurrection appearance tradition we have to rely almost exclusively on what can be gleaned from the traditions themselves. Here the personal testimony of Paul is crucial. He not only attests the tradition already established at the time of his conversion, within a year or two of the events themselves (1 Cor. 15.3-5/6/7).[174] But he also tells us what was regarded as the crucial identifying marks of a 'resurrection appearance' — a seeing of Jesus and a commissioning by Jesus. It was because his 'resurrection appearance' conformed to what was evidently already regarded as the 'norm' that his claim to a resurrection ap-

---

173. Cf. C. H. Dodd, 'The Appearances of the Risen Christ: An Essay in Form-Criticism of the Gospels', in D. E. Nineham, ed., *Studies in the Gospels: Essays in Memory of R. H. Lightfoot* (Oxford: Blackwell, 1955) 9-35. Dodd distinguishes 'concise' narratives (Matt. 28.8-10, 16-20; John 20.19-21) from the other 'circumstantial' narratives, with the implication that the former were 'drawn directly from the oral tradition handed down by the corporate memory of the Church' (10). But he also comments that John 20.11-17 'has something indefinably first-hand about it'; 'There is nothing quite like it in the Gospels. Is there anything quite like it in all ancient literature?' (20).

174. Within 'two or three years at most' (Funk, *Acts of Jesus* 466, though see n. 129 above).

pearance and to be an apostle was accepted by the leadership of the Jerusalem church, with whatever misgivings.[175]

Beyond that the origins of the tradition become much harder to discern. Particularly problematic is the question of locale. An appearance to women at or near the tomb has similar tradition-historical plausibility as the account of the discovery that the tomb was empty. But appearances to the eleven on Easter day run counter to the indication that they would see Jesus (first) in Galilee (Mark 16.7). The latter emphasis is confirmed by Matthew, a theological motivation is detectable in Luke's restriction of the appearances to Jerusalem, and the Fourth Gospel bears testimony to both traditions and suggests some attempt to rationalise the diversity (the appearance in John 21 as 'the third time' — 21.14). On this point, unfortunately, Paul gives us no assistance.

It is possible to envisage some sort of historical sequencing and coherence. For example, a women's tradition (empty tomb, appearance) emerged in Jerusalem, finding some confirmation in appearances claimed by male disciples who had remained in the Jerusalem area. It was met in further confirmation by reports of appearances to other disciples (the main body of the eleven) who had returned (despondently) to Galilee.[176] These traditions came together in the Jerusalem church and were given the more (but by no means completely) integrated and coherent shape which they have retained to this day.

If there is anything in this, then several important features should be highlighted. (1) Any merging of divergent traditions has been carried through only to a certain extent. The confusion regarding location and who was first is not removed in Matthew, in the Fourth Gospel or in the Markan longer ending. Only Luke has been bold enough to impose a pattern on his material by excluding all reference to Galilean appearances. (2) A core — empty tomb, third day, seeings, and commissionings — remains consistent, despite and through all the diversity. Here too, evidently, so long as the key point was being made through the various performances, the degree of divergence was not regarded as serious. (3) These key elements (core) probably go back to the (several) beginnings of the traditioning process. As consistently in the Jesus tradition, it was the *impact* made by discovery that the burial place of Jesus was empty, and by different experiences of seeing and hearing Jesus, which was embodied from the first telling

---

175. Gal. 1.18–2.10; 1 Cor. 9.1-2; 15.8-11. See further below, vol. 2.

176. The regular assumption that the disciples (all) fled to Galilee when Jesus was arrested (as in Gnilka, *Jesus* 293; Funk, *Honest* 223) lacks historical discrimination. As Wedderburn notes, it is equally as difficult to dispense critically with either one of the two sets (Jerusalem, Galilee) of traditions (*Beyond Resurrection* 55-57, 59-60). There are several reasons that those who saw Jesus in Galilee might then have returned to Jerusalem — e.g., to await Jesus' expected soon return (Sanders, *Historical Figure* 276: 'They did not give up his idea that the kingdom would come'). But fuller discussion is best left till vol. 2.

in the tradition and gave the tradition its essential shape.[177] (4) Several of the appearances were very personal in character and gave the tradition the character of personal testimony. Some of these (to Peter and James in particular) did not become church tradition until later or never. In these cases eyewitness testimony was not formulated in such a way as to become communal tradition.

18.5. Why 'Resurrection'?

Analysis of the history of the tradition only takes us so far — to first reports formulated as tradition. It does not explain the terms used, terms which defined the tradition as 'resurrection' appearances. We can be confident that there was a *visual* and *auditory* element to these seeings. That the seeing and hearing was a seeing and hearing of *Jesus* was a matter of doubt for some who shared the experience, but that memory of doubt has been retained in a tradition where no such doubt remained. That Jesus was *alive,* despite crucifixion and burial, was an understandable conclusion to draw from the experience. But why *'resurrection'?* Why was the further conclusion drawn, and why did it become the core interpretation, that God had raised Jesus from the dead?

The question arises for two reasons. First, because there were other categories which one would expect to have appealed to the disciples. Second, because 'resurrection' had a limited reference, that is, to what was expected to take place at the end of time, prior to the final judgment.[178] Both aspects require elucidation.

a. Why Did the First Witnesses Conclude That God Had Raised Jesus from the Dead?

Had they simply wanted to affirm his vindication or the vindication of his message,[179] they could have done so in other ways. Here, as in chapter 15, we need to take note of the options open to them.

(1) *Translation or rapture.* The most prominent examples in this category were Enoch (Gen. 5.24) and Elijah (2 Kgs. 2.11-12). They had been translated or raptured to heaven and remained there with the possibility of returning to earth. As already noted, there was considerable speculation current at the time of Jesus

---

177. 'We may reckon that the appearances of Jesus were talked about *immediately* after they happened' (Lüdemann, *Resurrection* 38, his emphasis).

178. See above, §17.6b.

179. So particularly Marxsen, *Resurrection* (see below, §18.5d).

regarding their current and future roles — Enoch as the 'scribe of righteousness'[180] and Elijah's return.[181] Josephus also reports speculation regarding Moses, whether he had died or been 'translated' *(metastēnai)* by God to himself *(Ant.* 3.96-97), or had gone back to the deity *(pros to theion anachōrēsai)* (4.326). And within a few decades of Jesus' death we find Ezra and Baruch both being spoken of as 'taken up' to live in heaven, 'until the times are ended' (*4 Ezra* 14.9), 'preserved until the end of times' (*2 Bar.* 13.3).[182]

A crucial difference, of course, is that translation excluded death: neither Enoch nor Elijah had died, and the speculation regarding Moses, Ezra, and Baruch saw translation as an alternative to death.[183] But the death of Jesus is central to the Jesus tradition. So a parallel here would not have been obvious; translation in that form was not so much of an option. I only pause to observe that it has been suggested as an option in the case of Mark's account of the empty tomb (lacking any account of a resurrection appearance)[184] and was subsequently drawn on (in effect) by the docetic claim that Christ had not in fact been crucified.[185]

(2) Vindication/exaltation. A much more likely category is that of the vindication or exaltation of a dead man.[186] We have already referred to the hope entertained by and for the righteous man, as classically expressed in Wis. 3.1-9 and 5.1-5 (§17.6a): he will be seen as numbered among the sons of God (5.5). Similarly the manlike figure of Daniel 7 represented the hopes of 'the saints' for (final) vindication before the throne of Yahweh. In 2 Macc. 15.13-14 Jeremiah appears to Judas Maccabeus in 'a trustworthy dream' (15.11)[187] as a figure of heavenly majesty. In *T. Job* 40.3 Job sees his dead children 'crowned with the splendour of the heavenly one'.[188] In *T. Abr.* 11, Adam (Recension A) or Abel (Recension B) is seen as sitting in final judgment. Jesus evidently reckoned that Abraham, Isaac, and Jacob were not (no longer?) dead but 'living' (Mark 12.26-27 pars.).

---

180. *Jub.* 4.17-19, 21-24; *1 En.* 12.4; 15.1.

181. See above, §15.6a.

182. *4 Ezra* 6.26; 14.9, 50; *2 Bar.* 13.3; 43.2; 46.7; 48.30; 76.2; see Stone, *Fourth Ezra* 172.

183. *4 Ezra* 6.26; *2 Bar.* 76.2.

184. See, e.g., E. Bickermann, 'Das leere Grab' (1924), in P. Hoffmann, ed., *Zur neutestamentlichen Überlieferung von der Auferstehung Jesu* (Darmstadt: Wissenschaftliche Buchgesellschaft, 1988) 271-84; Fuller, *Formation* 57; others in my *Jesus and the Spirit* 391 n. 113. Schillebeeckx sees the motif particularly in Luke's reuse of the Markan narrative (*Jesus* 340-44). See also Strecker, *Theology* 272-73.

185. Possibly implied already in 1 John 5.6-8, and probably in *Gos. Pet.* 5.19.

186. The difference in conceptualization between rapture and exaltation is not great.

187. Some textual witnesses add 'a sort of waking vision' *(hypar ti)*.

188. See also Müller, *Entstehung* 62-63.

This latter would have been the most obvious category for those who saw Jesus 'alive from the dead' to use as they attempted to articulate or make sense of (it amounts to the same thing) what they saw. The precedents were there. And indeed we do find various expressions of Christian belief to the effect that God vindicated or exalted Jesus directly from death.[189] But more typically the thought of exaltation is combined with (rather than understood as an alternative to) the predominant category of resurrection.[190] To be sure, it can be argued that the memory of Jesus himself predicting vindication for 'the Son of Man' in terms of resurrection (§17.6b) could have been stimulus enough to the disciples to see visions of the vindicated Jesus as resurrected Son of Man.[191] But the thesis stumbles on the absence of any reference to Jesus as the Son of Man in the accounts of resurrection appearances.[192]

(3) *Resurrection.* I have already indicated the character of resurrection hope in the Judaism of Jesus' day.[193] Also that the predominant expression of that hope was in terms of the general or final resurrection, prior to the final judgment. That might seem to rule out the category as relevant to understanding what had happened to Jesus.[194] In contrast, however, it seems to have been just this category, with its 'final' connotations, which provided the earliest articulation of resurrection faith.[195] Consider the following indications.

189. Acts 5.30-31; Phil. 2.8-9; in John's Gospel the 'lifting up' seems to be a single upward sweep through cross to heaven, as it were (John 12.32, 34); in Hebrews Jesus' death as (high) priest symbolizes him taking the blood of sacrifice (his own blood) into the heavenly sanctuary.

190. See, e.g., John 20.17-18; Acts 2.29-33; Rom. 10.9 (the resurrection made Jesus 'Lord'); 1 Cor. 15.20-28 (allusion to Ps. 110.1 [1 Cor. 15.25] set in the context of teaching on the resurrection); Heb. 13.20; 1 Pet. 3.21-22.

191. R. Pesch, 'Zur Entstehung des Glaubens an die Auferstehung Jesu. Ein neuer Versuch' (1983), in Hoffmann, ed., *Überlieferung* 228-55 (here 243-44).

192. Pesch ('Entstehung' 247-50) is able to point only to the visions of Stephen (Acts 7.55-56) and of John the seer (Rev. 1.13-16; 14.14), neither of which is usually reckoned a 'resurrection appearance', and the *Gos. Heb.* 7 account of the appearance to James, cited above (n. 171).

193. See above, §§17.6b and 18.2b.

194. As Wedderburn observes, the idea of an individual resurrection did not emerge so much from the disparate texts, which only with hindsight were seen so to speak, as from what was believed to have happened to Jesus (*Beyond Resurrection* 41). Müller reckons that 2 Maccabees 7 looked for an immediate resurrection (*Entstehung* 30-35; rightly questioned by Wedderburn 41-42), but then argues that this would not have provided a way of conceptualizing their visionary experiences for the first disciples; the decisive 'impulse' must have owed more to Jesus' own preaching of God's kingly rule (24-35) and personal expectation (Luke 12.49-50; 13.31-32; Mark 14.25) (36-46), which pointed to *eschatological* resurrection (55-60, 67-71).

195. 'That the completely alien reality experienced in these appearances could be understood as an encounter with one who had been raised from the dead can only be explained from

(i) One of the early confessional formulae which Paul echoes is Rom. 1.3-4: the gospel (not just Paul's gospel) concerns God's Son, 'who . . . was appointed Son of God in power . . . as from the resurrection of the dead'. The last phrase is striking. We would have expected 'the resurrection from the dead' *(anastasis ek nekrōn).*[196] Instead we have 'the resurrection of the dead' *(anastasis nekrōn),* the phrase used when it is the final resurrection which is in view.[197] The point is confirmed by the fact that elsewhere Paul is recalled as treating the Christian claims for Jesus' resurrection as a test case for the Pharisaic belief in the (final) resurrection.[198] The point is that Paul and those who articulated and used the formula regarded the resurrection of Jesus as of a piece with the final resurrection.[199]

(ii) Paul also uses the imagery of 'firstfruits *(aparchē)*' to describe the significance of Christ's resurrection (1 Cor. 15.20, 23). The imagery is of resurrection as a harvest of the dead; Paul returns to the agricultural metaphor in 15.37-38, 42-44 — resurrection as the emergence to new (different) life of the seed which has 'died' in the ground (15.36). But the *aparchē* is actually part of the harvest itself, the first sheaf of corn to be reaped and set aside to be offered up to God. There is no time-gap between the first sheaf and the rest of the harvest; the *aparchē* is the beginning of the whole harvest.[200] Such a metaphor could have been coined only if Jesus' resurrection had been regarded as the beginning of the final resurrection. In which case, it is equally unlikely that the metaphor was coined by Paul himself or coined some twenty years after the event. Its origin must surely go back to the earliest days, and it can have been coined only by those who did indeed regard Jesus' resurrection as the beginning of the (general) resurrection of (all) humankind (1 Cor. 15.21).

(iii) This line of thought probably illumines the otherwise completely puzzling report in Matt. 27.52-53 that Jesus' resurrection coincided with the resurrection of many of the saints (buried outside Jerusalem). To be more precise: the earthquake at the time of Jesus' death opened the tombs of the dead, many were

---

the presupposition of a particular form of the apocalyptic expectation of the resurrection of the dead'; 'Only as the beginning of the end . . . could Jesus' resurrection be understood as the confirmation of his pre-Easter claim to authority' (Pannenberg, *Jesus* 93, 106). Cf. Crossan and Reed, *Excavating Jesus* 258-62.

196. As in Luke 20.35; Acts 4.2; 1 Pet. 1.3.

197. Matt. 22.31; 1 Cor. 15.12-13, 42; Heb. 6.2. On Heb. 11.35 see above, chapter 17 n. 274.

198. Acts 23.6; 24.21. Similarly Acts 17.31; was part of the disbelief in 17.32 occasioned by the suggestion that the resurrection preparatory to judgment (17.31) had already happened?

199. See, e.g., Allison, *End of the Ages* 67-68; Dunn, *Romans* 15-16.

200. Further detail in my *Romans* 473-74.

raised, and after Jesus' resurrection 'they came out from the tombs, went into the holy city and appeared to many'.[201] The legend appears to be very old and whatever is to be made of it, it probably reflects the same very early perception of Jesus' resurrection as the start of the final resurrection.[202]

So our question returns with added force: why was the first articulation of post-Easter faith in just these terms — 'resurrection', the beginning of the resurrection of the dead? But the question itself still needs further clarification.

b. Does the Conceptualization of the Resurrection Body Bring Any Clarification?

In an earlier treatment, I suggested that a somewhat complex development in early Christian conceptualization of Jesus' resurrection is discernible. The basic line of the analysis still seems sound.[203]

(1) The initial conceptualization of 'resurrection' was most likely in quite physical terms — not so much a resuscitation (to a life later to be ended in death) as a raising (restoration?) to a life just like the present (that is, physical) life but now beyond the reach of death. That is what we would expect from what we know of resurrection hope in Herodian Palestine. It is suggested also by the conceptualization expressed in terms of 'coming out from the tomb'.[204] The empty tomb could have stimulated the thought of resurrection in these terms, but it may have been only a confirmation of the presuppositions built into the term itself.

(2) Paul's conceptualization of the resurrection body is clearly more 'spiritual' (his own term). As already noted, he envisages resurrection to/in a 'spiritual body *(pneumatikon sōma)*' which he explicitly contrasts with the 'soulish body *(psychikon sōma)*' of present, earthly existence (1 Cor. 15.44-50).[205] Moreover, if

201. Why the time gap between the rising and the coming out? Perhaps we should see a reflection of an immediate sense that Jesus' death and resurrection constituted a single event.

202. Jeremias, *Proclamation* 309-10; Allison, *End of the Ages* 40-46. Otherwise R. L. Troxel, 'Matt. 27.51-4 Reconsidered: Its Role in the Passion Narrative, Meaning and Origin', *NTS* 48 (2002) 18-29.

203. *Jesus and the Spirit* 116-17, 120-22; in contrast to the more typical view of a one-way development maintained, e.g., by Carnley: the initial belief was of resurrection 'in a less material way' = 'spiritual body' (*Structure* 58), and Wedderburn: a 'movement from the intangible to the tangible and thus to the demonstrable is likelier' (*Beyond Resurrection* 70-75), though neither takes sufficient account of all the key factors discussed in §18.2. Craig's critique of my earlier formulation (*Assessing* 326-27 n. 17) plays down the indications that Luke conceptualized spiritual experiences in very tangible terms (see above n. 99).

204. Matt. 27.52-53; John 5.28-29; cf. the use of Ps. 16.10 in Acts 2.26-27, 31 and 13.35-37 (Dunn, *Jesus and the Spirit* 118-20).

205. It should be recalled that Paul sees Jesus' resurrection as the pattern for the resur-

Paul believed that he had seen the resurrected body of Jesus on the Damascus road, then what he saw was more like a 'light body', something rather closer to the Hellenistic conception of a less substantial, more refined kind of post-mortem existence.[206] That was a conceptualization, presumably, easier to 'sell' in a Hellenistic milieu like Corinth. What is of interest here, however, is that Paul did not abandon either the idea of continued/re-created bodily existence, or the language of 'resurrection'. The reason, we may infer, was partly that his own thought was more constitutively Hebraic than Greek,[207] but also partly at least because the Christian faith in which he had been first instructed had already stamped the category of 'resurrection' firmly and indelibly on that faith. He gives ground to his Hellenized interlocutors (*spiritual* body) but remains true to his Jewish heritage (spiritual *body*).[208] Here again we are pointed to a conceptualization which was integral to the post-Easter faith from the first — which indeed *was* the post-Easter faith.

(3) It may well be that we should detect in Luke's strong emphasis on the physicality of Jesus' resurrected body (Luke 24.39) a reaction against what might have been regarded as Paul's dilution of the resurrection faith. The reaction is even stronger in Ignatius, *Smyrn.* 3.1,[209] where Paul's subtle distinction between 'body' and 'flesh' has already been lost to sight. Conceivably John's discourage-

---

rection of believers (1 Cor. 15.20, 23, 44-49); that is, his concept of resurrection body includes that of Jesus. On Paul's concept of 'body' and of the contrast here see my *Theology of Paul* 60-61, with further bibliography. *Pace* Grass, it is unlikely that Paul would have accepted the reformulation of his view in terms of a 'personal identity between the earthly and the eschatological I, not necessarily a continuity between earthly and heavenly body' (*Ostergeschehen* 185); for Paul 'identity' was never other than bodily identity.

206. D. B. Martin, *The Corinthian Body* (New Haven: Yale University, 1995) rightly points out that Paul's distinction would not have been understood as a distinction between material and non-material (123-29); even so, *pace* Craig *(Assessing passim),* a highly refined substance ('material') is not the same as the 'physical' body unavoidably destined for decay and death (1 Cor. 15.48; 2 Cor. 5.1).

207. I do not mean to evoke here the old outmoded antithesis between Hebraic and Greek thought. It is simply that Hebraic and Greek anthropologies were different in regard to the relation of soul/mind/spirit and body/flesh. See further my *Theology of Paul* chapter 3, where I argue that Paul introduces a key distinction between *sōma* and *sarx* (70-73): Paul does not speak of resurrection as spiritual(ized) *flesh* (on the contrary an antithesis between spirit and flesh is fundamental to his theology: 65-66, 477-82, 496-97), but only of spiritual *body.*

208. It is thanks to Paul that we can gain a clearer conception of the 'body', not as something distinct from the person, something within which the real person exists, but as the person embodied, whether in a three-dimensional context (physical body) or spiritual context (spiritual body). See further again my *Theology of Paul* chapter 3.

209. 'For I know and believe that he was in the flesh even after the resurrection' (*Smyrn.* 3.1), going on to cite Luke 24.39 and Acts 10.41 (3.2-3). See also Wedderburn, *Beyond Resurrection* 117-21.

ment of dependence on physical contact (John 20.17, 28-29) was an attempt at some sort of compromise (cf. 6.62). In any case, both Luke and John simply reinforce the earlier Christian conviction that post-Easter faith could be no other than resurrection faith, belief that Jesus had been raised bodily from the tomb.

If then the talk of 'core' belief is appropriate, the core belief of the first Christians was of Jesus' *bodily resurrection*. The different conceptualizations of the resurrection body were not a modification of that belief. The belief was accompanied or supplemented by equally firmly held beliefs in Jesus' vindication or exaltation. But resurrection, resurrection of the embodied person Jesus, was the heart of Easter faith and remained so.

c. What Kind of 'Seeing'?

If 'resurrection' and 'resurrection body' are problematic for conceptualization, no less is the character of the 'seeing' of the resurrected Jesus.[210]

(1) In the case of the sightings where the physicality of Jesus' presence is either assumed or stressed, the implication is of a normal seeing, as one would see a companion on the road or in the same room. Yet, at the same time, we have noted the persistent theme that Jesus was not at first recognized, and that 'some doubted' (above §18.4b). There is also the reported phenomenon of a Jesus who appeared (should we say 'materialized'?) in a locked room (John 20.19, 26) and disappeared ('dematerialized'?) just as abruptly (Luke 24.31). Are these simply story variations and embellishments? That is quite possible; they do not seem to belong to the core tradition. But do they (also) signal a recognition/assumption/instinct that Jesus' presence was not simply that of normal physical existence?

(2) The very early formulation, 'he appeared *(ōphthē)*', indicates by its passive form the assumption/impression that there was something to be seen.[211] They did not, as it were, create what they saw by their act of seeing. What they

---

210. My earlier discussion focused largely on this question — *Jesus and the Spirit* 104-109, 123-28.

211. The passive is used in an active sense 'become visible, appear' (BDAG, *horaō* 1d). *Pace* the famous attempt by W. Michaelis, *'horaō', TDNT* 5.355-61, to argue that *ōphthē* indicated 'revelation', a 'perception' of 'non-visionary reality', see again my *Jesus and the Spirit* 104-109; Carnley, *Structure* 208-11, 223-30. If Alsup is justified in talking of an 'appearance story Gattung', then it is important to note that the precedents (Genesis 18, Exodus 3, Judges 6 and 13, 1 Samuel 3, Tobit 5 and 12, and *T. Abr.*) involve a visual seeing, not a mental perception (*Post-Resurrection Appearance Stories* 239-63); similarly Schrage, *1 Korinther* 4.43-48. Lüdemann rightly objects that the language cannot be taken merely as a legitimation formula (*pace* U. Wilckens, above n. 152); that Paul had in mind an experience of 'seeing' is an inescapable conclusion (*Resurrection* 50-53).

saw was given them to see.[212] This is the basis of Hans Grass's often cited attempt to distinguish an 'objective vision' from a subjective vision.[213]

(3) The appearance to Paul sharpens these very issues. For his seeing is of a 'light body' in heaven (above n. 138) rather than of a companion on earth. The performance variations in Acts leave it unclear what if anything those with Paul on the road to Damascus saw or heard (Acts 9.7; 22.9). Luke does not hesitate to have Paul himself describing it as a 'heavenly vision' (Acts 26.19). And for his own part Paul describes it as God's revelation of his Son 'in me *(en emoi)*' (Gal. 1.16).[214] At the same time, however, it should be noted that Paul was no stranger to visionary experiences, including heavenly journeys (2 Cor. 12.1-7). Yet he was quite clear that the resurrection appearance to himself was of a different order from such experiences: it was the same 'seeing' as characterized the earlier resurrection appearances *(ōphthē);* and it was 'last of all', not to be confused with any subsequent 'visions and revelations'.[215] So it is hardly likely that Paul would have accepted that his seeing was a purely 'subjective vision'.

Given the core emphasis on 'seeing Jesus' we can hardly conclude other than that that is what they 'saw'. A more refined psychological analysis has no

212. I echo the formulation of Wilckens, 'Tradition-History' 67 ('the person who receives the appearance is passive, he experiences the appearance. In this sense, such an experience means something which is given to the seer to see'); but the attentive reader will also recognize an echo of the postmodern debate about meaning (§§5.6 and 6.4 above). See further A. C. Thiselton, *1 Corinthians* (NIGTC; Grand Rapids: Eerdmans, 2000) 1197-1203.

213. Grass, *Ostergeschehen* 189, 233-49, especially 247-49; he makes a point of noting that 'in distinction from the subjective vision hypothesis, it [the objective vision hypothesis] is a theological and not a historical hypothesis' (248). The argument which rooted belief in Jesus' resurrection in 'purely subjective' visions was classically expressed by Strauss, *Life of Jesus* 728-44, particularly 742-44. For the influence of the 'subjective vision' hypothesis see P. Hoffmann, 'Die historisch-kritische Osterdiskussion von H.S. Reimarus bis zu Beginn des 20. Jahrhunderts', in Hoffmann, ed., *Überlieferung* 15-67; and for a brief review see Lüdemann, *Resurrection* 54-59; others who follow the 'subjective vision' hypothesis in Carnley, *Structure* 69 n. 81, 152-53. Pannenberg takes care to point out that in his use also the term 'vision' 'can only express something about the subjective mode of experience, not something about the reality of an event experienced in this form' (*Jesus* 95); similarly Carnley, *Structure* 245-46.

214. However, Marxsen plays down the element of sight indicated in 1 Cor. 9.1 in order to interpret Paul's 'vision' as (only) 'revelation' (*Resurrection* 98-111).

215. Cf. Grass, *Ostergeschehen* 226-32; Pannenberg, *Jesus* 93-95; D. Kendall and G. O'Collins, 'The Uniqueness of the Easter Appearances', *CBQ* 54 (1992) 287-307; Schrage, *1 Korinther* 4.49. It should be recalled that Paul was writing these words some twenty years later; no other 'appearances' had evidently taken place in the interval. On the possibility of confusion between experiences of Jesus and experiences of the Spirit (cf. particularly Carnley, *Structure*) see further my *Jesus and the Spirit* 100-103; Wedderburn, *Beyond Resurrection* 77-85.

real basis in the data examined and would simply shift the discussion into quite a different context where other subject axioms and presuppositions are operative (and disputed).[216] All that can be said here is that the description of the 'seeing' was not unreflective but included an element of critical discernment.

d. Again, Why Resurrection?

So, once again, why 'resurrection'? It remains a question which we cannot answer with great confidence. But presumably there was something in what the first witnesses saw which they could bring to expression only with this term 'resurrection'. There seems to have been something about these Easter experiences which impacted in a determinative and decisive way in the affirmation, 'God has raised Jesus from the dead!'

(1) The most obvious alternative is in terms of hallucination, the projection of wishful thinking, the reaction of disappointed hope.[217] But does that provide a satisfactory answer to the question Why 'resurrection'?[218] There were precedents for visions of a dead hero, now seen as exalted to heaven. A vision which was the product of current ideas regarding exalted martyrs would more likely have seen Jesus clothed in heavenly majesty. We have such a vision in Rev. 1.12-16. But in all (most of) the early resurrection appearances Jesus seems to be still very earthbound. A self-projected vision would presumably be clothed in the imagery most closely to hand. That would include preeminently the imagery of Dan. 7.13-14, especially if it had been evoked by Jesus himself.[219] We would then anticipate visions of Jesus in apocalyptic garb, clothed in dazzling white, and/or riding on the clouds of heaven.[220]

But that is not what we find. On the contrary, it is the *unexpectedness* of the

216. Arguments based on the fear and despair of the disciples following Jesus' crucifixion, as portrayed in the Gospels, can be used in support of diverse and divergent psychological theories. On psychological explanations for Peter's seeing and reconstructions of Paul's mental state prior to his Damascus road vision (including Lüdemann, *Resurrection* 82-84, 97-100; Goulder, 'Did Jesus of Nazareth Rise from the Dead?' 58-63) see Wedderburn, *Beyond Resurrection* 75-77, 269 n. 205, and below, vol. 2. Contrast Pannenberg: 'The Easter appearances are not to be explained from the Easter faith of the disciples; rather, conversely, the Easter faith of the disciples is to be explained from the appearances' (*Jesus* 96).

217. See above, n. 213. J. J. Pilch, 'Appearances of the Risen Jesus in Cultural Context: Experiences of Alternate Reality', *BTB* 28 (1998) 52-60, suggests a further case of altered states of consciousness or experiences of alternate reality as an appropriate means of interpreting the biblical accounts (see also above, chapter 11 n. 171 and chapter 15 nn. 243, 338).

218. Catchpole, *Resurrection People* 208-10.

219. See above, §§16.4c and 17.4c.

220. P. Hoffmann, 'Auferstehung Jesu Christi', *TRE* 4.478-513 (here 496-97).

interpretation put upon the resurrection appearances which is so striking, compared with what was currently being envisaged in regard to exalted saints and martyred heroes of the past. Appearances of Jesus which impacted on the witnesses as *resurrection* appearances did not conform to any known or current paradigm.[221] Instead, they created their own.

(2) It also should be observed that 'resurrection' is indeed core belief from the beginning. The 'resurrection of Jesus' is itself the *beginning* of belief in Jesus as exalted, and not simply an elaboration of some other affirmation or prior belief. My own focus remains, as throughout, on the impact on the disciples and eschews any attempt to get behind that belief to some objectively conceived event. But it remains the case that 'the resurrection of Jesus', the articulation in a formulation in these terms, *is* the impact. It was by means of this language that they 'grasped' what had happened to Jesus, not just conceptualized their experience at some remove; rather we would better say that this was how they conceptually experienced what they experienced.[222]

This has to be said in face of the temptation to treat 'the resurrection of Jesus' as a secondary expression of some other impact, that is, as the way of giving eschatological significance to what actually made the difference to the first Christians. In recent decades the clearest exposition along these lines has been by Willi Marxsen. He argues that 'the resurrection of Jesus' was simply a way of saying that the significance of Jesus' teaching or mission could never die: 'the purpose of Jesus is continued . . . Jesus' *kerygma* continues to be preached';[223] 'the cause of Jesus lives on beyond Good Friday'.[224] The basic problem here is

---

221. Cf. my *Jesus and the Spirit* 132; Craig, *Assessing* 410-18; Barclay, 'Resurrection' 25-26.

222. Cf. Alsup's conclusion that it was 'the OT anthropomorphic theophany stories' which gave the Gospel appearance stories their form of expression (*Post-Resurrection Appearance Stories* 265).

223. W. Marxsen, 'The Resurrection of Jesus as a Historical and Theological Problem', in C. F. D. Moule, ed., *The Significance of the Message of the Resurrection for Faith in Jesus Christ* (London: SCM, 1968) 15-50 (here 38). Rowland gives hostages to this line of argument when he distinguishes 'appearances of Jesus alive to the disciples' from the conclusion reached subsequently, after reflection, 'that the resurrection of the dead must have occurred in the case of Jesus' (*Christian Origins* 190).

224. Marxsen, *Resurrection* 78; 'faith after Easter (faith in the risen Jesus) was no different in substance from the faith to which Jesus had already called men before Easter' (125-26); similarly Lüdemann, *Resurrection* 182-83 (falling back on quotations from Herrmann); despite earlier critique of such arguments (*Beyond Resurrection* 92-95), Wedderburn's own 'solution' is ultimately along the same lines (153-69); his view is similar to Geering's (*Resurrection* 213-33). The view, which could be characterized as belief in Jesus *past*, should be distinguished from Bultmann's belief in Christ *present*: 'To believe in the Christ present in the kerygma is the meaning of the Easter faith' (the final sentence of 'The Primitive Christian

that the first Christian preaching was not simply a repreaching of Jesus' *message;* it was a proclamation of Jesus' *resurrection.* That there was a turn from Jesus' gospel to the gospel about Jesus, from Jesus as proclaimer to Jesus as proclaimed,[225] remains a fundamental perception of the difference between pre-Easter Jesus tradition and post-Easter kerygma.[226]

In thus responding to Marxsen I do not for a moment retract my methodological principle, that our only viable subject matter for historical investigation is the impact made by Jesus as it has impressed itself into the tradition. I hope in what I have already written I have not been misunderstood to mean that nothing can be said about what (the one who) made that impact. So here, it is the impact summarized in the word 'resurrection' which requires us to conclude that there was a something which happened 'on the third day' which could only be apprehended/conceptualized as 'resurrection'. The tradition itself leaves no room, no time for the sort of reflection (Marxsen) or deception (Reimarus) which their hypotheses require. Despite the inconsistencies and tensions which the diversity of traditions evidences only too clearly, it is in the end of the day the tradition itself which pushes us to the conclusion that it was something perceived as having happened to *Jesus* (resurrection evidenced in empty tomb and resurrection appearances) and not just something which happened to the *disciples* (Easter faith) which provides the more plausible explanation for the origin and core content of the tradition itself.

18.6. The Final Metaphor

In conclusion two clarifications are called for.

a. 'Resurrection' as Interpretation

To return to the starting point of this chapter: in what sense, if any, can we speak of the resurrection of Jesus as historical? In terms of the distinction made earlier be-

---

Kerygma and the Historical Jesus', in C. E. Braaten and R. A. Harrisville, eds., *The Historical Jesus and the Kerygmatic Christ* [Nashville: Abingdon, 1964] 15-42 [here 42]). Schillebeeckx attempts to discern an 'Easter experience' of conversion, 'of grace as forgiveness', which was independent of and prior to the appearances and traditions of the empty tomb (*Jesus* 379-97). Carnley attempts a both-and: resurrection faith is based not only on 'a *memory* of the Jesus of the past', but also on 'a *knowledge* of the present Christ-Spirit' (*Structure* 298); see also his critique of Schillebeeckx (199-222).

225. I echo, of course, two of the classic slogans from the quest, from the Liberal quest (§4.3) and from Bultmann (§5.4).

226. 'The resurrected Jesus is not simply Jesus resumed, as if his death/resurrection had been a mere interruption' (Keck, *Who Is Jesus?* 110).

tween event, data, and facts (§6.3b), the resurrection certainly cannot be numbered among the data which have come down to us. Nor can we speak of empty tomb and resurrection appearances as data. The data are *reports* of empty tomb and of seeings/visions of Jesus. If historical facts are *interpretations* of the data, then the historical facts in this case, properly speaking, are at best the fact of the empty tomb, and the fact that disciples saw Jesus. The conclusion, 'Jesus has been raised from the dead', is further interpretation, an interpretation of interpreted data, an interpretation of the facts. The resurrection of Jesus, in other words, is at best a second order 'fact', not a first order 'fact' — an interpretation of an interpretation.[227]

To put the same point in a slightly different way: part of the data is the interpretation of the first disciples that 'God has raised Jesus from the dead'. The data include the interpretation made by the disciples. For the twenty-first-century quester, the conclusion that 'God has raised Jesus from the dead', as a conclusion of the quest, is a further act of interpretation — again an interpretation (evaluation) of the first-century interpretation. When we add the initial observation — that departure from this life (death) can indeed be described as a historical event, whereas entry on to some further existence can hardly be so described — it can be seen just how problematic it is to speak of the resurrection of Jesus as historical.[228]

A further aspect is that, as again we observed in §6.3c, the historical method inevitably works with some application of the principle of analogy. The resurrection of Jesus as 'understood' in the beginning, however, broke through the analogies given in the term itself — the analogy of waking or rising up from sleep, the analogy of resuscitation, that is, of reversal of death. Even as already used for the final resurrection, the claim that Jesus had been raised from the dead soon became a claim to something different. The resurrection of Jesus, in other words, did not permit itself to be explained in terms of current or previous analogies. On the contrary, the interpretation that God had raised Jesus from the dead became itself paradigmatic, that which defines rather than that which is defined.

---

227. Cf. Marxsen's repeated emphasis in 'Resurrection of Jesus', that 'the resurrection of Jesus' is an 'interpretation'. I leave unresolved the issue whether the interpretation 'resurrection' would have emerged without the discovery that Jesus' tomb was empty, as the considerations marshalled above (§18.2) would seem to suggest (cf. my *Jesus and the Spirit* 119-20). But the possibility cannot be ruled out that the initial 'seeings' were of a sufficiently earthy (tangible?) type (§18.5c) as to evoke the same interpretation. Craig, however, in talking of 'the historicity or historical fact or event of the resurrection' does not give enough weight to the interpretative jump involved *(Assessing passim)*.

228. Cf. Pannenberg's convoluted attempt to state in what sense the resurrection of Jesus can be designated as 'a historical event': it can be so designated in that 'the emergence of primitive Christianity, . . . traced back by Paul to appearances of the resurrected Jesus, can be understood . . . only . . . in the light of the eschatological hope for a resurrection from the dead' *(Jesus* 98).

In interpreting what they saw as 'the resurrection of Jesus', the first disciples were affirming that what had happened to Jesus afforded an insight into reality which was determinative for how reality itself should be seen. As interpretation, the resurrection of Jesus constituted a perspective on reality which determined how reality itself was conceived. As weak parallels I might cite $e = mc^2$ or the American Declaration of Independence, each of them a window through which physical reality itself and society itself are perceived. The most obvious strong parallel is creation. As belief that the cosmos is created determines how one perceives the cosmos and the place of the human species within it, so belief in the resurrection of Jesus determines how one perceives the significance of Jesus and the function of life and death.

In short, resurrection of Jesus is not so much a historical fact as a foundational fact or meta-fact,[229] the interpretative insight into reality which enables discernment of the relative importance and unimportance of all other facts.

b. 'Resurrection' as Metaphor

As Pannenberg also recognized, we can hardly avoid drawing on the category of 'metaphor' to characterize the concept 'resurrection'.[230] As noted above (§12.3c), the power of metaphor is the power 'to redescribe a reality inaccessible to direct description' (Ricoeur), 'reality depicting without pretending to be directly descriptive' (Martin Soskice). This point has been missed by those who want to see 'the resurrection of Jesus' as a way of saying something else, which could actually be said more easily and with less intellectual embarrassment than that 'God raised Jesus from the dead'. For to say that 'the resurrection of Jesus' is a metaphor is to recognize that the phrase is saying something *which could not otherwise be said.* In consequence, to translate 'resurrection' into something more 'literal' is not to translate it but to abandon it. To interpret the first Easter faith into the affirmation that Jesus' significance or message has long outlasted his life (Marxsen) is not to interpret the metaphor but to empty it. To reduce it to an accident of language[231] or to the mythical expression of deep human experience[232] is to lose the *extra nos* preserved by metaphorical reference. To re-

---

229. Cf. Fuller, *Formation* 22-24.

230. *Jesus* 74; cf. Theissen and Merz, *Historical Jesus* 508. Chester observes that 'the usage of resurrection terminology from an early stage in the Old Testament is strongly *metaphorical* in orientation, and serves especially as a symbol of *national* resurrection' ('Resurrection and Transformation' 77).

231. Geering prefers the inadequate alternative 'idiom' (alluding here to *Resurrection* 217).

232. N. Perrin, *The Resurrection Narratives: A New Approach* (London: SCM, 1977)

move any idea of personal survival from the concept 'resurrection'[233] is not to make the metaphor more meaningful but to destroy it. Reality grasped in and as metaphor is no less reality even if it cannot be expressed in other terms.

Christians have continued to affirm the resurrection of Jesus, as I do, not because they know what it means. Rather, they do so because, like the affirmation of Jesus as God's Son, 'the resurrection of Jesus' has proved the most satisfactory and enduring of a variety of options, all of them inadequate in one degree or other as human speech, to sum up the impact made by Jesus, the Christian perception of his significance. They do so because as a metaphor, 'resurrection' is perceived as referring to something otherwise inexpressible, as expressing the otherwise inchoate insight that this life, including Jesus' life, is not a complete story in itself but can be grasped only as part of a larger story in which God is the principal actor and in which Jesus is somehow still involved. In short, 'the resurrection of Jesus' is not so much a criterion of faith as a paradigm for hope.

---

suggests that Matthew and Luke have differently interpreted the 'primordial myth' of Mark's resurrection narratives into a 'foundation myth' of Christian origins — 'myth' being understood as 'the narrative expression of the deepest realities of human experience' (12).

233. Wedderburn, *Beyond Resurrection* 147-52.

CHAPTER 19

Jesus Remembered

19.1. A New Perspective on the Jesus Tradition

In the opening chapters I reviewed the 'quest of the historical Jesus' as an ongoing dialogue between 'faith' and 'history'. I pointed out that the roots of this quest, and in effect the opening exchanges of the contemporary dialogue, can be traced back to the emergence of 'a sense of history' in the Renaissance. The developments and fruits of *historical philology* and *textual criticism* from that time began the provision of a resource and base which is still fundamental to all scholarly work on the New Testament and life of Jesus research. The emergence of the model of scientific inquiry brought a rigorous methodology to historical study and raised many hopes regarding the objectivity of historical 'facts' which have in hindsight proved elusive, not to say illusory. But there is an equal danger of a postmodern over-reaction to the older historicist over-confidence. A model for historical study along the lines of *'critical realism',* which recognizes the dialogic nature of inquiry into that which may be known concerning persons and events of the past, seems to provide the most promising way forward.

The study of the past as a hermeneutical problem also highlighted a number of significant findings: the importance of recognizing a historical text as *historical* text; the importance of retaining an active concept of *'plain meaning'*, at least to the extent of endeavouring to listen to the text speak in its own language and idiom; the importance of respecting *the intention of the text* (entextualized), even when the questions being asked seek to draw other information from it or through it; and the importance, not least, of acknowledging and allowing for the nature of the hermeneutical process of *dialogue* between text and hearer/reader.

In addition, I argued that the source-critical findings of study of the Gospels in the second half of the nineteenth century (John as a much less direct historical source than the Synoptics, the two-source hypothesis for the Synoptics) still provide the best working hypothesis for an initial analysis of the Jesus tradition, however much they made need to be qualified, as to some extent I do wish to qualify them. On the other hand, the newer sources recently proposed and the attempts to stratify the hypothesized Q document are much overblown and draw firmer and more far-reaching conclusions than are justified by the data. Similarly, I have no doubt that any historical study of Jesus has to take seriously the character of the Judaism of the time and the social and political circumstances in which Jesus undertook his mission, as illuminated by archaeology. The use of sociological theory and generalisation, however, has always to be tempered by the realia of artefact and text.

All these, however, are in effect prolegomena to the main thrust of this book, which can be summed up in a number of bare propositions before being further elaborated below. (1) The only realistic objective for any 'quest of the historical Jesus' is Jesus *remembered*. (2) The Jesus tradition of the Gospels confirms *that* there was a concern within earliest Christianity to remember Jesus. (3) The Jesus tradition shows us *how* Jesus was remembered; its character strongly suggests again and again a tradition given its essential shape by regular use and reuse in oral mode. (4) This suggests in turn that that essential shape was given by the original and immediate *impact made by Jesus* as that was first put into words by and among those involved as eyewitnesses of what Jesus said and did. In that key sense, the Jesus tradition *is* Jesus remembered.

Let me restate this thesis in terms of the twofold new perspective on the Jesus tradition and its earliest transmission which the thesis embodies: (a) first regarding *the primary formative force* which gave the Jesus tradition its character, and (b) second, the character of oral tradition and of the *traditioning process* in the earliest disciple groups and churches. This has been united with (c) the methodological strategy of looking at the broad picture, focusing on *the characteristic motifs and emphases* of the Jesus tradition, rather than making findings overly dependent on individual items of the tradition.

a. *The primary formative force in shaping the Jesus tradition was the impact made by Jesus during his mission on his first disciples,* the impact which drew them into discipleship. (1) The initial formative impact was not Easter faith. The impulse to formulate tradition was not first effective in the post-Easter period. The tradition available to us, particularly in the Synoptic Gospels, has certainly been structured and regularly retold in the light of Easter faith. But again and again the characteristic motifs and emphases of the individual traditions show themselves to have been established without and therefore probably prior to any Easter influence. *The initiating impact was the impact of the pre-Easter call to faith.* (2) We can certainly hope to look behind that impact to *the one who made that impact.* But we cannot realistically expect to find a Jesus ('the historical Jesus') other than or different from the Jesus who made that impact. Any other 'historical Jesus' will, unavoidably and inevitably, be the consequence of inserting other factors and ideological concerns into the business of constructing 'the historical Jesus'. (3) The impact itself, in large part, *took the form of tradition.* For most of those who had been so decisively influenced by Jesus, who had found his challenge literally life-transforming, could not have failed to speak of that impact to others who shared the new appreciation of God's kingship and its consequences for their living in the here and now. That *impact-expressed-in-verbal-formulation* was itself the beginning of the Jesus tradition proper — as also of embryonic ritual, as the disciple groups met together to share that tradition, no doubt regularly in the context of the shared meals which had themselves been so characteristic of Jesus' mission.

b. The new perspective on the Jesus tradition as *oral* tradition dovetails into the new perspective on the initiating formative influence determining that tradition. It constitutes a deliberate attempt to break out from the centuries-old cultural conditioning of a literary, print-dominated mindset which has determined how the early transmission of the Jesus tradition has been conceived by NT scholarship generally. It does not deny literary interdependence between the Synoptic Gospels. But it questions whether the interrelations between the traditions utilized by the Synoptics are adequately conceptualized in exclusively literary and intertextual terms. It disputes a conceptualization of the Jesus tradition as in effect restricted within the bounds of two or four literary channels. It disputes even more fiercely any suggestion that any such channels were in effect independent of the others and exclusive to one or more churches. *It asks whether it is not more realistic in historical terms, in reference to groups/churches functioning initially in a highly oral society, to conceive of these groups/churches all having quite extensive repertoires of Jesus tradition, overlapping with that of other groups/churches and regularly shared by those (apostles, prophets and teachers) who moved among these groups/churches.* And it asks for a reconceptualization of the use made of Jesus tradition, including its transmission to new converts and other groups/churches, in terms of *oral performance* rather than of written editions.

The strength of this new perspective lies in *the conjunction of two factors.* One is *the character of oral tradition* as it has been illuminated by repeated studies of community tradition (quite different from personal reminiscence) as a combination of stability and flexibility, of stories and teaching material being maintained in identity of subject matter and/or structure and core content, in and through the diversity of detail in sequential performances. The other is *the character of the Jesus/Synoptic tradition* as attesting the same type of traditioning process. Characteristically in the Synoptic tradition we see traditions which were all important in one degree or other to the identity of the communities which rehearsed them. In the *stabilities* and *diversities* of the tradition, still evident in its permanent form (textual variations apart — or included!), we can trace the *conti-*

nuities and *variations* in the performances/retellings of the tradition. *In the stabilities we see the identity of the tradition; in the diversities its vitality.* The written Gospels are frozen (and extended) performances which commanded such assent, and such widening assent among the first churches, that they count as normative forms of the tradition. But initially, the Gospels were little different in character from the countless oral performances which had preceded them.

The two perspectives come together in the hypothesis that *the tradition's continuing identity was given in the first formation of the tradition and is to be seen as evidence of the impact made by the words or events thus recalled.*

c. I believe that the method followed in the above pages has confirmed the value of these perspectives. In the first place, the elements of the portrayal of the remembered Jesus have been drawn consistently from regular emphases and motifs in the Jesus tradition. A working rule of thumb has been that *a characteristic and relatively distinctive feature of the Jesus tradition is most likely to go back to the consistent and distinctive character of the impact made by Jesus himself.* In contrast, jarring and widespread features are unlikely to have been drawn into the tradition at a later stage precisely because they jarred and were thus unlikely to have received widespread acceptance among the communities that cherished the tradition.

In the second place, by regularly setting out the Jesus tradition synoptically I believe I have demonstrated the strength of the model of oral traditioning proposed. For again and again it has been clear that there is no consistency of interdependence between the parallel texts, some parts being closely parallel, others quite remote in vocabulary used. At the same time, again and again it has been clear that there is a stability of subject matter and of structure, and often of some core element (usually something said by Jesus), while the supporting details and particular applications demonstrate a considerable diversity. Such regularly recurring phenomena are not best explained by a uniform conception of *literary* dependency and redaction. They are best explained, in my view, in terms of *the oral character of the tradition and/or the oral mode of transmission* (even of read/heard written texts), where concern was for theme and core and where subsidiary details were treated as subject to the freedom of performance variation.

19.2. What Can We Say about Jesus' Aim(s)?

If the above methodological considerations are to the point, then, of course, the crucial question becomes What picture of Jesus emerges from this enquiry? What did the remembered Jesus look like? From the relatively clear outlines of the impact made by Jesus during his mission, as still sufficiently evident in the Jesus tradition, what can we say about the one who made the impact?

We started with *Jesus the Jew* — Jesus brought up to practise the religion of his forefathers and living out his mission within and as part of the diversity of Second Temple Judaism. *Nothing that has emerged from the above study of the Jesus tradition requires us to make substantial or serious modification of that starting assumption.* On the contrary, Jesus' engagement with the traditional priorities and concerns of Israel's prophets, the repeated indications of influence from Israel's Scriptures, and the frequent disputations regarding some of the issues which we know to have featured in the Jewish factionalism of the period all attest *a mission Jewish in character through and through.* Alternative suggestions of the principal resonating contexts for his mission, including that of a generalized Mediterranean peasant or a wandering Cynic philosopher, wholly fail to match in depth and extent the number and particularity of the distinctive resonances with and within first-century Palestinian Judaism. Given the range of first-century Judaism(s), and not yet looking to the subsequent partings of the ways between Christianity and Judaism, it is by no means clear that a description like 'marginal Jew' is appropriate for Jesus during his mission.

Circumstances of Jesus' *birth* and particularities of his upbringing are beyond historical reach. But it is clear that Jesus emerged from *the circle of John the Baptist* about the year 27. That Jesus was baptized by John is hard to dispute, and from early on that encounter with John was remembered by Jesus' disciples as marking out the point at which he was anointed by God for his mission. Whether Jesus is properly to be described as a disciple of the Baptist and how long he worked alongside (in partnership or competition with) John also remain obscure. So far as Jesus' own disciples were concerned, Jesus' distinctive mission began after John had been removed from the scene.

Again it is clear enough that the bulk of the Synoptic tradition is recalled as set within *Galilee.* This evidently involved a lot of travelling round Galilee's many villages, though to describe Jesus as permanently on the way with his (immediate) disciples (charismatic vagrancy) is much too exaggerated. Such geographical specificities as the Synoptic tradition retains are mainly grouped round the northern part of the lake and readily encompassable in one- or two-day journeys from a (principal) base in Capernaum. To what extent the much more extensive Jerusalem mission indicated in the Fourth Gospel is rooted in memory of periodic visits to Jerusalem (for pilgrim feasts) or of events during his final week there, or is elaborated from traditions not specific as to location is a question which likewise remains well short of a firm answer.

In trying to reach back through the memories of Jesus' mission to ascertain his aim, what motivated him, it remains true that we cannot avoid giving prime attention to his message of *the kingdom/kingship of God.* He certainly seems to have hoped for a *'coming'*, and a *soon* coming, of that royal rule. In the context of Jewish expectation, that must have been heard in terms of God visibly manifesting his authority in fuller and final fashion. The imminence of that coming constituted a *crisis* for Jesus' hearers. For God's rule would be characterized by eschatological reversal, the haughty humbled and the poor uplifted, the little ones made great, and the last given first place. And the kingdom's coming would be attended by great suffering, and followed by judgment, but also by rich reward (symbolized in the festive feast) for the penitent faithful.

To be more specific in deductions regarding the remembered Jesus at this point has proven impossible. The crisis of which Jesus spoke is not reducible to a social or political crisis. But the vision fleshed-out in his parables had clear social and political ramifications and consequences — this can hardly be denied. Nor is it any clearer whether Jesus envisaged a whole new order of human society (the end of time, resurrection, new creation) or used such language to express hope for a reconstituted society on earth. That it was hope in God, and for the future as God's — that is clear. But the 'what' of that hope remains in *metaphorically allusive language,* which still works to stir vision afresh and to evoke renewed hope but which can never be translated fully or adequately into descriptive prose without debilitating loss of content and power.

That the hope and evocative intention of Jesus' kingdom message were directed particularly to *Israel* is also clear. If Jesus' choice of twelve is any indication, then the hope and intention were in some sense for a restored Israel, for the scattered sheep to be gathered again under their true shepherd, or possibly for Israel to be reconstituted afresh as the assembly of Yahweh with a new focal point (Temple) for worship. But was it a hope for Israel to be liberated from an oppressive (Roman?) regime (to echo the language of Luke 24.21), or for the kingdom to be restored to Israel (to echo the question of Acts 1.6)? Was it a hope for the scattered of Israel (the two-thirds of Israel dispersed beyond Israel's borders) to be restored to the land (the end of exile), the meek to inherit (afresh) the land? Or was the call primarily a repetition of the call of prophets before him for the faithless of Israel to turn back to their God, to honour his name, and to live in accord with his priorities, all made possible, perhaps, by a (re)new(ed) covenant? The frustration at being unable to press finally for any one positive answer or to exclude finally any other positive answer is intense. But once again we should hesitate long and hard before insisting on either-or exegesis or that Jesus' kingdom message can be heard in only one way or as working on only one dimension.

The clearest fleshing out of Jesus' hope, the clearest indications of his aim at this point, is probably provided by the signals he is recalled as giving in regard to his own priorities: *his mission to bring good news for the poor and to call sinners.* Here the reconstituted Israel reaffirms what had always been Israel's constitutional priorities. From a kingdom perspective, a society in which the poor are uncared for is unacceptable to God: the self-indulgent rich and powerful stand in eternal peril of trusting in their riches, wheras the poor trusting in God have a far more secure future. So too, a religious community over-scrupulous in defining what is acceptable and unacceptable to God is more than likely by doing so to put *itself,* rather that those it condemns as sinners, beyond the reach of God's grace. Such an emphasis is not to be merely politicized into a vision for a reconstituted peasant or village society. It is rather a vision of society under God, where God's sovereign rule is at work, where his will is done; the political ramifications are inescapable but secondary. Nor can it be easily affirmed that Jesus' vision answered neatly to later concerns (mission to the Gentiles) or to modern concerns (liberation and feminist theology), though the tradition carries clear indications that Jesus valued women disciples highly and reacted sympathetically towards those Gentiles he encountered in the course of his mission. What can be said is that Jesus was recalled as encouraging and enacting a society which works to eliminate any unnecessary and hurtful boundaries between its members.

When attention is turned more directly to the other emphasis in Jesus' kingdom preaching, that God's (final) rule is already in evidence, the picture becomes still clearer. For Jesus is remembered as frequently pronouncing *the realisation of many long-term prophetic hopes:* the time fulfilled, the blessings of the age to come already being experienced. The Baptist's onesided emphasis on imminent and purgative judgment Jesus supplemented (not entirely replaced) with the complementary emphasis, drawn largely from the same prophet (Isaiah), of divine grace to the physically, socially, and religiously disabled. In the *liberation* he saw his exorcistic ministry bringing to demoniacs and in the *healing* (and forgiveness) he saw his ministry bringing (through the trust exercised) to those who were ill, he saw clear signs that God was exercising his rule already in the here and now. It was presumably such repeated experiences which confirmed for Jesus that his hope for the fuller (final) coming of God's kingdom could not be long delayed. God's royal rule had drawn near.

That Jesus' vision of the kingdom was not dependent on a specific time scale is strongly suggested by the fact he himself seems to have lived out his mission *in the light of the coming kingdom* and to have encouraged his disciples to do so. Kingdom priorities were not merely for the future, when in the fulness of God's purpose, no doubt, they would be fully realized. They were for the here and now; they provided the parameters for daily living: life to be lived as *subject* of a kingdom, loyalty to which superseded all other loyalties. Life lived as a *child* dependent on the goodness of God as Father, as a *learner* of Jesus, modelling his priorities, not least in service as the only true sign of success and of greatness. Life lived *in service of what is right,* by the spirit of the lawgiver rather than by the letter of the law, ever ready to read through the particular rule to discern the will of God where that rule was in danger of being too simplistically applied. Life lived out of *love of God* as the first priority, *love of neighbour* as second, and no further rule of thumb necessary where these two are lived out — even to the extent of recognizing that the neighbour in a particular instance may include the enemy. Life lived out of *forgiveness* — of error and failure humbly conceded, of forgiveness and acceptance readily offered and gladly received, a society bonded by acknowledgment of mutual need for forgiveness and experience of being forgiven, a society energised and empowered by the grace of forgiveness and gratitude for being forgiven. Such a community Jesus evidently saw as able to serve also as *a new family,* particularly for those disowned by their natural families. But the more dominant image Jesus used was that of *the open table,* not least as typifying the breaking down of boundaries between the religious and the nonreligious and as both imaging and to some extent already realising the hope of the great banquet of the coming kingdom.

Living out such a life-style marked out Jesus' circle of disciples from other groups of the time, differences which were bound to cause adverse comment. The contrast was greatest with the *Qumran* Essenes; but there are only a few hints that Jesus criticized Qumran's closed-in, purity-conscious community. The closer parallel, but also the greatest antipathy, is remembered in regard to *Pharisees'* criticism of Jesus' pattern of discipleship — particularly in regard to Jesus' failure to maintain separation from sinners and to observe the current halakhoth on Sabbath and purity. The antipathy may have spilled over into outright hostility on some occasions, but Luke also recalls friendly Pharisees, and Pharisaic involvement in Jesus' arrest and handing over to the secular power is not clearly attested.

However, someone who spoke frequently about the kingdom of God in ways critical of present social practices was bound to excite suspicion on the part of those who controlled and benefited from the status quo. We noted some hints that Jesus was alert to possible preemptive strikes by *Herod Antipas* during his Galilean mission. But those made most uneasy by Jesus' kingdom preaching and life-style seem to have been *the high priestly party* in their power base in Jerusalem. This becomes apparent only in the account of Jesus' last week in the Judean capital, but it is not hard to imagine that Jesus' casualness in regard to the prerogatives of the cult and the purity system focused on the Temple would have marked out Jesus as a troublemaker. Whether Jesus avoided Jerusalem prior to his final visit or visited it more frequently (as the Fourth Gospel indicates), the opposition to Jesus did not become deadly until that final week. In that final denouement it was evidently the perception that Jesus posed some sort of threat to the Temple, the cult, and/or those whose power base it was which proved the decisive reason or excuse for arresting Jesus and handing him over to Pilate for summary execution.

How did Jesus see his own role in all this? He was often hailed as *teacher* and responded positively to and in that role. His parables and aphorisms contained a critique of the current system of religious and social values and obviously made an enduring impression which still endures in the tradition. But in themselves they would probably not have been sufficient to trigger off Herodian or high priestly action against Jesus. *Prophet* was a category which Jesus seems to have fitted well, and found congenial to characterize much of his mission. He is clearly remembered as fully alive to the traditional fate of the prophet to be rejected, and his enemies were no doubt equally aware of that tradition! He was a famous *exorcist and healer* in his day, and many experienced miraculous happenings in his company. But he evidently resisted any temptation to take on the role of itinerant wonder-worker, and to call him 'magician' is as dismissive and denigratory now as it was then. It is also doubtful whether an accusation of sorcery played any part in the indictment eventually brought against him.

Of the more weighty terms used in relation to Jesus, it can hardly be doubted that he was executed as a claimant to the throne of David ('king of the Jews'). It is equally clear that the question whether he was the expected *royal Messiah* had become a crucial issue some time before his execution, not least among his disciples. Somewhat troublesomely for later Christian belief in Messiah/Christ Jesus, however, Jesus seems to have found no role model in the prevalent hope for a Davidic prince who would liberate the nation from Roman rule. He is remembered as forbidding talk of his role in such terms and as being unwilling to describe himself as such when the question was put to him formally at the end. His sense of what he was about, his own aim, was evidently not well served by the dominant imagery of the king of Israel, king of the Jews. If the title 'Messiah' subsequently proved indispensable in earliest Christian evaluation of Jesus, it is because his mission drew in other parts of Jewish expectation and gave the title new content, not because he fitted the hopes and expectations of the time.

The theme of *sonship* takes us much closer to the heart of Jesus' mission, though not, noticeably, in any conjunction, during his mission, with thought of the royal Messiah as God's son. Jesus' emphasis on God as a caring Father in his teaching is complemented by fairly clear indications of his own sense of intimate sonship. As he encouraged his disciples to live in trustful obedience before God as Father, so he encouraged them to echo his own habit of praying to God as *abba*. This does not tell us so much about Jesus' aim, but it certainly suggests the source of the inner strength by which he sustained that aim.

With one of his most characteristic and distinctive phrases, *'the son of man'*, we also hear resonances of self-understanding and possible implications for Jesus' understanding of what would be the outcome of his mission. For on the one hand, the idiomatic phrase bespeaks one not wishing to draw particular attention to himself ('someone', 'a man like me'), though conscious of his bound-up-ness with the frailty of the human condition. But on the other hand, if indeed Jesus also drew upon the particular use of the phrase in the vision of Daniel 7, then the very allusion suggests both the expectation of suffering, as Israel of old had suffered from its persecutors, and the anticipation of vindication following that suffering. The Jesus tradition certainly recalls Jesus as expressing such expectation and hope, and though open to the suspicion that precisely such a tradition reflects Christian interpretation of what they believed to have happened in the event, the tradition on this point is much more substantive than is often appreciated. That Jesus anticipated the likelihood of his being done away with, whether by underhand means or by formal execution, is highly probable. And that his message of God's kingly rule gave him equally firm hope that in that eventuality God would vindicate him, whether immediately or in the (imminent) final resurrection, is no less probable.

So, did Jesus see his calling as more than simply proclaiming the kingdom's coming and inculcating the kingdom life? Did he also intend somehow to 'bring in' the kingdom? Did he go to Jerusalem for what was his last (or first!) visit to challenge the leaders of Israel, a last do-or-die attempt to turn Israel back to its God? Did he see himself as lead-player in the final crisis which would result in God coming in his royal power to dispense judgment and blessing? Did he intend that his anticipated suffering and death would somehow serve to ensure that the penitent faithful would come through their final tribulation securely into the kingdom? To none of these questions can we give a firm Yes. But neither can we give a firm No. And it remains more likely than not that talk of rejection (the prophetic tradition), of the son of man suffering, and of a cup to be drunk and a baptism to be endured began in greater or less part with Jesus himself reflecting on his own destiny.

Of the hints still clearly recalled in the Jesus tradition, there are two which have captured most attention, both traditionally and in most recent discussion: the talk of the Temple's destruction and its rebuilding (in another form?) and the last supper's talk both of a (re)new(ed) covenant and of wine to be drunk new in the kingdom. Beyond that, firm data more or less cease, and we are left to speculate on the basis of such further reflection as the Evangelists provide. What we can say is that the open-endedness or ambiguity of the hopes or aims expressed in these utterances reached closure and achieved clarity in the earliest self-understanding of the first Christians and in the way they rooted what they went on to experience, understand, and practise in these utterances.

19.3. The Lasting Impact of Jesus' Mission

The lasting impact of Jesus' mission is most clear on two fronts: *Christianity* and the *Gospels*. However much or little we conclude it is possible to say about the mission and teaching and intention of Jesus, it is impossible reasonably to dispute that the movement which became known as Christianity has been the most direct and lasting effect of his work. The above study, however, makes it clearer that there was a very substantive *continuity* between Jesus' mission and what followed. Jesus' mission did not end in failure. What followed was not merely an attempt to counter disappointment, to eliminate cognitive dissonance. These assertions, of course, need to be further explored and properly tested in vol. 2. But already we begin to see the *future* in the way the story of Jesus *ends* — in *the resurrection of Jesus*.

Here again, whatever we may make of the facts (interpreted data), it is almost impossible reasonably to doubt that the sequel to Jesus' mission began with different members of his disciple group(s) seeing Jesus alive, seeing him as 'risen from the dead'. Not least, these experiences and the conviction which they embodied from their first articulation of them ('resurrection') must have signified God's confirmation of Jesus. Which is to say, the *hope* that Jesus was remembered as indicating in regard to his own future had been vindicated, as he himself had been vindicated; the son of man had indeed come on the clouds to the Ancient of Days and received his kingdom. Which is also to say that to that extent at least Jesus' hope and intention in regard to the kingdom of God had been realised. So too, we could go on to argue, the transmutation of the disciple band into 'the church of God' which soon attracted the ire of Saul the Pharisee (Gal. 1.13) was a recognizable realisation of Jesus' hope for a renewed Temple (supported on the 'pillar' apostles — Gal. 2.9), just as the Lord's Supper probably functioned more or less from the first as the continuation of Jesus' practice of table-fellowship and symbol of the new covenant inaugurated in his death. So too, it could be pointed out, the destruction of Jerusalem and its Temple, only forty years later, proved as accurate a fulfilment of Jesus' other forebodings as one could ask for. So there was *the continuity of fulfilment* between Jesus' aims and hopes and what in the event transpired.

Over all, of course, it was hardly a complete realisation of all that Jesus was remembered as forecasting and looking for: his resurrection was not the beginning of the harvest of resurrection of the dead; the mission soon to be undertaken to the Gentiles did not match very closely any expectation Jesus may have entertained regarding the eschatological pilgrimage to Zion of Gentile proselytes; the final judgment did not follow; the eschatological reversal which took place fell far short of the sort of hopes which Jesus' words must have engendered. But it was ever so with prophecy expressed in the images of human experience. And the measure of fulfilment and the continuity which that expressed were all that the first Christians needed to sustain their claim that God had vindicated Jesus' mission and was continuing that same mission in a new and different form through them.

The point is made all the stronger by the further indication of the lasting impact of Jesus' mission — *the Jesus tradition itself.* For, if I am right, the Jesus tradition was itself the very mode by which the impact made by Jesus on those he first called to discipleship was made communicable, a bond which united those who shared it, at the very core and formative of their corporate identity as 'Christ-ians', an occasion for celebration in their gatherings, an epitome of Jesus' mission and teaching, a means of instruction, apologetic, and evangelism in their interaction with others. There is no indication whatsoever that any of the Jesus tradition was experienced as in tension with the fuller appreciation of Jesus' significance which came with the revelation of his resurrection or with the gospel's focus on the cross (as in Paul). The Gospels themselves show no such signs of tension, with their story of a teaching and healing mission climaxing in death and resurrection. And the suggestions that various groupings of traditional material (Q^1, the tradition behind the *Gospel of Thomas*) would have been perceived as in tension with a gospel expressed only in terms of cross and resurrection actually have very little to commend them and depend to too great an extent on tendentious theses looking for evidence to support them. A fundamental fact of the Jesus tradition in its lasting form is that it was preserved precisely by those who preached Jesus' death and resurrection, *precisely as gospel.*

Not least of importance to be recognized at this point is the continuity of impression made regarding Jesus himself. For it is evident from the tradition that Jesus was heard as speaking from God, as a spokesman for God, for some at least as the eschatological representative of God. Nor does it appear that this conviction arose only with Easter hindsight. For it is enshrined in the Jesus tradition in not-yet-Christian terms and is expressed in terms which Easter faith broke through. As with the issue of Jesus' messianic status, it is hard to see how Easter faith could create such a weighty christological affirmation from the start, had the pre-Easter impact of Jesus not *already been measured in terms of divine authority and power.* The tradition indicates that Jesus' authority and role caused his disciples puzzlement and confusion. But the function of the Jesus tradition at this point is to retell these pre-Easter impressions, now clarified by the climax of the Jesus story and by the context of Easter faith in which the retelling took place within the communities of discipleship and faith. In short, it is not only the impression of Jesus' words and actions which is imprinted in the Jesus tradition, but also the impression of who Jesus *was.* And the unexpectedness of Jesus' 'resurrection' in the event only deepened the impact already made by Jesus in his pre-Easter mission.

We should simply add that the Jesus tradition's recollections of Jesus' teachings and manner of living and socializing evidently continued to serve the early Christian groupings as a *model* for any or all responsible living in community, as part of society. As Jesus himself lived in the light of the coming kingdom, so *the Jesus tradition continued to serve as a resource and inspiration for all car-*

ing and concerned living. Not as a blueprint for such a life, nor as an instruction manual for a complete social ethic or politically mature society. But as indicating the character of the deep personal relations and priorities, values, and motivations without which any social structure or political manifesto will fail to realise its best ambitions. The Jesus tradition heard responsively could and can still function as a test of the caring community, as a rebuke and challenge to any self-indulgent society arrogant in maintaining its own prerogatives and careless of the needs of others. But the same tradition shows that to hear Jesus speaking *only* in these terms is to diminish what Jesus himself stood for and to lose the key to the realisation of his vision of the kingdom. For, once again, we need to stress that Jesus is recalled as characteristically linking love of neighbour to love of God, the former presumably to large extent dependent on the latter. We need to stress that Jesus himself seems to have seen his expected death and hoped-for resurrection as of a piece with his kingdom preaching and living. And, again, we need to stress the retention of the Jesus tradition only within the Gospel format, and the wisdom of so retaining it. The lasting impact of Jesus in the Jesus tradition should not be fragmented but perceived afresh in its wholeness.

In short, *through the Jesus tradition the would-be disciple still hears and encounters Jesus* as he talked and debated, shared table-fellowship and healed. In hearing the Jesus tradition read from pulpit or stage, in sacred space or neighbour's sitting room, we sit with the earliest disciple and church groups as they shared memories of Jesus, nurtured their identity as his disciples, equipped themselves for witness and controversy, celebrated and learnt fresh lessons for life and worship from and in that celebration. Through that tradition it is still possible for anyone to encounter the Jesus from whom Christianity stems, the remembered Jesus.

Abbreviations

AB	Anchor Bible
ABD	*Anchor Bible Dictionary.* Ed. D. N. Freedman (New York: Doubleday; 6 vols. 1992)
AGAJU	Arbeiten zur Geschichte des antiken Judentums und des Urchristentums
Aland²⁶	*Novum Testamentum Graece.* Ed. K. Aland, et al. 26th edition (Stuttgart, 1979).
Aland²⁷	*Novum Testamentum Graece.* Ed. K. Aland, et al. 27th edition (Stuttgart, 1993).
An.Bib.	Analecta Biblica
ANRW	*Aufstieg und Niedergang der römischen Welt.* Ed. H. Temporini and W. Haase (Berlin, 1972-)
AOT	*The Apocryphal Old Testament.* Ed. H. F. D. Sparks (Oxford, 1984)
BA	*Biblical Archaeologist*
BAGD	W. Bauer, *A Greek-English Lexicon of the New Testament and Other Early Christian Literature.* ET and ed. W. F. Arndt and F. W. Gingrich. 2nd edition revised by F. W. Gingrich and F. W. Danker (University of Chicago, 1979)
BAR	*Biblical Archaeology Review*
BBB	Bonner biblische Beiträge
BBR	*Bulletin for Biblical Research*
BCE	Before Christian era
BDAG	W. Bauer, *A Greek-English Lexicon of the New Testament and Other Early Christian Literature.* 3rd edition of BAGD revised by F. W. Danker (Chicago: University of Chicago, 2000)

BDB	F. Brown, S. R. Driver and C. A. Briggs, *Hebrew and English Lexicon of the Old Testament* (Oxford: Clarendon, 1907)
BDF	F. Blass, A. Debrunner and R. W. Funk, *A Greek Grammar of the New Testament* (University of Chicago/University of Cambridge, 1961)
BETL	Bibliotheca ephemeridum theologicarum lovaniensium
Bib	*Biblica*
BJRL	*Bulletin of the John Rylands University Library of Manchester*
BJS	Brown Judaic Studies
BNTC	Black's New Testament Commentaries
BS	Biblical Seminar (Sheffield Academic Press)
BTB	*Biblical Theology Bulletin*
BWANT	Beiträge zur Wissenschaft vom Alten und Neuen Testament
BZ	*Biblische Zeitschrift*
BZNW	Beihefte zur *ZNW*
CBQ	*Catholic Biblical Quarterly*
CE	Christian era
cf.	*confer,* compare
ch(s).	chapter(s)
CIJ	*Corpus Inscriptionum Judaicarum*
COD	*Concise Oxford Dictionary*
ConB	Coniectanea biblica
ConBNT	Coniectanea biblica, New Testament
ConNT	*Coniectanea neotestamentica*
CR:BS	Currents in Research: Biblical Studies
CRINT	Compendia Rerum Iudaicarum ad Novum Testamentum
DJD	Discoveries in the Judean Desert
DJG	*Dictionary of Jesus and the Gospels.* Ed. J. B. Green and S. McKnight (Downers Grove: InterVarsity, 1992)
DSD	*Dead Sea Discoveries*
DSS	Dead Sea Scrolls
DSSB	*The Dead Sea Scrolls Bible.* Ed. M. Abegg, P. Flint and E. Ulrich (New York: HarperCollins, 1999)
EB	Études bibliques
ed(s).	edition, edited by, editor(s)
EDNT	*Exegetical Dictionary of the New Testament.* Ed. H. Balz and G. Schneider (Grand Rapids: Eerdmans; 3 vols. 1990-99)
e.g.	*exempli gratia,* for example
EKK	Evangelisch-katholischer Kommentar zum NeuenTestament
EncBr	*The New Encyclopaedia Britannica.* 15th edition. 30 vols. (Chicago University, 1978)

EncJud	*Encyclopaedia Judaica.* 16 vols. (Jerusalem, 1972)
ER	*The Encyclopedia of Religion.* Ed. M. Eliade. 16 vols. (New York, 1987)
ERE	*Encyclopaedia of Religion and Ethics.* Ed. J. Hastings. 13 vols. (New York: Scribner, 1908-27)
ET	English translation
et al.	*et alii,* and others
ETL	*Ephemerides theologicae lovanienses*
EvT	*Evangelische Theologie*
ExpT	*Expository Times*
FB	Forschung zur Bibel
FBBS	Facet Books, Biblical Series
FRLANT	Forschungen zur Religion und Literatur des Alten und Neuen Testaments
FS	Festschrift, volume written in honour of
García Martínez	F. García Martínez, *The Dead Sea Scrolls Translated: The Qumran Texts in English* (Leiden: Brill/Grand Rapids: Eerdmans, 1994, ^{2}1996)
GLAJJ	M. Stern, *Greek and Latin Authors on Jews and Judaism* (Jerusalem: Israel Academy of Sciences and Humanities; 3 vols. 1976, 1980, 1984)
GNB	Good News Bible
hap. leg.	*hapax legomenon,* sole occurrence
HBT	*Horizons in Biblical Theology*
HKNT	Handkommentar zum Neuen Testament
HNT	Handbuch zum Neuen Testament
HR	E. Hatch and H. A. Redpath, *Concordance to the Septuagint and Other Greek Versions of the Old Testament.* 2 vols. (Oxford, 1897)
HTKNT	Herders theologischer Kommentar zum Neuen Testament
HTR	*Harvard Theological Review*
ICC	International Critical Commentary
IDB	*Interpreter's Dictionary of the Bible.* Ed. G. A. Buttrick (Nashville: Abingdon; 4 vols. 1962)
IDBS	Supplementary volume to *IDB*
IEJ	*Israel Exploration Journal*
Int	*Interpretation*
JAAR	*Journal of the American Academy of Religion*
JANES	*Jorunal of the Ancient Near Eastern Society*
JBL	*Journal of Biblical Literature*
JBTh	*Jahrbuch für Biblische Theologie*

JJS	*Journal of Jewish Studies*
JR	*Journal of Religion*
JSJ	*Journal for the Study of Judaism*
JSNT	*Journal for the Study of the New Testament*
JSNTS	*JSNT* Supplement Series
JSOT	*Journal for the Study of the Old Testament*
JSOTS	*JSOT* Supplement Series
JSP	*Journal for the Study of the Pseudepigrapha*
JSPSupp	*JSP* Supplement Series
JSS	*Journal of Semitic Studies*
JTS	*Journal of Theological Studies*
KuD	*Kerygma und Dogma*
KEK	H. A. W. Meyer, Kritisch-exegetischer Kommentar über das Neue Testament
LD	Lectio divina
Loeb	Loeb Classical Library
LSJ	H. G. Liddell and R. Scott, *A Greek-English Lexicon.* Revised H. S. Jones (Oxford: Clarendon, ^{9}1940); with Supplement (1968)
LXX	Septuagint
Metzger	B. M. Metzger, *A Textual Commentary on the Greek New Testament* (London: United Bible Societies, 1975)
MM	J. H. Moulton and G. Milligan, *The Vocabulary of the Greek Testament* (London: Hodder, 1930)
Moule, *Idiom Book*	C. F. D. Moule, *An Idiom Book of New Testament Greek* (Cambridge: Cambridge University, 1953)
Moulton, *Grammar*	J. H. Moulton, *Grammar of New Testament Greek* (Edinburgh: Clark; 2 vols. 1906-29)
ms(s)	manuscript(s)
MT	Masoretic text (of the Old Testament)
NDIEC	G. H. R. Horsley, *New Documents Illustrating Early Christianity* (North Ryde, Australia, 1981-)
NEB	New English Bible (NT 1961; OT and Apocrypha 1970)
NF	Neue Folge = new series
NIGTC	New International Greek Testament Commentary
NIV	New International Version (1978)
NJB	New Jerusalem Bible (1985)
NovT	*Novum Testamentum*
NovTSup	Supplement to *NovT*
NRSV	New Revised Standard Version (1989)
NT	New Testament

NTAbh	Neutestamentliche Abhandlunger
NTOA	Novum Testamentum et Orbis Antiquus
NTG	New Testament Guides
NTS	*New Testament Studies*
NTTS	New Testament Tools and Studies
OBO	Orbis biblicus et orientalis
OCD	N. G. L. Hammond and H. H. Scullard, *Oxford Classical Dictionary* (Oxford: Clarendon, 1970)
ODCC	*The Oxford Dictionary of the Christian Church.* Ed. F. L. Cross and E. A. Livingstone. 2nd edition (Oxford: Oxford University, 1983)
OEANE	*The Oxford Encyclopedia of Archaeology in the Near East.* Ed. E. M. Meyers (New York: Oxford, 1997)
OT	Old Testament
OTP	*The Old Testament Pseudepigrapha.* Ed. J. H. Charlesworth (London: Darton; 2 vols. 1983, 1985).
pace	with due respect to, but differing from
par(s).	parallel(s)
passim	elsewhere
PG	*Patrologia graeca,* ed. J. P. Migne
PGM	*The Greek Magical Papyri in Translation.* Ed. H. D. Betz. 2nd edition (Chicago: University of Chicago, 1992)
QD	Quaestiones disputatae
RB	*Revue Biblique*
REB	Revised English Bible (1989)
RevQ	*Revue de Qumran*
RSV	Revised Standard Version (NT 1946, OT 1952, Apocrypha 1957)
SANT	Studien zum Alten und Neuen Testament
SBB	Stuttgarter biblische Beiträge
SBL	Society of Biblical Literature
SBS	Stuttgarter Bibelstudien
SBT	Studies in Biblical Theology
SBLDS	SBL Dissertation Series
SBLMS	SBL Monograph Series
SBM	Stuttgarter biblische Monographien
SCJ	Studies in Christianity and Judaism
SJT	*Scottish Journal of Theology*
SNTSMS	Society for New Testament Studies Monograph Series
SNTU	Studien zum Neuen Testament und seiner Umwelt
SR	*Studies in Religion/Sciences Religieuses*

ST	*Studia Theologica*
Str-B	H. Strack and P. Billerbeck, *Kommentar zum Neuen Testament* (München: Beck; 4 vols. 1926-28)
SUNT	Studien zur Umwelt des Neuen Testament
TDNT	*Theological Dictionary of the New Testament.* Ed. G. Kittel and G. Friedrich (ET Grand Rapids: Eerdmans; 10 vols. 1964-76)
TDOT	*Theological Dictionary of the Old Testament.* Ed. G. J. Botterweck and H. Ringgren (ET Grand Rapids: Eerdmans, 1974-)
TJT	*Toronto Journal of Theology*
TR	*Theologische Rundschau*
TRE	*Theologische Realenzyklopädie.* Ed. G. Krause and G. Müller (Berlin, 1977-)
TS	*Theological Studies*
t.t.	technical term
TynB	*Tyndale Bulletin*
TZ	*Theologische Zeitschrift*
UBS	The United Bible Societies, *The Greek New Testament.* 4th edition (New York, 1993)
v., vv.	verse, verses
VC	*Vigiliae christianae*
Vermes	G. Vermes, *The Dead Sea Scrolls in English* (London: Penguin, [4]1995)
v.l.	*varia lectio,* alternative reading
viz.	*videlicet,* namely
vol.	volume
WBC	Word Biblical Commentary
WMANT	Wissenschaftliche Monographien zum Alten und Neuen Testament
WUNT	Wissenschaftliche Untersuchungen zum Neuen Testament
ZNW	*Zeitschrift für die neutestamentliche Wissenschaft*
ZTK	*Zeitschrift für Theologie und Kirche*

Bibliography

The bibliography does not include commentaries and dictionary articles.

Abel, E. L. 'The Psychology of Memory and Rumour Transmission and Their Bearing on Theories of Oral Transmission in Early Christianity'. *JR* 51 (1971): 270-81.

Achtemeier, P. J. '"And He Followed Him": Miracles and Discipleship in Mark 10:46-52'. In *Early Christian Miracle Stories, Semeia* 11, edited by R. W. Funk, 115-45. Missoula: Scholars, 1978.

———. *'Omne verbum sonat:* The New Testament and the Oral Environment of Late Western Antiquity'. *JBL* 109 (1990): 3-27.

Ådna, J. 'The Encounter with the Gerasene Demoniac'. In *Authenticating the Activities of Jesus,* edited by B. Chilton and C. A. Evans, 279-301. Leiden: Brill, 1999.

———. *Jerusalemer Tempel und Tempelmarkt im 1. Jahrhundert n. Chr.* Wiesbaden: Harrassowitz, 1999.

———. *Jesu Stellung zum Tempel. Die Tempelaktion und das Tempelwort als Ausdruck seiner messianischen Sendung.* WUNT 2.119. Tübingen: Mohr Siebeck, 2000.

Aichele, G., et al. *The Postmodern Bible.* New Haven: Yale University, 1995.

Alexander, L. C. A. 'The Living Voice: Scepticism Towards the Written Word in Early Christianity and in Graeco-Roman Texts'. In *The Bible in Three Dimensions: Essays in Celebration of Forty Years of Biblical Studies in the University of Sheffield,* edited by D. J. A. Clines, S. E. Fowl, and J. R. Porter, 221-47. Sheffield: Sheffield Academic, 1986.

Alexander, P. S. 'Jesus and the Golden Rule'. In *Hillel and Jesus,* edited by J. H. Charlesworth and L. L. Johns, 363-88. Minneapolis: Fortress, 1997.

———. 'Orality in Pharisaic Judaism at the Turn of the Eras'. In *Jesus and the Oral Gospel Tradition,* edited by H. Wansbrough, 159-84. Sheffield: Sheffield Academic, 1991.

———. 'Rabbinic Judaism and the New Testament'. *ZNW* 74 (1983): 237-46.

Allison, D. C. 'Behind the Temptations of Jesus: Q 4:1-13 and Mark 1:12-13'. In *Authenticating the Activities of Jesus,* edited by B. Chilton and C. A. Evans, 195-213. Leiden: Brill, 1999.

———. *The End of the Ages Has Come: An Early Interpretation of the Passion and Resurrection of Jesus.* Philadelphia: Fortress, 1985.

———. *Jesus of Nazareth: Millenarian Prophet.* Minneapolis: Fortress, 1998.

———. *The Jesus Tradition in Q.* Harrisburg: Trinity, 1997.

———. 'The Pauline Epistles and the Synoptic Gospels: The Pattern of the Parallels'. *NTS* 28 (1982): 1-32.

———. 'Q 12:51-53 and Mark 9:11-13 and the Messianic Woes'. In *Authenticating the Words of Jesus,* edited by B. Chilton and C. A. Evans, 289-310. Leiden: Brill, 1999.

———. 'Q's New Exodus and the Historical Jesus'. In *The Sayings Source Q and the Historical Jesus,* edited by A. Lindemann, 395-428. Leuven: Leuven University, 2001.

Alsup, J. E. *The Post-Resurrection Appearance Stories of the Gospel-Tradition.* Stuttgart: Calwer, 1975.

Amir, Y. 'The Term *Ioudaismos:* A Study in Jewish-Hellenistic Self-Identification'. *Immanuel* 14 (1982): 34-41.

Andersen, Ø. 'Oral Tradition'. In *Jesus and the Oral Gospel Tradition,* edited by H. Wansbrough, 17-58. Sheffield: Sheffield Academic, 1991.

Antwi, D. J. 'Did Jesus Consider His Death to Be an Atoning Sacrifice?' *Interpretation* 45 (1991): 17-28.

Appleby, J., L. Hunt, and M. Jacob. *Telling the Truth about History.* New York: Norton, 1994.

Arens, E. *The ELTHON-Sayings in the Synoptic Tradition: A Historico-Critical Investigation.* Göttingen: Vandenhoeck und Ruprecht, 1976.

Arnal, W. E. *Jesus and the Village Scribes.* Minneapolis: Fortress, 2001.

———. 'Major Episodes in the Biography of Jesus: An Assessment of the Historicity of the Narrative Tradition'. *TJT* 13 (1997): 201-26.

Arnal, W. E., and M. Desjardins. *Whose Historical Jesus?* SCJ 7. Waterloo: Wilfrid Laurier University, 1997.

Atkinson, K. 'On Further Defining the First-Century CE Synagogue: Fact or Fiction?' *NTS* 43 (1997): 491-502.

Attridge, H. W. 'Reflections on Research into Q'. *Semeia* 55 (1995): 223-34.

Aune, D. E. 'Jesus and Cynics in First-Century Palestine: Some Critical Considerations'. In *Hillel and Jesus,* edited by J. H. Charlesworth and L. L. Johns, 176-92. Minneapolis: Fortress, 1997.

———.'Magic in Early Christianity'. In *ANRW* II.23.1, 1507-57, 1980.

———. *The New Testament in Its Literary Environment.* Philadelphia: Westminster, 1987.

———. 'Prolegomena to the Study of Oral Tradition in the Hellenistic World'. In *Jesus and the Oral Gospel Tradition,* edited by H. Wansbrough, 59-106. Sheffield: Sheffield Academic, 1991.

———. *Prophecy in Early Christianity and the Mediterranean World.* Grand Rapids: Eerdmans, 1983.

Avemarie, F. *Torah und Leben: Untersuchungen zur Heilsbedeutung der Tora in der frühen rabbinischer Literatur.* Tübingen: Mohr Siebeck, 1996.

Avemarie, F., and H. Lichtenberger. *Auferstehung — Resurrection.* WUNT 135. Tübingen: Mohr Siebeck, 2001.

Avery-Peck, A. J., and J. Neusner. *Judaism in Late Antiquity.* Part 4: *Death, Life-After-Death, Resurrection and the World-to-Come in the Judaisms of Antiquity.* Leiden: Brill, 2000.

Bailey, K. E. 'Informal Controlled Oral Tradition and the Synoptic Gospels'. *Asia Journal of Theology* 5 (1991): 34-54.

———. 'Middle Eastern Oral Tradition and the Synoptic Gospels'. *ExpT* 106 (1995): 563-67.

———. *Poet and Peasant: A Literary-Cultural Approach to the Parables in Luke.* Grand Rapids: Eerdmans, 1976.

———. *Through Peasant Eyes.* Grand Rapids: Eerdmans, 1980.

Baird, W. *History of New Testament Research.* Vol. 1: *From Deism to Tübingen.* Minneapolis: Fortress, 1992.

Baldensperger, W. *Das Selbstbewusstsein Jesu im Lichte der messianischen Hoffnungen seiner Zeit.* Strassburg: Heitz, 1888.

Balla, P. 'What Did Jesus Think about His Approaching Death?' In *Jesus, Mark and Q: The Teaching of Jesus and Its Earliest Records,* edited by M. Labahn and A. Schmidt, 239-58. Sheffield: Sheffield Academic, 2001.

Bammel, E. 'The Revolution Theory from Reimarus to Brandon'. In *Jesus and the Politics of His Day,* edited by E. Bammel and C. F. D. Moule, 11-68. Cambridge: Cambridge University, 1984.

Bammel, E., and C. F. D. Moule. *Jesus and the Politics of His Day.* Cambridge: Cambridge University, 1984.

Banks, R. *Jesus and the Law in the Synoptic Tradition.* SNTSMS 28. Cambridge: Cambridge University, 1975.

Barbour, I. G. *Issues in Science and Religion.* London: SCM, 1966.

Barbour, R. S. *Traditio-Historical Criticism of the Gospels.* London: SPCK, 1972.

Barclay, J. M. G. 'The Resurrection in Contemporary New Testament Scholarship'. In *Resurrection Reconsidered,* edited by G. D'Costa, 13-30. Oxford: Oneworld, 1996.

Bar-Ilan, M. 'Illiteracy in the Land of Israel in the First Centuries CE'. In *Essays in the Social Scientific Study of Judaism and Jewish Society,* edited by S. Fishbane and S. Schoenfeld, 46-61. Hoboken: Ktav, 1992.

Barker, M. *The Risen Lord: The Jesus of History as the Christ of Faith.* Edinburgh: Clark, 1996.

———.'The Time Is Fulfilled: Jesus and Jubilee'. *SJT* 53 (2000): 22-32.

Barnett, P. *Jesus and the Logic of History.* Grand Rapids: Eerdmans, 1997.

———. *Jesus and the Rise of Early Christianity: A History of New Testament Times.* Downers Grove: InterVarsity, 1999.

———. 'The Jewish Sign Prophets — AD 40-70 — Their Intentions and Origin'. *NTS* 27 (1981): 679-97.

Barr, J. 'Abba Isn't Daddy!' *JTS* 39 (1988): 28-47.

———. *Biblical Words for Time.* London: SCM, 1969, 2nd ed.

Barrett, C. K. 'The Background of Mark 10:45'. In *New Testament Essays: Studies in Memory of T. W. Manson,* edited by A. J. B. Higgins, 1-18. Manchester: Manchester University, 1959.

———. *Jesus and the Gospel Tradition.* London: SPCK, 1967.

Barth, K. *From Rousseau to Ritschl.* London: SCM, 1959.

Barton, S. C. 'Can We Identify the Gospel Audiences?' In *The Gospels for All Christians,* edited by R. Bauckham, 173-94. Grand Rapids: Eerdmans, 1998.

——. *Discipleship and Family Ties in Mark and Matthew.* SNTSMS 80. Cambridge: Cambridge University, 1994.

Barton, S. C., and G. N. Stanton. *Resurrection, L.* Houlden FS. London: SPCK, 1994.

Batey, R. A. *Jesus and the Forgotten City: New Light on Sepphoris and the Urban World of Jesus.* Grand Rapids: Baker, 1991.

Bauckham, R. 'Did Jesus Wash His Disciples' Feet?' In *Authenticating the Activities of Jesus,* edited by B. Chilton and C. A. Evans, 411-29. Leiden: Brill, 1999.

——. 'For Whom Were the Gospels Written?' In *The Gospels for All Christians,* edited by R. Bauckham, 13-22. Grand Rapids: Eerdmans, 1998.

——. 'Jesus' Demonstration in the Temple'. In *Law and Religion: Essays on the Place of the Law in Israel and Early Christianity,* edited by B. Lindars, 72-89. Cambridge: Clarke, 1988.

——. 'The Scrupulous Priest and the Good Samaritan: Jesus' Parabolic Interpretation of the Law of Moses'. *NTS* 44 (1998): 475-89.

——. 'The Son of Man: 'A Man in My Position' or 'Someone'?' *JSNT* 23 (1985): 23-33.

Bauckham, R., ed. *The Gospels for All Christians: Rethinking the Gospel Audiences.* Grand Rapids: Eerdmans, 1998.

Bauernfeind, O. *Die Worte der Dämonen im Markusevangelium.* Stuttgart: Kohlhammer, 1927.

Baumgarten, A. I. 'The Name of the Pharisees'. *JBL* 102 (1983): 411-28.

Baur, F. C. *Kritische Untersuchungen über die kanonische Evangelien.* Tübingen, 1847.

Bayer, H. F. *Jesus' Predictions of Vindication and Resurrection.* WUNT 2.20. Tübingen: Mohr Siebeck, 1986.

Beasley-Murray, G. R. *Baptism in the New Testament.* London: Macmillan, 1963.

——. *Jesus and the Kingdom of God.* Grand Rapids: Eerdmans, 1986.

——. *Jesus and the Last Days: The Interpretation of the Olivet Discourse.* Peabody: Hendrickson, 1993.

Becker, J. *Jesus of Nazareth.* Berlin: de Gruyter, 1998.

Bellinger, W. H., and W. R. Farmer, eds. *Jesus and the Suffering Servant: Isaiah 53 and Christian Origins.* Harrisburg: Trinity, 1998.

Ben-Chorin, S. *Brüder Jesus: Der Nazarener in jüdischer Sicht.* München: List, 1967.

Bergemann, T. *Q auf dem Prüfstand: Die Zuordnung des Mat/Lk-Stoffes zu Q am Beispiel der Bergpredigt.* FRLANT 158. Göttingen: Vandenhoeck und Ruprecht, 1993.

Berger, K. *Die Auferstehung des Propheten und die Erhöhung des Menschensohnes.* Göttingen: Vandenhoeck und Ruprecht, 1976.

——. *Die Gesetzauslegung Jesu I.* WMANT 40. Neukirchen-Vluyn: Neukirchener, 1972.

——. 'Die königlichen Messiastraditionen des Neuen Testaments'. *NTS* 20 (1973-74): 1-44.

——. 'Jesus als Nasoräer/Nasiräer'. *NovT* 38 (1996): 323-35.

——. 'Jesus als Pharisäer und frühe Christen als Pharisäer'. *NovT* 30 (1988) 231-62.

Betz, H. D. 'Jesus and the Cynics: Survey and Analysis of a Hypothesis'. *JR* 74 (1994): 453-75.

———. 'Jesus and the Purity of the Temple (Mark 11:15-18): A Comparative Religion Approach'. *JBL* 116 (1997): 455-72.

———. 'Magic in Greco-Roman Antiquity'. *ER* 9 (1995): 93-97.

———. *Nachfolge und Nachahmung Jesu Christi im Neuen Testament.* Tübingen: Mohr Siebeck, 1967.

———. *The Sermon on the Mount.* Hermeneia. Minneapolis: Fortress, 1995.

Betz, O. 'Die Frage nach dem messianischen Bewusstsein Jesu'. *NovT* 6 (1963): 24-37.

———. 'Probleme des Prozesses Jesu'. *ANRW* II.25.1 (1982): 565-647.

———. *What Do We Know about Jesus?* London: SCM, 1968.

Bietenhard, H. '"Der Menschensohn" — *ho huios tou anthrōpou.* Sprachliche und religionsgeschichtliche Untersuchungen zu einem Begriff der synoptischen Evangelien. I. Sprachlicher und religionsgeschichtlicher Teil'. *ANRW* II.25.1 (1982): 265-350.

Black, M. *An Aramaic Approach to the Gospels and Acts.* Oxford: Clarendon, 1967, 3rd ed.

Blackburn, B. L. 'The Miracles of Jesus'. In *Studying the Historical Jesus,* edited by B. Chilton and C. A. Evans, 353-94. Leiden: Brill, 1994.

Blinzler, J. *Der Prozess Jesu.* Regensburg: Pustet, 1969, 4th ed.

———. '*Eisin eunouchoi:* Zur Auslegung von Mt 19,12'. *ZNW* 48 (1957): 254-70.

Blomberg, C. L. 'The Parables of Jesus: Current Trends and Needs in Research'. In *John the Baptist and His Relationship to Jesus,* edited by B. Chilton and C. A. Evans, 231-54. Leiden: Brill, 1994.

———. '"Your Faith Has Made You Whole": The Evangelical Liberation Theology of Jesus'. In *Jesus of Nazareth: Lord and Christ,* I. H. Marshall FS, edited by J. B. Green and M. Turner, 75-93. Grand Rapids: Eerdmans, 1994.

Boccaccini, G. *Middle Judaism: Jewish Thought, 300 BCE to 200 CE.* Minneapolis: Fortress, 1991.

Bock, D. L. *Blasphemy and Exaltation in Judaism and the Final Examination of Jesus.* WUNT 2.106. Tübingen: Mohr Siebeck, 1998.

Bockmuehl, M. *Jewish Law in Gentile Churches: Halakhah and the Beginning of Christian Public Ethics.* Edinburgh: Clark, 2000.

Bockmuehl, M., ed. *The Cambridge Companion to Jesus.* Cambridge: Cambridge University, 2001.

Bode, E. L. *The First Easter Morning: The Gospel Accounts of the Women's Visit to the Tomb of Jesus.* AB 45. Rome: Biblical Institute, 1970.

Boff, L. *Jesus Christ Liberator: A Critical Christology for our Time.* Maryknoll, NY: Orbis, 1978.

Bolyki, J. *Jesu Tischgemeinschaften.* WUNT 2.96. Tübingen: Mohr Siebeck, 1998.

Bond, H. K. *Pontius Pilate in History and Interpretation.* SNTSMS 100. Cambridge: Cambridge University, 1998.

Booth, R. P. *Jesus and the Laws of Purity: Tradition History and Legal History in Mark 7.* JSNTS 13. Sheffield: JSOT, 1986.

Borg, M. J. *Conflict, Holiness and Politics in the Teachings of Jesus.* Harrisburg: Trinity, 1984, 1998, new ed.

———. *Jesus: A New Vision.* San Francisco: Harper and Row, 1987.

———. *Jesus in Contemporary Scholarship.* Valley Forge: Trinity, 1994.

———. 'An Orthodoxy Reconsidered: The "End-of-the-World Jesus"'. In *The Glory of Christ in the New Testament,* G. B. Caird FS, edited by L. D. Hurst and N. T. Wright, 207-17. Oxford: Clarendon, 1987.

Borg, M. J., ed. *Jesus at 2000.* Boulder, Colorado: Westview, 1997.

Boring, M. E. *Sayings of the Risen Jesus: Christian Prophecy in the Synoptic Tradition.* SNTSMS 46. Cambridge: Cambridge University, 1982.

Bornkamm, G. *Jesus of Nazareth.* ET London: Hodder and Stoughton, 1960 (1956).

Boslooper, T. *The Virgin Birth.* Philadelphia: Westminster, 1962.

Bousset, W. *Jesus.* London: Williams and Norgate, 1906.

———. *Jesus im Gegensatz zum Judentum: ein religionsgeschichtlicher Vergleich.* Göttingen: Vandenhoeck und Ruprecht, 1892.

———. *Kyrios Christos.* ET Nashville: Abingdon, 1970 (1913).

Bousset, W., and H. Gressmann. *Die Religion des Judentums im späthellenistischen Zeitalter.* HNT 21. Tübingen: Mohr Siebeck, 1925, 1966, 4th ed.

Bowden, J. *Jesus: The Unanswered Questions.* London: SCM, 1988.

Bowker, J. 'The Son of Man'. *JTS* 28 (1977): 19-48.

Braaten, C. E., and R. A. Harrisville. *The Historical Jesus and the Kerygmatic Christ.* Nashville: Abingdon, 1964.

Brandon, S. G. F. *The Fall of Jerusalem and the Christian Church.* London: SPCK, 1957, 2nd ed.

———. *Jesus and the Zealots: A Study of the Political Factor in Primitive Christianity.* Manchester: Manchester University, 1967.

———. *The Trial of Jesus of Nazareth.* London: Batsford, 1968.

Breech, J. *The Silence of Jesus: The Authentic Voice of the Historical Man.* Philadelphia: Fortress, 1983.

Brettler, M. Z. 'Judaism in the Hebrew Bible? The Transition from Ancient Israelite Religion to Judaism'. *CBQ* 61 (1999): 429-47.

Brooke, G. J. '4Q500 1 and the Use of Scripture in the Parable of the Vineyard'. *DSD* 2 (1995): 268-94.

Brooke, G. J., ed. *The Birth of Jesus: Biblical and Theological Reflections.* Edinburgh: Clark, 2000.

Brown, C. *Jesus in European Protestant Thought, 1778-1860.* Durham, NC: Labyrinth, 1985.

———. 'The Parable of the Rebellious Son(s)'. *SJT* 51 (1998): 391-405.

Brown, R. E. *The Birth of the Messiah: A Commentary on the Infancy Narratives in the Gospels of Matthew and Luke.* New York: Doubleday, 1977, 1993, 2nd ed.

———. *The Death of the Messiah: From Gethsemane to the Grave. A Commentary on the Passion Narratives in the Four Gospels,* 2 vols. New York: Doubleday, 1994.

———. 'The Gospel of Peter and Canonical Gospel Priority'. *NTS* 33 (1987): 321-43.

———. *An Introduction to the New Testament.* New York: Doubleday, 1997.

———. 'The Relation of 'The Secret Gospel of Mark' to the Fourth Gospel'. *CBQ* 36 (1974): 466-85.

———. *The Semitic Background of the Term 'Mystery' in the New Testament.* FBBS 21. Philadelphia: Fortress, 1968.

Bruce, F. F. 'Render to Caesar'. In *Jesus and the Politics of His Day,* edited by E. Bammel and C. F. D. Moule, 249-63. Cambridge: Cambridge University, 1984.

———. *The 'Secret' Gospel of Mark.* London: Athlone, 1974.

Buchanan, G. W. *Hermann Samuel Reimarus: The Goal of Jesus and His Disciples.* Leiden: Brill, 1970.

———. *Jesus: The King and His Kingdom.* Macon, GA: Mercer University, 1984.

Bühner, J. H. *Der Gesandte und sein Weg im 4. Evangelium.* Tübingen: Mohr Siebeck, 1977.

Bultmann, R. *The History of the Synoptic Tradition.* ET Oxford: Blackwell, 1963 (1921).

———. 'Is Exegesis Without Presuppositions Possible?' In *Existence and Faith,* 342-51. ET London: Collins, 1964 (1961).

———. *Jesus and the Word.* ET New York: Scribners, 1935 (1926).

———. 'The New Approach to the Synoptic Problem' (1926). In *Existence and Faith,* 39-62. London: Collins: Fontana, 1964.

———. 'New Testament and Mythology'. In *Kerygma and Myth,* edited by H. W. Bartsch, 1-44. ET London: SPCK, 1957 (1941).

———. 'The Primitive Christian Kerygma and the Historical Jesus'. In *The Historical Jesus and the Kerygmatic Christ,* edited by C. E. Braaten and R. A. Harrisville, 15-42. Nashville: Abingdon, 1964.

———. *Primitive Christianity in Its Contemporary Setting.* London: Thames and Hudson, 1956.

———. 'The Study of the Synoptic Gospels' (1934). In *Form Criticism,* 11-76. New York: Harper Torchbook, 1962.

———. *Theology of the New Testament,* Vol. 1. ET London: SCM, 1952 (1948).

Burger, C. *Jesus als Davidssohn.* FRLANT 98. Göttingen: Vandenhoeck and Ruprecht, 1970.

Burkett, D. 'The Nontitular Son of Man: A History and Critique'. *NTS* 40 (1994): 504-21.

———. *The Son of Man Debate: A History and Evaluation.* SNTSMS 107. Cambridge: Cambridge University, 1999.

Burkitt, F. C. *The Earliest Sources for the Life of Jesus.* London: Constable, 1922.

———. *The Gospel History and Its Transmission.* Edinburgh: Clark, 1906.

Burney, C. F. *The Poetry of Our Lord.* Oxford: Clarendon, 1925.

Burridge, R. A. *What Are the Gospels? A Comparison with Graeco-Roman Biography.* SNTSMS 70. Cambridge: Cambridge University, 1992.

Byrskog, S. *Story as History — History as Story: The Gospel Tradition in the Context of Ancient Oral History.* WUNT 123. Tübingen: Mohr Siebeck, 2000.

Cadbury, H. J. *The Peril of Modernizing Jesus.* London: Macmillan, 1937.

Cadoux, C. J. *The Historic Mission of Jesus.* London: Lutterworth, 1941.

Caird, G. B. *The Language and Imagery of the Bible.* London: Duckworth, 1980.

———. *New Testament Theology.* Oxford: Clarendon, 1994.

Cameron, R. *The Other Gospels: Non-canonical Gospel Texts.* Guildford: Lutterworth, 1983.

————. *Sayings Traditions in the Apocryphon of James.* Philadelphia: Fortress, 1984.

Camponovo, O. *Königtum, Königsherrschaft und Reich Gottes in den frühjüdischen Schriften.* OBO 58. Göttingen: Vandenhoeck und Ruprecht, 1984.

Caragounis, C. C. *The Son of Man.* WUNT 38. Tübingen: Mohr Siebeck, 1986.

Carnley, P. *The Structure of Resurrection Belief.* Oxford: Clarendon, 1987.

Carroll, J. T., and J. B. Green. *The Death of Jesus in Early Christianity.* Peabody: Hendrickson, 1995.

Carroll, R. P. *When Prophecy Failed: Reactions and Responses to Failure in the Old Testament Prophetic Traditions.* London: SCM, 1979.

Case, S. J. *Jesus: A New Biography.* Chicago: University of Chicago, 1927.

Casey, M. 'An Aramaic Approach to the Synoptic Gospels'. *ExpT* 110 (1999): 275-8.

————. *Aramaic Sources of Mark's Gospel.* SNTSMS 102. Cambridge: Cambridge University, 1998.

————. *From Jewish Prophet to Gentile God.* Cambridge: Clarke, 1991.

————. 'General, Generic and Indefinite: The Use of the Term "Son of Man" in Aramaic Sources and in the Teaching of Jesus'. *JSNT* 29 (1987): 21-56.

————. 'Idiom and Translation: Some Aspects of the Son of Man Problem'. *NTS* 41 (1995): 164-82.

————. 'The Jackals and the Son of Man (Matt. 8.20/Luke 9.58)'. *JSNT* 23 (1985): 3-22.

————. 'The Original Aramaic Form of Jesus' Interpretation of the Cup'. *JTS* 41 (1990): 1-12.

————. *Son of Man: The Interpretation and Influence of Daniel 7.* London: SPCK, 1979.

————. 'The Use of the Term *br ('*)*nsh(*'*)* in the Aramaic Translations of the Hebrew Bible'. *JSNT* 54 (1994): 87-118.

————. 'Where Wright is Wrong: A Critical Review of N. T. Wright's *Jesus and the Victory of God*'. *JSNT* 69 (1998): 95-103.

Casey, P. M. 'Culture and Historicity: The Cleansing of the Temple'. *CBQ* 59 (1997): 306-32.

Catchpole, D. R. *The Quest for Q.* Edinburgh: Clark, 1993.

————. 'The Question of Q'. *Sewanee Theological Review* 36 (1992): 3-44.

————. *Resurrection People: Studies in the Resurrection Narratives of the Gospels.* London: Darton, Longman and Todd, 2000.

————. *The Trial of Jesus.* Leiden: Brill, 1971.

————. 'The "Triumphal" Entry'. In *Jesus and the Politics of His Day,* edited by E. Bammel and C. F. D. Moule, 319-34. Cambridge: Cambridge University, 1984.

Cavallin, H. C. C. *Life after Death: Paul's Argument for the Resurrection of the Dead in 1 Cor 15. Part I: An Enquiry into the Jewish Background.* Lund: Gleerup, 1974.

Chadwick, H. *Lessing's Theological Writings.* London: Black, 1956.

Charlesworth, J. H. 'From Messianology to Christology: Problems and Prospects'. In *The Messiah,* edited by J. H. Charlesworth, 3-35. Minneapolis: Fortress, 1992.

————. 'Hillel and Jesus: Why Comparisons Are Important'. In *Hillel and Jesus,* edited by J. H. Charlesworth and L. L. Johns, 3-30. Minneapolis: Fortress, 1997.

————. *Jesus within Judaism: New Light from Exciting Archaeological Discoveries.* New York: Doubleday, 1988.

————. *The Old Testament Pseudepigrapha and the New Testament.* SNTSMS 54. Cambridge: Cambridge University, 1985.

————. 'The Righteous Teacher and the Historical Jesus'. In *Earthing Christologies: From Jesus' Parables to Jesus the Parable,* edited by W. P. Weaver and J. H. Charlesworth, 46-61. Valley Forge: Trinity, 1995.

Charlesworth, J. H., ed. *Jesus and the Dead Sea Scrolls.* New York: Doubleday, 1992.

————. *Jesus' Jewishness: Exploring the Place of Jesus in Early Judaism.* New York: Crossroad, 1991.

————. *The Messiah: Developments in Earliest Judaism and Christianity.* Minneapolis: Fortress, 1992.

Charlesworth, J. H., and C. A. Evans. 'Jesus in the Agrapha and Apocryphal Gospels'. In *Studying the Historical Jesus,* edited by B. Chilton and C. A. Evans, 479-533. Leiden: Brill, 1994.

Charlesworth, J. H., and L. L. Johns. *Hillel and Jesus: Comparative Studies of Two Major Religious Leaders.* Minneapolis: Fortress, 1997.

Charlesworth, J. H., H. Lichtenberger, and G. S. Oegema. *Qumran-Messianism: Studies on the Messianic Expectations in the Dead Sea Scrolls.* Tübingen: Mohr Siebeck, 1998.

Chiat, M. J. 'First-Century Synagogue Architecture: Methodological Problems'. In *Ancient Synagogues: The State of Research,* edited by J. Gutmann, 49-60. Chico, CA: Scholars, 1981.

Childs, H. *The Myth of the Historical Jesus and the Evolution of Consciousness,* SBLDS. Atlanta: SBL, 2000.

Chilton, B. *A Galilean Rabbi and His Bible: Jesus' Own Interpretation of Isaiah.* London: SPCK, 1984.

————. *God in Strength: Jesus' Announcement of the Kingdom.* SNTU B1. Freistadt: F. Plochl, 1979.

————. 'The Kingdom of God in Recent Discussion'. In *Studying the Historical Jesus,* edited by B. Chilton and C. A. Evans, 255-80. Leiden: Brill, 1994.

————. *Profiles of a Rabbi: Synoptic Opportunities in Reading about Jesus, BJS.* Atlanta: Scholars, 1989.

————. *Pure Kingdom: Jesus' Vision of God.* Grand Rapids: Eerdmans, 1996.

————. *Rabbi Jesus: An Intimate Biography.* New York: Doubleday, 2000.

————. '(The) Son of (the) Man, and Jesus'. In *Authenticating the Words of Jesus,* edited by B. Chilton and C. A. Evans, 259-87. Leiden: Brill, 1999.

————. *The Temple of Jesus: His Sacrificial Program within a Cultural History of Sacrifice.* University Park: Pennsylvania State University, 1992.

Chilton, B., ed. *The Kingdom of God.* London: SPCK, 1984.

Chilton, B., and C. A. Evans. *Authenticating the Activities of Jesus.* NTTS 28.2. Leiden: Brill, 1999.

————. *Jesus in Context: Temple, Purity and Restoration.* AGAJU 39. Leiden: Brill, 1997.

————. *Authenticating the Words of Jesus.* NTTS 28.1. Leiden: Brill, 1999.

————. *Studying the Historical Jesus: Evaluations of the State of Current Research.* Leiden: Brill, 1994.

Christ, F. *Jesus Sophia. Die Sophia-Christologie bei den Synoptikern.* Zürich: Zwingli, 1970.

Cohen, S. J. D. *The Beginnings of Jewishness: Boundaries, Varieties, Uncertainties.* Berkeley: University of California, 1999.

————. *From the Maccabees to the Mishnah.* Philadelphia: Westminster, 1987.

————. 'The Place of the Rabbi in Jewish Society of the Second Century'. In *The Galilee in Late Antiquity,* edited by L. I. Levine, 157-73. New York: Jewish Theological Seminary of America, 1992.

————. 'The Rabbinic Conversion Ceremony'. In *The Beginnings of Jewishness,* 198-238. Berkeley: University of California, 1999.

————. 'Were Pharisees and Rabbis the Leaders of Communal Prayer and Torah Study in Antiquity?' In *Evolution of the Synagogue,* edited by H. C. Kee and L. H. Cohick, 89-105. Harrisburg: Trinity, 1992.

Collingwood, R. G. *The Idea of History.* Oxford: Oxford University, 1946, 1961.

Collins, A. Y. 'The Empty Tomb and Resurrection According to Mark'. In *The Beginnings of the Gospel: Problems of Mark in Context,* 119-48. Minneapolis: Fortress, 1992.

————. 'From Noble Death to Crucified Messiah'. *NTS* 40 (1994): 481-503.

————. 'The Influence of Daniel on the New Testament'. In *Daniel,* edited by J. J. Collins, 90-112. Minneapolis: Fortress, 1993.

Collins, J. J. *The Apocalyptic Imagination: An Introduction to Jewish Apocalyptic Literature.* Grand Rapids: Eerdmans, 1984, 1998, 2nd ed.

————. *The Scepter and the Star: The Messiahs of the Dead Sea Scrolls and Other Ancient Literature.* New York: Doubleday, 1995.

————. 'The Son of Man in First-Century Judaism'. *NTS* 38 (1992): 448-66.

Conzelmann, H. *Jesus.* Philadelphia: Fortress, 1973.

————. *An Outline of the Theology of the New Testament.* London: SCM, 1969.

Cook, M. J. 'Jewish Reflections on Jesus: Some Abiding Trends'. In *The Historical Jesus Through Catholic and Jewish Eyes,* edited by B. F. Le Beau, L. Greenspoon, and D. Hamm, 95-111. Harrisburg: Trinity, 2000.

Corley, K. E. 'Women and the Crucifixion and Burial of Jesus. "He was Buried: On the Third Day He Was Raised"'. *Forum* 1 (1998): 181-225.

Cotter, W. *Miracles in Greco-Roman Antiquity.* London: Routledge, 1999.

Craig, W. L. *Assessing the New Testament Evidence for the Historicity of the Resurrection of Jesus.* Lewiston: Mellen, 1989.

Cross, F. M. *The Ancient Library of Qumran.* Sheffield: Sheffield Academic, 1995, 3rd ed.

Crossan, J. D. *The Birth of Christianity.* San Francisco: Harper, 1998.

————. *The Cross That Spoke: The Origins of the Passion Narrative.* San Francisco: Harper and Row, 1988.

————. 'Empty Tomb and Absent Lord (Mark 16:1-8)'. In *The Passion in Mark,* edited by W. H. Kelber, 135-52. Philadelphia: Fortress, 1976.

————. *Four Other Gospels.* Minneapolis: Winston, 1985.

————. *Fragments: The Aphorisms of Jesus.* San Francisco: Harper and Row, 1983.

————. *The Historical Jesus: The Life of a Mediterranean Jewish Peasant.* San Francisco: Harper, 1991.

————. *In Parables: The Challenge of the Historical Jesus.* New York: Harper and Row, 1973, 1985.

————. 'Itinerants and Householders in the Earliest Jesus Movement'. In *Whose Historical Jesus?,* edited by W. E. Arnal and M. Desjardins, 7-24. Waterloo, Ontario: Wilfrid Laurier University, 1997.

————. *Jesus: A Revolutionary Biography.* San Francisco: Harper, 1994.

————. *Sayings Parallels: A Workbook for the Jesus Tradition.* Philadelphia: Fortress, 1986.

————. *Who Killed Jesus? Exposing the Roots of Anti-Semitism in the Gospel Story of the Death of Jesus.* San Francisco: Harper, 1995 (paper 1996).

Crossan, J. D., and J. L. Reed. *Excavating Jesus: Beneath the Stones, behind the Text.* San Francisco: Harper, 2001.

Cullmann, O. *Baptism in the New Testament.* London: SCM, 1950.

————. *The Christology of the New Testament.* ET London: SCM, 1959 (1957).

————. *Jesus and the Revolutionaries.* New York: Harper and Row, 1970.

————. *Peter: Disciple, Apostle, Martyr.* London: SCM, 1962.

————. 'The Tradition'. In *The Early Church: Historical and Theological Studies,* 59-75. London: SCM, 1956.

Culpepper, R. A. *Anatomy of the Fourth Gospel: A Study in Literary Design.* Philadelphia: Fortress, 1983.

Dahl, N. A. 'The Crucified Messiah' (1960). In *Jesus the Christ: The Historical Origins of Christological Doctrine,* edited by D. H. Juel, 27-47. Minneapolis: Fortress, 1991.

————. 'The Problem of the Historical Jesus' (1962). In *Jesus the Christ: The Historical Origins of Christological Doctrine,* 81-111. Minneapolis: Fortress, 1991.

Dalferth, I. U. 'Volles Grab, leerer Glaube? Zum Streit um die Auferweckung des Gekreuzigten'. *ZTK* 95 (1998): 379-409.

Dalman, G. *The Words of Jesus Considered in the Light of Post-Biblical Jewish Writings and the Aramaic Language.* Edinburgh: Clark, 1902.

D'Angelo, M. R. '*Abba* and 'Father': Imperial Theology and the Jesus Tradition'. *JBL* 111 (1992): 611-30.

Danker, F. W. 'Luke 16.16 — An Opposition Logion'. *JBL* 77 (1958): 231-43.

Daube, D. *The New Testament and Rabbinic Judaism.* London: Athlone, 1956.

Davies, S. L. *Jesus the Healer: Possession, Trance, and the Origins of Christianity.* New York: Continuum, 1995.

Davies, W. D. '"Knowledge" in the Dead Sea Scrolls and Matt. 11.25-30'. In *Christian Origins and Judaism,* 119-44. London: DLT, 1953, 1962.

Davies, W. D., and E. P. Sanders. 'Jesus: from the Jewish Point of View'. In *The Cambridge History of Judaism.* Vol. 3: *The Early Roman Period,* edited by W. Horbury, W. D. Davies, and J. Sturdy, 618-77. Cambridge: Cambridge University, 1999.

Davis, S. T., D. Kendall, and G. O'Collins. *The Resurrection: An Interdisciplinary Symposium on the Resurrection of Jesus.* Oxford: Oxford University, 1997.

Dawes, G. W. *The Historical Jesus Question: The Challenge of History to Religious Authority.* Louisville: Westminster John Knox, 2001.

Dawes, G. W., ed. *The Historical Jesus Quest: Landmarks in the Search for the Jesus of History.* Leiderdorp: Deo, 1999.

D'Costa, G., ed., *Resurrection Reconsidered.* Oxford: Oneworld, 1996.

Deines, R. *Die Pharisäer: Ihr Verständnis im Spiegel der christlichen und jüdischen Forschung seit Wellhausen und Graetz,* WUNT 101. Tübingen: Mohr Siebeck, 1997.

de Jonge, M. *Early Christology and Jesus' Own View of His Mission.* Grand Rapids: Eerdmans, 1998.

———. *Jesus, The Servant-Messiah.* New Haven: Yale University, 1991.

Delobel, J. *Logia: Les Paroles de Jesus — The Sayings of Jesus.* BETL 59. Leuven: Leuven University, 1982.

DeMaris, R. E. 'Possession, Good and Bad — Ritual, Effects and Side-Effects: The Baptism of Jesus and Mark 1.9-11 from a Cross-cultural Perspective'. *JSNT* 80 (2000): 3-30.

de Moor, J. C. 'The Targumic Background of Mark 12:1-12: The Parable of the Wicked Tenants'. *JSJ* 29 (1998): 63-80.

den Heyer, C. J. *Jesus Matters: 150 Years of Research.* London: SCM, 1997.

Derrett, J. D. M. *Law in the New Testament.* London: Darton, Longman and Todd, 1970.

Dewey, J. 'The Gospel of Mark as an Oral-Aural Event: Implications for Interpretation'. In *The New Literary Criticism and the New Testament,* edited by E. S. Malbon and E. V. McKnight, 145-63. Sheffield: Sheffield Academic, 1994.

———. 'Oral Methods of Structuring Narrative in Mark'. *Interpretation* 43 (1989): 32-44.

Dexinger, F. 'Limits of Tolerance in Judaism: The Samaritan Example'. In *Jewish and Christian Self-Definition.* Vol. 2: *Aspects of Judaism in the Graeco-Roman Period,* edited by E. P. Sanders, et al., 88-114. London: SCM, 1981.

Dibelius, M. *From Tradition to Gospel.* ET London: Nicholson and Watson, 1934 (1919).

Dihle, A. *Die goldene Regel: Eine Einführung in die Geschichte der antiken und frühchristlichen Vulgarethik.* Göttingen: Vandenhoeck und Ruprecht, 1962.

———. 'The Gospels and Greek Biography'. In *Das Evangelium und die Evangelien,* ET *The Gospel and the Gospels,* edited by P. Stuhlmacher, 361-86. Grand Rapids: Eerdmans, 1991 (1983).

Dillon, R. J. *From Eye-Witnesses to Ministers of the Word: Tradition and Composition in Luke 24.* Rome: Biblical Institute, 1978.

Dodd, C. H. 'The Appearances of the Risen Christ: An Essay in Form-Criticism of the Gospels'. In *Studies in the Gospels: Essays in Memory of R. H. Lightfoot,* edited by D. E. Nineham, 9-35. Oxford: Blackwell, 1955.

———. *The Founder of Christianity.* London: Collins, 1971.

———. *Historical Tradition in the Fourth Gospel.* Cambridge: Cambridge University, 1963.

———. 'Jesus as Teacher and Prophet'. In *Mysterium Christi,* edited by G. K. A. Bell and A. Deissmann, 53-66. London: Longmans, 1930.

———. *The Parables of the Kingdom.* London: Religious Book Club, 1935, 1936, 3rd ed.

Donahue, J. R. *Are You the Christ? The Trial Narrative in the Gospel of Mark,* SBLDS. Missoula: SBL, 1973.

———. 'Tax Collectors and Sinners: An Attempt at Identification'. *CBQ* 33 (1971): 39-61.

Donaldson, T. L. *Jesus on the Mountain: A Study in Matthean Theology.* JSNTS 8. Sheffield: JSOT, 1985.

———. 'Proselytes or "Righteous Gentiles"? The Status of Gentiles in Eschatological Pilgrimage Patterns of Thought'. *JSP* 7 (1990): 3-27.

Downing, F. G. *Christ and the Cynics.* Sheffield: Sheffield Academic, 1988.

———. *Cynics and Christian Origins.* Edinburgh: Clark, 1992.

———. *Doing Things with Words in the First Christian Century.* JSNTS 200. Sheffield: Sheffield Academic, 2000.

———. 'Exile in Formative Judaism'. In *Making Sense in (and of) the First Christian Century,* 148-68. Sheffield: Sheffield Academic, 2000.

———. 'The Jewish Cynic Jesus'. In *Jesus, Mark and Q: The Teaching of Jesus and Its Earliest Records,* edited by M. Labahn and A. Schmidt, 184-214. Sheffield: Sheffield Academic, 2001.

Dschulnigg, P. *Sprache, Redaktion und Intention des Markus-Evangeliums.* SBB 11. Stuttgart: Katholisches Bibelwerk, 1986.

Duling, D. C. 'Solomon, Exorcism, and the Son of David'. *HTR* 68 (1975): 235-52.

Dungan, D. L. *A History of the Synoptic Problem.* New York: Doubleday, 1999.

Dunn, J. D. G. '"Are You the Messiah?" Is the Crux of Mark 14.61-62 Resolvable?' In *Christology, Controversy and Community,* D. R. Catchpole FS, edited by D. G. Horrell and C. M. Tuckett, 1-22. Leiden: Brill, 2000.

———. *Baptism in the Holy Spirit.* London: SCM, 1970.

———. 'The Birth of a Metaphor — Baptized in Spirit' (1977-78). In *The Christ and the Spirit.* Vol. 2: *Pneumatology,* 103-17. Grand Rapids: Eerdmans, 1998.

———. 'Can the Third Quest Hope to Succeed?' In *Authenticating the Activities of Jesus,* edited by B. Chilton and C. A. Evans, 31-48. Leiden: Brill, 1999.

———. *The Christ and the Spirit.* Vol. 1: *Christology.* Vol. 2: *Pneumatology.* Grand Rapids: Eerdmans, 1998.

———. *Christology in the Making.* London: SCM, 1980, 1989, 2nd ed.

———. 'The Danielic Son of Man in the New Testament'. In *The Book of Daniel: Composition and Reception,* 2 vols., edited by J. J. Collins and P. W. Flint, 528-49. Leiden: Brill, 2001.

———. 'Demythologizing — The Problem of Myth in the New Testament'. In *New Testament Interpretation: Essays on Principles and Methods,* edited by I. H. Marshall, 285-307. Exeter: Paternoster, 1977.

———. *The Evidence for Jesus.* London: SCM, 1985.

———. 'Jesus and Factionalism in Early Judaism'. In *Hillel and Jesus,* edited by J. H. Charlesworth and L. L. Johns, 156-75. Minneapolis: Fortress, 1997.

———. 'Jesus and Purity: An Ongoing Debate', *NTS* 48 (2002) 449-67.

———. 'Jesus and Ritual Purity: A Study of the Tradition-History of Mark 7.15' (1985). In *Jesus, Paul and the Law,* 37-60. London: SPCK, 1990.

———. *Jesus and the Spirit: A Study of the Religious and Charismatic Experience of Jesus and the First Christians as Reflected in the New Testament.* London: SCM, 1975.

913

————. *Jesus' Call to Discipleship.* Cambridge: Cambridge University, 1992.

————. *Jesus, Paul and the Law: Studies in Mark and Galatians.* London: SPCK, 1990.

————. 'Jesus, Table-Fellowship, and Qumran'. In *Jesus and the Dead Sea Scrolls,* edited by J. H. Charlesworth, 254-72. New York: Doubleday, 1992.

————. 'Jesus Tradition in Paul'. In *Studying the Historical Jesus,* edited by B. Chilton and C. A. Evans, 155-78. Leiden: Brill, 1994.

————. 'John and the Oral Gospel Tradition'. In *Jesus and the Oral Gospel Tradition,* edited by H. Wansbrough, 351-79. Sheffield: JSOT, 1991.

————. 'John the Baptist's Use of Scripture'. In *The Gospels and the Scriptures of Israel,* edited by C. A. Evans and W. R. Stegner, 118-29. Sheffield: Sheffield Academic, 1994.

————. 'Judaism in the Land of Israel in the First Century'. In *Judaism in Late Antiquity.* Part 2: *Historical Syntheses,* edited by J. Neusner, 229-61. Leiden: Brill, 1995.

————. *The Living Word.* London: SCM, 1987.

————. 'Mark 2.1–3.6: A Bridge between Jesus and Paul on the Question of the Law' (1984). In *Jesus, Paul and the Law.* London: SPCK, 1990.

————. 'Matthew 12:28/Luke 11:20 — A Word of Jesus?' (1988). In *The Christ and the Spirit.* Vol. 2: *Pneumatology,* 187-204. Grand Rapids: Eerdmans, 1998.

————. 'Matthew's Awareness of Markan Redaction'. In *The Four Gospels 1992,* F. Neirynck FS, edited by F. van Segbroeck, et al., 1349-59. Leuven: Leuven University, 1992.

————. 'Messianic Ideas and Their Influence on the Jesus of History'. In *The Messiah: Developments in Earliest Judaism and Christianity,* edited by J. H. Charlesworth, 365-81. Minneapolis: Fortress, 1992.

————. 'The Messianic Secret in Mark'. *TynB* 21 (1970): 92-117.

————. *The Partings of the Ways between Christianity and Judaism.* London: SCM, 1991.

————. 'Pharisees, Sinners and Jesus'. In *Jesus, Paul and the Law,* 61-88. London: SPCK, 1988, 1990.

————. 'Prophetic "I"-Sayings and the Jesus Tradition: The Importance of Testing Prophetic Utterances within Early Christianity'. *NTS* 24 (1977-78): 175-98.

————. 'The Question of Antisemitism in the New Testament Writings'. In *Jews and Christians: The Parting of the Ways AD 70 to 135,* edited by J. D. G. Dunn, 177-211. Tübingen: Mohr Siebeck, 1992.

————. '"Son of God" as "Son of Man" in the Dead Sea Scrolls? A Response to John Collins on 4Q246'. In *The Scrolls and the Scriptures: Qumran Fifty Years After,* edited by S. E. Porter and C. A. Evans, 198-210. Sheffield: Sheffield Academic, 1997.

————. 'Spirit-and-Fire Baptism'. *NovT* 14 (1972): 81-92.

————. 'Spirit and Kingdom'. In *The Christ and the Spirit.* Vol. 2: *Pneumatology,* 133-41. Grand Rapids: Eerdmans, 1970-71, 1998.

————. *The Theology of Paul the Apostle.* Grand Rapids: Eerdmans/Edinburgh: Clark, 1998.

————. *Unity and Diversity in the New Testament.* London: SCM, 1977, 1990, 2nd ed.

Dunn, J. D. G., and G. H. Twelftree. 'Demon-Possession and Exorcism in the New Testament (1980)'. In J. D. G. Dunn, *The Christ and the Spirit.* Vol. 2: *Pneumatology,* 170-86. Grand Rapids: Eerdmans, 1998.

Du Toit, D. S. 'Redefining Jesus: Current Trends in Jesus Research'. In *Jesus, Mark and Q: The Teaching of Jesus and Its Earliest Records,* edited by M. Labahn and A. Schmidt, 82-124. Sheffield: Sheffield Academic, 2001.

Ebner, M. *Jesus — ein Weisheitslehrer? Synoptische Weisheitslogien im Traditionsprozess.* Freiburg: Herder, 1998.

Eckstein, H.-J. 'Markus 10,46-52 als Schlüsseltext des Markusevangeliums'. *ZNW* 87 (1996): 33-50.

Eddy, P. R. 'Jesus as Diogenes? Reflections on the Cynic Jesus Thesis'. *JBL* 115 (1996): 449-69.

Edwards, D. *The Sign of Jonah.* London: SCM, 1971.

———. 'The Socio-Economic and Cultural Ethos of the Lower Galilee in the First Century: Implications for the Nascent Jesus Movement'. In *The Galilee in Late Antiquity,* edited by L. I. Levine, 53-73. New York: Jewish Theological Seminary of America, 1992.

Edwards, D. R., and C. T. McCollough. *Archaeology and the Galilee: Texts and Contexts in the Graeco-Roman and Byzantine Periods.* Atlanta: Scholars, 1997.

Egger, P. *"Crucifixus sub Pontio Pilato". Das "Crimen" Jesu von Nazareth im Spannungsfeld römischer und jüdischer Verwaltungs- und Rechtsstrukturen.* Neutestamentliche Abhandlungen NF 32. Münster: Aschendorff, 1997.

Ehrman, B. D. *Jesus: Apocalyptic Prophet of the New Millennium.* Oxford: Oxford University, 1999.

Eitrem, S. *Some Notes on the Demonology in the New Testament.* Uppsala: Almquist and Wiksells, 1966, 2nd ed.

Elliott, J. H. 'Social-Scientific Criticism of the New Testament and Its Social World'. *Semeia* 35 (1986): 1-33.

Ellis, E. E. 'The Historical Jesus and the Gospels'. In *Evangelium — Schriftauslegung — Kirche,* P. Stuhlmacher FS, edited by J. Ådna, 94-106. Tübingen: Mohr Siebeck, 1997.

———. *The Making of the New Testament Documents.* Leiden: Brill, 1999.

Eppstein, V. 'The Historicity of the Gospel Account of the Cleansing of the Temple'. *ZNW* 55 (1964): 42-57.

Ernst, J. 'Johannes der Täufer und Jesus von Nazareth in historischer Sicht'. *NTS* 43 (1997): 161-83.

———. *Johannes der Täufer: Interpretation — Geschichte — Wirkungsgeschichte.* BZNW 53. Berlin: de Gruyter, 1989.

Evans, C. A. 'Authenticating the Activities of Jesus'. In *Authenticating the Activities of Jesus,* edited by B. Chilton and C. A. Evans, 3-29. Leiden: Brill, 1999.

———. 'Did Jesus Predict His Death and Resurrection?' In *Resurrection,* edited by S. E. Porter, M. A. Hayes, and D. Tombs, 82-97. Sheffield: Sheffield Academic, 1999.

———. 'In What Sense "Blasphemy"? Jesus before Caiaphas in Mark 14.61-64'. In *Jesus and His Contemporaries: Comparative Studies,* 407-34. Leiden: Brill, 1995.

———. 'Jesus' Action in the Temple: Cleansing or Portent of Destruction?' *CBQ* 51 (1989): 237-70.

———. *Jesus and His Contemporaries: Comparative Studies.* Leiden: Brill, 1995.

———. 'Jesus and Predictions of the Destruction of the Herodian Temple'. In *Jesus and His Contemporaries: Comparative Studies,* 367-80. Leiden: Brill, 1995.

———. 'Jesus and the Messianic Texts from Qumran'. In *Jesus and His Contemporaries,* 83-154. Leiden: Brill, 1995.

———. 'Jesus and Zechariah's Messianic Hope'. In *Authenticating the Activities of Jesus,* edited by B. Chilton and C. A. Evans, 373-88. Leiden: Brill, 1999.

———. 'Jesus in Non-Christian Sources'. In *Studying the Historical Jesus,* edited by B. Chilton and C. A. Evans, 443-78. Leiden: Brill, 1994.

———. 'Jesus' Parable of the Tenant Farmers in Light of Lease Agreements in Antiquity'. *JSP* 14 (1996): 65-83.

———. 'The New Quest for Jesus and the New Research on the Dead Sea Scrolls'. In *Jesus, Mark and Q: The Teaching of Jesus and Its Earliest Records,* edited by M. Labahn and A. Schmidt, 163-83. Sheffield: Sheffield Academic, 2001.

———. 'Reconstructing Jesus' Teaching: Problems and Possibilities'. In *Hillel and Jesus,* edited by J. H. Charlesworth and L. L. Johns, 397-426. Minneapolis: Fortress, 1997.

———. *To See and Not Perceive: Isaiah 6.9-10 in Early Jewish and Christian Interpretation.* JSOTS 64. Sheffield: Sheffield Academic, 1989.

Evans, C. F. *Resurrection and the New Testament.* London: SCM, 1970.

Falk, H. *Jesus the Pharisee: A New Look at the Jewishness of Jesus.* New York: Paulist, 1979.

Farmer, W. R. *The Synoptic Problem.* New York: Macmillan, 1964, 1976, 2nd ed.

Fiensy, D. A. 'Jesus' Socioeconomic Background'. In *Hillel and Jesus,* edited by J. H. Charlesworth and L. L. Johns, 225-55. Minneapolis: Fortress, 1997.

Fine, S. 'A Note on Ossuary Burial and the Resurrection of the Dead in First-Century Jerusalem'. *JJS* 51 (2000): 69-76.

Fine, S., ed. *Jews, Christians, and Polytheists in the Ancient Synagogue: Cultural Interaction during the Greco-Roman Period.* London: Routledge, 1999.

Finnegan, R. *Oral Poetry: Its Nature, Significance and Social Context.* Cambridge: Cambridge University, 1977.

Fish, S. *Is There a Text in This Class? The Authority of Interpretive Communities.* Cambridge: Harvard University, 1980.

Fitzmyer, J. A. 'Abba and Jesus' Relation to God'. In *À Cause de L'Évangile,* J. Dupont FS, 15-38. Paris: Cerf, 1985.

———. 'Another View of the "Son of Man" Debate'. *JSNT* 4 (1979): 58-68.

———. 'Aramaic *Kepha'* and Peter's Name in the New Testament'. In *To Advance the Gospel: New Testament Studies,* 112-24. Grand Rapids: Eerdmans, 1981, 1998, 2nd ed.

———. 'The Languages of Palestine in the First Century A.D.'. In *A Wandering Aramean: Collected Aramaic Essays,* 29-56. Missoula: Scholars, 1979.

———. 'The New Testament Title 'Son of Man' Philologically Considered'. In *A Wandering Aramean: Collected Aramaic Essays.* Missoula: Scholars, 1974, 1979.

———. 'The Priority of Mark and the 'Q' Source in Luke'. In *Jesus and Man's Hope,* edited by D. G. Miller. Pittsburgh: Pittsburgh Theological Seminary, 1970.

————. 'The Qumran Community: Essene or Sadducean?' In *The Dead Sea Scrolls and Christian Origins,* 249-60. Grand Rapids: Eerdmans, 2000.

————. 'The Study of the Aramaic Background of the New Testament'. In *A Wandering Aramean: Collected Aramaic Essays,* 1-27. Missoula: Scholars, 1979.

Fleddermann, H. 'The Demands of Discipleship Matt 8,19-22 par. Luke 9,57-60'. In *The Four Gospels 1992,* F. Neirynck FS, edited by F. Van Segbroeck, et al., 541-61. Leuven: Leuven University, 1992.

Flusser, D. 'Hillel and Jesus: Two Ways of Self-Awareness'. In *Hillel and Jesus,* edited by J. H. Charlesworth and L. L. Johns, 71-107. Minneapolis: Fortress, 1997.

————. *Jesus.* Jerusalem: Magnes, 1969, revised 1998.

————. *Judaism and the Origins of Christianity.* Jerusalem: Magnes, 1988.

Foley, J. M. *Immanent Art: From Structure to Meaning in Traditional Oral Epic.* Bloomington: Indiana University, 1991.

————. *The Singer of Tales in Performance.* Bloomington: Indiana University, 1995.

Fortna, R. T. *The Fourth Gospel and Its Predecessor.* Philadelphia: Fortress, 1988.

Fowl, S. E. 'Reconstructing and Deconstructing the Quest for the Historical Jesus'. *SJT* 42 (1989): 319-33.

France, R. T. *Jesus and the Old Testament.* London: Tyndale, 1972.

————. 'Jesus the Baptist?' In *Jesus of Nazareth: Lord and Christ,* I. H. Marshall FS, edited by J. B. Green and M. Turner, 94-111. Grand Rapids: Eerdmans, 1994.

Francis, J. 'Children and Childhood in the New Testament'. In *The Family in Theological Perspective,* edited by S. C. Barton, 65-85. Edinburgh: Clark, 1996.

Fredriksen, P. *From Jesus to Christ: The Origins of the New Testament Images of Jesus.* New Haven: Yale University, 1988.

————. *Jesus of Nazareth, King of the Jews: A Jewish Life and the Emergence of Christianity.* New York: Knopf, 1999.

Freed, E. D. *The Stories of Jesus' Birth: A Critical Introduction.* Sheffield: Sheffield Academic, 2001.

Frei, H. W. *The Eclipse of the Biblical Narrative: A Study in Eighteenth and Nineteenth Century Hermeneutics.* New Haven: Yale University, 1974.

Freyne, S. 'Archaeology and the Historical Jesus'. In *Galilee and Gospel,* 160-82. Tübingen: Mohr Siebeck, 2000.

————. *Galilee and Gospel.* WUNT 125. Tübingen: Mohr Siebeck, 2000.

————. *Galilee from Alexander the Great to Hadrian, 323 BCE to 135 CE: A Study of Second Temple Judaism.* Wilmington: Michael Glazier, 1980.

————. *Galilee, Jesus and the Gospels: Literary Approaches and Historical Investigations.* Dublin: Gill and Macmillan, 1988.

————. 'The Geography, Politics, and Economics of Galilee and the Quest for the Historical Jesus'. In *Studying the Historical Jesus,* edited by B. Chilton and C. A. Evans, 75-121. Leiden: Brill, 1994.

————. 'Jesus and the Urban Culture of Galilee'. In *Galilee and Gospel,* 183-207. Tübingen: Mohr Siebeck, 2000.

Frickenschmidt, D. *Evangelium als Biographie. Die vier Evangelien im Rahmen antiker Erzählkunst.* Tübingen: Francke, 1997.

Fuchs, E. 'Jesus and Faith'. In *Studies of the Historical Jesus,* 48-64. London: SCM, 1964.

———. 'The Quest of the Historical Jesus'. In *Studies of the Historical Jesus,* 11-31. London: SCM, 1964.

Fuller, R. H. *The Formation of the Resurrection Narratives.* London: SPCK, 1972.

———. *The Foundations of New Testament Chrisotology.* New York: Scribner, 1965.

———. *The Mission and Achievement of Jesus.* London: SCM, 1954.

Funk, R. W. *The Acts of Jesus: The Search for the Authentic Deeds of Jesus.* San Francisco: Harper, 1998.

———. *Honest to Jesus.* San Francisco: Harper, 1996.

Funk, R. W., and R. W. Hoover, ed. *The Five Gospels: The Search for the Authentic Words of Jesus.* New York: Macmillan, 1993.

Furnish, V. P. *The Love Command in the New Testament.* Nashville: Abingdon, 1972.

Gadamer, H.-G. *Truth and Method.* New York: Crossroad, 1989.

Gärtner, B. *The Temple and the Community in Qumran and the New Testament.* SNTSMS 1. Cambridge: Cambridge University, 1965.

Gager, J. G. *Kingdom and Community: The Social World of Early Christianity.* Englewood Cliffs: Prentice-Hall, 1975.

Geering, L. *Resurrection — a Symbol of Hope.* London: Hodder, 1971.

Georgi, D. 'The Interest in Life of Jesus Theology as a Paradigm for the Social History of Biblical Criticism'. *HTR* 85 (1992): 51-83.

Gerhardsson, B. *The Gospel Tradition.* Lund: Gleerup, 1986.

———. 'Illuminating the Kingdom: Narrative Meshalim in the Synoptic Gospels'. In *Jesus and the Oral Gospel Tradition,* edited by H. Wansbrough, 266-309. Sheffield: Sheffield Academic, 1991.

———. *Memory and Manuscript: Oral Tradition and Written Transmission in Rabbinic Judaism and Early Christianity.* Lund: Gleerup, 1961, 1998.

———. *The Origins of the Gospel Traditions.* Philadelphia: Fortress, 1979.

———. *The Reliability of the Gospel Tradition.* Peabody: Hendrickson, 2001.

———. *The Testing of God's Son (Matt. 4.1-11 & Par.).* ConBNT 2/1. Lund: Gleerup, 1966.

———. *Tradition and Transmission in Early Christianity.* Lund: Gleerup, 1964.

Glasson, T. F. 'The Reply to Caiaphas (Mark xiv.62)'. *NTS* 7 (1960-61): 88-93.

———. 'Schweitzer's Influence — Blessing or Bane?' *JTS* 28 (1977): 289-302.

———. *The Second Advent: The Origin of the New Testament Doctrine.* London: Epworth, 1945, 1963, 3rd ed.

———. 'What Is Apocalyptic?' *NTS* 27 (1980-81): 98-105.

Gnilka, J. *Die Verstockung Israels. Isaias 6,9-10 in der Theologie der Synoptiker.* SANT 3. München: Kosel, 1961.

———. *Jesus of Nazareth: Message and History.* ET Peabody: Hendrickson, 1997 (1993).

———. 'Wie urteilte Jesus über deinen Tod?' In *Der Tod Jesu: Deutungen im Neuen Testament,* edited by K. Kertelge, 13-50. Freiburg: Herder, 1976.

Goguel, M. *Jesus the Nazarene — Myth or History?* London: Unwin, 1926.

———. *The Life of Jesus.* London: George Allen and Unwin, 1933.

Goodman, M. *The Ruling Class of Judaea: The Origins of the Jewish Revolt against Rome, AD 66-70.* Cambridge: Cambridge University, 1987.

Goppelt, L. *Theology of the New Testament.* Vol. 1: *The Ministry of Jesus in Its Theological Significance.* ET Grand Rapids: Eerdmans, 1981 (1975).

Goshen-Gottstein, A. 'Hillel and Jesus: Are Comparisons Possible?' In *Hillel and Jesus,* edited by J. H. Charlesworth and L. L. Johns, 31-55. Minneapolis: Fortress, 1997.

Goulder, M. 'Did Jesus of Nazareth Rise from the Dead?' In *Resurrection,* edited by S. C. Barton and G. N. Stanton, 58-68. London: SPCK, 1994.

Gourges, M. 'The Priest, the Levite, and the Samaritan Revisited: A Critical Note on Luke 10:31-35'. *JBL* 117 (1998): 709-13.

Grabbe, L. L. *Judaism from Cyrus to Hadrian,* 2 vols. Minneapolis: Fortress, 1992.

Grässer, E. 'On Understanding the Kingdom of God'. In *The Kingdom of God,* edited by B. Chilton, 52-71. ET London: SPCK, 1984 (1974).

Graf, F. *Magic in the Ancient World.* Cambridge: Harvard University, 1997.

Grant, M. *Jesus.* London: Weidenfeld and Nicolson, 1977.

Grass, H. *Ostergeschehen und Osterberichte.* Göttingen: Vandenhoeck und Ruprecht, 1961, 2nd ed.

Gray, R. *Prophetic Figures in Late Second Temple Jewish Palestine: The Evidence from Josephus.* Oxford: Oxford University, 1993.

Green, J. B. *The Death of Jesus: Tradition and Interpretation in the Passion Narrative.* WUNT 2.23. Tübingen: Mohr Siebeck, 1988.

Greene-McCreight, K. E. *Ad Litteram: How Augustine, Calvin, and Barth read the 'Plain Sense' of Genesis 1–3.* New York: Lang, 1999.

Grelot, P. *Jesus de Nazareth, Christ et Seigneur. Une lecture de l'Evangile.* Lectio Divina 167. Paris: Cerf, 1997.

Grimm, W. *Die Verkündigung Jesu und Deuterojesaja.* Frankfurt: $$$, 1981, 2nd ed.

Gruenwald, I. *Apocalyptic and Merkavah Mysticism.* Leiden: Brill, 1980.

Grundmann, W. *Jesus der Galiläer und das Judentum.* Leipzig: Wigand, 1941.

Guelich, R. A. *The Sermon on the Mount.* Waco: Word, 1982.

Gutmann, J. *Ancient Synagogues: The State of Research.* BJS 22. Chico: Scholars, 1981.

Hachlili, R. 'The Origin of the Synagogue: A Re-Assessment'. *JSJ* 28 (1997): 34-47.

Hagner, D. A. 'An Analysis of Recent "Historical Jesus" Studies'. In *Religious Diversity in the Graeco-Roman World: A Survey of Recent Scholarship,* edited by D. Cohn-Sherbok and J. M. Court, 81-106. Sheffield: Sheffield Academic, 2001.

————. *The Jewish Reclamation of Jesus: An Analysis and Critique of the Modern Jewish Study of Jesus.* Grand Rapids: Zondervan, 1984.

Hahn, F. *The Titles of Jesus in Christology.* ET London: Lutterworth, 1969 (1963, 1995, 5th ed.).

Hamerton-Kelly, R. *God the Father: Theology and Patriarchy in the Teaching of Jesus.* Philadelphia: Fortress, 1979.

Hamilton, W. *A Quest for the Post-Historical Jesus.* London: SCM, 1993.

Hampel, V. *Menschensohn und historischer Jesus. Ein Rätselwort als Schlüssel zum messianischen Selbstverständnis Jesu.* Neukirchen-Vluyn: Neukirchener, 1990.

Hanson, K. C., and D. E. Oakman. *Palestine in the Time of Jesus.* Minneapolis: Fortress, 1998.

Hare, D. R. A. *The Son of Man Tradition*. Minneapolis: Fortress, 1990.

Harnack, A. *The Sayings of Jesus*. London: Williams and Norgate, 1908.

―――. *What Is Christianity?* ET London: Williams and Norgate, 1901, 1904, 3rd edn. (1900).

Harrington, D. J. 'The Jewishness of Jesus: Facing Some Problems'. *CBQ* 49 (1987): 1-13.

Harris, H. *David Friedrich Strauss and His Theology*. Cambridge: Cambridge University, 1973.

Harris, W. V. *Ancient Literacy*. Cambridge: Harvard University, 1989.

Hartman, L. *Prophecy Interpreted: The Formation of Some Jewish Apocalyptic Texts and of the Eschatological Discourse Mark 13 par.* ConBNT 1. Lund: Gleerup, 1966.

Harvey, A. E. *Jesus and the Constraints of History*. London: Duckworth, 1982.

―――. *Strenuous Commands: The Ethic of Jesus*. London: SCM, 1990.

Harvey, G. *The True Israel: Uses of the Names Jew, Hebrew and Israel in Ancient Jewish and Early Christian Literature*. Leiden: Brill, 1996.

Harvey, V. A. *The Historian and the Believer*. London: SCM, 1966.

Havener, I. *Q: The Sayings of Jesus*. Collegeville: Liturgical, 1987.

Haverly, T. P. *Oral Traditional Literature and the Composition of Mark's Gospel*. Edinburgh PhD, 1983.

Hawkins, J. C. *Horae Synopticae: Contributions to the Study of the Synoptic Problem*. Oxford: Clarendon, 1898, 1909, 2nd edn.

Hay, D. M. *Glory at the Right Hand: Psalm 110 in Early Christianity*. SBLMS 18. Nashville: Abingdon, 1973.

Hedrick, C. W. *When History and Faith Collide: Studying Jesus*. Peabody: Hendrickson, 1999.

Hedrick, C. W., ed. *The Historical Jesus and the Rejected Gospels*. Semeia 44. Atlanta: Scholars, 1988.

Heil, J. P. *The Transfiguration of Jesus: Narrative Meaning and Function of Mark 9:2-8, Matt 17:1-8 and Luke 9:28-36*. Rome: Pontifical Biblical Institute, 2000.

Henaut, B. W. 'Is the "Historical Jesus" a Christological Construct?' In *Whose Historical Jesus?* edited by W. E. Arnal and M. Desjardins, 241-68. Waterloo: Wilfrid Laurier University, 1997.

―――. *Oral Tradition and the Gospels: The Problem of Mark 4*. JSNTS 82. Sheffield: Sheffield Academic, 1993.

Henderson, I. 'Didache and Orality in Synoptic Comparison'. *JBL* 111 (1992): 283-306.

Hengel, M. *The Atonement: The Origins of the Doctrine in the New Testament*. London: SCM, 1981.

―――. *The Charismatic Leader and His Followers*. ET Edinburgh: Clark, 1981 (1968).

―――. *Crucifixion*. London: SCM, 1977.

―――. 'Das Gleichnis von den Weingartnern. Mc 12:1-12 im Licht der Zenonpapyri und der rabbinischen Gleichnisse'. *ZNW* 59 (1968): 1-39.

―――. *The Four Gospels and the One Gospel of Jesus Christ*. London: SCM, 2000.

―――. *The 'Hellenization' of Judaea in the First Century after Christ*. London: SCM, 1989.

———. 'Jesus as Messianic Teacher of Wisdom and the Beginnings of Christology'. In *Studies in Early Christology*, 73-117. Edinburgh: Clark, 1995.

———. 'Jesus, the Messiah of Israel'. In *Studies in Early Christology*, 1-72. Edinburgh: Clark, 1995.

———. *Judaism and Hellenism*, 2 vols. London: SCM, 1974.

———. 'Maria Magdalena und die Frauen als Zeugen'. In *Abraham unser Vater*, O. Michel FS, edited by O. Betz, 243-56. Leiden: Brill, 1963.

———. *Property and Riches in the Early Church*. London: SCM, 1974.

———. 'Proseuche und Synagoge. Jüdische Gemeinde, Gotteshaus und Gottesdienst in der Diaspora und in Palästina'. In *Judaica et Hellenistica: Kleine Schriften I*, 171-95. Tübingen: Mohr Siebeck, 1971, 2000.

———. '"Sit at My Right Hand!" The Enthronement of Christ at the Right Hand of God and Psalm 110:1'. In *Studies in Early Christology*, 119-225. Edinburgh: Clark, 1995.

———. *The Son of God: The Origin of Christology and the History of Jewish-Hellenistic Religion*. London: SCM, 1976.

———. *Studies in the Gospel of Mark*. London: SCM, 1985.

———. *Was Jesus a Revolutionist?* Philadelphia: Fortress, 1971.

———. *The Zealots*. ET Edinburgh: Clark, 1989 (1961, 1976, 2nd ed.).

Hengel, M., and R. Deines. 'E. P. Sanders' "Common Judaism", Jesus, and the Pharisees'. *JTS* 46 (1995): 1-70.

Hengel, M., and A. M. Schwemer, eds. *Königsherrschaft Gottes und himmlischer Kult im Judentum, Urchristentum und in der hellenistichen Welt*. WUNT 55. Tübingen: Mohr Siebeck, 1991.

Herrenbruck, F. *Jesus und die Zöllner*. WUNT 2.41. Tübingen: Mohr Siebeck, 1990.

———. 'Wer waren die "Zöllner"?' *ZNW* 72 (1981): 178-94.

Herrmann, W. *The Communion of the Christian with God*. ET Philadelphia: Fortress, 1906, 1971 (1892).

Herzog, W. R. *Jesus, Justice and the Reign of God: A Ministry of Liberation*. Louisville: Westminster John Knox, 2000.

———. *Parables as Subversive Speech*. Louisville: Westminster John Knox, 1994.

Heschel, S. *Abraham Geiger and the Jewish Jesus*. Chicago: University of Chicago, 1998.

Hiers, R. H. *The Historical Jesus and the Kingdom of God*. Gainesville: University of Florida, 1973.

Higgins, A. J. B. *Jesus and the Son of Man*. London: Lutterworth, 1964.

———. *The Son of Man in the Teaching of Jesus*. SNTSMS 39. Cambridge: Cambridge University, 1980.

Hill, D. *New Testament Prophecy*. London: Marshall, Morgan and Scott, 1979.

———. 'On the Evidence for the Creative Role of Christian Prophets'. *NTS* 20 (1973-74): 262-74.

Hoffmann, P. 'Der Menschensohn in Lukas 12.8'. *NTS* 44 (1998): 357-79.

———. 'Jesus versus Menschensohn'. In *Salz der Erde — Licht der Welt*, A. Vögtle FS, edited by L. Oberlinner and P. Fiedler, 165-202. Stuttgart: KBW, 1991.

———. 'Mutmassungen über Q: zum Problem der literarischen Genese von Q'. In *The*

Sayings Source Q and the Historical Jesus, edited by A. Lindemann, 255-88. Leuven: Leuven University, 2001.

―――. 'The Redaction of Q and the Son of Man'. In *The Gospel behind the Gospels: Current Studies on Q,* edited by R. A. Piper. Leiden: Brill, 1995.

―――. *Studien zur Theologie der Logienquelle.* Münster: Aschendorff, 1972.

―――. *Zur neutestamentlichen Überlieferung von der Auferstehung Jesu.* Darmstadt: Wissenschaftliche Buchgesellschaft, 1988.

Hofius, O. 'The Lord's Supper and the Lord's Supper Tradition: Reflections on 1 Corinthians 11.23b-25'. In *One Loaf, One Cup: Ecumenical Studies of 1 Cor. 11 and Other Eucharistic Texts,* edited by B. F. Meyer, 75-115. Macon: Mercer University, 1993.

―――. 'Ist Jesus der Messias? Thesen'. *JBTh* 8, *Der Messias* (1993): 103-29.

Holladay, C. H. Theios Anēr *in Hellenistic Judaism: A Critique of the Use of This Category in New Testament Christology.* SBLDS 40. Missoula: Scholars, 1977.

Hollander, H. W. 'The Words of Jesus: From Oral Tradition to Written Record in Paul and Q'. *NovT* 42 (2000): 340-57.

Hollenbach, P. 'The Conversion of Jesus: From Jesus the Baptizer to Jesus the Healer'. In *ANRW* II.25.1, 196-219, 1982.

―――. 'The Historical Jesus Question in North America Today'. *BTB* 19 (1989): 11-22.

―――. 'Social Aspects of John the Baptizer's Preaching Mission in the Context of Palestinian Judaism'. In *ANRW* II.19.1, 850-75, 1979.

Holman, C. L. *Till Jesus Comes: Origins of Christian Apocalyptic Expectation.* Peabody: Hendrickson, 1996.

Holmén, T. 'The Alternatives of the Kingdom: Encountering the Semantic Restrictions of Luke 17,20-21 *(entos humōn)*'. *ZNW* 87 (1996): 204-29.

―――. 'Doubts about Double Dissimilarity: Restructuring the Main Criterion of Jesus-of-History Research'. In *Authenticating the Words of Jesus,* edited by B. Chilton and C. A. Evans, 47-80. Leiden: Brill, 1999.

―――. *Jesus and Jewish Covenant Thinking.* Leiden: Brill, 2001.

―――. 'The Jewishness of Jesus in the "Third Quest"'. In *Jesus, Mark and Q: The Teaching of Jesus and Its Earliest Records,* edited by M. Labahn and A. Schmidt, 143-62. Sheffield: Sheffield Academic, 2001.

Holtzmann, H. J. *Die synoptischen Evangelien. Ihr Ursprung und ihr geschichtlicher Charakter.* Leipzig: Engelmann, 1863.

―――. *Lehrbuch der historisch-kritischen Einleitung in das Neue Testament.* Freiburg: Mohr Siebeck, 1886.

Hooker, M. D. 'Christology and Methodology'. *NTS* 17 (1970-71): 480-87.

―――. 'On Using the Wrong Tool'. *Theology* 75 (1972): 570-81.

―――. *The Servant of God.* London: SPCK, 1959.

―――. *The Signs of a Prophet: The Prophetic Actions of Jesus.* London: SCM, 1997.

―――. *The Son of Man in Mark.* London: SPCK, 1967.

Horbury, W. *Jewish Messianism and the Cult of Christ.* London: SCM, 1998.

―――. 'The Messianic Association of "The Son of Man"'. *JTS* 36 (1985): 34-55.

―――. 'The Temple Tax'. In *Jesus and the Politics of His Day,* edited by E. Bammel and C. F. D. Moule. Cambridge: Cambridge University, 1984.

Horn, F. W. 'Die synoptischen Einlasssprüche'. *ZNW* 87 (1996): 187-203.

Horne, E. H. 'The Parable of the Tenants as Indictment'. *JSNT* 71 (1998): 111-16.

Horsley, R. A. *Archaeology, History and Society in Galilee: The Social Context of Jesus and the Rabbis.* Valley Forge: Trinity, 1996.

———. 'The Death of Jesus'. In *Studying the Historical Jesus,* edited by B. Chilton and C. A. Evans, 395-422. Leiden: Brill, 1994.

———. *Galilee: History, Politics, People.* Valley Forge: Trinity, 1995.

———. *Jesus and the Spiral of Violence: Popular Jewish Resistance in Roman Palestine.* San Francisco: Harper and Row, 1987.

———. 'Q and Jesus: Assumptions, Appoaches and Analyses'. In *Early Christianity, Q and Jesus, Semeia* 55, edited by J. S. Kloppenborg and L. E. Vaage, 175-209, 1992.

———. *Sociology and the Jesus Movement.* New York: Continuum, 1989.

———. 'Synagogues in Galilee and the Gospels'. In *Evolution of the Synagogue,* edited by H. C. Kee and L. H. Cohick, 46-69. Harrisburg: Trinity, 1991.

———. 'The Zealots: Their Origin, Relationship and Importance in the Jewish Revolt'. *NovT* 28 (1986): 159-92.

Horsley, R. A., and J. A. Draper. *Whoever Hears You Hears Me: Prophets, Performance, and Tradition in Q.* Harrisburg: Trinity, 1999.

Horsley, R. A., and J. S. Hanson. *Bandits, Prophets, and Messiahs: Popular Movements in the Time of Jesus.* Minneapolis: Seabury, 1985.

Howard, V. 'Did Jesus Speak about His Own Death?' *CBQ* 39 (1977): 515-27.

Hubbard, B. J. *The Matthean Redaction of a Primitive Apostolic Commissioning.* SBLDS 19. Missoula: Scholars, 1974.

Hübner, H. *Das Gesetz in der synoptischen Tradition.* Witten: Luther, 1973.

Hughes, J. H. 'John the Baptist: The Forerunner of God Himself'. *NovT* 14 (1972): 191-218.

Hultgren, A. J. *The Parables of Jesus.* Grand Rapids: Eerdmans, 2000.

Humphrey, E. M. 'Will the Reader Understand? Apocalypse as Veil or Vision in Recent Historical-Jesus Research'. In *Whose Historical Jesus?* edited by W. E. Arnal and M. Desjardins, 215-37. Waterloo: Wilfrid Laurier University, 1997.

Hurtado, L. W. 'A Taxonomy of Recent Historical-Jesus Work'. In *Whose Historical Jesus?* edited by W. E. Arnal and M. Desjardins, 272-95. Waterloo: Wilfrid Laurier University, 1997.

Iggers, G. G. *Historiography in the Twentieth Century: From Scientific Objectivity to the Postmodern Challenge.* Hanover: Wesleyan University, 1997.

Jacobson, A. D. *The First Gospel: An Introduction to Q.* Sonoma: Polebridge, 1992.

———. 'Jesus against the Family: The Dissolution of Family Ties in the Gospel Tradition'. In *From Quest to Q,* J. M. Robinson FS, edited by J. M. Asgeirsson, et al., 189-218. Leuven: Leuven University, 2000.

———. 'The Literary Unity of Q'. *JBL* 101 (1982): 365-89.

Jenkins, K., ed. *The Postmodern History Reader.* London: Routledge, 1997.

Jenkins, P. *Hidden Gospels: How the Search for Jesus Lost Its Way.* New York: Oxford University, 2001.

Jeremias, G. *Der Lehrer der Gerechtigkeit.* SUNT 2. Göttingen: Vandenhoeck und Ruprecht, 1963.

Jeremias, J. *The Eucharistic Words of Jesus.* ET London: SCM, 1966 (1960, 3rd ed.).

————. *Heiligengräber in Jesu Umwelt.* Göttingen: Vandenhoeck und Ruprecht, 1958.

————. *Jerusalem in the Time of Jesus.* London: SCM, 1969.

————. *Jesus' Promise to the Nations.* London: SCM, 1958.

————. *New Testament Theology.* Vol. One: *The Proclamation of Jesus.* London: SCM, 1971.

————. 'Paarweise Sendung im Neuen Testament'. In *Abba. Studien zur neutestamentlichen Theologie und Zeitgeschichte,* 132-39. Göttingen: Vandenhoeck und Ruprecht, 1966.

————. *The Parables of Jesus.* ET London: SCM, 1963 (1947, 1962, 6th ed.).

————. *The Prayers of Jesus.* ET London: SCM, 1967 (1966).

————. *The Problem of the Historical Jesus.* ET Philadelphia: Fortress, 1964 (1960).

Jeremias, J., and W. Zimmerli. *The Servant of God.* London: SCM, 1957, revised 1965.

Johnson, L. T. *The Literary Function of Possessions in Luke-Acts.* SBLDS 39. Missoula: Scholars, 1977.

————. *The Real Jesus.* San Francisco: Harper, 1996.

Juel, D. H. *Messianic Exegesis: Christological Interpretation of the Old Testament in Early Christianity.* Philadelphia: Fortress, 1988.

Kähler, M. *The So-Called Historical Jesus and the Historic Biblical Christ.* ET Philadelphia: Fortress, 1964 (1892).

Käsemann, E. 'The Beginnings of Christian Theology'. In *New Testament Questions of Today,* 82-107. London: SCM, 1960, 1969.

————. 'Is the Gospel Objective?' In *Essays on New Testament Themes,* 48-62. London: SCM, 1964.

————. 'The Problem of the Historical Jesus'. In *Essays on New Testament Themes,* 15-47. ET London: SCM, 1964 (1954).

————. 'Sentences of Holy Law in the New Testament'. In *New Testament Questions of Today,* 66-81. London: SCM, 1969.

Karrer, M. *Jesus Christus im Neuen Testament.* Göttingen: Vandenhoeck und Ruprecht, 1998.

Kautsky, K. *Foundations of Christianity.* ET London: George Allen and Unwin, 1925 (1908).

Kaylor, R. D. *Jesus the Prophet: His Vision of the Kingdom on Earth.* Louisville: Westminster/John Knox, 1994.

Kazen, T. *Jesus and Purity* Halakhah: *Was Jesus Indifferent to Impurity?* ConBNT 38. Stockholm: Almqvist and Wiksell, 2002.

Keck, L. E. *A Future for the Historical Jesus.* Nashville: Abingdon, 1971.

————. 'Oral Traditional Literature and the Gospels'. In *The Relationships among the Gospels,* edited by W. O. Walker, 103-22. San Antonio: Trinity University, 1978.

————. '"The Poor among the Saints" in Jewish Christianity and Qumran'. *ZNW* 57 (1966): 54-78.

————. *Who Is Jesus? History in the Perfect Tense.* Columbia: University of South Carolina, 2000.

Kee, H. C. 'Defining the First-Century Synagogue'. In *Evolution of the Synagogue,* edited by H. C. Kee and L. H. Cohick, 7-26. Harrisburg: Trinity, 1999.

————. 'Jesus: A Glutton and a Drunkard'. *NTS* 42 (1996): 374-93.

————. *Medicine, Miracle and Magic in New Testament Times.* SNTSMS 55. Cambridge: Cambridge University, 1986.

————. *Miracle in the Early Christian World.* New Haven: Yale University, 1983.

————. 'The Transformation of the Synagogue after 70 CE'. *NTS* 36 (1990): 1-24.

Kee, H. C., and L. H. Cohick, eds. *Evolution of the Synagogue: Problems and Progress.* Harrisburg: Trinity, 1999.

Kelber, W. H. 'Jesus and Tradition: Words in Time, Words in Space'. In *Orality and Textuality in Early Christian Literature, Semeia* 65, edited by J. Dewey, 139-67, 1994.

————. *The Oral and the Written Gospel.* Philadelphia: Fortress, 1983.

Kelber, W. H., ed. *The Passion in Mark.* Philadelphia: Fortress, 1976.

Keller, E, and M. Keller. *Miracles in Dispute: A Continuing Debate.* London: SCM, 1969.

Kelly, J. N. D. *Early Christian Creeds.* 2nd ed. London: Longmans, 1960.

Kendall, D., and G. O'Collins. 'The Uniqueness of the Easter Appearances'. *CBQ* 54 (1992): 287-307.

Kim, S. *'The Son of Man' as the Son of God.* WUNT 30. Tübingen: Mohr Siebeck, 1983.

Kirk, A. *The Composition of the Sayings Source: Genre, Synchrony and Wisdom Redaction in Q.* NovTSup 91. Leiden: Brill, 1998.

————. 'Examining Priorities: Another Look at the *Gospel of Peter*'s Relationship to the New Testament Gospels'. *NTS* 40 (1994): 572-95.

————. 'Upbraiding Wisdom: John's Speech and the Beginning of Q (Q 3:7-9, 16-17)'. *NovT* 40 (1998): 1-16.

Klassen, W. 'The Authenticity of Judas; Participation in the Arrest of Jesus'. In *Authenticating the Activities of Jesus,* edited by B. Chilton and C. A. Evans, 389-410. Leiden: Brill, 1999.

————. 'The Authenticity of the Command: "Love Your Enemies"'. In *Authenticating the Words of Jesus,* edited by B. Chilton and C. A. Evans, 385-407. Leiden: Brill, 1999.

————. *Judas: Betrayer or Friend of Jesus?* Minneapolis: Augsburg, 1996.

————. '"Love Your Enemies": Some Reflections on the Current Status of Research'. In *The Love of Enemy and Nonretaliation in the New Testament,* edited by W. M. Swartley, 1-31. Louisville: Westminster, 1992.

Klauck, H.-J. *The Religious Context of Early Christianity.* Edinburgh: Clark, 2000.

Klausner, J. *Jesus of Nazareth: His Life, Times and Teaching.* London: George Allen and Unwin, 1925.

Klawans, J. *Impurity and Sin in Ancient Judaism.* Oxford: Oxford University, 2000.

Klein, C. *Anti-Judaism in Christian Theology.* ET London: SPCK, 1978 (1975).

Kleinknecht, K. T. *Der leidende Gerechtfertigte. Die alttestamentlich-jüdische Tradition vom 'leidenden Gerechten' und ihre Rezeption bei Paulus.* WUNT 2.13. Tübingen: Mohr Siebeck, 1984.

Klinzing, G. *Die Umdeutung des Kultus in der Qumrangemeinde und im NT.* Göttingen: Vandenhoeck und Ruprecht, 1971.

Kloppenborg, J. S. '"Easter Faith" and the Sayings Gospel Q'. In *The Apocryphal Jesus and Christian Origins, Semeia* 49, edited by R. Cameron, 71-99, 1990.

———. *The Formation of Q*. Philadelphia: Fortress, 1987.

———. 'Literary Convention, Self-Evidence and the Social History of the Q People'. *Semeia* 55 (1992): 77-102.

———. *Q Parallels: Synopsis, Critical Notes and Concordance*. Sonoma: Polebridge, 1988.

———. 'The Sayings Gospel Q and the Quest of the Historical Jesus'. *HTR* 89 (1996): 307-44.

———. 'Tradition and Redaction in the Synoptic Sayings Source'. *CBQ* 46 (1984): 34-62.

Kloppenborg, J. S., ed. *The Shape of Q*. Minneapolis: Fortress, 1994.

Kloppenborg Verbin, J. S. 'Dating Theodotus (*CIJ* II 1404)'. *JJS* 51 (2000): 243-80.

———. 'Discursive Practices in the Sayings Gospel Q and the Quest of the Historical Jesus'. In *The Sayings Source Q and the Historical Jesus,* edited by A. Lindemann, 149-90. Leuven: Leuven University, 2001.

———. *Excavating Q: The History and Setting of the Sayings Gospel*. Minneapolis: Fortress, 2000.

Knohl, I. *The Messiah before Jesus. The Suffering Servant of the Dead Sea Scrolls*. Berkeley: University of California, 2000.

Koch, K. 'Messias und Menschensohn. Die zweistufige Messianologie der jüngeren Apokalyptik'. *JBTh* 8, *Der Messias* (1993) 73-102.

———. *The Rediscovery of Apocalyptic*. London: SCM, 1972.

Koester, H. *Ancient Christian Gospels: Their History and Development*. London: SCM, 1990.

———. 'GNOMAI DIAPHOROI: The Origin and Nature of Diversification in the History of Early Christianity'. In *Trajectories through Early Christianity,* by J. M. Robinson and H. Koester, 114-59. Philadelphia: Fortress, (1965) 1971.

———. 'The Historical Jesus and the Historical Situation of the Quest: An Epilogue'. In *Studying the Historical Jesus,* edited by B. Chilton and C. A. Evans, 535-45. Leiden: Brill, 1994.

———. *Introduction to the New Testament*. 2 vols. Philadelphia: Fortress, 1982.

———. 'Jesus the Victim'. *JBL* 111 (1992): 3-15.

———. 'One Jesus and Four Primitive Gospels'. In *Trajectories through Early Christianity,* by J. M. Robinson and H. Koester, 158-204. Philadelphia: Fortress, (1968) 1971.

———. 'The Sayings of Q and Their Image of Jesus'. In *Sayings of Jesus: Canonical and Non-Canonical,* T. Baarda FS, edited by W. L. Petersen, et al., 137-54. Leiden: Brill, 1997.

———. 'The Structure and Criteria of Early Christian Beliefs'. In *Trajectories through Early Christianity,* by J. M. Robinson and H. Koester, 205-31. Philadelphia: Fortress, 1971.

———. *Synoptische Überlieferung bei den apostolischen Vätern*. Berlin: Akadamie-Verlag, 1957.

———. 'Written Gospels or Oral Tradition?' *JBL* 113 (1994): 293-97.

Kollmann, B. *Jesus und die Christen als Wundertäter. Studien zu Magie, Medizin und*

Schamanismus in Antike und Christentum. FRLANT 170. Göttingen: Vandenhoeck und Ruprecht, 1996.

Kraemer, R. S. 'On the Meaning of the Term "Jew" in Greco-Roman Inscriptions'. *HTR* 82 (1989): 35-53.

Kraft, R. A., and G. W. E. Nickelsburg. *Early Judaism and Its Modern Interpreters.* Atlanta: Scholars, 1986.

Kümmel, W. G. 'Eschatological Expectation in the Proclamation of Jesus'. In *The Future of Our Religious Past,* R. Bultmann FS, edited by J. M. Robinson, 29-48. ET London: SCM, 1971 (1964).

————. *Introduction to the New Testament.* ET Nashville: Abingdon, 1975 (1973).

————. *The New Testament: The History of the Investigation of Its Problems.* Nashville: Abingdon, 1972.

————. *Promise and Fulfilment: The Eschatological Message of Jesus.* ET London: SCM, 1961, 2nd ed. (1956, 3rd ed.).

————. *The Theology of the New Testament.* Nashville: Abingdon, 1973.

————. *Vierzig Jahre Jesusforschung (1950-1990).* BBB 91. Weinheim: Beltz Athenaum, 1994.

Kuhn, H. W. *Ältere Sammlungen im Markusevangelium.* Göttingen: Vandenhoeck und Ruprecht, 1971.

Kvalbein, H. 'The Wonders of the End-Time: Metaphoric Language in 4Q521 and the Interpretation of Matthew 11.5 par'. *JSP* 18 (1998): 87-110.

Labahn, M., and A. Schmidt. *Jesus, Mark and Q: The Teaching of Jesus and Its Earliest Records.* JSNTS 214. Sheffield: Sheffield Academic, 2001.

Ladd, G. E. *Jesus and the Kingdom: The Eschatology of Biblical Realism.* London: SPCK, 1966.

Lampe, G. W. H. 'The Two Swords (Luke 22:35-38)'. In *Jesus and the Politics of His Day,* edited by E. Bammel and C. F. D. Moule, 335-51. Cambridge: Cambridge University, 1984.

Légasse, S. *The Trial of Jesus.* ET London: SCM, 1997 (1994).

Lehmann, K. *Auferweckt am dritten Tag nach der Schrift.* QD 38. Freiburg: Herder, 1968.

Leivestad, R. 'Exit the Apocalyptic Son of Man'. *NTS* 18 (1971-72): 243-67.

————. *Jesus in His Own Perspective.* Minneapolis: Augsburg, 1987.

Lemcio, E. E. *The Past of Jesus in the Gospels.* SNTSMS 68. Cambridge: Cambridge University, 1991.

Leroy, H. *Jesus. Überlieferung und Deutung.* Darmstadt: Wissenschaftliche Buchgesellschaft, 1978, 1999, 3rd ed.

Levine, A.-J. 'Jesus, Divorce and Sexuality: A Jewish Critique'. In *The Historical Jesus through Catholic and Jewish Eyes,* edited by B. F. LeBeau, L. Greenspoon, and D. Hamm, 116-29. Harrisburg: Trinity, 2000.

Levine, L. I. *The Ancient Synagogue: The First Thousand Years.* New Haven: Yale University, 2000.

————. 'The Sages and the Synagogue in Late Antiquity: The Evidence of the Galilee'. In *The Galilee in Late Antiquity,* edited by L. I. Levine, 201-22. New York: Jewish Theological Seminary of America, 1992.

———. 'The Second Temple Synagogue: The Formative Years'. In *The Synagogue in Late Antiquity,* edited by L. I. Levine, 7-31. Philadelphia: Fortress, 1987.

Levine, L. I., ed. *The Galilee in Late Antiquity.* New York: Jewish Theological Seminary of America, 1992.

Lichtenberger, H. 'Jesus and the Dead Sea Scrolls'. In *Hillel and Jesus,* edited by J. H. Charlesworth and L. L. Johns, 389-96. Minneapolis: Fortress, 1997.

Liebenberg, J. *The Language of the Kingdom and Jesus.* BZNW 102. Berlin: de Gruyter, 2001.

Lieu, J. 'The Women's Resurrection Testimony'. In *Resurrection,* edited by S. C. Barton and G. N. Stanton, 34-44. London: SPCK, 1994.

Lindars, B. 'All Foods Clean: Thoughts on Jesus and the Law'. In *Law and Religion: Essays on the Place of the Law in Israel and Early Christianity,* edited by B. Lindars, 61-71. Cambridge: Clarke, 1988.

———. *Jesus Son of Man: A Fresh Examination of the Son of Man Sayings in the Gospels.* London: SPCK, 1983.

———. *New Testament Apologetic.* London: SCM, 1961.

Lindblom, J. *Gesichte und Offenbarungen.* Lund: Gleerup, 1968.

Lindemann, A. 'Die Logienquelle Q: Fragen an eine gut begründete Hypothese'. In *The Sayings Source Q and the Historical Jesus,* 3-26. Leuven: Leuven University, 2001.

———. *The Sayings Source Q and the Historical Jesus.* BETL 158. Leuven: Leuven University, 2001.

Lindeskog, G. *Die Jesusfrage im neuzeitlichen Judentum. Ein Beitrag zur Geschichte der Leben-Jesu-Forschung.* Leipzig, 1938; reprinted Darmstadt: Wissenschaftliche Buchgesellschaft, 1973.

Loader, W. R. G. 'Challenged at the Boundaries: A Conservative Jesus in Mark's Tradition'. *JSNT* 63 (1996): 45-61.

———. *Jesus' Attitude to the Law.* WUNT 2.97. Tübingen: Mohr Siebeck, 1997.

Loffreda, S. 'The Late Chronology of the Synagogue of Capernaum'. In *Ancient Synagogues Revealed,* edited by L. I. Levine, 52-56. Jerusalem: Israel Exploration Society, 1981.

Lohfink, G. *Jesus and Community.* Philadelphia: Fortress, 1985.

Lohr, C. H. 'Oral Techniques in the Gospel of Matthew'. *CBQ* 23 (1961): 403-35.

Lohse, E. 'Die Frage nach dem historischen Jesus in der gegenwärtigen neutestamentlichen Forschung'. In *Die Einheit des Neuen Testaments,* 29-48. Göttingen: Vandenhoeck und Ruprecht, 1962, 1973.

———. *Märtyrer und Gottesknecht. Untersuchungen zur urchristlichen Verkündigung vom Sühntod Jesu Christi.* Göttingen: Vandenhoeck und Ruprecht, 1955, 1963, 2nd ed.

Loisy, A. *The Birth of the Christian Religion* (1933), and *The Origins of the New Testament* (1936). ET New York: University Books, 1962.

Lonergan, B. *Collection: Papers by Bernard Lonergan.* Toronto: University of Toronto, 1988.

———. *Method in Theology.* London: Darton, Longman and Todd, 1972.

Lord, A. B. 'The Gospels as Oral Traditional Literature'. In *The Relationships among the Gospels,* edited by W. O. Walker, 33-91. San Antonio: Trinity University, 1978.

928

————. *The Singer of Tales.* Cambridge: Harvard University, 1978.

————. *The Singer Resumes the Tale.* Ithaca: Cornell University, 1995.

Lüdemann, G. *The Great Deception and What Jesus Really Said and Did.* London: SCM, 1998.

————. *Jesus after Two Thousand Years: What He Really Said and Did.* London: SCM, 2000.

————. *The Resurrection of Jesus: History, Experience, Theology.* London: SCM, 1994.

————. *Virgin Birth? The Real Story of Mary and Her Son Jesus.* London: SCM, 1998.

Lührmann, D. 'Die Logienquelle und die Leben-Jesu-Forschung'. In *The Sayings Source Q and the Historical Jesus,* edited by A. Lindemann, 191-206. Leuven: Leuven University, 2001.

————. *Die Redaktion der Logienquelle.* WMANT 33. Neukirchen-Vluyn: Neukirchener, 1969.

————. 'The Gospel of Mark and the Sayings Collection'. *JBL* 108 (1989): 51-71.

Lundström, G. *The Kingdom of God in the Teaching of Jesus.* Edinburgh: Oliver and Boyd, 1963.

Maccoby, H. *Judas Iscariot and the Myth of Jewish Evil.* London: Halban, 1992.

————. 'Paul and the Eucharist'. *NTS* 37 (1991): 247-67.

————. 'The Washing of Cups'. *JSNT* 14 (1982): 3-15.

Machen, J. G. *The Virgin Birth of Christ.* London: Clarke, 1930.

Mack, B. L. *The Christian Myth: Origins, Logic and Legacy.* New York: Continuum, 2001.

————. *The Lost Gospel: The Book of Q and Christian Origins.* San Francisco: HarperCollins, 1993.

————. *A Myth of Innocence: Mark and Christian Origins.* Philadelphia: Fortress, 1988.

————. 'Q and a Cynic-Like Jesus'. In *Whose Historical Jesus?* edited by W. E. Arnal and M. Desjardins, 25-36. Waterloo: Wilfrid Laurier University, 1997.

Mackintosh, H. R. *Types of Modern Theology: Schleiermacher to Barth.* Edinburgh: Clark, 1937.

Madden, P. J. *Jesus' Walking on the Sea: An Investigation of the Origin of the Narrative Account.* BZNW 81. Berlin: de Gruyter, 1997.

Maier, J. *Jesus von Nazareth in der talmudischen Überlieferung.* Darmstadt: Wissenschaftliche Buchgesellschaft, 1978.

Malina, B. J. 'Assessing the Historicity of Jesus' Walking on the Sea: Insights from Cross-cultural Psychology'. In *Authenticating the Activities of Jesus,* edited by B. Chilton and C. A. Evans, 351-71. Leiden: Brill, 1999.

————. *The Social Gospel of Jesus: The Kingdom of God in Mediterranean Perspective.* Minneapolis: Fortress, 2001.

————. *The Social World of Jesus and the Gospels.* London: Routledge, 1996.

Manson, T. W. *The Sayings of Jesus.* London: SCM, 1949.

————. *The Teaching of Jesus.* Cambridge: Cambridge University, 1931.

Manson, W. *Jesus the Messiah.* London: Hodder and Stoughton, 1943.

Marcus, J. 'Mark 14:61: "Are You the Messiah-Son-of-God?"' *NovT* 31 (1989): 125-41.

————. 'The Beelzebul Controversy and the Eschatologies of Jesus'. In *Authenticating the Activities of Jesus,* edited by B. Chilton and C. A. Evans, 247-77. Leiden: Brill, 1999.

———. 'Entering into the Kingly Power of God'. *JBL* 107 (1988): 663-75.

———. 'The Old Testament and the Death of Jesus: The Role of Scripture in the Gospel Passion Narratives'. In *The Death of Jesus in Early Christianity,* edited by J. T. Carroll and J. B. Green, 205-33. Peabody: Hendrickson, 1995.

Marguerat, D., E. Norelli, and J.-M. Poffet. *Jesus de Nazareth. Nouvelles approches d'une énigme.* Geneva: Labor et Fides, 1998.

Marsh, C. 'Quests of the Historical Jesus in New Historicist Perspective'. *Biblical Interpretation* 5 (1997): 403-37.

Marsh, C., and S. Moyise. *Jesus and the Gospels.* London: Cassell, 1999.

Marshall, I. H. 'The Divine Sonship of Jesus'. In *Jesus the Saviour: Studies in New Testament Theology,* 134-49. London: SPCK, 1967, 1990.

———. *Jesus the Saviour: Studies in New Testament Theology.* London: SPCK, 1990.

———. *Last Supper and Lord's Supper.* Exeter: Paternoster, 1980.

———. *The Origins of New Testament Christology.* Leicester: IVP, 1976.

———. 'The Synoptic Son of Man Sayings in Recent Discussion'. In *Jesus the Saviour: Studies in New Testament Theology,* 73-99. London: SPCK, 1963, 1990.

Martin, D. B. *The Corinthian Body.* New Haven: Yale University, 1995.

Martin, R. *The Elusive Messiah: A Philosophical Overview of the Quest for the Historical Jesus.* Boulder: Westview, 1999.

Marxsen, W. 'The Resurrection of Jesus as a Historical and Theological Problem'. In *The Significance of the Message of the Resurrection for Faith in Jesus Christ,* edited by C. F. D. Moule, 15-50. London: SCM, 1968.

———. *The Resurrection of Jesus of Nazareth.* London: SCM, 1970.

Mason, S. 'Revisiting Josephus's Pharisees'. In *Judaism in Late Antiquity* 3.2: *Where We Stand: Issues and Debates in Ancient Judaism,* edited by J. Neusner and A. J. Avery-Peck, 23-56. Leiden: Brill, 1999.

Matthews, S. *Jesus on Social Institutions.* New York: Macmillan, 1928.

McArthur, H. K. 'On the Third Day'. *NTS* 18 (1971-72): 81-86.

McCane, B. R. '"Where No One Had Yet Been Laid": The Shame of Jesus' Burial'. In *Authenticating the Activities of Jesus,* edited by B. Chilton and C. A. Evans, 431-52. Leiden: Brill, 1999.

McCready, W. O. 'The Historical Jesus and the Dead Sea Scrolls'. In *Whose Historical Jesus?* edited by W. E. Arnal and M. Desjardins, 190-211. Waterloo: Wilfrid Laurier University, 1997.

McDonald, J. I. H. *The Resurrection: Narrative and Belief.* London: SPCK, 1989.

McDonnell, K., and G. T. Montague. *Christian Initiation and Baptism and the Holy Spirit.* Collegeville: Liturgical, 1991.

McKnight, E. V. *Jesus Christ in History and Scripture: A Poetic and Sectarian Perspective.* Macon: Mercer University, 1999.

McKnight, S. *A New Vision for Israel: The Teachings of Jesus in National Context.* Grand Rapids: Eerdmans, 1999.

———. 'Public Declaration or Final Judgment? Matthew 10:26-27 = Luke 12.2-3 as a

Case of Creative Redaction'. In *Authenticating the Words of Jesus,* edited by B. Chilton and C. A. Evans, 363-83. Leiden: Brill, 1999.

Meadors, E. P. *Jesus the Messianic Herald of Salvation.* Tübingen: Mohr Siebeck, 1995.

―――. 'The 'Messianic' Implications of the Q Material'. *JBL* 118 (1999): 253-77.

Meier, J. P. 'The Circle of the Twelve: Did It Exist during Jesus' Public Ministry?' *JBL* 116 (1997): 635-72.

―――. 'The Debate on the Resurrection of the Dead: An Incident from the Ministry of the Historical Jesus?' *JSNT* 77 (2000): 3-24.

―――. 'From Elijah-like Prophet to the Royal Davidic Messiah'. In *Jesus: A Colloquium in the Holy Land,* edited by D. Donnelly, 45-83. New York: Continuum, 2001.

―――. 'The Historical Jesus and the Historical Herodians'. *JBL* 119 (2000): 740-46.

―――. *A Marginal Jew,* Vol. 1: *The Roots of the Problem and the Person.* Vol. 2: *Mentor, Message, and Miracles.* Vol. 3: *Companions and Competitors.* New York: Doubleday, 1991, 1994, 2001.

―――. *A Marginal Jew,* New York: Doubleday, 1994.

―――. 'The Present State of the "Third Quest" for the Historical Jesus: Loss and Gain'. *Biblica* 80 (1999): 459-87.

―――. 'Reflections on Jesus-of-History Research Today'. In *Jesus' Jewishness,* edited by J. H. Charlesworth, 84-107. New York: Crossroad, 1991.

Mendels, D. *The Rise and Fall of Jewish Nationalism.* New York: Doubleday, 1992.

Merkel, H. 'Die Gottesherrschaft in der Verkündigung Jesu'. In *Königsherrschaft Gottes und himmlischer Kult im Judentum, Urchristentum und in der hellenistichen Welt,* edited by M. Hengel and A. M. Schwemer, 119-61. Tübingen: Mohr Siebeck, 1991.

―――. 'The Opposition between Jesus and Judaism'. In *Jesus and the Politics of His Day,* edited by E. Bammel and C. F. D. Moule, 129-44. Cambridge: Cambridge University, 1984.

Merklein, H. 'Die Umkehrpredigt bei Johannes dem Täufer und Jesus von Nazaret'. In *Studien zu Jesus und Paulus,* 109-26. Tübingen: Mohr Siebeck, 1987.

―――. *Jesu Botschaft von der Gottesherrscahft.* SBS 111. Stuttgart: KBW, 1989, 3rd ed.

―――. 'Wie hat Jesus seinen Tod verstanden?' In *Studien zu Jesus und Paulus II,* 174-89. Tübingen: Mohr Siebeck, 1998.

Meye, R. P. *Jesus and the Twelve.* Grand Rapids: Eerdmans, 1968.

Meyer, B. F. *The Aims of Jesus.* London: SCM, 1979.

―――. 'Appointed Deed, Appointed Doer: Jesus and the Scriptures'. In *Authenticating the Activities of Jesus,* edited by B. Chilton and C. A. Evans, 155-76. Leiden: Brill, 1999.

―――. *Critical Realism and the New Testament.* Princeton Theological Monographs 17. Allison Park: Pickwick, 1989.

―――. *Reality and Illusion in New Testament Scholarship: A Primer in Critical Realist Hermeneutics.* Collegeville: Liturgical, 1994.

Meyer, E. *Ursprung und Anfänge des Christentums.* Stuttgart: Cotta, 1921-23.

Meyer, M., and C. Hughes. *Jesus Then and Now: Images of Jesus in History and Christology.* Harrisburg: Trinity, 2001.

Meyer, R. *Der Prophet aus Galiläa. Studie zum Jesusbild der drei ersten Evangelien.* Darmstadt: Wissenschaftliche Buchgesellschaft, 1940, 1970.

Meyers, E. M. 'Roman Sepphoris in Light of New Archaeological Evidence and Recent Research'. In *The Galilee in Late Antiquity,* edited by L. I. Levine, 321-38. New York: Jewish Theological Seminary of America, 1992.

Meyers, E. M., and J. F. Strange. *Archaeology, the Rabbis and Early Christianity.* Nashville: Abingdon, 1981.

Michaels, J. R. 'The Itinerant Jesus and His Home Town'. In *Authenticating the Activities of Jesus,* edited by B. Chilton and C. A. Evans, 177-93. Leiden: Brill, 1999.

Michel, O. 'The Conclusion of Matthew's Gospel'. ET in *The Interpretation of Matthew,* edited by G. N. Stanton, 30-41. London: SPCK, 1983 (1950).

Milik, J. T. *Ten Years of Discovery in the Wilderness of Judaea.* London: SCM, 1959.

Millard, A. *Reading and Writing in the Time of Jesus.* BS 69. Sheffield: Sheffield Academic, 2000.

Miller, J. W. *Jesus at Thirty.* Minneapolis: Fortress, 1997.

Miller, R. J., ed. *The Complete Gospels.* San Francisco: Harper, 1994.

Moloney, F. J. 'The Fourth Gospel and the Jesus of History'. *NTS* 46 (2000): 42-58.

———. 'Matthew 19,3-12 and Celibacy'. *JSNT* 2 (1979): 42-60.

Momigliano, A. 'Religion in Athens, Rome and Jerusalem in the First Century BC'. In *Approaches to Ancient Judaism.* Vol. 5: *Studies in Judaism and Its Greco-Roman Context,* edited by W. S. Green, 1-18. Atlanta: Scholars, 1985.

Montefiore, C. G. *The Synoptic Gospels.* London: Macmillan, 1909, 1927, 2nd ed.

Montefiore, H. W. 'God as Father in the Synoptic Gospels'. *NTS* 3 (1956-57): 31-46.

Moo, D. J. 'Jesus and the Authority of the Mosaic Law'. *JSNT* 20 (1984): 3-49.

———. *The Old Testament in the Gospel Passion Narratives.* Sheffield: Almond, 1983.

Moore, G. F. *Judaism in the First Three Centuries of the Christian Era: The Age of the Tannaim,* 3 vols. Cambridge: Harvard University, 1927-30.

Moore, S. D. *Literary Criticism and the Gospels.* New Haven: Yale University, 1989.

Morgan, R. 'The Historical Jesus and the Theology of the New Testament'. In *The Glory of Christ in the New Testament,* G. B. Caird FS, edited by L. D. Hurst and N. T. Wright, 187-206. Oxford: Clarendon, 1987.

———. *The Nature of New Testament Theology.* London: SCM, 1973.

Morgan, R., and J. Barton. *Biblical Interpretation.* Oxford: Oxford University, 1988.

Morgan, R., and M. Pye. *Ernst Troeltsch: Writings on Religion and Theology.* Louisville: Westminster John Knox, 1990.

Morrice, W. G. *Hidden Sayings of Jesus: Words Attributed to Jesus outside the Four Gospels.* London: SPCK, 1997.

Moule, C. F. D. *The Birth of the New Testament.* London: Black, 1962, 1981, 3rd ed.

———. 'Fulfilment-Words in the New Testament: Use and Abuse'. In *Essays in New Testament Interpretation,* 3-36. Cambridge: Cambridge University, 1967-68, 1982.

———. 'The Gravamen Against Jesus'. In *Jesus, the Gospels and the Church,* W. R. Farmer FS, edited by E. P. Sanders, 177-95. Macon: Mercer University, 1987.

———. 'Neglected Features in the Problem of "the Son of Man"'. In *Neues Testament und Kirche,* R. Schnackenburg FS, edited by J. Gnilka, 413-28. Freiburg: Herder, 1974.

————. *The Origin of Christology*. Cambridge: Cambridge University, 1977.

————. *The Phenomenon of the New Testament*. London: SCM, 1967.

————. *The Significance of the Message of the Resurrection for Faith in Jesus Christ*. London: SCM, 1968.

————. '"The Son of Man": Some of the Facts'. *NTS* 41 (1995): 277-79.

Moxnes, H. 'The Historical Jesus: From Master Narrative to Cultural Context'. *BTB* 28 (1998): 135-49.

————. 'Jesus the Jew: Dilemmas of Interpretation'. In *Fair Play: Diversity and Conflicts in Early Christianity,* H. Räisänen FS, edited by I. Dunderberg et al., 83-103. Leiden: Brill, 2002.

Mueller-Vollmer, K. *The Hermeneutics Reader*. New York: Continuum, 1994.

Mulder, M. J. *Mikra*. CRINT 2.1. Assen: Van Gorcum, 1988.

Müller, M. *Der Ausdruck 'Menschensohn' in den Evangelien. Voraussetzungen und Bedeutung*. Leiden: Brill, 1984.

Müller, U. B. *Die Entstehung des Glaubens an die Auferstehung Jesu. Historische Aspekte und Bedingungen*. SBS 172. Stuttgart: KBW, 1998.

————. *Messias und Menschensohn in jüdischen Apokalypsen und in der Offenbarung des Johannes*. Gütersloh: Mohn, 1972.

Murphy, J. *The Religious World of Jesus: An Introduction to Second Temple Judaism*. Hoboken: Ktav, 1991.

Murphy-O'Connor, J. *The Holy Land, Oxford Archaeological Guides*. Oxford: Oxford University, 1998, 4th ed.

————. 'Jesus and the Money Changers (Mark 11:15-17; John 2:13-17)'. *RB* 107 (2000): 42-55.

Mussner, F. *Jesus von Nazareth im Umfeld Israels und der Urkirche. Gesammelte Aufsätze*. WUNT 111. Tübingen: Mohr Siebeck, 1999.

Myllykoski, M. *Die letzten Tage Jesu. Markus, Johannes. ihre Traditionen und die historische Frage*. Helsinki: Suomalainen Tiedeakatemia, 1994.

————.'What Happened to the Body of Jesus?'. In *Fair Play: Diversity and Conflicts in Early Christianity,* H. Räisänen FS, edited by I. Dunderberg, C. M. Tuckett, and K. Syreeni, 43-82. Leiden: Brill, 2002.

Neale, D. A. *None but the Sinners: Religious Categories in the Gospel of Luke*. JSNTS 58. Sheffield: Sheffield Academic, 1991.

Neill, S., and N. T. Wright. *The Interpretation of the New Testament, 1861-1986*. Oxford: Oxford University, 1964, 1988, 2nd ed.

Neirynck, F. 'The Apocryphal Gospels and the Gospel of Mark'. BETL 86 (1989): 123-75.

————. *Evangelica II*. Leuven: Leuven University, 1991.

Neugebauer, F. 'Geistsprüche und Jesuslogien'. *ZNW* 53 (1962): 218-28.

Neusner, J. '"First Cleanse the Inside"'. *NTS* 22 (1976): 486-95.

————. *From Politics to Piety: The Emergence of Rabbinic Judaism*. Englewood Cliffs: Prentice Hall, 1973.

————. *Judaism: The Evidence of the Mishnah*. Chicago: University of Chicago, 1981.

————. 'Mr Maccoby's Red Cow, Mr Sanders's Pharisees — and Mine'. *JSS* 23 (1991): 81-98.

————. *The Rabbinic Traditions about the Pharisees.* Leiden: Brill, 1971.

————. *Studying Classical Judaism: A Primer.* Louisville: Westminster, 1991.

Neusner, J., W. S. Green, and E. Frerichs. *Judaisms and Their Messiahs at the Turn of the Christian Era.* Cambridge: Cambridge University, 1987.

Neville, D. J. *Arguments from Order in Synoptic Source Criticism: A History and Critique.* Macon: Mercer University, 1994.

Newman, C. C., ed. *Jesus and the Restoration of Israel: A Critical Assessment of N. T. Wright's* Jesus and the Victory of God. Downers Grove: InterVarsity, 1999.

Newton, M. *The Concept of Purity at Qumran and in the Letters of Paul.* SNTSMS 53. Cambridge: Cambridge University, 1985.

Nickelsburg, G. W. E. *Resurrection, Immortality and Eternal Life in Intertestamental Judaism.* Cambridge: Harvard University, 1972.

Nielsen, H. K. *Heiligung und Verkündigung. Das Verständnis der Heiligung und ihres Verhältnisses zur Verkündigung bei Jesus and in der ältesten Kirche.* Leiden: Brill, 1987.

Nissen, A. *Gott und der Nächste im antiken Judentum. Untersuchungen zum Doppelgebot der Liebe.* WUNT 15. Tübingen: Mohr Siebeck, 1974.

Nolland, J. L. 'The Gospel Prohibition of Divorce: Tradition History and Meaning'. *JSNT* 58 (1995): 19-35.

Oakman, D. E. *Jesus and the Economic Questions of His Day.* Lewiston: Mellen, 1986.

————. 'The Lord's Prayer in Social Perspective'. In *Authenticating the Words of Jesus,* edited by B. Chilton and C. A. Evans, 137-86. Leiden: Brill, 1999.

Oberlinner, L. *Todeserwartung und Todesgewissheit Jesu. Zum Problem einer historischen Begründung.* SBB 10. Stuttgart: KBW, 1980.

O'Collins, G. *Christology: A Biblical, Historical and Systematic Study of Jesus.* Oxford: Oxford University, 1995.

————. 'The Resurrection: The State of the Questions'. In *The Resurrection: An Interdisciplinary Symposium on the Resurrection of Jesus,* edited by S. T. Davis, D. Kendall, and G. O'Collins, 5-28. Oxford: Oxford University, 1997.

Oegema, G. S. *The Anointed and His People: Messianic Expectations from the Maccabees to Bar Kochba.* JSPSupp 27. Sheffield: Sheffield Academic, 1998.

O'Neill, J. C. *The Bible's Authority: A Portrait Gallery of Thinkers from Lessing to Bultmann.* Edinburgh: Clark, 1991.

————. *Who Did Jesus Think He Was?* Leiden: Brill, 1995.

Ong, W. J. *Orality and Literacy: The Technologizing of the Word.* London: Routledge, 1982, 1988.

————. *The Presence of the Word: Some Prolegomena for Cultural and Religious History.* Minneapolis: University of Minnesota, 1967, 1981.

Osiek, C., and D. L. Balch. *Families in the New Testament World: Households and House Churches.* Louisville: Westminster John Knox, 1997.

Oster, R. E. 'Supposed Anachronism in Luke-Acts' Use of *synagōgē:* A Rejoinder to H. C. Kee'. *NTS* 39 (1993): 178-208.

Owen, P., and D. Shepherd. 'Speaking Up for Qumran, Dalman and the Son of Man: Was *Bar Enasha* a Common Term for "Man" in the Time of Jesus?' *JSNT* 81 (2001): 81-121.

Padgett, A. G. 'Advice for Religious Historians: On the Myth of a Purely Historical Jesus'. In *The Resurrection: An Interdisciplinary Symposium on the Resurrection of Jesus,* edited by S. T. Davis, D. Kendall, and G. O'Collins, 287-307. Oxford: Oxford University, 1997.

Paesler, K. *Das Tempelwort Jesu. Die Traditionen von Tempelzerstörung und Tempelerneuerung im Neuen Testament,* FRLANT. Göttingen: Vandenhoeck und Ruprecht, 1999.

Painter, J. 'When Is a House Not Home? Disciples and Family in Mark 3.13-35'. *NTS* 45 (1999): 498-513.

Pannenberg, W. *Jesus, God and Man.* London: SCM, 1968.

Paschen, W. *Rein und Unrein.* München: Kosel, 1970.

Patterson, S. J. *The God of Jesus: The Historical Jesus and the Search for Meaning.* Harrisburg: Trinity, 1998.

———. *The Gospel of Thomas and Jesus.* Sonoma: Polebridge, 1993.

Pawlikowski, J. T. *Christ in the Light of the Christian-Jewish Dialogue.* New York: Paulist, 1982.

Pelikan, J. *Jesus through the Centuries: His Place in the History of Culture.* New Haven: Yale University, 1985.

Perkins, P. *Resurrection: New Testament Witness and Contemporary Reflection.* London: Chapman, 1984.

Perrin, N. *Jesus and the Language of the Kingdom: Symbol and Metaphor in New Testament Interpretation.* Philadelphia: Fortress, 1976.

———. *The Kingdom of God in the Teaching of Jesus.* London: SCM, 1963.

———. 'Mark 14.62: The End Product of a Christian Pesher Tradition'. In *A Modern Pilgrimage in New Testament Christology,* 1-22. Philadelphia: Fortress, 1965-66, 1974.

———. *A Modern Pilgrimage in New Testament Christology.* Philadelphia: Fortress, 1974.

———. *Rediscovering the Teaching of Jesus.* London: SCM, 1967.

———. *The Resurrection Narratives: A New Approach.* London: SCM, 1977.

Person, R. F. 'The Ancient Israelite Scribe as Performer'. *JBL* 117 (1998): 601-609.

Pesch, R. 'Zur Entstehung des Glaubens an die Auferstehung Jesu. Ein neuer Versuch'. In *Zur neutestamentlichen Überlieferung von der Auferstehung Jesu,* edited by P. Hoffmann, 228-55. Darmstadt: Wissenschaftliche Buchgesellschaft, 1983, 1988.

Petersen, W. L., et al., eds. *Sayings of Jesus: Canonical and Non-canonical,* T. Baarda FS. NovTSup 89. Leiden: Brill, 1997.

Petuchowski, J. J., and M. Brocke, eds. *The Lord's Prayer and Jewish Liturgy.* London: Burns and Oates, 1978.

Pilch, J. J. 'Appearances of the Risen Jesus in Cultural Context: Experiences of Alternate Reality'. *BTB* 28 (1998): 52-60.

———. 'The Transfiguration of Jesus: An Experiment of Alternate Reality'. In *Modelling Early Christianity: Social Scientific Studies of the New Testament in Its Context,* edited by P. F. Esler, 47-64. London: Routledge, 1995.

Piper, J. *'Love Your Enemies': Jesus' Love Command in the Synoptic Gospels and the*

Early Christian Paraenesis. SNTSMS 38. Cambridge: Cambridge University, 1979.

Piper, R. A. *Wisdom in the Q-Tradition: The Aphoristic Teaching of Jesus.* SNTSMS 61. Cambridge: Cambridge University, 1989.

Piper, R. A., ed. *The Gospel behind the Gospels: Current Studies on Q.* NovTSup 75. Leiden: Brill, 1995.

Pixner, B. 'Jesus and His Community: Between Essenes and Pharisees'. In *Hillel and Jesus,* edited by J. H. Charlesworth and L. L. Johns, 193-224. Minneapolis: Fortress, 1997.

Poirier, J. C. 'Why Did the Pharisees Wash Their Hands?' *JJS* 47 (1996): 217-33.

Polag, A. *Fragmenta Q. Textheft zur Logienquelle.* Neukirchen-Vluyn: Neukirchener, 1979.

Porter, J. R. *Jesus Christ: The Jesus of History, the Christ of Faith.* Oxford: Oxford University, 1999.

Porter, S. E. *The Criteria for Authenticity in Historical-Jesus Research: Previous Discussion and New Proposals.* JSNTS 191. Sheffield: Sheffield Academic, 2000.

―――. 'Jesus and the Use of Greek in Galilee'. In *Studying the Historical Jesus,* edited by B. Chilton and C. A. Evans, 123-54. Leiden: Brill, 1994.

Powell, M. A. *Jesus as a Figure in History: How Modern Historians View the Man from Galilee.* Louisville: Westminster, 1998.

―――. *What Is Narrative Criticism?* Minneapolis: Fortress, 1990.

Pryke, E. J. *Redactional Style in the Marcan Gospel.* SNTSMS 33. Cambridge: Cambridge University, 1978.

Puig I Tàrrech, A. 'La recherche du Jesus historique'. *Biblica* 81 (2000): 179-201.

Räisänen, H. *The 'Messianic Secret' in Mark's Gospel.* Edinburgh: Clark, 1990.

―――. 'Zur Herkunft von Markus 7.15'. In *Logia: Les paroles de Jesus,* edited by J. Delobel, 477-84. Leuven: Leuven University, 1982.

Rappaport, U. 'How Anti-Roman Was the Galilee?' In *The Galilee in Late Antiquity,* edited by L. I. Levine, 95-102. New York: Jewish Theological Seminary of America, 1992.

Rau, E. 'Jesu Auseinandersetzung mit Pharisäern über seine Zuwendung zu Sünderinnen und Sündern. Lk 15,11-32 und Lk 18,10-14a als Worte des historischen Jesus'. *ZNW* 89 (1998): 5-29.

―――. *Jesus — Freund von Zollnern und Sundern. Eine methodenkritische Untersuchung.* Stuttgart: Kohlhammer, 2000.

Reed, J. L. *Archaeology and the Galilean Jesus.* Harrisburg: Trinity, 2000.

―――. 'The Sign of Jonah: Q 11:29-32 in Its Galilean Setting'. In *Archaeology and the Galilean Jesus,* 197-211. Harrisburg: Trinity, 2000.

Reicke, B. *The Roots of the Synoptic Gospels.* Philadelphia: Fortress, 1986.

Reimarus, H. *Concerning the Intention of Jesus and His Teaching* — see Talbert.

Reinbold, W. *Der älteste Bericht über den Tod Jesu. Literarische Analyse und historische Kritik der Passionsdarstellungen der Evangelien.* BZNW 69. Berlin: de Gruyter, 1994.

Reiser, M. 'Eschatology in the Proclamation of Jesus'. In *Jesus, Mark and Q: The*

Teaching of Jesus and Its Earliest Records, edited by M. Labahn and A. Schmidt, 216-38. Sheffield: Sheffield Academic, 2001.

———. *Jesus and Judgment.* Minneapolis: Fortress, 1997.

———. 'Love of Enemies in the Context of Antiquity'. *NTS* 47 (2001): 411-27.

Renan, E. *The Life of Jesus.* ET London: Truebner, 1864 (1863).

Rhoads, D. M. *Israel in Revolution, 6-74 CE.* Philadelphia: Fortress, 1976.

Riches, J. *A Century of New Testament Study.* Valley Forge: Trinity, 1993.

———. *Jesus and the Transformation of Judaism.* London: Darton, Longman and Todd, 1980.

Ricoeur, P. *Essays on Biblical Interpretation.* Philadelphia: Fortress, 1980.

———. 'The Hermeneutical Function of Distanciation'. In *From Text to Action: Essays in Hermeneutics II,* 75-88. Evanston: Northwestern University, 1991.

———. 'Preface to Bultmann'. In *Essays on Biblical Interpretation,* 49-72. Philadelphia: Fortress, 1980.

———. 'The Task of Hermeneutics'. In *From Text to Action,* 58-63. Evanston: Northwestern University, 1991.

———. *Time and Narrative* Vol. 1. Chicago: University of Chicago, 1984.

Riesenfeld, H. 'The Gospel Tradition and Its Beginning'. In *The Gospel Tradition,* 1-29. Philadelphia: Fortress, 1957, 1970.

Riesner, R. *Jesus als Lehrer.* WUNT 2.7. Tübingen: Mohr Siebeck, 1981.

———. 'Jesus as Preacher and Teacher'. In *Jesus and the Oral Gospel Tradition,* edited by H. Wansbrough, 185-210. Sheffield: Sheffield Academic, 1991.

———. 'Synagogues in Jerusalem'. In *The Book of Acts in Its Palestinian Setting,* edited by R. Bauckham, 179-210. Grand Rapids: Eerdmans, 1995.

Riley, G. J. 'Words and Deeds: Jesus as Teacher and Jesus as Pattern of Life'. *HTR* 90 (1997): 427-36.

Ringe, S. H. *Jesus, Liberation, and the Biblical Jubilee.* Philadelphia: Fortress, 1985.

Ristow, H., and K. Matthiae. *Der historische Jesus und der kerygmatische Christus.* Berlin: Evangelische, 1961.

Rivkin, E. *What Crucified Jesus?* Nashville: Abingdon, 1984.

Roberts, J. J. M. 'The Old Testament's Contribution to Messianic Expectations'. In *The Messiah,* edited by J. H. Charlesworth, 39-51. Minneapolis: Fortress, 1992.

Robinson, J. A. T. 'Elijah, John and Jesus'. In *Twelve New Testament Studies,* 28-52. London: SCM, 1962.

———. *The Human Face of God.* London: SCM, 1973.

———. *Jesus and His Coming: The Emergence of a Doctrine.* London: SCM, 1957.

Robinson, J. M. 'The Critical Edition of Q and the Study of Jesus'. In *The Sayings Source Q and the Historical Jesus,* edited by A. Lindemann, 27-52. Leuven: Leuven University, 2001.

———. 'Early Collections of Jesus' Sayings'. In *Logia. Les Paroles de Jesus — The Sayings of Jesus,* edited by J. Delobel, 389-94. Leuven: Peeters, 1982.

———. 'Galilean Upstarts: A Sot's Cynical Disciples?' In *Sayings of Jesus: Canonical and Non-Canonical,* T. Baarda FS, edited by W. L. Petersen, et al., 223-49. Leiden: Brill, 1997.

———. 'The History-of-Religions Taxonomy of Q: The Cynic Hypothesis'. In

Gnosisforschung und Religionsgeschichte, K. Rudolph FS, edited by H Preissler and H. Seiwert, 247-65. Marburg: Elwert, 1994.

―――. 'The Jesus of Q as Liberation Theologian'. In *The Gospel behind the Gospels,* edited by R. A. Piper, 259-74. Leiden: Brill, 1995.

―――. 'LOGOI SOPHON: On the Gattung of Q'. In *Trajectories through Early Christianity,* by J. M. Robinson and H. Koester, 71-113. Philadelphia: Fortress, (1964) 1971.

―――. *A New Quest of the Historical Jesus.* London: SCM, 1959.

―――. 'The Q Trajectory: Between John and Matthew via Jesus'. In *The Future of Early Christianity,* H. Koester FS, edited by B. A. Pearson, 173-94. Minneapolis: Fortress, 1991.

Robinson, J. M., P. Hoffmann, and J. S. Kloppenborg. *The Critical Edition of Q: Synopsis.* Leuven: Peeters, 2000.

Robinson, J. M., and H. Koester. *Trajectories through Early Christianity.* Philadelphia: Fortress, 1971.

Roloff, J. 'Anfänge der soteriologischen Deutung des Todes Jesu (Mk. x.45 und Lk. xxii.27)'. *NTS* 19 (1972-73): 38-64.

―――. *Das Kerygma und der irdische Jesus.* Göttingen: Vandenhoeck und Ruprecht, 1970.

Rordorf, W. 'Does the Didache Contain Jesus Tradition Independently of the Synoptic Gospels?' In *Jesus and the Oral Gospel Tradition,* edited by H. Wansbrough, 394-423. Sheffield: Sheffield Academic, 1991.

Rowland, C. *Christian Origins.* London: SPCK, 1985.

―――. *The Open Heaven: A Study of Apocalyptic in Judaism and Early Christianity.* London: SPCK, 1982.

Ruppert, L. *Jesus als der leidende Gerechte.* SBS 59. Stuttgart: KBW, 1972.

Russell, D. S. *The Method and Message of Jewish Apocalyptic.* London: SCM, 1964.

Safrai, S., ed. *The Literature of the Sages.* CRINT II.3.1. Assen: van Gorcum, 1987.

Safrai, S, and M. Stern. *The Jewish People in the First Century,* 2 vols. CRINT 1. Assen: van Gorcum, 1974, 1976.

Safrai, Z. *The Economy of Roman Palestine.* London: Routledge, 1994.

Saldarini, A. J. *Pharisees, Scribes and Sadducees in Palestinian Society.* Edinburgh: Clark, 1988.

Sanday, W., ed. *Studies in the Synoptic Problem.* Oxford: Clarendon, 1911.

Sanders, E. P. 'Common Judaism and the Synagogue in the First Century'. In *Jews, Christians, and Polytheists in the Ancient Synagogue,* edited by S. Fine, 1-17. London: Routledge, 1999.

―――. *The Historical Figure of Jesus.* London: Penguin, 1993.

―――. *Jesus and Judaism.* London: SCM, 1985.

―――. 'Jesus and the Kingdom: The Restoration of Israel and the New People of God'. In *Jesus, the Gospels and the Church,* W. R. Farmer FS, edited by E. P. Sanders, 225-39. Macon: Mercer University, 1987.

―――. 'Jesus' Galilee'. In *Fair Play: Diversity and Conflicts in Early Christianity,* H. Räisänen FS, edited by I. Dunderberg et al., 3-41. Leiden: Brill, 2002.

―――. *Jewish Law from Jesus to the Mishnah: Five Studies.* London: SCM, 1990.

————. *Judaism: Practice and Belief, 63 BCE–66 CE.* London: SCM, 1992.

————. *Paul and Palestinian Judaism.* London: SCM, 1977.

————. *The Tendencies of the Synoptic Tradition.* SNTSMS 9. Cambridge: Cambridge University, 1969.

Sanders, J. T. 'The Criterion of Coherence and the Randomness of Charisma: Poring through Some Aporias in the Jesus Tradition'. *NTS* 44 (1998): 1-25.

Sandmel, S. *The First Christian Century in Judaism and Christianity.* New York: Oxford University, 1969.

Sato, M. *Q und Prophetie. Studien zur Gattungs- und Traditionsgeschichte der Quelle Q.* WUNT 2.29. Tübingen: Mohr Siebeck, 1988.

Sawacki, M. *Crossing Galilee: Architectures of Contact in the Occupied Land of Jesus.* Harrisburg: Trinity, 2000.

Schaberg, J. *The Illegitimacy of Jesus: A Feminist Theological Interpretation of the Infancy Narratives.* San Francisco: Harper and Row, 1987.

————. 'Mark 14:62: Early Christian Merkabah Imagery?' In *Apocalyptic and the New Testament,* edited by J. Marcus and M. L. Soards, 69-94. Sheffield: JSOT, 1989.

Schams, C. *Jewish Scribes in the Second-Temple Period.* JSOTS 291. Sheffield: Sheffield Academic, 1998.

Schenke, L. *Auferstehungsverkündigung und leeres Grab. Eine traditionsgeschichtliche Untersuchung von Mk 16,1-8.* SBS 33. Stuttgart: KBW, 1969, 2nd ed.

Schiffman, L. H. 'Messianic Figures and Ideas in the Qumran Scrolls'. In *The Messiah,* edited by J. H. Charlesworth, 116-29. Minneapolis: Fortress, 1992.

————. *Who Was a Jew? Rabbinic and Halakhic Perspectives on the Jewish-Christian Schism.* Hoboken: Ktav, 1985.

Schillebeeckx, E. *Jesus: An Experiment in Christology.* ET London: Collins, 1979 (1974).

Schippers, R. 'The Son of Man in Matt. 12.32 = Luke 12.10 Compared with Mark 3.28'. In *Studia Evangelica,* 231-35, 1968.

Schleiermacher, F. D. E. *The Christian Faith.* ET Edinburgh: Clark, 1928 (1821-22).

————. *The Life of Jesus.* ET Philadelphia: Fortress, 1975 (1864).

————. *On Religion: Speeches to Its Cultured Despisers.* ET London: Routledge and Kegan Paul, 1893 (1799).

Schlosser, J. *Jésus de Nazareth.* Paris: Noesis, 1999.

————. *Le Règne de Dieu dans les dits de Jesus,* 2 vols. Paris: Gabalda, 1980.

————. 'Q et la christologie implicite'. In *The Sayings Source Q and the Historical Jesus,* edited by A. Lindemann, 289-316. Leuven: Leuven University, 2001.

Schmidt, K. L. *Der Rahmen der Geschichte Jesus: Literarkritische Untersuchungen zur ältesten Jesusüberlieferung.* Berlin: Trowitzsch und Sohn, 1919.

Schmidt, T. E. *Hostility to Wealth in the Synoptic Gospels,* JSNTS. Sheffield: JSOT, 1987.

Schmithals, W. 'Vom Ursprung der synoptischen Tradition'. *ZTK* 94 (1997): 288-316.

Schnabel, E. J. 'Jesus and the Beginnings of the Mission to the Gentiles'. In *Jesus of Nazareth: Lord and Christ,* I. H. Marshall FS, edited by J. B. Green and M. Turner, 37-58. Grand Rapids: Eerdmans, 1994.

Schnackenburg, R. *Die sittliche Botschaft des Neuen Testaments.* HTKNT Supplement 1. Freiburg: Herder, 1986.

————. *God's Rule and Kingdom.* Freiburg: Herder, 1963.

Schnelle, U. *The History and Theology of the New Testament Writings.* ET London: SCM, 1998 (1994).

Schottroff, L. *Lydia's Impatient Sisters: A Feminist Social History of Early Christianity.* Louisville: Westminster John Knox, 1995.

Schottroff, L., and W. Stegemann. *Jesus and the Hope of the Poor.* Maryknoll: Orbis, 1986.

Schrage, W. *The Ethics of the New Testament.* Philadelphia: Fortress, 1988.

Schreiber, S. *Gesalbter und König. Titel und Konzeptionen der königlichen Gesalbtenerwartung in frühjüdischen und urchristlichen Schriften.* BZNW 105. Berlin: de Gruyter, 2000.

Schröter, J. 'Die Frage nach dem historischen Jesus und der Charakter historischer Erkenntnis'. In *The Sayings Source Q and the Historical Jesus,* edited by A. Lindemann, 207-54. Leuven: Leuven University, 2001.

―――. *Erinnerung an Jesu Worte. Studien zur Rezeption der Logienüberlieferung in Markus, Q und Thomas.* WMANT 76. Neukirchen-Vluyn: Neukirchener, 1997.

―――. *Jesus und die Anfänge der Christologie.* Neukirchen: Neukirchener, 2001.

―――. 'Markus, Q und der historische Jesus. Methodische und exegetische Erwägungen zu den Anfängen der Rezeption der Verkündigung Jesu'. *ZNW* 89 (1998): 173-200.

Schulz, S. *Q: Spruchquelle der Evangelisten.* Zurich: Theologischer, 1972.

Schürer, E. *The History of the Jewish People in the Age of Jesus Christ,* revised and edited by G. Vermes and F. Millar, 4 vols. Edinburgh: Clark, 1973-87.

Schürmann, H. 'Die vorösterlichen Anfänge der Logientradition. Versuch eines formgeschichtlichen Zugangs zum Leben Jesu'. In *Der historische Jesus und der kerygmatische Christus,* edited by H. Ristow and K. Matthiae, 342-70. Berlin: Evangelische, 1962.

―――. *Gottes Reich — Jesu Geschick. Jesu ureigener Tod im Licht seiner Basileia-Verkündigung.* Freiburg: Herder, 1983.

―――. *Jesus. Gestalt und Geheimnis.* Paderborn: Bonifatius, 1994.

Schüssler Fiorenza, E. *In Memory of Her: A Feminist Theological Reconstruction of Christian Origins.* New York: Crossroad, 1983.

―――. 'Jesus and the Politics of Interpretation'. *HTR* 90 (1997): 343-58.

―――. *Jesus and the Politics of Interpretation.* New York: Continuum, 2000.

―――. *Jesus: Miriam's Child, Sophia's Prophet.* New York: Continuum, 1995.

Schwartz, D. R. *Studies in the Jewish Background of Christianity.* WUNT 60. Tübingen: Mohr Siebeck, 1992.

Schwarz, G. *'Und Jesus sprach'. Untersuchungen zur aramäischen Urgestalt der Worte Jesu.* BWANT 118. Stuttgart: Kohlhammer, 1987, 2nd ed.

Schweitzer, A. *The Mystery of the Kingdom of God: The Secret of Jesus' Messiahship and Passion.* ET New York: Macmillan, 1914 (1901).

―――. *The Quest of the Historical Jesus.* London: SCM, 1906, 2000, 2nd ed.

Schweizer, E. 'Der Menschensohn. Zur eschatologischen Erwartung Jesu'. In *Neotestamentica,* 56-84. Zurich: Zwingli, 1959, 1963.

―――. *Erniedrigung und Erhöhung bei Jesus und seinen Nachfolgern.* Zurich: Zwingli, 1962, 2nd ed. (ET 1960).

―――. *Jesus.* London: SCM, 1971.

————. *The Lord's Supper according to the New Testament.* ET Philadelphia: Fortress, 1967 (1956).

Schwemer, A. M. 'Der Auferstandene und die Emmausjünger'. In *Auferstehung — Resurrection,* edited by F. Avemarie and H. Lichtenberger, 95-117. Tübingen: Mohr Siebeck, 2001.

Scobie, C. H. *John the Baptist.* London: SCM, 1964.

Scott, B. B. *Hear Then the Parable: A Commentary on the Parables of Jesus.* Minneapolis: Fortress, 1989.

————. *Jesus, Symbol-Maker for the Kingdom.* Philadelphia: Fortress, 1983.

————. 'New Options in an Old Quest'. In *The Historical Jesus through Catholic and Jewish Eyes,* edited by B. F. Le Beau, L. Greenspoon, and D. Hamm, 1-49. Harrisburg: Trinity, 2000.

Scott, J. M., ed. *Exile: Old Testament, Jewish, and Christian Conceptions.* Brill: Leiden, 1997.

Segal, A. F. *The Other Judaisms of Late Antiquity.* Atlanta: Scholars, 1987.

Segundo, J. L. *The Historical Jesus of the Synoptics.* ET Maryknoll: Orbis, 1985 (1982).

Sellew, P. H. *Dominical Discourses: Oral Clusters in the Jesus Sayings Tradition.* Philadelphia: Fortress, 1989.

Setzer, C. 'Excellent Women: Female Witness to the Resurrection'. *JBL* 116 (1997): 259-72.

Sievers, J. 'Who Were the Pharisees?' In *Hillel and Jesus,* edited by J. H. Charlesworth and L. L. Johns, 137-55. Minneapolis: Fortress, 1997.

Slater, T. B. 'One like a Son of Man in First-Century CE Judaism'. *NTS* 41 (1995): 183-98.

Sloyan, G. S. *The Crucifixion of Jesus.* Minneapolis: Fortress, 1995.

Smith, D. M. *John among the Gospels: The Relationship in Twentieth-Century Research.* Minneapolis: Fortress, 1992.

Smith, M. *Jesus the Magician.* San Francisco: Harper and Row, 1978.

Snodgrass, K. *The Parable of the Wicked Tenants.* WUNT 27. Tübingen: Mohr Siebeck, 1983.

Sobrino, J. *Jesus the Liberator: A Historical-Theological Reading of Jesus of Nazareth.* Maryknoll: Orbis, 1993.

Soskice, J. M. *Metaphor and Religious Language.* Oxford: Clarendon, 1985.

Squires, J. T. *The Plan of God in Luke-Acts.* SNTSMS 76. Cambridge: Cambridge University, 1993.

Stanton, G. N. 'Early Objections to the Resurrection of Jesus'. In *Resurrection,* edited by S. C. Barton and G. N. Stanton, 79-94. London: SPCK, 1994.

————. 'Form Criticism Revisited'. In *What about the New Testament?* C. F. Evans FS, edited by M. D. Hooker and C. Hickling, 13-27. London: SCM, 1975.

————. 'Jesus of Nazareth: A Magician and a False Prophet Who Deceived God's People?' In *Jesus of Nazareth: Lord and Christ,* edited by J. B. Green and M. Turner, 164-80. Grand Rapids: Eerdmans, 1994.

Stauffer, E. 'Jesus, Geschichte und Verkündigung'. *ANRW* II.25.1 (1982): 3-130.

Steck, O. H. *Israel und das gewaltsame Geschick der Propheten.* WMANT 23. Neukirchen-Vluyn: Neukirchener, 1967.

Stegemann, E. W., and W. Stegemann. *The Jesus Movement: A Social History of Its First Century.* Minneapolis: Fortress, 1999.

Stegemann, H. *The Library of Qumran.* ET Grand Rapids: Eerdmans, 1998 (1993).

Stein, R. H. 'The Proper Methodology for Ascertaining a Markan Redaction History'. *NovT* 13 (1971): 181-98.

———. *The Synoptic Problem: An Introduction.* Grand Rapids: Baker, 1987.

Stemberger, G. *Jewish Contemporaries of Jesus: Pharisees, Sadducees, Essenes.* ET Minneapolis: Fortress, 1995 (1991).

Stone, M. E., ed. *Jewish Writings of the Second Temple Period.* CRINT 2.II. Assen: van Gorcum, 1984.

Strange, J. F. 'Ancient Texts, Archaeology as Text, and the Problem of the First-Century Synagogue'. In *Evolution of the Synagogue,* edited by H. C. Kee and L. H. Cohick, 27-45. Harrisburg: Trinity, 1999.

Strauss, D. F. *The Christ of Faith and the Jesus of History.* ET Philadelphia: Fortress, 1977 (1865).

———. *The Life of Jesus Critically Examined.* ET Philadelphia: Fortress, 1846, 1972 (1835-36, 1840, 4th ed.).

———. *A New Life of Jesus.* ET London: Williams and Norgate, 1879, 2nd ed. (1864).

Strecker, G. 'Schriftlichkeit oder Mündlichkeit der synoptischen Tradition?' In *The Four Gospels 1992,* F. Neirynck FS, edited by F. van Segbroeck, et al., 159-72. Leuven: Leuven University.

———. *Theology of the New Testament.* ET Berlin: De Gruyter, 2000 (1996).

———. 'The Theory of the Messianic Secret in Mark's Gospel'. In *The Messianic Secret,* edited by C. M. Tuckett, 49-64. ET London: SPCK, 1983 (1964).

Streeter, B. H. *The Four Gospels: A Study of Origins.* London: Macmillan, 1924.

Strobel, A. *Die Stunde der Wahrheit.* WUNT 21. Tübingen: Mohr Siebeck, 1980.

———. *Untersuchungen zum eschatologischen Verzögerungsproblem auf Grund der spätjüdisch-urchristlichen Geschichte von Habakuk 2,2ff.* NovTSup. Leiden: Brill, 1961.

Stroker, W. D. *Extracanonical Sayings of Jesus.* Atlanta: Scholars, 1989.

Stuckenbruck, L. T. *Angel Veneration and Christology: A Study in Early Judaism and in the Christology of the Apocalypse of John.* WUNT 2.70. Tübingen: Mohr Siebeck, 1995.

Stuhlmacher, P. *Biblische Theologie des Neuen Testaments.* Band 1: *Grundlegung von Jesus zu Paulus.* Göttingen: Vandenhoeck und Ruprecht, 1992.

———. 'Der messianische Gottesknecht'. *JBTh* 8, *Der Messias* (1993) 131-54.

———. 'Vicariously Giving His Life for Many, Mark 10:45'. In *Reconciliation, Law and Righteousness: Essays in Biblical Theology,* 16-29. Philadelphia: Fortress, 1986.

Suggs, M. J. *Wisdom, Christology and Law in Matthew's Gospel.* Cambridge: Harvard University, 1970.

Sweet, J. P. M. 'The Zealots and Jesus'. In *Jesus and the Politics of His Day,* edited by E. Bammel and C. F. D. Moule, 1-9. Cambridge: Cambridge University, 1984.

Talbert, C. H. *Reimarus Fragments.* Philadelphia: Fortress, 1970.

Talmon, S. 'The Concept of *Masiah* and Messianism in Early Judaism'. In *The Messiah,* edited by J. H. Charlesworth, 79-115. Minneapolis: Fortress, 1992.

Tan, K. H. *The Zion Traditions and the Aims of Jesus.* SNTSMS 91. Cambridge: Cambridge University, 1997.

Tatum, W. B. *In Quest of Jesus.* Nashville: Abingdon, revised 1999.

Taylor, J. E. *The Immerser: John the Baptist within Second Temple Judaism.* Grand Rapids: Eerdmans, 1997.

Taylor, V. *The Formation of the Gospel Tradition.* London: Macmillan, 1933.

———. *Jesus and His Sacrifice.* London: Macmillan, 1937.

Telford, W. R. 'Major Trends and Interpretive Issues in the Study of Jesus'. In *Studying the Historical Jesus: Evaluations of the State of Current Research,* edited by B. Chilton and C. A. Evans, 33-74. Leiden: Brill, 1994.

Theisohn, J. *Der auserwählte Richter. Untersuchungen zum traditionsgeschichtlichen Ort der Menschensohngestalt der Bilderreden des äthiopischen Henoch.* Göttingen: Vandenhoeck, 1969.

Theissen, G. 'The Beginnings of the Sayings Tradition in Palestine'. In *The Gospels in Context,* 25-59. Minneapolis: Fortress, 1991.

———. *The First Followers of Jesus: A Sociological Analysis of Earliest Christianity.* ET London: SCM, 1978 (1977).

———. *The Gospels in Context: Social and Political History in the Synoptic Tradition.* Minneapolis: Fortress, 1991.

———. 'Historical Scepticism and the Criteria of Jesus Research or My Attempt to Leap Across Lessing's Yawning Gulf'. *SJT* 49 (1996): 147-76.

———. 'Jesus im Judentum. Drei Versuche einer Ortsbestimmung'. *Kirche und Israel* 14 (1999): 93-109.

———. 'Jesus' Temple Prophecy'. In *Social Reality and the Early Christians,* 94-114. Minneapolis: Augsburg Fortress, 1992.

———. 'Jesus und die symbolpolitischen Konflikte seiner Zeit. Sozialgeschichtliche Aspekte der Jesusforschung'. *EvT* 57 (1997): 378-400.

———. 'The Legend of the Baptizer's Death'. In *The Gospel in Context,* 81-97. Minneapolis: Fortress, 1991.

———. *Lokalkolorit und Zeitgeschichte in den Evangelien: Ein Beitrag zur Geschichte der synoptischen Tradition.* NTOA 8. Freiburg: Universitätsverlag, 1989.

———. *Miracle Stories of the Early Christian Tradition.* ET Edinburgh: Clark, 1983 (1974).

———. 'Nonviolence and Love of Our Enemies (Matthew 5:38-44; Luke 6:27-38)'. In *Social Reality and the Early Christians,* 115-56. Minneapolis: Augsburg Fortress, 1992.

———. *The Shadow of the Galilean: The Quest of the Historical Jesus in Narrative Form.* London: SCM, 1987.

———. *Social Reality and the Early Christians.* Minneapolis: Augsburg Fortress, 1992.

———. 'The Wandering Radicals: Light Shed by the Sociology of Literature on the Early Transmission of Jesus Sayings'. In *Social Reality and the Early Christians,* 33-59. Minneapolis: Augsburg Fortress, 1992.

———. '"We Have Left Everything . . ." (Mark 10:28): Discipleship and Social Uprooting in the Jewish-Palestinian Society of the First Century'. In *Social Reality and the Early Christians,* 60-93. Minneapolis: Augsburg Fortress, 1992.

Theissen, G., and A. Merz. *The Historical Jesus: A Comprehensive Guide.* ET London: SCM, 1998 (1996).

Theissen, G., and D. Winter. *Die Kriterienfrage in der Jesusforschung: Vom Differenzkriterium zum Plausibilitätskriterium.* Freiburg: Universitätsverlag, 1997.

Thiselton, A. C. *New Horizons in Hermeneutics.* London: Marshall Pickering, 1992.

―――. *The Two Horizons.* Exeter: Paternoster, 1980.

Thomas, J. *Le mouvement baptiste en Palestine et Syrie (150 av. J.-C.–300 ap. J.-C.).* Gembloux: Duculot, 1935.

Thomas, R. *Literacy and Orality in Ancient Greece.* Cambridge: Cambridge University, 1992.

Thompson, M. B. 'The Holy Internet: Communication between Churches in the First Christian Generation'. In *The Gospels for All Christians,* edited by R. Bauckham, 49-70. Grand Rapids: Eerdmans, 1998.

Thompson, M. M. *The Promise of the Father: Jesus and God in the New Testament.* Louisville: Westminster John Knox, 2000.

Thyen, H. *'Baptisma metanoias eis aphesin hamartiōn'.* In *The Future of Our Religious Past,* R. Bultmann FS, edited by J. M. Robinson, 131-68. ET London: SCM, 1971 (1964).

Tilly, M. *Johannes der Täufer und die Biographie der Propheten. Die synoptische Täuferüberlieferung und das jüdische Prophetenbild zur Zeit des Täufers.* BZANT 137. Stuttgart: Kohlhammer, 1994.

Tödt, H. E. *The Son of Man in the Synoptic Tradition.* ET London: SCM, 1965 (1963).

Tomson, P. 'The Names Israel and Jew in Ancient Judaism and in the New Testament'. *Bijdragen* 47 (1986): 120-40, 266-89.

Trautmann, M. *Zeichenhafte Handlungen Jesu. Ein Beitrag zur Frage nach dem geschichtlichen Jesu.* Würzburg: Echter, 1980.

Trocmé, E. 'Historical and Dogmatic Method in Theology'. ET in *Historical Jesus Quest,* edited by G. W. Dawes, 29-53. Leiderdorp: Deo, 1999 (1913).

―――. 'Historiography'. In *ERE,* 716-23.

―――. *Jesus and His Contemporaries.* London: SCM, 1973.

―――. *The Social Teaching of the Christian Churches.* ET London: George Allen and Unwin, 1931 (1912).

Tuckett, C. M. 'Arguments from Order: Definition and Evaluation'. In *Synoptic Studies: The Ampleforth Conferences of 1982 and 1983,* edited by C. M. Tuckett, 197-219. Sheffield: JSOT, 1984.

―――. 'A Cynic Q?' *Biblica* 70 (1989): 349-76.

―――. 'The Historical Jesus, Crossan and Methodology'. In *Text und Geschichte,* D. Lührmann FS, edited by S. Schlarb and E. Maser, 257-79. Marburg: Elwert, 1999.

―――. *Nag Hammadi and the Gospel Tradition.* Edinburgh: Clark, 1986.

―――. 'On the Stratification of Q: A Response'. *Semeia* 55 (1992): 213-22.

―――. 'Q 22:28-30'. In *Christology, Controversy and Community,* D. R. Catchpole FS, edited by D. G. Horrell and C. M. Tuckett, 99-116. Brill: Leiden, 2000.

―――. *Q and the History of Early Christianity.* Edinburgh: Clark, 1996.

————. *The Revival of the Griesbach Hypothesis: An Analysis and Appraisal.* SNTSMS 44. Cambridge: Cambridge University, 1983.

————. 'The Son of Man and Daniel 7: Q and Jesus'. In *The Sayings Source Q and the Historical Jesus,* edited by A. Lindemann, 371-94. Leuven: Leuven University, 2001.

————. 'Thomas and the Synoptics'. *NovT* 30 (1988): 132-57.

Tuckett, C., ed. *The Messianic Secret.* London: SPCK, 1983.

Twelftree, G. H. *Jesus the Exorcist.* WUNT 2.54. Tübingen: Mohr Siebeck, 1993.

————. *Jesus the Miracle Worker.* Downers Grove: InterVarsity, 1999.

Urbach, E. E. *The Sages: Their Concepts and Beliefs,* 2 vols. Jerusalem: Magnes, 1979.

Uro, R. 'Thomas and Oral Gospel Tradition'. In *Thomas at the Crossroads,* edited by R. Uro, 8-32. Edinburgh: Clark, 1998.

Uro, R., ed. *Thomas at the Crossroads: Essays on the Gospel of Thomas.* Edinburgh: Clark, 1998.

Vaage, L. E. *Galilean Upstarts: Jesus' Followers According to Q.* Valley Forge: Trinity, 1994.

————. 'Jewish Scripture, Q and the Historical Jesus: A Cynic Way with the Word'. In *The Sayings Source Q and the Historical Jesus,* edited by A. Lindemann, 479-95. Leuven: Leuven University, 2001.

————. 'Q and Cynicism: On Comparison and Social Identity'. In *The Gospel behind the Gospels,* edited by R. A. Piper, 199-229. Leiden: Brill, 1995.

van der Horst, P. W. 'Can a Book End with *gar?* A Note on Mark xvi.8'. *JTS* 23 (1972): 121-24.

————. 'Was the Synagogue a Place of Sabbath Worship before 70 CE?' In *Jews, Christians, and Polytheists in the Ancient Synagogue,* edited by S. Fine, 18-43. London: Routledge, 1999.

Vanderkam, J. C. *The Dead Sea Scrolls Today.* Grand Rapids: Eerdmans, 1994.

————. 'Righteous One, Messiah, Chosen One, and the Son of Man in 1 Enoch 37-71'. In *The Messiah,* edited by J. H. Charlesworth, 169-91. Minneapolis: Fortress, 1992.

van der Loos, H. *The Miracles of Jesus.* NovTSup 9. Leiden: Brill, 1965.

van Henten, J. W. 'The First Testing of Jesus: A Rereading of Mark 1.12-13'. *NTS* 45 (1999): 349-66.

Vansina, J. *Oral Tradition as History.* Madison, Wisconsin: University of Wisconsin, 1985.

————. *Oral Tradition: A Study in Historical Methodology.* London: Routledge and Kegan Paul, 1965.

Van Voorst, R. E. *Jesus outside the New Testament.* Grand Rapids: Eerdmans, 2001.

Vermes, G. *Jesus the Jew.* London: Collins, 1973.

————. *The Religion of Jesus the Jew.* London: SCM, 1993.

————. '"The Son of Man" Debate'. *JSNT* 1 (1978): 19-32.

————. 'The Use of *bar nash/bar nasha* in Jewish Aramaic'. In *An Aramaic Approach to the Gospels and Acts,* edited by M. Black, 310-28. Oxford: Clarendon, 1967.

Via, D. O. *The Parables.* Philadelphia: Fortress, 1967.

Vielhauer, P. 'Gottesreich und Menschensohn in der Verkündigung Jesu'. In *Aufsätze zum Neuen Testament,* 51-79. München: Kaiser, 1957, 1965.

945

Vieweger, D., and A. Böckler. '"Ich gebe Ägypten als Lösegeld für dich". Mk 10,45 und die jüdische Tradition zu Jes 43,3b, 4'. *ZAW* 108 (1996): 594-607.

Viviano, B. T. 'Hillel and Jesus on Prayer'. In *Hillel and Jesus,* edited by J. H. Charlesworth and L. L. Johns, 427-57. Minneapolis: Fortress, 1997.

———. 'The Historical Jesus in the Doubly Attested Sayings: An Experiment'. *RB* 103 (1996): 367-410.

Vögtle, A. *Die 'Gretchenfrage' des Menschensohnproblems.* QD 152. Freiburg: Herder, 1994.

———. 'Todesankündigungen und Todesverständnis Jesu'. In *Der Tod Jesu: Deutungen im Neuen Testament,* edited by K. Kertelge, 80-88. Freiburg: Herder, 1976.

von Campenhausen, H. 'The Events of Easter and the Empty Tomb'. In *Tradition and Life in the Church,* 42-89. ET London: Collins, 1968 (1960).

Vouga, F. *Jesus et la Loi selon la tradition synoptique.* Geneva: Labor et Fides, 1988.

———. 'Mündliche Tradition, soziale Kontrolle und Literatur als theologischer Protest'. In *Logos und Buchstabe. Mündlichkeit und Schriftlichkeit im Judentum und Christentum der Antike,* edited by G. Sellin and F. Vouga, 195-206. Tübingen: Francke, 1997.

Wachob, W. H., and L. T. Johnson. 'The Sayings of Jesus in the Letter of James'. In *Authenticating the Words of Jesus,* edited by B. Chilton and C. A. Evans, 431-50. Leiden: Brill, 1999.

Walker, W. O., ed. *The Relationships among the Gospels.* San Antonio: Trinity University, 1978.

Wansbrough, H., ed. *Jesus and the Oral Gospel Tradition.* JSNTS 64. Sheffield: Sheffield Academic, 1991.

Watson, F. *Text and Truth: Redefining Biblical Theology.* Edinburgh: Clark, 1997.

Waubke, H.-G. *Die Pharisäer in der protestantischen Bibelwissenschaft des 19. Jahrhunderts.* Tübingen: Mohr Siebeck, 1998.

Weaver, W. *The Historical Jesus in the Twentieth Century, 1900-1950.* Harrisburg: Trinity, 1999.

Webb, R. L. 'John the Baptist and His Relationship to Jesus'. In *Studying the Historical Jesus,* edited by B. Chilton and C. A. Evans, 178-229. Leiden: Brill, 1994.

———. *John the Baptizer and Prophet: A Socio-Historical Study.* JSNTS 62. Sheffield: Sheffield Academic, 1991.

Wedderburn, A. J. M. *Beyond Resurrection.* London: SCM, 1999.

Weinfeld, M. 'Hillel and the Misunderstanding of Judaism in Modern Scholarship'. In *Hillel and Jesus,* edited by J. H. Charlesworth and L. L. Johns, 56-70. Minneapolis: Fortress, 1997.

Weiss, J. *Earliest Christianity: A History of the Period AD 30-150.* ET 1937; New York: Harper Torchbook, 1959 (1914).

———. *Jesus' Proclamation of the Kingdom of God.* ET Philadelphia: Fortress, 1971 (1892).

Wellhausen, J. *Einleitung in die drei ersten Evangelien.* Berlin: Georg Reimer, 1905.

Wells, G. A. *The Jesus Myth.* Chicago: Open Court, 1999.

Wenham, D. *The Rediscovery of Jesus' Eschatological Discourse.* Gospel Perspectives 4. Sheffield: JSOT, 1984.

Wenham, D., and C. L. Blomberg. *Gospel Perspectives.* Vol. 6: *The Miracles of Jesus.* Sheffield: JSOT, 1986.

Weren, W. J. C. 'The Use of Isaiah 5,1-7 in the Parable of the Tenants (Mark 12,1-12; Matthew 21,33-46)'. *Biblica* 79 (1998): 1-26.

Westerholm, S. *Jesus and Scribal Authority.* CBNTS 10. Lund: Gleerup, 1978.

Wilckens, U. *Resurrection.* Edinburgh: St Andrew, 1977.

―――. 'The Tradition-History of the Resurrection of Jesus'. In *The Significance of the Message of the Resurrection for Faith in Jesus Christ,* edited by C. F. D. Moule, 51-76. London: SCM, 1968.

Wilcox, M. 'Jesus in the Light of His Jewish Environment'. *ANRW* II.25.1 (1982): 131-95.

Willis, W., ed. *The Kingdom of God in 20th-Century Interpretation.* Peabody: Hendrickson, 1987.

Winger, M. 'Word and Deed'. *CBQ* 62 (2000): 679-92.

Wink, W. *John the Baptist in the Gospel Tradition.* SNTSMS 7. Cambridge: Cambridge University, 1968.

Wischmeyer, O. 'Herrschen als Dienen — Mark 10,41-45'. *ZNW* 90 (1999): 28-44.

Witherington, B. *The Christology of Jesus.* Minneapolis: Fortress, 1990.

―――. *The Jesus Quest: The Third Search for the Jew of Nazareth.* Downers Grove: InterVarsity, 1995, 1997, 2nd ed.

―――. *Jesus the Sage: The Pilgrimage of Wisdom.* Minneapolis: Augsburg Fortress, 1994.

―――. *Jesus the Seer: The Progress of Prophecy.* Peabody: Hendrickson, 1999.

―――. *Women in the Ministry of Jesus.* SNTSMS 51. Cambridge: Cambridge University, 1984.

Wolff, H. W. *Jesaja 53 im Urchristentum.* Berlin: Evangelische, 1950, 2nd edn.

Wood, H. G. *Did Christ Really Live?* London: SCM, 1938.

Wrede, W. *The Messianic Secret.* ET Cambridge: Clarke, 1971 (1901).

Wright, N. T. 'Five Gospels but No Gospel: Jesus and the Seminar'. In *Authenticating the Activities of Jesus,* edited by B. Chilton and C. A. Evans, 83-120. Leiden: Brill, 1999.

―――. *Jesus and the Victory of God.* London: SPCK, 1996.

―――. *The New Testament and the People of God.* London: SPCK, 1992.

Wright, S. *The Voice of Jesus: Studies in the Interpretation of Six Gospel Parables.* Carlisle: Paternoster, 2000.

Young, B. *Jesus the Jewish Theologian.* Peabody: Hendrickson, 1995.

―――. *The Parables: Jewish Tradition and Christian Interpretation.* Peabody: Hendrickson, 1998.

Zahrnt, H. *The Historical Jesus.* London: Collins, 1963.

Zeitlin, I. M. *Jesus and the Judaism of His Time.* Cambridge: Polity, 1988.

Zeitlin, S. *The Jews: Race, Nation, or Religion?* Philadelphia: Dropsie, 1936.

Zeller, D. 'Bedeutung und religionsgeschichtlicher Hintergrund der Verwandlung Jesu (Markus 9:2-8)'. In *Authenticating the Activities of Jesus,* edited by B. Chilton and C. A. Evans, 303-21. Leiden: Brill, 1991.

————. *Die weisheitlichen Mahnsprüche bei den Synoptikern.* Forschung zur Bibel 17. Würzburg: Echter, 1977.

Zias, J., and E. Sekeles. 'The Crucified Man from Givʿat ha-Mivtar: A Reappraisal'. *IEJ* 35 (1985): 22-27.

Zimmermann, J. *Messianische Texte aus Qumran. Königliche, priesterliche und prophetische Messiasvorstellungen in den Schriftfunden von Qumran.* WUNT 2.104. Tübingen: Mohr Siebeck, 1998.

Index of Authors

957

Index of Subjects

Index of Scriptures and
Other Ancient Writings

References to the Gospels printed in **bold** indicate that some exegesis or exposition is offered on these pages.

999